Encyclopedia of Latin American Theater

Encyclopedia of Latin American Theater

◆ ◆ ◆

Edited by Eladio Cortés
and Mirta Barrea-Marlys

Greenwood Press
Westport, Connecticut • London

Library of Congress Cataloging-in-Publication Data

Encyclopedia of Latin American theater / edited by Eladio Cortés and Mirta Barrea-Marlys.
    p. cm.
  Includes bibliographical references and index.
  ISBN 0–313–29041–5 (alk. paper)
    1. Latin American drama—Encyclopedias. 2. Dramatists, Latin
American—Biography—Encyclopedias. 3. Theater—Latin America—Encyclopedias. I.
Cortés, Eladio. II. Barrea-Marlys, Mirta.
  PQ7082.D7E63   2003
  862.009'98'03—dc21   2003049135

British Library Cataloguing in Publication Data is available.

Library of Congress Catalog Card Number: 2003049135
ISBN: 0–313–29041–5

First published in 2003

Greenwood Press, 88 Post Road West, Westport, CT 06881
An imprint of Greenwood Publishing Group, Inc.
www.greenwood.com

Printed in the United States of America

The paper used in this book complies with the
Permanent Paper Standard issued by the National
Information Standards Organization (Z39.48–1984).

10 9 8 7 6 5 4 3 2 1

Contents

List of Entries

Marchant [Lazcano], Jorge
Mayorga, Wilfredo
Meza [Wevar], Gustavo
Miranda, Jaime
Molleto [Labarca], Enrique
Moock [Bousquet], Armando
Morales, José Ricardo
Moreno, Gloria
Morgado, Benjamín
Neruda, Pablo
Orrego Vicuña, Eugenio
Parra, Marco Antonio de la
Pérez de Arce, Camilo
Pesutic, Mauricio
Petit [M.], Magdalena
Pineda [Devia], José
Radrigán [Rojas], Juan
Requena, María Asunción
Rivano, Luis
Roepke, Gabriela
Ruiz [Pino], Raúl
Sarah [Comandari], Roberto
Sharim [Paz], Nissim
Sieveking, Alejandro
Silva Endeiza, Víctor Domingo
Silva Gutiérrez, Jaime
Skármeta Vranicic, Antonio
Terbay, Andrés
Torres Villarrubia, Víctor
Vodanovic, Sergio
Wolff, Égon Raúl

Colombia

Acosta de Samper, Soledad
Afanador, Hugo
Alvarez Lleras, Antonio
Andrade Rivera, Gustavo
Angel, Albalucía
Ariza, Patricia
Assad, José
Bonnett, Piedad (Amalfi)
Buenaventura, Enrique
Buitrago, Fanny
Camargo, Beatriz
Díaz Díaz, Oswaldo
Díaz Vargas, Henry
Fernández de Solis y Valenzuela, Fernando
  (Bruno)
Fernández Madrid, José

Freidel, José Manuel
García, Luis Alberto
García, Santiago
García Piedrahita, Eduardo
Gaviria, José Enrique
González Cajiao, Fernando
Henriquez Torres, Guillermo
Laguado, Arturo
Mallarino, Víctor
Martínez, Gilberto
Moyano, Juan Carlos
Navajas, Esteban
Niño, Jairo Aníbal
Ortiz Rojas, José Joaquín
Osorio, Luis Enrique
Peñuela, Fernando
Porto de González, Judith
Reyes, Carlos José
Rodriguez de Moreno, Sofía
Samper, Gabriela
Torres, Carlos Arturo
Vargas, Enrique
Vargas Tejada, Luis
Viviescas, Victor
Zapata Olivella, Manuel

Costa Rica

Acuña, José Basilio
Arriaga, Guillermo
Barrionuevo, Joaquín
Calsamiglia, Eduardo
Cañas Escalante, Alberto F.
Carranza, Rafael
Carvajal, María Isabel
Castro Fernández, Héctor Alfredo
  (Marizancene)
Catania, Alfredo
Cavallini, Leda
Cruz Santos, Camilo
Echeverría, Aquileo
Elizondo, Víctor Manuel
Escalante, Manuel G.
Escalante Durán, Manuel G.
Fernández de Montagné, Aída
Fernández Ferraz, Juan
Fernández Guardia, Ricardo
Fernández Morua, Juan
Gagini, Carlos
Gallegos Troyo, Daniel

Preface

The *Encyclopedia of Latin American Theater* presents the history of the theater of Latin America as well as the history of the Nuyorican and Chicano theaters of the United States. It contains entries describing the most important playwrights, independent theaters, and cultural movements in Latin American theater. The preparation of this volume is the result of the cooperation of American and Hispanic scholars.

Specifically oriented toward the English-speaking public, this encyclopedia introduces the Latin American theater from its origin in a sociocultural context. The entries are of varying length, determined by the relative importance of the playwright or the literary movement. Each biographical entry contains factual information about the dramatist's life and works, a list of works, and a secondary bibliography. The more extensive entries also provide a critical perspective of the playwright. Translations are given for most Spanish titles.

The volume is divided into the following sections: Overview of Latin American Theater; Encyclopedia of Latin American Theater by country, in alphabetical order, including Nuyorican and Chicano theaters; General Bibliography; Index; and About the Contributors. The Overview discusses the general development of Latin American theater within a cultural and historical perspective. The development of theater across the centuries is presented at the beginning of each country. The biographical and topical entries are arranged alphabetically within each country section and place the author or movement within the context of international literature.

The entries of individuals are alphabetized by last name. Individuals with two last names are alphabetized under the first one. For instance, "Conrado Nalé Roxlo" is found under "Nalé." Birth and death dates, when known, follow the entry name. Each entry contains both a biographical note and most contain bibliographical information.

Citations of an author's plays include the following information, when known: title of the work with an English translation, date of first-staged performance, place of first-staged performance, place of publication, publisher, date of publication, and page numbers, where applicable. The works are listed in chronological order.

Bibliographical information appears in alphabetical order, by author's last name. The entries chosen are usually those that are most easily available in the United States. For authors about whom much has been written, a representative sample of bibliographical material is provided.

The entries for each country—except Mexico and Nicaragua—were authored by the individual whose name appears at the end of that country section. Mexico and Nicaragua are multiauthored; for these two countries, the entry author's name appears at the end of the entry.

This task would have been impossible without the help of many people. We would like to thank the contributors who so generously gave of themselves to make this encyclopedia possible, especially Denice Montesano, for her help with the introduction to the theater of Argentina (1955–present); Philippa Yin, for writing the Overview; and Gloria da Cunha-Giabbai, for her help and moral support. We would like to express our gratitude to our friends and colleagues Dr. Michèle Muncy and Dr. James Marlys for their unfailing help, support, and understanding. Our deepest gratitude goes to Dr. George Butler of Greenwood Press for his tireless efforts and patience. As editors, we assume responsibility for whatever mistakes there may be in fact and judgment. All that is worthy and useful in this encyclopedia is the result of the excellence of the contributors.

Overview of Latin American Theater

EARLY THEATER

Before the arrival of the Spanish in America, history, religion, great deeds, acts of heroes and devils, nature's marvels, and comic relief were acted, sung, danced, or all of these, with musical accompaniment, in the major population centers of what are now Mexico, Peru, and several other countries. The Spanish colonization fervor, beginning in the sixteenth century, almost completely did away with these accomplishments, and few had been depicted so that we might have a record of even their intent. In most places, the local customs have contributed a flavoring to the Spanish culture but have provided few clues for those who today might like to reconstruct an authentic cultural past. To the degree that we would esteem them, we must mourn their absence. But there were some pieces that were recorded by indigenous and Spanish observers of the rites and rituals of the pre-Columbian cultures of the Western Hemisphere.

In Mexico, the Aztec chronicler Fernando de Alva Ixtlixóchitl (1577–1648?) described the court of the king of Texcoco, Nezahualcóyotl (1648), including the information that there were "dancers and presentations of pleasure and entertainment." Presentations like these were often called *mitotes*, based on the Nahuatl word *mitotl* for "dance." And Hernán Cortés himself described that in the central plaza there was one area that served as a kind of stage where the actors gathered so that they could be seen from all around the area. Various representations of dance, recitation, and music are not uncommon in those few pre-Columbian codices that escaped the general burning of histories and texts by the Spanish, who saw all aspects of the indigenous culture as simply pagan. The Mexican love of theater, however, was immediately exploited by the Catholic clergy, who began writing plays in Nahuatl and other native languages to illustrate Christian doctrine and biblical stories.

In Peru, the Inca Garcilaso de la Vega described the activities in the court of his ancestors to the Spanish public. In the works performed, he noted, the actors were often nobles, and if they found favor with their audience, they were rewarded with jewels and other gifts. Further, added Garcilaso, the works were of two kinds, tragedies and comedies, but none were low or vile. Even when we take into consideration the fact that the genres of the Inca culture were likely to have had considerable differences with those designated by the same names in Spain, various accounts leave no doubt that there was a well-established theatrical tradition in the culture. In Puerto Rico and other Caribbean islands, the native (Taino) population was decimated by disease and the ravages of the colonization process by the middle of the sixteenth century. Thus, the activity known as the *areyto* (or *areíto*), involving narrative, music, song, and dance—an oral theater to transmit the tribal history and traditions—did not survive the onslaught. Nor was the *areyto* used to make it easier for the natives to understand and assimilate the Christian religion. It seems to have survived more as an idea than a reality, a love of celebratory music and dance in particular.

Together with remnants from the cultures mentioned above, there is at least one complete work, the *Rabinal Achí*, or Warrior of Rabinal, that was written in Quiché, the Mayan language of Central America. An inhabitant of Rabinal recited the play to a French cleric in 1855, and it was soon published in both French and Quiché. It has been performed in both Quiché and Spanish and widely studied. What becomes apparent very quickly is that in spite of the late date of its discovery it seems to have maintained considerable authenticity. The structure and the form, the rhetorical devices, the rhythm and the flow all point to its local genesis and provide a wealth of information and connection with those traditions that are now found primarily in folktales and poetry rather than in formal theater.

The Spanish colonial culture of the sixteenth century brought new diversions and more serious activities. In addition to bullfights and other games, both religious and secular plays were performed early in the colonies. As mentioned above, the Spanish clergy quickly began writing in whatever local language served their purposes of conversion and education. The Franciscan monk Toribio de Paredes (1490–1566), better known as Motolinía, described one such *auto*, or sacred play, performed by indigenous actors as having moved the audience deeply. Lay brotherhoods, the clergy, the indigenous converts, and, soon, the mestizo groups found that theater was a very satisfying activity for saints' days, government events, celebrations for visiting dignitaries, and other special occasions. Many Mexican churches were soon built with open chapels, large constructed spaces adjoining the church proper for the dual purpose of teaching and entertaining. This architectural feature is a principal contribution of the Mexican ideology that may stem from the original *teocalli* (place of instruction of the priests) and that facilitated widespread diffusion of the Catholic doctrine and the Spanish culture. In spite of the interest in and usefulness of this educational theater, the activity was also somewhat ephemeral. Most pieces were rapidly replaced with equivalents in Spanish or simply lost to posterity. The few that survived are Mexican, and there is no record of any survival of such theater in other areas, although there are reports of it in Central America and Peru. By 1575 this form of theater was already fading rapidly, as *creole* theater was beginning to make its ascent. As population in the colonies increased and diversified, Spanish theater troupes arrived, although infrequently, to play to overflow audiences. Local writers emulated the patterns they avidly absorbed as the latest fashion from the continent. In Mexico, Fernán González de Eslava (1534–1601) wrote more than twenty works, including a number of lively *entremeses* (one-act plays) on varied topics. Among these the *Ahorcado* (Hanged Man) stands out for its popular language and picaresque tone. Cristóbal de Llerena (1540?–1610?), a priest of Santo Domingo, wrote an *entremés* that earned his exile because of its biting satire. A writer of Chile, avoiding such social issues, wrote *El Hércules chileno* (The Chilean Hercules) in 1693, probably about Caupolicán, mighty chief of the Araucanians. These writers and others who paralleled their efforts provided the first steps in what will become Spanish American theater in the seventeenth century.

Of lesser influence is the scholastic theater, primarily written by Jesuits for the practice of young seminarians. The Companies of Jesus arrived in Mexico in 1572 and in Lima in 1578. Sometimes in Latin, but increasingly in Spanish, the intent of the scholastic theater was primarily didactic, and its audiences were limited. Nevertheless, it was customary for these groups to present recitations or plays at events of importance. While these plays were seldom very popular, the Jesuit academies and seminaries maintained the tradition of theater as good academic practice and so may have influenced other scholarly groups to do the same. Certainly, the universities supported some theatrical activity and the study of the theater in most Spanish American countries in the succeeding centuries.

The Siglo de Oro (Golden Age) of Spain led the colonies by example in its theater, with Lope de Vega, Tirso de Molina, and Calderón de la Barca. The fourth of the great dramatists of the period is the Mexican Juan Ruiz de Alarcón (1580–1639), claimed by both Mexico and Spain. Alarcón was born in Mexico City, went to Spain to study, returned to Mexico briefly, and remained in Spain after 1613. Hunched and red-bearded, he was shunned by the great Lope de Vega, and his plays were not well received. He was appointed to the Council of Indies in 1626, after which he stopped writing drama. His plays, however, reveal a writer of great skill. The proverbial Mexican courtesy and acute observations concerning Spanish society mark his works fairly uniformly. His most famous works remain *Las paredes oyen* (The Walls Have Ears) and *La verdad sospechosa* (The Truth Suspected), the latter of which became the basis for works by Corneille and Molière.

Sor Juana Inés de la Cruz (1648–1695) was another extraordinary Mexican writer, often called "The Tenth Muse." As a child, Juana showed an unexpected propensity for learning that marked her as a prodigy. Presented at the Viceroy's court, she showed a mastery of the scholarly domains—theology and Latin—quite beyond her seventeen years. For reasons still disputed, Juana de Azbache, as she was then known, renounced her worldly customs and entered a convent. There, befriended and still protected by the royal family, she accumulated a substantial library and wrote some of the most remarkable literature of the period, much of which is only now becoming fully appreciated. Her presence in the world of religious writers of the period is in itself a rebuke to the male-dominated hierarchy of the period. Her sometimes autobiographical *Respuesta a Sor Filotea* (Answer to Sister Filotea) (1691) is the first American defense of women's right to an education; and her *Primero sueño* (First Dream) was modeled after Góngora's *First Solitude* but owes no more than the impulse to this model. Her theatrical works, consisting of eighteen *loas* (dramatic poems), three *autos*, two *sainetes* (one-act farces), and two comedies, include *El divino Narciso* (The Divine Narcissus), which the critic José Juan Arrom acclaims as the best among all the sacramental plays. Unfortunately, her literary and intellectual efforts were condemned by the religious authority of the period, and she gave away her library, devoted herself to religious activities, and died soon afterward during an epidemic.

Juan de Espinosa Medrano (1639?–1688) came to prominence as professor of theology at the Seminary of San Antonio and archdeacon of the Cathedral of Cuzco. Son of a Spaniard and a Peruvian woman, Espinosa wrote works of great acuity in both Spanish and Quechua. He is also known for his *Apologética en favor de D. Luis de Góngora* (Apology in Defense of Don Luis de Góngora). His biblical drama, *Amar su propia muerte* (Loving Your Own Death), involves some of the most elegant theatrical language of the period. This, combined with the thematic and plot subtleties, makes it one of the most remarkable works of the period. Other writers who provided works in the American baroque period include Peruvian residents Juan del Valle y Caviedes (1652–1692) and Pedro de Peralta Barnuevo (1664–1743) and Mexicans Francisco Bramón and Matías de Bocanegra (1612–1668). Another writer, of more historic than artistic interest, lived in Cartagena de Indias:

Juan de Cueto y Mena (1604–1669). His dialogues, which are somewhat unpolished, nevertheless give vivid testimony of the level of literary culture available. In the early eighteenth century, Antonio Fuentes Arco, of Santa Fe, Argentina, wrote a *loa* to celebrate the lifting of a tax on *mate*, the popular herb tea. In the islands, literary activity included *El príncipe jardinero* (The Gardener Prince) (1730?), by the Cuban Santiago de Pita (?–1755). However, most plays were still brought from Spain and acted by visiting troupes or local residents. In Puerto Rico, for example, on the death of Philip V and the ascendancy of his son, Philip VI, in 1746, the lay brotherhood presented the Spanish play *El conde Lucanor* (Count Lucanor), by Calderón de la Barca; the merchants presented *Los españoles on Chile* (The Spaniards in Chile), by González de Bustos; and the free mulattos presented *El villano del Danubio* (The Villain of the Danube) and *El buen juez no tiene patria* (The Good Judge Knows No Country), by Hoz y Mota, which was followed by fireworks. On the last day the military garrison presented *Primero es la honra* (Honor Is First), by Agostín Moreto.

In the second half of the eighteenth century, neoclassic ideas found followers in the Spanish colonies, and a curious confluence of the aesthetic, social, and political ideas produced marked changes in the theater. While the scholastic or humanist theater of the Jesuits did not produce a rich lode of dramatic works, the same turning away from the Spanish authority and toward the Latin and Greek ideas of form, image, and personal, rather than imposed, authority encouraged the moves toward political independence that were growing. In fact, the expulsion of the Jesuits by Charles III in 1769 marked the end of continuous Jesuit education in Spanish America. But the shift away from the Church as sociopolitical authority had already begun. Toward the end of the eighteenth century and carrying on into the nineteenth, the first permanent theaters were being built throughout the Antilles and in every major city of the continent. Sources of funds included levies, taxes of various kinds (a tax on bread in Puerto Rico; a tax of seventeen pesos on each slave imported in Cuba), and even money earmarked for other purposes (the soldiers' regimental assets were appropriated in Montevideo). The shift to the primacy of theater as secular entertainment rather than religious instruction and celebration thus coincided with both the period of neoclassical taste and the inexorable movements toward national independence, even when these were not the reason for construction. The viceroy of the region of Buenos Aires (1784) and the town council of La Paz (Alto Peru) (1796) both justified the theater on the grounds that the works to be presented would provide forums for the honest portrayal of good behavior, language, and general civility, aims that differ from those of the Spanish baroque. This combination of neoclassic aesthetic and civil virtue of plays is made explicit in the 1799 petition of José de Cos Irberri in Santiago, Chile. He stated that the works of the period (in contrast to the Baroque) made a "wholesome impression," as well as observing the unities of time, place, and action; further, he said, the previous works were in bad taste and gave as example those in which the exalted love affairs of a daughter mock the father's vigilance. In Peru, continuing the strong literary tradition of the viceregal capitals, Fray Francisco del Castillo (1716–1770) wrote theater based on local history. Perhaps the most notable work of this period, however, is the anonymous *Ollántay* (Ollantay). Written originally in Quechua, this work has been the subject of considerable dispute. The date of its conception, its writing, and its structure have been considered pre-Hispanic, late indigenous colonial, or Spanish colonial, according to various scholars. An epic romance of apparently Spanish structure and rhyme with what some scholars consider typical pre-Hispanic melancholy, the work found considerable favor with the Peruvian public. But the date of its presentation, 1780, marked the rebellion of Túpac Amaru II, and further performances of the work were forbidden by the government.

THE DEVELOPMENT OF NATIONAL THEATER

While neoclassicism followed the Golden Age of Spain, Spanish America entered into the battles of independence from Spain at the same time. The works of the Spaniards Moratín and Ercilla were widely known and imitated in the Americas, although many works, once produced, were not published. The constant thirst for new plays, and the lack of an international press, left many plays unknown beyond their locality. Of those writers whose work is known, that of the Mexican-born Manuel Eduardo de Gorostiza (1789–1851) stands out. Taken to Spain after the death of his father in 1794, he grew up to become a political liberal. For this reason he suffered exile and the loss of his properties. Returning to Mexico in 1833, after serving the cause of the revolution in England, he served in a number of other distinguished positions. Gorostiza is best known for his play *Contigo, pan y cebolla* (Bread, Onions, and You) (1833), which was first performed in Mexico. His plays, in prose, are well constructed and always have a moral purpose. The Argentinean Manuel José de Lavardén (1754–1810?) wrote at least two plays, one of which, *Los Araucanos* (The Araucanians), in the style of Ercilla, was completely lost; the other, *Siripo* (Siripo), was destroyed in a fire. Nevertheless, this play was constructed with a conscious employment of Aristotle's principles and reconstructed for later performances. Neoclassic theater, however, was for the minority that could appreciate its finer points; whether because of its demands on the writer or because of the external demands of the politics of rebellion, fewer works were produced than one would expect in the light of the growth of traveling companies and the construction of theaters throughout the regions.

At the same time, popular theater provided both formal and informal theater for the growing cities and rural centers. Notable among writers of the period is the Mexican Juan de Medina, who wrote a number of works in schematic form, designed as the framework for comic pantomimes. Only two of these have survived. Another is the Cuban Buenaventura Pascual Ferrer (1772–1851), who wrote a *sainete, La mujer impertinente, el marido más paciente y el cortejo subteniente* (The Impertinent Woman, the Very Patient Husband and the Courtier). And in Argentina Juan Bautista Maciel, of Río de la Plata, wrote *El amor de la estanciera* (The Rancher's Love) (1790), a work with all the popular gaucho elements except mention of the gauchos themselves. The liberation of the theater from works in poetry, a growing emphasis on the value of the common man as subject for theatrical works, especially comedic works, and a bent for portraying regional customs or manners, *costumbrismo*, carried this popular theater into the nineteenth century. At that point the romantic movement, already in full force in Europe, came onto the local scene.

Spanish poets and playwrights such as the Duke of Rivas and José Zorrilla were met with tremendous enthusiasm. However, the nascent romanticism brought a fervor that also found ready response in the new countries. The influence of France and the United States, especially, on the politics and literature of the countries is obvious. We have only to mention the works of Rousseau, the constitutions and manifestos of independence, the poets Poe and Lamartine, to indicate this rich vein of thought and structure. But what is perhaps most interesting is that while Europe looked to past glories, real or imagined, and far-off lands for exotic images to strengthen their national images, the Latin American countries discovered themselves. They found the exotic on their doorsteps and their national images in their own making. The combination of romantic and *costumbrista* techniques enriched the nineteenth century and gave Spanish American countries their first authentic identities. The interplay of the sentiments of the romantic and the more historically accurate realism provided ample ground for most dramatists. In Mexico, always one of the most fruitful centers of culture, Fernando Calderón (1809–1845) wrote several historic dramas and a thoughtful satire, *A ninguna de las tres* (None of the Three). Another Mexican work, this one of marked romantic tendencies, is *La hija del rey* (The King's Daughter), by José Peón y Contreras (1843–1907). Alfredo Chavero (1841–1906) carried on the tradition of the *zarzuela* (a Spanish form of operetta in which spoken dialogue alternates with dances and songs), along with comic operas and some historic pieces. Other Mexican authors, dramatists of note, although they were better known as poets, include Hipólito Serán and José María Vigil. In many countries, however, the constant change of governments and their ideologies limited theatrical production, and it was still apparent that the Spanish playwrights of the period were, in most instances, more popular (or prestigious) than the locals.

In Argentina, romantic tendencies also followed hard upon the neoclassic. Following a very successful production of Lavardén's *Siripo* in 1813, in which he changed the native Indians into "noble savages," director Luis Ambrosio Morante also directed (and probably wrote) another play in the same vein, *Túpac Amarú*. At the same time, Governor Puyrredón formed the Sociedad del Buen Gusto (Society of Good Taste), with twenty-eight leading writers. One obvious goal for the new country was to encourage local drama; another was to provide translations of selected foreign plays. They also wanted to encourage and keep local acting talent. The arrival of dictator Juan Manuel Rosas (1829–1852) prevented the theater from developing its potential; in fact, he used the theater for heavy propaganda against the opposing factions. The liberals, in exile, were writing romantic works, but these had little effect on the national theater (e.g., Bartolomé Mitre [1821–1906], *Cuatro epocas* [Four Epochs]; José Mármol [1818–1871], *El cruzado* [The Crusade]). After the fall of Rosas, the works produced against the prior regime suffered from many of the same defects of excess. One of those who returned to Argentina was Pedro Echagüe (1821–1889). His drama *Rosas* (1860) was overbearing; another, *Amor y virtud* (Love and Virtue) (1868), was typically romantic. The Argentine theater limped toward the twentieth century with waves of gaucho works, popular circus productions, political drama, and a smattering of realist works. Among the last we may count the work of Nicolás Granada (1840–1915). The first work of a woman dramatist, Matilde Cuyas's *Contra soberbia humildad* (Humility against Pride), in 1877, was presented at a benefit performance. Together with the serious theater, the other most effective trend was that based on the gaucho. What was certainly a source of sometimes contentious politics had also become a mainstay of popular theater. Notable in this aspect was the *sainete criollo* (creole comedy), whose popularity reached numbers unheard of previously. The father of this genre was Nemesio Trejo (1862–1916), who wrote first for the Salesian schools. More than fifty of his plays received over one hundred performances each. With fifty-four houses throughout Argentina, their effect on the public was significant. The easily copied form became such a hit that more than 200 authors wrote them between 1890–1930. Among these, Enrique García Velloso, Ezequiel Soria, and especially Alberto Vacarezza figured prominently.

The writers of the contiguous area of Uruguay participated in many of the same areas of theatrical effort as those of Argentina. The same romantic, gaucho, and patriotic tendencies were shown in plays such as *Una víctima de Rosas* (A Victim of Rosas) (1845) by Francisco Xavier de Acha (1828–1888), *Amor y patria* (Love and Country) (1856) by Alejandro Magariños Cervantes (1825–1893), and *Julián Jiménez* (1890) by Abdón Aróztegui (1853–1926), the last of which had over a thousand performances. The Uruguayan Florencio Sánchez (1875–1910) was one of the period's foremost writers, acclaimed by both his nation and the larger region. Among his twenty extant works the best known are *M'hijo el dotor* (My Son the Lawyer) (1903) and *Barranca abajo* (Down the Cliff) (1905). His works gave a new sense of realism and social meaning to the theaters of both Uruguay and Argentina, where many of his plays were performed. Unfortunately, his fame took him to Italy, where he was quite unknown and could not achieve success. Poverty and tuberculosis caused his death at the age of thirty-five. His apparent successor in Uruguayan theater was Ernesto Herrera (1886–1917). His plays carried realism into naturalism and presented the first works of modern psychological acuity. His best work is probably *El león ciego* (The Blind Lion) (1911), which argues against the senseless national violence that had engulfed the country. Tragically, Herrera, like Sánchez, died young and also of tuberculosis.

Peru also presented interesting and productive theater in the same period. Two dramatists, Felipe Pardo y Aliaga (1806–1871) and Manuel Ascencio Segura (1805–1871) shared the stage, both writing numerous *costumbrista* plays. Their characters, at times reduced to typecasting, and their satiric take on society's foibles made them extremely popular. From 1830, with *Los frutos de la educación* (The Fruits of Education) of Pardo y Aliaga, to 1862, with Segura's *Na Catita* (Miss Catita), there was a play available by one of these popular authors. They were followed by Abelardo Gamarra (1857–1924), who included historic problems in plays such as *Ya vienen los Chilenos* (The Chileans Are Coming) (1886). The romantic Manuel Corpancho (1800–1863) and outstanding women authors gave the theater depth and variety. Clorinda Matto de Turner (1854–1909), for example, wrote an Inca play, *Hima Súmac* (1892), and one based on the exploits of conquistador Francisco Pizarro.

In Chile, Carlos Bello (1815–1854), the older son of critic and author Andres Bello, wrote what can be considered the first national play, *Los amores del poeta* (The Poet's Loves) (1842). The ups and downs of Chile's early theater scene were mostly downs. The new theater of Santiago, inaugurated in 1848, was held in the midst of gold fever; in fact, the play was titled *Ya no voy a California* (I'm Not Going to California Now). The theatergoing public favored the shorter *costumbrista* pieces and provided the background against which Daniel Barros Grez (1834–1904) rose to prominence, writing some twenty works. Several that dramatized proverbs met with considerable critical as well as popular success, such as *Cada oveja con su pareja* (Each Sheep with Its Mate) (1879), a comedy involving two couples. Of the Chilean historic pieces, *El tribunal del honor* (The Tribunal of Honor) (1877), by Daniel Caldera (1851–1896), was based on a public scandal and aroused such an outcry that he stopped writing plays altogether. *El jefe de la familia* (Head of the Family)

(1854), by Alberto Blest Gana (1830–1920), was published in 1858, although it was not performed until ten years later. Blest Gana, after this one piece, turned again to the novel, but his brother, Guillermo Blest Gana (1829–1904), enjoyed some acclaim with several works. The *zarzuela* was also popular in Chile, and in general, the tone of Chilean theater tended toward the lighter side. As in Argentina, *sainetes* were legion and popular well into the twentieth century. The most popular play of the period was *Don Lucas Gómez* (1885), a comedy by Mateo Martínez Quevedo (1848–1923). Using the idea of the *huaso* (bumpkin) in the city, he managed to combine a number of comic ideas that made everyone happy at the end. This work enjoyed twenty years of performances throughout the country.

Although there was significant theatrical activity in most of the developing countries throughout the nineteenth century, the general lack of theatrical facilities, the difficulties of developing audiences for local plays, and the political strife of the times deprived many countries, or more properly, their capital cities, of consistent theatrical development. Much the same can be said for development in the islands of the Caribbean. Thus, it is all the more remarkable to find outstanding dramatists in the face of these considerable economic, social, and political difficulties. The most eminent of the Bolivian writers bridges the period at the end of the nineteenth century. Ricardo Jaimes Freyre (1868–1933), Rubén Darío's Modernist poetry companion, wrote a colonial drama in three acts, *Los conquistadores* (The Conquistadors). In Colombia, romantic novelist Jorge Isaacs (1837–1895) also wrote three plays of historic interest. Cuban Gertrudis Gómez de Avellaneda (1814–1873) is another of those writers claimed by both Spain and their native country. Her first play, *Leoncia* (1844), provided encouraging success, and she eventually wrote plays in several genres, as well as adaptations of several French works. Her plays, romantic in their intense passions, include early psychological studies, as in *Baltasar* (1858) and the lighter *La hija de las flores* (Daughter of the Flowers) (1852). Her countryman José Martí (1853–1895) also wrote a romantic play at the early age of sixteen: *Abdala* (1869). In exile he wrote two more but realized that his oratorical skills were greater and so left the theater behind. The "Father of Puerto Rican Literature," Alejandro Tapia y Rivera (1826–1882), wrote several works, all of which presented serious historic or social themes. *La cuarterona* (The Quarteroon) (1867) treats the theme of love denied for differences of race, thus initiating a theme of long standing in Puerto Rico. The fundamental quest for a Puerto Rican identity was begun early in its theater and has continued to be one of the major themes. Puerto Rico also had, like Argentina, a characteristic and colorful subgenre, in this case, that of the *jíbaro*, or peasant theater. The genre was established with the works of Ramón Méndez Quiñones (1847–1889) and continued well into the twentieth century.

THE TWENTIETH CENTURY

Looking at the theater of the twentieth century and especially at that of recent decades, a number of trends become obvious that cut across or transcend national boundaries: expanded communication; pan-American aesthetic currents; and the constantly increasing number of artistic centers, dramatists, and plays that provide critical resources. There are also some interesting works or events that are worth examining in and of themselves. The critic Frank Dauster, in his *Historia del teatro hispanoamericano* (1966), discerned three stages in the general development of the theater in this century. The first thirty years consisted of late romanticism, realism, and short works. The next thirty years see considerable experimentation. Dauster refers to the last part of the century as the *florecimiento*, flowering, and he looks to this period as one of cosmopolitanization, with the best of each society providing new inspiration to others. This division provides a convenient way to look at examples characteristic of many of the countries, always bearing in mind that there are many cases that skew this neat classification.

First, the early century, full of comedy, with late romanticism and realism. The popularity of the *sainete* in Chile, Uruguay, Argentina, and Peru has been mentioned, as well as the evolution in Argentina of the *sainete criollo*. In Cuba, the *bufo* (from the Italian verb for mocking) was performed widely, including in theaters constructed especially for this form of comic theater. In Mexico, in spite of the generally destructive force of the revolution (1911–1921) and World War I, which kept many foreign companies from presenting in the Americas, the *zarzuela* and the *genero chico* (short works, either sung or spoken), both Spanish and in imitation, were performed when conditions permitted. Political reviews were also popular but normally not published, as they were often satirical to the point of danger to the author. Serious theater of social or political themes, realism, Ibsenian influence, and Pirandellian invention came into prominence alongside or supplanted the popular theater in some countries. Federico Gamboa (1864–1939) and Marcelino Dávalos (1871–1923) both wrote several important works. Gamboa's *La venganza de la gleba* (The Revenge of the Rabble) was Mexico's first rural drama. Dávalos's political stance earned his banishment, so his last works were written in the United States. The Cuban José Antonio Baralt (1885–1946) presented works of psychological and social impact, including *El hombre fuerte* (The Strong Man) (1915), about the classic strong-willed politician. In Paraguay, although playwrights complained that they could only use the theater when there was not a popular film playing, several plays gave evidence of the advancing cause of theater. Unfortunately, most of these were not published or otherwise conserved. Eloy Fariña Núñez (1885–1929), however, was a journalist who ended his career in Buenos Aires, where his plays were performed and printed by his newspaper. His works showed a serious side, with two dramas and a comedy, as well as a tragedy, *Entre naranjos y cocoteros* (Between Orange and Coconut Trees). Dr. Pedro Juan Caballero (1900–1946) was the most prolific of the Paraguayan writers, beginning early with *El pasado* (The Past) (1917). As founder of the Paraguayan Theater Company, he sought to produce plays with national themes. Several other authors followed suit, and into the 1940s and 1950s, there were efforts to establish repertory theater. It was still true, unfortunately, that both traveling players from Buenos Aires and films were more to the taste of the Asunción public. In Venezuela, a number of efforts by well-intentioned authors kept the Caracas Theater going, aided by the poet–politician Andrés Eloy Blanco (1899–1955). The most popular writer of the period was Leopoldo Ayala Michelena (1897–1962). Not a professional, he followed his dream of writing by night. His serious works are of the 1930s, including *Almas descarnadas* (Bare Souls), about family relations in society, along the lines of Arthur Miller's *Death of a Salesman*.

In the 1920s and 1930s, many vanguard movements point to a spirit of renovation in the theater. At the same time, sponsorship of the theater—its study, contests for outstanding works, and performance—often moved from government agencies to indirect sponsorship of groups and to the universities. In Mexico, the founding of the Union of Dramatic Authors (1923) led to the Ulises (Ulysses) group, which was followed by the Teatro Orientación

(Orientation Theater), supported by the government and under the direction of Celestino Gorostiza, an extremely capable director and organizer. All of these made efforts to bring world drama and works in translation to Mexico, which stimulated writing in Mexico. Additionally, the Orientation Theater group emphasized the ensemble over the star, which improved Mexican acting. However, as film became more popular, not only did the public abandon theaters for movie houses, but many of the best actors, directors, and writers did the same, including Gorostiza.

In Argentina, the decadence of the theater, on the one hand, and a sense of anticommercialism, on the other, resulted in the founding of a group known as *independents*. Their efforts crystallized in the Teatro del Pueblo (The People's Theater) in 1930, headed by Leónidas Barletta. The government offered its backing, and the theater flourished, offering both world and national drama at ticket prices competitive with movie theaters. Most of the eight works of Roberto Arlt (1900–1942), always avant-garde, were produced by the Teatro del Pueblo. Successive moves to ever larger theaters took place, but the last theater, which could seat 1,500, was burned for its opposition to Juan Perón's government. Other experimental theaters, the Juan B. Justo (1935) and the La Máscara (Mask) (1937), were part of perhaps the most active theatergoing movement of the century (in 1946, monthly attendance was 420,000).

Publication was also phenomenal: Complete plays were published in weekly magazines such as *La escena* (The Scene) for fifteen years and in biweekly magazines such as *Teatro moderno* (Modern Theater) for similar periods. These magazines alone account for the publication of over 1,000 new Argentine plays.

Chile presents another instance of the catalytic effect of independent theatrical effort. In Chile's case, it was labor theater early in the century that started the ball rolling. Then a student group took Spanish plays to groups in the south of the country. Some of these students went on to found the Teatro Experimental (Experimental Theater), which was incorporated into the University of Chile. With funding thus assured, the group evolved into the ITUCH, Instituto de Teatro de la Universidad de Chile (Institute of Theater of the University of Chile), which began sponsoring biannual festivals, including seminars in playwriting and production, and prizes to the winners. Shortly thereafter, another similar group sprang up as the Teatro Experimental de la Universidad Católica (Experimental Theater of the Catholic University), or TEUC. Soon both groups were producing in professional facilities and providing considerable encouragement to local groups and those in other cities, all of whom began to participate in the festivals.

Venezuela's theater was also invigorated in the 1930s by the Venezuelan Writers Association, which provided theatrical performances, among many other activities. Then, in the 1940s, the Ministry of Labor and Communications sponsored the Teatro Obrero (Workers' Theater), as they renamed the Bolívar Theater, and made it the site of an interesting experiment. Tickets to the theater were very inexpensive, and explanations were given over a loud speaker during the performances, with discussions held afterward. Even the small island of Puerto Rico had experimental theater and stimulated local production by means of contests. In 1938 the newly created Ateneo Puertorriqueño (Puerto Rican Atheneum) awarded prizes to three winning works. Emilio S. Belaval's 1939 manifesto for a Puerto Rican Theater, "Lo que podría ser un teatro puertorriqueño" (What a Puerto Rican Theater Might Be), and the *areyto* group led to the formation of the University Theater in that same year. Several developments over the next decade culminated in the formation of the government-sponsored Institute of Puerto Rican Culture in 1955 to create and support various forms of artistic expression in Puerto Rico. From 1958 on, the annual festivals are preeminent among these. With variations accounted for by differences of place, similar experimentation took place in many other countries. And while the search for quality theater in these countries usually meant serious local and/or international theater, there were also efforts to become more sophisticated in terms of presentation, technical aspects, and professional training for actors.

As we look at the efforts of the past thirty to forty years, it becomes apparent that there are as many differences as similarities in recent theater. Works of social realism and protest exist in most countries, for example. Women's voices—the natural response to increased roles for women in all areas of the arts and, indeed, in all professional areas—are apparent in all countries to a greater or lesser degree. At the same time, particularly strong national or regional theatrical tendencies set certain areas apart. The *carpa* (tent) theater of Mexico and the *campesino* (peasant) theater of Augusto Boal and his followers are but two of these phenomena. Fortunately, for the future, many of the authors, works, and movements are strong. A list of all these would be longer than is appropriate for such an overview, but a few can be mentioned that provide a sense of the quality and variety of the offerings in the last part of this century.

In Peru, *Collacocha* (1958), the best work of Enrique Solari Swayne (1915–   ), casts a civil engineer as epic hero, struggling to bring about a highway to connect the interior and coastal societies. Another writer who has given much to Peru's theater is Sebastián Salazar Bondy (1924–1965), in addition to his contributions as a writer of essays and poetry. However, there are several independent groups and theatrical companies that seem both willing and capable of carrying Peru's theater into the future. These groups, many of which have participated in the annual festivals such as that initiated by dramatist Sara Joffré, are trying to forge new alliances and funding for future efforts. Ecuador's famed writers of indigenist concerns, Jorge Icaza (1906–1978) and Demetrio Aguilera Malta (1906–1981), both wrote theatrical works with some success. However, they dealt primarily with social concerns of the city, not rural issues. Aguilera Malta's one-act play *El tigre* (The Tiger) (1956) is a well-anthologized exception. José Martínez Queirolo's (1931–   ) *Q.E.P.D.* (R.I.P.) presents the new, urban voice of Ecuadorian theater, critical of society in avant-garde works. Another interesting trend in Ecuador is that of street theater, collectives in the popular vein. Puerto Rico's Luis Rafael Sánchez (1936–   ) wrote *La pasión de Antígona Pérez* (The Passion of Antigona Pérez) in 1968. This and several other works have been successful explorations of societal relationships and are being presented both on the island and in the continental United States. Myrna Casas, director of many outstanding productions, drama professor of the University of Puerto Rico, artistic director of Producciones Cisne (Swan Production), and author of several works, including *La trampa* (The Trap) (1987), is among the most talented and influential playwrights. Also worthy of mention even in so brief a description as this are the Chileans Egon Wolff (1926–   ) and Sergio Vodanovich (1926–   ). Their works include realistic, comic, and symbolic aspects, bringing a high standard of quality to the contemporary stage.

In terms of sheer numbers of outstanding authors, though, Mexico and Argentina have dominated the field. The already mentioned Mexican writer Celestino Gorostiza is in excellent company with Rodolfo Usigli (1905–1979), whose works *El gesticulador* (The Gesturer), subtitled *Una pieza para demagogas* (A Work for Demagogues), and *Corona de sombra* (Crown of Shadows) highlight aspects of present and past society. Emilio Carballido (1925–) is another whose steady output of plays reflects and assesses modern society. Carlos Solórzano (1922–), born in Guatemala, has written several works that connect Mexican society to universal themes. *Las manos de Dios* (The Hands of God) (1957) is an excellent example of these. María Luisa Ocampo (1907–1974) was the first important Mexican woman dramatist of the century, with *Cosas de la vida* (Things of Life) (1926). The most prominent women of the new period—Luisa Josefina Hernández (1928–), Elena Garro (1920–1998), and Sabina Berman (1953–)—have continued not only to provide a woman's view of society but to take on issues of racial, ethnic, and political significance. An overview of feminist history is provided in the serious farce *El eterno femenino* (The Eternal Feminine) (1975) by Rosario Castellanos (1925–1974). A recent compilation (1994) by Kathleen O'Quinn of some 600 Spanish American women playwrights listed thirty-six authors of more than eighty plays, although the number of these that have been performed is considerably less. As elsewhere is the case, there are more Argentinean and Mexican authors in this listing than those from other countries.

Argentina's theater has enjoyed a fairly steady public, a number of prolific authors, and some outstanding literary contributions. The team of Camilo Darthés (1889–1974) and Carlos S. Damel (1890–1959), known simply as Darthés and Damel, provided a steady output of plays until the death of Damel. Germán Rozenmacher (1936–1971), Sergio de Cecco (1931–1986), and Roberto Cossa (1934–) are only a few of the many whose works evolved in the 1960s and 1970s. Griselda Gambaro (1928–) has given the theater a point of view toward a number of difficult themes where women, if they make mistakes, learn from them, and her brand of dark comedy makes for enjoyable theater in an unmistakably contemporary vein. Osvaldo Dragún (1929–) has bridged the gap between modern treatments and classic themes and continues to provide provocative ideas, such as his *El hombre que se volvió perro* (The Man Who Turned into a Dog). There are numerous official and independent theater schools as well as various regional centers of theater, all of which combine to provide many opportunities for new drama. The works of young writers such as Cristina Escofet (*Ritos del corazón*) (Rites of the Heart) (1994) and Carlos Izcovich (*Memorias*) (Memories) (1986) give evidence of the stimulus these have provided.

There are several aspects of recent theater that provide speculation for future directions aside from established commercial and professional serious theater, all based on the opening up of theater over the past thirty years. Elements as diverse as Vatican II, which opened the Church to greater participation, the Peruvian literacy policy, the U.S. hippie movement, and the California Farm Workers Strike all played a part in the broadening of the Spanish American theater. The Argentine Augusto Boal, with the Brazilian educator Paulo Freire, took to the countryside to make participants of the peasants and workers. By raising the consciousness of the spectators, they encouraged the workers to help shape and even participate in the presentations. In most cases, the works presented are based on short stories, folktales, or actual events. In Mexico in 1974, sixty-four Latin American theater groups met to exchange experiences and techniques and present their theatrical works. The Mexican Americans had formed a workers' theater under the direction of Luis Valdez, but the roots of this are the tent theaters (*teatro de carpa*) of lower-class urban areas and of rural Mexico.

Peasant activist theater was represented as well. In one sense, these movements represent a return to roots, but the elements of serious study by university groups as well as political parties have added a dimension that goes far beyond the popular basis. Another group, El Tajo del Alacrán (The Scorpion's Slash), a workers' group in Puerto Rico, routinely took to the streets in the 1960s, and several other groups have carried on in this spirit (Anamú, El Gran Quince). Especially notable is the work of Pedro Santaliz who, from 1978 on, worked with improvisational and workers' theater and continued the efforts with groups in New York. Another aspect of recent theater consists of efforts to reclaim indigenous culture, presenting theatrical works reconstructed or consistent with the cultures and often in the languages of the region. The Sna Jtz'ibajom project, a Tzotzil and Tzeltal nonprofit writers group, has presented theatrical works throughout Chiapas, Mexico, and several other regions. It may be viewed as exemplary of the success and problems of such groups. The participants have been successful, since their inception in 1983, in dramatizing folktales, presenting educational programs that argue for bilingual (Mayan first) schools, and reviving a degree of cultural pride in both the participants and the audiences. Yet the language of presentation is almost always Spanish, the common language of most Mayan-speaking communities. This not only goes against the stated aims of the group, but it often excludes all but the schooled or working men, who have learned Spanish as a second language. Similar efforts in Bolivia, Paraguay, and other areas are under way, with varied results.

At the end of this brief overview of Latin American theater, it is well to remind ourselves of the presence of theater and its role in society as the most public of the literary arts. Poets and novelists write as one individual to another, the reader. Theater, in contrast, is a public spectacle, in which the author, utilizing the talents of one actor or a company of many, writes for an audience. This audience vibrates in sympathy with the actors and their costumes, props, words, nuances, and gestures, sharing the same space. We recognize the authenticity of those works that touch the same vein, which are national in the best sense of the word. The chapters that follow will trace the histories and important elements of each country—authors, works, and movements—thus providing the reader with a sensitivity to the works that may approximate the national sympathy. Many works are outstanding, and many more than are presently known may cross their national cultural boundaries if readers are encouraged to delve more deeply into this rich storehouse.

Philippa Brown Yin

BIBLIOGRAPHY

Allen, Richard F. *Teatro hispanoamericano: una bibliografía anotada.* Boston: G. K. Hall, 1987.

Andrade, Elba, and Hilde F. Cramsie. *Dramaturgas latinoamericanas contemporáneas: antología crítica.* Madrid: Editorial Verbum, 1991.

Arrom, Juan José. *Historia del teatro hispanoamericano.* Mexico City: Ediciones de Andrea, 1967.

Boyle, Catherine M. *Chilean Theatre, 1973–1985: Marginality, Power, Selfhood.* Rutherford, NJ: Fairleigh Dickinson University Press, 1992.

Burguess, Ronald D. *The New Dramatists of Mexico, 1967–1985.* Lexington: University of Kentucky Press, 1991.

Cajiao Salas, Teresa, and Margarita Vargas. "An Overview of Contemporary Latin American Theatre." In *Philosophy and Literature in Latin America: A Critical Assessment of the Current Situation*, ed. Jorge J. E. Garcia and Mireya Camurati. Albany: State University of New York Press, 1989.

Correa, Gustavo, et al. *The Native Theatre in Middle America.* New Orleans: Tulane University Middle American Research Institute, 1961.

Dauster, Frank N. *Historia del teatro hispanoamericano: Siglos XIX y XX.* Mexico City: Ediciones de Andrea, 1966.

Dragún, Osvaldo. *Mesa redonda.* New York: Cinta Video, 1979

Eidelberg, Nora. *Teatro experimental hispanoamericano, 1960–1980: la realidad social como manipulación.* Minneapolis: Institute for the Study of Ideologies and Literature, 1985.

Flores, Yolanda. "The Drama of Gender: Feminist Theater by Women of the Americas." Ph.D. dissertation, Cornell University, Ithaca, NY, 1995.

Foppa, Tito Livio. *Diccionario teatral del Río de la Plata.* Buenos Aires: Ediciones de Carro de Tespis, 1961.

Foster, David William. *The Argentine teatro independiente, 1930–1955.* York, SC: Spanish Literature Publishing Co., 1986.

———. *Handbook of Latin American Literature.* New York: Garland, 1987.

Garzón Céspedes, Francisco, ed. *Recompilación de textos sobre el teatro latinoamericano de creación colectiva.* Havana: Casa de las Américas, 1978.

Gutiérrez, Sonia, ed. *Teatro popular y cambio social en América Latina: panorama de una experiencia.* Costa Rica: Editorial Universitaria Centro Americana, 1979.

Hebblethwaite, Frank P. *A Bibliographical Guide to the Spanish American Theatre.* Washington DC: Pan American Union, 1969.

Hoffman, Herbert H. *Latin American Play Index.* Metuchen, NJ: Scarecrow Press, 1983.

Hulet, Claude, ed. *Brazilian Literature.* 3 vols. Washington, DC: Georgetown University Press, 1974.

Jones, Willis Knapp. *Behind Spanish American Footlights.* Austin: University of Texas Press, 1966.

———. *Breve historia del teatro latinoamericano.* Mexico City: Ediciones de Andrea, 1956.

Kanellos, Nicolás, ed. *Mexican American Theatre: Then and Now.* Houston: Arte Público Press, 1989.

Luzuriaga, Gerardo, ed. *Popular Theatre for Social Change in Latin America.* Los Angeles: Latin American Center Publications UCLA, 1978.

Lyday, Leon F., and George W. Woodyand. *A Bibliography of Latin American Theater Criticism 1940–1974.* Austin: University of Texas Press, 1976.

———. *Dramatists in Revolt: The New Latin American Theater.* Austin: University of Texas Press, 1976.

Mohr, Eugene V. *The Nuyorican Experience: Literature of the Puerto Rican Minority.* Westport, CT: Greenwood Press, 1982.

Neglia, Erminio G., and Luis Ordaz. *Repertorio selecto del teatro hispanoamericano contemporáneo.* Tempe: Arizona State University, 1980.

Ordaz, Luis. *El teatro en el Río de la Plata.* Buenos Aires: Futuro, 1946.

Pellettieri, Osvaldo, ed. *Teatro y teatristas: estudios sobre teatro argentino e iberoamericano*. Buenos Aires: Editorial Galerna, 1992.

Perales, Rosalina. *Teatro hispanoamericano contemporáneo (1967–1987)*. Mexico City: Grupo Editorial Gaceta, 1993.

Pérez, Renard. *Escritores brasileiros contemporâneo; bibliografias, seguidas de antologia*. 2 vols. Rio de Janeiro: Editôra Civilição Brasileira, 1960–1964.

Ramírez, Elizabeth C. *Footlights across the Border: A History of Spanish Language Professional Theatre on the Texas Stage*. New York: Peter Lang, 1990.

Rizk, Beatriz J. *El nuevo teatro latinoamericano: una lectura histórica*. Minneapolis: Prisma Institute, 1987.

Rojas Garcidueñas, José. *El teatro de Nueva España en el siglo XVI*. Mexico City: SepSetentas, 1973.

Skidmore, Thomas E., and Peter H. Smith. *Modern Latin America*. New York: Oxford University Press, 1984.

Solórzano, Carlos. *El teatro latinoamericano en el siglo XX*. Mexico City: Editorial Pormaca, 1969.

Stern, Irwin, ed. *Dictionary of Brazilian Literature*. Westport, CT: Greenwood Press, 1988.

Suárez Radillo, Carlos Miguel. *El teatro barroco hispanoamericano: ensayo de una historia crítico-antológica*. Madrid: José Porrúa Turanzas, 1981.

Tatum, Charles M. *Chicano Literature*. Boston: Twayne, 1982.

Toro, Alfonso de, and Fernando de Toro, eds. *Hacia una nueva crítica y un nuevo teatro latinoamericano*. Frankfurt am Main: Vervuert, 1993.

Trenti Rocamora, José Luis. *El teatro en la América colonial*. Buenos Aires: Huarpes, 1974.

Weiss, Judith, et al. *Latin American Popular Theatre: The First Five Centuries*. Albuquerque: University of New Mexico Press, 1993.

Woodyard, George W., and Leon F. Lyday. "Studies on Latin American Theatre, 1960–69." *Theatre Documentation* 2 (1969–1970): 49–84.

Argentina

The theater of Argentina originated when the colonial communities of Buenos Aires contrived stages and open-air theaters to celebrate patron saints. The River Plate region regularly executed religious theatrical performances, with dates of presentations dating to 1610. The first manifestations of a secular theater in colonial Argentina are political satires. The first Argentine-born dramatist to be recorded by name was Antonio Fuentes del Arco. This writer of dialogue wrote and performed a *loa* in his native city of Santa Fe in gratitude to Philip V, who had just abolished a shipping tax on tea that profited Santa Fe.

The first permanent theatrical structure to be documented was founded in Buenos Aires by Pedro Aguilar and Domingo Sacomano in 1757. The second was established either in 1778 or 1783 and was called the Teatro de Ranchería. The edifice burned to the ground when its thatched roof caught fire on August 16, 1792. After the destruction of the Ranchería, no theatrical structure existed between 1792 and 1804. The Ranchería had spawned a love of the theater; thus performances continued to be given on makeshift stages. It is believed that the oldest antecedent of the gaucho theater, *El amor de la estanciera* (The Love of the Rancher), was performed on such a stage. A temporary theater was constructed in Buenos Aires in 1804 called the Coliseo Provisional de Comedias. The Coliseo Chico, as it was called (later, in 1828, the theater's name was changed to the Teatro argentino), marked its opening with *Zafira*, the Spanish interpretation of Voltaire's *Zaire*. The city's only theater was the focus of social events until the British invaded in 1806. On May 25, 1812, the temporary Coliseo was revamped and reopened with *El 25 de Mayo* (May 25), by Luis Ambrosio Morante (1775–1837), a Peruvian mestizo. Despite being written by a nonnative, the play is viewed as Argentine for its recreation of a historical event and patriotic theme.

The colonial period in the River Plate region created the foundation for a national Argentine theater. The roots of the gaucho theater and one-act *criollo* plays were established during this time. The construction of theatrical edifices in Buenos Aires gave the region exposure to European works by playwrights such as Calderón, Sotomayor, Goldoni, and Voltaire and the opportunity for the presentation of works by regional artists about and for Argentines to present.

The theater at the beginning of the nineteenth century in Argentina reflects the struggle for national independence and the resulting political dissension. Titles such as *La defensa y triunfo de Tucumán* (The Defense and the Triumph of Tucumán) and *El hipócrito político* (The Political Hypocrite) mirror the political situation. An important milestone of the times was the formation of a group called La Sociedad del Buen Gusto del Teatro (The Society of Good Theatrical Taste), which appeared around 1817. The goal of the society was to inspire the formation of a national theater. The ensuing patriotic works are a direct result of the group's effort toward reformation.

The nineteenth century is considered to be one of anarchy in Argentine history due to internal disorganization and civil discord. The theater undergoes a crisis due to the political situation and the appearance of the opera. The old Coliseo Provisional becomes an opera house until 1831, after which no opera is performed until 1848. During this time an important precursor to the gaucho theater appeared. The anonymous *sainete Las bodas de Chivico y Pancha* (The Wedding of Chivico and Pancha) (1826) resembles the primitive gaucho play *El amor de la estanciera* (The Love of the Rancher) for its wedding and details of the nuptial feast. Most important, the play continues the gaucho theme that will culminate with *Juan Moreira* toward the end of the nineteenth century.

The next phase in the history of Argentine theater is marked by the political period called the Rosas Era, which refers to the time of domination by Juan Manuel Rosas (1793–1877) between 1835 and 1852. The Argentine people were politically divided, and the atmosphere was one of conflict and violent oppression. The theater experienced a rise in the number of spectators, and theatrical activity remained uninterrupted for the following twenty-five years. In fact, the theater became big business and endured many conflicts among the organizers, actors, and other employees. Although there was an increase in attendance, there was a decrease in the quality of productions between 1829 and 1852.

Coinciding with the Rosas Era was the Romantic movement, introduced to the region by Esteban Echeverría. He inspired the youth to form literary groups, such as the Asociación de Mayo (1837), which met periodically. Around 1838, the political situation reached a critical point, and the followers of Romanticism, militant by nature, forced themselves into exile. Consequently, the formation of Argentine Romanticism occurs in places such as Uruguay, Chile, and Bolivia, countries where the Romantics migrated. Among the exiled were José Mármol, Juan B. Alberdi, Pedro Echagüe, and Bartolomé Mitre. In the meantime, the theater in Buenos Aires consisted mainly of the presentation of French and Spanish Romantic plays. There was little national theater under the dictatorship of Juan Manuel de Rosas. The few original plays that were performed dealt with European themes and lacked local language and color.

After the defeat of Rosas by Justo José de Urquiza at the Battle of Montecaseros in 1852, the country begins a period of reorganization that ultimately leads to national unity. Most ex-patriots returned to Argentina, but the national theater remained dormant, and foreign plays, performed by European companies, dominated the stage. Still, there was a desire for original Argentine works that received strong journalistic support when they appeared. Groups formed with the intention of protecting the national theater. The *Sociedad Protectora del Teatro Nacional*, founded in 1877, valued vernacular works such as *Solané*, a precursor to the Gaucho Theater.

Even so, the period between 1852 and 1884 is one of scarce local productions in the theaters of Buenos Aires. When a local play was staged, it was performed by Spanish companies or in Italian or French translations. However, the appearance of societies which called for a national theater indicated that theatrical growth was imminent. The end of the nineteenth century is distinctly marked by various types of vernacular theater, such as the gaucho theater and the national *sainete*. By the beginning of the twentieth century, the Argentine theater is finally thriving and expanding its horizons.

THE GAUCHO THEATER

The gaucho theater brings to the stage a character emblematic of the Argentine pampas: the gaucho. He is a historical and legendary figure in the Argentine nation. Always portrayed as a courageous defender of the cause, the gaucho suffered social prejudices and was forced to take refuge in new frontiers. His figure is simultaneously historical and legendary and he is embodied by characters such as Martín Fierro and Juan Moreira. The gaucho theater is preceded by plays such as *El amor de la estanciera, El detalle de la acción de Maipú, Las bodas de Chivico y Pancha*, and *Solané*. The gaucho theme culminates with works such as *Juan Moreira*, by Eduardo Gutiérrez (1851–1889), which first appeared as an insert in the daily paper *La patria argentina*. José J. Podestá (1858–1937), a famous clown also known as "Pepino el 88," portrayed the character through mime in 1884. The circus act was so successful that Gutiérrez later dramatized his own work in 1886. The work is considered by some critics to mark the beginning of Argentine drama. The story is about a valiant gaucho and his confrontations with his overseer and the police. The character's popularity among each class within Argentine society makes the play exemplary of a national theater.

Many gaucho plays emerged after the appearance of *Juan Moreira*. The cycle of the gaucho plays closes with the presentation of *Calandria* (1896), by Martiniano Leguizamón (1858–1935). The play focuses on a valiant and honorable gaucho and lacks the violence between the gaucho and police, typical of the gaucho theater. *Calandria* changes the image of the Argentine gaucho from idle vagabond to industrious worker, giving the vernacular theater a sense of optimism with the presentation of such a positive character.

THE NATIONAL *SAINETE*

The period between 1880 and 1930 brought to Buenos Aires millions of immigrants. The mixture of language, dialects, and culture began to be captured in *sainetes*, or one-act comedies, which attained an enormous popularity among spectators. Influenced by the popular Spanish genre called *género chico*, the *sainete* humorously exposes types living in the eclectic society of Buenos Aires. Writers of short musical comedies in the last decade of the nineteenth century are considered precursors of the theatrical phenomenon known as the *sainete criollo* or *sainete porteño*. López de Gomara (1859–1923), Emilio de Onrubia (1849–1907), Ezequiel Soria (1873–1936), Nemesio Trejo (1862–1916), and Enrique García Velloso (1880–1938) are among the most noteworthy pioneers of the genre. In 1918, José González Castillo (1885–1937) and Alberto T. Weisbach (1883–1929) presented *Los dientes del perro* (The Dog's Teeth), a *sainete* that included the tango *Mi noche triste* (My Sad Night). The production was so successful and continuously performed that it influenced other plays of the genre to include the tango. Thus, the *sainete porteño*, or one-act farce from the Rio Plate region, and the tango were born simultaneously in an age of migration to the area. The tango eventually separated from the theater and became an autonomous musical sensation.

The *sainete porteño* continued to follow two distinct lines of development: the purely comical, which was a reaction against the Spanish *género chico*, and the more traditional, which focused on dramatic content while maintaining zany characters. Among the playwrights from the first category are José González Castillo (1885–1937), Roberto Lino Cayol (1887–1927), and Roberto J. Payró (1867–1928). Following the more dramatic Spanish style are Enrique García Velloso (1880–1938), Florencio Sánchez (1875–1910), and Carlos Mauricio Pacheco (1881–1924). Finally, a third type of *sainete* appeared that joined the primitive *zarzuela criolla* (comic opera) and the dramatic *sainete*. Master of the style was Alberto Vacarezza (1888–1959), who played with names and sounds in order to distort daily language and produce a comic effect. The *sainete*, in all its forms, was probably the most popular genre among the immigrant population of Buenos Aires and lasted until 1930, when the Argentine theater began to reflect the destruction of national unity.

THE TWENTIETH CENTURY

The beginning of the twentieth century is known as the Golden Age of Argentine theater because theatrical performances captured the new social ideas expressed by intellectuals. Playwrights such as Roberto J. Payró and Florencio Sánchez present the conflicts and the struggle between the social classes. Another prolific playwright of the decade is David Peña, who is known for being the initiator of the historic Argentine theater, which disappeared with his death.

The gaucho theater and the urban theater are synthesized in the plays of Florencio Sánchez, who expressed his political and social criticism in *Barranca abajo* (The Gorge Below) (1905). Of Uruguayan origin, he and other compatriots living in Argentina enriched the theaters of Buenos Aires with their depictions of urban life. The Golden Age includes the success of the provincial comedy and the rural theater. Plays such as *La flor del trigo* (The Wheat Flower) (1908), by José de Maturana (1884–1917), and *Las campanas* (The Bells) (1908), by Julio Sánchez Gardel (1879–1937), are regional works that focus on the customs and hardships of provincial areas. Most of the regional plays were written and produced in the capital of Buenos Aires. Among the few playwrights who remained in the provinces was Julio Carri Pérez, whose many plays presented in his native Córdoba include *Tierra firme* (Firm Ground) (1913).

The prosperous period between 1910 and 1930 produced a national theater that successfully portrayed all aspects of Argentine life. The presentation of the different social types such as the gaucho, women, ranchers, and the middle and upper classes made the theater in Buenos Aires extremely prolific. The popularity of the theater, however, begins to decline after World War I (1914–1918). Around the year 1930 the political, social, and economic systems of Argentina began to deteriorate. The result is a period of creative decadence and negativity toward the theater that lasts until the middle of the century. The spectators had already began to abandon the theater during World War I. Later, the theater could not survive an era of political upheaval that presented the first radical government, the persecution of the lower classes, and a strong rift among intellectuals.

The *teatro por horas*, or hourly plays, renewed the popularity of the one-act farce. The quantity of plays outweighed the quality, as productions were taken over by *capocómicos* (leading comics). *Cabarets*, or musicals, were rapidly multiplying as a direct result of the orchestrated *sainete*. Also popular were plays that imitated Alberto Vacarezza's style of linguistic contortion and character satirization. The segmented theatrical performance, based on short plays and the *sainete*, eventually disappeared and was replaced with the more unified play, which consisted of three or four acts. Even so, the theater continued to lose spectators as the cinema and sporting events increased in popularity. Those dedicated to the theater formed independent companies committed to reviving the prestige the theater once enjoyed.

The decline in the theater's popularity did not stop the productivity of the many traditional and innovative playwrights active between 1910 and 1949. The supporters of the national drama include Ricardo Rojas, Paul Groussac, and Alejandro Berruti. Among the innovators of the theater are Roberto Arlt and Bernardo Canal Feijóo. Also representative of the experimental wave are three authors whose originality made them renowned: Francisco Defilippis Novoa, influenced by German expressionism; Samuel Eichelbaum, a fanatic of introspection; and Armando Discépolo, who was influenced by Luigi Pirandello and created a style identified as *grotesco criollo*. The period between 1910 and 1949 was also a collaborative one among playwrights. The team of Nicolás de las Llanderas and Arnaldo Malfatti produced numerous popular comedies. Another duo, Camilo Darthés and Carlos Damel, created enjoyable comedies by combining popular themes about love and marriage with an elevated artistic style.

The years between 1940 and 1955 continued to be ones of deterioration in the quantity and quality of theatrical productions. Theaters were converted to cinemas, and many playwrights turned to writing scripts for the screen. Many companies left to seek fame in the great theatrical capitals of New York, London, and Paris. Those still involved in the theater were forced to accommodate the few surviving theatrical companies and a public debauched by the war, the cinema, and thirty years of theatrical decadence. Poets such as Conrado Nalé Roxlo and Juan Oscar Ponferrada turned their interests to the stage and offered some attention to the deplorable state of the theater. Finally, in 1949, at the independent theater La Máscara, hope for revitalization was found in Carlos Gorostiza. The young playwright used the postwar Italian cinematic technique of "neorealism" in *El puente* (The Bridge). Although Gorostiza's play was successful, the theatrical crisis continued, paralleling the political and social conflicts that afflicted Argentina until 1955.

By the beginning of the 1950s, the independent theaters had formed as a reaction against commercialism and political control of the popular theater. Plays such as Palant's *El cerco* (The Hoop) were performed by amateur companies. The independent theater matured between 1950 and 1955 and established new theatrical standards. Playwrights of the midcentury theater captured the agitated political atmosphere by presenting plays that incorporated definite social criticism. Among the most notable authors dedicated to the cause were Agustín Cuzzani (1924–1987), Osvaldo Dragún (1929–), and Andrés Lizarraga (1919–1982). The political instability of the 1950s peaked with the revolution of 1955, which ended the political regime of Juan Domingo Perón (1895–1974), who had been in power since 1943. The sensation of newly found freedom among intellectuals gave hope that, culturally, Argentina would enter a period of growth, even though politically and economically the country regressed to the same postrevolutionary state it experienced in 1930.

By 1956 the independent theaters were extinct, thus marking the end of a twenty-six-year period of intense creativity on the Argentine stage. However, the spirit of these theaters is carried into the next generation with the emergence of Osvaldo Dragún and the premiere of his first play *La peste viene de Melos* (The Plague Comes from Melos) (1956). In the remaining years of the 1950s, Argentine realism continued to develop in the works of authors such as Juan Carlos Ghiano, Juan Carlos Ferrari, Agustín Cuzzani, and Andrés Lizarraga. These writers were the precursors of the fully evolved realism that would emerge in the following decade.

The 1960s were one of the most productive periods in the history of Argentine theater. They are marked by the appearance of renovated forms of realism, along with the simultaneous development of a powerful avant-garde movement. It was Ricardo Halac's *Soledad para cuatro* (Solitude for Four) that initiated this second adaptation of Argentine realism in 1961. His works, along with those of Roberto Cossa, best represent the tendencies of this period. Roberto Cossa is one of the central figures in contemporary Argentine theater. *El avión negro* (The Black Plane) (1970), a collaboration between Roberto Cossa, Carlos Somigliana, Ricardo Talesnik, and Germán Rozenmacher, proved to be a pivotal work in the new realist trajectory in that it was the first to fuse realism with other aesthetic impulses emerging at the time. This play provoked what Pellettieri has termed *critical realism*, which was fully embodied in Halac's *Segundo tiempo* (Second Period) (1976). This current continued throughout the 1970s, with other outstanding applications being Cossa's *La nona* (The Grandmother) (1977) and Halac's *El destete* (The Weaning) (1978).

The main difference between the realism ignited by the generation of 1960s dramatists and that of others was the influence of North American realism, most notably that of Arthur Miller, along with the theater of Chekhov and Stanislavski. The Argentine theater of this period differs from that of other Latin American countries in that it was not significantly molded by Brechtian theories. With the exception of Dragún's *Historias para ser contadas* (1957), there were no outstanding manifestations of the epic theater until the appearance of Ricardo Monti in the 1970s. The national influences that shaped the theater of this important decade were the aforementioned *grotesco criollo*, the naturalism of Florencio Sánchez, and the techniques of Roberto Arlt. Common thematic elements of the works included a dwelling on the past and not the future, frustration, society's influence on the life of man, and an absence of love. The main characters were antiheroes—failures in their attempts to set and achieve goals and therefore unable to improve their lot in life. The language, as in the traditional forms of realism, portrayed the dialects of the personages encountered in the plays.

The formation of an avant-garde movement rejected anything pertaining to realism and strove to invent a more innovative approach to drama. Imaginative ideas propelled the Argentine theater away from the long-standing realism and into a new revolutionary era. The birth of this movement can be traced to the opening of the Centro Experimental Audiovisual Instituto Torcuato Di Tella in Buenos Aires in 1958. Its patrons were strictly dedicated to theatrical experimentation and were always searching for ways to revitalize the theater. They somehow managed to circumvent the censure imposed by the Peronist government and thrived thirteen years until government officials forced them to close in 1971. Today the center is recognized as a major force in the evolution of the Argentine theater. The most outstanding dramatist associated with the Instituto Di Tella was Griselda Gambaro. From *El desatino* (The Folly) (1966) to *Penas sin importancia* (Unimportant Sorrows) (1990), she has consistently employed experimental techniques, making her theater, according to an array of critics, one of the most important, not only in Argentina but in Latin America as well.

Another critical figure in the development of this experimental theater was Eduardo

Pavlovsky, who founded the Grupo Yenesí in 1961. Theater experts agree that his work is similar to that of Gambaro's and that it also played a critical role in the formation and maintenance of the Argentine avant-garde. As with many Argentine plays of this period, both Pavlovsky's and Gambaro's serve as protests of the Argentine situation and that of all of Latin America as well. They depict unyielding dictators and governments, which are often symbolized but certainly never mentioned by name; acts of torture, kidnapping, murders, and rapes; and a myriad of unmentionable acts that transpired during these turbulent times in Latin American history.

Although the experimental theater flourished in the 1960s, it lost impetus in the 1970s with the closing of the independent theaters, the most important being the Nuevo Teatro and the Instituto Di Tella. This had a profound effect on the composition of Argentine drama since the theaters had served as a unifying force of the avant-garde movement of the previous decade. The playwrights of the early 1970s preferred to work independently and did not generate any specific theatrical movement during this period. There was a noticeable increase in street productions and in the use of nonconventional spaces, such as warehouses and churches, for theater activities. Also noted is an increased predilection for national themes. This is patent in the previously mentioned *El avión negro*, a transitional work, which for the first time deals openly with Peronism. Humor is the literary device of choice. Although there are several dramatists that merit acknowledgment, Alberto Adellach (1933–), Guillermo Gentile (1943–), and Ricardo Monti (1944–), are the most outstanding to emerge during the first half of the 1970s, with the contributions of Monti being the most significant.

The latter half of the 1970s saw the rise of the new dictatorship, which had an adverse effect on the theater. The gravity of the political and economical condition of the country caused such despair that theatrical production was greatly curtailed by Argentine standards. In fact, it was so unbearable for many theater professionals and writers that they felt it necessary to leave the country. Public attendance to performances was also extremely low. The dramatists that stayed behind to brave what historians have designated as the worst Argentine dictatorship of the twentieth century were known as *la generación fracturada* (the broken generation).

A sudden thematical shift brought on by the change in the political status quo, coupled with the incorporation of new technical influences, warrants the labeling of this mid-decade trend in the Argentine theater. In the ten years preceding the dictatorship, a variety of themes are explored. Generational conflicts are seen in Diana Raznovich's *Buscapiés*; family relationships, investigated in Sergio de Cecco's *El gran deschave* (The Great Fight) (1975); torture, which is most outstanding in Pavlovsky's *El señor Galíndez* (Mr. Galíndez) (1973); and manifestations of violence, prevalent in the works of several leading dramatists such as Gambaro, Pavlovsky, and Monti. The last two themes, which are controversial by nature, were often treated in a global manner, criticizing totalitarian practices in general. There was no direct mention of the latest wave of political violence in Argentina, but given the unrest that had been growing in the country since it yet again fell under complete military control in 1966, the true motivation behind these gruesome works is readily deciphered. Random tortures and executions grew to astronomic proportions around 1970, as both the Right and the Left participated in this destructive behavior. Unfortunately, this was only a dress rehearsal for the full-blown *proceso militar* that would begin in just a few short years.

After a brief reinstatement of Peronism from 1973 to 1976, the military returned again full force. This signaled the eruption of the infamous "Dirty War," in which the government at will began to arrest people they considered to be subversives. Playwrights became more restrained with their subject matter, as they were intellectually paralyzed by this government. The presentation of certain works—for example, Roma Mahieu's *Fuegos a la hora de siesta* (Fires at Siesta Time) and Pavlovsky's *Telarañas* (Cobwebs) (1977)—was prohibited. Some theaters were either closed or burned down (Picadero), and there were writers who were tortured, kidnapped, or murdered (Paco Urondo, Juan Gelman, Rodolfo Walsh). As is common in times of stringent censorship, the authors were forced to conceal their messages in metaphors and other creative manipulations of language. Also popular was a more psychological approach to the theater, which focused on behavioral analysis rather than social protest.

A problem that surfaced for theater scholars during this period was a lack of publications and articles pertaining to Argentine creations and productions. A technical shift is also noted during this period. The playwright and his play are no longer considered to be the center of the theatrical universe. The new focus is on the total development of the actor, the director, and the production itself. The manifestation of this trend in Argentina can be traced to three major figures, Eugenio Barba, Tadeusz Kantor, and Dario Fo, all of whom subscribed in one way or another to this holistic approach to the theater.

The influence of these theatrical personalities continued on into the 1980s due to their direct involvement in Argentine theater circles. In 1984, Fo directed two of his own plays, *Tutta casa, letto e chiesa* (All House, Bed and Church) and *Mistero buffo* (Comic Mystery), in the Teatro Municipal General San Martín. Kantor also paid a visit in September of the same year, presenting *Wielopole, wielopole* with his theater group Cricot II. There were no significant thematical changes in the Argentine theater until the fall of the dictatorship in 1983. With the rise of democracy came a great sense of liberation among artists. The most prevalent topic was the issue of the disappeared. Playwrights from every generation contributed works that dealt with this subject. Some of the most outstanding include Luis Arata's *Variaciones sobre un desayuno* (Variations over Breakfast) (1982), Halac's *Lejana tierra prometida* (The Far, Promised Land) (1981), and Gambaro's *Antígona furiosa* (Furious Antigone) (1988). The war in the Falkland Islands, which ultimately led to the final disintegration of the dictatorship, is encompassed in Gambaro's *Del sol naciente* (The Rising Sun) (1984) and Horacio del Prado's *Retaguardia* (1985). Some works, such as Germán González Arquati's *El fondo* (The Bottom) (1983), Milea's *Benemérita institución* (The Institution Benemérita) (1983), María José Campoamor's *008 se va con la murga* (008 Leaves with the Lees) (1984), and Carlos Izcovich's *Memorias* (Memories) (1986), deal directly with the dictatorship itself. Other related topics such as the kidnapping of children, torture, violence, and repression surfaced in the works of the time and were notably bolder than those of the previous era. However, these themes were quickly exhausted as both authors and the public became traumatized by the constant reliving of the tragedy. Much like post–Civil War Spain, many compatriots preferred to deny what had happened, and theatergoers sought refuge in the frivolity of commercial productions.

Aside from this thematical crisis, the 1980s were otherwise productive in Argentina, as old theatrical systems continued to thrive and new movements emerged. Since the 1950s, a constant stratification of theatrical trends had taken place. More specifically, leading dramatists of previous decades, as well as an array of actors and directors, were still active into the 1980s and even into the 1990s. As a result, a powerful substructure, derived from this accumulation and synthesis of styles, existed during the past decade, directly contributing to the strength and vigor of the Argentine theater.

Directly linked to this subsystem and its members was the establishment of the Teatro Abierto in 1981, a theatrical phenomenon whose main purpose was to covertly, yet overtly, question those in power. Although their criticisms were camouflaged in metaphors, they were easily deciphered by a receptive public who was experiencing the same gruesome reality. Although its success has been perceived by some critics as questionable at best, it is considered to be the culminating act of the generation in question. In its subsequent seasons, it also served as a forum for the introduction of a new generation of dramatists (Franco Franchi, Aarón Korz, Rodolfo Paganini, Gerardo Taratuto, Manual Cruz). Both the old and the new banded together with the public in opposition to the *proceso*. Its origin can be credited to Osvaldo Dragún, Agustín Cuzzani, and Patricio Esteve. They collected twenty-one works, all specifically written for the 1981 premiere of the Teatro Abierto. Some of the most outstanding were Halac's *Lejana tierra prometida*, Monti's *La cortina de abalorios* (The Beaded Curtain), Gambaro's *Decir sí* (To Say Yes), Pavlovsky's *Tercero incluído* (The Third Included), Cossa's *Gris de ausencia* (Grey Absence), and Dragún's *Mi obelisco y yo* (My Obelisk and I).

Teatro Abierto 1982 was not as successful as the previous year, although some stimulating works appeared on the program, such as *El oficial primero* (The First Official), by Carlos Somigliana. Teatro Abierto 1983 and 1984 proved to be even more difficult, and by the end of the 1986 season, it was no longer in existence. The main reason for its decline, according to many critics, was not organizational but political in nature. With the arrival of the new democracy, the Teatro Abierto had lost its reason for being. The greatest accomplishment of the festivals was to lurch theatergoers and dramatists out of their vegetative states that had been induced by the dictatorship. It proved that the Argentine theater and its public were still vital and ready to progress into the 1980s.

In 1985 a transition between the old and the new is noted in the works of Alberto Félix Alberto, Eduardo Rovner, and Mauricio Kartun. The main focus of their works lies within the images that they create. This presages a shift to the perception of a dramatic work as an art form, which does indeed occur in the final years of the decade. From 1987 on, a radical change is finally noted. Pellettieri has identified three individual tendencies that surfaced within the emergent subsystem: the theater of resistance; the new *sainete*; and the theater of parody and questioning (1994, 49). The common denominator between the three is the propensity for the use of parody and an intentional distancing from former models and styles. Some theater critics have erroneously identified this new generation as the *teatro joven*. Those involved in this theater are between the ages of twenty and thirty and are members of new theatrical groups such as El Clú del Claun, Los Macocos, Grupo Teatro Dorrego, Gambas al Ajillo, La Banda de la Risa, Los Melli, and La Organización Negra.

Thematically they are grounded to the conflicts and issues current in their society, as is any generation. The confrontation of feminism, "el machismo," and homosexuality have been popular topics. In contention with the traditional goals of the Argentine theater, this group finds itself in search of an artistic identity, as opposed to one that is defined by that which is Argentine. The originality of this system lies in its rejection of all formal theatrical structures, including the dramatic text itself. A resurgence of the Commedia dell'arte is noted, which greatly contrasts with the more formally structured theater of past decades. Although they have not completely abandoned the concept of the text, it is common to intersperse improvisations with prewritten dialogues or concepts. It is a comical theater that employs techniques used by clowns and may incorporate puppets or games. Another structural aspect that is unique is the hybridization of the genre with other disciplines, producing such combinations as dance theater, rock theater, video theater, and recital theater. Although at this moment it is too early to assess the impact that this emergent group has had on the Argentine theater, it can be observed that it has been extremely active and will no doubt leave its impression in the 1990s.

Through this examination of the trajectory of Argentine theater of the past few decades, it is evident that many of the changes have been more subtle than monumental and at times rather difficult to detect. Although the critics have painstakingly divided plays and dramatists into movements and generations, the fact is that a major transition in Argentine drama has not occurred since the 1960s, with the birth of the avant-garde. Furthermore, a number of the playwrights, Osvaldo Dragún, for example, were neither technically nor thematically compromised and preferred to adopt a more eclectic style. This is not to say that the plays emerging from Argentina were not of an extremely high quality. The country's status in the contemporary theater world confirms the creativity and originality of the works. Since the 1960s, traditional Argentine forms, such as realism and the *grotesco criollo*, have been present in some capacity in the theater, albeit modernized or synthesized with other styles. Gradually, the ideological struggle between the realism of this decade with the avant-garde was resolved, and toward the 1980s the two forms were frequently united in the same works. Instead of producing major trends, there was a constant meshing of the aforementioned Argentine forms with anything coming from the United States and Europe, which resulted in the consistent elaboration of original combinations that were considered to be revolutionary.

Regarding staging techniques, the most significant innovation to emerge has been the use of cinematographic techniques. In the history of the Argentine theater, this is first mentioned around 1970, with the appearance of Oscar Viale, who is considered to be a transitional dramatist bridging the 1960s and 1970s. Thematically, regardless of style and technique, the most prevalent theme of the past thirty-five years has been the quest to demythologize Argentine history. It has been a major preoccupation of dramatists who have relied on a variety of devices, such as metaphor, symbolism, or allegory, to accomplish this goal. As the 1990s unfolded, the Argentine theater continued to dominate the Latin American stage and there is no doubt its importance will carry on into the new millennium.

BIBLIOGRAPHY

Allen, Richard F. *Teatro hispanoamericano: una bibliografía anotada.* Boston: G. K. Hall, 1987.

Aloisi, Enzo. "Argentines Behind the Footlights: 20 Years of Independent Theaters." *Américas* 4 (1952): 21–23, 44–45.

Arancibia, Juana, and Zulema Mirkin, eds. *Teatro argentino durante el proceso (1976–1983).* Buenos Aires: Vinciguerra, 1992.

"Argentina." *Escenarios de dos mundos: inventario teatral de Iberoamérica.* Vol. 1. Madrid: Centro de Documentación Teatral, 1988, 123–197. Articles by scholars.

Arlt, Mirta. "Los '80—Gambaro-Monti—y más allá." *Latin American Theatre Review* 24.2 (Spring 1991): 49–58.

Beringuer Carisomo, Arturo. *Teatro argentino contemporáneo.* Madrid: Aguilar, 1960.

Bosch, Mariano G. *Historia de los orígenes del teatro nacional argentino y la época de Pablo Podestá.* Buenos Aires: Solar-Hachette, 1969.

Carella, Tulio. *El sainete criollo.* Buenos Aires: Hachette, 1957.

Carreira, André. "Teatro callejero en la ciudad de Buenos Aires después de la dictadura militar." *Latin American Theatre Review* 27.2 (Spring 1994): 103–131.

Castagnino, Raúl Héctor. *Literatura dramática argentina (1717–1967).* Buenos Aires: Pleamar, 1968.

———. *Sociología del teatro argentino.* Buenos Aires: Nova, 1963.

———. *Teatro argentino premoreirista (1600–1884).* Buenos Aires: Plus Ultra, 1969.

Cosentino, Olga. "El teatro de los años '70: una dramaturgia sitiada." *Latin American Theatre Review* 24.2 (Spring 1991): 31–39.

Dubatti, Jorge A. *Así se mira el teatro hoy.* Buenos Aires: Beas, 1994.

———. *El nuevo teatro de Buenos Aires en la postdictadura (1983–2001).* Buenos Aires: ATAUEL, 2002.

———. "Teatro abierto después de 1981." *Latin American Theatre Review* 24.2 (Spring 1991): 79–86.

Echagüe, Juan Pablo. *Teatro argentino.* Madrid: América, 1917.

Esteve, Patricio. "1980–1981 La prehistoria de teatro abierto." *Latin American Theatre Review* 24.2 (Spring 1991): 79–86.

Foppa, Tito Livio. *Diccionario teatral del Río de la Plata.* Buenos Aires: Carro de Tespis, 1961.

Foster, David William. *The Argentine Teatro Independiente, 1930–1955.* York, SC: Spanish Literature Publishing Co., 1986.

———. *Cultural Diversity in Latin American Literature.* Albuquerque: University of New Mexico Press, 1994.

———. "Krinsky de Jorge Goldenburg y la identidad étnica argentina." *Latin American Theatre Review* 24.2 (Spring 1991): 101–105.

Gallo, Blas Raúl. *Historia del sainete nacional.* Buenos Aires: Quetzal, 1958.

Ghiano, Juan Carlos. *Teatro argentino contemporáneo, 1949–1969.* Madrid: Aguilar, 1973.

———. *Teatro gauchesco primitivo.* Buenos Aires: Ediciones Losange, 1957.

Giella, Miguel Angel. "Teatro abierto 1981: de la desilusión a la alineación." *Latin American Theatre Review* 24.2 (Spring 1991): 101–105.

Giordano, Enrique. *La teatralización de la obra dramática: de Florencio Sánchez a Roberto Arlt.* Mexico City: Premia, 1982.

Javier, Francisco. "El teatro argentino, 1977–1983." *Latin American Theatre Review* 18.1 (Fall 1984): 113–115.

Jones, Willis Knapp. *Behind Spanish American Footlights.* Austin: University of Texas Press, 1966.

Kartun, Mauricio, and Osvaldo Pellettieri. *Teatro.* Buenos Aires: Ediciones Corregidor, 1999.

Neglia, Erminio G., and Luis Ordaz. *Repertorio selecto del teatro hispanoamericano contemporáneo.* Tempe: Arizona State University, Center for Latin American Studies, 1980.

Ordaz, Luis. *Aproximación a la travectoria de la dramática argentina*. Ottawa: Girol Books, 1992.

———. "Autores del nuevo realismo de los años '60 a lo largo de las tres últimas décadas." *Latin American Theatre Review* 24.2 (Spring 1991): 41–48.

———. *El teatro en el Río de la Plata*. Buenos Aires: Futuro, 1946.

Orgambide, Pedro, and Roberto Yahni, eds. *Enciclopedia de la literatura argentina*. Buenos Aires: Sudamericana, 1970.

Pagella, Angela Blanco Amores de. *Iniciadores del teatro argentino*. Buenos Aires: Ediciones Culturales Argentinas, 1972.

Paz, Marta Lena. *Proyecciones del teatro argentino en el fin del milenio*. Buenos Aires: Nueva Generación, 1999.

Pellettieri, Osvaldo. *Cien años del teatro argentino (1886–1990)*. Buenos Aires: Galerna, 1990.

———. "La puesta en escena argentina de los '80: realismo, estilización y parodia." *Latin American Theatre Review* 24.2 (Spring 1991): 117–131.

———. *Teatro argentino contemporáneo (1980–1990): crisis, transición y cambio*. Buenos Aires: Editorial Galerna, 1994.

———. *Teatro argentino de los '60: Polémica, continuidad y ruptura*. Buenos Aires: Corregidor, 1989.

———. "Teatro argentino (1980–1990)." *Latin American Theatre Review* 24.2 (Spring 1991): 9–12.

———, ed. *Teatro y teatristas: estudios sobre teatro iberoamericano y argentino*. Buenos Aires: Editorial Galerna, 1992.

Perales, Rosalina. *Teatro hispanoamericano contemporáneo (1976–1987)*. Mexico City: Grupo Editorial Gaceta, 1993.

Perinelli, Roberto. "La Escuela Municipal de Arte Dramático de Buenos Aires y su experiencia educativa (1984–1990)." *Latin American Theatre Review* 27.1 (Fall 1993): 15–21.

Podesta, Guido A. "La reescritura de la política en el teatro argentino." *Latin American Theatre Review* 25.1 (Fall 1991): 7–19.

Roster, Peter. "Generational Transitions in Argentina: From Fray Mocho to Teatro Abierto (1956–1985)." *Latin American Theatre Review* 25.1 (Fall 1991): 21–40.

———. "Impresiones de un investigador gringo en Buenos Aires." *Latin American Theatre Review* 24.2 (Spring 1991): 133–142.

Rovner, Eduardo. "Relaciones entre lo sucedido en la década y las nuevas tendencias teatrales." *Latin American Theatre Review* 24.2 (Spring 1991): 23–29.

Schanzer, George. *El teatro de Eduardo Pavlosky*. Buenos Aires: Ediciones Búsqueda, 1981.

Seibel, Beatriz. *Historia del teatro argentino: desde Los rituales hasta 1930*. Buenos Aires: Corregidor, 2002.

Seone, Ana. "Reportajes: Roberto Cossa, Alejandro Boero y Ricardo Bartis." *Latin American Theatre Review* 24.2 (Spring 1991): 107–115.

Skidmore, Thomas E., and Peter H. Smith. *Modern Latin America*. New York: Oxford University Press, 1984.

Toro, Fernando de. "El teatro argentino actual: entre la modernidad y la tradición." *Latin American Theatre Review* 24.2 (Spring 1981): 87–91.

Trastoy, Beatriz. "Entorno a la renovación teatral argentina de los años '80." *Latin American Theatre Review* 24.2 (Spring 1991): 93–100.

Tschudi, Lilian. *Teatro argentino actual (1960–1972)*. Buenos Aires: Fernando García Cambeiro, 1974.

Vázquez, Enrique. *La última: origen, apogeo y caída de la dictadura militar*. Buenos Aires: Eudeba, 1985.

Viñas, David. *Teatro rioplatense (1886–1930)*. Caracas: Biblioteca Ayacucho, 1977.

Zayas de Lima, Perla. *Diccionario de autores teatrales argentinos (1950–1980)*. Buenos Aires: Editorial Rodolfo Alonso, 1981.

———. *Diccionario de autores teatrales argentinos (1950–1990)*. Buenos Aires: Galerna, 1991.

♦

ADELLACH, Alberto (1933–). Pseudonym of Carlos Alberto Creste. Born in Buenos Aires, he was a journalist who became one of the initiators of the sociopolitical theater of the 1960s with the debut of *Homus dramaticus*. In 1971 he presented *¡Chau, papá!* (Goodbye, Papa!), written in the *grotesco político* (political grotesque) style. The mode presents the main character in self-conflict and focuses entirely on the local middle class. Adellach uses deformed parody and negative aspects of the country's history to alert the public of Argentina's political situation.

WORKS: *Criaturas* (Children) (s.1967). *Y entonces ¿qué?* (And Then What?) (s.1968). *Historia de desconocidos* (History of the Unknown) (s.1969), part of the trilogy *Homo dramaticus* p. in *Teatro* (Buenos Aires: Ediciones del Tablado, 1974). *Marcha* (March) (s.1969), part of the trilogy *Homo dramaticus* p. in *Teatro* (Buenos Aires: Ediciones del Tablado, 1974); *The Orgy, Modern One-Act Plays from Latin America* (Los Angeles: UCLA Latin American Center, 1974). *Palabras* (Words) (s.1969), part of the trilogy *Homus dramaticus* p. in *Teatro* (Buenos Aires: Ediciones del Tablado, 1974). *Primero ¿qué?* (What First?) (s.1970). *¡Chau, papá!* (Goodbye, Papa!) (s.1971) p. in *Teatro Argentino* (Buenos Aires: Teatro, 1970, 1973); *Teatro* (Buenos Aires: Ediciones del Tablado, 1974). *Esa canción es un pájaro lastimado* (That Song Is a Wounded Bird) (s.1971) p. in *Teatro* (Buenos Aires: Ediciones del Tablado, 1974). *Arena que la vida se llevó* (Sand That Life Took Away) (s.1976). *Vecinos y amigos* (Neighbors and Friends) (s.1976).

BIBLIOGRAPHY: Luis Ordaz, "Autores del 'nuevo realismo' de los años '60 a lo largo de las tres últimas décadas," *Latin American Theatre Review* 24.2 (Spring 1991):45. Osvaldo Pellettieri, "El teatro argentino del sesenta y su proyección en la actualidad," in *Cien años de teatro argentino 1886–1900* (Buenos Aires: Editorial Galerna, 1990), 138.

ALBERDI, Juan Bautista (1810–1884). Political thinker, philosopher, poet, musician, and playwright, Alberdi was born in Tucumán, Argentina. As a dramatist, Alberdi wrote two plays: the unfinished historical drama *La revolución de Mayo: Crónica dramática* (Dramatic Chronicle of the May Revolution) and *El gigante Amapolas* (The Giant Amapolas), a politically serious play described by the author as a one-act comedy. *El gigante Amapolas* combines the grotesque and the absurd by presenting Rosas as a straw puppet who conquers the enemy without moving. Luis Ordaz places Alberdi's play a century before its time owing to the absurd and the grotesque qualities of his characters.

WORKS: *La revolución de mayo: Crónica dramática* (Dramatic Chronicle of the May Revolution) (1839) p. (Montevideo, 1839); (Buenos Aires, 1925). *El gigante Amapolas y sus formidables enemigos, o Sea fastos dramáticos de una guerra memorable* (The Giant Amapolas and His Formidable Enemies, or Dramatic Shows of a Memorable War) p. (Chile, 1842); (Buenos Aires, 1925).

BIBLIOGRAPHY: Delfín Leocadio Garasa, "Juan Bautista Alberdi," in *Bibliografía de escritores hispanoamericanos 1609–1974* (New York: Gordian Press, 1975), 153–158. Angel Mazzei, *Dramaturgos post-Romanticos* (Buenos Aires: Ediciones Culturales Argentinas, 1970), 8–9. Luis Ordaz, *Aproximación a la trayectoria de la dramática argentina* (Ottawa: Girol Books, 1992), 15–18.

ARLT, Roberto (1900–1942). Arlt was born in Buenos Aires on April 7, 1900. He is considered one of Argentina's most innovative and prolific writers. Arlt became interested in the theater after seeing a chapter of his novel ("El humillado" in *Los siete locos*) staged by the Teatro del Pueblo, under the direction of Leónidas Barletta. The event inspired his first play, *Trescientos millones* (Three Hundred Million). The play is considered to be surreal and tragicomic with aspects of the grotesque as seen in Luigi Pirandello's plays. Critics describe all of Arlt's drama as nonconformist and unconventional. The representation of Arlt's plays was uniquely made possible by the independent theater movement and the Teatro del Pueblo, which allowed Arlt to become the principal force in renovating the theater of Argentina in the 1930s.

WORKS: *Trescientos millones* (Three Hundred Million) (s.1932) p. (Buenos Aires: Raño, 1932); (Buenos Aires: Futuro, 1950); in *Teatro completo* (Buenos Aires: Schapire, 1968). *El fabricante de fantasmas* (The Creator of Phantasms) (s.1936) p. (Buenos Aires: Futuro, 1950). *Saverio el Cruel* (Saverio the Cruel) (s.1936) p. (Buenos Aires: Futuro, 1950); (Buenos Aires: EUDEBA, 1964); in *Teatro completo* (Buenos Aires: Schapire, 1968). *Africa* (s.1938) p. in *Teatro completo* (Buenos Aires: Schapire, 1968); (Buenos Aires, 1938). *La isla desierta* (The Deserted Island) (s.1938) p. (Buenos Aires: Futuro, 1950); (Buenos Aires: EUDEBA, 1965); in *Teatro completo* (Buenos Aires: Schapire, 1968); in *Los clásicos del teatro hispanoamericano* (Mexico City: Fondo de Cultura Económica, 1975). *Separación feroz* (Fierce Separation) p. in *El Litoral* of Santa Fe (1938). *La fiesta del hierro* (The Feast of Iron) (s.1940) p. in *Teatro completo* (Buenos Aires: Schapire, 1968). *Prueba de amor* (Proof of Love) (s.1947) p. (Buenos Aires: Raño, 1932); (Buenos Aires: Futuro, 1950); in *Teatro completo* (Buenos Aires: Schapire, 1968). *El desierto entra en la ciudad* (The Desert Enters the City) p. (Buenos Aires: Futuro, 1952); in *Teatro completo* (Buenos Aires: Schapire, 1968). *La cabeza separada del tronco* (The Head Separated from the Trunk) (s.1964).

BIBLIOGRAPHY: Enzo Aloisi, "Argentines Behind the Footlights: Twenty Years of Independent Theaters, *Américas* 4 (1952): 22–23. Mirta Arlt, *Roberto Arlt, Saverio el cruel/La isla desierta* (Buenos Aires: Editorial Universitaria de Buenos Aires, 1964). Raúl Castagnino, *El teatro de Roberto Arlt* (La Plata: Universidad Nacional de la Plata,

1964), 88–89. Nira Etchenique, *Roberto Arlt* (Buenos Aires: La Mandrágora, 1962), 10–11. Osvaldo Pellettieri, "El intertexto de Pirandello en el teatro de Roberto Arlt," in *Cien años de teatro argentino (1886–1990)* (Buenos Aires: Editorial Galerna, 1990), 123–127.

BERRUTI, Alejandro E. (1888–1964). Born in Córdoba, Berruti was dedicated to all aspects of the theater for over forty years. He wrote over eighty plays, many of them *sainetes* (one-act plays). In addition to being a prolific playwright, Berruti was one of the founders of the Argentores organization in 1934 and worked at establishing a library of national plays. His most famous work, *Madre tierra* (Mother Earth), is a realistic representation of the struggle of farmers against the rich landowners. The tragedy was modernized by Osvaldo Dragún in 1955.

WORKS: *Madre tierra* (Mother Earth) (s.1920, Rosario, Teatro Polteama, performed by the Rivera–De Rosas Company); (s.1924, Buenos Aires, Teatro Nuevo, performed by the Enrique de Rosas Company) p. in *Argentores* 249 (1945). *Papá Bonini* (Papa Bonini) (s.1922). *La yunta brava* (The Ferocious Yoke) (s.1923). *El amigo Kraus* (The Friend Kraus) (s.1924). *Música barata* (Cheap Music) (s.1929, Teatro Apolo). *Tres personajes a la pesca de un autor* (Six Characters Fishing for an Author) (s.1929, Teatro Apolo). *Cuidado con las bonitas* (Careful with the Pretty Ones) (s.1931, Teatro Comedia by the Olinda Bazón Company). *Les llegó su San Martín* (Their Saint Martin Has Arrived) (s.1934) p. in *Argentores* 9 (1934).

BIBLIOGRAPHY: Blas Raúl Gallo, *Historia del sainete nacional* (Buenos Aires: Quetzal, 1958), 188–192. Willis Knapp Jones, *Behind Spanish American Footlights* (Austin: University of Texas Press, 1966), 147–148.

BETTI, Atilio (1922–). Born in Buenos Aires, Betti is described as a *poeta drámatico* (dramatic poet).

He is most known for his play *Fundación del desengaño, tragicomedia en dos partes* (Establishment of Disillusion, a Tragicomedy in Two Parts), which is about the founding of Buenos Aires by Mendoza.

WORKS: *La edad del hambre* (The Age of Hunger) (never staged) (Buenos Aires: Ed. Author, 1952). *Farsa del corazón* (Farce from the Heart) (s.1953) p. (Buenos Aires: Teatro Estudio, 1953); in *Talía* 19–20 (1960); (Buenos Aires: Huemul, 1970; 1972). *La culpa* (The Blame) (s.1957). *El buen glotón* (The Good Glutton) (s.1957) p. (Buenos Aires: Teatro Popular Independiente, 1957). *Maese amor* (Master Love) (w.1957). *El juego de la virtud* (The Game of Virtue) (s.1959) p. (Buenos Aires: Teatro Popular Independiente, 1957). *Fundación del desengaño, tragicomedia en dos partes* (Establishment of Disillusion, a Tragicomedy in Two Parts) (s.1960) p. (Buenos Aires: Talía, 1960); in *Teatro argentino contemporáneo* (Madrid: Aguilar, 1973). *Delta* (w.1961). *El duelo a bastonazos* (The Stick Duel) (w.1961) *Francisco Bernardone* (s.1964) p. (Buenos Aires: Teatro Expresión, 1955). *El nuevo David* (The New David) (s.1965) p. (Buenos Aires: Teatro Expresión, 1959). *Chaveta* (Penknife) (s.1966) p. in *Comentario* 32 (1962); (Buenos Aires: Carro de Tespis, 1966). *La selva y el reino* (The Forest and the Kingdom) (s.1969) p. (Buenos Aires: Huemul, 1969). *La avarcia* (Greed) (s.1970). *El hambre que no se ve* (Hidden Hunger) (w.1970). *Commedietta* (Little Comedy) (w.1971).

BIBLIOGRAPHY: Richard Allen, *Teatro hispanoamericano: Una bibliografía anotada* (Boston: G. K. Hall, 1987), 28. Juan Carlos Ghiano, *Teatro argentino contemporáneo, 1949–1969* (Madrid: Aguilar, 1973), 34–38; Betti gives opinion of his work, 258–259. Erminio Neglia and Luis Ordaz, *Repertorio selecto del teatro hispanoamericano contemporáneo* (Tempe: Arizona State University, 1980), 2.

BORTNIK, Aida (1938–). Born in Buenos Aires to Ukrainian parents, Bortnik first worked as a journalist. In 1972, she presented *Soldados y soldaditos* (Soldiers and Little Soldiers), which she wrote, produced, and directed. Bortnik is also involved in television and cinema, and her most famous movie script is for *La historia oficial* (The Official Story). In 1981 she became involved with Teatro Abierto (Open Theater) and presented *Papá querido* (Father Dear). In 1983 she offered Teatro Abierto *De a uno* (From One). The play is meant to show the hardships of the military dictatorship of Argentina from 1976 to 1983.

WORKS: *Soldados soldaditos* (Soldiers and Little Soldiers) (s.1972). *Tres por Chejov* (Three for Che-khov) (s.1974). *Dale nomás* (Do It) (s.1975). *Domesticado* (Domesticated) (s.1981), Argentores Prize. *Papá querido* (Father Dear) (s.1981). *De a uno* (From One) (s.1983). *Primaveras* (Springs) (s.1984).

BIBLIOGRAPHY: "Aida Bortnik," interview in *Teatro argentino durante el proceso (1976–1983)*, ed. Juana Arancibia and Zulema Mirkin (Buenos Aires: Vinciguerra, 1992), 243–246. Jean Graham-Jones, "Decir "no": El aporte de Bortnik, Gambaro y Raznovich al Teatro Abierto '81," in *Teatro argentino durante el proceso (1976–1983)*, ed. Juana Arancibia and Zulema Mirkin (Buenos Aires: Vinciguerra, 1992), 181–197. Nora Mazziotti, "Lo cotidiano enrarecido. *De a uno*, de Aida Bortnik," in *Teatro argentino durante el proceso (1976–1983)*, ed. Juana Arancibia and Zulema Mirkin (Buenos Aires: Vinciguerra, 1992), 91–97.

CANAL FEIJÓO, Bernardo (1897–1982). Canal Feijóo was born in the northern province of Santiago del Estero. In addition to being a dramatist, he was also a poet, lawyer, and great supporter of the arts. He believed that drama was a good vehicle for social communication. In *Pasión y muerte de Silverio Leguizamón* (The Passion and Death of Silverio Leguizamón) (1944), he dramatizes the life of a gaucho who rebels against the injustices committed against him and his people.

WORKS: *Pasión y muerte de Silverio Leguizamón* (The Passion and Death of Silverio Leguizamón) (s.1944) p. (Buenos Aires: Elan, 1944); (Buenos Aires: Centro Editor de América Latina, 1967). *Los casos de Juan el Zorro* (The Situations of John the Fox) (s.1954) p. (Buenos Aires: Talía, 1961); (Buenos Aires: Centro Editor de América Latina, 1967). *Tungasuka* (s.1963) p. (Buenos Aires: Carro de Tespis, 1968).

BIBLIOGRAPHY: Erminio G. Neglia and Luis Ordaz, *Repertorio selecto del teatro hispanoamericano contemporáneo* (Tempe: Arizona State University, 1980), 2. Luis Ordaz, *Aproximación a la trayectoria de la dramática argentina* (Ottawa: Girol Books, 1992), 56–61. Perla Zayas de Lima, *Diccionario de autores teatrales argentinos (1950–1980)* (Buenos Aires: Editorial Rodolfo Alonso, 1981).

CORONADO, Martín (1850–1919). Playwright, poet, novelist, and journalist, Coronado was born in Buenos Aires. After abandoning his study of law, he began writing plays of customs. Coronado was always involved in the quest for a national theater and for a time was president of the Argentine Academy of Letters. His first play, *La rosa blanca* (The White Rose), exhibits the remains of Romanticism. His masterpiece, *La piedra de escándalo* (The Scandalous Rock) (1902), shows his attention to national themes.

WORKS: *La rosa blanca* (The White Rose) (s.1877, Teatro de la Opera). *Luz de luna y luz de incendio* (Moonlight and Firelight) (s.1883). *Salvador* (s.1885). *Cortar por lo más delgado* (The Thinnest Cut) (s.1893). *Un soñador* (A Dreamer) (s.1896). *Justicia de antaño* (Justice in Days Gone By) (s.1897) p. (Buenos Aires: Comisión Nacional de Cultura. Inst. Nacional de Estudios de Teatro, 1950). *La piedra de escándalo* (The Scandalous Rock) (s.1902, by José Podestá) p. (Buenos Aires: Inst. Nacional de Estudios de Teatro, 1950). *Culpas ajenas* (Another's Faults) (s.1903). *Flor del aire* (The Air's Flower) (s.1904). *Los parásitos* (The Parasites) (s.1904). *Tormenta de verano* (Summer's Tempest). *El Sargento Palma* (Sergeant Palma) (s.1906) p. (Buenos Aires: Inst. Nacional de Estudios de Teatro, 1950). *Parientes pobres* (Poor Relatives) (s.1907). *La vanguardia* (The Vanguard) (s.1907). *Sebastián* (s.1908). *Vía libre* (Free Way) (s.1909). *Los curiales* (The Curials) (s.1910). *1810* (s.1910). *El hombre de la casa* (The Man of the House) (s.1911). *La chacra de Don Lorenzo* (Don Lorenzo's Ranch) (s.1918) p. in *La escena* 541 (1928). His plays are published in *Obras Completas. Teatro*, vols. 2–7 (Buenos Aires: Tall. Gráf. Argentinos, L. J. Rosso y Cía., 1925–1936).

BIBLIOGRAPHY: Mariano G. Bosch, *Historia de los orígenes del teatro argentino y la época de Pablo Podestá* (Buenos Aires: Solar-Hachette, 1969). Raúl Héctor Castagnino, *Literatura dramática argentina (1717–1967)* (Buenos Aires: Pleamar, 1968), 99–102. Castagnino, *Martín Coronado* (Buenos Aires, 1962).

COSSA, Roberto Mario (1934–). Born in Buenos Aires, Cossa began his theatrical career in 1956 as an actor at the San Isidro Theater. After his first play, *Nuestro fin de semana* (Our Weekend), Cossa was immediately associated with the new generation of realists, which included Somigliana, Halac, Talesnik, and Rozenmacher. Cossa is one of the initiators of the Teatro Abierto (Open Theater), together with Gorostiza, Dragún, and Somigliana, among others. *El avión negro* (The Black Plane), written in collaboration with Rozenmacher, Somigliana, and Talesnik, marks a change toward a freer style that integrates humor and the grotesque, qualities found in his later works. *La nona* (The Grandmother) illustrates his usage of the grotesque, the absurd, and black humor. His scrutiny of the immigrant, especially his longing to return to the homeland, continues in *Gris de ausencia* (Grey Absence).

WORKS: *Nuestro fin de semana* (Our Weekend) (s.1964), Argentores, Talía, and Semanario Teatral del Aire Awards, p. (Buenos Aires: Talía, 1972). *Los días de Julián Bisbal* (The Days of Julián Bisbal) (s.1966) p. (Buenos Aires: Talía, 1972). *La ñata contra el libro* (The Nose Against the Book) (s.1966), 3rd Municipal Prize, p. (Buenos Aires: Talía, 1967). *La pata de la sota* (The Jack's Leg) (s.1967), 2nd Municipal Prize, p. (Buenos Aires: Talía, 1972). *El avión negro* (The Black Plane) (s.1970), written in collaboration with Rozenmacher, Somigliana, and Talesnik, p. (Buenos Aires: Talía, 1971); in *Tres obras de teatro* (Havana: Casa de las Américas, 1970). *La nona* (The Grandmother) (s.1977). *No hay que llorar* (You Don't Have to Cry) (s.1979). *El viejo criado* (The Old Servant) (s.1980, Teatro Payró). *Gris de ausencia* (Grey Absence) (s.1981, Teatro del Picadero). *Tute Cabrero* (s.1981, Los Teatros de San Telmo). *El tío loco* (The Crazy Uncle) (s.1982). *Ya nadie recuerda a Frederic Chopin* (Already Nobody Remembers Frederick Chopin) (s.1982, Teatro Planeta). *De pies y manos* (Of Hands and Feet) (s.1984). *Los compadritos* (The Little Friends) (s.1985, Presidente Alvear Theater). *El Sur y después* (After the South) (s.1987). *Yepeto* (s.1987).

BIBLIOGRAPHY: Luis Ordaz, "Autores del 'nuevo realismo' de los años '60 a lo largo de las tres últimas décadas," *Latin American Theatre Review* 24.2 (Spring 1991): 41–48. Osvaldo Pellettieri, *Cien años de teatro argentina* (1986–1990) (Buenos Aires: Editorial Galerna, 1990), 145–151. Roberto Previdi Froelich, "América deshecha. El neogrotesco gastronómico y el discurso del fascismo en *La nona* de Roberto Cossa, in *Teatro argentino durante el proceso (1976–1983)*, ed. Juana Arancibia and Zulema Mirkin (Buenos Aires: Vinciguerra, 1992), 131–139. Perla Zayas de Lima, "Variables culturales e ideológicas en la respuesta de la crítica y los espectadores: El caso de *La nona*: América-europa (1977–1990)," in *Teatro y teatristas: Estudios sobre teatro argentino y iberoamericano*, ed. Osvaldo Pellettierí (Buenos Aires: Editorial Galerna, 1992).

CUZZANI, Agustín (1924–1987). Born in Buenos Aires, Cuzzani was a lawyer and a satirist. He developed a unique style called *farsátira* (a farcical satire) through which he expressed social criticism. His technique blended anachronisms and other elements of the expressionist theater with the modern farce. In his popular *Una libra de carne* (A Pound of Meat, s.1954), influenced by Shakespeare's *The Merchant of Venice*, the protagonist must pay his debts with a pound of his own flesh but has been so mistreated by society that he has no blood left in his veins.

WORKS: *Dalilah* (w.1942) p. (Buenos Aires: Pedestal, 1953). *Una libra de carne* (A Pound of Meat) (s.1954) p. (Buenos Aires: Quetzal, 1954); (Buenos Aires: Ariadna, 1957); (Buenos Aires: Quetzal, 1960); (Buenos Aires: Centro Editor de América Latina, 1967); in *Teatro argentino contemporáneo* (Madrid: Aguilar, 1973). *El centroforward murió al amanecer* (The Centerforward Died at Dawn) (s.1955) p. (Buenos Aires: Ariadna, 1955); (Buenos Aires: Quetzal, 1960); in *El centroforward murió al amanecer. Para que se cumplan las escrituras* (Buenos Aires: EUDEBA, 1966). *Los indios estaban cabreros* (The Indians Were Goatherds) (s.1958) p. (Buenos Aires: Talía, 1958); (Buenos Aires: Quetzal, 1960); (Buenos Aires: Centro Editor de América Latina, 1967). *Sempronio* (s.1962) p. (Buenos Aires: Quetzal, 1960); in *El teatro hispanoamericano contemporáneo*, vol. 2 (Mexico: Fondo de Cultura Económica, 1964). *Sempronio el peluquero y los hombrecitos* (Sempronio the Hairdresser and the Pansies) (s.1962). *El leñador* (The Woodman) (s.1965). *Para que se cumplan las escrituras* (So the Scriptures Can Be Fulfilled) (s.1965) p. (Buenos Aires: Quetzal, 1965); in *El centroforward murió al amanecer. Para que se cumplan las escrituras* (Buenos Aires: EUDEBA, 1966). *La envidia* (Envy) (s.1970). *El breve* (The Breve) (s.1976). *Disparen sobre el zorro gris* (Shoot Upon the Grey Fox) (s.1983, Teatro TFT). *Lo cortés no quita lo caliente* (Politeness Does not Take Away the Heat) (s.1985). *América año cero* (America Zero Year) (n.d.).

BIBLIOGRAPHY: Raúl Héctor Castagnino, *Literatura dramática argentina (1717–1967)* (Buenos Aires: Pleamar, 1968), 177–178. David William Foster, *A Dictionary of Contemporary Latin American Authors* (Tempe: Arizona State University, 1975), 31–32. Juan Carlos Ghiano, *Teatro argentino contemporáneo, 1949–1969* (Madrid: Aguilar, 1973), 30–34; Cuzzani gives opinion of his work, 208–209.

DAMEL, Carlos (1890–1959) and **DARTHÉS, Camilo** (1889–1974). The most successful and popular collaborators of the Argentine theater, both were born in Buenos Aires. Darthés was a businessman; Damel, an eye surgeon. They met as students and presented their first collaboration, *La última escena* (The Last Scene), in 1911. Together they wrote fifty-four plays depicting the changing customs of Argentine society. Their works were popular for suspense, authentic dialogues, and humor.

WORKS BY DAMEL AND DARTHÉS: *La última escena* (The Last Scene) (s.1911, Teatro Olimpo de Flores by the Juan Vidal Company). *La pipa de yeso* (The Plaster Pipe) (s.1912) p. in *Bambalinas* 202 (1922). *El novio de Martina* (Martina's Boyfriend) (s.1917) p. in *Bambalinas* 14 (1918). *La mascota del barrio* (The Neighborhood Mascot) p. in *Bambalinas* 65 (1919). *Hasta la hacienda baguala cai al jagüel con la seca* (s.1920). *El intruso* (The Intruder) (s.1920) p. in *Bambalinas* 98 (1920). *El loco Ruíz* (The Crazy Ruíz) (s.1920) p. in *Bambalinas* 65 (1919). *Las que van al infierno* (Those Who Go to Hell) p. in *Bambalinas* 98 (1920). *El autor* (The Author) (s.1921) p. in *Bambalinas* 195 (1921). *El viejo Hucha* (The Old Hucha) (s.1921) p. in *Bambalinas* 190 (1921). *Avanti foot-ball club* (Let's Go Soccer Club) p. in *Bambalinas*, n.231. *Hasta el pelo más delgado hace su sombra en el suelo* (Even the Thinnest Hair Casts Its Shadow on the Floor) (s.1922) p. in *Bambalinas* 119 (1922). *El botanazo* (s.1924) p. in *Bambalinas* 347 (1924). *Consultorio femenino* (Woman's Clinic) p. in *Bambalinas* 244 (1924). *El sostén de la familia* (The Support of the Family) (s.1931) p. (Buenos Aires: Carro de Tespis, 1966). *Como bola sin manija* p. in *La escena* 781 (1933). *El milagro de San Antonio* (The Miracle of Saint Anthony) p. in *La escena* 617 (1993). *El pavo de la boda* (The Wedding Turkey) p. in *La escena* 762 (1933). *Un bebé de París* (A Parisian Baby) (s.1934) p. in *Argentores* 7 (1934). *El señor X* (Mr. X) (s.1935) p. in *Bambalinas* 50 (1919). *Los chicos crecen* (The Children Grow) (s.1937, Teatro París) p. in *Argentores* 162 (1938); (Buenos Aires: Carro de Tespis, 1957). *La hermana Josefina* (The Sister Josephine) (s.1938) p. in *Argentores* 170 (1939). *Ni la quiero ni me importa* (I Don't Love Her and I Don't Care) (s.1940) p. in *Argentores* 194 (1940). *Un pucho en el suelo* (A Cigar Stub on the Floor) (s.1940) p. in *Argentores* 190 (1940). *¡Delirio!* (Delirium!) (s.1942) p. in *Argentores* 216 (1942). *Mi felicidad y tus amigas* (My Happiness and Your Girlfriends) (s.1942) p. *Argentores* 227 (1943). *Amparo* (s.1944) p. in *Argentores* 245 (1944). *Tres mil pesos* (Three Thousand Pesos) (s.1944) p. in *Argentores* 241 (1944). *Manuel García* (s.1946) p. in *Argentores* 258 (1941). *Quiero casarme de blanco* (I Want to Wed in White) p. in *Proscenio* 8 (1949). *¡Qué pequeño era mi mundo!* (How Small Was My World!) (s.1954) p. in *Argentores* (1954). *Escalera a dos puntas* (s.1955) p. (Buenos Aires: Carro de Tespis, 1964). *Envidia* (Envy) (s.1959) p. (Buenos Aires: Carro de Tespis, 1960).

WORKS BY DARTHÉS: *Mentiroso* (Liar) (s.1925) p. in *Bambalinas* 390 (1925). *El sueño de la casa propia* (The Dream of One's Own House) (s.1926) p. in *Bambalinas* 442 (1926). *El cadenero* (The Chain Man) (s.1928) p. in *La escena* 530 (1928).

BIBLIOGRAPHY: Willis Knapp Jones, *Behind Spanish American Footlights* (Austin: University of Texas, 1966), 142–144. Perla Zayas de Lima, *Diccionario de autores teatrales argentinos (1950–1980)* (Buenos Aires: Editorial Rodolfo Alonso, 1981), 55–57.

DE CECCO, Sergio (1931–1986). De Cecco was born in Buenos Aires and also known by the pseudonyms of Javier Sánchez and Amadeo Salazar. He received immediate success with the debut of his play *El reñidero* (The Quarrel Place) (w.1964). His following play, *Capocómico* (Head Comedian) (s.1965), lost some of the theatrical impact of *El reñidero*. The play is a melodrama about life in the old Creole circuses. Eleven years later, de Cecco presented *El gran deschave* (The Great Fight) (s.1976), written in collaboration with Armando Chulak, about a couple's verbal confrontation where nothing is withheld.

WORKS: *Prometeo* (Prometheus) (read in 1956). *El invitado* (The Guest) (s.1958, Ministry of Education Award). *El reñidero* (The Quarrel Place) (w.1964) p. (Buenos Aires: Talía, 1963; 1965). *Capocómico* (Head Comedian) (s.1965, Teatro General San Martín) p. (Buenos Aires: Talía, 1965). *El chou de la Chona* (s.1969, Rosario). *El gran deschave* (The Great Fight) (s.1976, Teatro Regina) p. (Buenos Aires: Talía, 1975). *Llegó el plomero* (The Plumber Arrived) (s.1980, Teatro Regina). *¡Moreira...!* (Moreira...!) (s.1984, Teatro Cervantes), written in collaboration with Carlos Páis and Peñarol Méndez.

BIBLIOGRAPHY: Raúl Castagnino, *Literatura dramática argentina (1717–1967)* (Buenos Aires: Pleamar, 1968), 199. Erminio G. Neglia and Luis Ordaz, *Repertorio selecto del teatro hispanoamericano contemporáneo* (Tempe: Arizona State University, 1980), 3. Luis Ordaz, "Autores del 'nuevo realismo' de los años '60 a lo largo de las tres últimas décadas," *Latin American Theatre Review* 24.2 (Spring 1991):45.

DEFILIPPIS NOVOA, Francisco (1890–1930). Born in Paraná (Entre Ríos), Defilippis Novoa was a rural teacher and journalist. He began his theatrical career writing *costumbrista* plays (plays of customs), such as the political satire *El diputado por mi pueblo* (The Representative of My Town), which debuted in 1918. He later makes the transition to romantic realism by developing characters who search for goodness and justice in order to construct a better world. The shift is exemplified by his play *La madrecita* (The Little Mother) (1920). The final stages of Defilippis Novoa's drama were experimental and influenced by local characters and places. He labeled his play *He visto a Dios* (I Have Seen God) (1930) as a "modern mystery." Luis Ordaz considers the play to be one of the most noteworthy contributions to the *grotesco criollo* trend, which was initiated a few years earlier by Armando Discépolo.

WORKS: *Crónica de policía* (Police Chronicle) (s.1913). *El día sábado* (The Day of Saturday) (s.1913) p. in *Nuestro teatro* 11 (1914); *Bambalinas* 178 (1921). *La casa de los viejos* (The House of the Old) (s.1914) p. in *El teatro nacional* 142 (n.d.); *Bambalinas* 303 (1924). *El diputado por mi pueblo* (The Representative of My Town) (s.1918) p. in *La escena* 18 (1918); *El apuntador* 6 (1931). *El conquistador de lo imprevisto* (The Conqueror of the Unforeseen) (s.1919) p. in *La escena* 49 (1919). *Un cable de Londres* (A Telegram from London) (s.1920) p. in *Bambalinas* 136 (1920). *El cacique blanco* (The White Indian Chief) (s.1920), written in collaboration with Claudio Martínez Payva, p. in *Bambalinas* 117 (1920). *La loba* (The Wolf) (s.1920)

p. in *La escena* 132 (1921). *La madrecita* (The Little Mother) (s.1920) p. in *Bambalinas* 129 (1920). *Santos y banditos* (Saints and Bandits) (s.1920), written in collaboration with Claudio Martínez Payva, p. in *Bambalinas* 142 (1920). *Cooperativa doméstica* (Domestic Co-Operative) (s.1921) p. in *Bambalinas* 177 (1921). *Los imigrantes* (The Immigrants) (s.1921) p. in *Teatro argentino* 42 (1921); in *Candilejas* 6 (1932). *Una vida* (A Life) (s.1921) p. in *Bambalinas* 168 (1921). *Los desventurados* (The Unlucky) (s.1922) p. in *Bambalinas* 257 (1923). *El turbión* (The Squall) (s.1922) p. in *Bambalinas* 219 (1922). *Hermanos nuestros* (Our Brothers) (s.1923) p. in *Bambalinas* 293 (1923). *La mariposa* (The Butterfly) p. in *Bambalinas* 257 (1923). *La samaritana* (The Samaritan) (s.1923) p. in *Bambalinas* 279 (1923). *Los caminos del mundo* (The Roads of the World) (s.1925). *Tu honra y la mía* (Your Honor and Mine) (s.1925) p. (Buenos Aires: Tommasi, 1925). *El alma de un hombre honrado* (The Soul of an Honest Man) (s.1926) p. (Buenos Aires: Luz, n.d.). *Yo tuve veinte años* (I Was Twenty Years Old) (s.1926) p. (Buenos Aires: Luz, n.d.). *María la tonta* (Silly Maria) (s.1927). *A mí me gustan las rubias* (I Like Blondes) (s.1929), written in collaboration with René Garzón. *Despiertate Cipriano* (Wake Up, Cipriano) (s.1929). *Tú, yo y el mundo después* (You and I and the World After) (s.1929) p. in *La escena* 596 (1929). *He visto a Dios* (I Have Seen God) (s.1930) p. in *El apuntador* 6 (1931); (Buenos Aires: Losange, 1953); (Buenos Aires: EUDEBA, 1965); (Buenos Aires: Centro Editor de América Latina, 1968). *Nosotros dos* (The Two of Us) (s.1930) p. in *Bambalinas* 630 (1930). *Sombras en la pared* (Shadows on the Wall) (s.1931) p. in *El apuntador* 9 (1931). *Ida y vuelta* (Departure and Return) (s.1941).

BIBLIOGRAPHY: Raúl Héctor Castagnino, *Literatura dramática argentina (1717–1967)* (Buenos Aires: Pleamar, 1968), 139–140. Erminio G. Neglia and Luis Ordaz, *Repertorio selecto del teatro hispanoamericano contemporáneo* (Tempe: Arizona State University, 1980), 3–4. Luis Ordaz, *El teatro en el Río de la Plata* (Buenos Aires: Futuro, 1946), 122–129.

DISCÉPOLO, Armando (1887–1971). Discépolo was born on Paraná Street in Buenos Aires on August 18, 1887. Discépolo began his dramatic career in 1908 as an actor and director of the Compañía Nacional de Aficionados (The National Company of Supporters). His early plays consisted of *sainetes* (one-act comedies),

dramas, and comedies. In 1923 he introduced the *grotesco* (grotesque) form to the Argentine theater with *Mateo* (Matthew), a one-act play with three scenes. Discépolo's *grotesco* plays were influenced by Italian playwrights Luigi Chiarelli and Luigi Pirandello, who uniquely combined drama with comedy to form plays characterized as "tragicomedies." The Pirandellian "ménage à trois" (the husband, wife, and lover) also influenced Discépolo's characters. Luis Ordaz classifies Discépolo's theater as *grotesco criollo* for its derivation from the Argentine *sainete* and its usage of social criticism. Through the *grotesco criollo*, Discépolo exposes the frustrations, failures, and poverty experienced by southern Italian immigrants living in Buenos Aires at the time.

WORKS: *Entre el hierro* (Among the Iron) (s.1910) p. (Montevideo: Bertani, n.d.); in *Bambalinas* 39 (1918); (Buenos Aires: Alvarez, 1969). *El rincón de los besos* (The Corner of Kisses) (s.1911) p. (Montevideo: Bertani, 1914); in *Bambalinas* 304 (1924). *La torcaz* (The Wild) (s.1911). *Espuma de mar* (Sea Foam) (s.1912), written in collaboration with Rafael José de Rosa. *La fragua* (The Forge) (s.1912) p. (Montevideo: Bertani, 1912); in *Bambalinas* 70 (1919); (Buenos Aires: Alvarez, 1969). *Mi mujer se aburre* (My Wife Gets Bored) (s.1914), written in collaboration with Rafael José de Rosa, p. in *La escena* 136 (1921). *El novio de mamá* (Mom's Boyfriend) (s.1914), written in collaboration with Rafael José de Rosa y Mario Folco, p. in *Bambalinas* 30 (1918). *El viaje aquel* (That Trip) (s.1914), written in collaboration with José de Rosa, p. (Montevideo: Bertrani, 1914). *El guarda 323* (The Guard 323) (s.1915) p. in *La escena* 17 (1920). *El patio de las flores* (The Flower Patio) (s.1915), written in collaboration with Federico Mertens. *La ciencie de la casualitat* (The Science of Chance) (s.1916), monologue from *El movimiento continuo* (Buenos Aires: Alonso, n.d.). *El movimiento continuo* (Continuous Motion) (s.1916) p. in *Bambalinas* 23 (1918); in *Teatro argentino* 35 (1920); in *Bambalinas* 3 (1924); (Buenos Aires: Alvarez, 1969). *El reverso* (The Reverse) (s.1916) p. in *Bambalinas* 304 (1924). *El chueco Pintos* (The Bow-Legged Pintos) (s.1917), written in collaboration with Rafael de Rosas and Mario Folco, p. in *La escena* 24 (1918); in *Bambalinas* 298 (1923). *Conservatorio "La armonía"* ("The Harmony" Conservatory) (s.1917), written in collaboration with Rafael de Rosa and Mario Folco, p. in *La escena* 13 (1918). *La espada de Dámocles* (Damocles' Sword) (s.1918), written in collaboration with Rafael de Rosa and Mario Folco), p. in *Bambalinas* 13 (1918). *El vértigo* (Vertigo) (s.1919) p. in *Bambalinas* 76 (1919); (Buenos Aires: Alvarez, 1969). *El clavo de oro* (The Golden Nail) (s.1920), written in collaboration with Rafael de Rosa and Mario Folco, p. in *La escena* 97 (1920). *Mustafá* (s.1921), written in collaboration with Rafael de Rosa, p. in *El teatro argentino* 40 (1921); in *La escena* 351 (1925); (Buenos Aires: Carro de Tespis, 1966); (Buenos Aires: Alvarez, 1969). *El príncipe negro* (The Black Prince) (s.1921), written in collaboration with Rafael De Rosa. *"L'Italia Unita" Ristorante* (The "United Italy" Restaurant) (s.1922), written in collaboration with Rafael de Rosa, p. in *El entreacto* 8 (1922). *Hombre de honor* (Man of Honor) (s.1923) p. in *Bambalinas* 291 (1923); (Buenos Aires: Alvarez, 1969). *Mateo* (Matthew) (s.1923) p. in *Bambalinas* 275 (1923); in *Argentores* 32 (1934); (Buenos Aires: Losange, 1958); (Buenos Aires: EUDEBA, 1965); (Buenos Aires: Alvarez, 1969). *Giácomo* (s.1924), written in collaboration with Rafael de Rosa, p. in *Bambalinas* 345 (1924); (Buenos Aires: Talía, 1970). *Muñeca* (Doll) (s.1924) p. in *Bambalinas* 345 (1924); (Buenos Aires: Carro de Tespis, 1965); Buenos Aires: Alvarez, 1969). *Babilonia* (Babylon) (s.1925) p. in *Bambalinas* 389 (1925); (Buenos Aires: Hachette, 1957); (Buenos Aires: EUDEBA, 1965); (Buenos Aires: Talía, 1970). *El organito* (The Little Organ) (s.1925), written in collaboration with Enrique Santos Discépolo, p. in *La escena* 407 (1926); (Buenos Aires: Losange, 1958); (Buenos Aires: Carro de Tespis, 1965); (Buenos Aires: Alvarez, 1969). *Patria nueva* (New Homeland) (s.1926) p. in *La escena* 415 (1926); (Buenos Aires: Alvarez, 1969). *Stéfano* (s.1928) p. in *La escena* 519 (1928); (Buenos Aires: Losange, 1958); (Buenos Aires: Carro de Tespis, 1965); (Buenos Aires: EUDEBA, 1965); (Buenos Aires: Centro Editor de América Latina, 1968); (Buenos Aires: Alvarez, 1969). *Levántate y anda* (Get Up and Go) (s.1929) p. in *La escena* 587 (1929); (Buenos Aires: Alvarez, 1969). *Amanda y Eduardo* (Amanda and Eduardo) (s.1931) p. (Buenos Aires: Carro de Tespis, 1966); (Buenos Aires: Alvarez, 1969). *Cremona* (s.1932) p. (Buenos Aires: Talía, 1970). *Relojero* (The Watchmaker) (s.1934) p. in *Argentores* 13 (1934); (Buenos Aires: Losange, 1958); (Buenos Aires: EUDEBA, 1965); (Buenos Aires: Alvarez, 1969).

BIBLIOGRAPHY: Luis Ordaz, *Aproximación a la trayectoria de la dramática argentina* (Ottawa: Girol Books, 1992), 43–45. Ordaz, *Armando Discépolo* (Buenos Aires: Talía, 1970). Ordaz, *El teatro en el Río de la Plata* (Buenos Aires: Futuro, 1946), 129–131. Osvaldo Pellettieri, "Armando Discépolo: Entre el grotesco italiano y el grotesco criollo," in *Cien años de teatro argentino (1886–1990)* (Buenos Aires: Galerna, 1990), 99–112. Pellettieri, "La primera época del teatro Armando Discépolo (1910–1923)," in *Cien años de teatro argentino (1886–1990)* (Buenos Aires: Galerna, 1990), 37–65. Pellettieri, "Las primeras obras de Armando Discépolo en colaboración (1914–1917)," in *Cien años de teatros argentino (1886–1990)* (Buenos Aires: Galerna, 1990), 67–98.

DRAGÚN, Osvaldo (1929–). One of the most famous contemporary Argentine dramatists, Dragún was born in 1929 in Paraná (Entre Ríos). He moved to Buenos Aires in 1944 and began to acquire his theatrical experience through acting, directing, and writing for local theater groups. He became affiliated with the independent theater company Fray Mocho in 1956, which catapulted Dragún's career. He became internationally known for his short plays, which he began writing in 1957. Disillusioned with post-Perón Argentina, he chose to focus on the dehumanization of man. The plays utilized an empty stage and popular music while focusing on the interaction between the actors and spectators. The themes treat various sociopolitical issues, such as insufficient money for medical attention, as seen in *Historia de un flemón, una mujer, y dos hombres* (The History of a Gumboil, a Woman, and Two Men). In 1958, Dragún deviated from his *historias* to write a musical drama, in collaboration with Andrés Lizarraga, called *Desde el 80* (Since 80). In 1964 he wrote a love story, *Amoretta* (Little Love), which contrasts with his previous plays by being a sentimental story with a happy ending. However, Dragún quickly returns to his world of dissolution and despair with the work he considers his masterpiece, *Heroica de Buenos Aires* (Heroical Buenos Aires). In 1981 he formed, together with his contemporaries, a new experimental theater called the Teatro Abierto (Open Theater). Today Dragún is considered to be one of the leaders of a movement that has created one of the richest and most forceful theaters in Latin America.

WORKS: *El gran duque ha desaparecido* (The Great Duke Has Disappeared) (w.1947). *La peste viene de Melos* (The Plague Comes from Melos) (w.1956, s.1966) p. (Buenos Aires: Ariada, 1956); in *Teatro '70* 26–29 (April–May 1972). *Historia de como nuestro amigo Panchito González se sintió responsable de la epidemia de peste bubónica en Africa* (The Story of How Our Friend Panchito González Felt Guilty About the Bubonic Plague Epidemic in South Africa) (s.1957) p. in *Historias para ser contadas* (Buenos Aires: Talía, 1957); in *Primer acto* 35 (1962); (Buenos Aires: Escorpio, 1965); (Buenos Aires: Austral, 1967); in *Teatro '70* 26–29 (April–May 1972); in *Teatro argentino* (Buenos Aires: Teatro '70, 1973). *Historia del hombre que se convirtió en perro* (The Story of the Man Who Turned into a Dog) (s.1957) p. in *Historias para ser contadas* (Buenos Aires: Talía, 1957); in *Primer acto* 35 (1962); (Buenos Aires: Escorpio, 1965); (Buenos Aires: Astral 1967); in *Teatro breve hispanoamericano contemporáneo* (Madrid: Aguilar, 1970); in *Teatro '70* 26–29 (April–May 1972); in *Teatro argentino* (Buenos Aires: Teatro '70, 1973); in *Teatro de la vanguardia* (Lexington: Heath, 1975). *Historia de un flemón, una mujer, y dos hombres* (The History of a Gumboil, a Woman, and Two Men) (s.1957) p. in *Historias para ser contadas* (Buenos Aires: Talía, 1957); in *Primer acto* 35 (1962); (Buenos Aires: Escorpio, 1965); (Buenos Aires: Astral, 1967); in *Teatro argentino* (Buenos Aires: Teatro '70, 1973). *Los de la mesa diez* (Those at Table Ten) (s.1957) p. (Buenos Aires: Talía, 1957); (Buenos Aires: Escorpio, 1965; (Buenos Aires: Astral, 1967); (Buenos Aires: Centro Editor de América Latina, 1968); in *Teatro '70* 26–29 (April–May 1972); in *Teatro argentino* (Buenos Aires: Teatro '70, 1973); in *Teatro argentino contemporáneo, 1949–1969* (Madrid: Aguilar, 1973). *Tupac Amarú* (s.1957) p. (Buenos Aires: Losange, 1957). *Desde el 80* (Since 80) (s.1958) w. in collaboration with Osualdo Dragún. *El jardín del infierno* (Hell's Garden) (s.1959) p. (Buenos Aires: Centro Editor de América Latina, 1966). *Historia de mi esquina* (The History of My Corner) (s.1960) p. (Buenos Aires: Escorpio, 1965). *Y nos dijeron que éramos inmortales* (And They Told Us We Were Immortal) (s.1963) p. (Buenos Aires: Los Monteagudos, 1963); (Madrid: Taurus, 1968); in *The Modern Stage in Latin America: Six Plays* (New York: Dutton, 1971). *Amoretta* (Little Love) (s.1964) p. (Buenos Aires: Carro de Tespis, 1965). *Heroica de Buenos Aires* (Heroical Buenos

Aires) (w.1964, s.1983) p. (Havana: Casa de las Américas, 1966); (Buenos Aires: Astral, 1967); in *Primer acto* 77 (1969). *Dos en la ciudad* (Two in the City) (s. as *El amasijo* [The Hodgepodge], 1968) p. (Buenos Aires: Calatayud, 1968); (Madrid: Taurus Ediciones, 1968) with title of El Maldito domingo (A Damned Sunday). *Historias con cárceles* (Prison Stories) (s.1972) p. in *Caminos del teatro latinoamericano* (Havana: Casa de las Américas, 1973). *Hoy se comen al flaco* (Today They'll Eat the Thin Man) (s.1976) p. in *Teatro: Hoy se comen al flaco; Al violador* (Ottawa, 1981). *Al violador* (For the Violator) (s.1984, Teatro Escuela) p. in *Teatro: Hoy se comen al Flaco; Al violador* (Ottawa, 1981). *Mi obelisco y yo* (My Obelisk and I) (s.1981) p. in *7 dramaturgos argentinos*, ed. Miguel Angel Giella, Peter Roster, and Leandro Urbina (Ottawa, 1983). *Al perdedor* (For the Loser) (s.1982, Teatro IFT). *El milagro en el mercado viejo* (The Miracle in the Old Market) (Casa de las Américas Award, 1963; s.1984, Teatro Margarita Xirgú) p. (Buenos Aires: Producciones Norte, 1963); (Havana: Casa de las Américas, 1963); (Madrid: Taurus, 1968). *Los hijos del terremoto* (The Sons of the Earthquake) p. in *Gestos* 2 (November 1986). *¡Arriba, Corazón!* (Uplift the Heart!) (s.1987, Teatro Municipal General San Martín). *Volver a La Habana* (Return to Havana) (s.1990).

BIBLIOGRAPHY: Juan Carlos Ghiano, *Teatro argentino contemporáneo, 1949–1969* (Madrid: Aguilar, 1973), 40–45, 316–317. Luis Ordaz, *Aproximación a la trayectoria de la dramática argentina* (Ottawa: Girol Books, 1992), 65–66. George Woodyard, "Osvaldo Dragún," in *A Dictionary of Latin American Authors*, ed. David William Foster (Tucson: Arizona State University, 1975), 1377–1381.

EICHELBAUM, Samuel (1894–1967). Eichelbaum was born on November 14, 1894, to Russian Jewish immigrants and wrote his first *sainete* (a one-act comedy), *El lobo manso* (The Tame Wolf), at the age of seven. In 1919 he began his professional dramatic career with the presentation of a one-act play, *La quietud del pueblo* (The Stillness of the Town), performed by the Muiño-Alippi players. Eichelbaum considered himself an initiator of a national theater that connected the gaucho tradition and universal themes. Rather than concentrate on folk tradition, he chose to capture the vigor and fortitude of the people. Eichelbaum offered another theatrical alternative to an audience that, until then, preferred a picturesque depiction of the Pampa. His works, which combine rustic language and psychological portrayals, make him a transitional author between the romantic gaucho *costumbrismo* and urban realism. Eichelbaum's theater has been noted for its psychological drama more so than for its action and spontaneity. He presents lonely characters searching for self-fulfillment within their social realms. In *Un guapo del 900* (A Gallant of 900), the juxtaposition of the macho, rural gaucho and the moral standards of urban Argentina contribute to the popularity of the play, which won the Municipal and National Drama Prizes in 1940.

WORKS: *El lobo manso* (The Tame Wolf) (n.s.) (n.d.). *El judío Aarón* (Aaron the Jew) (s.1926) p. in *Talía* 32 (1927). *Por el mal camino* (Along the Bad Road) (s.1911 in Yiddish). *Nadie la conoció nunca* (Nobody Ever Knew Her) (s.1926) p. in *Bambalinas* 461 (1927); (Buenos Aires: Carro de Tespis, 1956). *La quietud del pueblo* (The Stillness of the Town) (s.1919). *La mala sed* (Bad Thirst) (s.1920) p. in *La escena* 126 (1920); (Buenos Aires: Gleizer, 1932). *Un romance turco* (A Turkish Romance) (s.1920), written in collaboration with Pedro E. Pico, p. in *La escena* 9 (1920). *El dogma* (The Dogma) (s.1921) p. in *Bambalinas* 236 (1922). *La cáscara de nuez* (The Nut Shell) (s.1921) p. in *Teatro popular* 133 (n.d.). *El gato y su selva* (The Cat and Its Jungle) (s.1936) p. (Buenos Aires: Sudamericana, 1952). *La Juana Figueroa* (s.1921), written in collaboration with Pedro E. Pico. *Divorcio nupcial* (Nuptial Divorce) (s.1941) p. (Buenos Aires: Conducta, 1942). *Tejido de madre* (Mother's Weave) (s.1936) p. (Buenos Aires: Carro de Tespis, 1956). *Doctor* (s.1922) p. in *Bambalinas* 254 (1923), written in collaboration with Pedro E. Pico. *El camino del fuego* (The Fire Road) (s.1922) p. in *Bambalinas* 236 (1922). *Un hogar* (A Home) (s.1922) p. in *Bambalinas* 236 (1922); (Buenos Aires: Gleizner, 1923). *El ruedo de almas* (The Circle of Souls) (s.1923) p. in *La escena* 259 (1923). *Rostro perdido* (Lost Face) (s.1952) p. (Buenos Aires: EUDEBA, 1966). *La hermana terca* (The Stubborn Sister) (s.1924) p. in *Teatro nuevo* 1 (Buenos Aires, 1924). *Dos brasas* (Two Embers) (s.1955) p. (Buenos Aires: Sudamericana, 1952); in *Teatro argentino contemporáneo* (Madrid: Aguilar, 1959). *N. N. homicida* (Homicide N. N.) (s.1927) p. (Buenos Aires: Gleizner, 1928); (Buenos Aires:

Carro de Tespis, 1965). *Las aguas del mundo* (The Waters of the World) (s.1957) p. (Buenos Aires: Carro de Tespis, 1959). *Cuando tengas un hijo* (When You Have a Child) (s.1929) p. (Buenos Aires: El Inca, 1931). *Un cuervo sobre el imperio* (A Crow upon the Empire) (n.s.) p. (Buenos Aires: EUDEBA, 1966). *Señria* (Young Lady) (s.1930) p. in literary supplement to *La nación* (July 29, 1928); (Buenos Aires: El Inca, 1931). *Ricardo de Gales, príncipe criollo* (Richard of Wales, Creole Prince) (s.1931). *Gabriel, el olvidado* (Gabriel, the Forgotten One) (n.s.) p. (Buenos Aires: EUDEBA, 1966). *Soledad es tu nombre* (Solitude Is Your Name) (s.1932) p. (Buenos Aires: Gleizner, 1932). *Subsuelo* (Underground) (s.1967) p. (Buenos Aires: EUDEBA, 1966). *En tu vida estoy yo* (I Am in Your Life) (s.1934) p. (Buenos Aires: Gleizner, 1934). *Un patricio del 80* (A Patrician of the 80's) (n.s.), written in collaboration with Ulises Petit de Murat, p. (Buenos Aires: Talía, 1969). *Pájaro de barro* (Bird of Clay) (s.1940) p. (Buenos Aires: Sudamericana, 1952); (Buenos Aires: EUDEBA, 1965). *Un guapo del 900* (A Gallant of 900) (s.1940) p. (Buenos Aires: Colección Thespis, 1940); (Buenos Aires: Sudamericana, 1952); (Buenos Aires: Carro de Tespis, 1961); (Buenos Aires: Culturales Argentinas, 1967); (Buenos Aires: Centro Editor de América Latina, 1968); in *Los clásicos del teatro hispanoamericano* (Mexico City: Fondo de Cultura Económica, 1975). *Vergüenza de querer* (Ashamed to Love) (s.1941) p. (Buenos Aires: Conducta, 1942); (Buenos Aires: EUDEBA, 1965). *Un tal Servando Gómez* (Someone Named Servando Gómez) (s.1942) (Buenos Aires: Conducta, 1942); (Buenos Aires: Losange, 1954).

BIBLIOGRAPHY: Arturo Bereguer Carisomo, *Historia de la literatura argentina y americana* (Buenos Aires: Lasserre, 1967), 331. Bereguer Carisomo, *Teatro argentino contemporáneo* (Madrid: Aguilar, 1960), xi–xiv. Alejandro Berrutti, "Influencia del teatro gauchesco en la evolución del teatro argentino," *Lyra* 17 (1959): 174–176. Enrique Giordano, *La teatralización de la obra dramática: De Florencio Sánchez a Roberto Arlt* (Mexico City: Premia, 1982), 113–157. Willis Knapp Jones, "Three Great Latin American Dramatists: Eichelbaum, Usigli and Marqués," *Specialia* 1 (1969): 43–49.

FERRARI, Alfonso Amores (1903–   ). Ferrari Amores was born in Buenos Aires on February 7, 1903. A dramatist, poet, and novelist, he began his theatrical career with *La vida de Santa Teresita* (The Life of Saint Theresa) in

1934. He followed with *Espártaco* (Spartacus) (1939) and *El hombre que poda la parra* (The Man Who Prunes the Vine) (1943). His interest in radio-theater and journalism produced a long period of silence until 1963, when he wrote *A la sombra del alto manzano* (In the Shade of the Tall Apple Tree), about problems of a city neighborhood. In the same year, Ferrari presented *Las sábanas blancas* (The White Sheets), dealing with southern rural themes. In 1964 Ferrari won the Municipality of Buenos Aires Award for his theatrical experiment *La toma de la bohardilla* (The Taking of the Garret).

WORKS: *Austera* (Austere) (pamphlet p. 1929). *El voto femenino* (The Female Vote) (s.1933) p. in *El Hogar* (1933). *La vida de Santa Teresita* (The Life of Saint Theresa) (s.1934). *Tengo que matarte, Angela* (I Have to Kill You, Angela) (s.1934). *Espártaco* (Spartacus) (s.1939). *El hombre que poda la parra* (The Man Who Prunes the Vine) (s.1943). *La toma de la bohardilla* (The Taking of the Garret) (s.1962) p. (Buenos Aires: Carro de Tespis, 1963). *Los turistas* (The Tourists) (s.1967). *Las sábanas blancas* (The White Sheets) p. in *A la sombra del alto manzano*. *Las sábanas blancas* (Buenos Aires: Carro de Tespis, 1965). *Una anticuada máquina infernal* (An Antiquated Infernal Machine) (s.1968). *A la sombra del alto manzano* (In the Shade of the Tall Apple Tree) (s.1968) p. in *A la sombra del alto manzano*. *Las sábanas blanca* (Buenos Aires: Carro de Tespis, 1965). *Ritmo de puercoespín* (Porcupine Rythym) p. (Buenos Aires: Tálice, 1969). *El problema del oficial* (The Officer's Problem) (s.1970) p. (Buenos Aires: Talía, 1969).

BIBLIOGRAPHY: Richard Allen, *Teatro hispanoamericano: Una bibliografía anotada* (Boston: G. K. Hall, 1987), 68. Raúl Héctor Castagnino, *Literatura dramática argentina (1717–1967)* (Buenos Aires: Pleamar, 1968), 198. Tito Livio Foppa, *Diccionario teatral del Río de la Plata* (Buenos Aires: Carro de Tespis, 1961), 294. Perla Zayas de Lima, *Diccionario de autores teatrales argentinos (1950–1980)* (Buenos Aires: Editorial Rodolfo Alonso, 1981), 73–74.

FERRARI, Juan Carlos (1917–). Pseudonym for Enrique Grande, a medical doctor and professor. He is known for his urban comedy of customs, *Ese camino difícil* (That Hard Road), which consists of forty-eight scenes about problems of life in Buenos Aires. The play's performance in Nuevo Teatro was one of the greatest successes of the independent theaters. In 1958 Nuevo Teatro performed *Las nueve tías de Apolo* (Apollo's Nine Aunts), which projects a modern view of mythology. The play ends eighteen years from the start and concludes by addressing the situation of Argentina and World War II. Ferrari's theatrical production is full of authentic, local color.

WORKS: *Medio siglo* (Half a Century) (w.1950). *Cuando empieza el luto* (When the Mourning Begins) (s.1951) p. (Buenos Aires: La Máscara, 1951). *El tío Arguímedes* (Uncle Arguímedes) (s.1951) p. (Buenos Aires: La Máscara, 1951). *Ese camino difícil* (That Hard Road) (s.1952) p. in *Talía* 7 (1954). *Las campanas de Verona* (The Bells of Verona) (s.1956). *Canasta* (Basket) (s.1956). *El mazorquero* (The Cobman) (s.1956) p. (Buenos Aires: Meridiano, 1966). *Por arte de magia* (For the Art of Magic) (s.1956). *Las nueve tías de Apolo* (Apollo's Nine Aunts) (s.1958) p. (Buenos Aires: Talía, 1958). *Historia de Verano* (History of Summer) (s.1959). *La ñata* (The Flat Nosed Girl) (s.1959) p. (Buenos Aires: Talía, 1969). *Los culpables* (The Guilty) (s.1960). *Siempre vale la pena* (It's Always Worth It) (s.1960). *El desván* (The Garret) (w.1963). *Petit-Hotel* (Small Hotel) (s.1963). *Las ranas cantan de noche* (The Frogs Sing at Night) (s.1963) p. (Buenos Aires: Carro de Tespis, 1964). *Beatriz* (Beatrice) (s.1966). *Námun-Co* (s.1969). *Dos parejas y media* (Two Pairs and a Half) (s.1972). *Extraño episodio* (Strange Episode) (w.1973).

BIBLIOGRAPHY: Raúl Héctor Castagnino, *Literatura dramática argentina (1717–1967)* (Buenos Aires: Pleamar, 1968), 175. Willis Knapp Jones, *Behind Spanish American Footlights* (Austin: University of Texas Press, 1966), 153.

FERRETTI, Aurelio (1907–1963). Ferretti began his theatrical career as an actor and director. In 1929 he created the theatrical production, together with César Tiempo and Samuel Eichelbaum, *La mosca blanca* (The White Fly) from which the Teatro del Pueblo developed. Later Ferretti established and directed the Teatro Libre Tinglado. Ferretti soon presented a series of farces at which he excelled. *Fansa del cajero que fue hasta la esquina* (Farce of the Cashier Who Went to the Corner) is considered to be the best example of the playwright's outstanding skills as a satirist. The play, a satire of man's relationship to society, was a success in Buenos Aires and won the audience vote in the Ministry of Education drama contest.

WORKS: *Farsa del héroe y el villano* (Farce of a Hero and a Villain) (s.1946) p. in *Proscenio* 5 (1949); (Buenos Aires: Tinglado Libre Teatro, 1953). *La multitud* (The Multitude) (s.1946) p. (Buenos Aires: Tinglado Libre Teatro, 1946). *Las bodas del diablo* (The Weddings of the Devil) (s.1947) p. in *Argentores* 281 (1948). *Bonome, la farsa del hombre y el queso* (Bonome, Farce of the Man and the Cheese) (s.1949) p. in *Proscenio* 5 (1949); (Buenos Aires: Tinglado Libre Teatro, 1953). *La ilusión de Baltasar* (Baltasar's Illusion) (s.1949). *Farsa del consorte (Bertón y Bertina)* (Farce of the Partners [Bertón and Bertina]) (s.1950) p. (Buenos Aires: Tinglado Libre Teatro, 1953). *Farsa de farsas* (Farce of Farces) (s.1954) p. (Buenos Aires: Tinglado Libre Teatro, 1953). *La cama y el sofá* (The Bed and the Sofa) (s.1958) p. (Buenos Aires: Quetzal, 1963). *Farsa del cajero que fue hasta la esquina* (Farce of the Cashier Who Went to the Corner) (s.1958) p. (Buenos Aires: Ministerio de Educación y Justicia, 1958); (Buenos Aires: Centro Editor de América Latina, 1966). *Fidela* (s.1960) p. (Buenos Aires: Tinglado, 1953). *El café de Euterpe* (Euterpe's Café) (s.1961) p. (Buenos Aires: Quetzal, 1963). *Histrión* (Histrion) p. (Buenos Aires: Quetzal, 1963). *¡Pum . . . en el ojo!* (Bang . . . in the Eye!) (s.1964) p. (Buenos Aires: Quetzal, 1963). *Farsa del sexo opuesto* (Farce of the Opposite Sex) p. in *Talía* 31 (1967). *La pasión de Justo Pómez* (The Passion of Justo Pómez) (s.1970) p. (Buenos Aires: Quetzal, 1963).

BIBLIOGRAPHY: Richard Allen, *Teatro hispanoamericano: Una bibliografía anotada* (Boston: G. K. Hall, 1987), 69–70. Willis Knapp Jones, *Behind Spanish American Footlights* (Austin: University of Texas Press, 1966), 154. Erminio G. Neglia and Luis Ordaz, *Repertorio selecto del teatro hispanoamericano contemporáneo* (Tempe: Arizona State University, 1980), 11. Luis Ordaz, *Aproximación a la trayectoria de la dramática argentina* (Ottawa: Girol Books, 1992), 68–69.

GAMBARO, Griselda (1928–). Born in Buenos Aires, Griselda Gambaro is one of Latin America's most famous dramatists. Her plays have been performed throughout Europe and Latin America and in the United States.

The daughter of a postal worker, Gambaro attributes her theatrical skill to her early interest in the works of O'Neill, Pirandello, and Chekhov. Although she began her career as a short story writer, she emerged as a dramatist in the 1960s. Almost all of Gambaro's plays deal with the problems of passivity, suffering, and the nonassumption of individual responsibility within society. Many of her protagonists are victims in dependent relationships. *El campo* (The Camp) (1968) is considered to be Gambaro's most powerful and masterful play.

WORKS: *El desatino* (The Folly) (s.1965, Centro de Experimentación Audiovisual of the Di Tella Institute) p. (Buenos Aires: Instituto Di Tella, 1965); (Barcelona: Editorial Argonauta, 1979). *El viejo matrimonio* (The Old Married Couple) (s.1965, Teatro '35), later restaged as *Viaje de invierno* (A Winter Journey) (s.1985, Centro Cultural San Martín). *Las paredes* (The Walls) (s.1966). *Los siameses* (The Siamese Twins) (s.1967) p. (Buenos Aires: Editorial Insurrexit, 1967); (Barcelona: Editorial Argonauta, 1979); in *Nueve dramaturgos hispanoamericanos* (Ottawa: Girol Books, 1979). *El Campo* (The Camp) (s.1968, Teatro S.H.A., First Municipal Prize) p. (Buenos Aires: Editorial Insurrexit, 1967); (Buenos Aires: Centro Editor, 1981). *Cuatro ejercicios para actrices* (Four Exercises for Actresses) (s.1970). *Acuerdo para cambiar de casa* (Agreement to Move) (s.1971). *La gracia* (The Joke) p. in *El Urogallo* 17 (1972). *El miedo* (The Fear) (s.1972) *Nada que ver* (Nothing to Do with It) (s.1972, Teatro San Martín) p. (Ottawa: Girol Books: 1983). *Dar la vuelta* (To Take a Turn) (s.1973) p. (Buenos Aires, 1987). *Sólo un aspecto* (Only One Aspect) (s.1974) p. in *La palabra y el hombre* 8 (1973). *El nombre* (The Name) p. in *El Cronista*, Suplemento Cultural (September 6, 1975). *El viaje a Bahía Blanca* (The Trip to Bahía Blanca) (s.1975). *Sucede lo que pasa* (Whatever Happens, Happens) (s.1976, Argentores Prize) p. (Ottawa: Girol Books, 1983); (Buenos Aires, 1987). *Información para extranjeros* (Information for Foreigners) (s.1978, USA) p. (Buenos Aires, 1987). *Si tengo suerte* (If I'm Lucky) (s.1980). *Decir sí* (To Say Yes) (s.1981, Teatro del Picadero) (in Teatro Abierto 1981) p. in *Hispanoamérica* 7.21 (1978); in *Teatro: Las paredes. El desatino. Los siameses* (Barcelona: Editorial Argonauta, 1979); *21 estrenos argentinos* (Buenos Aires: Adans S.A., 1981). *La malasangre* (Bitter Blood) (s.1982, Teatro Olimpia) p. (Buenos Aires: Ediciones de la Flor, 1984). *Real envido* (s.1983) p. (Buenos Aires: Ediciones de la

Flor, 1984). *Del sol naciente* (The Rising Sun) (s.1984) p. (Buenos Aires: Ediciones de la Flor, 1984). *El despojamiento* (The Stripping) (s.1985) p. in *Tramoya* 21–22 (1981). *Nosferatu* (s.1986). *Puesta en claro* (Made Clear) (s.1986) p. (Buenos Aires, 1987). *Antígona furiosa* (Furious Antigone) (s.1988, Fundación de Tella Award). *Morgan* (s.1989). *Penas sin importancia* (Unimportant Sorrows) (s.1990, Sociedad de Críticos e Investigadores Teatrales Award).

BIBLIOGRAPHY: Mirta Arlt, "Los '80—Gambaro-Monti—y más allá," *Latin American Theatre Review* 24.2 (Spring 1991): 49–58. Joan Rea Boorman, "Contemporary Latin American Woman Dramatists," *Rice University Studies* 64.1 (1978): 69–80. Marta Contreras, *Griselda Gambaro: teatro de la descomposición* (Concepción: Ediciones Universidad de Concepción, 1994). David William Foster, "*La malasangre*, de Griselda Gambaro y la configuración dramática de un tema argentino," in *Teatro argentino de los '60—Polémica, continuidad y ruptura*, ed. Osvaldo Pellettieri (Buenos Aires: Corregidor, 1989), 199–206. Enrique A. Giordano, "*La malasangre* de Griselda Gambaro: Un proceso de reconstrucción y recodificación," in *Teatro argentino durante el proceso (1976–1983)*, ed. Juana Arancibia and Zulema Mírkin (Buenos Aires: Vinciguerra, 1992), 57–73. Kirsten Nigro, "Griselda Gambaro vista desde lejos: Primeros textos y contextos culturale," in *Teatro argentino de los '60—Polémica, continuidad y ruptura*, ed. Osvaldo Pellettieri (Buenos Aires: Corregidor, 1989), 169–181.

GARCÍA VELLOSO, Enrique (1880–1938).

Born in Rosario, Santa Fe, García Velloso was also a journalist, critic, professor, and theatrical director. He wrote more than 150 plays in different genres. He was also the founder and first president of Argentores (Sociedad Argentina de Autores Dramáticos–Argentine Society of Dramatists). Many of his plays are comedies, and his historical plays show his ability to present crowds on a stage. His play *Mamá Culepina* (1916) is considered one of the first to portray the true local color of Argentina.

WORKS: *Chin Yonk* (s.1893, Teatro de la Comedia), written in collaboration with Mauricio Nirenstein. *Instituto Frenopático* (Phrenopathic Institute) (s.1897). *Gabino el mayoral* (Gabino the Coachman) (s.1898, Teatro de la Comedia by the Company of Ramón Cebrián) p. in *El sainete criollo*

(Buenos Aires: Hachette, 1957). *Chiripá rojo* (Red Chiripá) (s.1900). *Jesús nazareno* (Jesus the Nazarene) (s.1902, Teatro Apolo) p. in *La escena* 52 (1919). *Caín* (s.1903). *Casa de soltero* (Bachelor's House) (s.1904, Teatro de la Comedia). *Fruta picada* (Chopped Fruit) (s.1907, Teatro Argentino). *El campo alegre* (The Happy Countryside) (s.1909). *Eclipse del sol* (The Sun's Eclipse) (s.1910, Teatro Apolo). *Tango en París* (Tango in Paris) (s.1913, Teatro Argentino). *Amores de la virreina* (The Loves of the Viceroy's Wife) (s.1914). *El zapato de cristal* (The Glass Shoe) (s.1915). *Mamá Culepina* (s.1916; 1941, Teatro Nacional de Comedia) p. (Buenos Aires: Colección Estrada, 1947), prologue by Martínez Cuitiño, includes *La cadena* (The Chain) and *Veinticuatro horas dictador* (Dictator for Twenty-four Hours). *La victoria de Samotracia* (Samotracia's Victory) (s.1917). *Las termas de Colo-colo* (The Hot Baths of Colo-Colo) (s.1918). *Morriña mía* (s.1921). *Una bala perdida* (A Lost Bullet) (s.1921). *Un hombre solo* (A Man Alone) (s.1925). *La sombra del pasado* (The Shadow of the Past) (s.1928). *El pasado renace* (The Past Is Reborn) (s.1938, Teatro Argentino, in homage after his death), third act written by Luis Rodríguez Acasuso. *El copetín* (The Aperitif) (s.1939, Teatro Argentino). For a list of complete works, see *Bibliografía de Enrique García Velloso* in *Boletín Academia Argentina de Letras* 6.21–22 (January–June 1938): 13–20.

BIBLIOGRAPHY: Tulio Carella, *El sainete criollo* (Buenos Aires: Hachette, 1957), 107. Blas Raúl Gallo, *Historia del sainete nacional* (Buenos Aires: Quetzal, 1958), 58–64. Willis Knapp Jones, *Behind Spanish American Footlights* (Austin: University of Texas, 1966), 155–156.

GHIANO, Juan Carlos (1920–).

Born in Nogoyá, Entre Ríos, Ghiano is a literary critic and notable dramatist of the 1950s. His play *La casa de los Montoya* (The Montoyas' House) was debuted in Buenos Aires in 1954 by a group from Paraná. Castagnino describes the work as a staged poem with elements of Valle-Inclán. The influence of the *esperpento* is more prominent in his next play, *Narcisa Garay, mujer para llorar* (Narcisa Garay, Woman Meant to Cry), which is characterized as a suburban tragicomedy.

WORKS: *La puerta al río* (The Door to the River) (s.1950). *La casa de los Montoya* (The Montoyas' House) (s.1954). *Narcisa Garay, mujer para llorar*

(Narcisa Garay, Woman Meant to Cry) (s.1959) p. (Buenos Aires: Talía, 1959); in *Teatro argentino contemporáneo* (Madrid: Aguilar, 1973). *La Moreira* (The Moreira) (s.1962) p. (Buenos Aires: Talía, 1962). *Los testigos* (The Witnesses) (s.1967) p. in *Actos del miedo* (Caracas: Monte Avila Editores, 1971), a collection of the following plays: *Los testigos, Los desmemoriados* (The Forgetful), *Los refugiados* (The Refugees), *Los sirvientes* (The Servants), *Los protegidos* (The Protected), *Los extraviados* (The Lost Ones), *Los devoradores* (Those Who Devour). *Corazón de tango* (The Heart of the Tango) (s.1968) p. (Buenos Aires: Talía, 1966). *La gula* (The Gluttony) (s.1970). *Antier* (The Day Before Yesterday) (s.1972) p. (Buenos Aires: Talía, 1966). *Explicación* (Explanation) p. in *Ceremonias de la soledad* (Buenos Aires: De la Flor, 1968), a collection of the following plays: *Explicación* (Explanation), *El abanico de Venecia* (The Venetian Fan), *R.S.I.V.P., Duelo por su conciencia* (Duel for His Conscience), *Nunca estaremos solas* (We Will Never Be Alone), *Pañuelo de llorar* (Handkerchief for Crying).

BIBLIOGRAPHY: Richard Allen, *Teatro hispanoamericano: Una bibliografía anotada* (Boston: G. K. Hall, 1987), 75–76. Raúl Héctor Castagnino, *Literatura dramática argentina (1717–1967)* (Buenos Aires: Pleamar, 1968), 178–179. Juan Carlos Ghiano, *Teatro argentino contemporáneo, 1949–1969* (Madrid: Aguilar, 1973), 45–49; Ghiano gives opinion of his work, 350–351.

GOROSTIZA, Carlos (1920–). Born in Palermo, a suburb of Buenos Aires. Gorostiza's first works were for his puppet theater. The plays were collected in *La clave encantada* (The Enchanted Clavichord) in 1942. At eighteen years of age he became involved as an actor in the independent Máscara Theater. Motivated by the lack of socially aware dramatists at the time, Gorostiza wrote *El puente* (The Bridge). The play shows the clash between the upper and lower classes in the Argentina of 1947. The reaction to *El puente* was enormous since the public enthusiastically identified with the play's local color and language.

WORKS: *El puente* (The Bridge) (s.1949, La Máscara), worked in collaboration with Pedro Doril, p. (Buenos Aires: Losange, 1954); (Buenos Aires: Talía, 1963); (Buenos Aires: Sudamericana, 1966); in *Teatro argentino contemporáneo* (Madrid: Agui-

lar, 1973). *El fabricante de piolín* (The Piolín Maker) (s.1950). *El caso del hombre de la valija negra* (The Case of the Man with the Black Suitcase) (s.1951) p. (Buenos Aires: La Máscara, 1951). *El juicio* (The Judgement) (s.1954). *Marta Ferrari* (s.1954). *El último perro* (The Last Dog) (s.1954), adaptation of the novel by Guillermo House. *El reloj de Baltasar* (Baltasar's Watch) (s.1955) p. (Buenos Aires: Losange, 1955). *El pan de la locura* (Bread of Insanity) (s.1958) p. (Buenos Aires: Talía, 1958; 1963); (Buenos Aires: Sudamericana, 1966); in *El teatro actual latinoamericano* (Mexico: Andrea, 1972). *Vivir aquí* (To Live Here) (s.1964) p. (Buenos Aires: Talía, 1964). *Los prójimos* (The Neighbors) (s.1967) p. (Buenos Aires: Sudamericana, 1966). *¿A qué jugamos?* (What Are We Playing?) (s.1968) p. (Buenos Aires: Sudamericana, 1969). *La clave encantada* (The Enchanted Clavichord), a collection of short plays for children p. (Buenos Aires: Talía, 1970). *La ira* (The Anger) (s.1970). *El lugar* (The Place) (s.1970) p. (Buenos Aires: Sudamericana, 1972). *Diálogo de dos sobrevivientes* (Dialogue of Two Survivors) (w.1972). *Los cinco sentidos capitales* (The Five Principal Senses) (s.1973). *Juana y Pedro* (s.1975). *La gallo y yo* (The Rooster and I) (s.1976). *Matar el tiempo* (Killing Time) (s.1982, Teatro Regina). *El acompañamiento* (The Accompaniment) (s.1981, Teatro del Picadero). *Hay que apagar el fuego* (The Fire Must Be Put Out) (s.1982, Teatro Abierto). *Papi* (Daddy) (s.1983). *El frac rojo* (The Red Dress-Coat) (s.1988, Teatro Ateneo). *Aeroplano* (Airplane) (s.1990).

BIBLIOGRAPHY: Rose Marie Armando, *Teatro argentino contemporáneo* (Buenos Aires: Revista Cultura, 1985), 37–43. Juan Carlos Ghiano, *Teatro argentino contemporáneo, 1949–1969* (Madrid: Aguilar, 1973), 24–29; Gorostiza gives opinion of his work, 58–59. William Knapp Jones, *Behind Spanish American Footlights* (Austin: University of Texas Press, 1966), 159–160.

GRIFFERO, Eugenio (1936–). A psychoanalyst, Griffero began his career as a dramatist in 1975 with the debut of *La fuerza del destino no trae mala suerte* (The Force of Destiny Doesn't Bring Bad Luck). In 1977 he presented a monologue, *Familia se vende* (Family for Sale). Five years later Griffero staged one of his most successful plays, *Principe azul* (Blue Prince), in the Argentine Teatro Abierto (Open Theater). Griffero's works are a mixture of opera, black humor, and the macabre.

WORKS: *La fuerza del destino no trae mala suerte* (The Force of Destiny Doesn't Bring Bad Luck) (s.1975). *Familia se vende* (Family for Sale) (s.1977). *La gripe* (The Flu) (s.1980, Teatro Municipal General San Martín). *Creatura* (Child) (s.1981). *Príncipe azul* (Blue Prince) (s.1982) p. in *Cuadernos de la Comedia Nacional* (June 1984). *El visitante extraordinario* (The Extraordinary Visitor) (s.1982, Teatro Margarita Xirgú). *El viento se los llevó* (The Wind Took Them Away) (s.1983), written in collaboration with Roberto Cossa, Francisco Anania, and Jacobo Lagsner. *Des tiempo* (Of Time) (s.1984, Teatro Cervantes), Molière Award. *Cuatro caballetes* (Four Little Horses) (s.1985). *La abeja en la miel* (The Bee in the Honey) (s.1991). *Pausa* (Pause) (s.1991). *Señora Beatriz* (Mrs. Beatrice) (s.1991). *Té de reinas* (Tea of Queens) (s.1991). *Viaje en globo* (A Trip by Balloon) (s.1991).

BIBLIOGRAPHY: Graciela Susana Puente, "Situación de re-encuentro en *Principe azul* de Eugenio Griffero," in *Teatro argentino durante el proceso (1976–1983)*, eds. Juana Arancibia and Zulema Mirkin (Buenos Aires: Vinciguerra, 1992), 141–153. Perla Zayas de Lima, *Diccionario de autores teatrales argentinos (1950–1980)* (Buenos Aires: Editorial Rudolfo Alonso, 1981), 88.

GROUSSAC, Paul (1848–1929). Born in Toulouse, France, Groussac arrived in Argentina at the age of eighteen. Author, essayist, and critic, he was a prominent figure in literary circles, and he founded the famous literary review *La biblioteca*. His only play, *La divisa punzó* (The Red Badge), establishes him as a valuable contributor to Argentine theater. The most popular play of 1923, it was revived in 1948 and had a run of over one hundred performances. The tragedy, whose title comes from the red badge worn by Rosas's followers, focuses on the dictator's trickery and egoism.

WORK: *La divisa punzó* (The Red Badge) (s.1923, Teatro de la Opera; s.1948, Teatro Nacional de la Comedia) p. (Buenos Aires: J. Menéndez, 1939).

BIBLIOGRAPHY: Tito Livio Foppa, *Diccionario teatral del Río de la Plata* (Buenos Aires: Carro de Tespis, 1961), 357–358. Roberto F. Giusti, "Paul Groussac," *La Prensa* (February 8, 1948). Willis Knapp Jones, *Behind Spanish American Footlights* (Austin: University of Texas Press, 1966), 160.

GUASTAVINO, Enrique (1898–1956). He began his dramatic career in 1927 with the debut of *Adriana y los cuatro* (The Four with Adriana). Guastavino's works are a faithful representation of good Argentine theater. His plays, mostly farces, are full of brilliant dialogue. In addition to being a critic, Guastavino also translated works by Rosso di San Secondo and Luigi Pirandello. He was director of the Argentino Theater in 1934.

WORKS: *Adriana y los cuatro* (The Four with Adriana) (s.1927). *Santa Fluvia* (Saint Fluvia) (s.1928). *La mujer más honesta del mundo* (The Most Honest Woman in the World) (s.1929). *El señor Pierrot y su dinero* (Mr. Pierrot and His Money) (s.1930). *La novia perdida* (The Lost Bride) (s.1941). *La importancia de ser ladrón* (The Importance of Being a Thief) (s.1942).

BIBLIOGRAPHY: Raúl Héctor Castagnino, *Literatura dramática argentina (1717–1967)* (Buenos Aires: Pleamar, 1968), 143. Luis Ordaz, *El teatro en el Río de la Plata* (Buenos Aires: Futuro, 1946), 138–139.

GUTIÉRREZ, Eduardo (1851–1889). Born in Buenos Aires to a prominent middle-class family, he began a career as a journalist and signed his pieces with the pseudonym "Hermenegildo Espumita." Around 1870 he joined the military, and for ten years he engaged in battles on the frontier against the Indians. After retiring from the military, Gutiérrez dedicated himself exclusively to writing, until his death from tuberculosis at the age of thirty-seven. The majority of his works consist of novels published in *folletines* (pamphlets) in various newspapers. Gutiérrez depicted the gaucho as victim of society in his novel *Juan Moreira* (published November 28, 1879–January 8, 1880, in *La Patria Argentina*). Four years later the actor José Podestá interpreted *Juan Moreira* in pantomime and received a favorable reception. Later in Chivilcoy, in 1886, Podestá and his troupe presented the work at the circus as a play, with dialogues extracted from the novel. The performance received an enthusiastic reception from the public, and most critics agree that from that moment the Argentine national theater was born.

WORKS: *Juan Moreira. Drama en dos actos* (s.1886), in collaboration with José J. Podestá, p. in *Orígenes del teatro nacional* (Buenos Aires: Instituto de Literatura Argentina, 1935); in *Teatro gauchesco primitivo* (Buenos Aires: Losange, 1957); in *Breve historia del teatro argentino*, vol. 2 (Buenos Aires: Editorial Universitaria de Buenos Aires, 1962); in *Enciclopedia Uruguaya*, n. 24 (Montevideo, 1968); in *Teatro rioplatense (1886–1930)* (Caracas: Biblioteca Ayacucho, 1977).

BIBLIOGRAPHY: Juan Carlos Ghiano, *Teatro gauchesco primitivo* (Buenos Aires: Ediciones Losange, 1957), 97–101. Luis Ordaz, *El teatro en el Río de la Plata* (Buenos Aires: Futuro, 1946), 35–37. David Viñas, *Teatro rioplatense (1886–1930)* (Caracas: Biblioteca Ayacucho, 1977), 1–19.

HALAC, Ricardo (1935–).

Born in Buenos Aires, Halac abandoned his studies of economics after receiving a scholarship from the Institute of Argentine-German Cultural Exchange in 1957. He lived in Munich and Berlin, and upon returning to Argentina, he wrote *Soledad para cuatro* (Solitude for Four). The play marks the beginning of the *nuevo realismo* (new realism) movement and deals with the deterioration of the middle-class family. For the first time the theater focuses on the anxiety, rebellion, and self-destruction of a whole generation of youth who function without moral guidance. Halac changes his style to the *nuevo grotesco* (new grotesque) with his later works. By 1983, with *Ruido de rotas cadenas* (The Sound of Broken Chains), Halac's characters show total despair and live in a world where love is almost nonexistent.

WORKS: *Soledad para cuatro* (Solitude for Four) (s.1961, La Máscara) p. in *Talía* 22 (1962); (Buenos Aires: Talía, 1962. *Estela de madrugada* (The Trail of Dawn) (s.1965) p. (Buenos Aires: The Angel Press, 1965). *Fin de Diciembre* (The End of December) (s.1965) p. (Buenos Aires: The Angel Press, 1965). *Tentempié I y II* (s.1969). *Segundo tiempo* (Second Period) (s.1976) p. (Buenos Aires: Ediciones Galerna, 1978). *El destete* (The Weaning) (s.1978). *Un trabajo fabuloso* (A Fabulous Work) (s.1980). *Lejana tierra prometida* (The Far, Promised Land) (s.1981). *Ruido de rotas cadenas* (The Sound of Broken Chains) (s.1983).

BIBLIOGRAPHY: Rose Marie Armando, *Teatro argentino contemporáneo* (Buenos Aires: Revista Cultura, 1985), 85–90. Luis Ordaz, *Aproximación a la trayectoria de la dramática argentina* (Ottawa: Girol Books, 1992), 72, 81. Ordaz, "Autores del 'nuevo realismo' de los años '60 a lo largo de las tres últimas décadas," *Latin American Theatre Review* 24.2 (Spring 1991): 42–43.

IMBERT, Julio (1918–).

Dramatist, poet, essayist, biographer, and director, Imbert was born in Rosario, Santa Fe. In 1951 he founded, together with his wife, actress Graciela Ensinck, Las Cuatro Tablas Theater in Rosario. His plays were performed both in Rosario and in Buenos Aires. One of his most significant works, *Los navegantes del Génesis* (The Navigators of the Genesis), a three-act tragedy, was shown on television in 1966. Earlier, his *Comedia de naranja* (Orange Comedy) was performed on the radio in 1953. Imbert wrote several one-act plays, of which *La noche más larga del año* (The Longest Night of the Year) won the 1957 University of La Plata contest. In another one-act play, *El diente*, a big incisor tooth symbolizes solidarity among men.

WORKS: *La lombriz* (The Worm) (s.1951). *Este lugar tiene cien fuegos* (This Place Has a Hundred Fires) (s.1952). *La mano* (The Hand) (s.1952) p. (Rosario: Ediciones Las Cuatro Tablas, 1953). *El reloj que no mide el tiempo* (The Watch That Doesn't Keep Time) (s.1953). *El diablo despide luz* (The Devil Throws Off Light) (s.1954). *Pelo de zanahoria* (Carrot's Hair) (s.1954). *La punta del alfiler* (The Point of the Pin) (s.1954). *Puyuta* (s.1955). *El diente* (The Tooth) (s.1956) p. (Buenos Aires: Losange, 1954). *Copelia* (s.1958). *La noche más larga del año* (The Longest Night of the Year) (s.1958) p. in *Comentario* 19 (April–June 1958). *Ursula duerme* (Ursula Sleeps) (s.1958) p. (Buenos Aires: Ediciones Hicancho, 1958). *Azor* (Goshawk) (s.1959) p. in *Comentario*: Act I in 26 (1960); Act II in 27 (1961); Act III in 28 (1961). *Comedia de naranja* (Orange Comedy) (s.1959). *Hesperidina para uno* (Hesperidin for One) p. in the *Clarín* of Buenos Aires (January 3, 1960) with the title of *Peppermint para uno* (Peppermint for One). *Panteras aquí* (Panthers Here) p. in *Revista de Teatro* 1 (November–December 1960). *La baba del diablo* (The Devil's Drool) (s.1961). *Electra* (s.1961) p. in *Los navegantes del Génesis*. *Electra* (Buenos Aires: Talía, 1964). *Los navegantes del Génesis* (The Navigators of the Genesis) (s.1961) p. (Buenos Aires: Talía, 1964). *Bio-*

grafía de estela transparente (Biography of a Transparent Stela) (s.1962). *Los hijos del verano* (Summer's Children) (s.1962) p. (Buenos Aires: Carro de Tespis, 1962). *El señor Comisario come pan* (Mr. Commissioner Eats Bread) (s.1962). *Día caprichoso* (Capricious Day) (s.1963). *Camila O'Gorman* p. (Buenos Aires: Talía, 1968). *Un ángel en la mantequería* (An Angel in the Grocer's Shop) (s.1969) p. (Buenos Aires: Talía, 1969).

BIBLIOGRAPHY: Willis Knapp Jones, *Behind Spanish American Footlights* (Austin: University of Texas Press, 1966), 161–162. Erminio G. Neglia and Luis Ordaz, *Repertorio selecto del teatro hispanoamericano contemporáneo* (Tempe: Arizona State University, 1980), 13–14. Perla Zayas de Lima, *Diccionario de autores teatrales argentinos (1950–1980)* (Buenos Aires: Editorial Rodolfo Alonso, 1981), 94–96.

INDEPENDENT THEATER MOVEMENT

The independent theater movement began in Argentina with the Teatro del Pueblo in 1930. Founded by the poet and writer Leónidas Barletta, it featured actors who distanced themselves from the commercial theater and its professional influence. Its purpose was to bring the community in touch with the best expressions of dramatic art by providing a stage for the most capable national writers. The movement aimed to train the actors and technicians and to place the actor at the service of the play instead of the other way around, which seemed customary at the time. Barletta's company inspired the formation of the following groups: Teatro Juan B. Justo, La Máscara, La Cortina, Teatro Experimental, Tinglado, Espondeo, Obra, Nuevo Teatro, Teatro Ensayo, El Gallo Petirrojo: M.E.E.B.A., Fray Mocho, Los Independientes, Di Tella, and finally the theater group of the Institute of Modern Art. The numerous groups (over fifty) supported an artistic and cultural movement that was capable of renovating the theater at every level. In a few years the groups multiplied and expanded throughout the Republic and at the same time influenced similar activity in the neighboring countries of Uruguay, Chile, Bolivia, Paraguay, and Peru.

BIBLIOGRAPHY: Enzo Aloisi, "Argentines Behind the Footlights: Twenty Years of Independent Theaters," *Américas* 4 (1952): 21–23, 44–45. David William Foster, *The Argentine teatro independiente, 1930–1955* (York, SC: Spanish Literature Publishing Co., 1986). Luiz Ordaz, *El teatro en el Río de la Plata* (Buenos Aires: Futuro, 1946), 163–194.

KARTUN, Mauricio (1946–). Born in San Martín, a suburb of Buenos Aires, Kartun is involved in theater, film, and radio in every aspect, from acting to writing. He gained popularity in the 1970s with the debut of *Civilización . . . O barbarie?* (Civilization . . . or Barbarism?). In 1980 he achieved popularity with *¡Chau, Misterix!* (Goodbye, Misterix!), about the frustrations of a ten-year-old boy who wants to be a fictional character. Kartun's following two works—*La casita de los viejos* (The Little House of the Old) and *Cumbia morena Cumbia* (Cumbia Dark Cumbia)—were part of the Argentine Teatro Abierto (Open Theater) in 1982 and 1983, respectively. *El partener* (The Partner) (1988) shows Kartun's ability to portray the individual in conflict with his surroundings.

WORKS: *Civilización . . . O barbarie?* (Civilization . . . or Barbarism?) (s.1973), w. in collaboration with H. Riva. *Gente muy así* (Snooty People) (s.1976). *El hambre da para todo* (Hunger Hits All) (s.1978). *¡Chau, Misterix!* (Goodbye, Misterix!) (s.1980, Teatro Auditorio Buenos Aires) p. in *4 Autores Teatro* (Buenos Aires: Argentores, 1985). *La casita de los viejos* (The Little House of the Old) (s.1982, Teatro Margarita Xirgú) p. in *8 Autores Teatro* (Buenos Aires: Argentores, 1985). *Cumbia morena Cumbia* (Cumbia Dark Cumbia) (s.1983) p. in *8 Autores Teatro* (Buenos Aires: Argentores, 1985). *Pericones* (Quadrille Dances) (s.1987). *El partener* (The Partner) (s.1988, Teatro Lorange).

BIBLIOGRAPHY: Darrell B. Lockhart, "Pasos para negar la realidad: *Cumbia morena Cumbia* de Mauricio Kartun," in *Teatro argentino durante el proceso (1976–1983)*, ed. Juana Arancibia and Zulema Mirkin (Buenos Aires: Vinciguerra, 1992), 75–90. Osvaldo Pellettieri, "La puesta en escena argentina de los '80: Realismo, estilización y parodia," *Latin American Theatre Review* 24.2 (Spring 1991): 117–131. Osvaldo Pellettieri, "El texto espectacular de *El partener* de Mauricio Kartun," in *Cien años de teatro argentino (1886–1990)* (Buenos Aires: Editorial Galerna, 1990), 153–173. Pellettieri, "Mauricio Kartun y el teatro nacional." *Teatro* Tomo II (Buenos Aires: Ediciones Corregidor, 1999), 9–28.

LAFERRÈRE, Gregorio de (1867–1913). Born in Buenos Aires, Laferrère's father was a rich Frenchman and his mother a descendant of Argentine nobility. Laferrère's sole intention as a playwright was to entertain. He felt no desire to express social criticism, and his writing was arbitrary. Even so, all his plays were successful. *Las de Barranco*, considered to be his masterpiece, displays a realistic conclusion instead of the commercial happy ending.

WORKS: *¡Jettatore!* (The Jinxer!) (s.1904). *Locos de verano* (The Insane of Summer) (s.1905). *Bajo la garra* (Under the Grip) (s.1906) p. in *Argentores* 100 (1936). *Las de Barranco* (Barranco's Women) p. in *Argentores* 165 (1939); in *Teatro rioplatense* (Caracas: Biblioteca Ayacucho, 1977). *Los invisibles* (The Invisible) (s.1911). Laferrère's works are published in: *Teatro completo* (Santa Fe, 1952), prologue and notes by E.M.S. Danero; *Obras escogidas* (Buenos Aires, 1953), prologue and notes by José María Monner Sans.

BIBLIOGRAPHY: Julio Imbert, *Gregorio de Laferrère* (Buenos Aires, 1962). Willis Knapp Jones, *Behind Spanish American Footlights* (Austin: University of Texas Press, 1966), 127–128. David Viñas, *Del apogeo de la oligarquía a la crisis de la ciudad liberal: Laferrère* (Rosario, 1965). Viñas, *Teatro rioplatense (1886–1930)* (Caracas: Biblioteca Ayacucho, 1977), 179.

LARRETA, Enrique (1873–1961). Born and died in Buenos Aires. Larreta was from a rich family of aristocratic landowners. He studied law and social sciences and later was a prominent diplomat. His plays, mostly sentimental dramas of the upper class, superficially develop themes from his novels. He made his theatrical debut in 1932 with a gaucho drama, *El linyera* (The Vagabond). He also wrote a historical play, *Santa María del Buen Aire* (Holy Mary of the Good Air) (s.1935), which was staged in Madrid one year before its debut in Buenos Aires. The play shows Larreta's ability to stage the history of the Spanish conquest.

WORKS: *El linyera* (The Vagabond) (s.1932, Teatro Ateneo by the Enrique de Rosas Company) p. (Buenos Aires: Sopena Argentina, 1940); (Buenos Aires: Espasa-Calpe Argentina, 1944); in *Obras completas* (Buenos Aires: Antonio Zamora, 1959). *La luciérnaga* (The Firefly) (s.1932, Teatro Cervantes). *Santa María del Buen Aire* (Holy Mary of the Good Air) (s.1935, Madrid-Teatro Español; s.1936, Buenos Aires) p. (Buenos Aires: Viau y Zona, 1936); (Buenos Aires: Espasa-Calpe Argentina, 1944). *Pasión de Roma* (Passion of Rome) (s.1937) p. (Buenos Aires: Espasa-Calpe Argentina, 1944); (Buenos Aires: Tall. Gráf. Argentinos L. J. Rosso, 1937). *La que buscaba Don Juan* (The One Don Juan Was Looking For) (s.1938) p. (Buenos Aires: Tall. Gráf. Argentinos L. J. Rosso, 1938). *Tenía que suceder* (It Had to Happen) (s.1943). *Jerónimo y su almohada* (Jeronimo and His Pillow) (s.1945) p. (Buenos Aires: El Ateneo, 1945). *Clamor* (s.1959). *Dramáticas personas* (a collection of four movie scripts and a three-act drama) p. (Buenos Aires: Kraft, 1959). All of Larreta's plays are published in *Obras completas* (Buenos Aires: Antonio Zamora, 1959).

BIBLIOGRAPHY: Arturo Berenguer Carisomo, *Los valores eternos en la obra de Enrique Larreta* (Buenos Aires, 1946). Carmelo Bonet, "Enrique Larreta, visión panorámica de su obra," *Boletín Academia Argentina de letras* 121 (1966): 419–449. Tito Livio Foppa, *Diccionario teatral del Río de la Plata* (Buenos Aires: Ediciones de Carro de Tespis, 1961), 396–397.

LAVARDÉN, Manuel José de (1754–1809). Dramatist and poet, he studied in Buenos Aires and Chuquisaca before going to Spain, where he obtained his law degree. While in Chuquisaca he wrote a theatrical piece called *Los Araucanos* (The Araucanians). His father's death hastened his return to Buenos Aires, where he became involved with a group of poets who organized La Sociedad Patriótica Literaria (The Patriotic Literary Society). Above all, Lavardén is known to be the first native dramatist to offer a play to the Argentine stage: *Siripo* was performed on a Sunday during the carnival season of 1789 in the Ranchería Theater. The neoclassic tragedy is important for establishing the cultured path of the Argentine theater. The popular course was initiated by *El amor de la estanciera* (The Ranch Woman's Love), an anonymous play that was probably also performed at the Ranchería Theater.

WORKS: *Los Araucanos* (The Araucanians) (n.d.). *Siripo* (s.1789, Ranchería Theater). *La muerte de Filipo de Macedonia* (The Death of Philip of Macedonia) (n.d.). *La pérdida de Jerusalem* (The Loss of Jerusalem) (n.d.).

BIBLIOGRAPHY: Arturo Berenguer Carisomo, "El neo-clasicismo (Lavardén)," in *Las ideas estéticas en el teatro argentino* (Buenos Aires: Instituto Nacional de Estudios de Teatro, 1947). Mariano G. Bosch, *Manuel de Lavardén, poeta y filósofo* (Buenos Aires: Sociedad General de Autores de la Argentina, 1944). Alberto Ghiraldo, "Un precursor del teatro en América, Manuel José de Lavardén," *Atenea* 142 (1937): 88–97.

LEGUIZAMÓN, Martiniano (1858–1935).

Born in Rosario del Tala, Entre Ríos, Leguizamón studied at the Colegio de Concepción del Uruguay in Entre Ríos and at eighteen wrote *Los apuros del sábado* (The Hardships of Saturday) for an improvisational acting group. After graduating, he moved to Buenos Aires, where he studied law and practiced journalism. His most important work, *Calandria*, was staged in 1896 by the Podestá-Scotti Company in a theater instead of at the circus, which was where gaucho plays were performed until then. *Calandria* ends the cycle of the gaucho drama that started in 1884 with the pantomime representation of *Juan Moreira*. Luis Ordaz describes the work as a rural comedy without tragic deaths or confrontations between the *milicos* and the "gauchos," a common portrayal in other plays before *Calandria*. The protagonist, Servando Cardoso, acquires the nickname of Calandria, which means "mockingbird," for his refusal to be caged in the army. Leguizamón solves the gaucho problem by turning him into a useful citizen, skilled at managing a ranch.

WORKS: *Los apuros del sábado* (The Hardships of Saturday) (s.1877, Teatro Colón, Entre Ríos). *Calandria* (s.1896, Teatro de la Victoria), p. in *Argentores* 8 (1919); (Buenos Aires: Ediciones Solar/Hachette, 1961), 26–108; in *Teatro rioplatense (1886–1931)* (Caracas: Biblioteca Ayacucho, 1977). *Del tiempo viejo* (From Old Times) (s.1915, Teatro San Martín). *La muerta* (The Dead Lady) (n.d.).

BIBLIOGRAPHY: Luis Ordaz, *Aproximación a la trayectoria de la dramática argentina* (Ottawa: Girol Books, 1992), 28. Ordaz, *El teatro en el Río de la Plata* (Buenos Aires: Futuro, 1946), 38–39. Osvaldo Pelletieri, *Cien años de teatro argentino (1886–1990)* (Buenos Aires: Galerna, 1990), 15–26. David Viñas, *Teatro rioplatense (1886–1930)* (Caracas: Biblioteca Ayacucho, 1977), 21.

LIZARRAGA, Andrés (1919–1982).

Born in La Plata, Lizarraga began his theatrical career in 1956. His most important contribution to the Argentine theater is a historical trilogy about the battles of the patriotic forces in northern Argentina during the period of the May Revolution of 1810 known as La Campaña del Alto Perú (The Campaign of High Peru). The trilogy consists of *Alto Perú* (High Peru), *Santa Juana de América* (Saint Joan of America), and *Tres jueces para un largo silencio* (Three Judges for a Long Silence). The plays share the same themes and cries for justice and freedom. Luis Ordaz considers Lizarraga as one of three authors of the 1960s (along with Agustín Cuzzani and Osvaldo Dragún) whose theater is characterized by its social criticism.

WORKS: *Desde el 80* (Since 80) (s.1958) w. in collaboration with Osvaldo Dragún. *Alto Perú* (High Peru) (s.1960) p. (Buenos Aires: Quetzal, 1962). *El carro eternidad* (The Eternity Car) (s.1960) p. (Buenos Aires: Quetzal, 1962). *Los Linares* (The Linares) (s.1960) p. (Buenos Aires: Talía, 1959); (Buenos Aires: Quetzal, 1962). *Santa Juana de América* (Saint Joan of America) (s.1960) p. (Havana: Casa de las Américas, 1960); (Buenos Aires: Quetzal, 1962). *Tres jueces para un largo silencio* (Three Judges for a Long Silence) (s.1960) p. (Buenos Aires: Quetzal, 1962); (Buenos Aires: Centro Editor de América Latina, 1966). *Un color soledad* (A Lonely Color) (s.1963) p. (Buenos Aires: Quetzal, 1962). *¡Y dale que va!* (There It Goes Again!) (s.1963) p. (Buenos Aires: Quetzal, 1962). *¿Quiere Ud. comprar un pueblo?* (Do You Want to Buy a Town?) p. (Buenos Aires: La Rosa Blindada, 1964). *Jack el destripador* (Jack the Ripper) (s.1967). *La cama y el emperador* (The Bed and the Emperor) (s.1970). *Romeo, Julieta y el tango* (Romeo, Juliette and the Tango) (s.1971).

BIBLIOGRAPHY: Erminio G. Neglia and Luis Ordaz, *Repertorio selecto del teatro hispanoamericano contemporáneo* (Tempe: Arizona State University, 1980), 14. Luis Ordaz, *Aproximación a la trayectoria de la dramática argentina* (Ottawa: Girol Books, 1992), 65–66. Perla Zayas de Lima, *Diccionario de autores teatrales argentinos (1950–1980)* (Buenos Aires: Editorial Rodolfo Alonso, 1981), 104–105.

LÓPEZ DE GOMARA, Justo S. (1859–

1923). Born in Spain, where he was a journalist

and director of the daily *El Español*. Upon arriving in Argentina, he settled in Rosario and became interested in the theater. There he debuted his first work, *Gauchos y gringos* (Gauchos and Foreigners), in 1884. His subsequent works were presented in Buenos Aires. López de Gomara is known as the first Argentine playwright to demand a percentage from the performance revenues. In 1889 he received 20 percent of the profits for *De paseo en Buenos Aires* (Promenading in Buenos Aires), a presentation of *porteños* (people from Buenos Aires) of various social classes. He is mostly remembered for his short political plays.

WORKS: *Gauchos y gringos* (Gauchos and Foreigners) (s.1884, in Rosario by the Juan Roigt Company). *La justicia de la tierra* (Justice of the Earth) (s.1887, Teatro Onrubia). *El submarino Peral* (The Peral Submarine) (s.1888, Teatro San Martín). *De paseo en Buenos Aires* (Promenading in Buenos Aires) (s.1889, Teatro Onrubia). *Valor cívico* (Civic Valor) (s.1890, Teatro Goldoni). *La sombra del prestigio* (The Shadow of Prestige) (s.1908, Teatro Argentino by the Florencio Parravicini Company).

BIBLIOGRAPHY: Raúl Héctor Castagnino, *Literatura dramática argentina (1717–1967)* (Buenos Aires: Pleamar, 1968), 93. Tito Livio Foppa, *Diccionario teatral del Río de la Plata* (Buenos Aires: Ediciones de Carro de Tespis, 1961), 413–414. Luis Ordaz, *El teatro en el Río de la Plata* (Buenos Aires: Futuro, 1946), 103.

MALFATTI, Arnaldo Mario Germán (1893–1968).

Born in Buenos Aires, Malfatti was one of Argentina's most prolific dramatists. He wrote over one hundred plays, either alone or in collaboration, spanning over three decades. His works include *sainetes* (one-act comedies), reviews, farces, operettas, and comedies. Most of his plays were successful, some having over one hundred consecutive performances. The comedy *Así es la vida* (Such Is Life) (s.1934) captures three decades of Argentine history through the presentation of middle-class family life. Malfatti also held various positions in the organizations of Argentores and Casa de Teatro.

WORKS: *¿Trabajar? ¡Nunca!* (Work? Never!) (s.1922, Teatro Opera by Roberto Casaux). *Los tres berretines* (Three Fits of Anger) (s.1932) p. (Buenos Aires: Carro de Tespis, 1965). *Así es la vida* (Such Is Life) (s.1934, Teatro Nacional by the Muiño-Alippi Company) p. in *Teatro argentino contemporáneo* (Madrid: Aguilar, 1962). *Al marido hay que seguirlo* (You Have to Follow Your Husband) (s.1943). *Una cándida paloma* (An Ingenuous Dove) (s.1945). *Vidas porteñas* (Lives of Buenos Aires) (s.1947). *¡Ah . . . si yo fuera rica!* (Oh . . . If I Were Rich!) (s.1951). *Valentía de pecar* (Courage to Sin) (s.1952). *Mi mujer, la nena . . . y pobre de mi* (My Wife, My Child . . . Poor Me) (s.1954). *Una viudita caprichosa* (A Capricious Little Widow) (s.1954). *Un escote que trae cola* (An Ascot That Carries a Tail) (s.1956). *El amor no pide permiso* (Love Doesn't Ask Permission) (s.1966).

BIBLIOGRAPHY: Arturo Bernguer Carisomo, *Teatro argentino contemporáneo* (Madrid: Aguilar, 1960), introduction. Tito Livio Foppa, *Diccionario teatral del Río de la Plata* (Buenos Aires: Ediciones de Carro de Tespis, 1961), 427–428. Luis Ordaz, *El teatro en el Río de la Plata* (Buenos Aires: Futuro, 1946), 140–144. Perla Zayas de Lima, *Diccionario de autores teatrales argentinos (1950–1980)* (Buenos Aires: Editorial Rodolfo Alonso, 1981), 110.

MARECHAL, Leopoldo (1900–1970).

Born in Buenos Aires to a middle-class family of Italian, French, and Spanish lineage. He was an outstanding figure in Argentine literature and wrote in various genres: novels, poetry, plays, essays, and epistles. Marechal began his dramatic career in 1950 with *El canto de San Martín* (San Martín's Chant), written in homage to the first centennial of the death of General San Martín. The dramatic oratory, with music by Julio Perceval, was performed in Mendoza. In 1951 he presented *Antígona Vélez*, based on the Greek myth of Antigone, transposed to Argentine territory. It won the first Culture Prize for 1951–1953.

WORKS: *El canto de San Martín* (San Martín's Chant) (s.1950, Mendoza). *Antígona Vélez* (s.1951, Teatro Nacional Cervantes) p. (Buenos Aires: Citerea, 1965). *Las tres caras de venus* (The Three Faces of Venus) (s.1952, Teatro Ateneo) p. (Buenos Aires: Citerea, 1966). *La batalla de José Luna* (José Luna's Battle) (s.1967) p. (Santiago de Chile: Ed. Univ., 1970).

BIBLIOGRAPHY: Graciela Maturo, "Leopoldo Marecha," in *Bibliografía de escritores hispanoam-*

ericanos 1609–1974 (New York: Gordian Press, 1975), 887–895. Rafael F. Squirru, *Leopoldo Marechal* (Buenos Aires: Ediciones Culturales Argentinas, 1961). Perla Zayas de Lima, *Diccionario de autores teatrales argentinos (1950–1980)* (Buenos Aires: Editorial Rodolfo Alonso, 1981), 112–113.

MARTÍNEZ CUITIÑO, Vicente (1887–1964).
Born in Astilleros, Uruguay, his family moved to Argentina in his youth. Martínez Cuitiño wrote *Rayito de sol* (A Little Ray of Sun) as a student in Geneva. The play was staged in Buenos Aires in 1909. He wrote in many genres, from plays of customs to vanguard experimentation, and always focused on the human condition of his times. He was also the first secretary of the Argentine Society of Authors and eventually became the group's president.

WORKS: *El único gesto* (The Only Gesture) (s.1908). *El derrumbe* (The Collapse) (s.1909). *Rayito de sol* (A Little Ray of Sun) (s.1909, Teatro Argentino). *Mate dulce* (Sweet Tea) (s.1911). *Los Colombini* (The Colombinis) (s.1912). *La fuerza ciega* (The Blind Force) (s.1917). *La fiesta del hombre* (The Man's Feast) (s.1919). *El malón blanco* (The White Raid) (s.1922), winner of the First Municipal Prize of 1922. *El espectador o la cuarta realidad* (The Spectator or the Fourth Reality) (s.1928). *Extraña* (Strange) (s.1929). *Atorrante o La venganza de la tierra* (Lazy or The Earth's Vengeance) (s.1932). *Horizontes* (Horizons) (s.1934). *Superficie* (The Surface) (s.1934).

BIBLIOGRAPHY: Tito Livio Foppa, *Diccionario teatral del Río de la Plata* (Buenos Aires: Carro de Tespis, 1961), 439–440. Luis Ordaz, *El teatro en el Río de la Plata* (Buenos Aires: Futuro, 1946), 140. Pedro Orgambide and Roberto Yahni, *Enciclopedia de la literatura argentina* (Buenos Aires: Sudamericana, 1970), 437–438.

MAURICIO, Julio (1919–   ).
Born in Buenos Aires, Mauricio was first a notable film director before he began a theatrical career. His first play, *Motivos* (Motives), received first prize from the Ministerial Department of Culture of Buenos Aires in 1964. His next play, *La valija* (The Suitcase) (1968), establishes him as one of the initiators of the local *nuevo grotesco* (new grotesque) movement. The play, which debuted in Nuevo Teatro, achieved immediate success. The scenes of *La valija* range from humorous to pathetic. Censorship forced Mauricio into a period of silence between 1972 and 1982, after which he presented *Elvira*.

WORKS: *Motivos* (Motives) (s.1964) p. (Buenos Aires: Talía, 1964). *La valija* (The Suitcase) (s.1968) p. (Buenos Aires: Talía, 1969). *En la mentira* (In the Lie) (s.1969) p. (Buenos Aires: Talía, 1969). *La depresión* (The Depression) (s.1970) p. (Buenos Aires: Talía 1970). *Un despido corriente* (A Fast Goodbye) (s.1972). *La puerta* (The Door) (s.1972). *Geón* (w. in 1973). *Los retratos* (The Pictures) (s.1974) p. in *Caminos del teatro latinoamericano* (La Habana: Casa de las Américas, 1973). *Elvira* (s.1982, Teatro Nacional Cervantes). *El enganche* (The Hook) (s.1982).

BIBLIOGRAPHY: Luis Ordaz, "Autores del 'nuevo realismo' de los años '60 a lo largo de las tres últimas décadas," *Latin American Theatre Review* 24.2 (Spring 1991): 46. Perla Zayas de Lima, *Diccionario de autores teatrales argentinos (1950–1980)* (Buenos Aires: Editorial Rodolfo Alonso, 1981), 117.

MERTENS, Federico (1886–1960).
Born in Buenos Aires, Mertens was an essayist, critic, and director of several important companies of actors. He made his transition from essayist to dramatist in 1908, with *Gente bien* (Good People) and *Las d'enfrente* (Those Opposite). Mertens is known as an important illustrator of middle-class customs of the beginning of the twentieth century. Mertens's comedies were enthusiastically received except for his experimental *Amor del sendero* (Love of the Pathway) (s.1946), in which he used his characters as puppets throughout the play.

WORKS: *Gente bien* (Good People) (s.1908). *Las d'enfrente* (Those Opposite) (s.1909) p. in *Talía* 8 (1936). *El orgullo de la casa* (The Pride of the House) (s.1911). *La carabina de Ambrosio* (A Dead Loss) (s.1918). *La familia de mi sastre* (My Tailor's Family) (s.1918). *El tren de las 10:30* (The 10:30 Train) (s.1918) p. in *Bambalinas* 17 (1919). *Mamá Clara* (Mother Clara) (s.1920) p. in *La Escena* 133 (1921). *La familia Pickaerpak* (The Pickaerpak Family) (s.1927). *La clase media* (The Middle Class) (s.1928). *Adán y Eva se divierten* (Adam and Eve Are Having Fun) (s.1929). *El padre Mediasuela* (Father Mediasuela) (s.1933). *Reformatorio Internacional de Señoritas* (International Reformatory for

Young Women) (s.1934). *La tragedia de un hombre feo* (The Tragedy of an Ugly Man) (s.1934). *La zarza en llamas* (The Burning Bush) (s.1941) p. in *Argentores* (1941), Second Prize of the National Cultural Commission. *Amor del sendero* (Love of the Pathway) (s.1946), Third Prize of the National Cultural Commission.

BIBLIOGRAPHY: Tito Livio Foppa, *Diccionario teatral del Río de la Plata* (Buenos Aires: Ediciones de Carro de Tespis, 1961), 453–454. Willis Knapp Jones, *Behind Spanish American Footlights* (Austin: University of Texas Press, 1966). Luis Ordaz, *Aproximación a la trayectoria de la dramática argentina* (Ottawa: Girol Books, 1992), 35.

MONTI, Ricardo (1944–). Born in Buenos Aires, Monti's interest in the theater began at the age of nine. Monti began his career as a playwright in 1970 with the debut of *Una noche con el señor Magnus e hijos* (An Evening with Mr. Magnus and His Children), performed by the Grupo Laboratorio (Laboratory Group). The play, which received three prizes, proposed to represent the middle class with the use of symbolic characters. Monti has been described as the dramatist of imagery, who strives to capture the essence of man, the meaning of reality, and the mood of the times. In *Marathón* (s.1980), an individual is trapped in a reality he wishes to escape. The play takes place during a dance marathon of tangos and milongas set in Buenos Aires during the crisis of the 1930s. Monti's plays have been performed throughout Argentina, Mexico, Costa Rica, Brazil, Spain, and Italy.

WORKS: *Una noche con el señor Magnus e hijos* (An Evening with Mr. Magnus and His Children) (s.1970), Argentores, Pilar de Luzarreta, and Pondal Ríos Prizes, p. (Buenos Aires: Talía, 1970). *Historia tendenciosa de la clase media argentina, de los extraños sucesos en que se vieron envueltos algunos hombres públicos, su completa dilucidación y otras escandalosas revelaciones* (The Tendentious History of the Argentine Middle Class, of the Strange Events in Which Some Public Men Found Themselves Involved, Its Complete Elucidation and Other Scandalous Revelations) (s.1971, Teatro Payró) p. (Buenos Aires: Talía, 1971). *Visita* (Visit) (s.1977), Carlos Arniches Award (Spain), p. (Buenos Aires: Talía, 1979). *Marathón* (s.1980, Los Teatros de San Telmo) p. in *El teatro argentino: Cierre de un ciclo,* ed. Luis Ordaz (Buenos Aires: CEAL, 1981). *La cortina de abalorios* (The Beaded Curtain) (s.1981, Teatro Abierto). *Una pasión sudamericana* (A South American Passion). *Marathon* (s.1990, Opera).

BIBLIOGRAPHY: Jorge J. Monteleone, "El teatro de Ricardo Monti," *Espacio* 2 (1987): 63–82. Peter L. Podol, "Surrealism and the Grotesque in the Theatre of Ricardo Monti," *Latin American Theatre Review* 14.1 (1980): 65–72. Mario Rojas, "*Marathon* y el discurso dramático del Proceso," in *Teatro argentino durante el proceso (1976–1983)*, ed. Juana Arancibia and Zulema Mirkin (Buenos Aires: Vinciguerra, 1992), 155–170. Julia Elena Sagaceta, "La dramaturgia de Ricardo Monti: La seducción de la escritura," in *Teatro argentino de los '60—Polémica, continuidad y ruptura*, ed. Osvaldo Pelletieri (Buenos Aires: Corregidor, 1989), 227–241. Beatriz Trastoy, "Teatro político: Producción y recepción (notas sobre *La cortina de abalorios*, de Ricardo Monti)," in *Teatro argentino de los '60—Polémica, continuidad y ruptura*, ed. Osvaldo Pelletieri (Buenos Aires: Corregidor, 1989), 217–223.

MOSQUERA, Beatriz (1936–). Mosquera studied acting, philosophy, and literature before presenting a children's play, *Tolón y Tolina*, in 1968. In 1970 she debuted *Mira lo que te está pasando* (Look What's Happening to You), a theatrical work of sketches and songs. Many of Mosquera's works are full of irony and humor. The debut of *La luna en la taza* (The Moon in the Cup) in 1979, during the military regime, shows her preoccupation with the country's destiny and human relationships.

WORKS: *Tolón y Tolina* (s.1968) w. in collaboration with Mara Lasio. *Un domingo después del lunes* (A Sunday After Monday) (s.1969). *Mira lo que te está pasando* (Look What's Happening to You) (s.1970). *Qué clase de lucha es la lucha de clases* (What Kind of Struggle Is the Class Struggle) (s.1972). *La luna en la taza* (The Moon in the Cup) (s.1979, Teatro del Centro) p. (Buenos Aires: Editorial Tierra Firme, 1987). *Ronda de encapuchados* (Round of the Hooded) (w.1979). *Despedida en el lugar* (Farewell at That Place) (s.1982, Teatro Odeón) p. (Buenos Aires: Editorial Tierra Firme, 1987). *Sábado a la noche* (Saturday Night) (s.1982). *Irredenta* (Unredempted) (s.1983) p. (Buenos Aires: Editorial Tierra Firme, 1987). *Otra vez la luna* (The Moon Again) (s.1984) p. (Buenos Aires: Editorial Tierra Firme, 1987). *En nuestro propio nombre* (In Our Own Name) (s.1986). *Violeta Parra y sus voces*

(Violeta Parra and Her Voices) (s.1988). *El último convento* (The Last Convent), debuted as *Bay Bay Buenos Aires* (Bye, Bye Buenos Aires) (s.1989). *Entre ustedes y yo (en ropa interior)* (Between All of You and I [in Underwear]) (s.1991). *Gotas de rocío sobre flores de papel* (Dew Drops on Paper Flowers) (s.1991). *La soga* (The Rope) (s.1991).

BIBLIOGRAPHY: Marta A. Lena Paz, *"La luna en la taza*: Fragmentación de la esperanza," in *Teatro argentino durante el proceso (1976–1983)*, ed. Juana Arancibia and Zulema Mirkin (Buenos Aires: Vinciguerra, 1992), 113–122. Perla Zayas de Lima, *Diccionario de autores teatrales argentinos (1950–1980)* (Buenos Aires: Editorial Rodolfo Alonso, 1981), 121–122.

NALÉ ROXLO, Conrado (1898–1971). Nalé Roxlo was born in Buenos Aires on February 15, 1898. He became a poet, humorist, and dramatist. His plays show a continuation of the themes found in his poetry and focus on the love relationships between male and female protagonists. Most of Nalé Roxlo's titles imply or refer to a female character since he seeks to explore, in a poetic and humorous way, the passionate aspects of feminine behavior.

WORKS: *La cola de la sirena* (The Mermaid's Tail) (s.1941) p. (Buenos Aires: Hachette, 1957); in *La cola de la sirena. Una viuda difícil. El pacto de Cristina. Judith y las rosas* (Buenos Aires: Sudamericana, 1957); (Buenos Aires: Huemul, 1973). *Una viuda difícil* (A Difficult Widow) (s.1944) p. (Buenos Aires: Poseidon, 1944); in *La cola de la sirena . . .* (Buenos Aires: Sudamericana, 1957). *El pacto de Cristina* (Cristina's Pact) (s.1945) p. in *La cola de la sirena . . .* (Buenos Aires: Sudamericana, 1957); in *La cola de la sirena . . .* (Buenos Aires: Huemul, 1973); in *Los clásicos del teatro hispanoamericano* (Mexico City: Fondo de Cultura Económica, 1975). *Judith y las rosas* (Judith and the Roses) (s.1956) p. in *La cola de la sirena . . .* (Buenos Aires: Sudamericana, 1957). *La culpa* (The Blame) (s.1957). *El juego de la virtud* (The Game of Virtue) (s.1957). *El nuevo David* (The New David) (s.1959). *El neblí* p. in *Teatro breve* (Buenos Aires: Huemul, 1964; 1969). *El pasado de Elisa* (Elisa's Past) p. in *Teatro breve* (Buenos Aires: Huemul, 1964). *El reencuentro* (The Reencounter) p. in *Teatro breve* (Buenos Aires: Huemul, 1964). *El vacío* (The Void) p. in *Teatro breve* (Buenos Aires: Huemul, 1964). *A la manera de . . .* (In the Way of . . .) (s.1969). *Cordelia la niña hada* (Cordelia the Fairy Child) (s.1969).

BIBLIOGRAPHY: Arturo Berenguer Carisomo, *Conrado Nalé Roxlo* (Buenos Aires: A-Z Editora, 1986). Enrique Giordano, *La teatralización de la obra dramática: De Florencio Sánchez a Roberto Arlt* (Mexico City: Premia, 1982), 161–182. María Hortensia Lacau, *El mundo poético de Conrado Nalé Roxlo* (Buenos Aires: Editorial Raigal, 1954), 263.

NOVIÓN, Alberto (1881–1937). Born in France, Novión's family first went to Montevideo before settling in Buenos Aires when he was fifteen. Novión began his theatrical career writing gaucho plays. In 1908 Novión's dramatic interests shifted with the play *La cantina* (The Canteen). The change led to his fame as Argentina's dramatist of immigrants, as well as one of the country's best writers of short plays. Novión was integral in popularizing the *sainete* (one-act comedy) in Buenos Aires, and his plays, whether comic or tragic, were always accepted by the audience. His dramatic works are viewed as live documents of his time and are written in a simple, fresh, and colorful style.

WORKS: *Doña Rosario* (s.1905, Teatro Nacional). *Jacinta* (s.1905, Teatro Apolo). *La tapera* (The Remains of an Abandoned House) (s.1905). *La tía Brigida* (Aunt Brigida) (s.1905). *Tierra adentro* (Inner Earth) (s.1905). *La gaucha* (The Gaucha) (s.1906) p. in *La escena* 74 (1919). *La cantina* (The Canteen) (s.1908). *La madriguera* (The Den) (s.1911). *La chusma* (The Gang) (s.1913). *Misia Pancha la brava* (The Brave Pancha) (s.1915) p. (Buenos Aires: Lib. Teatral Apolo, 1915). *La fonda del pacarito* (The Bird's Inn) (s.1916, Teatro Nacional by the Vittone-Pomar Company) p. in *El sainete criollo* (Buenos Aires: Hachette, 1957). *El vasco de Olavarría* (The Basque from Olavarría) (s.1920) p. in *Argentores* 114 (1936). *¡Bendita seas!* (Bless You!) (s.1921) p. in *La escena* 20 (1921) and 161 (1929); *Proscenio* 2 (1948); (Buenos Aires: Carro de Tespis, 1969). *En un burro tres baturros* (Three Peasants on a Donkey) (s.1923) p. in *Argentores* 76 (1935). *Don Chicho* (s.1933). *Tan chiquita y quiere casarse* (So Young, Yet She Wants to Marry) (s.1936, Teatro Corrientes). *El corazón en la mano* (Heart in Hand) (s.1938, Teatro París).

BIBLIOGRAPHY: Tulio Carella, *El sainete criollo* (Buenos Aires: Hachette, 1957), 251–269. Blas Raúl Gallo, *Historia del sainete nacional*

(Buenos Aires: Quetzal, 1958), 106–121. Willis Knapp Jones, *Behind Spanish American Footlights* (Austin: University of Texas Press, 1966), 163–164.

ONRUBIA, Emilio de (1849–1907). Born in Paraná, Entre Ríos, Onrubia is remembered as a political figure, philanthropist, novelist, journalist, and proprietor of the Onrubia Theater. He debuted *Lo que sobra y lo que falta* (Surplus and Shortage) in his theater during the revolution of 1890. The allusion to actual political figures caused quite a scandal. Among his most popular plays are *La hija del obispo* (The Bishop's Daughter) and *Vieja doctrina* (Old Doctrine).

WORKS: *La muerte de Rivadavia* (Rivadavia's Death) (s.1885, Teatro de la Opera). *Sin horizonte* (Without Horizon) (s.1885, Teatro de la Opera). *La copa de hiel* (The Bile Cup) (s.1886, Teatro de la Opera). *Vieja doctrina* (Old Doctrine). *Los cofrades de Pilatos* (Pilate's Accomplices). *La hija del obispo* (The Bishop's Daughter) (s.1907).

BIBLIOGRAPHY: Raúl Héctor Castagnino, *Literatura dramática argentina (1717–1967)* (Buenos Aires: Pleamar, 1968), 92. Tito Livio Foppa, *Diccionario teatral del Río de la Plata* (Buenos Aires: Ediciones de Carro de Tespis, 1961), 485–486. Luis Ordaz, *El teatro en el Río de la Plata* (Buenos Aires: Futuro, 1946), 28, 34, 53.

PACHECO, Carlos Mauricio (1881–1924). Born in Montevideo, where his father, an Argentine colonel, took refuge for political reasons. The family returned to Argentina when Pacheco was an infant. He showed interest in the theater at a young age and soon became an integral part of theatrical productions in Buenos Aires, offering more than seventy-eight plays to the public. *Los disfrazados* (The Disguised) is described by Luis Ordaz as one of the most enduring examples of the *sainete* genre and of Argentine drama in general. The play is noteworthy for introducing the tragicomic character of Don Pietro, who displays characteristics of the *grotesco criollo* style, which Armando Discépolo developed a decade later.

WORKS: *Blancos y colorados* (White and Colored) (w.1900, in collaboration with Héctor Bini). *Los disfrazados* (The Disguised) (s.1906, Teatro Apolo) p. in *Los disfrazados y otros sainetes* (Buenos Aires: EUDEBA, 1964); in *Teatro rioplatense* (Caracas: Biblioteca Ayacucho, 1977). *Música criolla* (Native Music) (s.1906, Teatro Apolo), w. in collaboration with Pedro Pico. *El batacazo* (The Cropper) (s.1907). *Los reos* (The Accused) (s.1907). *El patio de Don Simón* (The Patio of Don Simón) (s.1908). *Los fuertes* (The Strong) (s.1909). *La nota roja* (The Red Note) (s.1909). *La ribera* (The Shore) (s.1909, Teatro Argentino, by the Florencio Parravicini Company) p. in *El sainete criollo* (Buenos Aires: Hachette, 1957). *Las romerías* (The Pilgrimages) (s.1909). *De hombre a hombre* (From Man to Man) (s.1910). *Una juerga* (Revelry) (s.1912). *Las mariposas* (The Butterflies) (s.1912). *El cabaré* (The Cabaret) (s.1914). *El cerro* (The Ridge) (s.1915). *El diablo en el conventillo* (The Devil in the Convent) (s.1915). *La guardia de auxiliar* (The Auxiliary Guard) (s.1916). *La quinta de los Reyes* (The Kings' Country House) (s.1916). *Barracas* (The Barracks) (s.1918). *La boca del riachuelo* (The Mouth of the Small Stream) (s.1919). *Los piratas* (The Pirates) (s.1923). For a complete list of Pacheco's works with commentary, see Marta Lena Paz, *Bibliografía crítica de Carlos Mauricio Pacheco. Aporte para su estudio* in *Bibliografía Argentina de artes y letras*, n.14 (Buenos Aires: Fondo Nacional de las Artes, 1963).

BIBLIOGRAPHY: Tulio Carella, *El sainete criollo* (Buenos Aires: Hachette, 1957), 271–292. Blas Raúl Gallo, *Historia del sainete nacional* (Buenos Aires: Quetzal, 1958), 123–146. Luis Ordaz, *Aproximación a la trayectoria de la dramática argentina* (Ottawa: Girol Books, 1992), 26. David Viñas, *Teatro rioplatense (1886–1930)* (Caracas: Biblioteca Ayacucho, 1977), 153–177.

PAGANO, José León (1875–1964). Critic, dramatist, essayist, and art historian. His plays are valued for their technical excellence and clever plots. His most famous work, *Almas que luchan* (Battling Souls) (s.1906), is about a newspaperman and his involvement in the financial world. Pagano's plays have been presented both on stage and on radio.

WORKS: *Más allá de la vida* (Beyond Life) (s.1902, Theater of the Gran Vía in Barcelona). *El dominador* (The Dominator) (s.1903, in Rome, by the Ferrucio Garravaglia Company). *Nirvana* (s.1904). *Almas que luchan* (Battling Souls) (s.1906). *La ofrenda* (The Offering) (s.1914). *Los astros* (The Stars) (s.1916) p. (Buenos Aires: Carro de Tespis, 1965). *El sobrino de Malbrán* (Malbran's Nephew).

El tío Diego (Uncle Diego). *Cartas de amor* (Love Letters). *El zarpazo* (The Claw). *Lasalle. Blasón de fuego* (Arms of Fire). *El inglés de aquella noche se llamaba Aguirre* (The Englishman of That Night Was Named Aguirre). *El halcón* (The Falcon) (s.1921). *El secreto* (The Secret) (s.1921, Teatro Liceo) p. in *Teatro argentino contemporáneo* (Madrid: Aguilar, 1959). *Dos mujeres en una imagen* (One Image of Two Women). *El rescate* (The Ransom) (s.1950). *El día de la ira* (The Day of Anger) p. (Buenos Aires: Poseidon, 1959).

BIBLIOGRAPHY: Arturo Berenguer Carisomo, *Teatro argentino contemporáneo* (Madrid: Aguilar, 1959), xviii–xix. "Bibliografía de José Leon Pagano," *Boletín Academia Argentina de Letras* 29.114 (October–December 1964): 365–367. Raúl Héctor Castagnino, *Literatura dramática argentina (1717–1967)* (Buenos Aires: Pleamar, 1968), 115–116.

PALANT, Pablo (1914–1975). Born in Victoria, Entre Ríos, Palant was a dramatist, director, critic, and journalist. He was the theater critic for the daily paper *Noticias Gráficas* (Graphic News) while writing and directing for the theater. In May of 1950 he debuted *El cerco* (The Hoop), a sexual tragedy with existential tones reminiscent of Kafka and Sartre. The theme of unfulfilled love is always present in the works of Palant and appears in *La dicha impia* (The Impious Joy), which won the Argentores Prize and the Second National Award for the years 1954–1956. Pablo Palant is most noted for his play *El escarabajo* (The Scarab), which won the First National Theater Prize for 1959.

WORKS: *Diez horas de vida* (Ten Hours of Life) (s.1938) p. in *Teatro* 7–8 (May–June 1941). *Jan es antisemite* (Jan Is an Antisemite) (s.1939) p. in *Teatro* 3 (December 1940–January 1941). *La huída* (The Escape) (s.1941) p. in *Teatro* 2 (1940). *El amor muerto* (Dead Love) (s.1942) p. (Buenos Aires: Americana, 1942). *Los días del odio* (The Days of Hatred) (s.1946) p. in *Argentores* 262 (1946). *Esta mujer mía* (This Woman of Mine) (s.1947). *El cerco* (The Hoop) (s.1950). *Unos heredan y otros no* (Some Inherit and Others Don't) (s.1951), written in collaboration with Roberto Durán. *El ángel cruel* (The Cruel Angel) (s.1953) p. (Buenos Aires: Carro de Tespis, 1966). *La dicha impia* (The Impious Joy) (s.1956) p. in *Talía* 16 (1956); in *Argentores* 11 (1957). *Felicia fea* (Ugly Felicia) (s.1956). *El escar-*

abajo (The Scarab) (s.1959) p. (Buenos Aires: Talía, 1962). *El piano (y otros juegos)* (The Piano [And Other Games]) (s.1960) p. (Buenos Aires: Carro de Tespis, 1968). *El dedo gordo* (The Plump Finger) (s.1963). *Safo* (w.1964). *Sonata para trombón y amor* (Sonata for Trombone and Love) (s.1965). *María de los dos* (Maria of the Two) (s.1966) p. (Buenos Aires: Carro de Tespis, 1968). *Nos van a comer los piojos* (The Lice Are Going to Eat Us) (w.1966). *El trompo* (The Spinning Top) (s.1968). *¡Ojo que viene!* (Watch It's Coming!) (w.1970). *Triunfal reaparición de Quincón* (The Triumphal Reappearance of Quincón) (s.1970).

BIBLIOGRAPHY: Raúl Héctor Castagnino, *Literatura dramática argentina (1717–1967)* (Buenos Aires: Pleamar, 1968), 169. Erminio G. Neglia and Luis Ordaz, *Repertorio selecto del teatro hispanoamericano contemporáneo* (Tempe: Arizona State University, 1980), 15–16. Luis Ordaz, *El teatro en el Río de la Plata* (Buenos Aires: Futuro, 1946), 74, 176, 178, 180, 183, 186, 193.

PAVLOVSKY, Eduardo (1933–). Born in Buenos Aires, Pavlovsky received his medical degree with a specialty in psychoanalysis in 1957. Afterward, he studied theater with prominent directors and began his theatrical career as an actor. In 1962 he formed a theater group called Yenesí with Julio Tahier, which became one of the most important groups of the vanguard theater in Buenos Aires. Pavlovsky's first plays are short and psychoanalytical. They were mostly performed by the Yenesí group. With *Ultimo match* (The Final Match) (s.1970), written with Juan Carlos Hermes, Pavlovsky turns to a more concrete perception of the political situation in Argentina. He describes the shift as a change from absurdism to an exasperated realism. *El señor Galíndez* (Mr. Galíndez) (s.1973), considered to be Pavlovsky's best play, was written to denounce torture.

WORKS: *La espera trágica* (The Tragic Wait) (s.1962) p. (Buenos Aires: Cuadernos del Siroco, 1966). *Somos* (We Are) (s.1962) p. (Buenos Aires: Cuadernos del Siroco, 1966). *Camellos sin anteojos* (Camels Without Glasses) (s.1963). *El hombre* (The Man) (s.1963). *Imágenes, hombres y muñecos* (Images, Men and Puppets) (s.1963). *Un acto rápido* (A Rapid Act) (s.1965) p. (Buenos Aires: Cuadernos del Siroco, 1966). *El robot* (The Robot) (s.1966) p. (Buenos Aires: Cuadernos del Siroco, 1966). *La cac-*

ería (The Hunt) (s.1969) p. (Buenos Aires: Ed. de la Luna, 1967). *Circus-loguio* (s.1969), written in collaboration with Elena Antonietto. *Alguién* (Someone) (s.1970), written in collaboration with Juan Carlos Hermes, p. (Buenos Aires: Cuadernos del Siroco, 1966). *Ultimo match* (The Final Match) (s.1970), written in collaboration with Juan Carlos Hermes, p. (Buenos Aires: Ed. de la Luna, 1967); (Buenos Aires: Talía, 1970). *La mueca* (The Grimace) (s.1971) p. in *Tres obras de teatro* (Havana: Casa de las Américas, 1970). *El señor Galíndez* (Mr. Galíndez) (s.1973). *Telarañas* (Cobwebs) (s.1977, Teatro Payró; s.1985, Teatro del Viejo Palermo). *Cámara lenta; Historia de una cara* (Slow Camera; History of a Face) (s.1981, Teatro Olimpia). *Tercero incluído* (The Third Included) (s.1981, Teatro Abierto). *El señor Laforgue* (Mr. Laforgue) (s.1983, Teatro Olimpia). *Podestad* (s.1985). *Pablo* (s.1987, Teatro El Hanger). *Paso de dos* (Two Step) (s.1990).

BIBLIOGRAPHY: Rose Marie Armando, *Teatro argentino contemporáneo* (Buenos Aires: Revista Cultura, 1985), 99–105. Elena Cámara, *Del realismo exasperante de Eduardo Pavlovsky* (Chapel Hill: University of North Carolina, 1997). Jorge Dubatti, *Teatro, postmodernidad y política en Eduardo Pavlovsky* (Concepción, Uruguay: Ediciones de Ayllu, 1997). Jorge Dubatti, ed., *Teatro completo IV: Eduardo Pavlovsky* (Buenos Aires: ATUEL/TEATRO, 2002). Luis Ordaz, *Aproximación a la trayectoria de la dramática Argentina* (Ottawa: Girol Books, 1992), 72–73. George Schanzer, *El teatro de Eduardo Pavlovsky* (Buenos Aires: Ediciones Busqueda, 1981), 10. Estela Patricia Scipioni, *Torturadores apropiadores y asesinos: el terrorismo de estado en la obra dramática de Eduardo Pavlovsky* (Kassel, Germany: Reichenberger, 2000). Gabriela Toletti-Gong, *Dinámica grupal, familiar y política: una lectura psicosocial de la obra dramática de Eduardo Pavlovsky* (New York: State University of New York at Buffalo, 1994). George Woodyard, "Eduardo Pavlovsky, los años tempranos," in *Teatro argentino de los '60: Polémica, continuidad y ruptura,* ed. Osvaldo Pellettieri (Buenos Aires: Corregidor, 1989), 209–216.

PAYRÓ, Roberto Jorge (1867–1928).

Dramatist, novelist, short story writer, and journalist, Payró was born in Buenos Aires on April 19, 1867. His Catalonian father and his Uruguayan mother settled in Buenos Aires in 1828 during the regime of Manuel de Rosas. Payró's view of the world was shaped primarily by the difficulty his immigrant family experienced trying to become accepted into Argentine society. Payró became interested in the theater at the turn of the century. *Sobre las ruinas* (Upon the Ruins) (s.1904) and *Marco Severi* (s.1905) are considered to be part of the "thesis theater" or theater of ideas. The plays portray the social struggles that emerged from the conflict between progress and tradition. Payró is known as a true observer of the era when Argentina was shifting from a rural to an urban country.

WORKS: *Canción trágica* (Tragic Song) (s.1902). *Sobre las ruinas* (Upon the Ruins) (s.1904, Teatro Comedia by Jerónimo Podestá). *El triunfador* (The Winner) (s.1904). *Marco Severi* (s.1905). *El triunfo de los otros* (The Triumph of Others) (s.1907). *Vivir quiero contigo* (I Want to Live with You) (s.1923). *Fuego en el rastrojo* (Fire in the Stubble) (s.1925). *Alegría* (Joy) (s.1928). *Mientraiga* (While You Have Money in Your Pocket) (s.1937).

BIBLIOGRAPHY: Juan Carlos Ghiano, "Roberto J. Payró: Un testigo de excepción," *Al azar de las lecturas* (La Plata, Argentina, 1968), 19–31. Roberto F. Giusti, *Teatro completo* (Buenos Aires, 1956), 1–28. Eduardo González Lanuza, *Genio y figura de Roberto J. Payró* (Buenos Aires, 1965). S. M. Fernández de Vidal, "Bibliografía de Roberto J. Payró," *Bibliografía Argentina de Artes y Letras* 13 (January–March 1962).

PEÑA, David (1862–1930).

Peña was born in Rosario, Santa Fe. He began his theatrical career in 1883 with a romantic comedy, *¡Qué dirá la sociedad!* (What Will Society Say!), followed by a musical, *La lucha por la vida* (The Fight for Life). Following a period of theatrical inactivity, Peña presented *Próspera* (Prosperous) (s.1902), which was written to advocate his political party. In 1906 he began a series of national plays that led to his fame as the creator of the Argentine historical theater.

WORKS: *¡Qué dirá la sociedad!* (What Will Society Say!) (s.1883, Teatro de la Opera by the Juan Roig Company). *La lucha por la vida* (The Fight for Life) (s.1885). *Próspera* (Prosperous) (s.1902, Teatro San Martín, by the Carmen Cobeñas Company) p. (Buenos Aires: Adolfo Grau, 1903). *Inútil* (Useless) (s.1904, Teatro Apolo). *Facundo* (s.1906, Teatro Argentino). *Belgrano* (n.s.). *José Miguel Carrera* (n.s.). *Urquiza* (n.s.). *Dorrego* (s.1909). *Un cuerpo* (A Body) (s.1911). *Un loco* (A Crazy Man) (s.1911).

Liniers (s.1917). *La primera audición del himno nacional* (The First Hearing of the National Anthem) (s.1920, Consejo de Mujeres). *Una mujer de teatro* (A Theater Woman) (s.1921). *Don Félix de Montemar* (Don Felix of Montemar) (s.1923). *La madre del Cardenal* (The Cardinal's Mother) (s.1923). *Alvear* (s.1924). *El embrujo de Sevilla* (The Bewitchment of Seville) (s.1926, Teatro Sarmiento, by the Blanca Podestá Company). *Un tigre del Chaco* (A Tiger from Chaco) (s.1926).

BIBLIOGRAPHY: Tito Livio Foppa, *Diccionario teatral del Río de la Plata* (Buenos Aires: Carro de Tespis, 1961), 517–518. Willis Knapp Jones, *Behind Spanish American Footlights* (Austin: University of Texas Press, 1966), 94–95. Luis Ordaz, "David Peña," in *Enciclopedia de la literatura argentina*, ed. Pedro Orgambide and Roberto Yahni (Buenos Aires: Sudamericana, 1970), 497–498.

PICO, Pedro (1882–1945). Born in Buenos Aires, Pico studied at the University of Buenos Aires and received his law degree in 1907. He wrote in many categories ranging from his first *sainete* (one-act play) called *La polka del espiante* (The Spy's Polka) to the gaucho plays *Tierra virgen* (Virgin Land) and *La seca* (The Drought). He also wrote melodramas, political plays, and farces. Pico collaborated with eight other dramatists, including González Pacheco and Samuel Eichelbaum, which added to his repertoire of over one hundred plays. He is responsible for starting the royalty system in Argentina by demanding payment for each performance of *Del mismo barro* (From the Same Clay). Pico, a good illustrator of types and customs, is recognized as one of the most prolific and outstanding Argentine dramatists of the beginning of the twentieth century.

WORKS: *La polka del espiante* (The Spy's Polka) (s.1901, Teatro Apolo), written in collaboration with González Pacheco. *Para eso pago* (That's What I Pay For) (s.1903). *No hay novedad* (Nothing Is New) (s.1905). *Un robo* (A Burglary) (s.1905). *Ganarse la vida* (To Make a Living) (s.1907). *Tierra virgin* (Virgin Land) (s.1910). *La solterona* (The Old Maid) (s.1914). *La seca* (The Drought) (s.1917). *Del mismo barro* (From the Same Clay) (s.1918). *Pasa el tren* (The Train Passes By) (s.1919). *Las pequeñas causas* (The Small Causes) (s.1919). *No hay burlas con el amor* (There Are No Jokes in Love) (s.1921). *El dinero de mi mujer* (My Wife's Money) (s.1923). *La novia de los forasteros* (The Visitors' Girlfriend) (s.1926). *La luz de un fósforo* (A Match's Light). *Pueblerina* (The Villager) (s.1928). *Yo quiero que tú me engañes* (I Want You to Fool Me) (s.1931). *¡Caray, lo que sabe esta chica!* (Wow! What This Girl Knows!) (s.1932). *Yo no sé decir que no* (I Don't Know How to Say No) (s.1934). *Juan de Dios, milicio y paisano* (John of God, Militant Countryman) (s.1935), written in collaboration with González Pacheco. *Caminos en el mar* (Waterways) (s.1937). *Usted no me gusta, señora* (I Don't Like You, Madame) (s.1939). *Las rayas de la cruz* (The Stripes of the Cross) (s.1940) p. in *Teatro argentino*, vol. 7 (Buenos Aires: CEAL, 1980). *Querer y cerrar los ojos* (Love and Close Your Eyes) (s.1941). *Nace un pueblo* (A Town Is Born) (s.1943), written in collaboration with González Pacheco. *La historia se repite* (History Repeats Itself) (s.1945). *Novelera* (Keen on Novels or Fads) (s.1945). *Agua en las manos* (Water in the Hands) (s.1951, Teatro Versalles, by the Company of Arturo García Buhr) p. in *Teatro argentino contemporáneo* (Madrid: Aguilar, 1959).

BIBLIOGRAPHY: Richard Allen, *Teatro hispanoamericano: Una bibliografía anotada* (Boston: G. K. Hall, 1987), 116–118. Arturo Berenguer Carisomo, *Teatro argentino contemporáneo* (Madrid: Aguilar, 1959), li. Willis Knapp Jones, *Behind Spanish American Footlights* (Austin: University of Texas Press, 1966), 129–130. Luis Ordaz, *El teatro en el Río de la Plata* (Buenos Aires: Futuro, 1946), 107–108, 144–145.

PONFERRADA, Juan Oscar (1907–). Born in Catamarca, he is also known as a poet, essayist, and director. He moved to Buenos Aires in 1928. In 1940 he wrote *Pesebre* (The Manger), a one-act play in verse. He followed with a poetic tragedy, *El carnaval del diablo* (The Devil's Carnival), in 1943. The play takes place during La Chaya, a pagan festival in northern Argentina and combines folklore, superstition, the supernatural, and sex. The play won the first Municipal Prize in 1943 and the second prize of the National Commission of Culture for the years 1943–1945.

WORKS: *Pesebre* (The Manger) (w.1940). *El carnaval del diablo* (The Devil's Carnival) (s.1943) p. in *Tres obras dramáticas* (Buenos Aires: EUDEBA, 1970); *Teatro argentino contemporáneo* (Madrid: Aguilar, 1962). *El trigo de Dios* (God's

Wheat) (s.1947). *Los pastores* (The Shepherds) (s.1950) p. in *Tres obras dramáticas* (Buenos Aires: EUDEBA, 1970). *Un gran nido verde* (A Great Green Nest) (s.1966) p. in *Tres obras dramáticas* (Buenos Aires: EUDEBA, 1970).

BIBLIOGRAPHY: Willis Knapp Jones, *Behind Spanish American Footlights* (Austin: University of Texas Press, 1966), 167. Pedro Orgambide and Roberto Yahnigeds. *Enciclopedia de la literatura argentina* (Buenos Aires: Sudamericana, 1970), 514–515. Perla Zayas de Lima, *Diccionario de autores teatrales argentinos (1950–1980)* (Buenos Aires: Editorial Rodolfo Alonso, 1981).

ROJAS, Ricardo (1882–1957). Rojas was born in Tucumán on September 16, 1882. After secondary school, Rojas moved to Buenos Aires to study law. He proceeded to become president of the University of Buenos Aires, dean of the School of Philosophy, and chairman of the Departments of Spanish and Argentine Literature. In addition to teaching and literary criticism, Rojas wrote poetry, dramas, essays, and short stories. He aimed at continuing the tradition of the great writers of nineteenth-century Argentina. Rojas wrote four historical plays. The most popular, *Ollantay* (s.1939), shows his dedication to Argentine roots and culture before the Spanish conquests. Rojas sought to produce a national identity by remembering the Incan legend, an idea inspired by his pride in his own mixed blood. The tragedy, written in verse, was a great success among the public of all classes, and the critics applauded it as a national work that would endure time.

WORKS: *Elelín* (s.1929, Teatro Ateneo, by the Rivera-De Rosas Company) p. (Buenos Aires: Juan Roldán, 1929). *La casa colonial* (Colonial House) (s.1932, Teatro Liceo, by the Eva Franco Company). *Ollantay* (s.1939, Teatro Nacional de Comedia) p. (Buenos Aires: Losada, 1939). *La Salamanca* (Salamanca) (s.1943, Teatro Nacional de Comedia) p. (Buenos Aires, 1943). See *Obras de Ricardo Rojas*, vols. 7–15 (Buenos Aires: Losada, 1948–1949).

BIBLIOGRAPHY: Jorge Eduardo Becco, "Bibliografía de Ricardo Rojas," *Revista iberoamericana* 23.46 (1958): 335–350. Raúl H. Castagnino, "El teatro en la obra de Rojas," *Revista iberoamericana* 46 (July 1958): 227–238. Earl T. Glauert, "Ricardo Rojas and the Emergence of Argentine Cultural Nation-

alism," *Hispanic American Historical Review* 43.1 (1963): 1–13. "Homenaje a Ricardo Rojas," *Revista iberoamericana* 23.46 (1958): 221–448. Antonio Pagés Larraya, "Ricardo Rojas," *Bibliografía de escritores hispanoamericanos (1609–1974)* (New York: Gordian Press, 1975), 591–595.

ROVNER, Eduardo (1942–). Rovner began his theatrical career in 1976 with *Una pareja (qué es mío, qué es tuyo)* (A Couple [What Is Mine, What Is Yours]). The play presents humorous dialogue and common speech of the people from Buenos Aires. It gained notoriety for its similarity to *Who's Afraid of Virginia Woolf?* by Edward Albee. In most of his plays, Rovner seeks to explore human relationships and emotions through his characters. His plays combine elements from the theater of the absurd, black humor, satire, and cruelty. Rovner also participated in Teatro Abierto 1983 with *Concierto de aniversario* (Anniversary Concert), an absurd satire that, like other plays of Teatro Abierto, intended to criticize the authoritarianism of the military dictatorship.

WORKS: *Una pareja (qué es mío, qué es tuyo)* (A Couple [What Is Mine, What Is Yours]) (s.1976). *Una foto* (A Photograph) (s.1977). *La máscara (una familia, un tiempo)* (The Mask [A Family, a Time]) (s.1978). *Ultimo premio* (The Last Prize) (s.1981, Payró Theater). *Concierto de aniversario* (Anniversary Concert) (s.1983, Margarita Xirgú Theater). *Sueños de náufrago* (The Dreams of a Shipwrecked Person) (s.1985). *Y el mundo vendrá* (And the World Will Come) (s.1988). *Compañía* (Company) (s.1990, 2nd Municipal Prize). *Cuarteto* (Quartet) (s.1991). *Volvió una noche* (He Came Back One Night) (s.1991, Casa de las Américas Award).

BIBLIOGRAPHY: Osvaldo Pellettieri, "El teatro de Eduardo Rovner," in *Teatro argentino de los '60—Polémica, continuidad y ruptura*, ed. Osvaldo Pellettieri (Buenos Aires: Corregidor, 1989). Julia Elena Sagaseta, "*Concierto de aniversario* y *Cuarteto* de Eduardo Rovner: El poder de la imagen," in *Teatro argentino durante el proceso (1976–1983)*, ed. Juana Arancibia and Zulema Mirkin (Buenos Aires: Vinciguerra, 1992), 171–180.

ROZENMACHER, Germán (1936–1971). Born in Mar de Plata. Rozenmacher was a Hebrew professor and a short story writer. He became known as a dramatist in 1964 with the debut of his play *Réquiem para un viernes a la noche* (Requiem for a Friday Night), which deals with the racial and religious friction he experienced in his own life. In 1971 he presented the theatrical version of *El Lazarillo de Tormes* (Lazarillo of Tormes). His last play, *Simón Brumelstein, el Caballero de Indias* (Simon Brumelstein, the Knight of the Indies), was staged in 1982, more than ten years after his death.

WORKS: *Réquiem para un viernes a la noche* (Requiem for a Friday Night) (s.1964) p. Buenos Aires: Talía, 1965). *El avión negro* (The Black Plane) (s.1970), written in collaboration with Somigliana, Talesnik, and Cossa, p. (Buenos Aires: Talía, 1971). *El Lazarillo de Tormes* (Lazarillo of Tormes) (s.1971). *Simón Brumelstein, el Caballero de Indias* (Simon Brumelstein, the Knight of the Indies) (w.1971; s.1982).

BIBLIOGRAPHY: David William Foster, "Germán Rozenmacher: Escribiendo la experiencia contemporánea judia en Argentina," in *Teatro y teatristas: Estudios sobre teatro argentino y iberoamericano,* ed. Osvaldo Pellettieri (Buenos Aires: Editorial Galerna, 1992), 129–136. Perla Zayas de Lima, "Germán Rozenmacher: Un caballero en busca del *aor,*" in *Teatro argentino de los '60: Polémica, continuidad y ruptura,* ed. Osvaldo Pellettieri (Buenos Aires: Corregidor, 1989), 121–138.

SÁNCHEZ, Florencio (1875–1910). Born in Montevideo, Uruguay, on January 17, 1875, he was the first of thirteen children. His parents were from the middle class. Sánchez received little formal education and stopped attending school by the age of fifteen. He became a journalist and commuted between Uruguay and Argentina. His first important play, *M'hijo el dotor* (My Son the Doctor) was staged by Jerónimo Podestá in 1903 and resulted in immediate fame. The realism and authentic conversation were a refreshing change from most plays of the time. Although Sánchez did not introduce realism to Buenos Aires, his finishing touches ended the imitation of European plays and encouraged the movement toward a national Argentine theatre. After *M'hijo el dotor,* Sánchez wrote a total of twenty plays that included the play he considered to be his masterpiece, *La gringa* (The Gringa).

WORKS: See **Uruguay** under **Sánchez, Florencio** for a complete list of works and dates of performances. His works have been published in *Obras completas* (Buenos Aires: Schapire, 1968), 3 vols., with Introduction and Notes by Jorge Lafforgue.

BIBLIOGRAPHY: Enrique Giordano, *La teatralización de la obra dramática: De Florencio Sánchez a Roberto Arlt* (Mexico City: Premia, 1982), 71–110. Willis Knapp Jones, *Behind Spanish American Footlights* (Austin: University of Texas Press, 1966), 105–116. Luis Ordaz, *El teatro en el Río de la Plata* (Buenos Aires: Futuro, 1946), 68–84. David Viñas, *Teatro rioplatense (1886–1930)* (Caracas: Biblioteca Ayacucho, 1977), 91; includes the plays of *Canillita* and *Barranca abajo.*

SÁNCHEZ GARDEL, Julio (1879–1937). Born in Catamarca, Sánchez Gardel began his study of law in Buenos Aires in 1897. Unable to forget his native region, he is nostalgic in his second play, *Noche de luna* (Night of the Moon) (s.1907), which became an immediate success. His most noteworthy work, *La montaña de las brujas* (The Witches' Mountain) (s.1912), is renowed as Argentina's first lengthy play translated into English. Some critics proclaimed the play as one of the best of modern Argentine drama, whereas others criticized it as melodramatic and artificial, saved only by its excellent portrayal of local color.

WORKS: *Almas grandes* (Big Souls) (s.1904, performed by Jerónimo Podestá). *Noche de luna* (Night of the Moon) (s.1907) p. in *Teatro de Julio Sánchez Gardel* (Buenos Aires: Hachette, 1955). *Las campanas* (The Bells) (s.1908) p. in *Teatro de Julio Sánchez Gardel* (Buenos Aires: Hachette, 1955). *Después de misa* (After Mass) (s.1910). *Los mirasoles* (The Sunflowers) (s.1911) p. in *Argentores* 166 (1939); in *Teatro de Julio Sánchez Gardel* (Buenos Aires: Hachette, 1955). *La montaña de las brujas* (The Witches' Mountain) (s.1912) p. in *Teatro Argentino* 58 (1921); in *Teatro de Julio Sánchez Gardel* (Buenos Aires: Hachette, 1955); (Buenos Aires: Huemul, 1966); in *Teatro rioplatense* (Caracas: Biblioteca Ayacucho, 1977). *Sol de invierno* (Winter's Sun) (s.1914). *El zonda* (Hot Andean Wind) (s.1915).

BIBLIOGRAPHY: Juan Pablo Echagüe, *Teatro argentino* (Madrid: América, 1917), 1–9, 197–202. Juan Carlos Ghiano, *Teatro de Julio Sánchez Gardel* (Buenos Aires: Hachette, 1955), introduction. Willis Knapp Jones, *Behind Spanish American Footlights* (Austin: University of Texas Press, 1966), 170–171.

David Viñas, *Teatro rioplatense (1886–1930)* (Caracas: Biblioteca Ayacucho, 1977), 321.

SANDOR, Malena (1913–1968). Pseudonym for María Elena James de Terza. Born in Buenos Aires of Jewish extraction, she was a narrator and newswoman. Sandor began her theatrical career in 1937 with *Yo me divorcio, papá* (I'm Getting a Divorce, Dad), a one-act play of protest against social conventions. The next year she won the Culture Prize at the Nacional Theater for *Una mujer libre* (A Free Woman), about the emancipation of the protagonist, Liana Menéndez, who divorces her husband for a career.

WORKS: *Yo me divorcio, papá* (I'm Getting a Divorce, Dad) (s.1937). *Una mujer libre* (A Free Woman) (s.1938, Teatro Nacional Cervantes) p. in *Argentores* 221 (1942). *Yo soy la más fuerte* (I Am the Strongest One) (s.1943, Teatro Avenida) p. in *Argentores* 231 (1943). *Tu vida y la mía* (Your Life and Mine) (s.1945) p. in *Argentores* 252 (1945). *Ella y Satán* (Satan and Her) (s.1948). *Y la respuesta fue dada* (And the Answer Was Given) (s.1957) p. (Buenos Aires: Carro de Tespis, 1959); in *Teatro completo* (Buenos Aires: Talía, 1959). *Los dioses vuelven* (The Gods Return) (s.1958). *Dame tus labios Liette* (Give Me Your Lips Liette) (s.1959). *Un muchacho llamado Daniel* (A Boy Named Daniel) (s.1961). *Una historia casi verosímil* (Almost a True Story) (s.1966).

BIBLIOGRAPHY: Tito Livio Foppa, *Diccionario teatral del Río de la Plata* (Buenos Aires: Ediciones de Carro de Tespis, 1961), 612. Willis Knapp Jones, *Behind Spanish American Footlights* (Austin: University of Texas Press, 1966), 171–172. Perla Zayas de Lima, *Diccionario de autores teatrales argentinos (1950–1980)* (Buenos Aires: Editorial Rodolfo Alonso, 1981), 159–160.

SOMIGLIANA, Carlos (1932–1987). Born in Buenos Aires, he belonged to the realist generation of the 1960s. His first play, *Amarillo* (Yellow) (s.1965), is set in Rome, 123 A.C.E. and uses the character of Cayo Graco to expound the concepts of liberty and justice. Later, Somigliana actively participated in Teatro Abierto and wrote its manifesto. During this period, he presented two short plays, *El Nuevo Mundo* (The New World) (s.1981), which portrays the imaginary arrival of the Marquis de Sade to America, and *El oficial primero* (The First Officer) (s.1982), which condemns the atrocities occurring at the time in Argentina.

WORKS: *Amarillo* (Yellow) (s.1965, Teatro 35) p. (Buenos Aires: Falbo, 1965). *Amor de ciudad grande* (Love of a Big City) (s.1965, Teatro 35) p. (Buenos Aires: Falbo, 1965). *La bolsa de agua caliente* (The Hot Water Bag) (s.1966, Teatro Candilejas de Dolores) p. (Buenos Aires: Talía 1967). *De la navegación* (About Navigation) (s.1969). *El avión negro* (The Black Plane) (s.1970), written in collaboration with Roberto M. Cossa, Germán Rozenmacher, and Ricardo Talesnik, p. (Buenos Aires: Talía, 1970); in *Tres obras de teatro* (Havana: Casa de las Américas, 1970). *El ex-alumno* (The Former Student) (s.1978). *El Nuevo Mundo* (The New World) (s.1981, by Teatro Abierto). *El oficial primero* (The First Officer) (s.1982, by Teatro Abierto). *Inventario* (Inventory) (s.1983, by Teatro Abierto), written in collaboration with Hebe Serebrisky, Susana Torres Molina, and Peñarol Méndez. *Lavalle, historia de una estatua* (Lavalle, History of a Statue) (s.1983, Teatro Margarita Xirgu).

BIBLIOGRAPHY: Rose Marie Armando, *Teatro argentino contemporáneo* (Buenos Aires: Revista Cultura, 1985), 77–83. Luis Ordaz, "Autores del 'nuevo realismo' de los años '60 a lo largo de las tres últimas décadas," *Latin American Theatre Review* 24.2 (Spring 1991): 44–45. Ana Seoane, "El teatro de Carlos Somigliana: La historia y sus héroes," in *Teatro argentino de los '60: Polémica, continuidad y ruptura*, ed. Osvaldo Pellettieri (Buenos Aires: Corregidor, 1989), 145–154.

SORIA, Ezequiel (1873–1936). Born in Catamarca, Soria was also a theatrical director. He studied Law in Buenos Aires but never received his degree. Instead, he chose to pursue a theatrical career and wrote *El año 92* (The Year '92), a *zarzuela* (comic opera) with music by Andrés Abad y Antón. His inspiration was the Spanish *zarzuela El año pasado por aquí* (Last Year Around Here). In 1897 he presented a novelty to spectators, a serious *sainete* called *Justicia criolla* (Native Justice). The play is ranked highly among the *zarzuelas* of Argentina. Most of his plays allude to the economic and political situation of his time.

WORKS: *El año 92* (The Year '92) (s.1892, Teatro Alhambra). *Amor y lucha* (Love and Struggle) (s.1895, Teatro Olimpo) p. in *Zarzuelas criollas* (Buenos Aires: Padró and Rós, 1899). *El sargento Martín* (Sergeant Martín) (s.1896, Teatro Comedia de la Calle Artes), music by Eduardo García, p. in *Zarzuelas criollas* (Buenos Aires: Padró and Rós, 1899). *Amor y claustro* (Love and Cloister) (s.1897), music by Francisco Márquez, p. in *Zarzuelas criollas* (Buenos Aires: Padró and Rós, 1899). *Justicia criolla* (Native Justice) (s.1897, Teatro Olimpo) p. in *Zarzuelas criollas* (Buenos Aires: Padró and Rós, 1899). *La ley suprema* (The Supreme Law) (s.1897) p. in *Zarzuelas criollas* (Buenos Aires: Padró and Rós, 1899). *El deber* (Duty) (s.1898), music by Antonio Reynoso, p. in *Zarzuelas criollas* (Buenos Aires: Padró and Rós, 1899; (Buenos Aires: EUDEBA, 1965). *Política casera* (Domestic Politics) (s.1901) p. (Buenos Aires: EUDEBA, 1965). *La beata* (The Blessed) (s.1902). *Bravucho* (Brave) (s.1902). *El medallón* (The Medallion) (s.1902). *El escudo* (The Shield) (s.1906). *Diógenes* (s.1918). *Amor* (Love) (s.1920).

BIBLIOGRAPHY: Jacobo A. de Diego, prologue to *Política casera, drama en tres actos. El Deber, zarzuela en un acto y tres cuadros en prosa y en verso* (Buenos Aires: EUDABA, 1965). Blas Raúl Gallo, *Historia del sainete nacional* (Buenos Aires: Quetzal, 1958), 48–55. Ismael Moya, *Ezequiel Soria, zarzuelista criollo* (Buenos Aires: Imprenta de la Universidad, 1938). Oscar Ponferrada, *Ezequiel Soria, propulsor del teatro argentino* (Buenos Aires: Editiones Culturales Argentinas, Ministerio de Educación y Justicia, 1961).

TALESNIK, Ricardo (1935–). Born in Buenos Aires. Talesnik's first play, *La fiaca* (The Lazy) (s.1967), debuted first in Chile and then in Buenos Aires. The play was so successful that it was performed in Uruguay, Colombia, Venezuela, Mexico, Brazil, and Europe. In 1968 it was adapted to film. The play is a grotesque representation of the human condition. The protagonist, Nestor, is afflicted with *fiaca*, an Argentine slang for "laziness," and no one seems to understand why he does not get up and go to work. Talesnik's plays deal with social and political issues as well as personal relationships.

WORKS: *La fiaca* (The Lazy) (s.1967) p. (Buenos Aires: Talía, 1967); in *Primer Acto* 105 (February 1969). *El avión negro* (The Black Plane) (s.1970), written in collaboration with Roberto Cossa, Germán

Rozenmacher, and Carlos Somigliana, p. (Buenos Aires: Talía, 1970); in *Tres obras de teatro* (Havana: Casa de las Américas, 1970). *Cien veces no debo* (I Must Not for One Hundred Times) (s.1970) p. (Buenos Aires: Talía, 1972). *Solita y sola* (Alone and Lonely) (s.1972), written in collaboration with María Celina Parrondo. *Los japoneses no esperan* (The Japanese Don't Wait) (s.1973). *Traylesnik* (s.1974 in U.S.). *El chucho, una historieta musical* (The Chucho, a Musical History) (s.1976). *Cómo ser una buena madre* (How to Be a Good Mother) (s.1977). *Casi un hombre* (Almost a Man) (s.1979). *Yo la escribo y yo la vendo* (I Write and Sell It) (s.1979).

BIBLIOGRAPHY: Jorge A. Dubatti, "Ricardo Talesnik y el realismo: 'La fiaca' (1967)," in *Teatro argentino de los '60: Polémica, continuidad y ruptura*, ed. Osvaldo Pellettieri (Buenos Aires: Corregidor, 1989), 157–168. Luis Ordaz, *Aproximación a la trayectoria de la dramática argentina* (Ottawa: Girol Books, 1992), 73. Perla Zayas de Lima, *Diccionario de autores teatrales argentinos (1950–1980)* (Buenos Aires: Editorial Rudolfo Alonso, 1981), 167–169.

TALICE, Roberto (1902–). Talice began writing plays as an adolescent in Uruguay, his birthplace. At twenty-one years of age he moved to Buenos Aires, where he became an integral part of the theatrical scene, writing over one hundred plays, either alone or in collaboration. He was also president of Argentores (General Society of Argentine Authors). He wrote in many genres including comedies, *sainetes* (one-act comedies), farces, political satires, and dramas.

WORKS: *La nena* (The Child) (s.1915, Montevideo). *Asesinos* (Murderers) (s.1920, Montevideo). *Los infieles* (The Unfaithful) (s.1920, Montevideo, Teatro Solís). *Los puritanos* (The Puritans) (s.1923). *El secreto de la media moneda* (The Secret of the Half Coin) (s.1935), written in collaboration with L. Gassó and C. Schaeffer Gallo. *Ciudadano del mundo* (Citizen of the World) (s.1941) p. in *Argentores* 213 (1942). *Sábado del pecado* (Saturday of Sin) (s.1943), written in collaboration with Alejandro de Stefania, p. (Buenos Aires: Carro de Tespis, 1961). *John, Jean y Juan* (s.1944), received the Argentores Prize for that year, p. in *Argentores* 238 (1944). *La llama eterna* (The Eternal Flame) (s.1947), written in collaboration with Eliseo Montaine, p. in *Argentores* 272 (1947); (Buenos Aires: Carro de Tespis, 1963). *La oculta verdad* (Hidden Truth) (s.1948), written in collaboration with Eliseo Montaine, p. in *Proscenio* 3 (1948); *Argentores* (1961), (Buenos Aires: Carro de Tespis, 1961). *Siendo amor es primavera* (Making Love Is Springtime) (s.1949), written in collaboration with Eliseo Montaine. *Tempestad* (Tempest) (s.1950). *Juan sin sosiego* (John Without Rest) (s.1951) p. (Buenos Aires: Ed. by the Revista de Espectáculos, 1951). *Cuatro en el paraíso* (Four in Paradise) (s.1952), written in collaboration with Eliseo Montaine, p. in *Argentores* (1966). *El hombre prohibido* (The Prohibited Man) (s.1952), written in collaboration with Eliseo Montaine, p. in *Repertorio* 3 (1952–1953). *El ladrón del mar* (The Thief of the Sea) (s.1952). *La mujer incompleta* (An Incomplete Woman) (s.1952) p. in *Repertorio* 3 (1952–1953). *El amor comienza mañana* (Love Begins Tomorrow) (s.1953), written in collaboration with Eliseo Montaine. *Dos horas de amor* (Two Hours of Love) (s.1953). *La machorra* (The Barren Woman) (s.1953). *Enséñame a mentir* (Teach Me to Lie) (s.1955). *Noche en los ojos* (Night in the Eyes) (s.1957) p. in *Argentores* 209 (1957). *Luna de miel en el cielo* (Honeymoon in Heaven) (s.1959) p. in *Argentores* (1959). *Mi reino por un toro* (My Kingdom for a Bull) (s.1965). *Cinco para el amor* (Five for Love) (s.1967). *Los cammos de Dios* (The Ways of God) (s.1967). *Swing para una rosa de luto* (Swing for a Mourning Flower), (1967), written in collaboration with Eliseo Montaine, p. (Buenos Aires: Carro de Tespis, 1967). *Libra, Leo y Sagitario* (Libra, Leo and Sagittarius) (s.1973). *¡Viva la Pepa!* (Long Live Pepa!) (s.1977).

BIBLIOGRAPHY: Richard F. Allen, *Teatro hispanoamericano: Una bibliografía anotada* (Boston: G. K. Hall, 1987), 134–136. Willis Knapp Jones, *Behind Spanish American Footlights* (Austin: University of Texas Press, 1966), 174. Perla Zayas de Lima, *Diccionario de autores teatrales argentinos (1950–1980)* (Buenos Aires: Editorial Rodolfo Alonso, 1981), 169–170.

TIEMPO, César (1906–1980). Pseudonym for Israel Zeitlin. Born in Ekaterinoslav, Ukraine, his family moved to Argentina before his first birthday. In addition to being a dramatist, Tiempo was a journalist, poet, narrator, theater critic, and scriptwriter for movies. In 1933 he debuted his first major work, *El teatro soy yo* (I Am the Theater), a satire about racial and religious intolerance. *Pan criollo* (Native Bread) won the first National Theater prize in 1937 and was performed by famous actors throughout Argentina, Paraguay, and Uruguay. The play shows the bonding love between a Jew and a Christian. His sentimental comedy *El ilustrador de manzanas* (The Apple Illustrator) successfully debuted in 1957 and boasts over 300 performances in a two-year period.

WORKS: *El diablo se divierte* (The Devil Has Fun) (s.1922). *El teatro soy yo* (I Am the Theater) (s.1933, Teatro Smart, by the Company of Enrique Guastavino) p. (Buenos Aires: Anaconda, 1933). *Alfarda* (s.1935, Teatro Argentino). *Pan criollo* (Native Bread) (s.1937, Teatro Nacional) p. (Buenos Aires: Tall, Graf. Porter Hnos., 1938). *Clara Beter vive* (Clara Beter Lives) (s.1941, Teatro Argentino). *Zazá porteña* (s.1945, Teatro Casino), written in collaboration with Arturo Cerretani. *La dama de las comedias* (The Leading Lady of Comedies) (s.1951, Teatro Municipal) p. (Buenos Aires: Carro de Tespis, 1971), written in collaboration with Arturo Cerretani. *El ilustrador de manzanas* (The Apple Illustrator) (s.1957, Teatro Comedia of Rosario; s.1957, Teatro Marconi of Buenos Aires) p. in *Argentores* 20 (1958); (Buenos Aires: Carro de Tespis, 1958). *Se llamaba Clara Beter* (Her Name Was Clara Beter) (s.1978).

BIBLIOGRAPHY: Tito Livio Foppa, *Diccionario teatral del Río de la Plata* (Buenos Aires: Ediciones de Carro de Tespis, 1961), 656–657. Willis Knapp Jones, *Behind Spanish American Footlights* (Austin: University of Texas Press, 1966), 177–178. Perla Zayas de Lima, *Diccionario de autores teatrales argentinos (1950–1980)* (Buenos Aires: Editorial Rodolfo Alonso, 1981), 172–173.

TREJO, Nemesio (1862–1916). Born in San Martín, Buenos Aires, Trejo was a journalist, *payador* (a minstrel who accompanies himself with a guitar), and a writer of one-act comedies. As a *sainetero* (writer of one-act comedies), Trejo combines the Spanish art form with Argentine attributes. His most popular play, *Los políticos* (The Politicians) (s.1897), blends the chorus and duets, which are typically Spanish, with the characters and language of Argentina. Trejo wrote more than fifty-five *sainetes*.

WORKS: *La fiesta de Don Marcos* (The Party of Don Marcos) (s.1890, Pasatiempo Theater, Paraná, by the Rogelio Juárez–Abelardo Lastra Company). *Los óleos del chico* (The Child's Oils) (s.1892 by the Podestá Family). *Los políticos* (The Politicians) (s.1897) p. in *Teatro argentino* (Buenos Aires: Casa

Editora A. Pérez); in *Siete sainetes norteños* (Buenos Aires: Losange, 1958); in *Teatro rioplatense* (Caracas: Biblioteca Ayacucho, 1977). *La esquila* (The Small Bell) (s.1899). *Los vividores* (The Good Timers) (s.1902). *Los inquilinos* (The Tenants) (s.1907). *Las mujeres lindas* (The Pretty Women) (s.1916, Teatro Nacional, by the Vittone-Pomar Company).

BIBLIOGRAPHY: Luis Ordaz, *El teatro en el Río de la Plata* (Buenos Aires: Futuro, 1946), 55–58. David Viñas, *Teatro rioplatense (1886–1930)* (Caracas: Biblioteca Ayacucho, 1977), 61, 63.

VACAREZZA, Alberto (1888–1959). Born in Buenos Aires, Vacarezza debuted his first *sainete, El juzgado* (The Court), at the age of eighteen. He ends the cycle of writers of the *creole sainete* (one-act comedy) that began with Nemesio Trejo. Vacarezza mostly used the dialect of the lower class in his plays. He also invented his own vocabulary, such as puns on proper names, which added to the humor of his works. He had a vast repertoire and boasted to have written a hundred works. His most popular play was *Tu cuna fue un conventillo* (Your Crib Was a Tenement House) (s.1920), which broke all records with its 3,000 performances.

WORKS: *El juzgado* (The Court) (s.1904). *Los escruchantes* (The Pests) (s.1911, Teatro Nacional) p. in *Teatro rioplatense* (Caracas: Biblioteca Ayacucho, 1977). *Los villanos* (The Villains) (s.1912, Teatro Argentino). *Los cardales* (The Thistle Garden) (s.1913). *El comité* (The Committee) (s.1914, Teatro Argentino, by the Vittone-Pomar Company). *La ley Palacios* (The Palacios Law) (s.1915, Teatro Argentino). *El último gaucho* (The Last Gaucho) (s.1915). *La casa de los Batallán* (The Batalláns' House) (s.1917). *El buey corneta* (The Ox-Horn) (s.1918). *La otra noche en los Corrales* (The Other Night at the Corrales) (s.1918). *¡Va . . . cayendo gente al baile!* (People Are Falling at the Dance!) (s.1919, Teatro Nacional). *Tu cuna fue un conventillo* (Your Crib Was a Tenement House) (s.1920, Teatro Nacional, by the Arata-Simari-Franco Company) p. in *La escena* 114 (1920); *Argentores* 32 (1920); *El sainete criollo* (Buenos Aires: Hachette, 1957). *Cuando un pobre se divierte* (When a Poor Man Has Fun) (s.1921, Teatro Nacional). *El arroyo Maldonado* (The Maldonado Stream) (s.1922), written in collaboration with Carlos Pacheco. *El cambalache de la buena suerte* (The Shop of Good Luck) (s.1925). *La vida es un sainete* (Life Is a Sai-

nete) (s.1925). *La fiesta de Santa Rosa* (The Feast of Saint Rose) (s.1926). *El cabo Rivero* (The Chief Rivero) (s.1928). *Juancito de la Ribera* (Johnny of the Ribera) (s.1928). *El conventillo de la Paloma* (Paloma's Tenement House) (s.1929) p. in *La escena* 282 (1930). *El camino a la Tablada* (The Road to Tablada) (s.1930). *La china Dominga* (The Chinese Woman, Dominga) (s.1932). *La comparsa se despide* (The Appearance Is Over) (s.1932, Teatro Cómico, by the Cicarelli-Busto-Mutarelli Company). *San Antonio de los Cobres* (s.1938). *Lo que pasó a Reynoso* (What Happened to Reynoso) p. in *Argentores* 115 (1936). *Allá va el resero Luna* (There Goes Luna, the Cowboy) p. in *Argentores* (1942).

BIBLIOGRAPHY: Tulio Carella, *El sainete criollo* (Buenos Aires: Hachette, 1957), 353. Blas Raúl Gallo, *Historia del sainete nacional* (Buenos Aires: Quetzal, 1958), 195–207. Luis Ordaz, *El teatro en el Río de la Plata* (Buenos Aires: Futuro, 1946), 93–98. David Viñas, *Teatro rioplatense (1886–1930)* (Caracas: Biblioteca Ayacucho, 1977), 297.

VIALE, Oscar (1932–). Pseudonym for Gerónimo Oscar Schissi. Born in Buenos Aires, Viale began his theatrical career as an actor at the age of thirteen. Viale's plays focus on the problems of a complex Argentine society. His first plays are burlesque sketches that combine comedy, political satire, the absurd, the grotesque, and the *sainete* (one-act comedy) as well as regional language and customs. *El grito pelado* (At the Top of Ones's Voice) (s.1967) was an immediate success. It was followed by *La pucha*, a combination of various styles including the musical revue.

WORKS: *El grito pelado* (At the Top of One's Voice) (s.1967, Teatro del Bajo). *La pucha* (s.1969, Teatro Municipal General San Martín). *Chúmbale* (s.1971, Teatro Margarita Xirgu). *¿Yo?, . . . Argentino* (Me? . . . Argentinean) (s.1976, Los Teatros de San Telmo). *Encantada de conocerlo* (Pleased to Meet You) (s.1978, Teatro Regina). *Convivencia* (Living Together) (s.1979, Teatro Regina). *Intimas amigas* (Close Friends) (s.1981, Colón de Mar de Plata). *Periferia* (Periphery) (s.1982, Teatro Municipal Gral. San Martín). *Ahora vas a ver lo que te pasa* (Now You'll See What Will Happen to You) (s.1983, Teatro Abierto). *Antes de entrar dejen salir* (Let Them Leave Before Entering) (s.1983, Teatro Blanca Podestá). *Camino negro* (Black Road) (s.1983, Teatro Blanca Podestá), written in collaboration with Alberto Alejandro. *Visitante nocturno* (Nocturnal Visitor) (s.1984), written in collaboration with Alberto Alejandro. *Trátala con cariño* (Treat Her with Love) (s.1985). *Convivencia femenina* (Feminine Coexistence) (s.1985, Teatro Lorange).

BIBLIOGRAPHY: Rose Marie Armando, *Teatro argentino contemporáneo* (Buenos Aires: Revista Cultura, 1985). Luis Ordaz, "Autores del 'nuevo realismo' de los años '60 a lo largo de las tres últimas décadas," *Latin American Theatre Review* 24.2 (Spring 1991): 41–48. Osvaldo Pellettieri, "El teatro argentino del sesenta y su proyección en la actualidad," in *Teatro argentino de los '60: Polémica, continuidad y ruptura*, ed. Osvaldo pellettier (Buenos Aires: Corregidor, 1989), 75–97. Perla Zayas de Lima, *Diccionario de autores teatrales argentinos (1950–1980)* (Buenos Aires: Editorial Rodolfo Alonso, 1981), 178–179.

Mirta Barrea-Marlys

Bolivia

Even before the arrival of the Spaniards to this area of South America, there had been dramatic performances in Quechua and Aymara. These plays, for the most part, have disappeared. We know about them through references recorded by missionaries and by other chroniclers such as the Inca Garcilaso de la Vega. We also have references to plays staged in Spanish in the thriving silver town of Potosí as early as 1550. These were secular plays from Spain via Lima. The missionaries, in the endeavor to evangelize and teach the doctrine of the Catholic Church, used didactic forms as a didactic instrument. This religious theater in Upper Peru, also known as the province of the Charcas, bears great similarity to what the church was doing in the other regions of the Spanish colonies. To reach those who did not know Spanish, the native tongues were used in these dramatic presentations. In this colonial province the languages were Quechua and Aymara.

In 1859, Felix Reyes Ortiz's drama *Odio y Amor* (Hate and Love) reflected the influence of the French playwright Alexandre Dumas and was well accepted by the spectators. Two years before, Reyes Ortiz staged in La Paz his first known play *Plan de una representación* (Plan for a Dramatic Presentation). The dialogue is well written, the plot well crafted, and the satirical descriptions of the society of his day biting and elegant at the same time. The plot deals with a group of students who are trying to stage a play dealing with politicians and other members of society; because of this metatheatrical dimension, this comedy has been compared favorably with Pirandello's *Six Characters in the Search of an Author*. But Ortiz is remembered in the history of the Bolivian theater because shortly after the success of his *Odio y Amor*, he produced a historical drama, *Los lanzas*, exalting the heroic accomplishments of the brothers García Lanza during the war of independence against Spain. This three-act play became one of his favorites among the Bolivian elite.

The usage of historical events has been one of the constants found in the Bolivian theater. These historical events were not limited to Bolivia, but they moved in time and geography in the Americas. Such is the case of *Iturbide o ambición y amor* (Iturbide or Ambition and Love) by Rosendo Gutiérrez (1840–1883). In this 1862 play, the main character is Agustín Iturbide who, shortly after declaring the independence of Mexico, proclaimed himself the emperor of that country. The same can be said of José Pol, who in 1869 staged for a very brief period his drama *Atahualpa*, an attempt in five acts to give a tragic dimension to the figure of Atahualpa, the Inca killed treacherously by Pizarrro. A year earlier, in 1868, Hermógenes Jofré published a drama, *Los mártires* (The Martyrs), that, as far as it is known, was never staged. The drama takes place in Haiti, and it deals with the brutal killing of political prisoners, including a former president of the country. While such an event did not occur in Haiti, this was a way to veil a Bolivian event that took place in 1861, when Colonel Plácido Yañez ordered the execution of political prisoners including the former president of the republic, Joe Córdoba. Benjamín Lenz (1836–1878), a contemporary and friend of Ortiz Reyes, also wrote historical plays such as *El guante negro* (The Black Glove), depicting the Rosas tyrannical era in Argentina. He also wrote *La mejicana* (The Mexican Woman), *El hijo natural* (The Illegitimate Child), *Borrascas del corazón* (Heart's Storm), his drama *Celos y venganza* (Jealousy and Revenge), and many others.

Chronologically straddling the nineteenth and twentieth centuries, there is Ricardo Jaimes Freyre (1868–1933), the son of well-known literary parents. His father was Julio Lucas Jaimes (1843–1914), a dramatist contemporary of Reyes Ortiz and Lenz, who like them, wrote comedies: his best known are *Un hombre en apuros* (A Man in Trouble) (1855), and a historical drama, *Morir por la patria* (Dying for the Motherland) (1882). His mother was Carolina Freyre de Jaimes (1884–1916) who, like her husband, wrote plays but was more interested in feminine themes. Because she was born in Peru, both countries have claimed her as one of their writers. Their son Ricardo, both a poet and a dramatist, wrote several plays, and his best known are *Los conquistadores* (The Conquistadors) and the biblical drama *La hija de Jefthé* (The Daughter of Jephtha) (1889). *Los conquistadores* was written in verse closely resembling Romantic Spanish dramatists such as Duque de Rivas, Hartenzbuch, Zorrilla, and others. The historical setting is the time of the Spanish conquest of America, as the title suggests. It seems that he wrote it with the hope that famous Spanish actress María Guerrero (1868–1929) would play the role of Catalina de Enciso. It is not clear whether or not the play was ever staged.

The twentieth century continued to see periods of great dramatic activity. The group of writers who tried to renovate the Bolivian letters in the years before the Chaco war have been the "Generación del 21" (The 1921 Generation), and some dramatists are among them. Some of the most important playwrights of this generation are Antonio Díaz Villamil, who wrote *La rosita* (Little Rose) and a three-act play, *La hoguera* (The Bonfire), with its patriotic plot set during the Pacific war; and Alberto Saavedra Pérez, author of *La huelga de los mineros* (The Miners' Strike). Another dramatist of the period was Mario Flores, who, although a prolific and successful author, was more appreciated in Argentina, where he spent the greater part of his life.

These writers, particularly Saavedra Pérez, introduced themes and plots relevant to the problems of social justice of the times, with a great deal of local color. Although the Chaco halted all dramatic activities for a while, shortly after the end of the hostilities between Bolivia and Paraguay Díaz Villamil resumed his dramtic production. Also, in 1943, Joaquín Gantier, who had written some plays about the Chaco war, published a comedy, *El Molino* (The Mill), with dialogue partly in Spanish and partly in Quechua. Its setting is rural Bolivia, and the dialogue reflects local color.

In the early 1950s Guillermo Francovich, already known as a man of letters, began to convey his philosophical ideas through the medium that the stage offered him. In 1961, *La lanza capitana* (The Point Lance), by Raúl Botelho Gosálvez, was recognized as one of the best dramas of the decade. It received the Premio Nacional de Teatro 1961 (First National Prize for the Theater of 1961). This drama, like many other Bolivian plays, bases its plot on a historical event and portrays the 1781 revolt against colonial authorities led by Aymara leader Tupac Katari.

In 1956 in a Paris theater, the play *Les Etandards du roi* (The King's Banners) was staged and its author was Bolivian Adolfo Costa Du Rels (1881–1980). In 1972 this play received the Gulbenkian Prize, the prestigious award that recognizes the best dramatists in the Latin World. Its Spanish version, *Los estandartes del rey*, was staged in La Paz in 1968. It was published in a bilingual edition (French and Spanish) in 1974, and in 1977, it was produced in Cochabamba during the VI Festival Departamental de Teatro "Julio Travesí" (The VI Regional Theater Festival "Julio Travesí"), with the playwright present on that ocassion. Costa Du Rels has written several dramas, and his best known are *Les Forces du Silence* (The Forces of Silence), staged in Buenos Aires in 1944; *El signo del fuego* (The Sign of Fire) (1957); and *El quinto jinete* (The Fifth Horseman) (1963). In his plays, Costa Du Rels broaches the universial existential themes, particularly those reflecting human anguish.

Another important dramatist is Raúl Salmón Tapias, who contributed to the theater of those years with his keen portrayals of a greedy and unjust society. He, as well as others whose plays convey similar ideas and deal with similar themes, founded the "teatro social" (social theater). Because he continued using this blending of history and social criticism in his plays, his theater is known as "teatro histórico social" (historical social theater). Three of his best known plays, *Viva Belzu* (Long Live Belzu) (1952), *Juana Sánchez* (1966), and *Tres generales* (late 1960s), are based on three historical figures emerging from the nineteenth century. Initially, it appears as if Salmón follows the traditional historical drama so prevalent in that country for generations; yet a careful examination of the plots and characters shows that he uses certain moments of the Bolivian past under three military dictators to address the sociopolitical problems of today's Bolivia and, for that matter, present-day Latin America. His dramatic techniques are modern, both in language as well as psychological approach to the characters. His dramas are very useful for those interested in studying the culture and civilization of present-day Bolivia. The themes and dialogues give important insights into how Bolivian intellectuals see themselves and the sociopolitical problems that ail the country. Dramatically the plays fall short because of obvious didactic tendencies. Other younger writers joined this kind of theater in the 1970s and 1980s and produced more or less meritorious plays dealing with the problems of social conscience and the consciousness of class struggle. One of the most recent authors portraying the evils of today's Bolivian society is Carlos Urquizo Huici.

Since the late 1950s, several cities in Bolivia have seen an increase in dramatic productions, particularly Cochabamba, La Paz, and Santa Cruz. This latter urban center saw the founding of the Teatro Experimental Universitario (The University Experimental Theater) in 1959 with a program that trained a select group of actors. La Paz theaters, although they have continued to stage some works written by Bolivians, have had a tendency to produce foreign plays, particularly from Europe. According to some critics, the last ten or fifteen years have seen a decrease in the interest shown toward the Bolivian theater.

BIBLIOGRAPHY

Allan, Richard F. *Teatro hispanoamericano: una bibliografía anotada.* Boston: G. K. Hall, 1987.

Arrom, José Juan. *Historia del teatro hispanoamericano (época colonial).* Mexico City: Editorial de Andrea, 1966.

Dial, Eleanore Maxwell. "The Military in Government in Bolivia: A View from the Theater of Raúl Salmón." *Latin American Theatre Review* 9.1 (Fall 1975): 47–53.

Díez Medina, Fernando. *Literatura boliviana*. Madrid: Aguilar, 1959.

Echazu, Edgar Avila. *Literatura pre-hispánica y colonial*. La Paz. Editorial Gispert y Cia, 1974.

Finot, Enrique. *Historia de la literature boliviana*. La Paz: Gisbert y Cía, 1964.

Gisbert, Teresa. *Teatro virreinal en Bolivia*. La Paz Dirección Nacional de Informaciones de la Presidencia de la República, 1962.

Gómez-Martínez, José Luis. "Guillermo Francovich: una faceta de su pensamiento y un apéndice bibliográfico." *Revista iberoamericana* 52.134 (1986): 293–303.

Guzmán, Augusto. *Biografías de la literatura boliviana (1525, 1925)*. Cochabamba, La Paz: Editorial Los Amigos del Libro, 1982.

———. *Biografías de la nueva literatura boliviana*. Cochabamba, La Paz: Editorial Los Amigos del Libro, 1982.

———. *Panorama de la literatura boliviana del siglo XX*. Cochabamba, La Paz: Editorial Los Amigos del Libro, 1967.

Hellmer, Marie. *Apuntes sobre el teatro en la villa imperial de Potosí: documentos del Archivo de Potosí, 1572–1636*. Potosí: Universidad Tomás Frías, 1960.

Jones, Willis Knapp. *Behind Spanish American Footlights*. Austin: University of Texas Press, 1966.

Muñoz, Willy Oscar. "Precursores del teatro boliviano." *Alba de América* 7.12–13 (1989): 97–104.

———. "Producción dramática boliviana: las últimas dos décadas." *Diógenes: anuario crítico del teatro latinoamericano 1987*, ed. Marina Pianca. Ottawa: Girol Books, 1988, 31–36.

———. *Teatro boliviano contemporáneo*. La Paz: Ediciones Casa Municipal de la Cultura "Franz Tamayo," 1981.

———. "Teatro boliviano contemporáneo." *Revista Iberoamericana* 52.134 (January, March 1986): 181–194.

———. "El teatro boliviano en la década de los 80." *Latin American Theatre Review* 25 2 (Spring 1992): 13–21.

———. "Teatro boliviano 1989." *Diógenes: anuario crítico del teatro latinoamericano*, ed. Marina Pianca. Buenos Aires: Grupo Editor Latinoamericano, 1991, 33–39.

———. "Teatro boliviano 1990." *Gestos* 12 (1991): 182–189.

———. "Teatro boliviano 1992." *Diógenes: anuario crítico del teatro latinoamericano*. Mexico City: Grupo Editorial Gaceta, 1994, 21–29.

———. "Teatro boliviano: 1994." *Diógenes: anuario crítico del teatro latinoamericano 1993–1994*, ed. Marina Pianca. Riverside: Department of Spanish and Portuguese, Univrsity of California, 1995, 15–26.

———. "El teatro boliviano en la década de los ochenta." *Latin American Theatre Review* 25.2 (1992): 13–22.

———. "Teatro boliviano en la década de los 90." *Latin American Theatre Review* 34.1 (2000): 25–41.

———. "El teatro boliviano: la última época, 1967–1985." *Bolivia: 1952–1986*. Special issue of *Los ensayistas* 20–21 (1986): 175–187.

———. "El teatro nacional en busca de un punto de partida." *Tendencias actuales en la literatura boliviana*, ed. Javier Sanjinés C. Minneapolis/Valencia: Institute for the Study of Ideologies and Literature/Instituto de Cine y Radio-Televisión, 1985, 135–169.

Rivadeneira Prada, Raúl. *Historia del TEU*. La Paz: Ediciones Signo, 1999.

Salmón, Raúl. *Teatro boliviano*. Madrid: Editorial Paraninfo, 1972.

Soria, Mario. *El teatro boliviano en el siglo XX.* La Paz: Biblioteca Popular Boliviana de "Ultima hora," 1980.

———. *Teatro boliviano: 1980–1998 (cena dramática).* Santa Cruz: Fondo Editorial Municipal, 1999.

Ugarte Chamorro, Guillermo. *Las primeras representaciones teatrales en el Alto Perú.* Lima: Servicio de Publicaciones del Teatro Universitario de San Marcos, 1963.

◆

BOTELHO GOSÁLVEZ, Raúl (1917–1967). Although Botelho Gosálvez is basically known as a novelist, he left an indelible mark on Bolivian theater with his one outstanding theatrical work, *La lanza capitana*, first performed in 1961. Based on the historical rebellion in the late eighteenth century against the Spaniards led by the Aymara warrior Tupai Katari, Botelho Gosálves's play is important for its exhaltation of the role played by indigenous figures in the resistance to Spanish rule. In the process of mounting a complicated dramatic spectacle, which won the author the Primer Premio Nacional de Teatro in 1961, the author provides, at a crucial time for the recognition of indigenous culture in the Americas, an energetic defense of the historical role of indigenous peoples. Tupac Katari's proud rejection of Hispanic culture—and especially its version of Christianity through his refusal of the sacrament of confession—as he is led to his public execution, is of great dramatic impact.

WORK: *La lanza capitana* (1967).

BIBLIOGRAPHY: Willy Oscar Muñoz, "*La lanza capitana*: texto y contexto." *Gestos* 11 (1991): 135–145.

CRESPO PANIAGUA, Renato (1922–). Crespo Paniagua has had a long political and professional career, serving on the Bolivian Supreme Court. His "Ciclo Autóctono," as its name indicates, focuses on themes relating to the countryside, the land, and national types; they include both a historical and a folkloric dimension and a part of a Latin American dramaturgy designed to counter "Creole" versions of European themes. His historic comedy, *Cuidado . . . que viene España!*, is the attempt to recreate what might have been the indigenous reaction to the arrival of the Spanish conquerors; the play has an allegorical dimension, in the sense that a critique of the failure of the Incas to resist the Spanish invasion is, by extension, a critique of current Bolivian institutions in the face of new foreign interventions.

WORKS: *Narciso (comedia en tres actos)* (1968); *Cuidado . . . que viene España!* (1971); *La promesa verde* (1972); *Morir un poco* (1977); *Dar posada al peregrino (comedia en 3 actos)* (1981).

FRANCOVICH, Guillermo (1901–1990). Guillermo Francovich was born in Sucre in 1901. A lawyer by training, he began his career in 1929 as an officer for the Bolivian foreign service and as a diplomat representing his country abroad, particularly in Brazil. As a writer he is better known as an essayist, a critic, and a thinker. He wrote on many modern thinkers as well as philosophical and literary movements. His essays delve in depth into both existentialism and structuralism. In Bolivia as well as abroad, he is well known by his *El pensamiento boliviano en el siglo XX* (Bolivian Thought in the Twentieth Century) (Mexico: Fondo de Cultura Económica, 1956). His thesis in this work on the worth of Bolivian culture before the 1952 Revolution contrasts sharply with the view held by another respected thinker and essayist, Augusto Céspedes.

Already well established as a man of letters, he began writing plays. From the early 1950s on, he published over twenty dramatic works. In the introduction to his *Teatro completo I* (Complete Theater I) Francovich expresses his concern for the view of the world and humanity as presented by French existentialism and also his reactions to structuralism. There seems to be a logical evolution that led this author to move from the abstract ideas expressed in his essays to a literary genre where these ideas spring out of characters and situations in society. Francovich seemed to possess the same desire that led thinkers and philosophers such as Unamuno, Camus, and Sartre to express their intellectual, sociological, and philosophical ideas by using dramatic dialogue to portray the human condition.

The twelve plays included in his *Teatro completo I* cover a twenty year span. *Soledad y tiempo* (Time and Solitude) was written in 1951, and the last one, *El reencuentro* (The Reencounter), in 1971. In his theater, the plays are arranged according to their historical chronology, rather than ordered by the dates of their publication or staging. The first play, *El monje de Potosí* (The Monk from Potosi), takes place in 1635, and the last, *Monseñor y los poetas* (Monsignor and the Poets), in modern times.

Many of these are one-act plays that are subdivided (cuadros) allowing changes in space and time in the plot. Although not all of these plays have been staged, several were radio broadcast in Bolivia. In 1957, *Como los gansos* (Like Geese) was well received by the public during a theater festival in Habana (Cuba).

Francovich uses Bolivian history and legends of his native land as the background for his plays, but his themes are universal. The monk who accidentally is shot and dies is believed to be a saintly hermit until it is discovered that the skull he carries with him is not a reminder of death as the ultimate reality but the remains of an enemy that he has killed, and it is a constant reminder of his hatred. The people of Potosí believed him to be a saintly monk, and they were deeply surprised and then angered when they discovered the truth. People and events in a Pirandellean way are not always as they seem.

WORKS: *El monje de Potosí* (La Paz/Cochabamba: Editorial Signo, 1962). *Teatro completo II* (La Paz/Cochabamba: Editorial "Los Amigos del Libro," 1983). *Teatro completo I* (La Paz/Cochabamba: Editorial "Los Amigos del Libro," 1983).

BIBLIOGRAPHY: Allen, Richard F. *Teatro hispanoamericano: una bibliografía anotada* (Boston: G. K. Hall, 1987). Fernando Díez Medina, *Literatura boliviana* (Madrid: Aguilar, 1959). José Luis Gómez-Martínez, "Guillermo Francovich: una faceta

de su pensamiento y un apéndice bibliográfico," *Revista iberoamericana* 52.134 (Jan., March, 1986): 293–303. Willis Knapp Jones, *Behind Spanish American Footlights* (Austin: University of Texas Press, 1966). Willy Oscar Muñoz, "El teatro boliviano en la década de los 80." *Latin American Theater Review* 25 (Spring 1992): 13–21. Willy Oscar Muñoz, "Teatro boliviano contemporáneo." *Revista iberoamericana* 52.134 (Jan., March, 1986): 181–194. Oscar Muñoz Cadima, "El Teatro Nacional en busca de un punto de partida," *Tendencias actuales en la literatura boliviana*, ed. Javier Sanjinés C. (Minneapolis/Valencia: Institute for the Study of Ideologies and Literature/Instituto de Cine y Radio-Televisión, 1985), 135–169. Mario Soria, *El teatro boliviano en el siglo XX* (La Paz: Biblioteca Popular Boliviana de "Ultima Hora," 1980).

MAROF, Tristán, psued. of Gustavo A. Navarro (1898–1979). Marof was basically a political polemisist, credited with being the founder of Bolivian Trotskism. He utilized many literary genres as platforms for the espousal of his militant criticism of Bolivian social life and political institutions. His play *El jefe* (The Chief, 1965) is about the pretenses of power, ridiculous authoritarian posturing, and the vanity of political ambitions. It is noteworthy that, as a leftist, Marof chose the vehicle of comedy (one would have expected grim social realism), but it is in line with other satirical works he produced.

WORK: *El jefe* (La Paz: Talleres Gráficos Bolivianos, 1965).

SALMÓN, Raúl (1925–1990). Salmón is the author of dozens of plays that are variously called "teatro social" (social theater) and "comedia criolla" (national comedy). His work is local-color in nature, and his characters are popular types, where everyday citizens or examples of political power. He himself served as a populist mayor of La Paz (Salmón studied political science at George Washington University), and turned his conversations with people in his press-the-flesh political style into witty dialogues that were of a whole with his extensive radio work (he owned Radio Nacional América, the largest station in Bolivia). Mario Vargas Llosa has claimed that Salmón is the model for the Bolivian radio scriptwriter in his *La tía Julia y el escribidor* (1977; *Aunt Julia and the Scriptwriter*).

WORKS: *El canillita* (1943); *Busch* (1944); *El infierno* (1944); *Mi made fue una chola* (1944); *Parricidio* (1944); *Potosí en la sangre* (1944); *Prisionera de guerra* (1944); *Sangre indígena* (1944); *Albores de libertad* (1945); *Los viejos saben mś que los diablos* (1945); *Cachito* (1947); *Caparelly (1948); El fugitivo* (1948); *Flor de barro* (1948); *Saturnito Calderón* (1948); *Escuela de pillos, Joven, rica y plebeya. Los hijos del alcohol* (195?); *Un argentino en La Paz* (1950); *Fuga de la ley* (1952); *Noches de La Paz* (1952); *Siembra* (1955); *Cuatro comedias cortas y populares* (1975); *Diálogos con el vecindario paceño; gestión del Jefe de la Comuna* (1980); *La computadora hablante* (1985); *Redención* (1985); *El estaño era Limachi; drama en 7 cuadros* (1989); *Miss Ch'i-jini; comedia dramática de ambiente criolla* (1989); *El partido de la contrapartida* (1989); *Plato paceño* (1989); *Las dos caras de Olañeta* (1990); *Seis obras de teatro breve* (1990); *Hijo de chola* (1991); *Linares, dictador civil* (1991); *Mi compadre el ministro* (1991).

TEATRO DE LOS ANDES. Founded in Yotala, a city near Sucre, by the Argentine César Brie in 1991, this theater collective places emphasis on forming professional, creative actors in a community of interlocking artistic activities grouped around the concept of theater as spectacle, with an emphasis on humor and memory. The collective's journal, *El tonto del pueblo* (1995–), is a formal published platform for the discussion of these issues. Of particular importance is the group's commitment to Andean cultural roots and the relationship between theater and traditional spectacles such as feasts and rituals, as well as the heterogeneous and hybrid nature of Andean culture and its artistic expression. The group has participated extensively in theater festivals in the United States and Europe, as well as all over Latin America. In addition to Brie, other prominent artists associated with the Teatro de los Andes are Maritz Wilde and David Mondaca. Since 1999, Teatro de los Andes, along with other theater collectives, form part of TIBO, Teatro Independiente Boliviano.

BIBLIOGRAPHY: Willy Oscar Muñoz, "César Brie: nueva forma de hacer teatro en Bolivia," Gestos 20 (1995): 140–145. Willy Oscar Muñoz, "Teatro de los Andes: en busca de un nuevo teatro boliviano," *Latin American Theatre Review* 27.1 (Fall 1993): 23–27; Mario T. Soria, *Teatro boliviano: 1980–1998 (cena dramática).* Santa Cruz: Fondo Editorial Municipal, 1999, 134–139.

NOTE: Adolfo Costa du Rels (1891–1980) is not covered here, since his major literary work, including the play produced in Spanish as *Los estandartes del rey*, was published in French.

Brazil

The theater in Brazil emerges—as in all of Latin America—associated with the Church. In the sixteenth century the Jesuits introduce the theater in Brazil, and they do so with a specific purpose: to evangelize the Indians. The theater is used as a vehicle to carry out what is considered a mission of higher value—that of catechizing the natives.

Manuel da Nóbrega (1519–1570) arrived in Brazil in 1549, and in 1553, José de Anchieta (1534–1597). With their arrival, the enormous Jesuit cultural and religious contribution is consolidated. On the one hand (and this is applicable to the Jesuits in general), their cultural contribution is unquestionable, and on the other, they bring a thirst, an anxiety, for learning the languages, religious practices, and habits of the indigenous world. It is precisely the Jesuits who will take advantage of the natural inclination that the Indians felt toward music—singing and dancing, specifically—in order to introduce them to European theater, with which the Jesuits were so familiar. In this manner, they begin the whole process of contact, knowledge, and integration of the Indian into the Western world, as well as initiating the process of converting the natives to Catholicism. Therefore, the plays assumed pragmatic, educational, and religious features. The first play that was staged by the Jesuits took place eight years after the arrival of Manuel da Nóbrega, *Diálogo, conversão do gentio* (Dialogue, Conversion of the Gentile). Ten years later, José de Anchieta's first work is staged, *Auto da pregação universal* (Play of Universal Preaching), in 1567. The goal of the theater during this period was almost exclusively evangelization, in which the priests were the protagonists. Parallel to this activity, laymen also staged plays, following a tradition that already existed in the Iberian Peninsula. However, they were connected in one way or another to the religious world, both by the location (churches or convents) as well as by the plot; for example, the *Auto de Santiago* (Play of Saint James), staged in 1564. One can see that the beginning of the theater in Brazil always assumes an underlying religious and educational goal, following, as mentioned above, the medieval traditions of the Iberian Peninsula. Consequently, the plot and the characters are very limited, excluding, for example, women or any romantic manifestation that does not carry an allegorical reading of religious nature. Also, the goal of evangelization is coordinated with the intention of dignifying and even mythicizing the image of the priest and of religion.

The religious theater develops throughout the seventeenth century, experiencing both a noticeable decline and an evolution, as one can verify in the works of Luis Figueira (1575–1643) and José Borges de Barros (1657–1719), where we observe the integration of indigenous languages in the latter's works. On the other hand, the theater is also used by the politicians, in public stagings, in order to ensure the colonial power by celebrating important political events with parades, as seen in the ceremony that took place in Rio de Janeiro in 1641 to celebrate the crowning of King João IV.

The eighteenth century brings new trends into the theater, as a consequence of the Enlightenment. At the beginning of the century, we find that the scenery is not much different from that of the previous period, since the theater continues to depend—up to a certain extent—on the Church, by still using churches and convents for stagings; it also depends still on the political power, by staging plays at palaces. This situation continues until the end of the 1720s, when the Church decides to forbid the staging of plays at places of worship. In 1729, the bishop of Pernambuco, José Fialho, banned all stagings at churches. Thus, we see how the religious authority reacted in view of the degradation experienced by the religious theater as a consequence of the excesses that were taking place and because their initial goals had been lost.

Furthermore, new ideas of the Enlightenment began to spread throughout Latin America, which valued the theater not only for its capacity as a training and didactic tool. The direct consequence of this is that numerous theaters are created. The year 1760 is a fundamental year for the development of the theater in Brazil, as can be seen by the construction of the Teatro da Praia, in Bahia, considered the first Brazilian public theater house. The creation of permanent theater companies, such as the one directed by Manuel Luis Ferreira, and the arrival of foreign companies contribute to this period of renewal. At the same time, Rio de Janeiro becomes the center of Brazilian theater, replacing Bahia.

The repertoire of the eighteenth century continues to maintain its total dependence on Europe. During the sixteenth and seventeenth centuries, Spanish and Portuguese works dominate the theater, and now the French achieve major importance, especially with Molière, although the Italians, like Goldini, also staged plays. Spanish works, particularly by Calderón, are staged, because of their enormous prestige during the Siglo de Oro. Theatrical activity in the eighteenth century ends based on the works of foreign playwrights, the continuation of the religious theater with little social impact (directed by the Franciscans), intense activity with marionettes, and an event of transcendence for the Brazilian theater. For the first time, as Cacciaglia states, we see an attempt at creating an "embryo" of local dramaturgy, initiated by Luis Alves Pinto (1719–1789). In 1780, Alves Pinto debuts with a comedy titled *Amor mal correspondido* (Unreciprocated Love), which is considered the first work to be staged by a national playwright.

The nineteenth century is much more complex, being characterized by abundant activity, both creative and critical and some of it excellent, as, for example, the work developed by Machado de Assis in the field of criticism. As in other parts of Latin America, one will find the coexistence of different literary and stylistic movements, even within one author's works. The theater, however, continues to depend on Europe, and at the beginning of the century, no important changes are observed in relation to the end of the eighteenth century. The content is still insignificant. People want to be entertained. It is an amateur theater with a varied but superficial repertoire, from historical dramas to comedies. The Italian operas achieve great success. At the same time, construction of theater houses continues.

At the beginning of the nineteenth century, a significant event occurs to enrich the Brazilian theater: the exile of the Royal Family from Portugal as a consequence of the Napoleonic invasion. Escorted by their Court, they establish themselves in Rio de Janeiro. The arrival of the Court significantly contributes to the development of the theater, as verified in the construction of a new theater house in order to substitute the obsolete Manuel Luis

Theatre. The new theater house, the Teatro Real de São João, was inaugurated in 1813. The Royal Family attends many plays, and with their support, the theater has a major impact on society. Many operas are staged.

The enormous success that the period of Romanticism reached beginning in the 1830s will also enhance the theater in Brazil, by bringing in new perceptions of freedom and innovation while at the same time emphasizing national values and patriotism. The new romantic values are consolidated with the staging in 1838 of the tragedy *Antônio José ou O poeta e a Inquisição* (Antônio José or The Poet and the Inquisition), by Gonçalves de Magalhães (1811–1882), in which both the plot and playwright are totally Brazilian, and it is considered the first Brazilian historical drama. At the same time, Luís Carlos Martins Pena (1815–1848) creates the *comédia de costumes*, while other authors write about themes that soon cause a major repercussion in Brazilian literature—like that of patriotism, as seen in Casimiro de Abreu's (1839–1860) *Camões e o jau* (Camões and the Man of Java); or the attack on slavery, carried out by Antônio de Castro Alves (1847–1871) in *Gonzaga ou Revolução de Minas* (Gonzaga or the Revolution of Minas) in 1862.

The theme and setting of the Brazilian romantic writers strictly followed the principles of this literary movement. Thus, we find the battle for freedom in Antônio de Castro Alves's *Gonzaga ou Revolução de Minas*, based on the Inconfidentes conspiracy in 1789, or works set in the Middle Ages, such as *O cavaleiro teutônico ou a A feira de Mariemburg* (The Teutonic Knight or The Mariemburg Market) in 1855, by Antônio Gonçalves Teixeira e Souza (1812–1861). Barata Ribeiro (1843–1910), like Castro Alves, returned to the topic of slavery; that is, the attack he makes on slavery is portrayed in his works *Segredo do lar* (Home Secret) in 1881 and *O divórcio* (The Divorce) in 1882; slavery is also reflected in Agrário de Menezes's (1834–1863) work *Calabar* (1858). And as happened with Martins Pena, Francisco José Pinheiro Guimarães (1809–1857) became well known for his *comédia de costumes*: *A ciumenta* (The Jealous Woman) in 1841 and *O brasileiro em Lisboa* (The Brazilian in Lisbon) in 1844. There are several other playwrights worthy of mention. For example, Luís Carlos Martins Pena, creator of the *comédia de costumes*, was a prolific writer. He based his works on the reality of the country in order to create superficial and amusing plays. Another prominent romantic author was Antônio Gonçalves Dias (1823–1864), who rebels against prejudices, egotism, and backward attitudes. Another romantic author is Manuel Antônio Álvares de Azevedo (1831–1852), whose play *Macário* (1851) is structured as a dialogue between Macário and the devil, covering topics such as love and philosophy, in which he develops the contrast between fiction and reality. Other outstanding writers of this period are Manuel de Araújo Porto Alegre (1806–1879) and Joaquim Norberto da Silva (1820–1891).

With the peak of Romanticism, many significant theater houses are built throughout Brazil, such as the Pedro II in Porto Alegre in 1838, the Melpomene in Alagoas in 1846, the Teatro Lírico Fluminense in Rio de Janeiro in 1852, and the Tivoly also in Rio in 1847. During this period, one observes how the popular theater houses constructed at the beginning of the century have changed in appearance as a consequence of intense theatrical activity and the prestige achieved by the theater. This allows the emergence of professional actors, such as João Caetano dos Santos (1808–1863), who dominated the theater in Brazil and introduced innovative features in the staging.

Romanticism ends during the first half of the nineteenth century, giving way to Realism, which brings to the stage aspects of daily life and breaks away from the previous exoticism, which had produced a certain weariness in the public. At the same time, realism focuses on characters in daily life who are frequently portrayed from a caricatural perspective. Realism pays special attention to the psychological analysis of its characters, who belong mostly to the bourgeoisie. During this period, the most influential Brazilian writers of the nineteenth century are José de Alencar and especially Joaquim Maria Machado de Assis, who are considered the most significant authors of Brazilian literature.

Joaquim Manuel de Macedo (1820–1882) was a leader of Realism in Brazil. His importance lies in his capacity to reflect the Brazilian bourgeoisie of his time, although one should remember that he also produced romantic works, such as the Indianist *Cobé* (1852). His most prominent work, no doubt, is *O primo da Califórnia* (The Cousin from California) (1858), as it was considered the first Realist play of Brazilian theatre.

Joaquim José de França Júnior (1838–1890), having much in common with Martins Pena, focused his work on reflecting the society of his time. His works contain a strong criticism of the snobbishness, superficiality, and immorality of the Brazilian bourgeoisie, above all in plays with a clear political purpose: *Caiu o ministério!* (The Government Has Fallen!) (1884) and *Como se fazia um deputado* (How a Deputy Used to Be Made) (1882).

Important to the theater of the time is Artur Azevedo (1855–1908). He was a prolific and witty writer who developed his theatrical activity in a variety of fields. He not only wrote comedies with great success, but he also wrote *revistas* called *bambochatas* and operettas. His major contributions to the theater were humor, his portrayal of social concerns, energy, variety, and irony. His social concerns are reflected in the antislavery themes of two plays: *O liberato* (Liberato) (1871) and *A família Salazar* (The Salazar Family) (1882).

Other important playwrights of this period are: Moreira Sampaio (1851–1901), author of *revistas* and comedies; Artur Rodrigues da Rocha, and especially José Joaquim Campos Leão (1829–1883), better known as Qorpo Santo. He produced approximately fifteen short works, and their importance, according to Cacciaglia, lies in the fact that they are predecessors of Jarry and Ionesco and of the theater of the Absurd.

During the second half of the nineteenth century, even though Realism prevails, one can still encounter works written with characteristics of Romanticism. And parallel to this, lyrical opera reaches prominence, dominated by the Italian tenors and foreign conductors, mostly Italian. However, there is still concern and interest in building a national lyrical theater. In 1858, the Academia de Música e Ópera Nacional is inaugurated in Rio de Janeiro, and that same year, local actors stage the first lyrical representation in Portuguese (the *zarzuela A estréia de um artista* [An Artist's Debut]). Children's theater begins to emerge during this period, reaching success in the twentieth century. Also the French operetta, usually interpreted by French companies, achieved success, although there were also German, Spanish, and Italian companies.

At the turn of the century the theater experiences major changes. It is a period when the theater is more accommodating, even going to the extreme of creating plays for specific artists, with no technical innovation nor variation in theme. The criticism toward the bourgeoisie continues, as well as a slight social criticism. This period is overshadowed by

Henrique Coelho Neto (1864–1934), an author of vast production, having written comedies, dramas, libretos, fables, dramatic poems, among others. One can observe a direct influence of the European writers in Coelho Neto's works, mostly of D'Annunzio.

At the beginning of the twentieth century, the majority of the Brazilian playwrights were not well known for their contributions to the theater; however, their importance lies in the fact that they allow us to see to what extent they were influenced by foreign authors. Among them are Roberto Gomes (1882–1922), the symbolist Paulo Gonçalves (1897–1927), and the parnassian José Maria Goulart de Andrade (1881–1936). There is also another trend during this period that continues to be based on national reality, in which we find Oliveira Lima (1867–1928), with *O secretário del-Rei* (The King's Secretary) (1904), and Afonso Arinos (1868–1916), who wrote *O contratador de diamantes* (The Diamond Contractor) (1913). Graça Aranha (1868–1931), a significant writer of this period, also ventured into the theater, with his dramatic poem *Malasarte*.

Brazilian literature had lived many years under the direct influence of European literature and ideology. This trend was finally broken at the beginning of the Modernist movement, which took place during the first few decades of the twentieth century. Specifically, the Week of Modern Art in 1922 is a milestone. From this point on, Brazilian literature experiences a fundamental qualitative change by integrating literary techniques and ideologies that reflect Brazilian reality. Since then, one can talk about an authentic Brazilian literature. However, this did not necessarily happen in the theater, since, on the one hand, not much attention was paid to it since it was overshadowed by the novel and poetry, and it continued to depend on foreign plays until the 1940s, when the Teatro Brasileiro de Comédias (TBC), the Teatro Universitário, and the Os Comediantes companies emerge. However, the works of Oswald de Andrade were an exception. He wrote three plays: *O homem e o cavalo* (Man and Horse) (1934), *A morta* (The Dead Woman) (1937), and *O rei da vela* (The Candle King) (1937); in these there is an attempt to free Brazilian literature from its dependence. These works are irreverent, satirical, and antithetical and criticize the established values in society.

The first years of the 1920s are not of major importance in terms of the theater, where we see Viriato Correa and Oduvaldo Viana continuing with the *comédias de costumes*. However, the second half of this decade brings interesting contributions. In 1927, Alvaro Moreyra and his wife Eugênia inaugurate the Teatro de Brinquedo in Rio de Janeiro. This was a turning point in terms of innovative trends in Brazilian theater. The Teatro de Brinquedo is elitist and amateur. In it one encounters an awareness toward social concerns, an attempt to alert the spectator to the real problems of this period and to make him or her confront reality. It also focused on the establishment of critical thinking. The first play performed in this theater is a comedy: *Adão, Eva e outros membros da família* (Adam, Eve and Other Members of the Family) (1927). Ten years later the Moreyras inaugurate the Companhia de Arte Dramática Álvaro Moreyra where the works of foreign and Brazilian authors were staged: Ibsen and Pirandello, Benjamin Lima, Carlos Lacerda, and José Carlos Liboa, among others.

Much of the interest in renewing the theater not only originates in the new precepts of Modernism but also arises from the public. The critics are also weary and wish to improve the outdated theater of this period. The search is for new themes and forms, which are achieved in 1932 with the debut of *Deus lhe pague* (May God Repay You), by Joracy

Camargo (1898–1973), an author whose works are related to the Teatro de Brinquedo. Here social concern is clearly evident, and very current concepts are presented, such as Marxism.

The ideologizing of these works also covers Freudian theories, which appear in *Sexo* (Sex), by Renato Vianna (1894–1953). Critics, such as Décio de Almeida, questioned the "modernity" of this kind of theater because they were based on works of the nineteenth century. Therefore, in the 1920s there has been a major attempt at renovation, but this is not necessarily generalized, as historical works continue to be successful. In 1938, the play *Marquesa de Santos* (The Marquise of Santos), by Viriato Correa (1884–1967), is quite successful, and so is *Carlota Joaquina* (1939) by R. Magalhães, Jr. (1907–1982). Although in decline, the operetta continues to have many enthusiasts.

At the end of the 1930s, new companies emerge, such as the Teatro do Estudante in 1937; the Grupo de Teatro Experimental in 1939; and Os Comediante, which was initiated in 1938 but was not officially inaugurated until 1940. These companies, with the contribution of European directors, will become the foundation of modern dramaturgy. The Teatro do Estudante do Brasil (TEB), founded by Paschoal Carlos Magno, consisted of university students. The first play they staged was *Romeo and Juliet* by Shakespeare. This company's main traits were its aesthetic concerns. They also emphasized the use of Brazilian Portuguese (instead of Luso).

Os Comediantes consisted of aficionados when it emerged, but it did not limit its actors to university students; it also had an affinity with the Teatro de Brinquedo. The Polish director Zbigniew Ziembinski made his debut in Brazil with this group. His major contributions to the theater were innovative techniques. In 1943 he directed Nelson Rodrigues's *Vestido de noiva* (Bridal Gown), which, in the opinion of most of the critics (Álvaro Lins, Yan Michalski, and Almeida), encompassed a key moment in the authentic renovation and modernization of Brazilian theater. This process of renewal is consolidated in the 1940s with the creation of several companies, such as Teatro Brasileiro de Comédias, O Teatro Universitário, the Grupo Universitário do Teatro de São Paulo, the Teatro de Câmara, and the Companhia Fernando de Barros.

In 1958 the Seminário Permanente de Dramaturgia is created, and they stage a very successful play by Gianfrancesco Guarnieri (1936–   ) in 1959, *Eles não usam black-tie* (They Don't Wear Tuxedos). Guarnieri is also an actor in this play. The setting is the shantytowns (*favelas*) where problems of the marginalized classes are presented. This play opens the way to a trend in which the themes and writers are exclusively Brazilian, and they portray the reality of the marginalized. Writers such as Oduvaldo Vianna Filho, Augusto Boal, Flávio Migliacci, Roberto Freire, Edy Lima, and Benedito Rui Barbosa portray reality with leftist and populist views. Their goal, which was to acknowledge the works of modern Brazilian playwrights and to attain an authentic Brazilian theater, emerged during the Week of Modern Art. Plays that become hits during this period are Guarnieri's *Eles não usam black-tie* and Oduvaldo Vianna Filho's *Chapetuba F.C.* (1959).

The Arena company developed a very creative theater, with a strong social component. It maintained these characteristics without any pertinent changes, even after the establishment of the military dictatorship in 1964. It closed down at the end of the 1960s. In terms of theatrical companies, the Arena predominantly focused on the Brazilian social and political reality. At the individual level, two writers who were also successful in achieving this goal were Alfredo Dias Gomes, with *O pagador de promessas* (Payment as Pledged)

(1967), which contrasts the urban and rural world of northeastern Brazil; and Ariano Suassuna, with *O auto da compadecida* (The Rogue's Trial) (1956), which faced Brazilian reality in a very personal manner, mixing religion, traditions, and literature in an attempt to reflect a deeper side of Brazil by using legends, *romanceiros*, the *literatura de cordel*, and folklore. Undoubtedly Dias Gomes is an important author in Brazilian contemporary theater. The TBC staged *O pagador de promessas* in 1960. His plays strongly criticize the established powers, especially the Church, attack social hypocrisy, and defend popular values.

Another playwright within this group is Jorge Andrade, author of *A moratória* (The Moratorium) (s.1955), who criticizes the dehumanization of progress. The marginalized world is also reflected in Antônio Callado's work *Pedro Mico* and in Guarnieri's *Gimba, o presidente dos valentes* (Gimba, the President of the Brave) (1973).

In 1958 the "Oficina" group, which is closely related to the Arena group in terms of objectives, emerges. The Oficina company was originally composed of amateurs, and their goal was, as with other companies, to stage the works of unknown Brazilian authors and noncommercial foreign writers. They did theatrical research and experimented with new activities. Their debut was at the Teatro Novos Comediantes, with the staging of two unknown Brazilian playwrights—*A ponte* (The Bridge), by Carlos de Queiroz Teles, and *Vento forte para um papagaio subir* (Strong Wind for a Parrot to Ascend), by José Celso Martínez Correa—and the poem *Anti-Rio*, by Jorge Cunha Lima.

The theater at the beginning of the 1960s is predominantly political, but it maintains its social component. This kind of theater was not well received by the military, who had taken over the government in 1964 and regarded the theater as an enemy. This compelled the theater to become a strong front of resistance against the regime, especially after the approval of the "Ato Institucional No. 5" (AI-5) in 1968, which institutionalized censorship.

One of the most significant forms of resistance toward the military regime was the staging of *Shows opinião* (Opinion Shows), which made its debut in 1964 by the group Opinião, directed by Augusto Boal. They adopted a literary-musical form of collage, based on texts by Armando Costa, Oduvaldo Vianna Filho, and Paulo Pontes. One year later they staged *Liberdade, liberdade* (Freedom, Freedom), based on texts by Flávio Rangel and Millôr Fernandes. Shortly after, censorship forbade the staging of *Brasil pede passagem* (Brazil Requests Change). These plays were characterized by their desire for freedom and their social orientation, which were based on Brazilian reality.

The consequences of the military coup did not immediately affect the theater, for its fame continued for approximately four years. Many fascinating plays transmitting a provocative and aggressive message were staged; for example, Oswald de Andrade's *O rei da vela* (The Candle King) in 1967 and Chico Buarque's *Roda viva* (Commotion) in 1968. These represented the rejection of the military dictatorship by Brazilian intellectuals. In 1965 the Teatro da Universidade Católica de São Paulo (TUCA) staged a new play based on the poem *Morte e vida Severina* (Death and Life Severina) by João Cabral de Melo Neto. This company consisted of university students under the direction of Roberto Freire. It was a major success both in Brazil and France. One year later, following the provocative attitude and opposition that characterized these years, other plays made their debut: *Eu sou vida: Eu não sou morte* (I Am Life: I Am Not Death) and *Mateus e Mateusa* (Matthew and Female Matthew), by Qorpo Santo (José Joaquim de Campos Leão).

Plínio Marcos also staged another important work in 1965: *Dois perdidos numa noite*

(Two Men Lost in a Dirty Night). Marcos's characters are usually at the limit of social marginalization—prostitutes, homosexuals, the homeless, the unemployed—and he presents how they confront each other in order to survive. Other writers who follow this line of thought are Isabel Câmara, Consuelo de Castro, José Vicente, and Antônio Bivar.

Although during the first years of the dictatorship there was apparently total freedom to stage new plays, the truth is that censorship affected the theater from the very beginning of the military coup. In 1965 some plays were forbidden, such as *O vigário* (The Vicar), by Rolf Hochluth. And political and social theater, which had been one of the most productive areas of the Brazilian theater, was limited in the extreme during this period.

The Movimiento de Cultura Popular (MCP) in Pernambuco and the Centro Popular de Cultura (CPC) in Rio de Janeiro, which had strong political components, had their work curtailed. Both groups traveled throughout Brazil, making the theater approachable to the public, adding to it new values. The MCP group also contributed to the diffusion of music in the country. The CPC, which emerged in the União Nacional de Estudantes in Rio, also dedicated itself to presenting plays and music to different neighborhoods of the city, establishing direct contact with the public.

In 1968 the Oficina group just about disappeared, and during the 1970s, the Teatro de Arena followed the same fate, ending one of the most brilliant endeavors carried out by the avant-garde in Brazil. Because of the intensification of censorship, writers such as Augusto Boal, José Celso, and Ferreira Gullar were forced to seek exile, whereas others, such as Guarnieri and Vianna, were confronted with major difficulties in introducing new plays to the public.

Surprisingly, plays of political content were constantly staged. For example, Roberto Athayde achieved great success in 1973 with *Apareceu a Margarida* (Daisy Appeared), and Dias Gomes staged *O túnel* (The Tunnel) in 1972 and *As primícias* (First Fruits) in 1978. These plays openly criticized the Brazilian political regime. In 1977 Jorge Andrade also staged *Milagre na cela* (Miracle in the Prison Cell), which deals with torture. During this period, we also find authors that take an independent stand, with no connection to theater companies; for example, Millôr Fernandes and João Bethencourt.

It is important to note that during the 1970s there is a great proliferation of independent and alternative theater groups, such as Asdrúbal Trouxe o Trombone, which staged a play that portrayed the carioca youth, *Trate-me leão* (Treat Me Lion), in 1976. Also, the group O Pessoal do Victor staged *Na carreira do divino* (Divine Career), which is based on Carlos Alberto Sofredini's text. The greatest success that this alternative theater reached, however, was in 1978, with the staging of Mário de Andrade's *Macunaíma*, directed by Antunes Filho.

Although the AI-5 was abolished in 1979, the military still maintained their control during the 1980s. Thus, the 1980s and 1990s in Brazilian theater could be characterized as lacking definition, specific goals, direction, and the organization that previous groups such as TBC, Arena, or Opinião had provided. Consequently, the theater during this period is not of extraordinary quality, although one should mention Antunes Filho and his debut of *Nelson Rodrigues, o eterno retorno* (Nelson Rodrigues, the Eternal Return), in 1982, and the contribution of Naum Alves de Souza. Independent groups with young actors continue to emerge, such as O Pessoal do Cabaré, O Poleiro dos Anjos (directed by Busa Ferraz, 1981), O pessoal do Despertar, and O Teatro dos Quatro, but they usually do not last very long. Currently, the Brazilian theater scene is suffering an important crisis, in part caused by the lack of theater houses, the reduction in the number of spectators, and the smaller number of authors in comparison to previous decades.

BIBLIOGRAPHY

Abreu, Brício de. *Esses populares tão desconhecidos.* Rio de Janeiro: Editora Rapaso Carneiro, 1963.

Azevedo, Manuel Duarte Moreira de. *O Rio de Janeiro.* Rio de Janiero: B. L. Garnier, 1877.

Boal, Augusto. *Legislative Theatre: Using Performance to Make Politics.* London; New York: Routledge, 1998.

Boccanero, Silio. *O theatro brasileiro.* Bahia: Imprensa Econômica, 1906.

Borba Filho, Herrmilio. *Historia do teatro.* Rio de Janeiro: Livraria Editors de Casa do Estudante do Brasil, 1950.

Bosi, Alferdo. *História concisa da literatura brasileira.* São Paulo: Editora Cultrix, 1985.

"Brasil." *Escenarios de dos mundos: inventario teatral de Iberoamérica.* Vol. 1. Madrid: Centro de Documentación Teatral, 1988, 228–301. Articles by scholars.

Cacciaglia, Mário. *Pequena história do teatro no Brasil.* São Paulo: EDUSP, 1980, 1986.

Câmara Cascudo, Luís da. *Dicionário do folclore brasileiro.* 6th ed. Belo Horizonte: Editora Itatiaia, EDUSP, 1988.

Cândido, Antônio, and José Aderaldo Castello. *Presenca da literatura brasileira.* 3 vols. São Paulo: Difusão Européia do Livro, 1966.

Clark, Fred M., and Ana Lucía Gazolla de García. *Twentieth-Century Brazilian Theatre: Essays.* Chapel Hill, Estudios de Hispanófila, 1978.

Correa, Viriato. "Origens e desenvolvimiento do teatro brasileiro." *Jornal do Comércio* (Rio de Janeiro), June 27, 1954.

Coutinho, Afrânio. *A literatura no Brasil.* 6 vols. Rio de Janeiro: Editorial Sul Americana, Livraria São José, 1971.

Cruz, Osmar Rodrigues. "Origem de renovacão do teatro brasileiro." *Revista Brasiliense* (November–December 1956).

Doria, Gustavo Alberto Acioli. *Moderno teatro brasileiro, crônica de suas raízes.* Rio de Janiero: Serviço Nacional de Teatro, Ministério de Educaçao e Cultura, 1975.

Faria, Joao Roberto. *O teatro realista no Brasil, 1855–1865.* São Paulo: Editora Perspectiva, 1993.

Fleiuss, Max. "O teatro no Brasil." *Dyonisos* (Rio de Janeiro), February 1955.

Galante de Sousa, J. *O teatro no Brasil.* 2 vols. Rio de Janeiro: Ministério de Educação e Cultura, Instituto Nacional do Livro, 1960.

George, David Sanderson. *The Modern Brazilian Stage.* Austin: University of Texas Press, 1992.

Gonçalves, Augusto de Freitas Lopes. *Dicionário histórico e literário do teatro no Brasil.* 4 vols. Rio de Janeiro: Livraria Editora Cátedra, 1982.

Hessel, Lothar Francisco. *O teatro jesuítico no Brasil.* Porto Alegre: URGS, 1972.

———. *O teatro no Brasil da colônia à regência.* Porto Alegre: URGS, 1974.

———. *O teatro no Brasil sob Dom Pedro II.* Port Alegre: URGS, 1979.

Hollanda, Sérgio Buarque de. "Teatro jesuítico." *Diário Carioca,* September 28, 1951.

Hulet, Claude. *Brazilian Literature.* 3 vols. Washington, DC: Georgetown University Press, 1974.

Jacobbi, Ruggero. *A expressão dramática*. Rio de Janeiro: Instituto Nacional do Livro, 1956.

———. *Teatro in Brasile*. Bolonha: Cappelli, 1961.

Leite, Serafim. *Historia da Companhia de Jesus no Brasil*. Rio de Janeiro: Instituto Nacional do Livro, 1950.

Litrernto, Oliveiros. *Apresentacão da literatura brasileira*. 2 vols. Rio de Janeiro: Editora Forense-Universitária Ltd. 1978.

Magaldi, Sábato. *Panorama do teatro brasileiro*. São Paulo: Disfusão Européia do Livro, 1962.

Marinho, Henrique. *O teatro brasileiro*. Paris-Rio: Garnier, 1904.

Mendes, Miriam García. *O negro e o teatro brasileiro*. São Paulo: Fundação Cultural Palmares, 1993.

Mendonça, Carlos Sussekind de. *Historia do teatro brasileiro*. Rio de Janeiro: Mendonça, 1926.

Michalski, Yan. *O teatro sob pressão, uma frente de resistência*. Rio de Janeiro: Jorge Zahar Editor, 1985.

Moisés, Massaud. *História da literatura brasileira*. 4 vols. São Paulo: EDUSP, 1984.

Moisés, Massaud, and José Paulo Paes. *Pequeno dicionário de literatura brasileira*. São Paulo: Editores Cultrix, 1980.

Morais Filho, Melo. "O teatro de Anchieta." Arquivo do Districto Federal. Rio de Janeiro, January 1943.

Neves, Orlando. *Trinta anos de teatro*. Portugal: Sol XXI, 1993.

Nunes, Mário. *40 anos de teatro*. Rio de Janeiro: Serviço Nacional de Teatro, 1956.

Oliveira, Valdemar de. *Eça Machado, Casto Alves, Nabuco . . . e o Teatro*. Recife: Universidad Federal de Pernambuco, 1967.

———. *O teatro brasileiro*. Salvador: Aguiara e Souza, 1958.

Paixão, Múcio da. *O teatro no Brasil*. Rio de Janeiro: Brasília Editora, 1936.

Peixoto, Fernando. *Teatro em questão*. São Paulo: Editora Hucitec, 1989.

Peregrino Júnior, João. *O teatro de costumes no Brasil*. Rio de Janeiro: MEC, Serviço de Documentação, 1959.

Perez, Renard. *Escritores brasileiros contemporâneos*. 2 vols. Rio de Janeiro: Editora Civilização Brasileira. 1960.

Pontes, Joel. *O teatro moderno em Pernambuco*. São Paulo: São Paulo Editora, 1966.

Prado, Décido de Almeida. *Apresentação do teatro brasileiro moderno*. São Paulo: Martins Ed., 1956.

———."A evolução da literatura dramática." *A literatura no Brasil* 6 (1971): 7–37.

———. *O teatro brasileiro moderno*. São Paulo: EDUSP, 1988.

Prado, Décio de Almeida. *História concisa do teatro brasileiro*. São Paulo: EDUSP, 1999.

Romero, Sílvio. *História da literatura brasileira*. 6th ed. Rio de Janeiro: José Olympio, 1960.

Silva, Armando Sérgio da. *Oficina: do teatro ao te-ato*. São Paulo: Editora Perspectiva, 1981.

Silva, Lafayette. *História do teatro brasileiro*. Rio de Janeiro: Serviço Gráfico do Ministério de Educação e Saúde, 1938.

Silveira, Miroel. *A contribuição italiana ao teatro brasilero (1895–1964)*. São Paulo: Edições Quiron, 1976.

Soares, José Carlos de Macedo. *O teatro jesuita no Brasil*. Rio de Janeiro: Serviço Nacional de Teatro, MEC, 1956.

Sousa Bastos, Antônio. *Carteira do artista*. Lisboa: J. Bastos, 1898.

Stegagno Picchio, Luciana. *La letteratura brasiliana*. Milão: Sansoni, Accademia, 1972.

Stern, Irwin, ed. *Dictionary of Brazilian Literature*. Westport, CT: Greenwood Press, 1988.

Veríssimo, José. *História da literatura brasileira: De Bento Teixeira a machado de Assis*. 5th ed. Rio de Janeiro: José Olympio, 1969.

Weiss, William. *Theatre in Brazil*. Ottawa: University of Ottawa, Institute for International Co-operation, 1980.

◆

ALENCAR, José de

ALENCAR, José de (1832–1877). Born in Mecejana, Ceará, he was a lawyer, a journalist, and a politician. He worked as a government employee and later became Minister of Justice. Alencar was a prolific writer, having written novels, plays, poems, and literary criticism. In his writing he tried to portray Brazil in its totality, including the rural and urban world. His theatrical works are characterized by a variety of themes, even though the dialogues are declamatory and unnatural, and lack fluency. This, together with his moralizing tone, was his main flaw. Alencar's best play made its debut in 1857, *O demônio familiar* (The Family Demon), a comedy that focuses on the bourgeois family. He also developed and attacked slavery in his drama *Mãe* (Mother) and even wrote a historical drama, his last work, *O Jesuíta* (The Jesuit).

WORKS: *O demônio familiar* (The Family Demon) (Rio, 1857). *A noite de São João* (The Night of Saint John) (Rio, 1857). *O Rio de Janeiro verso e reverso* (Rio de Janeiro Back and Reverse) (Rio, 1857). *As asas de um anjo* (The Wings of an Angel) (Rio, 1860). *Mãe* (Mother) (Rio, 1862). *A expiação* (The Atonement) (Rio, 1868) (sequel to *As asas de um anjo*). *O Jesuíta* (The Jesuit) (Rio, 1875) (Alencar's only historical drama, written in 1862 and staged in 1875). *O credito* (The Credit) (1895).

BIBLIOGRAPHY: Anônimo, "Literatura dramática," *Revista Popular* 15 (1862), pp. 158–165, 219–227. T. A. Araripe Júnior, *Literatura brasileira*, José de Alencar, 2nd ed. (Rio, 1894). Flavio Aguilar, *A comedia nacional no teatro de José de Alencar* (São Paulo: Atica, 1984). Machado de Assis, "Revista dramática," *Diário do Rio de Janeiro* (Rio), March 29, 1860. Sacramento Blake, *Diccionario bibliographico brasileiro*, vol. 5 (Rio, 1899), pp. 74–82. Joao Roberto Faria, *José de Alencar e o teatro* (São Paulo: Perspectiva, Editora da Universidade de São Paulo, 1987). Luis Gastão d'Escragnolle Dória, "Cousas do passado," *Revista do Instituto Histórico e Geográfico Brasileiro* 71, pt. 2 (1908), pp. 310–315 (study on *As asas de um anjo*). Joaquim Manoel de Macedo, *Anno bibliographico brasileiro* (Rio) vol. 3 (1873), pp. 297–301. *Obra completa*, 4 vols. (Rio, 1958–1960). S. Saraiva, "O Jesuíta," *Gazeta de Noticias* (Rio), September 19, 1875. *Obras de ficção*, 16 vols., Rio, 1951. *Obras*, São Paulo, 1960. "Semana literária," *Diário do Rio de Janeiro* (Rio), March 6, 13, and 27, 1866. Guilherme Studart, *Diccionário bio-bibliográphico cearense*, vol. 2, Rio, 1913, pp. 158–167. *Teatro completo*, 2 vols. (Rio, 1977) (introduction and comments by R. Magalhães Júnior and Marlene de Castro Correia). José Veríssimo, *Estradas brasileiras*, 2nd series (1889–1893) (Rio, 1894), pp. 153–164. José Veríssimo, ed., *Estudos de literatura brasileira*, 3rd series (Rio, 1903), pp. 135–163 (study on *O Jesuíta*). José Veríssimo, *História da literatura brasileira* (Rio, 1916), pp. 270–283, 381–383.

ÁLVARES DE AZEVEDO, Manuel Antônio

ÁLVARES DE AZEVEDO, Manuel Antônio (1831–1852). Born in São Paulo, he died of tuberculosis at the young age of twenty-one, unable even to finish his studies at law school. He was an excellent Romantic poet. For the theater he wrote the drama *Macário* (1851), which, in the first part, is a fantastic dream, and the topics of love, philosophy, and women are covered in a dialogue between Macário and the devil. The conclusion of the first part shows the impossibility of finding answers to the major themes that worry man. The second part is also a dialogue, this time between Macário and The Thinker, who ends up committing suicide. At the end, the devil deceives Macário.

WORKS: *Macário* (São Paulo, 1851). See also *Obras de Manuel Antônio Alvares de Azevedo (Works)*, 4th ed., vol. 3 (Rio de Janeiro, 1873).

BIBLIOGRAPHY: Severino João Albuquerque, "A Brazilian Intermediary in the Transmission of European Romantic Ideas: Alvares de Azevedo," *Romance Notes* 23.3 (Spring 1983): 220–226. Malcolm Bátchelor, "Alvares de Azevedo: A Transitional Figure in Brazilian Literature," *Hispania* 39.2 (1956): 149–156. Edgard Cavalheiro, *Alvares de Azevedo*. Veiga Miranda, *Alvares de Azevedo* (São Paulo, 1931). Homero Pires, *Alvares de Azevedo. Ensaio bio-bibliográfico* (Rio, 1931).

ANCHIETA, Father José de (1534–1597). Born in Spain (Canary Islands) and educated at Coimbra, he entered the Companhia de Jesus in 1551 and arrived in Brazil in 1553. He was extremely interested in the customs, language, and religion of the Indians. He learned the Tupi language and later wrote a grammar entitled *Arte de gramática da língua mais usada na costa do Brasil* (Grammar of the Language Most Used on Brazil's Coast) in 1595. He wrote poetry and plays (*autos*) in Spanish and Portuguese. The theme in his poetry and plays is always religious. Father Anchieta's plays were based on religious works of the Middle Ages of the Iberian Peninsula, and his goal was to catechize the Indians. His best play was *Auto na-fest de São Lourenço* (Play for Saint Lawrence), which was staged in 1583. It is a good example of the religious theater of the sixteenth century in Brazil.

WORKS: *Auto da Vila da Vitória ou de São Maurício* (Play for Victory Village or Saint Maurice's Village), published in *Boletim do Museu Paulista*, 3. *Auto de pregação universal* (Play of Universal Preaching), found in Simão de Vasconcelos, *Vida do venerável Pe. José de Anchieta*, (vol. 1 Rio, 1943), pp. 34, 56–58. *Auto de São Lourenço* (Play for Saint Lawrence), published in *Primeiras letras. Publicações da Academia Brasileira de Letras* (Rio, 1923), pp. 143–190. *Auto de Ursula* (Play for Saint Ursula), published in *Primeiras Letras. Publicações da Academia Brasileira de Letras* (Rio, 1923), pp. 40–66. *Auto do Crisma* (Play for Chrism), published in *Primeiras letras. Publicações da Academia Brasileira de Letras* (Rio, 1923), pp. 67–74. *Boletim do Museu Paulista*, vol. 1, (Documentação Lingüística, 1948). *Diálogo de Guaraparim* (Dialogue of Guaraparim), published in *Primeiras letras. Publicações da Academia Brasileira de Letras* (Rio, 1923), pp. 92–108. Melo Morais Filho, *Os escravos vermelhos*, (Rio, n.d.), pp. 154–169. *Poesias* organized by Maria de Lurdes de Paula Martins (São Paulo, n.d.), pp. 67–70. Joaquim Ribeiro, *Estética da língua portuguesa* (Rio, n.d.), pp. 288–296.

BIBLIOGRAPHY: Leodegário Amarante del Azevedo, "Anchieta e a Literatura Barroca em Latim," *Revista Letras* 35 (1986), 37–47. Leodegário Amarante de Azevedo, "Anchieta—Humanista de contra-reforma," *Boletim de Filologia*, (Lisbon) 30 (1985); 69–75. Jarbas de Carvalho, "Teatro Anchietano," in *Pedro Timóteo, antologia do jornalismo brasileiro* (Rio, 1944), pp. 244–252. Oscar Fernández, "José de Anchieta and Early Theatre Activity in Brazil," *LBR* (Summer 1978): 26–43. Helen Dominian, *Apostle of Brazil: The Biography of Padre José de Anchieta* (New York, 1958). Melo Morais Filho, "O teatro de Anchieta," *Arquivo do Distrito Federal*, vol. 1 (Rio, 1897). Juan Francisco Recalde, "Teatro tupi de Anchieta," *Revista do Arquivo Municipal* (São Paulo), 98 (1944): 131–141. Claude-Henri Frêches, "Le théatre du P. Anchieta: Contenu et structures," *Annali Istituto Universitario Orientale* (Nápoles) 3 (1961): 47–70. Joseph E. Gillet, "José de Anchieta, the First Brazilian Dramatist," *Hispanic Review* 21.2 (1953): 155–160. D. Lee Hamilton, "A vida e as obras de José de Anchieta," *Hispania* 26.4 (1953): 407–424. Lothar Hessel and Georges Raeders, *O teatro jesuítico no Brasil* (Porto Alegre: Editora da URGS, Universidade Federal do Rio Grande do Sul, 1972). Maria de Lurdes de Paula Martins, "Contribuição para o estudo do teatro tupi de Anchieta," *Boletim da Faculdade de Filosofia da Universidade de São Paulo* 24 (1941). Renata R. Mautner Wasserman, "The Theater of Jose de Anchieta and the Definition of Brazilian Literature," *Luso-Brazilian Review* 36.1 (Summer 1990): 71–85. José Augusto Mourão, "José de Anchieta, missionário e trovador do Brasil: Literatura e evangelização," *Broteria* (Lisboa) 111.6 (December 1980): 475–489. Joaquim Tomás, "Anchieta e o nosso teatro religioso," *Jornal do Comércio* (Rio), August 23, 1953. Richard Preto-Rodas, "Anchieta and Vieira: Drama as Sermon, Sermon as Drama," *LBR* (December 1970): 96–103. Joel Pontes, *Teatro de Anchieta* (Rio, 1978).

ANDRADE, Jorge (1922–1984). Born in Barretos, São Paulo, he studied at the Escola de Arte Dramática de São Paulo. His works are dramas of social protest. He wrote a trilogy based on the decadence of the rural aristocracy: *O telescópio* (The Telescope) (s.1954), in which he studies the destruction of a family on a farm. *A moratória* (Moratorium) (s.1955), set in the last years of the 1920s, portrays the devastation farmers experienced during the coffee crisis; and *Pedreira das almas* (Quarry of Souls) (s.1958) is set in the nineteenth century in Minas Gerais during the mining crisis. In *Vereda de Salvação* (Path of Salvation) (s.1954), he portrays the world of the oppressed. In 1977 Andrade makes the debut of *Milagre na cela* (Miracle in the Prison Cell), which covers the theme of torture.

WORKS: *O faqueiro de prata* (The Silver Knife Case) (1954). *O telescópio* (The Telescope) (s.1954) (Rio, 1960). *Vereda de Salvação* (Path of Salvation) (s.1954) (São Paulo, 1963). *A moratória* (Moratorium) (s.1955) (São Paulo, 1956). *Pedreira das almas* (Quarry of Souls) (s.1958) (Rio, 1960). *A escada* (The Stairs) (s.1961) (São Paulo, 1964). *Os ossos do barão* (The Baron's Bones) (s.1963), (São Paulo, 1964). *Rastro atrás* (Backward Track) (São Paulo, 1967). *A receita* (The Recipe) (s.1968). *Marta, a árvore e o relógio* (Marta, the Tree and the Watch) (includes *As confrarias, Pedreira das almas, A moratória, O telescópio, Vereda da Salvação, Senhora da Boca do Lixo, A escada, Os ossos do barão, Rasto atrás e O sumidouro*) (São Paulo, 1970). *Milagre na cela* (Miracle in the Prison Cell) (Rio, 1977). *O incêndio* (The Fire) (São Paulo, 1978).

BIBLIOGRAPHY: Fred M. Clark, "Tragedy and the Tragic: Andrade's *Pedreira das almas*," *Latin American Theatre Review* 15.1 (Fall 1981): 21–30. Delmiro Gonçalves, "Drama do café encontrou seu autor," *Visão*, no. 24 (June 19, 1964): 20–23. Richard A. Mazzara, "Two New Plays by Jorge Andráde," *Latin American Theatre Review* 2.1 (1968): 49–52. Richard A. Mazzara, "The Theater of Jorge Andrade," *Latin American Theatre Review* 1.1 (1967): 3–18. Benedicta S. Monsen, "Plantation Playwright, Jorge Andrade of Brasil," *Américas* 8.8 (August 1956): 8–12. Gerald M. Moser, "Jorge Andrade's São Paulo Cycle," *Latin American Theatre Review* 5.1 (1971): 17–24. Décio de Almedia, *Apresentação do teatro brasileiro moderno* (São Paulo, 1956), pp. 148–151. Anatol Rosenfeld, "Jorge Andrade," *Palco + Platéia*, no. 3 (1970): 48–50. Silviano Sandago, "A moratória em processo," *PMLA* 83.2 (May 1968): 332–339.

ANDRADE, Oswald de (1890–1954). Born in São Paulo, he was a lawyer and journalist. He was a Modernist who wrote poetry, literary manifestos, novels, and plays. He was one of the organizers of the Week of Modern Art in 1922. Andrade was a Marxist (until 1945), and his theater is expressionist. He published *O rei da vela* (The Candle King) in 1937. It was not staged at that time, but in 1967 the Teatro Oficina staged it with enormous success. It is a very critical satire of capitalism, of dishonest intellectuals, and of the corrupt bourgeoisie. In 1937 he wrote *A morta* (The Dead Woman), a very aggressive text (which is a characteristic of his plays) in which he attacks the existing corruption in society.

WORKS: *Théatre brésilien, mon coeur balance* (Brazilian Theatre, My Trembling Heart) (São Paulo, 1916). *O homem e o cavalo* (Man and Horse) (São Paulo, 1934). *A morta* (The Dead Woman), in Teatro (Rio, 1937). *O rei da vela* (The Candle King), in *Teatro* (1937). *O rei floquinhos* (The Fluffy King), for children (São Paulo, 1957).

BIBLIOGRAPHY: Ronald Burgess, "Birth. Life. A Morta. de Andrade," *LBR* (Winter 1985); 103–110. Haroldo de Campos, "A estrutura de 'O rei da vela': Da vela à vala," *Correio da Manhã*, September 10, 1967. Fred M. Clark, "Oswald and Mayakovsky: *O homem e o cavalo* and Mystery-Bouffe," *REH* (May 1982): 241–256. David Sanderson George, "Anthropophagy and the New Brazilian Theatre," *DAI* 42.12 (June 1982): 5137A. Ruggero Jacobbi, "Teatro de Oswald de Andrade," *O espectador apaixonado* (Porto Alegre, 1962). Sábato Magaldi, *Panorama do teatro brasileiro*, 2nd ed. (Rio, 1976), pp. 189–192. Luciana Stegagno Picchio, *La letteratura brasiliana* (Milão, 1972), pp. 511–513. Samuel Rawet, "Teatro no Modernismo," in "Modernismo, estudos críticos," *Revista Branca* (Rio, 1954). Sérgio Tapajós, "Oswald e Mário de Andrade," *Correio da Manhã*, December 31, 1967.

ASSIS, Joaquim Maria Machado de (1839–1908). Born in Rio de Janeiro, he was a journalist and government employee at the Ministry of Industry and Commerce. He was also a mulatto. Poet, short story writer, dramatist, and literary critic, he was also one of the founding members of the Academia Brasileira de Letras. He stands out as a novelist and wrote three fundamental novels of Brazilian literature. His theater works did not reach the same standard as his novels. He translated several plays from the French, and some of his own plays consist of only one act. *Lição de botânica* (Botany Lesson) is his best play mostly because of the fluidity of the dialogues. Another significant play is *Não consultes médico* (Don't Check with the Doctor), which focuses on the overcoming of the loss of a romantic love.

WORKS: *Hoje avental, amanhã luva* (Today an Apron, Tomorrow a Glove) (Rio, 1860). *Odisséia dos vinte anos* (Odyssey of a Twenty-Year-Old) (Rio, 1860). *Desencantos* (Disenchantments) (Rio, 1861). *Gabriela* (Gabrielle) (São Paulo, 1862). *O caminho da porta* (The Pathway of the Door) (Rio, 1863). *O protocolo* (Protocol) (Rio, 1863). *Quase ministro* (Almost a Government Official) (Rio, 1864). *O pomo da discórdia* (Bone of Contention) (1864). *Os deuses de casaca* (The Gods in Tails) (Rio, 1866). *O remorso vivo* (Live Remorse) (Rio, 1867). *Cenas da vida do Rio de Janeiro* (Scenes of Life in Rio de Janeiro) (Rio, 1873). *Antes da Missa. Conversa de duas damas* (Before Mass. Conversation of Two Ladies) (Rio, 1878). *Tu, só tu, puro amor . . .* (You, Only You, Pure Love . . .) (Rio, 1880). *Não consultes médico* (Don't Check with the Doctor) (Rio, 1896). *Lição de botânica* (Botany Lesson) (Rio, 1908). *As forcas Caudinas* (The Caudinas Forces) (Rio, n.d.). See also *Teatro completo* (Complete Plays) (Rio, 1982).

BIBLIOGRAPHY: Modesto de Abreu, *Machado de Assis* (Rio, n.d.). Modesto de Abreu, "O teatro de Machado de Assis," *Jornal do Comércio* (Rio), August 5, 1934. Fernando Mendes de Almeida, "O teatro e a poesia de Machado de Assis," *Roteiro* (São Paulo), June 21, 1930. José Maria Bello, *Retrato de Machado de Assis* (Rio, n.d.). Sacramento Blake, *Diccionário bibliográphico brasileiro*, vol. 4 (Rio, 1898), pp. 195–198. Edgard Cavalheiro, "Machado de Assis e o teatro," *A Gazeta* (Vitória), June 20, 1939. Pinheiro Chagas, "Letras e Artes," *Annuário do Archivo Pitoresco* (Lisbon), March 1866. João Carlos de Sousa Ferreira, "Páginas menores," *Correio Mercantil* (Rio), September 21, 1862. Benjamin Lima, "O teatro de Machado de Assis," *Jornal do Brasil* (Rio), May 18, 1940. Edoardo Limoeiro, "Crônicas," *A Saudade* (Rio), September 21, 1862. Quintino Bocaiúva, "Carta ao autor," *Theatro de Machado de Assis*, vol. 1 (Rio, 1862). Ari Martins, "Machado de Assis teatrólogo," *Federação das Academias de Letras do Brasil* (Rio, 1940). Mário Matos, *Machado de Assis* (Rio, 1939). Salvador de Mendonça, "O barbeiro de Sevilha," *Diário do Rio de Janeiro* (Rio), September 9, 1866. J. Ferreira de Meneses, "Machado de Assis e O Caminho da Porta," *Imprensa Acadêmica* (São Paulo), August 14, 1864. Raimundo Morais, *Machado de Assis* (Belém, 1939). Sílvio Vieira Peixoto, "Quintino, crítico de Machado de Assis," *Annuário Brasileiro de Literatura* (Rio, 1938), pp. 349–351. Alfredo Pujol, *Machado de Assis* (São Paulo, 1917). Lafayette Silva, "O teatro de Machado de Assis," *Revista da Academia Brasileira de Letras* (Rio), 37.120 (1931): 462–471. Orris Soares, "O teatro de Machado de Assis," *Revista do Brasil* (Rio), June 1939. Inocêncio F. da Silva, *Diccionário bibliográphico português*, vol. 12 (Lisbon, 1884), pp. 107–109, 391–392. Cláudio de Sousa, "Clássicos no Teatro," *Revista de Língua Portuguesa* (Rio), no. 19 (September 1922). Vercingetorix (Antônio José Vitorino de Barros?), "Os deuses de casaca," *Semana Ilustrada* (Rio), January 7, 1866.

AZEVEDO, Artur (1855–1908). Born in the state of Maranhão, he was the brother of Aluízio Azevedo. He wrote short stories and was the author of *revistas* called *bambochatas*, operettas, and criticism of the theater. One of the main playwrights of the second half of the nineteenth century, a defender of the national theater, he supported the need to build the National Theatre of Rio, which was inaugurated after his death. In his works, we find the influence of European and Brazilian writers, such as Martins Pena and França Júnior. His numerous plays are mainly comedies in which he uses a rich and varied language, but they are usually superficial in theme. Azevedo also wrote plays that covered several different themes, such as marriage in *O dote* (The Dowry) (1907), which reflects different aspects of the dark side of the society of his time; slavery is portrayed in *O escravocrata* (The Slavocrat) (1884), *O liberato* (Liberato) (1881), and *A família Salazar* (The Salazar Family) (1882). His best work was *A capital federal* (The Federal Capital) (1897), which contrasts urban and rural life.

WORKS: *Amor por anexins* (Love for Popular Sayings) (Lisbon, 1872); (Rio, 1879). *O capadócio* (The Imposter), parody of *Trovatore* (Rio, 1872). *A casadinha de fresco* (The New Wife), parody of *La petite mariée*, by Lecoq (Rio, 1876). *A filha de Maria Angu* (Maria Angu's Daughter), parody of *La Fille de Mme. Angot*, by Lecoq (Rio, 1876). *Uma* *véspera de Reis* (The Eve of Three King's Day) (Rio, 1876). *Abel Helena* (Abel Helena), imitation of *La belle Hélène*, by Offenback (Rio, 1877). *A pele do lobo* (The Wolf's Skin), *Revista do Rio de Janeiro* (Rio) 6 (1877); *Revista de Teatro* (Rio) 289 (January–February 1956). *A jóia* (The Jewel) (Rio, 1879); *Revista de Teatro* (Rio) 286 (July–August 1955). *Os doidos* (The Insane), *Revista dos Teatros* (Rio), July 1879. *Os noivos* (The Engaged) (Rio, 1880). *A princesa dos cajueiros* (The Princess of the Cashew Trees) (Rio, 1880). *O liberato* (Liberato), *Revista Brasileira* 10 (Rio) (1881): 199–227. *A flor de lis* (Fleur-de-lis) (Rio, 1882). *A mascote na roça* (The Mascot in Rural Country) (Rio, 1882). *O escravocrata* (The Slavocrat) (Rio, 1884). *O mandarim* (Mandarin) (Rio, 1884). *Cocota* (Cocota) (Rio, 1885). *O bilontra* (The Scoundrel) (Rio, 1886, 1896). *A donzela Teodora* (The Damsel Teodora) (Rio, 1886). *Herói à força* (Hero by Force) (Rio, 1886). *A terra das maravilhas* (The Marvelous Land) (Rio, 1886). *O carioca* (The Carioca) (Rio, 1887). *Mercúrio* (Mercury) (Rio, 1887). *A almanjarra* (The Odd One) (Rio, 1888). *Fritzmac* (Fritzmac) (Rio, 1889). *Viagem ao Parnaso* (Trip to Parnassus), *Correio do Povo*, March 1891. *O tribofe* (The Cheater) (Rio, 1892). *Como eu me diverti* (How I Had Fun), *Album* (Rio) 37 (1893): 291. *O major* (The Major) (Rio, 1895). *A fantasia* (The Fantasy) (Rio, 1896). *A capital federal* (The Federal Capital) (Rio, 1897). *O badejo* (The Grouper) (Rio, 1898). *Confidências* (Secrets), *Revista Brasileira* (Rio) 16 (1898). *O jagunço* (The Hired Assassin) (Rio, 1898). *Gavroche* (Gavroche) (Rio, 1899). *A viúva Clark* (The Clark Widow) (Rio, 1900). *A Estação* (The Station) (Rio), March 31, 1901. *Comem!* (Eat!) (Rio, 1902). *A fonte Castália* (The Castália Fountain) (Rio, 1904). *O dote* (The Dowry) (Rio, 1907). *Entre a missa e o almoço* (Between Mass and Lunch), *O Século* (Rio), December 6, 1907. *O oráculo* (The Oracle) (Rio, 1907). *Vida e morte* (Life and Death) (Rio, 1932). *Entre o vermute e a sopa* (Between Vermouth and Soup), *Revista de Teatro* (Rio) 285 (May–June 1955). *O retrato a óleo* (The Oil Painting), *Boletim da Sociedade Brasileira de Autores Teatrais* (Rio) 283 (January–February 1955). *Casa de orates* (Madhouse), *Revista de Teatro* 289 (January–February 1956). *O genro de muitas sogras* (The Son-in-Law with many Mothers-in-Law), *Revista de Teatro* (Rio) 291 (May–June 1956). *O mambembe* (The Cheapie), *Revista de Teatro* (Rio) 292 (March–April 1956). *Uma consulta* (The Appointment) (n.d.).

BIBLIOGRAPHY: Modesto de Abreu, "Artur Azevedo," *Revista das Academias de Letras* (Rio) 56 (March–April 1945). Modesto de Abreu, "Popularidade de Artur de Azevedo," *Boletim da Sociedade Brasileira de Autores Teatrais* (Rio) 283 (January–February 1955). Modesto de Abreu, "A técnica teatral do Badejo," *Boletim da Sociedade Brasileira de Autores Teatrais* (Rio) 288 (November–December 1955). Pedro Moniz Aragão, "A arte no teatro popular," *Boletim da Sociedade Brasileira de Autores Teatrais* (Rio) 234 (April 1947). Pedro Moniz de Aragão, "Artur Azevedo e a sua paixão pelo teatro," *Boletim da Sociedade Brasileira de Autores Teatrais* (Rio) 259 (January–February 1951). Pedro Moniz de Aragão, "Artur Azevedo," *Dionysos* (Rio), no. 2 (June 1952). V. de Algerana (Alvarenga Fonseca), "Artur Azevedo," *Almanack dos theatros* (Rio, 1909), pp. 5–8. Artura Azevedo, "As minhas primeiras peças," *Almanaque Brasileiro Garnier* (Rio, 1903), pp. 188–191. Raul de Azevedo, "Os três Azevedo (Artur, Aluísio e Américo)," *Jornal do Commércio* (Rio), October 5, 1952. Plínio Barreto, "Um grande homem de teatro," *Revista de Teatro* (Rio) 288 (November–December 1955). Sacramento Blake, *Diccionário bibliográphico brasileiro*, vol. 1 (Rio, 1883), pp. 338–341. Adolfo Caminha, *Cartas literárias* (Rio, 1895), pp. 193–200. Joracy Camargo, "Artur Azevedo e a realidade brasileira do seu tempo," *Boletim da Sociedade Brasileira de Autores Teatrais* (Rio) 284 (March–April 1955). Raul Cardoso, "Artur Azevedo e Moreira Sampaio," *Autores e Livros* (Rio) 1 (October 19, 1941), p. 179. Batista Coelho, "Ribaltas e gambiarras," *Jornal do Brasil* (Rio), November 19, 1908. Ciro Vieira da Cunha, *No tempo de Paulo Ney* (São Paulo, 1950), pp. 37–39. Armando Erse (João Luso), *Elegias* (Porto, 1916), pp. 53–61. Gryphus (Visconti Coaracy), *Galeria theatral* (Rio, 1884), pp. 215–217. Múcio Leão, "Quatro aspectos de um escritor," *Letras Brasileiras* (Rio), no. 1 (May 1943). Joaquim Madureira, *Impressões de theatro* (Lisbon, 1905), pp. 215–218. R. Magalhães Júnior, *Artru Azevedo e sua época* (São Paulo, 1955). Mário Martins, *A evolução da literatura brasileira* (Rio) 2 (1945), pp. 173–202. Múcio da Paixão, *Espírito alheio* (São Paulo, 1916), pp. 97–100. Garcia Redondo, *Artur Azevedo* (Sociedade de Cultura Artística, Conferências, São Paulo, 1914), pp. 97–148. Antônio Simões dos Reis, *Poetas do Brasil*, vol. 2 (Rio, 1951), pp. 263–271. Abadie Faria Rosa, "O teatro no Distrito Federal," *Biblioteca da Academia Carioca de Letras. Aspectos do Distrito Federal* (Rio, 1943), pp. 208–211. Moreira Sampaio, "Artur Azevedo," *A Semana* (Rio), December 12, 1887. Miguel Santos, "Sobre Artur Azevedo," *Boletim da Sociedade Brasileira de Autores Teatrais*

(Rio) 273 (May–June 1953). Roberto Seidl, *Artur Azevedo. Ensaio bio-bibliográphico* (Rio, 1937). Inocêncio F. da Silva, *Diccionário bibliográphico português*, vol. 20 (Lisbon, 1911), pp. 275–276. Oliveira e Silva, "Escola dos Maridos," *A Estação* (Rio), March 15, 1891. J. F. Velho Sobrinho, *Dicionário bio-bibliográfico brasileiro*, vol. 1 (Rio, 1937), pp. 577–582. José Verissimo, "Bibliografia," *Revista Brasileira*, vol. 3 (Rio, 1895), p. 125. Eduardo Vitorino, *Actores e actrizes* (Rio, 1937), pp. 151–161.

BLOCH, Pedro (1914–). Born in the Ukraine, he became a doctor and musician. A member of the Academia Brasileira de Letras, he wrote a comedy for the radio, *Marilena versus destino* (Marilena versus Destiny) (1940). His main work, *As mãos de Eurídice* (Eurídice's Hands) (1951), is a monologue that has reached world success. Another successful work is *Dona Xepa* (Mrs. Xepa) (1955), which was later adapted for television in 1977. It reflects the efforts of a *favela* (woman from the slums) to help her family overcome poverty.

WORKS: *Marilena versus destino* (Marilena versus Destiny) (São Paulo, 1940). *O grande Alexandre* (The Great Alexander) (São Paulo, 1948). *As mãos de Eurídice* (Eurídice's Hands) (Rio, 1951). *Um cravo na lapela* (A Carnation on the Coat Lapel) (Rio, 1953). *Irene* (Irene) (Rio, 1953). *A camisola do anjo* (The Angel's Nightgown) (Rio, 1954). *Leonora* (Leonora) (Rio, 1954). *O torreão de pedra* (The Stone Turret) (Rio, 1961). *Brasileiros em Nova Iorque* (Brazilians in New York) (Rio, 1962). *Miquelina* (Miquelina) (Rio, 1962). *Roleta paulista* (The Paulista Rolette) (Rio, 1963). *Esta noite choveu prata* (Last Night It Rained Silver) (Petrópolis, 1964). *Os inimigos não mandam flores* (Enemies Do Not Send Flowers) (Petrópolis, 1964). *Soraia posto dois* (Bus Stop at Soraia [Copacabana]), (Rio, 1964). *Amor a oito mãos* (Eight-Hands Love) (Rio, 1965). *Morreu um gato na China* (A Cat Died in China) (Rio, 1966). *LSD e o contrato azul* (LSD and the Blue Contract) (Rio, 1971). *Dona Xepa* (Mrs. Xepa) (Rio, 1973). *Karla, valeu a pena* (Karla, It Was Worth It) (Rio, 1976). *A mancha* (The Stain) (n.d.). *Um anão chora baixinho* (A Dwarf Cries Quietly) (n.d.). *A xícara do imperador* (The Emperor's Cup) (n.d.). *Procura-se uma rosa* (Somebody Is Looking for a Rose) (São Paulo, n.d.).

BIBLIOGRAPHY: Joanna Courteau, "The Search for Authentic Man in *As mãos de Eurídice*," *Mester* 13.2 (Fall 1984): 55–62. "O espetáculo não pode parar," *Comentário* 3 (1962): 67–72.

BOAL, Augusto (1931–). Educated at Columbia University, he belonged to the Teatro Arena. An actor and dramatist, in 1970 he published a *teatro jornal*. He was imprisoned and tortured by the military regime in 1971. After being released, he went into exile, then returned to Brazil in 1985. Boal began his debut with comedies such as *Sortilégio* (Sortilege) (1952) and *Marido magro, mulher chata* (Skinny Husband, Nagging Wife) (s.1956). He achieved success and recognition with a work staged by the Teatro de Arena in 1960, *Revolução na América do Sul* (Revolution in South America), which is a political and social satire with a Marxist point of view focusing on the South American revolutions. Boal is an excellent director and researcher.

WORKS: *Sortilégio* (Sortilege) (1952). *Marido magro, mulher chata* (Skinny Husband, Nagging Wife) (s.1956) (São Paulo, 1956). *Revolução na América do Sul* (Revolution in South America) (São Paulo, 1960). *José do parto à sepultura* (José, From Childbirth to the Grave) (1962). *A lua muito pequena e a caminhada perigosa* (Very Small Moon and the Dangerous Walk) (São Paulo, 1968). *Tio Patinhas* (Uncle Scrooge) (1977). *Murro em ponta de faca* (Acting Foolishly) (1978). *Arena conta Tiradentes* (Tiradentes Tells Arena) (n.d.).

BIBLIOGRAPHY: Judith I. Bisset, "Victims and Violaters: The Structure of Violence in *Torquemada*," *Latin American Theatre Review* 15.2 (Spring 1982): 27–43. Augusto Boal, "Que pensa você da arte de esquerda?" *Latin American Theatre Review* 3.2 (Spring 1970): 45–53. Boal, "The Joker System: An Experiment by the Arena Theater for São Paulo," *The Drama Review* 14.2 (Winter 1970): 91–96. Boal, "El teatro popular en Brasil," *Revista Teatro* 14.7 (1971): 37–41. Boal, "Teatro Jornal: Primeira edição," *Latin American Theatre Review* 4.2 (Spring 1971): 47–60. *Categorias de teatro popular* (Buenos Aires, 1972). Boal, "Caminos del teatro latinoamericano," *Conjunto*, no. 16 (April–June 1973): 77–78. Boal, *200 exercícios e jogos para o ator e o não ator com vontade de dizer algo através do teatro* (Rio, 1977). Boal, *Teatro do oprimido* (Rio, 1977). Boal, *Técnicas latino-americanas de teatro popular*

(São Paulo, 1979). Boal, "Un teatro di poveri," *Il corriere UNESCO* 36.5–6 (May–June 1983): 4–7. Augusto Boal, *Legislative Theatre: Using Performance to Make Politics* (London: Routledge, 1998). Ross E. Butler, "Social Themes in Selected Contemporary Brazilian Dramas," *RomN* (Autumn 1973): 52–60. Kay Ellen Capo, "Performance of Literature as Social Dialectic," *Literature in Performance* 4.1 (November 1983): 31–36. Charles Driskell, "An Interview with Augusto Boal," *Later American Theatre Review* (Fall 1975): 71–78. Selma Calasans Rodrigues, "Arena conta Tiradentes: Uma experiência de teatro político," *Revista Iberoamericana* 50.126 (January–March 1984): 221–228. Mady Schutzman and Jan Cohen-Cruz, *Playing Boal: Theatre, Therapy, Activism* (London: Routledge, 1994).

BUARQUE DE HOLLANDA, Chico (Francisco) (1944–).

Composer, singer, novelist, and playwright. In 1969 he went into exile because of political persecution under the military dictatorship. In 1971 he made his debut with *Roda viva* (Commotion), a musical that was later adapted for television. In it he attempted to involve the public in the play and performance. Three years later he wrote *Calabar* with Ruy Guerra, a kind of musical acting mixed with singing and dancing. At a later date he debuted two more musicals. The first was *Gota d'água* (Drop of Water), in 1975, with Paulo Pontes, and the second, *A ópera do malandro* (Opera of the Vagabond), in 1978.

WORKS: *Roda viva* (Commotion) (1971). *Calabar, ou o elogio da traição* (Calabar, the Ode to Betrayal) (Rio, 1974). *Gota d'água* (Drop of Water) (Rio, 1975). *A ópera do malandro* (Opera of the Vagabond) (Rio, 1978).

BIBLIOGRAPHY: Ida Fátima Garritano, "Uma anatomia teatral da malandragem," *Minas Gerais, Suplemento Literário* 18.862 (April 9, 1983): 6–8. Lisa Oliveira-Joue, "Entrevista com Chico Buarque de Hollanda sobre *Gota d'água*," *Langues Neo Latines* 79.3 (1985): 141–154. Daphne Patai, "Race and Politics in Two Brazilian Utopias," *LBR* 19.1 (Summer 1982): 66–81. Maria do Carmo Peixoto Pandolfo, "Gota d'água—a trajetória de um mito," *Serviço Nacional de Teatro, Monografias 1977* (Rio, 1979), pp. 146–224. Anazildo Vasconcelos da Silva, *A poética de Chico Buarque* (Rio, 1974). Selma Suely Teixeira, "Análise da dramaturgia de Chico Buarque de Hollanda," *Estudos Brasileiros* 7.12

(1981): 37–68. George Woodyard, "The Dynamics of Tragedy in *Gota d'água*," *LBR* Supplementary Issue (1978), pp. 151–160.

CAMARGO, Joracy (1898–1973).

Born in Rio de Janeiro, he was a lawyer, customs official, journalist, actor, and theater director. In 1932 he made his debut with *Deus lhe pague* (May God Repay You), which was a major success because it broke the ties with previous forms of theater, such as vaudeville and light comedies. This work focuses on important social questions, such as poverty and marginalization, although it is not a profound study. We also find social concerns in *O bobo do rei* (The King's Jester) (1930), *O juízo final* (The Final Judgement), and *O sindicato de mendigos* (Beggars' Union) (1939). He also wrote historical dramas, such as *A retirada da Laguna* (The Retreat from Laguna) and *Tamandaré* (Tamandaré, the Victor), the latter written for the radio. Family dramas, such as *A pupila dos meus olhos* (Apple of My Eye) (1940), also comprise his works.

WORKS: *Me leva, meu bem* (Take Me, My Dear) (1924). *Calma no Brasil* (Calm in Brazil) (1925). *O macaco azul* (The Blue Monkey) (1927). *De quem é a vez?* (Whose Turn Is It?) (1928). *O amigo da família* (The Family's Friend) (1929). *Bazar de brinquedos* (Toy Bazaar) (1929). *Chauffeur* (Chauffeur) (1929). *Mania de grandeza* (Greatness Compulsion) (1929). *Santinha de pau oco* (The Little Saint of Hollow Wood) (1929). *Tenho uma raiva de você . . .* (I Am So Mad at You . . .) (1929). *O bobo do rei* (The King's Jester) (1930). *O sol e a lua* (The Sun and the Moon) (1930). *A velha guarda* (The Old Generation) (1930). *Boneco de trapo* (Rag Doll) (1931). *Uma semana de prazer* (A Week of Pleasure) (1931). *Anastácio* (Anastácio) (1932). *O anjo da meia noite* (The Midnight Angel) (1932). *Deus lhe pague* (May God Repay You) (1932). *O neto de Deus* (God's Grandson) (1932). *O homem que voltou da posteridade* (The Man That Returned from Posterity) (1933). *Maktub* (Maktub) (1933). *Maria Cachucha* (Maria Cachucha) (1933). *O sábio* (The Wise Man) (1933). *Em nome da lei* (In the Name of the Law) (1934). *Marabá* (Marabá) (1934). *A máquina infernal* (The Infernal Machine) (1935). *O duque de Caxias* (The Duke of Caxias) (1937). *Fora da vida* (Outside of Life) (1938). *Mocidade* (Youth) (1938). *O sindicato de mendigos* (Beggars' Union) (1939).

A pupila dos meus olhos (Apple of my Eye) (1940). *Bonita demais* (Too Beautiful) (1943). *Mocinha* (Young Woman) (1943). *Nós, as mulheres* (We, the Women) (1943). *Encruzilhada* (Crossroads) (1944). *Lili do 47* (Lili of 47) (1945). *Bagaço* (Bagasse) (1946). *Bodas de Aurora* (Aurora's Wedding) (1953). *Rainha Elizabeth* (Queen Elizabeth) (1953). *A figueira do inferno* (Hell's Fig Tree) (1954). *A Santa Madre* (Mother Superior) (1954).

BIBLIOGRAPHY: Edison Carneiro, "Deus lhe pague," *Boletim de Ariel* (Rio) (January 1934). Bandeira Duarte, "Joracy Camargo e a comédia da sua vida," *Boletim da Sociedade Brasileira de Autores Teatrais* (Rio) 239 (September 1947). Sábato Magaldi, *Panorama do teatro brasileiro*, 2nd ed. (Rio, 1976), pp. 187–189. Décio de Almeida Prado, *Apresentação do teatro brasileiro moderno* (São Paulo, 1956), pp. 65–74. Zora Seljam, *Vida e obra de Joracy Camargo* (Rio de Janeiro: Academia Brasileira de Letras, 1998).

COELHO NETO, Henrique (1863–1934). Born in Caxias, his father was Portuguese, and his mother, Indian. He went to medical and law school but pursued a career in journalism and teaching. He was also a federal deputy and diplomat. He opposed the Modernist movement. Writing over one hundred works, he produced novels and numerous plays. He also wrote short stories, fables, *crônicas*, legends, and literary criticism. He was one of the most prolific writers of Brazilian literature. His work is characterized by eclectism and a powerful imagination. He possessed an extremely rich vocabulary and was a writer concerned with form (aesthetic). Coelho Neto wrote seventeen works for the theater. His best play was *Quebranto* (Breakdown) (1908), a social drama that attacks egotism, hypocrisy, and social conventions.

WORKS: *Indenização ou República* (Compensation or Republic) (1889). *Carneiro preto* (Black Sheep) (1890). *Os raios-X* (The X-Rays) (1897). *Pelo amor!* (For Sake of Love!) (1897). *Ao luar* (In the Moonlight) (1898). *Relicário* (Reliquary) (1899). *Fim da raça* (End of the Race) (1900). *Saldunes* (Saldunes) (Lisbon, 1900). *Artemis* (Artemis) (1898). *As estações* (The Seasons) (1898). *Hóstia* (Host) (1898). *Ironia* (Irony) (1898). *O diabo no corpo* (Devil in the Body) (1905). *A muralha* (The Wall) (1905). *Pastoral* (Pastoral) (Lisbon, 1905). *Theatro infantil* (Children's Plays) (Rio, 1905). *Nuvens* (Cloud) (1908). *Quebranto* (Breakdown) (1908). *Bonança* (Calm) (1909). *O dinheiro* (Money) (1912). *A borboleta negra* (The Black Butterfly) (1915). *O intruso* (The Intruder) (1915). *Fogo de vista* (Fire) (1924). *O desastre* (The Disaster) (1928). See also *Teatro* (Plays), vol. 1 (Porto, 1911). *Teatro*, vol. 2 (Porto, 1907). *Teatro*, vol. 3 (Rio, 1907). *Teatro*, vol. 4 (Porto, 1908). *Teatro*, vol. 5 (Porto, 1917). *Teatro*, vol. 6 (Porto, 1924).

BIBLIOGRAPHY: Modesto de Abreu, "O teatro de Coelho Neto," *Revista de Teatro* (Rio) 295 (January–February 1957). Mario Cacciaglia, *Quattro secoli di teatro in Brasile* (Rome, 1980), pp. 100–104. Péricles de Morais, *Coelho Neto e sua obra* (Porto, 1926). Artur Mota, *Vultos e livros* (São Paulo, 1921), pp. 33–48. Coelho Netto, *Coelho Netto* (Rio, 1942). Paulo Coelho Netto, *Bibliografia de Coelho Netto* (Rio, 1956). Luciana Stegagno Picchio, *La letteratura brasiliana* (Milão, 1972), pp. 449–450. Colin Pierson, "Coelho Neto: Introduction of African Culture into Brazilian Drama," *Latin American Theatre Review* (Spring 1976): 57–62. J. Galante de Sousa, *O teatro no Brasil* (Rio, 1960), pp. 180–183. Eduardo Vitorino, *Actores e actrizes* (Rio, 1937).

DIAS, Antônio Gonçalves (1823–1864). Born in Sítio Boa Vista, Caxias, son of a Portuguese and a woman of Indian and African origin. This mixture of races would influence his personal life and is reflected in his writing. A teacher and journalist, he published his first poetry book, *Primeiros cantos* (First Songs), in 1847. As a diplomat he traveled extensively throughout Europe. Gonçalves Dias had a profound knowledge of the European writers of his time. His first play, *Patkull* (1843), is set in Europe, and the protagonist is the prince of Livonia, who faces a tragic destiny. His next work, *Beatriz Cenci* (1844), is a tragic love story. In 1847 he wrote a historical drama, *Leonor de Mendonça*, set in Portugal. That same year, he wrote his last play, *Boabdil*, a love story set during the Middle Ages in Granada, Spain. He died in a shipwreck in 1864.

WORKS: *Patkull, drama do ano 1707* (Patkull, Drama of the Year 1707) (1843). *Beatriz Cenci* (1844). *Boabdil* (1847). *Leonor de Mendonça* (1847). *A noiva de Messina* (Messina's Fiancée) (1862). See also *Teatro completo* (Complete Plays) (Rio, 1979).

BIBLIOGRAPHY: Antônio Soares Amora, "Gonçalves Dias: Dramaturgo," *Comentário* 6 (1965): 366–368. Manoel Bandeira, *Gonçalves Dias* (Rio, 1952). Manuel Bandeira, "A poética de Gonçalves Dias," *Poesia completa e prosa escolhida de Gonçalves Dias* (Rio, 1959). M. Pinheiro Chagas, "Antônio Gonçalves Dias (Esboço Crítico)," *Revista contemporânea de Portugal e Brasil*, vol. 5 (Lisbon, 1865), pp. 173–185. Pinheiro Chagas, *Gonçalves Dias e Castro Alves* (Rio, n.d.). Eugênio Gomes, "Os dramas de Shelley e Gonçalves Dias sobre Beatriz Cenci," *Revista Brasileira* (Rio), no. 9 (April 1944). Ruggero Jacobbi, *Goethe, Schiller, Gonçalves Dias* (Porto Alegre, 1958), pp. 46–84. Ruggero Jacobbi, *Teatro in Brasile* (Bolonha, 1951), pp. 62–68. Hélio Lopes, "O Romantismo faz 150 anods de Brasil, desde Gonçalves de Magalhães," *Minas Gerais, Suplemento Literário* 21.1035 (September 1986): 2. Sábato Magaldi, *Panorama do teatro brasileiro* (São Paulo, 1962). Lúcia Miguel Pèrerra, *A vida de Gonçalves Dias* (Rio, 1943). Décio de Almeida Prado, "Leonor de Mendonça [literary supplement of the journal]," Suplemento Literário do Jornal, *O Estado de São Paulo*, November 7–14, 1964.

FIGUEIREDO, Guilherme (1915–). Born in Campinas, he became a lawyer, diplomat, teacher, and translator. He was also a poet, novelist, essayist, musical and theatrical critic, and playwright. He received the Martins Pena Award for Drama with *O asilado* (The Asylum Seeker) (1962), which tells the story of a political activist. Most of his theater is inspired in the Greco-Latin tradition. An example is *A raposa e as uvas* (The Fox and the Grapes) (s.1950). It is an allegory about freedom, and Aesop is the main character. His debut in 1942 was with *Lady Godiva*, which is also an allegory about sex. Still referring to the classics, he wrote *Greve geral* (General Strike) in 1949, based on Aristophanes, and *Um deus dormiu lá em casa* (A God Slept at Home) (s.1949), based on the story of Amphitryon.

WORKS: *Napoleão* (Napoleon) (1941). *Lady Godiva* (1942). *Pantomina trágica* (Tragic Pantomime) (1948). *Greve geral* (General Strike) (1949). *Um deus dormiu lá em casa* (A God Slept at Home) (s.1949) (Rio, 1964). *A raposa e as uvas* (The Fox and the Grapes) (s.1950) (Rio, 1964). *Don Juan* (1951). *Os fantasmas* (The Ghosts) (São Paulo, 1956). *A menina sem nome* (The Girl with No Name) (Rio, 1958). *Tragédia para rir* (Tragedy to Laugh

At) (Rio, 1958). *O asilado* (The Asylum Seeker) (Rio, 1962). *Balada para satã* (Ballad for Satan) (São Paulo, 1962). *A muito curiosa história da virtuosa matrona de Éfeso* (The Very Curious Story of the Matron of Ephesus) (Rio, 1964). *Maria da ponte* (Maria of the Bridge) (Rio, 1970). *Seis peças em um ato* (Six Plays in One Act) (n.d.) (includes: *O princípio de Arquimedes* [Archimedes' Principle], *Meu tio Alfredo* [My Uncle Alfredo], *Fim de semana* [Weekend], *Uma visita* [A Visit], *Cara e coroa* [Heads or Tails], *Juízo final* [The Final Judgement]).

BIBLIOGRAPHY: Luro Bro, "Visita a Guilherme Figueiredo," *Mundo Nuevo*, no. 4 (Autumn 1966): 71–73. Luís Correia de Melo, *Dicionário de autores paulistas* (São Paulo, 1954), p. 223. Décio de Almeida Prado, *Apresentação do teatro brasileiro moderno* (São Paulo, 1956), p. 75.

FRANÇA JÚNIOR, Joaquim José de (1838–1890). Born in Rio de Janeiro, he was a lawyer and journalist. As a journalist he wrote his famous *crônicas*, a good documentation of his time. He was influenced by Martins Pena and exerted influence over Artur Azevedo. França Júnior was a famous playwright with a special talent to depict and satirize the most representative characters of his time: immigrants, students, the *fazendeiro paulista*, the Portuguese, the politicians, women professionals, the *mulata*. His most important work is *As doutoras* (The Women Doctors) (1889) in which he satirizes the incipient feminism of that time. The rich *paulista* appears in the comedy *Typos de atualidade* (Current Characters) (1862); the foreigner is portrayed in the comedy *O tipo brasileiro* (The Brazilian Characters) (1877); and examples of political satire are *Caiu o ministério!* (The Government Has Fallen!) (1882) and *Como se fazia um deputado* (How a Deputy Used to Be Made) (1882).

WORKS: *Meia hora de cynismo* (A Half-hour of Cynicism) (São Paulo, 1861). *A República modelo* (The Model Republic) (São Paulo, 1861). *Tipos de actualidade* (Current Characters) (São Paulo, 1862). *Ingleses na costa* (English on the Coast) (Rio, 1864). *Amor com amor se paga* (One Pays for Love with Love) (Rio, 1871). *O defeito de família* (The Family Fault) (Rio, 1871). *Direito por linhas tortas* (Straight Through Crooked Ways) (Rio, 1871). *Entrei para o Club Jacome* (I Entered the Jacome Club) (Rio, 1877). *O tipo brasileiro* (The Brazilian Character)

(Rio, 1877). *Caiu o ministério!* (The Government Has Fallen!) (Rio, 1882). *Três candidatos* (Three Candidates) (Rio, 1882). *Um carnaval no Rio de Janeiro* (Carnaval in Rio de Janeiro) (Rio, 1882). *Como se fazia um deputado* (How a Deputy Used to Be Made) (Rio, 1882). *Dous proveitos em um sacco* (Eat Your Cake and Keep It) (Rio, 1883). *De Petrópolis a Paris* (From Petrópolis to Paris) (Rio, 1884). *A lotação dos bonds* (Overflow of the Trolleys) (Rio, 1885). *As doutoras* (The Women Doctors) (Rio, 1889). *Portugueses às direitas* (Portuguese the Right Way) (Rio, 1890). See also *Teatro de França Júnior*, 2 vols. (Rio, 1980).

BIBLIOGRAPHY: Aluísio Azevedo, "França Júnior," *O Globo* (Rio), April 5, 1882. Artur de Azevedo, "França Júnior," *Autores e Livros* (Rio) 1 (September 21, 1941): 83. Manuel Bandeira, "O sonho de França Júnior," *Boletim do Rio* (Autumn 1934). Sousa Bastos, *Carteira do artista* (Lisbon, 1898), pp. 151–152. Sacramento Blake, *Diccionário bibliográphico brasileiro* (Rio, 1883). Luís Gastão d'Escragnolle Dória, "Cousas do passado," *Revista do Instituto Histórico e Geográfico Brasileiro* (Rio) 2, (1908). Gryphus (J. Visconti Coaracy), *Galeria teatral* (Rio, 1884), pp. 233–234. Rubem Gill, "O centenário de 'As doutoras,'" *Anuário da Casa dos Artistas* (Rio, 1939). Armando Gonzaga, "Nomes imortais do teatro brasileiro," *Boletim da SBAT* (Rio), no. 223 (March 1947). Artur Mota, "Perfis acadêmicos," *Revista da Academia Brasileira de Letras* (Rio) 28 (1928). Lafayette Silva, *História do teatro brasileiro* (Rio, 1938), pp. 161–162. X.Y.Z. (Artur Azevedo), "Teatros," *O álbum* (Rio), no. 6 (February 1893).

GOMES, Alfredo Dias

GOMES, Alfredo Dias (1922–   ). He began law school but then went to work for radio and television. In 1960 he staged *O pagador de promessas* (Payment as Pledged), which contains a strong antireligious component, mixing popular mysticism with the intolerance of the Church. Two years later, he wrote *A revolução dos beatos* (The Revolution of the Religious), which carries the same theme. In both of these works, set in northeastern Brazil, he portrays the search for justice while he also strongly criticizes religion. In plays such as *A invasão* (The Invasion) (1962), he covers the topic of urban marginalization. *Odorico, o bem amado* (Odorico, the Beloved) is a political critique whose protagonist is a politician of a small city; in *Dr.*

Getúlio, sua vida e sua glória (Dr. Getúlio, His Life and His Glory) (1968), the focus is on a samba school; and in *O túnel* (The Tunnel) (1972), with humor he strongly criticizes the Brazilian authorities. Another work that criticizes the government is *As primícias* (First Fruits), staged in 1978.

WORKS: *A invasão* (The Invasion) (Rio, 1962). *A revolução dos beatos* (The Revolution of the Religious) (Rio, 1962). *O berço do herói* (The Cradle of the Hero) (Rio, 1965). *O santo inquérito* (The Holy Inquisition) (Rio, 1966). *O pagador de promessas* (Payment as Pledged) (Rio, 1967). *Dr. Getúlio, sua vida e sua glória* (Dr. Getúlio, His Life and His Glory) (Rio, 1968). *As primícias* (First Fruits) (Rio, 1977). *O rei de Ramos* (The King of Ramos), *Campeões do mundo* (World Champions) (Rio, 1980). See also *Teatro de Dias Gomes* (Dias Gomes' Theatre), 2 vols. (Rio, 1972) (includes: *O pagador de promessas; A invasão; A revolução dos beatos; Odorico, o bem amado; O berço do herói; O santo inquérito; Dr. Getúlio, sua vida e sua glória; O túnel; Vamos soltar os demônios* [Let's Untie the Demons]).

BIBLIOGRAPHY: Anônimo, "Dias Gomes assiste em Lisboa ao êxito de O Santo inquérito," *Revista de Teatro* (Rio), no. 419 (September–October 1977). Anônimo, "O pagador de promessas," *Anhembi* 40.118 (September 1960): 192–193. Fernando Millán Chivite, "Breve introducción al teatro brasileño en España y Mundo mental y Sociológico de O Pagador de promessas," *Revista de Cultura Brasileña* (Madrid), no. 22 (September 1967): 281–300. Francis A. Dutra, "The Theatre of Dias Gomes: Brazil's Social Conscience," *Cithara* 4.2 (May 1965): 3–13. Alfredo Dias Gomes, "O berço do herói e as armas do Carlos," *Revista Civilização Brasileira*, no. 4 (September 1965): 257–268. Ida Fátima Garritano, "Uma anatomia teatral da malandragem," *Minas Gerais, Suplemento Literário* 18.862 (April 9, 1983): 6–8. Randal Johnson, "Deus e o Diabo na Terra da Globo: (God and the Devil in the Land of Globo): Roque Santeiro and Brazil's 'New Republic,'" *Studies in Latin American Popular Culture* 7 (1988): 77–88. Richard A. Mazzara, "Psychological and Social Change in Some Recent Works by Brazilian Authors," *Journal of Evolutionary Psychology* 7.1–2 (1986): 84–90. Armando Moreno, "Como vi El pagador de promessas," *Primer Acto*, no. 75 (1966): 21. Carlos de la Rica, "Anotaciones en torno a O Pagador de promessas," *Revista de Cultura Brasileña*, no. 19 (December 1966): 390–395. George

Woodyard, "A Metaphor for Repression: Two Portuguese Inquisition Plays," *LBR* 10. 1 (1973): 68–75. Woodyard, *The Modern Stage in Latin America; Six Plays* (New York, 1971).

GUARNIERI, Gianfrancesco (1936–   ). Of Italian origin, he is an actor and belonged to the Teatro Arena, having made his debut with *Eles não usam black-tie* (They Don't Wear Tuxedos). From a Marxist point of view, he criticizes the industrialization that took place in Brazil, which created enormous poverty. The play is set in a shantytown (*favela*) in Rio; love relationships are mixed within the social classes in this politically defined work. *Gimba* (1973) is also set in the *favelas* and focuses on the relationships between social classes. In *A semente* (The Seed), the protagonist is a fanatic Marxist union leader who wants to carry out the revolution at any cost. He also criticizes the dictatorship in *O grito parado no ar* (The Scream Holding in Mid-air) in 1973.

WORKS: *Eles não usam black-tie* (They Don't Wear Tuxedos) (Rio de Janeiro, 1959). *Animália* (São Paulo, 1968). *Marta Saré* (Rio, 1968). *Arena conta Zumbi* (Rio, 1970). *Gimba, o presidente dos valentes* (Gimba, the President of the Brave) (Rio de Janeiro, 1973). *O grito parado no ar* (The Scream Holding in Mid-air) (São Paulo, 1973). *Janelas abertas* (Open Windows) (São Paulo, 1978). *Ponto de partida* (Point of Departure) (São Paulo, 1979). *A semente* (The Seed) (São Paulo, n.d.). See also *Teatro de Gianfrancesco Guarnieri* (Rio de Janeiro, 1978) (includes: *A semente, Eles não usam black-tie* [They Don't Wear Tuxedos], *Gimba, O filho do cão* [The Dog's Puppy], *O cimento* [The Cement]).

BIBLIOGRAPHY: Edgard de Oliveira Bárros, "Teatro paulista descobre a periferia," *Revista de Teatro* 453 (January–March 1985): 5–9. Elizabeth Anne Fonseca-Downey, "The Theater of Gianfrancesco Guarnieri as an Expression of Brazilian National Reality," *Dissertation Abstracts International* 43.4 (October 1982), pp. 1159A–1160A. G. Guarnieri, "O teatro como expressão da realidade nacional," *Revista Brasiliense*, no. 25 (September–October 1959): 121–126. "Guarnieri e o Teatro," *Minas Gerais-Suplemento Literário* 18.889 (October 15, 1983): 1. Paulo F. Pinto, "Eles não usam black-tie," *Revista Brasiliense*, no. 16 (March–April 1958): 179–182. Selma Calasans Rodrigues, "Arena conta Tiradentes: Uma experiência de Teatro Político,"

Revista Iberoamericana 50.126 (January–March 1984): 221–228.

MACEDO, Joaquim Manuel de (1820–1882). Born in Itaboraí, Rio de Janeiro, he was a doctor, professor, and government deputy. Novelist, poet, historian, and playwright, he wrote a total of twenty novels, twelve dramas, and ten other books, in which we find *crônicas*, biographies, and didactic and travel works. Macedo was a romantic author with a special talent to define the character of his protagonists. In 1849, together with Manuel de Araújo Porto Alegre and Gonçalves Dias, he founded the magazine *Guanabara*. He creatively reflected the life of the Brazilian bourgeoisie of the second half of the nineteenth century. In the play *O cego* (The Blind Man) (1849), he criticizes the situation of oppression that women were living at that time in Brazil. His best work, *O primo da Califórnia* (The Cousin from California), is considered the first work of Realist theater in Brazil, in which he criticizes society for not being able to value people adequately, allowing false appearances. He also wrote an Indianist play (*Cobé*) (1852) and romantic plays, such as *Amor e pátria* (Love and Fatherland) (1863).

WORKS: *O cego* (The Blind Man) (Niterói, 1849). *Cobé* (Cobé) (Rio, 1852). *O fantasma branco* (The White Ghost) (Rio, 1856). *O primo da Califórnia* (The Cousin from California) (Rio, 1858). *O sacrifício de Isaac* (Isaac's Sacrifice) (Rio, 1859). *Luxo e vaidade* (Luxury and Vanity) (Rio, 1860). *Amor e pátria* (Love and Fatherland) (Rio, 1863). *Lusbela* (Lusbela) (Rio, 1863). *O novo Otelo* (The New Othello) (Rio, 1863). *A torre em concurso* (The Tower Under Inquiry) (Rio, 1863). *Remissão de pecados* (Forgiveness of Sins) (Rio, 1870). *Cincinnato quebra-louças* (The Cincinnato China Breaker) (Rio, 1873). *Vingança por vingança* (Revenge for Revenge) (Rio, 1877). *Antonica da Silva* (Rio, 1880). *Romance de uma velha* (An Old Lady's Romance) (Rio, n.d.). See also *Teatro completo* (Complete Plays), 2 vols. (Rio, 1979).

BIBLIOGRAPHY: Antônio Soares Amora, *História da literatura brasileira* (São Paulo, 1955), pp. 64–65. Machado de Assis, "Semana literária," *Diário do Rio de Janeiro*, May 1–8, 1866. Sousa Bastos, *Carteira do artista* (Lisbon, 1898), p. 237. Sacramento Blake, *Diccionário bibliográphico brasileiro*, vol. 4 (Rio, 1898), pp. 183–190. Ronald de Carvalho, *Pequena história da literatura brasileira*, 3rd ed. (Rio, 1925), pp. 279–290. R. Magalhães Jumor, "O Mistério do Macaco," *Revista do Teatro* (Rio), no. 292 (May–June 1956). Evaristo de Morals, "A esravidão nas belas letras," *Revista Americana* (Rio) (October 1917), pp. 47–64. Artur Morta, "Perfis acadêmicos," *Revista Brasileira de Letras* (Rio), no. 113 (193). Edmundo Muniz, "O teatro de Macedo," *Boletim da Sociedade Brasileira de Autores Teatrais* (Rio), no. 261 (May–June 1951). Astrojildo Pereira, "Romancistas da cidade," *Interpretações* (Rio, 1944). Joaquim Caetano Fernandes Pinheiro, *Curso elementar de literatura nacional*, 2nd ed. (Rio, 1883), p. 592. Sílvio Romero, *História da literatura brasileira*, 3rd ed. (Rio, 1943), pp. 11–73. Lery Santos, *Pantheon fluminense* (Rio, 1880), p. 497. Tanio Rebelo Costa Serra, *Joaquin Manuel de Macedo, ou os dois Macedos: a luneta magica do II Reinado*. (Rio Edições do Departamento Nacional do Libro, Fundação. Biblioteca Nacional, 1994). Lafayette Silva, *História do teatro brasileiro* (Rio, 1938), pp. 10–143. José Verissimo, *História da literatura brasileira* (1916), pp. 237–242, 285–286, 381–383. Ferdinand Wolf, *O Brasil literário* (São Paulo, 1955), pp. 262–289, 334–336, 340–341, 346–348.

MAGALHÃES, Domingos José Carlos Gonçalves de (1811–1882). Born in Rio de Janeiro, he became a doctor in 1832. He was also a diplomat. He wrote the first Brazilian historical drama, titled *Antônio José ou O poeta e a Inquisicão* (Antônio José or The Poet and the Inquisition) (1839). Antônio José, a Brazilian Jew, is the protagonist. Many of Gonçalves de Magalhães's works were written and staged in Portugal. His second tragedy, *Olgiato* (1841), is set in Italy and focuses on the conspiracy against Galeazzo Maria Sforza, in Milan, during the fifteenth century. He also wrote *Oscar, o filho de Ossian* (Oscar, Son of Ossian) and translated Shakespeare's *Othello* (1842).

WORKS: *Antônio José ou O poeta e a Inquisição* (Antônio José or The Poet and the Inquisition) (Rio, 1839). *Olgiato* (Olgiato) (Rio, 1841). *Othello* (Othello) (Rio, 1842). See also *Obras de Domingos José de Magalhães*, 8 vols. (Rio, 1864–1865).

BIBLIOGRAPHY: Machado de Assis, "Semana literária," *Diário do Rio de Janeiro* (Rio), February 27, 1866. Sacramento Blake, *Diccionário bibliográphico brasileiro*, vol. 2 (Rio, 1893), pp. 217–221, 478. Otto Maria Carpeaux, *Pequena bibliografia crítica da literatura brasileira*, 2nd ed. (Rio, 1955), pp. 75–77. José de Alcântara Machado, *Gonçalves de Magalhães ou o romântico arrependido* (São Paulo, 1936). Alcântara Machado, "Gonçalves de Magalhães," *Revista da Academia Brasileira de Letras* (Rio), 42–44. Sábato Magaldi, *Panorama do teatro brasileiro*, (São Paulo, 1962), pp. 33–39. Artur Mota, "Perfis acadêmicos," *Revista da Academia Brasileira de Letras* (Rio) 27 (1928), pp. 37–79. Luciana Stegagno Picchio, *La letteratura brasiliana* (Milão, 1972), pp. 146–149. Sílvio Romero, *História da literatura brasileira*, 2nd ed., vol. 2, (Rio, 1903), pp. 14–41. Inocêncio Francisco da Silva, "Domingos José Gonçalves de Magalhães," *Revista Contemporânea de Portugal e Brasil* (Lisbon) 5 (1865), pp. 285–301. J. F. Velho Sobrinho, *Diccionário bio-bibliográphico brasileiro*, vol. 1 (Rio, 1907), p. 501. J. Galante de Sousa, *O teatro no Brasil*, vol. 2 (Rio, 1960), pp. 323–325. Ferdinand Wolf, *O Brasil literário* (São Paulo, 1955), pp. 208–250, 328–331.

MARCOS, Plínio (1935–). Born in Santos, he became an actor. His work concentrates on the marginalized sector of society. He transposed the world of the *favelas* to the theater, a world dominated by ignorance, selfishness, and violence, while at the same time the language he used reflects each character—coarse and aggressive. His first work, *Barrela* (1963), was censored by the government. It is set in a prison and reflects the brutalizing effect it has on the prisoners due to the extremely violent environment in which they find themselves. Even more representative of his theater is *Navalha na carne* (Razor in the Flesh), written in 1966. The main characters are a prostitute, a homosexual, and a pimp who live in a terribly miserable and egotistical world. Another work that was censored is *Abajur lilás* (Lilac Lamp), set in a brothel; its three main characters are prostitutes. During the 1980s he covered existentialist themes in such works as *Jesus homem* (The Man Jesus).

WORKS: *Barrela* (s.1963) (São Paulo, 1976). *Dois perdidos numa noite suja* (Two Men Lost in a Dirty Night) (s.1965) (São Paulo, 1978). *Navalha na carne* (Razor in the Flesh) (s.1966) (São Paulo, 1978). *Verde que te quero verde* (Green, I Want You Green) (s. in São Paulo, 1968). *Homens de papel*

(Paper Men) (São Paulo, 1977). *Na barra do catimbó* (In the Mud of the Backwoods) (São Paulo, 1978). *Quando as máquinas param* (When the Machines Stop) (São Paulo, 1978). *Oração para um pé de chinelo* (Prayer for a Very Poor Person) (São Paulo, 1979).

BIBLIOGRAPHY: Benedito Antunes, "Plínio Marcos: Entre o fácil o difícil," *Minas Gerais, Suplemento Literário* 22.1103 (August 6, 1988), p. 2. Joel Pontés, "Plínio Marcos, dramaturgo da violência," *Latin American Theatre Review* 3.1 (Autumn 1969): 17–27. Elzbieta Szoka, "Permanent Distress: Towards a Semiotic Interpretation of Three Plays by Plínio Marcos," *Dissertation Abstracts International* 52. (Jan. 1992), p. 2570A. Szoka, "The Spirit of Revolution in Contemporary Brazilian Theatre: An Interview with Plínio Marcos," *The Drama Review* 34.1 (Spring 1990): 70–83.

MARTINS PENA, Luís Carlos (1815–1848). Born in Rio de Janeiro, he was an employee of the Court. He wrote twenty-two comedies and six dramas. His first comedy was *O juiz de paz na roça* (The Rural Justice of the Peace), presented in 1842. He exerted strong influence on the Brazilian theater of the nineteenth century, where he portrayed the concerns, customs, and events of that period. Another important comedy, which followed the patterns established in *O juiz de paz na roça*, is *O Judas em Sábado de Aleluia* (Judas on Holy Saturday) (1846). His dramas are set in foreign countries, like Spain (*O Nero da Espanha* [Spain's Nero]) and clearly follow the romantic models. He also wrote an Indianist drama, *Itaminda*, in 1858. Martins Pena exerted influence over José Joaquim França Júnior, Artur Azevedo, and many others. He also introduced the *comédia de costumes* in Brazil.

WORKS: *O juiz de paz na roça* (The Rural Justice of the Peace) (Rio, 1842). *A família e a festa da roça* (The Family and the Rural Party) (Rio, 1842). *O diletante* (The Amateur) (Rio, 1846). *O Judas em Sábado de Aleluia* (Judas on Holy Saturday) (Rio, 1846). *O caixeiro da taverna* (The Cashier at the Tavern) (Rio, 1847). *Os irmãos das almas* (Brothers of the Souls) (Rio, 1847). *Quem casa quer casa* (Whomever Marries Wants a House) (Rio, 1847). *O noviço* (The Apprentice) (Rio, 1853). *Os dous ou O inglês maquinista* (The Two or the English Machinist) (Rio, 1871). See also *Teatro* (Plays) (Rio, 1898); *Teatro de Martins Pena*, 2 vols. (Rio, 1956).

BIBLIOGRAPHY: Sacramento Blake, *Diccionário bibliográphico brasileiro*, vol. 5, pp. 377–380. Joracy Camargo, "O Molière brasileiro," *Dionysos* (Rio) 1 (Autumn 1949). Otto Maria Carpeaux, *Pequena bibliografia crítica da literatura brasileira*, 2nd ed. (Rio, 1955), pp. 81–82. Guilherme de Figueiredo, "Introdução a Martins Pena," *Dionysos* (Rio) (Autumn 1949), pp. 73–86. Ernâni Fornari, "Martins Pena, seu tempo e seu teatro," *Província de São Pedro* (Puerto Alegre) 11 (March–June 1948). Ernâni Fornari, "O namoro e o casamento através da obra de Martins Pens," *Dionysos* (Rio) 1 (Autumn 1949). Raimundo Magalhães Junior, "Martins Pena e seus seguidores," *Dionysos* (Rio) 1 (Autumn 1949). Leon F. Lyday, "Satire in the Comedies of Martins Pena," *LBR* (December 1968), pp. 67–70. Sábato Magaldi, *Panorama do teatro brasileiro* (São Paulo, 1962), pp. 40–58. Heitor Moniz, *Vultos da literatura brasileira* (1933), pp. 41–61. Haroldo Paranhos, *História do Romantismo no Brasil (1830–1850)* (São Paulo, n.d.), pp. 245–254. Luciana Stegagno Picchio, *La letteratura brasiliana* (Milão, 1972), pp. 216–220. Colin Pierson, "Martins Pena: A View of Character Types," *Latin American Theatre Review* (Spring 1978): 41–48. Décio de Almeida Prado, *A literatura no Brasil*, vol. 6 (Rio, 1971), pp. 10–11. Jaime Rodriguez, "As idéias e as palavras. Notas sobre a identidade cultural de Luís Carlos Martins Pena," *Serviço Nacional de Teatro* (Rio, 1977), pp. 225–278. Sílvio Romero, *Vida e obra de Martins Pena* (Porto, 1901). Lafayette Silva, "O criador da comédia brasileira," *Ilustração brasileira* (Rio) (August 1926). Lafayette Silva, "Martins Pena, o comediógrafo dos nossos costumes," *Anais do 3rd Congresso de História Nacional*, vol. 7 (Rio, 1942), pp. 255–269. Cláudio de Sousa, "Martins Pena," *Revista da Academia Brasileira de Letras* (Rio) 76 (1948), pp. 157–179. Mário de Vasconcellos, "Ensaio sobre o teatro no Brasil," *Revista Americana* (Rio) (March 1910), pp. 432–455. Luís Francisco da Veiga, "Carlos Martins Pena o criador da comédia nacional," *Revista do Instituto Histórico e Geográfico Brasileiro* (Rio, 1877), pp. 375–407. José Verissimo, "Martins Pena e o teatro brasileiro," *Revista Brasileira* (Rio) 15 (1898), pp. 47–64.

MOREYRA, Álvaro (1888–1965). Born in Porto Alegre, he was a lawyer, a journalist, and an author of plays and children's books. In 1927 he founded the Teatro de Brinquedo with his wife Eugênia in Rio de Janeiro. In 1937 he directed the Companhia de Arte Dramática. His initial works were influenced by Symbolism and later by Modernism. He was active in the Week of Modern Art in 1922. His main contributions to the theater were to close the distance between the theater and the public and to stage unknown Brazilian writers. His most important work, *Adão, Eva e outros membros da família* (Adam, Eve and Other Members of the Family), made its debut in 1927 at the inauguration of the theatre Teatro de Brinquedo. It is a comedy, apparently superficial, but he attacks the capitalist system. The characters are a thief and a beggar, who end up victorious in society.

WORKS: For Children's Theatre, Moreyra wrote *Adão, Eva e outros membros da família* (Adam, Eve and Other Members of the Family) (Rio, 1927). *Espetáculo do arco da velha* (Rainbow Show) (Rio, 1927). *Jardim sem grades* (Garden with No Fence) (n.d.).

BIBLIOGRAPHY: Gustavo A. Dória, *Moderno teatro brasileiro* (Rio, 1975), pp. 17–37. Sábato Magaldi, *Panorama do teatro brasileiro*, 2nd ed. (Rio, 1976), pp. 185–186.

QORPO SANTO (1829–1883). Born in Villa do Triunfo, his original name was José Joaquim de Campos Leão. A merchant, teacher, and policeman, he is one of the most fascinating characters of Brazilian literature. He became mentally ill at the age of thirty-four, at which time he began to call himself "Qorpo Santo." He created his own orthography and was a poet and author of dramas. Qorpo Santo exerted influence over Mário de Andrade and Oswald de Andrade, and he was one of the predecessors of the theater of the Absurd. His plays were very successfully staged in the 1960s. The plays themselves are very short, and one observes the concerns he had in relation to sex, the Church, and women. Most of all, he emphasizes the topic of sex, as in *A separação dos dois esposos* (Separation of the Two Spouses) and in the satire *Um credor da Fazenda Nacional* (A Creditor from the National Treasury). In his works he fights against traditional conventions and the mixing of reality with fiction. He also strongly criticizes the values of the bourgeoisie.

WORKS: *Ensiglopédia ou Seis meses de uma enfermidade* (Encyclopedia or Six Months of an Ill-

ness) (Porto Alegre, 1877). *As relações naturais e outras comédias* (Natural Relations and Other Comedies) (Porto Alegre, 1969) (includes: *As relações naturais, Mateus e Mateusa* [Mathew and Female Mathew], *Hoje sou um e amanhã outro* [Today I Am One and Tomorrow, Another], *Eu sou vida e não sou morte* [I Am Life and Not Death], *Um credor da Fazenda Nacional* [A Creditor from the National Treasury], *Um assovio* [A Whistle], *Certa entidade em busca de outra* [One Certain Entity Seeking Another], *Um parto* [Childbirth]).

BIBLIOGRAPHY: Diário de Bittencourt, "Algumas idéias de Qorpo Santo," *Correio do Povo* (Porto Alegre) (August 28, 1966). Guilhermino Cesar, "Qorpo Santo, autor de vanguarda do século XIX," *Correio do Povo* (Porto Alegre) (August 19, 1966). Guilhermino Cesar, "Do mito à realidade," *Jornal do Brasil* (Rio) (May 4, 1969). Cesar, *História da literatura do Rio Grande do Sul*, Porto Alegre, 1971. Fernando Cristovão, "Qorpo-Santo," *Correio do Povo* (Porto Alegre) (April 24, 1971). Pedro Laretti, "Qorpo-Santo," *Pasquim* (Rio), no. 79 (December 6, 1971). Berenice Otero, "O teatro do absurdo como alternativa," *Zero Hora* (Porto Alegre) (January 17, 1970). Décio Pignatari, "Qorpo Santo," *Contracomunicação*, São Paulo, 1971. Olinto de Sanmartin, "O precursor," *Estado do Rio Grande* (Porto Alegre) (December 3, 1955). Olinto de Sanmartin, "O poeta Qorpo Santo," *Correio do Povo* (Porto Alegre) (November 1957). Múcio Teixeira, "Não foi Marinetti o fundador do Futurismo? A obra esquecida de Joaquim ou José Leão do Corpo Santo," *A Reação* (Bagé), no. 138 (January 18, 1930).

RODRIGUES, Nelson (1912–1980). Born in Recife, he was a playwright, journalist, and novelist. He sometimes used the pseudonym Suzana Flag. He portrayed the lower bourgeoisie in the theater. The themes of his works revolve mostly around marginalization—prostitution, abortion, and incest. An example is *Álbum de família* (Family Portrait) (s.1945), in which incest is portrayed. His first play, *Uma mulher sem pecado* (Woman without Sin), was staged in 1939. Four years later, in Rio, *Vestido de noiva* (Bridal Gown) made its debut. This work is considered the turning point of Brazilian theater into Modernism. It is an expressionist work with Freudian influences.

WORKS: *A mulher sem pecado* (Woman without Sin) (Rio de Janeiro, 1944) (1939). *Vestido de noiva*

(Bridal Gown) (Rio de Janeiro, 1944) (s.1943). *Album de família* (Family Album) (Rio de Janeiro, 1948) (s.1945). *Anjo alegre* (Merry Angel) (Rio de Janeiro, 1948) (s.1946). *Dorotéia* (Dorothy) (Rio de Janeiro, 1948). *A valsa no 6* (Valse No. 6) (Rio de Janeiro, 1951). *Senhora dos afogados* (Lady of the Drowned) (Rio de Janeiro, 1955). *A falecida* (The Dead Woman) (Rio de Janeiro, 1956) (s.1954). *Perdoa-me por me traíres* (Forgive Me for Your Betrayal) (Rio de Janeiro) (s.1957). *Viúva porém honesta* (Widow But Honest) (Rio de Janeiro) (s.1957). *Os sete gatinhos* (The Seven Kittens) (Rio de Janeiro) (s.1958). *Boca de ouro* (Mouth of Gold) (Rio de Janeiro) (s.1959). *O beijo no asfalto* (Kiss on the Asphalt) (Rio de Janeiro) (s.1960). *Bonitinha mas ordinária* (Cute But Mediocre) (Rio de Janeiro) (s.1961). *Toda nudez será castigada* (All Nudity Will Be Punished) (Rio de Janeiro) (s.1962). *O anti-Nelson Rodrigues* (The Anti-Nelson Rodrigues) (Rio de Janeiro, 1975). *A serpente* (The Serpent) (Rio de Janeiro, 1978).

BIBLIOGRAPHY: Anônimo, "Nelson Rodrigues: Um debate," *Cadernos Brasileiros* 8.35 (May–June 1966): 46–52. Anónimo, "Vestido de Noiva," *Anhembi* 31.92 (1958): 401–404. José Arrabal, "À margem de Nelson," *O Jornal*, December 28, 1970. Walmir Ayala, "Nelson Rodrigues: Depoimento," *Jornal do Comércio* (Rio), July 27, 1967. Roberto Lamar Bledsoe, "The Expressionism of Nelson Rodrigues" (Ph.D. diss., University of Wisconsin, 1971). Marcelo Câmara, "O moralista Nelson Rodrigues," *O Fluminense*, December 9, 1973. Paul B. Dixon, "Scenic Space and Psychic Space in Nelson Rodrigues' *Vestido de Noiva* and Rene Marques' *El apartamiento*," *Papers on Romance Lit. Relations* (1983), 15–23. Victor Giudice, "Nelson Rodrigues: Nudez e diálogo," *Tribuna da Imprensa*, June 8, 1973. Angela Maria Dias de Brito Gomes, "O teatro de Nelson Rodrigues," *Revista Brasileira de Língua e Literatura* 2.6 (1980): 57–59. Randal Johnson, "Nelson Rodrigues as Filmed by Arnaldo Jabor," *Latin American Theatre Review* 16.1 (Fall 1982): 15–28. Raimundo Magalhães Júnior, "A farsa erótica do Sr. Nelson Rodrigues," *Boletim da Sociedade Brasileira de Autores Teatrais* (Rio) no. 229 (April–August 1946). Paulo Lara, "Nelson Rodrigues, censura não é desculpa," *Folha da Tarde* (São Paulo), December 24, 1975. Alvaro Lins, "Nelson Rodrigues," *Jornal de Crítica*, 5th ser. (1947): 176. Ronaldo Lima Lins, *O teatro de Nelson Rodrigues* (Rio, 1979). Franklin de Oliveira, "No fim de dezembro deixou este mundo Nelson Rodrigues," *Revista de Teatro* (Rio), no. 436 (October–December 1980). A. Fonseca Pimentel, *O teatro de Nelson Rodrigues* (Rio, 1951). Léo Gilson Ribeiro, "O sol sobre o pântano: Nelson Rodrigues, um expressionista brasileiro," *Cadernos Brasileiro* 6.1 (January–February 1964): 50–65. Nelson Rodrigues, *Teatro quase completo*, 4 vols. (Rio de Janeiro, 1966). Maria Flora Sussekind, "Nelson Rodrigues e o teatro falso," *Serviço Nacional de Teatro. I Concurso Nacional de Monografias, 1976* (Brasília, 1977), pp. 5–42. Lucy Serrano Vereza, "A moral dos nossos dias," *O Globo*, (Rio), October 25, 1972.

SUASSUNA, Ariano (1927–   ). Born in Paraíba, he became a lawyer. He is a novelist, journalist, playwright, poet, and professor of aesthetics at the Universidade de Recife. In 1946 he founded the Pernambuco Student Theater. His works contain a strong religious component, approximating themselves to the progressive sector of the Catholic Church in Brazil. He was influenced by Plato, the Comedia dell'Arte Italiana, Calderón de la Barca, and Gil Vicente. His works revolve around the rural world of the Northeast, using the legends and popular traditions of this area, while he also mixes real and fictitious characters and events. His best and most representative work is *O auto da compadecida* (The Rogue's Trial) (1956), in which he mixes popular religion with Catholicism, which results in a syncretism that seeks justice as its goal.

WORKS: *E de Tororó* (It's of Tororó) (Rio, 1950). *Ode* (Ode) (Recife, 1955). *Auto da compadecida* (The Rogue's Trial) (Rio, 1957). *O casamento suspeito* (The Suspicious Marriage) (Recife, 1961). *O santo e a porca* (The Saint and the Pig) (Recife, 1964). *Uma mulher vestida de sol* (A Woman Dressed in the Sun) (Recife, 1967). *A pena e a lei* (The Punishment and the Law) (Rio, 1971). *Farsa da boa preguiça* (Farce of the Good Sloth) (Rio, 1973).

BIBLIOGRAPHY: Victor Auz, "Auto da Compadecida," *Revista de la Cultura Brasileña* 4 (1965): 350–355. Augusto Boudoux, "Entrevista com Ariano Suassuna," *Revista do Globo*, no. 815 (March 3–16, 1962): 30–33. Paulo Dantas, "Na compadecida alma do Nordeste," *Revista Brasiliense* 14 (1957): 80–97. Jose Augusto Guerra, "El mundo mágico y poético de Ariano Suassuna," *Revista de Cultura Brasileña* (Madri) 35 (1973): 56–71. Leon Lyday, "The *Barcas* and the *Compadecida: Autos* Past and Present," *LBR*

(Summer 1974): 84–88. Wilson Martins, "Poetic Humor and Universality of Suassuna's Compadecida," *Ball State University Forum* 10.3 (1969): 25–30. Aldo Obino, "A obra fabulosa de Suassuna," *Revista de Teatro* (Rio), no. 385 (1972): 26. L. H. Quackenbush, "The 'Auto' Tradition in Brazilian Drama," *Latin American Theatre Review* 5.2 (Spring 1972): 29–43. Dillwin F. Ratcliff, "Folklore and Satire in a Brazilian Comedy," *Hispania* 44.2 (1961): 282–284. Ratcliff, "Representative Play of Northeastern Brazil," *Kentucky Foreign Language Quarterly* 9.2 (1962): 86–92.

Lizabeth Souza Fuertes

Chicano

In the XIV canto of the epic poem *Historia de la Nueva México* (History of New Mexico), Gaspar Pérez de Villagrá points out that one of the captains of Juan de Oñate's expedition to New Mexico composed a play that recreated the reception given by the Indians to Christianity. Chicano scholars agree that this is the first known play dealing with southwestern reality; therefore, it should be considered a precedent to what later became known as Chicano theater.

As a matter of fact, theater presentations have always been part of Hispanic southwestern history. In colonial time, religious plays were very common. Some of them—*Los pastores* (The Shepherds), *Las cuatro apariciones de la Virgen de Guadalupe* (The Four Appearances of the Virgin of Guadalupe), and *Los reyes magos* (The Three Wise Men)—have been performed through the years. Also from the same time period is *Los Moros y los Cristianos* (Moors and Christians), a play known for being the second one whose performance has been documented. With variations, these plays are still being performed and they are part of southwestern Hispanic folklore. A good example of the presence of such plays is Luis Valdez's television production *La pastorela* (The Shepherds' Tale).

Toward the end of the eighteenth century and the beginning of the nineteenth century, a type of theater that recreated episodes of recent history began to appear. Such is the case of *Los Comanches* (The Comanches), a heroic drama written at the end of the eighteenth century that deals with the military campaigns conducted by the Spanish against the Comanche Indians. *Los Tejanos* (The Texans), a text written around 1845, is the first theatrical testimony of a topic that would later be the most important feature theme of Chicano literature, the cultural and political clash between Anglos and Hispanics.

Although there is evidence that throughout the nineteenth century there was a constant Hispanic theatrical activity in the Southwest, it is not until the middle of the century that we find evidence of such activity. Nicolás Kanellos and John Brokaw, among others, have studied the work of the professional theater companies that traveled the Southwest giving Spanish performances. These companies were usually from Mexico, although the actors and actresses were from different Hispanic origins, and the plays that formed their repertoires were both Spanish and Spanish American.

At the beginning of the twentieth century, the Mexican Revolution caused a series of migratory waves that intensified the Hispanic element in the Southwest and brought with them an intense Spanish theatrical activity. Cities such as San Antonio, El Paso, Tucson, and Los Angeles had a large number of theaters that regularly offered performances in Spanish. During this period, the *carpas* (tent shows) and *tandas de variedades* (vaudevilles) were also very common. These types of itinerant theaters toured the Southwest, reaching distant Hispanic communities. The *carpas* offered a variety of entertainment. Their repertoires included *corridistas*, mimes, acrobats, and comic sketches of all kinds. The *tandas de variedad* featured opera performances, *zarzuelas*, operettas, and *números de revista* (musical numbers).

The first decades of the twentieth century were a period of great theatrical activity in Spanish in the American Southwest. Nicolás Kanellos pointed out that in the 1920s the city of Los Angeles became a blooming center of theatrical production. Also from this period is the Mexican expansion to the North and the Midwest of the United States, especially to cities such as Chicago, Detroit, and Seattle, which became required stops in any touring Spanish-language company.

Unfortunately, a few years later, the Great Depression and the massive deportation of Hispanics gave a serious blow to this Spanish theatrical activity. It was a moment when young playwrights were starting to produce original plays, and had Spanish production continued, it would have certainly given an important contribution to the Latin American stage. It was not until two decades later, in the mid-1960s, that Mexican American theater played an important role in the cultural life of the Hispanics in the United States. In 1965, Luis Valdez, who had just received his theater degree from San José State University, founded the Teatro Campesino (Farmworkers Theater) to help César Chávez's campaign to improve the working conditions on the farms in the San Joaquín Valley. The Teatro Campesino brought together all the features of the collective and independent theatrical groups of the 1970s. It was a revolutionary theater both in its content and in its presentation. It was lively, spontaneous, heterogeneous, satirical, and politically compromised. The language was that of the audience, a mixture of Spanish, English, and Chicano slang.

The example of the Teatro Campesino spread rapidly. In a very short time, other theater groups were formed by laborers, workers, and students. Like Valdez, these groups saw in the theater a suitable means by which to fulfill an urgent social function. In 1971, TENAZ (National Theatre of Aztlan), a coalition of Chicano groups, was formed. TENAZ's initial goals were the organization of annual meetings, the coordination of festivals and theater workshops, and the publication of a Chicano theater journal.

Among the Chicano theater groups of the time the most important were: El Teatro de la Esperanza (The Theatre of Hope), formed in 1971 by Jorge Huerta; El Teatro Urbano (The Urban Theatre of East Los Angeles), under the direction of René Rodríguez; El Teatro de la Libertad (Liberty Theatre), of Tucson; La Compañía de Teatro de Albuquerque (Theatre of Albuquerque), created by José Rodríguez; and El Teatro Desengaño del Pueblo (Theatre Telling It Like It Is), founded by Nicolás Kanellos in Gary, Indiana. For some, the 1980s were years of crisis for the Chicano stage; for others they were simply years of reorientation and change. It is true that the theater groups did not have the same kind of social involvement that those of the 1960s and 1970s did. It is also true that the use of bilingualism decreased. Nevertheless, the 1980s were important years for the diffusion of Chicano drama through mass media channels.

The 1980s was also a remarkable period for the important role played by Chicanas. Authors such as Cherríe Moraga successfully staged plays of feminist content; others like the poet Lucha Corpi and Barbara Brinson-Pineda explored theatrical forms like the *teatropoesía*, a combination of poetry and drama. A good example of the variety of objectives and interests of the Chicano theater of the 1980s can be seen in the XIV meeting of TENAZ, which took place in San Antonio in 1988. During this festival, collective plays and single author plays and performances that ranged from musicals to monologues were put on stage. The plays presented dealt as much with Chicano problems as with general Latin American issues. The creation of a committee whose main purpose was the international promotion of Latino theater is significant to the new conception of Chicano production.

Following this line of action, the Chicano theater of the 1990s carried out a clear process of diversification. While some independent groups insisted on their original social objectives, there was a constant production of feminist plays, and as part of a phenomenon that starts to be known as Latino theatre, Chicano plays of all kinds are part of the regular repertoire of many American cities.

BIBLIOGRAPHY

Arrizón, Alicia. *Latina Performance: Traversing the Stage*. Bloomington: Indiana University Press, 1999.

Boland, Mary Denning. "An Analysis of the Theater of Luis Valdez." Ph.D. dissertation, Saint Louis University, 1983 (University Microfilms International, 1987).

Brokaw, John W. "A Mexican-American Acting Company, 1849–1939." *Educational Theatre Journal* 27.1 (March 1975): 23–29.

Broyles-González, Yolanda. *El Teatro Campesino: Theater in the Chicano Movement*. Austin: University of Texas Press, 1994.

Flores, Arturo C. *El Teatro Campesino de Luis Valdez (1965–1980)*. Madrid: Pliegos, 1990.

González-T, César A. *A Sense of Place: Rudolfo A. Anaya: An Annotated Bio-bibliography*. Berkeley: Ethnic Studies Library Publications Unit, University of California, Berkeley, 2000.

Huerta, Jorge A. *Chicano Theater: Themes and Forms*. Ypsilanti, MI: Bilingual Press/ Editorial Bilingüe, 1982.

Kanellos, Nicolás. "The Flourishing of Hispanic Theatre in the Southwest." *Latin American Theatre Review* 16.1 (Fall 1983): 29–40.

———. *Hispanic Theatre in the United States*. Houston: Arte Público Press, 1984.

———. *Mexican American Theatre: Then and Now*. Houston: Arte Público Press, 1983.

———. "Nineteenth-Century Origins of the Hispanic Theatre in the Southwest." *Crítica* 1.1 (1984).

———. "El teatro professional hispánico: orígenes en el suroeste." *La Palabra* 2.1 (1980): 16–24.

Kourilisky, Françoise. "Approaching Quetzalcoatl: The Evolution of *El Teatro Campesino*." *Performance* 2.1 (Fall 1973): 37–46.

Ramírez, Elizabeth C. *Footlights Across the Border*. New York: Peter Lang, 1990.

———. "A History of Mexican American Professional Theatre in Texas, 1875–1935." Ph.D. dissertation, University of Texas, Austin, 1982.

Shirley, Carl R., and Paula W. Shirley. *Understanding Chicano Literature*. Columbia: University of South Carolina Press, 1988.

Tatum, Charles M. *Chicano Literature*. Boston: Twayne, 1982.

Valdez, Luis. *Early Works: Actos, Bernabé and Pensamiento Serpentino*, Houston, TX: Arte Público Press, 1990.

Vega, Manuel de Jesús. "El Teatro Campesino chicano y la vanguardia teatral, 1965–

1975. Ph.D. dissertation, Middlebury College, 1983 (University Microfilms International, 1984).

◆

ANAYA, Rudolfo A. (1937–). Born in Pastura, New Mexico, Anaya is one of the most important Mexican American writers. His bestseller novel *Bless Me, Ultima* (1972) was awarded the Premio Quinto Sol, and it has been translated into different languages. Although Anaya is mainly known for his narrative, he has also produced a play, *The Season of la Llorona* (1987), which deals with the Mexican and Mexican American legend of *la Llorona*, a recurrent theme in his work.

WORK: *The Season of la Llorona* (s.1987) (p. Albuquerque, El Teatro de la Compañía de Albuquerque).

BIBLIOGRAPHY: Cordelia Candelaria, "Rudolfo A. Anaya," in *Chicano Writers*, ed. Francisco A. Lomelí and Carl R. Shirley (Detroit: Gale Research, 1989), 24–35. César A. González-T. and Phyllis S. Morgan, *A Sense of Place: Rudolfo A. Anaya, an Annotated Bibliography*. Berkeley: Ethnic Studies Library Publications Unit, University of California, 2000. "Rudolfo A. Anaya," in Juan Bruce Novoa's *Chicano Authors: Inquiry by Interview* (London and Austin: University of Texas Press, 1980), 183–202.

AVENDAÑO, Fausto (1941–). Born in Culiacán, Mexico, Avendaño came to the United States at the age of four. He is the author of many short stories and a three-act historical play, *El corrido de California* (California's Ballad), which studies the social and ideological changes in Mexican life during the American invasion of California in 1846.

WORK: *El corrido de California* (California's Ballad) (Berkeley: Editorial Justa, 1979).

BIBLIOGRAPHY: Grace M. Bearse, review of *El corrido de California, Revista Chicano-Riqueña* 9.4 (Fall 1981): 74. Armando Miguélez, "Aproximaciones al nuevo teatro de autor único," in *Literatura hispana en los Estados Unidos*, ed. F. Avendaño (Sacramento: ETL-Hispanic, 1987), 8–18. Jorge Santana, "Fausto Avendaño," in *Chicano Writers*, ed. Francisco A. Lomelí and Carl R. Shirley (Detroit: Gale Research, 1989), 45–47. María Herrera Sobek, review of *El corrido de California, La Palabra* 2.1

(Spring 1980): 89–90. Oscar U. Somoza, review of *El corrido de California, Explicación de textos literarios* 9 (Spring 1981): 204.

BACA, Jimmy Santiago (1952–). Born in Santa Fe, New Mexico, Baca is a celebrated award-winning poet who, in 1991, staged his first play, *Los tres hijos de Julia* (Julia's Three Sons). Baca's works are strongly influenced by his troubled youth and his later commitment to the New Mexican Chicano community.

WORK: *Los tres hijos de Julia* (Julia's Three Sons) (s.1991) (p. Los Angeles Theatre Center).

BIBLIOGRAPHY: A. Gabriel Meléndez, "Carrying the Magic of His People's Heart: An Interview with Jimmy Santiago Baca," *Americas Review: A Review of Hispanic Literature and Art of the USA* (1991). Meléndez, "Jimmy Santiago Baca," in *Chicano Writers*, 2nd ed., ed. Francisco A. Lomelí and Carl R. Shirley (Detroit, MI: Gale Research, 1992), 21–29.

BARRIOS, Gregg (1945–). Born in Victoria, Texas, Gregg Barrios's poems are better known than his only play, *Dale Gas Cristal* (Step on It Crystal) (1977), which was produced when Barrios was working as a teacher in Crystal City. The play reflects the influence of Barrios's political involvement in the Chicano movement.

WORK: *Dale Gas Cristal* (Step on It Cristal) (s.1977) (p. Albuquerque, Floricanto IV Festival).

BIBLIOGRAPHY: Nuria Bustamantes, "Gregg Barrios," in *Chicano Writers*, 2nd ed., ed. Francisco A. Lomelí and Carl R. Shirley (Detroit, MI: Gale Research, 1992), 30–34.

CHÁVEZ, Denise (1948–). Born in Las Cruces, New Mexico, Chávez is a professor of drama who became known as a playwright in the 1970s. Chávez has written more than twenty plays, which include religious, social, and children's topics. Her most successful play, *Plaza*, was staged during the same year (1984) in Albuquerque, New York, and Edinburgh, Scotland. The play explores identity problems as well as the loss of Hispanic values in modern Hispanic communities in the United States. Chávez's interest in psychological and social problems is also the subject of *Hecho en México* (Made in Mexico) (s.1983), a play dealing with the problems of immigrant workers, and *Nacimiento* (Birth) (s.1980), in which four women remember moments of their youth in a process of self-identification. A very lyrical play, *Nacimiento* was later developed by Chávez into a short story book, *The Last of the Menu Girls* (1986).

WORKS: *Novitiates* (s.1973) (p. Dallas Theatre Center). *The Flying Tortilla Man* (s.1975) (p. Española, NM, Northern New Mexico Community College). *The Mask of November* (s.1975) (p. Española, NM, Northern New Mexico Community College). *Elevator* (s.1977) (p. Santa Fe, Theatre Arts Corporation). *The Adobe Rabbit* (s.1980) (p. Taos, Taos Community Auditorium). *Nacimiento* (Birth) (s.1980) (p. Albuquerque, Nuestro Teatro). *Santa Fe Charm* (s.1980) (p. Santa Fe Actors' Lab). *El santero de Córdova* (Córdova's Santero) (s.1981) (p. Albuquerque, Feria Artesana, 1981). *An Evening of Theatre* (s.1981) (p. Santa Fe, New Mexico School for the Visually Handicapped). *How Junior Got Thrown in the Joint* (s.1981) (p. Santa Fe, State Penitentiary of New Mexico). *Sí, hay posada* (Yes, There Is Room) (s.1981) (p. Albuquerque, Nuestro Teatro). *The Green Madonna* (s.1982) (p. Santa Fe Council for the Arts). *Francis!* (s.1983) (p. Las Cruces, NM, Immaculate Heart of Mary Cathedral). *Hecho en México* (Made in Mexico), in collaboration with Nita Luna (s.1983) (b. Albuquerque, Kimo Theatre). *La morenita* (The Little Brunette) (s.1983) (p. Las Cruces, NM, Immaculate Heart of Mary Cathedral, 1983). *Plaza* (s.1984) (p. Albuquerque, Kimo Theatre; New York, Festival Latino de Nueva York; Edinburgh, Scotland, Scotland Arts Festival, September 1984). *Plague-Time* (s.1985) (p. Albuquerque, Kimo Theatre). *Novena Narrative* (s.1987) (p. New Mexico Tour of 6 Cities). *The Step* (s.1987) (p. Houston, Museum of Fine Arts). *Language of Vision* (s.1988) (p. Albuquerque, Fiesta Artística). *Women in the State of Grace* (s.1989) (p. Grinnell, IA, Grinnell College).

BIBLIOGRAPHY: Annie O. Eysturoy, "Denise Chávez," in *This Is About Vision: Interviews with Southwestern Writers*, ed. William Balassi, John F. Crawford, and Annie O. Eysturoy (Albuquerque: University of New Mexico Press, 1990), 156–169.

Martha E. Heard, "The Theatre of Denise Chávez: Interior Landscapes with *sabor nuevomexicano*," *Americas Review* 16.2 (Summer 1988): 83–91. Rowena A. Rivera, "Denise Chávez," in *Chicano Writers*, 2nd ed., ed. Francisco A. Lomelí and Carl R. Shirley (Detroit: Gale Research, 1992), 70–76.

DE LEÓN, Nephtalí (1945–). Born in Laredo, Texas, de León is a prolific and multifaceted Chicano writer. His work consists of plays, essays, poems, and children's stories usually illustrated by himself. In 1972, de León published his book *5 Plays*, which includes a series of bilingual dramas: *The Death of Ernesto Nerios*; *Chicanos, the Living and the Dead*; *Play Number 9*; *The Judging of Man*; and *The Flies*.

The Death of Ernesto Nerios was staged in 1978 as *La muerte de Ernesto Nerios*, and it tells the tragic death of a young Chicano murdered by the police in 1971. In the style of the Chicano ideology of the 1970s, *Chicanos, the Living and the Dead* is an original combination of social criticism and phantasy. Realistic scenes depict Chicano complaints and demands to the U.S. government, and Ernesto "Che" Guevara and a dead Chicano journalist discuss politics while in Limbo. *Play Number 9* parallels the myth of Prometheus with the Chicano attempt to change the American educational system. In *The Judging of Man*, de León's most abstract and least political play, the characters are personifications of human virtues and defects at the moment of the final judgment of mankind. *The Flies* is a fable in which the story of three young flies, victims of forces beyond their own control, works as an analogy with the Chicano people reality.

In 1979, de León published another play, *Tequila Mockingbird, Or the Ghost of Unemployment*, which is a satire on illegal Mexican immigration. The border patrol mistakes the owner of a fruit company, his assistant, and Uncle Sam for illegal workers and sends them to Mexico. In Mexico they experience the hard reality of the Mexican poor people, they suffer a complete transformation, and eventually they become Brown Berets.

El segundo de Febrero (The Second of February), a historical play written by de León,

Carlos González, and Alfredo Alemán, was published in 1983. The play, which shows de León's concern for young Chicano education, is an account of the history of Mexico and the creation of the American Southwest. Also a result of de León's interest in education is the 1979 stage production of his children's story *I Will Catch the Sun.*

WORKS: *5 Plays* (Denver: Totinem, 1972). *The Flies* (s.1973) (p. El Paso, University of Texas at El Paso). *Chicanos! The Living and the Dead* (s.1974) (p. Hagerman, NM). *El tesoro de Pancho Villa* (Pancho Villa's Treasury) (s.1977) (p. Lubbock, TX). *La muerte de Ernesto Nerios* (Ernesto Nerios's Death) (s.1978) (p. San Antonio, San Pedro Playhouse). *I Will Catch the Sun* (s.1979) (p. San Antonio, Thiry Auditorium, Our Lady of the Lake University). *Tequila Mockingbird, Or the Ghost of Unemployment* (San Antonio: Trucha, 1979).

BIBLIOGRAPHY: Rafael C. Castillo, "Nephtalí de León: A Profile," *Viaztlán* 3 (Summer 1985): 7–8. Jean S. Chittenden, "Nephtalí de León," in *Chicano Writers*, ed. Francisco A. Lomelí and Carl R. Shirley (Detroit: Gale Research, 1989), 98–106. Sabino Garza, "Nephtalí de León," *La Luz* 6.12 (December 1977): 15–19. Moises Sandoval "Sandy," "Chicano Arts Theatre," *Caracol* 4.10 (June 1978): 17.

DOMÍNGUEZ, Sylvia Maida (1935–   ). Sylvia Maida Domínguez is a native of the Rio Grande valley of south Texas. Domínguez holds a Ph.D. in Spanish from the University of Arizona and works as a Spanish professor at the Pan American University in Edinburgh, Texas. Domínguez's plays, which are written in Spanish, have been staged in different Texas local and national institutions. However, her last work, *Tres aguilas de la Revolución Mexicana* (Three Eagles of the Mexican Revolution) (s.1990), was produced in Reynosa, Mexico. *La comadre María* (Mary the Gossip) (1979) and *Samuel la carretilla* (Samuel the Wheelbarrow) (s.1974) address problems of daily life. *Tres aguilas de la Revolución Mexicana* examines the problems of Mexican peasantry through the eyes of Emiliano Zapata, Pancho Villa, and Francisco Madero, and *Tesoro español de obras originales* (Spanish Treasury of Original Works) (s.1971) is a series of sketches on classical and historical figures.

WORKS: *Tesoro español de obras originales* (Spanish Treasury of Original Works) (s.1971) (p. Edinburg, TX, Pan American University Ballroom). *La comadre María* (s.1972) (p. San Juan, TX: Saint John's School Auditorium). *La comadre María* (Mary the Gossip) (p. Austin, TX, American Universal Art Forms, 1973). *Samuel la carretilla* (Samuel the Wheelbarrow) (s.1974) (p. Edinburg, TX, Pan American University Fine Arts Auditorium). *Tres aguilas de la Revolución Mexicana* (s.1990) (p. Reynosa, Mexico, Restaurante Elegante).

BIBLIOGRAPHY: Patricia de la Fuente, "Sylvia Maida Domínguez," in *Chicano Writers*, 2nd ed., ed. Francisco A. Lomelí and Carl R. Shirley (Detroit: Gale Research, 1992), 87–89.

HERNÁNDEZ, Alfonso C. (1938–   ). Alfonso C. Hernández was born in Atotonilco, Mexico. He came to the United States in 1960, where he obtained an M.A. in French at Claremont McKenna College, California, where he also became involved in the Chicano movement.

Although Hernández studied the theater of Luis Valdez and staged some of his plays, Hernández's plays do not reflect a clear influence of the Chicano political movement of the 1960s and 1970s. His first plays, *The Lemon Tree, The Wedding Dress*, and *The Potion* (published in the Chicano journal *El Grito* in 1974), are erotic and pessimistic stories with little dialogue. The use of pantomime, music, and theatrical effects are the most important aspects of these plays. In 1979, Hernández published three more plays: *The False Advent of Mary's Child, Every Family Has One*, and *The Imperfect Bachelor*. These plays denounce the hypocrisy of bourgeois society, its obsessions, sins, and corruption. They differ from earlier plays in that the characters' psychology is developed more in depth and the stories depend on dialogue rather than on technical effects. They also contain the eroticism and explicit sexual content of his earlier plays.

WORKS: *The Lemon Tree, The Potion, The Wedding Dress*, in *El Grito* 7 (June–August 1974): 38–54. *The False Advent of Mary's Child and Other Plays* (Berkeley: Justa, 1979).

BIBLIOGRAPHY: Nuria Bustamante, "Alfonso C. Hernández," in *Chicano Writers*, 2nd ed., ed. Francisco A. Lomelí and Carl R. Shirley (Detroit: Gale Research, 1992), 127–131. Charles M. Tatum, *Chicano Literature* (Boston: Twayne, 1982), 75–76.

HERNÁNDEZ, Inés (1947–   ). Born in Galveston, Texas, Hernández is known for her Spanish and English poetry, which reflects her Chicano and Native American heritage. Her only play, *El día de Guadalupe* (Guadalupe's Day), was staged in 1984.

WORK: *El día de Guadalupe* (Guadalupe's Day) (s.1984) (p. Fresno, California State University).

BIBLIOGRAPHY: Clara Lomas, "Inés Hernández," in *The Longman Anthology of International Women Writers 1895–1975*, ed. Marian Arkin and Barbara Shollar (White Plains, NY: Longman, 1989), 1019–1020. Laura Gutiérrez Spencer, "Inés Hernández," in *Chicano Writers*, 2nd ed., ed. Francisco A. Lomelí and Carl R. Shirley (Detroit: Gale Research, 1992), 132–136.

MARES, E. A. (1938–   ). Ernesto Gustavo Mares was born in Albuquerque, New Mexico. A poet and essayist, Mares became known as a playwright in 1979 with the successful production of his bilingual play *Lola's Last Dance*. The play tells the story of Lola, an aging prostitute who, while remembering her lovers, gives an ironic view of Albuquerque's past.

Lola's Last Dance marks the beginning of Mares's collaboration with the Compañía de Teatro de Albuquerque. The presence of New Mexico history is one of the most characteristic aspects of Mares's theater. *El corrido de Joaquín Murieta* (The Ballad of Joaquin Murieta) (s.1984) was the result of Mares's attempt to do a bilingual adaptation for the Compañía de Teatro de Albuquerque of Pablo Neruda's *Fulgor y muerte de Joaquín Murieta* (Splendor and Death of Joaquin Murieta). Instead, Mares wrote an original play based on his own research on this legendary hero. In Mares's play, Joaquín Murieta is a native from New Mexico who goes to California to trade horses. Also in the line of historical drama, *Santa Fe Spirit* (s.1989) is a musical based on the history of Santa Fe. Finally, *Padre Antonio José Martínez de Taos* (Father Antonio José Martínez from

Taos) (s.1983) is a monologue on this decisive but usually discredited figure of New Mexican history. Mares's *The Shepherd of Pan Duro* (s.1989) is not a historical drama but, rather, a traditional *posada* turned into a parable on homeless people in modern time.

WORKS: *Lola's Last Dance* (s.1979) (p. Albuquerque, Compañía de Teatro de Alburquerque). *Padre Antonio José Martínez de Taos* (Father Antonio José Martínez from Taos) (s.1983) (p. Ratón, NM, New Mexico Endowment for the Humanities Chautauqua Program). *Vista del puente*, bilingual adaptation of Arthur Miller's *View from the Bridge* by Mares and Cecilio García-Camarillo (s.1983) (p. Albuquerque). *El corrido de Joaquín Murieta* (The Ballad of Joaquin Murieta) (s.1984) (p. Albuquerque, Compañía de Teatro de Alburquerque). *Santa Fe Spirit* (s.1989) (p. Santa Fe Spirit Company). *The Shepherd of Pan Duro* (s.1989) (p. Albuquerque, Compañía de Teatro de Albuquerque).

BIBLIOGRAPHY: Mary Montaño Army, "New Life for an Old Myth," *Impact Albuquerque Journal* (May 1985): 5–14. Enrique R. Lamadrid, "E. A. Mares," in *Chicano Writers*, 2nd ed., ed. Francisco A. Lomelí and Carl R. Shirley (Detroit: Gale Research, 1992).

MORAGA, Cherríe (1952–   ). Cherríe Moraga was born in Whittier, California. She is known for her polemic work as a poet, essayist, and playwright. The book Moraga coauthored with Gloria Anzaldúa, *This Bridge Called My Back: Writings by Radical Women of Color*, has become a classic of Women's Studies in the United States. Her plays reflect her social concerns dealing with aspects of feminism, lesbianism, racism, and classism. *Giving Up the Ghost* (s.1987) and *Shadow of a Man* (s.1990) explore the relationship between men and women, the imposition of gender roles, and the discrimination against women in a male chauvinistic society. Her other play, *Heroes and Saints* (s.1992), was inspired by the protest that took place in the San Joaquin Valley in 1988. The play shows the influence of social activist César Chávez and of playwright Luis Valdez and his Teatro Campesino.

WORKS: *Giving Up the Ghost: Teatro in Two Acts* (Los Angeles: West End Press, 1986). *Giving Up the Ghost* (s.1987) (p. Seattle, Front Room Theater). *Shadow of a Man* (s.1990) (p. San Francisco, Women in the Arts and the Eureka Theatre Company). *Heroes and Saints* (s.1992) (p. Teatro Misión of San Francisco, Women in the Arts). *Heroes and Saints and Other Plays* (Albuquerque: West End Press, 1994).

BIBLIOGRAPHY: Norma Alarcón, "Interview with Cherríe Moraga," *Third Woman* 3.1–2 (1986): 127–134. Yvonne Yarbro-Bejarano, "Cherríe Moraga," in *Chicano Writers*, ed. Francisco A. Lomelí and Carl R. Shirley (Detroit: Gale Research, 1989), 165–177. Yvonne Yarbro-Bejarano, "Cherrie Moraga's *Giving Up the Ghost*: The Representation of Female Desire," *Third Woman* 3.1–2 (1986): 113–120. Jorge Huerta, review of *Giving Up the Ghost, Americas Review* 15.2 (Summer 1987): 104–105. Raquel Aguilú de Murphy, review of *Giving Up the Ghost, Americas Review* 15.2 (Summer 1987): 105–107. Luz María Umpierre, "Interview with Cherríe Moraga," *Americas Review* 14 (Summer 1986): 54–67.

MORTON, Carlos (1942–   ). Carlos Morton was born in Chicago, Illinois. He received a B.A. in English from the University of Texas at El Paso in 1975, and from 1979 to 1981, he worked as a playwright with the San Francisco Mime Troupe. In 1987, he completed his doctorate in drama at the University of Texas at Austin with a dissertation on his own work: "Three Plays on the Latin Experience in America: *Johnny Tenorio, Malinche,* and *The Savior.*" Currently Morton works as a professor in the Department of Theatre at the University of California, Riverside.

Morton's plays show the strong influence of Bertold Brecht and of Luis Valdez and El Teatro Campesino. Through a combination of irony, carnavalesque humor, and social protest, Morton reviews Chicano history, myth, and religion. In *El jardín* (The Garden) (s.1975) and *Pancho Diablo* (s.1984), Morton draws a parallel between biblical subjects and characters and Chicano reality. *Rancho Hollywood* (s.1980) and *Los dorados* (The Golden) (s.1978) are metatheatrical plays that question Anglo history and stereotypes of the Hispanic Southwest. In *La Malinche* (s.1984), Morton approaches this legendary Mexican figure and shows her as an American Medea, a woman victim of her own destiny. Intertextuality is also the technique used in *Johnny Tenorio* (s.1983), Morton's adaptation of José Zorrilla's *Don Juan Tenorio* to Chicano modern times.

Las Muchos Muertes de Danny Rosales (The Many Deaths of Danny Rosales) (originally called *Las Many Muertes de Richard Morales*) is probably Morton's most popular play. It is based on a true story, the 1975 murder of a young Chicano by a Texas police chief. The play denounces the racism and discrimination with which minority groups are being treated and condemns the impunity of American police crimes.

The Savior (s.1988) tells the story of Archbishop Oscar Arnulfo Romero, murdered in San Salvador, El Salvador, in 1980. *The Savior* differs from the rest of Morton's plays in that it considers recent Latin American history instead of Chicano history. However, Morton points out the participation of the United States in the events that took place in El Salvador and relates the Chicano troubled experience in the United States to the American political role in Central America.

WORKS: *El jardín* (s.1975) (p. Iowa City, University of Iowa). *Las Many Muertes de Danny Rosales* (s.1976) (p. San Diego, University of California). *Los dorados* (The Golden) (s.1978) (p. San Diego, California-Pacific Theater). *Rancho Hollywood* (s.1980) (p. San Francisco, Teatro Gusto). *Johnny Tenorio* (s.1983) (p. San Antonio, TX, Centro Cultural de Aztlán). *The Many Deaths of Danny Rosales and Other Plays* (Houston: Arte Público Press, 1983). *La Malinche* (s.1984) (p. Austin, University of Texas). *Pancho Diablo* (s.1984) (p. Los Angeles, University of California). *The Savior* (s.1988) (p. Seattle Group Theatre).

BIBLIOGRAPHY: M. Alicia Arrizón, "Carlos Morton," in *Chicano Writers*, 2nd ed., ed. Francisco A. Lomelí and Carl R. Shirley (Detroit: Gale Research, 1992), 186–190. Juan Bruce-Novoa, "Round Table on Chicano Literature," *Journal of Ethnic Studies* 3.1 (Spring 1975): 99–103. Lee Daniel, "Un pocho en México. Una entrevista con Carlos Mortón," *Confluencia* 7.1 (Fall 1991): 115–118. Marco A. Franco, "His Work Is All Play," *Vista* 3.12 (August 1988): 32. Erlinda González-Berry, review of *The Many Deaths of Danny Rosales and Other Plays, Latin American Theatre Review* 22.2 (Spring 1989): 132–133. William A. Henry, "Visions from the Past: Emerging Playwrights Trade Anger for Dialogue," *Time*, July 1988, 82–83. Carlos Morton, "Los dioses y los diablos en el teatro chicano," *Rayas* 1.4 (July–August 1978): 10. Edith E. Pross, "A Chicano Play and Its Audience," *Americas Review* 14.1 (Spring 1986): 71–79. Abel Markos Salas, review of *La Malinche, National Hispanic Journal* 4.1 (Spring 1985): 28–29. Teatroscope: Review of *Johnny Tenorio, National Hispanic Journal* 3.4 (Winter 1984): 26.

PORTILLO TRAMBLEY, Estela (1936–). Born in 1936 in El Paso, Texas, Estela Portillo Trambley is a prolific playwright, poet, and short story writer. In her plays, Portillo avoids ideological flags, attempting instead to inject in her characters and subjects a strong dramatic intensity, which induces her audience and readers to reflect on social problems, such as repression, intolerance, and injustice. Her best-known play, *The Day of the Swallows*, relates the problems and suffering of Josefa, a lesbian who lives in a rural traditional Hispanic community. Victim of her own fears, the protagonist mutilates a young man when he discovers her relationship with a prostitute, and she finally kills herself when her lover deserts her. The most interesting aspect of the play is the psychological complexity of the characters. In the same psychological line, *Sor Juana* approaches the life of Sor Juana Inés de la Cruz. In Portillo's play, Sor Juana is seen as an arrogant woman, sheltered in her studies and totally detached from the problems of Mexico and her compatriots. *Puente Negro* and *Black Light*, also included in *Sor Juana and Other Plays*, deal with problems closer to the Chicano reality, whereas her fourth play, *Autumn Gold*, is a comedy detached from any specific Mexican American issue.

Portillo is also a Chicana pioneer of musicals, a genre that was very popular among Chicano audiences before World War II that has been neglected by later Chicano playwrights. *Morality Play* (s.1974) and *Sun Images* (s.1976) are two interesting three-act musicals in which we can appreciate Portillo's ability to approach this lighter theatrical genre.

WORKS: *The Day of the Swallows, El Grito* 4.3 (Spring 1971): 4–47; *The Day of the Swallows*, in *Nuevos pasos*, Chicano and Puerto Rican Drama, ed. Nikolás Kanellos and Jorge Huerta (Houston: Arte Público Press, 1989). *Morality Play* (s.1974) (p. El Paso, Chamizal National Theatre). *Black Light* (s.1975) (p. El Paso, Chamizal National Theatre). *El hombre cósmico* (Cosmic Man) (s.1975) (p. Chamizal National Theatre). *Sun Images* (s.1976) (p. El Paso, Chamizal National Theatre). *Isabel and the Danzing Bear* (s.1977) (p. El Paso, Chamizal National Theatre). *Sor Juana and Other Plays* (Houston: Bilingual Press, 1983).

BIBLIOGRAPHY: Juan Bruce-Novoa, "Estela Portillo-Trambley," in *Chicano Authors: Inquiry by Interview* (Austin: University of Texas Press, 1980), 164–181. Armando Miguélez, "Aproximaciones al nuevo teatro chicano de autor único," *Explicación de Textos Literarios* 15.2 (1986–1987): 8–18. Faye Nell Vowell interview with Estela Portillo-Trambley, *Melus* 9.4 (Winter 1982).

RECHY, John (1934–). John Rechy is a very polemic Chicano writer from El Paso, Texas, who, in spite of his frequent writings on Chicano issues, has not always been considered a Chicano writer. However, he is unquestionably one of the most important gay writers of the United States. Rechy deals mainly with narrative, but his two plays *Momma as She Became . . . But Not as She Was* and *Tigers Wild* were staged in New York in 1978 and 1986.

WORKS: *Momma as She Became . . . But Not as She Was* (s.1978) (p. New York). *Tigers Wild* (s.1986) (p. New York).

BIBLIOGRAPHY: Stephen Holden, "Emotional Scar Tissue," review of *Tigers Wild* in the *New York Times*, October 22, 1986. Didier T. Jaén, "John Rechy," in *Chicano Writers*, 2nd ed., ed. Francisco A. Lomelí and Carl R. Shirley (Detroit: Gale Research, 1992), 212–219. William Leyland, "John Rechy," in *Gay Sunshine Interviews*, vol. 2 (San Francisco: Gay Sunshine, 1978), 251–268.

SIERRA, Rubén (1946–). Born in San Antonio, Texas, Rubén Sierra is one of the most complete Chicano theater playwrights. He is an actor, writer, director, and producer of plays. Sierra's first plays were clearly influenced by the Teatro Campesino. Due to its polemical content, the premiere in San Antonio of Sierra's first play, *La raza pura*, or *Racial, Racial* (s.1968), a satire of racism in the United States, received a strong reaction from conservative Anglo groups, who even threatened to bomb the theater. The play was, however, a success. In 1988, Sierra again approached this subject in *Say, Can You See*. More in the vein of the allegorical acts of the Teatro Campesino are *The Conquering Father* (s.1972) and *Articus and the Angel* (s.1983), while *La capirotada de los espejos* (The Mixture of the Mirrors) (s.1973) follows the historical tendency that is also a characteristic of the Teatro Campesino. *The Millionaire y el pobrecito* (s.1979) is an adaptation of Mark Twain's *The Prince and the Pauper* (1881) to Chicano reality. *I Am Celso* is an adaption of Leo Romero's poem of the same name. Basically, all of Sierra's plays cover ethnic and minority problems. However, with *Manolo*, a three-act play dealing with the drug addiction problem among Vietnam veterans, Sierra succeeded in reaching larger audiences.

WORKS: *La raza pura (Racial, Racial)* (s.1968) (p. San Antonio, St. Mary's University). *The Conquering Father* (s.1972) (p. San Antonio, Downstage Theatre). *La capirotada de los espejos* (The Mixture of the Mirrors) (s.1973) (p. Seattle, Teatro del Piojo). *Manolo* (s.1975; s.1983) (p. Seattle, Teatro Quetzalcóatl; Northridge, California State University). *The Millionaire y el pobrecito* (s.1979) (p. Los Angeles, Public Theatre). *Articus and the Angel* (s.1983) (p. Seattle, Group Theatre). *I Am Celso*, adapted by Sierra and Jorge Huerta from Leo Romero's *Celso*, (s.1985) (p. Los Angeles, University of California). *Say, Can You See* (s.1988) (p. Seattle, Group Theatre).

BIBLIOGRAPHY: Arthur Ramírez, "Rubén Sierra," in *Chicano Writers*, 2nd ed., ed. Francisco A. Lomelí and Carl R. Shirley (Detroit: Gale Research, 1992), 259–263. Carl R. Shirley and Paula W. Shirley, *Understanding Chicano Literature* (Columbia: University of South Carolina Press, 1988), 82–83. Charles M. Tatum, *Chicano Literature* (Boston: Twayne, 1982), 73–74.

TEATRO CAMPESINO. See VALDEZ, Luis Miguel.

TEATRO DE LA ESPERANZA. Initially named Teatro MECHA, it began as a student group at the University of California at Santa Barbara in 1969. The group participated in the formation of TENAZ (El Teatro Nacional de Aztlán). In 1971, as a consequence of ideological differences, the group became El Teatro de la Esperanza (Theater of Hope) and, under Jorge Huerta's direction, started performing at La Casa de la Raza. El Teatro de la Esperanza shows the clear influence of Bertold Brecht's theories and of Latin American independent groups such as El Teatro Experimental de Cali and El Teatro Campesino.

El Teatro de la Esperanza has staged plays written by authors not belonging to the group; nevertheless, they frequently write and produce their own plays. Among the most important plays are *Guadalupe*, *La víctima* (The Victim), *Trampa sin salida* (No Way Out), *Pánfila la curandera* (Panfila the Healer), and *Brujerías* (Witchcraft). *Guadalupe* is a documentary play based on the social problems of a Chicano community; *La víctima* deals with the Mexican American deportation policies of the 1970s; and *Trampa sin salida* is an *acto* condemning police brutality. *Pánfila la curandera* and *Brujerías* are short plays that verge on comedy.

TEATRO LIBERTAD. Created in Tucson, Arizona, in 1975 by a group of farmworkers, students, and Chicano activists, El Teatro Libertad tended toward collective play creation. The plays were written after a detailed research of cases of social injustice involving Chicano people. Among the Teatro Libertad's more important plays are *El vacil del 76* (The Waiver of 76) which is a revision of Mexican American history through the eyes of three Chicanos, a Mexican worker, and an Irish American who are traveling from Tucson to Phoenix. *Los cabrones* (The Bastards), a farce about the maltreatment of undocumented workers; and *Los pelados* (The Underdogs), a play dealing with the problems of urban Chicano families.

VALDEZ, Luis Miguel (1940–). Born in Delano, California, where he later worked with César Chávez to unionize the farmworkers, Valdez is the most important Chicano playwright. With El Teatro Campesino, Valdez created a whole concept of theater that was followed by many playwrights and theatrical Chicano groups. According to Valdez, the main objective of Chicano theater is to propagate a sense of nationalism among Chicano audiences by dealing with Chicano issues and becoming a channel through which Chicanos will reflect on their problems and explore their solutions. To this effect, Valdez created two different kinds of plays, *el mito* (the myth) and *el acto* (the act). With *el mito*, Valdez approaches Amerindian art and insists on the pre-Colombian roots of Chicano essence, whereas *el acto* shows a clear influence of the spontaneous sixteenth-century Spanish *pasos* and the Italian Renaissance commedia dell'arte. Usually, the *actos* are short dramatic sketches with a humor close to the grotesque and the absurd of Brechtian theater, which combine dance, music, dialogues, and pantomime to express, in a concise and effective way, a polemic social message.

Valdez's plays have been both published and produced. *Las dos caras del patroncito* (The Two Faces of the Owner) (s.1965), *Vietnam campesino* (s.1970), *La quinta temporada* (The Fifth Season) (s.1966), *Huelguistas* (Strikers) (s.1970), and *The Militants* (s.1969) are plays more clearly related to the problems of the *campesinos*. *Vietnam campesino, Dark Root of a Scream* (s.1971), and *Soldado Razo* (s.1971) deal with the effect that war has had in the Chicano communities *Los vendidos* (The Sellouts) (s.1967), *No saco nada de la escuela* (I Don't Get Anything Out of School) (s.1969), and *I Don't Have to Show You No Stinking Badges* (s.1986) denounce the discrimination of Chicanos in American society. *The Shrunken Head of Pancho Villa, Bernabé, La conquista de México* (The Conquest of Mexico) (s.1968), *La gran carpa de la familia Rascuachi* (The Great Tent of the Rascuachi Family) (s.1971), *Zoot Suit* (s.1978), *Bandido* (Bandit) (s.1981), and *Corridos* (s.1982) cover different aspects of Chicano history, culture, tradition, and lore.

Valdez's last play, *I Don't Have to Show You No Stinking Badges*, bespeaks his involvement with mainstream entertainment. For the first time in his career, he examines the conflicts faced by Chicanos working as actors in Hollywood. Valdez's relationship with Hollywood started in the 1980s, when his success with *Zoot Suit* in Los Angeles's mainstream theaters led him to arrange for the screen and direct a film version. The film was well received, but it was not a success. However, a few years later, Valdez came back to Hollywood to direct *La Bamba*, a film about the life of rock singer Ritchie Valens. Although this time it was a success, the film received some negative reviews due to the romantization of Valens's life. Valdez received similar criticism when he staged *La gran carpa de la familia Rascuachi*, a play that insists on Valdez's mystical conception of Chicano people. *Corridos*, Valdez's dramatization of the Mexican folk ballads, was also accused of perpetuating Mexican stereotypes. For many critics Valdez has betrayed the goals he once traced for Chicano theater; for others, he is a consistent and innovative playwright that, at the time, was able to create a sense of a national Chicano theater.

WORKS: *The Shrunken Head of Pancho Villa* (s.1963) (p. San José, San José State College Drama Department). *Las dos caras del patroncito* (The Two Faces of the Owner) (s.1965) (p. Delano, CA). *La quinta temporada* (The Fifth Season) (s.1966) (p. Delano, CA, Filipino Hall). *Los vendidos* (The Sellouts) (s.1967) (p. Los Angeles, Elysian Park). *La conquista de México* (The Conquest of Mexico) (s.1968) (p. Del Rey, CA, Centro Campesino Cultural). *The Militants* (s.1969) (p. Fresno, CA). *No saco nada de la escuela* (I Don't Get Anything Out of School) (s.1969) (p. Fresno, CA, St. John's Church). *Bernabé* (s.1970) (p. Fresno, CA) *Huelguistas* (Strikers) (s.1970) (p. Fresno, CA). *Vietnam campesino* (s.1970) (p. Delano, CA, Guadalupe Church). Actos by Valdez and *El Teatro Campesino*, (San Juan Bautista: Cucaracha, 1971). *Dark Root of a Scream* (s.1971) (p. Los Angeles). *La gran carpa de la familia Rascuachi* (The Great Tent of the Rascuachi Family) (s.1971). *Soldado Razo* (Chicano Soldier) (s.1971) (p. Fresno, CA, Chicano Moratorium on the War on Vietnam). *El fin del mundo* (The End of the World) (s.1972). *El baile de los gigantes* (Danze of Giants) (s.1974) (p. México City, Quinto Festival). *The Shrunken Head of Pancho Villa* (San Juan Bautista: Cucaracha, 1974). *Zoot Suit* (s.1978) (p. Los Angeles, Mark Taper Forum). *Bandido* (Bandit) (s.1981) (p. San Juan Bautista, CA). *Corridos* (s.1982) (p. San Juan Bautista, CA). *I Don't Have to Show You No Stinking Badges* (s.1986) (p. Los Angeles Theater Center). *Luis Valdez—Early Works*: Actos, Bernabé *and* Pensamiento serpentino (Houston: Arte Público 1990). *Zoot Suit and Other Plays* (Houston: Arte Público, 1992).

BIBLIOGRAPHY: Maria Alicia Arrizon, Review of *I Don't Have to Show You No Stinking Badges*, *Ambiente* (October 1990), 11–12. Mary Denning Boland, "An Analysis of the Theater of Luis Valdez." Ph. D. dissertation, Saint Louis University, 1983 (University Microfilms International, 1987). Yolanda Broyles-González, *El Teatro Campesino: Theater in the Chicano Movement* (Austin: University of Texas Press, 1994). Arturo C. Flores, *El Teatro Campesino de Luis Valdez (1965–1980)* (Madrid: Pliegos, 1990). Víctor Fuentes, "Luis Valdez, Hollywood y Tezcatlipoca," *Chiricú* 5.2 (1988): 35–39. Nicolás Kanellos, "Luis Miguel Valdez," in *Chicano Writers*, 2nd ed., ed. Francisco A. Lomelí and Carl R. Shirley (Detroit: Gale Research, 1992), 281–292. Françoise Kourilsky, "Approaching Quetzalcoatl: The Evolution of *El Teatro Campesino*," *Performance* 2 (Fall 1973): 37–46. Carlos Morton, "The Many Masks of *Teatro Chicano*" (a review of the play *Zoot Suit*), *Caracol* 5.1 (September 1978): 12-16-21. Rosaura Sánchez, Review of *Corridos, Crítica* 1.2 (Spring 1985): 131–133. Yvonne Yarbro-Bejarano, "From *Acto* to *Mito*: A Critical Appraisal of the Teatro Campesino," in *Modern Chicano Writers*, ed. Joseph Sommers and Tomás Ybarra-Frausto (Englewood Cliffs, NJ: Prentice-Hall, 1979), 176–185.

VENEGAS, Daniel (n.d.). Daniel Venegas is a good example of the rich Mexican American theatrical production of the 1920s. Unfortunately, very little is known of this writer, considered by Nicolás Kanellos as a precursor of today's Chicano literature. As it happened with the majority of the plays produced in the 1920s, Venegas's plays have been lost, and the only references we have to them are a series of positive reviews published in Los Angeles's newspapers *La Opinión* and *El Heraldo de México*.

WORKS: *¿Quién es el culpable?* (Who Is to Blame?) (s.1924) (p. Los Angeles). *Nuestro egoísmo* (Our Selfishness) (s.1926?) (p. Los Angeles). *Esclavos* (Slaves) (s.1930?) (p. Los Angeles). *El maldito jazz* (That Darned Jazz) (s.1930?) (p. Los Angeles, 1930). *Revista astronómica* (The Astronomic Review) (s.1930?) (p. Los Angeles). *El con-su-lado* (s.1932) (p. Los Angeles). *El establo de Arizmendi* (Arizmendi's Stable) (s.1933) (p. Los Angeles).

BIBLIOGRAPHY: Nicolás Kanellos, "Daniel Venegas," in *Chicano Writers*, ed. Francisco A. Lomelí and Carl R. Shirley (Detroit: Gale Research, 1992), 271–274. Kanellos, introduction to *Las aventuras de don Chipote o Cuando los pericos mamen* (The Adventures of Don Chipote or When Parakeets Suckle Their Young) (Mexico City: SEP, 1984), 7–15.

Juan Torres Pou

Chile

In terms of a Chilean theater tradition, there is very little to discuss until the nineteenth century when amateur theater groups began to appear and writers like Andrés Bello began to translate into Spanish the classical French plays of Racine and Molière, as well as writing their own. Theater written during the latter half of the nineteenth century and the first forty years of the twentieth century demonstrated a marked preference for themes particular to Chile, its history, and culture. Also prevalent because of their popularity were light comedies, usually in the form of *costumbrista* works, or the comedy of manners. These, along with plays about Chile's history, endured well into the twentieth century, composed by authors like Antonio Acevedo Hernández, Daniel Barros Grez, Armando Moock, René Hurtado Borne, and Germán Luco Cruchaga. Some of these plays have become Chilean classics (e.g., Acevedo Hernández's *Un 18 típico*, Barros Grez's *Como en Santiago*, Luco Cruchaga's *La viuda de Apablaza*, or Moock's *Pueblecito*) that are still being performed. Departing from the norm during the first third of the twentieth century, Acevedo Hernández's works are particularly significant, since themes of social concern are introduced (e.g., *La canción rota, En el suburbio*, or *Almas perdidas*).

With the support of governmental funding, university theaters and theater programs were founded in the 1940s. These would provide professional training, bring about a major renovation in Chilean theater, and foster the development of a national theater. The first of these university theaters to be established was the Teatro Experimental (Experimental Theater) under the direction of Pedro de la Barra at the University of Chile in 1941. Eventually this theater program would become known as the best in all of Latin America. Similarly, Pedro Mortheiru and others founded the Teatro de Ensayo in 1943 at the Catholic University of Chile, also located in Santiago. Yet other university theaters were established in Concepción (TUC, 1947), Valparaíso (Catholic University, 1958), Antofagasta (1962), and Santiago (TEKNOS, State Technical University, 1962). These university theaters would lead to a Chilean theater legacy that would produce a group of internationally acclaimed playwrights, the so-called Generation of 1957: Isidora Aguirre, Fernando Cuadra, Fernando Debesa, Jorge Díaz, Luis Alberto Heiremans, Gabriela Roepke, Alejandro Sieveking, Sergio Vodanovic, and Égon Wolff, among others. This group of playwrights, who created a "boom" in Chilean theater in the 1950s and 1960s, composed a wide variety of works: those dealing with historical or folkloric themes; those written in the vein of psychological or social realism; those that were Brechtian in nature and committed to a cause; as well as theater of the Absurd.

By the late 1960s Chilean theater was in a state of crisis with declining audiences, due in part to the influence of television. Coinciding with university reform movements intended to democratize the universities, theater programs there also were restructured. As a consequence of this democratic spirit, new groups (e.g., Taller de Experimentación and the Taller de Creación Teatral) were formed to produce collective creations, which thus more equally involved the collaboration of the entire team, making the director an equal partner in the production, rather than a tyrant. From this concept—and coinciding with the political climate that was to lead to the formation of the Popular Unity coalition—was born popular theater. This legacy led to the formation of collective theater groups like El Aleph and Ictus, which came to be known internationally for their innovative approach to creating theater. Moreover, this climate fostered the emergence of amateur theater groups (e.g., ANTACH, or the National Association of Amateur Theater of Chile). Independent theater companies like the Teatro El Ángel and El Túnel were prospering. Also, new playwrights— those of the Generation of 1972—were beginning to appear on the scene: David Benavente, José Chesta, Ariel Dorfman, José Pineda, Juan Radrigán, Raúl Ruiz, and Antonio Skármeta, to name only a few.

With the military coup of 1973 and the ousting of Salvador Allende and his Popular Unity ideals, everything changed. From the military's perspective, their role was to rid the country of its Marxist enemies, which would enable them to cleanse and heal Chilean society. A "cultural blackout" occurred as actors, directors, and writers were detained or exiled. Military officers replaced democratically elected rectors at universities throughout the country, resulting in the closure and/or reorganization of many departments and university theaters. The Theater of the University of Concepción, for example, was one of the first to be abolished since it had been so closely associated with popular social theater and its leftist political stance. Theater programs at both the University of Chile and the Catholic University underwent profound changes. Since their economic survival depended on their exemption from a new theater tax imposed by the military government (22 percent of the gross take of the box office), they were obliged to perform works that the military government considered to be of significant cultural value—works from classical French drama or from the Golden Age of Spain. As theater professors were dismissed from their university positions, some (e.g., Gustavo Meza) formed their own independent theater groups and, for the most part, performed works by modern international playwrights, so long as these works did not convey sociopolitical messages that would endanger them. Several actors, directors, authors, and theater companies went into exile of their own volition (e.g., Alejandro Sieveking and his Teatro del Ángel, Jaime Miranda, Antonio Skármeta, the Compañía de los Cuatro); however, others like the group El Aleph were not so fortunate. In 1974 when they presented a satire of the military coup (*Y al principio existía la vida*), its members were all detained, one of them was killed, and after two years of imprisonment, the others were permitted to seek exile in France. The Teatro La Feria also experienced milder forms of repression when it staged *Hojas de Parra* in 1977, but other well-known groups like Ictus did not experience any real difficulties. As one might expect under these precarious circumstances, very few new works by Chilean dramatists were created. At this stage it seemed as though the authoritarian military regime had been successful in silencing voices of protest.

In 1977 many of the independent theater companies that had been performing plays by contemporary playwrights from other countries found themselves in dire straits when these authors refused to allow their works to be performed in Chile as a means of protesting the human rights abuses of the military regime. Directors like Gustavo Meza of the Teatro Imagen resolved this problem by turning to writing the works themselves, by moving to collaborative theater, and by holding competitions to showcase new works by Chilean playwrights (Krugh, Interview with Meza). It was thus that the voices of three Chilean playwrights were discovered: Marco Antonio de la Parra, Juan Radrigán, and Luis Rivano. This period of time (roughly from 1976 to 1980) marks one of the richest periods of theater production in Chile's history, rivaled perhaps only by the late 1950s and 1960s. It generated landmark works that documented the events and socioeconomic conditions of the time in Chile, dealt with the subject of exile, and called into question issues of power. Many theater companies were involved in the production of such works at this time: Ictus, Teatro La Feria, Teatro Imagen. Playwrights of all ages also addressed the same topics: Jorge Díaz, Ramón Griffero, Jaime Miranda, Marco Antonio de la Parra, Juan Radrigán, Égon Wolff.

The return of democratization to Chile has brought differing reactions from Chilean playwrights. On the one hand, authors like Ariel Dorfman (*La muerte y la doncella*) and Isidora Aguirre (*Retablo de Yumbel*) directly address the atrocities that occurred during the military regime, posing the dilemma of how Chileans are to effect a reconciliation when amnesty allows torturers and murderers to go unpunished. Other authors like Juan Radrigán, who wrote so prolifically during the regime as he championed the cause of the poor and oppressed, now seem paralyzed as they face the quandary of what to write about: On the one hand, not to write about events that occurred during the authoritarian military regime would be to betray history, to deny that it ever happened; on the other hand, it is impossible to write honestly about that history because the full truth of those events has never been revealed (Krugh, Interview with Radrigán). Still other playwrights like Gustavo Meza note that the transition has been difficult, partly because the military regime provided a unifying element for the theater world as they raised their voices in protest (Krugh, Interview with Meza). Finally, for yet another group of playwrights, democratization seems to have fostered a spirit of liberating innovation, freeing them—along with directors and all participants in the staging of a work—to experiment with language, space, lighting, music, dance, symbols, icons, and intertextuality. Most critics agree that the Gran Circo Teatro's debut of Andrés Pérez's *La negra Ester* (The Black Esther) in 1988 marks the beginning of this trend (Pereira Poza 115). Also displaying these characteristics of renovation are works by Víctor Carrasco and Santiago Ramírez (*KM 69 Are You Lonesome Tonight*), Mauricio Celedón (*Transfusión* [Tranfusion]), Andrés del Bosque (*Los socios* [The Partners]), Claudia Donoso (*La manzana de Adán* [Adam's Apple]), and Inés Stranger (*Cariño malo* [Evil Affection]). The presence of these recent arrivals on the Chilean theater scene, along with that of the still-active playwrights of the Generation of 1957 (Isidora Aguirre, Jorge Díaz, Alejandreo Sieveking, Sergio Vodanovic, and Égon Wolff) and those of the Generation of 1987 (Gregory Cohen, Ramón Griffero, Jaime Miranda, and Marco Antonio de la Parra), who are just now reaching the peak of their careers, suggests that Chilean theater will continue to play a leading role in the development of Latin American theater, just as it has since the 1950s.

BIBLIOGRAPHY

Abascal Brunet, M. *Apuntes para la historia del teatro en Chile*. 2 vols. Santiago: Editorial Universitaria, 1941.

————, and E. Pereira Salas. *Pepe Arias o la zarzuela chica en Chile*. Santiago: Editorial Universitaria, 1955.

Acevedo, Patricio. *Cuerpo y cultura autoritaria: Dos experiencias de expresión corporal en grupos de base. Testimonios*. Santiago: CENECA, 1984.

Acevedo Hernández, Antonio. "Consideraciones sobre el teatro chileno." *Ateneo* 95 (March 1933): 146–158, 196; (April 1933): 309–319.

————. "Cuarenta años de teatro." *En viaje* 30.257 (March 1995).

Alegría, Fernando. "Chile's Experimental Theatre." *Interamerican* 4.10 (October 1945): 24.

————. *Literatura chilena del siglo XX*. 2nd ed. Santiago: Zig-Zag, 1962.

Amunátegui, Miguel Luis. *Las primeras representaciones dramáticas en Chile*. Santiago: Nacional, 1888.

Boyle, Catherine M. *Chilean Theater, 1973–1985: Marginality, Power Selfhood*. Rutherford, NJ: Fairleigh Dickinson Press, 1992.

————. "From Resistance to Revelation: The Contemporary Theatre in Chile." *New Theatre Quarterly* 4.15 (1988): 209–221.

————. "Images of Women in Contemporary Chilean Theatre." *Bulletin of Latin American Studies* 5.2 (1986): 81–96.

————. *Thematic Development in Chilean Theatre Since 1973: In Search of the Dramatic Conflict*. Cranbury, NJ: Fairleigh Dickinson Press, 1992.

Bravo-Elizondo, Pedro. *Cultura y teatro obrero en Chile. 1900–1930*. 3 vols. Madrid: Ediciones Michay, 1986.

————. *Raíces del teatro popular en Chile*. Guatemala City: Impresos D & M, 1991.

Brncic Juricic, Zlatko. *Historia del teatro en Chile*. Santiago: Editorial Universitaria, 1953.

————. "El Teatro chileno a través de cincuenta años." *Anales de la Universidad de Chile* 111 (1952): 113–169. Rpt. in *Desarrollo de Chile en la primera parte del siglo*. Santiago: Universidad de Chile, 1953, 358–416.

Cajiao Salas, Teresa, and Margarita Vargas. "An Overview of Contemporary Latin American Theater." In *Philosophy and Literature in Latin America: A Critical Assessment of the Current Situation*, ed. Jorge J. E. Gracia and Mireya Camurati. Albany: State University of New York Press, 1989.

Campbell, Margaret V. *The Development of the National Theater in Chile to 1842*. Gainesville: University of Florida, 1958.

Cánepa Guzmán, Mario. *Gente de teatro*. Santiago: Arancibia Hermanos, 1969.

————. *Historia del teatro en Chile*. Santiago: Editorial Universidad Técnica del Estado, 1974.

————. *El teatro obrero y social en Chile*. Santiago: Ediciones Cultura y Publicaciones del Ministerio de Educación, 1971.

Canovas, Rodrigo. *Lihn, Zurita, ICTUS, Radrigán: literatura chilena y experiencia autoritaria*. Santiago: FLASCO, 1986.

Castedo-Ellerman, Elena. *El teatro chileno de mediados del siglo XX*. Santiago: Andrés Bello, 1982.

Céspedes, Sergio. "Theatre in the Concentration Camps of Chile." *Theatre Quarterly* 6.24 (1976–1977): 13–21.

————. "Chilean Theater 1973–1993: The Playwrights Speak." (A roundtable discussion with Isidora Aguirre, Gregory Cohen, Ramón Griffero, and Égon Wolff.) *Review: Latin American Literature and Arts* 49 (Fall 1994): 84–89.

"Chile." *Escenarios de dos mundos: inventario teatral de Iberoamérica*. Vol. 2. Madrid: Centro de Documentación Teatral, 1988, 64–121. Articles by scholars.

Cristóbal, Juan. *La vida romántica de Alejandro Flores*. Santiago: Zig-Zag, n.d.

Díaz, Jorge. "Reflections on the Chilean Theatre." *Drama Review* 14.2 (1970): 84–86.

Durán-Cerda, Julio. "Actuales tendencias del teatro chileno." *Revista Interamericana de Bibliografía* 13 (1963): 152–175.

———. *Panorama del teatro chileno, 1842–1959*. Santiago: Editorial del Pacífico, 1959. (Prologue and six plays).

———. *Repertorio del teatro chileno, bibliografía, obras inéditas y estrenadas*. Santiago: Instituto de Literatura Chilena, 1962.

———. "El teatro en las tareas revolucionarias de la independencia de Chile." *Anales de la Universidad de Chile* 119 (3rd Quarter 1960): 227–235.

———, ed. *El teatro contemporáneo chileno*. Mexico City: Aguilar, 1970.

Ehrmann, Hans. "Chilean Theatre, 1970." *Latin American Theatre Review* 4.2 (1971): 65–68.

———. "Chilean Theatre: 1971–1973." *Latin American Theatre Review* 7.2 (Spring 1974): 39–43.

———. "Theatre in Chile: A Middle-Class Conundrum." *Drama Review* 14.2 (1970): 77–83.

Eidelberg, Nora. *Teatro experimental hispanoamericano, 1960–1980: la realidad social como manipulación*. Minneapolis: Institute for the Study of Ideologies and Literature, 1985.

Escudero, Alfonso María. *Apuntes sobre el teatro chileno*. Santiago: Editorial Salesiana, 1967.

Falino, L. P., Jr. "Theatre Notes from Chile." *Latin American Theatre Review* 3.2 (1970): 67–71.

Fernández, Teodosio. *El teatro chileno contemporáneo (1941–1973)*. Madrid: Playor, 1982.

Fernández Fraile, Maximino. *Historia de la literatura chilena*. 2 vols. Santiago: Editorial. Salesiana, 1994.

———. *Literatura chilena de fines del siglo xx*. Santiago: Editorial Don Bosco, 2002.

Fernández Navas, Luis. *Teatro visto a tontos y a locos*. Antofagasta, Chile: Taller de Liceo de Hombres, 1956.

Gamir Aparicio, Manuel. *Compendio histórico del teatro*. Santiago de Chile: Nacional, 1902.

García, Lautaro. "Anotaciones sobre el teatro en Chile." *Zig-Zag* (Special Issue) (December 1955): 248–253.

Garzón Céspedes, Francisco, ed. *Recopilación de textos sobre el teatro latinoamericano de creación colectiva*. Havanna: Casa de las Américas, 1978.

Gerez, Vicente. *La vida santiaguina*. Santiago: Gutenberg, 1879. Chapter 5 deals with "Nacimiento de la escena dramática."

Guerrero del Río, Eduardo. "Historia generacional del teatro chileno en el siglo XIX, a partir del discurso de Lastarria." *Cuadernos hispanoamericanos* 409 (July 1984): 117–128.

Gutiérrez, Sonia, ed. *Teatro popular y cambio social en América Latina*. Ciudad Universitaria Rodrigo Facio, Costa Rica: EDUCA, 1979.

Guzmán, Eugenio. "La violencia en el teatro de hoy." *Conjunto* 6 (January–March 1968): 25–35. Also published in *Textos* 1.4 (May 1971): 1–8.

Hernández, Roberto. *Los primeros teatros de Valparaíso*, Valparaíso, Chile: San Rafael, 1928.

Huneus Gana, Jorge. "Bosquejo histórico del teatro chileno." *Cuadro histórico de la producción intelectual de Chile*. Santiago: Universidad, 1910.

Hurtado, Maria de la Luz. *La dramaturgia chilena: 1960–1970*. Santiago: CENECA, 1983.

———. *Sujeto social y proyecto histórico en la dramaturgia chilena actual, 1 parte: constantes y variaciones entre 1960–1973*. Santiago: CENECA, 1983.

———. "Teatro y sociedad chilena: la dramaturgia de la renovación universitaria en 1950 y 1970." *Apuntes* 94 (March 1986): 7–64.

———, and Carlos Ochsenius. *Maneras de hacer y pensar el teatro en el Chile actual: el teatro ICTUS*. Santiago: CENECA, 1980.

———. *Seminario teatro chileno en la década del 80*. Santiago: CENECA, 1980.

Jara, René. Entry on Chile. Trans. David William Foster. *Handbook of Latin American Literature*. 2nd ed. Ed. David William Foster. New York and London: Garland, 1992, 123–128.

Jofré, Manuel Alcides. "Culture, Art, and Literature in Chile: 1973–1985." *Latin American Perspectives* 16.2 (Spring 1989): 70–95.

———. *Literatura chilena en el exilio*. Santiago: CENECA, 1986.

Jones, Willis Knapp. *Behind Spanish American Footlights*. Austin: University of Texas Press, 1966.

———. *Breve historia del teatro latinoamericano* Mexico City: Ediciones de Andrea, 1956.

———. "Chile's Dramatic Renaissance." *Hispania* 44.1 (March 1961): 89–94.

———. "New Life in Chile's Theater." *Modern Drama* 2.1 (May 1959): 57–62.

Krugh, Janis L. Interview with Gustavo Meza. June 16, 1994.

———. Interview with Juan Radrigán. June 26, 1994.

Latchman, Ricardo A. "Curtain Time in Chile." *Las América* 4.9 (September 1952): 16–19.

Latorre, Mariano. "Apuntes sobre el teatro chileno contemporáneo." *Atenea* (August 1948): 254–272, 281–282; (November–December 1948): 92–114.

———. "El teatro chileno en la colonia." *Atenea* 93.288 (June 1949): 462–472, 93.289 (July 1949): 138–151; 93.290 (August 1949): 291–302.

Layera, Ramón. "After the Coup; Four Dramatic Versions of Allende's Chile." *Latin American Theatre Review* 12.1 (Fall 1978): 39–42.

Literature Chilena 36–37 (Spring 1986–Summer 1986). Special issue on Chilean theater.

Luzuriaga, Gerardo, ed. *Popular Theatre for Social Change in Latin America*. Los Angeles: UCLA Latin American Center Publications, 1978.

María y Campos, Armando de. *Breve historia del teatro en Chile*. Mexico City: CEPSA, 1940.

Mora, Gabriela. "Notas sobre el teatro chileno actual." *Revista Iberoamericana de Bibliografía* 18 (1968): 415–421.

Morel Montes, Consuelo. "La escuela de teatro de la Universidad Católica de Chile: Principios pedagógicos." *Latin American Theatre Review* 27.1 (Fall 1993): 39–42.

Morgado, Benjamín. *Eclipse parcial del teatro chileno*. Santiago: Senda, 1943.

———. "El movimiento teatral chileno." *Conjunto* 7 (April–June 1968): 75–78.

Noguera, Héctor. "Hacia un teatro auténticamente chileno." *Conjunto* 13 (May–August 1972): 89–90.

———. "Notas para un panorama de teatro en Chile." *Primer Acto* 69 (1965): 27–30.

Norris, Ginjer Leanne. "Ariel Dorfman's "Death and the Maiden": Artistic Interpretations of a Politically Inspired Drama." B.A. dissertation, Madison University, 1995.

Ochsenius, Carlos. *Expresión teatral poblacional 1973–1982*. Santiago: CENECA, 1983.

———. *Teatros universitarios de Santiago, 1940–1973. El estado de la escena*. Santiago: CENECA, 1982.

Orrego Vicuña, Eugenio. *El nacionalismo en el teatro chileno*. Santiago: Universidad de Chile, 1927.

Peña, Nicolás. *Teatro dramático nacional*. Vol. IX. *Biblioteca de Escritores de Chile*. Santiago, Barcelona, 1912 and 1923. (Prologue and Seven Early Chilean Plays. 1817–1877.)

Perales, Rosalina. *Teatro hispanoamericano contemporáneo (1967–1987)*. Mexico City: Grupo Editorial Gaceta, 1993.

Pereira Poza, Sergio. "Prácticas teatrales innovadoras en la escena nacional chilena." In *Hacia una nueva crítica y un nuevo teatro latinoamericano*, ed. Alfonso de Toro and Fernando de Toro. Frankfurt am Main: Vervuert, 1993, 115–126.

Pereira Salas, Eugenio. *El teatro en Santiago de Nuevo Extremo, 1709–1809*. Santiago: Universitaria, 1941.

Pérez Coterillo, Moisés, ed. *Teatro chileno Contemporáneo*. Madrid: Fondo de Cultura Económica, 1992. (Anthology)

Petit, Magdalena. "The Little Theatres of Chile." *Bulletin of the Pan American Union* 82.10 (1948): 560–565.

Piga, Domingo. *Dos generaciones del teatro chileno*. Santiago: Editorial Bolívar, 1963.

———, and Orlando Rodríguez. *El teatro chileno del siglo XX*. Santiago: Imprenta Lathrop, 1964.

———. "El teatro obrero y social." *Teatro chileno del siglo veinte*. Santiago: Publicaciones de la Escuela de Teatro, Universidad Católica de Chile, 1964.

Piña, Juan Andrés, ed. *Teatro chileno en un acto (1955–1985)*. Santiago: Teatro Taller, 1989.

Rau Alliende, Erwin. "Breve reseña histórica del teatro aficionado chileno." *Conjunto* 13 (May–August 1972): 86–89.

Rela, Walter. *Contribución a la bibliografía del teatro chileno, 1804–1960*. Noticia preliminar de Ricardo A. Latchman. Montevideo: Universidad de la República, 1960.

Rizk, Beatriz. *El nuevo teatro latinoamericano: Una lectura histórica*. Minneapolis, MN: Prisma Institute, 1987.

Rodríguez, Orlando. "El teatro chileno contemporáneo." *Apuntes* 64 (November–December 1966): 1–41.

———. *Teatro chileno del siglo XX (Su dimensión Social)*. Quimantú: Editorial Nacional, 1973.

Rojo, Grínor. "Muerte y resurrección del teatro chileno: Observaciones preliminares." *Caravelle: Cahiers du Monde Hispanique et Luso-Brésilien* 40 (1983): 67–81.

———. *Muerte y resurrección del teatro chileno, 1972–1983*. Madrid: Libros del Meridión, 1985.

———. *Los orígenes del teatro hispanoamericano contemporáneo. La generación de dramaturgos de 1927: Dos direcciones*. Valparaíso: Ediciones Universitarias, 1972.

———. "Le Théâtre chilien contemporain." Trans. François López. *Europe* 570 (1976): 253–266.

Sienna, Pedro. *La vida pintoresca de Arturo Bührle*. Santiago: Osiris, 1933.

Sieveking, Alejandro. "Teatro chileno antifascista." In *Primer coloquio sobre la litera-*

tura chilena (de la resistencia y el exilio), ed. Poli Délano. Mexico City: Editorial Universitaria Autónoma, 1980, 97–113.

Silva, Victor Domingo. "Panorama del teatro chileno." *Máscaras* 1 (June 1930): 3–4; 3 (August 1930): 3–4; 4 (September 1930): 3–4.

Silva Castro, Raúl. "El drama." *Panorama literario de Chile*. Santiago: Universitaria, 1961.

Sotoconil, Rubén, ed. *Teatro escolar (manual y antología)*. Santiago: Austral, 1965.

———. *Teatro para escolares y aficionados*. Santiago: Ernesto Toro, 1952. (Anthology)

Suárez Radillo, Carlos Miguel. "El teatro chileno actual y las universidades como sus principales fuerzas propulsoras." *Inter-American* 1 (January–March 1972): 18–29.

Teatro chileno actual. Santiago: Zig-Zag, 1966.

Teatro chileno del siglo veinte. Santiago: Publicaciones de la Escuela de Teatro, Universidad Católica de Chile, 1964.

Tessier, Domingo. "El teatro experimental de la Universidad de Chile." *Revista de la Universidad de México* 11.3 (November 1956): 15–19.

"The Theatre in Chile: Before the Coup and After." *Theatre Quarterly* 5.20 (1976): 103–107.

Thomas, Charles P. "Chilean Theatre in Exile: The Teatro del Ángel in Costa Rica, 1974–1984." *Latin American Theatre Review* 19.2 (Spring 1986): 97–101.

Toro, Fernando de. "El teatro en Chile: ruptura y renovación. Perspectiva semiológica de los fenómenos de producción y recepción en los últimos doce años." *Le Théatre sous la contrainte*. Aix-en-Provence: Université de Provence, 1988. 237–248.

Torre, Guillermo de. "Nuevas direcciones del teatro." *Atenea* 299 (May 1950): 125–135.

Torres-Rivera, Rebeca. "The Theatre in Chile from 1941 to 1981." Ph.D. dissertation, University of California, Riverside, 1984.

Vargas de A., and Laura Ruth, eds. *Seis ensayos teatrales*. Santiago: Imprenta El Esfuerzo, 1934.

Vega, Daniel de la. *Luz de Candilejas: El teatro y sus miserias: 1920–1930*. Santiago: Nacimiento, 1930.

Vidal, Hernán. *Dictadura militar, trauma social e inaguración de la sociología del teatro en Chile*. Minneapolis: Institute for the Study of Ideologies and Literature, 1991.

———. *Poética de la población marginal: El teatro poblacional chileno, 1978–1985. Antología crítica*. Minneapolis: Institute for the Study of Ideologies and Literature, 1987.

———. *Teatro chileno de la crisis institucional (1973–1980). Antología crítica*, ed. María de la Luz Hurtado and Carlos Oschsenius. Santiago: CENECA, 1982.

Villegas, Juan. "Los marginados como personajes: teatro chileno de la decada de los sesenta." *Latin American Theatre Review* 19.2 (Spring 1986): 85–95.

———. "Teatro chileno y afianzamientos de los sectores medios." *Ideologies and Literature* 4.17 (September–October 1983): 306–319.

Vodanovic, Sergio. "La experimentación teatral chilena: Ayer, hoy mañana." *Revista EAC* 1 (1972): 8–16. Also published in *Popular Theater for Social Change in Latin America*, ed. Gerardo Luzuriaga. Los Angeles: UCLA, 1979, 102–115.

Yánez Silva, Nathanael. "Panorama de 150 años de teatro nacional." *La Nación* 18 (September 1960).

———. "Veinte años de teatro chileno." *Atenea* 90 (August 1932): 206–228.

Yrarrázaval, Paz D., Giselle Munizaga S. De Z., and Consuelo Morel M. "El teatro chileno en la segunda mitad del siglo XIX." *Apuntes* (Special Issue) (1981): 1–482.

◆

ACEVEDO HERNÁNDEZ, Antonio (1886–1962). Born in 1886, Acevedo Hernández was raised in southern Chile among the rural poor. A self-taught man, he worked for a time on a farm and saw firsthand the exploitation of tenant farmers by the oligarchy. In search of work he migrated in 1903 to Santiago, where he began writing. Acevedo Hernández is known as one of the most important Chilean playwrights of the first four decades of the twentieth century. His more than fifty works reflect the dialect, folklore, and the life of the rural poor of southern Chile and have been labeled as *costumbrista* (or theater of manners). Other plays deal with the problems of the urban poor. Nearly all demonstrate his preoccupation with issues of social justice in Chilean society. Essentially, his message deals with the need to educate the poor in order to improve their lot in life. One of his best known works, a four-act play titled *Chañarcillo* (Chañarcillo), was first staged in 1933 and was a box office hit.

WORKS: *El inquilino* (The Tenant), 1913. *El rancho* (The Hut), 1913. *La peste blanca* (The White Plague), 1914. *En el suburbio* (In the Slums), 1914. *Carcoma* (Woodworm), 1919. *Cain* (Cain) (Santiago: Nascimento, 1927); also in his *Teatro*. *Caín* (Cain), 1928. *Teatro* (Theater) (Santiago: Nascimento, 1927–1934). *Cabrerita* (Cabrerita) (Santiago: Nascimento, 1929); publ. in English with the same title, tr. Wilbur E. Bailey, in *Plays of the Southern Americas* (Stanford, CA: Stanford University Press 1942), reprinted under the same title (Freeport, NY: Books for Libraries Press 1971). *Camino de flores* (Bed of Flowers) (Santiago: Nascimento, 1929); also in his *Teatro*. *De pura cepa* (Of Pure Stock) (Santiago: Nascimento, 1929); also in his *Teatro*. *Un 18 típico* (A Typical Independence Day) (Santiago: Nascimento, 1929); also in his *Teatro*. *Quién quiere mi virtud!* (Who Wants My Virtue!) (Santiago: Nascimento, 1929); also in his *Teatro* and in *Apuntes* 25 (December 1962). *El milagro de la montaña* (Mountain Miracle), 1932. *Por el atajo* (The Shortcut) (Santiago: Nascimento, 1932); also in his *Teatro*. *Almas perdidas* (Lost Souls), 4th ed. (Santiago: Nascimento, 1932); also in his *Comedias*. *Angelica* (Angelica) (Santiago: Nascimento, 1933; also in his *Comedias*. *Arbol viejo* (The Old Tree) (Santiago:

Nascimento, 1934); also in his *Teatro* and in *Apuntes* 69 (April 1968). *La cancion rota* (The Chilean Song) (Santiago: Nascimento, 1933); in his *Teatro*; and in Julio Durán Cerda, ed., *Panorama del teatro chileno, 1842–1959* (Santiago: Ed. del Pacífico, 1959). *Cardo negro* (Black Thistle) (Santiago: Nascimento, 1933); also in his *Comedias* and *Teatro*. *Comedias* (Comedies) (Santiago: Nascimento, 1932–1933). *Joaquín Murieta* (Joaquín Murieta), in *Excelsior* 1, supp. 1 (August 1936): 3–30. *El torrente* (The Torrent), 1952. *Cuando la muerte habló* (When Death Spoke), 1953. *El triangulo tiene cuatro lados* (The Triangle Has Four Sides) (Santiago: Ediciones A. Acevedo Hernández, 1963). *Los caminos de Dios* (God's Ways), 1955. *Chañarcillo* (Chañarcillo) (Santiago: Ed. Ercilla, 1970); also in *Excelsior* 1.25 (1936): 32–66; in *Apuntes* 63 (October 1966); and in Willis Knapp Jones, ed., *Antología del teatro hispanoamericano* (Mexico City: Andrea, 1959); excerpt publ. in English under the same title in Willis Knapp Jones, ed., *Spanish American Literature in Translation: A Selection of Prose, Poetry, and Drama Since 1888*, vol. 2 (New York: Frederick Ungar, 1963).

BIBLIOGRAPHY: Raúl Barrientos, "Relación mítica entre el campesino y la tierra en tres dramas chilenos," *Antar* 1.1 (1974): 14–25. Juan Villegas, "Teatro chileno y afianzamiento de los sectores medios," *Ideologies and Literature* 4.17 (September–October 1983): 306–318.

AGUIRRE, Isidora (1921–). Aguirre, one of Chile's most highly acclaimed female playwrights, was born in 1921 in Santiago. A member of the Generation of 1957, she took classes in play writing at the Ministry of Education's Chilean Academy and studied film in France. Her career as a playwright was established in 1955 when the University of Chile's Experimental Theater staged three of her plays, one of which was *Carolina* (Express for Santiago). Primarily known as a playwright, Aguirre has authored and illustrated children's books and has written two novels. She has taught theater both in Chile and abroad. Several of her plays have won prestigious national and international prizes. One of Aguirre's first works to receive praise was *Población esperanza* (A Shanty Town Called Hope), a tragedy she wrote in collaboration with Manuel Rojas. This play deals with the plight of the poor and oppressed in Santiago and opened in 1959.

WORKS: *Carolina* (*Express for Santiago*) (Santiago: Teatro Experimental de la Universidad de Chile, 1955); also in *Apuntes* 46 (March 1965); in *Teatro chileno actual* (Santiago: Zig-Zag, 1966); in Juan Andrés Piña, ed., *Teatro chileno en un acto (1955–1985)* (Santiago: Teatro Taller, 1989); tr. as *Express for Santiago* by Stanley Richards, in Margaret Gardner Mayorga, ed., *Best Short Plays of 1959/60* (Dodd-Mead, 1961). *Anacleto Chinchín* (Anacleto Chinchin), 1956. *Pacto de medianoche* (Midnight Pact), 1956. *Las Pascualas* (The Pascualas) (Santiago, 1957). *Dos y dos son cinco* (Two and Two Are Five), 1957. *Población Esperanza* (A Shanty Town Called Hope), written in collaboration with Manuel Rojas, 1959. *Entre dos trenes* (Between Two Trains), in *Apuntes* 20 (April 1962). *La dama del canasto* (The Lady with the Basket), 1965. *Don Anacleto Avaro* (Don Anacleto Miser), 1965. p. in *Cinco obras en un acto* (Santigao: Ministerio de Educación Publica, 1982). *Las tres Pascualas* (The Three Pascualas), in *Poet Lore* 59.4 (1965); excerpt publ. in English in Willis Knapp Jones, ed., *Spanish American Literature in Translation: A Selection of Prose, Poetry, and Drama Since 1888*, vol. 2 (New York: Frederick Ungar, 1963). *La micro* (The Bus), in *Apuntes* 65 (December 1966). *El periodista* (The Journalist), in *Apuntes* 65 (December 1966). *Las sardinas o La supresión de Amanda* (Sardines, or Suppressing Amanda), in *Apuntes* 65 (December 1966). *Los que van quedando en el camino* (Ranquil or Those Left by the Wayside) (Santiago: Imprenta Müller, 1970); also (Santiago: Universidad de Chile, 1969); and in *Conjunto* 8 (1970): 61–98; (English tr. by Francis Horning Barraclough in preparation); p. in German as *Die Guten Tage, die Schlechten Tage* (Berlin: Ed. Dialog, 1974). *En aquellos locos aquellos locos años veinte* (In Those Crazy 1920s), 1974. *La pérgola de las flores* (The Flower Market) (Santiago: Andrés Bello, 1981); a radio adaptation appears in Carlos Miguel Suárez Radillo, ed., *Temas y estilos en el teatro hispanoamericano contemporáneo* (Madrid: Ed. Litho-Arte, 1975). *Lautaro* (Lautaro) (Santiago: Nascimento, 1982); also in *Apuntes* 89 (November 1982); and in Moisés Pérez Coterillo, ed., *Teatro chileno contemporáneo* (Madrid: Fondo de Cultura Económica, 1992), 1107–1193. *El amor a la africana* (Love African Style), 1986. *Federico hermano* (Brother Federico), 1986. *Retablo de Yumbel* (Altarpiece of Yumbel) (Havana: Casa de las Américas, 1987) and (Concepción: Ediciones Literatura Americana Reunida, 1987); (English translation by Teresa Cajiao Salas and Margarita Vargas in preparation). *Tía Irene, yo te amaba* (Aunt Irene, I Loved You), 1988. *Diálogos de fin de siglo* (End-of-the-Century Dialogues), in collaboration with Ictus (Santiago: Torsegel, 1989). *Los papeleros* (The Paper Collectors) (Santiago: Torsegel, 1989); also published in *Mapocho* 2.1 (1964): 57–93; and 245–290 in Carlos Solórzano, ed., *El teatro actual latinoamericano*, vol. 1 (México: Ediciones de Andrea, 1972). *Magy ante el espejo* (Maggy in Front of the Mirror), in *Tramoya* 30 (January–March, 1992): 3–15. *Los Liberatores: Bolivar y Miranda* (The Liberators: Bolivar and Miranda) (Santiago: Lar, 1993). *Los mancebos* (The Young Men), n.d.

BIBLIOGRAPHY: Marjorie Agosín, "Aguirre, Isidora: 'Carolina o la eterna enmascarada,' " *Letras Femeninas* 5.1 (1979): 97–100. Elba Andrade, "Isidora Aguirre," *Critical Survey of Drama* (Salem Press, Foreign Language Series) 1 (1986): 31–38. Enrique Bello, "Isidora Aguirre define los móviles de su teatro," *Ultramar* 4 (April 1960): 1–9. Judith Ishmael Bisset, "Delivering the Message: *Gestus* and Aguirre's *Los papeleros*," *Latin American Theatre Review* 17.2 (Spring 1984): 31–37. Pedro Bravo-Elizondo, "*Ranquil* y *Los que van quedando en el camino*," *Texto Crítico* 10 (1978): 76–85. Elena Castedo-Ellerman, *El teatro chileno de mediados del siglo XX* (Santiago: Andrés Bello, 1982), 179–187. Eleanora Maxwell Dial, "Brechtian Aesthetics in Chile: Isidora Aguirre's *Los papeleros* (The Garbage Collectors)," in *Latin American Women Writers: Yesterday and Today*, ed. Yvette E. Miller and Charles M. Tatum (Pittsburgh: Latin American Literary Review, 1977), 85–90. Inés Dolz Blackburn, "La historia en dos obras de teatro chileno contemporáneo," *Confluencia: Revista Hispánica de Cultura y Literatura* 6.2 (Spring 1991): 17–24.

ARRAU CASTILLO, Sergio (1928–). Arrau was born in Santiago in 1928 and is the cousin of internationally known pianist Claudio Arrau. A member of the Generation of 1957, he has written more than fifty plays, which mostly have been performed outside Chile. His work has won several awards, including the prestigious Andrés Bello Prize. *Santa María del Salitre* (St. Mary of Saltpeter), an example of documentary theater, won the Eugenio Dittborn Prize at the Third National Theater Competition in 1985. The play deals with the salt miners' strike and subsequent massacre at Iquique in 1907.

WORKS: *La multa* (The Fine), in *Apuntes* 77 (July 1969). *Orllie-Antoine de Tounens*, n.d. *Ruca-pequenización del membrillo* (The Cutting of the Quince Tree), in *Apuntes* 77 (July 1969). *Digo que norte sur corre la tierra* (I Say the Land Runs North and South) (Lima: Lluvia Editores, 1982); also in *Tramoya* 33 (October–December 1992): 158–213; and in Supplement to *El Público* 92 (1992). *El padre del teatro venezolano y Entre ratas y gorriones* (The Father of Venezuelan Theater and Between Rats and Sparrows) (Caracas: Concurso Andrés Bello, 1983). *El rey de la Araucanía* (The King of Araucania), in *Caravelle* 40 (1983). *Santa María del Salitre* (St. Mary of Saltpeter), 1985. *Marijuana*, n.d. *El limbo* (The Limb), n.d. *Lisístrata González* (Lysistrata González), n.d. *Manuel viene galopando por las alamedas* (Here Comes Manuel Galloping Down the Boulevards), n.d. *Secretario de Estado* (Secretary of State), n.d. *El rey jabonero* (The Soap King), n.d.

BIBLIOGRAPHY: Pedro Bravo-Elizondo, "Gradación y degradación intertextual en *Digo que norte sur corre la tierra*," *Alba de América* 10.18–19 (July 1992): 135–140. Bravo-Elizondo, "Sergio Arrau, el dramaturgo ignorado," *Latin American Theater Review* 23.1 (Fall 1989): 135–142. Bravo-Elizondo, "*Santa María del Salitre*: Recuperación de un drama de la historia," *Literatura Chilena: Creación y Crítica* 10.2–3 (April–September 1986): 17–20.

BARELLA, Carlos (1893–1961). Even though he was a journalist, editor of journals, poet, and novelist, Barella was known mostly as a playwright, writing plays for both children and adults in poetry and prose. He served as vice president of the Association of Theater Authors of Chile, as well as the director of the National Theater. He was awarded Chile's annual prize for theater in 1960. Most of his plays date from the first quarter of the twentieth century, but a few were written in the 1930s and 1940s. He sometimes wrote works in collaboration with other Chilean playwrights (e.g., René Hurtado Borne or Roberto López). Most of his plays were social or historical in nature. His most significant work was undoubtedly *Manuel Rodríguez*, which won the Municipal Prize in the historical category in 1941.

WORKS: *Fatalidad* (Fate), 1912. *El triunfo de la vida* (The Triumph of Life), 1915. *Los culpables* (The Guilty Ones), 1916. *También la gente del pueblo . . .* (The Townspeople Too . . .), 1918. *Un drama vulgar* (An Ordinary Drama), 1920. *Hotel Chile, atendido por su propio dueño* (The Chile Hotel, Served by Its Owner), 1928. *Rajadiablos* (Devils), 1928. *Papú, papú* (Papuan, Papuan), 1934. *Lo llamaban Agitador* (He Was Called Agitator), 1939. *Manuel Rodríguez* (Manuel Rodríguez), 1941.

BARRA, Pedro de la (1912–1978). Barra was born in Talca in 1912. Having studied at the University of Chile, he and some associates from Santiago put together a theater company that traveled to southern Chile, performing classical Spanish plays by Lope de Rueda and Cervantes. In 1941 he was involved in the founding of the Experimental Theater at the University of Chile, where he was its first director. His work as director was noteworthy, winning him the National Art Prize in the theater category in 1953. He later became the director of the Theater of Antofagasta, a position he occupied until 1975 when he was removed from his position by the military. He died in exile in Caracas, Venezuela, on July 6, 1978. In 1980 the Actors' Union SINDARTE organized the Pedro de la Barra Theater Festival to be held annually in his memory. Barra believed that in order to have a truly national theater national themes must be presented in the works staged. His best-known play was undoubtedly *Viento de proa* (Headwind), which was first performed in London in 1948. Although he was primarily known as a director, Barra also authored a few plays; however, most of his works remain unpublished.

WORKS: *La feria* (The Fair), 1939. *Viento de proa* (Headwind), 1948. *La piojera*, 1958.

BARRIOS, Eduardo (1884–1963). Barrios was born in Valparaíso on October 25, 1884, and died on September 13, 1963. He had a long, distinguished career as a public servant in Chile, where he worked as the director of libraries, archives, and museums. He also served as Minister of Education during the administration of President Carlos Ibáñez (1927–1931). In literature he was primarily known for his psychological novels, but he also wrote several plays that were critical of Chile's social system. The theater works also contain psychological development of characters that is so typical of his best novels. *Por el decoro* (For the Sake of a Good Reputation), a one-act comedy that satirizes bureaucracy and the Chilean elites, was first produced in 1913.

WORKS: *Mercaderes en el templo* (Merchants in the Temple), 1911. *Vivir* (To Live) (Santiago: Imp. Universitaria, 1916). *Lo que niega la vida* (What Life Denies), in *Teatro escogido* (Santiago, 1947). *Por el decoro* (For the Sake of a Good Reputation), in *Teatro escogido* and in *Apuntes* 29 (June 1963); English tr. in Willis Knapp Jones ed., in *Short Plays of the Southern Americas* (Stanford, CA: Stanford University Press, 1944). *Teatro escogido: Vivir. Lo que niega la vida. Por el decoro* (Selected Theater: To Live. What Life Denies. For the Sake of a Good Reputation) (Santiago, 1947).

BIBLIOGRAPHY: Ned J. Davidson, *Eduardo Barrios* (New York: Twayne, 1970). Juan Villegas, "Teatro chileno y afianzamientos de los sectores medios," *Ideologies and Literature* 4.17 (September–October 1983): 306–319.

BARROS GREZ, Daniel (1834–1906). Barros Grez was the best known Chilean playwright of the last quarter of the nineteenth century. *Costumbrismo*, or the comedy of manners, was an important part of his work. Many of his plays were comedies about the fickleness of love among characters representing the middle class (e.g., *La colegiala* [The Schoolgirl]). *El casi casamiento* (The Almost Marriage), first staged in 1881, is an adaptation of a chapter from his novel *El huérfano* (The Orphan), which also deals with the theme of love. His most memorable play is undoubtedly *Como en Santiago* (As They Do in Santiago), a three-act comedy of manners that takes place in a provincial town where residents wish to imitate life in Santiago. As a young woman from the town is duped by the city slicker, the clash of rural and urban values is clearly seen.

WORKS: *La colegiala* (The Schoolgirl), in *Revista de Chile* 3 (1873): 277–291. *El tejedor, o La batalla de Maipú* (The Weaver, or The Battle of Maipú) (Talca: Imp. de La Opinión, 1873). *Cada oveja con su pareja* (Every Jack Has His Jill), 1879, in his *Teatro*. *Como en Santiago* (As They Do in

Santiago) (Santiago: Imp. Gutenberg, 1881); (Santiago: Ed. Universitaria, 1954); (Santiago: Nascimento, 1983); in his *Teatro*; in Gerardo Luzuriaga et al., *Los clásicos del teatro hispanoamericano* (Mexico City: Fondo de Cultura Económica, 1975); and in Julio Durán Cerda, ed., *Panorama del teatro chileno, 1842–1959* (Santiago: Ed. del Pacífico, 1959). *El casi casamiento* (The Almost Marriage), in *El casi casamiento o mientras más vieja más verde* and *El vividor* (Santiago: Nuevo Extremo, 1959). *El vividor* (The Opportunist), in *El casi casamiento* and *El vividor* (Santiago, 1959); and in his *Teatro*. *El tribunal del honor* (The Court of Honor), in *Apuntes* 63 (October 1966). *El ensayo de la comedia* (The Play Rehearsal), in his *Teatro* (1975). *Teatro* (Theater) (Santiago: Nascimento, 1975). *El avaro* (The Miser), in *Apuntes* 85 (November 1979).

BIBLIOGRAPHY: Eduardo Jiménez Tornatore, "Aproximación actancial a *Como en Santiago*," *Anales del Instituto Ibero-Americano* 1.3–4 (1991–1992): 39–52.

BENAVENTE P., David (1941–). Benavente was born in Santiago in 1941 and thus is considered a member of the Generation of 1972. He was educated at the Catholic University of Chile, where he specialized in sociology and became interested in theater. He studied theater, film, and television in the United States and in Europe. Benavente's *Tengo ganas de dejarme barba* (I Feel Like Letting My Beard Grow) depicts the world of adolescence in which Nacho faces his uncertainties about what to do in life and the differences between the values of the young and the old. Most of his later works are critical views of the political and economic conditions in Chile during the latter part of the 1970s.

WORKS: *La ganzúa* (The Thief), in *Apuntes 58* (May 1966). *Tengo ganas de dejarme barba* (I Feel Like Letting My Beard Grow), in *Mapocho 17* (1968): 97–152. *Tejado de viario* (Glass Roof), 1972. *Pedro, Juan y Diego* (Tom, Dick and Harry), in collaboration with Ictus, 1976. *Pedro, Juan y Diego/Tres Marías y una Rosa* (Tom, Dick, and Harry/ Three Marías and One Rosa) (Santiago: CESOC, 1976). *Bienaventurados los pobres* (Blessed Are the Poor), in collaboration with Jaime Vadell and José Manuel Salcedo (Santiago: Ediciones Aconcagua, 1978). *Tres Marías y una Rosa* (Three Marías and One Rosa), in Moisés Pérez Coterillo ed., *Teatro chi-*

leno contemporáneo (Madrid: Fondo de Cultura Económica, 1992), 877–960; and in María de la Luz Hurtado et al., eds., *Teatro chileno de la crisis institucional* (Minneapolis: University of Minnesota and Santiago: CENECA, 1982), 196–248. *Hug*, in collaboration with Jorge Cánepa, n.d.

BIBLIOGRAPHY: Catherine M. Boyle, *Chilean Theater, 1973–1985* (Cranbury, NJ: Fairleigh Dickinson University Press, 1992) (pp. 64–70 on *Pedro Juan y Diego*, pp. 78–84 on *Tres Marías y una Rosa*). "Conversando con David Benavente," *Teatro en las Américas* 1.1 (Spring 1981): 9–10. Hans Ehrmann, "Teatro postgolpe: Pedro, Juan, María y Rosa," *Gestos* 4.8 (November 1989): 155–161. W. Nick Hill, "Signos de la modernidad como autoreflexión crítica en el teatro chileno contemporáneo," *Alba de América* 8.14–15 (July 1990): 245–251.

BUNSTER, Enrique (1912–1976). Born in 1912, Bunster was the descendant of an English sailor who had come ashore in Chile in the eighteenth century to steal pigs. He began his career as an author writing short stories but turned to writing plays. Bunster was particularly interested in historical topics dealing with the sea and travels, as his two most remembered plays, *Un velero sale del puerto* (A Sailing Ship Leaves Port) and *La isla de los bucaneros* (The Island of the Buccaneers), illustrate.

WORKS: *Teatro verosímil* (Credible Theater), 1933. *Casa de locos* (Insane Asylum), 1937. *Un velero sale del puerto* (A Sailing Ship Leaves Port), 1937. *El hombre y sus recuerdos* (The Man and His Memories), 1938. *El tren de carga* (The Freight Train), 1938. *La isla de los bucaneros* (The Island of the Buccaneers), in *Teatro* 1.1 (November 1945): 17–74. *Nadie puede saberlo* (No One Can Know About It), 1953. *Teatro breve: Un velero se hace a la mar. Nadie puede saberlo* (Short Plays: A Sailing Ship Goes to Sea. No One Can Know About It), 1953. *El ministro salteador* (The Thieving Minister), 1962.

CAMPAÑA, Gustavo (1902–1958). Most of Campaña's work was written between 1921 and 1941 and is in a light, comical vein. Although these kinds of works were popular in Chile at the time, they have lost much of their appeal since the reforms of university theaters in the 1950s. Campaña sometimes wrote in collaboration with Pedro J. Malbrán. His production includes some radio plays. He was honored for his lifetime achievement in theater in 1956 with Chile's annual prize. One of his most memorable works, written in 1938, is probably *Tarzán en el matadero* (Tarzan in the Slaughterhouse), a one-act comedy in which Jane takes a room in a boarding house, promising to pay the rent as soon as her husband arrives.

WORKS: *La casa del tío* (The Uncle's House), 1921. *¡Que viene el lobo!* (The Wolf Is Coming!), 1922. *Superavit* (Surplus), 1931. *Departamento de lujo* (Deluxe Apartment), 1936. *Esta copia feliz del Edén* (This Happy Copy of Eden), 1939. *Yo quiero ser gigoló* (I Want to Be a Gigolo), in *Revista Teatral. La Escena* 66 (1941): 1–16. *La cola de la Bencina* (The Last of the Benzine), 1942. *Tarzán en el matadero* (Tarzan in the Slaughterhouse), in *Apuntes* 51 (August 1965); and in *Revista Teatral. La Escena* 63 (1938): 1–14.

CÁNEPA [GUZMÁN], Mario (1919–   ). Although he has written both poetry and fiction, Cánepa is especially well known for his research on Chilean theater, having authored such works as *Historia del teatro chileno* (History of Chilean Theater) (1974); *El teatro en Chile desde los indios hasta los teatros universitarios* (Theater in Chile from the Indians to the University Theaters) (1966); *Gente de teatro* (Theater People) (1969); and *El teatro obrero y social en Chile* (Social and Workers' Theater in Chile, 1971). Cánepa also wrote several plays in the 1950s and 1960s.

WORKS: *Bendita sea mi suegra* (Blessed Be My Mother-in-Law), 1951. *El indiecito valiente* (The Brave Little Indian), 1953. *El amor llama una vez* (Love Comes Along Only Once), 1954. *Se rematan mujeres* (Putting Women out of Their Misery), 1954. *Yo no puedo vivir sin tu mujer* (I Can't Live without Your Wife), 1955. *El salario de Judas* (Judas' Salary), 1964.

CARIOLA [VILLAGRÁN], Carlos (1895–1960). Known as an actor, playwright, and theater critic, Cariola was one of the founders of the Association of Theater Authors of Chile. In addition to the comedies of manners so typical of his period, Cariola also wrote theater for children, as well as musical reviews. He also was involved in silent movies. In 1953 Chile awarded him its annual prize for his work in theater. His most memorable work is undoubtedly *Entre gallos y medianoche* (At an Unearthly Time), a comedy performed in 1919 by Enrique Báguena's theater company. The play was subsequently popularized by Rafael Frontaura and has become one of Chile's most popular and classical comedies, having been performed more than 200 times by a variety of groups.

WORKS: *Entre gallos y medianoche* (At an Unearthly Time) (Santiago: Imp. Universitaria, 1920); and in *Finis Terrae* 4.13 (1957): 35–61. *On parle français (se habló castellano)* (One Speaks French [One Speaks Spanish]) (Santiago: Nascimento, 1923). *Agua que no has de beber* (Water You Don't Have to Drink), n.d. *Dieta parlamentaria* (Parliamentarian Diet), n.d. *Doña Dorotea Dueñas dueña* (Doña Dorothy Dueñas, Proprietress), n.d. *Estos muchachos de cincuenta años* (These Fifty-Year-Old Boys), n.d. *¡Qué vergüenza para la familia!* (What a Disgrace for the Family!), n.d. *Todo lo arreglan los gringos* (The Gringos Will Arrange Everything), n.d. *El tuerto es rey* (The One-Eyed Person Is King), n.d.

CASTRO, Oscar (19?–   ). Known as a playwright, actor, and director, Castro founded the group El Aleph in 1968. This theater group was one of the first to experiment with collective creation in Chile and had a large following there. He, along with others in the group, spent at least ten years (1976–1986) in exile in Paris during the military regime, but he returned to Chile afterward. His best known play is *La increíble y triste historia del general Peñaloza y del exiliado Mateluna* (The Incredible and Sad Story of General Peñaloza and the Exile Mateluna), which was the group's first production in France in 1976 under the title *L'incroyable et triste histoire du Général Peñaloza et de l'exilé Mateluna*. The play in its original form intertwined the stories of the dictator General Peñaloza and a political refugee, Fernando Mateluna Rojas, living in Paris.

WORKS: *Casimiro Peñafleta, preso político* (Casimiro Peñafleta, Political Prisoner), 1978. *Sálvese quien pueda* (Whoever Can, Save Yourself), coauthor with Carlos Genovese, in *Apuntes* 86 (July 1980). *La guerra* (War), n.d. *La increíble y triste historia del general Peñaloza y del exiliado Mateluna* (The Incredible and Sad Story of General Peñaloza and the Exile Mateluna), n.d. *La noche suspendida* (Suspended Night), n.d.

BIBLIOGRAPHY: Jacqueline Baldran, "Entretien avec Oscar Castro," *Cahiers du Monde Hispanique et Luso-Brésilien: Caravelle* 40 (1983): 69–77. Oscar Castro, "La increíble y triste historia del Teatro Aleph, escrita por su propio director," *Apsi* 5.100 (June 2–15, 1981): 14–16. Ariel Dorfman, "In the Concentration Camps of Chile," *Canadian Theater Review* 22 (Spring 1979): 48–66. Dorfman, "El teatro en los campos de concentración: Entrevista a Oscar Castro," *Araucaria de Chile* 6 (1979): 115–146. Fernando de Toro, "Entrevista de Fernando de Toro con Oscar Castro del Teatro Aleph," *Iberoamericana* 22–23 (1984): 153–162.

CERDA, Carlos (1942–   ). Like many other contemporary Chilean writers, Cerda spent more than ten years in exile during the military regime. A member of the Generation of 1972, Cerda has written novels, essays, and theater. Cerda's two most significant plays were productions staged by the group Ictus. *Lo que está en el aire* (What Is in the Air) premiered in Santiago on January 6, 1986, under the direction of Delfina Guzmán and Nissim Sharim. This work was originally written as a radio play by Cerda and Omar Saavedra Santis, which they titled *Un tulipán, una piedra, una espada . . .* (A Tulip, a Stone, a Sword . . .) and which was broadcast in West Germany.

WORKS: *Lo que está en el aire* (What Is in the Air), in collaboration with Ictus (Santiago: Sinfronteras, 1986). *Este domingo* (This Sunday), in collaboration with José Donoso (Santiago: Andrés Bello, 1990), in *Apuntes* 100 (June 1990).

BIBLIOGRAPHY: Inés Dolz Blackburn, "La historia en dos obras de teatro chileno contemporáneo," *Confluencia* 6.2 (Spring 1991): 17–24. Manuel Jofré, "Carlos Cerda narrador: Chile y el exilio: dos mitades de silencio," *Apsi* 3–9 (April 1984): 34–35. Ursula Sydow, "Carlos Cerda: Kein Reisender ohne Gepack," *Weimarer Beitrage: Zeitschrift für Literaturwissenschaft, Asthetik und Kulturtheorie* 36.2 (1990): 325–334.

CHESTA [ARÁNGUIZ], José (1936–1962). Born in Temuco in 1936, Chesta showed great promise as a playwright before his untimely death in 1962. All of his works are social in nature, mostly dealing with the real problems of fishermen or miners living near Concepción. *Las redes del mar* (The Nets from the Sea) premiered in 1959 in a production by the Theater of the University of Concepción and was restaged in 1963. This theater group also performed his two-act play *El umbral* (The Threshold) in 1967 and again in the early 1970s. This work depicts the violence of a strike by miners in Lota and Coronel.

WORKS: *Las redes del mar* (The Nets from the Sea, 1959) (Concepción: Imp. de la Universidad de Concepción, 1963). *El umbral* (The Threshold), 1960. *Cruces hacia el mar* (Crossings Towards the Sea, 1961) (Santiago: Ed. Universitaria, 1962).

BIBLIOGRAPHY: Teodosio Fernández, *El teatro chileno contemporáneo (1941–1973)* (Madrid: Playor, 1982), 102–105.

COHEN, Gregory (1953–). A member of the Generation of 1987 (or the "Lost Generation"), Cohen is known as a poet, novelist, actor, playwright, and director. He has been associated with the Teatro de Cámara (Chamber Theater) and has appeared as an actor in productions of Josseau's *Demencial Party* (Demented Party) in 1983 and *Su Excelencia el Embajador* (His Excellency the Embassador) in 1982. *Adivina la comedia*, a surrealistic play dominated by the themes of oppression, the absurd, and the lack of communication, was staged in 1981 by the Grupo del Teniente Bello under Cohen's direction and was sponsored by the French-Chilean Institute of Culture. The play won a prize in the Fourth Theater Festival of the University Cultural Association (Agrupación Cultural Universitaria).

WORKS: *Lily, yo te quiero* (Lily, I Love You), 1980. *Adivina la comedia*, 1981. *Estación los héroes* (Heroes' Station), 1982. *Diálogos de Napoleón y Bolívar* (Dialogues of Napoleon and Bolivar), 1983. *La pieza que falta* (The Missing Part), in collaboration with Roberto Brodsky, 1986. *A fuego lento* (On Low Heat), 1988. *Bienvenidos todos* (Everyone Welcome), 1994.

BIBLIOGRAPHY: Pedro Bravo-Elizondo, "El discurso crítico metateatral de Gregory Cohen y Marco Antonio de la Parra, dramaturgos de la 'Generación Perdida,' " *Confluencia* 5.1 (Fall 1989): 31–34. Bravo-Elizondo, "Teatro de Cámara, Gregory Cohen y *A fuego lento*," *Gestos: Teoría y práctica del Teatro Hispánico* 6.12 (November 1991): 189–192.

CÓRDOBA, Lucho (?–1981). Born in Peru, Córdoba emigrated to Chile and became known as an actor, director, and playwright. In 1937, he, along with Olvido Leguía, set up a theater company that was recognized for its light entertainment in the 1930s and 1940s. He continued to be an active participant in Chilean theater until his death in 1980. In 1969 the Córdoba-Leguía theater company performed his sarcastically humorous play *¿Qué haremos con los momios?* (What Shall We Do with the Conservatives?), in which the author pokes fun of Chile's right-wing politicians.

WORKS: *A mí me lo contaron* (They Told Me), coauthor with Américo Vargas, in *Apuntes* 47 (April 1965). *¿Qué haremos con los momios?* (What Shall We Do with the Conservatives?), 1969. *No me atropelle, soy de la UNCTAD* (Don't Run Over Me, I'm From the United Nations Commission on Trade and Development), 1972. *El aprendiz de Drácula* (Dracula's Apprentice), in *Apuntes* 92 (September 1984). *La última noche que pasé contigo* (The Last Night I Spent with You), n.d.

CUADRA PINTO, Fernando (1925–). Born in Rancagua in 1925, Cuadra studied at the University of Chile. He is also a professor of literature and dramaturgy there, as well as the dean of the Department of Arts. A member of the Generation of 1957, he is one of Chile's well-known contemporary playwrights and directors, as well as the director and founder of the theater school "La Casa." Many of his works are realistic in tone and deal with social themes. Cuadra's most successful and memorable plays are *La niña en la palomera* (The Girl in the Attic) and *La familia de Marta Mardones* (Martha Mardones' Family). The latter, a three-act play staged by TEKNOS in 1976, later became a television serial that reflected traditional values of Chile's middle class.

WORKS: *Cinco lagartos* (Five Lizards), 1943. *Encrucijada* (The Crossroads), 1945. *Las Medeas* (The Medeas), 1948. *La ciudad de Dios* (The City of God), 1949. *Las murallas de Jerico* (The Walls of Jericho) (Santiago: Sec. Publ. del ITUCH, 1952). *Elisa* (Elise), 1953. *La desconocida* (The Stranger), 1954. *La vuelta al hogar* (The Return Home), 1956. *El diablo está en Machalí* (The Devil Is in Machalí), 1958. *Los sacrificados* (The Sacrificed), 1959. *El mandamás* (The Bigwig), 1960. *Rancagua 1814* (Rancagua 1814), 1960. *Las avestruces* (The Ostriches), 1962. *Pan amargo* (Bitter Bread), 1964. *Coloquios para una tarde de otoño* (Conversations for an Autumn Afternoon), 1965. *Doña tierra* (Doña Land), in *Apuntes* 64 (November 1966) and in his *Teatro*. *Los últimos días* (The Last Days), adaptation of Fernando Rivas's novel, 1966. *El romance de Miguel con la María* (Miguel's Romance with María), 1968. *Con el sol en las redes* (With the Sun in the Nets), in *Apuntes* 75 (May 1969). *Los ocelotes* (The Ocelots), 1969. *Galileo Galilei*, 1970. *La niña en la palomera* (The Girl in the Attic) (Santiago: Ed. Ercilla, 1970); (Santiago: Pehuén, 1987); and in his *Teatro*. *Chilean Love*, 1975. *El corderito dorado y la princesa Mañunga* (The Little Golden Lamb and Princess Mañunga), theater for children, 1975. *Preludio y fuga para dos* (Prelude and Fugue for Two), 1975. *La familia de Marta Mardones* (The Family of Marta Mardones) (Santiago: University of Chile, 1976); in his *Teatro* (Santiago: Nascimento, 1979); and in *Mapocho* 24 (1977): 103–166. *Un día en la vida de Amelia Riquelme* (A Day in the Life of Amelia Riquelme), 1978. *Teatro* (Theater) (Santiago: Nascimento, 1979). *El día que comenzó la investigación de la muerte de Lidia Fernández* (The Day They Began the Investigation into the Death of Lydia Fernández), 1980. *Ultimo balance* (Last Balance Sheet), 1985. *Huinca emperador* (Emperor Huinca), 1986.

DEBESA [MARÍN], Fernando (1921–). Born in Santiago in 1921, Debesa is associated with the Generation of 1957. Having studied architecture at the Catholic University of Chile, he was one of the founders of the Teatro de Ensayo at that institution. He extended his training in the theater in the mid-1950s when he studied drama at Yale University. His works tend to be *costumbrista*, historical, or psychological in nature. Debesa's most famous play, *Mama Rosa* (Mama Rosa), a five-act *costumbrista* tragedy, is considered one of the classics of contemporary Chilean theater. Written in 1956 while he was studying at Yale University, the play outlines fifty years in the life of a bour-

geois family and their loyal servant, Mama Rosa.

WORKS: *Bernardo O'Higgins*, in *Escenario* 1.3 (June 1961): 7–29. *Primera persona, singular* (First Person, Singular), in *Apuntes* 33 (October): 4–22. *El enemigo de los perros* (The Dogs' Enemy), in *Apuntes* 41 (August 1964). *El guaraapelo* (The Locket), in *Mapocho* 4.1 (1965): 57–66. *Persona y perro* (Person and Dog), in *Teatro chileno actual* (Santiago: Zig-Zag, 1966). *Mama Rosa* (Nanny Rosa) (Santiago: Ed. Universitaria, 1969, 1983, 1990); (Santiago: Nuevo Extremo, 1958); in *Apuntes* 64 (November 1966); and 113–214 in *Teatro chileno contemporáneo*, ed. Moisés Pérez Coterillo (Madrid: Fondo de Cultura Económica, 1992). *El árbol Pepe* (The Tree Joe), in *Teatro chileno contemporáneo* (Santiago: Ed. Andrés Bello, 1982). *El guerrero de la paz* (The Warrior of Peace) (Santiago: Ed. Universitaria, 1984) and in *Mapocho* 18 (Summer 1969): 113–164.

BIBLIOGRAPHY: Elena Castedo-Ellerman, *El teatro chileno de mediados del siglo XX* (Santiago: Andrés Bello, 1982), 187–200.

DEL CAMPO, Santiago (1916–1962). Born in 1916, del Campo was known as a playwright, drama critic, and journalist. Undoubtedly, his greatest success as a playwright was *Martín Rivas*, which was based on Blest Gana's nineteenth-century novel by the same name. This play was performed by the Teatro de Ensayo at the Catholic University in 1954. *California*, a poetic play, was awarded the Municipal Prize in 1939 and was staged in Argentina and Mexico, as well as in Chile.

WORKS: *Paisaje en destierro* (Countryside in Exile), 1937. *California* (California), 1939. *Que vienen los piratas* (The Pirates Are Coming), 1942. *No siempre amanece* (Day Doesn't Always Break), 1946. *Tres comedias de guerra* (Three War Comedies), 1946. *El hombre que regresó* (The Man Who Came Back), 1947. *Morir por Catalina* (Dying for Catalina), 1948. *El depravado Acuña* (Depraved Acuña), 1953. *Martín Rivas* (Martín Rivas), 1954. *La casada infiel* (The Unfaithful Wife), 1961. *K. O. Ramírez* (K. O. Ramírez), 1961. *Otra vez como antes* (Again Like Before), in *Apuntes* 26 (May 1963).

DÍAZ [GUTIÉRREZ], Jorge (1930–). Born of Spanish parents in Córdoba, Argentina, in 1930, Díaz was a young child when his family moved to Chile in 1934. He later became a Chilean citizen. In 1955 he completed his university studies in architecture at the Catholic University in Santiago, where he subsequently studied theater. In 1959 he joined the professional theater company Ictus, working first as an actor and set designer. A few years later he began writing works for the group to perform, including *El cepillo de dientes* (The Toothbrush). In 1965 Díaz emigrated to Spain, where he has, for the most part, continued to live. He has held dual citizenship (Chilean-Spanish) since 1975.

A member of the Generation of 1957, Díaz is one of Chile's most prolific and internationally renowned playwrights, appreciated for his theater of the Absurd, use of black humor and irony, and integration of lighting and musical effects, set design, and costuming. Predominant themes in his theater revolve around solitude, the lack of—perhaps even the impossibility of—real communication, and the inadequacy of language as a vehicle for communication, alienation, marginalization, and sociopolitical concerns. The use of ritual and cyclical time are hallmarks of his works. Díaz's best-known play in the Absurd vein, already a classic in Latin American theater, is *El cepillo de dientes* (The Toothbrush). Originally written as a one-act play, this work premiered in Santiago in 1961 in a production by Ictus. This play was staged at a Latin American theater festival/symposium at the University of Kansas in 1982 by the New York–based group Nuestro Teatro. It was also performed by another group at the First Theater Festival in Los Angeles in August 1982. Expanded to two acts in a 1966 revision, the work is a farce that presents a day in the life of a young married couple. Through it Díaz shows the lack of communication and values so prevalent in contemporary society.

WORKS: *La paloma y el espino* (The Dove and the Hawthorn), 1956. *Manuel Rodríguez* (Manuel Rodríguez), 1957. *El cepillo de dientes, o Náufragos en el parque de atracciones* (The Toothbrush, or Shipwrecked People in the Amusement Park), first version (1961) in *Apuntes* 16 (October 1961); second version (1966) in Julio Durán-Cerda, ed., *Teatro contemporáneo chileno* (Mexico City: Aguilar,

1970); also in Frank Dauster, Leon Lyday, and George Woodyard, eds., *9 dramaturgos hispanoamericanos: Antología del teatro del siglo XX*, vol. 3 (Ottawa, Ontario: Girol Books, 1979), 63–120; in Elena Paz and Gloria Waldman, eds., *Teatro contemporáneo* (Boston: Heinle & Heinle, 1983); and in Díaz's collection *Teatro: La víspera del degüello . . .* (Madrid: Taurus, 1967). *Un hombre llamado Isla* (A Man Called Island), 1961. *Réquiem por un girasol* (Requiem for a Sunflower), 1961, in Díaz's *Teatro: La víspera del degüello . . .* (Madrid: Taurus, 1967). *El lugar donde mueren los mamíferos* (The Place Where the Mammals Die) (Santiago: Teatro Ictus, 1963), in *Mapocho* 3.3 (1965): 107–142; in L. Howard Quackenbush, ed., *Teatro absurdo hispanoamericano* (Mexico City: Editorial Patria, 1987); and English tr. by Naomi Nelson, in George Woodyard, ed., *The Modern Stage in Latin America: Six Plays; An Anthology* (New York: E. P. Dutton, 1971). *El velero en la botella* (The Sailboat in the Bottle), in *Mapocho* 1.1 (March 1963): 53–84; in *Primer Acto* 69 (1965): 38–54; and in *El velero en la botella / El cepillo de dientes* (Santiago: Ed. Universitaria, 1967; 1973). *Canciones para sordos: Variaciones para muertos en percusión* (Songs for the Deaf: Variations for the Percussive Dead), in *Conjunto* 1 (July–August 1964): 17–48. *La mala noche de don Etcétera* (Don Et Cetera's Bad Night), in *Apuntes* 45 (December 1964). *Variaciones para muertos en percusión* (Variations for the Percussive Dead), in *Conjunto* 1 (July–August 1964): 17–48. *El nudo ciego* (The Blind Knot), 1965. *Canción de cuna para un decapitado* (Lullaby for a Decapitated Man), 1966. *Teatro: La víspera del degüello, El cepillo de dientes, Réquiem por un girasol* (Madrid: Taurus, 1967). *Topografía de un desnudo* (Topography of a Nude Man) (Santiago: Editora Santiago, 1967); in *Apuntes* 64 (November 1966); and in Moisés Pérez Coterillo, ed., *Teatro chileno contemporáneo* (Madrid: Fondo de Cultura Económica, 1992), 459–522. *La víspera del degüello o La génesis fue mañana* (The Eve of the Execution, or Genesis Was Tomorrow), in Díaz's collection *Teatro: La víspera del degüello . . .* (Madrid: Taurus, 1967); in Frank Dauster and Leon Lyday, eds., *En un acto* (New York: Van Nostrand, 1974); in *Teatro chileno actual* (Santiago: Zig-Zag, 1966); English tr. in Gerardo Luzuriaga and Robert S. Rudder, eds. and trans., *The Orgy: Modern One-Act Plays from Latin America* (Los Angeles: University of California, Latin American Center, 1974). *Introducción al elefante y otras zoologías* (Introduction to the Elephant and Other Zoologies), 1968. *La orgástula* (not translatable), 1969, in *Latin American*

Theatre Review 4.1 (Fall 1970): 79–85. *La Costacosa* (The Thingumajig), 1970. *Liturgia para cornudos* (Liturgy for Cuckolds); revised version's title is *Ceremonia ortopédica*, 1970. *La pancarta, o Está estrictamente prohibido todo lo que no es obligatorio* (The Placard, or Everything That Isn't Obligatory Is Strictly Forbidden), 1970, in *Teatro difícil* (Madrid: Escelicer, 1971); the second version's title was changed to *Amaos los unos sobre los otros. Americaliente* (Hot America) (Santiago: Universidad de Chile, 1972). *Los alacranes* (The Scorpions), in collaboration with Francisco Uriz, 1973. *Amaos los unos sobre los otros* (Love Yourselves Above All Others), English translation in Francesca Colecchia and Julio Matas, eds. and trans., *Selected Latin American One-Act Plays* (Pittsburgh: University of Pittsburgh Press, 1973), 177–204. *Antropofagia de salón* (Drawing Room Cannibalism), 1973. *Las hormigas* (The Ants), in collaboration with Francisco Uriz, 1973. *Algo para contar en Navidad* (Something to Tell on Christmas) (Barcelona: Ed. Don Bosco, 1974); and in *Apuntes* 61 (August 1966). *La corrupción del ángel cibernético* (The Corruption of the Cybernetic Angel), 1974. *Mear contra el viento: Los documentos secretos de la ITT* (Pissing into the Wind: The Secret Documents of ITT), written for TV by Díaz and Francisco Uriz, in *Conjunto* 21 (July–September 1974): 8–50. *Algo para contra en Navidad* (Barcelona: Ediciones Don Bosco, 1974). *Ceremonia ortopédica* (Orthopedic Ceremony), 1976, revised version of *Liturgia para cornudos*, in Díaz's *Teatro, ceremonias de la soledad. El locutorio* (The Locutory), in Jorge Díaz et al., *Teatro . . .* (Valladolid: Caja de Ahorros Provincial de Valladolid, 1976); and in his *Teatro, ceremonias de la soledad. Serapio y Yerbabuena* (Barcelona: Ediciones Don Bosco, 1976). *Mata a tu prójimo como a ti mismo* (Kill Thy Neighbor as Thyself) (Madrid: Cultura Hispánica, 1977); also in L. Howard Quackenbush, ed., *Teatro absurdo hispanoamericano* (Mexico City: Editorial Patria, 1987); and in Díaz's *Teatro, ceremonias de la soledad*; the revised version's title changed to *Esplendor carnal de la ceniza. La puñeta* (Screwing Things Up), 1977. *Teida, historias para contar por el aire* (Teida, Stories to be Told Through the Air) (Barcelona: Ediciones Don Bosco, 1977). *Un día es un día, o Los sobrevivientes* (A Day Is a Day, or The Survivors), 1978. *El espantajo: Collage grotesco para representar con rabia* (The Scarecrow: Grotesque Collage to Be Presented with Fury), in *Conjunto* 38 (October–December 1978). 97–118. *El generalito: Fábula para niños acerca del poder absoluto y la lucha popular* (The Little General: Fa-

ble for Children About Absolute Power and the People's Struggle), in *Conjunto* 38 (October–December 1978): 80–96. *Teatro, ceremonias de la soledad: El locutorio, Mata a tu prójimo como a ti mismo, Ceremonia ortopédica* (Theatre, Ceremonies of Solitude: The Locutory, Kill Thy Neighbor as Thyself, Orthopedic Ceremony) (Santiago: Nascimento, 1978). *Ceremonias de soledad* (Solitary Ceremonies) (Santiago: Nascimento, 1978). *Contrapunto para dos voces cansadas, o El locutorio* (Counterpoint for Two Tired Voices, or the Locutory), 1979, English tr. in *Travesía* 1.2. *Ecuación* (Equation), 1979, in *Estreno* 11.2 (Autumn 1983): 17–23. *La manifestación* (The Demonstration), 1979. *¿Estudias o trabajas?* (Do You Study or Work?), in collaboration with Rafael Herrero, 1981. *El extraterrestre* (The Extraterrestrial), n.d. *Toda esta targa noche* (This Whole Night Long), 1981; later revised as *Canto subterráneo para blindar una paloma. Ligeros de equipaje* (Traveling Light), 1982, in *XV Festival Internacional de Teatre de Sitges* (Barcelona: Depto. de Cultura de la Generlitat de Catalunya, 1983); and in *Teatro latinoamericano en un acto* (Havana: Casa de las Américas, 1986), 37–71. *Piel contra piel* (Skin Against Skin), 1982. *Un ombligo para dos* (A Navel for Two), 1982, in *Estreno* 11.2 (Autumn 1983). *Desde la sangre y el silencio, o Fulgor y muerte de Pablo Neruda* (From Blood and Silence, or Splendor and Death of Pablo Neruda), in *XV Festival Internacional de Teatre de Sitges* (Barcelona: Dept. de Cultura de la Generlitat de Catalunya, 1983). *El génesis fue mañana* (Genesis Was Tomorrow, later revised as *La víspera del degüello o La génesis fue mañana*), in Frank Dauster and Leon F. Lyday, eds., *En un acto*, 2nd ed. (Boston: Heinle & Heinle, 1983), 159–181. *Antropofagia* (Anthropophagy), 1984. *Esplendor carnal de la ceniza* (Carnal Glow of the Ashes), revised version of *Mata a tu projimo como a ti mismo*, 1984. *La pandilla del arcoiris* (The Rainbow's Gang), 1985. *Canto subterráneo para blindar una paloma* (Subterranean Chant to Shield a Dove), in *Conjunto* 70 (October–December 1986). *Las cicatrices de la memoria* (The Scars of Memory) (Madrid: Cultura Hispánica, 1986). *Crónica* (Chronicle), 1986. *Dicen que la distancia es el olvido* (They Say That Distance Is Forgetting), 1986. *Ayer, sin ir más lejos* (Yesterday, Without Going Any Further), 1987, new title given to *Las cicatrices de la memoria. Matilde* (Matilda), 1987. *Instrucciones para hacer una donación voluntaria* (Instructions on Making Voluntary Donations), 1988, later retitled *Muero, luego existo. Muero, luego existo* (I Die, Therefore I Exist), 1988, revised version of *Instruc-*

ciones para hacer una donación voluntaria, in Juan Andrés Piña, ed., *Teatro chileno en un acto (1955–1985)* (Santiago: Teatro Taller, 1989). *Oscuro vuelo compartido* (Shared Dark Flight), in *Apuntes* 97 (December 1988). *La otra orilla* (The Other Shore), 1988. *Ayer, sin ir más lejos* (Yesterday, Without Going Any Further) (Madrid: Ediciones Antonio Machado, 1988). *Míster Humo no más: Al centro de la energía* (Mr. Smoke No More: At the Center of Energy), 1990. *El mundo es un pañuelo* (The World Is a Handkerchief), 1990. *Los ángeles ladrones* (The Thieving Angels), in collaboration with Vittorio Cintolesi, 1991. *Pablo Neruda viene volando* (Here Comes Pablo Neruda Flying), in collaboration with Ictus, 1991. *Un corazón lleno de lluvia* (A Heart Full of Rain) (Salamanca: Junta de Comunidades Castilla-La Mancha, 1992). *El guante de hierro* (The Iron Glove), 1992. *El jaguar azul* (The Blue Jaguar) (Menorca: Al-les Cardona, S.A., 1992). *Un corazón lleno de lluvia* (A Heart Full of Rain) (Toledo: Servicio de Publicaciones, Junta de Comunidades de Castilla-La Mancha, 1992). *De boca en boca* (From Mouth to Mouth), 1993. *Del aire al aire* (From Air to Air), 1993. *El estupor* (The Stupor), 1993. *Percusión* (Percussion) (Guadalajara: Minaya, S.A., 1993). *Del aire al aire* (From Air to Air) (Santiago: Universitaria, 1993). *Historia de nadie* (No One's History). *El jaguar azul* (The Blue Jaguar) (Menorca: Societat Cercle Artístic de Ciutadella de Menorca, 1993). *Percusión* (Percussion) (Guadalaiara: Patronato Municipal de Cultura, Ayuntamiento de Guadalajara, 1993). *The Rebellious Alphabet*, trans. of *Alfabeto rebelde* by Geoffrey Fox (New York: Holt, 1993). *Antología subjetiva: teatro 1963–1995* (Subjective Anthology: Theater 1963–1995) (Santiago: Red Internacional del Libro, 1996). *Textículos ejemplares de Jorge Díaz: absolutamente todo acerca de nada* (Jorge Díaz's Exemplary Texticles: Absolutely Everything about Nothing) (Santiago: Ediciones RIL, 1997). *Todas las fiestas del mañana* (All Tomorrow's Parties), n.d.

BIBLIOGRAPHY: Becky Boling, "Crest or Pepsodent: Jorge Díaz's *El cepillo de dientes*," *Latin American Theatre Review* 24.1 (Fall 1990): 93–103. Ronald D. Burgess, "*El cepillo de dientes*: Empty Words. Empty Games?" *Estreno* 9.2 (Autumn 1983): 29–31. Fernando Burgos, "Estética de la ironía en el teatro de Jorge Díaz," *Revista Chilena de Literatura* 27–28 (April–November 1986): 133–141. Elena Castedo-Ellerman, *El teatro chileno de mediados del siglo XX* (Santiago: Andrés Bello, 1982), 124–141. Julio Durán-Cerda, "El teatro chileno de nuestros días," *El teatro chileno contemporáneo* (Mexico

City: Aguilar, 1970), 52–57. *Estreno* 11.2 (Autumn 1983), special issue devoted to Jorge Díaz. Priscilla Meléndez, "Silencios y ausencias en *Historie nadie* de Jorge Díaz," *Estreno: Cuadernos del Teatro Español Contemporáneo* 2 (Spring 1995): 11–13. José Monleón, "Diálogo con Jorge Díaz," *Primer Acto* 69 (1965): 32–37. Monleón, "Otra vez con Jorge Díaz," *Primer Acto* 153 (1973): 59–66. Nancy Dale Nieman, "Dos estrenos de Jorge Díaz en Madrid," *Hispania* 70.3 (September 1987): 549. Kirsten F. Nigro, "Stage and Audience: Jorge Díaz's *El lugar donde mueren los mamíferos* and *Topografía de un desnudo*," *Estreno* 9.2 (Autumn 1983): 36–40. L. Howard Quackenbush, "Dos autos del absurdo de Arreola y Díaz," *La Palabra y el Hombre* 71 (July–September 1989): 176–185. Quackenbush, "Jorge Díaz: La desmitificación religiosa y el culto a la vida," *Estreno* 9.2 (Autumn 1983): 9–12. María A. Salgado, "*El cepillo de dientes* and *El apartamiento*: Two Opposing Views of Alienated Man," *Romance Notes* 17.3 (Spring 1977): 247–254. Eduardo Thomas, "Ficción y creación en cuatro dramas chilenos contemporáneos," *Revista Chilena de Literatura* 33 (April 1989): 61–72 (on *El cepillo de dientes* and *El locutorio*). Juan Villegas, "Teatro y público: El teatro de Jorge Díaz," *Estreno* 9.2 (Autumn 1983): 7–9. Leland A. Walser, "*Ship in a Crystal Jar* by Jorge Díaz: Communication Crisis in a Technological World," *Language Quarterly* 21.1–2 (Fall–Winter 1982): 7, 12. George W. Woodyard, "Jorge Díaz," in *Latin American Writers*, 3 vols., ed. Carlos Solé and María Isabel Abreu (New York: Macmillan, 1989), 1393–1397. Woodyard, "Jorge Díaz and the Liturgy of Violence," in *Dramatists in Revolt: The New Latin American Theatre*, ed. Leon F. Lyday and George W. Woodyard (Austin: University of Texas Press, 1976), 59–76. Woodyard, "Ritual as Reality in Díaz's *Mata a tu prójimo como a ti mismo*," *Estreno* 9.2 (Autumn 1983): 13–15. Woodyard, "The Theatre of the Absurd in Spanish America," *Comparative Drama* 3.3 (Fall 1969): 183–192. Woodyard, "The Two Worlds of Jorge Díaz," *Estreno* 18.1 (1992). Daniel Zalacaín, "*El cepillo de dientes y el humorismo en el teatro absurdista*," *Symposium* 42.1 (Spring 1988): 62–71. Zalacaín, "La mudez del lenguaje en tres piezas absurdistas de Jorge Díaz," *Explicación de Textos Literarios* 14.1 (1985–1986): 15–24.

DÍAZ MEZA, Aurelio (1879–1933). Known as a journalist, historian, playwright, theater critic, and entrepreneur, Díaz Meza organized the Chilean Theater Company (Compañía de

Teatro Chileno) in 1915. His work with this company was later to bring to the forefront Alejandro Flores, who would become one of the most important figures in Chilean theater in the 1930s. Díaz Meza was also known for his collections of Chilean legends and traditions. Díaz Meza's career as a playwright began in 1908 when *Rucacahuiñ*, a *zarzuela* or comic operetta of indigenous theme with music by Alberto García, premiered. In addition to operettas, he also wrote comedies and *sainetes* (or one-act comic pieces used as curtain raisers). Díaz Meza also composed one drama, *Bajo la selva* (Under the Forest), in 1914.

WORKS: *Rucacahuiñ* (1908). *Bajo la Selva* (Under the Forest) (1914). *Martes, jueves y sábados* (Tuesdays, Thursdays and Saturdays) (Santiago: ITUCH, 1953); also in *Apuntes* 30 (July 1963). *Amorcillos* (Cupids), in *Apuntes* 32 (September 1963).

DITTBORN, Eugenio (1915–1979). One of the founders of the Teatro de Ensayo Universidad Católica (TEUC) at the Catholic University in 1943, Dittborn became the director of this experimental theater and later of the Theater Center (Centro de Teatro) at that university. Teaching theater courses at the Catholic University, Dittborn emphasized the importance of establishing a national theater and training Chileans to be theater professionals. He directed productions of Luis Alberto Heiremans's *Versos de ciegos* (Verses of the Blind) and *El tony chico* (The Little Clown), as well as Juan Guzmán Améstica's *El Wurlitzer*. A few years after his death, the Catholic University established a national theater competition and prize that were named in his honor.

DONOSO [YÁÑEZ], José (1924–1996). Donoso was born in Santiago on October 5, 1924, and died there of cancer on December 7, 1996. He was internationally known as one of the major authors of the Latin American "Boom" whose outstanding talents in the narrative merited his being awarded several prestigious literary prizes, as well as Chile's National Literature Prize in 1990. In addition to writing

short stories and novels, more recently in his career he had turned to poetry and theater.

Having received a scholarship in 1949, he traveled to the United States to continue pursuing studies at Princeton University, completing his B.A. in English there in 1951. It was during this period that his first short stories were published. After returning to Chile, Donoso continued to write but earned his living teaching English at the Kent School in Santiago and lecturing at the Catholic University. In 1958 he left Chile to work in Buenos Aires, where he was to meet María Pilar Serrano, the woman who was later to become his wife. Donoso returned to Chile in 1960, leaving again in 1963 for what was to be a long, self-imposed exile. From 1963 to 1965 Donoso was a writer-in-residence at the University of Iowa. In 1965 Donoso moved his family to Spain, where they were to remain for many years. It was not until 1981 that he and his family moved back to Santiago, Chile. One of Donoso's better known theater works is *Sueños de mala muerte* (Miserable Dreams), a collaborative creation with Ictus, which deals with the theme of thwarted hopes and dreams and illustrates well Donoso's black humor.

WORKS: *Sueños de mala muerte* (Miserable Dreams), in collaboration with Ictus (Santiago: Editorial Universitaria, 1985). *Este domingo* (This Sunday), in collaboration with Carlos Cerda (Santiago: Editorial Andrés Bello, 1990); in *Apuntes* 100 (June 1990).

BIBLIOGRAPHY: Guillermo Castillo-Feliú, "José Donoso," in *Spanish American Authors: The Twentieth Century*, ed. Angel Flores (New York: H. W. Wilson Co., 1992), 271–277. Carlos Genovese, "El espacio escénico y su influencia modificadora de la puesta en escena: Una experiencia del Teatro Ictus de Chile," *Latin American Theatre Review* 25.1 (Fall 1991): 41–50 (about *Sueños de mala muerte*). Cedomil Goic, "José Donoso," in *Latin American Writers*, vol. 3, ed. Carlos A. Solé and María Isabel Abreu (New York: Charles Scribner's Sons, 1989), 1277–1288. Thomas Kozikowski, "José Donoso," in *Hispanic Writers: A Selection of Sketches from Contemporary Authors*, ed. Bryan Ryan (Detroit: Gale Research, 1991), 165–168.

DORFMAN [ZELICOVICH], Ariel (1942–). Born on May 6, 1942, in Buenos Aires, Dorfman moved to New York with his family at age two when his father began working for the United Nations. The Dorfman family moved again in 1954, settling in Chile, where he completed his education at the University of Chile with a major in literature, becoming a naturalized Chilean citizen in 1967. Dorfman married María Angélica Malinarich in 1966 and worked in Chile as a writer and journalist until 1973 when, after the military coup, his Chilean citizenship was revoked because of his activism; like other exiled Chileans, he sought refuge in France. Having received a fellowship from the Woodrow Wilson Center for International Scholars, Dorfman moved his family to Washington, D.C. in 1980. The military government eventually gave Dorfman permission to return to Chile. Since 1987 he has divided his time between teaching at Duke University and living in Santiago.

A member of the Generation of 1972, Dorfman is internationally known as an author of essays, short stories, novels, poems, and most recently, plays. In all of these genres he has raised his voice in protest against the brutality of dictatorial regimes. His most successful play to date has been *La muerte y la doncella* (Death and the Maiden), which premiered in March 1991 at the Teatro de la Esquina in Santiago under the direction of Ana Reeves, with music by Andreas Bodenhöfer. In New York City Mike Nichols directed a production in English, in which Richard Dreyfuss, Gene Hackman, and Glenn Close starred. Close won a Tony Award for her portrayal of Paulina. The play was also produced in Vienna and London, where it was equally successful, winning the Sir Laurence Olivier Prize for Best Play in 1991. A film version directed by Roman Polanski was released early in 1995.

WORKS: *Lector* (Reader), play based on his short story of the same title; *Teatro 1: La muerte y la doncella* (Death and the Maiden) (Buenos Aires: Ediciones de la Flor, 1992); English tr. (New York: Penguin Books, 1992) and (London: Nick Hern Books, 1991). *Viudas* (Widows), novel on which his play was based (México: Siglo XXI, 1981; rev. ed., 1985); English tr. Stephen Kessler (New York: Pantheon Books, 1983) and (New York: Penguin Books,

1989). *Reader* (trans. of *Lector*) (London: Nick Hern Books, 1995). *Lector/Viudas* (Reader/Widows) (Buenos Aires: Ediciones de la Flor, 1996). *La muerte y la doncella* (Death and the Maiden) (Santiago: LOM Ediciones, 1997). *The Resistance Trilogy: Widows, Death and the Maiden, Reader* (London: Nick Hern Books, 1998); *Viudas* (Widows) (Madrid: Alfaguara/ Santillana, 1998).

BIBLIOGRAPHY: Peggy Boyers and Juan Carlos Lertora, "Ideology, Exiles, Language: An Interview with Ariel Dorfman," *Salmagundi* 82–83 (Spring–Summer 1989): 142–163. Angel Flores, ed., "Ariel Dorfman," in *Spanish American Authors: The Twentieth Century* (New York: H. W. Wilson Co., 1992), 280–282. Eduardo Galán, "*La muerte y la doncella.* ¿Perdonar los crímenes del fascismo?" *Primer Acto* 249 (May–June 1993): 116–117. John Incledon, "Liberating the Reader: A Conversation with Ariel Dorfman," *Chasqui: Revista de Literatura Latinoamericana* 20.1 (May 1991): 95–107. Incledon, "New Play by Ariel Dorfman," *Hispania* 75.5 (December 1992): 1224–1225. Emily J. McMurray, "Ariel Dorfman," in *Hispanic Writers: A Selection of Sketches from Contemporary Authors*, ed. Bryan Ryan (Detroit: Gale Research, 1991), 168–171. Silverio Muñoz, "Entrevista a Ariel Dorfman," *Prismal-Cabral: Revista de Literatura Hispánica, Cuaderno Afro-Brasileiro Asiático Lusitano* 3–4 (Spring 1979): 60–76.

ERNHARD, James. *See* PÉREZ DE ARCE, Camilo.

FLORES, Alejandro (1896–1962). Having written comedies mostly in the 1920s and 1930s, Flores sometimes wrote in collaboration with Carlos Cariola (e.g., *Don Juan se casa* [Don Juan Gets Married], 1930) or with Rafael Frontaura (e.g., *La compañerita* [The Little Companion], 1932). Flores also wrote poetry and was known in Chile as an actor both in theater and film. His contributions to Chilean theater were recognized in 1946 when he was awarded that country's National Arts Prize.

WORKS: *El derrumbe* (The Collapse), 1919. *Malhaya tu corazón* (Cursed Be Your Heart), 1921. *Match de amor* (Love Match), 1922. *La comedia trunca* (The Truncated Comedy), 1926, in *Revista Teatral. La Escena* 1.6 (September 10, 1932): 1–47. *¡Cuídate, hermano!* (Take Care of Yourself, Brother!), 1926. *La película roja* (The Red Film),

1931. *A toda máquina* (At Full Speed), 1934, in *Revista Teatral. La Escena* 30 (1934): 1–35. *El brindis* (The Toast), 1935. *Y paz en la tierra* (And Peace on Earth), 1936. *La nueva marsellesa* (The New Woman from Marseilles), 1937. *Gran candidato para el 58* (Great Candidate for '58), 1956. *Los megatones del sultán* (The Sultan's Megatons), n.d.

BIBLIOGRAPHY: Luis Enrique Délano, *La vida romántica y novelesca de Alejandro Flores* (Santiago, 1937).

FRANK, Miguel (1920–). A lawyer and playwright, in 1948 Frank founded a theater company that initially performed plays by foreign authors. He later began writing his own plays, mostly humorous in tone, although some were dramas. *Los trasplantados* (The Transplants) (1963) is an adaptation of a novel by Chile's well-known author Alberto Blest Gana.

WORKS: *Tiempo de vals* (Waltz Time), 1952. *Punto muerto* (Stalemate), 1953. *La terrible Catalina* (Terrible Kathleen), 1954. *Matrimonio para tres* (Marriage for Three), 1955. *Aquí hay gato encerrado* (There Is a Caged Cat Here), 1961. *Los trasplantados* (The Transplants), 1963. *Hola, muchachos* (Hello, Boys), 1964. *Mi querido Presidente* (My Dear President), 1964. *Duérmete, Gabriela* (Go to Sleep, Gabrielle), 1965. *Finita*, winner of the Gabriela Mistral Prize, 1968. *El hombre del siglo* (The Man of the Century), English tr. in Willis Knapp Jones, ed. and trans., *Men and Angels: Three South American Comedies* (Carbondale: Southern Illinois University Press, 1970). *Amores de ayer y amores de hoy* (Yesterday's Loves and Today's Loves), 1971. *La primera piedra* (The First Stone), n.d.

FRONTAURA, Rafael (1896–1966). Known primarily for his work as an actor, Frontaura won Chile's National Art Prize in 1949 and the Annual Prize for Theater Work in 1962 in recognition of his lifetime achievement in, and contributions to, Chilean theater. He wrote many plays in collaboration with others (e.g., Carlos Cariola, Alejandro Flores, and Armando Moock). He wrote one silent movie in collaboration with Cariola, *El hombre de acero* (The Man of Steel), as well as several plays (e.g., *Abajo las castas, El tuerto es rey,* and *Doña Dorotea Dueñas dueña*).

WORKS: *Como se pide* (As Requested), 1918. *La oveja negra* (The Black Sheep), 1920.

GARCÍA, Lautaro (1895–1982). Also an author of short stories, García primarily wrote comedies of manners and humorous *sainetes* (i.e., one-act farces used as curtain raisers) on historical or *costumbrista* themes. His works were popular during the 1920s and 1930s when this type of theater prevailed in Chile. He was also the author of an adaptation (for theater) of Thomas Mann's *The Blue Angel.* His *Una sola vez en la vida* (Once in a Lifetime) won Santiago's Municipal Prize in 1941. His lifetime dedication to Chilean theater was recognized in 1958 when he was awarded the Annual Prize for Theater Work.

WORKS: *El peuco*, 1920. *El rancho del estero* (The Ranch of the Estuary), 1920. *La voluntad de los muertos* (The Will of the Dead), 1920. *La maestra rural* (The Rural Teacher), 1921. *El alma de las máscaras* (The Soul of the Masks), 1922. *Una pareja inverostmil* (An Unlikely Couple), 1927. *Nuestro amor Q.E.P.D.* (Our Love, May It Rest in Peace), 1928. *Margarita y la crinolina* (Maguerite and the Crinoline), 1930. *El vendedor de sueños* (The Dream Vendor), 1932. *Una sola vez en la vida* (Once in a Lifetime), 1941. *Ya nadie se llama Deidamia* (No One Is Named Deidamia Anymore), 1957.

GENOVESE, Carlos (1947–). Playwright, director, and actor, Genovese has been associated since 1980 with the theater company Ictus, which is known for its collaborative creations. Works in which he has participated in the creative process with Ictus include *Primavera con una esquina rota* (Spring with a Broken Corner) (1984), based on Mario Benedetti's novel. His *Dos en el desván* (Two on the Sofa) debuted in April 1991 at the Teatro Taller Siglo XX (Twentieth Century Theater Workshop) under his direction.

WORKS: *Sálvese quien pueda*, co-author with Óscar Castro, in *Apuntes 86* (July 1980). *La lección de Barba*, in *Ictus Informa* (January–February 1989).

GRIFFERO [SÁNCHEZ], Ramón (1953–). Griffero was born in Santiago in 1953. A member of the Generation of 1987, he is known as a playwright, director, and actor. After a nine-year absence, he returned to Chile in 1982, founding and directing the Teatro Fin de Siglo (End-of-the-Century Theater). In 1985 he was awarded the Art Critics' Prize for his work. Perhaps Griffero's best known works are a trilogy consisting of *Cinema Utoppia* (Cinema Utoppia) (1985), *Historias de un galpón abandonado* (Stories of an Abandoned Cellar), (1984), and *99-La Morgue* (99, The Morgue) (1986), all of which were performed by his theater company in Santiago.

WORKS: *Antes del fin o recuerdos del hombre con su tortuga* (Before the End or Memories of Man and His Tortoise) (Santiago: 1982). *Historias de un galpón abandonado* (Santiago de Chile: Teatro Fin de Siglo, 1983). *Cinema Utoppia*, in Moisés Pérez Coterillo, ed., *Teatro chileno contemporáneo* (Madrid: Fondo de Cultura Económica, 1992), 1203–1235. *3 Obras de Ramón Griffero S.: Historias de un galpón abandonado. Cinema Utoppia. 99-La Morgue* (Santiago: Instituto Internacional de Teoría y Crítica de Teatro Latinoamericano [IITCTL]/Neptuno Editores, 1992). *Rio abajo* (Thunder River) (Santiago: Dolmen Edicime, 1996).

BIBLIOGRAPHY: Catherine M. Boyle, *Chilean Theater, 1973–1985: Marginality, Power, Selfhood* (Rutherford, NJ: Fairleigh Dickinson University Press, 1992), 171–176, on *Cinema Utoppia*. Pedro Bravo-Elizondo, "Ramón Griffero: Nuevos espacios, nuevo teatro," *Latin American Theatre Review* 20.1 (Fall 1986): 95–101. Eduardo Guerrero, "Espacios y poética en Ramón Griffero: Análisis de su trilogía: *Historias de un galpón abandonado, Cinema Utoppia, y 99-La Morgue*," in *Hacia una nueva crítica y un nuevo teatro latinoamericano*, ed. Alfonso de Toro and Fernando de Toro (Frankfurt: Klaus Dieter Vervuert Verlag, 1992), 127–135. María de la Luz Hurtado, "Más allá de la estética de la disidencia oficial. Entrevista con Ramón Griffero," *La Escena Latinoamericana* 2 (1989): 83–88. Grínor Rojo, "Teatro chileno: 1983–1987: Observaciones preliminares," *Alba de América* 7.12–13 (July 1989): 159–186. María Teresa Salinas, "Griffero, una nueva perspectiva: El teatro de imágenes," *Literatura Chilena: Creación y Crítica* 10.2–3 (April–September 1986): 27–30. Alfonso de Toro, "Prólogo," *3 Obras de Ramón Griffero S.: Historias de un galpón abandonado. Cinema Utoppia. 99-La Morgue*, by Ramón Griffero S. (Santiago: Instituto Internacional de Teoría y Crítica de Teatro Latinoamericano [IITCTL]/Neptuno Editores, 1992), 24–36.

GUZMÁN AMÉSTICA, Juan (1931–). Born in Santiago in 1931, Guzmán Améstica studied theater at the University of Chile (ITUCH [Instituto de Teatro de la Universidad de Chile]) and became a professor at the University of Valdivia. Known as a playwright in the Generation of 1957, his works were among the first in Latin America to deal with the theme of the generation gap. Although nearly all of his works from the 1960s deal with this subject, undoubtedly the most remembered of these plays is *El Wurlitzer* (The Jukebox), a two-act "comedy-drama" that was Chile's entry in the first Latin American Play Competition held in March 1962. Written in the vein of social realism, the play deals with the conflict of values between middle-class youths and their parents.

WORKS: *El caracol* (The Snail), 1960. *Juanito* (Johnny), 1960. *Sin vivir, sin morir* (Without Living, Without Dying), 1960. *Trigo morado* (Purple Wheat), 1960. *El Wurlitzer* (The Jukebox), in *Mapocho* 19 (Winter 1969): 119–175. *Cáncer en la familia* (Cancer in the Family), n.d.

BIBLIOGRAPHY: Elena Castedo-Ellerman, *El teatro chileno de mediados del siglo XX* (Santiago: Andrés Bello, 1982), 63–65.

GUZMÁN CRUCHAGA, Juan (1895–1979). Guzmán Cruchaga was both a poet and a playwright, although he was better known for his poetry. His first plays were *La sombra* (The Shadow) (1919), *La princesa que no tenía corazón* (The Princess Who Didn't Have a Heart) (1920), and *El maleficio de la luna* (The Moon's Curse) (1922). After writing these plays, Guzmán Cruchaga abandoned the genre until 1951 when he wrote *María Cenicienta, o La otra cara del sueño* (Mary Cinderella, or The Other Side of the Dream), a four-act play that won first prize at the University of Chile's theater competition that year. This play presents the unfortunate events after Cinderella married the prince.

WORKS: *María Cenicienta, o La otra cara del sueño* (Mary Cinderella, or The Other Side of the Dream) (Santiago: Imp. Chile, 1952); 2nd ed. (San Salvador: Ministerio de Cultura, 1959).

HEIREMANS, Luis Alberto (1928–1964). Born into a wealthy family in Santiago on July

14, 1928, Heiremans was a member of the Generation of 1957. He completed studies in medicine at the Catholic University but changed his focus afterward to theater. In addition to his reputation as a playwright, Heiremans was known as an actor, director, and professor associated with the Catholic University's Teatro de Ensayo. He died of cancer in 1964 at age thirty-six, abruptly ending a promising career as one of Chile's most important playwrights. Critics generally consider his best works to be those of the 1960s—*El abanderado* (The Outlaw), *Versos de ciego* (Blind Man's Ballads), and *El tony chico* (The Little Clown). Each of these plays combine Heiremans' neo-Christian viewpoint with Chilean folklore, popular tradition, and poetic language and use of symbolism, which has resulted in comparisons between his theater production and that of Federico García Lorca.

WORKS: *La simple historia* (The Simple Story), 1951. *La jaula en el árbol* (The Cage in the Tree), in *Finis Terrae* 4.13 (1957): 5–33; and in *Teatro* (Santiago: Ed. del Nuevo Extremo, 1959). *Moscas sobre el mármol* (Flies on Marble) (Santiago: Editorial del Nuevo Extremo, 1958). *Sigue la estrella* (Follow the Star), in *Apuntes* 17 (November 1961); also in *Teatro chileno actual* (Santiago: Zig-Zag, 1965). *El abanderado* (The Outlaw), in his *Teatro* (Santiago: Nascimento, 1982); in his collection *Versos de ciego* (Santiago, 1962); in Julio Durán-Cerda, ed., *El teatro contemporáneo chileno* (Mexico City: Aguilar, 1970); in his *El abanderado. Versos de ciego* (Santiago: Ercilla, 1970); and in Moisés Pérez Coterillo, ed., *Teatro chileno contemporáneo* (Madrid: Fondo de Cultura Económica, 1992), 223–290. *Dos piezas teatrales de Luis A. Heiremans: Versos de ciego y El abanderado* (Two Theatrical Pieces of Luis A. Heiremans: Verses of the Blind and Standard-Bearer) (Santiago: Imp. Mueller, 1962). *La eterna trampa* (The Eternal Trap), in *Mapocho* 23 (Spring 1970): 259–301. *La ronda de la buena nueva* (The Good News Serenade), in *Apuntes* 23 (October 1962). *Versos de ciego* (Blind Man's Ballads), in *Escenario* (1962); in his collection *Versos de ciego* (Santiago: Imp. Mueller, 1962); in his *El abanderado. Versos de ciego* (Santiago: Ercilla, 1970); and in his *Teatro* (Santiago: Nascimento, 1982); Eng. tr. by Virginia L. Iverson, 1964. *El mar en la muralla* (The Sea on the Wall), in *Apuntes* 43 (October 1964); in *Mapocho* 3.1 (1965); and in Juan Andrés Piña, ed., *Teatro chileno en un acto (1955–1985)* (Santiago: Teatro Taller, 1989). *El año repetido* (The Repeated Year), in *Mapocho* 3.1 (1965). *Arpeggione*, in *Mapocho* 3.1 (1965). *Buenaventura* (Good Fortune) (Santiago: Ed. Pehuén, 1990); and in *Mapocho* 3.1 (1965): 67–106. *Cuentos y canciones de la mamá* (Mom's Stories and Songs), in *Apuntes* 53 (October 1965). *El tony chico* (The Little Clown), in his *Teatro* (Santiago: Nascimento, 1982); in *Apuntes* 64 (November 1966); in *Mapocho* 16 (Autumn 1968): 123–178; and in *Teatro chileno contemporáneo* (Santiago: Ed. Andrés Bello, 1982). *El palomar a oscuras* (Pigeonhouse in the Dark), in *Anales de la Universidad de Chile* 125.141–144 (January–December 1967): 148–183.

BIBLIOGRAPHY: Elba M. Andrade, "El *leitmotiv* del mar en *El tony chico* de Luis Alberto Heiremans," *Explicación de Textos Literarios* 16.2 (1987–1988): 93–105. Teresa Cajiao Salas, *Temas y símbolos en la obra de Luis Alberto Heiremans* (Santiago: Editorial Universitaria, 1970). Elena Castedo-Ellerman, *El teatro chileno de mediados del siglo XX* (Santiago: Andrés Bello, 1982), 89–103, on Heiremans. Fernando Debesa, "Apuntes sobre la obra dramática de Luis Alberto Heiremans," *Apuntes* 43 (October 1964): 22–28. Eugenio Dittborn, "Constantes en la trilogía dramática de Luis Alberto Heiremans," *Boletín de la Universidad de Chile* 56 (1965): 70–80. Patricio Estellé, "Apuntes a la obra de Luis Alberto Heiremans," in *Memoria del Décimosegundo Congreso del Instituto de Literatura Iberoamericana* (Mexico City, 1966), 73–84. Teodosio Fernández, *El teatro chileno contemporáneo (1941–1973)* (Madrid: Playor, 1982), 123–133. Tomás P. MacHale, "Notas sobre Luis Alberto Heiremans," *Mapocho* 3.1 (1965): 59–106. Margaret Sayers Peden, "The Theater of Luis Alberto Heiremans: 1928–1964," in *Dramatists in Revolt: The New Latin American Theater*, ed. Leon F. Lyday and George W. Woodyard (Austin: University of Texas Press, 1976), 120–132. Grinor Rojo, "Explicación de Luis Alberto Heiremans," *Literatura Chilena: Creación y Crítica* 10.2–3 (April–September 1986): 23–26. "Luis Alberto Heiremans," in *Latin American Writers*, vol. 3, ed. Carlos A. Solé and María Isabel Abreu (New York: Charles Scribner's Sons, 1989), 1347–1352.

HUIDOBRO, Vicente (1893–1948). Best known as a poet associated with *creacionismo*, Huidobro was born in Santiago on January 10, 1893. Born into an aristocratic Chilean family, he was able to spend time in Europe during his youth, learning much about European arts and literature. In addition to poetry, Huidobro also wrote essays, some prose fiction, and two plays: *Gilles de Raíz* and *En la luna* (On the Moon). The former was a surrealistic work based on the figure and legend of Bluebeard.

WORKS: *Gilles de Raíz*, 1932. *En la luna* (Santiago: Ercilla), 1934.

BIBLIOGRAPHY: Lidia Neghme Echeverría, "El creacionismo político de Huidobro en *En la luna*," *Latin American Theatre Review* 18.1 (1984): 75–82.

HURTADO BORNE, René (1887–1960). One of the founders of, and an active participant in, the Chilean Association of Dramatists (1915), Hurtado Borne was one of the most prolific Chilean playwrights of the first three decades of the twentieth century. He also translated into Spanish works of foreign dramatists. Having written more than eighty plays in his lifetime, he received Chile's Annual Theater Prize in 1957. Most of his plays deal with the sociopolitical problems of his day (e.g., class structure, the decadence of the oligarchy, corrupt business practices of the aristocracy). Probably Hurtado Borne's best play, *Su lado flaco* (Her Weak Point), was first brought to the stage in 1922. The work is the story of an old maid who is fulfilling her duty to support her sister and her sister's children.

WORKS: *Primeros pasos. ¿Por qué se ama? La otra. Entre las brumas* (First Steps. Why Does One Love? The Other Woman. In the Fog) (Santiago: Imp. y Encuadernación de Chile, 1913). *El asedio. El mal ejemplo* (The Siege. The Bad Example) (Santiago: Soc. Imp. y Lit. Universo, 1915). *Damas de noche* (Ladies of the Night), 1915. *La señorita Risa* (Miss Laugh), 1916. *El culpable de siempre* (The Same Culprit as Ever), 1918. *Mal hombre* (Bad Man) (Santiago: Soc. Imp. y Lit. Universo, 1918). *Tierra nuestra* (Our Land), 1920. *Vida nueva* (New Life), 1920. *El derecho a la felicidad* (The Right to Happiness), 1922. *La culpa bendita* (Blessed Fault), in *Mapocho* 1.5–6 (October–November 1930): 1–38. *Su lado flaco* (Her Weak Point), in *Revista Teatral. La Escena* 1.9 (October 10, 1932): 1–68. *La mala pasión* (Evil Passion), 1936. *La insidia* (The Trap), 1941.

ICTUS. Probably Chile's best known independent theater group known for its collective creations, Ictus was founded in 1956 when a group of actors left the Catholic University's Teatro de Ensayo. It functioned as a collective group from 1969 to 1973 with its television program *La manivela*. Ictus was awarded the Ollantay Prize in 1979 by the Latin American Center of Creation and Theater Research (Centro Latinoamericano de Creación e Investigación Teatral, or CELCIT) in recognition of the group's contributions to a collective approach to popular theater. Since 1962 Ictus performances have been held in the Teatro La Comedia in Santiago. The group has toured internationally. In the early years of its existence, Ictus performed plays by foreign playwrights but soon turned to a collaborative approach, working with Chilean authors such as Jorge Díaz, José Donoso, Isidora Aguirre, David Benavente, Sergio Vodanovic, Marco Antonio de la Parra, and others. Since the group's work tends to deal with sociopolitical issues, Ictus was one of the voices of protest against the military regime. Currently, Nissim Sharim and Delfina Guzmán are two of the directors/actors who are the moving forces behind the group's work. Others who are associated with the group are Carlos Cerda, Carlos Genovese, and Claudio di Girólamo.

WORKS: *¿Cuántos años tiene un día?* (How Many Years Are There in a Day?), in collaboration with Sergio Vodanovic, in *Tramoya* 12 (July–September 1978): 16–75; also in *Teatro chileno de la crisis institucional, 1973–1980*, ed. María de la Luz Hurtado et al. (Minneapolis and Santiago: University of Minnesota and CENECA, 1982), 139–195. *Lo que está en el aire* (What's in the Air), in collaboration with Carlos Cerda (Santiago: Ed. Sinfronteras, 1986). *Primavera con una esquina rota* (Spring with a Broken Corner), in *Conjunto* 67 (January–March 1986). *Amor de mis amores* (Love of My Loves), in collaboration with Patricio Contreras, in *Teatro chileno en un acto (1955–1985)*, ed. Juan Andrés Piña (Santiago: Teatro Taller, 1989). *Lindo país esquina con vista al mar* (Pretty Country on the Corner with a View of the Sea), in collaboration with Marco Antonio de la Parra, Darío Osses, and Jorge Gajardo, in Moisés Pérez Coterillo, ed., *Teatro chileno contemporáneo* (Madrid: Fondo de Cultura Económica, 1992), 969–1039.

BIBLIOGRAPHY: Catherine M. Boyle, *Chilean Theater, 1973–1985: Marginality, Power, Selfhood* (Rutherford, NJ: Fairleigh Dickinson University Press, 1992), 155–160 on *¿Cuántos años tiene un día?*, 160–165 on *Primavera con una esquina rota*. Rodrigo Canovas, *Lihn, Zurita, ICTUS, Radrigán* (Santiago: FLACSO, 1986). Carlos Genovese, "El espacio escénico y su influencia modificadora de la puesta en escena: Una experiencia del Teatro ICTUS de Chile," *Latin American Theatre Review* 25.1 (Fall 1991): 41–50. Genovese, "Ficción y realidad: Crónica de un caso chileno," *Latin American Theatre Review* 21.2 (Spring 1988): 99–104 (about life imitating art as Ictus staged *Primavera con una esquina rota* and a subsequent production, *Lo que está en el aire*). Flora González, "*Primavera con una esquina rota* de Mario Benedetti: De la novela del exilio a la representación comprometida," *Hispania* 75 (March 1992): 38–49. "Ictus," *Literatura Chilena* 10.2–3 (April–September 1986): 67. María de la Luz Hurtado and Carlos Ochsenius, *Maneras de hacer y pensar el teatro en el Chile actual: Teatro ICTUS* (Santiago: CENECA, 1980). Nissim Sharim, "¿Quiénes somos? El ICTUS y la creación colectivo," *Tramoya* 12 (July–September 1978): 4–13.

JODOROWSKY, Alejandro (1929–). Born in Chile in 1929, Jodorowsky is known as an actor, director of both theater and film, playwright, and novelist. He began his career in acting with the Teatro de Ensayo at the Catholic University in Santiago. With Enrique Lihn he founded the Theater of Marionettes at the University of Chile's Experimental Theater. He worked with Marcel Marceau in Paris and wrote at least two works for his mimes: *El fabricante de máscaras* (The Mask Maker) and *La jaula* (The Cage). Jodorowsky, along with Arrabal and Toper, formed a theater group called El Grupo Pánico, for which he wrote *El juego que todos jugamos* (The Game We All Play) and *Juegos pánicos* (Ghastly Games). Jodorowsky has lived abroad since the mid-1950s. In Mexico, where he currently resides, he has been very successful as a director of both theater and film productions.

WORKS: *El fabricante de máscaras* (The Mask Maker). *La jaula* (The Cage). *El juego que todos jugamos* (The Game We All Play). *Juegos pánicos* (Ghastly Games). *El túnel que se come por la boca* (The Tunnel Swallowed by the Mouth).

BIBLIOGRAPHY: Fernando Burgos, "Modernidad y neovanguardia hispanoamericanas," *Revista de Estudios Hispánicos* 18.2 (May 1984): 207–220. Winifred Harner, "Polycentric Framing Devices and Dramatic Structure in Alejandro Jodorowsky's *El túnel que se come por la boca*," *Tinta* 1.3 (December 1983): 11–17.

JOSSEAU, Fernando (1924–). Born in southern Chile in 1924, Josseau studied theater in Margarita Xirgú's academy, after which he enrolled at the University of Chile, where he specialized in direction. He has become known as a theater critic, director, playwright, and novelist. A member of the Generation of 1957, he is one of a few Chilean playwrights whose works are consistently written in the vein of the Absurd. *El prestamista* (The Moneylender) is undoubtedly Josseau's best-known work because it enjoyed enormous international success, having been staged in more than fifty countries. In the play the audience hears the voice of a police detective interrogating three characters—played by one single actor—who are suspects in a murder case. None of the characters is really what he seems to be, a play with the theme of appearance and reality that Josseau repeats in many of his works.

WORKS: *Esperar el amanecer* (Waiting for the Dawn), 1950. *El César* (Caesar), 1951. *El prestamista* (The Moneylender), 1956 (Buenos Aires: Talía, 1957). *La torre de marfil* (The Ivory Tower), 1957. *La gallina* (The Her), 1974, in Moisés Pérez Coterillo, ed., *Teatro chileno contemporáneo* (Madrid: Fondo de Cultura Económica, 1992), 703–730. *La mano* (The Hand, 1974), in Moisés Pérez Coterillo, ed., *Teatro chileno contemporáneo* (Madrid: Fondo de Cultura Económica, 1992), 683–701. *El estafador Renato Kauman* (The Swindler Renato Kauman), 1976. *S Excelencia, el Embajador* (His Excellency, the Ambassador), 1982. *Demencial Party* (Demented Party), 1983. *Alicia en el país de las zancadillas* (Alice in the Land of Tricks), 1986. *Los pianistas mancos* (The One-Handed Pianists), 1991. *Las goteras* (The Bedskirt), n.d.

BIBLIOGRAPHY: Teodosio Fernández, *El teatro chileno contemporáneo (1941–1973)* (Madrid: Playor, 1982), 56–58.

LAMBERG, Fernando (1928–). Known as a professor, playwright, and poet, Lamberg has received both the Gabriela Mistral Prize and the Municipal Prize. His best-known work is probably *El periodista* (The Journalist) (1954), a one-act play dealing with a journalist in search of a human interest story. The journalist is too shortsighted to see such a story occurring in his own son's life.

WORKS: *El juicio* (The Judgment), 1952. *El que construyó su propio infierno* (The Man Who Made His Own Hell), 1954. *El periodista* (The Journalist) (Santiago: Teatro Experimental de la Universidad de Chile, 1954). *Una antigua belleza* (An Old Beauty), 1958. *Una madeja para tejer* (A Skein to Weave), 1959. *Aprendices de la vida* (Apprentices in Life), 1960.

LARRAÍN DE IRARRÁZAVAL, Ester (1906–). Born in 1906, Larraín de Irarrázaval was the daughter of Chilean diplomats. One of Chile's first women playwrights, she used the pseudonym "Gloria Moreno." Some of her plays are in the *costumbrista* vein so typical of Chilean theater before the formation of the universities' experimental theaters (e.g., *La breva pelá*, about Chilean customs of courtship in rural areas); others were intended for a youthful audience (e.g., all of the plays included in the collection *Amor y polizón*); and still others are historical in nature (e.g., *La última victoria*, about Chilean independence and Bernardo O'Higgins). Several plays (e.g. *Niña, Aguas abajo*, and *Instituto de la felicidad*) deal with married couples. *Instituto de la felicidad*, for example, is about a young couple already tired of married life who through the Institute of Happiness farcically regain their happiness.

WORKS: *Mar* (Sea) (Santiago: Empresa Periodística "El Imparcial," 1936). *Instituto de la felicidad* (The Institute of Happiness), 1938 (Puente Alto: Imp. La Libertad, 1943). *Niña. Aguas abajo* (Girl. Downstream) (Santiago: Nascimento, 1940). *La última victoria* (The Last Victory), 1942 (Santiago: Zig-Zag, 1945). *Amor y polizón, teatro para la juventud* (Love and the Stowaway, Theater for the Young) (Santiago: Zig-Zag, 1945). *La breva pelá* (The Plain Stroke of Luck), in *Apuntes* 57 (April 1966).

BIBLIOGRAPHY: Willis Knapp Jones, *Behind Spanish American Footlights* (Austin: University of Texas Press, 1966), 232–233. Jones, "New Life in Chile's Theatre," *Modern Drama* 2.1 (1959): 57–62. Jones, "Notaricio de Ulyses," *Atenea* 450 (1984): 159–163.

LIHN, Enrique (1929–1988). One of Chile's best-known poets of the twentieth century, Lihn also wrote some short stories, novels, and plays. Along with Alejandro Jodorowsky, he founded the Theater of Marionettes at the University of Chile's Experimental Theater. His plays include *La Meka* (performed by the Teatro Imagen under the direction of Gustavo Meza in Santiago in 1984) and *Niú York, cartas marcadas* (staged in Santiago in 1985).

WORKS: *La Meka*, 1984. *Niú York, cartas marcadas* (New York, Marked Letters), 1985.

LITTÍN [KUKUMIDIS], Miguel (1942–). Having studied theater at the University of Chile, Littín began his career as a playwright and even wrote at least one novel, but in the early 1970s, he turned to film as a means of reaching larger audiences. As a film director, he has been very successful. Although one of Littín's plays, *Los hijos de Isabel* (Isabel's Children) (1963), is an example of realism, most of his theater pieces are in the vein of the avant-garde. Both *El hombre de la estrella* (The Man from the Star) (1962) and *La sonrisa* (The Smile) (1964) deal with social problems. *Me muero de amor por tus palancas, o Cómo hacer la revolución jugando al luche* (I Am Dying of Love for Your "Palancas" or How to Have a Revolution Playing "Luche") (1966) was performed by the El Callejón theater group.

WORKS: *El hombre de la estrella* (The Man from the Star), 1962. *Los hijos de Isabel* (Isabel's Children), 1963. *Tres para un paraguas* (Three for One Umbrella), 1963, in *Apuntes* 48 (May 1965). *La sonrisa* (The Smile), 1964. *La mariposa debajo del zapato* (The Butterfly under the Shoe), 1965. *Me muero de amor por tus palancas, o Cómo hacer la revolucion jugatido al luche*, 1966. *Conflicto* (Conflict), n.d., in collaboration with Enrique Gajardo Velázquez.

BIBLIOGRAPHY: Teodosio Fernández, *El teatro chileno contemporáneo (1941–1973)* (Madrid: Playor, 1982), 105–107, 168–170.

LÓPEZ [MENESES], Roberto (1882–1942). López's works of the 1920s and 1930s were well accepted during that time but have left little impact on the Chilean theater in subsequent years. López wrote mostly light comedies dealing with topics familiar to the lower and middle classes of Chilean society. He wrote some works in collaboration with Carlos Barella (e.g., *Fray Andresito*) and José Rojas (e.g., *El padre Bernabé*). Among his light comedies are *A la luz de la luna* (By the Light of the Moon), *La señorita Lulú* (Miss Lulu), and *El puñal roto* (The Broken Dagger). López also wrote some theater for children.

WORKS: *A la luz de la luna* (By the Light of the Moon), 1926. *Ha venido el amor* (Love Has Come), 1926. *La señorita Lulú* (Miss Lulu), 1928. *Del mismo barrio* (From the Same Neighborhood), 1931. *Pero qué quieres, Joaquín?* (But What Do You Expect, Joaquín?), 1932. *La cena de los sacristanes* (The Sacristans' Dinner), 1933. *El puñal roto* (The Broken Dagger), in *Revista Teatral. La Escena* 31 (1935): 1–52.

LUCO CRUCHAGA, Germán (1894–1936). A journalist, novelist, and playwright of aristocratic origins, Luco Cruchaga traveled throughout Chile in search of material about which he could write. In spite of the fact that he authored only a few plays, he is still considered one of the most important Chilean *costumbrista* playwrights during the early part of the twentieth century. Works like *Amo y señor* (Lord and Master) (1926) deal with the moral decadence of the upper class and the power of money. His masterpiece, considered one of the classics of Chilean theater, is *La viuda de Apablaza* (The Widow of Apablaza). First performed in 1928 with Elsa Alarcón and Evaristo Lillo in the starring roles, it has been revived several times: in 1956 and 1960, by the University of Chile's Experimental Theater, and again in April 1991, by the Teatro del Arte (Art Theater Group) under the direction of Rolando Valenzuela.

WORKS: *Amo y señor*, in his *Teatro* (Santiago: Nascimento, 1979). *Bailabuén*, in his *Teatro* (Santiago: Nascimento, 1979). *La viuda de Apablaza* (The Widow of Apablaza) (Santiago: Nuevo Extremo, 1958); in *Apuntes* 63 (October 1966); and in his *Teatro* (Santiago: Nascimento, 1979).

BIBLIOGRAPHY: Raúl Barrientos, "Relación mítica entre el campesino y la tierra en tres dramas chilenos," *Antar* 1.1 (1974): 14–25. Julio Durán-Cerda, "Germán Luco Cruchaga y el teatro chileno moderno," *Texto Crítico* 7.22–23 (July–December 1981): 292–309. Durán-Cerda, "Luco Cruchaga, iniciador del realismo crítico en el teatro chileno," *Ideologies and Literature* 4.17 (September–October 1983): 78–93. Luis Merino Reyes, "Aproximación a Germán Luco Cruchaga y su *Viuda de Apablaza*," *Literatura Chilena* 10.2–3 (April–September 1986): 21–22.

MALBRÁN A., Pedro J. (1900–1955). Malbrán wrote several light, humorous plays for theater and radio, sometimes collaborating with Gustavo Campaña (e.g., *A última hora*) or José Martínez (e.g., *Las diez de última, Le llegó el Colo-Colo, El santo de la comadre*). Among his works are *El hombre que casi maté* (The Man I Almost Killed), *El marido de la doctora* (The Doctor's Husband), and *La ruleta de la risa* (The Wheel of Laughter). *El arreglo de Washington* (Washington's Arrangement) was staged as recently as April 1992 when it was performed by the Compañía de Teatro Chileno Sindicato de Actores y Artistas de Chile under direction of Hermógenes Méndez.

WORKS: *El marido de la doctora* (The Doctor's Husband), in *Revista Teatral. La Escena* 61 (1938): 1–19. *El hombre que casi maté* (The Man I Almost Killed) (Santiago: Ercilla, 1940). *Antropófagos por fuerza* (Anthropophagites of Necessity), in *Revista Teatral. La Escena* 25 (n.d.): 1–14. *El arreglo de Washington* (Washington's Arrangement) n.d. *Los dos quesos de Balta Marín* (Balta Marín's Two Cheeses) (Santiago: Nascimento, n.d.). *La guerra de don Ladislao* (Don Ladislao's War), n.d. *Liquidación de maridos* (Clearance Sale on Husbands), n.d. *Los muertos mandan* (The Dead Rule), n.d. *Peñaranda la revuelve. La ruleta de la risa* (Peñaranda Turns It. The Wheel of Laughter), n.d.

MARCHANT [LAZCANO], Jorge (1950–). Journalist, novelist, and playwright, Marchant is a member of the Generation of 1987. *Gabriela*, based on the life of the famous Chilean poet Gabriela Mistral, is his best-known work to date. As Quinteros notes, the idea for the play originated with actress Alicia Quiroga, reflecting her desire to use theater to raise consciousness to contributions that Chilean women have made to culture (103). Marchant authored the text for the production. Music for it was composed by Guillermo Riffo. The production premiered in Santiago on July 17, 1981, with Alicia Quiroga playing the role of Mistral.

WORKS: *Gabriela* (Santiago: Ediciones Cerro Santa Lucía, 1981). *Ultima edición* (Late Edition), 1983. *Como tú me quieras* (However You Love Me), 1984.

BIBLIOGRAPHY: Fernando Josseau, review of "Gabriela," in *El Mercurio*, July 26, 1981, C15. Isis Quinteros, "*Gabriela*: Personaje dramático, personaje teatral," *Latin American Theatre Review* 23.1 (Fall 1989): 103–110.

MAYORGA, Wilfredo (1912–   ). A successful playwright, Mayorga began writing in the latter part of the 1930s. Several of Mayorga's works reflect his fascination with Chilean folklore. His prize-winning plays include *La marea* (The Tide), which won the Municipal Prize in 1939; *La bruja* (The Witch), which won the Quadricentennial Prize in 1941; and *La gran familia* (The Great Family), which won the Gabriela Mistral Prize in 1963. *Un señor de clase media* (A Middle-Class Gentleman), which made its debut in 1963, was revived in October 1990 in a production under the direction of T. Rodríguez.

WORKS: *La marea* (The Tide), 1939. *La bruja* (The Witch), 1941, in his *Teatro*. *El mentiroso* (The Liar), 1942. *El eterno enemigo* (The Eternal Enemy), 1944. *El hermano lobo* (The Half-Breed Brother), (Santiago: Smirnow, 1945) (Valparaíso: Umbral, 1995). *La bruja del maule* (The Witch of the Swindle), 1946. *Los emperadores* (The Emperors), 1949. *El corazón limita con el mar* (The Heart Is Bounded by the Sea), 1950. *Gerardo y sus cuatro temores* (Gerardo and His Four Fears). 1950. *La gran famuta* (The Great Family), 1963. *Por el camino del alba* (Along the Path of Dawn), in his *Teatro*, 1982. *Un señor de clase media* (A Middle-Class Gentleman), in his *Teatro*, 1982. *Teatro* (Theater) (Santiago: Nascimento, 1982). *La comedia de los juglares* (The Comedy of the Minstrels), n.d. *El viajero oportuno* (The Timely Traveler), n.d. *El viento* (The Wind), n.d.

MEZA [WEVAR], Gustavo (1938–   ). Born in Osorno in 1938 and raised in Santiago, Meza completed his theater studies at the University of Chile. Initially, Meza focused his career on directing, but in a personal interview, he commented that after the coup he became a playwright out of sheer necessity, because so many writers had gone into exile (Krugh). In 1974 he founded the Teatro Imagen, an independent professional theater company and school that he has directed since that time. Meza has directed a number of important, hallmark works in contemporary Chilean theater, such as *El último tren* (The Last Train). When Meza writes, it is usually in collaboration with others, and the works are performed by the Teatro Imagen. *Viva Somoza* (Long Live Somoza), for example, was written in collaboration with Juan Radrigán and premiered in 1980.

WORKS: *Cero a la izquierda* (Zero to the Left), 1980. *Viva Somoza* (Long Live Somoza), in collaboration with Juan Radrigán, 1980. *¿Quién dijo que el fantasma de don Indalicio había muerto?* (Who Said the Ghost of Don Indalicio Had Died?), 1982. *El último tren* (The Last Train), collective creation with Teatro Imagen, in María de la Luz Hurtado, Carlos Ochsenius, and Hernán Vidal, eds., *Teatro chileno de la crisis institucional* (Santiago: CENECA, 1982), 102–138. *Cartas de Jenny* (Letters from Jenny), in *Apuntes* 99 (October 1989). *Osorno 1897: Murmuraciones acerca de la muerte de un juez* (Osorno 1897: Rumors About the Death of a Judge), 1993.

BIBLIOGRAPHY: W. Nick Hill, "Signos de la modernidad como autoreflexión crítica en el teatro chileno contemporáneo," *Alba de América* 8.14–15 (July 1990): 245–251. Janis L. Krugh, Interview with Gustavo Meza, June 16, 1994. Héctor Noguera, "Desde Chile," *Latin American Theatre Review* 17.1 (Fall 1983): 65–67. Juan Andrés Piña, "Chile: Intimidad y exploración en *Cartas de Jenny*," *El Público* 67 (April 1989).

MIRANDA, Jaime (1956–   ). Miranda was born in northern Chile on October 4, 1956, and forms part of the Generation of 1987. After the coup, he left for Venezuela—a self-imposed exile—where he received most of his theater training. He later spent some time at Cornell University, directing a workshop on popular theater. Having returned to Venezuela, Miranda wrote *Por la razón o la fuerza* (With Cause or of Necessity)—a play about people who live in exile for economic reasons—which was staged by the Company of Four (Compañía de los Cuatro) under the direction of Humberto Duvauchelle in Venezuela and in Europe. It was also performed at the University of Kansas in 1982 for a Latin American theater festival/symposium and finally in Chile in 1985. It was this work that established Miranda's reputation as a playwright.

WORKS: *Kalus* (Kalus), 1980. *Por la razón o la fuerza. Regreso sin causa* (Santiago: Sinfronteras, 1986).

BIBLIOGRAPHY: Catherine M. Boyle, *Chilean Theater, 1973–1985: Marginality, Power, Selfhood* (Rutherford, NJ: Fairleigh Dickinson University Press, 1992), 165–171, on *Regreso sin causa*. Pedro Bravo-Elizondo, "*Regreso sin causa*: Jaime Miranda y sus razones," *Latin American Theatre Review* 19.2 (Spring 1986): 79–84.

MOLLETO [LABARCA], Enrique (1923–). Known both as a novelist and playwright, Molleto's production is limited. In general, it could be said that his plays deal with themes of sin and regeneration. Although his works are few in number, at least two of them won major Chilean prizes. *La torre* (The Tower) (1961), about a family that has a monster living in the tower of their house, won the Gabriela Mistral Prize. *El sótano* (The Cellar), a two-act, realistic play dealing with the end of World War II and the Germans' persecution of Jews, won the Alerce Prize given by the Association of Chilean Writers in 1963 and the Municipal Prize in 1964.

WORKS: *El telescopio* (The Telescope), 1958, in his collection *Un cambio importante. Un cambio importante* (An Important Change), in his collection *Un cambio importante* (Santiago: Editorial del Pacífico, 1960). *La torre* (The Tower) (Santiago: Editorial del Pacífico, 1961). *El sótano* (The Cellar) (Santiago: Sociedad de Escritores de Chile, 1963); also in *Teatro chileno actual* (Santiago: Zig-Zag, 1966). *La llamada* (The Call), in his collection *Un cambio importante*, 1960. *La confesión* (The Confession), in *Mapocho* 5.1 (1966): 102–105.

BIBLIOGRAPHY: Teodosio Fernández, *El teatro chileno contemporáneo (1941–1973)* (Madrid: Playor, 1982), 53–55.

MOOCK [BOUSQUET], Armando (1894–1942). Considered one of the three most important Chilean playwrights in the first four decades of the twentieth century, Moock also wrote short stories and novels, as well as a few radio plays. Although he began studies to be an architect, he abandoned them to devote himself to writing, a decision that alienated him from his family. In 1919 he moved to Buenos Aires, where the economic situation was better and where his work was better received. At times he had to act in order to earn a living, as was the case during 1918 when he was part of the theater troupe of Enrique Báguena and Arturo Bührle. His success in Argentina was impressive. In 1921—only two years after his arrival—four of his plays were in production there simultaneously. After 1926 Moock served Chile as consul in a number of cities: in the Argentine cities of La Plata, Mendoza, and Buenos Aires; in Vigo and Barcelona (Spain); as well as in Paris and Rome. Although Moock authored more than fifty plays, many of them were never published. Most of his vast theater production is in the *costumbrista* vein with touches of realism or naturalism.

WORKS: *Crisis económica* (Economic Crisis), 1914. *Isabel Sandoval, modas* (Isabel Sandoval, Fashions) (Santiago: Imp. Univ., 1915); also (Santiago: Nascimento, 1929); and in *Apuntes* 50 (July 1965). *Los demonios* (The Demons), 1917. *Un negocio* (A Business), 1918. *Mundial pantomín* (World Pantomime), in his collection *Teatro seleccionado*, vol. 2, 1937; and in *Revista Teatral: Teatro Popular* 1.6 (November 1919): 1–32. *Los siúticos* (The Very Genteel), 1919. *Rosa Espinoza* (Rosa Espinoza), 1921. *La araña gris* (The Gray Spider), in *Revista Teatral: La Escena* 5.213 (July 27, 1992): 1–23. *Era un muchacho alegre* . . . (He Was a Happy Boy . . .), in *Revista Teatral: La Escena* 5.201 (May 4, 1922): n.p. *Monsieur Ferdinand Pontac* (Monsieur Ferdinand Pontac), in *Revista Teatral: La Escena* 5.211 (July 13, 1922): 1–32. *Primer amor* (First Love), in *Revista Teatral: La Escena* 5.221 (July 13, 1922): 33–40. *Un loco escribió este drama o la odisea de Melitón Lamprocles* (A Madman Wrote This Drama or the Odyssey of Melitón Lamprocles),

1923. *El castigo de amar* (The Penalty of Loving), in *Revista de Teatro: Bambalinas* 7.321 (May 31, 1924): 3–46. *La fiesta del corazón* (The Heart's Festival), 1925. *Canción de amor* (Love Song), 1926. *Alzame en tus brazos* (Lift Me in Your Arms), 1927. *Un casamiento a la Yankee* (Marriage Yankee Style), in *Revista de Teatro: Bambalinas* 10.498 (October 29, 1927): 1–31. *Del amor y del odio* (Of Love and Hatred), 1927. *El mundo y yo no estamos de acuerdo* (The World and I Do Not Agree), 1928. *Yo no soy yo* (I Am Not I), in *Revista de Teatro: Bambalinas* 12.579 (May 17, 1928): 2–20. *La conspiración de los lobos o el duelo de las barcas* (The Wolves' Conspiracy or the Duel of the Boats), 1929. *Cuando venga el amor* (When Love Comes) (Santiago: Nascimento, 1929); also in his *Teatro seleccionado*, vol. 1, 1937. *Estoy solo y la quiero* (I'm Alone and I Love Her), in *Revista Teatral: La Escena* 12.558 (March 7, 1929): n.p. *Mocosua* (Buenos Aires: Imp. Márquez, 1929). *Pueblecito* (Little Town) (Santiago: Nascimento, 1929); in his *Teatro seleccionado*, vol. 1; in *Apuntes* 63 (October 1966); and in Julio Durán-Cerda, ed., *Panorama del teatro chileno, 1842–1959* (Santiago: Editorial del Pacífico, 1959). *Los amigos de don Juan* (Don Juan's Friends), 1932. *El miedo de los pingüinos* (The Fear of the Penguins), 1933. *Cóctel* (Cocktail), 1934. *Rigoberto* (Buenos Aires: Argentores, 1935); in *Argentores* 2.58 (May 30, 1935): 1–48; in Willis Knapp Jones, ed., *A Play of Contemporary Argentina* (Boston: D. C. Heath, 1954); and in his *Teatro* (Santiago: Nascimento, 1971). *Un crimen en mi pueblo* (A Crime in My Town) (Santiago: Cultura, 1936); in *Revista Teatral: La Escena* (1936): 1–30; and in *Apuntes* 21 (May 1962). *Alpern*, in his *Teatro seleccionado*, vol. 1, 1937. *El cancionero del niño* (The Child's Collection of Lyrical Poems) (Santiago: Cultura, 1937); also in *Revista Teatral: La Escena* 42 (1937): 1–28. *Del brazo y por la calle* (Arm in Arm and Down the Street) (Buenos Aires: Argentores, 1939); also in (Madrid: Gráficas Arba, 1948); and in *Argentores* 6.173 (December 15, 1939): 1–39. *Natacha*, in his *Teatro seleccionado*, vol. 2, 1937; also in his *Teatro* (Santiago: Nascimento, 1971). *La serpiente* (The Serpent), in his *Teatro seleccionado*, vol. 1, 1937; in Hymen Alpern and José Martel, eds., *Teatro hispanoamericano* (New York: Odyssey Press, 1956); and in Gerardo Luzuriaga et al., *Los clásicos del teatro hispanoamericano* (México: Fondo de Cultura Económica, 1975). *Teatro seleccionado* (Selected Theater), 2 vols. (Santiago: Cultura, 1937). *La viuda de Zumárraga* (The Widow Zumárraga), 1937. *No dejan surgir al criollo* (The Native Is Not Allowed to

Arise), 1938. *Verdejo agradece* (Verdejo Is Grateful), 1939. *Algo triste que llaman amor* (Something Sad They Call Love), 1941. *La señorita Charleston* (Miss Charleston), in his *Teatro seleccionado*, vol. 2; and in *Apuntes* 67 (June 1967). *Teatro* (Theater) (Santiago: Nascimento, 1971). *Los perros* (The Dogs), n.d. *Casimiro Vico primer actor* (Casimiro Vico, Leading Man), n.d.

BIBLIOGRAPHY: Raúl H. Castagnino, "El sentido de la universalidad en el teatro de Armando Moock," *Boletín de Estudios de Teatro* 14 (September 1945): 134–136. Willis K. Jones, "Armando Moock, Forgotten Chilean Dramatist," *Hispania* 22 (1939): 41–50. Raúl H. Silva Cáceres, *La dramaturgia de Armando Moock* (Santiago: Editorial Universitaria, 1964). Silva Cáceres, *Estructura y temática en la dramaturgia de Moock* (Santiago: Universidad de Chile, 1960). Roberto A. Tálice, "La comedia de Moock que rechazaron todas las actrices," *Argentores* 56 (October 1946): 29–30. Juan Ventura Agudiez, "Armando Moock y el sainete argentino," *Duquesne Hispanic Review* 3 (1964): 139–164. Ventura Agudíez, "El concepto costumbrista de Armando Moock," *Revista Hispánica Moderna* 29.2 (April 1963): 148–157.

MORALES, José Ricardo (1915–). Morales was born in Málaga, Spain, in 1915. He began his higher education at the University of Valencia, receiving his degree in history and geography in Chile in 1942. He became a Chilean citizen in 1962. He has taught at both the Catholic University and the University of Chile. Morales was one of the founders of the University of Chile's Experimental Theater, directing the first work staged by that group. In addition to his activities as a director, he has also edited some anthologies of poetry and has authored a number of plays. He received the García Lorca Prize in Spain in October 1990 for his significant contributions to the relationship of Spain with the Americas in the field of theater. Most of his plays are in the Absurd vein, much like the theater of Beckett and Ionesco. His is a theater of ideas where the works have no real plot. Humor is also almost always present in his plays, as are word plays and linguistic games. His plays have been performed in Chile, the United States, Canada, Spain, and France.

WORKS: *Bárbara Fidele* (Faithful Barbara) (Santiago: Ediciones Cruz de Sur, 1952). *El juego de la verdad* (The Game of Truth), 1953. *A ojos cerrados* (With Eyes Closed) (Santiago: Ediciones Espadaña, 1955). *Burlilla de don Berrendo* (Don Berrendo's Little Joke) (Santiago: Imp. Carmelo Soria, 1955). *De puertas adentro* (At Home) (Santiago: Ediciones Espadaña, 1955). *Pequeñas causas* (Little Causes) (Santiago: Ediciones Espadaña, 1955). *La vida imposible* (Impossible Life), 1958 (Santiago: Ed. Universitaria, 1958, 1962). *Los culpables* (The Guilty Ones), in *Anales de la Universidad de Chile* 122.131 (July–September 1964). *La adaptación al medio* (Adapting to the Environment), in his *Teatro de una pieza* (1965). *El canal de la Mancha* (The Canal of La Mancha), in his *Teatro de una pieza* (1965). *La grieta* (The Crack), in his *Teatro de una pieza* (1965). *La Odisea* (The Odyssey), in his *Teatro de una pieza* (1965). *Prohibida la reproducción* (Reproduction Forbidden), in his *Teatro de una pieza* (1965). *Teatro de una pieza* (One-Act Plays) (Santiago: Ed. Universitaria, 1965). *La teoria y el método* (Theory and Method), in his *Teatro de una pieza* (1965). *La cosa humana* (The Human Thing), in *Anales de la Universidad de Chile* 194.138 (April–June 1966). *Hay una nube en su futuro* (There Is a Cloud in Your Future), in *Anales de la Universidad de Chile* (1966); and in *Teatro chileno actual* (Santiago: Zig-Zag, 1966). *Oficio de tinieblas* (Office of Darkness) in *Análes de la Universidad de Chile* (1966). *Un marciano sin objeto* (A Useless Martian), 1967. *Las horas contadas* (Numbered Hours), in *Árbol de Letras* 8 (July 1968). *Cómo el poder de las noticias nos da noticias del poder* (How the Power of the News Gives Us News About Power), in *Primer Acto* 122 (July 1970). *El segundo piso* (The Second Floor), in *Revista de Occidente* 91 (October 1970). *No son farsas: Cinco anuncios dramáticos* (They Are Not Farces: Five Dramatic Announcements) (Santiago: Ed. Universitaria, 1974). *Orfeo y el desodorante o el último viaje a los infiernos* (Orpheus and the Deodorant, or the Last Journey to Hell), in *No son farsas: Cinco anuncios dramáticos* (Santiago: Ed. Universitaria, 1974), 13–78. *Teatro inicial* (Initial Theater) (Santiago: Ed. Universitaria, 1976). *La imagen* (The Image), 1977, in his *Teatro en libertad* (1985). *Nuestro norte es el sur* (Our North Is the South), in his *Teatro en libertad* (1983). *Este jefe no le tiene miedo al gato* (This Boss Isn't Afraid of the Cat), in his *Teatro en libertad* (1983). *Teatro en libertad* (Theater in Freedom) (Madrid: Colección La Avispa, 1983).

BIBLIOGRAPHY: Elena Castedo-Ellerman, *El teatro chileno de mediados del siglo XX* (Santiago: Andrés Bello, 1982), 141–162, 225. Teodosio Fernández, *El teatro chileno contemporáneo (1941–1973)* (Madrid: Playor, 1982), 170–175. José Monleón, "Encuentro tardío y necesario con el exilio de José Ricardo Morales," *Primer Acto* 122 (July 1970).

MORENO, Gloria *See* LARRAÍN DE IRARRÁZAVAL, Ester.

MORGADO, Benjamín (1909–). Known as a poet and author of short stories, novels, essays, and theater for children (e.g., *El rey Midas*, 1935; *Trasgolisto*, 1935) and adults. His theater works won him the Municipal Prize and the prize for Direction of National Theater, among others. Most of his works (e.g., *Tempestad sin sollozos* [Tempest Without Sobs], *Te querré toda la vida* [I Will Love You All My Life], *Trébol de cuatro hojas* [Four-Leaf Clover]) are sentimental comedies, which were popular in the 1930s but have left no lasting impression.

WORKS: *El hombre del brazo encogido* (The Man with the Withered Arm), 1936. *Trébol de cuatro hojas* (Four-Leaf Clover) (Santiago: Ed. "Senda," 1938). *Petroleo* (Oil) (Santiago: Ediciones Senda, 1941). *La sombra viene del mar* (The Shadow Comes from the Sea), 1943. *Te querré toda la vida* (I Will Love You All My Life), in *Tempestad sin sollozos* (1945). *Tempestad sin sollozos* (Tempest Without Sobs, 1945) (Santiago: Gutenberg Imp., 1946). *X.X. saluda atte. a Ud.* (Sincerely Yours) (Santiago: Ed. "Senda," 1950). *Hoy comienza el olvido* (Forgetting Begins Today), 1954. *¿Qué prefiere Ud.?* (What Do You Prefer?), 1958. *7-4-2* (Santiago: Ediciones Senda, 1937). *Los viejos deben descansar* (The Elderly Should Rest), 1974. *La maestra era pobre* (The Teacher Was Poor), 1976.

NERUDA, Pablo (1904–1973). Neruda was born of humble origins on July 12, 1904, in Parral, a small town in southern Chile. Christened Neftalí Eliecer Ricardo Reyes Basoalto, he changed his name to Pablo Neruda in 1920. Although he was not able to complete his university studies, he was already highly regarded as a poet by the time he was twenty years old. He traveled extensively, and from 1952 on, he mostly made his home in Chile, although he continued to travel. After Allende became president, he named Neruda the Chilean ambassador to France. In 1971 while serving in that capacity, he was awarded the Nobel Prize for Literature. In 1972, suffering from cancer, he returned to Chile and his home on Isla Negra, where he continued to write. He died on September 23, 1973—just a few days after the military coup that overthrew the Allende government.

Although Neruda has been almost exclusively known for his poetry, he wrote one noteworthy play, *Fulgor y muerte de Joaquín Murieta* (Splendor and Death of Joaquín Murieta), which made its debut under the direction of Pedro Orthous at the University of Chile in 1967. As one might expect, the play is a mixture of poetry and theater. Brechtian in structure and in its use of the V-effect, the play also shows the influence of the Japanese Noh and Kabuki dramatic forms, with its intermittent dances, songs, orchestal interludes, and choruses.

WORKS: *Fulgor y muerte de Joaquín Murieta* (Santiago: Zig-Zag, 1967) and (Buenos Aires: Losada, 1974); German tr., *Glanz und Tod des Joaquin Murieta*, in *Theater Heute* 4 (April 1971); English tr. by Ben Belitt, *Splendor and Death of Joaquín Murieta* (New York, 1972).

BIBLIOGRAPHY: Elena Castedo-Ellerman, *El teatro chileno de mediados del siglo XX* (Santiago: Andrés Bello, 1982), 200–202. Ivan Droguett, "Apuntes sobre *Fulgor y muerte de Joaquín Murieta* de Pablo Neruda," *Latin American Theatre Review* 2.1 (1968): 39–48.

ORREGO VICUÑA, Eugenio (1900–1959). The son of playwright Luis Orrego Luco, Eugenio Orrego Vicuña was born in 1900. Many of his early plays are sentimental plays based on the theme of love, such as *El amo de su alma* (Her Soul's Master) (1924). Other works are historical in nature. His *Ensayos dramáticos* (Dramatic Experiments) (1948) was awarded the Municipal Prize. He also authored a book about nationalism in the theater of Chile.

WORKS: *La rechazada* (The Rejected Woman) (Santiago: Editorial Hispánica, 1923). *El amo de su alma* (Her Soul's Master) (Santiago: Chile Nuevo,

1924). *Tragedia interior* (Internal Tragedy) (Santiago, 1925). *Del nacionalismo en el teatro chileno* (On Nationalism in Chilean Theater), 1927. *Vírgenes modernas* (Modern Virgins) (Santiago: Imprenta Universitaria, 1930). *Mujeres, paisajes y templos* (Women, Landscapes and Temples), 1931. *El lobo* (The Wolf) (Santiago: Nascimento, 1933). *San Martín* (San Martín) (Santiago: Ed. Cultura, 1938). *El alba de oro* (The Golden Dawn), in *Apuntes* 99.41 (1941): 46–192. *Camino adelante* (Straight On), in collaboration with Max Jara (Santiago: Universidad de Chile, 1941). *O'Higgins* (O'Higgins), 1942. *Carrera* (Carrera) (Santiago: Universidad de Chile, 1943). *El reino sin término* (The Endless Kingdom) (Santiago: Universidad de Chile, 1946). *El amigo de Hamlet, o El manicomio* (Hamlet's Friend, or the Insane Asylum), in his *Ensayos dramáticos* (1948). *Catalina Isabel, o Cuando Chile era reino* (Catherine Elizabeth, or When Chile Was a Kingdom), in his *Ensayos dramáticos* (1948). *En el tiempo de los virreyes* (In the Time of the Viceroys), in his *Ensayos dramáticos* (1948). *En el umbrat* (On the Threshold), in his *Ensayos dramáticos* (1948). *Ensayos dramáticos* (Dramatic Experiments) (Santiago: Universidad de Chile, 1948). *La niña sonrisa* (The Little Smile), in his *Ensayos dramáticos* (1948). *La noche de San Silvestre* (The Night of St. Sylvester), in his *Ensayos dramáticos* (1948).

PARRA, Marco Antonio de la (1952–). Parra was born in Santiago in 1952. A member of the Generation of 1987, Parra is known as a director, playwright, and author of short stories and novels. A psychiatrist by profession, he wrote his first plays (*Quiebrespejos* [Cracked Mirrows] and *Brisca* [Brisque]) in 1974 while he was still a medical student. Torn between his desire to be a doctor and his desire to write, Parra has managed to do both quite successfully. The play that established Parra as one of Chile's foremost contemporary playwrights was *Lo crudo, lo cocido y lo podrido* (The Raw, the Cooked and the Rotten), which made its debut under the direction of Gustavo Meza at the Catholic University on June 30, 1978. In 1979 this play won a shared first prize at New York's Theater of Latin America competition. Most of Parra's plays deal in some way with the theme of power and how it corrupts and mix a wide variety of elements from popular culture. His messages, as well as the form they take, have set him apart as one of Chile's most outstanding playwrights at the present time. Most recently he has written *Heroína (El mito del nacimiento del héroe)* (Heroine [The Myth of the Hero's Birth]), *La pequeña historia de Chile* (Brief History of Chile), *El continente negro* (The Black Continent), *Madrid/Sarajevo, Tristán e Isolda (Bolero estático)* (Tristan and Isolde [Static Bolero]), and *Ofelia* (Ophelia).

WORKS: *Quiebrespejos* (Cracked Mirrows), 1974. *Brisca* (Brisque), 1974. *Matatangos* (Tango Killer), 1978 (Santiago: Nascimento, 1983). *Lo crudo, lo cocido y lo podrido* (The Raw, the Cooked and the Rotten) (Santiago: Nascimento, 1983); also in Moisés Pérez Coterillo, ed., *Teatro chileno contemporáneo* (Madrid: Fondo de Cultura Económica, 1992), 809–865; and in María de la Luz Hurtado, Carlos Echsenius, and Hernán Vidal, eds., *Teatro chileno de la crisis institucional, 1973–1980* (Minneapolis and Santiago: University of Minnesota and CENECA, 1982), 250–286. *King Kong Palace y La secreta obscenidad de cada día* (King Kong Palace and Secret Obscenities), suplemento de *El Público*, 1985. *El deseo de toda ciudadana* (The Desire of Every Female Citizen), 1987. *La secreta obscenidad de cada día / Infieles / Obscenamente (in)fiel* (The Secret Obscenity of Every Day / The Unfaithful / Obscenely [Un]Faithful) (Santiago: Planeta, 1988). *La noche de los volantines* (The Night of the Kites), 1989. *Infieles* (The Unfaithful); in *La secreta obscenidad de cada día / Infieles / Obscenamente (in)fiel*; English tr. by Charles Philip Thomas, *Latin American Literary Review* 40 (January–June 1989): 34–47. *King Kong Palace (o El exilio de Tarzán) y Dostoievski va a la playa* (King Kong Palace or Tarzan's Exile and Dostoyevski Goes to the Beach) (Santiago: Pehuén Editores, 1990). *Límites* (Limits), 1991. *El padre muerto* (The Dead Father), 1991. *La secreta obscenidad de cada día* (Secret Obscenities), in *Teatro CELCIT* 1.2 (1991); English tr. by Charles Philip Thomas, in *Latin American Literary Review* 16.32 (July–December 1988): 67–113. *Dédalus en el vientre de la bestia (Sudamérica)* (Dedalus in the Belly of the Beast [South America]), 1992. *Lindo país esquina con vista al mar* (Pretty Country on the Corner with a View of the Sea), in collaboration with Darío Osses, Jorge Gajardo, and Ictus, in Moisés Pérez Coterillo, ed., *Teatro chileno contemporáneo* (Madrid: Fondo de Cultura Económica, 1992), 969–1039 (Parra authored segment titled "Toda una vida" [An Entire Life]). *Telémaco* (Telemachus), 1993.

Tristán e Isolda (Bolero estático) (Tristan and Isolde), 1993.

BIBLIOGRAPHY: Jacqueline Eyring Bixler, "Kitsch and Corruption: Referential Degeneration in the Theatre of Marco Antonio de la Parra," *Siglo XX: 20th Century* 11.1–2 (1993): 11–29. Catherine M. Boyle, *Chilean Theater, 1973–1985: Marginality, Power, Selfhood* (Rutherford, NJ: Fairleigh Dickinson University Press, 1992), 98–107 on *Lo crudo, lo cocido y lo podrido*, and 178–184 on his segment "Toda una vida" in *Lindo país esquina con vista al mar*. Boyle, "La obra dramática de Marco Antonio de la Parra o la representación de un juego hamletiano," *Alba de América* 7.12–13 (July 1989): 145–150. Enzo Cozzi, "Political Theatre in Present-Day Chile: A Duality of Approaches," *New Theatre Quarterly* 6.22 (May 1990): 119–127. Marco Antonio de la Parra, "El teatro del cambio," *Primer Acto* 240 (September–October 1991): 44–49. Grínor Rojo and Sara Rojo, "Teatro chileno: 1983–1987: Observaciones preliminares," *Alba de América* 7.12–13 (July 1989): 31–34.

PÉREZ DE ARCE, Camilo (1912–1970). Born in 1912, Pérez de Arce wrote detective novels under the pseudonyms of James Ernhard and Guillermo Blanco. With few exceptions his theater is also in this vein: *Bajo el signo de la muerte* (Under the Sign of Death) (1951); *Raza de bronce* (Bronze Race) (1954); and his best-remembered work, *Comedia para asesinos* (Comedy for Murderers), (1957), a melodrama that was awarded the Teatro de Ensayo Prize in 1957. One exception to the murder mystery genre was *El Cid* (The Cid), a surrealistic drama about the Spanish hero. This play was produced by the Teatro de Ensayo in 1950 and won Santiago's Municipal Prize that year.

WORKS: *El Cid* (The Cid), 1950. *Bajo el signo de la muerte* (Under the Sign of Death), 1951. *La rebelión de la aldea* (The Town's Rebellion), 1952. *El túnel* (The Tunnel), 1953. *Raza de bronce* (Bronze Race), 1954. *El correo del rey* (The King's Mail), 1955. *Comedia para asesinos* (Comedy for Murderers), in *Finis Terrae* 4.13 (1957): 63–103. *Visitantes de la muerte* (Visitors of Death), 1959. *La Plaza de los Cuatro* (The Plaza of the Four), 1964. *Sesentaiséis trece* (Sixty-six Thirteen), n.d.

PESUTIC, Mauricio (19?–). One of Chile's rising directors and playwrights, Pesutic collaborated with Raúl Osorio in the writing of *Los payasos de la esperanza* (Clowns of Hope), which premiered in 1977 in a production of the Theater Research Workshop (Taller de Investigación Teatral) under Osorio's direction. Undoubtedly his best-known work, this play is about three unemployed clowns who are waiting to hear if their proposal to entertain children eating in soup kitchens will be accepted by the church office responsible for the soup kitchens. Under the author's direction *Antonio, no sé, Isidro, Domingo* (Anthony, I Don't Know, Isidore, Dominic) made its debut in 1984 at the Catholic University in Santiago.

WORKS: *Los payasos de la esperanza* (Clowns of Hope), 1977. *Antonio, no sé, Isidro, Domingo* (Anthony, I Don't Know, Isidore, Dominic), 1984. *Marengo* (Marengo), 1988.

BIBLIOGRAPHY: Catherine M. Boyle, *Chilean Theater, 1973–1985: Marginality, Power, Selfhood* (Rutherford, NJ: Fairleigh Dickinson University Press, 1992), 70–78, on *Los payasos de la esperanza*.

PETIT [M.], Magdalena (1900–1968). Known primarily for her historical novels, Petit also wrote theater. Her best-known play was *La Quintrala* (1935)—an adaptation of her novel of the same title—which deals with the legend of a demon-possessed murderess of the colonial period. A film version of this work also exists. *El hijo del Caleuche* (Caleuche's Son) won the Municipal Theater's competition in 1940 and was subsequently adapted into a novel Petit entitled *El Caleuche* (1946). She also wrote a few plays for children.

WORKS: *La Quintrala* (Santiago: Imp. "El Esfuerzo," 1935). *El hijo del Caleuche* (Caleuche's Son), 1940.

BIBLIOGRAPHY: Marjorie Agosín, "Una bruja novelada: 'La Quintrala' de Magdalena Petit," *Chasqui* 12.1 (1982): 3–13.

PINEDA [DEVIA], José (1937–). A member of the Generation of 1972, Pineda completed his studies in acting at the Theater School of the University of Chile in 1959. He has worked with several theater groups (e.g., Ictus, Theater Institute at the University of

Chile [ITUCH], and the Theater of the University of Concepción). Currently, he is on the faculty of the University of Chile's School of Theater. His work has also included adaptations for television, as well as theater for children. *Coronación* (Coronation) (1966), his adaptation of the novel by José Donoso, was staged in 1966 in a production of the Theater School at the University of Chile. *Los marginados* (The Dispossessed) (1967), which won first prize at a competition organized by the Association of Chilean Writers (Sociedad de Escritores de Chile), takes a critical view of the superficiality of the wealthy who decide to help the poor without really understanding the problems they face.

WORKS: *Pensión para gente sola* (Boardinghouse for Lonely People), 1959. *El robot Ping-Pong* (The Ping-Pong Robot), in *Apuntes* 38 (May 1964); and in *Teatro infantil* (Santiago: Ministerio de Educacion Pública, 1990). *Coronación* (Coronation), 1966. *Los marginados* (The Dispossessed) (Santiago: Ed. Universitaria, 1967). *Peligro a 50 metros* (Danger 50 Meters Ahead), coauthor with Alejandro Sieveking, in *Apuntes* 70 (June 1968) (Pineda wrote the first part called *Las obras de misericordia* [Works of Pity], 1968). *La Kermesse*, 1974. *Cabaret Bijoux* (Bijoux Cabaret), coauthor with Zimmer, 1976. *El boquete* (The Narrow Opening), 1980. *80 mil hojas* (80,000 Leaves), 1980. *El fantasma de la Avda. España* (The Phantom of Spain Avenue), 1986. *¡Cierra esa boca, Conchita!* (Close That Mouth, Conchita!), 1992.

BIBLIOGRAPHY: Elena Castedo-Ellerman, *Teatro chileno de mediados del siglo XX* (Santiago: Andrés Bello, 1982), 206–208, on *Las obras de misericordia*.

RADRIGÁN [ROJAS], Juan (1937–). An author of short stories, novels, poetry, and plays, Radrigán was born on January 23, 1937, in Antofagasta. Of humble origins, Radrigán had to work from a very young age. He began writing theater in the last few years of the 1970s, achieving recognition and success with his first play, *Testimonio de las muertes de Sabina* (Testimony Regarding Sabina's Deaths), which the Teatro del Angel staged in 1979. For the next decade he would be considered one of Chile's most outstanding playwrights, and his works were performed—most often by the group El Telón—in cities throughout Chile, reaching not only traditional audiences attending professional theater but also schools, labor unions, and the urban poor. His works have also been performed in other countries of the Americas and in Europe. In 1982 he won the Municipal Prize, as well as the Art Critics' Prize for Best Dramatist of the Year. His most recent play, *La contienda humana* (The Human Struggle), was written and staged in 1987. Radrigán has not written any new plays since the end of the military regime, citing the problem of what to write about. He questions how one can write without dealing with the facts about what happened during the military dictatorship. Nevertheless, Radrigán's creative energy is still at work as he writes the lyrics for a national opera to be called *El encuentramiento*. With music by Patricio Solovera, this popular opera will incorporate rhythms from all over Latin America (Krugh, interview).

WORKS: *Los olvidados* (The Forgotten Ones), 1982. *La felicidad de los García* (The Garcías's Happiness), 1983. *Made in Chile*, 1984. *Teatro de Juan Radrigán* (Juan Radrigán's Theater), 1st ed. (Santiago and Minneapolis: CENECA and University of Minnesota, 1984). *Las voces de la ira* (Voices of Wrath), 1984. *La contienda humana* (The Human Struggle) (Santiago: Ediciones Literatura Alternativa, 1989). *Isabel desterrada en Isabel* (Isabel Exiled in Isabel), in Juan Andrés Piña, ed., *Teatro chileno en un acto (1955–1985)* (Santiago: Teatro Taller, 1989). *Hechos consumados* (When All Is Said and Done), in Moisés Pérez Coterillo, ed. *Teatro chileno contemporáneo* (Madrid: Fondo de Cultura Económica, 1992), 1049–1097; also in *Teatro de Juan Radrigán (11 obras)*, 211–244. *Las brutas* (The Oafish Women), in *Teatro de Juan Radrigán (11 obras)*, (1993), 97–135. *Informe para indiferentes* (Report for the Indifferent), in *Teatro de Juan Radrigán (11 obras)*, (1993), 285–316. *Islas de porfiado amor* (Islands of Obstinate Love), in *Teatro de Juan Radrigán (11 obras)*, (1993), 317–351. *El loco y la triste* (The Crazy Man and the Sad Woman), in *Teatro de Juan Radrigán (11 obras)*, (1993), 137–173. *Redoble fúnebre para lobos y corderos: Isabel desterrada en Isabel, Sin motivo aparente, El invitado* (Funeral Knell for Lambs and Wolves: Isabel Exiled in Isabel, For No Apparent Reason, The Guest), in *Teatro de Juan Radrigán (11 obras)*, (1993), 175–209. *Teatro de Juan Radrigán (11 obras)* (Juan Radrigán's Theater [11 Plays]), 2nd ed. (Santiago: LOM Ediciones, 1993). *Testimonio de las muertes de Sabina* (Testimony Regarding Sabina's Deaths), in *Teatro de Juan Radrigán (11 obras)*, (1993), 51–82. *El toro por las astas* (The Bull by the Horns), in *Teatro de Juan Radrigán (11 obras)*, (1993), 245–283. "¡¡Viva Somoza!!" (Long Live Somoza!!), in collaboration with Gustavo Meza, 3rd episode of *Cuestión de ubicación*, in *Teatro de Juan Radrigán (11 obras)*, (1993), 83–96. *Los borrachos de luna* (Moondrunk), in *Pueblo del mal amor/Los borrachos de luna* (Santiago: Editorial Ñuke Mapu, n.d.). *Cuestión de ubicación* (A Question of Position), n.d. *Memorias del olvido* (Memories of Forgetting), n.d. *Pueblo del mal amor / Los borrachos de luna* (Town of Bad Love/ Moondrunk) (Santiago: Editorial Ñuke Mapu, n.d.). *Tengo aparición de la verdad* (I Have a Vision of the Truth), n.d.

BIBLIOGRAPHY: *Apuntes* 95 (Spring 1987) contains some articles on and an interview with Radrigán. Catherine M. Boyle, *Chilean Theater, 1973–1985*: Marginality, Power, Selfhood (Rutherford, NJ: Fairleigh Dickinson University Press, 1992), 122–127 on *Testimonio de las muertes de Sabina*, 127–131 on *El invitado*, and 131–139 on *El toro por las astas*. Pedro Bravo-Elizondo, "El dramaturgo de *Los olvidados*: Entrevista con Juan Radrigán," *Latin American Theatre Review* 17.1 (Fall 1983): 61–63. Janis L. Krugh, Interview with Juan Radrigán, June 26, 1994. Lidia Neghme Echeverría, "La resistencia cultural en *El toro por las astas* de Radrigán," *Latin American Theatre Review* 22.1 (Fall 1988): 23–28.

REQUENA, María Asunción (1915–1986). Born in 1915, Requena spent much of her childhood in Punta Arenas in southern Chile. A dentist by profession, she began writing plays as a form of relaxation and was affiliated with the Catholic University in Santiago. Like many of her compatriots, she and her husband—Raúl Rivera, the former director of the theater group TEKNOS at the Technical University—went into exile in France after the military coup in 1973. Still in exile, Requena died in Lille on March 18, 1986. Her works are mostly social or historical in nature and usually take place in the southern part of Chile. One of Requena's most remembered plays is *El camino más largo* (The Longest Road), which relates the story of Dr. Ernestina Pérez, the first woman to practice medicine in Chile. In general, it could be said that Requena's theater production made significant folkloric contributions and encouraged other playwrights to consider Chile and its history as suitable topics for theater.

WORKS: *Míster Jones llega a las ocho* (Mr. Jones Arrives at Eight O'Clock), 1952. *Fuerte Bulnes* (Fort Bulnes) (Santiago: Premio Teatro Experimental de la Universidad de Chile, 1953); also in *Teatro* 5 (August 1955): 37–79; and in Requena's *Teatro. Cuento de invierno* (Winter Story), later retitled *El criadero de zorros de Magallanes* (The Foxes' Breeding Grounds of Magellan), 1957. *El camino más largo* (The Longest Road), 1958. *Pan caliente* (Hot Bread), 1958 (Santiago: Sociedad de Escritores de Chile, 1961); and in *Apuntes* 71 (June 1968). *Piel de tigre* (Tiger Skin), 1961. *Ayayema* (Santiago: Sociedad de Escritores de Chile, 1964); also in Julio Durán-Cerda, ed., *Teatro chileno contemporáneo* (Mexico City: Aguilar, 1970); and in Requena's *Teatro. Aysén*, n.d. *Chiloé, cielos cubiertos* (Chiloé, Gray Skies, 1972), in Moisés Pérez Coterillo, ed., *Teatro chileno contemporáneo* (Madrid: Fondo de Cultura Económica, 1992), 599–674 also in Requena's *Teatro*, 202–293. *Homo chilensis*, 1973. *Teatro* (Theater) (Santiago: Nascimento, 1979). *La Chilota*, n.d.

BIBLIOGRAPHY: Nora Eidelberg, "*Ayayema* de María Asunción Requena," in *Teatro experimental hispanoamericano, 1960–1980: La realidad social como manipulación* (Minneapolis: Institute for the Study of Ideologies and Literature, 1985), 147–151. Willis Knapp Jones, "Chile's Dramatic Renaissance," *Hispania* 44.1 (1961): 89–94. Jones, "New Life in Chile's Theatre," *Modern Drama* 2.1 (1959): 57–62. Juan Villegas, "María Asunción Requena: Exito e historia del teatro," *Latin American Theatre Review* 28.2 (Spring 1995): 19–37.

RIVANO, Luis (1933–). Born in Cauquenes in 1933, Rivano is known as an author of novels, short stories, plays, and poetry. Until 1965, when his first novel (*Esto no es el paraíso*) was published, he was a policeman—a *carabinero*. With the appearance of that novel, he was abruptly fired. When asked if writing wasn't a rather unusual pastime for a policeman, Rivano responded that the truly odd thing was that he had never been a policeman at all (Krugh, Interview). Since 1965 he has operated a successful bookstore in Santiago, has continued to

write, and has been an active participant in the production of several of his plays. Rivano currently resides in Santiago with his wife, Beatriz. Rivano's works are noteworthy for their realism, use of humor, strong language, and slang. The characters who inhabit his theatrical world are mostly from the seamier side of life: pimps, prostitutes, gigolos, thieves, prisoners. Nearly all of Rivano's plays to date have been performed. *Sexy boom* (Sexy Boom) premiered in 1985. *El rucio de los cuchillos* (The Knife Maker), based on his book of short stories by same title, premiered in May 1991 in a production of the Buvas Company at the Teatro El Conventillo II under the direction of Silvia Santelices.

WORKS: *Te llamabas Rosicler* (Your Name Was Rosicler) (Santiago: Ediciones de la Librería de Luis Rivano, 1976); in *Te llamabas Rosicler. Por sospecha. ¿Dónde estará la Jeannette?* (Santiago de Chile: Pehuén Editores, 1990), 7–74; and in Moisés Pérez Coterillo, ed., *Teatro chileno contemporáneo* (Madrid: Fondo de Cultura Económica, 1992), 739–797. *Un gasfíter en sociedad* (A Plumber in Society), 1977. *Los matarifes* (The Butchers), 1977. *Por sospecha* (Under Suspicion), 1979), in *Te llamabas Rosicler. Por sospecha. ¿Dónde estará la Jeannette?* (Santiago: Pehuén Editores, 1990), 75–115. *La ultima canción* (The Last Song), 1981. *Casados y descasados* (Married and Divorced), 1982. *Remigio o el hombre que compraba y vendía cosas* (Remigio, or The Man Who Bought and Sold Things), 1982. *Míster Espectáculo* (Mr. Spectacle), 1983. *¿Dónde estará la Jeannette?* (I Wonder Where Jeannette Is?), 1984, in *Te llamabas Rosicler. Por sospecha. ¿Dónde estará la Jeannette?* (Santiago: Pehuén Editores, 1990), 117–193. *Sexy boom* (Sexy Boom), 1985. *La miseria y el show* (Wretchedness and the Show), 1991. *El rucio de los cuchillos* (The Knife Maker), 1991.

BIBLIOGRAPHY: Pedro Bravo-Elizondo, "Historias de marginalidad a ritmo de tango," in Moisés Pérez Coterillo, ed., *Teatro chileno contemporáneo* (Madrid: Fondo de Cultura Económica, 1992), 733–737. Janis L. Krugh, Interview with Luis Rivano, (June 25, 1994). Juan Andrés Piña, "El teatro de Luis Rivano: Historias de la otra marginalidad," in Luis Rivano, *Te llamabas Rosicler. Por sospecha. ¿Dónde estará la Jeannette?* (Santiago: Pehuén Editores, 1990), 197–205.

ROEPKE, Gabriela (1920–). Roepke was born in Santiago in 1920. A member of the Generation of 1957, she was one of the founders of the Teatro de Ensayo at the Catholic University of Chile. Known especially for her psychological dramas, she has also written plays for children, as well as two collections of poetry. She began her theater studies in Chile, continuing them in the United States (at the University of North Carolina) and France (at the Sorbonne). She has taught at the Catholic University of Chile, the University of Kansas, Kansas State University, and the Julliard School. Residing in New York, she has turned to opera and teaching voice. In general, Roepke's works tend to be more universal in theme than those of other Chilean playwrights of her generation, not dealing with issues particular to Chile. Although Castedo-Ellerman considers *Martes 13* (Tuesday, the 13th)—a trilogy of Absurd, one-act plays—to be Roepke's most original and successfully developed work (163), her best-known play is undoubtedly *Una mariposa blanca* (The White Butterfly), a one-act play that was written and first performed in the United States in 1957. The Catholic University's Teatro de Ensayo staged another production of it in Santiago in 1959. This work was transformed into an opera that was presented at New York City's Lincoln Center in 1971 (Dauster and Lyday, 70).

WORKS: *La invitación* (The Invitation), 1954. *Los culpables* (The Guilty), 1955; later titled *Juegos silenciosos* (Silent Games), 1959. *Las santas mujeres* (The Holy Women), 1955. *Una mariposa blanca* (The White Butterfly), 1957, in *Apuntes* 13 (July 1961): 20–45; also in *Teatro chileno actual* (Santiago: Zig-Zag, 1966); and in Frank Dauster and Leon F. Lyday, eds., *En un acto*, 2nd ed. (Boston: Heinle & Heinle, 1983), 69–88; English tr. by Thomas and Mary Patterson, in Margaret Gardner Mayorga, ed., *Best Short Plays 1959/60* (New York: Dodd-Mead, 1961). *Los peligros de la buena literatura* (The Dangers of Good Literature), 1957, in *Apuntes* 18 (1961): 24–40. *La telaraña* (The Spider's Web), 1958, in *Apuntes* 54 (November 1965): 8–50. *Casi en primavera* (Almost in Springtime), 1959. *Dúo* (Duet), 1959. *Juegos silenciosos* (Silent Games), 1959, revised version of *Los culpables*, 1955. *El bien fingido* (The Feigned Interest), 1964. *Un castillo sin fantasmas* (A Castle without Ghosts), 1965. *Martes 13* (Tuesday, the 13th), in *Mapocho* (1970).

BIBLIOGRAPHY: Elena Castedo-Ellerman, *El teatro chileno de mediados del siglo XX* (Santiago: Andrés Bello, 1982), 163–172. David Dávila, "The Life and Theater of Gabriela Roepke" (Ph.D. diss., University of Cincinnati, 1973). Hans Ehrmann, "Theatre in Chile: A Middle-Class Conundrum," *Drama Review* (1970): 77–86. Willis Knapp Jones, "Chile's Dramatic Renaissance," *Hispania* 44.1 (March 1961): 89–94.

RUIZ [PINO], Raúl (1941–). A member of the Generation of 1972, Ruiz was born in 1941. Like Miguel Littín, he turned to the film industry in the early 1970s as a means of reaching a larger audience than was possible with the theater. In general, Ruiz's works tend to revolve around some rite or ceremony associated with daily life. His plays are consistently in the Absurd vein, but here the absurd is employed not to underline the futility of life but rather to criticize tradition and authority and to suggest the possibility of social change (Castedo-Ellerman, 175). In this sense, his work could be considered a form of social protest, following the lines of Jorge Díaz's theater. The influence of Genet, Ionesco, and Arrabal are also evident in Ruiz's theater. *La maleta* (The Suitcase) (1962), performed by the Company of Four in 1962, is perhaps his best-known play.

WORKS: *El automóvil* (The Automobile), 1959. *Babel*, 1960. *La estatua* (The Statue), 1960. *El sillón* (The Armchair), 1960. *A escape* (At Full Speed), 1961. *La ciudad se construye de noche* (The City Is Built at Night), 1961. *El niño que quiere hacer las tareas* (The Boy Who Wants to Do His Homework), 1961, in *Apuntes* 14 (August 1961): 16–32. *Zoológico* (Zoo), 1961, in *Teatro. Boletín Oficial del ITUCH* 3 (1961): 6–12. *Cambio de guardia* (Change of Guard), 1962. *El equipaje* (The Baggage), 1962. *El estafador* (The Cheater), 1962, in Miller Williams, ed., and trans., *Chile: An Anthology of New Writing* (Kent, OH: Kent State University Press, 1968). *La maleta* (The Suitcase), 1962. *Trilogía sobre el tema de Ulises* (Trilogy on the Theme of Ulysses), 1962.

BIBLIOGRAPHY: Elena Castedo-Ellerman, *El teatro chileno de mediados del siglo XX* (Santiago: Andrés Bello, 1982), 172–176.

SARAH [COMANDARI], Roberto (1918–). A psychiatrist by profession, Sarah writes under the pseudonym of Andrés Terbay and is the author of novels, short stories, and plays. Particularly successful during the early years of the 1950s, Sarah's plays tend to deal with Chilean life. Sarah's best-known work is undoubtedly *Algún día* (Some Day) (1949), a sad drama about the monotonous life of an Italian immigrant family, hoping to better their lifestyle. This play made its debut in Santiago on December 25, 1949, and won the Experimental Theater competition in that year.

WORKS: *Las idólatras* (The Idolaters), 1938. *Por encima de los dioses* (Above the Gods), 1941. *Algún día* (Some Day), 1949 (Santiago: Escuela Nacional de Artes Gráf., 1950). *Mi vida es para ti* (My Life Is for You), 1952. *El viajero parte al alba* (The Traveler Leaves at Dawn), 1952. *El collar rojo* (The Red Necklace), 1954. *La sombra prohibida* (The Forbidden Shadow), 1955. *Una luz en la lluvia* (A Light in the Rain), 1959. *La voz dulce* (The Sweet Voice), 1959.

SHARIM [PAZ], Nissim (1932–). Trained as a lawyer, Sharim is known as an actor, director, playwright, and critic. He began his association with the theater group Ictus as an amateur actor. He and Delfina Guzmán have served as directors for the group.

WORKS: *Cuestionemos la cuestión* (Let's Question the Matter), 1969, in *Mapocho* 20 (Summer 1970): 131–180. *La mar estaba serena* (The Sea Was Calm), in collaboration with Claudio di Girólamo, Carlos Genovese, Sergio Vodanovic, and Ictus, 1981. *Prohibido suicidarse en democracia* (No Committing Suicide in Democracy), in collaboration with Carlos Genovese, n.d.

BIBLIOGRAPHY: Juan Andrés Piña, "Entrevista con Nissim Sharim de Ictus: Las razones de una primavera," *Apsi* (July 17–30, 1984): 34–35.

SIEVEKING, Alejandro (1934–). Born in Chile in 1934, Sieveking is known as an actor, director, and one of Chile's most prolific playwrights. A member of the Generation of 1957, he began his studies in architecture at the University of Chile but later changed his focus to acting and theater. Having married well-known Chilean actress Bélgica Castro, he founded a theater company known as the Teatro del Ángel. While the company was on tour in 1974, Sieveking went into voluntary exile in Costa Rica, where he founded (in San José) a new theater group, also called the Teatro del Ángel. Sieveking and his wife remained in exile in Costa Rica for ten years (1974–1984). He directed all of the plays performed at the Teatro del Ángel during this time and performed as an actor in most of them. In Costa Rica Sieveking remained active as a playwright, writing *Pequeños animales abatidos* (Small Game Hunt) (1974), *Volar con sólo un ala* (Flying on Only One Wing) (1976), *La diablada* (The She-Deviled) (1975), *La comadre Lola* (Godmother Lola) (1982), and *El uno para el otro* (For One Another) (1979). In November of 1984 he and his wife returned to Santiago and began preparations for filming a television series titled *Amigos del alma*.

WORKS: *Encuentro con la sombra* (Encounter with the Shadow), 1955. *Una plaza sin pájaros* (A Plaza Without Birds), 1955. *El fin de febrero* (The End of February) (Santiago: ITUCH, 1957). *Mi hermano Cristián* (My Brother Christian), 1957 (Santiago: ITUCH, 1958); also in *Apuntes* 64 (November 1966) and in *Teatro chileno actual* (Santiago: Zig-Zag, 1966). *La abuelita encantada* (The Bewitched Grandma), 1958. *Donde no está la pared* (Where There Is No Wall), 1958, in *Apuntes* 42 (September 1964). *Asunto sofisticado* (Sophisticated Matter), 1959. *Honorato, el caballo del circo* (Honorato, the Circus Horse), 1959. *Parecido a la felicidad* (Something Like Happiness), 1959 (Santiago: ITUCH, 1959). *La coronación de Pierrot* (Pierrot's Coronation), 1960. *Los hermanastros* (The Stepbrothers), 1960; revised versions in 1963. *La cama en el medio de la pieza* (The Bed in the Middle of the Room), 1961. *La gran batalla del living* (The Great Battle of the Living Room), 1961. *La madre de los conejos* (The Rabbits' Mother), 1961, in *Escenario* 1.1 (April 1961): 1–25. *Dionisio* (Dionysus), 1962. *El paraíso semi-perdido* (Paradise Semi-Lost), in *Apuntes* 19 (March 1962); Aurelio Diaz Meza, *Animas de día claro* (Spirits by Daylight), in *Teatro chileno contemporáneo*, ed. Julio Durán-Cerda (Mexico City: Aguilar, 1970), 357–423; and in *Mapocho* 1.2 (July 1963): 40–66. *Piel de asno* (Donkey's Hide), 1964. *La remolienda* (Rave-up), 1964, in Alejandro Sieveking's *Ingenuas palomas y otras obras de teatro* (Santiago: Ed. Universitaria, 1993), 135–201; and in his *Tres obras de teatro: La remolienda, Tres tristes tigres, La mantis religiosa* (Santiago: Ed. Universitaria, 1974). *El cheruve* (The Fire Stone), 1966, in *Mapocho* 5.2–3 (1966): 41–56. *Todo se irá-se fuese va al diablo* (Everything Will Go-Went-And Is Going to Hell), 1968, English tr. in *The Praying Mantis and Other Plays*, trans. Charles Philip Thomas (Oshkosh, WI: GMW Publications, 1986). *Una vaca mirando el piano* (A Cow Watching the Piano), 1968, second part of *Peligro a 50 metros*, in collaboration with José Pineda, in *Apuntes* 70 (June 1968). *La sal del desierto* (The Salt of the Desert), 1972. *Cama de batalla* (Bed Battleground), 1973. *La virgen del puño cerrado* (The Virgin with the Clenched Fist), 1973; also known as *La virgen de la manita cerrada* in 1974. *Pequeños animales abatidos* (Small Game Hunt) (Havana: Casa de las Américas, 1975); also in his *Pequeños animales abatidos y otras obras* (Arce, Costa Rica: Ed. Fernández, 1977); English tr. in *The Praying Mantis and Other Plays*, trans. Charles Philip Thomas (Oshkosh, WI: GMW Publications, 1986). *Volar con sólo un ala* (Flying on Only One Wing), 1976. *El uno para el otro* (For One Another), 1979. *La diablada* (The She-Deviled), 1981. *La comadre Lola* (Godmother Lola), 1982. *La mantis religiosa* (The Praying Mantis), English tr. in *Modern International Drama* 17.1 (Fall 1983): 7–35 and in *The Praying Mantis and Other Plays*, trans. Charles Philip Thomas (Oshkosh, WI: GMW Publications, 1986). *Manuel Leonidas Donaire y las cinco mujeres que lloraban por él* (Manuel Leonidas Donaire and the Five Women Who Cried for Him), 1984, in *Cuadernos de Teatro* 11 (March 1985): 11–78. *Libres de polvo y paja* (Free, of Dust and Straw), in collaboration with Nelly Meruane, 1988. *El chinchinero*, 1989. *El cometa Vita-Zeta* (The Vita-Zeta Comet), 1989. *Directo al corazón* (Straight to the Heart), 1989. *Ingenuas palomas* (Innocent Doves), 1989), in Alejandro Sieveking's *Ingenuas palomas y otras obras de teatro* (also includes *Tres tristes tigres* and *La remolienda*) (Santiago: Ed. Universitaria, 1993), 19–75. *Max y Ma* (Max and Ma), 1990. *Tres tristes tigres* (The Ragged Rascals Ran), in Moisés Pérez Coterillo, ed., *Teatro chileno contemporíneo* (Madrid: Fondo de Cultura Económica, 1992), 533–590; in Alejandro Sieveking's *Ingenuas palomas* (Santiago: Ed. Universitaria, 1993), 77–133; and in his *Tres obras de teatro: La remolienda, Tres tristes tigres, La mantis religiosa* (Santiago: Ed. Universitaria, 1974); English tr. by Charles Philip Thomas, in *The Praying Mantis and Other Plays* (Oshkosh, WI: GMW Publications, 1986).

BIBLIOGRAPHY: Pedro Bravo-Elizondo, "Entrevista a Bélgica Castro y Alejandro Sieveking, teatristas chilenos (November 25, 1989, San José, Costa Rica)," *Alba de América* 9.16–17 (1991): 371–379. Elena Castedo-Ellerman, *El teatro chilena de mediados del siglo XX* (Santiago: Andrés Bellow, 1982), 69–89. César Cecchi, "El teatro de Alejandro Sieveking," prologue to Sieveking's *Tres obras de teatro: La remolienda, Tres tristes tigres, La mantis religiosa* (Santiago: Ed. Universitaria, 1974). Cecchi, Prologue to Sieveking's *Pequeños animales abatidos y otras obras* (Arce, Costa Rica: Ed. Fernández, 1977). Bravo-Elizondo, "Entrevista con Alejandro Sieveking," *Latin American Theatre Review* 12.2 (1979): 55–59. Bravo-Elizondo, "Entrevista con Alejandro Sieveking," *Latin American Theatre Review* 14.2 (Spring 1981): 65–70.

SILVA ENDEIZA, Víctor Domingo (1882–1960). Having served in the political posts of representative from Iquique (1915–1918) and as a Chilean consul in both Argentina and Spain, Silva was also known as a journalist, novelist, poet, and playwright. In 1954 he was awarded the National Prize in Literature, which was followed in 1959 by the annual Prize for Theater. Primarily performed in Chile, Argentina, and Uruguay, most of Silva's plays date from the first third of the twentieth century and tended to be *costumbrista*, political, historical, or social in nature. *Fuego en la montaña* (Fire on the Mountain), which deals with Chile's indigenous peoples, won the Municipal Prize in 1938.

WORKS: *El pagó de una deuda* (The Payment of a Debt), 1908. *La ilusión que vuelve* (The Returning Illusion), 1909. *El primer acto* (The First Act), 1909. *Como la ráfaga* (Like a Flash) (Valparaíso: Soc. Imp. y Lit. Universo, 1910). *Nuestras víctimas* (Our Victims), 1911. *La vida cruel* (Cruel Life), 1913. *Aires de la pampa* (Breezes from the Pampa), 1916. *La vorágine* (The Vortex), 1916. *El grito de la sangre* (The Blood's Cry), 1918. *Junto a la cuna* (Next to the Cradle), 1918. *Los buenos muchachos* (The Good Boys), 1919. *El hombre de la casa* (The Man of the House), 1919. *La victoria es nuestra* (Victory Is Ours), 1919. *Viento negro* (Black Wind), 1919. *Las aguas muertas* (Neap Tide), 1920. *Más allá del honor* (Beyond Honor), 1923. *Muñequitas* (Little Dolls), 1924. *Lucecitas en la sombra* (Little Lights in the Dark), also known as *Las luciérnagas* (Fireflies), 1927. *Cabeza de ratón* (Head of a Rat), 1928. *Una alhaja sin estuche* (A Piece of Jewelry without a Jewelry Box), 1933. *No me hable Ud. de amor* (Don't Speak to Me of Love), 1933. *La dama de la Cruz Roja* (The Lady from the Red Cross), 1934. *Fuego en la montaña* (Fire on the Mountain), 1938. *Los balcones floridos* (Flowered Balconies), n.d.

SILVA GUTIÉRREZ, Jaime (1934–). Born in 1934, Silva became known primarily for his plays directed to juvenile audiences: a musical comedy in collaboration with Luis Advis, *La princesa Panchita* (Princess Panchita), debuted in 1958 and revived in 1981 in a production of the Itinerant Theater; *Los grillos sordos* (The Deaf Crickets), a one-act comedy; and *Arturo y el ángel* (Arthur and the Angel, 1961), dealing with the historical figure of Arturo Prat, the Chilean hero of the War of the Pacific, a one-act play intended for adolescents, performed by the Theater of the University of Concepción in 1966. Without doubt, Silva's most important and most widely known work to date is *El evangelio según San Jaime* (The Gospel According to Saint James), which was first staged in 1969 in a production of the University of Chile under direction of Pedro Orthous.

WORKS: *Edipo* (Oedipus), 1953, in Roque Esteban Searpa, ed., *El joven laurel* (Santiago: Ed. Universitaria, 1953). *El otro avaro* (The Other Miser) (Santiago: Imp. Univ. Ediciones del Joven Laurel, 1954). *La princesa Panchita* (Princess Panchita), 1958, with music by Luis Advis (Santiago: ITUCH, 1958); also in *Mapocho* 1.3 (1963): 125–152. *Las beatas de Talca* (The Devout Women from Talca) (Santiago: Universidad de Chile, 1959). *Los niños en el desván* (The Children in the Attic), 1960. *Arturo y el ángel* (Arthur and the Angel), 1961, in *Apuntes* 39 (June 1964); also in *Mapocho* 3.2 (1965): 103–116. *Los grillos sordos* (The Deaf Crickets), in *Apuntes* 27 (April 1963). *El evangelio según San Jaime* (The Gospel According to Saint James) (Santiago: ITUCH, 1969). *Apocalipsis* (Apocalypse), in collaboration with Gabriel Rojo, in *Mapocho* 25 (1977): 173–195. *La fantástica isla de los casi animales* (The Fantastic Island of the Almost Animals), in *Mapocho* 25 (1977): 145–171. *Juegos de niños* (Children's Games), in Aurelio Díaz Mesa, *Cinco obras en un acto* (Santiago: Ministerio de Educación Publica, 1982). *El muchacho y las alas* (The Boy

and the Wings), n.d. *La rebelión* (The Rebellion), n.d. *Las travesuras de don Dionisio* (Don Dionysus' Pranks), n.d.

BIBLIOGRAPHY: Catherine M. Boyle, *Chilean Theater, 1973–1985: Marginality, Power, Selfhood* (Rutherford, NJ: Fairleigh Dickison University Press, 1992), 33–34. Elena Castedo-Ellerman, *El teatro chileno de mediados del siglo XX* (Santiago: Andrés Bello, 1982), 117–120. Teodosio Fernández, *El teatro chileno contemporáneo (1941–1973)* (Madrid: Playor, 1982), 116–117.

SKÁRMETA VRANICIC, Antonio (1940–). Born in Antofagasta to parents of Yugoslavian origin on November 7, 1940, Skármeta experienced poverty throughout much of his childhood. In spite of these humble origins, he has achieved international acclaim as an author of novels and short stories and has also written a number of radio plays and film scripts. He attended the University of Chile, where he acted in and directed some productions of an experimental theater group. He subsequently obtained a Master of Arts degree from Columbia University. During the early years of the 1970s—before the coup—he taught contemporary Latin American literature at the University of Chile and narrative technique at the Catholic University. After the military coup, while visiting West Berlin, Skármeta opted to seek exile in Germany, where he remained until democratic rule returned to Chile. He currently resides in Santiago.

WORKS: *La victoria* (The Victory), 1973. *Reina la tranquilidad en el país* (Tranquility Reigns in the Nation), 1975. *La búsqueda* (The Search), 1976. *No pasó nada* (Nothing Happened), 1976. *La mancha* (The Sleeve), 1978. *La insurrección* (The Insurrection), 1979. *La composición* (The Composition), 1980. *Desde lejos veo este país* (I See This Country from Far Away), in collaboration with Christian Ziewer, 1980. *La huella del desaparecido* (The Trail of the Disappeared), 1980. *Ardiente paciencia* (Burning Patience), 1982; English tr. by Marion Peter Holt, in George W. Woodyard and Marion Peter Holt, eds., *Drama Contemporary: Latin America* (New York: PAJ Publications, 1986), 63–91. *Muertos mientras tanio* (Meanwhile Dead), 1982.

BIBLIOGRAPHY: Angel Flores, *Spanish American Authors: The Twentieth Century* (New York: H.

W. Wilson Co., 1992), 808–811. Bryan Ryan, ed., *Hispanic Writers* (Detroit: Gale Research, 1991), 443–444.

TERBAY, Andrés (1918–   ). *See* SARAH [COMANDARI], Roberto.

TORRES VILLARRUBIA, Víctor (1934–   ). Born in Santiago in 1934, Torres Villaurrubia became associated with the leftist Central Única de Trabajadores (CUT) and its theater in 1966. Consequently, many have viewed his theater as political propaganda. Brechtian influence is evident in his best-known works, *Una casa en Lota Alto* (A House in Lota Alto) (1973) and *Los desterrados* (The Exiles) (1973). The former deals with the personal and political discord in a family in the coal-mining town of Lota; the latter, with the poverty to be found in a nitrate mining region in northern Chile.

WORKS: *Jornada presidencial* (Presidential Visit), 1965. *Testigo marginal* (Marginal Witness, 1965). *La clínica* (The Clinic), 1966. *Los electores* (The Voters), 1966. *El futbolista* (The Soccer Player), 1967. *El krumiro*, 1967. *Una casa en Lota Alto* (A House in Lota Alto) (Havana: Casa de las Américas, 1973). *Los desterrados* (The Exiles), 1973.

BIBLIOGRAPHY: Teodosio Fernández, *El teatro chileno contemporáneo (1941–1973)* (Madrid: Playor, 1982), 110–111. Ramón Layera, "After the Coup: Four Dramatic Versions of Allende's Chile," *Latin American Theatre Review* 12.1 (1978): 39–42.

VODANOVIC, Sergio (1926–   ). Born in Yugoslavia in 1926, Vodanovic was a small child when his family emigrated to Chile. A member of the Generation of 1957 that revitalized Chilean theater, Vodanovic studied theater in the United States during the latter part of the 1950s. During the early years of the Pinochet regime, he lived in exile in Colombia. Vodanovic's career as playwright dates from 1947 when his first play, *El príncipe azul* (The Blue Prince), was performed at the Municipal Theater in Santiago. During the military regime, Vodanovic collaborated with Ictus on two works: *¿Cuántos años tiene un día?* (How Many Years Are in One Day?) (1978) and *La mar estaba serena* (The Sea Was Calm) (1981), a box office hit.

Among Vodanovic's most recent plays are *El mal espíritu* (The Evil Spirit) (1990) and *La hora del Ángelus* (The Hour of the Angelus) (1994). The latter, staged in Santiago in 1994 by the Teatro Espejo under the direction of Juan Cuevas, revolves around issues and problems of adolescents in contemporary society.

WORKS: *El príncipe azul* (The Blue Prince), 1947. *El senador no es honorable* (The Untrustworthy Senator), 1951. *Mi mujer necesita marido* (My Wife Needs a Husband), 1953. *La cigüeña también espera* (The Stork Is Also Waiting), 1955. *Deja que los perros ladren* (Let the Dogs Bark) (Santiago: Ed. del Nuevo Extremo, 1960); also in *Apuntes* 64 (November 1966); in *Primer Acto* 26 (September 1964); in his *Teatro* (Santiago: Nascimento, 1978); and in his *Deja que los perros ladren. Nos tomamos la universidad* (Santiago: Ed. Universitaria, 1972). *Los fugitivos* (The Fugitives), in *Mapocho* 2.3 (1964): 114–154. *Los traidores* (The Traitors), 1964. *El delantal blanco* (The White Apron) (Santiago: Editorial Universitaria, 1965); in *Mapocho* 4.2 (1965): 32–41; in Frank Dauster and Leon Lyday, eds., *En un acto: Diez piezas hispanoamericanas*, 2nd ed. (Boston: Heinle & Heinle, 1983), 1–14; and in Juan Andrés Piña, ed., *Teatro chileno en un acto (1955–1985)* (Santiago: Teatro Taller, 1989). *Las exiliadas* (The Exiled Women), in *Teatro chileno actual* (Santiago: Zig-Zag, 1966). *La gente como nosotros* (People Like Us), in *Mapocho* 5.4 (1966): 92–100. *Perdón . . . ¡Estamos en guerra!* (Excuse Me . . . We're at War!), in *Anales de la Universidad de Chile* 124.139 (July–September 1966): 148–195; in his *Teatro* (Santiago: Nascimento, 1978); and in Moisés Pérez Coterillo, ed., *Teatro chileno contemporáneo* (Madrid: Fondo de Cultura Económica, 1992), 369–430. *Nos tomamos la universidad* (We Took over the University), in collaboration with the Taller de Experimentación Teatral (Santiago: Editorial Universitaria, 1969) and (Santiago: Ed. Nascimento, 1972); also in his *Deja que los perros ladren. Nos tomamos la universidad* (Santiago: Ed. Universitaria, 1972). *Igual que antes* (Same as Ever), 1972. *¿Cuántos años tiene un día?* (How Many Years Are in One Day?), in collaboration with Ictus, 1978. *Viña: Tres comedias en traje de baño* (Viña: Three Beach Plays), in his *Teatro* (Santiago: Nascimento, 1978); and in Julio Durán-Cerda, ed., *Teatro contemporáneo chileno* (Mexico City: Aguilar, 1970); and English tr. in William I. Oliver, ed. and trans., *Voices of Change in the Spanish American Theater: An Anthology* (Austin: University of Texas Press, 1971). *La mar estaba* *serena* (The Sea Was Calm), in collaboration with Ictus, 1981. *El mal espíritu* (The Evil Spirit), 1990. *La hora del Ángelus* (The Hour of the Angelus), 1994.

BIBLIOGRAPHY: Marjorie Agosín, "Entrevista con Sergio Vodanovic," *Latin American Theatre Review* 17.2 (Spring 1984): 65–71. Elba Andrade, "Discurso político y axiología social-cristiana en *Nos tomamos la universidad*," *Gestos* 4.8 (November 1989): 99–108. Catherine M. Boyle, *Chilean Theater, 1973–1985: Marginality, Power, Selfhood* (Rutherford, NJ: Fairleigh Dickinson University Press, 1992). Elena Castedo-Ellerman, *El teatro chileno de mediados del siglo XX* (Santiago: Andrés Bello, 1982), 50–63. Teodosio Fernández, *El teatro chileno contemporáneo (1941–1973)* (Madrid: Playor, 1982), 78–81, 136–141. W. Nick Hill, "Signos de la modernidad como autoreflexión crítica en el teatro chileno contemporáneo," *Alba de América* 8.14–15 (July 1990): 245–251. Willis Knapp Jones, *Behind Spanish American Footlights* (Austin: University of Texas Press, 1966), 239. Andrea G. Labinger, "The Cruciform Farce in Latin America: Two Plays," in *Farce*, ed. James Redmond (Cambridge: Cambridge University Press, 1988), 219–226.

WOLFF, Égon Raúl (1926–). Born to German immigrants in Santiago on April 13, 1926, Wolff is a member of the Generation of 1957 and is considered to be one of the most distinguished playwrights of Latin America. Although he holds a degree in chemical engineering, he began writing plays because of an annual theater competition sponsored by the University of Chile's Experimental Theater. His fascination for theater was to lead to his receiving a scholarship to study drama at Yale University and to his becoming an internationally well-known figure in the renovation of Latin American theater. He was elected to the Chilean Academy of Language in 1984. Almost without exception his works deal with the middle sectors—often the *siúticos*, or "yuppies"—of Chilean society, their values, and their fears of losing their social position.

Generally considered to be Wolff's masterpieces are *Los invasores* (The Invaders) (1964), *Flores de papel* (Paper Flowers) (1970), and *La balsa de la Medusa* (Medusa's Barge) (1984). One of the best-known classics of twentieth-century Latin American theater, *Los invasores* makes use of some fantastic/surrealistic elements to present a clear social message, which is at the same time a fear of the bourgeoisie: That is, if something is not done to rectify the great social injustices that exist in Latin America, the poor masses will undoubtedly revolt against the established order.

WORKS: *Los invasores* (The Invaders) (Santiago: Ercilla, 1970); in Julio Durán-Cerda, ed., *El teatro contemporáneo chileno* (Mexico City: Aguilar, 1970), 131–209; in Carlos Solórzano, ed., *El teatro hispanoamericano contemporáneo*, vol. 1 (Mexico City: Fondo de Cultura Económica, 1964), 126–190; in Moisés Pérez Coterillo, ed., *Teatro chileno contemporáneo* (Madrid: Fondo de Cultura Económica, 1992), 299–360; in *Three Contemporary Latin-American Plays*, comp. by Ruth Lamb (Waltham, MA: Xerox College Publ., 1971). *Mansión de lechuzas* (Mansion of Owls), in *Teatro chileno actual* (Santiago: Zig-Zag, 1966). *Niñamadre* (A Touch of Blue) (Santiago: Instituto Chileno-Norteamericano de Cultura, 1966) and in his *Teatro* (Santiago: Nascimento, 1978). *Flores de papel* (Paper Flowers), in his *Niñamadre* (Santiago: Nascimento, 1978); in Frank Dauster, Leon Lyday, and George Woodyard, eds., *9 dramaturgos hispanoamericanos: Antología del teatro del siglo XX*, vol. 2 (Ottawa, Ontario: Girol Books, 1979), 149–221; in Roberto Cossa et al., *Tres obras de teatro* (Havana: Casa de las Américas, 1970); and in Orlando Rodríguez-Sardiñas et al., *Teatro contemporáneo hispanoamericano* (Madrid: Escelicer, 1971); English tr. by Margaret Sayers Peden (Columbia: University of Missouri Press, 1971). *Discípulos del miedo* (Disciples of Fear), in his *El signo de Caín. Discípulos del miedo* (Santiago: Ediciones Valores Literarios, 1971). *El signo de Caín* (The Sign of Cain) (Santiago: Ed. Universitaria, 1971); and in his *El signo de Caín. Discípulos del miedo* (Santiago: Ediciones Valores Literarios, 1971). *Kindergarten* (Kindergarten), in *Teatro* (Santiago: Nascimento, 1978). *José*, 1980. *Espejismos* (Mirror Images), in *Apuntes* 88 (October 1981). *Alamos en la azotea* (Poplars in the Terrace), in *Teatro chileno contemporáneo* (Santiago: Ed. Andrés Bello, 1982). *El sobre azul* (The Blue Envelope), in *Caravelle* 40 (1983). *La balsa de la Medusa* (Medusa's Barge), in *Apuntes* (Special Issue) (1984): 81–215. *Háblame de Laura* (Speak to Me of Laura), in *Apuntes* 96 (October 1988): 125–171. *Parejas de trapo/La balsa de la Medusa* (Rag Couples/Medusa's Barge) (Santiago:

Ed. Universitaria, 1988). *Teatro completo* (Complete Theater) (Boulder, CO: Society of Spanish and Spanish-American Studies, 1990). *Cicatrices* (Scars), (Santiago: Editorial Universitaria, 1995).

BIBLIOGRAPHY: Pedro Bravo-Elizondo, ed., *La dramaturgia de Égon Wolff* (Santiago: Nascimento, 1985). Bravo-Elizondo, "Reflexiones de Égon Wolff en torno al estreno de *José*," *Latin American Theatre Review* 14.2 (Spring 1981): 65–70. Iván Carrasco, "*Flores de papel* de Égon Wolff: La crisis de la identidad," *Revista Chilena de Literatura* 20 (November 1982): 113–132. Elena Castedo-Ellerman, "Égon Wolff," in *Latin American Writers*, vol. 3, ed. Carlos Solé and María Isabel Abreu (New York: Macmillan, 1989), 1311–1315. Castedo-Ellerman, "Variantes de Égon Wolff: Fórmulas dramática y social," *Hispamérica* 5.15 (December 1976): 15–38. Joseph Chrzanowski, "Theme, Characterization and Structure in *Los invasores*," *Latin American Theatre Review* 11.2 (Spring 1978): 5–10. Frank Dauster, "Concierto para tres: *Kindergarten* y el teatro ritual," *Cahiers du Monde Hispanique et Luso-Brésilien: Caravelle* 40 (1983): 9–15. Diógenes Fajardo, "Teatro: China entre los invasores," *El Café Literario* 5.26 (March–April 1982): 33–36. Teodosio Fernández, *El teatro chileno contemporáneo (1941–1973)* (Madrid: Playor, 1982), 82–88, 141–151. Teodosio Fernández Rodríguez, "El teatro de Égon Wolff," in *XVII Congreso del Instituto Internacional de Literatura Iberoamericana: El barroco en América, literatura hispanoamericana, crítica histórico-literaria hispanoamericana* (Madrid: Cultura Hispánica del Centro Iberoamericano de Cooperación, Universidad Complutense de Madrid, 1978), 1247–1257. Myra S. Gann, "Meaning and Metaphor in *Flores de papel*," *Latin American Theatre Review* 22.2 (Spring 1989): 31–36. Norma Helsper, "The Ideology of Happy Endings: Wolff's *Mansión de lechuzas*," *Latin American Theatre Review* 26.2 (Spring 1993): 123–130.

Janis L. Krugh

Colombia

The Colombian cultural evolution can be analyzed through the various stages of its theater. We start with a European theater in theme and form, and we reach a theater that searches for a national identity within its rich cultural and ethnic roots. Colombian theater takes elements that are nourished by indigenous, African, and Hispanic traditions, revealing our cultural *mestizaje*. The techniques of Occidental, Oriental, or pre-Columbian theater are used to enrich our own traditions and to recover stories, characters, and issues that are of interest to the Colombian audience.

In pre-Columbian America, there already existed a ritual or paratheatrical form of theater, where music, dance, and recitations were indispensable elements of the ceremonial act. Some celebrations of religious character existed in the region of the Chibchas. One such celebration was the ceremony of the Moja, which was practiced by the Muisca Indians in honor of the sun. The sacrifice of the Moja was a ritual event where an adolescent, chosen as a child, was immolated in the temple of Sugamuxi. Fernando González Cajiao sees these celebrations as pre-Columbian paratheatrical forms, because of the chants, dances, and other elements present in the religious ceremony.

A new conception of theater that incorporated ethnocultural elements was originated from the cultural shock of the Conquest. Many pre-Hispanic cultural elements had to be mimicked so that they could survive within the civilization of the conquerors. The first American pieces followed the Spanish dramatic forms in a *mestizo* language that united the two cultures in conflict. In Colombia, these works, which still persist in some rural areas, took the form of dances like the *Cuadrillas de San Martín* (Saint Martin's Cuadrillas) and the *Juego de los caballeros* (The Games of the Cavalier). These representations emerged from the "Moorish and Christian" traditions and were theatrical performances that expressed the cultural shock and the encounter of two distinct worlds. It is essentially street theater with costumes that grab the attention of passers-by, a masquerade that recreates jocosely the victory of the cross over the devil.

The first play that we know of in the history of the Colombian theater is a piece that mocks baroque language but, nevertheless, remains within the peninsular cultural tradition. Fernando Fernández de Valenzuela was the first playwright in New Granada, and he wrote the *Láurea crítica* (The Critical Laurel Wreath) in 1629. It is a one-act play in baroque-style verse with typical characters of the epoch, acting as a satire on false Gongorism and euphuism.

In the beginning of the nineteenth century, the theatrical and commercial activity in Colombia limited itself to following the canons of European fashion. This was the century of the Romantic theater and the opera, the century when Creole descendants of the Spanish identified themselves more with European styles and foreign culture than with the American world. When political power was obtained, the Creole elite wished to conserve economic control. They defended this right in the written culture inherited from Europe. And at the same time, they ignored the autochthonous illiterate and oral culture.

In 1820, José Domínguez Roche wrote *La pola*, a play that had at least three representations. The 1826 representation was performed in the capital of the Republic, and it created one of the most famous episodes in the history of national theater. The audience so furiously protested the execution of the famous Independence War heroine that the theater manager was forced to change the historical events in the play by turning a death penalty into exile to the Llanos Orientales. This piece, as others from the same time period, recreates a mix of styles and tendencies that often came late to the colonies. *Atala* and *Guatimoc* by José Fernández Madrid are pieces that also follow the European canons, even though they are set in America. The author accepted the criticisms of Simón Bolívar. Bolívar thought that his plays lacked authenticity since he only cared to follow the tragic Italian system. He even changed some of the historical events to reconcile with the rigid demands of the neoclassic patterns.

The most well-known piece of Colombian theater in the last century is *Las convulsiones* (The Convulsions) (1828) by Luis Vargas Tejada. It is a comedy that represents life in the capital after the War of Independence, satirizing the conduct of young women who feigned convulsions to escape severe family control. In 1833, José Joaquín Ortiz Rojas's *Sulma*, a neoclassic tragedy, enjoyed very little acceptance from its audience because it was inclined toward Romanticism. What is considered interesting about this tragedy is the theme, its dramatization of the cult of the Moja, and the ceremonies that preceded the ritual.

Another comedy of manners was *Un alcalde a la antigua y dos primos a la moderna* (An Old-Fashioned Mayor and Two Modern Cousins) (1857) by José María Samper, a play that criticizes the abuse of authority and the foolishness of the village mayor. At the same time, it represents the conflict created by arranged marriage. In this play, we begin to see the elements of a bourgeois ideology, where liberty and love are primary and indispensable elements for the happiness of the individual. In 1864, the entertaining play *El espíritu del siglo* (The Spirit of the Century) by José María Vergara y Vergara was published in *El mosaico* (The Mosaic). This piece confronts two different moments in Western civilization, in an attempt to criticize the hypocrisy, greed, and vanity of its contemporaries. Adam sends Abel and Cain to visit the world to see the progress of their descendants. Cain and Abel come to realize that men kill each other and greedily search for small golden pebbles, the only sign of value in the world.

Candelario Obeso published *Secundino el zapatero* (Secundino the Cobbler) in 1880, a comedy that presents the vices of the epoch and the opportunism of the city dwellers. The manual laborers—a workforce that continued to be underrated by the upper class—are lauded for their handicraft and honest attitudes. In 1891, *Lope de Aguirre* by Carlos Arturo Torres was presented for the first time in Bogotá, borrowing the history of the famous Spanish conqueror and his rebellion against the Spanish Crown.

In Colombia, the early theater movement did not have the vigor of the movement of Argentina or Mexico, where independent theater groups created an audience, critics, and playwrights. There was not an established commercial theater that would support the development of companies, regular shows, criticism, actors, authors, and directors. This obliged the few national authors—like Luis Enrique Osorio and Antonio Alvarez Lleras—to occupy themselves with the training of actors. They wrote plays with national themes that had to compete with the visiting companies whose repertoire was foreign to the reality of Colombia. This imported theater was an escape for the elite who had access to the creation of art. The national theater depended on this class for its precarious subsistence, and regardless of the social and critical interest of the authors, they had to make concessions to the elite on whom they depended. Among the Colombian authors of the first half of the twentieth century, Alvarez Lleras and Osorio are the most prominent figures. Their works are inscribed in the social and political currents of the time. Another author that should be remembered is Emilio Campos "Campitos" who presented political caricatures within musical vaudeville. During this period, *La violencia* profoundly transformed the country. With rural and provincial Colombia, this sort of *costumbrista* theater, a mixture of Spanish comedy and one-act farce, disappeared.

With World War II and the advent of industry, a new phase of Latin American theater began. Drama opened itself to universal preoccupations. The Absurd and existentialist philosophy gained ground in Colombia's theater. In their work, Third World authors reflected the existential anguish, the alienation, the vacuum that the developed society produced in human beings. And they also showed the problems from underdeveloped regions devastated by violence and social conflicts. The characters became symbolic and lost their individuality. They were transformed into numbers or pronouns. The works reflect inequality and injustice in the countryside and in the city, in the state or the church, in society or the human condition. The contradictions manifest themselves in the characters and the situations, whose antagonistic positions are a projection of the Latin American reality: oppressed and oppressors, slaves and masters, colonialism and self-determination, dependency and political or cultural independence.

At this time, the theater in Latin American caught up with Western theater. The new themes demanded experimentation in the theatrical discourse. Some authors hoped to restore the original mythical/ceremonial level to theater, and they sought nourishment from an internal reality and in the genuine expressions of popular culture. The bourgeois theater—essentially based on the mechanical repetition of a discourse that was not responsive to the "here and now"—was rejected. The playwrights incorporated all theatrical tendencies, from the theater of the Absurd to political theater to epic theater, in order to recreate the historical moment.

Colombian theater suffered a series of transformation that, in part, had their origin in the European and North American vanguard movements. But these changes were also a response to the social and political transformations of the country and all of Latin America. The Cuban Revolution had a profound effect at the ideological and political level of the country, creating enthusiasm in the leftist groups and the Colombian youth who saw the possibility of change in the government system. The playwrights and theater people felt the need to propitiate a direct and current communication with the public through themes of common interest. They did not reject universal theater but, instead, assimilated the contributions of Bertold Brecht, Konstantin Stanislavsky, Antonin Artaud. Also, they adapted the expressive techniques and aesthetic resources of universal theater to their own reality. The basic objective of the Colombian dramatists was to recover the cultural patrimony and utilize it as a shield against the cultural colonialism that threatened (and still threatens) to destroy autonomous values. In this way, the New Colombian theater was conceived in the 1960s as a reflection of the political and social changes experienced by the country.

THE NEW COLOMBIAN THEATER

Although it was the "literary" genre that took the most time in gaining independence from European cultural currents, Colombian theater became a bastion of the cultural and multiethnic patrimony of the country. The New Theater was the crystallization of the popular and marginal culture that has resisted the repression exercised by the dominant official culture—the culture that controlled all means of communication, regulated the educational programs, and defined the national political culture.

One of the characteristics of the New Theater that defined its dramaturgy was the way it was tightly linked to the interests of the Colombian public. The findings of a formal type were directed toward the creation of a new theatrical language, linking it to the social and cultural context in which it was generated. The defenders of the "here and now" confronted the defenders of the imported cosmopolitan culture, a culture that had fomented alienation and loss of identity within Colombia. The principal objective of the New Theater was the recuperation of identity. Therefore, it implemented new expositions on historical, political, and social processes that contributed to the formation of the cultural patrimony of the country. From the social and real surroundings of each community emerged the themes. These were realities that had been denatured and/or veiled, and it was necessary to return them to their real significance. In this way, the cultural values belonging to the masses, which have been reduced to the oral and unknown to the majority for years, were now saved.

The playwrights who lived through *La violencia* felt the need to give a testimony of this dramatic era. Within their works, they analyzed the causes and consequences of this brutality and protested the useless sacrifice of the Colombian people. The significant works of the movement were Manuel Zapata Olivella's *El retorno de Caín* (The Return of Cain) and *Caronte liberado* (Charon Liberated), Gustavo Andrade Rivera's *Historias para quitar el miedo* (Stories to Take Away the Fear) and *Remington 22*, Enrique Buenaventura's *Los papeles del Infierno* (Documents from Hell), and Jairo Aníbal Niño's *Alguien muere cuando nace el alba* (Someone Dies When Dawn Begins) and *Golpe de estado* (Coup d'Etat).

The theories of Stanislavsky and Brecht were brought to the Colombian theater scene by Enrique Buenaventura and Santiago García. They created a national dramaturgy, a critical discourse, and their works represented the New Theater and the more stable independent groups in the country. Buenaventura has directed El Teatro Experimental de Cali (TEC) since 1963, and García has directed the collective La Candelaria in Bogotá since 1972. For the younger generation, the theories of Jerzy Grotowski, Antonin Artaud, and Eugenio Barba have driven theater in new directions, bringing about different objectives, themes, and attitudes within the national theater movement. A cultural polemic has been opened that allowed an evolution of theater that has achieved diffusion, diversification, and implantation in the nation. Despite the divergences and differences between groups and theater people, there are points of confluence and encounter in an attempt to recover the popular traditions. The folklore and characters of history have been incorporated into Colombian theater. The national lifestyle and the events of everyday life are analyzed within dramatic works.

Colombian theater has collected themes, styles, and attitudes that had not been dramatized before. In collective creations, in collective montages, in the versions of other national authors, these themes, styles, and attitudes have found their channel of expression. Colombian theater has not produced better works, but it *has* enriched the theatrical space with new characters, stories, and situations that had been ignored from theater and culture until now. It is a vigorous movement that continues to nourish itself from its cultural roots, from its assimilation of universal theater elements, from other artistic forms, expanding its horizon into the next millennium.

The history of the New Colombian theater can be grouped in four stages. The first period was a school or university theater that was undoubtedly academic. The public was shaped by the minority elite who had access to the university and to the culture of the status quo. The second period corresponded to the time of official repression and the trimming of the budget. It was a popular stage that looked for its audience in the poor neighborhood and in the rural areas. It was the movement's time of expansion, and a new public was created. The third period was marked by the organization of trade unions and the founding of La Corporación Colombiana de Teatro (Colombian Theatre Organization). This organization of syndical character reunited the independent theater groups, sponsored festivals, workshops, and publications, and supported the theater movement in the country. Furthermore, the theater workers linked themselves with the other trade unions. During this stage, the theater became involved with the process of social development. It researched the history of Colombia and the themes essential to the community, representing them with veracity so the audience could confront their conflicts and contradictions. The fourth period corresponded to the professionalism of theater, when there were members who had graduated from drama schools and authors who were able to stage their plays. The commercial theater also experienced a resurgence. It benefited itself from the theatrical public and movement that had been able to establish itself within the country. The stage was characterized by pluralism and tolerance. As a show of the vitality of the movement and the broad spectrum of interests, we can mention the presence of theater schools, independent theater groups, workshops, publications, specialized criticism, and national and international festivals.

Theater Schools

Presently, there are four theater schools with the approbation of a higher education degree: The Theater School of La Universidad de Antioquia grants a Masters in Dramatic Art, where dramatists and directors like Mario Yepes and Henry Díaz work. There is the Theater School of La Universidad del Valle, where Enrique Buenaventura has taught. The Department of Dance and Theater of La Universidad de Nariño offers a Bachelor's in Theater. Finally, there is the National School of Dramatic Art (ENAD [Escuela Nacional Arte Dramático]), founded in 1951 by Victor Mallarino. This school has been dedicated to the formation of actors and directors and, in addition to its academic function, has staged a number of plays from the national and international repertory.

Independent Theater Groups

There are more than 300 theater groups distributed throughout the nation. The more established ones have their own theater, and others work in rented auditoriums. There are a number of theaters that support international festivals of great magnitude. In March 1994, Bogotá's Ibero-American Festival presented more than 400 shows in ten days. Some of the theater groups with a trajectory of various years and whose plays merit attention are the following: Acto Latino was founded in Bogotá in 1967; La Candelaria was founded by Santiago García in 1972; Esquina Latina was founded by Orlando Cajamarca in Cali in 1972; Hilos Magicos is a marionette and puppet theater founded in 1974 in Bogotá and is directed by Ciro Gómez; La Libelula Dorada is one of the most appreciated children's theater groups in Colombia, founded by Iván Dario and César Santiago Alvarez in 1976; El Local was founded in 1970 by Miguel Torres; La Mama was founded in 1968; La Mascara was founded in 1972, but it was transformed in 1983 by a group of women who sought to analyze the problems of women through theater (abortion, infanticide, prostitution); El Taller de Artes de Medellin was founded by Samuel Vásquez in 1975; Teatro Experimental de Cali was founded by Enrique Buenaventura in 1963; Teatro Libre de Bogotá was founded in 1973 by Ricardo Camacho, Jorge Plata, and Germán Moure; El Teatro Matacandelas was founded in Medellín by Cristóbal Peláez in 1979; El Teatro Nacional was founded by Fanny Mickey in 1981, and it has invited theater groups from other countries; El Teatro Taller de Colombia is directed by Jorge Vargas and Mario Matallana and was founded in 1972; El Teatro Popular de Bogota was founded in 1968 by Jorge Alí Triana, Jaime Santos, and Rosario Montaña.

Theater Workshops

There are a series of workshops in Colombia that seek to train actors, directors, and authors. Other workshops seek an audience of children to initiate them in corporal expression and artistic creation. It is also a means of subsistence for the theater groups and schools. For example, El Taller de Dramaturgia, founded in 1975, helped the development of the New Theater. From here, playwrights were trained and important works emerged. Such works as *La agonía del difunto* (The Agony of the Deceased) by Esteban Navajas, *La huelga* (The Strike) and *Tiempo de vidrio* (Time of Glass) by Sebastián Ospina were staged in El Teatro Libre. El Taller de la Corporación Colombiana de Teatro has fomented various investigations and then edited the critical/theoretical results, making them accessible to interested readers. The theater group Esquina Latina from Cali has developed systematic theatrical workshops in various neighborhoods, which seeks to consolidate groups interested in theater and integrate them into creative activities. At the same time, the links of the theater group are strengthened within its medium.

Specialized Publications

Among the periodicals published in Colombia are *Teatro* (Theater), edited by Gilberto Martínez in Medellín, and *Actuemos* (Let's Act), a publication by Dimensión Educativa, edited by Jairo Santa in Bogotá. The publications of the group La Candelaria and El TEC have developed a theatrical theory on collective creation and Colombian dramaturgy. With the success of the national and international theater festivals, other publications like *Gestus* from the ENAD and *Quiropterus* from La Libélula Dorada have emerged. Texts have begun to be published that facilitate the study and diffusion of theater. In response to the growing demand for specialized works and texts, La Universidad de Antioquia has initiated a theater collection in its Publications Department.

Theater Criticism

In addition to the playwrights and theater directors who have theorized and written about theater (Enrique Buenaventura, Santiago García, Gilberto Martínez, and Carlos José Reyes), there is a group of scholars who have done important critical publications about theater. Scholars such as Fernando González Cajiao, Beatriz Rizk, Giorgio Antei, Héctor Orjuela, Misael Vargas, Gonzalo Arcila, and María Mercedes Jaramillo have written extensively about Colombian theater. In criticism and review of the shows the following stand out: Guillermo González Uribe, Eduardo Marceles Daconte, Hugo Afanador, Juan Carlos Moyano, Juan Monsalve, Adolfo Chaparro, and Iván Dario Alvarez in children's theater.

Festivals

The presence of university festivals was the major catalyst for the emergence of the New Theater. Additionally, the festival in Manizales has helped to develop the national theater by providing an arena of exchange with other theater groups. The national and regional festivals support the provincial theater groups by giving them the opportunity to show their work. Finally, the Ibero-American Festival, which we hope continues to take place, has brought to the country works from the universal repertory, styles and themes that enrich the national movement. The Ibero-American Festival allows the work of unrecognized theater groups to be known at the international level. It foments criticism and publications, it is an open space for the reexamination of culture, and it has created an audience.

BIBLIOGRAPHY

Antei, Giorgio, ed. *Las rutas del teatro*. Bogotá: Centro Editorial de la Universidad Nacional, 1989.

Arcila, Gonzalo. *Nuevo teatro en Colombia: Actividad creativa y política cultural*. Bogotá: Ediciones CEIS, 1983.

Baycroft, Bernardo. "Brecht in Colombia the Rise of the New Theatre." Ph.D. dissertation, Stanford University, Stanford, CA, 1986.

Buenaventura, Enrique. "Actor, creación colectiva y dramaturgia nacional." *Boletín Cultural y Bibliográfico del Banco de la República* 22.4 (Bogotá 1985): 42–46.

———. "Apuntes para un Método." *Primer Acto* (1980): 183.

———. "El arte no es un lujo." In *Teatro y política*, ed. Emile Cooperman. Buenos Aires: Ediciones La Flor, 1969.

———. "L'Art n'est pas un luxe." *Partisans* (1967): 36–80.

————. *El arte nuevo de hacer comedias*. Cali: Comisión de publicaciones del TEC, n.d.

————. "Artistas y obreros en el nuevo teatro." *Documentos Políticos* (1978): 40–43.

————. "Brecht y el Nuevo Teatro Colombiano." *International Brecht Society: Communications* 19.3 (1990): 43–48.

————. "En busca de un método para la enseñanza teatral." *Periódico del Teatro Escuela de Cali*. TEC Archives, 1962.

————. "In Colombia: An Invisible Theatre." *International Theatre Information* (1972): 18–19.

————. "La creación colectiva como una vía del teatro popular." TEC Archives, n.d.

————. "El debate del teatro nacional." *Conjunto* 43 (1980): 14–23.

————. "De Stanislavsky a Brechet." *Mito* (1958): 21.

————. "La dramaturgia en el Nuevo Teatro." *Conjunto* 59 (1984): 32–37.

————. "La dramaturgia nacional y la práctica social." *Actuemos* 3.17 (September 1, 1985): 12–18.

————. "Ensayística." *Máscaras y ficciones*. Cali: Centro editorial de la Universidad del Valle, 1992, 195–263. (It contains: "De Stanislavsky a Bertoldo Brecht," "Teatro épico y teatro didáctico de Bertoldo Brecht," "Brecht y el teatro dialéctico," "A través de las piezas de Brecht," "La Formación de los temas constantes de Bertold Brecht," and "Visión histórico-estética de la aparición y presencia de Bertold Brecht en América Latina.")

————. "The Impact of Two Cultures." *International Theatre Informations* (1976).

————. "El movimiento teatral colombiano en 1978." *El Pueblo* (Cali), December 24, 1978, 1.

————. "El Nuevo Teatro." Publicación del CEDRA (Centro de documentación e investigación de dramaturgia nacional y latinoamericana). Bogotá, 1988.

————. "El Nuevo Teatro y el movimiento de liberación cultural." TEC Archives, May 1980.

————. "El Nuevo Teatro y su relación con la estética." Cali: Comisión de Publicaciones del TEC, 1979.

————. *Primer Acto* (1972): 145.

————. "El problema de la dramaturgia nacional." *Boletín Cultural y Bibliográfico del Banco de la República* (Bogotá) (1985).

————. *Qué es la CCT*. Cali: Comisión de Publicaciones del TEC, 1977.

————. "Teatro e identidad cultural." TEC Archives, 1988.

————. "El teatro un fin en sí mismo." (Interview). *Revista Nueva* 77 (1981): 75–76.

————. "Teatro y la historia." *Primer Acto* 163–164 (1973–1974): 28–35.

————. "Teatro y política." *Conjunto* 22 (1974): 90–96.

————. "Theatre and Culture." *Drama Review* 14.2 (1970): 151–156.

————. "Trayectoria y originalidad del teatro colombiano." *Diógenes* 87 (1988): 57–63.

————. "Visión histórica de la aparición y presencia de Bertold Brecht en América Latina." TEC Archives, 1975.

Buitrago, Fanny. "A la diestra y a la siniestra." *Latin American Theatre Review* 20.2 (1987): 77–80.

Chaparro, Adolfo. "Los placeres de la dispersión." *Gaceta* (Bogotá) (1990): 9.

"Colombia." *Escenarios de dos mundos: inventario teatral de Iberoamérica*. Vol. 1. Madrid: Centro de Documentación Teatral, 1988, 302. Articles by scholars.

García, Santiago. "En busca de nuevas relaciones con un nuevo público." In *Materiales para una historia del teatro en Colombia*, ed. Carlos José Reyes and Maida Watson. Bogotá: Colcultura, 1978, 482–492.

———. "Dramaturgia nacional y público." *El Espectador* (Bogotá) 146 (1986): 10–13.

———. "Sobre la urgencia de una dramaturgia." *Tramoya* 16–17 (1988): 61–70.

———. *Teoría y práctica del teatro.* Bogotá: CEIS, 1983.

———. "La ubicación de la ideología en el proceso creativo." *Conjunto* 47 (1981): 5–13.

González, Patricia. "El Nuevo Teatro en Colombia." Ph.d. dissertation, University of Texas, Austin.

González Cajiao, Fernando. "Adiciones a la bibliografía del teatro colombiano de Héctor H. Orjuela, 1978." *Materiales para una historia del teatro en Colombia*, 690–713.

———. "Los años 80 en Colombia: El derecho a ser distintos." *Latin American Theatre Review* 25.2 (1992): 37–58.

———. *Historia del teatro en Colombia.* Bogotá: Instituto Colombiano de Cultura, 1986.

———. *Teatro popular y callejero colombiano.* Santafé de Bogotá: Cooperativa Editorial Magisterio, 1997.

González Uribe, Guillermo. "Catorce espectáculos para la memoria." *Escenario de dos mundos.* Vol. 1. Madrid: Centro de documentación teatral, 1988.

Jaramillo de Velasco, María Mercedes. "La creación colectiva y la colonización cultural." *Gestos* 4.7 (1989): 75–79.

———. *El Nuevo Teatro Colombiano y la colonización cultural.* Bogotá: Editorial Memoria, 1987.

———. *El Nuevo Teatro Colombiano: Arte y política.* Medellín: Universidad de Antioquia, 1992.

———. "La mujer en la dramaturgia colombiana." *Teatro, Revista de Estudios Teatrales (Alcalá de Henares)* 2 (1992): 89–104.

Lamus, Marina. "La búsqueda de un teatro nacional 1830–1890." *Boletín Cultural y Bibliográfico del Banco de la República* 29.31 (1992): 57–84. La Libélula Dorada. *El dulce encanto de la isla Acracia* (The Sweet Charm of Acracia Island), *Los espíritus lúdicos* (The Ludicrous Spirits), *Ese chivo es puro cuento* (That Gota Is Made Up) *Delirium titerensis.* Bogotá: Arango editores, 1991.

Lamus Obregón, Marina. *Bibliografía del teatro colombiano: siglo índice analítico de las publicaciones periódicas.* Santafé de Bogotá: Instituto Caro y Cuervo, 1998.

———. *Estudios sobre la historia del teatro en Colombia.* Santafé de Bogotá: Alcaldía Mayor de Bogotá, 2000.

———. *Teatro en Colombia, 1831–1886: práctica teatral y sociedad.* Santafé de Bogotá: Editorial Ariel, 1998.

Luna, Maria del Pilar. "La mujer busca su escenario." *El Tiempo* (Bogotá), April 14 1992, 1B+.

Marceles Daconte, Eduardo. "El método colectivo en el teatro colombiano." *Latin American Theatre Review* 11.1 (1977): 91–96.

Marín, Beatriz. *Ritos, tardes abrazadas.* Medellín: Asociación de Teatro El Chisme, 1992.

Martínez, Gilberto. "Hacia una auténtica creación colectiva." In *El teatro latinoamericano de creación colectiva*, ed. Francisco Garzón Céspedes. Havana: Casa de las Américas, 1978.

———. *Teatro, teoría y práctica.* Medellín: Autores Antioqueños, 1986.

Orjuela, Héctor. *Bibliografía del teatro colombiano.* Bogotá: Instituto Caro y Cuervo, 1974.

————. *El teatro en la Nueva Granada: siglos XVI–XVIII*. Santafé de Bogotá: Kelly, 2000.

Ortega de Peñalosa, Beatriz. *La candidata. Teatro colombiano*. Colección Alba, Bogotá: Ediciones de la Idea, 1964.

Ortega Ricaute, José Vicente. *Historia crítica del teatro en Bogotá*. Bogotá: Ediciones Colombia, 1927.

Ovadia Andrade, Reneé. "El nuevo teatro en Colombia." Ph.D. dissertation, University of California, 1982.

Parra Flórez, Eliceo Antonio. *Historia del teatro en el Meta*. Villavicencio: Ministerio de Cultura de Colombia, 2000.

Peña Gutiérrez, Isaías. *El teatro colombiano a fin de siglo: acotaciones y codas*. Cali, 1996.

Reyes, Carlos José. "Aspectos del teatro colombiano en los siglos XIX y XX." In *Teatro colombiano*, ed. Misael Vargas. Bogotá: Ediciones El Alba, 1985, 59–87.

————. "Cien años de teatro en Colombia." *Nueva historia de colombia* 6 (1989): 213–236.

————. *Materiales para una historia del teatro en Colombia*. Ed. Maida Waston and Carlos José Reyes. Bogotá: Instituto Colombiano de Cultura, 1978.

————. "Métodos de creación colectiva en un trabajo teatral contra el sistema." *Conjunto* 20 (1974): 21–37.

————. "Proyección del TEC en el teatro nacional." *Letras Nacionales* 86 (1966): 33–34.

————. "Teatro e Historia." *Conjunto* 61–62 (1984): 146–156.

Rizk, Beatriz J. *La dramaturgia de la creación colectiva*. Mexico City: Grupo Editorial Gaceta, 1991.

Vargas, Misael B. "Cinco siglos de teatro colombiano." *Teatro colombiano*. Bogotá: Ediciones del Alba, 1985.

◆

ACOSTA DE SAMPER, Soledad (1833–1913). A writer, essayist, and playwright. Acosta was the most prolific woman writer of the last century. As a journalist she wrote many articles about family and the role of women in society.

WORKS: *Las desdichas de Aurora. Comedia de costumbres* (The Misfortunes of Aurora. Comedy of Customs) (Four Acts), *La mujer* (Bogotá, November 1880, January 1881). *Una educación útil* (A Useful Education) (Dialogue for Schools), *La mujer* (Bogotá, 1880). *La familia* (The Family) (Bogotá, December 1884). *El viajero. Comedia de costumbres nacionales* (The Traveller. Comedy of National Customs) (Two Acts), *La mujer* (Bogotá, 1890). *Las víctimas de la guerra* (The Victims of War) (Drama in Five Acts), n.d.

BIBLIOGRAPHY: Fernando González Cajiao, *Historia del teatro en Colombia* (Bogotá: Instituto Colombiano de Cultura, 1986). Carlos José Reyes, "Aspectos del teatro colombiano en los siglos XIX y XX," in *Teatro colombiano*, ed. Misael Vargas (Bogotá: Ediciones El Alba, 1985), 58–87.

AFANADOR, Hugo (1949–). A director, actor, and playwright. In 1980 Afanador founded Centro Cultural García Márquez with José Assad, where they stage plays that deal with Colombian society and reality. Afanador has participated in national and international festivals of theater; also, he has taught workshops and seminars about the actor's role. For him, the actor is a creative subject that enriches the performance rather than a subject that repeats already approved dramatic formulas.

La boda rosa de Rosa Rosas (Rosa Rosas' Rose Wedding) recreates the life of the middle class during El bogotazo, when political leader Jorge Eliécer Gaitán was killed in Bogotá in

1948. This event transformed the city and the country, and Rosa's wedding shows the world that is dying. *La pandilla del cuarto menguante* (The Gang of the Last Quarter of the Moon) is a wedding that takes place in 1003. Through the union of two powerful families (vampires), Afanador shows how the elite conserves its political and economical position.

WORKS: *La boda rosa de Rosa Rosas* (Rosa Rosas' Rose Wedding). *Cuestión de honor* (Honor Issue). *Más allá de la guerra* (Beyond the War). *El menú de los recuerdos* (Menu of Memories). *La pandilla del cuarto menguante* (The Gang of the Last Quarter of the Moon). *A la topa tolondra* (Without Attention). *Venganza en el año 2092* (Revenge in the Year 2092). *Vía lactea* (Milky Way).

BIBLIOGRAPHY: Misael B. Vargas, "Cinco siglos de teatro colombiano." In *Teatro colombiano* (Bogotá: Ediciones del Alba, 1985).

ALVAREZ LLERAS, Antonio (1892–1956). Poet, literary critic, and playwright. He founded and directed the theater company Renacimiento. He was one of the promoters of national theater at the beginning of the century. His most important critical work is *El teatro visto por un comediógrafo* (The Theater as Seen by a Comedy Writer). He wrote such farces as *El Angel de Navidad* (The Christmas Angel), *De año nuevo* (Of New Year's Eve), *El marido de Mimí* (Mimi's Husband), and *Por teléfono* (By Telephone). Among his dramatic works are the following: *Alejandría, la pagana* (Alexandria, the Pagan); *Alma joven* (Young Soul) (1912), which premiered in Bogotá; *Los Benavides* (The Benavides); *Como los muertos* (Like the Dead), (1916), which also premiered in Bogotá; *Los de Altamora* (Those from Altamora); *El doctor Bacanotas* (Doctor Bacanotas); *Don Luis Velásquez*; *Fuego Extraño* (Strange Fire) (1912), which premiered in Caracas and then traveled to Spain and Bogotá; *Los mercenarios* (The Mercenaries) (1924), which premiered in El Teatro Municipal de Bogotá; *El sí de los cocacolos* (The "Yes" of the "Young-ones"); *Sirena pesca marido* (A Siren Fishes a Husband); *La toma de Granada* (The Taking of Granada); *Los traidores de Puerto Cabello* (The Traitors from Puerto Cabello); *Ví-*

boras sociales (Social Vipers) (1911); *El Virrey Solis* (The Viceroy Solis); and *Zarpazo* (Smack) (1927), which was his most successful play and was presented in Colombia, Mexico, New York, Paris, Puerto Rico, and Seville. The piece is about a family conflict where José kills his mother's alleged lover, an intriguing politician. From a modern perspective, the filial feelings appear to be exaggerated.

WORKS: *Víboras sociales* (Social Vipers) (1911). *Alma joven* (Young Soul) (1912). *Fuego Extraño* (Strange Fire) (1912). *Alejandría, la pagana* (Alexandria, the Pagan). *El Angel de Navidad* (The Christmas Angel). *De año nuevo* (Of New Year's Eve). *Los Benavides* (The Benavides). *Como los muertos* (Like the Dead). *El doctor Bacanotas* (Doctor Bacanotas). *Don Luis Velásquez. El sí de los cocacolas* (The "Yes" of the "Young-ones"). *Los de Altamora* (Those from Altamora). *El marido de Mimí* (Mimi's Husband). *Los mercenarios* (The Mercenaries) (1924). *Por teléfono* (By Telephone). *Sirena pesca marido* (A Siren Fishes a Husband). *La toma de Granada* (The Taking of Granada). *Los traidores de Puerto Cabello* (The Traitors from Puerto Cabello). *El Virrey Solis* (The Viceroy Solis). *Zarpazo* (Smack) (1927). *El teatro visto por un comediógrafo* (The Theater as Seen by a Comedy Writer).

BIBLIOGRAPHY: Frank Dauster, *Historia del teatro hispanoamericano; Siglo XIX y XX*, 2nd ed. (Mexico City: Ediciones de Andrea, 1973), 144. Fernando González Cajiao, *Historia del teatro colombiano* (Bogotá: Colcultura, 1986). Juan Guerrero Zamora, *Historia del teatro contemporáneo*, vol. 4 (Barcelona: Juan Flores, 1961), 543. Willis Knapp Jones, *Breve historia del teatro latinoamericano* (Mexico City: Ediciones de Andrea, 1956), 127. Leon Lyday, "Antonio Alvarez Lleras and His Theatre," *Latin American Theatre Review* 2.2 (Spring 1969): 29. Lyday, *The Dramatic Art of Alvarez Lleras* (University of North Carolina, 1966). José A. Núñez Segura, *Literatura colombiana* (Medellín: Editorial Bedout, 1966), 729–735. Héctor Orjuela, *Bibliografía del teatro colombiano*, vol. 7 (Bogotá: Caro y Cuervo, 1974). José Vicente Ortega Ricaute, *Historia crítica del teatro en Bogotá* (Bogotá: Ediciones Colombia, 1927). Nicolás Bayona Posada, *Panorama de la literatura colombiana* (Medellín: Ediciones la Tertulia, 1963), 110. Daniel Samper Ortega, *Selección Samper Ortega de literatura colombiana*, vol. 5 of 100 vols. (Bogotá: Editorial Minerva, 1937). Agustín del Saz, *Teatro hispanoamericano*, vol. 2 (Barcelona: Editorial Vergara, 1963),

341. *Teatro social hispanoamericano* (Barcelona: Editorial Labor, 1967), 92.

ANDRADE RIVERA, Gustavo (1921–1974). He was a playwright and among the first authors to incorporate *la violencia* into his pieces in an objective way without the melodrama other authors prefered. His plays have been staged at both national and international theater festivals. *El camino* (The Path) won the prize in El Festival de Arte de Cali in 1964 and later was staged in Spain by Miguel Suárez Radillo. *Remington 22* is his most famous piece and has been published and presented many times. It also won first prize in La Corporación Festival de Teatro in 1961 and was staged at El Primer Festival de Teatro Latinoamericano in Mexico. It was later translated into English at Pittsburg University.

WORKS: *Remington 22 y otras piezas de teatro* (Bogotá: Instituto Colombiano de Cultura, 1973), which includes: *Farsa de la ignorancia y la intolerancia en una ciudad alejada de provincia que bien puede ser está* (Farce of Ignorance and Intolerance in a City Far from the Province That Could Very Well Be This One), *El hombre que vendia talento* (The Man Who Sold Talent), *El propio veredicto* (The Proper Verdict). *Farsa para dormir en el parque* (Farce to Sleep in the Park). *El hijo de Candido se quita la camisa* (Candido's Son Takes Off His Shirt). *Historias para quitar el miedo* (Stories to Take Away the Fear). *Hola allá adentro* (Hello in There).

BIBLIOGRAPHY: Frank Dauster, *Historia del teatro hispanoamericano; Siglo XIX y XX*, 2nd ed. (Mexico City: Ediciones de Andrea, 1973), 146. Fernando González Cajiao, *Historia del teatro colombiano* (Bogotá: Colcultura, 1986). Héctor Orjuela, *Bibliografía del teatro colombiano* (Bogotá: Caro y Cuervo, 1974), 14.

ANGEL, Albalucía (1939–). Angel is the most well-known Colombian feminist writer. In her narrative and plays, Angel analyzes the modern problems that affect women's lives. *La manzana de piedra* (The Stone Apple) recreates the lives of three generations of women in the same family. Each character confronts different problems within the family and community, but all are refrained by a patriarchal society.

WORKS: *La manzana de piedra* (The Stone Apple) (1983). *Siete lunas y un espejo* (Seven Moons and One Mirror) in *Voces en escena: Antología de dramaturgas latinoamericanas*, eds. María Mercedes Jaramillo and Nora Eidelberg (Medellín: Universidad de Antioquia, 1991), 13–79.

BIBLIOGRAPHY: María Mercedes Jaramillo, "Albalucía Angel: El discurso de la insubordinación," in *¿Y las mujeres? Ensayos sobre literatura colombiana*, ed. María Mercedes Jaramillo, Angela Inés Robledo, and Flor María Rodríguez (Medellín: Universidad de Antioquia, 1991), 203–238. Jaramillo, "Albalucía Angel y Fanny Buitrago por la insubordinación," *Conjunto* 92 (1992): 47–54. Jaramillo, "Del drama a la realidad en Albalucía Angel y Fanny Buitrago," in *Escritura y diferencia: Autoras colombianas del siglo XX*, ed. María Mercedes Jaramillo, Betty Osorio, and Angela Robledo (Bogotá: Universidad de los Andes and Medellín, Universidad de Antioquia).

ARIZA, Patricia (1945–). Patricia Ariza is an actress in the group La Candelaria. In recent years, Ariza has gained fame as an author, a theater director, and contributor to women's theater groups like La Máscara from Cali and Teatro Trama Luna from Bogotá. These theater groups have also been dedicated to the investigation of a feminine dramaturgy. *El viento y la ceniza* (Wind and Ashes) (1987) was the first play she wrote to commemorate the five hundreth anniversary of the encounter of Europe and the Americas. In 1991, she staged *Mi parce, monólogo para una pelada* (My Buddy, Monolog for a Girl), where she deals with the youths from the marginal neighborhoods of Medellín and presents their language and experience. *Cuarto menguante* (Waning of the Moon) (1992) is her most recent piece, and in it she explores the diverse periods of womanhood through the vital cycles (menstruation, motherhood, menopause).

WORKS: *El viento y la ceniza* (Wind and Ashes), in *Cuatro obras del teatro La Candelaria* (Bogotá: Ediciones Teatro La Candelaria, 1987), 335–394; also in *Voces en escena: Antología de dramaturgas latinoamericanas*, ed. Nora Eidelberg and María Mercedes Jaramillo (Medellín: Universidad de Antioquia, 1991), 81–132. *Mi parece, monólogo para una pelada* (My Buddy, Monolog for a Girl) (1991). *Cuarto menguante* (Waning of the Moon) (1992).

BIBLIOGRAPHY: Nora Eidelberg, "Patricia Ariza: Entre la transgresión y el compromiso," *Escritura y diferencia: Autoras colombianas del siglo XX*, ed. María Mercedes Jaramillo, Betty Osorio, and Angela Robledo (Bogotá: Universidad de los Andes and Medellín, Universidad de Antioquia). Guillermo González Uribe, "IX Festival de teatro de Manizales, llegaron el juego y la estética," *El Espectador* (September 1987). Pilar Quiñones, "De *El viento y la ceniza*," *Vanguardia Liberal*. Martina Uris, "*El viento y la ceniza*," *Voz* (October 1986).

ASSAD, José (1958–   ). Assad is a director and playright. Assad studied at the Escuela Nacional Arte Dramático (ENAD) and founded Centro Cultural García Márquez with Hugo Afanador in 1980. *Juan Pueblo cuentero* (John Smith Storyteller) is a collective creation based on different events about Colombian history. *Biofilo Panclasta* (1983) presents the life of a Colombian anarchist who shared moments with Lenin and Gorki. *Cenizas sobre el mar* (Ashes over the Sea) (1989) recreates the episodes of the Conquest and the confrontation of two very different worlds. In *Un pecado muy original* (A Very Original Sin) (1987), the biblical characters Adam, Eve, the Devil, and the Angel stage modern problems.

WORKS: *Ascensor para tres* (Elevator for Three) (1981). *La pantalla* (The Screen) (1981). *Biofilo Panclasta* (1983). *Los juegos de la luna* (The Games of the Moon) (1987). *Un pecado muy original* (A Very Original Sin) (1987). *Cenizas sobre el mar* (Ashes over the Sea) (1989). *Cenizas sobre el mar* (Ashes over the Sea), in *Antología del teatro colombiano contemporáneo* (Madrid: Fondo de Cultura Económica, 1992), 907–946. *Eroplástica* (1992). *Cinco por ocho cuarenta* (Five Times Eight Forty) (n.d.).

BIBLIOGRAPHY: Jorge Prada, "Entre lo absurdo y lo imaginario," in *Antología del teatro colombiano contemporáneo* (Madrid: Fondo de Cultura Económica, 1992), 899–905.

BONNETT, Piedad (Amalfi) (n.d.). Bonnett is a playwright. One of her plays, *Noche de epifanía* (Night of Epiphany), was staged at El Teatro Libre de Bogotá in 1988. In 1991, Bonnett analyzed women's identity and their social position in *Gato por liebre* (Sell a Pig in a Poke) (1991), based on the story by Manfred Karge, *Jacke wie Hose*. This piece was directed by Ricardo Camacho. Laura García played the role of a woman who takes her husband's identity and clothing in order to keep his job. The play deconstructs women's roles in traditional and patriarchal societies through the situations the protagonist confronts with her husband's friends, including going to bars and brothels to keep her secret and her new job. Bonnett highlights gender issues and reveals the gender ideology that permeates Colombian society.

WORKS: *Noche de epifanía* (Night of Epiphany) (1988). *Gato por liebre* (Sell a Pig in a Poke) (1991), in *Antología crítica del teatro hispanoamericano en un acto*, eds. María Mercedes Jaramillo and Mario Yepes (Medellín: Universidad de Antioquia).

BIBLIOGRAPHY: Betty Osorio, "*Gato por liebre* de Piedad Bonnett," in *Antología crítica del teatro hispanoamericano en un acto*, ed. María Mercedes Jaramillo and Mario Yepes (Medellín: Universidad de Antioquia). Beatriz J. Rizk, "Hacia una poética feminista: La increíble y triste historia de la dramaturgia femenina en Colombia," in *Escritura y diferencia: Autoras colombianas del siglo XX*, ed. María Mercedes Jaramillo, Betty Osorio, and Angela Robledo (Bogotá: Universidad de los Andes and Medellín, Universidad de Antioquia).

BUENAVENTURA, Enrique (1925–   ). He has been called—and rightly so—the father of the New Colombian theater because of his untiring efforts as director, critic, and author. Buenaventura has struggled for the creation of an ideologically independent dramaturgy in tune with the national reality. Precarious economic conditions forced Colombian theater people to depend more on human resources than on modern technology. This limitation became an aesthetic virtue, thanks to the artistic ability and universal knowledge about theater of playwrights such as Buenaventura. His cultural objective was to create a new relationship with the audience, and this has fundamentally directed his theater achievements. To obtain the audience's participation, it was indispensable to represent themes of popular interest and to create a new artistic language. These were the basic elements to develop a new method of work known as "Collective Creation." This method of work involves the actors in an active way during the staging of a play, and it changes the dynamism between audience and scene, between director and author, and between actors and director. Since the "here and now" was sought, it became indispensable to know the opinion of the spectator in order to represent his or her interests and attitudes. This methodology did not eliminate the author or the director, but it brought out the full participation of the actors through the improvisations they made during the montage of the play.

Buenaventura's first play is *A la diestra de Dios Padre* (To the Right Hand of Father God) (1958), which collects the popular legends of the "Blacksmith and Death." It is an adaptation of the version by Tomás Carrasquilla. This is his most well-known version of another author's work and one of the plays that remained for the longest period of time in the repertory of the group. It has seen five versions between 1958 and 1984 because the group actualized the play according to the circumstances at the moment of representation. It is essentially a popular play with a festive tone that uses mythical and religious topics within a social and political context. *A la diestra de Dios Padre* is one of the most well known plays of the New Theater. Buenaventura's work as author and theorist is known not only in Colombia but worldwide. His theoretical contributions established the development of Collective Creation, the foundation for a national dramaturgy, and the emergence of the New Theater.

WORKS: *El monumento: Farsa en un acto, seis visitas y un desagravio* (The Monument: Farce in One Act, Six Visits and One Ammends), in *Mito* 5.26 (1959): 11–127. *A la diestra de Dios Padre* (To the Right Hand of Father God), 3rd version, *Teatro* (Bogotá: Ediciones Tercer Mundo, 1963); *Teatro*, ed. Carlos Solórzano (Mexico City: Fondo de Cultura Económica, 1964); *Teatro*, ed. Carlos José Reyes (Bogotá: Colcultura, 1977); 4th version, *Teatro*, ed. Francisco Garzón Céspedes (Havana: Casa de las Américas, 1980); 5th version, *Teatro colombiano contemporáneo* (Bogotá: Tres Culturas Editores, 1985), 51–87. *Un requiem por el padre Las Casas* (A Requiem for Father Las Casas), 1st version, *Teatro* (Bogotá: Tercer Mundo, 1963); 2nd version, *Los papeles del infierno y otros textos* (Mexico City: Siglo XXI, 1990), 279–342, 2nd version, *Máscaras y ficciones* (Cali: Centro editorial de la Universidad del Valle, 1992), 27–81; 2nd version, *Antología de Teatro colombiano contemporáneo* (Prologue of Fernando González Cajiao, Madrid: Fondo de Cultura Económica, 1992), 193–247; *San Antoñito, Semanario Cultural*, May 6, 1979, 11–12. *La tragedia del rey Christophe* (The Tragedy of King Christophe), in *Teatro* (Bogotá: Tercer Mundo, 1963). *Los inocentes* (The Innocents) (TEC Archives, 1967). *El presidente* (The President) in *Letras nacionales* (1967): 43–55. *La trampa* (The Trap) (TEC Archives, 1967). *Los papeles del infierno: La autopsia* (Documents from Hell: The Autopsy), in *Revista casa de la cultura* (1968): 65–77; *Letras nacionales* 32–33 (1977): 107–113. *Teatro* (Bogotá: Colcultura, 1978), *Teatro* (Havana: Casa de las Américas, 1980); *Los papeles del infierno y otros textos* (Mexico City: Siglo XXI, 1990), 29–40. *Los papeles del infierno: El entierro* (Documents from Hell: The Burial), in *Razón y fábula* (1968): 11–121; *Primer acto* (1972). *Los papeles del infierno: La maestra* (Documents from Hell: The Teacher), *Revista casa de la cultura* (1968): 79–85; *Primer acto* (1980): 105–107; *Cuadernos de teatro 3 y 4* (Cali: Publicación de la CCT, n.d); *Teatro* (Bogotá: Colcultura, 1977); *Teatro* (Havana: Casa de las Américas, 1980); *Los papeles del infierno y otros textos* (Mexico City: Siglo XXI, 1990), 15–20; *Máscaras y ficciones* (Cali: Centro editorial de la Universidad del Valle, 1992), 109–116. *Los papeles del infierno: El menú* (Documents from Hell: The Menu), in *Conjunto* 3.10 (1968): 12–44; *Teatro actual latinoamericano*, ed. Carlos Solórzano (Mexico City: Ediciones de Andrea, 1972); *Teatro* (Havana: Casa de las Américas, 1980); *Los papeles del infierno y otros textos* (Mexico City: Siglo XXI, 1990), 143–219. *Los papeles del infierno: La orgía* (Documents from Hell: The Orgy) in *Revista casa de la cultura* (1968): 87–113; *Primer acto* (1972); *Teatro* (Havana: Casa de las Américas, 1980); *Teatro latinoamericano en un acto* (Col. La Honda. Havana: Casa de las Américas, 1980); *Los papeles del infierno y otros textos* (Mexico City: Siglo XXI, 1990), 105–142; *The Orgy, Modern One Act Plays from Latin America*, Ed. Johannes Wilbert et al. (Los Angeles: University of California Press, 1974); *Máscaras y ficciones* (Cali: Centro editorial de la Universidad del Valle, 1992), 83–108. *Tirano Banderas* (The Tyrant Banderas) (TEC Archives, 1968); *Máscaras y ficciones* (Cali: Centro editorial de la Universidad del Valle, 1992), 117–193. *Historia de una bala de plata* (The Story of a Silver Bullet) (Cali: Comisión de publicaciones del TEC, 1969). *El padre* (The Father) (TEUSACA. Universidad Santiago de Cali, 1969). *Seis horas en la vida de Frank Kulak* (Six Hours in the Life of Frank Kulak) (TEC Archives, 1969). *El convertible rojo* (The Red Convertible) (TEC Archives, 1970). *Los papeles del infierno: La audiencia* (Documents from Hell: The Audience), in *Tramoya* (1970); *Teatro* (Bogotá: Colcultura, 1978); *Teatro* (Havana: Casa de las Américas, 1988); *Los papeles del infierno y otros textos* (Mexico City: Siglo XXI, 1990), 41–69. *The Twisted State*, in *Drama Review* 14.2 (1970): 151–156. *Los papeles del infierno: La requisa* (Documents from Hell: The Search), in *Primer acto* (1972); *Revista Eco* (1975): 538–583; *Teatro* (Bogotá: Colcultura, 1977); *Tramoya* (1979); *Los papeles del infierno y otros textos* (Mexico City: Siglo XXI, 1990), 71–104. *Los papeles del infierno: El sueño* (Documents from Hell: The Dream), in *Primer acto* (1972). *Los papeles del infierno: La tortura* (Documents from Hell: The Torture), in *Primer acto* (1972); *Tramoya* (1979); *Teatro* (Havana: Casa de las Américas, 1980); *Los papeles del infierno y otros textos* (Mexico City: Siglo XXI, 1990), 21–28. *La denuncia* (The Denunciation), in *Conjunto* 19 (1974): 41–80; *Primer acto* 163–164 (1973): 40–59. *Se hizo justicia* (Justice Was Served) (Cali: Publicación de la Universidad del Valle, 1977); *Los papeles del infierno y otros textos* (Mexico City: Siglo XXI, 1990), 221–236. *Vida y muerte del fantoche lusitano* (The Life and Death of the Lusitanian Nincompoop), in *Teatro* (Havana: Casa de las Américas, 1980). *La encrucijada* (The Crossroads) (TEC Archives, 1982). *Opera bufa* (Buffoonery Opera) (Cali: Comisión de publicaciones del TEC, 1984). *El encierro* (The Enclosure) (TEC Archives, 1986). *Escuela para viajeros* (School for Travellers) (TEC Archives, 1988). *El ánima sola* (The Lonely Soul), in *Los papeles del infierno y otros textos* (Mexico City: Siglo XXI, 1990), 343–383. *Crónica* (Chronic), in *Los papeles del infierno y otros textos* (Mexico City: Siglo XXI, 1990), 237–277. *Proyecto piloto* (Pilot Project), in *Gestos* (1991): 213–236; *Antología crítica del teatro hispanoamericano en un acto*, ed. María Mercedes Jaramillo and Mario Yepes (Medellín: Universidad de Antioquia). *Máscaras y ficciones* (Masks and Fictions) (Cali: Centro editorial de la Universidad del Valle, 1992).

TEATRO EXPERIMENTAL DE CALI: Enrique Buenaventura, "Esquema general del método de trabajo colectivo del TEC," in *Cuaderno de teatro 3 y 4: Teoría y práctica del teatro* (Cali: Comisión de publicaciones del TEC, 1970). "Esquema general del trabajo colectivo del TEC," in *Materiales*, 314–346.

"Gira por San Francisco y México," *Trabajo teatral* 3 (1973): 76–81. "El TEC habla de su propio estreno," *Trabajo teatral* 3 (1973): 67–75. "El teatro y la clase obrera," *Trabajo teatral* 4 (1975): 106–107. "Tercer taller nacional de formación teatral" (Cali: Comisión de publicaciones del TEC). *La denuncia, teatro documental latinoamericano* (Mexico City: UNAM, 1982), 29–89.

BIBLIOGRAPHY: Giorgio Antei, "Un paradigma teatral: Notas sobre *Historia de una bala de plata*," *Contexto* 5 (1979). Antei, ed., *Las rutas del teatro* (Bogotá: Centro editorial de la Universidad Nacional, 1989). Gonzalo Arcila, *Nuevo Teatro en Colombia: Actividad creadora y política cultural* (Bogotá: Ediciones CEIS, 1983). Ramón de la Campa, "The New Latin American Stage: An Interview with E. Buenaventura," *Theater* 12.1 (1980): 19–21. Castagnino, "Teatro colombiano. Enrique Buenaventura: *En la diestra de Dios Padre*," in *Semiótica, ideología y teatro hispanoamericano contemporáneo* (Buenos Aires: Nova, 1974), 197–204. Raúl Castagnino, "Descripción semiótica de un texto dramático hispanoamericano contemporáneo: *En la diestra de Dios Padre* de Enrique Buenaventura," in *Semiología del teatro*, ed. José M. Diez Borque and Luciano García Lorenzo (Barcelona: Editorial Planeta, 1975). Alberto Castilla, "*Tirano Banderas*, version teatral de Enrique Buenaventura," *Latin American Theatre Review* 10.2 (1977): 65–71. Oscar Collazos, "Buenaventura quince años de trabajo creador," *Conjunto* 3.10 (1968): 6–11. Collazos, "Trayectoria del Teatro Escuela de Cali," *Letras nacionales* 2.8 (1966): 25–27. Luis A. Diez, "Entrevista con Enrique Buenaventura," *Latin American Theatre Review* 14.32 (1981): 49–57. Manuel Drezner, "Enrique Buenaventura, hombre de teatro," *Letras nacionales* 1 (1965): 81–84. Nora Eidelberg, "La ritualización de la violencia en cuatro obras de teatro hispanoamericanas," *Latin American Theatre Review* 13.1 (1979): 29–37. Mario Escobar, "Buenaventura lleva su teatro a la Olimpiada," *El Occidente* (Cali) (September 19, 1968). Maida Watson Espener, "Enrique Buenaventura's Theory of the Committed Theatre," *Latin American Theatre Review* 9.2 (1976): 43–47. Maida Watson Espener, "The Social Theatre of Enrique Buenaventura" (Master's thesis, University of Florida, 1971). Gabriel Flores Arzayús, "Prólogo," *Teatro*, de Enrique Buenaventura (Bogotá: Tercer Mundo, 1963). Víctor Fuentes, "La creación colectiva del TEC," in *Popular Theater for Social Change in Latin America*, ed. Gerardo Luzuriaga (Los Angeles: UCLA, Latin American Center Publications, 1978), 338–349. Roberto Gacio Suárez, "Historia y realidad social en el teatro de Enrique Buenaventura," *Conjunto* 45 (1980): 108–109. Manuel Galich, "*La denuncia*: Actual y continental," *Conjunto* 19 (1974): 36–39. Luis Alberto García, "Apuntes para abrir un debate sobre las ponencias de Enrique Buenaventura," *El Espectador* (Magazín Dominical, October 15, 1978), 9. Francisco Garzón Céspedes, "Prólogo," *Teatro*, by de Enrique Buenaventura (Havana: Casa de las Américas, 1980). Fernando González Cajiao, "Enrique Buenaventura: El maestro," *Letras nacionales* 32.33 (1977): 103–106. Natividad González Freire, "A propósito de Enrique Buenaventura," *Bohemia* (1970). Oscar González, "*La denuncia*, segunda versión," *Estravagario, El pueblo*, May 26, 1975, 3. Patricia González, "El evangelio, la evangelización y el teatro: El Nuevo Teatro Colombiano," *Conjunto* 61 (1984): 45–49. González, "Hacia un teatro popular y político," *Textos* 3.16 (1973): 4. González, "El Nuevo Teatro en Colombia" (Ph.D. diss., University of Texas, 1981). Philippe Hammon, "La cuestión militar: *Soldados*," *Trabajo teatral* 4 (1975): 26–30. Francisco Javier Higuero, "Dialéctica de un cambio," *palpitar hispano* 1.10 (1983): 10. María Mercedes Jaramillo de Velasco, "La creación colectiva y la colonización cultural," *Gestos* 4.7 (1989): 75–95. Jaramillo de Velasco, "La función popular y social de las versiones de una obra de Enrique Buenaventura," in *Expresiones colectivas en el teatro y en los espectáculos teatrales*, ed. Lucía Fox (East Lansing: Imprenta La Nueva Crónica, 1990). Jaramillo de Velasco, *El Nuevo Teatro Colombiano y la colonización cultural* (Bogotá: Editorial memoria, 1987). Jaramillo de Velasco, *El Nuevo Teatro Colombiano: Arte y política* (Medellín: Universidad de Antioquia, 1992). Jaramillo de Velasco, "La proyección teatral de la masacre de las bananeras," *Latin American Theatre Review* 23.1 (1989): 89–103. Jaramillo de Velasco, "*Proyecto piloto* de Enrique Buenaventura: Una visión apocalíptica," in *Antología crítica del teatro hispanoamericano en un acto*, ed. María Mercedes Jaramillo and Mario Yepes (Medellín: Universidad de Antioquia). Oscar Jurado, "*Soldados*," *Textos* 2.7 (1972): 4. Fernando Luzuriaga, "*En la diestra de Dios Padre* y la contextualización histórica del folclor," in *Narradores latinoamericanos 1929–1979* (Caracas: Ediciones del Centro de Estudios Latinoamericanos Rómulo Gallegos, 1980), 2. Luzuriaga, "Enrique Buenaventura: Un nuevo teatro para un nuevo público," in *Introducción a las teorías latinoamericanas del teatro* (Mexico City: Universidad Autónoma de Puebla, 1980). Eduardo Marceles Daconte, "El método de creación colectiva en el teatro colombiano," *Latin American Theatre Review* (1977): 91–96. Marceles Daconte, "La farsa equivocada del TEC," *El Espectador* (September 1984). Octavio Marulanda, "Teatro 65: Un año de premoniciones," *Letras nacionales* 6 (1966): 57. Christine McIntyre, Emma Buenaventura, and Abril Trigo, "Charlando con Enrique Buenaventura," *Prismal Cabral* 9 (1983): 10. Rubén Monasterio, "Entrevista con Enrique Buenaventura," *Primer acto* 145 (1972): 22–32. Alvaro Monroy Caicedo, "*La tragedia del rey Christophe*," *El Tiempo*, March 5, 1963, 11. Reneé Ovadia Andrade, "El nuevo teatro en Colombia" (Ph.D. diss. University of California, 1982). Nohra Parra Martínez, "Ante todo teatro popular propone Enrique Buenaventura," *El Tiempo*, April 28, 1963, 11. Carlos José Reyes, "Enrique Buenaventura el dramaturgo," 1 *Letras nacionales* (1965): 85. Reyes, "Proyección del TEC en el teatro nacional," *Letras nacionales* 2.8 (1966): 33–36. Reyes, "El teatro de Enrique Buenaventura: El escenario como mesa de trabajo," in *Teatro* by Enrique Buenaventura (Bogotá: Colcultura, 1977). Rómulo Rivas, "Entrevista a Enrique Buenaventura director del TEC," *Aquí. La noticia*, August 13, 1973. Beatriz Rizk, *La dramaturgia de la creación colectiva* (Mexico City: Grupo Editorial Gaceta, 1991). Rizk, "Un maestro que duda," in *Antología del teatro colombiano contemporáneo* (prologue of Fernando González Cajiao, Madrid: Fondo de Cultura Económica, 1992), 183–192. Rizk, *El nuevo teatro latinoamericano: Una lectura histórica* (Minneapolis: Prisma Institute, 1987). José Luis Alonso de Santos, "Enrique Buenaventura y su método de creación colectiva," *Primer acto* 183 (1980): 73–82. Diana Taylor, "Destruyendo la evidencia: La supresión como historia en *La maestra*," 5.10 *Gestos* (1990): 91–101.

BUITRAGO, Fanny (1946–   ). Buitrago is a writer and playwright. Buitrago recreates Colombian history in her plays and analyzes the violence that has permeated society. The events that take place in *El final del Ave María* (The End of the Hail Mary) denounce the military regimes, the corruption of the ruling class, and the violence of the drug lords. The main plaza is the site where mothers, widows, beggars, unemployed people, and street sellers come together and project the misery and misfortune of the Colombian poor.

WORKS: *El hombre de paja. Las distancias doradas* (The Man of Straw. The Golden Distances) (Bogotá: Espiral, 1964) (won the award at El IV

Festival de Teatro in Cali in 1964). *El final del Ave María* (The End of the Hail Mary), in *Gestos* 6:12 (1991): 115–163. *El trébol de cuatro hojas* (The Lucky Clover), n.d. *El angelito Tito* (The Little Angel Tito), n.d.

BIBLIOGRAPHY: Elba Andrade and Hilda Cramsie, eds., *Dramaturgas latinoamericanas contemporáneas* (Madrid: Editorial Verbum, 1991). Lucía Garavito, *El hombre de paja*: Una aproximación semiótica y hermenéutica," *Revista de estudios colombianos* 5 (1988): 35–40. María Mercedes Jaramillo, "Fanny Buitrago: La desacralización de lo establecido," *¿Y las mujeres? Ensayos sobre literatura colombiana*, ed. María Mercedes Jaramillo, Angela Inés Robledo, and Flor María Rodríguez (Medellín: Universidad de Antioquia, 1991), 239–281. Jaramillo, "Albalucía Angel y Fanny Buitrago por la insubordinación," 92 *Conjunto* (1992): 47–54. Jaramillo, "Del drama a la realidad en Albalucía Angel y Fanny Buitrago," in *Escritura y diferencia: Autoras colombianas del siglo XX*, ed. María Mercedes Jaramillo, Betty Osorio, and Angela Robledo (Bogotá: Universidad de los Andes & Medellín, Universidad de Antioquia). Beatriz J. Rizk, "Hacia una poética feminista: La increíble y triste historia de la dramaturgia femenina en Colombia," in *Escritura y diferencia: Autoras colombianas del siglo XX*, ed. María Mercedes Jaramillo, Betty Osorio, and Angela Robledo (Bogotá: Universidad de los Andes and Medellín, Universidad de Antioquia, in print).

CAMARGO, Beatriz (n.d.). Camargo is an actress, director, and playwright. Camargo was once a member of La Candelaria and other theater groups in Bogotá. Her performances are related to Mother Nature and such feminine topics as creation and reproduction. In 1983, along with Bernardo Rey, she founded the group Teatro Itinerante del sol; they staged *La Bacante* (The Maenad). She has worked in Europe, Bali, and Java, where she has become familiar with ritual and ceremonial theatre. *María de la Candelaria* (Maria of the Candlemass) was a procession through the main streets of Bogotá. It was a performance that brought together profane and sacred elements with propitiatory intentions. *El siempreabrazo* (The Alwayshug) was selected for the fourth Ibero-American Festival in 1994. This piece is based on pre-Columbian mythology; it is a ritual performance that searches for connections and har-

mony with the Mother Earth. *Eva-I-Io* (Eve-I-Io), staged in Germany and in Bogotá in 1986, portrays the feminine characters who are the victims of patriachal oppression (God, Zeus), wars, and violence, in the past and present. *Eart* (1986) is again a junction between sacred and profane elements and characters. Here, Camargo defends matriarchy and creates a feminine character that is a mother, a witch doctor, and a soothsayer. In 1988, Bernardo Rey directed this play at the women's jail, El Buen Pastor, in Bogotá. *Muysua-sueño* (Muysua-Dream) premiered in 1993, during the Second International Encounter, Mujeres en Escena in Cali. This play projects the powers of (re)creation of Mother Earth.

WORKS: *La Bacante* (The Maenad) (1983). *Eva-I-Io* (1986). *Eart* (1986). *Muysua-sueño* (Muysua-Dream) (1993). *El siempreabrazo* (The Alwayshug) (1994). *María de la Candelaria* (Maria of the Candlemass) (n.d.).

BIBLIOGRAPHY: Juan Carlos Moyano, "El eterno femenino en las obras de Beatriz Camargo," *El Espectador* 309 (Magazín Dominical, Bogota) (1989): 3–6.

DÍAZ DÍAZ, Oswaldo (1910–1967). A lawyer, playwright, and novelist, he was one of the founders of the radio-theater in Colombia. His fecund dramatic productions cover four decades, from 1927 until 1967, and range from historical themes to children's plays such as *Blondinete*—a farce done with puppets. *La jaula de cristal* (The Crystal Cage) (1949) expresses the anguish of enslavement to technology. Its characters are symbolic: Eblis is the exploiter; Ariel is the spirit; and Flora is Nature, known as D-5 43D in the world of science. *El Fenix y la tórtola* (The Phoenix and the Ring Dove) (1951) dramatizes the problems of the person who loses his or her liberty to a state that takes over science and all possible social spaces.

Among his works are the following plays: *Blondinete* (1941), represents the struggle for power and the intrigues of human beings. *La boda de caperucita* (Little Red Riding Hood's Wedding) (1932) premiered in 1940. *Cada mayo una rosa* (Each May a Rose) was staged by Fausto Cabrera at El Teatro Colón in 1955. *Claver* won an award in the first Festival de Arte de Cali in 1961. *La comedia famosa de doña Antonia Quijana* (The Famous Comedy of Doña Antonia Quijana) was transmitted by radio in 1947 and later was directed by Bernardo Romero Lozano at El Teatro Experimental de la Universidad Nacional. *Desdémona ha muerto* (Desdémona Has Died) (1955) won an award in Barranquilla in 1956. *Diana Váldez* was written in 1954, and *Dos estampas del 20 de julio* (Two 20th of July Stamps) appeared in 1949. *En vela* (In a Vigil) (1941) premiered at El Teatro de la Comedia, and *Expreso* (Express) was written in 1934. *Galán* and *La gaitana* (1937) recreate the history of the famous national heroes. *Hora azul, 3 a.m.* (The Blue Hour, 3 a.m.) premiered in the second Festival de Teatro in 1958. *Reina Juana* (Queen Juana) was written in 1952. *La señal de caín* (Cain's Signal) (1958) obtained the prize at El Tercer Festival de Teatro in 1959. *La sopa del soldado* (The Soldier's Soup) premiered at La Universidad Pedagógica in 1962. *Sueño de una noche de septiembre* (A September Night Dream) (1965) never premiered, and *El pretor* (The Praetor) (1967) and *Vida plena* (Full Life) were published in 1967.

WORK: *Teatro* (Bogotá: Publicaciones Editoriales, 1967).

BIBLIOGRAPHY: Juan José Arrom, *Certidumbre de América* (Madrid: Editorial Gredos, 1977), 178. Frank Dauster, *Historia del teatro hispanoamericano; Siglos XIX y XX* (2nd ed. Mexico City, Ediciones de Andrea, 1973), 144. Agustín del Saz, *Teatro hispanoamericano* (Barcelona: Editorial Vergara, 1963), 2, 366. Fernando González Cajiao, *Historia del teatro colombiano* (Bogotá: Colcultura, 1986). Héctor Orjuela, *Bibliografia del teatro colombiano* (Bogotá: Instituto Caro y Cuervo, 1974), 59.

DÍAZ VARGAS, Henry (1948–   ). He is an autodidact and has dedicated himself to writing, acting, and directing theater. In 1979, he founded the group Las Puertas, with which he staged his first plays. In 1981, he founded La Academia Teatral de Antioquia with Marta Ofelia Pisa, which is an institution dedicated to the teaching of theater. Many of Díaz's plays are about the underdogs, their lives, and struggles to survive in a society that ignores them. *El cumpleaños de Alicia* (Alicia's Birthday) recreates the life and conflicts of two lesbian lovers. The main causes of their disagreements are their different social status and backgrounds. Alicia uses her position to exploit/to punish her lover and servant. Their deformed relationship reflects the homophobia in a patriarchal society. *La sangre más transparente* (The Most Transparent Blood) won the national theater prize in 1992. It takes place in a *barrio* in Medellín where violence and crime are drug related and where adolescents are the victims and the executioners. Their tragic destinies show the lack of alternatives that fatherless children have. The father abandonment also reflects the state negligency toward the Colombian poor. Other plays written by Díaz are about Colombian history during colonial times, where he recreates the conflicts between Spaniards and Creoles.

WORKS: *La candileja* (The Lampion) (1970). *Los honores* (The Honors) (1970). *El mimeógrafo* (The Mimeograph) (1975). *La máléfica serpiente de siete cabezas* (The Malefic Serpent with Seven Heads) (1976). *El puño contra la roca* (The Fist Against the Rock) in *Revista de la Universidad de Antioquia* (Medellín, March 1976). *Simeón Calamaris* (1983). *El cumpleaños de Alicia* (Alicia's Birthday) *Teatro* (Medellín: Revista de la Universidad de Medellín, 1985), 9–46, which won the prize given by El Primer Concurso Nacional de Obras Dramáticas de la Universidad de Medellín in 1985. *Maduras tinieblas* (Mature Tenebrae) (Medellín: Revista de la Universidad de Antioquia, 1985), 215. *Más állá de la ejecución* (Beyond the Execution), in *Teatro* (Medellín: Revista de la Universidad de Medellín, 1985), 91–121. *Antología del teatro colombiano contemporáneo* (Prólogo de Fernando González Cajiao, Madrid: Fondo de Cultura Económica, 1992), 733–765. *De golpe elúltimogolpeymisión cumplida* (The Blow "Thelastblowandmission" Accomplished) (1986). *El siguiente* (The Next One) (1988). *El salto y las voces* (The Jump and the Voices) (1989). *La encerrona del miedo* (Enclosed by Fear) (Medellín: Universidad de Antioquia, 1991), 161–183. *Josef Antonio Galán o de cómo se sublevó el común* (Josef Antonio Galán or How the People Revolted) (Medellín: Universidad de

Antioquia, 1991), 79–159. *Las puertas* (The Doors) (Medellín: Universidad de Antioquia, 1991), 27–77. *La vasija de cristal* (The Crystal Vase) (1993). *La sangre más transparente* (The Most Transparent Blood) (n.d.), in *Antología crítica del teatro hispanoamericano en un acto*, Ed. María Mercedes Jaramillo and Mario Yepes (Medellín: Universidad de Antioquia).

BIBLIOGRAPHY: Marleny García Sánchez, "Cuestionar las vivencias," *Antología del teatro colombiano contemporáneo* (Prólogo de Fernando González Cajiao, Madrid: Fondo de Cultura Económica, 1992), 729–733. María Mercedes Jaramillo de Velasco, Review: *Las puertas, Josef Antonio Galán o de cómo se sublevó el común, La encerrona del miedo, Gestos* (1992), 7, 13, 179–181. Jaramillo de Velasco, "*La sangre más transparente* de Henry Díaz: Una existencia en vilo," in *Antología crítica del teatro hispanoamericano en un acto*, Ed. María Mercedes Jaramillo & Mario Yepes (Medellín: Universidad de Antioquia, in print). Mario Yepes, "Henry Díaz, dramaturgo: Uno de los sobrevivientes," *Las puertas, Josef Antonio Galán o de cómo se sublevó el común, La encerrona del miedo* (Medellín: Universidad de Antioquia, 1991), 9–24.

FERNÁNDEZ DE SOLIS Y VALENZUELA, Fernando (Bruno) (1616–1677). He was a priest, a poet, and the first Colombian playwright. He wrote *Láurea crítica* (The Critical Laurel Wreath) (1629) when he was only thirteen years old. This play shows the close cultural connections that existed between Spain and its colonies.

WORK: *Láurea crítica* (The Critical Laurel Wreath) (1629).

BIBLIOGRAPHY: Juan José Arrom, *Esquemas generacionales de las letras hispanoamericanas* (Bogotá: Ediciones del Instituto Caro y Cuervo, 1977), 70. José Juan Arrom and José Manuel Rivas Sacconi, "La *Láurea crítica* de Fernando Fernández de Valenzuela: Primera obra teatral colombiana," *Materiales* (85–93). Eduardo Camacho Guizado, "Una sátira al gongorismo," *Materiales* (94–102). Antonio Gómez Restrepo, *Historia de la literatura colombiana* (Bogotá: Ministerio de Educación Nacional, 1945), 1, 281; 2, 301–309. Fernando González Cajiao, *Historia del teatro colombiano* (Bogotá: Colcultura, 1986). Héctor Orjuela, *Bibliografía del teatro colombiano* (Bogotá: Instituto Caro y Cuervo, 1974), 74. José Vicente Ortega Ricaute, *Historia crítica del teatro en Bogotá* (Bogotá:

Ediciones Colombia, 1927), 1. Sergio Elías Ortiz, "Notas sobre el teatro en el Nuevo Reyno de Granada," *Boletín de Historia y antigüedades* (Bogotá), 57, 414. José María Vergara y Vergara, *Historia de la literatura en la Nueva Granada* (Bogotá: Ediciones del Banco Popular, 1976), 1, 75.

FERNÁNDEZ MADRID, José (1789–1830). Fernández Madrid was a doctor, a journalist, a poet, and a playwright. He founded the newspaper *Argos americano* and collaborated on *El semanario*. Fernández Madrid was one of the founders of Colombian theater and his neoclassic tragedies, which were in vogue at that time, recreate the idealized vision of the American Indian. He wrote, staged, and published *Atala* in Havana in 1822. It is a play in hendecasyllabic verses that dramatizes the subject of Chateaubriand. *Guatimoc* recreates the historic episodes of the conquest of the Aztec Empire and the death of its last emperor. This play was written during the time of independence, and the confrontation between Spaniards and Aztecs is used as a metaphor for the Colombian War of Independence. The betrayal of the Tazcaltecs is used to critize the Latin Americans who supported the Spaniards. In this play the political and social interests of the Creole class appear; this class wanted economic independence from the metropolis without severing cultural ties. These two tragedies were presented in Bogotá only after independence in 1825.

WORKS: *Atala* (Havana: Imprenta Fraternal, 1822). *Atala, Guatimoc* (Int. Alvaro Garzón Marthá, Bogotá: Arango Editores, 1988).

BIBLIOGRAPHY: Javier Arango Ferrer, "Raíz y desarrollo de la literatura colombiana," in *Historia extensa de Colombia* (Bogotá: Ediciones Lerner, 1965), 19, 132–160. Juan José Arrom, *Esquema generacional de las letras hispanoamericanas* (Bogotá: Ediciones del Instituto Caro y Cuervo, 1977), 139. Agustín del Saz, *Teatro hispanoamericano* (Barcelona: Editorial Vergara, 1963), 1, 277. Fernando González Cajiao, *Historia del teatro colombiano* (Bogotá: Colcultura, 1986). Willis Knapp Jones, *Breve historia del teatro latinoamericano* (Mexico City: Ediciones de Andrea, 1956), 51. Isidoro Laverde Amaya, *Bibliografía colombiana* (Bogotá: Talleres gráficos del Banco de la República). Héctor Orjuela, *Bibliografía del teatro colombiano* (Bogotá:

Instituto Caro y Cuervo, 1974), 75. José Vicente Ortega Ricaute, *Historia crítica del teatro en Bogotá* (Bogotá: Ediciones Colombia, 1927), 7.

FREIDEL, José Manuel (1957–1990). Freidel abandoned his studies in law at La Universidad de Medellín to engage in theater. He was the founder of La Corporación Artística La Fanfarria with Nora Quintero in 1976 in Medellín, a theater group that in 1988 became La Asociación Ex-Artística Fanfarria Teatro. Freidel directed the theater groups of La Universidad Nacional and La Escuela Popular de Arte. His plays premiered in Bogotá, Ecuador, and at the festivals in Manizales. The majority were staged with La Fanfarria. He was a playwright and a director and created a series of noteworthy plays. *A-E-I-O-U* (1975) premiered with the theater group A-E-I-O-U, where he deconstructs school desertions through the rural instructor who teaches ants how to read. *Amantina o la historia de un desamor* (Amantina or the Story of Lack of Love) (1976) is a play that inaugurated Freidel's style and broke with the sociopolitical styles of the moment. The play revolves around the story of a beggar whose routine creates loneliness and a lack of love for the helpless.

Other plays include: *Las arpías* (The Harpies) (1981), staged by La Fanfarria; *Ciudad, ciudad* (City, City) (1983), staged by La Escuela Popular de Arte. *Contratiempos* (Setbacks) (1988), staged by La Fanfarria. *Cuatro sonajas de fierro* (Four Iron Timbrels) (1976), staged by La Fanfarria; *Desenredando* (Untangling) (1973), staged by the U Group; *En casa de Irene* (In Irene's House) (1984), staged by La Fanfarria; *Soledad quiere bailar* (Soledad Wants to Dance) (1988), staged by La Fanfarria; and *24 horas en la vida de K* (24 Hours in K's Life) (1989), presented by La Escuela Popular de Arte. *La fábula de Hortensia la flor más petulante y tal vez la más perversa* (The Fable of Hortensia the Most Haughty Flower But Perhaps the Most Perverse) (n.d.); *Monólogo de una actriz triste* (The Monologue of a Sad Actress) (1986), staged by La Fanfarria, *Un raya en la vida de Lucrecia* (A Stripe in Lucrecia's Life) (n.d.).

WORKS: *Los infortunios de la bella Otero y otras desdichas* (The Misfortunes of Beautiful Otero and Other Afflictions) (Medellín: Ediciones otras palabras, 1985). *Las tardes de Manuela* (Manuela's Afternoons), *Antología del teatro colombiano contemporáneo* (Prólogo de Fernando González Cajiao, Madrid: Fondo de Cultura Económica, 1992), 777–801.

BIBLIOGRAPHY: Adela Donadia, "Un poeta intenso y desbordante," in *Antología del teatro colombiano contemporáneo* (Prólogo de Fernando González Cajiao, Madrid: Fondo de Cultura Económica, 1992), 767–775.

GARCÍA, Luis Alberto (1937–). García is a director and playwright. His most famous play is *I Took Panama*. It is one of the most popular plays of the New Colombian theatre. It was premiered by El Teatro Popular de Bogotá in 1974 and was on stage almost a decade. The play shows the conflicts between Colombia and the United States during the separation of Panama from Colombia and jocosely reflects the cultural and political differences between the two countries and presidents. *La Gaitana* (The Gaitana) (1980) recreates the story of the famous cacique who killed Pedro de Añasco to avenge the death and torture of her son. Other plays are: *El gorro de cascabeles* (Jingle Bell Hat) (n.d.); *Michín el gato bandido* (Michin the Bandit Cat), staged by El Teatro Popular de Bogotá in 1971; *Otro extraño ha llegado a nuestros predios* (Another Stranger Has Come to Our Land) (1969); *La primera independencia* (The First Independence) (1975), presented by El Teatro Popular de Bogotá in 1977; *El sueño de Gettysburg* (The Dream of Gettysburg) (1968); *Toma tu lanza Sintana* (Take Your Spear Sintana) (1972), staged by El Teatro Popular de Bogotá in 1973; *Tras las huellas de la historia* (In Search of the Prints of History) (1970); *La viuda del celador* (The Watchman's Widow) (1982); *Vivir en paz* (To Live in Peace) (1984), adapted by Enrique Pulecio; and *Cien años de soledad* (One Hundred Years of Solitude) (n.d.).

WORKS: *I Took Panama*, in *Teatro colombiano contemporáneo* (Bogotá: Tres Culturas Editores, 1985), 89–156; *Antología del teatro colombiano* *contemporáneo* (Madrid: Fondo de Cultura Económica, 1992), 421–506.

BIBLIOGRAPHY: Fernando González Cajiao, *Historia del teato en Colombia* (Bogotá: Instituto Colombiano de Cultura, 1986). Jorge Manuel Pardo, "Entre la sátira y el comic," in *Antología del teatro colombiano contemporáneo* (Madrid: Fondo de Cultura Económica, 1992), 417–420.

GARCÍA, Santiago (1928–   ). The theater La Candelaria was founded by Santiago García in 1972 with the help of his friends from La Casa de la Cultura. Today, La Candelaria is one of the most outstanding theater groups in the country, and it is a bastion for independent theater. García initiated Collective Creation plays using a different methodology from that used by El TEC. The group's objective is the collective montage of a piece: They penetrate the theme by investigating the historical and social conditions of the characters and the events. For this, La Candelaria counts on professionals from different fields: sociologists, historians, musicians, painters, and the people, from which the themes, the language, the tone, and the gestures emerge.

La ciudad dorada (The Golden City) (1972) is the second Collective Creation play, and it brings together the theme of peasant migration to the city. It was made in collaboration with a group of *campesinos* from the Llanos Orientales. The third Collective Creation play is *Guadalupe años sin cuenta* (Guadalupe Years Without Count) (1975), and it is one of the most renowned plays of the New Colombian theater. The advent of this play was a trip to the Llanos Orientales, where the theater group heard *corridos* that told the story of the Revolution of the Llanos in the 1950s and of its legendary leader, Guadalupe Salcedo Unda.

This theater group and its director have made decisive contributions to the development of the national dramaturgy with their publications, essays about theater, and training of actors, directors, and authors, such as Fernando Peñuela and Patricia Ariza.

WORKS BY LA CANDELARIA: *Guadalupe años sin cuenta* (Guadalupe Years Without Count), in *Teatro colombiano contemporáneo* (Bogotá: Tres Culturas Editores, 1985), 183–244. *Cinco obras de creación colectiva* (Five Collective Creation Plays) (Bogotá: Ediciones del teatro La Candelaria, 1986). (It has: *La ciudad dorada* [The Golden City], *Los diez días que estremecieron al mundo* [The Ten Days That Shook the World], *Golpe de suerte* [Strike of Luck], *Guadalupe años sin cuenta* [Guadalupe Years Without Count], and *Nosotros los comunes* [We the People].)

WORKS BY SANTIAGO GARCÍA: *Corre, corre Carigüeta* (Run, Run Carigüeta), in *Cuatro obras del teatro La Candelaria* (Bogotá: Ediciones teatro La Candelaria, 1987), 263–334. *El diálogo del rebusque* (The Dialogue of the Search for Livelihood), in *Cuatro obras del teatro La Candelaria* (Bogotá: Ediciones La Candelaria, 1987), 9–115. *Maravilla Estar* (Wonderful Star), in *Tres obras del teatro La Candelaria* (Bogotá: Ediciones teatro La Candelaria, 1991), 59–140. *El paso* (The Passage), in *Antología del teatro colombiano contemporáneo* (Madrid: Fondo de Cultura Económica, 1992), 257–286. *La trifulca* (The Squabble), in *Tres obras del teatro La Candelaria*, 141–201.

BIBLIOGRAPHY: "Un quevedo visto por los colombianos de La Candelaria," *ABC* (Madrid, September 11, 1984). Ricardo Almeida, *El diálogo del rebusque*, *Revista de Hoy* (Ecuador, May 22, 1983). Giorgio Antei, ed., *Las rutas del teatro* (Bogotá: Centro Editorial de la Universidad Nacional, 1989). Liliana Alzate, "Una trifulca para repetir," *El Nuevo Siglo* (Bogotá, August 13, 1991). Willmarck Arango, "*El paso* de La Candelaria . . . de puro milagro," *El Occidente* (Cali, May 9, 1989). Claudia Arcila, "*La trifulca*: Entre carnaval y cuaresma," *El Espectador* (August 11, 1991). Gonzalo Arcila, *La imagen teatral en La Candelaria* (Bogotá: Ediciones Teatro La Candelaria, 1992). Arcila, *Nuevo Teatro en Colombia: Actividad creadora y política cultural* (Bogotá: Ediciones CEIS, 1983). Bernard Baycroft, "Entrevista con Santiago García," *Latin American Theatre Review* (Spring 1982): 77–82. Gilberto Bello, "Un paso adelante," *El Espectador* (March 8, 1989). Bello, "Rebuscando en la palabra," *El Espectador* (March 29, 1989). Bello, "Carnaval teatral," *El Espectador* (July 28, 1991). Nicolás Buenaventura, "Un país entre la soledad y la violencia," in *Antología del teatro colombiano contemporáneo* (Madrid: Fondo de Cultura Económica, 1992), 251–255. Orlando Cajamarca, "Alicia Maravilla," *El País* (Gaceta Dominical, Cali, October 21, 1990). Cajamarca, "Alicia *Maravilla Estar*, búsqueda de la felicidad. Ultimo montaje del teatro La Candelaria," *Impacto* (New York) (July 18–24, 1989). Alfonso

Carvajal, "Búsqueda y riesgo en *La trifulca*," *La Patria* (Manizales, August 30, 1991). Gabriel Castillo, "*El diálogo del rebusque*. Quevedo revivido y hoy actual," *La opinión Torreón* (Cohavila, México, October 12, 1983). Julio Daniel Chaparro, "Del otro lado del espejo," *El Espectador* (April 9, 1990). Jorge Child, "El rebusque," *El Espectador* (October 1982). Ileana Dieguez, "*El paso* de La Candelaria por Cadiz: Parábola en el tiempo," *Conjunto* (1989), 79. Fernando Duque Mesa, "*Maravilla Estar* en el laberinto de la postmodernidad," *Cuadernos Corporación Colombiana de Teatro* (Bogotá, 1992). Lisandro Duque, "Acerca de *El diálogo del rebusque*," *Documentos políticos* (Bogotá, 1981), 148, 9. Mario Escobar, "Telones y ceniza," *La Patria* (Manizales, September 5, 1989). Carlos Espinosa Dominguez, "*Guadalupe*: Un ajuste de cuentas con la historia," *Conjunto* (1976), 29, 84–88. Aníbal Gallego, "Qué *Maravilla Estar* en este mundo," *Revista Consigna* (June 30, 1990), 389. María Margarita García, "País de las mil máscaras," *La Prensa* (Manizales, September 3, 1989). Eduardo Gómez, "Un montaje colectivo. *El paso*," *El Tiempo* (July 22, 1989). Alfredo González, "*El paso* saca la cara," *El Espectador* (May 27, 1988). Angela María González, "Estreno en La Candelaria," *El Espectador* (May 15, 1985). Patricia González, "El Nuevo Teatro en Colombia" (Ph.D. diss., University of Texas, 1981). Fernando González Cajiao, *Historia del teatro en Colombia* (Bogotá: Instituto Colombiano de Cultura, 1986). Carlos Gutiérrez, "La Candelaria *Maravilla Estar*. Otro paso para afianzar la dramaturgia nacional," *Nueva Frontera* (October 26, 1989). Fernando de Ita, "Quevedo y un experimento colombiano," *Uno más uno* (México, October 6, 1983), 6, 21–23. María Mercedes Jaramillo de Velasco, *El nuevo teatro colombiano: Arte y política* (Medellín: Universidad de Antioquia, 1992). Jaramillo de Velasco, *El nuevo teatro colombiano y la colonización cultural* (Bogotá: Editorial Memoria, 1987). María Mercedes Jaramillo de Velasco and Betty Osorio, "La trifulca y el carnaval," in *Texto y contexto* (Bogotá: Universidad de los Andes, 1991), 17, 218–219. Oscar Jurado, "Santiago García y el teatro latinoamericano: En busca de un lenguaje propio," *Conjunto* (1973), 15, 122–127. Rine Leal, "Santiago y la memoria," *Conjunto* (1988), 75, 93–95. Gaspar León, "Un teatro cercano, *El paso (parábola del camino)*," *Colombia hoy informa* (Bogotá, July 1989), 59. Eduardo Marceles Daconte, "*Diálogo del rebusque* o la fantasía de la realidad," *Latin American Theatre Review* (Fall 1982), 19, 105–108. Marceles Daconte, "Detrás del escenario de La Candelaria," *El Espectador* (July 1984), 19. Olga Marín and Rafael Chaparro, "Juegue el único sueño posible en el absurdo. El circo de los sueños," *La Prensa* (October 26, 1989). Carlos Alberto Martínez, "Una aproximación poética," *El Siglo* (Bogotá, May 26, 1988). Martínez, "*El paso*: Un nuevo salto de La Candelaria," *Conjunto* (1989), 78, 73–74. Martínez, "*Maravilla Estar* o la lucidez de lo imposible," *El Espectador* (Magazín Dominical, May 20, 1990), 369. Armando Neira, "*La trifulca* en rock," *Credencial* (Bogotá, August 1, 1991). "Estreno de la Candelaria. *Corre, corre Carigüeta*," *Nueva Frontera* (Bogotá, May 27–June 2, 1985). "La parábola del camino," *Nueva Frontera* (Bogotá, June 27–July 3, 1988), 689.

GARCÍA PIEDRAHITA, Eduardo (1903–?).
García was an essayist, a journalist, and a playwright. The style of his plays is realistic. In *Pasiones en pugna* (Passions in Conflict), García analyzes the struggles and problems of the workers during their strike. *Estampas de rebeldes* (Rebelds' Stamps) is a historic play that takes place in 1560 in Peru when Pizarro's soldiers revolted against his tyrannic rule.

WORKS: *Teatro* (Bogotá: Instituto Colombiano de Cultura, 1981). (It has: *Pasiones en pugna* [Passions in Conflict], which won the first prize in 1977 during the contest Teatro Abierto sponsored by La Secretaría de Educación of Antioquia; and *Estampas de rebeldes* [Rebelds' Stamps], which won the prize given by La Universidad del Valle and El Instituto Colombiano de Cultura in 1978.)

BIBLIOGRAPHY: Fernando González Cajiao, *Historia del teatro en Colombia* (Bogotá: Instituto Colombiano de Cultura, 1986).

GAVIRIA, José Enrique (?–1959).
Gaviria was a playwright. He was a diplomat in the Dominican Republic, and the cultural traditions and religious practices of Haiti and the Dominican Republic impacted him. In *Kaiyou* (1942), his first play, he recreated Haitian history and the social and political problems of the blacks and mulattos on the island. *El llanto de los muertos* (Deaths' Weeping) takes place during the seventeenth century in Cartagena, where dogmatism was ruling and destroying people's lives. *Ejército de hormigas* (Ants' Army) recreates *La violencia* that affected and afflicted Colombia during the 1950s. *Caminos de niebla*

(Paths in the Mist) was staged by Víctor Mallarino at El Teatro Colón in Bogotá in 1957.

WORKS: *Caminos en la niebla y otras piezas teatrales* (Bogotá: Instituto Caro y Cuervo, 1978). (It includes: *Caminos en la niebla* [Paths in the Mist], *El llanto de los muertos* [Deaths' Weeping], *La sombra siguió adelante* [The Shadow Followed Ahead], *Ejército de hormigas* [Ants' Army], and *Kaiyou.*)

BIBLIOGRAPHY: Fernando González Cajiao, *Historia del teatro en Colombia* (Bogotá: Instituto Colombiano de Cultura, 1986). Héctor Orjuela, *Bibliografía del teatro colombiano* (Bogotá: Instituto Caro y Cuervo, 1974), 87.

GONZÁLEZ CAJIAO, Fernando (1938–).
He is a playwright and a well-known critic. He is also a historian of Colombian theatre. One of the main objectives of González Cajiao's plays is to recover pre-Columbian history and legends.

WORKS: *La comadreja* (The Weasel), in *Revista Universidad de Antioquia* (1961), 145, 321. *La auténtica y edificante fábula del conejo y los animales poderosos* (The Authentic and Instructive Fable of the Rabbit and the Powerful Animals) (1971). *Cómo el conejo decidió las elecciones en el reino de los animales* (How the Rabbit Decided Elections in the Kingdom of the Animals) (1971). *Conjunto* (1977), 32. *Atabí o la última profecía de los Chibchas* (Atabí or the Last Prophecy of the Chibchas) (Bogotá: Instituto Colombiano de Cultura, 1984). *Popón el brujo y el sueño de Tisquesusa* (Popón, the Warlock and the Dream of Tisquesusa), in *Tramoya* (Mexico City: Universidad Veracruzana, 1992), 33, 214–253. *La familia armadillo* (The Armadillo Family) (n.d.). *Él globo* (The Globe) (n.d.). *Huellas de un rebelde* (Footprints of a Rebel) (n.d.).

ESSAYS: *Historia del teatro en Colombia* (Bogotá: Instituto Colombiano de Cultura, 1986). "Los años 80 en Colombia: El derecho a ser distintos," *Latin American Theatre Review* (1992), 25, 2. Ed., *Antología del teatro colombiano contemporáneo* (Madrid: Fondo de Cultura Económica, 1992).

BIBLIOGRAPHY: Leon F. Lyday, "Fernando González Cajiao, en busca de una modalidad dramática," *Revista El café literario* (January–February 1979), 7.

HENRIQUEZ TORRES, Guillermo (1940–).
He is a writer, essayist, and playwright. He has made an important contribution to contemporary Colombian theater and continues to play an active role in its development.

WORKS: *Academia de baile* (Dance Academy) (n.d.). *El cuadrado de astromelias* (The "Astromelia" Square), in *Antología del teatro colombiano contemporáneo* (Madrid: Fondo de Cultura Económica, 1992), 517–547. *Detras del abanico* (Behind the Fan) (n.d.). *Escarpín de señoras* (Women's Pumps) (n.d.). *Hora de César* (Cesar's Hour) (n.d.). *Marta Cibelina* (Marten Cebellina) (n.d.). *La pianola* (The Pianola) (n.d.). *Reunión de Tiaras* (The Reunion of the Tiaras) (n.d.). *Las tentaciones de sor Mariana de Montes* (The Temptations of Sister Mariana de Montes) (n.d.). *Trece maneras de mirar un mirlo* (Thirteen Ways to Look at a Blackbird) (n.d.).

BIBLIOGRAPHY: Fernando González Cajiao, "Entre la vigilia y el sueño," in *Antología del teatro colombiano contemporáneo* (Madrid: Fondo de Cultura Económica, 1992), 509–515.

LAGUADO, Arturo (1919–).
Laguado is a journalist, a lawyer, and a playwright. Among his comedies and tragedies are *El entremés de los fantasmas cándidos* (The Candid Phantoms' One-Act Play) (n.d.); *La jaula* (The Cage) (n.d.); *Pericardias* (n.d.); *Se permite la aventura* (Adventure Is Allowed) (n.d.); and *El tratado* (The Treaty) (n.d.).

WORKS: *El gran guiñol* (The Great Puppet), in *Antología del teatro colombiano contemporáneo* (Madrid: Fondo de Cultura Económica, 1992), 297–346.

BIBLIOGRAPHY: Marina Lamus, "La obra de un precursor," in *Antología del teatro colombiano contemporáneo* (Madrid: Fondo de Cultura Económica, 1992), 289–296.

MALLARINO, Víctor (1909–1967).
Born in Bogotá, Mallarino was a poet and playwright. He was a valid contributor to the Colombian theater of the first half of the twentieth century.

WORKS: *La casa del olvido* (The House of Oblivion) (n.d.). *Un poeta de ayer y una niña de hoy* (A Poet of Yesterday and a Girl of Today) (n.d.).

MARTÍNEZ, Gilberto (1934–).
Born in Medellín, Martínez studied medicine at La Universidad de Medellín and at the University of California. He is an author, director, and the-

ater theorist. Martínez has developed his work in Medellín, where he has promoted and directed various theater groups such as El Triángulo, La Carreta, Teatro Libre de Medellín, El Tinglado, La Casa del Teatro, and La Escuela Municipal de Teatro. Since the 1960s, he has sustained the magazine *Teatro*, where he analyzes national theater performances and makes critical and theoretical contributions. He is one of the pioneers of theater criticism in the nation. Among his critical essays are: *Hacia un teatro dialéctico* (1979) and *Citas y reflexiones sobre Bertold Brecht* (1991). Among his montages the following are remembered: *Las monjas* (The Nuns), by the Cuban Eduardo Manet, and *La historia de una muñeca abandonada* (The Story of an Abandoned Doll), by Alfonso Sastre. Among his dramatic plays we can highlight *El grito de los ahorcados* (The Outcry of the Hung) (1965), which recreates the people's insurrection of 1781, when the tobacco peasant workers, upset by excessive taxation, decided to rebel against the tax collectors. With this play he won the National Theater Contest in Medellín in 1966. This piece has been presented by theater groups from Argentina, Bulgaria, Canada, Colombia, Cuba, and Mexico.

WORKS: *El Zarpazo* (The Smack) (Medellín: Revista Teatro, 1974). *El grito de los ahorcados* (The Outcry of the Hung), in *Antología colombiana del teatro de vanguardia* (Bogotá: Instituto Colombiano de Cultura, 1975); *Antología del teatro colombiano contemporáneo* (Madrid: Fondo de Cultura Económica, 1992), 355–414. *Teatro, teoría y práctica* (Medellín: Autores antioqueños, 1986) (it has: *La ceremonia* [The Ceremony], *El horóscopo* [The Horoscope], *Las vicisitudes del poder* [The Vicissitudes of Power], and *El Zarpazo* [The Smack]). *El tren de las cinco no sale a las cinco en punto* (The Five O'Clock Train Does Not Leave at Five O'Clock) (Medellín: Revista Teatro #12 n.d.). *Dos minutos para dormirse* (Two Minutes to Fall Asleep) (Medellín: Revista Teatro #12 n.d.). *Doña Pánfaga o el sanalotodo* (Doña Pánfaga or the "Cure-all") (Medellín: Revista Teatro #10 n.d.).

BIBLIOGRAPHY: Fernando González Cajiao, *Historia del teatro en Colombia* (Bogotá: Instituto Colombiano de Cultura, 1986). María Mercedes Jaramillo de Velasco, *El Nuevo Teatro Colombiano: Arte y política* (Medellín: Universidad de Antioquia,

1992). Héctor Orjuela, *Bibliografía del teatro colombiano* (Bogotá: Instituto Caro y Cuervo, 1974), 123, Rodrigo Zuluaga, "Volver a contar la historia," in *Antología del teatro colombiano contemporáneo* (Madrid: Fondo de Cultura Económica, 1992), 349–353.

MOYANO, Juan Carlos (1959–). Moyano is a poet, actor, director, and one of the most prominent young playwrights. He is best known for his street plays. *Cuando las marionetas hablaron* (When the Marionettes Spoke) (1975) analyzes human vices and virtues through the puppets' conduct.

WORKS: *Hoy, no hay función* (There Is No Show Today), *El profesor Prometeo* (Prometheus the Teacher) (1978), and *La cabeza de Gupuk* (Gupuk's Head) (1979) were all staged by El Teatro Taller de Colombia. *La bruja o el sueño de las tormentas* (The Sorcerer or the Tempests' Dream) was staged in 1993 during the Second International Encounter, Mujeres en Escena in Cali.

NAVAJAS, Esteban (1948–). Navajas is an anthropologist and playwright. Born in Bogotá, he has been an important contributor to the contemporary Colombian theater.

WORKS: *La agonía del difunto* (The Agony of the Deceased), in *Teatro colombiano contemporáneo* (Bogotá: Tres Culturas Editores, 1985), 21–50; in *Antología del teatro colombiano contemporáneo* (Madrid: Fondo de Cultura Económica, 1992), 691–726. *Canto triste a una sombra de boxeo* (A Sad Song to the Shadow Boxing) (Medellín: Universidad de Antioquia, 1982). *La comparsa del juicio final* (The Chorus of the Final Judgement) (n.d.). *El pionero* (The Pioneer) (n.d.). *Trilogía del trueno y el fango* (Trilogy of Thunder and Mud) (n.d.).

BIBLIOGRAPHY: Jorge Plata, "Un macabro memorial de agravios," in *Antología del teatro colombiano contemporáneo* (Madrid: Fondo de Cultura Económica, 1992).

NIÑO, Jairo Aníbal (1941–). Born in Moniquirá, Niño is a director, playwright, and poet. His first experience with theater was in the puppet group Juan Pueblo from Medellín. He has been linked to the Dramaturgy Workshop of El Teatro Libre de Bogotá. Niño was the theater director of the La Universidad Nacional theater group in Medellín, of El Teatro de Arte of Cartagena, and of La Escuela Distrital de Teatro. His plays have been translated into various languages and have been represented in diverse countries. Niño has won awards such as El Festival de Teatro Universitario in 1966, 1967, and 1968 and the contest for the best Author of Theater in 1968. From his Dramaturgy Workshop emerged important plays that were staged by El Teatro Libre. *La agonía del difunto* (The Agony of the Deceased) (1976) is a well-known piece by Esteban Navajas. It is a solid tragicomedy that recreates the problems between landowners and peons. Popular elements and ritual ceremonies were added to enrich the play. Among the plays written by Niño the following stand out: *El Monte Calvo* (The Barren Mount) (1975) was presented by the theater of La Universidad Libre and is one of the most well-known pieces of Colombian theater. This play explores the theme of war through forgotten and perturbed veterans. The excellent quality of the dramatic language contains elements of the Absurd theater. The veterans' dialogue projects the alienation that war produces in human beings. *El sol subterráneo* (The Subterranean Sun) (1978) is another of the plays that works the theme of the banana plantations. Niño charges the drama using elements of the Greek tragedies: The three feminine characters, like the Furies, confront the lieutenant and succeed in destroying him.

WORKS: *Las bodas de lata o el baile de los arzobispos* (The Tin Wedding or the Dance of the Archbishops) (Bogotá: Albón, 1968). *Los inquilinos de la ira* (The Tenants of Rage) (Bogotá: Punto y coma, 1975). *El Monte Calvo* (The Barren Mount), in *Antología colombiana del teatro de vanguardia* (Bogotá: Instituto Colombiano de Cultura, 1975), 101–135; in *Actuemos* (1982), 2; in *Antología del teatro colombiano contemporáneo* (Madrid: Fondo de Cultura Económica, 1992), 655–679. *La agonía del difunto* (The Agony of the Deceased) (1976). *La madriguera* (The Burrow), in *Teorema* (Bogotá, 1978), 14–20. *El sol subterráneo* (The Subterranean Sun) (Bogotá: Carlos Valencia Editores, 1978); in *Teatro colombiano contemporáneo* (Bogotá: Tres culturas, 1985), 157–182.

BIBLIOGRAPHY: "Entrevista con Jairo Aníbal Niño," *Actuemos* (1982), 2, 2. Gonzalo Arcila,

Nuevo Teatro en Colombia: Actividad creadora y política cultural (Bogotá: Ediciones CEIS, 1983). Guillermo Arévalo, "Jairo Aníbal Niño, trabajador del teatro colombiano," in *Materiales* (546–563). Alberto Castilla, "Participación latinoamericana en el VII Festival Mundial de Nancy," *Latin American Theatre Review* (Fall 1969), 3, 1, 62. Eduardo Gómez, "Un juego trágico y esquizoide," in *Antología del teatro colombiano contemporáneo* (Madrid: Fondo de Cultura Económica, 1992), 647–653. Fernando González Cajiao, *Historia del teatro en Colombia* (Bogotá: Instituto Colombiano de Cultura, 1986). González, "El Nuevo Teatro en Colombia" (Ph.D. diss., University of Texas, 1981). Patricia González, "Jairo Aníbal Niño, un dramaturgo colombiano," *Latin American Theatre Review* (Spring 1982); 35–43. María Mercedes Jaramillo de Velasco, "Autonomía cultural en el teatro colombiano," in *Colombia: Literatura y cultura en el siglo XX*, ed. Isabel Vergara (UNESCO, 1994). Jaramillo de Velasco, *El Nuevo Teatro Colombiano y la colonización cultural* (Bogotá: Editorial Memoria, 1987). Jaramillo de Velasco, *El Nuevo Teatro Colombiano: Arte y política* (Medellín: Universidad de Antioquia, 1992). Jaramillo de Velasco, "La proyección teatral de la masacre de las bananeras," *Latin American Theatre Review* (1989), 23, 1, 89–103. Héctor Orjuela, *Bibliografía del teatro colombiano* (Bogotá: Instituto Caro y Cuervo, 1974), 134.

ORTIZ ROJAS, José Joaquín (1814–1892). Born in Tunja, Ortiz Rojas was a poet and a journalist. In 1834, his play *Sulma* was staged at a friend's house in Bogotá. It is a neoclassic tragedy that recreates the Muysca ceremonies to the sun.

WORK: *Sulma* (Int. Alvaro Garzón Marthá, Bogotá: Arango Editores, 1988).

OSORIO, Luis Enrique (1896–1966). Osorio was born in Bogotá. He was a sociologist, novelist, and playwright. He was the founder of the magazines *La novela semanal* and *El cuento semanal* and also of La Compañía Dramática Nacional, Escuela de Arte Dramático, Compañía Bogotana de Comedias, and La Escala; and with Rómulo Betancur he created El Teatro de la Comedia. The best plays by Osorio are based on *La violencia* in Colombia. *Nube de abril* (April Cloud) (n.d.) is based on the events of April 9, 1948, when popular leader Jorge

Eliécer Gaitán was assassinated. *El doctor Manzanillo* (Doctor Manzanillo) (n.d.) recreates the conflict between the traditional parties in Colombia. *El iluminado* (The Enlightened) (n.d.) is, according to González Cajiao, one of his best plays. It is a historical parody of an imaginary country, Tartuja, but it evokes Colombia of the middle of the nineteenth century.

WORKS: *Flor tardía* (Late Flower) (1917) was his first play, and it premiered at El Teatro Municipal de Bogotá. *La ciudad alegre y coreográfica* (The Happy and Choreographic City) (1919) is a Spanish operetta. *La sombra* (The Shadow) (1920) premiered in Caracas in the Company of Manolo Puértolas. *El beso del muerto* (The Kiss of the Deceased) (1921) and *Los celos del fantasma* (The Jealousy of the Phantom) (1921) premiered in Buenos Aires. *Sed de justicia* (Thirst for Justice) (1921) premiered in Bogotá. *Tragedia íntima* (Intimate Tragedy) premiered in Paris in 1927. *Al amor de los escombros* (To the Love of Rubble) (n.d.) premiered in Mexico. *Los creadores* (The Creators) (n.d.) premiered in French. *Las rápsodas* (The Rhapsodes) (n.d.) was staged at El Teatro Ideal de México. *Nube de abril* (April Cloud) (n.d.). *El doctor Manzanillo* (Doctor Manzanillo) (n.d.). *El iluminado* (The Enlightened) (n.d.).

BIBLIOGRAPHY: Ernesto Barrera, "Algunos aspectos en el arte dramático de Luis Enrique Osorio," *Materiales* (263–272). *Barrera, Realidad y fantasía en el drama social de Luis Enrique Osorio* (Madrid: Playor, SA, 1973). Fernando González Cajiao, *Historia del teatro en Colombia* (Bogotá: Instituto Colombiano de Cultura, 1986). José A. Nuñez Segura, *Literatura colombiana* (Medellín: Editorial Bedout, 1966), 735–743. Héctor Orjuela, *Bibliografía del teatro colombiano* (Bogotá: Instituto Caro y Cuervo, 1974), 146.

PEÑUELA, Fernando (1948–). Peñuela is a director, an actor, a playwright, and a member of La Candelaria. Peñuela promotes theater in the *barrios* as well as in factories and is an active member of El Taller Permanente de Investigación Teatral. *La tras-escena* (Behind the Scenes) (s.1984) is about theater, and the play projects the similarities between art and reality.

WORKS: *La tras-escena* (Behind the Scenes), staged by La Candelaria in 1984; in *Antología del teatro colombiano contemporáneo* (Madrid: Fondo de Cultura Económica, 1992), 811–895. *Asunto de honor* (A Matter of Honor) (1987). *La ingenuidad* (Ingenuity), premiered in 1988. *Cotidianidades* (Daily Life) staged in 1989. *Claro de luna* (Moonlight) (1991). *Pleito maternal* (Maternal Conflict) (1991). *Camisa de once varas* (Shirt of Eleven Rods) (n.d.). *Carta de recomendación* (Letter of Recommendation) (n.d.).

BIBLIOGRAPHY: Gonzalo Arcila, "El teatro se mira a sí mismo," in *Antología del teatro colombiano contemporáneo* (Madrid: Fondo de Cultura Económica, 1992), 805–809. Ileana Cidoncha, "Plano y doble juego de *La tras-escena*," *El Nuevo Día* (San Juan, December 9, 1988). Heriberto Ferrer, "*La tras-escena* de Fernando Peñuela," *Revista en Rojo* (San Juan, December 23–29, 1988). "Qué pasa detrás del telón," *Nueva Frontera* (Bogotá, May 28, 1984). Fernando Ramírez, "*Tras-escena* nueva experiencia de La Candelaria," *La República* (Bogotá, June 2, 1984). Richard Shepard, "*Tras-escena* por un grupo colombiano," *New York Times*, August 14, 1986. Allan Wallack, "*Tras-Escena* Anarchy Stages Anarchy," *Newsday* (New York, August 13, 1986).

PORTO DE GONZÁLEZ, Judith. Born in Cartagena, Porto de González is a very prolific playwright and a writer. As Beatriz Rizk rightly affirms, her plays are realistic and reproduce the dominant ideology in issues of gender and class. In *40 grados bajo 0* (40 Degrees Below 0) a woman is frozen for seven years because she is afraid of losing her younger lover if she gets old. *Lily llamó el sábado* (Lily Called on Saturday) recreates the life of a schizophrenic wife who kills herself after telling her husband about the affair she had with her doctor while she was sick. The moral order is thus restored. Lily's husband had numerous affairs while she was in the hospital, yet his behavior is never questioned.

WORKS: *Al convento y para mí un pirata* (To the Convent and for Me a Pirata) staged in 1964 at La Sala de Orientación Artística (Cartagena: Publicaciones La Baranda, 1966). *La casa de don Benito* (Don Benito's House), comedy in one act (Bogotá, 1965). *Pasan los años en la tierra* (The Years Pass on Earth) (Cartagena: La Baranda, 1965). *Pilares vacíos* (Empty Pilars) won the prize at El Festival de Arte de Cali in 1966. *Son los chinos* (It's the Chinese) (1966). *Mesa de juego* (Game Table) (1967) (Cartagena: La Baranda, 1979); also in *Narrativa y teatro* (Bogotá: Ministerio de Educación Nacional,

Instituto Colombiano de Cultura Hispánica, 1972). *Teatro* (Five plays) (Cartagena: La Baranda. 1968). *Teatro* de Judith Porto de González (The Theater of Judith Porto de González) (Cartagena: Editorial Bolívar, 1968). *La obra literaria de Judith Porto de González* (The Literary Works of Judith Porto de González) (Bogotá: Editorial ABC, 1972) (includes: *40 grados bajo 0*; *Pasan los años en la tierra*; *Son los chinos*). *Antoñito el milagrero* (Antoñito the Miracle Worker), in *Lecciones de teatro* (Cartagena: La Baranda, 1983), 165–188. *Teatro actual: Comedias y dramas* (Modern Theater: Comedies and Dramas) (Cartagena: La Baranda, 1990). *40 grados bajo 0* (40 Degrees Below 0) (n.d.). *El galeote* (The Galley Slave) (n.d.). *Lily llamó el sábado* (Lily Called on Saturday) (n.d.). *En un pasillo oscuro* (In a Dark Passage) (n.d.). *Una reunión clandestina* (A Clandestine Reunion) (n.d.).

BIBLIOGRAPHY: Roberto Burgos Ojeda, Prólogo to *Teatro* de Judith Porto de González (Cartagena: Editorial Bolívar, 1968). Beatriz J. Rizk, "Hacia una poética feminista: La increíble y triste historia de la dramaturgia femenina en Colombia," in *Escritura y diferencia: Autoras colombianas del siglo XX*, ed. María Mercedes Jaramillo, Betty Osorio, and Angela Robledo (Bogotá: Universidad de los Andes and Medellín, Universidad de Antioquia).

REYES, Carlos José (1941–   ). His uninterrupted work as author, director, and critic has made him one of the most outstanding playwrights in the national panorama. He began his theater career with university theater groups like El Buho (1958), which provided a cultural space independent from the limits imposed by the status quo. El Buho is one of the pioneer groups in the New Colombian theater. In 1964, with Carlos Perozzo, he founded El Teatro de Arte Popular. This group was one of the first theater groups that created an audience for the national theater. Its plays analyzed the social problems of the country. Further, Reyes wrote and staged plays for children, such as: *Dulcita y el burrito* (Dulcita and the Little Donkey) (1964); *El globito manual* (The Little Manual Balloon) (1974); and *El hombre que escondió el sol y la luna* (The Man Who Hid the Sun and the Moon) (1974). These two last plays won awards and were published by Casa de las Américas in 1976. The children's plays initi-

ated a children's dramaturgy where the peripeteia of the characters responds to the cultural and social background of Colombian children. These plays were presented at La ventana del Alacrán, which was a stage created by Reyes's group, El Alacrán, exclusively for children. Among his productions the following stand out: *Soldados* (Soldiers) (1966) is one of the most represented pieces in the Colombian New theater. The play is based on the novel by Alvaro Cepeda Samudio and deals with the banana plantation strike of 1928. It belongs to the cycle of plays that deal with the theme of the banana plantations. In 1968, *Los viejos baúles empolvados que nuestros padres nos prohibieron abrir* (The Old Dusty Trunks That Our Parents Forbade Us to Open) premiered. It exposes the spiritual and material misery that afflict the middle class. In 1992, La Universidad de Antioquia published an anthology of his works, where *La antesala* (The Vestibule) and *La mudez* (Muteness) should be noted.

WORKS: *Dulcita y el burrito* (Dulcita and the Little Donkey (1964). *Soldados* (Soldiers) (s.1966), in *Teatro* de Enrique Buenaventura (Bogotá: Instituto Colombiano de Cultura, 1977), 161–194. *Teatro para niños* (Theatre for Children) (Bogotá: Biblioteca Colombiana de Cultura, 1972) (includes: *Dulcita y el burrito* [Dulcita and the Little Donkey], *La fiesta de los muñecos* [The Puppets' Party] and *La piedra de la felicidad* [The Rock of Happiness]). *Los viejos baúles empolvados que nuestros padres nos prohibieron abrir* (The Old Dusty Chests That Our Parents Prohibited Us to Open) (Bogotá: Instituto Colombiano de Cultura, 1973); also in *Antología del teatro colombiano contemporáneo* (Madrid: Fondo de Cultura Económica, 1992), 559–644. *El arca de Noé* (Noah's Ark), *Antología de teatro infantil* (Ed. Emilio Carballido, México: Editores Mexicanos Unidos, 1979), 215–231. *El carnaval de la muerte alegre* (The Carnival of the Cheerful Dead) (Int. María Mercedes Jaramillo, Madrid: El público, Centro de documentación teatral, 1992). *Dentro y fuera* (Inside and out) (Int. María Mercedes Jaramillo, Medellín: Universidad de Antioquia, 1992) (includes: *La antesala* [The Vestibule], *Función nocturna* [Nocturnal Function], *La mudez* [Muteness], *Recorrido en redondo* [Round Trip Journey], *Los viejos baúles empolvados que nuestros padres nos prohibieron abrir* [The Old Dusty Trunks That Our Parents Forbade Us to Open], and *La voz* [The Voice]).

BIBLIOGRAPHY: Frank Dauster, *Historia del teatro hispanoamericano; Siglos XIX y XX*, 2nd ed. (Mexico City: Ediciones de Andrea, 1973), 147. Eduardo Gómez, "El II Festival de Teatro: Tres obras para niños," *Nueva Frontera* (Santafé de Bogotá, 1975), 10, 14. Gomez, "Tres obras para niños," *Materiales* (397–400). Fernando González Cajiao, *Historia del teatro en Colombia* (Bogotá: Instituto Colombiano de Cultura, 1986). Patricia González, "El Nuevo Teatro en Colombia" (Ph.D. diss., University of Texas, 1981). María Mercedes Jaramillo de Velasco, "Autonomía cultural en el teatro colombiano," in *Colombia: Literatura y cultura en el siglo XX*, ed. Isabel Vergara (UNESCO, 1994). Jaramillo de Velasco, "En busca de una dramaturgia nacional," in *Antología del teatro colombiano contemporáneo* (Madrid: Fondo de Cultura Económica, 1992), 551–557. Jaramillo le Velasco, "La labor teatral de Carlos José Reyes," in *Dentro y fuera* (Medellín: Universidad de Antioquia, 1992), 9–28. Jaramillo de Velasco, *El Nuevo Teatro Colombiano y la colonización cultural* (Bogotá: Editorial memoria, 1987). Jaramillo de Velasco, *El Nuevo Teatro Colombiano: Arte y política* (Medellín: Universidad de Antioquia, 1992). Jaramillo de Velasco, "La proyección teatral de la masacre de las bananeras," *Latin American Theatre Review* (1989), 23, 1, 89–103. Jaramillo de Velasco, "Una trayectoria fecunda," in *El carnaval de la muerte alegre* (Madrid: El público, Centro de documentación teatral, 1992), 9–19. José Monleón, "Conversación con Carlos José Reyes: Nadie paga la boleta para que lo insulten todo el tiempo," *Primer Acto* (1984), 203, 204, 41. Héctor Orjuela, *Bibliografía del teatro colombiano* (Bogotá: Instituto Caro y Cuervo, 1974), 163. Antonio Orlando Rodríguez, "El compañero Globito," *Conjunto* (1979), 40, 118–121.

RODRIGUEZ DE MORENO, Sofía. An actress and playwright, she founded and directed La Academia y Teatrino Don Eloy with her husband, Angel Alberto Moreno. Her style was realistic, and most of her plays were dedicated to children. Moreno also wrote the music for her plays. *José Dolorcitos* (José "Littlepains") (1965) won the prize Teatro Escolar de *El Tiempo*. The main character is a peasant child whose only entertainment is playing with the stars; eventually, they help him obtain peace. *El abuelo Rin Ron* (The Grandfather Rin Ron) (n.d.) premiered at El Teatro Colón. Rin Ron, the tadpole's grandfather, held a convention with other animals to judge human beings for the destruction of the environment. *Brujas modernas* (Modern Witches) (n.d.) won *El Tiempo*'s theater prize. The play is about street children and the people who take advantage of them to make money.

WORKS: *La culpable* (The Guilty One) (n.d.). *El chatico* (The Chatico) (n.d.). *La estrella milagrosa* (The Miraculous Star) (n.d.). *José Dolorcitos* (José "Littlepains") (Colombia: Ediciones La Idea). *Los niños y el poeta* (The Children and the Poet) (n.d.). *El niño que soñaba* (The Child Who Dreamt) (n.d.).

SAMPER, Gabriela (1918–1974). Born in Bogotá, Samper was a writer. Her vivid stories about jailed women, *La mojana* (n.d.) and *La Marimunda* (n.d.), were dramatized. In 1961, Samper founded a theater group for children, El Burrito. She was also the director of El Teatro Cultural del Parque Nacional, where plays by Colombian playwrights were staged.

WORKS: *La mojana* (n.d.). *La Marimunda* (n.d.).

TORRES, Carlos Arturo (1867–1911). Torres was a poet, essayist, and diplomat. In 1891, he wrote *Lope de Aguirre*, which premiered at El Teatro Municipal de Bogotá. Aguirre's adventures in America with his followers, *los Marañones*, were depicted by Torres as the first rebellion in the Spanish colonies against Felipe II.

WORK: *Lope de Aguirre* (Prol. Rubén Sierra Mejía, Bogotá: Arango Editores, 1989).

BIBLIOGRAPHY: Héctor Orjuela, *Bibliografía del teatro colombiano* (Bogotá: Caro y Cuervo, 1974), 188. José Vicente Ortega Ricaute, *Historia crítica del teatro en Bogotá* (Bogotá: Ediciones Colombia, 1927), xxii. Daniel Samper Ortega, *Selección Samper Ortega de literatura colombiana*, 100 vols. (Bogotá: Editorial Minerva, 1937), 81, 507; 9, 5; 37, 137.

VARGAS, Enrique (1944–). Born in Manizales, Vargas is an actor, author, and director of theater. Vargas is also a professor at La Universidad Nacional in Santafé de Bogotá, where he directs a workshop on representing and investigating imagery in theater and a workshop on puppet theater. Vargas's work covers stories of ordinary people and makes excellent use of vernacular language. His recent plays demonstrate a continuous experimentation with techniques and elements that enrich his theater. In some of Vargas's plays, the scenery, which supports the narration of the story, has been reduced to the manipulation of paper that can be transformed into a mountain, a cave, or the universe.

Sancocho de cola (Tail Stew) (1985) is a carpet play where a minimal stage allows the narrator to become a Demiurge who tells the story, creates the rain and wind, raises clouds of dust over the town, and represents the different characters including the bull. His interest in popular Romances brought him to collect the different versions of the Romance *Conde Lirio*. Vargas recreates the story in its different perspectives, reflecting the tragedy of the lovers. The one who opposes the union of the couple is metamorphosed differently according to the land (a serpent, a fast-flowing river, a violent city); this change is supported by the music of each region.

WORKS: *Sancocho de cola* (Tail Stew) (1985). *Conde Lirio* (Count Lirio) (n.d.).

VARGAS TEJADA, Luis (1802–1829). Vargas Tejada, a playwright and poet, was author of the most outstanding comedy of the nineteenth century, *Las convulsiones* (The Convulsions) (n.d.). Vargas Tejada also wrote neoclassic tragedies where he explores pre-Columbian history: *Sacresazipa* (n.d.), *Witikindo* (n.d.), *Aquimín* (n.d.), and *Sugamuxi* (n.d.). Even though his plays were not strictly historical, they recreated the environment and attitudes of the Indians. The only tragedies by Vargas Tejada that have been conserved are *La madre de Pausanias* (Pausanias' Mother) (1928) and *Doraminta* (1929). The first play is a short dialogue in verse where the tyrant's mother laments about her luck and joins the Spartan people to annihilate their common enemy. This play alludes to the tyranny of the Liberator and invites people to rebel against the hero, now turned into a villain. The second play has autobiographical elements that correspond to the flight of the writer after a failed attempt against Simón Bolívar. Other plays by Vargas

Tejada are *Catón en Utica* (Caton in Utica) (n.d.) and *El Parnaso transferido* (Transferred Parnassus) (n.d.).

WORKS: *Las convulsiones* (The Convulsions) (Bogotá: Arango Editores, 1989). *La madre de Pausanias* (Pausanias' Mother) (Bogotá: Arango Editores, 1989). *Doraminta* (n.d.).

BIBLIOGRAPHY: José Caicedo Rojas, *Apuntes de ranchería* (Bogotá: Imprenta Nacional, Biblioteca Popular de Cultura Colombiana, 1945), 245. Caicedo Rojas, "Luis Vargas Tejada," in *Discuros académicos* (Bogotá: Editorial ABC, Biblioteca de la presidencia de Colombia, 1955), 1, 191. Frank Dauster, *Historia del teatro hispanoamericano: Siglos XIX y XX*, 2nd ed. (Mexico City: Ediciones de Andrea, 1973), 10. Agustín del Saz, *Teatro hispanoamericano* (Barcelona: Editorial Vergara 1963), 1, 153. Antonio Gómez Restrepo, *Historia de la literatura colombiana* (Bogotá: Ministerio de Educación Nacional, 1945). Fernando González Cajiao, *Historia del teatro colombiano* (Bogotá: Colcultura, 1986). Willis Knapp Jones, *Breve historia del teatro latinoamericano* (Mexico City: Ediciones de Andrea, 1956), 50. Isidoro Laverde Amaya, *Ojeada histórico crítica sobre los orígenes de la literatura colombiana* (Bogotá: Biblioteca Luis Angel Arango, Talleres gráficos del Banco de la República, 1963), 112. Héctor Orjuela, *Bibliografía del teatro colombiano* (Bogotá: Instituto Caro y Cuervo, 1974), 195. José Vicente Ortega Ricaute, *Historia crítica del teatro en Bogotá* (Bogotá: Ediciones Colombia, 1927), 6. Vicente Pérez Silva, "Casi poeta, un poco comediógrafo, político y conspirador," *Materiales* (167–172). Daniel Samper Ortega, *Selección Samper Ortega de literatura colombiana*, 100 vols. (Bogotá: Editorial Minerva, 1937), 83, 273.

VIVIESCAS, Victor (1958–). Viviescas is an actor, a director, and a playwright. Since 1975, Viviescas has been working with different theater groups in Medellín, such as La Escuela Popular de Arte, La Casa del Teatro, and El Tinglado. He won El Premio de Dramaturgia Nacional Bogotá 450 años in 1988, with *Crisanta sola, Soledad Crisanta* (Crisanta Alone, Soledad Crisanta). Soledad is the main character; she wants to be a singer, but violence and fatality leave her alone in the city.

WORKS: *Aníbal es un fantasma que se repite en los espejos* (Anibal Is a Ghost Who Has a Reflection in Mirrors) (1986). *Prométeme que no gritaré*

(Promise Me That I Won't Scream) (1988). *Tríptico del dolor* (Tryptic of Pain) (1989). *Monólogo a dos voces en siete pecados capitales* (Monologue in Two Voices in Seven Capital Sins) (1990). *Veneno* (Poison) (1990). *Crisanta sola, Soledad Crisanta* (Crisanta Alone, Soledad Crisanta), in *Antología del teatro colombiano contemporáneo* (Madrid: Fondo de Cultura Económica, 1992), 955–986.

BIBLIOGRAPHY: Gloria Carmenza Arias, "Una personal poética de la violencia," in *Antología del teatro colombiano contemporáneo* (Madrid: Fondo de Cultura Económica, 1992), 949–953. Carlos José Reyes, "El teatro de Víctor Viviescas," *Revista de la Universidad de Antioquia* (Medellín, October–December 1991), 226.

ZAPATA OLIVELLA, Manuel (1920–   ). He is a doctor, writer, essayist, and anthropologist and has dedicated a great part of his literary creation to the cultural and oral traditions of black Colombians. He has received two awards for his dramatic creations: the El Espiral award in 1954 and El Festival de Arte de Cali award in 1962. His narrative work is well known in Colombian literature with pieces such as *Changó, el gran putas* (Shango, the Great S.O.B.) (1983), which is his most recognized work. It presents the epic of the black Africans enslaved in America, and with it, he won the Francisco Matarazzo Sobrinho literary award in Brazil.

Hotel de vagabundos (Hotel for Vagabonds) (s. 1954) won the El Espiral award, and it presents the life of New York City prostitutes and sailors in marginal neighborhoods. *Los pasos del indio* (The Steps of an Indian) (1958), staged by the theater group El Buho, exposes the precarious life of the Wayuu people from La Guajira. The play denounces the exploitation of Wayuu chiefs by foreign companies as well as the social and economic inequality of the region. The direct accusation precipitated controversy about the function of theater, and as a consequence, El Buho lost indispensable economic support and disappeared from the national panorama. *Caronte liberado* (Charon Liberated) (1959) and *El retorno de Caín* (The Return of Cain) (1962) are plays that present the theme of *La violencia* of the 1950s in Colombia. Some of his other plays include *Tres veces libertad* (Freed Three Times) (1966) and *Malonga el liberto* (Malonga the Free Black) (1966).

WORKS: *Hotel de vagabundos* (Hotel for Vagabonds) (s. 1954), (Bogotá: Espiral Colombia, 1955). *Caronte liberado y La bruja de Pontezuela* (Bogotá: Instituto Colombiano de Cultura, 1972). *Los pasos del indio* (The Steps of an Indian), in *Antología del teatro colombiano contemporáneo* (Madrid: Fondo de Cultura Económica, 1992), 153–182.

BIBLIOGRAPHY: Yvonne Captain Hidalgo, *The Culture of Fiction in the Works of Manuel Zapata Olivella* (Columbia and London: University of Missouri Press, 1993). José Luis Díaz Granados, "La olvidada e inmediata semejanza," in *Antología del teatro colombiano contemporáneo* (Madrid: Fondo de Cultura Económica, 1992), 1143–1151. Fernando González Cajiao, *Historia del teatro en Colombia* (Bogotá: Instituto Colombiano de Cultura, 1986). Héctor Orjuela, *Bibliografía del teatro colombiano* (Bogotá: Instituto Caro y Cuervo, 1974), 206.

María Mercedes Jaramillo

Costa Rica

A glance at the literary history of Costa Rica shows that the Costa Rican theater did not begin to flourish until the 1950s with the establishment of the Teatro Universitario. Interest in the theater reached its zenith during the decade of the 1970s. Some critics believe that the delay in the development of a Costa Rican national theater was due to the lack of an indigenous theater, such as existed, for example, in Mexico, Peru, and Guatemala (Arron; Jones; Henríquez Ureña). But others do not consider this assertion to be a valid one. Anita Herzfeld and Teresa Cajiao Salas, in *El teatro de hoy en Costa Rica*, maintain that the late development of the Costa Rican theater was due to the country's cultural isolation (9). Stoyan Vladich concurs with Herzfeld and Cajiao Salas and blames the cultural isolation on geographical and economic problems, a poor system of transportation, and slow urban growth (Vladich, 40).

The first theatrical performances to take place on Costa Rican soil, and for which there is historical documentation, occurred on October 25, 1722, at the Plaza of Cartago, during the celebrations of the marriage of the Prince of Asturias to the Princess of Orleans. The performances consisted of *loas* (prologues), *comedias* (comedies), and *entremeses* (short plays or interludes). In 1725, to celebrate the crowning of Luis I, the comedy *Afectos de odio y amor* was staged outside the house of the governor of the Province of Costa Rica, Don Diego de la Haya Fernández. It is believed that Don Diego authored the *loa* and the comedy staged for the occasion.

The themes of the first plays written in Costa Rica were of a religious nature or were intended specifically to flatter the Spanish Crown. The religious plays were known as *auto sacramentales*. They were staged at convents under the auspices of religious institutions, in keeping with Spanish tradition. Very few copies of the *auto sacramentales* written during the colonial period have been preserved. Herzfeld and Cajiao Salas note that one of the *autos*, *La infancia de Jesu-Cristo* (The Infancy of Jesus Christ), written by the Spanish priest Gaspar Fernández y Avila and published in 1833, had a continuous staging throughout the country well into the twentieth century.

Among the playwrights at the beginning of the nineteenth century, one finds the name of Joaquín de Oreamuro, whose *Una loa y dos entremeses* (A Prologue and Two Interludes) was first presented in 1809. The play's theme reflected the political and historical period in which it was written. The playwright's intention was to honor Fernando VII, who had been captured by the French. The *loa* attacked Napoleon's invasion of Spain, whereas the *entremeses* exalted the virtues of the monarch. Other dramatists associated with the Costa Rican theater of the first half of the century were the Panamanian playwright Victor de la Guardia y Ayala, a resident of Costa Rica and author of *La usurpación del poder* (Usurpation of Power), and Daniel Castillo, who wrote several *autos sacramentales*.

During the second half of the nineteenth century, Costa Rican playwrights began to move away from themes related to the Church and Spain and instead reflected upon and integrated into their writings national themes and traits that the audience could identify. Examples of this new form of expression are found in the works of Pilar Jiménez, a young actor who in 1869 wrote the comedy *Gracias a Dios que está puesta la mesa* (Thank Heavens That the Table Is Set), and in the writings of the Colombian José Manuel Lleras (1843–1879). Lleras wrote the *zarzuela La guarda del campamento* (The Camp's Guard) (1873), which dealt with Costa Rica's war of 1856 against pirate aggression. The *zarzuela* was well liked by President Tomás Guardia, but it was less popular with the public, perhaps because of the numerous historical inaccuracies and anachronisms that appeared in his works.

The name of Rafael Carranza (1840–1930) also stands out. He authored *Un duelo a la moda* (A Fashionable Duel) (s.1885), *Un desafío* (A Defiance), and *Un duelo a muerte* (A Duel to Death), which was staged at the Teatro Municipal (Vladich, 38, 39; Herzfeld and Cajiao Salas, 12). In 1890, the comedy *Los pretendientes* (The Suitors), written by Carlos Gagini, was presented at the Gran Hotel. Other playwrights who contributed to the Costa Rican stage during the nineteenth century include the Spanish Jesuit León Tornero, a resident of Costa Rica and whose *Daniel* was staged in 1878 at the San Luis Gonzaga School; the Spaniard Juan Fernández Ferraz, also a resident of Costa Rica, who staged Benito Pérez Galdós' *Gloria* at the Teatro Municipal in 1882; and Emilio Pacheco Cooper, Joaquín Barrionuevo, Ernesto Martén, Manuel Escalante, and Gonzálo Sánchez Bonilla.

The Catholic Church played an important role in the incipient Costa Rican theater, largely because of censorship. Plays written in the country were expected to be submitted to the Church's censors, and the clergy took it upon itself to criticize from the pulpit the works of playwrights that it did not deem "proper" for a good Christian. But in reality, the priests were unable to fully control what their congregations saw on the stage. Curiously, plays written by foreign playwrights did not have to pass before the censors of the Church. On many occasions, reprimands from the pulpits regarding specific plays helped increase those plays' popularity. This was the case regarding a play with the actress Lelia Castillo (Herzfeld and Cajiao Salas, 14). Her debut in 1846 created a great controversy among the clergy because the Catholic Church deemed it immoral to have a woman appear on stage.

During the twentieth century, Costa Rican playwrights attempted to capture the national character by including in their works popular language, local humor, historical events, and typical political and social situations. The stage was used to criticize the army, the press, and the foreign elements present in the country. But although playwrights looked to, and drew from, Costa Rican history and society for inspiration, with regard to technique they failed to produce an authentic theater. It was not until the appearance of the writings of Héctor Alfredo Castro Fernández that Costa Rican playwrights began to place attention on the structure of the play and various writing techniques (Fernández, 142).

At the beginning of the twentieth century, the plays of Costa Rican dramatists projected their nation on the stage. This literary manifestation of local customs and manners, known as *costumbrismo*, was followed by realism and then experimental theater. During the decade of the 1980s there was a resurgence of *costumbrismo*. Albino Chacón in "Características neocostumbristas del teatro actual en Costa Rica" (*Neocostumbristas* Characteristics of Contemporary Costa Rican Theater) labels the current Costa Rican national theater as *neocostumbrista* (Chacón, 54).

Among the major playwrights of the present century, one finds the name of Ricardo Fernández Guardia, whose play *Magdalena* (s.1902) was the first Costa Rican play to be staged in a Costa Rican theater (Herzfeld and Cajiao Salas, 13). The list of prominent early playwrights is completed with mention of the names of Carlos Gagini, Eduardo Calsamiglia, José Fabio Garnier, and Francisco Soler. These men were members of Costa Rica's intellectual elite. Most of them were educated in Europe. According to Herzfeld and Cajiao Salas, their works have not been able to withstand the test of time. Their works lack a true sense of theatrical technique: "todos desconocían la técnica teatral." Only Gagini's plays might be of some interest to a contemporary audience (Herzfeld and Cajiao Salas, 13).

Prominent authors of the 1920s and the first half of the 1930s were Raúl Salazar Alvarez, whose play *San José en camisa* (San José Wears a Shirt) was performed 110 at the Teatro Trébol, and José Marín Cañas, who studded his plays with national and regional themes. The name of Héctor Alfredo Castro is also bracketed with noteworthy playwrights of the period. His personal wealth allowed him to publish his plays simultaneously in Spanish and French and to finance the stage productions. Many of his works were presented at the Teatro Trébol, Teatro Adela, and Teatro América. According to the critics, they were too cerebral and intellectual for a public that was easily entertained with situations that involved action and intrigue. Documentation regarding Castro's works comes to us secondhand, mainly through the history of the theater; the texts have not survived.

During the Great Depression, the Costa Rican theater saw a lull in its development. Two reasons might account for this: Foreign theatrical companies ceased to visit the country during that period, and theatergoers became tired of the *costumbristas* plays and their regional themes. After World War II, when foreign theatrical companies returned to the country, the public seemed to prefer foreign plays, especially those written by Federico García Lorca, Tennessee Williams, and Jean Paul Sartre, among other authors. The enthusiasm previously shown for Costa Rican authors had vanished (Herzfeld and Cajiao Salas, 70).

The Little Theater Group of Costa Rica was the first permanent theatrical group to be established in Costa Rica. It was founded by English-speaking residents during the decade of the 1950s. The plays were presented in English, and the proceeds of the performances were given to charity. The group's first performance was *Claudia*, written by Rose Franken and staged at Teatro Nacional. Salvador Solís (in "El movimiento teatral costarricense [1951–1971]" [Costa Rica's Theatrical Movement (1957–1971)]) denies the Little Theater Group of Costa Rica a major role in the development of the Costa Rican theater (Solís, 70). Around the same time as the formation of the Little Theater Group of Costa Rica, the intellectual elite of Costa Rica saw the need for creating national theatrical companies that would promote the works of national authors. The upper and middle classes shared this sentiment.

In 1951, the Costa Rican writer Alfredo Sancho Colombarí presented to the president of the Universidad de Costa Rica a blueprint to establish at the university a faculty for the dramtic arts. Although the plan gave evidence of careful thought, it did not materialize. To fill the void with regard to the dramatic arts, the university instead hired members of the Spanish theatrical company Compañía Lope de Vega to work with the newly formed Teatro Universitario. Under the direction of José Tamayo the Compañía de Lope de Vega had received the Eduardo Marquina Award (Solís, 70). The cast of the Teatro Universitario, consisting of José Carlos Rivera, Pilar Biernet, Luis Felipe Lazcano, and Conchita Montijano, was directed by Alfredo Sancho. The first performances of the Teatro Universitario were Miguel de Cervantes's plays *El retablo de las maravillas* (The Altar of the Marvels), *La guarda cuidadosa* (The Careful Guard), and *La cueva de Salamanca* (The Cave of Salamanca). In 1953 the Italian Luccio Ranucci became director of the company. Ranucci then established a Teatro Cámara Universitario with the intent of presenting works written by the students as well as the classic dramatists (Herzfeld and Cajiao Salas, 14–15).

In 1957 the University of Costa Rica created its first professorship of dramatic arts with the appointment of Guido Sáenz as member of its faculty as well as director of the Teatro Universitario. Several plays written by the Spanish playwright Alejandro Casona were staged by the Teatro Universitario, who toured with their performances to several urban centers and throughout the countryside. In 1968, upon the return to Costa Rica of the playwright Daniel Gallegos Troyo, who had been trained in Europe and in the United States, the University of Costa Rica made a serious attempt to incorporate into its curriculum the field of dramatic arts by creating the Department of Dramatic Arts, with Gallegos Troyo as its director.

In 1955 a group of Costa Rican artists formed the Teatro Arlequín, later known as Asociación Cultural del Teatro Arlequín. Members of the cast went on to establish a playhouse by the same name. Guido Saénz and the Belgian actor Jean Moulaert, who was married to the actress Ivette Castro, daughter of the playwright Alfredo Castro, were the driving forces behind the Teatro Arlequín. Luccio Ranucci also played an important role within the group. The original cast of El Arlequín consisted of Lenín Garrido and his wife Anabelle, José Trejos, Kitiko Moreno, Virginia Grüter, and Ana Poltonieri. According to Salvador Solís, the group premiered with plays by Eugene O'Neill and Susan Glasspell (Solís, 74). Herzfeld and Cajiao Salas write that the first plays presented by Teatro Arlequín were works by Noel Coward and Quintero (Herzfeld and Cajiao Salas, 15). Salvador Solís in his article "El movimiento teatral costarricense (1951–1971)," and Guido Fernández in *Los caminos del teatro costarricense*, point out how the Teatro Arlequín helped in the formation of a new generation of Costa Rican actors, among whom one finds Daniel Gallegos, Guido Saénz, and José Trejos. It is worth noting that Moulaert demanded from the cast of Teatro Arlequín complete memorization of their roles, thus setting the standards for a more disciplined theatrical performance. Actors were no longer allowed to rely on prompters, as they had done in the past. The Teatro Arlequín was to become a model for future theatrical groups such as Las Máscaras (1956–1962) and the Grupo Israelita de Teatro (1966–1970). The Teatro Arlequín disbanded when Luccio Ranucci resigned his position as director of the Teatro Universitario. The theater hall named after the group closed, not to reopen until 1956 at the insistence of Lenín Garrido. The group Teatro de Bolsillo gave the opening performance (Solís, 75).

Costa Rica saw a proliferation of theatrical groups in the late 1950s and 1960s. Two of these were Teatro de la Prensa, composed of journalists, and Las Máscaras. The original cast of Las Máscaras consisted of Ana Poltronieri, Lenín Garrido, Anabelle Garrido, Oscar Castillos, Virginia Fernández, Roberto Fernández, and Marcelita Petain (Herzfeld and Cajiao Salas, 16). Las Máscaras presented foreign as well as Costa Rican plays. Among the latter was *El luto robado* (Stolen Sorrow), written by the Costa Rican Alberto Cañas. José Tasiés served as artistic director. In 1961 Las Máscaras dissolved, and many of its members joined El Arlequín, which had regrouped. Other performing troupes founded around the same time were the theatrical association of the Instituto Costarricense de Electricidad [ICE]

(1965 to 1968); the Teatro de la Caja de Seguro (1966–1973), under the directorship of Alfredo Sancho; DECA (1964–1965); Las Brujas (1964–1967); Teatro Estudio de Costa Rica (1966–1968), directed by the Mexican Hernán de Sandozequi; Teatro de Costa Rica (1966); Estudio de las Artes y las Letras [AECA] (1966); Compañía Nacional de Comedias (1966–1968); and Grupo Israelita de Teatro (GIT) (1966–1970) (Solís, 76). GIT was founded by the Argentinean actress Haydee de Lev in 1966. Its main thrust was to create an experimental theater that would give venue to the works of national playwrights. The GIT chose to inaugurate its performances with Alberto Cañas's *En agosto hizo dos años* (Two Augusts Ago). Other Costa Rican playwrights of the period are Héctor Alfredo Castro, Carlos Luis Saénz, María del Rosario Ulloa Zamora, Aída Fernández de Montagné, Lilia Ramos, Albertina Fletis de Ramírez, Alfredo Saborío, Raúl Salazar, Abel Robles Chacón, Gonzalo Chacón Trejos, Manuel Escalante, Ricardo Jímenez Alpizar, Carlos Orozco, Manuel Segura Méndez, and José Basileo Acuña.

Foreign theatrical groups had an important role in the development of Costa Rican actors during the nineteenth and twentieth centuries. At a time when local theatrical companies were not established in Costa Rica, foreign troupes permitted Costa Rican actors to join their performances while they were on tour in the country, thus giving Costa Rican actors an opportunity to acquire professional acting experience. In the second half of the twentieth century, foreign actors once again played a major part in the development of the dramatic arts in Costa Rica. Actors from abroad, such as Argentineans Alfredo and Gladys Catania, members of Teatro 21, an independent group of actors from the province of Santa Fe, Argentina, were invited in 1968 by the Argentinean embassy of Costa Rica to give acting lessons in Costa Rica. Along with them came Carlos Catania, the accomplished actor/director/playwright. Herzfeld and Cajiao Salas regard the presence of the Catanias in the Central American country as a watershed in the development of a national theater inasmuch as they were the first to provide formal training in acting technique, "comenzó el verdadero auge en el aprendizaje formal organizado, de la técnica de actuación" (Herzfeld and Cajiao Salas, 17). This contributed further to the development of the dramatic arts in Costa Rica.

Two additional developments in Costa Rica in the late 1960s and early 1970s served to further encourage the dramatic arts. One was the First Central American Cultural Festival, held in Costa Rica. The other was the establishment of national awards for outstanding figures of the Costa Rican stage. The Costa Rican theater received further impetus in 1971 when President José Figueres created the Ministerio de Cultura, Juventud y Deportes (Ministry of Culture, Youth, and Sports). Two prominent figures of the Costa Rican theater, Alberto Cañas and Guido Saénz, were named, respectively, minister and vice minister of the Ministry. Under the auspices of the Ministerio de Cultura, Juventud y Deportes, the Compañía Nacional de Teatro was organized, with the Spaniard Esteban Polls serving as director (Solís, 79).

The government's efforts led to a greater interest in the theater among the population at large. Theatrical groups made up of bureaucrats, factory workers, and even farmers emerged throughout the country. Their artistic efforts were subsidized by monies from the municipalities as well as the national government. In 1971 the Spaniard Carlos Suárez Radillo was hired to form neighborhood theaters. Under the initiative of the plan Teatros de Barrios (Neighborhood Theaters), Radillo was to create a new public of theatergoers from which future actors, playwrights, and directors were to be formed. For this mission, national playwrights were asked to write plays with Costa Rican themes that would be of special interest to the public at large. Another requirement imposed on the playwrights was the use of streamlined settings, thereby permitting the cast of the Teatro Universitario to tour the entire country. The first play selected for this endeavor was Samuel Rovinski's *Las fisgonas de Paso Ancho* (The Snoopers of Paso Ancho) (1971).

The government's efforts were not without success. During the 1970s the number of theatergoers increased at an impressive rate. In the 1960s a good play would draw about 2,000 spectators, in the 1970s, this figure would grow to about 30,000. The popularity of newly formed open air theaters contributed to the rise in number, as did public transportation from the neighborhoods to the theaters. Also, this was a decade in which it was cheaper to buy a theater ticket than a movie ticket (Rovinski, 59).

Ironically, political unrest throughout Latin America during the 1970s contributed to the growth in Costa Rica's theater, not to mention the country's intellectual life in general. Many Latin American political exiles settled in Costa Rica, where they found freedom of expression and intellectual and political openness denied them in their own countries. In 1975, as the result of Chile's political unrest, several Chileans arrived in the small Central American country. Among the group was the director/actor/playwright Alejandro Sieveking, Lucho Barahona, Angélica Castro, and Ana González, all accomplished members of the Chilean Teatro del Angel. In Costa Rica, these actors and actresses founded a second Teatro del Angel, which they named Teatro del Angel de Costa Rica. By the time Bélgica Castro and Alejandro Sieveking returned to Chile in 1984, they had left an indelible imprint on the Costa Rican theater, having trained a new generation of actors, actresses, and directors ("Teatro del Angel," 69). Argentinean and Uruguayan actors, actresses, and directors also made their way to Costa Rica during the decade of the 1970s.

With the 1980s, the intellectual boom that Costa Rica had experienced in the 1970s came to a halt. Several causes might account for this. Conservative groups of Costa Rican society began to challenge the liberal ideas of members of the exiled communities. As a result, theatrical productions presenting controversial topics were avoided. Economic belt tightening at the national level led to a reduction of government subsidies for many private theatrical companies. This in turn forced many troupes to increase the price of admission in order to stay solvent, making attendance to theatrical productions prohibitive for the vast majority of the population.

According to Albino Chacón, in his article "Características neocostumbristas del teatro actual en Costa Rica," the majority of the Costa Rican theatergoers of the 1980s tired of experimental and intellectual theater and clamored for a return to classic Costa Rican themes. Chacón has theorized that with regard to the theater the 1980s in Costa Rica should be labeled as *neocostumbrista*. An example of revived *neocostumbrismo* is found in Rovinski's play *Las fisgonas de Paso Ancho*. Many of the productions presented at the Teatro Chaplin, and written by Eduardo Zúñiga, Marcia Saborío, Merina Carmona, Walter Fernández, or Ronald Villar, are considered *neocostumbristas*.

In the *neocostumbrismo* of the 1980s one sees the same anecdotal characters of the *costumbrismo*. The plays present situations that pertain to the countryside or to urban elements as they might have appeared in the urban theater, or *teatro urbano*, also known as *neocostumbrismo urbano*, which manifested itself during the decades of the 1930s and 1940s. Marginal groups have a voice in *neocostumbrismo*. The works of Melvin Méndez are the most representative of this category (Chacón, 59–60). But not all the playwrights that wrote during the decade of the 1980s fall under the rubric of *neocostumbristas*. Exceptions may be seen in the works of Alberto Cañas, Daniel Gallegos, Antonio Yglesias, and in some of the plays by Samuel Rovinski, Ana Istarú, Guido Saénz, Miguel Rojas, Leda Cavallini and Guadalupe Pérez. The names of Guillermo Arriaga, Alejandro Tosatti, and Juan Cerdas should be also added to the list of contemporary writers (Rojas, 37).

Like many other national theaters throughout Latin America, Costa Rican theater is still looking for its own identity. The playwright Samuel Rovinski best summarizes the present Costa Rican theater when he states that Costa Rica is still in the process of searching for an authentic means of expression to reflect its own national reality, its own identity (Rovinski, 56).

BIBLIOGRAPHY

Arrom, Juan José. *Historia del teatro hispanoamericano*. Mexico City: Ediciones de Andrea, 1967.

Barzuna, Guillermo. "Presencia del teatro costarricense en 1982." *Káñina, Revista Artes y Letras. Universidad de Costa Rica* 7.1 (1983).

Bonilla, Abelardo. *Historia y antología de la literatura costarricense*. San José: Hermanos Tresjos, 1957.

Chacón, Albino. "Características neocostumbristas del teatro actual en Costa Rica." *Escena* (1991–1992): 13–14, 28–29.

———. "El público costarricense rechaza el teatro serio." *Revista Aportes* 65 (April 1990).

"Costa Rica." *Escenarios de dos mundos: inventario teatral de Iberoamérica*. Vol. 1. Madrid: Centro de Documentación Teatral, 1988, 382–403. Articles by scholars.

Durán Bunster, Rodrigo. "De la narración al drama: Experiencias para el análisis." *Escena* 11.21 (1989).

Fernández, Guido. *Los caminos del teatro en Costa Rica*. San José: Educa, 1977.

Fumero, Patricia. *Base de datos: las compañiás y las representaciones teatrales en San José (1850–1915)*. San José: Universidad de Costa Rica, Centro de Investigaciones Históricas de América Central, 1994.

———. *Teatro, público y estado en San José, 1880–1914: una aproximación desde la historia social*. San José: Editorial de la Universidad de Costa Rica, 1996.

González Salas, Roberto. *Una etapa del teatro en Costa Rica: grupo de teatro La Caja*. San José: Editorial Nacional de la Salud y Seguridad Social, 1992.

Henríquez Ureña, Pedro. *Las corrientes literarias en la América hispánica*. Mexico City: Fondo de Cultura Económica, 1954.

Herzfeld, Anita, and Teresa Cajiao Salas. *El teatro de hoy en Costa Rica*. San José: Editorial Costa Rica, 1973.

Jones, Willis Knapp. *Behind Spanish American Footlights*. Austin: University of Texas Press, 1966.

Loaiza, Norma. "Los setenta y dos años del Teatro Nacional." *La Nación* (San José de Costa Rica), October 21, 1969:

Martín, Flora. "Resumen Cartelera teatral 1991." *Escena* 14.30 (1992): 115–128.

Morales, Carlos. "El teatro en Costa Rica." *Escena* 3.5 (1981).

Quesada, Alvaro. "La dramaturgia costarricense de las dos últimas dos décadas." *Escena* 15.31 (1993).

Quesada Soto, Alvaro. "Guía bibliográfica para un estudio del teatro costarricense (1890–1950)." *Escena* 12.24–25 (1989).

———. "El teatro nacional y la cultura nacional." *Escena* 13.27 (1991).

Rodó, Manuel P., and Alfonso Ulloa Zamora. *El Teatro Nacional.* San José: Instituto costarricense de turismo, 1967.

Rojas, Miguel. *Puntos de vista en el teatro.* San José: Ediciones Guayacán, 1989.

———. "Un acercamiento a la perspectiva de tres dramaturgos en Costa Rica." *Escena* 14.30 (1992).

———. "¿Para qué queremos un teatro sin teatro nacional?" *Escena* 15.31 (1993).

Rovinski, Samuel. "El teatro y el cine contemporáneo en Costa Rica." *Confluencias* 1.1 (Fall 1985).

Sandoval, Virginia. *Resumen de la literatura costarricense.* San José: Editorial Costa Rica, 1979.

———. "Dramática costarricense." *Revista Iberoamericana* 53 (1987): 138–139.

Solís, Salvador. "Movimiento teatral costarricense (1951–1971)." *Escena* 28–29 (1991–1992): 70.

Sotela, Rogelio. *Escritores de Costa Rica.* San José: Imprenta Lehman, 1942.

Thomas, Charles. "Chilean Theatre in Exile: The Teatro del Angel in Costa Rica, 1974–1984." *Latin American Theatre Review* 19.2 (Spring 1986): 97–101.

Valdeperas Acosta, Jorge. *Para una nueva interpretación de la literatura constarricense.* San José: Editorial Costa Rica, 1979.

Valembois, Victor. *Teatro y sociedad en Costa Rica (1968–1977).* Proyecto de la vicerectoria de investigación. San José: Universidad de Costa Rica, 1980.

Vásquez, Magdalena, and José Angel Vargas. "Reseña del drama en Costa Rica a partir de 1950." *Escena* 10 (1988): 19–20.

Vladich, Stoyan. "Notas para una historia del teatro costarricense." *Escena* 9.18 (1987): 40.

Závala, Magda. "La compañía nacional de teatro y la promoción de una dramaturgia nacional y popular." *Escena* 3.5 (1981).

◆

ACUÑA, José Basilio Poet, playwright, and translator of the works of William Shakespeare and recipient in 1983 of the Premio Magón (Magón Award). Acuña has written *Initada, Poema sagrado del sol* (Initada, the Sun's Sacred Poem), for which he was granted the Aquileo J. Echeverría award in 1970. This play portrays the emergence of the Inca Empire, from the time that the survivors of the legendary *Atlandida* appeared to the arrival of the Incas and the foundation of Cuzco by Manco Cápac and *mama* Ocllo. In *Máscaras y candilejas* (Masks and Footlights), written between 1965 and 1971, Acuña presents nine one-act plays and one three-act play. These plays satirize the social, economic, and political life of the country as well as its oligarchy. Among the best plays of the collection one finds *Chica-Pica, Tiquismiquis, Venta de cachivaches* (Sale of Knick-knacks), and *Dante Alighieri.*

WORKS: "Ganimedes," in *Repertorio Americano,* Vol. 19, no. 3 (1929), 102–103. *Máscaras y candilejas* (Masks and Footlights) (San José: Lehmann, 1972). *Initada, Poema sagrado del sol* (Initada, The Sun's Sacred Poem) (n.p., n.d.).

BIBLIOGRAPHY: Virginia Sandoval de Fonseca, "Dramaturgia costarricense," *Revista Iberoamericana* 53.138–139 (1987): 173–192.

ARRIAGA, Guillermo. Contemporary playwright. Author of *La última noticia* (The Last News) (1983), *Inquilino* (The Tenant) (1984), and *La guerra como consecuencia* (War as an Outcome) (1986). These plays deal with contemporary social problems and generational clashes. Arriaga also wrote *Límite de velocidad* (Speed Limit) (1990), a play representative of the theater of the Absurd that explores alienation and manipulation of modern culture.

BARRIONUEVO, Joaquín. Author of the two-act play *El grito de la conciencia* (The Cry of the Conscience). This play was well received by the critics but not by the public. Barrionuevo also wrote the three-act play *El cuarto mandamiento* (The Fourth Commandment) (n.d.).

WORKS: *El grito de la conciencia* (The Cry of the Conscience), in *Albores* (San José: Alsina, 1906). *El cuarto mandamiento* (The Fourth Commandment) (n.d.).

BIBLIOGRAPHY: Faisán, "El drama de Barrionuevo," *Arte y vida* 1.3 (1910).

CALSAMIGLIA, Eduardo (1880–1918). Considered to be one of the first major playwrights of Costa Rica. Most of his plays were comedies written in verse. Calsamiglia is remembered for *El combate* (The Combat) and *Poderes invisibles* (Invisible Powers). This latter work was staged by the theatrical group Compañía Iris at the Teatro Nacional. In *El combate*, the reader notices the influence of positivism. Its theme portrays the antagonistic relationship that exists between passion and scientific reasoning. Other plays by Calsamiglia are: *¡El!* (He!); *Ni en el cielo* (Not Even in Heaven); *Resoluciones externas* (External Decisions), a one-scene work written in verse and prose; *El vapor* (The Steamer), written in verse; *Las opiniones de San Pedro* (Saint Peter's Opinions), also written in verse; *La comedia de la vida* (The Comedy of Life), a one-act satire written in prose and verse; *Vindicta* (Vindicated), staged by the Compañía Cuevas; *Altavismo*, a three-act play written in verse and staged by the Compañía de Armas; *Doña Restituta*, a zarzuela staged by Barrajón; *La tormenta* (The Storm), a parody staged by Alfredo del Diestro; *El hombre malo* (The Evil Man), a comedy, staged by Díaz de Mendoza; and *Bronces de antaño* (Bronces of Yesteryear), a one-act posthumous work, written in verse. Cal-

samiglia was working at the time of his death on *La presencia del pasado* (The Presence of the Past), a four-act drama, and *Corazón artificial* (Artificial Heart), a three-act play.

WORKS: *Gordos y flacos* (Fat and Thin People) (Heredia, Costa Rica: Imprenta L. Cartín, 1904 and in San José: Imprenta Moderna, 1974). *El combate y otras obras dramáticas* (The Combat and Other Plays) (San José: Imprenta Moderna, 1914) (this book includes: *Poderes invisibles, Ni en el cielo, El combate, Resoluciones externas, El vapor, Un pecado mortal, Las opiniones de San Pedro*, and *La comedia de la vida; proceso cómico en verso* [Invisible Powers, Not Even in Heaven, The Combat, External Decision, The Steamer, A Mortal Sin, The Opinions of St. Peter, and The Comedy of Life], coauthored with O. Baudrit, P. Pacheco, A. Echeverría, and T. Sáenz). *El combate*, in *Antología del teatro costarricense (1890–1950)*, ed. Alvaro Quesada et al. (San José: Editorial de la Universidad de Costa Rica, 1993).

BIBLIOGRAPHY: Olga Marta Barrantes, "La pugna entre el bien y el mal en *Poderes invisibles* de E. Calsamiglia," *Káñina* 4.2 (1981), 9–14. Camilo Cruz Santos, "El libro de Calsamiglia," *Pandemonium* 8.10 (1914), 265–270. Cruz Santos, "Obras teatrales de Eduardo Calsamiglia" and "Prólogo a la manera antigua," in *De mi vida inquieta* (San José: Alsina, 1930), 31–42, 51–61. Aquileo J. Echeverría, "Un drama de Calsamiglia," in *Crónicas y cuentos míos* (San José: Studium, 1981). M. E. Rodríguez Valerín, "Eduardo Calsamiglia: Poeta lírico romántico, dramaturgo y poeta humorístico satírico" (Ph.D. diss., Universidad de Costa Rica). Gastón de Silva, "Parloteos," *Páginas Ilustradas* 5.202 (1908), 3428. Joaquín Vargas Coto, "Calsamiglia," *Lecturas*, 2.21, 336. Virginia Sandoval de Fonseca, "Dramaturgia costarricense," *Revista Iberoamericana*, 53.138–139 (1987), 173–192.

CAÑAS ESCALANTE, Alberto F. (1920–). Member of a distinguished Costa Rican family, Cañas has held the positions of lawyer, journalist, literary critic, drama professor, diplomat, and member of the Academia Costarricense de la Lengua (Costa Rican Academy of the Language). The playwright has the distinction of breaking away from caricaturesque *costumbristas* themes and launching Costa Rican theater into a new direction. He has written poetry, plays, and essays, as well as novels and short stories in which national themes are prevalent. His work has been greatly influenced by Italian playwright Pirandello. Cañas's works include: *Hay que besar a la niña* (The Girl Ought to Be Kissed) (1942), a three-act play; *Dónde termina la calle* (Where the Street Ends) (1943), a one-act play; *Don Juan pusilámine* (Pusillanimous Don Juan) (1943), a three-act play; *El héroe* (The Hero) (1956); *Los pocos sabios* (A Few Wise Men), presented by *El Arlequín* in 1959; and *El luto robado* (Stolen Sorrow), staged by *Las Máscaras* in 1959 and granted the Aquileo J. Echeverría theater prize in 1962. *El luto robado* portrays the absurdity of social conventions. Cañas also wrote: *Algo más que dos sueños* (Something More Than Just Two Dreams), written in 1963 and staged for the first time by Grupo Israelita de Teatro in 1967 at the Teatro de la Calle 4. This play was revised and staged again at the Olympic Festival in Mexico City in 1968. *En agosto hizo dos años* (Two Augusts Ago) was staged in 1966, also by the Grupo Israelita de Teatro, and directed by Andrés Saénz. It saw the stage again in October 1969 at the Seventh Guatemalan Theater Festival, sponsored by the Universidad Popular and the Dirección de Cultura y Bellas Artes (Office of Culture and Fine Arts). The play deals with the existential concepts of life and death, present and past, being and existence. During the decade of the 1980s Cañas wrote *Escena de la torturada y el gorila* (Scene of the Tortured Woman and the Gorila) (1980), *Tarantela*, and *Ni mi casa es ya mi casa* (Not Even My House Is Mine Any Longer) (1982). This last work portrays the country's economic hardship during the depression. *Murámonos* (Let's Die), another play by Cañas, was based on the novel of the same title written by Federico Gutiérrez. His play *Cosas de mujeres* (Women's Things) was staged by Manuel Ruiz in 1988.

WORKS: *Algo más que dos sueños* (Something More Than Just Two Dreams), in *Teatro hispanoamericano*, ed. Carlos Solórzano (Madrid: Aguilar, 1969); in *Revista Pórtico* 1.1 (1963), 108–128; and in *El teatro de hoy en Costa Rica*, eds. Anita Herzfeld and Teresa Cajiao Salas (San José: Editorial Costa Rica, 1973). *El luto robado* (Stolen Sorrow) (San José: Editorial Costa Rica, 1963). *En agosto hizo dos años* (San José: 1968). *El héroe* (The Hero), in *Obras breves del teatro costarricense*, vol. 2 (San José: 1971), 123–161. *La segua y otras piezas* (The Segua and Other Works) (San José: Editorial Textos, 1974) (this edition includes *La segua, En agosto hizo dos años, El luto robado*, and *El héroe* [The Segua, Two Augusts Ago, Stolen Sorrow, and The Hero]); 2nd ed. (San José: EDUCA, 1976); 3rd ed. (San José: EDUCA, 1977). *Tarantela* (San José: Editorial Costa Rica, 1978). "Una reafirmación académica," *Escena* 2.12 (1979), 6–7. *Una bruja en el río* (A Witch in the River) (San José: Editorial Costa Rica, 1978). *Uvieta* (San José: Editorial Costa Rica, 1980). "Teatro costarricense en el teatro costarricense," *Escena* 2.2 (1980), 13–14. "Dos notas al vuelo," *Escena* 3.5 (1981), 22–23. *Los pocos sabios*, in *Escena* 4.7 (1982), i–viii. *Acotaciones a un índice, Escena* 1.2 (1982), 4. *Valle Inclán 50 años después, Escena* 8.15 (1986), 40. *Resumen cartelera teatral 1986, Escena* 9.17 (1987), 11–15.

BIBLIOGRAPHY: María Bonilla, "La vigencia de *Oldemar y los coroneles*," *Escena* 5.11: 21–22. María Lourdes Cortés, "Lectura de la producción de sentido de Alberto Cañas, Daniel Gallegos y Samuel Rovinski" (Ph.D. diss., Universidad de Costa Rica, 1987). Virginia Sandoval de Fonseca, "Dramaturgia costarricense," *Revista Iberoamericana*, 53.138–139 (1987), 173–192.

CARRANZA, Rafael (1840–1930). Considered to be the forerunner of the *costumbrista* theater of Costa Rica. Carranza authored several satirical comedies, among which one finds *Un duelo a la moda* (A Fashionable Duel), staged in 1885. Other works by Carranza are *Un desafío* (The Duel) and *Un duelo a muerte* (A Duel to Death), which was presented at the Teatro Municipal. Carranza is also remembered for being the founder of several newspapers and writer of satiric poetry.

WORKS: *Un duelo a la moda* (A Fashionable Duel) (San José: Imprenta Greñas, 1890); in *Antología del teatro costarricense (1890–1950)*, ed. Alvaro Quesada et al. (San José: Editorial de la Universidad de Costa Rica, 1993); and in Olga Marta Barrantes, *Antología comentada de la literatura costarricense del período comprendido entre 1809 hasta 1920* vol. 1. (Universidad de Costa Rica, 1978).

CARVAJAL, María Isabel. *See* LYRA, Carmen.

CASTRO FERNÁNDEZ, Héctor Alfredo (Marizancene) (1888–1966). Born in San José but lived in France until 1935. Upon his return to Costa Rica, Castro started writing plays in French under the pseudonym Marizancene. Castro Fernández's work was influenced by surrealism and deals with psychological and ideological crises. He has authored the one-act comedies *Pounette* and *El amero*, as well as *Espíritu de rebeldía* (A Rebellious Spirit), a one-act drama published in 1930; *El vitral* (The Stained-Glass Window), a three-act drama published in 1937; *El punto muerto* (Stalemate), a three-act drama; *La horma de su zapato* (His Match), a one-act play; and the three-act plays *El calvario* (The Calvary). His best-known work, *Aguas negras* (Black Waters), is a complex play that deals with human passions and an inhospitable region. This play, considered to be one of his best works, was never staged. Castro Fernández also wrote literary critical essays on Costa Rican playwrights.

WORKS: *Le point Mort* (Stalemate), ed. Abelardo Bonilla (San José: Imprenta Trejos, 1915). *Chaussure a son pied* (His Match) (San José: Imprenta Trejos, 1937). *El vitral* (The Stained-Glass Window), trans. Mario Fernández Callejas (San José: Imprenta Española, 1937); and in *Antología del teatro costarricense (1890–1950)*, Alvaro Quesada et al., eds. (San José: Editorial de la Universidad de Costa Rica, 1993). *Pounette*, trans. Gonzalo Chacón Trejos (San José: Imprenta Trejos, 1938); (San José: Editorial Costa Rica, 1937); in *Teatro*, trans. M. Rosa de Bonilla and Rafael R. Odín, ed. Lorenzo Vives (San José: Editorial Falcó) (this book contains: *Fragata Bar, Juego limpio, Una noche, esta noche*). *Une soir, ce soir* (San José: Imprenta Trejos, 1938). *La horma de su zapato* (His Match), trans. Gonzalo Chacón (San José: Imprenta Trejos, 1938). *El punto muerto* (Stalemate), trans. and ed. Abelardo Bonilla (San José: Imprenta Trejos, 1938). *Espíritu de rebeldía* (Spirit of Rebellion), trans. Mario Fernández Callejas (San José: Imprenta Trejos, 1938). *El amero* (San José: Imprenta Trejos, 1938). *Una noche, esta noche*, trans. Rafael R. Odín, ed. Lorenzo Vives (San José: Imprenta Falcó, 1939). *Aguas negras* (Black Waters), trans. M. Rosa Picado and Abelardo Bonilla (S.P.I., 1947). *La rama de Salzburgo* (The Branch of Salzburg) (San José: Editorial Falcó, 1956). "El teatro de José Fabio Garnier," in *Brecha* 1.3 (1956), 15. "El teatro de Carlos Orozco," in *Brecha* 2.2 (1957), 2–6. "El teatro de M. G. Escalante Durán" in *Brecha* 2.12 (1957). *Juego limpio* (Fair Play), trans. M. Rosa de Bonilla, in *Obras breves del teatro costarricense*, vol. 1 (San José: Editorial Costa Rica, 1969).

BIBLIOGRAPHY: Alfonsina Camacho Suárez, "Estudio de la obra de H. Alfredo Castro" (Ph.D. diss., Universidad de Costa Rica, San José, 1966). Moisés Vincenzi, *El teatro de H. Alfredo Castro Fernández* (San José: Trejos, 1957). Vincenzi, "*El vitral*," in *Brecha* 2.4 (1957), 21–22. Lorenzo Vives, "Para una exégesis teatral marizanceniana," in *Brecha* 5.5 (1961), 2–7.

CATANIA, Alfredo. Author of the play *Puerto Limón* (Port of Limón), based on the novel of the same title written by Joaquín Gutierrez.

WORK: *Puerto Limón* (Port of Limón), in *Conjunto* 36 (1978).

CAVALLINI, Leda. Contemporary writer, coauthor with Lupe Pérez Rey of *Ellas en la maquila* (Women at the Machine), *Pinocho* (Pinocchio), and *Pancha Carrasco reclama* (Pancha Carrasco Asks for What She Deserves). For *Pinocho*, Cavallini and Pérez Rey were awarded the 1989 Aquileo J. Echeverría theater prize. *Pancha Carrasco reclama* attempts to reconstruct the conflicts faced by women in the nineteenth century and their attempt to establish themselves as social entities.

WORK: *Pancha Carrasco reclama* (Pancha Carrasco Asks for What She Deserves), in *Escena* 10.19–10 (1988), 20–38.

BIBLIOGRAPHY: Emilio Arias Astúa, "Leda Cavallini: Premio compartido Aquileo J. Echeverría en Teatro 1989," *Escena* 12.24–25 (1990).

CRUZ SANTOS, Camilo. Author of the play *La iniciación* (The Initiation), written in collaboration with Francisco Soler.

WORK: *La iniciación* (The Initiation), coauthored with Francisco Soler, in *Renovación* 4.81–82 (1914); 129–152; in *Escena* 11.20–21 (1989), 91–118; and in *Antología del teatro costarricense (1890–1950)*, Alvaro Quesada et al., eds. (San José: Editorial de la Universidad de Costa Rica, 1993).

BIBLIOGRAPHY: Rogelio Sotela, "Camilo Cruz Santos," *Athenea* 4.7 (1920), 830–833.

ECHEVERRÍA, Aquileo. Author of the one-act tragicomedy *Pan francés* (French Bread), staged in 1909 at the Teatro Variedades.

WORK: *Pan francés* (French Bread), in *El gato negro* (n.p., n.d.).

ELIZONDO, Víctor Manuel. Author of *El granuja* (The Rouge); *Los próceres hablan* (The Leaders Speak), a patriotic fantasy; *Bolívar y la española* (Bolívar and the Spaniard); *El milagro* (The Miracle); *El pleito de las muñecas* (The Doll's Fight); *La muñeca negra* (The Black Doll), a comedy for children; *El huevo de Colón* (Columbus's Egg); *La última ilusión* (The Last Illusion); *El cuento de mamá* (Mother's Story); and *Tío Conejo castigado* (Uncle Rabbit Has Been Punished).

ESCALANTE, Manuel G. (1867–1943). Author of the three-act comedy *Final de Norma* (Norma's Ending), based on Pedro de Alarcón's work.

WORK: *Final de Norma* (Norma's Ending) (San José: Editorial María V. de Lines, 1911).

ESCALANTE DURÁN, Manuel G. (1905–?). Author of the three-act plays *Jeannine* and *Bruma*.

WORKS: *Jeannine* (San José: Editorial Trejos, 1945). *Bruma* (San José: Imprenta Trejos, 1948).

BIBLIOGRAPHY: H. Castro Fernández, "El teatro de M. G. Escalante Durán," *Brecha* 2.12 (1957).

FERNÁNDEZ DE MONTAGNÉ, Aída. Author of *Once de abril* (April Eleventh), staged in Costa Rica on April 10, 1936, and in El Salvador in 1937; *El día de las Américas* (The Day of the Americas); *Primero de mayo de 1857* (May 1st, 1857); *Sembremos, sembremos* (Let's Plant, Let's Plant); *Fue un 14 de julio* (It Was on a Fourth of July); *¿Quién es mi madre?* (Who Was My Mother?); *Carta al niño Dios* (A Letter to a Young Jesus), staged in 1937; *Manos feas* (Ugly Hands), staged August 15, 1936; *Mi madre murió para que yo viviera . . . !* (My Mother Died So That I Could Live . . . !); *La paz* (Peace); *Patria* (Country); *Costa Rica y sus artes* (Costa Rica and Her Arts); *Doce de octubre* (October 12th), staged

in 1936; and *Allá en el arroyo* (By the Stream). Other works by Fernández de Montagné include *La lluvia* (The Rain); *Buscando mariposas* (Looking for Butterflies); *25 de diciembre* (December 25th); *Fases de la luna* (Phases of the Moon); *Día de invierno* (A Winter's Day); *Por palacios de princesas* (Through Princesses' Palaces); *!No hay que querer volar sin tener alas!* (One Should Not Want to Fly without Wings!), a two-act play staged November 21, 1937; *Fue un sueño* (It Was a Dream), a three-act play; *Sueño de gitana* (A Gypsy's Dream); *Las hadas premian a los buenos* (The Fairies Reward Those Who Have Been Good); and *Avaricia* (Greed).

FERNÁNDEZ FERRAZ, Juan. Spanish author living in Costa Rica. He wrote *Gloria*, a play based on Benito Pérez Galdós's novel by the same title. It was staged at the Teatro Municipal in 1882.

WORK: *Gloria* (San José: Imprenta de La Paz, 1882).

FERNÁNDEZ GUARDIA, Ricardo (1867–1950). Historian and author of three books of short stories. His only play, *Magdalena*, staged at the Teatro Nacional on August 7, 1902, and again in 1984 by the Compañía Nacional de Teatro, portrays Costa Rican coffee growers and their newly acquired taste for refined European goods and critically examines the role of women and society's conventionalism. Fernández Guardia also demonstrated throughout his life an interest in politics, history, and diplomacy.

WORK: *Magdalena* (San José: Imprenta M.V. de Lines, 1902); also in *Antología del teatro costarricense (1890–1950)*, Alvaro Quesada et al., eds. (San José: Editorial de la Universidad de Costa Rica, 1993); and in *Escena* 5.1 (1986), 4–16; "Prólogo a Magdalena" (San José: Impresa y Librería Española, 1902); *Crónicas coloniales* (San José: Editorial Costa Rica, 1967).

BIBLIOGRAPHY: Gastón Alvarez Gaínza, "Apuntes para el estudio del contenido de *Magdalena*," *Escena* 3.5 (1981), 40–45. María Bonilla, "La vigencia de Magdalena," *Escena* 5.1 (1983), 2. María Lourdes Cortés, "De Magdalena a Eva: Tres momentos de la mujer en la dramaturgia nacional," *Escena* 11.22–23 (1989), 49–54. Víctor Hugo Fernández, *Ricardo Fernández Guardia* (San José: Ministerio de Cultura, 1978). Teodoro Picado, "Don Ricardo Fernández Guardia," *Brecha* 5.8 (1961), 7. Alvaro Quesada Soto, "*Magdalena* de Fernández Guardia: El liberalismo, la oligarquía y el matrimonio," *Escena* 5.12 (1984), 2. Quesada Soto, "Temas y variaciones en los inicios del teatro costarricense: Fernández Guardia, Gagini, Garnier," *Escena* 9.16 (1986), 39. Alberto Segura M., "Lectura ideológica de *Magdalena*" (Ph.D. diss., Universidad de Costa Rica, 1983). Rogelio Sotela, "Fernández Guardia," *Athenea* 4.1 (1920), 846. Virginia Sandoval de Fonseca, "Dramaturgia costarricense," *Revista Iberoamericana* 53.138–139 (1987), 173–192.

FERNANDEZ MORUA, Juan. Author of the dramatic play *Que no suceda* (That It Doesn't Happen), published in 1920.

GAGINI, Carlos (1865–1925). Author of *Don Concepción*, a one-act comedy written in verse and prose, first staged at the Teatro Nacional on August 24, 1902, by the Compañía E. Serrador. *Don Concepción* portrays a peasant family in San José and its desire to become incorporated into the social and political life of the city. Through the use of satire, Gagini ridicules ignorance and political corruption. *Don Concepción* is considered to be Costa Rica's national classic play. Other plays by Gagini are: *Los pretendientes* (The Suitors), a play that criticizes a father who, together with his daughter's suitors, is only interested in her marriage to obtain social and economic gains, staged in 1890 at the Gran Hotel; *El Marqués de Talamanca* (The Marquis of Talamanca), a three-act *zarzuela* written in verse and staged at the Teatro Nacional on November 24, 1900; the comedies *Las cuatro y tres cuartos* (Four and Three-Fourths) and *El candidato* (The Candidate); and *Toño*. The playwright also authored the children's plays *Trocitos de carbón* (Bits of Coal) and *Madre modelo* (Exemplary Mother). Gagini also wrote poetry, novels, and essays and is remembered as well for his pedagogical work and for being one of the first to investigate and study the indigenous languages of Costa Rica.

WORKS: *El Marqués de Talamanca* (The Mar-

quis of Talamanca) (Santa Ana, El Salvador: Imprenta de Angel Delgado, 1905) (this book includes: *Don Concepción, El Marqués de Talamanca, Los pretendientes*). *Los pretendientes* (The Suitors) (Santa Ana, El Salvador: 1905). *Cuentos y otras prosas* (Short Stories and Other Narratives) (San José: Imp. Lehmann, 1917). *El árbol enfermo* (The Sick Tree) (San José: Editorial Costa Rica, 1979). *La ciencia metafísica* (Metaphysical Science) (San José: Falcó y Borrasé, 1918). *Las cuatro y tres cuartos* (Four and Three-Fourths), in *Selección de cuatro autores costarricenses*, ed. Cecilia Valverde Barrenechea (San José: Imprenta Trejos, 1959), 62–77. *Don Concepción*, in *Selección de cuatro autores costarricenses*, ed. Cecilia Valverde Barrenechea (San José: Imprenta Trejos, 1959), 3–61; and in *Antología del teatro costarricense (1890–1950)*, Alvaro Quesada et al., eds. (San José: Editorial de la Universidad de Costa Rica, 1993). *Madre modelo* (Exemplary Mother), in Lilia Rama's *Luz y bambalinas* (Lights and Flies) (San José: Ministerio de Educación Pública, 1961), 347–349. *Teatro*, ed. Francisco Marín Cañas (San José: Editorial Costa Rica, 1963) (this book includes: *El Marqués de Talamanca, Los pretendientes, Don Concepción, Las cuatro y tres cuartos, El reino de Flora*, and *Trocitos de carbón*).

BIBLIOGRAPHY: María Eugenia Acuña, "Carlos Gagini: Su vida y su obra en el contexto nacional e hispanoamericano" (Ph.D. diss., Universidad de Costa Rica, San José, 1984). María Eugenia Acuña, "Carlos Gagini," *Cilampa* 7 (1985), 7–10. María Eugenia Acuña, "Carlos Gagini y el romanticismo en Costa Rica," *Revista Iberoamericana* 53.138–139 (1987), 121–138. María Eugenia Acuña, "La influencia del costumbrismo en los primeros relatos y el en teatro de Carlos Gagini," *Kañina* 12.1 (1988), 11–18. Cecilia Ureña de Molina, "Carlos Gagini Chavarría: Hechos y obras," *Revista de Filología y Lingüística de la Universidad de Costa Rica* 3.5 (1979), 3–4. Virginia Sandoval de Fonseca, "Dramaturgia costarricense," *Revista Iberoamericana* 53.138–139 (1987), 173–192. Alvaro Quesada Soto, "Temas y variaciones en los inicios del teatro cotarricense: Fernández Guardia, Gagini, Garnier," *Escena* 9.16 (1986), 39.

GALLEGOS TROYO, Daniel (1930–). Gallegos was born in San José, Costa Rica, and attended primary school in Costa Rica and secondary school in Long Beach, California. He started his higher education in the United States and returned to Costa Rica to pursue a law degree at the Universidad de Costa Rica. Gallegos did postdoctoral work at Columbia University and studied theater at Yale University and at the New York Actors' Studio from 1959 to 1960. While living in Europe, Gallegos performed with the Royal Shakespeare Company, the British Drama League, and the ORTF in Paris. He also performed professionally in Mexico. Upon his return to Costa Rica, Gallegos was named director and professor of the Department of Dramatic Arts at the University of Costa Rica. The playwright has authored the following works: *Ese algo de Dávalos* (That Dávalos), a three-act comedy, winner in Guatemala of the Premio Certamen Nacional de Bellas Artes "15 de septiembre" (Fine Arts Award "September 15") in 1960 and of the Aquileo J. Echeverría award in 1964. Other plays by Gallegos are *Los profanos* (The Laymen), winner of the "15 de septiembre" award; *El hacha de plata* (The Silver Ax), written in English; and *La colina* (The Hill), considered to be one of the best dramatic plays written in Costa Rica, also awarded the Aquileo J. Echeverría prize in 1968. The play caused great controversy due to religious and metaphysical questions, since six characters confront, reject, and accept the concept of the death of God. To this list of plays one should add *La casa* (The House), which presents generational conflicts; and the two-act play *Punto de referencia* (Reference Point), which brings forth the problems encountered in a couple's relationship as well as those dealing with identity. *Punto de referencia* was staged at the Sala Vargas Calvo of the Teatro Nacional in 1984. *El séptimo círculo* (The Seventh Circle) is a 1982 play that portrays the antagonism that exists between generations and the absurdity of life. The characters in Gallego's plays usually present moral, social, and political conflicts that are identifiable by his audience. His plays have universal themes.

WORKS: *Ese algo de Dávalos* (That Dávalos) (San José: Editorial Costa Rica, 1967). *La colina* (The Hill) (San José: Editorial Costa Rica, 1969); also in *El teatro actual latinoamericano*, ed. Carlos Solórzano (Mexico, 1972). *Shakespeare . . . a ritmo de tango* (Shakespeare . . . to the Rhythm of the Tango), in *Escena* 10.19–20 (1988), 8–9. *Los Profanos* (The Profane), in *Repertorio Centroamericano* 14 (1969), 75–101. *Giradoux 1980*, in *Escena* 3.3 (1980), 8. *Prestigio y determinación de Richard Salvat: Mago de Sitges*, (The Prestige and Determination of Richard Salvat: Magician of Sitges), I part, in *Escena* 5.9 (1983), 12. *Saludo a un colega dramaturgo*, in *Escena* 5.11 (1984), 20.

BIBLIOGRAPHY: Carmen Naranjo, "La violencia en escena: Obra y gracia de Daniel Gallegos," *Escena* 4.7 (1982), 9. Virginia Sandoval de Fonseca, "Dramaturgia costarricense," *Revista Iberoamericana* 53.138–139 (1987), 173–192. María Lourdes Cortés, "Lectura de la producción de sentido de la obra dramatúrgica de Alberto Cañas, Daniel Gallegos y Samuel Rovinski" (Ph.D. diss., Universidad de Costa Rica, San José, 1987).

GARNIER, José Fabio (1884–1956). Garnier is considered to be one of the most prolific writers of Costa Rica. Garnier studied in Italy and wrote plays following the style of the Italian Renaissance. His plays present human conflicts but lack local color. He authored about forty plays, among them: *El retorno* (The Return) (1912), a drama dedicated to the actress María Melato and staged in 1906; *La última escena* (The Last Scene), a one-act comedy dedicated to Evangelina Adams and staged at the Teatro Nacional on October 13, 1910; *Pasa el ideal* (The Ideal Passes By) (1918); *¡Nada!* (Nothingness) (1918), a study of a one-act play written in Venice; *Boccaccesca* (1919), inspired by Boccaccio's *Decameron; A la sombra del amor* (At the Shadow of Love), a three-act comedy, staged by Compañía Soler Adams y Jambrina y Tordesillas, in 1921; *La sombra hermana* (The Faithful Shadow), also a three-act comedy; and *Agua santa* (Holy Water), staged October 1, 1921, by Compañía Soler. Other works include: *Con toda el alma* (With All of One's Heart), a three-act drama staged in 1933; *El talismán de Afrodita* (Aphrodite's Talisman), a comic drama staged June 9, 1929, by Compañía Herrero-Tordesillas; *Si el marido engaña* (If the Husband Cheats), presented in 1954; *Si el diablo sopla* (If the Devil Blows), a play from 1955; *La doncella que quiso volver* (The Maiden Who Wanted to Come Back) (1955); *Campanitas de plata* (Silver Bells), a two-act play; and *Umbral invisible* (Invisible Threshold). Garnier also wrote children's theater such as *El dulce secreto* (Sweet Secret), as well as literary criticism and two novels.

WORKS: *La primera sonrisa* (The First Smile) (San José: Imprenta Lines, 1904); and (Paris: Casa Editorial Garnier, 1906). *¡Nada!* (Nothingness!) (San José: Tipografía Nacional, 1906). *Día de fiestas* (Holidays), in *Páginas Ilustradas* 4.137 (1907), 2190–2194. *La vida inútil* (The Senseless Life) (Paris: Casa Editorial Garnier, 1910). "Segundo Coloquio que pasó entre Cipión y Berganza, perros del Hospital de Valladolid, diálogo" (Second Colloquium between Cipión and Berganza, Dogs of the Hospital of Valladolid, a Dialogue), in *A la sombra del amor* (San José: Imprenta M.V. de Lines, 1921); and in "Segundo Coloquio que pasó entre Cipión y Berganza, perros del Hospital de Valladolid, diálogo," in *Colección Ariel*, 76–77 (1916), 67–84. *Teatro*, vol. 1 (San José: Imprenta Española, 1912) (this book includes: *El retorno, La última escena, Nada* [The Return, The Last Scene, and Nothingness]. *Literatura patria* (San José: Tipografía Nacional, 1913). *¡Nada!*, in *Teatro*, vol. I (San José: Librería Española, 1912). *Pasa el ideal* (The Ideal Passes By) (San José: Imprenta Lehman, 1918). *Boccaccesca* (San José: Imprenta Alsina, 1919); and (San José: Imprenta Minerva, 1981). *Agua santa* (Holy Water) (San José: Editorial Alsina, 1921). *A la sombra del amor* (At the Shadow of Love) (San José: María V. de Lines, 1921); and in *Antología del teatro costarricense (1890–1950)*, Alvaro Quesada et al., eds. (San José: Editorial de la Universidad de Costa Rica, 1993). *El dulce secreto*, in *Educación* 10.57 (1938), 142–154, and in *Repertorio Americano* 3.11 (1924), 164–167. *Con toda el alma* (With All of One's Heart) (San José: Imprenta Reyes y Cía., 1929). *El talismán de Afrodita* (Aphrodite's Talisman) (San José: Imprenta Lines, A. Reyes, 1929).

BIBLIOGRAPHY: "Justicia al mérito," *Páginas Ilustradas* 5.201 (1907), 3409. "Una esperanza costarricense," *Páginas Ilustradas* 5.189 (1908), 3204. "José Fabio Garnier. Clise," *Arte y vida* 3 (1909), 5. "José Fabio Garnier," *Anales del Ateneo de Costa Rica* 1.6 (1912), 5. "Otro reportaje," *Reproducción* 11.174 (1929), 83. H. Alfredo Castro Fernández, "El teatro de José Fabio Garnier," *Brecha* 1.3 (1956), 15. Justo A. Facio, "José Fabio Garnier," *Páginas Ilustradas* 3.115 (1906), 1850. *José Fabio Garnier, el ingeniero, el maestro, el literato* (San José: Lemann, 1963). Giuseppe Lipparini, "Letteratura latinoamericana," *Repertorio Americano* 3.29 (1922), 396. Al-

varo Quesada Soto, "Temas y variaciones en los inicios del teatro costarricense: Fernández Guardia, Gagini, Garnier," *Escena* 9.16 (1986), 39. Rogelio Sotela, "José Fabio Garnier," *Athenea* 1.13 (1918), 274. José María Zeledón, "José Fabio Garnier. Un esbozo," *Páginas Ilustradas* 7.248 (1910), 2. José María Zeledón, "Notas breves," *Páginas Ilustradas* 7.248 (1910), 2.

GUARDIA Y AYALA, Victor de la (1722–1823). Author of *La política del mundo* (The World's Politics), published in Costa Rica in 1902 by his grandson Ricardo Fernández Guardia. The three-act play written in verse premiered in Penomé, Panamá, in 1908. It deals with the imperialistic policies of Julius Caesar and Napoleon. The play has several anachronisms, one of which appears in the last act, when the characters who live in the first century make reference to people living in the nineteenth century. It should be noted that this literary license was acceptable at the time that the play was written.

WORK: *La política del mundo* (The World's Politics) (San José: Imprenta y Librería Española, 1902).

ISTARÚ, Ana (1960–   ). Contemporary actress, playwright, and poet. Author of the plays *Madre nuestra que estás en la tierra* (Our Mother Who Is on Earth), a three-act play staged in March 1988 in San José by the Compañía Nacional de Teatro and later by Teatro Trova, and *El vuelo de la grulla* (The Flight of the Crane). In both plays, women are presented as suffering entities. In 1980 Istarú won the award for Mejor Actriz Debutante (Best First Performance) for her interpretation of the character of Areusa, in the production of *La Celestina* staged by Teatro del Angel. Istarú has published five books of poetry, among which are *La estación fiebre*, for which she won the Premio Certamen Latinoamericano EDUCA in 1982, and *La muerte y otros efímeros agravios* (1984).

WORKS: *El vuelo de la grulla* (The Flight of the Crane), in *Escena* 5.11 (1984), 15–19. *Madre nuestra que estás en la tierra* (Our Mother Who Is on Earth), in *Escena* 11.20–21 (1989), 23–45.

JIMÉNEZ, Pilar. Author of *Gracias a Dios que está puesta la mesa* (Thank Heavens That the Table Is Set), staged by the theatrical group Saturnino Blen.

JIMÉNEZ ALPIZAR, Ricardo. His works include *Alacrán* (Scorpion) (1933), a three-act drama; *Un cuento de la tía Panchita* (Aunt Pachita's Story) (1936), a one-act children's play; *La muerte de la mariposa* (The Death of the Butterfly) (1937), a one-act lyric fantasy; and *Veintiocho de diciembre* (December 28th) (1939), a one-act comic skit.

JINESTA, Ricardo. Author of *La mueca del destino* (The Face of Destiny), a two-act drama.

WORKS: *La mueca del destino* (The Face of Destiny). *Páginas de amor* (Love Pages) (San José: Falcó y Borrasé, 1919), 75–119.

LYRA, Carmen. Pen name of María Isabel Carvajal, author of children's theater. Her plays include *La cigarra y la hormiga* (The Cicada and the Ant); *Ponerle el cascabel al gato* (To Put the Bell on the Cat); *Los recuerdos de la abuelita* (Grandma's Remembrances); the dramatized short story *Salir con un domingo siente* (To Go Out on a Sunday); *El violín mágico* (The Magic Violin); *La caperucita roja* (Little Red Riding Hood), a *zarzuela*; *Ensueños de nochebuena* (A Christmas Eve Fantasy); *La virgen y los ángeles* (The Virgin and the Angels); *El granito de maíz* (The Kernel of Corn), published in the magazine *San Serlín*; *¿Quiere usted quedarse a comer?* (Would You Like to Stay for Dinner?); *La mina sol* (The Sun Mine), a comedy; and *Había una vez* (Once Upon a Time), a three-act comedy presented at the Escuela Normal. Other works by Lyra are *Balada de doña Rota* (The Ballad of Doña Rota) and, with Francisco Soler, *La ilusión eres tú* (You Are My Illusion).

WORKS: *La ilusión eres tú* (You Are My Illusion), coauthored with Francisco Soler, in *Pandemonium* 8.108 (1914), 14. *La niña sol* (The Girl Sun), in *Lecturas* 2.23 (1919), 366–367. *Ponerlé el cascabel al gato* (To Put the Bell on the Cat), in *Repertorio Americano* 4.15 (1922), 206–207; and in *Educación* 4.8 (1958), 17–19. *Julián Marchena y Francisco Soler*, in *Repertorio Americano* 10.21 (1925). *Balada de doña Rota* (The Ballad of Doña Rota), in *Triquitraque* 33 (1939), 8–9. *Ensueños de nochebuena* (Christmas Eve Fantasy), in *Repertorio Americano* 12.513 (1930), 2169–2172. *Ensueños de Navidad*, in *Carmen Lyra*, Luisa González and Carlos Luis Saénz, eds. (San José: Ministerio de Cultura, Juventud y Deportes, Dept. de Publicaciones, 1972).

BIBLIOGRAPHY: Luisa González and Carlos Luis Saénz, eds., *Carmen Lyra* (San José: Ministerio de Cultura, 1977). Ministerio de Cultura, Juventud y Deportes, "II Festival Nacional de Teatro para niños, Carmen Lyra," *Escena* 10.19–20 (1984), 15.

MARÍN CAÑAS, José (1904–1980). Marín Cañas wrote the one-act play *Como tú* (Like You). A longer version was staged in March 1929 at San José's Teatro Americano. Marín Cañas also wrote *En busca de un candidato* (In Search of a Candidate) (1935). This play deals with the regional customs of San José. Other plays by Marín Cañas are *El O.K.* (The O.K.), the short comedy *El valor de la moneda* (The Value of Money); the burlesque play *El tesoro de la Isla del Coco* (The Treasure of Coco Island); and *Un pic-nic delikatessen*. *Como tú* (Like You) and *Una tragedia de ocho cilindros* (A Tragedy of Eight Cylinders), both staged in 1938, are the only works by Marín Cañas that have survived.

WORKS: *Como tú* (Like You) (San José: Imprenta Borrasé, 1929); reprinted as a one-act play in *Escena* 3.5 (1981), i–v. *Una tragedia de ocho cilindros* (A Tragedy of Eight Cylinders), in *Excelsior* (1978).

MARTÉN (MARTÍN), Ernesto. Martén is the author of the successful comedy *Cuento de amor* (A Love Story), staged by the Compañía Adams at the Teatro Nacional on November 3, 1910.

WORKS: *Cuento de amor* (A Love Story) (San José: Imprenta del Comercio, 1910); and in *Páginas Ilustradas* 7.258 (1910), 10.

BIBLIOGRAPHY: "*Cuento de amor*. Comedia de don Ernesto Martén," *Páginas Ilustradas* 7.262 (1910), 8. Oscar Padilla, "Un *Cuento de amor*," *Páginas Ilustradas* 7.262 (1910), 12. Claudio González Rucavado, "*Cuento de amor*," *Páginas Ilustradas* 8.270 (1911), 6–7. Roberto Valladares, "Teatro pa-trio. *Cuento de amor*, por el Lic. Ernesto Martín," *Páginas Ilustradas* 7.257 (1910), 10–13.

MÉNDEZ, Melvin (1958–). Contemporary actor and playwright. Méndez studied at the School of Dramatic Arts of the Universidad de Costa Rica and has taught at the Universidad Nacional's School of Dramatic Arts. Méndez has acted in films, radio, and television. In 1980 he received the Premio Nacional (National Prize) for a first performance on the stage and in 1986 the Premio Nacional for best actor. His play *Eva, sol y sombra* (Eva, Sun and Shadow) portrays a woman who feels overwhelmed by her husband. This work was presented at the Teatro Municipal. Other plays by Méndez are *Con el alfiler en las alas* (Pinned Wings); *Méteme el hombro* (Reset My Shoulder); *San Zapatero* (Saint Shoemaker), staged by Grupo Brecha; and *Villa Nueva de la Boca del Monte*, coauthored with Rodolfo Cisneros. His short story "El loco del violín" (The Madman of the Violin) obtained first place in 1983 in the Certamen Brunca (Brunca Competition) of the Universidad Nacional de Pérez Zeldón. His most current writing is "Adiós candidato" (Good-Bye Candidate), which shows solidarity with marginal groups.

WORKS: *Con el alfiler en las alas* (Pinned Wings), in *Escena* 9.17 (1987), 27–37. *Eva, sol y sombra* (Eva, Sun and Shadow), in *Teatro para el teatro* (San José: Teatro Nacional, 1989).

MONESTEL, José. Monestel was winner in 1984 of the Certamen Siete Provincias (Seven Provinces Contest) sponsored by the Ministerio de Cultura, Juventud y Deportes (Ministry of Culture, Youth, and Sports) with the one-act comedy of historical background, *Siempre lo mismo* (Always the Same).

WORK: *Siempre lo mismo* (Always the Same), in *Escena* 10.19–20 (1988), 39–57.

MURILLO PORRAS, José Neri. Murillo Porras is author of the following plays: *Ambición* (Ambition), a play presented in El Salvador in 1943; *Madre del mundo* (Mother of the World); *El retorno de las águilas* (The Return of the Eagles); and *Tierra y paz* (Land and Peace).

NARANJO, Carmen (1928–). Naranjo is a writer and poet. She studied at the Universidad de Costa Rica and completed postgraduate work at Mexico's Universidad Nacional Autónoma and in Iowa. Naranjo has held the position of minister at the Ministry of Culture, Youth and Sports and is currently director of Editorial Universitaria Centroamericana (EDUCA). She has been the recipient of numerous national awards for literature. Naranjo has published *La voz* (The Voice), *Nunca hubo alguna vez* (There Never Was a Once Upon a Time) (1984), and *Otro rumbo para la rumba* (Another Way to the Rumba) (1989).

WORKS: *La voz*, in *Obras breves del teatro costarricense*, vol. 2 (San José: Editorial Costa Rica, 1971). "*La violencia en escena*: Obra y gracia de Daniel Gallegos," in *Escena* 4.7 (1982), 9.

OREAMURO, Joaquín de (1755–1827). Oreamuno wrote *Una loa y dos entremeses* (A Prologue and Two Interludes) for the festivities honoring Fernando VII in 1809. The *loa* attacked Napoleon's invasion of Spain, whereas the *extremeses* exalted the virtues of the monarch.

OROZCO, Carlos. The following works are attributed to Orozco: *Río de sangre* (Bloody River), a play critical of communism that was staged by the Compañía María Teresa Montoya; *Ya no iré a tu casa* (Now I Won't Go to Your House), staged at the Teatro Nacional by the Compañía de Silvia Villalaz; *Locutas*, a tragic play; *Experiencia peligrosa* (A Dangerous Experience), a three-act drama; *El embrujo de mi tierra* (The Magic of My Country), a historic play; *El caballero del guante gris* (The Grey Gloved Gentleman), a play with philosophical undertones.

BIBLIOGRAPHY: Sonia Benedictus, "Del *Río de sangre*, el drama intenso," *Repertorio Americano* 26.9 (1933), 41. H. Alfredo Castro Fernández, "El teatro de Carlos Orozco," *Brecha* 2.2 (1957), 2–6.

OROZCO CASTRO, Jorge. Orozco Castro is author of *Germinal*, which premiered at the Teatro Nacional in 1938.

WORK: *Germinal*, in *Obras breves del teatro*

costarricense, vol. 1 (San José: Editorial Costa Rica, 1969).

PACHECO COOPER, Emilio (1865–1905). Pacheco Cooper is author of the dramas *Calumniada* (Slandered) and the well-received *Venganza de un poeta* (Vengeance of a Poet), which was staged at the Teatro Nacional on January 14, 1900. According to Fernando Borges, the play was staged in 1905. *Venganza de un poeta* presents the theme of intellectual pursuits.

PÉREZ REY, Guadalupe. Pérez Rey is a contemporary actress, director, and playwright. Pérez Rey was the first woman to graduate from the School of Civil Engineering of the Universidad de Costa Rica. The author has written about twenty-three plays, of which twelve have been staged. Her work includes: *Astucia femenina* (Female Astuteness), staged in 1966 by the Grupo de Teatro de la Caja at the Clínica Carlos Durán; *Pancha Carrasco reclama* (Pancha Carrasco Asks for What She Deserves); and *Ellas en la maquila* (Women and Machine) and *Pinocho* (Pinocchio), two plays that were coauthored with Leda Cavallini. *Ellas en la maquila* portrays the lives and plights of women employed in a textile factory. For *Pinocho*, Pérez Rey and Cavellini were awarded the Aquileo J. Echeverría theater award in 1989. Other works of Pérez Rey are: *Pobre chico* (Poor Kid); *Fermín*, a one-act play; *El audífono* (The Earphones); *Celos* (Jealosy); *Estrategia maternal* (Maternal Strategy); *La trampa* (The Trap), a 1985 play with detectivesque theme; *La cabaña* (The Cabin); *Veinte manzanas* (Twenty Apples); *Los maridos de Lucrecia* (Lucrecia's Husbands); *Operación Lucrecia* (Operation Lucretia); *Como mi mujer ninguna* (No One Compares to My Wife); *El brindis de la muerte* (Death's Toast); *¿Qué le pasó a Victoria Eugenia?* (What Happened to Victoria Eugenia?); *Algo más que dos sueños* (Much More Than Two Dreams), written in 1963 and staged for the first time by Grupo Israelita de Teatro in 1967 at the Teatro de la Calle 4. A second staging of *Algo más que dos sueños* was revised and presented at the Olympic Festival in Mexico City in 1968.

WORKS: *Algo más que dos sueños* (Much More Than Two Dreams), in *Revista Pórtico* 1 (1963), 108–128; and in *Teatro breve hispanoamericano*, ed. Carlos Solórzano (Madrid: Editorial Aguilar, 1970). *Astucia femenina* (Female Astuteness), in *Obras breves de teatro costarricense*, vol. 1 (San José: Editorial Costa Rica, 1969).

BIBLIOGRAPHY: María Pérez Yglesias, "Una vida para reconstruir," *Escena* 11. 22–23 (1989), 84–98.

REUBEN, William (1947–). Reuben started his literary life by writing poetry. His only known play to date is *Teófilo Amadeo: Una biografía* (Teófilo Amadeo: A Biography), which was staged by Teatro Grupo. The play was directed by Antonio Yglesias. Reuben has said that Alfredo and Carlos Catania as well as Antonio Yglesias have greatly influenced his work.

WORK: *Teófilo Amadeo: Una biografía* (Teófilo Amadeo: A Biography), in *El teatro de hoy en Costa Rica*, eds. Anita Herzfeld and Teresa Cajiao Salas (San José: Editorial Costa Rica, 1973).

ROJAS, Miguel (1952–). Rojas studied dramatic arts at the Universidad de Costa Rica, where he currently teaches. His first play to be staged was *Los días nublados* (Cloudy Days); in 1985, by the Compañía Nacional de Teatro. This play, like other plays by Rojas, presents historical themes. Here in *Los días nublados*, Rojas portrays the impact of Costa Rica's Civil War of 1823 and the triumph of liberty and progress. The play *Armas tomar* (Call to Arms) is part of the same historical trilogy to which *Los días nublados* belongs. According to the author, the third play of the trilogy will deal with the role that President Juan Mora had on Costa Rican history. Other plays by Mora are *Lo que somos* (As We Are), winner of the Festival de Teatro Grano de Oro (Golden Grain) in 1977; *Granada real* (Majestic Granada); *Dónde canta el mar* (Where the Sea Sings); *El anillo del pavo real* (The Peacock's Ring); and *La tropa de Pepe Candela* (Pepe Candela's Troop), a children's play. Rojas's most recent work is *De tiempo en tiempo sin importancia* (Inconsequentially from Time to Time).

WORKS: "*A propósito de la dramaturgia costarricense*," *Escena* 4.8 (1982), 6–7. *Aquí abajo estamos* (Here We Are Below), *Escena* 5.12 (1984), 12–17. *Donde canta la mar* (Where the Sea Sings), *Escena* 5.12 (1984), 7–11. *A cada quien su flor* (A Flower for Everyone), *Escena*, 5.12 (1984), 18–22. *El maravilloso mundo del teatro infantil*, *Escena* 6.13 (1985), 15. *Los buscadores del alma escondida* (Seekers of a Hidden Soul), *Escena* 7.14 (1985), 3–4. *Obras teatrales* (San José: Editorial de la Universidad de Costa Rica, 1988). *Alas del futuro* (Wings of the Future), *Escena* 11.22–23 (1989), 37–38. *De tiempo en tiempo sin importancia* (Inconsequentially From Time to Time), in *Teatro para el teatro* (Theater for the Theater), vol. 1 (San José: Teatro Nacional, 1989). "El viejo arte del autor dramático," *Escena* 12.24–25 (1990). "*Gulliver dormido* de Samuel Rovinski: una parodia del discurso del poder," *Latin American Theatre Review*, 21.1 (1990), 51–63. "Un acercamiento a la perspectiva de tres dramaturgos en Costa Rica, 1990," *Escena* 14.30 (1992), 35–39.

ROSALES CHACON, Mario Enrique (1948–). Rosales Chacon studied at the Universidad de Costa Rica. He is the author of *La otra cara de la luna* (The Other Face of the Moon), which received an honorary mention in 1972 in the Concurso del Teatro Breve (Competition of Brief Theatrical Plays), and in 1973 was awarded the Revista Tertulia prize granted by the Ministerio de Cultura, Juventud y Deportes (Ministry of Culture, Youth and Sports).

ROVINSKI, Samuel (1932–). Rovinski attended primary and secondary schools in San José and obtained a degree in civil engineering from the Universidad Nacional Autónoma of Mexico. Rovinski founded and manages one of the most important construction companies in Costa Rica. He is also a very active member of the Costa Rican intellectual community. Rovinski has authored the following plays: *La Atlántida* is a three-act play written in 1960 and recipient of honorary mention at the Juegos Florales Centroamericanos (Literary Competition of Central America) held in Guatemala in 1960. *Los agitadores* (The Agitators), written in 1964, earned the playwright honorary mention. *Gobierno de alcoba* (Bedroom Government) is a play in which Rovinski portrays how rightist and leftist dictators manipulate the people of their countries. *Gobierno de alcoba* was staged in 1967 at the Teatro Nacional. The play was directed by Andrés Saénz and Daniel Gallegos. A second staging of this play was presented by the Grupo Israelita de Teatro (GIT). *El laberinto* (The Labyrinth) (1967) was staged at the Teatro Nacional in 1969 under the direction of Esteban Polls, and *Las fisgonas de Paso Ancho* (The Snoopers of Paso Ancho) (1971) was staged that same year at the Escuela República de Haití in Paso Ancho by the Teatro Estudiantil Universitario (Student's University Theater). Alfredo Catania directed this satirical play, and Rovinski was awarded first prize at the Festival de Teatro Centroamericano. *Gobierno de alcoba* and *Las fisgonas de Paso Ancho* helped popularize the theater in Costa Rica. *Un modelo para Rosaura o la manera de acomodar una historia a nuestro gusto* (A Model for Rosaura or How to Manipulate History to Our Liking), a three-act play, won the Premio Editorial Costa Rica (Editorial Award of Costa Rica) and the Aquilo J. Echeverría awards. *Un modelo* (A Model) falls into the category of experimental theater. With this play, Rovinski criticizes the upper middle class. As part of the action, the author, director, and actors interrupt the performance to give their opinions regarding the conventional marriage portrayed and to suggest an outcome. Other plays by Rovinski are *El martirio del pastor* (The Martyrdom of the Shepherd) (1984), whose theme centers around the assassination of Monsignor Oscar Romero and the relationship between church and state, and *Guillermo dormido* (Guillermo Asleep). *Las fisgonas de Paso Ancho* and *Guillermo dormido* are considered Rovinski's best attacks on the ruling class.

WORKS: "*Gobierno de alcobas*" (Bedroom Government), in *Obras breves del teatro costarricense*, vol. 2 (San José: Editorial Costa Rica, 1971), 41–81. *El laberinto* (The Labyrinth), in *El teatro de hoy en Costa Rica*, ed. Anita Herzfeld and Teresa Cajiao Salas (San José: Editorial Costa Rica, 1973), 59–113.

Las fisgonas de Paso Ancho (The Snoopers of Paso Ancho) (San José, Costa Rica: Editorial Costa Rica, 1975). *Un modelo para Rosaura o la manera de acomodar una historia a nuestro gusto* (A Model for Rosaura or How to Manipulate History to Our Liking) (San José: Editorial Costa Rica, 1975). "La obra teatral: ¿Creación individual o colectiva?" *Escena* 3.5 (1981), 16–20. "Dramatización de lo inmediato," *Escena* 4.7 (1982), 24–25. "El martirio del pastor en los Estados Unidos de Norteamérica," *Escena* 9.17 (1987), 17–19. "En busca del público perdido," *Escena* 9.18 (1987), 49–54. "Dramatización de lo inmediato," *Escena* 10.19–20 (1988), 111–118. "Dramatización de lo inmediato. El sentido de lo cómico," *Escena* 11.20–21 (1989), 126–133.

BIBLIOGRAPHY: "*Gulliver dormido* de Samuel Rovinski: Una parodia del discurso del poder," *Latin American Theatre Review* 21.1 (1990), 51–63. María Lourdes Cortés, "Lectura de la producción de sentido de la obra dramática de Alberto Cañas, Daniel Gallegos y Samuel Rovinski" (Ph.D. diss., Universidad de Costa Rica, 1987). Arnaldo Mora, "*El martirio del pastor*," *Escena* 9.18 (1987), 11–12.

SABORIO, Alfredo Montenegro. Saborio is the author of the mystic play *La Virgen de los Angeles* (The Virgin of the Angels) and the heroic drama *Juan Santamaría*. Both plays were staged at the Teatro Nacional in 1938.

WORKS: *Teatro costarricense* (San José: Imprenta Nacional, 1942) (this volume includes *Juan Santamaría* and *La Virgen de los Angeles*).

SAÉNZ, Carlos Luis. Saénz is an author of children's theater and the anthology *Navidades* (Christmas) (1929). The book includes the following plays by the author: *Zánganos y obreras* (Lazy Men and Working Women), *Recuerdos de Navidad* (Christmas Remembrances), *Fantasía de Navidad* (Christmas Fantasy), *Así fue* (That's the Way It Was), *Cuento inocente* (Innocent Story), and *El frailecito duende* (The Gremlin Friar). Other plays are *Las hojas* (The Leaves), *Isidro el labrador* (Isidoro: Laborer), *La ladrona del sueño* (The Thief of Dreams) (dedicated to mothers), *El 15 de septiembre* (September 15th), *El cepillo de dientes* (The Toothbrush), *Juego de pastores ante el portal de Belén* (Shepherds' Games at the Crèche),

and *En lo que paró el baile* (How the Dance Ended Up).

SALAZAR ALVAREZ, Raúl. He is the author of *El hombre que buscaba el verdadero amor* (The Man Who Sought True Love), a comedy dedicated to María Teresa Montoya and published in 1929. This play portrays the problems encountered by Costa Rican women who marry foreigners. Salazar also wrote *La mujer que tenía en la boca el corazón* (Scared Woman), a one-act dramatic comedy published in 1920 and based on a short story written by Sir Arthur Conan Doyle; *San José en camisa* (San José Wears a Shirt), a comedy that depicts the night life of San José; and the popular *Ciento diez veces* (One Hundred and Ten Times), staged at the Teatro Trébol. Other works attributed to Salazar Alvarez are *Amor, lazo divino* (Love, Divine Bondage), a two-act play; *Mañana primavera* (Tomorrow, Spring), a one-act comedy; *Yo soy un descubritore* (I, the Discoverer), a comedy that deals with the discovery of America; and *El despertar de don Juanito* (Juanito's Awakening), also a comedy. Salazar coauthored with Roberto Valladeres the play *La fea* (The Ugly Woman).

WORKS: *Amor, lazo divino* (Love, Divine Bondage), in *Lecturas* 1.13 (1918), 194–196. *La fea* (The Ugly Woman), in *Lecturas* 2.287 (1919), 446–447. *Mañana primavera* (Tomorrow, Spring), in *Nous* 2.12 (1919), 13–16. *La mujer que tenía en la boca el corazón* and *El hombre que buscaba el verdadero amor* (Scared Woman and The Man Who Sought True Love) (San José: La Tribuna, 1929); and in *Antología del teatro costarricense (1890–1950)*, Alvaro Quesada et al., eds. (San José: Editorial de la Universidad de Costa Rica, 1993).

BIBLIOGRAPHY: Justo A. Facio, "Dos comedias dramáticas," *Repertorio Americano* 9.7 (1929), 102–103.

SÁNCHEZ BONILLA, Gonzalo. His reputation as a playwright rests on his work *El pobre manco* (The Unfortunate One-Armed Man), based on a short story by the same title. Sánchez Bonilla also wrote the musical *La bachillera*, a two-act *zarzuela* staged in 1916; *El amor es triunfo* (Love Is Triumphant), a one-act comedy staged in 1917; and *Cuando las rosas mueren* (When the Roses Die).

WORKS: *En el aniversario* (The Anniversary), *Selenia*, 9 (1910), 67. *Cuando las rosas mueren* (When the Roses Die), in Rogelio Sotela, ed., *Escritores de Costa Rica* (San José: Imprenta Lehman; 1942). O. M. Barrantes, *El pobre manco* (The Unfortunate One-Armed Man), in *Antología comentada de la literatura dramática costarricense*, Diss. Universidad de Costa Rica, 1978.

SANCHO COLOMBARÍ, Alfredo. Sancho is Mexican by birth but lived in Costa Rica from 1950 to 1967, then returned to Mexico. Sancho was the founder of the Teatro Experimental de Costa Rica and professor of dramatic arts from 1950 to 1967. While in Costa Rica, Sancho wrote *Débora*, a play that premiered in 1951 at the Teatro Municipal with a staging by the Teatro Experimental de Costa Rica under the direction of the author and Lucio Ranucci. He also wrote and directed *Taller de reparaciones (Se reparan seres humanos)* (Body Shop: Humans Repaired), which was staged by the Teatro de la Prensa de Costa Rica in 1956. Other plays are *Las alemeonidas*, staged in 1962, and *Las tres carátulas* (The Three Masks) (1970).

WORKS: *Débora* (San José: Imprenta Nacional, 1955). *Taller de reparaciones (Se reparan seres humanos)* (Body Shop: Humans Repaired) (San José: Imprenta Vargas, 1956). *Las alemeonidas* (San Salvador, El Salvador: Ministerio de Educación Pública Departamento Editorial, 1961). *Las tres carátulas* (The Three Masks), ed. C. Suárez Rodillo (Mexico City: Finisterre, 1970).

SOLER, Francisco (1893–1920). Soler was a playwright, short story writer, and journalist. He was born in Costa Rica and died in Paris at an early age. He wrote *El único cuento de hadas* (The Only Fairy Tale) and *La ilusión eres tú* (You Are a Fantasy). This last work was written in collaboration with Carmen Lyra. With Camilo Cruz Santos he wrote the comedy *La iniciación* (The Initiation). Soler also wrote *El último madrigal* (The Last Madrigal) (1919), a short story written as a dialogue, and a novel entitled *El esplandor del Ocaso* (Splendorous End) (1918). He also contributed to *Actuali-*

dades and *La linterna*. His conferences were published under the titles *Los siete pecados capitales* (Seven Capital Sins) and *Musgo de ruinas* (Mossy Ruins).

WORKS: *La ilusión eres tú* (You Are a Fantasy), in *Pandemonium* 8.108 (1914), 328–332. *La iniciación* (The Initiation), in *Renovación* 4.81–82 (1914), 129–152; in *Escenas* 11.20–21 (1989), 91–118; and in *Antología del teatro costarricense (1890–1950)*, ed. Alvaro Quesada et al. (San José: Editorial de la Universidad de Costa Rica, 1993). *El último madrigal* (The Last Madrigal) (San José: Imprenta Falcó y Borrasé, 1918); and in (San José: Imprenta Nacional, 1919). *El único cuento de hadas* (The Only Fairy Tale), in *Athenea* 3.15 (1920), 834–839; in *Escritores de Costa Rica*, ed. Rogelio Sotela (San José: Imprenta Lehman, 1942), and in *Cultura* 1.15 (1929), 5–7. "Dos cartas de Francisco Soler," *Escena* 11.20–21 (1989), 80.

BIBLIOGRAPHY: Carmen Lyra, "Julián Marchena y Francisco Soler," *Repertorio Americano* 10.21 (1925). Flora Ovares, "Paco Soler," *Escena* 11.20–21 (1989), 80–81. Cristián Rodríguez, "In memorian Paco Soler," *Escena* 11. 20–21 (1989), 84–90. Rodríguez, "Paco Soler," *Brecha* 1.9 (1957), 2–4. Margarita Rojas et al., "Paco Soler," *Escena* 11.20–21 (1989), 80–81. Mario Sancho, "Paco Soler," *Brecha* 1.9 (1959), 10–11. Carlos Santander et al., "Paco Soler," *Escena* 11.20–21 (1989). Rogelio Sotela, "Francisco Soler," *Athenea* 3.15 (1920), 830–833. Jenaro Valverde, "Paco Soler. Apuntes de su vida y su obra," *Athenea* 3.15 (1920), 826–827.

TORNERO, León. Tornero, a Spanish priest, was author of a five-act tragedy with biblical themes entitled *Daniel* (1879). *Daniel* was staged in 1878 at the Colegio San Luis Gonzaga of Cartago.

WORK: *Daniel* (San José: Imp. Nacional, 1879).

ULLOA ZAMORA, María del Rosario. Ulloa Zamora is author of *Rayo de sol* (Ray of Light); *La carta de Dios* (The Letter from God), a dramatization of a short story; *El baúl de la abuela* (The Grandmother's Trunk); *Lo que es la Patria* (What is the Motherland); *El buscador de nidos* (The Searcher of Nests); *Entre las hadás* (Among the Fairies); *La nietecita* (The Little Niece); *Las dos rosas* (The Two Roses), a philosophical dialogue; *Una linda* *historia* (A Beautiful Story); *Princesas y pateres* (Princesses and Fathers); *Inocencia* (Innocence); *Galas de hermana* (The Sister's Regalia); *Golondrinas viajeras* (Traveling Swallows); *Homenaje de las provincias de Costa Rica a la bandera* (Homage to the Provences of Costa Rica to the Flag); *Los cantones de la provincia de San Jose* (The Cantons of San Jose Provence); *Viaje imaginario a Puntarenas* (Imaginary Journey to Puntarenas).

URBANO, Victoria. Urbano is author of *El fornicador* (The Fornicator). This play reopened the theater season of the Teatro Universitario in 1988, after a two-year closure.

UREÑA, Daniel (1876–1933). Ureña was a playwright, director, and actor for the Compañía Dramática, which he founded in 1903. Ureña directed his three-act drama *María del Rosario*, staged in 1906 at the Teatro Variedades by Compañía Dramática Nacional; the actor Emilio Thuiller played the role of the protagonist. His philosophical play *Los huérfanos* (The Orphans) was staged on June 6, 1909, at the Teatro Nacional. Other works by Ureña include: *Sombra y luz* (Shadow and Light), written in verse; the one-act plays *De la estación al hipódromo* (From the Station to the Hippodrome) (1903) and *San José alegre* (The Joyful San José), (1903); *El sueño de una noche* (The Dream of a Night) (n.d.), and *Muñequerías* (Overdressing) (n.d.).

WORKS: *María del Rosario* (San José: Imprenta Alsina, 1907); and in *Antología del teatro costarricense (1890–1950)*, ed. Alvaro Quesada et al. (San José: Editorial de la Universidad de Costa Rica, 1993). *Sombra y luz* (San José: 1907). *Los huérfanos* (San José: Imprenta Alsina, 1910).

BIBLIOGRAPHY: Lorenzo Celada, "*María del Rosario*," *Páginas Ilustradas* 6.173 (1909), 2876. "Daniel Ureña," *Arte y vida* 1.1 (1910), 3. Justo A. Facio, "*Sombra y luz*," *Páginas Ilustradas* 4.163 (1907), 2638. Virginia Sandoval de Fonseca, "Dramaturgia costarricense," *Revista Iberoamericana*, 53.138–139 (1987), 173–192.

VALDELOMAR MORA, Víctor (1957–   ). Born in Golfito, Valdelomar has been an avid promoter of the Compañía Nacional de Teatro and is considered to be one of the most outstanding playwrights of his generation. The play that has given Valdelomar fame is *Como semilla e'coyol*, a play that deals with the theme of violence and drugs. Other works by Valdelomar are *La parábola de la riqueza* (The Parable of the Riches) (1981) and *Macedonio el viejo* (The Old Macedonio) (1984).

WORKS: *La parábola de la riqueza*, in *Escena* 3.5 (1981), vi–viii. *Como semilla e'coyol*, in *Escena* 5.9 (1983), i–viii. *Macedonio el viejo*, in *Escena* 5.11 (1984), 12–14.

BIBLIOGRAPHY: Elenco de *Como semilla e'coyol*, "Apuntes sobre la experiencia dramatúrgica de *Como semilla e'coyol*," *Escena* 4.8 (1982), 4–5.

YGLESIAS (IGLESIAS), Antonio (1943–   ). Yglesias studied architecture in Italy and Germany. Upon his return to Costa Rica, Yglesias became director of Teatro Grupo and professor of film appreciation at the Universidad de Costa Rica. While living in Italy, Yglesias coauthored the play *Historia de una vida* (History of a Life), written as a group project. Back in Costa Rica he wrote *Las hormigas* (The Arts), staged in 1969 by the Teatro Grupo at the Universidad de Costa Rica. In *Las hormigas*, Yglesias proposes through humor and caricature the thesis that a revolution should come from the masses, and like ants, united, they should strive for the freedom that has been usurped from them by the oligarchy. In 1980 Yglesias wrote *El gran Tividavo* (The Great Tivadavo). He also authored *Pinocho rey* (The Pine-Cone King). In general, his plays deal with grotesque and satirical parodies that denounce power, politics, and ideological manipulation. Yglesias sees the theater as a means to express passion, anguish, and contradiction.

Gladys M. Varona-Lacey

Cuba

While the first indigenous dramatic compositions that we know of were called *areitos*, and they were mainly Indian chants with some acting, the first recorded plays presented in Cuba are mentioned in the Minutes of the City Council of May 18, 1570, in which the parties involved discuss the payment to a Juan Pérez de Vargas for a play to be presented in Havana. Soon *entremeses* and *comedias*, shorter comic plays, were also discussed. The proliferation of secular theater to the apparent neglect of religious theater prompted a law in 1681 that prohibited the presentation of secular plays in churches. Plays were staged not only in Havana but also in cities such as Santiago, Santa Clara, and Matanzas. In January 1765, *El maestro Alejandro de Zárate* (The Teacher Alejandro of Zárate) was presented. Ventura Pascual Ferrer, "El regañón" (The Scolder), was not only a playwright but also one of Cuba's first theater critics in the eighteenth century. In 1776 the first commercial theater, El Coliseo, was built. In 1800 a second theater, El Circo de Marte, was built, and in 1827, the Diorama playhouse was built.

In the first half of the eighteenth century an anonymous Cuban wrote *El príncipe jardinero y fingido Cloridano* (The Gardener Prince and the Pretend Cloridano). In the second half of this century the first theater of importance was built on the island, El Coliseo. Most of the plays presented, with the exception of *El príncipe*, were by peninsular playwrights. Cuban authors penned *entremeses* and *sainetes* presented after the first act and songs performed at the end of the second act. During the first years of the nineteenth century the plays most often presented were by Spaniards of translations from the French. When Foxá wrote *Don Pedro de Castilla* in 1836, he became the first Romantic playwright in America. (It was first staged in 1838.) Soon after this, Milanés staged his *Conde Alarcos*, which transcended Romanticism. Then Crespo y Borbón, Millán, and others wrote historical dramas and plays dealing with local customs. In this vein, though most of her plays were written and performed in Spain, G. Gómez de Avellaneda stands out. Joaquín Lorenzo Luaces, who published *Aristodemo* in 1867, is the next important playwright. After Cuba won its independence from Spain and became a republic, the names of Ramón S. Varona, José Antonio Ramos, Sánchez Galarraga, and others surface.

During the nineteenth century, authors such as Joaquín Lorenzo Luaces, Gertrudis Gómez de Avellaneda, José Jacinto Milanés, José María Heredia, and Agustin Millán stand out. The only nineteenth-century tradition that was kept alive during the first thirty years of the twentieth century was the incorporation of the buffoon or trickster, a technique found mainly at the Teatro Alhambra. Even though some authors such as Marcelo Salinas, Salvador Salazar, Ramón Sánchez Varona, and Luis Varal wrote many plays, it was Gustavo Sánchez Galarraga who dominated the stage with over thirty works in prose and verse. He was known as the Cuban Benavente. During these years, there were several composers who wrote the music and words to *zarzuelas* such as *Cecilia Valdés, La Habana que vuelve* (The Habana That Turns), *Amalia Batista, María la O* (María the O), and others.

José Antonio Ramos, creator of a social theater, was perhaps the best-known playwright of these four decades or the first forty years of the twentieth century. Ramos wrote about the oppression of women and men, the exploitation of the worker, and the corruption of local politicians. His best-known work is *Tembladera* (Earth Shaking) (1918). Unfortunately, other such talented playwrights have not followed him. In 1936 the founding of the theater La cueva, under the direction of Luis Baralt, marked the initiation of the modern theater in Cuba. Many theatrical groups proliferated between 1938 and 1950, as never before. Popular theater has always been a main staple among Cuban playwrights. Paco Alfonso was the main writer of *Teatro popular*. *Teatro popular* was created by the Partido Socialista Popular and the Confederación de Trabajadores de Cuba. Alfonso's theater was a theater of political satire. A new generation of playwrights such as Nora Badía, Eduardo Manet, Raúl González, Flora Díaz Parrado, and others appeared. Three playwrights who stand out since the 1940s are Virgilio Piñera, Carlos Felipe, and Rolando Ferrer. Virgilio Piñera is believed to have brought Cuban theater to the twentieth century with an adaptation of *Electra* to the Cuban stage. *Electra Garrigó* (1941) was the most successful play staged by a Cuban playwright up to that time. Virgilio Piñera embodies the Cuban spirit of not taking anything seriously; his theater has been referred to as theater of the Absurd. Carlos Felipe was born and raised in a poor Havana neighborhood, and his theater is full of low-life characters. One of his most famous early plays was *El chino* (The Chinese Man) (1947). In this play Felipe plays with past and present time and develops his characters. *El chino* is one of the most widely presented Cuban plays. Rolando Ferrer began writing and presenting plays in the early 1950s. *Laila la mariposa* (Lila, the Butterfly) (1954) is one of his best and better-known works. In this play, mythology and religion are mixed, and Federico García Lorca's influence is ever present. His main protagonists are three women: a black, a mulatto, and a white.

The 1950s is known as the period of the *salitas*, or small stages, because of the many *salitas* that were created. During this period, works of Cuban playwrights were not staged frequently. However, new playwrights such as Fermín Borges, Antona Rufat, and Virgilio Piñera began to appear. Other authors of these years who deserve to be mentioned are Matías Montes Huidobro and Gloria Parrado. The first ten years of the Cuban Revolution saw a flourishing of the theater in Cuba. In 1959 alone, forty-eight works by Cuban playwrights were staged—more than what was staged between 1952 and 1958. There are two main groups in this period: The Realist authors include Abelardo Estorino, Reguera Samuel, José Brene, and Quintero. The other group consists of authors who preferred experimental theater and includes such authors as José Triana, Antón Arrufat, and Andorr. Several important playwrights such as Matías Montes Huidobro, Borges, Raúl de Cárdenas, and Ferreira opted to leave the island and wrote their plays abroad. Carlos Felipe and Virgilio Piñera stand out between the first years of the Revolution. *Aire frío* (Cold Air) and *Dos viejos pánicos* (Two Old Panics) are Piñera's most successful plays of these years.

Antón Arrufat staged *El vivo al pollo* (True to the Chicken) in 1961, a grotesque farce that deals with abstract subjects such as the search for immortality. *Todos los domingos* (Every Sunday) and *Los siete contra Tebas* (Seven Against Thebes) are two important

Arrufat plays during these years. José Triana and Abelardo Estorino did not stage plays until 1959. Triana's 1966 play *La noche de los asesinos* (The Criminals) gained worldwide recognition. Estorino with his play *El robo del cochino* (The Stolen Pig) in 1961 became one of the most promising Cuban young dramatists. The play deals with the last few years of the Batista regime, and it presents the conflict between generations, the exploitation of women, and the machismo. Manuel Reguera Saumell staged *Recuerdo de Tulipa* (Remembrance of Tulipa) in 1962, which deals with a woman who struggles to present her nude body as an artistic event. In *La soga al cuello* (The Rope on the Neck) (1968), Reguera Saumell returns to his rural roots and his family problems. José R. Brene (1927–1991) in *Santa Camila de La Habana Vieja* (Saint Camila of the Old Habana) (1963) presents the Cuban Revolution for the first time. Another successful playwright is Héctor Quintero, who mixes humor with bitter satire in plays such as *Contigo pan y cebolla* (With You, Bread and Onion) (1964) and *El premio flaco* (The Thin Prize) in 1966.

As a playwright, Eugenio Hernández Espinoza (1937–   ) has given us the most authentic image of the black in Cuba. The black man's religion, beliefs, and emotions are present in his plays. In *Santa Camila de La Habana Vieja* he uses elements of Afro-Cuban culture in a poetic manner in which the isolation of this man is always present. *María Antonia* (1967) was seen by over 20,000 persons during its first eighteen presentations.

BIBLIOGRAPHY

Adellach, Alberto. *Cordelia de pueblo en pueblo: teatro*. Havana: Casa de las Américas, 1982.

Aguirre, Yolanda. *Apuntes en torno al teatro colonial en Cuba (1790–1833)*. Havana: Universidad de La Habana, Dirección de Publicaciones, 1969.

Alvárez-Borland, Isabel, and David George. "La noche de los asesinos: textos, Staging and Audience." *Latin American Theatre Review* 20.1 (1986): 37–48.

Arenal, Humberto. "El teatro cubano: crisis material o de valores?" *Gaceta de Cuba* (March 1990): 7–8.

Arróm, Juan José. *Historia de la literatura dramática cubana*. New Haven, CT: Yale University Press, 1944.

Artiles, Freddy. *Teatro y dramaturgia para los niños en la Revolución*. Editorial Letras Cubanas, 1970.

Azor, Ileana. "Hacia una nueva época en el teatro cubano." *Gestos: teoría y práctica del teatro hispanoamericano* 5.9 (April 1990): 135–139.

Barrios, Lygia A. "Teatro contemporáneo cubano en la primera mitad del siglo veinte piezas maestras." M.A. dissertation, Florida State University, 1967.

Bissell, Sally Joan. "Manuel Areu and the Nineteenth-Century Zarzuela in México and Cuba." *Dissertation Abstracts International* 49.4 (1988): 651.

Cao, Antonio F. *Elementos comunes en el teatro cubano del exilio: Marginalidad y patriarcado*. Ed. Pedro Monge Rafuls. New York: Ollantay, 1994.

Colechan, Francesca. "Matías Montes Huidobro: His Theater." *Latin American Theatre Review* 13.2 (1980): 77–80.

Correa, Armando. El teatro cubano de los 80: creación vs. africalidad. *Latin American Theatre Review* 25.2 (1992): 67–78.

Cowley y Albirle, Angel José. *Indice de las piezas dramáticas permitidas sin atajos ni correcciones, de las permitidas con ellos y de las absolutamente prohibidas: pre-*

sentado al gobernador superior civil de la isla por el censor principal de teatros de esta capital en cumplimiento de la disposición superior por la que se superior por la que se recomendó la formación de este registro. Havana: Imprenta del Gobierno y Capitania General, 1852.

"Cuba." *Escenarios de dos mundos: inventario teatral de Iberoamérica.* Vol. 2. Madrid: Centro de Documentación Teatral, 1988, 12–63. Articles by scholars.

Escarpenter, José A. "Veinticinco años de teatro cubano en el exilio." *Latin American Theatre Review* 19.2 (1986): 57–66.

Espinoza Domínguez, Carlos. "Festival de teatro de La Habana: Balance." *Latin American Theatre Review* 15.2 (1982): 65–72.

———. "Nueva dramaturgia Cubana: Tres entrevistas." *Latin American Theatre Review* 15.1 (1981): 59–68.

Franklin, Lillian Cleamons. "The Image of the Black in the Cuban Theatre." Ph.D. dissertation, Ohio State University, 1998.

Gibbs, Charles L. *Luis A. Baralt and the Cuban Theater.* Carbondale: Southern Illinois University, 1969.

González Freire, Natividad. *Teatro cubano del siglo XIX. Sel y Prol.* Havana: Arte y Literatura, 1963.

———. *Teatro cubano (1927–1961).* Havana: M. De Relaciones Exteriores, 1961.

Hernández García, Lissette. "Críticas sobre cine y teatro cubano: Arturo Arias Polo." *La palabra y el hombre* 75 (July–September 1990): 195–206.

Leal, Rine. "Asumir la totalidad del teatro cubano." *Ollantay Theater Magazine* 1.2 (July 1993): 26–39.

———. *Breve historia del teatro cubano.* Havana: Ed. Letras Cubanas, 1980.

———. *Un cuarto de siglo de dramaturgia.* Havana: Literatura Cubana, 1985.

———. *El teatro cubano actual.* Havana: Casa de las Américas, 1964.

———. *Teatro cubano en un acto.* Havana: Ed. R, 1963.

———. *Virgilio Piñera.* Havana: Institución del Libro, 1967.

Martí de Cid, Dolores. *Teatro cubano contemporáneo.* Madrid: Aguilar, 1959.

Martin, Randy. "Cuban Theater under Rectification: The Revolution after the Revolution." *The Drama Review* 34.1 (Spring 1990): 38–59.

———. *Realist Ensembles: Theater and State in Cuba and Nicaragua.* Minneapolis: University of Minnesota Press, 1994.

———. "Theater after the Revolution: Refiguring the political in Cuba and Nicaragua." In *On Edge: The Crisis of Contemporary Latin American Culture*, ed. George Yudice et al. Minneapolis: University of Minneapolis Press, 1992, 115–140.

Martín, Eleonor Jean. "*Dos viejos pánicos*: A Political Interpretation of the Cuban Theater of the Absurd." *Revista/Review Interamericana* 9 (1979): 50–56.

Meléndez, Priscilla. "El espacio dramático como signo: *La noche de los asesinos* de José Triana." *Latin American Theatre Review* 17.1 (1983): 25–36.

Monge Rafuls, Pedro R. "On Cuban Theater." Trans. Clydia A. Davenport. *Ollantay Theater Magazine* (Winter–Spring 1994): 101–113.

Montes Huidobro, Matías. *Persona, vida y máscara en el teatro cubano.* Miami: Ediciones Universal, 1973.

———. *Teatro bufo cubano.* Miami: Editorial Persona, 1987.

———. El teatro cubano en el vórtice del compromiso 1959–1961. Miami: Ediciones Universal, 2002.

———. "Teatro en *Lunes de Revolución*." *Latin American Theatre Review* 18.1 (1984): 17–34.

Muguercia, Magaly. "El grupo Prometeo: Algunos criterios para la valoración de su labor en la etapa 1954–1958. "*Universidad de La Habana* 227 (1986): 315–325.

———. *El teatro cubano en vísperas de la revolución.* Havana: Editorial Letras Cubanas, 1988.

Muñoz, Elias Miguel. "Teatro cubano de transición (1958–64), Piñera y Estorni." *Latin American Theatre Review* 19.2 (1986): 45–57.

Nigro, Kristen F. "*La noche de los asesinos*: Playscript and Stage Enactment." *Latin American Theatre Review* 11.1 (1977): 45–57.

Palls, Terry L. "El carácter del teatro cubano contemporáneo." *Latin American Theatre Review* 13.2 (1980): 51–58.

———. "El teatro de lo absurdo en Cuba." *Latin American Theatre Review* 11.2 (1978): 25–32.

———. "The Theater 1900–1985." *Dictionary of Twentieth Century Cuban Literature.* Westport, CT: Greenwood Press, 1990, 458–466.

Pianca, Maura. "El teatro cubano en la década de los ochetenta." *Latin American Theatre Review* 24.1 (1990): 121–134.

Pogolotti, Graciela. *Literatura y arte nuevo en Cuba.* Havana: Ed. Laia, 1977.

Rey Alfonso, Francisco. *Gran teatro de La Habana: cronología mínima, 1834/1987.* Havana: Talleres de impresión del Banco Nacional de Cuba, 1988.

Rizk, Beatriz J. "Taller Internacional de Nuevo Teatro (Cuba 1983)." *Latin American Theatre Review* 16.2 (1983): 73–80.

Rivero Muñíz, José. *Bibliografía del teatro cubano.* Havana: Biblioteca Nacional, 1957.

Robreño, Eduardo. *Historia del teatro popular cubano.* Havana: Oficina del Historiador de la ciudad de La Habana, 1961.

Rodríguez, Antonio Orlando. "Children's Theater: A Cuban Experience." *Theater* (1980): 26–29.

Scheneider, Larussa A. "*Ramona*: Quinta Essential Cuban Drama." *Latin American Theatre Review* 19.1 (1985): 27–32.

Trives, Toni. "Race, Gender, and Humanism in Cuba's Socialist Theater." *Dissertation Abstracts International* 51.7 (1991): 2349. University of California, Los Angeles.

Vitier, Cintio. *Eros en los infiernos* Havana: Editorial Unión, 1971.

Watson, Maida. "The Search of Identity in the Theater of Three Cuban American Female Dramatists." *Bilingual Review/La Revista Billingüe* 16.2–3 (May–Dec. 1991): 188–196.

Watson Espener, Maida. "Ethnicity and the Hispanic American Stage: The Cuban Experience." *Hispanic Theater in the United States* (Houston: Arte Público Press, 1984): 34–44.

Wess, Judith A. "Cuba's Teatro Nuevo: First National Festival." *Latin American Theatre Review* (1979): 87–92.

Woodyard, George, et al. *The Cambridge Guide to African and Caribbean Theater.* New York: Cambridge University Press, 1994.

Woodyard, George W. "Perspectives on Cuban Theater." *Revista/Review Interamericana* 9 (1979): 42–49.

◆

ARRUFAT, Antón (1935–   ). He was born in Santiago de Cuba. He is a playwright, journalist, poet, and short story writer. He fled to the United States during the Batista regime in 1957 but returned to his country after the Castro revolution. There he has contributed to journals such as *Lunes de revolución*, *Revista Casa de las Américas*, and *Gaceta de Cuba*. His tendency to write experimental theater has put him at odds with a revolutionary regime that became increasingly intolerant of writers who did not promote revolutionary values. He was criticized for his play *Los siete contra Tebas* (Seven Against Thebes) for its alleged antirevolutionary ideas. The Jury first awarded the play the UNEAC theater prize and agreed to publish it, then rejected its ideology and banned its presentation in Cuba. His themes deal with death and man's inability to communicate.

WORKS: *El caso se investiga* (The Case Is Under Investigation) (1957). *El último tren* (The Last Train) (1957). *La zona cero* (Zero Zone) (1959). *La repetición* (The Repetition) (1963). *Teatro: El caso se investiga, El vivo al pollo, El último tren, La repetición, La zona cero* (Theater: The Case Is Under Investigation, Have Fun If You Are Alive) (Havana: Ed. Nacional de Cuba, 1963). *Todos los domingos* (Every Sunday) (1965) (Havana: Ed. Revolución 1965). *Los siete contra Tebas* (Seven Against Thebes) (1968). *La caja está cerrada* (The Box Is Closed) (Havana: Letras Cubanas, 1984).

BIBLIOGRAPHY: Frank N. Dauster, "The Theater of Antón Arrrufat," in *Dramatists in Revolt*, ed. G. Woodyard and L. F. Lyday (Austin: University of Texas Press, 1976), 3–18. David W. Foster, "Antón Arrufat," in *Cuban Literature: A Research Guide* (New York: Garland, 1985), 95–98. Manuel Galich, "Arrufat en el teatro experimental," *La Gaceta de Cuba* 29 (1963): 15. Rine Leál, *Teatro cubano en un acto* (Havana: Ed. Revolucíon. 1963), 56. *En primera persona* (Havana: Instituto del libro, 1967), 177–80. Dolores Martí de Cid and María A. Wellington," Antón Arrufat," in *Dictionary of Twentieth Century Cuban Literature*, ed. Julio A. Martínez (Westport, CT: Greenwood Press, 1990), 34–38. Matías Montes Huidobro, *Persona, vida y máscara en el teatro cubano* (Miami: Ed. Universal, 1973), 378–88. Rodney Karl Reading, "The Renewal of Traditional Myth and Form in the Works of Antón Arrufat," *Revista/Review Interamericana* 10 (1980): 357–77. José Triana, "Apuntes sobre un libro de Arrufat," *La Gaceta de Cuba* 18 (1963): 12–13.

BARALT, Luis A. (1892–1969). He was born in New York and probably died in the United States. He was a playwright, teacher, and translator. He studied literature and law at the University of Havana, where he taught history, philosophy, and aesthetics from 1914 until 1960, when he defected to the United States, where he continued teaching. He served as secretary of education in 1934 and became president of the National Authors Guild in his native country. He was cofounder of the Teatro de Arte de la Cueva in 1936. His plays are philosophical and deal with Indo-Cuban themes.

WORKS: *Taowami* (1920). *La luna en el pantano* (The Moon on the Marsh) (Havana: UCAR, 1936). *Meditación de tres por cuatro* (Three by Four Meditation) (1950). *Tragedia indiana* (Indian Tragedy), in *Teatro cubano contemporaneo* (Madrid: Aguilar, 1959). *Junto al río* (Next to the River) (n.d.).

BIBLIOGRAPHY: José J. Arrom, *Historia de la literatura dramática cubana* (New Haven: Yale University Press, 1944), 84–85. Frank N. Dauster, *Historia del teatro hispanoamericano (Siglos XIX y XX)* (Mexico City: De Andrea, 1966), 66. Natividad González Freire, *Teatro cubano contemporáneo (1928–1957)* (Havana: Sociedad Colombista Panamericana, 1958), 63–67. *Teatro cubano (1927–1961)* (Havana: Ministerio de Relaciones Exteriores, 1961), 43. Charles L. Gibbs, *Luis A. Baralt and the Cuban Theater* (Carbondale: Southern Illinois University, 1969). Francisco Ichaso, "*Junto al río* de Luis A. Baralt," in *Escenario y pantalla*, *Diario de la Marina* (March 19, 1938), 6. Willis Knapp Jones, *Breve historia del teatro latinoamericano* (Mexico City: Ediciones de Andrea, 1956), 157. Dolores Martí de Cid, "Luis A. Baralt," in *Teatro cubano contemporáneo* (Madrid: Aguilar, 1959), 43–48. Esther Sánchez-Grey-Alba, "El sentido poético de *La luna en el río* de Luis A. Baralt," *Círculo: Revista de cultura* 4 (1985): 61–67.

BRENE, José R. (1927–1991). He was born in Cárdenas, province of Matanzas, Cuba. He was a playwright and a sailor who studied theater arts at the Seminario de Dramaturgia del Teatro Nacional in Havana at the Institute of Matanzas and in the United States and Mexico. In 1949, José Brene returned to Cuba, where he wrote four novels. He became a prolific playwright. Critics see two different stages in Brene's theater: before and after the Castro revolution. His first plays criticize official corruption and other social ills such as the lack of morals. After the triumph of the 1959 revolution his plays have a definite social-realist orientation. His plays explore the themes of machismo and political corruption in his native country as well as in all of Latin America. His plays caricaturize inept *caudillos*, the Catholic Church, and North American economic imperialism. Brene's greatest asset, according to some critics, is his ability to write effective dialogues. Others say that his theater is maniqueist, that his characters are completely good or bad, according to the sociopolitical message he wishes to convey.

WORKS: *Santa Camila de La Habana vieja* (Saint Camila of the Old Havana) (1962). *Pasado a la Criolla* (Creole Past) (1963). *El gallo de San Ysidro* (The Rooster of San Ysidro) (1964). *El ingenioso criollo don Matias Pérez* (The Ingenuous Creole don Matias Pérez) (1965). *La fiebre negra* (The Black Fever) (1965). *Los demonios de Remedios* (Remedios's Devils) (1965). *El bohío de Mamá Yaya* (Mama Yaya's Hut) (n.d.). *Teatro de José R. Brene* (Havana: Ed. Unión, 1965). *Fray Sabino* (1970). *El camarada don Quijote, el de Guanabacuta arriba, y su fiel compañero, Sancho Panza, el de Guanabacuta abajo* (Comrade Don Quijote, the One from Upper Guanabacuta, and His Loyal Companion, Sancho Panza, the One from Lower Guanabacuta) (1970). *Miss Condonga* (1982). *José R. Brene, Teatro* (Havana: Letras cubanas, 1982).

BIBLIOGRAPHY: "José R. Brene," in *Dictionary of Twentieth Century Cuban Literature*, ed. Julio A. Martínez (Westport, CT: Greenwood Press, 1990), 80–84. Instituto de Literatura y Lingüística, Academia de Ciencias de Cuba (Havana: Editorial Letras Cubanas, 1980), 156. David Camps, "Teatro de José R. Brene," *Unión* 4.4 (October/December 1965), 173–75. Matías Montes Huidobro, *Persona, vida y máscara en el teatro cubano* (Miami: Ed. Universal, 1973), 303–36. Terry L. Palls, "El arte y la realidad: El teatro de José Brene y la realidad socio-política cubana," *National Symposium on Hispanic Theatre* (Iowa: University of Northern Iowa, 1965), 183–90.

COVARRUBIAS, Francisco (circa 1780–1850). He was born and died in Havana and was an accomplished actor and playwright. He is credited with Cubanizing the traditional Spanish *pasos, sainetes*, and *entremeses*, all Spanish one-act plays. He exchanged the traditional Spanish colloquial speech and characters for typical Cuban types. Covarrubias is credited with the foundation of the Teatro Na-

cional in Havana and another one in Matanzas. For many, he is the father of Cuban theater. Although all we have left of his copious production of short one-act plays are fragments, the titles and other pertinent information available point to an energetic, creative individual who made a significant contribution to the development of Cuban theater in the first decades of the nineteenth century.

WORKS: *Las tertulias de La Habana* (Conversations in Havana) (1914). *La feria de Carraguao* (The Carraguao Fair) (1815). *Este sí que es chasco* (This Is Really a Disappointment) (1816). *Los velorios de La Habana* (Havana's Wakes) (1818). *El tío Bartolo y la tía Catana* (Uncle Bartolo and Aunt Catana) (1820). *El montero en el teatro* (The Mountaineer in the Theater) (1829). *El peón de tierra adentro* (The Inland Laborer) (n.d.). *La valla de gallos* (The Cockpit) (n.d.) *El rastro por la mañana* (The Slaughter House in the Morning) (n.d.).

BIBLIOGRAPHY: José J. Arróm, *Historia de la literatura dramática cubana* (New Haven: Yale University Press, 1944), 35–37. José Agustín Millán, *Biografía de don Francisco Covarrubias* (Havana: n.p., 1851). Matías Montes Huidobro, "Historia del imposible," in *Persona, vida y máscara del teatro cubano* (Miami: Ed. Universal, 1973), 209–10.

ESTORINO, Abelardo (1925–). He was born in Unión de Reyes, a small town in Matanzas. Though he graduated and practiced dentistry for several years, he has gained acclaim as a playwright and theater critic. He began his theatrical career when he became part of Teatro Universitario, assisted the playwright Julio Matas, and studied directing at Teatro Estudio. His final change into a playwright came after the Revolution of 1959. His plays *El robo del cochino* (The Stolen Pig) and *La casa vieja* (The Old House) won praise from the prestigious Casa de las Américas. He is one of a handful of playwrights to achieve recognition in postrevolutionary Cuba. His plays deal with the problems of machismo, sex, magic, and the fraticidal struggles before and after the Castro revolution. His most popular and accomplished play is *Morir del cuento* (To Die by Cheating).

WORKS: *El robo del cochino* (The Theft of the Pig) (1961). *La casa vieja* (The Old House) (Havana:

Casa de Las Américas, 1964). *La dolorosa historia del amor secreto de Don José Jacinto Milanés* (The Painful Story of the Secret Love of Mr. José Jacinto Milanés) (1974). *Ni un sí ni un no* (Neither a Yes or a No) (1979). *Morir del cuento* (To Die by Cheating) (1984). *Que el diablo te acompañe* (May the Devil Go with You) (1987). *El peine y el espejo* (The Comb and the Mirror) (n.d.) *Hay un muerto en la calle* (There Is a Dead Body in the Street) (n.d.). *Los mangos de Caín* (The Mangoes of Cain) (n.d.).

BIBLIOGRAPHY: Wilfredo Cancio Isla, "Abelardo Estorino en la maestría de sus textos," *Conjunto* 64 (April–June 1985), 163–66. Frank N. Dauster, *Historia del teatro hispanoamericano (Siglos XIX y XX)* (Mexico City: De Andrea, 1966), 128–29. "Diálogo con Estorino," *Bohemia* 56.44 (October 30, 1964), 23. Rine Leal, *En primera persona (1954–1966)* (reviews published in the Cuban press) (Havana: Instituto del Libro, 1967). Vivian Martínez Tabares, "Aproximación a un texto teatral," *Tablas* 1.84 (January–March 1984), 28–34. Matías Montes Huidobro, *Persona, vida y máscara en el teatro cubano* (Miami: Ed. Universal, 1973), 261–83, 387–400. Magaly Muguercia, (On *Morir del cuento*), *Revolución y Cultura* 8 (August 1984), 2–9. Lorraine Elena Roses, "Abelardo Estorino," in *Dictionary of Twentieth-Century Cuban Literature*, ed. Julio A. Martínez (Westport, CT: Greenwood Press, 1990), 158–160.

FELIPE, Carlos (1911–1975). He was born in Havana, Cuba and was a playwright, singer, and actor. He graduated from the Catholic Escuelas Pías (Pious Schools) as a mercantile specialist. Felipe became initiated in the theater with a group called Agrupación Artística Gallega (Galician Artistic Group). One of his better-known and most accomplished works is *El chino* (The Chinese Man). According to some critics, this play embodies the essence of the *teatro bufo cubano*: a combination of sex, humor, and social commentary.

WORKS: *Esta noche en el bosque* (Tonight in the Forest) (1939). *Tambores* (Drums) (1943). *El chino* (The Chinese Man) (1947). *Capricho en rojo* (Caprice in Red) (1948). *Ladrillos de plata* (Silver Bricks) (1956). *Réquiem por Yarini* (Requiem for Yarini) (1960).

BIBLIOGRAPHY: Armando Correa, "Carlos Felipe: En encuentro con la imagen," *Tablas* 1 (January–March 1984), 26–27. José A. Escarpanter and Linda S. Glaze, "Carlos Felipe," in *Dictionary of Twentieth-Century Cuban Literature*, ed. Julio A. Martínez (Westport, CT: Greenwood Press, 1990), 166–70. José A. Escarpanter, "El teatro de Carlos Felipe," *Revista Nacional de Teatro* 1.1 (1961), 26–27. "*Requiem por Yarini* de Carlos Felipe: Una tragedia cubana," in *Festschrift Jose Cid Pérez*, ed. Alberto Gutierrez de la Solana and Elio Alba-Buffil (New York: Senda Nueva de Ediciones, 1981), 103–9. Francisco Garzón Céspedes, "Prologo" in *Teatro*, ed. Carlos Felipe (Havana: Letras Cubanas, 1967), 5–19. Rine Leal, "Un Carlos llamado Felipe" in *Primera persona (1954–1966)* (La Habana Instituto del Libro, 1967), 189–201. Eduardo Manet, "Actitud y obra de Carlos Felipe," *Estudios* 5 (August 1950), 46–47. Dolores Martí and Jose Cid Perez, eds. "Carlos Felipe," in *Teatro cubano contemporaneo* (Madrid: Aguilar, 1958), 157–63. Julio Matas, "Pirandello, Proust and *El chino* by Carlos Felipe," *Hispanic Journal* 5.1 (1983), 43–47. Matías Montes Huidobro, *Persona, vida y máscara en el teatro cubano* (Miami: Ed. Universal, 1973), 113–39, 284–302. Cintio Vitier, "Eros en el infierno," *Revista de la Biblioteca Nacional José Marti* 59.10.2 (1968), 169–75.

FERRER, Rolando (1925–1976). He was born in Santiago de Cuba and died in Havana. He was a playwright, scriptwriter, and director. He studied law and medicine before experimenting with the theater in 1946, when he joined the Grupo Escénico Libre. Ferrer won worldwide recognition with *Lila la mariposa* (Lila the Butterfly) in 1954. In 1960 he won a scholarship to study theater in Paris. After *El que mató al responsable* (The One Who Killed the Responsible Man), his theater became politicized.

WORKS: *Cita en el espejo* (A Date with the Mirror) (1949). *La hija de Nacho* (Nacho's Daughter) (1951). *Lila la mariposa* (Lila, the Butterfly) (1954). *La taza de café* (The Cup of Coffee) (1959). *Los próceres* (The Leaders) (1959). *Función homenaje* (Homage Performance) (1960). *El corte* (The Cut) (1961). *Fiquito, un nombre para un caballito* (Fiquito, a Name for a Colt) (1961). *El que mató al responsable* (The One Who Killed the Responsible Man) (1962). *Teatro* (Havana: Ed. Unión, 1963). *Las de enfrente* (The Girls Across the Street) (1964). *Cosas de Platero* (Platero's Things) (1965). *Teatro* (Havana: Letras Cubanas, 1983). *Busca buscando* (Search by Searching) (n.d.).

BIBLIOGRAPHY: Eberto García Abreu, "Una tragedia en tono doméstico," in *Teatro Cubano Contemporáneo: Antología* (Mexico City: FCE, 1992), 285–291. Matías Montes Huidobro, *Persona, vida y máscara en el teatro cubano* (Miami: Ed. Universal, 1973), 203–211.

GOMÉZ DE AVELLANEDA, Gertrudis

(1814–1873). She was born in Puerto Príncipe, Camagüey, Cuba, and died in Spain. She was a playwright, a novelist, and a poet. She began writing at an early age, and when she was twenty-two, she traveled to Spain, where she gained fame as a playwright. After having established herself as a playwright in Spain, she returned to Cuba in 1859 but left again for Spain five years later. She seems to have preferred Spain, perhaps due to the relative freedom she found there as a writer. Her first known play, *Leoncia*, was not allowed to be presented in Cuba but won critical acclaim when it was staged in Seville in 1840. Perhaps her most successful play was *La hija de las flores* (The Daughter of the Flowers), which played for over two months. Gómez de Avellaneda's most accomplished play, however, is *Baltasar* (1858). Her plays deal with historical themes and with the traditional relationships between men and women.

WORKS: *Leoncia* (1840). *El príncipe de Viana* (The Prince of Viana) (1844). *Munio Alfonso* (1844). *Egilona* (1845). *Saúl* (1846). *Flavio Recaredo* (1851). *La verdad vence apariencias* (Truth Overcomes Appearances) (1852). *Errores del corazón* (Mistakes of the Heart) (1852) *El donativo del diablo* (The Devil's Donation) (1852). *Tres amores* (Three Loves) (1858) *Baltasar* (1858). *La hija de las flores o Todos están locos* (The Daughter of the Flowers or Everyone Is Crazy), staged at Teatro del Príncipe in Madrid in 1852. *La aventurera* (The Adventurer) (1853). *La hija del rey René* (King René's Daughter) (1855). *Simpatía y antipatía* (1855). *Los oráculos de Talía o Los duendes en Palacio* (Talia's oracles or The Gremlins in the Palace) (1855). *El millonario y la maleta* (The Millionaire and the Suitcase) (1870).

BIBLIOGRAPHY: José J. Arrom, *Historia de la literatura dramática cubana* (New Haven: Yale University Press, 1944), 54–58. J. A. Escoto, *Gertrudis Gómez de Avellaneda* (Matanzas: n.p., 1911). E. B. Williams, *The Life and Dramatic Works of Gertrudis Gómez de Avellaneda* (Philadelphia: n.p., 1924).

HEREDIA Y HEREDIA, José María (1803–

1839). He was born in Santiago, Cuba, and probably died in his native country. He was a poet, playwright, translator, and publisher. He founded and directed two of the first literary journals in Spanish America dedicated almost exclusively to literary criticism but was exiled because of his independentist ideas. After a few months in 1824 in the United States, he moved to Mexico, where he wrote and translated plays from the English and French. He was allowed to return to Cuba in 1836 but left again three months later in 1837.

WORKS: *Eduardo IV o El usurpador clemente* (Edward IV or The Clement Usurper), staged in Matanzas in 1819. *Los últimos romanos* (The Last Romans) (1829). *Aristodemo* (n.d.). *Guillermo Tell* (William Tell) (n.d.). *Moctezuma o Los mexicanos* (Moctezuma or The Mexicans) (n.d.). *El campesino espantado* (The Scared Farmer) (n.d.).

BIBLIOGRAPHY: F. González del Valle, *Cronología herediana* (Havana: n.p., 1938). P. J. Guiteras, "Don José María Heredia," *Revista de Cuba* 9 (1881).

HERNÁNDEZ ESPINOZA, Eugenio

(1937–). He was born in Havana. He is a playwright, director, and literary consultant. His first play, *María Antonia*, won wide acclaim in 1967, and ten years later, he won the prestigious Casa de las Américas Theater Award with *La Simona* (The Simona Woman). Two of his plays, *Patakín* and *María Antonia*, have been filmed.

WORKS: *María Antonia* (1967) (Havana: Letras cubanas, 1979). *La Simona* (Havana: Casa de las Américas, 1977). *Calixta comité* (Calixta Committee) (1980). *Oba y Shangó* (1983), *Odebí, el cazador* (Odebí, the Hunter) (1984). *Mi socio Manolo* (My Partner Manolo) (1988). *Emelina Cundiamor* (1989).

BIBLIOGRAPHY: Inés María Martiatu, "Una Carmen caribeña," in *Teatro cubano contemporáneo: Antología* (Mexico City: FCE, 1992), 935–41.

LUACES, Joaquín Lorenzo (1821–1867). He

was born and died in Havana. He was a playwright and a poet. Although he wrote many plays, according to José Juan Arrom, only two were published, but we have a handful of the manuscripts of the others. *Aristodemo* is often cited as the playwright's attempt to protest the Spanish tyrannical colonial regime by pretending to adhere to the plot lines of a classical play.

WORKS: *El mendigo rojo* (The Red Beggar) (1859). *Aristodemo* (1867). *Teatro* (Havana: Ed. del Consejo Nacional de Cultura, 1964). *El becerro de oro* (The Golden Calf) (Havana, 1967). Plays in manuscript form from Osberg's book: *El conde y el capitán* (The Count and the Captain), *El fantasmón de Aravaca* (The Big Ghost from Aravaca), *La escuela de los parientes* (School for Relatives), *Dos amigas* (Two Lady Friends), *A tigre y zorra bull-dog* (To a Tiger and Foxy Bull-Dog).

BIBLIOGRAPHY: José J. Arróm, *Historia de la literatura dramática cubana* (New Haven: Yale University Press, 1944), 58–60. Arturo de Osberg, *Joaquín Lorenzo Luaces* (Havana: Ed. Letras Cubanas, 1983). E. Piñeyro, "Una tragedia griega por un poeta cubano," in *Estudios y conferencias de historia y literatura* (New York: n.p., 1880), 233–246.

MARTÍN, Manuel, Jr. (1934–   ). He was born in Artemisa and defected to the United States in 1956. He is a playwright, director, actor, and teacher. He studied theater arts at Hunter College and the American Academy of Dramatic Arts in New York and also in Europe. In New York, together with Magaly Alabau, he founded the Duo Theater in 1969, where he served as director for twenty years. The themes of his early plays deal mainly with the painful realization that an exile lives in a world that is alien to his culture and upbringing. He has also attempted to find common ground between his original and adopted countries as in *Rita and Bessie*, a play dealing with two pillars of popular Cuban and American music: Rita Montaner and Bessie Smith.

WORKS: *Francesco: The Life and Time of the Cenci* (1973). *Rasputin* (1976). *Carmencita* (1978). *Swallows* (1980). *Sangivin en Union City* (Union City Thanksgiving) (1983). *Fight!* (1986). *The Legend of the Golden Coffee Bean* (1987). *Lección de historia en Sorocabana* (History Lesson in Sorocabana) (1987). *Rita and Bessie* (1988). *Platero y yo* (Platero and I) (1989).

BIBLIOGRAPHY: Juan Carlos Martínez, "Volver del revés las apariencias," in *Teatro cubano contemporáneo: Antología* (Mexico City: FCE, 1992), 783–788.

MONTES HUIDOBRO, Matías (1931–   ). He was born in Sagua la Grande. He is a playwright, teacher, journalist, and television commentator. He published the periodical *Nueva Generación* with other intellectuals. He was a member of the cultural society Nuestro Tiempo (1951). He studied pedagogy at the Universidad de La Habana and taught school for several years in his native country before defecting to the United States. He was a commentator for CMBF television and professor at the National School of Journalism in 1960. He emigrated to the United States in 1961, and he became the founder of the periodical *Caribe* (1976–1977). At present, he teaches at the University of Hawaii.

WORKS: *Los acosados* (The Accused Ones) (1960). *La botija* (The Earthen Jug) (1960). *Las vacas* (The Cows) (1960). *El tiro por la culata* (Backfire) (1960). *Gas en los poros* (Gas in the Pores) (1961). *La sal de los muertos* (The Dead Men's Salt) (1971). *Ojos para no ver* (Eyes That Do Not See) (1979). *Su cara mitad* (His Better Half) (1992).

BIBLIOGRAPHY: Francesca Colecchia, "Matías Montes Huidobro: His Theatre," *Latin American Theatre Review* 13.2 (1980): 77–80. José A. Escarpanter, Veinticinco años de teatro cubano en el exilio," *LATR* 19.2 (1986): 57–66. José A. Escarpenter and Linda S. Glaze," Matías Montes Huidobro," in *Dictionary of Twentieth-Century Cuban Literature*, ed. Julio A. Martínez (Westport, CT: Greenwood Press, 1990), 309–314. Jorge Febles, "La desfiguración enajenante en *Ojos para no ver*," *Crítica Hispánica* 4.2 (1982): 127–36. Luis González Cruz, "Matías Montes Huidobro, the Poet: Selected Poems and an Interview," *Latin American Theatre Review* 2.1 (1974): 163–70. Mireya Jaimes Freyre, "Review of *Desterrados al fuego*," *Latin American Literary Review* 4.9 (1976): 96–98. Rine Leal, *Teatro cubano en un acto* (Havana: Ed. Revolución, 1963), 217–20. Julio Matas, Prólogo to Matías Montes Huidobro's *Persona, vida y máscara en el teatro cubano* (Miami: Ed. Universal, 1973), 9–18. Gemma Roberts, "Review of *Desterrados del fuego*," *Revista Iberoamericana* 42.96–97 (1976): 642–44. Orlando Rodríguez-Sardinas and Carlos Miguel Suárez Radillo, *Teatro selecto contemporáneo hispanoamericano*, vol. 3 (Madrid: Escelicer, 1971), 117–24.

William Siemens, "Parallel Transformations in *Desterrados al fuego*," *Términos* 2.6 (1984): 17–18.

PIÑERA LIERA, Virgilio (1912–1979). He was born in Cárdenas, a city of Matanzas, Cuba, and died in his native country. He was a playwright, novelist, short story writer, and journalist. Although he suffered the scorn and persecution of Castro's revolution due to his sexual preferences, he wrote for and directed the daily *Revolución*. His plays, for the most part, are associated with existentialism and the theater of the Absurd. Since the time he wrote his dissertation in 1941, which he refused to give his teachers to read, Piñera Liera became known as a brilliant, marginated author. During the 1940s he wrote plays such as *Electra Garrigó, Jesús*, and *Falsa alarma*. Piñera's theater explores the fears and absurdity of man's existence. His play *Dos viejos pánicos* (Two Old Panics) received the prestigious annual award of Casa de las Américas in 1968. *Una caja de zapatos vacía* (An Empty Shoebox), spirited out of Cuba and published in Miami, deals with oppression, and it is difficult to establish a link to life in Cuba as an outsider. Piñera is recognized as one of Cuba's best playwrights, and his works are represented throughout the Spanish-speaking world.

WORKS: *Electra Garrigó* (1943). *Jesús* (1948). *Falsa alarma* (False Alarm) (1948). *Aire frío* (Cold Air) (Havana: Ed. Pagran, 1959). *Teatro completo* (Havana: Ed. Erre, 1960). *Dos viejos pánicos* (Two Old Panics) (Havana: Casa de las Américas, 1968). *Estudio en blanco y negro* (Study in Black and White), in *Teatro breve hispanoamericano contemporáneo* (Madrid: Aguilar, 1970). *Una caja de zapatos vacía* (An Empty Shoebox) (Miami: Ed. Universal, 1986). *La boda* (The Wedding) (n.d.). *El flaco y el gordo* (The Skinny One and the Fat One) (n.d.).

BIBLIOGRAPHY: Reinaldo Arenas, "La isla en peso con todas sus cucarachas," *Mariel* 2 (1983): 20–24. José Bianco, Prólogo, "Piñera, narrador," in *El que vino a salvarme* (Buenos Aires: Sudamericana, 1970), 7–19. Guillermo Cabrera Infante, "Vidas para leerlas," *Vuelta* 41 (April 1980): 4–16. Calvert Casey, "Una segunda mirada de *Aire frío*," *Gaceta de Cuba* 16 (1963): 14. "*Dos viejos pánicos* en Colombia," *Conjunto* 7 (n.d.): 60–71. José A. Escarpenter, "Review of *Una caja de zapatos vacía*," *Linden Lane Magazine* 5.4 (October–December 1986): 30. Roberto Fernández Retamar, "Virgilio Piñera," in *La poesía contemporánea en Cuba* (1927–1953). *Orígenes*, 1954. 99–101. Ambrosio Fornet, "Anatomía de una cucaracha (Pequeñas maniobras)," in *En tres y dos* (Havana: Ed. Revolución, 1964), 73–78. David William Foster, "A Bibliography," in *Cuban Literature: A Research Guide* (New York: Garland, 1985), 426–27. Read G. Gilden, "Virgilio Piñera and the Short Story of the Absurd," *Hispania* 63 (1980): 348–55. Luis F. González-Cruz, "Virgilio Piñera, in *Dictionary of Twentieth-Century Cuban Literature*, ed. Julio A. Martínez (Westport, CT: Greenwood Press, 1990), 361–68; "Virgilio Piñera y el teatro del absurdo en Cuba," *Mester* 5.1 (November 1974): 52–58; "Arte y situación de Virgilio Piñera," *Caribe* 2.2 (Fall 1977): 77–86; "Trayectoria intelectual de Virgilio Piñera," prologue to Virgilio Piñera's *Una caja de zapatos vacía*, Critical ed. (Miami: Ed. Universal, 1986). Rine Leal, "Dos farsas cubanas del absurdo," *Ciclón* 3.2 (1957): 65–67 (Virgilio Piñera, *Falsa alarma*, and Antón Arrufat, *El caso se investiga*); "Virgilio Piñera o el teatro como ejercicio mental," *Gaceta de Cuba* 34 (1964): 2–3. Rogelio Llopis, "Pequeñas maniobras," *Casa de las Américas* 24 (1964): 106–7. César López, "El aire en el remolino (*Aire frío*)," *Gaceta de Cuba* 58 (1967): 11, 15; "Chiclets, canasta, presiones y diamantes," *Unión* 6.3 (1967): 131–34. Tomás López Ramírez, "Virgilio Piñera y el compromiso del absurdo," *Areíto* 9.34 (1983): 38–40. Ainslee McLees-Armstrong, "Elements of Sartrian Philosophy in *Electra Garrigó*," *Latin American Theatre Review* 7.1 (1973): 5–11. Eleanor Jean Martin, "*Dos viejos pánicos*: A Political Interpretation of the Cuban Theater of the Absurd," *Revista Interamericana* 9 (1979): 50–56. Julio Matas, "Infiernos fríos de Virgilio Piñera," *Linden Lane Magazine* 4.2 (April–June 1985): 22–25. Ernesto Méndez y Soto, "Piñera y el tema del absurdo," *Cuadernos Hispanoamericanos* 299 (1975): 448–53. Matías Montes Huidobro, *Persona, vida y máscara en el teatro cubano* (Miami: Ed. Universal, 1973), 140–88; "Virgilio Piñera: Un proceso de anulación verbal," in *Texto y contexto en la literatura Iberoamericana*, Memorias del XIX Congreso del Instituto Internacional de Literatura Iberoamericana (1980), 265–74.

RAMOS, José Antonio (1885–1946). He was born and died in Havana. He was a playwright, novelist, diplomat, and journalist who became one of the most famous writers of his time. He was instrumental in the creation of the Society of Cuban Authors and served as his country's consul in Madrid and Philadelphia. He studied in Paris and lived in Mexico City during the dictatorship of Machado in the 1930s. His themes blend social and political criticism with individual concerns. According to critics, Ramos quickly overcame an early tendency to allow his ideological concerns to interfere with his plays and became one of the main figures in the development of Cuban theater. His play *Tembladera* (Earth Shaking), is often cited as his finest and one of the pillars of Cuban theater in our century.

WORKS: *Almas rebeldes* (Rebel Souls) (1906). *Una balada perdida* (A Lost Ballad) (1907). *La hidra* (The Hydra) (1908). *Nanda* (1908). *A La Habana me voy* (I'm Leaving to Havana) (1909). *Liberta* (1911). *Satanás* (Satan) (1913). *Calibán Rex* (1914). *El hombre fuerte* (The Strong Man) (1915). *El traidor* (The Traitor) (1915). *Tembladera* (Earth Shaking) (1918). *Coabay* (1929). *En las manos de Dios* (On God's Hands) (1933). *La leyenda de las estrellas* (The Legend of the Stars) (1934). *La recurva* (The Curve) (1941). *FU-3001* (1944).

BIBLIOGRAPHY: Imeldo Alvarez García, "Prólogo," in *Coaybay* (Havana: Arte y Literatura, 1975), 9–25. José J. Arrom, "El teatro de José Antonio Ramos," *Revista Iberoamericana* 24 (June 30, 1947): 263–71. Salvador Bueno, "José Antonio Ramos, frustración y rebeldía," *Universidad de La Habana* 70–72 (January–June 1947): 220–22. David William Foster, *Handbook of Latin American Literature* (New York: Garland, 1987), 223–24, 226. Natividad González Freire, *Teatro cubano contemporáneo* (1927–1961) (Havana: Ministerio de Relaciones Exteriores, 1961), 113–15. Max Henríquez Ureña, "Evocación de José Antonio Ramos," *Revista Iberoamericana* 12 (June 1947): 251–61; *Panorama histórico de la literatura cubana* (Mexico City: Las Américas, 1963), 338–39, 347–49. Matías Montes Huidobro, *Persona, vida y máscara en el teatro cubano* (Miami: Ed. Universal, 1973), 80–99; "Técnica dramática de José Antonio Ramos," *Journal of Inter-American Studies and World Affairs* 12.2 (April 1970): 229–41; "José Antonio Ramos," in *Dictionary of Twentieth-Century Cuban Literature*, ed. Julio A Martínez (Westport, CT: Greenwood Press, 1990), 395–401. José A. Portuondo, "El contenido político y social de las obras de José Antonio Ramos," *Revista de la Biblioteca Nacional José Martí* 60.1 (January–April 1969): 5–58; "El prag-

matismo y las impurezas de la realidad," in José Antonio Ramos's *Coaybay* (Havana: Arte y Literatura, 1975), 361–85. Esther Sánchez-Grey Alba, *Tres obras dramáticas de José Antonio Ramos* (New York: Senda Nueva de Ediciones, 1983), 9–28, 39–43, 99–106, 125–31.

TRIANA, José (1931–   ). He was born in Hatuey, studied acting at the Círculo de Bellas Artes de Madrid, where he began writing for the theater, and has lived in Paris since 1980. He is a playwright, actor, and editor. Upon his return to Cuba in 1959, he staged his first two plays, *El mayor general hablará de teogonía* (The Major General Will Speak About Theogony) and *La visita del Angel* (The Angel's Visit). He also served as literary adviser to the Consejo Nacional de Cultura, the Instituto Cubano del Libro, and the publishing house Letras Cubanas. Adhering to its classical model, the protagonist in *Medea en el espejo* (Medea in the Mirror) murders her children and her lover's girlfriend in order to marry him and ascend the social ladder. In 1967 he went to Europe in order to stage his *La noche de los asesinos* (The Murderers). This work has attracted universal critical attention and has been translated and presented in many European and Asian countries. It won the coveted Casa de las Américas prize in 1965. It is a play within a play that deals with the tensions brought about when a new order appears. Some children plan to assassinate their parents, symbol of the old order, of established authority, in order to fulfill their aspirations. Ironically, the symbolic assassination of the parents only leads to chaos. According to theater critics, Triana's main themes deal with the irrationality of human behavior, but the absurdity of his characters does not raise metaphysical questions.

WORKS: *El mayor general hablará de teogonía* (The Major General Will Speak About Theogony) (s. in Sala Arlequín, 1955). *La visita del Angel* (The Angel's Visit) (s. in Sala Arlequín, 1955). *Medea en el espejo* (Medea in the Mirror) (s. 1960). *El parque de la fraternidad* (Fraternity Park) (Havana: Unión, 1962). *La muerte del Ñeque* (The Death of Ñeque) (1963). *La noche de los asesinos* (The Murderers) (s. at the 6th Havana Festival of Latin American Theater, 1966). *La casa ardiendo* (The Burning House) (n.d.).

BIBLIOGRAPHY: Román V. de la Campa, *José Triana: Ritualización de la sociedad cubana* (Minneapolis: University of Minnesota Institute for the Study of Ideologies and Literature, 1979). Frank N. Dauster, "The Game of Chance: The Theater of José Triana," in *Dramatists in Revolt: The New Latin American Theater*, ed. Leon F. Lyday and George W. Woodyard (Austin: University of Texas Press, 1976), 167–189. José A. Escarpenter and Linda S. Glaze, "José Triana," in *Dictionary of Twentieth-Century Cuban Literature*, ed. Julio A. Martínez (Westport, CT: Greenwood Press, 1990), 466–70. Abelardo Estorino, "Destruir los fantasmas, los mitos de las relaciones familiares. Entrevista a José Triana y Vicente Revuelta," *Conjunto* 2.2 (August–September 1967): 6–14. Rine Leal, *Teatro cubano en un acto* (Havana: Ed. Revolución, 1963); *En primera persona (1954–1966)* (Havana: Instituto del Libro, 1967). Julio Miranda, *Nueva literatura cubana* (Madrid: Taurus, 1971). Matías Montes Huidobro, *Persona, vida y máscara en el teatro cubano* (Miami: Ed. Universal, 1973), 327–341, 413–427. Anne C. Murch, "Genet-Triana-Kopit: Ritual as Dance Macabre," *Modern Drama* 15 (March 1973): 369–379. Erminio G. Neglia, "El asedio a la casa: Un estudio del decorado en *La noche de los asesinos*," *Revista Iberoamericana* 110–111 (January–June 1980): 139–149. Kirsten F. Nigro, "*La noche de los asesinos*: Playscript and Stage Enactment," *Latin American Theatre Review* 11.1 (1977): 45–57.

Mirta A. González

Dominican Republic

Immediately after the discovery of the New World, during the busiest phase of the Spanish conquest, the island of Hispaniola was the focus of Western culture in the Americas. Charles V founded there the first two universities on the continent; at the same time, the religious culture was being spread by Franciscan, Dominican, and Mercedarian convents.

This initial splendor, however, was short-lived; soon the *conquistadores* turned their attention to exploring the mainland, and before the sixteenth century was out, Santo Domingo (the capital city) had become a mere port of call. Repeated attacks by Spain's foes since the end of the sixteenth century, the division of the island, the western portion of which fell to France (1697), and during the first half of the nineteenth century, several invasions by the Haitians (the former French slaves) spelled the ruin of the Spanish colony and, while reducing it to extreme poverty, nearly destroyed its cultural institutions. One of the plausible (but as yet only conjectural) roots of Dominican theater is *areito*, a ritual performed by the indigenous Tainos, which is said to have been richly expressive in gestures, costumes simulating gods, and narrations about their mythological origin and their past; this ceremony touched on the tribe's ideals, feelings, and customs, such as tilling, fishing, and collecting fruits.

We have no details about theatrical performances in the island before 1588, when documents on Cristóbal de Llerena's *entremeses* (interludes) refer to comedies as customary events. Llerena (who was born in Santo Domingo around 1540 and died around 1610), a canon of the cathedral and a university professor, wrote dramatic pieces for the ecclesiastical festivities. These, according to a medieval custom, included not only edifying works meant to enliven doctrine and history but also comic works intended to retain the fleeting attention of the faithful. The only sample of Llerena's production that we have is the aforementioned interlude, which alludes to the sacking of Santo Domingo by Francis Drake (January 10, 1586) and to the local authorities' frivolity and baseness.

According to Marcio Veloz Maggiolo (223), this interlude was the first instance of socially critical drama to appear in the Americas, while the ensuing scandal and trial was the first instance of intellectual pressure and political repression against a writer. At any rate, voicing sociopolitical concerns has been, throughout history, the distinctive feature of most Dominican plays.

Tirso de Molina, one of the greatest among Spanish playwrights, was in Santo Domingo from 1616 to 1618, while a member of a group entrusted with reforming the Mercedarian convent. In his *Historia de la Orden de la Merced* (History of the Order of Mercy), Tirso narrates this group's activities; on the other hand, in his book *Deleitar aprovechando* (To Make Good Use of Pleasure) he describes a poetry contest, honoring Our Lady of Mercy, which took place in September 1616: he himself submitted eight works, one of which was awarded a prize. There are lexical traces of this visit to Santo Domingo in at least three comedies by Tirso: *La villana de Vallecas* (The Peasant Woman from Vallecas), *Amazonas en las Indias* (Amazon Women in the Indies), and *La lealtad contra la envidia* (Loyalty against Envy).

What we know about the theatrical activity in Santo Domingo during the seventeenth century comes mainly in the form of ecclesiastical prohibitions. In 1610 the archbishop Rodríguez Xuárez established that no *auto*, comedy, or farce should be performed in the churches belonging to his archbishopric without consent from the prelate or his vicar general. This consent would not be granted without carefully examining what was to be said and performed and considering how holy, Catholic, and decent the performance would be. A few burlesque interludes were allowed in these performances, as long as they were not indecent or "too profane" (Utrera, 113).

In August 1663 the Archbishop Francisco de la Cueba y Maldonado prohibited the seminary students from participating in the performance of comedies. According to him, in the festivities honoring Our Lady of the Rosary, celebrated every year in October, the students presented comedies that had been commissioned to them for the occasion. This distracted the seminarians from their studies for more than two months. Again, in 1679, the Archbishop Domingo Fernández y Navarrete complained to the king that many bullfights were celebrated and many comedies staged; that these were addressed to women, performed by night, and ended very late, from which nothing good could be expected. As a result, in 1680, the governor Francisco Segura Sandoval y Castillo received a royal order prohibiting bullfights from being so frequent and comedies from being performed at night.

Our information about the theatrical activities in Santo Domingo during the eighteenth century is equally scarce. It is known, however, that public interludes were as popular as ever among people of all classes and that José Solano y Bote, governor of the island from 1771 to 1779, had young amateurs perform numerous comedies, by native and Spanish authors, in the gubernatorial palace. These performances, just as gala balls, were attended by the main figures and families of the time. Henríquez Ureña speculates that Calderón de la Barca and Agustín Moreto were the authors whose comedies were staged the most often by theatrical amateurs (443).

When Spain's vast empire disintegrated, at the end of the eighteenth century, there began for Santo Domingo an era of almost constant sociopolitical upheaval, which continues even today. The capital city was in possession of the French from 1795 to 1809. The occupation army formed a dramatic society that staged French comedies in the Regina church, modified for this purpose. We know that sixteen officers and five ladies played all of the roles; unfortunately, we do not know which comedies they performed.

Then, in February 1822, the former Spanish colony was taken by Haiti (founded in 1804). Many people fled the country; the university was closed for good; palaces and convents were deserted. Still, the Dominicans refused to mingle with the invaders. The Spanish-speaking society continued to meet, to read its old books, and to write poetry for the religious festivities.

The Dominicans put an end to the Haitian occupation on February 27, 1844; among the main factors leading to this outcome were the separatist activities of La Filantrópica, a cultural society that used theater as a means of propaganda. It staged foreign plays that brought to mind the country's predicament, such as *La viuda de Padilla*, by Francisco Martínez de la Rosa, which condemns the French invasion of Spain.

Francisco Javier Foxá (1816–c. 1865), chronologically the first Romantic playwright of America, must be mentioned here. A Dominican by birth, Foxá lived in Cuba, where he wrote the historic drama *Don Pedro de Castilla* in 1836, only one year after Rivas's *Don Alvaro o la fuerza del sino* (Don Alvaro or the Force of Destiny) (the first Romantic drama of Spain) was premiered. Clearly influenced by Victor Hugo, Foxá also wrote the chivalrous drama *El templario* (The Knight Templar) and the comic play *Ellos son* (They Are).

The liberation from the Haitians brought about a protracted internal struggle between independence-minded Dominicans and proponents of a return to Spanish rule. The killing of patriot Antonio Duvergé, ordered by President Pedro Santana, is the subject of the first play by Félix María del Monte, a turning point in the history of Dominican theater, which pointed the way to a nationalistic literature by renewing Llerena's critical approach to social problems. Del Monte (1819–1899), deeply influenced by European Romantic writers, particularly Chateaubriand, is now regarded as the father of Dominican theater.

The new republic was annexed to Spain in 1861, which caused a four-year Restoration War, subject of *Tilema*, by Manuel de Jesús Rodríguez Montaño (1847–1915), and *Cacharros y manigüeros*, by Javier Angulo Guridi (1816–1884), the first Dominican play to portray the peasant language. A general reaction against Spain was manifest in the drama *Iguaniona*, also by Angulo Guridi, which inaugurated a series of *indigenista* plays: *Ozema*, by Félix María del Monte; *Anacaona*, by José Joaquín Pérez (1845–1900); *Higüenamota*, by Américo Lugo (1870–1952); *La muerte de Anacaona*, by Ulises Heureaux, Jr. (1876–1938); *Los quisqueyanos*, by Julio Arzenio (1894–1932); and *Leyenda india*, by Manuel de Jesús García (1912–   ). It has been argued that this *indigenista* trend is out of place in the Dominican Republic, where most of the native population was exterminated by the first Spanish settlers; but while criticizing the conquerors, it reveals a search for national identity in the Spanish American context.

In the late nineteenth century, the heyday of the post-Romantic, nationalistic theater of manners, the most important plays include *El hombre epopeya* (The Epos Man) and *La hija del hebreo* (The Hebrew's Daughter), by Federico Henríquez y Carvajal (1848–1952); *El que menos corre vuela*, by José Francisco Pellerano (1844–1879); *Los viejos verdes* (Merry Old Men), by César Nicolás Pensón (1855–1901); and *Una flor del Ozama* (A Flower from Ozama) and *Amor y expiación* (Love and Expiation), by the novelist Francisco Gregorio Billini (1844–1898), regarded as one of the greatest Dominican playwrights of the time, together with Angulo Guridi and del Monte.

At the turn of the century, we must mention the drama *Maldito amor* (Cursed Love) and the comedy *Pedir peras al olmo* (Request Pears of the Elm Tree), by José María Jiménez (1861–1942); the *zarzuela Las feministas* (The Feminists), by the poetess Virginia Elena Ortea (1866–1903); *La justicia y el azar* (Justice and Chance) and *Vidas tristes* (Sad Lives), by Rafael A. Deligne (1863–1902); *Fuerzas contrarias* (Opposite Forces) and *De la vida* (Of Life), by Arturo Pellerano Castro (1865–1916), an emulator of José Echegaray; the opera libretto *María de Cuéllar* and the humoristic play *Soldado, pulpera y comendador* (Soldier, Grocer Woman, and Commander), by the illustrious poet Gastón F. Deligne (1861–1913).

By the second decade of our century a new art was emerging. The prolific Ulises Heureaux, Jr. (1876–1938), educated in Paris, was displaying a technical mastery that time after time earned him unprecedented box office success. Then, in 1916, the celebrated humanist Pedro Henríquez Ureña (1884–1946) wrote *El nacimiento de Dionisos* (The Birth of Dionysus), a brilliant attempt at re-creating preclassical Greek drama. This is a crucial work in the country's literature, since it initiates an exploration that continues even today. The critic and essayist Max Henríquez Ureña (1885–1968), author of the comedy *La combinación diplomática* (Diplomatic Plot), also belongs to the new trend, as does the poet Federico Bermúdez (1884–1921), who wrote the monologue *El fantasma* (The Ghost).

The United States occupied the republic from 1916 to 1924, rekindling the tradition of socially critical theater. There appeared, in rapid succession, such plays as *La inmolación* (The Inmolation) and *El hijo del héroe* (The Son of the Hero), by Ricardo Pérez Alfonseca; *Así marcha la justicia* (That's the Way Justice Marches), by Renato d'Soto; *Orgullo de raza* (Pride of Race), by Miguel Angel Jiménez; and *Quisqueya y la ocupación americana* (Quisqueya and the American Occupation), by Delia M. Quesada. Especially productive were Apolinar Perdomo, author of *En la hora del dolor* (In Time of Grief), *Un cuento de amor* (A Story of Love), *En el manicomio* (In the Madhouse), and *Sonámbulo* (Sleepwalker); and Rafael Damirón, who wrote *Alma criolla* (Creole Soul), *Mientras los otros ríen* (While the Others Laugh), *La trova del recuerdo* (Memory's Love Song), *Tres minutos de otro tiempo* (Three Minutes from Another Time), *Como cae la balanza* (As the Scales Fall), and, in collaboration with Arturo Logroño, *Los yanquis en Santo Domingo* (The Yankees in Santo Domingo) and *Una fiesta en el Castine* (A Party at the Castine).

Shortly after the U.S. Navy withdrew from Santo Domingo, General Rafael Leónidas Trujillo took power, which he held for thirty years. The theatrical world remained apparently unaffected by this change until 1942; from that time on, the official censorship tended to stifle every creative effort. The influence of Pedro Henríquez Ureña's only play began to be felt also around that time; since then, all of the foremost dramatists in the country have followed in his footsteps. The first one was Franklin Mieses Burgos, author of *El héroe* (The Hero) (1949) and *La ciudad inefable* (The Ineffable City) (1954). Marcio Veloz Maggiolo, the country's chief novelist, wrote a play titled *Creonte* (1963), and the well-known poet Héctor Incháustegui Cabral created the trilogy *Miedo en un puñado de polvo* (Fear in a Handful of Dust), which includes *Filoctetes*, *Prometeo*, and *Hipólito*. Carlos Esteban Deive wrote *El hombre que nunca llegaba* (The Man Who Wouldn't Arrive); Carlos Acevedo, *Momo* and *Sísifo*; Franklin Domínguez, the nation's most prolific playwright, used this genre to satirize Dominican politics in his plays *Antígona humor* (1968) and *Lisístrata odia la política* (Lisístrata Hates Politics) (1981); Iván García Guerra, the best-known figure in theater after Domínguez, set his play *Andrómaca* (1983) against a Dominican backdrop by placing the black president Ulises Heureaux (popularly dubbed "Lilís") in an ingenious symbiosis of history and Greek drama. Not even younger writers have escaped this Hellenistic obsession; suffice it to mention *El horno de la talega* (The Sack Furnace) (1988), by Haffe Serrulle.

According to Angel Mejía, given the Dominican Republic's turbulent history, its intellectuals have felt the need to preserve the Spanish language and to adhere to purer, more universal values, such as those perceived to be embodied in classical Greek culture. While this form of expression helps in avoiding censorship, it does not promote the faithful representation of Dominican people on the stage or the formation of a theatregoing public.

A psychological brand of drama involving the problems of middle- and upper-class characters was also written during the Trujillo Era and immediately afterward. Among the most anthologized plays of this sort we find *La trinitaria blanca* (The White Pansy) and *La tía Beatriz hace un milagro* (Aunt Beatriz Works a Miracle) (both published in 1968), by Manuel Rueda. The former, probably the best play written in the 1950s, is particularly interesting for depicting the frustrations of a spinster as she is denied freedom to express her sexuality in a society fixated on appearances and gossip. Of similar impact are Máximo Avilés Blonda's *Las manos vacías* (Empty-handed) (1959) and *La otra estrella en el cielo* (The Other Star in the Sky) (1963), and Franklin Domíngez's *El último instante* (The Last Moment) (1958). Somewhat later comes *Los ojos grises del ahorcado* (The Green Eyes of the Hanged Person), by Rafael Añez Bergés. Considering the repressive times, these dramatists did what they could to obliquely question, in a family setting, the institution of power and the consequences of its exertion, thus criticizing Trujillo's regime.

The years 1960–1965 were extremely disappointing for most Dominicans. The high expectations raised by Juan Bosch, the first democratically elected president, were thwarted by yet another coup d'état, and the ensuing revolution was stopped by the American invasion of May 1965. This military intervention brought back the nightmare of 1916–1924; to many people's minds, it was a symbolic rape. Strangely enough, this shattering event did not motivate any of the established dramatists to write an all-encompassing work that would mirror it. Only Manuel Rueda tried to capture an aspect of this invasion in a very weak and somewhat melodramatic play titled *Entre alambradas* (Barbed Wire All Around) (1968).

In order to portray the people's frustration and helplessness, dramatists resorted to abstract symbolism and existential pessimism. In *La fábula de los cinco caminantes* (The Fable of Five Travelers), Iván García turned to universal symbols to show the relation between power and ambition. This work is one of the finest Dominican plays and the best of its kind; another jewel is *Se busca un hombre honesto* (Wanted: Honest Man) (1965), by Franklin Domínguez. Other important plays in the same style are: *¿Estamos de acuerdo? . . . Sí señor* (Are We in Agreement? . . . Yes Sir), by Rafael Vásquez; *Los señores impertinentes* (The Impertinent Gentlemen), by Carlos E. Deive; and *La muñeca de Gysina* (Gysina's Doll), by Efraín Castillo.

The invasion, with all its implications, brought about an upsurge of artistic energy in the late 1960s and attempts to create an authentic Dominican theater in the 1970s. In 1967 Iván García published an important volume titled *Más allá de la búsqueda* (Beyond the Search), which includes the eponymous play, as well as *Don Quijote de todo el mundo* (Don Quixote from All Over the World) *Un héroe más pará la mitología* (One More Hero for Mythology), *Los hijos del Fénix* (Children of Phoenix), and *La fábula de los cinco caminantes* (The Fable of Five Travelers). In 1968 Manuel Rueda penned *La tía Beatriz hace un milagro* (Aunt Beatriz Works a Miracle), *Vacaciones en el cielo* (Vacation in the Sky), and *Entre alambradas* (Barbed Wire All Around), while Franklin Domínguez gave us *Espigas maduras* (Rope Spikes), *Antígona humor, Los actores*, and *El encuentro* (The Encounter). First performed in 1958, *Espigas maduras* is among the best plays written by a Dominican author. It portrays, through the use of a familial setting, the abuse of authority embodied in the figure of the father. Also in 1968, Efraín Castillo came out with *Viaje de regreso* (Return Voyage), and Avilés Blonda published three important works in one volume: *La otra estrella en el cielo* (The Other Star in the Sky); *Yo, Bertolt Brecht* (I, Bertold Brecht), and *Pirámide 179* (Pyramid 179).

In the 1970s young playwrights began to try themes and forms reflecting the Dominican experience. For instance, Jaime Lucero dealt with issues that concern the common person in a realistic fashion. Reworking historical events, Lucero created such plays as *Mamasié, Los gavilleros* (The Row of Sheaves), *Papá Liborio*, and *Cuentos del callejón La Yaya* (Stories from the La Yaya Alley). Jimmy Sierra, Ignacio Nova, Aquiles Julián, and Reynaldo Disla organized yearly shows at carnival time; they managed to incorporate short critical plays dealing also with historical occurrences (such as *Retablo vivo del 12 de octubre* [Live Presentation of October 12]) to the processions. In large measure, these young authors are disciples of Venezuelan director Rómulo Rivas, who promoted amateur theater in the Republic at the beginning of the decade. His teachings on collective writing and creation paved the way for the 1976–1979 and 1984–1985 street theater events, which added vitality to the Dominican scene.

Such groups as Taller, Arte Juvenil, Floreshuno, La Rueda, Texpo, Grupo Cristo Rey, and Teatro del Liceo Juan Pablo Duarte were among the *comparsas* (Masquerades) that animated the 1976–1979 street theater experiments. As to the 1984–1985 Festivales de Teatro Callejero, they were enriched by collective works like *Ni David ni Goliat* (Neither David nor Goliath), by the group Gayumba; *La guerra de las galaxias* (The War of the Galaxies) and *La primera carga al machete* (The First Charge to the Machete), by Los Teatreros; *Estela, la mujer del plomero* (Estela, the Plumber's Wife), by Teatro UASD; and *La multa* (The Fine), by Cantera.

Reynaldo Disla, whose technical mastery increased considerably as a result of this experience, was able to apply it to his first play, *Las despoblaciones* (The Depopulations) (1980), dealing with the exodus from the northern region, which took place in 1605–1606. Haffe Serrulle tried to incorporate popular themes, myths, and rituals to theater in *Leyenda de un pueblo que nació sin cabeza* (Legend of a People That Was Born Headless) (1974), *Prostitución en la casa de Dios* (Prostitution in the House of God) (1977), *La danza de Mingo* (Mingo's Dance) (1977), and *Bianto y su señor* (Bianto and His Lord) (1984). The creations of the different troupes that emerged in the 1970s and early 1980s are even more significant in the search for an authentically Dominican theater. Among the many plays written and performed by these groups, we must mention *Mi primera manifestación* (My First Manifestation) and *Regina exprés* (Regina Express), by Gratey; *El terrateniente* (The Landowner), by Teatro Obrero; *Las artimañas* (The Traps) and *La urna* (The Urn), by Gayumba; *La mariposa que quiso viajar a la luna* (The Butterfly That Wanted to Travel to the Moon), by Hombre-Escena; *Así en el cielo como en la tierra* (It Is in the Sky as It Is on the Earth), by Chispa; and *Panobrero* (Breadworker), by Tetraico.

The collective inspiration of the 1970s practically disappeared in the late 1980s, giving way to a more individualized activity. Angel Mejía attributes this to a lack of economic development and to a growing discontent with the political system. In this period of separate efforts, a few dramatists have achieved some degree of success. To begin, Reynaldo Disla was awarded the prestigious Premio Casa de las Américas for his outstanding *Bolo Fran-*

cisco, a play rooted in the popular custom of street theater. Arturo Rodríguez authored and staged several interesting plays in the psychological vein of Manuel Rueda, incorporating fiction-writing and movie-making techniques: *Cordón umbilical* (Umbilical Cord) (1983), *Refugio para cobardes* (Refuge for Cowards) (1989), *Parecido a Sebastián* (Similar to Sebastian) (1989), *Todos menos Elizabeth* (Everyone Except Elizabeth) (1991), and *Hoy toca la pianista gorda* (Today the Fat Pianist Plays) (1993). Carlos Castro shows an interest in marginal themes and popular characters in *El gran juego* (The Great Game) (1988) and *Roca tumba* (Rock Tomb) (1993); so does Frank Disla's *El último son* (The Last Son) (1987), which depicts prostitutes and policemen. The time-honored tradition of picaresque narrative informs part of Manuel Chapuseaux's work. William Mejía has published four plays: *Batallando* (Fighting) (1989), *Encuentro en la astronave* (Encounter on the Spaceship) (1991), *Cosas de tierra adentro* (Things of the Inner Earth) (1993), and *La vision del paladín* (The Vision of the Paladin) (1993). Two important plays have been published by women: *La hierba no da fruto* (Grass Does Not Give Fruit) (1991), by Germana Quintana, and *Por hora y a-piece work* (By Hour and a Piece Work) (1993), by Elizabeth Ovalle. Finally, we have to mention Giovanny Cruz, one of the country's most talented dramatists. His *Amanda* (1990) depicts race, gender, and other cultural legacies, including voodoo, to confront the problems of creating a Dominican identity.

Since 1985, Casa de Teatro has awarded an important biennial prize and published the work of the winning dramatist, thus promoting a greater interest in theater. The Shell Oil Company has sponsored the performance of significant plays as well. There are, in the city of Santo Domingo alone, two national theaters (Teatro Nacional and Palacio de Bellas Artes) and two private ones (Nuevo Teatro and Casa de Teatro). There are two national theater companies (Teatro de Bellas Artes and Teatro Rodante), three university groups (Teatro de la Universidad Autónoma de Santo Domingo, Teatro de la Universidad Católica Madre y Maestra, and Teatro del Instituto de Tecnología), as well as several independent troupes, including Teatro Gayumba, Teatro Cucaramácara, Alta Escena, Teatro Piloncito, and Papalote. The nation boasts several outstanding directors, such as Rafael Villalona, Bienvenido Miranda, Basilio Nova, Manuel Chapuseaux, Franklin Rodríguez, Víctor Checo, Kenedy Olguín Vera, and Radhamés Polanco, not to mention directing playwrights such as Franklin Domínguez, Iván García, Giovanny Cruz, and Haffe Serrulle. These facts attest that theater is alive and well in the Dominican Republic, in spite of the economic problems that are common to most developing nations. In order to achieve a healthy balance and growth, however, the state, the private sector, and the public at large need to support independent groups at least as much as they currently support commercial theater.

BIBLIOGRAPHY

Alcántara Almánzar, José. *Antología de la literatura dominicana*. 2nd ed. Santo Domingo: Taller, 1988.

———. *Narrativa y sociedad en Hispanoamérica*. Santo Domingo: Instituto Tecnológico de Santo Domingo, 1984.

Alvarez de Icaza, Francisco. "Cristóbal de Llerena y los orígenes del teatro en la América española." *Revista de filología española* 8 (April 1921): 121–130.

Arrom, José Juan. *Historia del teatro hispanoamericano (época colonial)*. 2nd ed. Mexico City: Ediciones de Andrea, 1967.

Aybar, Robinson. "El teatro dominicano en la década del 80." *Latin American Theatre Review* 25.2 (Spring 1992): 169–172.

Chapuseaux, Manuel. *Manual de teatrero: Guía de trabajo para grupos aficionados de teatro popular.* Santo Domingo: Corripio, 1987.

Cruzado, Américo. *El teatro en Santo Domingo (1905–1929).* Ciudad Trujillo: Montalvo, 1952.

Disla, Reynaldo. "El teatro dominicano en cuatro tiempos." *Diógenes: Anuario crítico del teatro latinoamericano* 3 (1987): 137–140.

———. "Teatro dominicano: Poner el dedo sobre la calle." *Diógenes: Anuario crítico del teatro latinoamericano* 2 (1986): 187–193.

Ginebra, Danilo. *Panorama del teatro dominicano.* Santo Domingo: Teatro Gratey, 1984.

Henríquez Ureña, Pedro. *Obra crítica.* Ed. Emma Susana Speratti Piñero. México City: Fondo de Cultura Económica, 1960.

Johnson, Julie Greer. "Cristóbal de Llerena and His Satiric Entremés." *Latin American Theatre Review* 22.1 (Fall 1988): 39–45.

Jones, Willis Knapp. *Behind Spanish American Footlights.* Austin: University of Texas Press, 1966.

Lockward, Jaime A. *Teatro dominicano, pasado y presente.* Ciudad Trujillo: La Nación: 1959.

Mejía, Angel. "Del Partenón al Faro del Colón, teatro dominicano." In Margarita Vallejo de Paredes, *Antología del teatro iberoamericano.* Vol. dedicated to Central America and the Dominican Republic.

Molinaza, José. *Historia crítica del teatro dominicano, 1924–1930.* 2 vols. Santo Domingo: Editora Universitaria UASD, 1984.

———. *Historia del teatro dominicano.* Santo Domingo: Editora Universitaria, 1998.

———. "El teatro en República Dominicana durante 1989." *Diógenes: Anuario crítico del teatro latinoamericano* 2 (1986): 167–175.

"República Dominicana." *Escenarios de dos mundos: inventario teatral de Iberoamérica* Vol. 4. Madrid: Centro de Documentación Teatral, 1988, 142–167. Articles by scholars.

Sánchez, Federico. *El teatro dominicano en su historia.* Santo Domingo: Casa Weber, 1986.

Teatro Gratey. *Panorama del teatro dominicano.* Santo Domingo: Corripio, 1984.

Utrera, Fray Cipriano de. *Universidades de Santo Domingo de la Paz y de Santo Tomás de Aquino y Seminario Conciliar de la ciudad de Santo Domingo de la Isla Española.* Santo Domingo: Padres Franciscanos Capuchinos, 1932.

Valldeperes, Manuel. *El arte de nuestro tiempo.* Ciudad Trujillo: Librería Dominicana, 1957.

Vallejo de Paredes, Margarita, ed. *Antología literaria dominicana.* Vol. 3. *Teatro.* Santo Domingo: Corripio, 1972.

Veloz Maggiolo, Marcio. *Cultura, teatro y relatos en Santo Domingo.* Santiago de los Caballeros: Universidad Católica Madre y Maestra, 1972.

Villalona, Rafael. "República Dominicana." *Diógenes: Anuario crítico del teatro latinoamericano* 2 (1986): 177–185.

◆

ANGULO GURIDI, Javier (1816–1884). Writer, journalist, and soldier who fought for Dominican independence; member of the Senate. Alongside these professional activities, he managed to write several plays; his comedies are especially noteworthy for their pioneering use of rural dialect.

WORKS: COMEDIES: *Cacharros y manigüeros* (*entremés*, 1867). *Don Junípero* (1868). *Los apuros de un destierro* (Troubles of Exile) (1868). VERSE DRAMAS: *Iguaniona* (1867). *El conde de Leos* (Count of Leos) (1868). PROSE PLAYS: *La ciguapa* (The Owl) (n.d.). *El fantasma de Higuey* (The Ghost of Higuey) (n.d.). OTHER WORKS: *Ensayos poéticos* (Poetical Essays) (n.d.) *Geografía de la isla de Santo Domingo* (Geography of Santo Domingo Island) (n.d.).

BIBLIOGRAPHY: Pedro Henríquez Ureña, *Obra crítica*, ed. Emma Susana Speratti Piñero (Mexico City: FCE, 1960). Willis Knapp Jones, *Behind Spanish American Footlights* (Austin: University of Texas Press, 1966). José Molinaza, *Historia crítica del teatro dominicano, 1492–1930*, 2 vols. (Santo Domingo: Editora Universitaria UASD, 1984).

AVILÉS BLONDA, Máximo (1931–). Poet, actor, playwright, lawyer, and educator. He has been theater director of the Universidad Autónoma de Santo Domingo and general director of Fine Arts.

WORKS: POETRY: *Centro del mundo* (Center of the World) (1952). *Cantos a Helena* (Songs for Helena) (1971). PLAYS: *Las manos vacías* (Empty-handed) (1959). *La otra estrella en el cielo* (The Other Star in the Sky) (1963). *Yo, Bertolt Brecht* (I, Bertold Brecht.) (1966). *Pirámide 179* (Pyramid 179) (1966).

BIBLIOGRAPHY: José Alcántara Almánzar, *Antología de la literatura dominicana* (Santo Domingo: Taller, 1988). Willis Knapp Jones, *Behind Spanish American Footlights* (Austin: University of Texas Press, 1966). Fernando de Toro, "Análisis actancial de *Pirámide 179*, de Máximo Avilés Blonda," *Revista iberoamericana* 54 (1988): 271–287.

BILLINI, Francisco Gregorio (1844–1898). Politician, educator, and writer. In 1884 he succeeded Ulises Heureaux, Sr., as president of the Republic; he created the "Travelling Teacher" institution and oversaw the publication of the periodical *El eco de la opinión*.

WORKS: *Una flor del Ozama* (A Flower from Ozama, verse play), (1867). *Amor y expiación* (Love and Expiation, historical play) (1882). *Habeas corpus* (articles on constitutional law, previously published in *El eco de la opinión*) (1886). *Bani o Engracia y Antoñita* (*costumbrista* novel.) (1892).

BIBLIOGRAPHY: José Alcántara Almánzar, *Antología de la literatura dominicana* (Santo Domingo: Taller, 1988). Pedro Henríquez Ureña, *Obra crítica*, ed. Emma Susana Speratti Piñero (Mexico City: FCE, 1960). Willis Knapp Jones, *Behind Spanish American Footlights* (Austin: University of Texas Press, 1966). José Molinaza, *Historia crítica del teatro dominicano, 1492–1930*, 2 vols. (Santo Domingo: Editora Universitaria UASD, 1984).

CRUZ, Giovanny. One of the most talented directors and playwrights of the Dominican Republic. He studied chemistry and children's literature. In Colombia, Cruz studied theater production and became acquainted with the work of Buenaventura and Santiago García. He has been director of Teatro de Bellas Artes. He has received several prizes for his work, including best director. In this capacity he is probably the most innovative director of the Dominican theater. His most important plays are *Amanda* and *Virgen de los Narcisos* (The Virgin of the Daffodils), both of 1990. *Amanda* is particularly interesting in the way Cruz employs elements of the Dominican culture to confront the problem of language, race, gender, and identity. This author, with his commitment to stage authentic Dominican motifs, appears to be most promising.

WORKS: *Amanda* (1990). *Virgen de los Narcisos* (The Virgin of the Daffodils) (1990).

DAMIRÓN, Rafael (1882–1956). Damirón was a *costumbrista* playwright and novelist. His theatrical production is a landmark in Dominican literature insofar as it attests to a growing interest in accurately portraying and criticizing the national reality.

WORKS: *Alma criolla* (Creole Soul) (1916). *Mientras los otros ríen* (While the Others Laugh) (1917). *La trova del recuerdo* (Memory's Love

Song) (n.d.). *Tres minutos de otro tiempo* (Three Minutes from Another Time) (n.d.). *Como cae la balanza* (As the Scales Fall) (n.d.). Also, collaborating with Arturo Logroño, *Una fiesta en el Castine* (A Party at the Castine) (n.d.) and *Los yanquis en Santo Domingo* (The Yankees in Santo Domingo) (n.d.).

BIBLIOGRAPHY: Willis Knapp Jones, *Behind Spanish American Footlights* (Austin: University of Texas Press, 1966). José Molinaza, *Historia crítica del teatro dominicano, 1492–1930*, 2 vols. (Santo Domingo: Editora Universitaria UASD, 1984).

DEIVE, Carlos Esteban (1935–). He is a dramatist, short story writer, journalist, essayist, literary critic, and educator. He has won the Popular Theatre Contest (1957), the National Prize for Literature (1963), and the Reserve Bank Theatre Prize (1970).

WORKS: *Los señores impertinentes* (Impertinent Gentlemen) (1957). *Tendencias de la novela contemporánea* (Trends in Contemporary Novel.) (1963). *Museo de diablos* (Devil Museum) (1966). *El líder máximo, El antropófago, y el hombre que nunca llegaba* (The Supreme Leader, The Man Eater, and The Man Who Wouldn't Arrive) (1970).

BIBLIOGRAPHY: José Alcántara Almánzar, *Antología de la literatura dominicana*, 2nd ed. (Santo Domingo: Taller, 1988).

DELIGNE, Gastón Fernando (1861–1913). Deligne was a *modernista* poet who committed suicide, desperate at suffering from leprosy. He provided the lyrics for the opera *María de Cuéllar* and for the comic skit *Soldado, pulpera y comendador* (Soldier, Grocer Woman, and Commander).

WORKS: *Soledad* (Loneliness) (1887). *Galaripsos* (1908). *Romances de la Hispaniola* (Ballads from Hispaniola) (1931). *Páginas olvidadas* (Forgotten Pages) (1944).

BIBLIOGRAPHY: José Alcántara Almánzar, *Antología de la literatura dominicana*, 2nd ed. (Santo Domingo: Taller, 1988). Pedro Henríquez Ureña, *Obra crítica*, ed. Emma Susana Speratti Piñero (Mexico City: FCE, 1960). Willis Knapp Jones, *Behind Spanish American Footlights* (Austin: University of Texas Press, 1966). José Molinaza, *Historia crítica del teatro dominicano, 1492–1930*, 2 vols. (Santo Domingo: Editora Universitaria UASD, 1984).

DELIGNE, Rafael Alfredo (1863–1902). Deligne was a poet, critic, playwright, and short story writer. He died of leprosy, an illness that also plagued the life of his brother, Gastón Fernando.

WORKS: *La justicia y el azar* (Justice and Chance, verse drama) (1894). *Milagro* (Miracle) (1896). *A Dios* (To God, poetry). *Vidas tristes* (Sad Lives, prose play) (1901). *En prosa y en verso* (Prose and Verse, anthology) (1902).

BIBLIOGRAPHY: José Alcántara Almánzar, *Antología de la literatura dominicana*, 2nd ed. (Santo Domingo: Taller, 1988). Pedro Henríquez Ureña, *Obra crítica*, ed. Emma Susana Speratti Piñero (Mexico City: FCE, 1960). Willis Knapp Jones, *Behind Spanish American Footlights* (Austin: University of Texas Press, 1966). José Molinaza, *Historia crítica del teatro dominicano, 1492–1930*, 2 vols. (Santo Domingo: Editora Universitaria UASD, 1984).

DISLA, Reynaldo. Disla is a young dramatist from the Dominican Republic. He is a fervent promoter of the popular theater, particularly street theater. He participated in the 1976–1979 street theater performed during carnival and the 1984–1985 Festivales de Teatro Callejero in Santo Domingo. His works reflect a strong desire to incorporate authentic Dominican themes, especially popular material. His first work, *Las despoblaciones* (The Depopulations) (1980), deals with the fleeing of the population from the northern region of the country in 1605 and 1606. In 1985 he won the prestigious Premio Casa de las Américas with his play *Bolo Francisco* (1983). This play depicts elements of police brutality in a rural setting in which the protagonist, a poor one-legged musician, is killed for hitting a policeman and for talking to a former Communist who visits him. The police as well as the rest of society is presented in a state of degradation. His latest play is *La muerte aplaudida* (The Death Applauded) (1989). Disla's contribution to Dominican drama lies mainly in his use of popular characters and street language.

WORKS: *Las despoblaciones* (The Depopulations) (1980). *Bolo Francisco*, (1983). *La muerte aplaudida* (The Death Applauded) (1989).

DOMÍNGUEZ, Franklin (1931–). Born in Santiago de Caballeros, Domínguez is the most prolific and successful of twentieth-century Dominican playwrights; he is five-time winner of the National Prize for Theatre; his works have been translated to English, French, German, Portuguese, and other languages. He directed *La silla* (The Chair), the first Dominican feature film. He has authored more than sixty plays. Some of his plays deal with the abuse of power; others with political corruption. He is without a doubt the best known of the contemporary Dominican playwrights.

WORKS: *El vuelo de la paloma* (The Pigeon's Flight) (1952). *Alberto y Ercilia* (Alberto and Ercilia) (1954). *Tertulia de fantasmas* (Gathering of Ghosts) (1956). *La niña que quería ser princesa* (The Girl Who Would Be a Princess) (1957). *Un amigo desconocido nos aguarda* (An Unknown Friend Awaits Us) (1958). *El último instante* (The Last Moment) (1958). *La broma del senador* (The Senator's Joke) (1958). *La espera* (The Wait) (1959). *Espigas maduras* (Ripe Spikes) (1960). *Se busca un hombre honesto* (Wanted: Honest Man) (1965). *Omar y los demás* (Omar and the Others) (1975). *Lisístrata odia la política* (Lysistrata Hates Politics) (1979). *Los borrachos* (The Drunkards) (1983). *Drogas* (Drugs) (1986). *Las extrañas presencias* (Strange Presences) (1992).

BIBLIOGRAPHY: José Alcántara Almánzar, *Antología de la literatura dominicana*, 2nd ed. (Santo Domingo: Taller, 1988). Willis Knapp Jones, *Behind Spanish American Footlights* (Austin: University of Texas Press, 1966). Daniel Zalacaín, "Dinámica dramática en *Omar y los demás* de Franklin Domínguez," *Latin American Theatre Review* 23 (1989): 119–126.

FOXÁ, Francisco Javier (1816–1865). Foxá was a Cuban playwright, born in Santo Domingo. He was the first Romantic dramatist of the New World.

WORKS: *Don Pedro de Castilla* (1836). *El templario* (The Knight Templar) (1838). *Ellos son* (They Are, verse comedy).

BIBLIOGRAPHY: Pedro Henríquez Ureña, *Obra crítica*, ed. Emma Susana Speratti Piñero (Mexico City: FCE, 1960). Willis Knapp Jones, *Behind Spanish American Footlights* (Austin: University of Texas Press, 1966).

GARCÍA GUERRA, Iván (1938–). He is a narrator, journalist, playwright, actor, and director. He has won the Best Director Prize (1966) and the short story contest sponsored by La Máscara (1968).

WORKS: *Más allá de la búsqueda* (Beyond the Search) (1967), which includes the eponymous play, as well as *Don Quijote de todo el mundo* (Don Quixote from All Over the World), *Un héroe para la mitología* (A Hero for Mythology), *Los hijos del Fénix* (Children of Phoenix), and *La fábula de los cinco caminantes* (The Fable of Five Travelers). *Andrómaca* (1983). *Solitud* (1993).

BIBLIOGRAPHY: José Alcántara Almánzar, *Antología de la literatura dominicana*, 2nd ed. (Santo Domingo: Taller, 1988). Raquel Aguilu de Murphy, "Soledad e incomunicabilidad en la obra teatral de Iván García," *Revista iberoamericana* 54 (1988): 259–269.

HENRÍQUEZ UREÑA, Max (1885–1968). He was a politician, poet, and writer, born in Santo Domingo. He was a member of the International Tribunal of The Hague; minister of Foreign Relations (1931–1933); delegate to the Society of Nations (1936–1939); ambassador to Brazil and Argentina, and the author of the comedy *La combinación diplomática* (Diplomatic Complot) (1916).

WORKS: *Anforas* (Amphoras, poetry) (1914). *Panorama histórico de la literatura dominicana* (Historical Panorama of Dominican Literature) (1945). *Episodios dominicanos* (Dominican Episodes) (1951). *Breve historia del modernismo* (A Brief History of Modernism) (1954). *Garra de luz* (Talon of Light, verse) (1958). *Panorama histórico de la literatura cubana* (Historical Panorama of Cuban Literature) (1963).

BIBLIOGRAPHY: Willis Knapp Jones, *Behind Spanish American Footlights* (Austin: University of Texas Press, 1966). José Molinaza, *Historia crítica del teatro dominicano, 1492–1930*, 2 vols. (Santo Domingo: Editora Universitaria UASD, 1984).

HENRÍQUEZ UREÑA, Pedro (1884–1946). A humanist, critic, and writer, he was born in Santo Domingo and died in Buenos Aires. He was one of the leading figures of literary research in Latin America and author of the extremely influential Hellenizing play *El* *nacimiento de Dionisos* (The Birth of Dionysus) (1909).

WORKS: *Ensayos críticos* (Critical Essays) (1905). *Horas de estudio* (Hours of Study) (1910). *Tablas cronológicas de la literatura española* (Chronological Tables of Spanish Literature) (1913). *Seis ensayos en busca de nuestra expresión* (Six Essays in Search of Our Expression) (1928). *La versificación irregular en la poesía castellana* (Irregular versification in Castilian Poetry) (1920). *Historia de la cultura en la América hispánica* (History of Culture in Spanish America) (1947). *Las corrientes literarias en la América hispánica* (Literary Currents in Spanish America) (1949). *La utopía de América* (Utopia of America (n.d.).

BIBLIOGRAPHY: Willis Knapp Jones, *Behind Spanish American Footlights* (Austin: University of Texas Press, 1966). José Molinaza, *Historia crítica del teatro dominicano, 1492–1930,* 2 vols. (Santo Domingo: Editora Universitaria UASD, 1984).

HENRÍQUEZ Y CARVAJAL, Federico
(1848–1952). A writer, educator, and patriot who was born in Santo Domingo, he collaborated with Eugenio María de Hostos and supported Cuban independence. He founded the periodicals *El mensajero* and *Letras y ciencias.* He presided over the Supreme Court of Justice, and in 1916, during the U.S. military occupation, he refused to be president of the Republic.

WORKS: *El hombre epopeya o De flor en flor* (The Epos Man or From Flower to Flower) (1870). *La hija del hebreo* (The Hebrew's Daughter) (1878). *Rosas de la tarde* (Afternoon Roses) (n.d.). *Guaracuya, el monólogo de Enriquillo* (Guaracuya, Enriquillo's Monologue) (n.d.). *Del amor y del dolor* (Of Love and Sorrow) (n.d.) *El derecho internacional y la guerra* (War and International Law) (n.d.) *Ética y estética* (Ethics and Esthetics) (n.d.). *Romancero dominicano* (Dominican Ballad Book) (n.d.). *Todo por Cuba* (Everything for Cuba) (n.d.) Also, in collaboration with Manuel de Jesús Rodríguez Montaño (1847–1915): *Tilema* (poetic drama) (1873). *Amores de dos zagalas o Los cálculos de un tutor* (Loves of Two Girls or Calculations of a Legal Guardian, *zarzuela*) (1871). *La promesa cumplida* (Promise Kept, *zarzuela*) (1874).

BIBLIOGRAPHY: Pedro Henríquez Ureña, *Obra crítica,* ed. Emma Susana Speratti Piñero (Mexico City: FCE, 1960). Willis Knapp Jones, *Behind Spanish American Footlights* (Austin: University of Texas

Press, 1966). José Molinaza, *Historia crítica del teatro dominicano, 1492–1930,* 2nd ed. (Santo Domingo: Editora Universitaria UASD, 1984).

HEUREAUX, Ulises, Jr. (1876–1938). Heureaux, the son of the Negro dictator, was a prolific dramatist.

WORKS: *De director a ministro* (From Manager to Minister) (1926). *Consuelo. Amor que emigra* (Emigrating Love) (n.d.). *El grito de 1844* (The Declaration of 1844) (n.d.). *Genoveva. Lo inmutable* (What Never Changes) (n.d.). *El artículo 291* (Article 291) (n.d.). *El jefe* (The Chief) (n.d.). *La fuga de Clarita* (Little Claire's Escape) (n.d.). *Entre dos fuegos* (Caught between Two Fires), (n.d.). *La noticia sensacional* (The Scoop) (n.d.). *El enredo* (Entanglement) (n.d.) *Blanca* (n.d.). *La muerte de Anacaona* (Anacaona's Death) (n.d.). *En la hora superior* (In a Superior Time) (n.d.). *Alfonso XII.* (n.d.). *En la copa del árbol* (In the Treetop, novel) (n.d.)

BIBLIOGRAPHY: Willis Knapp Jones, *Behind Spanish American Footlights* (Austin: University of Texas Press, 1966). José Molinaza, *Historia crítica del teatro dominicano, 1492–1930,* 2 vols. (Santo Domingo: Editora Universitaria UASD, 1984).

INCHÁUSTEGUI CABRAL, Héctor
(1912–   ). He is a poet, essayist, playwright, literary critic, educator, and diplomat. He is regarded as one of the most representative poets of his generation. Incháustegui Cabral was awarded the Pedro Henríquez Ureña Prize in 1952. He is a member of Spain's Royal Academy of Language and president of the National Society of Writers.

WORKS: *Poemas de una sola angustia* (Poems of a Single Anguish) (1940). *Rumbo a la otra vigilia* (Towards the Other Vigil) (1942). *En soledad de amor herido* (Lonely and Hurt by Love) (1943). *De vida temporal* (Of Temporary Life) (1944). *Canciones para matar un recuerdo* (Songs for Killing a Memory) (1944). *Versos 1940–1950* (Verse 1940–1950) (1950). *Memorias del olvido* (Memories from Oblivion) (1950). *Muerte en el Edén* (Death in Eden) (1951). *Casi de ayer* (Almost from Yesterday) (1952). *Las ínsulas extrañas* (Strange Islands) (1952). *Rebelión vegetal* (Vegetal Rebellion) (1956). *El pozo muerto* (The Dead Fountain) (1960). *Miedo en un puñado de polvo* (Fear in a Handful of Dust) (1964). *Por Copacabana buscando* (Searching in Copacabana) (1964). *Diario de la guerra* and *Los* *dioses ametrallados* (Diary of the War and Bullet-Ridden Gods) (1967). *De literatura dominicana siglo XX* (On 20th Century Dominican Literature) (1968). *Teatro* (Theatre) (1968).

BIBLIOGRAPHY: José Alcántara Almánzar, *Antología de la literatura dominicana*, 2nd ed. (Santo Domingo: Taller, 1988). Willis Knapp Jones, *Behind Spanish American Footlights* (Austin: University of Texas Press, 1966).

LLERENA, Cristóbal de (1540–1610?). He was a canon and music director of the Santo Domingo cathedral and rector of the Gorjón university. He is now regarded as the first playwright (and composer) born in the Americas. Of his plays, only an *entremés* (1588) is known.

BIBLIOGRAPHY: Francisco Alvarez de Icaza, "Cristóbal de Llerena y los orígenes del teatro en la América Española," *Revista de Filología Española* 8 (April 1921): 121–130. Pedro Henríquez Ureña, *Obra crítica*, ed. Emma Susana Speratti Piñero (Mexico City: FCE, 1960). Julie Greer Johnson, "Cristóbal de Llerena and His Satiric *Entremés*," *Latin American Theatre Review* 22.1 (Fall 1988): 39–45. Willis Knapp Jones, *Behind Spanish American Footlights* (Austin: University of Texas Press, 1966). José Molinaza, *Historia crítica del teatro dominicano, 1492–1930*, 2 vols. (Santo Domingo: Editora Universitaria UASD, 1984).

LUGO, Américo (1870–1952). Lugo was a lawyer and a historian, born in Santo Domingo. He wrote on political and historical matters, as well as for the theater.

WORKS: PLAYS: *Ensayos dramáticos* (Dramatical Essays) (1906), which includes *Víspera de boda* (Eve of a Wedding), *Elvira, En la pena pobre* (In Grief and Poverty), and *El avaro* (The Miser). *Higüenamota* (Indian drama, 1907). OTHER WORKS: *Camafeos* (Cameos) (n.d.). *Heliotropo* (Heliotrope) (n.d.). *El nacionalismo dominicano* (Dominican Nationalism) (n.d.).

BIBLIOGRAPHY: Pedro Henríquez Ureña, *Obra crítica*, ed. Emma Susana Speratti Piñero (Mexico City: FCE, 1960). Willis Knapp Jones, *Behind Spanish American Footlights* (Austin: University of Texas Press, 1966). José Molinaza, *Historia crítica del teatro dominicano, 1492–1930*, 2 vols. (Santo Domingo: Editora Universitaria UASD, 1984).

MIESES BURGOS, Franklin (1907–1976). He was a poet and lawyer, and cofounder of the journal *La poesía sorprendida* in 1943.

WORKS: *Sin mundo ya y herido por el cielo* (Left with No World and Hurt by the Sky) (1944). *Clima de eternidad* (Climate of Eternity) (1947). *Presencia de los días* (Presence of Days) (1948). *Seis cantos para una sola muerte* (Six Songs for a Single Death) (1948). *El héroe* (The Hero, play) (1949). *Antología* (Anthology) (1952). *La ciudad inefable* (The Ineffable City, play) (1954).

BIBLIOGRAPHY: José Alcántara Almánzar, *Antología de la literatura dominicana*, 2nd ed. (Santo Domingo: Taller, 1988). Willis Knapp Jones, *Behind Spanish American Footlights* (Austin: University of Texas Press, 1966).

MONTE, Félix María del (1819–1899). Monte was a writer and politician. He served as Minister of Justice and of Public Instruction. As a lyrical poet, he was inspired by native themes. He is best remembered for penning the country's national anthem.

WORKS: *El general Antonio Duvergé o las víctimas del 11 de abril* (General Antonio Duvergé or The Victims of April 11) (1855). *Ozema o la joven indiana* (Ozema or The Indian Girl) (1866). *El último abencerraje* (The Last of the Abencerrages) (n.d.). *El mendigo de la catedral de Lyon* (The Beggar of Lyon's Cathedral) (n.d.). *Un vals de Strauss* (A Strauss Waltz) (n.d.). *El artista Antonio Brito* (Antonio Brito, Artist) (n.d.). *La juventud* (Youth) (n.d.). *El premio de los pichones* (The Pigeons' Prize) (n.d.).

BIBLIOGRAPHY: Pedro Henríquez Ureña, *Obra crítica*, ed. Emma Susana Speratti Piñero (Mexico City: FCE, 1960). Willis Knapp Jones, *Behind Spanish American Footlights* (Austin: University of Texas Press, 1966). José Molinaza, *Historia crítica del teatro dominicano, 1492–1930*, 2 vols. (Santo Domingo: Editora Universitaria UASD, 1984).

PELLERANO AMECHUZARRA, Fernando Arturo (1889–1933). He was the son of Arturo Pellerano Castro and an important playwright in the beginning of the twentieth century. His plays helped the development of the Dominican theater.

WORKS: *El más fuerte* (The Strongest One). *Un cobarde* (A Coward). *Grandezas efímeras* (Ephemeral Grandeur). *Los defensores del pueblo* (The People's Protectors). *La hoz* (The Sickle). *En la casa del loco* (In the Madman's House). *La fuga de los árboles* (The Trees' Escape). *Bueno es cuidar la pierna, pero* . . . (Minding Your Leg Is One Thing, But This . . .).

BIBLIOGRAPHY: Willis Knapp Jones, *Behind Spanish American Footlights* (Austin: University of Texas Press, 1966). José Molinaza, *Historia crítica del teatro dominicano, 1492–1930*, 2 vols. (Santo Domingo: Editora Universitaria UASD, 1984).

PELLERANO CASTRO, Arturo (1865–1916).

He was a poet and playwright, known as "Byron," his pen name. Born in Curaçao on May 13, 1865, Pellerano Castro was a popular playwright at the turn of the century. He died in Santo Domingo on May 5, 1916.

WORKS: POETRY: *La última cruzada* (The Last Crusade) (1888). *Criollas* (Creole Women) (1907). PLAYS: *Fuerzas contrarias* (Opposite Forces) (n.d.). *Antonia*. (n.d.). *De mala entraña* (Evil Heart) (n.d.). *De la vida* (Of Life) (n.d.).

BIBLIOGRAPHY: José Alcántara Almánzar, *Antología de la literatura dominicana*, 2nd ed. (Santo Domingo: Taller, 1988). Pedro Henríquez Ureña, *Obra crítica*, ed. Emma Susana Speretti Piñero (Mexico City: FCE, 1960). Willis Knapp Jones, *Behind Spanish American Footlights* (Austin: University of Texas Press, 1966). José Molinaza, *Historia crítica del teatro dominicano, 1492–1930*, 2 vols. (Santo Domingo: Editora Universitaria UASD, 1984).

PENSON, César Nicolás (1855–1901).

Penson was a journalist, essayist, philologist, and poet. He was founder of *El telegrama*, the first Dominican newspaper, and is best remembered for his stories drawing on the country's traditions and episodes, in the manner of Ricardo Palma's *tradiciones*.

WORKS: *Los viejos verdes* (Merry Old Men, verse comedy) (1879). *Cosas añejas* (Yesteryear) (1891). *Reseña histórico-crítica de la ciudad de Santo Domingo* (Historico-Critical Review of Santo Domingo City) (1892). *Compendio de las partes de la oración francesa* (Compendium of French Grammar). *Biografías de dominicanos ilustres* (Biographies of Illustrious Dominicans).

BIBLIOGRAPHY: José Alcántara Almánzar, *Antología de la literatura dominicana*, 2nd ed. (Santo Domingo: Taller, 1988). Pedro Henríquez Ureña,

Obra crítica, ed. Emma Susana Speretti Piñero (Mexico City: FCE, 1960). Willis Knapp Jones, *Behind Spanish American Footlights* (Austin: University of Texas Press, 1966). José Molinaza, *Historia crítica del teatro dominicano, 1492–1930*, 2 vols. (Santo Domingo: Editora Universitaria UASD, 1984).

PERDOMO, Apolinar (1882–1918).

He was a lyric poet who was a significant contributor to the development of the Dominican theater.

WORKS: *En la hora del dolor* (In Time of Grief) (n.d.). *Un cuento de amor* (Love Story) (n.d.). *En el manicomio* (In the Madhouse) (n.d.). *Sonámbulo* (Sleepwalker) (n.d.).

BIBLIOGRAPHY: Willis Knapp Jones, *Behind Spanish American Footlights* (Austin: University of Texas Press, 1966). José Molinaza, *Historia crítica del teatro dominicano, 1492–1930*, 2 vols. (Santo Domingo: Editora Universitaria UASD, 1984).

RODRÍGUEZ, Arturo.

Rodríguez is a young dramatist who started writing plays in the middle 1980s. He writes very much in the psychological vein of Manuel Rueda. In his plays he employs narrative and cinematographic techniques. The cinema is the major source of influence on his plays. He is very well received by Dominican audiences, especially by the middle classes. Rodríguez published *Cordón umbilical* in 1985, followed by *Refugio para cobardes* and *Parecido a Sebastián*, both in 1989. In 1991 he wrote *Todos menos Elizabeth*, and most recently, *Hoy no toca la pianista gorda*. *Cordón umbilical* is Rodríguez's most important drama thus far. This work depicts the crisis children undergo upon the death of their mother. It is also a bitter criticism of the hypocrisy of family relations. Rodríguez can be seen as the Neil Simon of Dominican theater, given his success with the middle class.

WORKS: *Cordón umbilical* (Umbilical Cord) (1985). *Refugio para cobardes* (Refuge for Cowards) (1989). *Parecido a Sebastián* (Sebastian's Lookalike) (1989). *Todos menos Elizabeth* (All But Elizabeth) (1991). *Hoy no toca la pianista gorda* (The Fat Pianist Is Not Playing Today) (n.d.).

BIBLIOGRAPHY: Bonnie Hildebrand Reynolds, "La semiótica y la supervivencia en *Cordón umbil-*

ical de Arturo Rodríguez Fernández," *Gestos* (November 1991): 85–95.

RUEDA, Manuel (1921–). Born in Montecristi, he is a poet, playwright, pianist, educator, and critic. In 1957 he was awarded the National Prize for Literature for his play *La trinitaria blanca* (The White Pansy), a play dealing with the social and sexual frustrations of a woman in a society dominated by moral intransigencies. Rueda was again awarded the National Prize for Literature in 1994 for his overall productivity. He has been director of the National Conservatory of Music and of the Folklore Research Institute (Universidad Nacional Pedro Henríquez Ureña).

WORKS: *Las noches* (The Nights) (1949). *Tríptico* (Tryptich) (1949). *La criatura terrestre* (The Terrestrial Creature) (1963). *Teatro* (Theatre) (1968), a volume that includes *La trinitaria blanca*, as well as *La tía Beatriz hace un milagro* (Aunt Beatrice Works a Miracle), *Vacaciones en el cielo* (Vacation in the Sky), and *Entre alambradas* (Barbed Wire All Around). *El rey Clinejas* (King with Tresses, play) (1979).

BIBLIOGRAPHY: José Alcántara Almánzar, *Antología de la literatura dominicana*, 2nd ed. (Santo Domingo: Taller, 1988). Grace Alvarez-Altman, "Literary Onomastic Typology in Manuel Rueda's Dramas," *Literary Onomastics Studies* (1983): 285–299. Willis Knapp Jones, *Behind Spanish American Footlights* (Austin: University of Texas Press, 1966).

SERRULLE, Haffe (1947–). Serrulle is a playwright and director who currently heads the theater department of the Universidad Autónoma de Santo Domingo. In the late 1960s he went to Spain to study theater, returning in 1970 to his country, where he involved himself in writing and directing plays.

WORKS: *Leyenda de un pueblo que nació sin cabeza* (Legend of a People That Was Born Headless) (1974). *Duarte* (1975). *La danza de Mingo* (Mingo's Dance) (1977). *Bianto y su señor* (Bianto and His Lord) (1984). *El horno de la talega* (The Sack Furnace) (1988).

BIBLIOGRAPHY: Joan T. Eldridge, "The Existential, Socialist, and Folkloric Themes in *La danza de Mingo*," *Afro-Hispanic Review* 13 (1994): 10–15. Federico Sánchez, *El teatro dominicano en su historia* (Santo Domingo: Casa Weber, 1986).

VELOZ MAGGIOLO, Marcio (1936–). Born in Santo Domingo, he is a novelist, playwright, short story writer, journalist, diplomat, educator, and archeologist. He has been awarded the National Prize for Literature (1962) and that of the William Faulkner Foundation (University of Virginia) for his novel *El buen ladrón* (The Good Thief).

WORKS: *El sol y las cosas* (Sun and Things, 1962). *El buen ladrón* (The Good Thief, novel) (1963). *Creonte* (1963). *Intus* (n.d.). *El cáncer nuestro de cada día* (Our Daily Cancer) (n.d.). *Y después las cenizas* (And Then Ashes) (n.d.).

BIBLIOGRAPHY: José Alcántara Almánzar, *Antología de la literatura dominicana*, 2nd ed. (Santo Domingo: Taller, 1988).

Alfonso Montelongo

El Ecuador

The first examples of Ecuadoran drama of the 16th century are the colonial *autos* performed on the plaza Matriz in Quito and Santo Domingo's plaza in Guayaquil. The *crónicas* refer to the representations of colonial drama, a pantomimic theater, which present very emotive fights between Indians and Spaniards. Those episodes, although dull and unevenly performed, gained great interest as evidenced in Modesto Chávez Franco's and Armando de María Campos's chronicles (*Entre cómicos de ayer*, 1950, 174–181.)

There is no doubt that by the seventeenth and eighteenth centuries, the theater had already become a popular form of entertainment. Plays continued to be generally directed toward the sophisticated Spanish and Creole audiences rather than at the indigenous populations. Various types of Spanish Golden Age drama, especially the *comedia*, monopolized colonial theaters, while Ecuadoran playwrights endeavored to imitate such dramatizations by putting aside aborigine theater.

On January 3, 1857 the *Teatro de Guayaquil*, an edifice built for drama's performances, was inaugurated by the theatrical Company of Fedriani-Ramírez. In 1880, the *Teatro Nacional Sucre* marked the beginning of the theater in Quito. These events justify the shifting focus from performing plays of Peninsular origin and breaking away from Spanish literary models to creating a uniquely Ecuadoran theater.

One of the first playwrights to appear as an important literary figure was Juan Montalvo with his first play *La leprosa* [The Leprous Woman] on April 6, 1872. This play was followed by *Jara* [Jara] written in June, *Granja* [Granja] on May 20, 1873, *El descomulgado* [The Excommunicated] and *El dictador* [The Dictator], the latter written two years before President Gabriel García Moreno, the protagonist in the play, was killed in Quito. Ironically, President García Moreno was killed in a way very similar to the one described in Montalvo's play. Montalvo's drama is indicative of his intention to express the tortured reality of human existence.

Yet, however dramatic the theater of the nineteenth century was, the plays did not sufficiently represent ordinary people. Something more was needed; something that would orient Ecuadoran people into the future. At that juncture, a *comedy of manners* entered the marketplace, which was best exemplified by the playwright Francisco Aguirre Guarderas (1875–1904), who gave theater the highly-acclaimed play *Receta para viajar* [A Prescription for Traveling]. Led by Aguirre, a man of immense theatrical skill, the satiric *estampa quiteña* drew upon the popular formula and arranged the story to capture and hold the interest of the general audience.

Although Ecuadoran women writers were more frequently involved in writing poetry and short stories, they were not totally absent from theater at the turn of the XIXth century. Mercedes González de Moscoso (1860–1911), born in Guayaquil, is considered the first woman dramatist in Ecuador who created a sensational drama—*Abuela* [The Grand-mother]—filled with strong emotions and unequivocal moral sentiments.

By the end of the nineteenth century, there was an increasing interest in the dramatic Spanish genre known as the *sainete*. Víctor Manuel Rendón (1859–1940), who held a diplomatic position in France, reconceptualized the Ecuadoran drama as it was imagined by his predecessors and contemporaries, and produced perfect pictures of Ecuadoran human life in a French environment. Thus Rendón contributed to the renovation of theater by creating portraits of Ecuadoran life that not only rivaled each other but that were aimed primarily at overturning the prevailing Spanish comedy and "sainete." Generally, this model of drama was a rebellion against romantic situations and characterization, and sought to put on stage that which the dramatist could verify through the observation of ordinary life.

Most important for Rendón was the necessary linkage of homeland and history. If the self could not be wholly circumscribed by nationality, as he demonstrated in his plays of French atmosphere, neither could it possibly be understood without nationalist referents. In searching for that national identity for his theater, he wrote *Salus Populi* [The Well-Being of the People] where a great figure of Ecuadoran history—Gabriel García Moreno—was reconstructed. One would have to wait several years to see another model of historical theater with the playwright Francisco Tobaron on the stages of Ecuador, particularly in his *Los dioses y el caballo* [The Gods and the Horse].

This process of turning human life into a theme of literary art was followed by Carlos Arturo León (1886–1967?). León's theater was born of a marriage between national life and moral principles. The driving force behind his emphasis on the scene might be explained very simply. If the environment was essential to the realism which inspired the new drama, then the immediate setting in which its characters lived and moved was equally important. Undoubtedly this attitude helps to account for his writing of *El recluta* [The Soldier], *La huérfana* [The Orphan Girl], and *La mujer de tu prójimo* [Somebody Else's Wife] which stand as illustrating examples of his defense of the ethics of daily life.

The establishment of the National Conservatory of Quito gave birth to three important theatrical groups: the *Compañía dramática*, the *Cuadro Albornoz*, and the *Compañia de ópera*. It is interesting to note that the plays performed by the Compañía Dramática were written by Spanish authors: Alvarez Quintero and the "first" Benavente. Eventually however, all three groups disbanded. The only survivor, actor Ernesto Albán, gave life to the famous *Evaristo Corral y Chancleta*, the main figure of his *Estampas quiteñas*, a series of sketches representing Ecuadoran life through the Evaristo character. Similarly, Raúl Andrade (1905–1983) mercilessly set out to expose in his play *Suburbio* [The Outskirts] the bitter taste of the hidden, painful, and depressing reality of the people living on the outskirts of Quito.

The complex, literary, social, and political matrix of feelings about ordinary people in their natural setting provided a historical perspective on the powerful forces governing human life, forces of which one might not be fully aware and over which one might have little control. Jorge Icaza's *Barro de la sierra* [Mountain Soil] and *Flagelo* [The Lash] represent a poignant contribution to the dramatic discourse about the injustice committed against the Indians. For Icaza, the Indian, the peasant is distanced as a completely different physical type, someone wholly Other.

Enrique Avellán Ferrés further developed the sociological poetics to produce a true Ecuadoran social theater. No play, however, better exemplifies the new direction of the social drama than *Manos de criminal* [Criminal Hands] which is a gloomy play of brutal and psychological realism, which depicts human hate and universal poverty.

In 1956, Pedro Jorge Vera (1914–1999), a novelist and the author of *Los animales puros* [Pure Animals], translated the elements of description present in his novel to the stage. He published a volume containing four plays: *La mano de Dios* [God's Hand], *Luto eterno* [Eternal Mourning], *Los ardientes caminos* [The Burning Paths] and *El Dios de la selva* [Jungle's God]. However atmospheric the darkness of the social theater, however closely observed their inner struggles, however inevitable the play's end, its mechanics conformed with the pattern of the well-made play.

Vera's stated philosophy, both of the novel and the drama, was one of absolute objectivity, with setting, characterization, and dialogue rendered so close to actual life that an audience would be convinced by the illusion of its reality. In *El Dios de la selva*, the dramatist creates not only a grandiose protagonist but a scenario similar to the one in the famous novel *La vorágine* by the Colombian writer José Eustasio Rivera, in which the protagonist is surrounded by the tropic. Unlike the novel, however, nature is not the dominating element, but rather the dominated one.

In tracking the trajectory of social theater, Ricardo Descalzi, the well-known Ecuadoran critic, provides another powerful model. His play *Portovelo* [Portovelo], written within the philosophical discourse of modernity, exploits the medium of a gold mine to denounce the alienation of the miners.

The last important movement in the Ecuadoran theater began on December 18, 1954. According to Hernán Rodríguez Castelo (*Teatro contemporáneo*, Clasicos Ariel 96, p. 5), it occurred with the creation of the *Teatro íntimo* whose primary objective was to recover the pure values of comedy for the Ecuadoran theater.

A small number of playwrights, inspired by the tenets of the *Teatro íntimo*, put their work on the stage. Among them, the novelist and playwright Demetrio Aguilera Malta stands out. In 1936, Aguilera Malta went to Spain. While there, the Spanish Civil War broke out and he enlisted on the Republican side as a reporter. His play *España leal* [Loyal Spain] presents his vision of the city of Madrid during wartime. Perhaps his most memorable dramatic creation is *Infierno negro* [Black Hell], a terrifying portrait of man in an industrial society, which shows how human idealism is defeated again and again by the mechanisms of the dominating power.

In spite of the apparent success of *Teatro íntimo*, Ecuadoran dramatists were filled with doubts. They felt that they had become trapped by the very realism they had set out to achieve. Compared with other arts, the theater seemed antiquated. It was necessary to seek something new, something more contemporary and modern in spirit.

In 1956 the *Teatro íntimo* disintegrated and was substituted by several theatrical groups, such as the *Teatro independiente* (1954–1970), created by the dramatist Francisco Tobar García, Teatro Experimental Universitario (TEU, 1955–1963), Compañía Gómez Albán, and particularly the Grupo Tzántzico which was both a theatrical group and a movement inspired by the Cuban revolution.

In the view of the theatrical critics Hernán Rodríguez Castelo and Franklin Rodríguez Abad, the theater of the 1960s is one of rebellion and reaction, with new forms challenging the old, and old forms, in turn, providing the basis for the new. The air was thick with idiosyncratic labels such as existentialism, surrealism, and the Absurd. However, the threads of the many different styles were interwoven within a single play in performance.

It is always interesting to trace the influences of any great writer, and none more than those of Tobar García. Son of the famous historiographer Julio Tobar Donoso, his career as playwright developed rapidly. He travelled to Europe and his direct contact with English literature exerted influence on his theater. In 1974, his first drama *Casa de naipes* [The House of Cards], inspired by Shiller's *The Bandits*, was performed.

Two main subjects dominate Tobar's writing: solitude and death, with the exception of the historical and epic drama *Los dioses y el caballo*. Beginning with *Todo lo que brilla es oro* [Everything that Shines is Gold], particular characteristics and techniques appear in his drama, especially an atmosphere that was often vividly dreamlike and a nightmarish reality.

Tobar's most extraordinary achievement is his *En los ojos vacíos de la gente* [The People's Blank Stare], a tragedy depicting the sordid case of one woman, Carmen, who suffers a calvary in a small, provincial town. Tobar himself has declared that Carmen represents for him what Emma represented for Flaubert in *Madame Bovary*. The critical question is to what extent the writing of this play permitted Tobar to pursue more subtly his pessimistic philosophy of determinism. Carmen, the protagonist, mocked and tormented on all sides, feels completely lost. The end of the drama is bitter, but necessary in order to denounce the hypocrisy and the Pharisaism of people. This outlook is no more cynical nor fatalistic than the everyday tragedy suffered by ordinary people.

Perhaps Aguilera Malta and Tobar's interest in expressionistic techniques was the immediate cause of the disastrous results of social theater as such. Both dramatists portray a desire in their work to find ways to counteract realism by manipulating reality so that their audience might perceive it afresh. Both wrote prolifically and had international success.

During the 1970s the theater in Ecuador changed notably. It was the time for Ecuador's impressive industrial growth because of the oil "boom." In one decade a handful of writers set their stamp upon the Ecuadoran theater with all the zest of political and social revolution: Demetrio Aguilera Malta, Pedro Jorge Vera, Jorge Icaza, Jorge Enrique Adoum. Their plays were of great historical interest because they attest to the failure of social and political structures. The "mise-en-scène" of Jorge Icaza's novel *Huasipungo* is a good example of this movement.

Without a doubt, Ecuadoran theater has a new generation of playwrights: Jorge Enrique Adoum, Juan Andrade, Simón Corral, Pedro Cruz Rodríguez, José Martínez Queirolo, Hugo Salazar Tamariz, and Alvaro San Félix among others. Not to mention that female playwrights are attracting the attention of scholars, Saranelly Toledo de Lamas and Eugenia Viteri for example, have been the subject of several studies.

All of these dramatists and their work, however, do not as yet indicate what the future of Ecuadoran theater will be; although it is agreed that these writers reveal a profound anxiety. Experiments with sociopolitical styles meant that by the end of the decade the Ecuadoran theater scene was set to catch the spirit of the times.

While it is certain that we are living in an era of transition—a time in which almost all of the established modes of existence have disintegrated—what remains to be seen is how the emerging modes will become clearly recognized. The plays of the 1980s and the 1990s depict the "inner significance" of events and depart from objective reality to employ signs, condensations, and a dozen devices which, to the conservative, must seem arbitrarily fantastic. It is an approach to theater which is hard to define but very well represented by two experimental groups: Malayerba (Weeds) in Quito and El Juglar (The Jongleur) in Guayaquil, both characterized by their power to call up the astonishing symbolic and parabolic forces of the stage.

In the midst of such chaos, in a world torn by conflicts and rotten with corruption, it is no wonder that both dramatists and scholars are anxious about the future of Ecuadoran theater. We are expecting the moment when the anxious waiting is over.

BIBLIOGRAPHY

Almeida Naveda, Eduardo. "Breve panorama del teatro en Ecuador durante los años 80." *Latin American Theatre Review* 25.2 (1992): 87–92.

Andino, Peky. *Kito con K.; Ceremonia con sangre; Ulises y la máquina de perdices.* Quito: Eskeletra Editorial, 1998.

Araujo Sánchez, Diego. "Panorama del teatro ecuatoriano." *Cultura* 2.5 (1979): 101–112.

Arias, Augusto. *Panorama de la literatura ecuatoriana.* Quito: Imprenta de la Universidad, 1948.

Barrera, Isaac J. *Historia de la literatura ecuatoriana.* Quito: LIBRESA, 1979.

Barriga López, Franklin, and Leonardo Barriga López. *Diccionario de la literatura ecuatoriana.* Quito: Casa de la Cultura Ecuatoriana, 1973.

Breilh, Alfredo. "Autores y tendencias del teatro ecuatoriano en la década de los '90." *Latin American Theatre Review* 34.1 (2000): 87–101.

Descalzi, Ricardo. *Diccionario bibliográfico ecuatoriano.* Vol. 2. Quito: Biblioteca Ecuatoriana, "Aurelio Espinosa Polit," 1990.

———. *Historia crítica del teatro ecuatoriano.* 6 vols. Quito: Casa de la Cultura Ecuatoriana, 1968.

Eidelberg, Nora. "La ritualización de la violencia en cuatro obras teatrales hispanoamericanas." *Latin American Theatre Review* 13.1 (1979): 29–37.

Estrella, Ulises. "Situación y proyecciones del teatro en el Ecuador." *Conjunto* 11.12 (1972): 62–65.

García Jaime, Luis. *Teatro.* Guayaquil: Casa de la Cultura Ecuatoriana, 1997.

Handelsman, Michael H. "*El secuestro del general, El pueblo soy yo* y la desmitificación del caudillo." *Revista Review Interamericana* 10.2 (1980): 135–142.

Luzariaga, Gerardo. *Bibliografía del teatro ecuatoriano, 1900–1982.* Quito: Casa de la Cultura Ecuatoriana, 1984.

———. "La generación del 60 y el teatro." *Caravelle-Cahiers du Monde Hispanique et Luso-Brésilien* 34 (1980): 158–168.

Merino, Oswaldo. *Reflexiones sobre el teatro popular en el Ecuador.* Quito: Instituto Andino de Artes Populares del Convenio de Andrés Bello, 1992.

Murgueytio, Reinaldo. *Plaza vencido (El Chulquero).* Quito: Editorial Espejo, 1963.

Pimentel, Rodolfo Pérez. *Diccionario biográfico del Ecuador.* Guayaquil: Imprenta de la Universidad de Guayaquil, 1994.

Ribadeneyra Aguirre, Santiago. "Algunas reflexiones e irreverencias hacia el próximo teatro ecuatoriano." *Revista iberoamericana* 54 (1988): 959–967.

Rodriguéz Castelo, Hernán. "Teatro ecuatoriano." *Cuadernos hispanoamericanos* 172 (1964): 104–106.

San Félix, Alvaro. "Teatro de intención política en el Ecuador." *Cultura* 5.13 (1982): 209–225.

Simmonds, Adolfo H. "La formación del teatro ecuatoriano." *Revista Colegio Vicente Rocafuerte* 53 (1949): 8–9.

Teatro ecuatoriano. Guayaquil-Quito: Publicaciones Educativas "Ariel," n.d.

Tobar García, Francisco. "Teatro durante los años 1944 a 1956 vistos por un autor." In *Trece años de cultura nacional. Ensayos de varios autores.* Quito: Casa de la Cultura, Ecuatoriana, 1957.

◆

ADOUM AUD, Jorge Enrique (1923–). Adoum was born in Ambato on June 29, 1923. He studied at the Colegio San Gabriel of the Jesuits in Quito. Later, he traveled to Chile were he met Pablo Neruda and became his secretary. Jorge Adoum is one of the most well-known and respected Ecuadoran writers. His poetry *Ecuador amargo* (Bitter Ecuador) is an excellent example of his poetics on the reality of Ecuador—a land made of shadows, gray events, where only the act of protesting prevails as a redemption vehicle. In spite of being a militant Communist and recognizing the need for greater social awareness, his writings do not represent an act of propaganda but an attempt to illustrate his aspirations for peace and freedom.

He was very successful as a poet and novelist—he wrote the novel *Entre Marx y una mujer desnuda* (Between Marx and a Naked Woman). His theatrical works *El sol bajo las patas de los caballos* (The Sun Trampled Beneath Horses' Hooves), on the colonization of America, and *La subida a los infiernos* (The Climb to Hell), focusing on the relation of society and Christianity, have been highly praised, despite their controversial character. Most of the performances of his plays have been critically acclaimed.

WORKS: *Le soleil foulé par les chevaux*, trad., performed in Universidad, July 14, 1970. *El sol bajo las patas de los caballos*, in *Conjunto* 14 (1972): 43–85; also in *La última rueda* 1 (1975): 55–83; and in *La gran literatura ecuatoriana del 30* (Quito: Editorial El Conejo, 1984). *The Sun Trampled Beneath Horses' Hooves*, in *The Massachusetts Review* 15.1–2 (1974): 285–324. *La subida a los infiernos* (Quito: Casa de la Cultura Ecuatoriana, 1976). *Teatro* (Quito: Editorial Casa de la Cultura Ecuatoriana, 1981). *La africana* (The African Woman) (Quito: Imprenta de Julio Sáenz, n.d.).

BIBLIOGRAPHY: María Dolores Aguilera, "Jorge Enrique Adoum: El dintorno de la escritura, el precipicio," *Quimera* 5 (1981): 9–10. Aguilera, "Entrevista: La poesía sudamericanamente malherida," *Quimera* 5 (1981): 10–15. Jean Andreu, "Entretiens. Interview," *Caravelle* (Toulouse) 42 (1984): 151–180. Diego Araujo Sanchez, "Panorama del teatro ecuatoriano," *Cultura* 2.5 (1979): 108. Isaac J. Barrera, *Historia de la literatura ecuatoriana* (Quito: LIBRESA, 1979), 1172–1173. Franklin Barriga López and Leonardo Barriga López, *Diccionario de la literatura ecuatoriana* (Quito: Casa de la Cultura Ecuatoriana, 1973). Carlos Calderón Chico, *Jorge Enrique Adoum: entrevista en dos tiempos* (Quito: Editorial Universitaria, 1988). Lenore V. Gale, "Poesía y comunicación en la lírica contemporánea hispanoamericana," *DAI* (1978): 360–361A. Eduardo Giordano, "Entrevista a Jorge Enrique Adoum," *Revista Cultural de Excelsior* 187 (1987): 8–17. Laura Hidalgo, "Acercamiento a *Entre Marx y una mujer desnuda*," *Cultura* 3 (1979): 66–82. Hidalgo, "*Entre Marx y una mujer desnuda*, de Jorge Enrique Adoum," *Revista iberoamericana* 54 (1988): 144–145. Gerardo Luzuriaga, *Bibliografía del teatro ecuatoriano. 1900–1982* (Quito: Casa de la Cultura Ecuatoriana, 1984), 15. Luzuriaga, "La generación del 60 y el teatro," *Caravelle-Cahiers du Monde Hispanique et Luso-Brésilien* 34 (1980): 168. Cecilia Mafla Bustamante, "Los apareamientos y la matriz convencional en el poema "Destrucciones" de Jorge Enrique Adoum," *Revista de la Pontificia Universidad Católica del Ecuador* 22.58 (1964): 83–93. Pablo Martínez, "Strategies of (Re)presentation in the New Ecuadorian Novel: *Between Marx and a*

Naked Woman and the Aesthetics of Violence," *New Novel Review* 3.1 (1995): 83–106. Pablo Arturo Martínez Arévalo, "Jorge Enrique Adoum: Ideología, estética e historia (1944–1990)," *DAI* 52.3 (1991): 933A. Martinez Arévalo, "Niveles teórico-estructurales de un 'Texto sin personajes,' " *Cultura* 3 (1979): 83–101. Jean O'Bryan-Knight, "Jorge Enrique Adoum," *Hispamérica* 27.79 (1998): 41–50. O'Bryan-Knight, "Love, Death, and Other Complications in Jorge Enrique Adoum's *Ciudad sin ángel.*" *Hispanic Journal* 20.2 (1999): 291–309. José Olivio Jiménez, "Crónica de poesía: Adoum y Becerra," *Cuadernos americanos* 205 (1976): 246–254. Rodolfo Perez Pimentel, *Diccionario biográfico del Ecuador*, vol. 6 (Guayaquil: Imprenta de la Universidad de Guayaquil, 1994), 6. Hernán Rodríguez Castelo, "Jorge Enrique Adoum," *Teatro contemporáneo* (Guayaquil-Quito: Publicaciones Educativas "Ariel," n.d.), 38–39. Oscar Rodríguez Ortiz, *Sobre narradores y héroes: A propósito de Arenas, Scorza y Adoum* (Caracas: Monte Avila, 1988). Victor Rodríguez, "Entre la lírica y la épica: la poesía enciclopédica de Pablo Neruda, Jorge Enrique Adoum y Ernesto Cardenal," *DAI* 54.10 (1994): 3765A. Genevieve Rozenthal, "Jorge Adoum en París," *Latin American Theatre Review* 8.2 (1975): 74. (About *The Sun Trampled Beneath the Horses' Hooves*.) San Félix, "Teatro de intención política en el Ecuador," *Cultura* 5.13 (1982): 209–225. Selva, Mauricio, "Tres poetas revolucionarios: Ecuador, Venezuela, Colombia," *Cuadernos americanos* 205 (1976): 246–254. León Vieira, *12 escritores ecuatorianos contemporáneos, una glosa* (n.p., 1984). C. Michael Waag, "Frustration and Rage in Jorge Enrique Adoum's *Entre Marx y una mujer desnuda*," *Perspectives on Contemporary Literature* 10 (1984): 95–101. Daniel Waksman Schina, "Adoum en Europa: El primer desembarco de los Marines," *Letras del Ecuador* 148 (1972): 3–5.

AGUILERA MALTA, Demetrio (1909–1981). Born in Guayaquil on May 24, 1909, he studied at the Colegio Vicente Rocafuerte. After graduation he enrolled in law school. His initiation as a writer is illustrated in his book *El libro de los Manglares* (The Book of Manglares). In 1936 he went to Spain to learn about the offset printing system. While in Spain the Spanish Civil War broke out, and he enlisted on the Republican side as a reporter. His vision of the war is illustrated in his book *Madrid:*

Reportaje novelado de una retaguardia heroica (Madrid: A Novelistic Report on a Heroic Rearguard), which was published for the first time in Barcelona. Long an American traveler, his book *Canal Zone* reflects a journalistic vision of the Panamanian Canal zone under U.S. rule. After journeying throughout America and Spain, he returned to Ecuador and was appointed Subsecretario of Public Education. Later, he was cultural attaché to the Ecuadoran embassies in Chile, Argentina, Uruguay, Brazil, and Mexico.

He published *La caballeresa del sol* (The Sun's Damsel) on Manuelita Sáenz, the most important woman in the life of Simón Bolívar. As a novelist he wrote *La isla Virgen* (The Virgin Island), which reflects the reality of the jungle; *Don Goyo* (Mr. Goyo), published in 1933, on the myth of the teluric force of the jungle; and *Siete lunas y siete serpientes* (Seven Moons and Seven Serpents), published in 1970. Aguilera Malta is one of the most well-known and respected writers in Ecuador and has also been one of the most influential promoters of theater. He attracted critical attention for his strong social drama in which the element of social criticism enhances its tragic properties. His plays *Lázaro* (Lazarus) and *Dientes blancos* (White Teeth) also reflect his knowledge of the often-neglected art of scenography.

WORKS: *España leal* (Republican Spain), performed in Guayaquil, September 1938. *Sátiro encadenado*, performed in 1939. *Lázaro* (Lazarus), in *Revista del Colegio "Vicente Rocafuerte"* 53 (1941): 15–42. *Sangre azul* (Blue Blood), in *Anales de la Universidad de Guayaquil* 1.1 (1949): 230–271; also (Washington, D.C.: Unión Panamericana, 1948); and in *Dos comedias fáciles* (Two Simple Comedies), coauthor W. H. Jones (Boston: Houghton Mifflin, 1950). *No bastan los átomos* (Atoms Are Not Enough), in *Revista de la Casa de la Cultura Ecuatoriana* 7.15 (1954): 333–412; also (Quito: Casa de la Cultura Ecuatoriana, 1955). *Dientes blancos* (White Teeth) Quito: Casa de la Cultura Ecuatoriana, 1955; and in *Base* 1 (1936): 49–65. *Honorarios, Dientes blancos, El tigre* (Honorariums, White Teeth, The Tiger) (Mexico: Ediciones de Andrea, 1959). *Infierno negro* (Black Hell) (Xalapa, Mexico: Universidad Veracruzana, 1967), translated into English by Elizabeth Lowe in *Modern International Drama* 10.2 (1977): 7–42.

BIBLIOGRAPHY: Jorge Enrique Adoum, *"No bastan los átomos y Dientes blancos," Letras del Ecuador* 101 (1955): 25. Jaime Alazraki, Roland Grass, and Russell O. Salmon, "Hacia la 'negritude'; las ediciones *variorum* de *Dientes blancos,"* in *Homenaje a Andrés Iduarte* (Clear Creek, IN: The American Hispanist, 1976), 285–300. Richard F. Allen, "El simbolismo empleado en *El secuestro del general," Explicación de textos literarios* 8 (1979–1980): 145–151. Richard F. Allen, "La obra literaria de Demetrio Aguilera Malta," *Mundo Nuevo* 41 (1969): 52–62. Richard F. Allen and Eugene M. Decker, *Infierno negro* and *Casa Grande e Senzala: A Comparison in Social Conflict*, (Evanston, IL: Northwestern University Press, 1970), 17–31. Pedro F. de Andrea, "Demetrio Aguilera Malta: Bibliografía," *Comunidad Latinoamericana de Escritores* 5 (1969): 23–58; also in *El tiempo*, October 14, 1971. Maria Elena Angulo, " 'Realismo maravilloso' and Social Context in Five Modern Latin American Novels," *DAI* 50.10 (1990): 3243A. Augusto Arias, *Panorama de la literatura ecuatoriana* (Quito: Imprenta de la Universidad, 1948), 415. Isaac J. Barrera, *Historia de la literatura ecuatoriana* (Quito: LIBRESA, 1979), 1201–1202, 1269. Franklin Barriga López and Leonardo Barriga López, *Diccionario de la literatura ecuatoriana* (Quito: Casa de la Cultura Ecuatoriana, 1973). V. L. Benites, Notas del arte: *Lázaro*, de Aguilera Malta en escena," *El universo*, August 16, 1941. Alberto Borges, "Entrevista a Demetrio Aguilera Malta," *Vistazo* 13.151 (1969): 134–138. John S. Brushwood, "El criollismo 'de esencias' en *Don Goyo y Ecue-Yamba-O." Estudios de literatura hispánica en honor de José J. Arrom*, ed. Andrew P. Debicki (Chapel Hill: University of North Carolina Press, 1974), 215–225. Lynn Carbon Gorell, "Demetrio Aguilera Malta," *Latin American Theatre Review* 15.2 (1982): 12. Juan Carrión, "Reseña de *El tigre* de Demetrio Aguilera Malta," *Letras del Ecuador* 106 (1956): 25. Boyd G. Carter, "La novelística de Aguilera Malta: enfoques y pareceres," *Chasqui* 3.3 (1974): 66–70. Emmanuel Carvallo, *Teatro completo de Demetrio Aguilera Malta* (Mexico City: Finisterre, 1970). Carvallo, Prólogo, *Trilogía ecuatoriana: Teatro breve* (Mexico City: Andrea, 1959). Juan R. Castellano, "Demetrio Aguilera Malta: *España leal," Books Abroad* 14.2 (1940): 197–198. Ricardo Descalzi, "Demetrio Aguilera Malta, señor de la escena," *El Universo*, April 13, 1966. Descalzi, *Historia crítica del teatro ecuatoriano*, 6 vols. (Quito: Casa de la Cultura Ecuatoriana,

1968), 1146–1171. Luis A. Díez. "The Apocalyptic Tropics of Aguilera Malta," *Latin American Literary Review* 10.20 (1982): 31–40. Nora Eidelberg, "La ritualización de la violencia en cuatro obras teatrales hispanoamericanas," *Latin American Theatre Review* 13.1 (1979): 29–37 (includes an analysis of *Infierno negro* by Demetrio Aguilera Malta). Antonio Fama, "Entrevista con Demetrio Aguilera Malta." *Chasqui* 7.3 (1978): 16–23. Fama, *Realismo mágico en la narrativa de Aguilera Malta* (Madrid: Nova Scholar, 1977–1978). Renan Flores Jaramillo, "Demetrio Aguilera Malta," *Cuadernos hispanoamericanos* 348 (1979): 623–638. Michael H. Handelsman, "*El secuestro del general, El pueblo soy* y la desmitificación del caudillo," *Revista Review Interamericana* 10.2 (1980): 135–142. Aida Heredia, "*Dientes blancos* o la perfecta seducción de la sonrisa," *Afro-Hispanic Review* 16.1 (1997): 32–37. Phillip Koldewyn, "Protesta guerrillera y mitología: novela nueva de Aguilera Malta," *Nueva narrativa hispanoamericana* 5.1–2 (1975): 199–205. Kevin S. Larsen, "*Los fantoches* de Demetrio Aguilera Malta," *Texto crítico* 9.30 (1984): 136–143. Gerardo Luzuriaga *Del realismo al expresionismo: El teatro de Aguilera Malta* (Madrid: Plaza Mayor, 1971). Luzuriaga, "La evolución estilística del teatro de Aguilera Malta," *Latin American Theatre Review* 3.2 (1970): 39–44. Luzuriaga, "La generación del 60 y el teatro," *Caravelle-Cahiers du Monde Hispanique et Luso-Brésilien* 34 (1980): 162. Luzuriaga, "Permanencia y renovación en el teatro de Aguilera Malta," *Cuadernos del Guayas* 32–33 (1970): 36, 43. A. Magaña Esquivel, "Teatro: *Dientes blancos* en la Universidad," *Nacional* 17 (1962): n.p. William W. Megenney, "Problemas raciales y culturales en dos piezas de Aguilera Malta," *Cuadernos americanos* 176 (1971): 221–228. Carlos H. Monsato, "*Infierno negro*: Drama de protesta social," *Duquesne Hispanic Review* 10.1 (1971): 11–22. Mart Morello-Frosch, "El realismo integrador de *Siete lunas y siete serpientes* de Demetrio Aguilera Malta," *Memoria del XVI Congreso Internacional de Literatura Iberoamericana*, ed. Donald A. Yates (East Lansing: Michigan State University Latin American Studies Center, 1975–1977), 387–392. Margaret Sayers Peden, "Aguilera Malta's *Seven Serpents and Seven Moons," Translation Review* 5 (1980): 37–41. Rodolfo Pérez Pimentel, *Diccionario biográfico del Ecuador*, vol. 4 (Guayaquil: Imprenta de la Universidad de Guayaquil, 1987), 3–8. Blasco Perkins, "Demetrio Aguilera Malta: *Infierno negro," Zona Franca* 5.65 (1969): 53. Elide Pittarello, "Conversando con Demetrio Aguilera Malta," *Studi de Letteratura Ispano*

Americana 12 (1982): 31–47. Clementine Christos Rabassa, *Demetrio Aguilera Malta and Social Justice* (Rutherford, Madison, Teaneck, NJ: Fairleigh Dickinson University Press, 1980). Clementin C. Rabassa, "El aire como materia literaria: la épica, la nueva narrativa y Demetrio Aguilera Malta," *Nueva narrativa hispanoamericana* 4 (1974): 261–268. Rabassa, *En torno a Aguilera Malta* (Guayaquil: Casa de la Cultura Ecuatoriana, Núcleo del Guayas, 1981). Rabassa, "El espíritu épico de Aguilera Malta," *Cultura* 5.13 (1982): 17–22. Rabassa, "Prolegómeno al tema del negro en la obra de Demetrio Aguilera Malta," *Comunidad latinoamericana de escritores* 15 (1974): 22–25. Rabassa, "Teatro de la experiencia negra: Una comparación temática y estructural de *Infierno negro* y *¡Yari-Yari, Mamá Olúa!*" Northeast Modern Language Association, Pittsburgh, April 1977. Rabassa, "Zoomorfosis y la trayectoria épico-cristiana en *Siete lunas y siete serpientes* de Demetrio Aguilera Malta," *Vistazo* (July 1970): 103–105. Hernán Rodríguez Castelo, "Demetrio Aguilera Malta, infatigable autor," in *Teatro ecuatoriano* (Guayaquil-Quito: Publicaciones Educativas "Ariel," n.d.) 33–40. Rodríguez Castelo, "Teatro ecuatoriano," *Cuadernos hispanoamericanos* 172 (1964): 104–106. Antonio Sacoto, "*Siete lunas y siete serpientes*," *Cultura* 5.13 (1982): 45–56. Alvaro San Félix, "Teatro de intención política en el Ecuador," *Cultura* 5.13 (1982): 215. Agustín del Saz, "La obsesión del miedo mortal, *El tigre* (1957) de Demetrio Aguilera Malta," in *Teatro social hispanomericano* (Barcelona: Labor, 1967), 146–167. George O. Schanzer, "El teatro hispanoamericano de post mortem," *Latin American Theatre Review* 7.2 (1974): 5–16 (includes an analysis of *Infierno negro* by Aguilera Malta). Mauricio de la Selva, "Demetrio Aguilera Malta," *Diálogo con América*. Mexico City: Cuadernos americanos, (1964): 11–17. William L. Siemens, "The Antichrist Figure in Three Latin American Novels," in *The Power of Myth in Literature and Film*, Selected Papers from the 2nd Annual Florida State University Conference on Literature and Film, ed. Victor Carrabino (Tallahassee: University Press of Florida, 1980). William L. Siemens, "The Devouring Female in Four Latin American Novels" [includes *Siete lunas y siete serpientes*], *Essays in Literature* 1 (1974): 118–129. Siemens, "Witchcraft and Alternative Reality in *Siete lunas y siete serpientes*," *West Virginia University Philological Papers* 28 (1997): 74–81. Teresa Parrish Smotherman, "Desde el indigenismo al pensamiento de la liberación: la obra de Demetrio Aguilera Malta," *DAI* 58.2 (1997):470–471A. Vicente Francisco Torres,

"Demetrio Aguilera Malta," *La palabra y el hombre* 95 (1995): 153–158. Guillermo Antonio Villegas, "Mecanismos de dramatización de un mito: *El tigre* de Aguilera Malta," *Thesaurus* 33.2 (1978): 247–253. C. Michael Waag, "Sátira política a través de la historia mitificada: *El secuestro del general*, de Demetrio Aguilera Malta," *Revista iberoamericana* 54 (1988): 144–145, 771–778. Kenneth Wishnia, "Myth, Non-Linear Time and Self-Negation: Demetrio Aguilera Malta's *El Tigre* and Eugene O'Neill's *The Emperor Jones*," *Hispanic Journal* 15.2 (1994): 257–269.

AGUIRRE GUARDERAS, Francisco (1875–1904).

Aguirre Guarderas was a man of literary gatherings and gave theater the highly acclaimed theatrical work *Receta para viajar* (Prescription for Traveling), a comedy of manners, which was performed on June 11, 1892. Despite some trouble with censoring, the play places him as one of Ecuador's most outstanding playwrights. The time had come for the stage to present characters with genuine roots and authentic Ecuadoran backgrounds. Thus in *Receta para viajar*, we find characters making brilliantly incisive remarks about themselves and other people. Yet the remarks are made in such a way and are put into such an incongruous context that one does not stop to take them seriously.

WORKS: *Receta para viajar* (Prescription for Traveling) (Quito: Biblioteca Ecuatoriana Mínima, 1892). *Receta para heredar* (Prescription for Inheritance) (play has been lost). *Receta para viajar*, comedia inédita en cuatro actos y en verso, in *Orígenes del teatro nacional* (Puebla, Mexico: Editorial Cajica, 1960), 673–827; also in *Teatro ecuatoriano* (Guayaquil-Quito: Publicaciones Educativas "Ariel," n.d.), 71–186.

BIBLIOGRAPHY: Francisco Aguirre Váscones, "Francisco Aguirre Guarderas," *Cultura* 2 (1979): 108 ff. Raúl Andrade, "Claraboya," *El Comercio*, May 16, 1970 (on *Receta para viajar*). Diego Araujo Sánchez, "Panorama del teatro ecuatoriano," *Cultura* 2.5 (1979): 101. Augusto Arias, *Panorama de la literatura-ecuatoriana* (Quito: Imprenta de la Universidad, 1948), 412. Franklin Barriga López and Leonardo Barriga López, *Diccionario de la literatura ecuatoriana* (Quito: Casa de la Cultura Ecuatoriana, 1973). Barriga López and Barriga López, *Conceptos emitidos por la prensa sobre la comedia*

Receta para viajar *coleccionados por los amigos del autor*. (Quito: Imprenta Católica, 1892). Ricardo Descalzi, *Historia crítica del teatro ecuatoriano*, 6 vols. (Quito: Editorial Casa de la Cultura Ecuatoriana, 1968), 285–306. Hernán Rodríguez Castelo, "Conceptos sobre la comedia *Receta para viajar*," in *Teatro ecuatoriano*, vol. 1 (Guayaquil-Quito: Publicaciones Educativas "Ariel," n.d), 29–35. Rodríguez Castelo, *Teatro ecuatoriano*, vol. 2 (Guayaquil-Quito: Publicaciones Educativas "Ariel," n.d), 12. Rodríguez Castelo, "Teatro ecuatoriano," *Cuadernos hispanoamericanos* 172 (1964): 83–84.

ALBÁN GÓMEZ, Ernesto (1937–).

Born in Quito, he studied law at the Universidad Católica del Ecuador. His first publication was a collection of short stories entitled *Salamandra* (Salamander) (1960). Three years later *Teatro* (Theater) appeared, which includes the plays *Jueves* (Thursday), an interpretation of the inner conflict felt by Judas, *El pasaporte* (The Passport)—both performed—and *La verdadera historia de Notre-Dame* (Notre-Dame's True Story). He also produced *Es prohibido leer a Maquiavelo* (It Is Prohibited to Read Machiavelli), a political farce where irony serves to break the dramatic tension. The well-known critic Descalzi has said that from his childhood Albán knew all the details about the theatrical "mystery" (1721). In addition to his work as a dramatist, he collaborated on several of Quito's journals, newspapers, and supplements and has been subdirector of *El tiempo*.

WORKS: *Salamandra* (Salamander) (Quito: Editorial Casa de la Cultura Ecuatoriana, 1960). *Jueves* (Quito: Editorial Ateneo Ecuatoriano, 1963). *Teatro* (Quito: Editorial Ateneo Ecuatoriano, 1963). *La verdadera historia de Notre-Dame* (Quito: Editorial Ateneo Ecuatoriano, 1963). *El pasaporte* (Guayaquil: Editorial Casa de la Cultura. Núcleo del Guayas, 1970), 7–19.

BIBLIOGRAPHY: Diego Araujo Sánchez, "Panorama del teatro ecuatoriano," *Cultura* 2.5 (1979): 107. Franklin Barriga López and Leonardo Barriga López, *Diccionario de la literatura ecuatoriana* (Quito: Casa de la Cultura Ecuatoriana, 1973). Ricardo Descalzi, *Historia crítica del teatro ecuatoriano*, 6 vols. (Quito: Casa de la Cultura Ecuatoriana, 1968), 1721–1735. Francisco Febres Cordero, "En busca de destino," *Cultura* 6.18 (1984): 247–248. Gerardo Luzuriaga, *Bibliografía del teatro ecuatoriano. 1900–1982* (Quito: Casa de la Cultura Ecuatoriana, 1984), 20–21. Luzuriaga, "La generación del 60 y el teatro," *Caravelle-Cahiers du Monde Hispanique et Luso-Brésilien* 34 (1980): 168. Hernán Rodríguez Castelo, "Ernesto Albán Gómez," in *Teatro contemporáneo* (Guayaquil-Quito: Publicaciones Educativas "Ariel," n.d), 57. Rodríguez Castelo, "Micro Ensayo," *El tiempo*, November 5, 1966. Alvaro San Félix, "Teatro de intención política en el Ecuador," *Cultura* 5.13 (1982): 212–223.

ALBÁN MOSQUERA, Ernesto (1912–1984).

Born in Ambato, he is considered to be Ecuador's first national actor. He initiated his dramatic life with the "Moncayo-Barahona" company, where he always performed comical characters. Later he established his own company, which he named after his wife and himself, La Compañía Gómez-Albán. He gave life to the famous Ecuadoran character Evaristo Corral y Chancleta, the main figure of his *Estampas quiteñas* (Impressions from Quito), a series of sketches representing the Evaristo character, who is a very ingenious figure, ready to make fun of everybody. "Evaristo" was very popular among the people because in him they found understanding of their own joys and frustrations. He is known as the Aristophanes of the theater in Quito. As director of the Compañia Ecuatoriana de Comedias Gómez-Albán, Albán Mosquera has journeyed throughout Europe and America.

WORKS: *Evaristo inspector de subsistencias* (Evaristo Subsistence Inspector). *Evaristo teniente político* (Evaristo Political Lieutenant). *Modelo de revolución* (Revolution Model). *El chuchaque de Evaristo. Por andar bebiendo . . . agua* (For Drinking . . . Water). *Evaristo académico de la lengua* (Evaristo Academician). *Jesusa se dedica al deporte* (Jesusa Dedicates Herself to Sports). *Aquí se empeña hasta el alma* (Here Even the Soul Is Pawned). *La voz de la conciencia* (The Voice of the Conscience). *Merienda familiar* (Snack with the Family). *A las puertas del cielo* (At Heaven's Gate). *Evaristo con siete treinta* (Evaristo at Seven Thirty). *Amor a la moderna* (Modern Love). *El purgante* (The Purgative). In *Estampas quiteñas* (Editorial Fray Jodoco Ricke, 1949), a series of sketches representing the "Evaristo" character. *Picardía ecuatoriana-Política en broma* (Quito: Impreso en Offsetec, 1968).

BIBLIOGRAPHY: Raúl Andrade, "Cuarentena de Evaristo," *Cultura* (1984): 303–304. Diego Araujo Sánchez, "Panorama del teatro ecuatoriano," *Cultura* 2.5 (1979): 107. Franklin Barriga López and Leonardo Barriga López, *Diccionario de la literatura ecuatoriana* (Quito: Casa de la Cultura Ecuatoriana, 1973). Ricardo Descalzi, *Historia crítica del teatro ecuatoriano*, 6 vols. (Quito: Casa de la Cultura Ecuatoriana, 1968), 984–1018. Francisco Febres Cordero, "Claveles para Evaristo," *Cultura* (1984): 305–307. Febres Cordero, "En busca de destino," *Cultura* 6.18 (1984): 247–248. Gerardo Luzuriaga, *Bibliografía del teatro ecuatoriano, 1900–1982* (Quito: Casa de la Cultura Ecuatoriana, 1984), 22. Hernán Rodríguez Castelo, "Micro Ensayo," *El tiempo*, November 5, 1966. Alvaro San Félix, "Mito y realidad de Evaristo," *Cultura* 5.13 (1982): 222–223. San Félix, "Teatro de intención política en el Ecuador," *Cultura* 5.13 (1982): 215.

ANDRADE, Raúl (1905–1983). Andrade was born in Quito on October 4, 1905. He became a journalist and playwright. Being from a family of means, he was able to travel throughout Mexico and Colombia, where he worked as a journalist for *El tiempo* (Bogotá, Colombia) and published his book *La internacional negra en Colombia* (The Black International in Colombia), a collection of articles on the crisis in Colombia. He represented the Ecuadoran government in a number of countries, including Spain, Chile, and other European countries. Because of his merits he received several decorations: "Al Mérito" (Ecuador), "Orden de San Carlos" (Colombia), and "Comendador de la Orden de Leopoldo" (Belgium). As a dramatist, Andrade published *Suburbio* (The Outskirts), a romantic evocation on the suburbs of Quito. In this piece Andrade achieves what we can most demand from a writer: He transplants the bitter taste of a hidden reality to the theater, when that reality is so painful and depressing. Andrade is undoubtedly a great author, a symbol of the Ecuadoran writer. He has been called "el genial Raúl Andrade."

WORKS: *Suburbio: Evocación romántica del arrabal quiteño* (Quito: Imprenta de la Universidad, 1931); also in *Rieles* (Quito) 3.14 (1931); appendix. *Lápida sobre un silencio* (Stone over Silence), in *Cuadernos del Guayas* 47 (1979): 49–51.

BIBLIOGRAPHY: Abelardo Moncayo, *Raúl Andrade: crónica de un cronista* (Quito: Casa de la Cultura Ecuatoriana, 1991). Augusto Arias, "El teatro," in *Panorama de la literatura ecuatoriana* (Quito: Imprenta de la Universidad, 1948), 414. Isaac J. Barrera, *Historia de la literatura ecuatoriana* (Quito: LIBRESA, 1979), 1258, 1269. Franklin Barriga López and Leonardo Barriga López, *Diccionario de la literatura ecuatoriana* (Quito: Casa de la Cultura Ecuatoriana, 1973). Ricardo Descalzi, *Historia crítica del teatro ecuatoriano*, 6 vols. (Quito: Casa de la Cultura Ecuatoriana, 1968), 888–898. Descalzi, *Diccionario bibliográfico ecuatoriano*, vol. 2 (Quito: Biblioteca Ecuatoriana "Aurelio Espinosa Polit," 1990), 41–47. Gerardo Luzuriaga, *Bibliografía del teatro ecuatoriano, 1900–1982* (Quito: Casa de la Cultura Ecuatoriana, 1984), 23. Hernán Rodríguez Castelo, "De las aventuras únicas: *Suburbio* de Raúl Andrade," *Teatro ecuatoriano* no 55, Clásicos Ariel (Guayaquil: Publicaciones Educativas "Ariel," n.d.), 22. Rodríguez Castelo, *Teatro ecuatoriano*, vol. 2, Col. Clásicos Ariel no 36. (Guayaquil-Quito: Publicaciones Educativas "Ariel," n.d), 19. Rodríguez Castelo, "Teatro ecuatoriano," *Cuadernos hispanoamericanos* 172 (1964): 89. Adolfo H. Simmonds, "La formación del teatro ecuatoriano," *Revista Colegio Vicente Rocafuerte* 53 (1949): 8–9.

ANDRADE HEYMANN, Juan (1945–). Born in Quito on December 18, 1945, he distinguished himself as a short story writer and published *Cuentos extraños* (Strange Stories) in 1961. In 1972 the play *Cuentos del día siguiente* (Stories for the Following Day) appeared. According to critics, he preferred universal rather than local topics of *indigenista* literature. As a poet, he wrote *Coros* (Chorus) along the lines of existentialism. A man of many talents, Andrade Heymann also created dramatic works. Ricardo Descalzi notes that among the stories included in his book *El lagarto en la mano* (An Alligator in the Hand), there are also two short plays entitled *El caracol se envuelve al revés* (The Snail Hides in His Shell) and *Clodia*. In both works the inner life of the characters is depicted through very clever dialogues. Over the years, Andrade Heymann has relied more and more on local life to provide him with anecdotal material. The author employs theatrical devices to ironically criticize state institutions.

WORKS: *Cuentos extraños* (Quito: Casa de la Cultura Ecuatoriana, 1961). *Cuentos del día siguiente* (Quito: Su Imprenta, 1972). *El caracol se envuelve al revés*, in *El lagarto en la mano* (Quito: Talleres Gráficos Minerva, 1975); also (Quito: Editorial El Conejo, 1984). *Clodia*, in *El lagarto en la mano* (Quito: Talleres Gráficos Minerva, 1975). *¿Y el diablo se encargará del resto . . . o no?* (And the Devil Will Take Care of the Rest . . . Right?) (Unpublished).

BIBLIOGRAPHY: Franklin Barriga López and Leonardo Barriga López, *Diccionario de la literatura ecuatoriana* (Quito: Casa de la Cultura Ecuatoriana, 1973). Ricardo Descalzi, *Historia crítica del teatro ecuatoriano*, 6 vols. (Quito: Casa de la Cultura Ecuatoriana, 1968), 1754–1757. Descalzi, *Diccionario bibliográfico ecuatoriano*, vol. 2 (Quito: Biblioteca Ecuatoriana "Aurelio Espinosa Polit," 1990), 24. Gerardo Luzuriaga, *Bibliografía del teatro ecuatoriano, 1900–1982* (Quito: Casa de la Cultura Ecuatoriana, 1984), 23–24. Hernán Rodríguez Castélo, ed., *Teatro contemporáneo*. Col. Ariel no 96 (Guayaquil-Quito: Publicaciones Educativas "Ariel," n.d), 25.

ARROYO, César E. (1887–1937). Arroyo was born in Quito and was a poet, journalist, playwright, and diplomat. He traveled extensively representing his country. While in Madrid, he was appointed director of the academic journal *Cervantes*. Inspired by the Romantic movement, Arroyo's early poetry *Flores de trapo* (Artificial Flowers) is classified as romantic. Innovative, well-defined, César Arroyo built solidly on his perceptions gained throughout his travels. His works summarize in their own way, through the microcosm of his personal experience, the development of Ecuadoran letters: first, an evocation of his country in *Retablo* (Frontispiece); later the feeling of the Gothic style in *Catedrales de Francia* (France's Cathedrals), and finally his work as a dramatist—*La canción de la vida* (Life's Song); *El caballero, la muerte y el diablo* (The Gentleman, Death, and the Devil), based on fantasy and inspired by Gustavo Durero's design. This drama represents an example of the literature between the last Parnasianism and the early Modernism. Arroyo is not the sum of influences but rather a happy conjunction of other temperaments and facets of his own personality.

WORKS: *Flores de trapo*, in *Altos relieves* 1.16 (1907): 285–286; also in *La ilustración ecuatoriana* 2.21 (1910): 343. *La canción de la vida*, in *Letras* (Quito) 1.1 (1912): 18–23. *El caballero, la muerte y el diablo*, in *Letras* (Quito) 4.35 (1916):328–337. *La noche blanca* (White Night), in *Ecuatorial* (Quito) 2 (1924). *Asamblea de sombras* (Gathering of Shadows) (Quito: Editorial Artes Graficas, 1931).

BIBLIOGRAPHY: Augusto Arias, "El teatro," in *Panorama de la literatura ecuatoriana* (Quito: Imprenta de la Universidad, 1948), 414. Isaac J. Barrera, *Historia de la literatura ecuatoriana* (Quito: Ediciones LIBRESA, 1979), 1134–1135, 1209. Franklin Barriga López and Leonardo Barriga López, *Diccionario de la literatura ecuatoriana* (Quito: Casa de la Cultura Ecuatoriana, 1973). Ricardo Descalzi, *Historia crítica del teatro ecuatoriano*, 6 vols. (Quito: Casa de la Cultura Ecuatoriana, 1968), 888–1898. Descalzi, "Maeterlinck en España," *Letras* 6.46 (1917): 322–328, also in *Diccionario bibliográfico ecuatoriano*, vol. 2 (Quito: Biblioteca Ecuatoriana "Aurelio Espinosa Polit," 1990). Gerardo Luzuriaga, *Bibliografía del teatro ecuatoriano, 1900–1982* (Quito: Casa de la Cultura Ecuatoriana, 1984), 24–25. Hernán Rodríguez Castelo, *Teatro ecuatoriano*, vol. 12. Col. Clásicos Ariel no 36 (Guayaquil-Quito: Publicaciones Educativas "Ariel," n.d), 11, 19–20. Rodríguez Castelo, "Teatro ecuatoriano," *Cuadernos hispanoamericanos* 172 (1964): 91–92.

AVELLÁN FERRÉS, Enrique (1908–). A poet and dramatist, he was born in Guayaquil on December 11, 1908. Avellán Ferrés learned to write very early, and his first novel, *La enorme pasión* (Enormous Passion), was published in Riobamba in *Los Andes* and *La nación*. He studied at the University of Guayaquil, where he received degrees in social and political sciences. He received multiple literary prizes and served in many national and international political posts. Widely traveled, he presented his plays in many American and European countries: *Como los árboles* (Like the Trees), a markedly realistic drama; *El mismo caso* (The Same Case), which reminds us of *The Waivers* by Gerhart Hauptmann; *Manos de criminal* (Criminal Hands), which draws on the stock situations of tragedy; *Clarita la negra* (Black Clarita); and *La rebelión del museo* (Rebellion in the Museum), reflecting children's fantasy. Avellán's method of juxtaposing individuals' attitudes in order to reveal a vital and problematic situation is another reason for his profound impact as a realist writer.

WORKS: *Como los árboles* (Guayaquil: Imprenta La Rápida, 1927); also (Quito: Imprenta de la Universidad Central, 1940, 2nd ed.). *El mismo caso* (Quito: Imprenta del Ministerio de Educación, 1938). *Sin caminos* (Without Direction) (Quito: Imprenta del Ministerio de Educación, 1939). *Manos de criminal* (Quito: Talleres Gráficos de Educación, 1939); also in *La semana* (Guayaquil) 2.58 (1960). *Clarita la negra* (Children's Theater) (Quito: Talleres Gráficos Nacionales, 1966); also in *América* 35.108 (1965): 160–175. *Album musical de Clarita la negra* (Quito: Talleres Gráficos Nacionales, 1966). *Tiempo y ausencia* (Time and Absence), in *Teatro*, vol. 1 (Quito: Talleres Gráficos Nacionales, 1969) 3–50. *Correntada* (River Current), in *Teatro*, vol. 1 (Quito: Talleres Gráficos Nacionales, 1969), 51–142. *La rebelión del museo* (Quito: Talleres Gráficos Nacionales, 1969). *Teatro para niños* (Quito: Talleres Gráficos Nacionales, 1973).

BIBLIOGRAPHY: Augusto Arias, "El teatro," in *Panorama de la literatura ecuatoriana* (Quito: Imprenta de la Universidad, 1948), 414–415. Franklin Barriga López and Leonardo Barriga López, *Diccionario de la literatura ecuatoriana* (Quito: Casa de la Cultura Ecuatoriana, 1973) Campanero, "Clarita la negra," *El tiempo*, November 19, 1966. Ricardo Descalzi, *Diccionario bibliográfico ecuatoriano*, vol. 2 (Quito: Biblioteca Ecuatoriana "Aurelio Espinosa Polit," 1990). Descalzi, *Historia crítica del teatro ecuatoriano*, 6 vols. (Quito: Casa de la Cultura Ecuatoriana, 1968), 745–769. Joaquin Gallegos Lara, "A propósito de teatro. Prólogo a *El mismo caso* de Enrique Avellán Ferrés" (Quito: Imprenta del Ministerio de Educación, 1938), 3. Gerardo Luzuriaga, *Bibliografía del teatro ecuatoriano, 1900–1982* (Quito: Casa de la Cultura Ecuatoriana, 1984), 25–26. Hernán Rodríguez Castelo, "Entre el dramón y lo social: Avellán," *Teatro ecuatoriano*, Col. Clásicos Ariel no 55 (Guayaquil-Quito: Publicaciones Educativas "Ariel," n.d), 16–18. Rodríguez Castelo, *Teatro ecuatoriano*, vol. 2, Col. Clásicos Ariel no 36 (Guayaquil-Quito: Publicaciones Educativas "Ariel," n.d), 12, 19. Rodríguez Castelo, "Teatro ecuatoriano," *Cuadernos hispanoamericanos* 172 (1964): 90–91. Alvaro San Félix, "Teatro de intención política en el Ecuador," *Cultura* 5.13 (1982): 215.

BARRERA, Isaac E. (1884–1970). Barrera was born in Otavalo on February 4, 1884. He is valued as one of Ecuador's major intellectuals, a historian, poet, journalist, dramatist, and literary critic. His poetry appeared in such prestigious literary journals as *La ilustración ecuatoriana, Letras*, and *Hojas dispersas*. He used the pen name Juan de la Cuesta in some of his writings. Barrera's main work is *Historia de la literatura ecuatoriana*. Although his work is representative of various genres, all have the stamp of difficulty, which the writer establishes and then resolves. His theatrical contributions, *Historia relatada por Pierrot* (Story Told by Pierrot)—comedia dell'arte style—and *La melancolía de una tarde* (The Melancholy of an Evening) represent an innovative conception for romantic drama, which is reinforced by an appropriately rhetorical dialogue, strong with sententiae to convey clear indications of the social and moral conditions of his characters.

WORKS: *Historia relatada por Pierrot*, in *Letras* 2.15 (1913): 79–82. *La melancolía de una tarde* (Quito: Imprenta de la Universidad, 1914); also in *Letras* 2.16 (1914): 109–117; 2.17 (1914): 134–141; and 2.18 (1914): 182–190.

BIBLIOGRAPHY: Franklin Barriga López and Leonardo Barriga López, *Diccionario de la literatura ecuatoriana* (Quito: Casa de la Cultura Ecuatoriana, 1973). Ricardo Descalzi, *Historia crítica del teatro ecuatoriano*, 6 vols. (Quito: Casa de la Cultura Ecuatoriana, 1968), 442–448. Gerardo Luzuriaga, *Bibliografía del teatro ecuatoriano, 1900–1982* (Quito: Casa de la Cultura Ecuatoriana, 1984), 27. Hernán Rodríguez Castelo, Introducción, *Teatro ecuatoriano*, vol 2. Col. Clásicos Ariel no 36 (Guayaquil-Quito: Publicaciones Educativas "Ariel," n.d), 10. Barbara Schlutar, "Historias literarias en el Ecuador: una revisión," *Revista de crítica literaria latinoamericana* 15.30 (1989): 319–324.

CORRAL, Simón (1946–   ). This poet and dramatist was born in Quito on January 5, 1946. He studied sociology at the Universidad Central del Ecuador and was president of the Federación de Estudiantes Universitarios del Ecuador (FEUE) (Federation of University Students of Ecuador). He is a professor at the Universidad Central de Quito. As a member of the theatrical group Teatro Popular Ecuatoriano, he took an interest in writing. First, he published various poems in different journals:

Pocuna, Bufanda del sol, and *Revista Americas*. After having journeyed extensively in the rural zones of the jungle, he wrote the play *El cuento de don Mateo* (Don Mateo's Story), a work based on the life of the farmworkers and their love of agricultural life. By using short dialogues, he dramatizes his criticism of the new rich through "docudramas" on the rural life.

WORKS: *El cuento de don Mateo*, performed in Quito, 1966, and published in *Teatro ecuatoriano contemporáneo*, no 1 (Guayaquil: Casa de la Cultura Ecuatoriana, 1970), 21–34. *El ejército de Runas* (The Runas' Army), performed in Quito during the Third National Theater Festival, in 1970.

BIBLIOGRAPHY: Franklin Barriga Lópéz and Leonardo Barriga López, *Diccionario de la literatura ecuatoriana* (Quito: Casa de la Cultura Ecuatoriana, 1973). Ricardo Descalzi, *Historia crítica del teatro ecuatoriano*, 6 vols. (Quito: Casa de la Cultura Ecuatoriana, 1968), 1768–1774. Ulises Estrella, "Situación y proyecciones del teatro en el Ecuador," *Conjunto* 11.12 (1972): 62–65. Gerardo Luzuriaga, *Bibliografía del teatro ecuatoriano. 1900–1982* (Quito: Casa de la Cultura Ecuatoriana, 1984), 32. Luzuriaga, "La generación del 60 y el teatro," *Caravelle-Cahiers du Monde Hispanique et Luso-Brésilien* 34 (1980): 163. Hernán Rodríguez Castelo. *Teatro contemporáneo ecuatoriano*, Col. Clásicos Ariel no 96) (Guayaquil-Quito: Publicaciones Educativas "Ariel," n.d.), 25.

CRUZ RODRÍGUEZ, Pedro (1953–   ). He is an actor and playwright, born in Guayaquil on April 29, 1953. He graduated from the Colegio Nacional Eloy Alfaro. Although he attended law school, he decided to pursue a career in literature instead, working as an actor. He is therefore most noted for his achievements in the theater. In 1979, while he was still a student at the Colegio Vicente Rocafuerte, he received an award for his drama *Lágrimas de pobre* (Poor Man's Tears); he also received the Primer premio and Medalla de Oro in Guayaquil for his play *Rumipata Pacobamba*. In 1975 he wrote *Los cargadores* (The Porters), which was performed in Guayaquil in 1976. Following the footsteps of Enrique Buenaventura in Colombia, he experimented with the theater of *creación colectiva*. Utilizing this method, he wrote *Artículo 25* (Article 25), which deals with the problem of agrarian reform. He is also known for his puppet theater, such as *Diálogo en la noche de los caídos* (Dialogue in the Night of the Fallen), and the grotesque farce *Los zapatos de la Cenicienta* (Cinderella's Slippers).

WORKS: *Diálogo en la noche de los caídos*, in *Cuadernos del Guayas* 46 (1978): 92–108. *Los zapatos de la Cenicienta*, in *Cuadernos del Guayas* 46 (1978): 109–122. *Los cargadores*, in *Teatro de expresión popular* (Guayaquil: Casa de la Cultura Ecuatoriana, Núcleo del Guayas, 1980), 87–106. *Historia nuevamente a contar (Las alcabalas)* (A Story to Be Told Again [The Escises]), in *Teatro de expresión popular* (Guayaquil: Casa de la Cultura Ecuatoriana, Núcleo del Guayas, 1980), 17–60. *Rumipata* (new version of *Rumipata Pacobamba*), in *Teatro de expresión popular* (Guayaquil: Casa de la Cultura Ecuatoriana, Núcleo del Guayas, 1980), 61–85. *Un cuento de Montesdeoca* (Montesdeoca's Story) (teatro infantil) and *El señor sol* (Mr. Sun) (teatro infantil), in *Teatro de expresión popular* (Guayaquil: Casa de la Cultura Ecuatoriana, Núcleo del Guayas, 1980).

BIBLIOGRAPHY: Jorge Astudillo y Astudillo, "Cruz: hombre nuevo y un teatro diferente," in *Teatro de expresión popular* (Guayaquil: Casa de la Cultura Ecuatoriana, Núcleo del Guayas, 1980), 10–15. Gerardo Luzuriaga, *Bibliografía del teatro ecuatoriano. 1900–1982* (Quito: Casa de la Cultura Ecuatoriana, 1984), 32–33.

DESCALZI DEL CASTILLO, Ricardo (1912–1990). Descalzi was a playwright and theatrical critic, born in Riobamba on September 22, 1912. Descalzi attended the Instituto Nacional Mejía in Quito, where he was noted for his love of literature. In Ambato he founded the well-known literary journal *Riscos* and was director of the university journal. In 1978, he was appointed director of the National Library. He began his dramatic career very early with his play *Los caminos blancos* (White Roads). In 1947, he wrote *En el horizonte se alzó la niebla* (Fog on the Horizon), a psychological drama, and in 1951 he published *Portovelo* (Portovelo) and won first prize with *Clamor de sombras* (A Cry in the Shadows), which presents the Oedipus and Electra complexes. Later, he traveled to Paris to study oncology. When he returned to Quito, he published his collection of short stories *Los murmullos de Dios* (God's Whispering) and a novel *Saloya*, which takes place in the Ecuadoran jungle. As a physician he published two books on oncology and another on biological sciences. Descalzi has distinguished himself in the field of theater for many years. He has been successful even in the comic arena, with *Un quiteño en Nueva York* (A Man from Quito in New York), a sketchy play in which he developed the character of the "quishca" from the capital Quito. In 1966 he was appointed president of the Instituto Ecuatoriano de Teatro, and his tragedy *Una quimera en París* (A Chimera in Paris) was also published. In 1981 he adapted *Huasipungo* for the theater, which appeared under the title of *El huasipungo de Andrés Chiliquinga*. As a theatrical critic, he wrote *Historia crítica del teatro ecuatoriano*, in which he highlights a number of nationally acclaimed dramatists who have been instrumental in Ecuadoran theatrical life.

WORKS: *Los caminos blancos* (unpublished), performed in Quito, 1939. *Anfiteatro* (Amphitheater) (Quito: Imprenta Fernández, 1950). *Portovelo* (Quito: Casa de la Cultura Ecuatoriana, 1951). *En el horizonte se alzó la niebla* (Quito: Casa de la Cultura Ecuatoriana, 1961). *Clamor de sombras* (Quito: Casa de la Cultura Ecuatoriana, 1961). *Una quimera en París* (A Chimera in Paris), in *Revista Casa de la Cultura Ecuatoriana* 24 (1966). *Un quiteño en Nueva York* (unpublished). *Historia crítica del teatro ecuatoriano*, 6 vols. (Quito: Casa de la Cultura Ecuatoriana, 1968).

BIBLIOGRAPHY: Diego Araujo Sánchez, "Panorama del teatro ecuatoriano," *Cultura* 2.5 (1979): 104. Augusto Arias, *Panorama de la literatura ecuatoriana* (Quito: Imprenta de la Universidad, 1948), 415. Isaac J. Barrera, *Historia de la literatura ecuatoriana* (Quito: LIBRESA, 1979), 1269. Franklin Barriga López and Leonardo Barriga López, *Diccionario de la literatura ecuatoriana* (Quito: Casa de la Cultura Ecuatoriana, 1973). Ricardo Descalzi, *Historia crítica del teatro ecuatoriano*, 6 vols. (Quito: Casa de la Cultura Ecuatoriana, 1968), 1083–1123. Gerardo Luzuriaga, *Bibliografía del teatro ecuatoriano. 1900–1982* (Quito: Casa de la Cultura Ecuatoriana, 1984), 40–41. Luzuriaga "Ricardo Descalzi: *Historia crítica del teatro ecuatoriano*," *Revista iberoamericana* 37.75 (1971): 470–472. Luzuriaga, "La generación del 60 y el teatro,"

Caravelle-Cahiers du Monde Hispanique et Luso-Brésilien 34 (1980): 158. Rodolfo Pérez Pimentel, *Diccionario gráfico del Ecuador*, vol. 3 (Guayaquil: Editorial de la Universidad de Guayaquil, 1987), 92–94. Domingo Piga, "Ricardo Descalzi y el teatro ecuatoriano," *El Comercio* (Lima), December 15, 1974, 31. Hernán Rodríguez Castelo, "Descalzi: Más sicoanálisis y *Portovelo*," in *Teatro ecuatoriano*, Clásicos Ariel, no 55 (Guayaquil-Quito: Publicaciones Educativas "Ariel," n.d.), 22–24. Rodríguez Castelo, "Teatro ecuatoriano," *Cuadernos hispanoamericanos* 172 (1964): 99–101. Alvaro San Félix, "Teatro de intención política en el Ecuador," *Cultura* 5.13 (1982): 215. Francisco Tobar García, "Teatro durante los años 1944 a 1956 vistos por un autor," In *Trece años de cultura nacional. Ensayos de varios autores* (Quito: Casa de la Cultura Ecuatoriana, 1957), 91–92.

DÍAZ YCAZA, Rafael (1925–   ). Díaz Ycaza was born in Guayaquil on October 24, 1925. Poet, short story writer, and dramatist, he studied journalism at the Escuela de Periodismo, Universidad de Guayaquil. He has been vice president of the César Borja Lavayen college; president of the Ecuadoran Writers Committee for the Peace, university professor, and member of the generation group entitled Madrugada. He has won several literary prizes at both the national and international levels. Even though he is known as a poet and short story writer, he has made a new career as a playwright. *Ella en el infierno* (She's in Hell) demonstrates a very advanced attitude toward the theater by contributing to modern drama with his constant insight into the incongruities and contradictions of human motives. Díaz Ycaza has had to face the assumption that the rational is relatively unimportant and that the irrational is the dominant mode of life.

WORKS: *El miedo*, performed in Guayaquil in the Teatro del Patronato Municipal de Bellas Artes, July 1966. *Christus*, performed in Guayaquil, October 1968. *Ella en el infierno* (She's in Hell), in *Teatro ecuatoriano contemporáneo*, vol. 1 (Guayaquil: Casa de la Cultura Ecuatoriana 1970), 65–74.

BIBLIOGRAPHY: Isaac J. Barrera, *Historia de la literatura ecuatoriana* (Quito: LIBRESA, 1979), 1172. Franklin Barriga López and Leonardo Barriga López, *Diccionario de la literatura ecuatoriana* (Quito: Casa de la Cultura Ecuatoriana, 1973). Ricardo Descalzi, *Historia crítica del teatro ecuatoriano*, 6 vols. (Quito: Casa de la Cultura Ecuatoriana, 1968), 1873. Gerardo Luzuriaga, *Bibliografía del teatro ecuatoriano. 1900–1982* (Quito: Casa de la Cultura Ecuatoriana, 1984), 42. Luis Montoya Andrade, "A propósito de *Tierna y violentamente*, de Rafael Díaz Ycaza," *Situación del relato ecuatoriano*, ed. Manuel Corrales Pascual, vol. 2. (Quito: Ediciones de la Universidad Católica, 1977–1979), 91–111. 2 vols. Galo René Pérez, *Pensamiento y literatura del Ecuador* (N.p., n.d.). Rodolfo Pérez Pimentel, *Diccionario biográfico del Ecuador*, vol. 5 (Guayaquil: Imprenta de la Universidad de Guayaquil, 1988), 112–119. Hernán Rodríguez Castelo, "Rafael Díaz Ycaza," in *Teatro contemporáneo*, Col. Clásicos Ariel no. 96 (Guayaquil-Quito: Publicaciones Educativas "Ariel," n.d.), 39. Benjamín Sántangel, *Rafael Díaz Ycaza, autor de Cuaderno de Bitácora* (N.p., 1949).

GONZÁLEZ DE MOSCOSO, Mercedes

(1860–1911). She used Rosa del Valle as a pen name. She was born in Guayaquil on October 12, 1860. A poet and playwright, González de Moscoso is considered to be Ecuador's first woman writer. Her poetical production appeared in *Cantos del hogar* (Songs from Home) and *Rosas de otoño* (Autumn Roses). Being the sister of the literary writer Nicolás Augusto González, she continued the family's theatrical tradition by writing three plays: *Martirio sin culpa* (Guiltless Martyrdom), *Abuela* (Grandmother), and *Nobleza* (Nobility). Despite their vast differences in tone and dramatic technique, her plays share an emotional-volitional tone. For her, only love was aesthetically productive, for only in love could she truly appreciate the complex and varied multiplicity of feminine values.

WORKS: *Martirio sin culpa*, performed in Quito, ca. 1905. *Abuela* (Guayaquil: Imprenta Mercantil, 1907). *Nobleza* (unpublished).

BIBLIOGRAPHY: Soledad Acosta de Samper, *La mujer en la sociedad moderna* (Paris: Garnier Hnos., 1895), 402. Augusto Arias, *Panorama de la literatura ecuatoriana* (Quito: Imprenta de la Universidad, 1948), 413. Cesar E. Arroyo, "A la Sra. Mercedes G. de Moscoso," *Guayaquil artístico* 9.175 (1911): 107. Arroyo, "A Mercedes González de Moscoso," *El hogar cristiano* 5.25 (1911): 418. Franklin Barriga López and Leonardo Barriga López, *Diccionario de la literatura ecuatoriana* (Quito: Editorial Casa de la Cultura, 1973). Luis Eduardo Bueno, "Martirio sin culpa," in *Horas perdidas* (Quito: Casa de la Cultura Ecuatoriana, 1958). Morayma Ofyr Carvajal, "Mercedes González de Moscoso," in *Galería del espíritu. Mujeres de mi patria* (Quito: Editorial Fray Jodoco Ricke, 1949), 193–197. Francisco José Correa Bustamante, "Mercedes González de Moscoso," in *Joyel poético ecuatoriano* (Guayaquil: Editorial Arquidiocesana Justicia y Paz, 1987), 84. Ricardo Descalzi, *Historia crítica del teatro ecuatoriano*, 6 vols. (Quito: Casa de la Cultura Ecuatoriana, 1968), 2008. Gerardo Luzuriaga, *Bibliografía del teatro ecuatoriano. 1900–1982* (Quito: Casa de la Cultura Ecuatoriana, 1984), 49. Rodolfo Pérez Pimentel, *Diccionario biográfico del Ecuador*, vol. 3 (Guayaquil: Imprenta de la Universidad de Guayaquil, 1987), 178–179. Rodrigo Pesantez Rodas, *Presencia de la mujer ecuatoriana en la poesía* (Guayaquil: Universidad de Guayaquil, 1960), 61–62.

ICAZA CORONEL, Jorge

(1906–1978). A novelist and playwright, Icaza was born in Quito on June 10, 1906. He received his secondary education from the Instituto Nacional Mejía and went on to study medicine at the University of Ecuador. The death of his father marked a turning point in his career, and he eventually worked in the national theater with the Compañía Dramática Nacional. In 1929, he founded the dramatic company Marina Moncayo, which he named after his fiancée. Encouraged by his success, he turned from actor to playwright and later to novelist. His first literary work was *Barro de la Sierra* (Mountain Soil), published in 1933, where he explores the injustices committed against the Indians. The injustices that Icaza observed furnished the thematic material for his novels *Huasipungo*, *En las calles* (In the Streets), which won an award in a national contest, and *Cholos*, which has been translated into many languages. No play, however, better exemplifies the *teatro indigenista* and the new direction of the realistic theater than *Flagelo* (The Lash) in which the life of the Indians is discussed as an obscure nightmare.

WORKS: *El intruso* (The Intruder), performed in Quito, September 9, 1928. *La comedia sin nombre* (The Comedy without a Name), performed in Quito, May 23, 1929. *Por el viejo* (Because of the Old

Man), performed in Quito, August 19, 1929. *¿Cuál es?* (Which One Is It?) (Quito: Editorial Bolívar, 1931). *Como ellos quieren* (As They Wish) (Quito: Editorial Bolívar, 1931). *Sin sentido* (Nonsense) (Quito: Editorial Labor, 1932). *Barro de la sierra*, performed in 1933. *Flagelo* (The Lash) (Guayaquil-Quito: Teatro ecuatoriano, Clásicos Ariel no 55, n.d.), 65–87.

BIBLIOGRAPHY: Jorge Enrique Adoum, "El indio, persona o personaje," *Casa de las Américas* 22.127 (1981): 22–29. Raúl Andrade, "Relieve de Jorge Icaza," *Cuadernos del Guayas* 46 (1978): 165–166. Augusto Arias, *Panorama de la literatura ecuatoriana* (Quito: Imprenta de la Universidad, 1948), 414. Isaac J. Barrera, *Historia de la literatura ecuatoriana* (Quito: LIBRESA, 1979), 1192–1195, 1200. Franklin Barriga López and Leonardo Barriga López, *Diccionario de la literatura ecuatoriana* (Quito: Casa de la Cultura Ecuatoriana, 1973). Agustín Cueva, *Jorge Icaza* (Buenos Aires: Centro Editor de América Latina, 1968). Ricardo Descalzi, *Historia crítica del teatro ecuatoriano*, 6 vols. (Quito: Casa de la Cultura Ecuatoriana, 1968), 788–821. Mario Campana, "Nucancic *Huasipungo* caraju," *Quimera* 131–132 (1994): 85–87. Adina Cruz, "Similitud y contraste en las novelas *Huasipungo y The Pearl*," *Kañina* 4.2 (1980): 109–115. Bernard M. Dulsey, "El teatro de Jorge Icaza," *Revista de estudios hispánicos* 7.1 (1973): 23–37. Dulsey, "Icaza sobre Icaza," *Modern Language Journal* 54.4 (1970): 233–245. Niza Fabre-Maldonado, *Americanismos, indigenismos, neologismos y creación literaria en la obra de Jorge Icaza* (Ecuador: Abrapalabra, 1993). F. Ferrándiz Alborz, "Jorge Icaza," in *Teatro ecuatoriano*, Clásicos Ariel no 55 (Guayaquil-Quito: Publicaciones Educativas "Ariel," n.d.), 43–63. Armando González Pérez, "Social Protest and Literary Merit in *Huasipungo* and *El mundo es ancho y ajeno*," *Revista interamericana de bibliografía* 38 (1988): 329–338. Deborah C. Footer, "Survival of the Fittest: Animal Imagery in Jorge Icaza's *Huasipungo* and the Reader's Perception of the Indian," *Beyond Indigenous Voices*, ed. Mary H. Preuss. (Lancaster, CA: Laberynthos, 1996), 139–142. Gerardo Luzuriaga, *Bibliografía del teatro ecuatoriano. 1900–1982* (Quito: Casa de la Cultura Ecuatoriana, 1984), 51–52. Luzuriaga, "La generación del 60 y el teatro," *Caravelle-Cahiers du Monde Hispanique et Luso-Brésilien* 34 (1980): 162, 168. Cecilia Mafla Bustamante, "A Study of the English Translation of Jorge Icaza's *Huasipungo, The Knowledges of the Translator. From Literary Interpretation to Machine Classification*, Malcom Coulthard and Patricia

Baubeta, ed. New York: Mellen, 1996. 259–278. Kathleen N. March, "El bilingüismo literario y la verosimilitud," *Revista de literatura* 46.92 (1984): 109–116. Kathleen March and Luis Martul-Tobio, "Las sorpresas del virtuoso compromiso: El indigenismo de Jorge Icaza," *Ideologies and Literature* 4:17 (1983): 163–180. David L. Nielson, "The Word, The Beast, the Indian: Animal Codes in the Literary Characterization of the Native American in *Cumandá, Huasipungo and El indio*," *DAI* 57.9 (1997): 3931A. James Earl Norman, "Ortiz' Juyungo and Icaza's *Huasipungo*: A Comparative Study of Narrative and Theme," *DAI* 44.9 (1984): 2781A. J. Enrique Ojeda, "Elementos picarescos en la novela *El chulla Romero y Flores*, de Jorge Icaza," *Actas del I Congreso Internacional sobre la picaresca*, ed. Manuel Criado de Val Madrid: Fundación Universitaria española, 1979), 1117–1122. Rodolfo Pérez Pimentel, *Diccionario biográfico del Ecuador*, vol. 5 (Guayaquil: Imprenta de la Universidad de Guayaquil, 1988), 157–163. Hernán Rodríguez Castelo, "Icaza: Del dramón al sicoanálisis y a *Flagelo*," in *Teatro ecuatoriano*, Clásicos Ariel no 55 (Guayaquil-Quito: Publicaciones Educativas "Ariel," n.d.), 18–20. Rodríguez Castelo, "Jorge Icaza por él mismo," *El tiempo* (Quito), September 6, 1970. Rodríguez Castelo, *Teatro ecuatoriano*, vol. 2, Col. Clásicos Ariel no 36 (Guayaquil-Quito: Publicaciones Educativas "Ariel," n.d), 19. Rodríguez Castelo, "Teatro ecuatoriano," *Cuadernos hispanoamericanos* 172 (1964): 89–90. Theodore Allan Sackett, "Metaliteratura e intelectualidad en la última ficción de Jorge Icaza," *Revista iberoamericana* 54.144–145 (1988): 753–762. Miguel Sáinz de los Terreros, "Funciones narrativas en la narrativa indigenista," *Anales de la literatura hispanoamericana* 13 (1984): 57–67. Alvaro San Félix, "Teatro de intención política en el Ecuador," *Cultura* 5.13 (1982): 215. Armin Shonberger-Rosero, "Introducción histórico-social a la obra de Icaza," *Bibliografía ecuatoriana* 7 (1976): 96–126. Universidad Central del Ecuador, "Bibliografía sobre Jorge Icaza," *Bibliografía ecuatoriana* 7 (1976): 127–146. Anthony J. Vetrano, "Imagery in Two of Jorge Icaza's Novels: *Huasipungo* and *Huairapamushcas*," *Revista de estudios hispánicos* 6 (1972): 293–301. Martí Vilumara, "La 'opera omnia' de Jorge Icaza," *Camp del'Arpa* (1973): 6–25.

LARREA ANDRADE, Hugo (1907–). Larrea Andrade was a poet, fiction writer, and playwright. Born in Ibarra, on September 4, 1907, Larrea Andrade published in 1927 his first book of poems under the title *Alma en éxtasis* (Soul in Ecstasy), followed by *Fontana* (Little Fountain), a narrative book, and the fictional essay *Destino* (Destination), published in Quito in 1942. Although he was successful as a poet and essayist, he is noted for his achievements in the theater. In 1955 his historical drama *Paccha* (Paccha) first appeared. Despite being well acquainted with history, with the exception of a few anachronisms, it seems that *Paccha* represents an effort to transform literature for reading into literature for the theater. Later, this writer–playwright continued writing prose and published *Breviario del recuerdo* (Breviary of Memories), an anthology of Ecuadoran writers. In 1960 a collection of his plays was published with the generic title *Teatro*, although his first drama was written around 1929. While one would claim that any of his plays was a great dramatic work, his plays have raised issues concerning historical theater and some of its problems.

WORKS: *El cansancio de la vida* (The Drudgery of Life), in *Teatro* (Quito: Tirso de Molina, 1960). *Dignidad y pobreza* (Dignity and Poverty), in *Teatro* (Quito: Tirso de Molina, 1960). *Patria* (Homeland), in *Teatro* (Quito: Tirso de Molina, 1960). *Paccha*, in *Teatro* (Quito: Tirso de Molina, 1960). *Atahualpa* (Atahualpa), in *Teatro* (Quito: Tirso de Molina, 1960). *La ruta de las almas* (The Path of Souls), in *Teatro* (Quito: Tirso de Molina, 1960). *Sacrificio heroico* (Heroic Sacrifice), in *Teatro* (Quito: Tirso de Molina, 1960).

BIBLIOGRAPHY: Isaac J. Barrera, *Historia de la literatura ecuatoriana* (Quito: LIBRESA, 1979), 1269. Franklin Barriga López and Leonardo Barriga López, *Diccionario de la literatura ecuatoriana* (Quito: Casa de la Cultura Ecuatoriana, 1973). Ricardo Descalzi, *Historia crítica del teatro ecuatoriano*, 6 vols. (Quito: Casa de la Cultura Ecuatoriana, 1968), 851–870. Gerardo Luzuriaga, *Bibliografía del teatro ecuatoriano. 1900–1982* (Quito: Casa de la Cultura Ecuatoriana, 1984), 54–55.

LEÓN, Carlos Arturo (1886–1967). Born in Riobamba, he studied law and later became an attorney. He began his theatrical career as a youth. He began writing *En pos de la felicidad* (In Pursuit of Happiness), representing children's fantasy. His very first drama was *Repar-*

ación (Reparation), performed in 1914, and in the following years, he developed into an important dramatist. Other published works are *El recluta* (The Soldier), which stirred such nationalism that the government eliminated the indiscriminate custom of drafting of soldiers; *La huérfana* (The Orphan Girl), in which his Christian thesis of charity and forgiveness are made manifest; *La mujer de tu prójimo* (Somebody Else's Wife), with an explosive subject matter similar to that of *A Doll's House* by Ibsen; and *La civilizada* (The Civilized Woman). In his plays he deals with the lives of the people and satirizes their customs and way of life. It is worthwhile to note that poetic justice always takes place in his dramas.

WORKS: *El recluta* (Riobamba: Imprenta Artística, 1916). *En pos de la felicidad* (Riobamba: Tipografía La Buena Prensa, 1927). *Reparación* (Riobamba: La Buena Prensa del Chimborazo, 1928). *Fuego entre cenizas* (Fire Among the Ashes) (Riobamba: La Buena Prensa del Chimborazo, 1928). *La huérfana* (Riobamba: La Buena Prensa del Chimborazo, 1928). *Segundas nupcias* (Second Nuptials) (Riobamba: La Buena Prensa del Chimborazo, 1928). *Ya estoy civilizada* (I Am Already Civilized) (Quito: Gráficas Boli, 1928). *La mujer de tu prójimo* (Riobamba: n.p., 1936) *Viva la libertad* (Long Live Freedom) (Unpublished). *El amor no se compra* (Love Can't Be Bought) (Unpublished). *El Duque de Gandía* (The Duke of Gandia) (Unpublished).

BIBLIOGRAPHY: Augusto Arias, *Panorama de la literatura ecuatoriana* (Quito: Imprenta de la Universidad, 1948), 413. Isaac J. Barrera, *Historia de la literatura ecuatoriana* (Quito: LIBRESA, 1979), 1210. Ricardo Descalzi, *Historia crítica del teatro ecuatoriano*, 6 vols. (Quito: Casa de la Cultura Ecuatoriana, 1968), 448–485. Gerardo Luzuriaga, *Bibliografía del teatro ecuatoriano, 1900–1982* (Quito: Casa de la Cultura Ecuatoriana, 1984), 56–57. Hernán Rodríguez Castelo, *Teatro ecuatoriano*, vol. 2, Col. Clásicos Ariel no 36 (Guayaquil-Quito: Publicaciones Educativas "Ariel," n.d.), 11, 13–14. Rodríguez Castelo, "Teatro ecuatoriano," *Cuadernos hispanoamericanos* 172 (1964): 84–85.

MARTÍNEZ QUEIROLO, José (1931–). He is a dramatist and short story writer. Born in 1931, this playwright surely owes much of his knowledge of new theatrical techniques to the new theories of space and truth in performance, theories that he not only assimilated but put into practice. Martínez Queirolo is a writer involved with daily events, a writer who takes a position and knows how to dramatize it. In 1962, his plays *La casa del qué dirán* (What Will They Say About That House) and *Las faltas justificadas* (The Justified Mistakes) were a sensational novelty in a contest that took place at the Instituto Ecuatoriano de Teatro de la Casa de la Cultura Ecuatoriana. In essence, these two plays are the portrait of a society that denies room for sincerity. *Requiem por la lluvia* (Requiem for the Rain) is another example of a dramatic examination of society that reveals an intense poetic force. *La balada de la cárcel de Reading* (The Ballad of the Reading's Prison) shows undeniable points of contact with the poem by the same title written by Oscar Wilde. The solid and modern construction of his plays is enough to give him a reputation as a dramatist.

WORKS: *La casa del qué dirán* and *Las faltas justificadas*, in *4 piezas en 1 acto* (Quito: Talleres Gráficos del Ministerio de Educación 1962), 1–49, 101–123. *Requiem por la lluvia* (Quito: Editorial de la Revista *Pocuna 3*, 1963). *El baratillo de la sinceridad* (The Street Sale of Sincerity), in *Teatro* (Guayaquil: Editorial Oro, 1965). *Goteras* (Roof Leaks), in *Teatro* (Guayaquil: Editorial Oro, 1965). *Montesco y su señora* (Montesco and His Wife), in *Teatro* (Guayaquil: Editorial Oro, 1965). *Q.E.P.D.* (Revista *Fundateatros*, 1970). *R.I.P.*, trans. of *Q.E.P.D.*, Gerardo Luzuriaga and Robert S. Rudder, trans., in *The Orgy: Modern One-Act Plays from Latin America* (Los Angeles: University of California, Latin American Center, 1974), 53–68. *Los unos vs. los otros* (Ones vs. the Others), in *Antología teatro selecto hispanoamericano* (Madrid: Escelicer, 1970). *La dama meona* (Quito: Editorial Universitaria 1977).

BIBLIOGRAPHY: Diego Araujo Sánchez, "Panorama del teatro ecuatoriano," *Cultura* 2.5 (1979); 106. Franklin Barriga López and Leonardo Barriga López, *Diccionario de la literatura ecuatoriana* (Quito: Casa de la Cultura Ecuatoriana, 1973). Jorge Dávila Vázquez, "Aproximación al teatro ecuatoriano contemporáneo," *Cultura* 3 (1979): 391–396; also in *La última rueda* (Ecuador) 7 (n.d.): 22–26. Ricardo Descalzi, *Historia crítica del teatro ecuatoriano*, 6 vols. (Quito: Casa de la Cultura Ecuatoriana, 1968), 1656–1687. Carlos Espinosa Domínguez, "En-

trevista a Ilonka Vargas," *Latin American Theatre Review* 16 (1983): 64. Renán Flores Jaramillo, "An Opinion . . ." *Latin American Theatre Review* 10.1 (1976): 22 (review of *Los unos vs. los otros*) Gerardo Luzuriaga, *Bibliografía del teatro ecuatoriano. 1900–1982* (Quito: Casa de la Cultura Ecuatoriana, 1984), 58–64. Luzuriaga, "La generación del 60 y el teatro," *Caravelle-Cahiers du Monde Hispanique et Luso-Brésilien* 34 (1980): 162, 164. Luzuriaga, "Notas sobre el teatro ecuatoriano 1977," *Latin American Theatre Review* 11.2 (1978): 91–93. Raúl Márquez, "El teatro: Una necesidad social," *Puño* 1 (1974): 61–63. Márquez, "Martínez Queirolo, José," Interview, *La razón*, October 8, 1965. Hernán Rodríguez Castelo, "José Martínez Queirolo," in *Teatro contemporáneo*, Col. Clásicos Ariel no 96 (Guayaquil-Quito: Publicaciones Educativas "Ariel," n.d.), 42–47. Rodríguez Castelo, "Teatro ecuatoriano," *Cuadernos hispanoamericanos* 172 (1964): 117. Carlos Miguel Suarez Radillo, "Síntesis panorámica del teatro ecuatoriano de hoy y studio crítico sobre José Martínez Queirolo (con su pieza Q.E.P.D)," *Fundateatros* 4 (1971): 127–146.

MERA, José Trajano (1862–1919). Mera came from a literary family and cultural lineage. He went to Europe as an Ecuadoran consul. Many of Mera's writings are scattered in a variety of journals and literary supplements published in Europe. In 1909, in Madrid, he published *Sonetos y sonetillos* (Sonnets and Little Sonnets), a poetic collection. In 1910 *Cónsules y consulados* (Consuls and Consulates) appeared, inspired by his job experiences in different European countries. Mera began his dramatic career in 1911 with the play *Guerra y paz* (War and Peace). He also wrote *La visita del poeta* (The Poet's Visit) and later, in 1917, his controversial play *Los virtuosos* (The Virtuous), a socially committed drama against those whose behavior becomes a series of postures that no longer correspond to any moral feelings. The author's introduction to this play aroused a tremendous commotion.

WORKS: *Guerra y paz* (Quito: Tipografía y Encuadernación Salesiana, 1915). *La visita del poeta* (Quito: Tipografía y Encuadernación Salesiana, 1915). *Los virtuosos*, performed in Quito in 1917 (unpublished). *Silvia* (Quito: Revista de la Sociedad Jurídico-Literaria 71–72–73, 1919). *Transformación* (Transformation) (Unpublished). *¿De tal palo tal as-*

tilla? (The Apple Doesn't Fall Far from the Tree?) (Unpublished). *Quiero ser algo* (I Want to Be Something) (Unpublished). *El bar de la Candelaria* (Candelaria's Bar) (Unpublished).

BIBLIOGRAPHY: Diego Araujo Sánchez, "Panorama del teatro ecuatoriano," *Cultura* 2.5 (1979): 102. Augusto Arias, *Panorama de la literatura ecuatoriana* (Quito: Imprenta de la Universidad, 1948), 414. Isaac J. Barrera, "J. Trajano Mera. Rodrigo Pachano Lalama," *Boletín de la Academia Nacional de Historia* 36.87 (1956): 143. Franklin Barriga López and Leonardo Barriga López, *Diccionario de la literatura ecuatoriana* (Quito: Casa de la Cultura Ecuatoriana, 1973). Ricardo Descalzi, *Historia crítica del teatro ecuatoriano*, 6 vols. (Quito: Casa de la Cultura Ecuatoriana, 1968), 405–429. Gerardo Luzuriaga, *Bibliografía del teatro ecuatoriano. 1900–1982* (Quito: Casa de la Cultura Ecuatoriana, 1984), 65. Hernán Rodríguez Castelo, *Teatro ecuatoriano*, vol. 2, Col. Clásicos Ariel no 36 (Guayaquil-Quito: Publicaciones Educativas "Ariel," n.d.), 16. Alvaro San Félix, "Teatro de intención política en el ecuador," *Cultura* 5.13 (1982): 209–225.

MOLESTINA MATHEUS, J. Eusebio (ca. 1850–?).

He was born in Guayaquil. This poet and playwright initiated his theatrical career in 1898, although by 1878 he had already written and published a play entitled *Eufemia la costurera* (Eufemia the Dressmaker), dedicated to a lady whose name is unknown but with the initials F.M.M. In 1883 he published the play *El poeta y la coqueta* (The Poet and the Flirt) in *El Telégrafo Press* and in the same year *Las penas del trovador* (The Troubadour's Hardships). Some of his plays show an exotic atmosphere of bad taste. The musical comedy *La Duquesa y la aldeana* (The Duchess and the Country Woman), which takes place in Madrid, *El Conde y el Marqués* (The Count and the Marquis), and *El hijo de la Duquesa* (The Son of the Duchess) are good examples of an entirely artificial environment. *Espinas y abrojos* (Thistles and Thorns), performed in Guayaquil in 1898, exemplifies the theater known as *criollista* and is considered as a precursor of the realist and social theater.

WORKS: *Eufemia la costurera* (Guayaquil: Imprenta de Ezequiel Gómez, s.f.). *Las penas del trovador* (Guayaquil: Imprenta de "El Telégrafo," 1883).

El poeta y la coqueta (Guayaquil: Imprenta de "El Telégrafo," 1883). *Espinas y abrojos* (Guayaquil: Tipografía "El Vigilante," 1910). *La Duquesa y la aldeana* (Guayaquil: Librería e Imprenta Gutemberg, 1910).

BIBLIOGRAPHY: Ricardo Descalzi, *Historia crítica del teatro ecuatoriano*, 6 vols. (Quito: Casa de la Cultura Ecuatoriana, 1968), 322–332; 1996–1997. 9. Gerardo Luzuriaga, *Bibliografía del teatro ecuatoriano. 1900–1982* (Quito: Casa de la Cultura Ecuatoriana, 1984), 66. Rodolfo Pérez Pimentel, *Diccionario biográfico del Ecuador*, vol. 1 (Guayaquil: Imprenta de la Universidad de Guayaquil, 1987), 327–333. Hernán Rodríguez Castelo, *Teatro ecuatoriano*, vol. 1, Col. Ariel no 17 (Guayaquil-Quito: Publicaciones Educativas "Ariel," n.d.), 22–23. Rodríguez Castelo, *Teatro ecuatoriano*, vol. 2, Col. Clásicos Ariel no 36 (Guayaquil-Quito: Publicaciones Educativas "Ariel," n.d.), 12–13. Rodríguez Castelo, "Teatro ecuatoriano," *Cuadernos hispanoamericanos* 172 (1964): 83.

MONTALVO FIALLOS, Juan (1832–1889).

Montalvo was an Ecuadoran premier essayist, polemist, and political critic, born in Ambato on April 13, 1832. Montalvo was the founder of the newspaper *El cosmopolita* and the author of *Siete tratados* (Seven Treaties) and *Las catilinarias* (The Catilinarians). Exiled in Ipiales, Colombia, he wrote his tragedies. In his *Teatro ecuatoriano*, Descalzi mentions that of the seven plays that Montalvo wrote, five were published in Havana, Cuba. It appears that *La leprosa* (The Leprous Woman) was his first drama, although in 1872 he also wrote another play, *Jara* (Jara). His plays were not written to be presented but rather to imitate Plato, Schiller, Renán, and other writers who simply wrote dramas. His intention was to express the tortured reality of human existence in a time when man could not live by any other means but by those passions that molded his life and became his destructive destiny. His *El dictador* (The dictator) on his political enemy García Moreno is of great importance in spite of some historical flaws. These five plays appeared in *El libro de las pasiones*. According to the title, each play represents a different passion: *Jara* represents "revenge"; *El descomulgado*, "love"; *Granja*, "jealousy"; *La leprosa*, "virtue"; and finally, *El dictador*, a sum of all passions.

WORKS: *La leprosa*, dated February 6, 1872, published in *Libro de las pasiones* (Book of Passions) (Havana: Cultura, 1935), also in (Ambato: Editorial Pío XII, 1970). *El descomulgado* (The Excommunicated) (Ambato: Publicaciones de la Biblioteca de Autores Nacionales, 1921); also in *Libro de las pasiones* (Havana: Cultura, 1935). *Jara*, in *Libro de las pasiones* (Havana: Cultura, 1935). *Granja* (Granja), in *Libro de las pasiones* (Havana: Cultura, 1935). *El dictador* (The Dictator), in *Libro de las pasiones* (Havana: Cultura, 1935).

BIBLIOGRAPHY: José L. Abellán, "En torno a la figura, la obra y la significación intelectual de Juan Montalvo," *Cuadernos hispanoamericanos* 320–321 (1977): 249–277. Roberto D. Agramonte, "Preámbulo de los *Siete tratados* de Montalvo," *Circulo* 19 (1990): 39–46. Enrique Anderson Imbert, "El arte de la prosa de Juan Montalvo," *Explicación de textos literarios* 3 (1975): anexo 210 pp. Diego Araujo Sánchez, "Panorama del teatro ecuatoriano," Cultura 2.5 (1979): 100. Augusto Arias, *Panorama de la literatura ecuatoriana* (Quito: Imprenta de la Universidad 1948), 143–164, 412. Isaac Barrera, *Juan Montalvo* (Quito: Casa de la Cultura Ecuatoriana, 1954). Franklin Barriga López and Leonardo Barriga López, *Diccionario de la literatura ecuatoriana* (Quito: Casa de la Cultura Ecuatoriana, 1973). Benjamín Carrion, *Unamuno y Montalvo* (Quito: Casa de la Cultura Ecuatoriana, 1954), 29–34. Salvador Bueno, "A propósito del sesquicentenario de Juan Montalvo," *Casa de las Américas* 135 (1982): 140–46. Ricardo Descalzi, *Historia crítica del teatro ecuatoriano*, 6 vols. (Quito: Casa de la Cultura Ecuatoriana, 1968), 203–214, 226–228, 1202–1203. L. R. Gallo, *Literatos ecuatorianos* (Riobamba: n.p., 1927). Eloy R. González and Jennifer T. Roberts, "Montalvo's Recantation, Revisited," *Bulletin of Hispanic Studies* 55 (1978): 203–210. Plutarco Naranjo, "Los escritos de Montalvo," in *Juan Montalvo. Estudio biobibliográfico*, vol. 1 (Quito: Casa de la Cultura Ecuatoriana, 1966), 311–334. Plutarco Naranjo and Carlos Rolando, *Juan Montalvo. Estudio biobliográfico*, vol. 2 (Puebla, Mexico: Editorial José M. Cajica, 1971). Marcela Ochoa Penroz, "Juan Montalvo: una reescritura del Quijote en América," *Inti* 46–47 (1997–1998): 57–70. Rodolfo Pérez Pimentel, *Diccionario biográfico del Ecuador*, vol. 8 (Guayaquil: Imprenta de la Universidad de Guayaquil, 1994), 228–236. J. S. Rodó, *Hombres de América* (Barcelona: Editorial Cervantes, 1924). Hernán Rodríguez Castelo, *Teatro ecuatoriano*, vol. 1, Col. Ariel no 17 (Guayaquil-Quito: Publicaciones Educativas "Ariel," n.d.), 23–28. Antonio Sacoto, "Amplitud de la obra literaria de Montalvo: lo francés," *Revista hispánica moderna* 35 (1969): 237–247. Sacoto, "García Moreno y la política en la obra de Montalvo," *Cuadernos americanos* 164 (1969): 137–155. Sacoto, "El pensamiento de Montalvo sobre el indio y el negro," *Cuadernos americanos* 158 (1968): 171–178. Sacoto, "Veintimilla en *Las catilinarias* de Montalvo," *Cuadernos americanos* 182 (1972): 157–167. Edmund S. Urbanski, "Ecuadorian Literary War over Juan Montalvo," *Hispania* 52 (1969): 102–109. Alvaro San Félix, "Teatro de intención política en el Ecuador," *Cultura* 5.13 (1982): 213. Miguel Antonio Vasco, "The Mighty Pen," *Americas* 41.2 (1989): 57

PALACIO, Pablo Gonzalo Zaldumbide, *Cuatro grandes clásicos americanos* (Buenos Aires: Academia Argentina de Letras, 1947).

PALACIO, Pablo (1906–1947). Palacio was born in Loja. In 1918 he enrolled at the Colegio Bernardo Valdivieso, and in 1921 he participated in the Juegos Florales (Floral Contest). He published the short story *Un hombre muerto a puntapiés* (A Man Kicked to Death), which sparked considerable interest among the intellectual youth. Among a myriad of other activities, he was secretary of the Department of Education and dean of the College of Philosophy and Letters. He was a polemic writer, and his writings express the feelings of a transitional period. His emphasis on the unexpected leads him to what is seemingly a marginal area. His literary obsessions are characterized by borderline situations: madness, death, illness. Palacio experimented with language and criticized reality implacably, but his literature cannot be explained without taking into account the writer's own life, since the former only reflected his vital concerns. His play *Comedia inmortal* (Immortal Comedy) represents a satiric rebellion against romantic situations and characterization.

WORKS: *Comedia inmortal*, in *Revista Esfinge* 1.2 (1926); also in *Pablo Palacio. Obras escogidas* (Guayaquil: Clásicos Ariel, no. 8, n.d., 185–192). *Obras completas* (Complete Works) (Quito: Casa de la Cultura Ecuatoriana, 1964); also in Colección Letras del Ecuador, 31 (Guayaquil: Casa de la Cultura Ecuatoriana, núcleo del Guayas, 1976).

BIBLIOGRAPHY: Hugo Alemán, "Pablo Palacio," in *Presencia del pasado*, vol. 2 (Quito: Casa de la Cultura Ecuatoriana, 1953), 66–78. Franklin Barriga López and Leonardo Barriga López, *Diccionario de la literatura ecuatoriana* (Quito: Casa de la Cultura Ecuatoriana, 1973). Jozef Bell, "Pablo Palacio: un renovador," *Minas-Gerais suplemento literário* 30 (1975): 9. Rubén Darío Buitrón, Pablo Palacio: *Vida del ahorcado* (Mexico City: Premiá Editora, 1982). Fernando Burgos, "La vanguardia hispanoamericana y la transformación narrativa," *Nuevo texto crítico* 2.3 (1989): 157–169. Benjamin Carrion, "Pablo Palacio en *Mapa de América* (Madrid: SGEL, 1931). Wilfredo H. Corral, "Colindantes sociales y literarias de *Débora* de Pablo Palacio," *Texto crítico* 14 (1979): 188–199. Wilfrido Corral, "La recepción canónica de Palacio como problema de la modernidad y la historiografía literaria hispanoamericana," *Nueva revista de filología hispánica* 35.2 (1987): 773–788. Louise T. Crissman, "The Works of Pablo Palacio: An Early Manifestation of Contemporary Tendencies in Spanish American Literature," *DAI* (1973): 86–87A. Mari Dahl, "Reacciones frente al espejo palaciano: La condena, la locura y la modernidad," *Dactylus* 12 (1993): 71–83. Ricardo Descalzi, *Historia crítica del teatro ecuatoriano*, 6 vols. (Quito: Casa de la Cultura Ecuatoriana, 1968), 730–735. Renato Flores Jaramillo, "Dos novelistas enloquecidos en la mitad del mundo," *Cuadernos hispanoamericanos* 303 (1975): 677–692. Renén Flores Jaramillo, "Pablo Palacio o la magnífica locura," *Cultura* (1984): 29–62. Michael Hendelsman, "Una doble y única lectura de 'Una doble y única mujer' de Pablo Palacio," *Chasqui* 24.2 (1995): 3–23. Miriam Julia Kohen, "Sociología de la función social en la obra de Pablo Palacio," *Cultura* (1984): 103–128. Pierre López, Daniel Meyran, and Adriana Castillo de Berchenko, eds. *Pablo palacio: Entre le drame et la folie: Le Cas d'un narrateur equatorien des années 30.* Perpignan, France: Centre de recherches Iberiques et Latino-Americaines, 1993. Gerardo Luzuriaga, *Bibliografía del teatro ecuatoriano. 1900–1982* (Quito: Casa de la Cultura Ecuatoriana, 1984), 72–73. Alfredo Pareja Diezcanseco, "El reino de la libertad en Pablo Palacio," *Casa de las Américas* 22.127 (1981): 3–20. Rodolfo Pérez Pimentel, *Diccionario biográfico del Ecuador*, vol. 3 (Guayaquil: Imprenta de la Universidad de Guayaquil, 1987), 315–321. Renato Prada-Oropeza, "La metaliteratura de Pablo Palacio," *Hispamérica* 10.28 (1981): 3–17. David Quintero, "Ideología y representación en Pablo Palacio," *DAI* 51.9 (1991): 3094A, University of Washington. David Quintero, "*Un hombre muerto a puntapiés*: lectura introductoria," *Revista iberoamericana* 54.144–145 (1988): 725–737. Humberto Robles, "Pablo Palacio: El anhelo insatisfecho," *Cultura* (1984): 63–78. Hernán Rodríguez Castelo, "Otro caso aparte," in *Teatro ecuatoriano*, no. 55 (Guayaquil-Quito: Publicaciones Educativas "Ariel," n.d.), 15. Rodríguez Castelo, *Teatro ecuatoriano*, vol. 2. Col. Clásicos Ariel no. 36 (Guayaquil-Quito: Publicaciones Educativas "Ariel," n.d.), 19. Jorge Ruffinelli, "Pablo Palacio: Literatura, locura y sociedad," *Revista de crítica literaria latinoamericana* (Lima) 5.10 (1979): 47–60. Ruffinelli, "Pablo Palacio: retrato de un precursor maldito," *Revista de Bellas Artes* 27 (1976): 20–23. Francisco Tobar García, "Pablo Palacio, el iluminado," *Homenaje a Pablo Neruda y Miguel Angel Asturias*, ed. Francisco Sánchez Castaner and Luis Sáinz de Medrano (Madrid: Consejo Superior de Investigaciones Científicas, 1973–1974), 657–665.

PALACIOS, Carlos Alberto. Born in Loja, Palacios cultivated lyric poetry, although one of his most noteworthy achievements was his allegoric play *El despertar de la selva* (The Jungle's Awakening). He took great pride in exulting the work of the Catholic missionaries in the Amazon region of Ecuador.

WORK: *El despertar de la selva* (Loja: Editorial Bolívar, 1965).

BIBLIOGRAPHY: Ricardo Descalzi, *Historia crítica del teatro ecuatoriano*, 6 vols. (Quito: Casa de la Cultura Ecuatoriana, 1968), 1748–1750. Gerardo Luzuriaga, *Bibliografía del teatro ecuatoriano. 1900–1982* (Quito: Casa de la Cultura Ecuatoriana, 1984), 73.

PROAÑO, Juan Félix (1850–1938). Proaño was born in Riobamba on July 20, 1850. He entered the religious life and was dean of the Cathedral of Riobamba. Well known in historical and archeological circles, Proaño was inspired by the Indian folklore, especially the Indians of Licán. A humanist, he was a member of the Academy of History. In the literary field, he is noted for his theatrical production. In 1919 he wrote *Quizquiz* (an Incan tragedy), on the life of General Quizquiz and his fighting against the conquerors, and *Condorazo* (Condorazo) (king of Puruhá), a prehistorical Ecuadoran drama, which presents the history of Régulo de Puruhá. He also wrote *Arengas* with which the ambassadors of the Tihuantinsuyo

(Cuzco and Quito) went to Licán to congratulate the Emperor Huayna-Capac on his marriage to Princess Pacha de Puruhá. Juan Félix Proaño is a point of reference for the modern historical dramatists.

WORKS: *Quizquiz o el desastre de una raza* (Quizquiz or The Disaster of a Race) (Riobamba: Imprenta de "El Observador," 1919). *Condorazo* (Riobamba: Tipografía Prensa Católica, 1925).

BIBLIOGRAPHY: Augusto Arias, *Panorama de la literatura ecuatoriana* (Quito: Imprenta de la Universidad, 1948), 413. Franklin Barriga López and Leonardo Barriga López, *Diccionario de la literatura ecuatoriana* (Quito: Casa de la Cultura Ecuatoriana, 1973). Ricardo Descalzi, *Historia crítica del teatro ecuatoriano*, 6 vols. (Quito: Casa de la Cultura Ecuatoriana, 1968), 572–583. Gerardo Luzuriaga, *Bibliografía del teatro ecuatoriano. 1900–1982* (Quito: Casa de la Cultura Ecuatoriana, 1984), 76. Rodolfo Pérez Pimentel, *Diccionario biográfico del Ecuador*, vol. 1 (Guayaquil: Imprenta de la Universidad de Guayaquil, 1987), 381. Hernán Rodríguez Castelo, ed., "Introduccíon. *Arengas*," in *Teatro ecuatoriano*, vol. 1., Col. Clásicos Ariel no. 17 (Guayaquil-Quito: Publicaciones Educativas "Ariel," n.d.), 41–59. Rodríguez Castelo, "Folk-loore de los indígenas de Lican," *El telégrafo* (Guayaquil), March 3, 1930. Rodríguez Castelo, *Literatura ecuatoriana*, Col. Clásicos Ariel no. 100 (Guayaquil-Quito: Publicaciones Educativas "Ariel," n.d.), n.p.

RENDÓN PÉREZ, Víctor Manuel (1859–1940). Víctor Manuel Rendón, a noted playwright, was born in Guayaquil on December 2, 1859. He died in 1940 after a long and fulfilling career. Throughout his lifetime, he held a number of important positions of public service: member of the Academia Ecuatoriana and correspondent for the Academia Española; academic for the Academia Hispanoamericana de Ciencias y Artes de Cádiz; and member of the Academia Diplomática Internacional de Paris. Physician, diplomat, dramatist, and poet, he went to France, where he held a diplomatic post in the Ecuadoran embassy in Paris. He lived there for several years, which explains why some of his plays were written in French, and then later performed in Quito, Guayaquil, and Riobamba. Rendón was a prolific writer, credited with twenty-nine books written in Spanish and sixteen in French. Perhaps the most interesting aspect of his literary personality is his capacity as a dramatist. Unfortunately, his first play, *La muerte de Veleda* (Veleda's Death), written while he was attending secondary school, has been lost. *Le revenant*, written in French and later translated into Spanish with the title *Cuadro heróico* (Heroic Picture), was performed in Paris during World War I. Upon his return to Ecuador, he continued with his dramatic work: *Con Victoria y Gloria Paz* (With Victoria and Gloria Paz); *El matrimonio eugénico* (Eugenic Marriage), which was written in honor of the dramatist Carlos Arturo León; *Charito* (Charito); and *Las tres Victorias* (The Three Victoria Girls), where with only one name for three different characters the author presents this dramatic farce. Compared to the romantic drama of his time, the emphasis in Rendón's plays is all on a perfect picture of life. In more concrete terms, his production has all the French earmarks, rather than the Ecuadoran *costumbrismo*, with the exception of *Salus populi* (The Well-Being of the People), which has a national theme—Gabriel García Moreno; it is set in Guayaquil, and it is considered his best drama because of the historical precision of the stated events. Within this line of Ecuadoran themes some *sainetes* written in the last years of his life might be placed. In this aspect, it can be seen as part of a dramatic tradition whose most glorious ancestors are the French dramatists.

WORKS: *Cuadro heroico* (Guayaquil: Reed & Reed, 1937). *Madrinas de guerra* (Godmothers of War) (Guayaquil: Reed & Reed, 1937). *Hoy, ayer y mañana* (Today, Yesterday and Tomorrow) (Guayaquil: Reed & Reed, 1937). *El matrimonio eugénico* (Guayaquil: Reed & Reed, 1937). *El ausentismo* (Absenteeism) (Guayaquil: Reed & Reed, 1937). *Con Victoria y Gloria Paz* (Guayaquil: Reed & Reed, 1937). *Periquín o la noche sabrosa* (Periquín or a Delightful Night) (Guayaquil: Reed & Reed, 1937). *En fuente florida* (In Fuente Florida Resort) (Guayaquil: Reed & Reed, 1937). *Salus populi* (Guayaquil: Reed & Reed, 1937). *Charito* (Charito) (Guayaquil: Reed & Reed, 1937). *Almas hermosas* (Beautiful Souls) (Guayaquil: Reed & Reed, 1937). *El billete de lotería* (The Lottery Ticket) (Guayaquil: Reed & Reed, 1937). *Las tres Victorias* (The Three

Victoria Girls) (Guayaquil: Reed & Reed, 1937). *La carretilla* (The Wheelbarrow) (Guayaquil: Reed & Reed, 1937).

BIBLIOGRAPHY: Augusto Arias, *Panorama de la literatura ecuatoriana* (Quito: Imprenta de la Universidad, 1948), 413. Franklin Barriga López and Leonardo Barriga López, *Diccionario de la literatura ecuatoriana* (Quito: Casa de la Cultura Ecuatoriana, 1973). "Biobibliografía," Colección Letras no. 82 (Guayaquil: Casa de la Cultura Ecuatoriana del Guayas, 1979), 5. Ricardo Descalzi, *Historia crítica del teatro ecuatoriano*, 6 vols. (Quito: Casa de la Cultura Ecuatoriana, 1968), 526–566. Gerardo Luzuriaga, *Bibliografía del teatro ecuatoriano. 1900–1982* (Quito: Casa de la Cultura Ecuatoriana, 1984), 76–80. Rodolfo Pérez Pimentel, *Diccionario biográfico del Ecuador*, vol. 2 (Guayaquil: Imprenta de la Universidad de Guayaquil, 1987), 262–266. Victor Manuel Rendón, *Teatro; obras representadas en el Ecuador (1922–1936)* (Guayaquil: Reed & Reed, 1937). Hernán Rodríguez Castelo, *Teatro ecuatoriano*, vol. 2, Col. Clásicos Ariel no. 36 (Guayaquil-Quito: Publicaciones Educativas "Ariel," n.d.), 14–15, 18. Rodríguez Castelo, "Teatro ecuatoriano," *Cuadernos hispanoamericanos* 172 (1964): 85. Alvaro San Félix, "Teatro de intención política en el Ecuador," *Cultura* 5.13 (1982); 215.

RODRÍGUEZ CASTELO, Hernán (1933–   ).

A playwright and bibliographer, Rodríguez Castelo was born in Quito, on June 1, 1933. He holds degrees in classical humanities and philosophy, in addition to having studied theology and religious studies. He is a member of the Academia Ecuatoriana de la Lengua and founder and director of the Cine-Club of criticism. He is also professor in several colleges and has participated in critical roundtables at colleges and universities. He received the highest laurels in recognition of his work as writer and educator. Among his important dramatic works are *Canción de Navidad* (Christmas Song), an adaptation of Dickens's play; *El pobre hombrecillo* (The Poor Man), his longest and most ambitious work, an example of Calderonian theater; *La noche aquella* (That Night), based upon a short story written by Selma Lagerlot; *La fiesta*, his best theatrical creation; and *El hijo* (The Son), in which the author advances the examination of human solitude. Rodríguez Castelo succeeds in making clear his vision ex-

ploring religious themes. As a critic, he has edited various texts on theatrical criticism. Among them are *Teatro contemporáneo*, *Teatro ecuatoriano*, and *Teatro social ecuatoriano*.

WORKS: *Canción de Navidad* (Quito: Talleres Gráficos "Royal Print," 1959). *La noche aquella* (That Night), in *Mi colegio*, December 1960. *El Decreto 21–29* (The Decree 21–29), in *El catolicismo* (Guayaquil, 1965). *El pobre hombrecillo* (The Poor Man), *La fiesta* (The Party), and *El hijo* (The Son), in *Teatro* (Quito: Casa de la Cultura Ecuatoriana, 1967). *Casandra, el payaso y el vagabundo* (Casandra, the Clown and the Vagabond), performed in the II Festival Nacional de Teatro on August 16, 1969. *Teatro ecuatoriano*, Col. Clásicos Ariel no. 36 (Guayaquil-Quito: Publicaciones Educativas "Ariel," ca. 1971). *Teatro contemporáneo*, Col. Clásicos Ariel no. 96 (Guayaquil-Quito: Publicaciones Educativas "Ariel," ca. 1972). *Teatro social ecuatoriano*, Col. Clásicos Ariel no. 55 (Guayaquil-Quito: Publicaciones Educativas "Ariel," ca. 1972). *El principito* (The Little Prince), based on *La conquista del reino* (The Kingdom's Conquest) and *Feliz día señor San José* (Good Day, Mr. San José) (unpublished).

BIBLIOGRAPHY: Diego Araujo Sánchez, "Panorama del teatro ecuatoriano," *Cultura* 2.5 (1979): 94–109. Franklin Barriga López and Leonardo Barriga López, *Diccionario de la literatura ecuatoriana* (Quito: Casa de la Cultura Ecuatoriana, 1973). Ricardo Descalzi, *Historia crítica del teatro ecuatoriano*, 6 vols. (Quito: Casa de la Cultura Ecuatoriana, 1968), 1581–1605. Gerardo Luzuriaga, *Bibliografía del teatro ecuatoriano. 1900–1982* (Quito: Casa de la Cultura Ecuatoriana, 1984), 81–82. Luzuriaga, "La generación del 60 y el teatro," *Caravelle Cahiers du Monde Hispanique et Luso-Brésilien* 34 (1980): 164. Rodolfo Pérez Pimentel, *Diccionario biográfico del Ecuador*, vol. 5 (Guayaquil: Imprenta de la Universidad de Guayaquil, 1988), 262–268. Ernesto Proaño, *Literatura ecuatoriana* (Cuenca: Editorial Don Bosco, n.d.), 439–440. Hernán Rodríguez Castelo, "Hernán Rodríguez Castelo," in *Teatro contemporáneo*, Col. Clásicos Ariel no. 96 (Guayaquil-Quito: Publicaciones Educativas "Ariel," n.d.), 48–51. Rodríguez Castelo, "Teatro ecuatoriano," *Cuadernos hispanoamericanos* 172 (1964): 102. Francisco Tobar García, "Teatro durante los años 1944 a 1956 vistos por un autor," in *Trece años de cultura nacional. Ensayos de varios autores* (Quito: Casa de la Cultura Ecuatoriana, 1957), 97.

RODRÍGUEZ S., Antonio. This poet and religious playwright's dramatic production is im-

pressive. Rodríguez stresses the role of the two elements that have contributed to the production of his dramas: Ecuadoran history and legends beginning with colonial events. *El terremoto* (The Earthquake), based on the earthquake that struck Riobamba, Ambato, and Latacunga, on February 4, 1797, and *La sed de oro* (The Gold Fever), about the tragedy of Cajamarca, with the sacrifice of the last Inca, Atahualpa, among others, demonstrate Rodríguez's concern to depict and to interpret the life of his country.

WORKS: *El terremoto* (Quito: Editorial Chimborazo, 1926). *La emboscada de Berruecos* (The Berrueco Ambush), written in 1926 (Quito: Escuela Tipográfica Salesiana, 1933). *La sed de oro* (Quito: Prensa Católica, 1928). *Tarqui* (Tarqui's Plain) (Revista *El centinela*, s.n., 1929). *Las vírgenes del sol* (Goddesses of the Sun) (Latacunga: Imprenta America, 1932). *La virgen de la selva* (The Jungle's Virgin), a dramatic adaptation of Juan León Mera's novel *Cumandá* (Quito: Escuela Tipográfica Salesiana, 1932). *La mejor conquista el corazón* (The Best Conquest Is the Heart) (Quito: Escuela Tipográfica Salesiana, 1938).

BIBLIOGRAPHY: Ricardo Descalzi, *Historia crítica del teatro ecuatoriano*, 6 vols. (Quito: Casa de la Cultura Ecuatoriana, 1968), 2001. Gerardo Luzuriaga, *Bibliografía del teatro ecuatoriano. 1900–1982* (Quito: Casa de la Cultura Ecuatoriana, 1984), 82–83. Hernán Rodríguez Castelo, *Teatro ecuatoriano*, vol. 2, Col. Clasicos Ariel n. 167 36 (Guayaquil-Quito: Publicaciones Educativas "Ariel," n.d.), 18.

ROMÁN, Sergio (1934–). Román is a playwright and poet born in Guayaquil in 1934. He holds a Licenciatura in social sciences. A sharp political critic, he is specially known for his defense of the Cuban revolution. In 1962 he went into exile in Costa Rica, where he was professor of scenography—the art of representing drama—at the Conservatorio de Castella, in San José, and later university professor, particularly in the area of theatrical arts. In Costa Rica he found the opportunity to dedicate himself completely to theater. As theatrical director, he produced *La zapatera prodigiosa* by Federico García Lorca, *La visita de la vieja dama* by Dürrenmatt, *El mar trajo la flor* by the Ecuadoran dramatist Eugenia Viteri, and

others. His play *Un extraño en la niebla* (A Stranger in the Fog) revitalized the Ecuadoran drama precisely because this author believed that significant social issues should be dealt with there.

WORKS: *Un extraño en la niebla* (Guayaquil: Casa de la Cultura Ecuatoriana, 1970); also in *Teatro ecuatoriano contemporáneo*, vol. 2 (Guayaquil: Casa de la Cultura Ecuatoriana, 1971), 1–54. *Función para butacas* (Function for Armchairs) (Guayaquil: Casa de la Cultura Ecuatoriana, 1972); also in *Teatro ecuatoriano contemporáneo*, vol. 3 (Guayaquil: Casa de la Cultura Ecuatoriana, 1973), 135–179.

BIBLIOGRAPHY: Franklin Barriga López and Leonardo Barriga López, *Diccionario de la literatura ecuatoriana* (Quito: Casa de la Cultura Ecuatoriana, 1973). Gerardo Luzuriaga, *Bibliografía del teatro ecuatoriano. 1900–1982* (Quito: Casa de la Cultura Ecuatoriana, 1984), 83. Hernán Rodríguez Castelo, "Sergio Román," in *Teatro contemporáneo*, Col. Ariel no. 96 (Guayaquil-Quito: Publicaciones Educativas "Ariel," n.d.), 52–54.

SACOTO ARIAS, Augusto (1907–1979). He was a poet and playwright, born in Azogues on September 18, 1907. He studied his secondary school at the Colegio Nacional Juan Bautista Vázquez. In 1927 he began his studies in law and social science at the University in Cuenca; then he traveled to Quito during the revolution of the "Cuatro días," where he completed his career. He devoted himself to literature, particularly to poetry, and undertook the artistic and literary project of producing poetic theater. The *Velorio del albañil* (The Bricklayer's Wake), of elegiac style, and *La furiosa Manzanera* (The Furious Manzanera), a tragedy that received the Premio Nacional de Literatura in 1942, have been considered within the literature of social concern. Both plays show how Sacoto tuned his voice to the Spanish dramatist García Lorca, although recognizing his distinction. In all his work we have a testimony of his taste for the magical aspect of popular tradition.

WORKS: *Velorio del albañil* (The Bricklayer's Wake) (Quito: Litografía e Imprenta Romero, 1938); also in Hernán Rodríguez Castelo, ed., *Clásicos Ariel* no. 36 (Guayaquil: Publicaciones Educativas "Ariel," 1971), 125–133. *La furiosa Manzanera* (Quito: Litografía e Imprenta Romero, 1942); also in (Quito: *Re-*

vista del Mar Pacífico, 1943); and in Hernán Rodríguez Castelo, ed., Clásicos Ariel no. 36 (Guayaquil: Publicaciones Educativas "Ariel," 1971), 135–169. *Adah* (unpublished).

BIBLIOGRAPHY: Diego Araujo Sánchez, "Panorama del teatro ecuatoriano," *Cultura* 2.5 (1979): 105. Augusto Arias, *Panorama de la literatura ecuatoriana* (Quito: Imprenta de la Universidad, 1948), 436–439. Franklin Barriga López and Leonardo Barriga López. *Diccionario de la literatura ecuatoriana* (Quito: Casa de la Cultura Ecuatoriana, 1973). Ricardo Descalzi, *Historia crítica del teatro ecuatoriano*, 6 vols. (Quito: Casa de la Cultura Ecuatoriana, 1968), 1136–1146. Aurelio Espinosa Polit, Prólogo (Quito: Editorial Revista del Mar Pacífico, 1936), 8–9. Gerardo Luzuriaga, *Bibliografía del teatro ecuatoriano. 1900–1982* (Quito: Casa de la Cultura Ecuatoriana, 1984), 85. Luzuriaga, "La generación del 60 y el teatro," *Caravelle-Cahiers du Monde Hispanique et Luso-Brésilien* 34 (1980): 162. Hernán Rodríguez Castelo, ed., *Teatro ecuatoriano*, vol. 2, Col. Clasicos Ariel no. 36 (Guayaquil-Quito: Publicaciones Educativas "Ariel," n.d.), 19. Rodríguez Castelo, "Teatro ecuatoriano," *Cuadernos hispanoamericanos* 172 (1964): 92. Humberto Vacas Gómez, "Augusto Sacoto Arias," *Cuadernos del Guayas* 47 (1979): 51–53.

SALAZAR TAMARIZ, Hugo (1923–   ). Salazar is a poet and playwright, born in Cuenca on September 2, 1923. He traveled extensively throughout America, Europe, Asia, and Africa. In 1940 he moved to Guayaquil, where he is currently residing, and became a university professor in Ecuadoran literature and contemporary drama. As an actor, he participated in the theatrical group Horizonte. In 1962 he published the play *La llaga* (The Ulcer). In this play Salazar condemns political corruption and the hope for a new order of justice, in addition to offering a good example of critical realism. In 1968 he published three plays in one volume: *La falsa muerte de un ciclista* (The Faux Death of a Bicyclist), *Toque de queda* (Curfew), and *Por un plato de arroz* (Because of a Dish of Rice). *La falsa muerte de un ciclista* is a balance between farce and the grotesque where the Pirandellian influence is quite obvious. In *Por un plato de arroz* the author underlines the importance of the genre as an essential expression of the stage of life.

WORKS: *La llaga* (Cuenca: Editorial Casa de la Cultura Ecuatoriana, Núcleo del Azuay, 1962). *La falsa muerte de un ciclista*, in *Teatro* (Guayaquil: Casa de la Cultura Ecuatoriana, 1968), 7–53. *Por un plato de arroz*, in *Teatro* (Guayaquil: Casa de la Cultura Ecuatoriana, 1968), 105–123; also in *Teatro ecuatoriano contemporáneo*, vol. 2 (Guayaquil: Casa de la Cultura Ecuatoriana, 1961), 221–256. *Teatro* (Guayaquil: Casa de la Cultura Ecuatoriana, 1968). *La falsa muerte de un ciclista*, *Toque de queda*, and *Por un plato de arroz* in *Teatro. El habitante amenazado*, in *Teatro ecuatoriano contemporáneo*, vol. 3 (Guayaquil: Casa de la Cultura Ecuatoriana, 1973), 181–236. *En tiempos de la colonia* (Babahoyo: Universidad técnica de Babahoyo, 1979).

BIBLIOGRAPHY: Franklin Barriga López and Leonardo Barriga López, *Diccionario de la literatura ecuatoriana* (Quito: Casa de la Cultura Ecuatoriana, 1973). Ricardo Descalzi, *Historia crítica del teatro ecuatoriano*, 6 vols. (Quito: Casa de la Cultura Ecuatoriana, 1968), 1700–1708. Carlos Espinosa Domínguez, "Entrevista a Ilonka Vargas," *Latin American Theatre Review* 16 (1983): 64. Gerardo Luzuriaga, *Bibliografía del teatro ecuatoriano. 1900–1982* (Quito: Casa de la Cultura Ecuatoriana, 1984), 86–87. Rodolfo Pérez Pimentel, *Diccionario biográfico del Ecuador*, vol. 5 (Guayaquil: Imprenta de la Universidad de Guayaquil, 1988), 281–287. Hernán Rodríguez Castelo, "Otros autores: Hugo Salazar Tamariz," in *Teatro contemporáneo*, Col. Clasicos Ariel no. 96 (Guayaquil-Quito: Publicaciones Educativas "Ariel," n.d.), 37.

SALGADO VIVANCO, Manuel. Salgado published his works with two pen names, Juan Gil and Juan Jacobo. A talented journalist, he published his political articles in *El Dia* in Quito. His lack of sentimentality in confronting reality face to face, when that reality is so painful and depressing, is undoubtedly his greatest quality as a writer and satirist. *El delito legendario* (Legendary Crime), a sharp criticism of judges and social conventions, *Un potaje comunista* (A Communist Porridge), and *La casa del crimen* (The House of Crime), where he deals with the problem of abortion, are a few examples of the author's most secret and passionate ambition: to modify people's nature.

WORKS: *El delito legendario*, performed in Quito, on May 17, 1928 (unpublished). *Un potaje* *comunista*, performed in Quito, on May 23, 1931 (unpublished). *La casa del crimen* (Quito: Tipografía Fernández, 1935). *Política de faldas* (Women in Politics) (unpublished). *El sexto no adulterar* (The Sixth Doesn't Commit Adultery) (unpublished). *Los abolengos* (Noble Lineages) (unpublished). *La promesa del traidor* (The Traitor's Promise) (unpublished).

BIBLIOGRAPHY: Ricardo Descalzi, *Historia crítica del teatro ecuatoriano*, 6 vols. (Quito: Casa de la Cultura Ecuatoriana, 1968), 821–851. Gerardo Luzuriaga, *Bibliografía del teatro ecuatoriano. 1900–1982* (Quito: Casa de la Cultura Ecuatoriana, 1984), 88. Alvaro San Félix, "Teatro de intención política," *Cultura* 5.13 (1982): 215.

SAN FÉLIX, Alvaro (1931–   ). Pen name of Carlos Benavides Vega, a playwright. Born in Guayaquil, he is considered the master of the dramatic conceit. He is a numerary member of the Instituto Otavaleño de Antropología. A tireless traveler, San Félix wrote *En lo alto, grande laguna* (Way Up High, Great Lagoon), where it is not the official history that is presented but rather the true history of one land, Otavalo. As an authentic man of theater, he dedicated himself to acting and writing theater, touring not only his country but Latin America as well. One of the pioneers of historical drama, he wrote *Caudillo en llamas* (Chief on Fire), *Espejo, alias Chushig* (Espejo, Alias Chushig), and *La herida de Dios* (The Wound from God), about the historical figure of Gabriel García Moreno. This play received the award Aurelio Espinosa Polit, Premio Nacional de Literatura, in 1978. In *La muerte viene de Dallas* (Death Comes from Dallas), he is a stern judge of the atomic bomb world. Ecuadoran characters as Montalvo, Manuela Sáenz, González Suárez, and García Moreno have a place in his dramas. With Pedro Saad Herrería, he wrote *Una loca estrella* (A Crazy Star), a play of historical theater on Manuelita Sáenz.

WORKS: *Las ranas y el mar* (The Frogs and the Sea) (Quito: Talleres Gráficos del Ministerio de Educación, 1962), 101–123; also in *Teatro ecuatoriano contemporáneo*, vol. 2 (Guayaquil: Casa de la Cultura Ecuatoriana, 1971), 192–220. *Teatro ecuatoriano: Cuatro piezas en un acto* (Quito: Editorial Ministerio de Educación, 1962). *Un caballo para Elena* (A Horse for Helen), in *La última rueda*

(Quito) 3–4 (1976): 82–108. *La herida de Dios* (The Wound from God) (Quito: Universidad Católica, 1979). *Caudillo en llamas* (Chief on Fire) (Guayaquil: Casa de la Cultura Ecuatoriana, Núcleo del Guayas, 1980); also with *Espejo, alias Chushig* (Otavalo: Editorial Gallo Capitán, 1979). *La muerte viene de Dallas* (Death Comes from Dallas) (unpublished).

BIBLIOGRAPHY: Diego Araujo Sánchez, "Panorama del teatro ecuatoriano," *Cultura* 2.5 (1979): 108. Franklin Barriga López and Leonardo Barriga López, *Diccionario de la literatura ecuatoriana* (Quito: Casa de la Cultura Ecuatoriana, 1973). Jorge Dávila Vásquez, "Aproximación al teatro ecuatoriano," *Cultura* 2.3 (1979): 383–384. Dávila Vásquez, "Aproximación al teatro ecuatoriano contemporáneo," *La última rueda* (Quito) 7 (n.d.): 15–18. Ricardo Descalzi, *Historia crítica del teatro ecuatoriano*, 6 vols. (Quito: Casa de la Cultura Ecuatoriana, 1968), 1688–1695. Carlos Espinosa Domínguez, "Entrevista a Ilonka Vargas," *Latin American Theatre Review* 16 (1983): 64. Gerardo Luzuriaga, *Bibliografía del teatro ecuatoriano. 1900–1982* (Quito: Casa de la Cultura Ecuatoriana, 1984), 90. Manolo F. Medina, "La metahistoria en *La herida de Dios*: Otro juicio público de García Moreno," *Verdad* (Universidad del Azuay) 6 (1990): 189–204. Hernán Rodríguez Castelo, *Teatro contemporáneo*, Col Clásicos Ariel no. 96 (Guayaquil-Quito: Publicaciones Educativas "Ariel," n.d.), 47–48. Rodríguez Castelo, "Teatro ecuatoriano," *Cuadernos hispanoamericanos* 172 (1964): 117. Alvaro San Félix, "Nos quedamos inéditos," *Difusión cultural* 1.1 (1984): 36–37. San Félix, "Teatro de intención política en el Ecuador," *Cultura* 5.13 (1982): 209–225. San Félix, "Teatro: pronóstico reservado," *Espejo* (Quito) 1.1 (1979): 24–28. Carlos Miguel Suárez Radillo, "Síntesis panorámica del teatro ecuatoriano de hoy," *Fundateatros* (Caracas) 4 (1970): 2.

SOLA FRANCO, Eduardo (1915–   ). A painter and playwright, he was born in Guayaquil on October 16, 1915. He began his life as a dramatist in Lima. After traveling through America and Europe, he presented his first play in Guayaquil in 1966. While in Lima he wrote *Las bodas que prepara el diablo* (Weddings Prepared by the Devil) and *Regreso al recuerdo* (Return to Memories). In Hamilton (Bermuda Islands), he produced *Habitación sin tiempo* (Room without Time). *Trampa al inocente* (Trick for the Innocent) was performed in Paris, and finally, having returned to Lima, he published *Los caminos oscuros* (Dark Roads), *El silencio* (Silence), as well as the novel *Latitud cero* (Zero Latitude) and *Del otro lado del mar* (On the Other Side of the Sea), a book of short stories. In 1966, commemorating the anniversary of the city of Guayaquil, he wrote *El Apocalipsis* (Apocalypse), where he depicts a tormented man who is condemned to live an everyday life. Another play, *El árbol de tamarindo* (The Tamarind Tree), was written in Guayaquil and is an example of a tropical spell manifested in the local and rural environment. Sola Franco's theater can be characterized for its tendency to utilize all forms of allegory. The high aesthetic value of his artistic production—as both a painter and dramatist—makes him one of the most important artists of the twentieth century.

WORKS: *El Apocalipsis*, performed in Guayaquil, July 26, 1966 (unpublished). *El árbol de tamarindo*, performed in Guayaquil, April 26, 1967 (unpublished). *La mujer enclaustrada en el Ritz*, performed in 1988. His last plays *La habitación en sombra* (The Shadowed Room), *Lucha con el ángel* (Fighting with the Angel), *Palacio de espejos* (The Palace of Mirrors), *El zafarrancho* (1988, a surrealist drama), and *Ojos de los gatos en la noche* have not been performed yet.

BIBLIOGRAPHY: Ricardo Descalzi, *Historia crítica del teatro ecuatoriano*, 6 vols. (Quito: Casa de la Cultura Ecuatoriana, 1968), 1780–1800. Gerardo Luzuriaga, *Bibliografía del teatro ecuatoriano. 1900–1982* (Quito: Casa de la Cultura Ecuatoriana, 1984), 91–93. Rodolfo Pérez Pimentel, *Diccionario biográfico del Ecuador*, vol. 8 (Guayaquil: Imprenta de la Universidad de Guayaquil, 1994), 330–345.

TOBAR GARCÍA, Francisco (1928–). A poet and playwright, he was born in Quito in November 1928. His father was the famous historiographer Julio Tobar Donoso. He attended the Jesuit school Colegio San Gabriel in which a theatrical tradition was well developed. In 1947, his first drama, *Casa de naipes* (The House of Cards), inspired by Schiller's *The Bandits*, was performed. In 1954 he created his own theatrical group, and his plays *El miedo* (Fear), *Las mariposas* (Butterflies), and *En una sola carne o La trampa* (In One Flesh Only or

The Trap) were performed. According to Tobar himself, *El miedo* is a kind of anticipation of his production. Two subjects dominated Tobar's writing: solitude and death. Intertwined with these two ample topics are the genres of autobiography and biography. That is the case of his play *Amargo misterio* (Bitter Mystery), unpublished owing to the author's desire, because of its biographical character. Without attempting to analyze his works, we should point out that his theatrical production encompasses both tragedy and comedy and that his passion to depict the anguish of contemporary man is an underlying force in his dramas. In the play *La parábola* (The Parable) of Kafkian atmosphere, the characters reach the line of symbolical order. However, in *Todo lo que brilla es oro* (Everything That Shines Is Gold) a bitter irony serves as aesthetic catalyst. In sum, Tobar's theater could be characterized for its intellectual approach and his fatalist tendency. He has been called "the prophet of the middle class," and no play better exemplifies this title than his dramatic trilogy *Trilogía del mar* (Trilogy of the Sea), where the three plays included are interwoven by the human context of their characters: a photographic record of human failure.

WORKS: *Un hombre de provecho* (A Useful Man), performed in Quito in 1951 (unpublished). *El miedo* (Fear), in *Teatro*, vol. 1 (Quito: Casa de la Cultura Ecuatoriana, 1962). *Las mariposas* (The Butterflies), in *Teatro*, vol. 1 (Quito: Casa de la Cultura Ecuatoriana, 1962). *En una sola carne o La trampa* (One Flesh Only or The Trap), in *Teatro*, vol. 1 (Quito: Casa de la Cultura Ecuatoriana, 1962). *La res* (The Cattle), in *Teatro*, vol. 1 (Quito: Casa de la Cultura Ecuatoriana, 1962). *Atados de pies y manos* (Tied Hands and Feet), in *Teatro*, vol. 1 (Quito: Casa de la Cultura Ecuatoriana, 1962). *El limbo* (The Limbo) or *Todo lo que brilla es oro* (Everything that Shines is Gold), in *Teatro*, vol. 1 (Quito: Casa de la Cultura Ecuatoriana, 1962). *La parabola*, in *Teatro*, vol. 1 (Quito: Casa de la Cultura Ecuatoriana, 1962). *Transmigración del avaro* (The Avaricious' Transmigration), in *Teatro*, vol. 2 (Quito: Casa de la Cultura Ecuatoriana, 1962). *Los dioses y el caballo* (The Gods and the Horse), in *Teatro*, vol. 2 (Quito: Casa de la Cultura Ecuatoriana, 1962). *El silencio* (Silence), in *Teatro*, vol. 2 (Quito: Casa de la Cultura

Ecuatoriana, 1962). *Ares y Mares o La noche no es para dormir* (Ares and Mares or The Night Is Not for Sleeping), in *Teatro*, vol. 2 (Quito: Casa de la Cultura Ecuatoriana, 1962), translated into German and French. *La llave del abismo* (The Key for the Abyss), in *Teatro*, vol. 2 (Quito: Casa de la Cultura Ecuatoriana, 1962). *Alguien muere la víspera* (Somebody Will Die the Eve), performed in Quito in June 1962 (unpublished). *Una gota de lluvia en la arena* (A Raindrop on the Sand), performed in Quito, in May 1963 (unpublished). *El arca de Noé* (Noah's Ark), performed in Quito, in June 1963 (unpublished). *Trilogía del mar* (Trilogy of the Sea), performed in Quito (1963–1964–1965), includes *Una gota de lluvia en la arena*, *El ave muere en la orilla*, and *Las ramas desnudas*. *El ave muere en la orilla* (The Bird Dies on the Shore), performed in Quito, in May 1964 (unpublished). *El César ha bostezado* (Cesar Has Yawned), performed in Quito, in November 1964 (unpublished). *Las ramas desnudas* (Naked Branches), performed in Quito, in May 1965 (unpublished). *La gallina de los huevos de oro* (The Hen of the Golden Eggs), performed in Loja, on May 8, 1966 (unpublished). *Extraña ocupación* (Strange Occupation), in *Tres piezas de teatro* (Quito: Casa de la Cultura Ecuatoriana, 1967). *Cuando el mar no existe* (When the Sea Does Not Exist), in *Tres piezas de teatro* (Quito: Casa de la Cultura Ecuatoriana, 1967). *Un león sin melena* (A Lion without a Mane), performed in Quito, on May 5, 1967 (unpublished). *La dama ciega* (The Blind Lady) (Quito: Casa de la Cultura Ecuatoriana, 1967). *El recreo* (The Break), performed in Quito, in June 1974 (unpublished). *En los ojos vacíos de la gente* (The People's Blank Stare), in *Teatro contemporáneo*, Col. Clásicos Ariel no. 96 (Guayaquil-Quito: Publicaciones Educativas "Ariel," n.d.) 67–149.

BIBLIOGRAPHY: Diego Araujo Sánchez, *La literatura ecuatoriana en los últimos treinta años (1950–1980)* (Quito: Editorial El Conejo, 1983). Franklin Barriga López and Leonardo Barriga López, *Diccionario de la literatura ecuatoriana* (Quito: Casa de la Cultura Ecuatoriana, 1973). Francesca Colecchia, "Un ejemplo del diálogo angustiado en el teatro," *Espiral* 104 (1967): 5–13. Carla Dávalos, Entrevista. "Paco Tobar, ¿vividor, loco o genio?" *Hoy* (Quito), February 20, 1988. "Vivir" Supplement. Jorge Dávila Vàzquez, "Aproximación al teatro ecuatoriano contemporáneo," *Cultura* 2.3 (1979): 381–396; also in *La última rueda* 7 (n.d.): 19–22. Ricardo Descalzi, *Historia crítica del teatro ecuatoriano*, 6 vols. (Quito: Casa de la Cultura Ecuatoriana, 1968), 1411–1577. Zulema Echegarry, "Usigli, To-

bar y Carballido," *Vértice* (1992): n.p. Francisco Febres Cordero, "En busca de destino," *Cultura* 18 (1984): 248. Renato Flores Jaramillo, "Dos novelistas enloquecidos en la mitad del mundo," *Cuadernos hispanoamericanos* 303 (1975): 677–692. Gerardo Luzuriaga, *Bibliografía del teatro ecuatoriano. 1900–1982* (Quito: Casa de la Cultura Ecuatoriana, 1984), 93–100. Luzuriaga, "La generación del 60 y el teatro," *Caravelle-Cahiers du Monde Hispanique et Luso-Brésilien* 34 (1980): 160. Herminio G. Neglia, "La escenificación del fluir psíquico en el teatro hispanoamericano," *Hispania* 58 (1975): 884–889. José Maria Oyuela Cantos, "El teatro de Francisco Tobar García," *Arco* 9.75 (1967): 38–44. Julio Pazos Barrera, "Tres piezas de teatro de Paco Tobar García (*La esperanza a pesar de la muerte*)," Thesis (Quito, Universidad Católica, 1968). Hernán Rodríguez Castelo, "Introducción," in *Teatro contemporáneo*. Col. Clásicos Ariel no. 96 (Guayaquil-Quito: Publicaciones Educativas "Ariel," n.d.), 26–36. Rodríguez Castelo, "Teatro ecuatoriano," *Cuadernos hispanoamericanos* 172 (1964): 107, 108–115. Rodríguez Castelo, *Teatro ecuatoriano*, vol. 2. Col. Clásicos Ariel no. 36 (Guayaquil-Quito: Publicaciones Educativas "Ariel," n.d.), 18–19, 27. Kessel Schwartz, "Francisco Tobar García and *Un hombre de provecho*," *Romance Notes* 14.2 (1972): 252–257. Francisco Tobar García, "Francisco Tobar, por él mismo, "*El Tiempo* (Quito), May 6, 1969. Tobar García, "*La noche no es para dormir*," *Arco* 2, 8–9 (1960): 253–254. Tobar García, "El teatro durante los años de 1944 a 1956 vistos por un autor," In *Trece años de cultura nacional. Ensayos de varios autores* (Quito: Casa de la Cultura Ecuatoriana, 1957), 83–100. Rodrigo Villacis Molina, "Francisco Tobar, hombre de teatro," in *Transparencias* (Quito: Casa de la Cultura Ecuatoriana, 1963), 9–34.

TOLEDO DE LAMAS, Saranelly (1933–   ). Born in Riobamba, she is a poet and playwright. She has also contributed to cultural journalism and began writing a section entitled "Agenda cultural" (Cultural Agenda) in an Ecuadoran newspaper. As a poet she published *Los peces de jade cantan a la paz* (The Jade Fish Sing About Peace) and *Orfeo y otros cantos* (Orpheus and Other Songs). As a dramatist, she wrote *El viaje y el féretro* (The Trip and the Coffin), *Las noches de la bruja* (Witch Nights), *Martin Luther King*, and the monologue *Poda*.

WORKS: *Martin Luther King* in *Razón y fábula*

(Revista de la Universidad de los Andes, Bogotá) 12 (1967): 131–148. *Poda*, performed in Casa de la Cultura, Guayaquil, 1968 (unpublished). *Orfeo y otros cantos* (Quito: Casa de la Cultura Ecuatoriana, 1971). *Las noches de la bruja* (Guayaquil: Casa de la Cultura Ecuatoriana, Núcleo del Guayas, 1977). *Los peces de jade cantan a la paz* (Guayaquil: Imprenta Municipal, 1984). *El viaje y el féretro* (unpublished).

BIBLIOGRAPHY: Morayma Ofyr Carvajal, *Galería del espíritu. Mujeres de mi patria* (Quito: Editorial Fray Jodoco Ricke, 1949), n.p. Gerardo Luzuriaga, *Bibliografía del teatro ecuatoriano. 1900–1982* (Quito: Casa de la Cultura Ecuatoriana, 1984), 54. Rodrigo Pesantez Rodas, *Presencia de la mujer ecuatoriana en la poesía* (Guayaquil: Universidad de Guayaquil, 1960), n.p. Hernán Rodríguez Castelo, "Saranelly de Lamas," in *Teatro contemporáneo*. Col. Clásicos Ariel no. 96 (Guayaquil-Quito: Publicaciones Educativas "Ariel," n.d.), 51–52.

UBIDIA, Abdón (1944–). Abdón Ubidia is generally considered one of the greatest living Ecuadorian writers. He was born in Quito in 1944. A novelist, short story writer, poet, essayist, and playwright, Ubidia has become well-known in literary circles and among the general Ecuadorian public for his literary production. At a young age, he was a member of the "Tzántzico" movement and one notes in his first works a profound interest for social transformation. Ubidia has published studies of oral literature, including *El cuento popular* (The Popular Short Story, 1977) and *La poesía popular ecuatoriana* (The Ecuadorian Popular Poetry, 1982). *Bajo el mismo extraño cielo* (Under the Same Strange Sky), a collection of stories, won the National Literary prize José Mejía. His novel *Sueño de lobos* (Wolves' Dreams) (1986), written under the most modern literary tendencies, was awarded the same prize and was declared by the critics the best novel published that year. In 1989 he published *Divertinmentos o Libro de fantasías y utopías* (1989) a collection of short fiction, and in 1996 appeared *El palacio de los espejos* (The Mirrors' Palace). His most recent works are *Referentes*, a collection of essays dealing with the loss of the traditional values, and *El cristal con que se mira*,

a book on literary criticism. Some of his works have been translated into English, French, German, and Russian. His novel *Ciudad de invierno* (Winter City), whose protagonist is the city of Quito, is now in its tenth edition. At the turn of the century, Ubidia shows his intellectual sharpness in writing the play *Adiós, Siglo XX* (Good-bye, Twentieth Century). In this piece, although he acknowledges the theatrical value of the "epic"—the play is an enormous parable—he rejects its rational assumptions as a form of facile optimism. In *Adiós, Siglo XX*, Ubidia's use of alienation techniques to disillusion, measures up to the complexities of the twentieth century existence which can no longer be clarified. At present, Abdón Ubidia directs the renowned publishing house "El Conejo" in Quito.

WORKS: *El cuento popular* (The Popular Short Story) (Quito: IADAP, 1977). *Bajo el mismo extraño cielo* (Under the Same Strange Sky) (Bogotá: Círculo de Lectores, 1979). *Sueño de lobos* (Wolves' Dreams) (Quito: Editorial El Conejo, 1986). *Divertinmentos, libro de fantasías y utopías* (Divertinmentos: A Book of Fantasies and Utopias) (Quito: Grijalbo, 1989). *El palacio de los espejos* (The Mirrors' Palace) (Quito: Editorial El Conejo, 1996). Mary Ellen Fiewegar, trans., *Wolves' Dream* (Pittsburgh, PA: Latin American Literary Review Press, 1997). *Ciudad de invierno y otros relatos* (Winter's City and Other Short Stories) (Quito: Eskeletra, 1999). *Referentes* (Referents) (Quito: Editorial El Conejo, 2000). *Adiós, Siglo XX* (Good-bye, Twentieth Century) (Quito: Colección Antares, 2002).

BIBLIOGRAPHY: Cecilia Ansaldo, *Literatura ecuatoriana de los últimos treinta años* (Quito: Editorial El Conejo, 1983). Jorge Dávila Vázquez y Alexandra Astudillo Figueroa, "Estudio introductorio." In *Cuentos escogidos* (Quito: Libresa, 1993). Lupercio González, "Realidad desnuda. Entrevista a Abdón Ubidia, escritor." (Internet: *Fusión*: Revista mensual, January 30, 2003). Gladys Jaramillo, et al., *Indice de la narrativa ecuatoriana* (Quito: Editora Nacional, 1992). Laura Hidalgo, "Epílogo." In *Ciudad de invierno* (Cuenca: Casa de la Cultura Ecuatoriana, 1983) 139+. Alberto Rengifo, *La gillete, un cuento de Abdón Ubidia* (Quito: Departamento de Letras de la Universidad Católica del Ecuador, 1987. Pedro Saad, "*Adiós, Siglo XX* (Quito: Colección Antares. 2002. Raúl Vallejo, *Una gota de* *inspiración, toneladas de transpiración* (Quito: Libresa, n.d.).

VARGAS, Arístides (1954–). Born in Córdoba, Argentina, 1954. He started acting onstage when he was very young. At the age of twenty-one he was forced into exile because of the Argentinian military coup d'état. During the exile he went first to Perú, and then to Ecuador, taking up residence in Quito in 1977. He acted in *Apareces*, a film directed by Carlos Naranjo and in *Entre marx y una mujer desnuda* (1996), an adaptation of Jorge Enrique Adoum's novel by Camilo Luzuriaga, a film full of intrigue, satire, and magical realism. However, Arístides Vargas is above all a man of theater. In seeking to better the Latin American theater, he founded with other professionals the theatrical group Malayerba (Weeds) in 1979. He is an award-winning author and actor. His first dramatic text was *Jardín de pulpos* (The Octopuses Garden), followed by *La edad de la ciruela* (The Age of the Plum), and *Pluma y la tempestad* (Pluma and the Storm) where he explores the significance of identity constructs. In June 2002, in the Berlin House of World Cultures, the Grupo Malayerba gave the European premiere of *Nuestra Señora de las Nubes* (Our Lady of the Clouds), written in 1998 and considered a masterpiece of Latin American theater. Its success is attributed to its political treatment of exile. A man of great talent, Vargas knew how to portray a society in process of change. In his plays, memories are creative and recapture past time reliving impressions of past experiences. On looking closer at his last plays, one finds that in *La casa de Rigoberta mira al sur y El deseo más canalla* characters are not the subjects of the play but symbols, examples through which many critical questions can be analyzed.

WORKS: *La fanesca* (The Ecuadoran Soup "Fanesca"), 1984 (Festival de Grenoble, August 2002). *Jardín de pulpos* (Octopuses Garden), 1992. (Teatro Iré de Puerto Rico, 2001). *La edad de la ciruela* (The Age of the Plum), 1994 (Festival de Cádiz, 1998). *Pluma y la tempestad* (Pluma and the Storm), 1995 (Festival de Cádiz, 1997; Festival de Bogotá, 1998; Universidad del Valle, Colombia, 1999). *Teatro. Jardín de pulpos. La edad de la ciruela. Pluma y la*

tempestad (Quito: Eskeletra Editorial, 1997). *Nuestra Señora de las Nubes* (Our Lady of the Clouds), 1998 (*Primer acto* 275 (1998): 57–72) (Temporada Teatral de Chile, 1999; X Festival de Teatro de La Habana, 2000; Panamá, Teatro Nacional, 2001; Berlin: House of World Cultures, 1ˢᵗ May–1ˢᵗ June, 2002). *Nuestra Señora de las Nubes, Donde el viento hace buñuelos, El deseo más canalla.* (Madrid: Consorcio Casa de América, 2000). *La casa de Rigoberta mira al sur* (Dallas, Teatro Dallas, 2000; Managua, Nicaragua, Teatro Rufino Garay, 2000; Festival Vallenato, Colombia, 2001; La Habana, Festival Mayo Teatral 2001).

BIBLIOGRAPHY: David Ladra, "*Pluma y la tempestad*, de A. Vargas" (*Primer acto* 271 (1997): 104–105). Ladra, "El teatro de Arístides Vargas" (*Primer acto* 275 [1998]: 56). Ania Martí, "Otra apuesta latinoamericana por el arte escénico" (*La jiribilla*, Havana, May 2001). *Jardín de pulpos y Pluma y la tempestad*, in *Postmodernismo y teatro en América Latina*, ed. Beatriz J. Rizk (Madrid: Iberoamericana, 2001). Sara Torres, "Tres espectáculos latinoamericanos" (*Primer acto* 286 (2000): 136–137). L. Teresa Valdivieso, "Ecuador: trayectoria de un teatro" (II Congreso Internacional de Caminerías Iberoamericanas. Universidad Nacional de Rosario, Argentina, August 1999). Valdivieso, "Las encrucijadas de la escena: innovación en el teatro latinoamericano," *Voces y textos literarios del Ecuador* (Quito: Editorial El Conejo, 2003). Arístides Vargas, "*La casa de Rigoberta mira al sur*," *Conjunto* 121 [2001]: n.p.). Vargas, "La dramaturgia de lo invisible" (Talleres, Astarté Films. Costa Rica, 2001). Vargas, "Evolucíon formal en el teatro latinoamericano" (*Primer acto* 275 [1998]: 51–55). Emily Zhukov, "Malayerba" (⟨http://www.villaconcordia-pma.com⟩. January 30, 2003).

VERA, Pedro Jorge (1914–). He was born in Guayaquil on June 16, 1914. A poet, novelist, and playwright, he studied social sciences at the universities of Guayaquil and Quito, and became a university professor. He traveled throughout America, Europe, and Asia and has lived in Chile and Cuba. He initiated himself as a writer by publishing poetic books, such as *Nuevo itinerario* (New Itinerary) in 1937 and *Romances madrugadores* (Early Ballads) in 1939. While in Chile, he published his first play, *El Dios de la selva* (The Jungle God), performed in Santiago in 1941. A novelist, he produced his first novel, *Los animales puros* (Pure Animals), in 1946. In 1952 Vera wrote his second play, *Hamlet resuelve su duda* (Hamlet Resolves His Doubt), which was reprinted four years later under the title *Los ardientes caminos* (The Burning Paths). Back in Quito, he was enthused with theater, especially with the group Teatro Intimo whose actors performed Vera's play *Luto eterno* (Eternal Mourning). In 1956 he furthered his career as a playwright by publishing the volume *Teatro*, which included four plays: *La mano de Dios* (God's Hand) is within the parameters of the theater of ideas, although the characters are symbolic. *Luto eterno* underscores the lack of authenticity in modern society. Vera himself classified this play as a "grotesque farce." In the third play of this volume, *Los ardientes caminos*, Vera excels in dramatizing within a character the myth of a large sector of Ecuador. In *El Dios de la selva*, his best play, the dramatist creates a scenario similar to the one in the famous novel *La Vorágine*, in which the protagonist is surrounded by the tropics. Unlike the novel, however, nature is not the dominating element but, rather, the dominated.

WORKS: *El Dios de la selva* (Quito: Anales de la Universidad Central, 1943). *Hamlet resuelve su duda* (Quito: Casa de la Cultura Ecuatoriana, 1952). *La mano de Dios*, in *Teatro* (Quito: Casa de la Cultura Ecuatoriana, 1956). *Luto eterno*, in *Teatro* (Quito: Casa de la Cultura Ecuatoriana, 1956). *Los ardientes caminos*, in *Teatro* (Quito: Casa de la Cultura Ecuatoriana, 1956). *Los animales puros*, vols. 1 and 2, Col. Clásicos Ariel no. 26 and no. 27 (Guayaquil-Quito: Publicaciones Educativas "Ariel," n.d.); also (Quito: Editorial El Conejo, Col. Biblioteca de literatura ecuatoriana, no. 4, 1986).

BIBLIOGRAPHY: Franklin Barriga López and Leonardo Barriga López, *Diccionario de la literatura ecuatoriana* (Quito: Casa de la Cultura Ecuatoriana, 1973). Francesca Colecchia, *"Luto eterno," Duquesne Hispanic Review* 2 (1963): 77–83 (comparison of *Luto eterno* by Pedro Jorge Vera with *La casa de Bernada Alba* by Federico García Lorca). Ricardo *Descalzi, Historia crítica del teatro ecuatoriano*, 6 vols. (Quito: Editorial Casa de la Cultura Ecuatoriana, 1968), 1267–1295. Mary J. Haritos, "Las novelas de Pedro Jorge Vera." *DAI* 46.11 (1986): 3366A. Michael H. Hendelsman, *"El secuestro del general, El pueblo soy yo* y la desmitificación del caudillo," *Revista/Review interamericana* 10.2 (1980): 135–142. Gerardo Luzuriaga, *Bibliografía del teatro ecuatoriano. 1900–1982* (Quito: Casa de la Cultura Ecuatoriana, 1984), 103–104. Luis Martul Tobio, "La construcción del dictador populista en *El pueblo soy yo*," *Revista iberoamericana* 58.159 (1992): 489–500. Herminio Neglia, "Dos aspectos de lo heroico en la literatura hispanoamericana del siglo XX," *Revista interamericana de bibliografía* 33 (1983): 231–236. Enrique Novoa Arizaga and Laura de Crespo, *Antología del relato ecuatoriano* (Quito: Casa de la Cultura Ecuatoriana, 1973), 227–229. Rodolfo Pérez Pimentel, *Diccionario biográfico del Ecuador*, vol. 4 (Guayaquil: Imprenta de la Universidad de Guayaquil, 1987), 275–281. Isabel Robles and Jaime Montañez, "Entre la política y la literatura: las novelas de Pedro Jorge Vera," *Cuadernos hispanoamericanos* 328 (1977): 130–143. Hernán Rodríguez Castelo, "Entrevista." *El tiempo*, March 21, 1971. Rodríguez Castelo, "Pedro Jorge Vera y su gran *Dios de la selva*," in *Teatro ecuatoriano*, Col. Clásicos Ariel no. 55 (Guayaquil-Quito: Publicaciones Educativas "Ariel," n.d.), 29–33. Rodríguez Castelo, Prólogo a *Los animales puros*, Col. Clásicos Ariel no. 26 (Guayaquil-Quito: Publicaciones Educativas "Ariel," n.d.). Rodríguez Castelo, "Teatro ecuatoriano," *Cuadernos hispanoamericanos* 172 (1964): 95–97. Antonio Sacoto, "La novela ecuatoriana del 70," *Cuadernos americanos* 230 (1980): 200–209. Enrique Vázquez López, "Dos miradas a los últimos relatos de Pedro J. Vera: "Los mandamientos de la ley de Dios" y "La semilla estéril," *Situación del relato ecuatoriano*, ed. Manuel Corrales Pascual (Quito: Ediciones de la Universidad Católica, 1977–1979).

VILLASÍS ENDARA, Carlos (1930–). He is a poet, short story writer, and playwright. Born in Manabí, Villasís founded the Museo de Arte Latinoamericano and was appointed secretary for the Biennial of Quito in 1967. He was also the founder of the Galaxia group in Cotopaxi, in addition to organizing the first meeting of young writers in the city of Latacunga. Villasís has written mostly poetry and also a collection of historical short stories compiled in his book *Cuna de héroes* (Cradle of Heroes). However, he has also published a book entitled *Teatro* that includes four plays: *El hombre de la máscara* (The Masked Man), *En cualquier lugar del mundo* (Anywhere in the World), *El* *hombre que cambió su sombra* (The Man Who Traded His Shadow), and *San Juan de las manzanas* (Saint John of Apples). This latter work is an *auto popular*, which in 1967 received an award at the Second Festival of the Arts in Guayaquil. According to Villasís it is inspired by the short story "La muerte tiene permiso" (Death Has Permission) by the Mexican writer Edmundo Valadés. The work *En cualquier lugar del mundo* is a tragedy based on the anguish suffered by Spain when two atomic bombs were dropped on the Spanish sea.

WORKS: *El hombre en la máscara, En cualquier lugar del mundo, El hombre que cambió su sombra,* and *San Juan de las manzanas,* in *Teatro* (Quito: Casa de la Cultura, 1967). *Anatomía del disparate* (Quito: Casa de la Cultura Ecuatoriana, 1978). *Los caminos oscuros de la gloria,* in *Los caminos oscuros de la gloria y otras piezas de teatro* (Quito: Casa de la Cultura Ecuatoriana, 1978). *La ciudad en una trampa, Las ratas huyen del sol, Los caminos oscuros de la gloria, El director de fracasos,* and *Anatomía del disparate,* in *Los caminos oscuros de la gloria y otras piezas de teatro* (Quito: Casa de la Cultura Ecuatoriana, 1978).

BIBLIOGRAPHY: Franklin Barriga López and Leonardo Barriga López, *Diccionario de la literatura ecuatoriana* (Quito: Casa de la Cultura Ecuatoriana, 1973). Ricardo Descalzi, *Historia crítica del teatro ecuatoriano,* vol. (Quito: Casa de la Cultura Ecuatoriana, 1968), 1834–1850. Gerardo Luzuriaga, *Bibliografía del teatro ecuatoriano. 1900–1982* (Quito: Casa de la Cultura Ecuatoriana, 1984), 105–107. Galo René Pérez, *Pensamiento y literatura del Ecuador* (Quito: Casa de la Cultura Ecuatoriana, 1972), n.p. Hernán Rodríguez Castelo, "Carlos Villasís Endara," in *Teatro contemporáneo,* Col. Clásicos Ariel no. 96 (Guayaquil-Quito: Publicaciones Educativas "Ariel," n.d.), 41–42. Rodríguez Castelo, *Literatura ecuatoriana 1830–1980* (Otavalo: Editorial Gallocapitán, 1980), 146–147.

VITERI, Eugenia (1932–). Born in Guayaquil on June 2, 1932, she attended the School of Philosophy at the University of Guayaquil. Later she was appointed editor of the journal *Mañana* and traveled throughout Mexico, Chile, Cuba, France, Spain, Italy, former USSR, and Korea. With her husband Jorge Vera, she has undertaken diverse journalistic projects while devoting herself to writing short stories and theater. Her first book was a collection of short stories entitled *Diez cuentos universitarios* (Ten Stories from the University), which includes "El anillo" (The Ring) in which she explores a theme that she would later use in elaborating her drama. Politically a socialist, she never abandons popular realism. In 1962, she received a prize for her play *El mar trajo la flor* (The Flower Was Brought by the Sea), based on the short story "El anillo." This play, in which Viteri's art acquired a more symbolic vision, emphasizes her ability to explore human relations. No doubt that in the development of theater written by women, Viteri has been an outstanding example of a writer setting the pace for women's literature.

WORKS: *El mar trajo la flor,* in *Teatro ecuatoriano: Cuatro piezas en un acto.* José Martínez Queirolo et al. (Quito: Ministerio de Educación Pública, 1962), 125–143.

BIBLIOGRAPHY: Franklin Barriga López and Leonardo Barriga López, *Diccionario de la literatura ecuatoriana* (Quito: Casa de la Cultura Ecuatoriana, 1973). Benjamín Carrión, "Los zapatos y los sueños," *Los zapatos y los sueños* 34 (1977): 9–10. Ricardo Descalzi, *Historia crítica del teatro ecuatoriano,* 6 vols. (Quito: Casa de la Cultura Ecuatoriana, 1968), 1695–1700. Herberto Espinoza. "Voces y espacios femeninos en *Las alcobas negras* de Eugenia Viteri". *Letras femeninas* 21.1 (1995): 47–56. Gerardo Luzuriaga, *Bibliografía del teatro ecuatoriano. 1900–1982* (Quito: Casa de la Cultura Ecuatoriana, 1984), 107. Consuelo Navarro. "Sexo y literatura: mito y realidad". *Kañina* 9.2 (1985): 25–29. Hernán Rodríguez Castelo, "Los autores y las obras," in *Teatro contemporáneo,* Col. Clásicos Ariel no. 96 (Guayaquil-Quito: Publicaciones Educativas "Ariel," n.d.), 24.

Teresa Valdivieso

El Salvador

El Salvador is a country of painting, poetry, and short story. Other genres, such as the novel or the theater, have received less attention. But more than any other artistic expression, Salvadoran character is defined by unexpressed thoughts. If Fuentes (27) views Argentina as the place where ideas are put into words in Latin America, González y Contreras (33–35), in one of the rare essays on the Salvadoran national spirit, claims that silence, mutilated expressions, and tragic beauty are the basic features of El Salvador's "underground human being." According to González, El Salvador is a country of artistic muteness. It is therefore not accidental that since Gallegos Valdés's essay on Salvadoran literature there have been very few attempts to develop a critique of the country's history of the arts. Even in the United States, where since the mid-1970s an interest in the sociopolitical history exists due primarily to the civil war, there is neither an extensive analysis of Salvadoran literature and arts nor a single work on what Salvadorans often judge to be the country's primary contribution to the current Latin American canon: regionalist painting and narrative. This lack of information is accentuated by the exclusion that most academic works on Latin American arts have perpetuated until the present—the silence of any reference to the country's history of the arts. There is therefore a close correspondence between the Salvadoran tendency toward artistic muteness and the silence of criticism about Salvadoran culture. One of the scarce works on Salvadoran literature is Beverley and Zimmerman's chapter on the use of poetry as an ideological channel for the diffusion of revolutionary ideas thoughout the country (115–143). Nevertheless, their approach is so ideologically Marxist that it excludes any reference to poets like David Escobar Galindo, who has published more than thirty books, or to other highly influential literary publications, such as *Taller de Letras* of the Universidad Centroamericana (UCA), and to the weekly literary page of the various newspapers of the capital city.

Salvadoran literature is thus still waiting for its critics. And the same lack is true for more specific studies on particular artists. There are no descriptive monographs on the main writers—Francisco Gavidia, Salarrué, or Roque Dalton—nor for the most relevant painters—José Mejía Vides, Valero Lecha, Carlos Cañas. A cultural history of the country has yet to be written.

The pre-Columbian text that would legitimate El Salvador's claim to having been one of the great centers of Central American native cultures has yet to be found, such as the *Güegüense* for Nicaragua or Guatemala's *Rabinal Achí*. Nevertheless, more than the drama of an extinct past civilization, what characterizes Salvadoran rural culture is the presence of a syncretic colonial legacy. There are indeed multiple "dances" that can be considered as traditional popular theater.

The *historiantes*, or rehearsed masked plays that tell battle stories between medieval

Moors and Spaniards, date back to the colonial period and are kept alive by Indian and Mestizo communities in the countryside, as well as in certain important cities. Similarly, *La danza del tigre y del venado* (The Dance of the Tiger and the Deer), *La partesana*, the *Procesiones de Semana Santa* (Holy Week Processions), and *La yegüita* (The Little Mare), just to mention a few, are examples of the syncretism of Salvadoran popular culture. María de Baratta's *Cuzcatlán típico* represents the most classical ethnographic account on the "theater-dances"; one may also consult Marroquin's ethnographies *San Pedro Nonualco* (1964) and *Panchimalco* (1959), the *Calendario de fiestas religiosas tradicionales* (Dirección), as well as Herrera Vega's *Expresión literaria* (Literary Expression). All of these texts present detailed information on the "dances," although they lack the interpretative dimension that characterizes the current works on cultural studies in the United States. These seasonal rehearsals, produced sometimes by an entire community, as is the case for the Passion stories during the Holy Week, are testimony to the rich medieval culture still alive in the country. Even though literary scholars have usually abandoned their study, it would not be difficult to state the relationships of these dances to several "high-literary" works such as *La chanson de Rolland* and the *Codex Calixtinus* or *Liber Sancti Jacobi*, as well as to the *Stabat Mater* or the *Passion*. Indeed, medieval and Renaissance forms of musical theater are salient traits of what today city-dwellers refer to as "Indian" and peasant culture. But as a matter of fact, their syncretic character has accentuated regional features, thanks to which local history is recorded through biblical or literary symbols. The works of anthropologists and musicologists point in the same direction (Bricker; Cohen, 16). While Bricker has demonstrated how in the Chiapas Highlands Indian historiography is encoded in their seasonal festivities, Cohen has raised the question of what the role of Aztec perception was in the rehearsal of the *Lamentation of Jeremiah*, based on Don Juan de Lienas's version of 1650. For Salvadoran popular theater, the identification of Christ, the savior, and the name of the country is so obvious that the Passion, in its theatrical and musical form, has been used innumerable times by popular and high-literary culture, as well as by Liberation Theology, in order to offer an encoded interpretation of current tragic events. Following a similar metaphorical bias, the Transfiguration of the Christ, celebrated on August 6, has traditionally offered a symbolic pattern to those interested in a more romantic vein.

To go beyond pure descriptive ethnographic accounts, that is, toward a more interpretative analysis, is perhaps the most important task of future criticism. Salarrué's final work, his only novel *Catleya luna* (1974), has opened the path to future research on the cryptic Indian historiography encoded in those theater-dances. He claims that the figure of the deer in *La danza del tigre y del venado*, as performed in the Izalco region, may be viewed as a scapegoat figure. The simple ethnographic account of a mere hunting ceremonial assumes a deep religious meaning in his novel. The deer is recognized as a nagual, or double animal, that represents a Quetzalcoatl or Christ-like figure, whose immolation is required for the well-being of the community. Nevertheless, given the contemporary academic convention that assigns the study of popular theater to the realm of anthropology, we will concentrate ourselves on high-literary works.

Independence from Spain in 1821 marks the beginning of El Salvador's national theater. Touring companies from Mexico and Spain began performing in the country before Independence. By the mid-nineteenth century they had become constant visitors. From 1842 on, theaters were built for their performances. The most important plays of the first half of the century—*Mournful Nights* (1827), author unknown, and *La tragedia de Francisco Morazán* (Francisco Morazán's Tragedy) (only published in 1894), by Francisco Díaz—establish a close link between the writing and acting of theater and the foundation of the Salvadoran nation. They both portray the deeds of the nation's founders, Manuel José Arce and Francisco Morazán.

At the end of the nineteenth century, the Liberal Reform confiscated the land from the Indian communities and from the Church, starting a process of land concentration where coffee flourished. This period saw the emergence of the first truly literary movement in Central America in general, as Ramírez has noted (306–307). Nevertheless, if in the rest of the peninsula the emergent national literatures developed by a conflict between regionalism and modernism, in El Salvador the works of Francisco Gavidia, a literary corpus that spanned over fifty years, facilitated their reconciliation. Gavidia is the founder of Salvadoran national literature, writing in all genres except for the novel. Anticipating the role of modernist poets, he translated French poetry and playwrights into Spanish and introduced French metric techniques in order to create a new Latin American language. Nonetheless, he remained loyal to regional history, and his writing was never seduced by the modernist vogue of using an exotic thematic. All his plays are characterized by what Góchez Sosa and Canales (603) have called "the search of the nation through its historical past."

By the dawn of the twentieth century, El Salvador boasted five legitimate Italian theaters, three in San Salvador and one each in Santa Ana and San Miguel. The touring companies' influence on Salvadoran theater was immeasurable. They established a melodramatic style that was to last the entire twentieth century, generations after the original performances. They greatly encouraged local authors by producing their works.

From 1859 to 1931, the Mariano Luque, Evangelina Adams-Bravo, Virginia Fábregas, María Teresa Montoya, and Gerardo de Nieva companies produced and directed in San Salvador. In their wake, local talents emerged, and in 1929, the first state-sponsored drama school opened. While José María Peralta Lagos's play *Candidato* (Candidate) (1931) offers the most important artistic and historical account of this period, Gerardo de Nieva, a Spanish author and stage director who founded the Escuela de Artes Escénicas, 1928–1935, continued to produce a nationally oriented theater based on Gavidia's influence.

The 1929 Depression hit El Salvador brutally. In 1931, the first democratically elected government was replaced by a military regime that lasted until 1944. The following year, the Martínez dictatorship confined theater to the schoolyard, and theaters were converted into movie houses. His regime also exerted a very harmful influence on popular theater-dances. After suppressing an Indian revolt in the western part of the country, known in the United States as "Matanza" (Anderson), he forbade any reference to a cultural link with the Izalco group.

It was not until the late 1940s, with the advent of a process of industrialization and development after the 1948 revolution, that a National Theater Company was created. In 1957, the Universidad Nacional opened its own theater. Talented directors from France, Mexico, Italy, and Spain directed classical and contemporary works. Military reformism created the model of government that lasted until the end of the 1970s. Moreover, the coffee price increase during the 1950s propitiated a transfer of capital to industry and a development of the infrastructure. It is during this period that the four comprehensive works on the literary history of the country were written (Membreño, 1959; Toruño, 1958; Gallegos Valdés, 1958/1962; and López Vallecillos, 1964). It is also during these years that the novel emerged with the publication of more than fifteen novels in a country that had never practiced this modern and "bourgeois" genre.

Throughout the 1960s Edmundo Barbero, who had worked with Federico García Lorca of Spain, introduced Salvadoran audiences to the European and avant-garde theater. Sponsored by the Direccíon General de Artes, Barbero worked at the Direccíon de Teatro from 1952 and produced some classic plays of Calderón, Molière, Gogol, Pirandello, García Lorca, and surprisingly, Sartre and Camus. The presentation of Sartre's *A puerta cerrada* (Huit clos) provoked such an impact on Salvadoran society that a wide polemic on morality and art lasted more than two months in the newspapers of the capital. After a few years in Mexico, Barbero returned to San Salvador in 1963 and directed the Teatro Universitario at the Universidad Nacional. During this second period, he produced plays of Lope de Vega, Shakespeare, Machiavelli, Alberti, Beckett, Albee, and Brecht, alternating with national authors. Barbero's enormous influence on Salvadoran theater is the most clear example of the rapid development of Salvadoran urban literary culture, thanks largely to the inclusion of the middle classes in political bureaucracy. Around him appeared a new generation of playwrights, all born in the 1930s. Their preoccupations are political, to be sure, but more than that, existential, greatly influenced by Sartre and Camus. The early 1960s is El Salvador's most productive era in playwriting. Here below, we offer a brief commentary on the main playwrights of the period. Roberto Arturo Menéndez, author, actor, and stage director, wrote *Los desplazados* (The Displaced Ones) (1952), *La ira del cordero* (The Lamb Madness) (1959), and *Nuevamente Edipo* (Oedipus Again) (1966). While the first play relates the deeds of a disqualified old actor, the last two re-create classical myths, the biblical Cain and Abel and the Theban Oedipus.

Walter Béneke wrote *El paraíso de los imprudentes* (The Imprudent's Paradise) (1955) and *Funeral Home* (1958), set, respectively, in Paris and in the United States. Both deal with people at the end of their paths, forced to make decisions regarding the future. A similar vision to that of Béneke is offered by the plays of Alvaro Menen Desleal, author of *Luz negra* (Black Light) (1967). This is Menen Desleal's most important Beckett-inspired drama. *El cielo no es para el reverendo* (Heaven Is Not for the Priest) recreates the tradition of El partideño, a Salvadoran Robin Hood, which had previously inspired Gavidia's *Ursino at the Turn of the Century*. Italo López Vallecillos wrote two plays: *Las manos vencidas* (Defeated Hands), (1964), inspired by Sartre's *A puerta cerrada* (Huit clos), and *Burudy sur* (1969), a political farce. José Roberto Cea's *Las escenas cumbres* (The High Scenes) (1967) explores loneliness and uses the Icarus myth as a springboard for the story. Roberto Armijo recovered the legends of the *Popul Vuh* in his *El príncipe no debe morir* (The Prince Should Not Die) (1970) and uses a traditional children's game as a title for a play on political repression, *Jugando a la gallina ciega* (Playing the Blind Hen Game) (1970). Finally, José Napoleón Rodríguez Ruíz's *Anastacio Rey* (1970) belongs to this same prolific generation. Rodríguez Ruíz's recovery of an Indian uprising in the mid-nineteenth century, as a predecessor of today's revolutionary movement, won the first prize at the Concurso de Cultura in Guatemala in 1969.

Nevertheless, power struggles that effectively anticipated the civil war eventually caused the collapse of both the national and university companies in the early 1970s. The military intervention and closing of the Universidad Nacional, considered a stronghold of the guerrilla in the heart of the capital, was the most visible consequence of the forthcoming war. In this climate of repression and lack of funds for artistic creation, it was therefore not a coincidence that such a significant work as Barbero's *Panaroma del teatro en El Salvador*, which was planned as a complete anthology of Salvadoran theater, from Francisco Gavidia until the young playwrights in the late 1960s, was published in 1972–1979 only in its first volume.

In 1968, the National Arts Center (CENAR), a school for the performing arts within the secondary program of education, was opened. Collective creation became the dominant force in Salvadoran theater. Existing drama with plot and character development was rejected in favor of revisiting history from the point of view of the oppressed. Literary works were adapted for the theater. Many groups formed around innovative productions, but no playwrights appeared. Raw, young, angry graduates arrived on the scene at the outbreak of the civil war. Because of increasing polarization in the political arena and radicalism of the artists, many died or left the country. Since 1990, they have been returning, bringing with them techniques learned abroad. During the civil war, in the late 1980s, a new, independent movement was born, seeking, on the one hand, an all-out diversion for war-tired audiences and, on the other, trying to deal with the war itself.

Since the signing of the Chapultepec Peace Accords (1992), many attempts have been made to create theater on a new set of rules: Private theaters are opening constantly, companies are becoming more professional, and there is renewed audience interest. The government has just inaugurated a brand-new complex of buildings for the Performing Arts (CENAR), and theater has a salient role in this new state-sponsored institution. In 1993, Sol del Río, one of the most renowned groups in the country, organized a very successful Latin American Festival, with the participation of Mexico, Venezuela, all Central American countries, and even Denmark. This group has produced several of the biggest theatrical successes since the end of the war: *San Salvador después del eclipse* (San Salvador after the Eclipse) (1991) and *Tierra de cenizas y esperanzas* (Land of Ashes and Hope) (1992); Carlos Velis, an actor who specializes in adapting material for the stage, has coauthored these two plays. A recent publication, *Teatro* (1992), compiles three works of Velis's: *La misma sangre* (Same Blood) (1990), *La flor que se fue* (The Flower That Disappeared) (1991), and *San Salvador después del eclipse* (1992); written in a very colloquial language, the first and last one attempt to capture the uncertainty as well as the popular festivities for the signing of the Peace Accords. The second one is a children's play. Velis is also the author of one of the most complete histories on Salvadoran theater published by the Instituto Chiapaneco de Cultura. Young playwrights such as José Luis Ayala, Miguel Angel Chichilla, author of *Las abejas* (The Bees) (1985), and Giovani Galeas, who has already published *La conferencia* (The Conference) and *Diálogos eternos* (Eternal Dialogues) (1990) are all working on projects.

Regarding Salvadoran theaters, it is important to make the following concluding remarks. Performance conditions in El Salvador are extremely poor. When halls are built, little or no attention is given to performance needs, from the point of view of either stage or audience. By the end of World War II, the traditional italianate built at the end of the nineteenth century had become rat-infested third-rate movie houses. Interest in restoring them began to be expressed in the 1960s and actually started in the 1970s. Renovation of

San Salvador's National Theater was begun in 1976. The work was directed by Ricardo Jiménez Castillo, with Roberto Salomón and Simón Magaña as theatrical counsel. The theater, a technical gem, was completed at the outbreak of the civil war and has not yet been used to its full potential. Its magnificent murals were painted by Carlos Cañas. The Santa Ana National Theater was restored in the mid-1990s. The San Miguel National Theater restoration failed, and the theater is in shambles. None of the universities have theaters, and performances are held in big halls and classrooms. Private enterprise has undertaken the building of multipurpose auditoriums, but with the exception of the CAES (auditorium built in 1970), they rarely serve theater at all. In 1979, Actoteatro was built: A cultural center as a forum for all the arts around a central stage was a concept that seemed right for San Salvador. But as the war raged on, Actoteatro was closed. Since the end of the civil war, Actoteatro's concept is once again being attempted, and San Salvador boasts over a dozen new performing spaces—La Luna and Sol del Río are the most representative. In 1993, the Teatro circulante opened, conceived as a traveling company, within its own walls.

BIBLIOGRAPHY

Alas, Javier, *Piedras en el huracán poesía joven salvadoreña década de los 80.* San Salvador: Dirección de Publicaciones, 1993.

Anderson, Thomas. *El Salvador's Communist Revolt of 1932.* Lincoln: University of Nebraska Press, 1971.

Argueta, Manlio. *Poesía de El Salvador.* San José, Costa Rica: EDUCA, 1983.

Baratta, María de. *Cuzcatlán típico. Ensayo sobre etnofonía de El Salvador, folklore, folkwisa y folkway.* San Salvador: Publicaciones del Ministerio de Cultura, 1991. First edition: 1951.

Barbero, Edmundo. *Panorama del teatro en El Salvador.* San Salvador: Editorial Universitaria, 1979. First edition: 1972.

———. *El teatro: historia informal del mismo a través de lo anecdótico y pintoresco.* San Salvador: Dirección de Publicaciones, 1976.

Beverley, Jhon, and Marc Zimmerman. *Literature and Politics in the Central American Revolutions.* Austin: University of Texas Press, 1990.

Borgeson, Paul W., Jr. "El Salvador." In *Handbook of Latin American Literature*, ed. David William Foster. New York: Garland, 1987, 517–528.

Bricker, Victoria Reifler. *The Indian Christ, the Indian King. The Historical Substrate of Maya Myth and Ritual.* Austin: University of Texas Press, 1981.

Cea, José Roberto. *Teatro en y de una comarca centroamericana: Ensayo histórico-crítico.* San Salvador: Canoa Editores. 1993.

Dirección del Patrimonio Cultural. *Calendario de fiestas religiosas tradicionales de El Salvador.* San Salvador: Dirección de Publicaciones, 1978.

"El Salvador." *Escenarios de dos mundos: inventario teatral de Iberoamérica.* Vol. 2. Madrid: Centro de Documentación Teatral, 1988, 160–185. Articles by scholars.

Escobar Galindo, David. *Antología del relato costumbrista en El Salvador.* Cultura, Revista del Ministerio de Educación de El Salvador No. 74 (January–December 1989).

Fuentes, Carlos. *Valiente nuevo mundo. Épica, utopía y mito en la novela. hispanoamericana.* Mexico City: Fondo de Cultura Económica, 1990.

Galeas, Giovanni. *La conferencia y diálogos eternos.* Mexico City: Correo Escénico/ Artteatro, 1990.

Gallegos Valdés, Luis. *Panorama de la literatura salvadoreña.* San Salvador: UCA-Editores. 1981. First edition: 1958. Second revised edition: 1962.

Gallegos Valdés, Luis, and David Escobar Galindo, eds. *Poesía femenina en El Salvador (Breve Antología).* San Salvador: Dirección de publicaciones, 1976.

Góchez Sosa, Rafael, and Tirso Canales. *100 años de poesía en El Salvador (1800–1900).* San Salvador: Impresora Pipil, S.A., 1978.

González y Contreras, Gilberto. *Hombres entre lava y pinos.* Mexico City: B. Costa Amic Editor-Impresor, 1946.

Hernández, Edgar Iván, Mauricio Paz, Edgar Alfaro, Rafael Lara Valle, E. C anonymous, Eduardo Romero, and Oscar Aguilar. *Cuando el silencio golpea las campanas.* San Salvador: Editorial Sombrero Azul, 1991.

Herrera Vega, Adolfo. *Expresión literaria de nuestra vieja raza.* San Salvador: Dirección de Publicaciones, 1961.

Huezo Mixco, Miguel, ed. *Pájaro y volcán.* San Salvador: UCA-Editores, 1989.

López Vallecillos, Italo. *El periodismo en El Salvador.* San Salvador: Editorial Universitaria, 1964.

Marroquín, Alejandro Dagoberto. *Panchimalco.* San Salvador: Dirección de Publicaciones, 1959.

———. *San Pedro Nonualco.* San Salvador: Editorial Universitaria, 1964.

Membreño, María B. *Literatura de El Salvador.* San Salvador: Tipografía Central, 1959.

Ramírez, Sergio. "Balcanes y volcanes (aproximaciones al proceso cultural contemporáneo en Centroamérica)." *Centroamérica hoy.* Mexico City: Siglo XXI Editores, 1975, 279–366.

Rodríguez Díaz, Rafael Arturo. *Cinco estudios sobre literatura salvadoreña.* San Salvador: UCA-Editores, 1989.

Toruño, Juan Felipe. *Desarrollo literario de El Salvador.* San Salvador: Departamento Editorial del Ministerio de Cultura, 1958.

Velis, Carlos. Teatro. *La misma sangre (1990) La flor que se fue (1991), San Salvador después del eclipse (1992).* San Salvador: Ediciones La Luna Casa y Arte, 1992.

———. *Historia del teatro en El Salvador*, Vol. 1, De la Colonia a 1900. Tuxtla Gutiérrez, Chiapas, México: Gobierno del Estado de Chiapas, DIF—Chiapas/Instituto Chiapaneco de Cultura, 1993.

◆

ARAGÓN, Emilio J. (1884–1938). Aragón was one of the leading Salvadoran actors of the turn of the century. His play *Los contrabandistas* (The Contrabandists) was successfully produced by the Adams Bravo Company in 1911. Family honor is saved and lost through lawless behavior.

WORKS: *Los contrabandistas* (play, 1911). *La propia vida* (One's Own Life) (play, 1926).

ARMIJO, Roberto (1937–). Armijo is a poet, playwright, essayist, and university professor. In the 1950s, he integrated the group Generación comprometida (Engaged Genera-

tion), whose more important members are Italo López Vallecillos, Waldo Chávez Velasco, and Alvaro Menen Desleal. As an avant-garde circle, its original statement highlighted the rupture with the literary values of the past. Later, he was a member of the Circulo Literario Universitario Salvadoreño (1956), which gathered such figures as Roque Dalton, Manlio Argueta, Napoleón Rodríguez Ruíz, and José Roberto Cea. This group proclaimed a very critical political position toward the social problems of the country and assumed that art and literature had a social function. The *Anthology poetas jóvenes de El Salvador* (1960), edited by Cea, has compiled the early works of this generation. The formation of the group was in effect a renewal for Salvadoran literature. Its works were diffused to the general public in public acts, as well as in magazines that have become the model of literary journals in the country. The two most relevant magazines of this generation are *Hoja* and *La pájara pinta*. *Hoja* was edited by López Vallecillos; *La pájara pinta*, a collage of social criticism and avant-garde writing, has been considered until now a model of cultural diffusion and critical art. Armijo cultivates poetry and essays but has also written plays and a novel. As a critical essayist, in 1965 he won the prize República de El Salvador with his work *Francisco Gavidia, la odisea de su genio* (Francisco Gavidia, the Odyssey of His Genius). It is an erudite and inmense work that recovers the historical value of the classical Salvadoran writer. Two years later, he received the prize 15 de Septiembre in Guatemala, for his work *Rubén Darío y su intuición del mundo* (Rubén Darío and His Idea of the World). During the fifty-year celebration of Rúben Darío in Nicaragua he received the first prize with his essay "T. S. Eliot, el poeta más solitario del mundo." His plays have also received several prizes. *Jugando a la gallina ciega* (Playing the Blind Hen Game) (1969) won the first prize at the Juegos Florales de Quezaltenango, Guatemala, in 1969. Armijo's lyrical poetry is blended with the cruelty and absurdity of the contemporary world. The same year, *El príncipe no debe morir* (The Prince Should Not Die) won the third prize in Guatemala. He also wrote two other plays, the *Absalon* and *Los escarabajos* (The Beetles), both not yet published. He has also written the novel *El asma de Leviatán* (Leviatan's Asthma) (1990). He lives in Paris, where he teaches at the Université de Paris-Nanterre.

WORKS: *La noche ciega al corazón que canta* (The Night Blinds a Singing Heart) (1959). *Elegías* (1965). *Francisco Gavidia, la odisea de su genio* (Francisco Gavidia, the Odyssey of His Genius) (1965–1967). *El príncipe no debe morir* (The Prince Should Not Die) (1967). *Jugando a la gallina ciega* (Playing the Blind Hen Game) (1969). *El asma de Leviatán* (Leviatan's Asthma) (1990).

ARRIETA YUDICE, Ernesto (189?–194?). A lawyer and playwright, he was well known for his genre comedies, or *cuadros de costumbres*, inspired on regional motifs of the turn of the century. According to Barbero (18), his better comedies are *El inspector de hacienda* (The Tax Inspector), an adaptation of one of Arturo Ambrogi's regional stories, and *El padre Eusebio . . .* (Father Eusebio . . .). His plays were produced by Gerardo de Nieva, director of the Escuela Nacional de Prácticas Escénicas, during the 1930s.

WORKS: *Nuevo método de cobrar* (A New Method of Collecting) (play, 1929). *El padre Eusebio o las píldoras del Doctor Naranja* (Father Eusebio or the Pills of Doctor Orange) (play, 1935). *El inspector de hacienda* (play, 1936).

BIBLIOGRAPHY: Edmundo Barbero, *Panorama del teatro en El Salvador* (San Salvador: Editorial Universitaria 1979).

BARATTA, María de (1890–1970). A musician and ballet, dance, and theater director, Baratta studied music at the Conservatorio Nacional de Música with its director, Juan Aberle, as well as piano composition with Agustín Roig, disciple of the famous Spanish composer Enrique Granados. She investigated and compiled Salvadoran traditional music and theater-dances. Besides her remarkable work on Salvadoran popular theater, *Cuzcatlán típico* (Typical Cuscatlan) (1950/1991), she composed several original dances—"Los tecomatillos," "Can-Calugui-Tunal," "Ofrenda de la Elegida," "Nagualismo"—as well as stylized folk dances—"La yegüita" and the Indian ballet "En el teocalli." Her works have received several distinctions. "Twelve Folk Songs," from *Cuzcatlán típico*, received a prize from the Ministerio de Instrucción in 1930; in 1934, in Piedras Negras, Coahuila, Mexico, her compositions "Ofrenda de la elegida" (Offering to the Chosen) and "Bacanal indígena" received a similar prize. At the Juegos Florales de Santa Ana, El Salvador, in 1939, she won the golden medal for her prose *Collar de dientes* (Necklace of Teeth). And finally, in 1949, she received the prize José María Peralta Lagos of the Beneficencia Española for her work *Historia de moros y cristianos* (History of Moors and Christians).

WORKS: *Cuzcatlán típico* (1950/1991).

BÉNEKE, Walter (1928–1980). Béneke has been considered one of the most outstanding Salvadoran playwrights, although he has only written two plays, *El paraíso de los imprudentes* (The Imprudents' Paradise) (1955) and *Funeral Home* (1958), which received a prize at the Concurso Nacional de Cultura in 1958. He was Minister of Education and carried out several diplomatic missions. His plays are inspired by French existentialism.

WORKS: *El paraíso de los imprudentes* (1955). *Funeral Home* (1958).

CEA, José Roberto (1939–   ). He is a self-taught writer who stands out mainly for his poetic works, even though he has also written plays, short stories, and novels. His publications date from 1956, when he became a member of the Círculo Literario Universitario Salvadoreño. From an early age, his participation in this group imbued his poetry with a social and political character. His writings have had ample diffusion in the country, because he has never lived in exile. He published a compilation of his generation's poetry in the volume *Poetas jóvenes de El Salvador* (Young Poets of El Salvador) (1960). He has also published several books of poems. The first was *Los días enemigos* (The Unfriendly Days) (1965). According to the critics, his most elaborate work is *Todo el códice* (All the Codex) (1967), which won the second *Accesit* of the Premio Adonis in Madrid in 1966. Cea's originality consists in contrasting ancient pre-Hispanic myths with current events. He attempts to recover the historical memory of his native Indian town, Izalco, in order to give an account of the present. He has won several regional prizes, such as honorable mention in the 13th Concurso Nacional de Cultura in El Salvador with his book *Naugrafio genuino* (Genuine Shipwreck) in 1969. He has also published two anthologies of Salvadoran poetry: *Antología general de la poesía en El Salvador* (General Anthology of the Poetry in El Salvador) (1971) and *Poesía revolucionaria y de la otra* (Revolutionary Poetry and the Other One) (1972). In 1974, Cea won the first prize in the Concurso Latino Americano de Poesía Pablo Neruda, owing to his book *Poeta del tercer mundo* (Poet of the Third World). More recently he has received the Premio Rubén Darío, in 1981, with his book *Los herederos de Farabundo* (Farabundo's Heirs). It is a "collage-poem" that relates the stories of the Salvadoran hero Farabundo Martí through multiple proverbs, choirs, and popular testimony. In 1984, he received the prize in poetry at the Concurso Latino Americano, held by the Editorial Universitaria Centroamericana (EDUCA) in San José, Costa Rica, with his book *Los pies sobre la tierra de preseas* (The Feet on the Land of Gems). In these poems, the clear reference to Gavidia's elegy is transformed into an exaltation of the Salvadoran revolutionary movement. In theater, he also received the second prize in the Juegos Florales de Quetzaltenango, Guatemala, in 1969, with his play *Las escenas cumbres* (The High Scenes). This work has been published several times and is frequently played in the country. In 1993 he published one of the most complete histories of theater in the country. A trip to Argentina's capital in the 1970s acquainted Cea with the publishing industry. He decided to found a publishing house in El Salvador. Canoa Editores, directed by Cea, has the very ambitious project of offering universal and Latin American literature to the general Salvadoran public. Thanks to Canoa Editores, Cea plays a very important role in Salvadoran society today, that of disseminating literary works in a country where foreign books are luxury goods.

WORKS: *Amoroso poema en golondrina a la ciudad de Armenia* (Love Poem to the City of Armenia) (1958). *Los días enemigos* (1965). *Casi el encuentro* (The Almost Meeting) (1965). *Códice liberado* (Freed Codex) (1966). *De perros y hombres* (Of Dogs and Men) (1967). *Las escenas cumbres* (play, 1969). *Todo el códice* (All the Codex) (1967). *Naufragio genuino* (1969). *El potrero* (The Horseman) (1969). *El solitario de la habitación* 5–3 (The Solitary Man of Room 5–3) (play, 1971). *Toda especie de retratos* (All Kind of Portraits) (1976). *Mester de picardía* (Master of Roguery) (1977). *Misa-Mitin* (Mass-Meeting) (1977). *Los herederos de Farabundo* (1981). *Los pies sobre la tierra de preseas* (1984), in *Teatro de y en una comarca centroamericana* (Theater from and in a Central-American Territory) (1993).

CHÁVEZ VELASCO, Waldo (1932–   ). A lawyer, poet, and playwright, he studied law in Italy, where he became familiar with existential philosophy. His poetry first appeared in the compilation entitled *La bomba de hidrógeno* (The Hydrogen Bomb) (1950). While his poetic works are influenced by Neruda, his plays have an existential or regionalist vein. He has received several regional prizes for his works. In 1962, he won the Certamen Nacional de Cultura in El Salvador for his book *Cuentos de hoy y mañana* (Short Stories of Today and Tomorrow). He received the second prize at the Juegos Florales Centroamericanos de Quetzaltenango, Guatemala, for his play *El sombrero de otoño* (Autumn's Hat) the same year.

WORKS: *Fábrica de sueños* (Dreams Factory) (play, 1957). *Ruth de Moab* (play, 1958). *El zipitín* (play, 1960). *Cuentos de hoy y mañana* (1962). *El sombrero de otoño* (play, 1962).

DÍAZ, Francisco (1812–1845). Díaz is traditionally recognized as the first Salvadoran playwright, although several texts existed prior to his. The best known is *Mournful Nights* (1827), author unknown, one of the oldest existing texts. It narrates the deeds of Manuel José Arce, one of the nation's founders. A similar relationship between writing theater and forming nations can be discovered in Díaz's *La tragedia de Francisco Morazán*, published in 1894. It relates the last days of General Francisco Morazán (1842), whom the author fought alongside with in Costa Rica. During the civil war, Díaz was also recognized as the prototype of the engaged writer, a sort of guerilla-fighter avant-la-lettre. Nevertheless, his writing is characterized by a deep "nostalgia of death" and by a quest for a violent end.

WORKS: *Epístola* (1842). *Poesías* (1848). *La tragedia de Francisco Morazán* (Francisco Morazán's Tragedy) (play, 1894).

ESCOBAR GALINDO, David (1943–   ). A lawyer, poet, playwright, and university professor, his vocation as a poet came early. He has a doctorate in law and has carried out multiple official missions: director of the National Library (1971), secretary of the National Cooperation Commission with UNESCO (1971–1973), director of International Affairs of the Minister of Foreign Affairs (1972–1973), and member of the Commission for Peace with Honduras (1973) and of the General Treaty of Peace with Honduras (1980). More recently, he was one of the government members who signed the Peace Accords in Chapultepec in 1992. He publishes a weekly column for *La Prensa Gráfica* and also for the literary magazine of *Diario Latino* in San Salvador. He is currently rector of the Universidad José Matías Delgado. His writings are numerous and multifaceted, although his poetic works are more abundant. In narrative, he has published the novel *Una grieta en el agua* (A Crack in the Water) (1972) and several books of short stories: *La rebelión de las imágenes* (The Rebellion of Images) (1976), *Matusalén el abandónico* (The Defeated Methuselah) (1980), *Los sobrevivientes* (The Survivors) (1980), and *La tregua de los dioses* (The Truce of the Gods) (1981). His play *Las hogueras de Itaca* (The Fires of Ithaca) (1987) won the Theater Prize at the Concurso Centro Americano de Quetzaltenango Guatemala, in 1984. Using ancient techniques of the classical Greek art, Escobar Galindo offers a dramatic allegory of the Salvadoran conflict. He has also written children's stories, *Fabulas* (Fables) (1979) and his book of poems *La ronda de las frutas* (The Serenade of Fruits) (1979). He is one of El Salvador's leading poets. His poetry is characterized by a "thirst of plenitude" and by a "passion for time," with very strong roots in a metaphysical humanism. The critics have considered him as a lyric poet because his internal quest informs a very elegant and refined form. Since 1974, after the kidnapping of his father, Escobar Galindo has demonstrated a sensibility deep enough to understand the Salvadoran conflict and the origins of random violence in the country. This change of attitude is all the more manifest in his recent works. He is one of the authors of the current Peace Treaty.

WORKS: *El bronce y la esperanza* (Bronze and Hope) (1963). *Las manos en el fuego* (Hands in the Fire) (1969). *Extraño mundo del amanecer* (The Strange World of Dawn) (1970). *Duelo ceremonial por la violencia* (Ceremonial Duel for Violence) (1971). *Destino manifiesto* (Obvious Destiny) (1972). *Vigilia memorable* (Memorable Vigil) (1972). *Memoria de España* (Memory of Spain) (1973). *Cornamusa* (Brass Horn) (1975). *La barca de papiro* (The Papyrus Boat) (1975). *Coronación furtiva* (Clandestine Coronation) (1975). *Arcanus* (1976). *Trenes por la violencia* (Trains for Violence) (1977). *Discurso secreto* (Secret Lecture) (1977). *Las nubes en el confín* (Clouds in the Horizon) (1978). *Diario de una ciudad destruida* (Diary of a Destroyed City) (1978). *Sonetos penitenciales* (Penitential Sonnets) (1980). *El guerrero descalzo* (The Shoeless Warrior) (1980). *Los fuegos del azar* (The Fires of Hazard) (1983). *Las hogueras de Itaca* (play, 1987). *Gente que pasa. Historias sin cuento* (People Passing By. Histories Without Stories) (1988). *Jazmines heredados* (Inherited Jasmines) (1992).

GAVIDIA, Francisco (1864–1955). The most important Salvadoran writer of the turn of the century, he represents the classical Renaissance figure, or *nuestro señor barroco*, who attempts to cover the total knowledge of Latin American culture. During his passage through El Salvador in 1882, he initiated Rubén Darío to the renewed forms of the Castillian verse. Although he applied the French metric and hendecasyllabic verse from his early works, Gavidia never succumbed to the modernist temptation to thematize the exotic. On the contrary, regionalism and modernism merge in the figure of *Soter*, the Greek name of the country, in order to write the first fictionalized history of El Salvador. His most relevant plays—*Júpiter, Ursino de Orbajena, Lucía Lasso o los piratas* (Lucía Lasso or the Pirates), *La princesa Citalá* (Princess Citalá), *Los juramentos* (The Oaths), *Amor e interés* (Love and Interest), *Ramona, La torre de márfil* (Ivory Tower)—even if they are all inspired by a classical European form and style, deal with Salvadoran historical subjects. His plays continue to be produced in the coun-

try; in 1990, Sol del Río presented *Júpiter*, a very personal account of Salvadoran independence.

WORKS: *Poemas* (Poems) (1884). *Versos* (Verses) (1885). *Júpiter* (historical drama, 1895). *Gramática del idioma Salvador* (Grammar of the Salvador Language) (1909). *Los aeronautas* (1909). *Obras* (Works) (the most complete compilation of lyrical poetry, essays, plays, and conferences, 1913). *Historia moderna de El Salvador* (Modern History of El Salvador) (1917). *Héspero* (play, 1931). *Los juramentos* (1943). *La princesa Citalá* (dramatic poem, 1944). *Cuentos de marinos* (Seamen Stories) (1947). *La torre de marfil* (play, 1949). *Sooter o tierra de preseas* (Sooter or Land of Gems) (1949). *Cuentos y narraciones* (Short Stories and Narrations) (1960). *Obras completas* (Complete Works), vols. 1–2 (1974–1976).

GUSTAVE, Edgar (1967–   ). Gustave is one of the leading young playwrights in the country. During the civil war, he published several short symbolic dramas dealing with the daily realities of war.

WORKS: *Morir ahora* (To Die Now) (1985). *El laberinto de la verdad* (The Labyrinth of Truth) (1986). *La última cena* (The Last Supper) (1989).

LINDO, Hugo (1917–1985). A lawyer, poet, novelist, playwright, and diplomat, he is one of the greatest literary figures of the 1940s and 1950s. His poetic works are inspired by metaphysical, social, and intimate subjects; his narrative follows a twofold trend: regional realism and universal fiction. He introduced science fiction to the country and had an enormous influence owing to the important official missions that he fulfilled. He was Minister of Education, ambassador in Chile, Colombia, and Spain, as well as member of the Academia Salvadoreña de la Lengua, of Cultura Hispánica, and of the Organización de los Estados Centroamericanos (ODECA). Even though his play *Una pieza francamente celestial* (A Play Frankly Celestial) received "honorable mention" at the Concurso Nacional de Cultura in 1966, Lindo's main contribution to Salvadoran literature is in poetry. His play is a satire of Latin American politics and of false religious beliefs.

WORKS: *Prima al sol* (Song to the Sun) (1933). *Clavelia* (1936). *Poema eucarístico y otros* (Eucharistic Poems and Others) (1943). *Guaro y champaña* (Guaro and Champagne) (1947). *Libro de horas* (Prayer Book) (1947). *Antología del cuento moderno centroamericano* (Anthology of the Modern Central-American Short Story) (1949–1950). *Sinfonía del límite* (Symphony to the Limit) (1953). *El anzuelo de Dios* (God's Fish-Hook) (1956). *Aquí se cuentan cuentos* (Short Stories Are Told Here) (1959). *Trece instantes* (Thirteen Instants) (1959). *¡Justicia señor Governador!* (Justice, Mister Governor!) (1960). *Varia poesía* (Various Poems) (1961). *Navegante río* (Navigating River) (1963). *Cada día tiene su afán* (Each Day Has Its Eagerness) (1965). *Una pieza francamente celestial* (A Play Frankly Celestial) (play, 1966). *Solo la voz* (1968). *Maneras de llover* (Ways of Raining) (1969). *Ese pequeño siempre* (That Little Always) (1971). *Espejos paralelos* (Parallel Mirrors) (1974). *Resonancia de Vivaldi* (Vivaldi's Resonance) (1976). *Aquí mi tierra* (Here My Land) (1979).

LLERENA, José (1884–1938). His plays were produced by the Mercedes Navarro, Virginia Fábregas, and Fernando Soler companies in different theaters of the capital. He is one of the most successful playwrights of the 1920s. His works present honorable city characters who confront corruption and abuse of political and economic power. He founded the Editorial Cuzcatlania (1927), which played an enormous role in disseminating scientific and literary works.

WORKS: *El corazón de los hombres* (play, 1921). *Los tatuados* (play, 1922). *El derecho de los otros* (play, 1924). *La miseria alegre* (play, 1925). *Nuestra sombra* (play, 1926). *La raza nueva* (play, 1927). *Espigas de Gloria* (1937).

LÓPEZ, Matilde Eleña (1922–). A poet, essayist, playwright, and university professor, she has published since her adolescence in the country's newspapers and magazines. In 1944, López went into exile in Guatemala, where she started her studies in literature. Later, she prepared her doctorate in philosophy and literature at the Central University of Quito in 1956. After living a year in Panama, she returned to El Salvador in 1957. She has worked at the University of El Salvador in which she has fulfilled several administrative and teaching positions.

She is one of the most important members of the Generation of 44, also known as the Generation of the Dictatorship. The year 1944 was a key year for El Salvador; after thirteen years of military dictatorship, the government collapsed owing to a series of peaceful protests. The Generation of 44 envisaged the project of developing a wide program of cultural criticism, which covered literature, painting, sculpture, and music. Its project consisted of disseminating all genres of artistic expression to the general public. Thanks to a "renaissance" provided by the leading essay *Minimum vital* (1928) of Alberto Masferrer, the aim of the arts was to contribute to the social and cultural development of the country. Other members of the group were Antonio Gamero, Cristobal Humberto Ibarra, Osvaldo Escobar Velado, Alfonso Morales, and Ricardo Trigueros de León. Having stated the social function of the arts, this generation was the direct predecessor of the Generación comprometida in the 1950s. Currently, López publishes in Taller de Letras and in the newspapers of the capital, *Diario Latino* and *El Mundo*.

WORKS: *Masferrer, alto pensador de Centroamérica* (1954). *Interpretación social del arte* (1962). *Dante, poeta y ciudadano del futuro* (1965). *Cartas a Groza* (1970). *Estudios de poesía* (1972). *La balada de Anastacio Aquino* (play, 1976). *El momento perdido* (1976). *Refugio para la soledad* (1978). *Los sollozos oscuros* (1982).

LÓPEZ VALLECILLOS, Italo (1932–1986). López was a historian, playwright, poet, and journalist. Nothing characterizes his works better than the clear division that exists between his poetry and his prose. While his poetic production derives from his intimate, existential, and erotic experience, his other works are socially and politically oriented. He studied journalism in Spain and carried out several positions as an editor at the Editorial Centroamericana, EDUCA, San José, and at UCA-Editores in San Salvador. He named his generation as *comprometida* (engaged), following the influence of French existentialism. He wrote two plays. *Las manos vencidas* (1964) received the first prize at the Juegos Florales de

Quetzaltenango, Guatemala. The play deals with a philosophical conflict between existentialism and Marxism and was produced by the Teatro Universitario in 1967. *Burudy sur*, a political irony of Salvadoran life, received honorable mention at the Concurso de Cultura in San Salvador in 1966.

WORKS: *Biografía del hombre triste* (1954). *Imágenes sobre el otoño* (1962). *El periodismo en El Salvador* (1964). *Las manos vencidas* (play, 1964). *Gerardo Barrios y su tiempo* (1965). *Burudy sur* (play, 1966). *Puro asombro* (1970). *Celda noventa y seis* (play, 1975). *Inventario de soledad* (1977). *Poesía completa* (1987).

MENDEZ, José María (1916–). A lawyer, university professor, and writer, he has been attorney, vice-rector, and rector of the Universidad Nacional. His best-known work is *Tres mujeres al cuadrado*, which won the second prize at the 8th Concurso Nacional de Cultura in 1962. He has also directed the journal *Patria Nueva* and, under the pen name of Flirt, wrote a very successful column entitled "Flirteando." His brief farce *Este era un rey* was produced as part of the repertoire of the Teatro Universitario during the early 1970s. This play, as well as *El sargento y el borracho* and *La ronda del adulterio*, are all included in the section "Mini-Teatro" of his book *Disparatario* (1957, 151–176).

WORKS: *Disparatario* (1957). *Tres mujeres al cuadrado* (1962). *Tiempo irredimible* (1977).

MENEN DESLEAL, Alvaro (1931–). Although he was a member of the Círculo Literario Universitario Salvadoreño, his works do not reflect the same kind of political commitment that characterizes Cea, Dalton, or Argueta. Menen Desleal is one of the leading Salvadoran writers of fantastic literature. His narrative and theater seem closer to Jorge Luis Borges than to those of his generation. His poetry is defined by a clear existential orientation, although lately he has been shifting toward a poetry of concrete images. His play *Luz negra* (1967), a Beckett-inspired drama, is the most often performed play in Salvadoran history.

WORKS: *La llave* (1962). *Cuentos breves y mar-* *avillosos* (1963). *El extraño habitante* (1964). *El circo y otras piezas falsas* (play, 1966). *Luz negra* (play, 1967). *Ciudad, casa de todos* (1968). *Una cuerda de nylon y oro* (1968). *Revolución en el país que edificó un castillo de hadas* (1971). *La ilustre familia androide* (1972). *Los vicios de papá* (1978).

MENÉNDEZ, Roberto Arturo (1930–). An actor, stage director, and playwright, he belongs to the generation that, since the early 1950s, worked under the leading Spanish playwright Edmundo Barbero. His works deal mainly with mythical subjects, which are nevertheless put into a Salvadoran context.

WORKS: *La ira del cordero* (play, 1959). *Nuevamente Edipo* (play, 1966).

PERALTA LAGOS, José María (1873–1944). An engineer, general, and satiric writer, he was Minister of War and a diplomat. T. P. Mechín, as he used to sign his works, represents the culminating point of the nineteenth-century *costumbrismo*. His literary style is informed by everyday regional and national customs, the content of which is represented ironically. He also recreates Salvadoran colloquial language. His play *Candidato* (1931) relates the political climate that prevailed in the country after the 1929 depression, the rise of the Labor Party in the 1931 election, and the military coup d'état that put an end to the first democratically elected government in Salvadoran history.

WORKS: *Burla burlando* (1923). *Brochazos* (1925). *Doctor Gonorreitigorrea* (1926). *Candidato* (play, 1931). *La muerte de la tórtola* (1933).

RIVAS BONILLA, Alberto (1891–1985). A physician, university professor, journalist, and writer, Rivas Bonilla's early poetry is modernist in style, inspired by Lugones, while his narrative follows a more regionalist mood, close to the picaresque novel. His comedies were successfully produced by Gerardo Nieva; *Andanzas y malandazas* and *Me monto en un potro* are his two most praised regionalist works, as bear witness their numerous editions.

WORKS: *Versos* (1926). *Andanzas y malandanzas* (1936). *Me monto en un potro* (1943). *Una chica moderna* (play, 1945). *Celia en vacaciones* (play,

1947). *Alma de mujer* (play, 1949). *El libros de los sonetos* (1971).

RODRÍGUEZ RUÍZ, J. Napoleón (1930–). A lawyer and playwright, he has been dean of the Law School, as well as vice rector of the Universidad Nacional. He has received several regional distinctions. His play *Rambó* won a prize at the Juegos Florales de Quetzaltenango, Guatemala, in 1968, as did his *Anastacio Rey* in the capital of Guatemala in 1969. Since he was a member of the Teatro Universitario, his plays have been produced by this group on several occasions, especially *Anastacio Rey* because of its political content as well as its musical scores and dances that make it more appealing to the public.

WORKS: *Rambó* (play, 1969). *Anastacio Rey* (play, 1970). *Los helicopteros* (play, 1980).

Rafael Lara Martínez

Guatemala

Guatemala is the home of the oldest authentic extant play from pre-Columbian America and the birthplace of the first woman dramatist of Central America. Notable from the early colonial period are religious plays unique to Guatemala, called *loas del diablo* (Scenes of the Devil). Jones points out that this type of noisy dramatic entertainment involving the devil's temptation of the Christians, who are ultimately saved by the Virgin Mary, can occasionally still be seen today (437). Extant from the late colonial period is the anonymous dramatic piece written in 1772 titled *Historia de la conversión de San Pablo* (History of the Conversion of Saint Paul). Considering these works, and other dramatic activity of the time, Jones writes that Ramón A. Salazar dates the beginnings of Guatemala's modern theater from the end of the eighteenth century (447). The pre-Columbian *Rabinal Achí*, however, is the most famous and most important early dramatic piece in the history of the theater of Guatemala. Richard Callan reminds us in his study on Miguel Angel Asturias that the Maya Quiché text of this only surviving play from the pre-Hispanic theater, a drama-ballet also called "Dance of the Drum," was discovered in the mid-nineteenth century. He goes on to say that it was later studied and translated by Georges Raynaud, Miguel Angel Asturias's professor at the Sorbonne (121). Not only is the *Rabinal Achí* important for its historic value but also for its influence on later dramas such as *Soluna* (Sunmoon) by Asturias. A modernized version of the play, according to Jones, was successfully staged in 1950 as *Quiché-Achí* (Quiche Man) by Carlos Girón Cerna (453).

Among other early Guatemalan dramatists figure Juan Fermin Aycinena (1838–1898); Miguel Ángel Urrutia (1852–1931); Ismael Cerna (1856–1901), who is considered to be the founder of the national theater of Guatemala (271); Manuel Valle (1861–1913); his son, Rafael Valle (1894–1922); and a couple of women dramatists, Trinidad Coronado (n.d.) and Mercede Tejada Milla (n.d.). Not prolific, but of note in the Guatemalan theater, are Máximo Soto Hall (1871–1944), along with Rafael Arévalo Martínez (1884–1975). In the following generation Adolfo Drago Bracco (1894–   ) and Miguel Marsicovétere y Durán (1913–   ) focus a great deal on the theater. According to Jones, the latter is the founder of the group Tepeus (Messengers) of the Generación de 1930 (44).

George R. McMurray, in *Spanish American Writing Since 1941*, suggests that Guatemala's modern theater began in 1944 after the fall of the dictator Jorge Ubico. The nation's three leading playwrights since then are Carlos Solórzano, the Nobel Prize–winning Miguel Angel Asturias, and Manuel Galich. The years from 1944 to 1954 were a time of peace and stability in Guatemala that allowed much social progress. Among other things, the Universidad Popular was founded, and the Teatro de Arte Universitario of the University of San Carlos was established. This is also the time that the following were formed: the Academia Dramática (Drama Academy) and the Compañía de Teatro de la Universidad

Popular (Theater Company of the Universidad Popular); the first Festival de Teatro de Aficionado (Theatre Festival of Amateurs); the Compañía de Teatro para Niño ((Theater Company for Children); and the first Compañía Nacional de Teatro de Bellas Artes (National Theater Company of Fine Arts). Concurrently there were the "Festivales de Antigua" and those of the Teatro Guatemalteco, the "Festivales de Barrios," and other activities of independent groups. Also during this period, according to Carrillo, many theaters were established ranging from seating capacities of 115 seats in the Teatro Gadem to 2,005 seats in the Teatro Nacional (95).

Although an era of military repression, the theater manages to continue in the period between 1954 and 1974. During the 1960s and until 1974, the theatergoer was primarily from the middle class, and a play never had more than 3,000 spectators to view it over a three-, four-, or in the case of a very successful play, five-week run. Theater critics during these decades also wrote for a limited readership. Among the dramatists writing and staging plays during this time were Manuel José Arce, Víctor Hugo Cruz, Augusto Medina, Manuel Galich, Ligia Bernal, Enrique Campag, René García Mejía, Miguel Ángel Asturias, María del Carmen Escobar, and Hugo Carrillo.

A turning point in contemporary Guatemalan theater came, however, in 1974 with the production of Hugo Carrillo's dramatic version of Asturias's *El señor presidente* (Mister President). Carrillo writes that the play was performed during the XII Festival de Teatro Guatemalteco (XII Festival of Guatemalan Theatre) in posthumous homage to Miguel Angel Asturias (96). The play was a resounding critical and box office success, as it ran for ten consecutive months, setting a record for Central America. Carrillo points out that the play also received all the prizes awarded the theater in Guatemala (97). When one considers Guatemala's theater of this period, it is clear that there is a theatrical movement before *El señor presidente* and another after it. Following this event, which similarly affected the theater, as did the overthrow of the dictator Ubico in 1944, there is an explosive production of plays by new Guatemalan dramatists. The young writers worked feverishly to meet the demands of the rapidly growing theater public. This activity resulted in what is now labeled the Golden Age of Guatemalan theater. However, by 1975 many of the theatrical works being written and staged were critical of the government. Carrillo lists the following as some of the more representative dramatists and works of the period: *Un niño llamado Paz* (A Child Called Peace), by Enrique Campag; *Delito, condena y ejecución de una gallina* (Crime, Conviction and Execution of a Chicken), by Manuel José Arce; the symbolic plays *La pierda en el pozo* (The Stone in the Well) and *Tus alas, Ariel* (Your Wings, Ariel), by Ligia Bernal; and *Lo que el viento nos dejó* (What the Wind Left Us), a collective creation by the university group called Nalga y Pantorrilla (Buttock and Calf) (97). The Gilded Era ended, however, shortly after the Universidad Popular Theatre mysteriously burned. Carrillo's *El corazón del espantapájaros* (The Scarecrow's Heart) was playing at the theater of the Universidad Popular when the theater received death threats against the director, crew, and actors. The theater "mysteriously" burned, and an actor was shot as he entered the building. Other hostile activity involving the police resulted in the disbanding of *teatristas*, self-imposed exile, and a significant decline in theater activity among those who wrote original works. Carrillo points out that those dramatists still writing and staging plays avoided openly addressing social and political issues, and greater attention was given children's theater. Also collective works void of any social or political content began to be produced (97).

Thus, the Golden Age of Guatemalan theater came to a sudden close. Arce went into exile in France, Galich left and later died in Cuba, and Asturias's plays were no longer staged. Others such as Ligia Bernal remained silent, and Carrillo worked abroad or tended to write only dramatized classic Guatemalan novels. Curiously, the theater public continued to grow. However, it was not until 1985, under the administration of Vinicio Cerezo Arévalo, that plays by national dramatists were staged again. At this time, according to Carrillo, the theater of the Universidad Popular was named Sala Manuel Galich, and his plays began to be performed once more (98). Works by Arce and Carrillo also have been presented, but all dramatic pieces pass a prudent self-censorship before being performed.

Stable theatrical groups active during the decade of the 1980s include La Compañía de teatro de la Universidad Popular; Grupo 7–79; Teatro-Club (an independent group without their own theater); and El Grupo Diez (another independent group but with their own theater). And in the last years of the decade, a group of *café-teatros* have begun to mount successfully a number of productions on an irregular basis (Carrillo, 99). Also during the 1980s El Patronato de Bellas Artes (Organization to Encourage the Fine Arts) began to award "El Opus" each year to the most outstanding Guatemalan *teatristas*, and starting in 1991, the prize has been awarded to all artists regardless of the cultural area. A number of other positive endeavors were initiated in the 1980s that help support theater activity in Guatemala. For example, the *Revista de las Naciones* (Journal of the Nations) annually recognizes theatrical talent. The bimonthly journal *Arteatro* (Theater Art) is another manifestation of the good health of Guatemalan theater. In 1985 the government created the Ministerio de la Cultura (Culture Ministry). In 1988, AGTTEA (Asociación Guatemalteca de Trabajadores del Teatro—Guatemalan Association of Theater Workers) was organized. It is also notable that the more important daily and weekly newspapers usually have theater news in their culture pages. On the other hand, few works and studies on the Guatemalan theater were published during the 1980s. Among those that were, we can cite *Obra dramática de Manuel Galich* (Dramatic Work of Manuel Galich), by Víctor Hugo Cruz (1989); *La intensa y brillante vida de Manuel Francisco Galich López* (The Intense and Brilliant Life of Manuel Francisco Galich López), which appeared in the *Revista de la Universidad de San Carlos* (Journal of the University of Saint Charles); *Ideas políticas en el teatro de Manuel Galich* (Political Ideas in the Theater of Manuel Galich), a 1982 thesis by Mario Alberto Carrera; and Silvia Ana Herrera Ubico's *El teatro en Guatemala en el siglo XX* (Guatemalan Theater in the Twentieth Century), published in 1980.

The decade of the 1980s showed progress with the return of the staging of Guatemalan works, and into the 1990s the theater public is large and continues to grow. Currently the AGTTEA is active; and theaters that are constantly performing plays include the Teatro de la Universidad Popular; Teatro de Cámara del Centro; Cultural M. A. Asturias; Teatro Gadem; Teatro Metropolitano; Teatro de Bellas Artes; and the Teatro Abril. Among the stable theater groups figure the CIA. de Teatro de la Universidad Popular; Grupo 7-79; Grupo Diez; and Teatro Gadem. Five *café-teatros* have opened in the last few years, and the more outstanding are La Terraza and La Fonda de Don Pepe.

Notable among the prominent personalities of the Guatemalan theater of the 1980s are

Manuel Galich, Manuel José Arce, Víctor Hugo Cruz, Manuel Corleto, Ricardo Martínez, Jorge Hernández Vielman, Juan Carlo(Roda), Lui Escobedo, and Hugo Carrillo. One Guatemalan theater group in exile is the Teatro Vivo, which is currently headquartered in Paris. From among the more important young Guatemalan *teatristas*, largely from the Academia de Arte Dramático of the Universidad Popular, we can mention Guillermo Ramírez Valenzuela (director); Ricardo Martínez (author and director of children's theater); Fran Lepe (director); Juan Carlo(Roda) (author); Antonio Guitron (director and author); Leonel Vaccaro (author); and Oswaldo Ortega (author).

At the present time the theater of Guatemala is generally in good health. Complete freedom on the stage, due to government "oversight," is not completely enjoyed. However, theatrical activity is fueled largely by the healthy appetite of the public. Plays by mature dramatists such as Carrillo and the late Galich enjoy continued success, whereas younger artists have reason to be encouraged to contribute to a vital theater whose presence is manifest in large commercial theaters as well as university houses and also the ever popular *café-teatros*.

BIBLIOGRAPHY

Bernal de Samayoa, Ligia. *Hugo Carrillo: un teatro para estudiantes*. Tesis de Licenciatura en Letras. Universidad del Valle, 1986.

Callan, Richard. *Miguel Angel Asturias*. New York: Twayne Publishers, 1970.

Carrillo, Hugo. "El teatro de los ochenta en Guatemala." *Latin American Theatre Review* 25.2 (Spring 1992): 93–106.

Díaz Vasconcelos, Luis Antonio. *Apuntes para la literatura guatemalteca*. Guatemala: Secretaría de Educación, 1942.

Fernández Molina, Manuel. *Dos estudios históricos sobre el teatro en Guatemala*. Guatemala: Dirección General. Cultura y Bellas Artes, 1982.

"Guatemala." *Escenarios de dos mundos: inventario teatral de Iberoamérica* Vol. 3. Madrid: Centro de Documentación Teatral, 1988, 12–53. Articles by scholars.

Hugo Cruz, Victor. *Obra drámatica de Manuel Galich*. Guatemala: Universidad San Carlos, 1989.

Johnson, Harvey L. "La historia de la conversion de San Pablo." *Nueva Revista de Filología Hispánica*. 4 (1950): 115–160.

Jones, Willis Knapp. *Behind Spanish American Footlights*. Austin: University of Texas Press, 1966.

———. *Breve historia del teatro latinoamericano*. Mexico City: Ediciones de Andrea, 1956.

Paz Hernández Aragón de Tavera, Ma. de la. *Teatro indígena prehispánico*. Morelia: Universidad Michoacana de San Nicolás de Hidalgo, 1996.

Salazar, Ramón A. *Historia del desenvolvimiento intelectual de Guatemala*. Guatemala: Tipografía Nacional, 1897.

Shillington, John. *Grappling with Atrocity: Guatemalan Theatre in the 1990s*. London: Associated University Presses, 2002.

Solórzano, Carlos. *Panorama general del movimiento teatral guatemalteco*. Guatemala: Ministerio de Cultura y Deportes, 1986.

———. *Teatro breve*. Mexico City: Lecturas Mexicanas, 1986.

————. *El teatro latinoamericano en el siglo XX*. Mexico City: Editorial Pormaca, 1964.

————, ed. *Teatro guatemalteco contemporáneo*. Madrid: Editorial Aguilar, 1964.

◆

ARÉVALO MARTÍNEZ, Rafael (1884–1975). Arévalo Martínez wrote little for the theater. A journalist, professor, and ambassador, he published poetry, novels, short stories, philosophical essays, and plays. In 1940 he published his first drama, *Los duques de Endor* (The Dukes of Endor). It is a fantastic piece in three acts that treats the abdication of Edward VII, known as the Duke of Windsor. In 1956 he published his second drama, *El hijo pródigo* (The Prodigal Son).

WORKS: *Los duques de Endor* (The Dukes of Endor) (Guatemala: Talleres de la Imprenta del "Centro Editorial," 1940). *El hijo pródigo* (The Prodigal Son) (Guatemala: Tipografía Nacional, 1956).

BIBLIOGRAPHY: Willis Knapp Jones, *Behind Spanish American Footlights* (Austin: University of Texas Press, 1966), 454. Carlos Solórzano, *El teatro latinoamericano en el siglo XX* (Mexico City: Editorial Pormaca, 1964), 90–91.

ASTURIAS, Miguel Ángel (1899–1974). Asturias is best known as a novelist, but he also wrote five plays for the theater. His *Soluna* (Sunmoon) (1955) blends ancient myths and modern everyday life into a dreamlike magical realism. The theme, according to McMurray, is that man cannot live by reason alone but that in order to attain psychic wholeness he must retain contact with the myths of his ancestral and telluric origins (272). Another dramatic work by Asturias is *La audiencia de los confines* (Tribunal of the Frontiers) (1957). This play, whose title refers to the most remote courts of justice when Guatemala was under Spanish rule, dramatizes the struggles of Bishop Bartolomé de las Casas to prohibit slavery among the Indians. The implication of the work is that the exploitation of the Guatemalan Indian continues unabated into the twentieth century. The vitality and persistence of Mayan myths is evident in *Cuculcán*, which draws on the *Annals of the Cakchiquels*, and the *Popol Vuh*, as well as the Yucatecan *El libro de los libros de Chilam Balam* (The Book of Books of Chilam Balam); the latter is among the most recondite of all Mayan records. The play is a chromatic ballet based on the three daily positions of the sun: morning, afternoon, and night. *Cuculcán* (usual spelling is Kukulkán) is one of the supreme gods and is pitted against Guacamayo, a false god and deceiver. The Guatemalan playwright Solórzano has summarized *Cuculcán* as the advent, plenitude, and setting sun "amid the voices that people and Nature daily manifest their amazement at the phenomenon of passing time" (Solórzano, 21). Of the two other plays by Asturias, *Chantaje* (Blackmail) with its thirty-odd speaking parts is perhaps the most difficult to classify. A prostitute, a business tycoon, and a policeman figure in this noisy, complex work in which absurdity dominates. *Dique seco* (Dry Dock), perhaps set in Italy, is the only play by Asturias that doesn't take place in Guatemala. This two-act comedy is a farce with strikingly visual qualities. In general, the plays of Asturias are open to numerous interpretations since it is difficult to distinguish any single decisive meaning for them. Callan has stated that "the influence of unconscious archetypes on human behavior, the basic myths which man endlessly relives, these are the fundamental themes that give meaning to his [Asturias's] work" (151).

WORKS: *Soluna* (Sunmoon); (Buenos Aires: Losange, 1955). *La audiencia de los confines* (Tribunal of the Frontiers) (Buenos Aires: Ariadna, 1957). *Teatro: Chantaje, Dique Seco, Soluna, La audiencia de los confines* (Buenos Aires: Losada, 1964).

BIBLIOGRAPHY: Richard Callan, *Miguel Angel Asturias* (New York: Twayne Publishers, 1970), 120–151. Willis Knapp Jones, *Behind Spanish American Footlights* (Austin: University of Texas Press, 1966), 456. George R. McMurray, *Spanish American Writing Since 1941: A Critical Survey* (New York: Ungar, 1987), 272–273. Carlos Solórzano, ed., *Teatro guatemalteco contemporáneo* (Madrid: Editorial

Aguilar, 1964), 21. Carlos Solórzano, *El teatro latinoamericano en el siglo XX* (Mexico City: Editorial Pormaca, 1964), 174–175.

AYCINENA, Juan Fermín (1838–1898). Aycinena made his theatrical debut in Lima with a poetic comedy in verse, *El hombre de bien* (Honest Man). The piece's eight characters are essentially Guatemalan, and the loss of a coffee crop due to a hailstorm is the subject of the prize-winning effort. Jones writes that the play won the Ateneo de Lima prize in 1887 and was printed in the *Revista* of the Guatemala Academy the following year (452). When he returned to Guatemala, Aycinena wrote several other plays such as *La locura literaria* (Literary Madness), which suggests that not everyone should attempt to be a writer; *La semilla de bien* (The Seed of Good) (1890), about the orphan Perico who is reared by a bandit but still turns out well; and the three-act *Esther*, based on the biblical story of Xerxes and Queen Vasti, which was later written as a *zarzuela*. Aycinena also wrote, according to Jones, a *juguete* in two acts about an orphan, an untitled *sainete* about women in the eighteenth century, and a prose dramatic piece, *Quedarse con los crespos hechos* (Left with Styled Curls) (453).

WORKS: *El hombre de bien* (Honest Man) (1888). *La semilla de bien*, (The Seed of Good) (1890). *La locura literaria* (Literary Madness). *Esther. Quedarse con los crespos hechos* (Left with Styled Curls).

BIBLIOGRAPHY: Willis Knapp Jones, *Behind Spanish American Footlights* (Austin: University of Texas Press, 1966), 452.

CARRILLO, Hugo (1928–1994). Hugo Carrillo was a director and a committed playwright who studied in Paris and the United States. He was one of the founders of the University Art Theatre (1950). He directed the National Theatre Company until 1968 and was the artistic director of the independent Theatre Club beginning in 1972. Carrillo's major works include *El corazón del espantapájaros* (The Scarecrow's Heart) (1962); *La herencia de la Tula* (Tula's Inheritance) (1964); *Mortaja, sueño, y autopsia para un teléfono* (Shroud, Dream and Autopsy

for a Telephone) (1972), three one-act plays; and *El señor presidente* (Mr. President) (1989), based on the novel of the same title by Guatemala's Nobel Prize–winning novelist Miguel Angel Asturias (161). Other of his works are *¡La chalana!* (The Barge!), *La calle del sexo verde* (The Street of Smutty Sex), *El lorito fantasioso* (The Conceited Parrot), and *María* (dramatic version of Jorge Isaacs's novel). Carrillo founded the Educational Theatre for school and college students for which he adapted classic Latin American novels to the stage. His plays are translated into many languages and presented widely.

WORKS: *El corazón del espantapájaros* (The Scarecrow's Heart) (1962). *La herencia de la Tula* (Tula's Inheritance) (1964). *Mortaja, sueño, y autopsia para un teléfono* (Shroud, Dream, and Autopsy for a Telephone) (1972). *El lorito fantasioso* (The Conceited Parrot) (Guatemala: Serviprensa Centroamericana, 1982). *María* (Guatemala: Ediciones Teatro-Club, Serviprensa Centroamericana, 1984). *El señor presidente* (Mr. President) (Guatemala: Delgado Impresos, 1989). *¡La Chalana!* (The Barge!) (n.d.). *La calle del sexo verde* (The Street of Smutty Sex) (n.d.).

BIBLIOGRAPHY: Hugo Carrillo, "El teatro de los ochenta en Guatemala," *Latin American Theatre Review* (Spring 1992); 93–106. Willis Knapp Jones, *Behind Spanish American Footlights* (Austin: University of Texas Press, 1966), 459. Ligia Bernal de Samayoa, *Hugo Carrillo: Un teatro para estudiantes* (Tesis de Licenciatura en Letras. Univ. del Valle. 1986). Carlos Solórzano, *El teatro latinoamericano en el siglo XX* (Mexico City: Editorial Pormaca, 1964), 172–173.

CERNA, Carlos Girón. Carlos Cerna, although a diplomat by profession, wrote many plays. Among the more notable are *Ixquix* (1935), which is a three-act tragedy based on the *Popol Vuh; Quiché-Achí* (Quiche Man), successfully staged in 1950; *Tututicutu*, also inspired in the past; *La fotografía de los signos* (The Photograph of the Signs); and the play that won the 1951 Ministry of Education contest, *Al tercer día* (On the Third Day).

WORKS: *Ixquix* (1935). *Quiché-Achí* (Quiche Man) (1950). *Al tercer día* (On the Third Day)

(1951). *Tututicutu* (n.d.). *La fotografía de los signos* (The Photograph of the Signs) (n.d.)

BIBLIOGRAPHY: Willis Knapp Jones, *Behind Spanish American Footlights* (Austin: University of Texas Press, 1966), 453–454.

CERNA, Ismael (1856–1901). Ismael Cerna is considered to be the founder of the national theater of Guatemala (271). Jones suggests that autobiographic details can be gleaned from two of his plays—*Vender la pluma* (Selling the Pen) and *La muerte moral* (The Moral Death), both influenced by José Echegaray. Jones states that Cerna's masterpiece is *La penitenciaria de Guatemala* (The Penitentiary of Guatemala) (453). This play in verse was written and first performed in El Salvador. It was published serially in *La República* and later in 1891 in book form.

WORKS: *La penitenciaria de Guatemala* (The Penitentiary of Guatemala) (1891). *Vender la pluma* (Selling the Pen) (n.d.). *La muerte moral* (The Moral Death) (n.d.).

BIBLIOGRAPHY: Willis Knapp Jones, *Behind Spanish American Footlights* (Austin: University of Texas Press, 1966), 453.

CORONADO, Trinidad. Trinidad Coronado first published *Ensayos dramáticos* (Dramatic Essays) in Antigua in 1893 and later *Los héroes de Alcalá* (The Heroes of Alcala) in 1897.

WORKS: *Ensayos dramáticos* (Dramatic Essays) (1893). *Los héroes de Alcalá* (The Heroes of Alcala) (1897).

BIBLIOGRAPHY: Willis Knapp Jones, *Behind Spanish American Footlights* (Austin: University of Texas Press, 1966), 454.

DRAGO BRACCO, Adolfo (1894–   ). *Entre nieblas* (In the Fog) (1918) was the first of some twenty plays by Drago Bracco, and interestingly, all were performed. *Colombina quiere flores* (Colombina Wants Flowers) (1928) was first performed in the Teatro Municipal of Quetzaltenango in December 1923. Concerning Colombina's birthday party, this commedia dell' arte is probably, Jones concludes, the only Central American play ever performed in an English translation (455). Most of Drago Bracco's plays have foreign settings. Examples are *En la noche mil y dos* (In the One Thousand and Second Night), *La danza de los cerezos en flor* (The Dance of the Cherry Tree in Bloom), set in a fanciful Japan, and *Se han deshojado en el jardín las rosas* (The Roses Have Lost Their Petals in the Garden), published in 1938 and considered by Solórzano to be his masterpiece (89).

WORKS: *Entre nieblas* (In the Fog) (1918). *Colombina quiere flores* (Colombina Wants Flowers) (1928). *Se han deshojado en el jardín las rosas* (The Roses Have Lost Their Petals in the Garden) (1938). *En la noche mil y dos* (In the One Thousand and Second Night) (n.d.) *La danza de los cerezos en flor* (The Dance of the Cherry Tree in Bloom) (n.d.).

BIBLIOGRAPHY: Willis Knapp Jones, *Behind Spanish American Footlights* (Austin: University of Texas Press, 1966), 454–455. Jones, *Breve historia del teatro latinoamericano* (Mexico City: Ediciones de Andrea, 1956), 144. Carlos Solórzano, *El teatro latinoamericano en el siglo XX* (Mexico City: Editorial Pormaca, 1964), 89–90.

GALICH, Manuel (1913–1984). Galich belongs to the trio formed by himself, Carlos Solórzano, and Miguel Angel Asturias, although he wrote and staged works prior to 1944. The prolific playwright, often considered to be the father of contemporary Guatemalan theater, was a left-wing professor, statesman, and diplomat. He spent years in exile mainly in Argentina and later in Cuba, where he died. While Minister of Education, he began to write plays about the history of Guatemala for the schools (Jones, 145). Works from this early period are *El retorno* (The Return) (1938); *El señor Gukup-Cakix* (Mister Sunbird) (1939), which is based on an episode found in the *Popul Vuh* that deals with the Gukup or Sunbird; *Canciller Cadejo* (Chancellor Cadejo) (1940); and the three historic works—*Carta a su ilustrísima* (Letter to His Grace), which is set in the early seventeenth century, *Belem, 1813*, and *15 de septiembre* (15th of September), which dramatize Guatemala's struggle for independence—from *Historia a escena* (Scenes from History) (1949). *Papá Natas* (1938) whose title is based on the word *papanatas*, or simpleton, and its sequel *La mugre* (Filth) (1953) treat a weak father and a most unpleasant family. *M'hijo el bachiller* (My Son the Graduate) (1939) is a violent denunciation of the education system in Guatemala. *De lo vivo a lo pintado* (From the Living to the Painted) (1947), performed in the Palace Theatre and on the open-air Ministry of Education stage in 1947, inveighs against the corrupt legal profession and injustices to women. His personages are clearly unpleasant, but Galich's contribution to the stage is unquestionable. Beginning in the early 1950s, he began to publish plays that deal with social problems. *El tren amarillo* (The Yellow Train) (1954) is a sensational and hard-hitting attack of the foreign banana companies operating in Guatemala, *Entre cuatro Paredes* (Among Four Paredes) (1964) is a comedy of manners satirizing upper-middle-class hypocrisy, and *El último cargo* (The Last Charge) (1974) is a guerrilla drama that is based on the confrontation between the conservative establishment and revolutionaries attempting to seize power and institute social justice for the common people. Jones reminds us that *Ida y vuelta* (Round Trip), a trilogy depicting the poverty and wars of nineteenth-century Guatemala, won for Galich the Central American Drama Competition of 1948 (458). *Pascual Abaj, Mister John Tenor y yo* (Mister John Tenor and I), and *El pescado indigesto* (The Undigested Fish) (1960) are examples of his later plays and belong to political and social criticism.

WORKS: *M'hijo el bachiller* (My Son the Graduate) (1939). *De lo vivo a lo pintado* (From the Living to the Painted) (1947). *El tren amarillo* (The Yellow Train) (1954). *Entre cuatro Paredes* (Among Four Paredes) (1964). *El último cargo* (The Last Charge) (1974).

BIBLIOGRAPHY: Víctor Hugo Cruz, *Obra dramática de Manuel Galich* (Guatemala: Universidad San Carlos, 1989). Manuel Galich, *Obras de teatro* (Guatemala: Comité Nacional de Alfabetización, 1946). Willis Knapp Jones, *Behind Spanish American Footlights* (Austin: University of Texas Press, 1966), 457–459. George R. McMurray, *Spanish American Writing Since 1941: A Critical Survey* (New York: Ungar, 1987), 273–274. Carlos Solór-

zano, *El teatro latinoamericano en el siglo XX* (Mexico City: Editorial Pormaca, 1964), 127–129.

LA PARRA DE LA CERDA, Vicenta (1834–1905). Not only is Vicenta la Parra de la Cerda a pioneer in Guatemala's national theater; she is also the first woman dramatist of Central America. Her first play, the four-act *Angel caído*, (Fallen Angel) was written in 1880, but according to Jones, it was not staged until July 18, 1886, in the Teatro Nacional by a group of visiting players from Spain (143). For the 1886 performance, she revised the play into three acts but published it in its original form in 1888. The play is about an unfaithful wife who deserts her husband Alberto and their daughter for the husband's best friend. The two lovers get shot, and although Alberto calls her a "fallen angel," he forgives her before she dies. Another play, *Hija maldita* (Damned Daughter), treats a "willful daughter" who attempts to escape marrying the husband of her family's choice. *Los lazos del crimen* (The Traps of Crime) (1897) is another work concerning a woman who suffers. Jones sees the characters of Guatemala's first woman dramatist as puppets more than as real characters (452). Nonetheless, de la Cerda is important as a forerunner of the country's female dramatists.

WORKS: *Angel caído* (Fallen Angel) (s.1886). *Los lazos del crimen* (The Traps of Crime) (1897). *Hija maldita* (Damned Daughter) (n.d.).

BIBLIOGRAPHY: Willis Knapp Jones, *Behind Spanish American Footlights* (Austin: University of Texas Press, 1966), 451–452. Jones, *Breve historia del teatro latinoamericano* (Mexico City: Ediciones de Andrea, 1956), 143.

MARSICOVÉTERE Y DURÁN, Miguel (1913–). In Guatemalan theater Marsicovétere y Durán is important for having founded the Tepeus group among the Generation of 1930. *Tepeus* is a Quiché word meaning "messengers" and is a reference to the group's desire to carry forward the literary tradition of the Indian. He also wrote a number of plays, and some are rather interesting in style and content. Jones points out that in *El espectro acróbata* (The Acrobatic Ghost) (1953) the reader, after finishing the work, turns the book upside down and, starting from the other end, reads a "tragedy of masks" (455). He goes on to say that *El camino blanco y el camino negro* (The White Road and the Black Road) (1938) has two characters who talk "only when the spectators seem to be getting bored" (455).

WORKS: *El camino blanco y el camino negro* (The White Road and the Black Road) (1938). *El espectro acróbata* (The Acrobatic Ghost) (1953). *La mujer y el robot* (The Woman and the Robot). *El evangelio de Odolán* (The Gospel of Odolán). *Cada quien con su fantasma* (Each One with His Ghost). *Señorita Dama* (Miss Dama). *La noche sin dioses* (The Night without Gods). *El espejo roto* (The Red Mirror).

BIBLIOGRAPHY: Willis Knapp Jones, *Behind Spanish American Footlights* (Austin: University of Texas Press, 1966), 455. Jones, *Breve historia del teatro latinoamericano* (Mexico City: Ediciones de Andrea, 1956), 144. Carlos Solórzano, *El teatro latinoamericano en el siglo XX* (Mexico City: Editorial Pormaca, 1964), 89–90.

SOLÓRZANO, Carlos (1922–   ). Solórzano, one of Latin America's foremost dramatists, was born in San Marcos, Guatemala, but has received degrees, published, and lived in Mexico for much of his life. After earning his doctorate, Solórzano traveled to France, where he took specialized courses in dramatic art during the period 1948–1950. After returning to Mexico he was named director of the Teatro Universitario Profesional of the University of Mexico in 1952. Solórzano held this post until 1962, and since then he has lectured on drama and Latin American literature at his alma mater. Therefore, some consider him to be a Mexican dramatist, whereas others label him as Guatemalan-Mexican. At any rate, some discussion of Solórzano is required when the theater of Guatemala is considered. In addition to his *Teatro guatemalteco contemporáneo* (1964), he has written and staged the following works: *Doña Beatriz la sin ventura* (The Unhappy Miss Beatriz) (1951), a three-act play that dramatizes an episode of the Spanish conquest of Guatemala; *La sin ventura* (The Unhappy One) (1952); *El hechicero* (The Magician) (1954), a carefully structured tragedy

that takes place in a starving medieval town; *Las manos de Dios* (The Hands of God) (1956), which has been translated into various languages; *Los fantoches* (The Puppets) (1958), based on the Mexican ritual known as the "Burning of Judas" the Saturday before Easter; *Mea culpa* (My Fault), a play that treats the confessions of a judge and a priest; *El crucificado* (The Crucifixion) (1958), a play combining biblical myth and Mexican folklore to express Solórzano's denunciation of Christianity, which is depicted as a bloody, sacrificial cult of fanatics; *El sueño del ángel* (The Angel's Sleep) (1960), a dialogue between an elderly woman and her cruel guardian angel; *Cruce de vías* (Railroad Crossing) (1960), an Absurdist, expressionistic piece; and *Los falsos demonios* (The False Demons) (1963), which was published in 1966 as a novel. Another one-act play is *El zapato* (The Shoe), which is published in Carlos Solórzano's *Teatro breve* (1986). McMurray concludes that Solórzano, whether considered to be a Mexican or Guatemalan dramatist, is "one of Latin America's foremost dramatists and has been instrumental in the development of an avant-garde theatre of ideas designed to replace realistic regionalism with a more poetically conceived, universal art form" (215).

WORKS: *Doña Beatriz* (Miss Beatriz), *El hechicero* (The Magician), and *Las manos de Dios*, (The Hands of God), in Carlos Solórzano, *El teatro hispanoamericano contemporáneo* (Mexico City: Fondo de Cultura Económica, 1964), 301–358. *Las manos de Dios* is also in Elena Paz and Gloria F. Waldman, *Teatro contemporáneo* (Boston: Heinle & Heinle, 1983), 91–135. *Los fantoches* (The Puppets), in Carlos Solórzano, *Teatro breve hispanoamericano* (Madrid: Aguilar, 1969), 327–342; also in Frank Dauster and Leon Lyday, *En un acto* (Boston: Heinle & Heinle, 1990), 20–33. *El crucificado* (The Crucifixion), in Gerardo Luzuriaga and Robert S. Rudder, eds., *The Orgy: Modern One-Act Plays from Latin America* (1974). *Los fantoches, Mea culpa* (My Fault), *Cruce de vías* (Railroad Crossing), *El sueño del ángel* (The Angel's Sleep), *El zapato* (The Shoe), and *El crucificado*, in Carlos Solórzano, *Teatro breve* (Mexico City: Joaquín Mortiz, 1977).

BIBLIOGRAPHY: Frank Dauster, "The Drama of Carlos Solórzano," *Modern Drama* 7 (May 1964);

89–100. Willis Knapp Jones, *Behind Spanish American Footlights* (Austin: University of Texas Press, 1966), 456–457. George R. McMurray, *Spanish American Writing Since 1941: A Critical Survey* (New York: Ungar, 1987), 212–216, 272. Douglas Radcliff-Umstead, "Solórzano's Tormented Puppets," *Latin American Theatre Review* (Spring 1971); 5–11. Esteban Rivas, *Carlos Solórzano y el teatro hispanoamericano* (Mexico: 1970), 127. Peter J. Schoenbach, "La libertad en *Las manos de Dios*," *Latin American Theatre Review* (Spring 1970); 21–29. Carlos Solórzano, *Teatro breve* (Mexico City: Lecturas Mexicanas, 1986). Solórzano, *Teatro guatemalteco contemporáneo* (Madrid: Editorial Aguilar, 1964). Solórzano, *El teatro hispanoamericano* (Mexico City: Fondo de Cultura Económica, 1964). Solórzano, *Teatro latinoamericano del siglo XX* (Buenos Aires: Nueva visión, 1961). Solórzano, *El teatro latinoamericano en el siglo XX* (Mexico City: Editorial Pormaca, 1964), 183–187.

SOTO HALL, Máximo (1871–1944). The poet laureate of Guatemala made a very brief incursion into the theater with two theatrical pieces, *Madre* (Mother), which was performed but never published, and *Por un nombre* (By One Name).

WORKS: *Madre* (Mother). *Por un nombre* (By One Name).

BIBLIOGRAPHY: Willis Knapp Jones, *Behind Spanish American Footlights* (Austin: University of Texas Press, 1966), 454. Willis Knapp Jones, *Breve historia del teatro hispanoamericano* (Mexico City: Ediciones de Andrea, 1956), 144.

TEJADA MILLA, Mercedes. Mercedes Tejada Milla is the author of two extant plays. The first is *Dolor* (Pain), and the other is a three-act play titled *Una vida* (A Life), which was performed on October 9, 1924.

WORKS: *Dolor* (Pain) (n.d.). *Una vida* (A Life) (s.1924).

BIBLIOGRAPHY: Willis Knapp Jones, *Behind Spanish American Footlights* (Austin: University of Texas Press, 1966), 454.

URRUTIA, Miguel Ángel (1852–1931). Urrutia is the author of several plays. His first effort was the four-act poetic tragedy *La expiación* (The Atonement) (1884). Urrutia also wrote *Un conflicto en el hogar* (A Conflict in the Home), which was performed at the Teatro Nacional in 1903. His last play is *Silencio heroico* (Heroic Silence), a three-act tragedy in prose that was not published until 1924. Marital fidelity is the theme of *La expiación* in which the son Ernesto discovers his mother in the garden with her lover Julián, the father's best friend. Ernesto, outraged by what he saw, murders the fleeing Julián. His predicament is that the truth will shame his mother, and because he shot Julián in the back, he is unable to claim self-defense. Jones suggests that the mother eventually attempted to save her convicted son by confessing all to the magistrate, but her words are drowned out by the shots of the firing squad (452).

WORKS: *La expiación* (The Atonement) (1884). *Un conflicto en el hogar* (A Conflict in the Home) (s.1903). *Silencio heroico* (Heroic Silence) (1924).

BIBLIOGRAPHY: Willis Knapp Jones, *Behind Spanish American Footlights* (Austin: University of Texas Press, 1966), 452. Knapp Jones, *Breve historia del teatro latinoamericano* (Mexico City: Ediciones de Andrea, 1956), 143–144. Carlos Solórzano, *El teatro latinoamericano en el siglo XX* (Mexico City: Editorial Pormaca, 1964), 47.

VALLE, Manuel (1861–1913). Manuel Valle wrote a few plays. *Flor del café* (Coffee Plant) exalts the beauty of the Guatemalan countryside and one of its natural products, coffee. *Del colegio a los quince* (From School at Fifteen) is about a young lady's trials in the real world after leaving school.

WORKS: *Flor del café* (Coffee Plant). *Del colegio a los quince* (From School at Fifteen).

BIBLIOGRAPHY: Willis Knapp Jones, *Behind Spanish American Footlights* (Austin: University of Texas Press, 1966), 453.

VALLE, Rafael (1894–1922). Rafael Valle, the son of Manuel Valle, wrote *El retorno* (The Return) (1921). His *Rayo de luz* (Ray of Light) and *La alegría de producir* (The Joy of Producing) were both published posthumously in 1922.

WORKS: *El retorno* (The Return) (1921). *La al-*

egría de producir (The Joy of Producing) (1922). *Rayo de luz* (Ray of Light) (1922).

BIBLIOGRAPHY: Willis Knapp Jones, *Behind Spanish American Footlights* (Austin: University of Texas Press, 1966), 453. Carlos Solórzano, *El teatro latinoamericano en el siglo XX* (Mexico City: Editorial Pormaca, 1964), 47–48.

Lee A. Daniel

Honduras

Honduran theater has endured many difficulties since colonial times in Central America, and to this day, it struggles for mere existence. As described by director Candelario Reyes in his 1992 article, theater in Honduras reflects the same lack of national identity that most other art forms in this impoverished country reveal. Indeed, the National Academy of Theater is an itinerant institution that is unable to provide much support for actors, playwrights, directors, and artists associated with stage production.

The situation in Honduras is long-standing, as this country has been mired in poverty since its independence as a republic in 1838. Prior to this date, Honduran theater in colonial Central America was not distinguishable from that of its Guatemalan or Salvadoran neighbors. Ileana Azor traces the origins of theater in her study *Origen y presencia del teatro en nuestra América*, stating that the predisposition and receptivity of pre-Columbian tribes to all live performances in a sense prepared the way for the evangelizing Spaniards to introduce their own dramatic forms in the New World and thus for the Conquest to take a sure foothold in the indigenous cultures. She does not distinguish, however, any particular Central American indigenous theatrical tradition, other than to list the various anonymous works authored in Nahuatl as well as Spanish.

The founding father of theater, and indeed, the first cultivator of intellectual life in Honduras, is Father José Trinidad Reyes (1797–1855), who also founded the National University in Tegucigalpa. He is best known for his pastoral dramas, called *pastorelas*, which were intended, as is much contemporary Honduran theater, for consumption by a public of lower literary pretentions (Hoffman, 94). In them, he revived a theatrical genre cultivated by Renaissance dramatists, such as Juan del Encina and Garcilaso de la Vega, with classical roots in Virgil, and adapted it for a less learned public, with political and satirical elements, musical compositions, Nativity themes, and didactic purposes.

Mentioned by at least one historian of Honduran theater is the fable-teller Luís Andrés Zúñiga, whose 1915 *Los Conspiradores* (The Conspirators), a drama in three acts, exalts the moral character and magnanimous heart of the Central American military hero General Morazán (Ardón, 122). Other theatrical activity in the first two decades of this century is scarcely mentioned. This is another reflection of the lack that dominates the Honduran stage.

Among those who do merit naming are Alonso A. Brito, who died prematurely in 1926, a poet whose major contribution was children's theater. José María Tobías Rosa, a moralist whose work was generally not well received because of the overbearing nature of his moral message, was the author of a number of plays that also leaned onto the didactic sphere. Additionally, Víctor F. Ardón closes his 1958 historical review of Honduran theater by naming a few of the plays that he himself has written, highlighting the recourse that he also points out from Father Trinidad Reyes's work—the use of standard Castillian by upper-class characters, in contrast to the Central American dialect spoken in Honduras among characters representing the lower class.

In 1961, Spanish Valencian native Andrés Morris (1928–) took up residence in Honduras and made a name for himself as the premier playwright in the nation. While criticized for being excessively melodramatic, Morris is still the best-known and most widely praised author for the stage in the country. His work is also of a socially critical nature, employing parody and sarcasm to ridicule a bureaucracy that frustrates an honest working person's efforts to escape poverty.

In the aforementioned article of Candelario Reyes, the contemporary playwright and theorist spoke of Honduran theater as a movement whose goals have never reached fruition. Despite the founding of the National Theatre in 1965, there is still no stable, accessible forum for the presentation of stage productions. In 1982, the founding of the Comunidad Hondureña de Teatristas (Honduran Theater Community, or COMHTE) offered a brief moment of optimism to those interested in forming an artistic and cultural platform from which to launch positive social changes in Central America. It had as a slogan *Por un nuevo teatro para una nueva sociedad* (For a new society through new theater) and was dedicated to organizing national theater festivals, regional symposia, and workshops that would aid in the development of a theater of national identity. Its demise, only six years later, was due to governmental apathy and overt opposition to a genre that the bureaucracy viewed as subversive. The Festival de Teatro por la Paz (Theatre Festival for Peace), founded by Candelario Reyes as part of COMHTE, is one of the few aspects of the movement known as *campesino* theater that continues to function, held every two years in Santa Barbara. He himself does not see much room for hope in Honduran theater. Reyes concludes that national theater in Honduras amounts to an oxymoron, as not only is support for productions authored by Hondurans limited but support is also scarce for works imported to Honduras from neighboring countries.

Finally, the group receiving attention and plaudits from observers of artistic endeavor in Honduras is Teatro La Fragua, founded in 1979 by American Jesuit priest Jack Warner and currently headquartered in El Progreso, Honduras's third-largest city. His mission in Honduras responds to the need, identified and reiterated by numerous critics of Honduran society, for a national identity. Warner speaks of the tripartite methods of La Fragua: staging (1) secular drama, (2) *El Evangelio en Vivo!*—representations from the Gospel; and (3) *cuentos Hondureños*, Honduran myth and folklore presented dramatically (Fleming, 140). Taking into account the illiteracy of the general theatregoing public, La Fragua seeks also to serve as a vehicle for teaching its audience some rudiments of reading and writing, history, and politics. With that in mind, director Warner seeks to maintain a balance between the number of secular and religious pieces that the Teatro performs. The secular plays tend to appeal to a more middle-class audience, situated in the cities, while the religious cycle is more a part of the *teatro campesino*, a traveling theater company that reaches into the remote, rural regions of the country. Warner calls this sector of Honduran society the core (Fleming, 145).

BIBLIOGRAPHY

Ardón, Victor F. "*La producción dramática en Honduras.*" *Humanismo* 48–49 (May–June 1958): 116–126.

Azor, Ileana. *Origen y presencia del teatro en nuestra América*. Havana: Letras Cubanas, 1988.

Fleming, John. "Forging a Honduran Identity: The people's Theatre of Teatro La Fragua." *Latin American Theatre Review* 28.1 (Fall 1994): 139–152.

"Honduras." *Escenarios de dos mundos: inventario teatral de Iberoamérica*. Madrid: Centro de Documentación Teatral, 1988. 3.54–85. Articles by scholars.

Reyes, Candelario. "Una década de búsqueda del teatro hondureño." *Latin American Theatre Review* 25.2 (Spring 1992): 107–111.

Suárez Radillo, Carlos Miguel. *Temas y estilos en el teatro hispanoamericano*: una experiencia radiofónica de difusión teatral: selección de textos programados por Radio Nacional de España en sus emisiones para el exterior. Zaragoza: Litho Arte, 1975.

Toro, Fernando de, and Peter Roster. *Bibliografía del teatro hispanoamericano. (1900–1980)*. VerlaKlaus: Dieter Vervuert, 1985.

Weiss, Judith, et al. *Latin American Popular Theatre: The First Five Centuries*. Albuquerque: University of New Mexico Press, 1993.

◆

BRITO, Alonso A. (?–1926). Brito was a poet whose theatrical pieces were written mainly to be performed by young people, containing recitable works, dialogues, and monologues suited to a youthful audience. If José Trinidad Reyes is to be known as a fabulist by vocation, then Brito should be noted for his dramatic capability.

WORKS: *La tristeza de la cumbre* (The Sadness of the Summit) (1917). *Las ínfulas del dinero* (The Whims of Wealth) (n.d.), *Un caballero de industria* (An Industrious Gentleman) (n.d.), *El corazón del pueblo* (The Heart of the People) (n.d.).

BIBLIOGRAPHY: Victor F. Ardón, "La producción dramática en Honduras," *Humanismo* 48–49 (May–June 1958): 116–126.

MORRIS, Andrés (1928–) A native of Valencia, Spain, Andrés Morris resided in Madrid, Stockholm, and London, where he was involved in radio transmissions in Spanish, before settling in Tegucigalpa in 1961. He is a professor of literature at the university there. He is best known for his *Trilogy of the Isthmus*, which is made up of three plays: *El Guarizama* (1967), *Oficio de hombres* (Men's Work) (1968), and *La miel del aberrojo* (The Bee's Honey) (1969). Morris's plays depict the difficulties and small triumphs of the people in their day-to-day existence in a country overwhelmed by foreign interests and influences.

WORKS: *La tormenta* (The Storm) (1955). *Ras de las gentes* (1957). *Los ecos dormidos* (The Sleeping Echos) (1957). *La ascensión del busito* (The Climb of the Little Bus) (1965). *El Guarizama* (1967). *Oficio de hombres* (Men's Work) (1968). *La miel del aberrojo* (The Bee's Honey) (1969).

BIBLIOGRAPHY: Pedro Shimose, ed, *Diccionario de autores iberoamericanos* (Madrid: Dirección General de Relaciones Culturales, Institución de Cooperación Iberoamericana, 1982). Carlos Miguel Suárez Radillo, *Temas y estilos en el teatro hispanoamericano contemporáneo. Una experiencia radiofónica de difusión teatral* (Zaragoza: Litho Arte, 1975).

REYES, José Trinidad (1797–1855). A Honduran statesman and churchman, promoter of feminist causes, literacy, art, and intellectual life in Honduras, he founded the University of Honduras and contributed greatly to the establishment of its library. He is the author of the first Spanish-language drama written in Central America. His works were never published, circulating instead in manuscript form. The final work mentioned exists only in fragmentary form. Reyes is praised for his upholding of the classical Spanish language, his integrating his drama with music, and his wit.

WORKS: Nine *pastorelas* are attributed to him: *Noemi* (before 1838). *Micol* (1838). *Neftalia* (1840). *Elisa* (1851). *Albano* (1851). *Olimpia* (1855). *Floro, o sea, la Pastorela del Diablo* (n.d.). *Zelfa* (n.d.). *Rubenia* (n.d.).

BIBLIOGRAPHY: E. Lewis Hoffman, "The Pastoral Drama of José Trinidad Reyes," *Hispania* 46.1 (1963): 93–101.

TEATRO LA FRAGUA. Although no one playwright is featured in the repertoire of this *campesino* theater, the company itself merits an entry here because of its importance as the single surviving professional theater group to have come out of COMHTE (Comunidad Hondureña de Teatristas), an umbrella organization under which numerous theater groups were formed in the mid-1980s. La Fragua's adaptations of commedia dell'arte pieces, such as Molière's *Scapino*, have proven effective in depicting for the people their own trying social and economic situations in modern-day Honduras. In a religious vein, La Fragua does performances of Bible stories such as the Three Wise Men and the Passion of Jesus Christ, again adapting the biblical original to the Honduran environment.

BIBLIOGRAPHY: John Fleming, "Forging a Honduran Identity: The People's Theatre of Teatro La Fragua," *Latin American Theatre Review* 28.1 (Fall 1994): 139–152. Judith A. Weiss et al., *Latin American Popular Theatre: The First Five Centuries* (Albuquerque: University of New Mexico Press, 1993).

ZUÑIGA, Luís Andrés. A playwright who continued in the fabulist tradition of Father Trinidad Reyes, Zuñiga is known for his prize-winning historical drama *Los Conspiradores* (The Conspirators) (1915) (another edition in Mexico in 1954), which recounts the plot against the president of the Central American Republic, General Morazán. The play is said to give adequate and appropriate depictions of Morazán's moral character and maganimous heart. Comments critical of the play point out the sophisticated linguistic expressions of people in all different social classes and the lengthy dissertations on stage that force the attention of the audience.

WORKS: *Los Conspiradores* (The Conspirators) (1915).

BIBLIOGRAPHY: Victor F. Ardón, "La producción dramática en Honduras," *Humanismo* 48–49 (May–June 1958): 116–126.

Helena Antolin Cochrane

Mexico

The writers featured in this dictionary include mainly playwrights. Excluded are such authors as Carlos Fuentes, José Agustín, and Octavio Paz, who have written plays but have not gained recognition in this field or spent a substantial amount of time in the theater. Although they have had a significant impact on the theater, we have also excluded directors, set designers, screenwriters, authors, and directors of musicals, *pastorelas* (Nativity plays), and vaudeville. These exclusions are not meant to diminish their importance in the development of Mexican theater. Any study of colonial Mexican theater would have to rely on critics such as Joaquín García Icazbalceta, Irving Roth, José Rojas Garcidueñas, and Armando de María y Campos. Our knowledge of nineteenth-century theater has been enhanced greatly by the efforts of Enrique de Olavarría y Ferrari and Luis Reyes de la Maza. While the dean of twentieth-century drama critics is Armando de María y Campos, Antonio Magaña Esquivel, Ruth Lamb, Frank Dauster, and Ron Burgess, among others, have also made a significant contribution to our knowledge of modern Mexican theater. Theater directors such as Ignacio Retes, Héctor Mendoza, Juan José Gurrola, Luis de Tavira, and many others have made significant contributions to the current high status of Mexican theater.

THEATER IN COLONIAL MEXICO

The theater in Mexico flourished during the colonial period like few other art forms. Fueled by the existence of a pre-Hispanic theatrical tradition and by the missionaries' zeal to teach the Catholic faith, a form of religious theater, in Indian or Spanish languages, was in operation a few years after the conquest of Mexico in 1521. Although secular theater appears as early as 1539, the nonreligious plays that have survived date from the 1560s. A more scholarly type of theater was that written in Spanish and/or in Latin by students and faculty at the Jesuit schools after 1572. All three manifestations of theater were written and staged throughout the Spanish domination of Mexico.

The first Mexican theatrical representations in Indian dialects and in Spanish were *autos*, religious dramatic allegories. Directed for the most part by the priests and represented by the Indians and/or Spaniards, these *autos* were very popular among the Indian population during the Spanish rule. Indians represented biblical characters, allegorical figures, or themselves. The resulting performances, as described by the chroniclers, were funny, inspirational, and quite different from anything that a cast of Spaniards alone might have produced. Almost all *autos*, in Spanish or in a native language, ended with a "Tocotín," an Indian dance accompanied by indigenous instruments. These *autos* not only instructed but also entertained their audience. Short farces, jokes, songs, dances, or one-act secular compositions often were performed at the beginning or the end of the play or both, and between acts. An example of this type of play is *The Final Judgment*, written by Andrés de Olmos during the first half of the sixteenth century. These plays were staged in the *atrio* or court-yard of a church in order to accommodate a large number of spectators.

Although the handwriting, vocabulary, and historical facts found in several of these *autos* clearly place them in the sixteenth or seventeenth centuries, several of them were not printed or translated into Spanish and other languages until the eighteenth and, in some instances, the nineteenth and twentieth centuries. An example of this is *The Sacrifice of Isaac*, written by Bernabé Vásquez in the second half of the eighteenth century and translated into Spanish in 1899. *The Merchant*, a secular play written by Don José Gaspar in 1687, was translated into English in 1970.

The first known play by an American-born playwright is Juan Pérez Ramírez's *Desposorio espiritual entre el pastor Pedro y la iglesia mexicana* (Spiritual Wedding of the Shepherd Peter and the Mexican Church). It was written and performed in Spanish in order to celebrate the presentation of the Archbishop's pallium to Don Pedro Moya de Contreras in 1574. The oldest secular drama that we have notice of was presented in 1539, *La conquista de Rodas* (The Conquest of Rhodes), to celebrate the peace treaty between Charles V of Spain and Francis I of France. During the second half of the sixteenth century, livelier, more popular forms of theater appeared. These were the *entremeses*, *sainetes*, and *coloquios*. The first two were one-act plays, with or without music, in which local affairs were addressed. The *coloquios* varied in length from one to seven acts and were concerned with current historical events, biblical themes, and local mores. The short dramas were presented at the beginning, between acts, or at the end of longer, more serious plays, as in the case of the *autos*. Fernán González de Eslava, a Spaniard who came to the New World in 1558, excelled in these short dramatic genres.

With the arrival of the Jesuits in 1572, a more frequent and scholarly kind of theater appeared. As a rule they had dramatical representations at the beginning and at the end of the school term, during the festivities of Corpus Christi and its patron saints, and in order to celebrate an important event such as the arrival of a new viceroy or the birth of a child to the Queen or the Vicereine. As a requirement, the students were asked to write and act out dialogues, eclogues, and longer plays in Latin or Spanish at the main *colegios* and *universidades* of Mexico. These plays, also written by faculty, were based on classical models. For the most part they were rhetorical exercises that catered to small audiences. One such play is *El triunfo de los santos* (The Triumph of the Saints), written by Pedro Morales in 1579 to celebrate the arrival of some important Catholic relics; another one is the *Dialogus in adventu inquisitorium factus . . .* (Dialogue upon the Arrival of the Inquisitors . . .), written by Bernardino de Llanos in 1589 to honor the visit of the Inquisitors.

Mexico was the first Spanish colony in the Americas to have commercial theater. Professional actors were imported as early as 1574, and by the end of the sixteenth century, there were two *corrales de comedias* (Theater Houses) in operation: one, next door to the Hospital de Nuestra Señora and the other in the patio of the Hospital Real de Indios. As in Spain, hospitals in Mexico supplemented their income by renting out space for theatrical presentations. Gonzalo de Riancho was the first lay director hired to oversee and stage plays during religious festivities and at other times. He served in this capacity from 1595 to 1618.

WOMEN *CAZUELAS*

The seventeenth century is highlighted by a playwright who was known mainly in Spain, Juan Ruiz de Alarcón, and by a Hieronymite nun, Sor Juana Inés de la Cruz. Ruiz de Alarcón, a major Golden Age author, is considered to be one of the first Western writers preoccupied with the psychological development of his characters and with morality. *La verdad sospechosa* (The Truth Suspect) deals with the moral and psychological implications of lying. He is said to be the founder of the Comedy of Character. Writers such as Moreto, Moratín, Corneille, Molière, and López de Ayala are indebted, in one way or another, to Juan Ruiz de Alarcón. Since colonial times women in Mexican theater have played a key role as actresses, directors, or playwrights. The history of women in Mexican theater parallels that found in other parts of the world during the sixteenth, seventeenth, and eighteenth centuries. At first they were allowed to watch secular theater, but only in special sections hidden by partitions called *cazuelas de mujeres* so that they could see but not be seen. Although at first female parts were played by men dressed as women, women were later allowed to act on stage, provided they were married. It appears that by the middle of the eighteenth century women had established their right to write, direct, and act in plays whether they were married or single.

Although better known for her poetry and feminist views, Sor Juana Inés de la Cruz's contribution to Mexican theater is significant. She wrote mainly one-act plays (*loas, coloquios, entremeses, sainetes*). She also wrote one comedy, *Los empeños de una casa* (The Travails of a Household). It is an entertaining play in which one of the characters, Doña Leonor, shares some of the characteristics of the author. She is an educated, eloquent, and independent woman. Sor Juana's success seems to have made an impact on the way men regarded women, for, in 1687, María de Celi, an actress, was named director of the Coliseo, the official Theater House, by the Viceroy. During the eighteenth century, several women held this post. Sor Juana is arguably the greatest Mexican poet during colonial times, but her influence in the theater has not yet been completely recognized or established. Besides the success of her play *Los empeños de una casa*, the mixture of music, singing, dance, and acting we find in her *villacincos* and her *loas* are perhaps among the first samples of the beginnings of the musical theater or opera in Mexico.

Other seventeenth-century playwrights include Cristóbal Gutiérrez de Luna who wrote a play about the Christianization of the Indian nobility, *Coloquio de la nueva conversión y bautismo de los últimos reyes de Tlaxcala* (Dialogue of the New Conversion and the Baptism of the Last Kings of Tlaxcala). Matías de Bocanegra wrote a fictionalized account of Francisco de Borja's life in 1640, *Comedia de San Francisco de Borja*. Francisco de Acevedo wrote *El pregonero de Dios y patriarca de los pobres* (The Announcer of God and Patriarch of the Poor). It is a comedy about the life of St. Francis of Assisi, which was censured by the Inquisition for not adhering to historical truth.

The first half of eighteenth-century Mexican secular theater is dominated by Eusebio Vela, an actor, director, and playwright who came to the New World in 1713 to work in his brother's theatrical company. Only three of fourteen works that he reportedly wrote have reached us: *Si el amor excede al arte . . .* (If Love Surpasses Art . . .), *La pérdida de España* (The Loss of Spain), and *Apostolado de las Indias y martirio de un cacique* (Apostolate of the Indies and Martyrdom of a Cacique). Vela paid more attention to scenography than to poetry, ideas, or didacticism. He had a penchant to awe and terrify his audience by having, on stage, representations of rocks that turned into mythological monsters such as the furies, or the Devil riding a dragon to meet St. James on a white stallion. There were thunders in the dark, screams, the sound of chains being dragged, foul smells. Because of his scenography and his intent to shock his audience, he may well be regarded as an early Romantic or late Baroque. Ana María de Castro assumed directorship of the Coliseo after Vela's death in 1737.

During this same period, Cayetano Javier de Cabrera y Quintero, a Bethlehem Hospitaller priest, distinguished himself as a playwright and a poet. He wrote several short dramatic compositions, an example of which is *Los empeños de la casa de sabiduría* (The Travails of the House of Wisdom), written as an introduction to the presentation of Sor Juana's *Los empeños de una casa* (The Travails of a Household). One of his longer dramatic works that has survived is *El iris de Salamanca* (The Iris of Salamanca), which deals with the life of St. John Sahagún. His narrative work *Escudo de Armas* (Coat of Arms) was censured in 1746. In it, he documents the Virgin of Guadalupe's right to be called the Patron Saint of Mexico, but he also derides the Indians, the medical profession, and the royalties that City Hall received from *pulque*, a pre-Hispanic alcoholic drink.

The second half of the eighteenth century up to the Mexican Independence in 1821 witnessed the rise of secular popular theater and somewhat of a decline in religious dramas. Recently imported ideas from the United States and France were discussed; new theaters were built in Mexico City, 1753, and in Puebla, 1760. Of many "pantomine dances" by Juan de Medina, two of them written in 1796 have survived. *Los juegos de Eglea* (The Games of Eglea) and *Muerte trágica de Muley-Eliacid, emperador de Marruecos* (The Tragic Death of Muley-Eliacid, Emperor of Morocco).

Also, a more nationalistic type of theater began to emerge. Fernando Gavila, sometimes known as Fernando de Dávila, wrote and had staged *La mexicana en Inglaterra* (The Mexican Girl in England) in 1792. He also wrote *La lealtad americana* (American Loyalty) in 1796 and the *zarzuela*, a short musical dramatic composition, *La linda poblana* (The Beautiful Girl from Puebla), in 1802. José Agustín de Castro is the author of *loas*, *autos*, and two one-act plays: *El charro* (The Cowboy) and *Los remendones* (The Shoemakers). The first is a monologue by a *charro*, a not-so-bright prototype of masculinity, who finds himself in the patio of a convent. The second is a light satire on the empty claims to nobility by two poverty-stricken shoemakers. Typical Mexican dances such as the "Jarabe," and the "Bamba poblana" were featured in place of the more traditional *entremeses*. Religious drama, though not as prevalent as before, was still popular among certain audiences. Manuel Quiroz Campo Sagrado's *Certamen poético en argumentos entre los cinco sentidos* (Poetic Contest in Dialogues Amongst the Five Senses), a dramatic panegyric of the Virgin Mary, is an example.

MEXICAN THEATER IN THE NINETEENTH CENTURY

The outstanding literary figure during the Wars of Independence (1810–1821) was José Joaquín Fernández de Lizardi, a journalist who began writing stories, novels, and plays after his newspaper, *El Pensador Mexicano* (The Mexican Thinker), was closed by the government. His dramatic production during these years includes *El fuego de Prometeo*

(The Fire of Prometheus), *Auto mariano* (Marian "Auto"), *La noche más venturosa* (The Most Fortunate Evening), and *Todos contra el payo* (Everyone Against the Simpleton).

Unlike fiction or poetry, which after Independence were influenced by non-Hispanic literatures, Mexican theater closely followed its Spanish models. Judging from published reports, theatrical activity in nineteenth-century Mexico was vibrant and popular. In 1831, under President Bustamante, the Mexican Academy of Dramatic Arts was founded. Although there were many playwrights, three who received the most critical attention during the first half of the century are Ignacio Rodríguez Galván (1816–1842), Manuel Eduardo de Gorostiza (1789–1851), and Fernando Calderón (1809–1845). For the most part, all three wrote romantic historical dramas and comedies of manners. In the second half of the century, the following dramatists stand out: Manuel José Othón (1858–1906), who wrote sentimental dramas in both verse and prose; Alfredo Chavero (1841–1906), who wrote about pre-Hispanic themes as well as comic operettas known as *zarzuelas*; and José Peón y Contreras (1843–1907), who wrote historical plays and was one of the most prolific Mexican dramatists in the nineteenth century.

As the capital city, Mexico City had the most theaters. The Teatro de Santanna, later known as El Nacional, was built in the early 1840s and lasted until 1900. The Coliseo Nuevo, built during colonial times, became the Teatro de México and subsequently became the Teatro Principal. The gas-lit Teatro de Iturbide, the site of three plays by Pantaleón Tovar, later became the Teatro Nacional and lasted until 1900. Some twenty years later, in 1875, the Teatro Arbeu was completed. Although there were several theaters in the capital, the two major venues were the Teatro Principal and the Teatro Nacional.

Although the focus of Mexican theatrical activity was Mexico City, it was not limited to that metropolis. Since colonial times, plays, gymnastics competitions, important trials, and political events have been staged in spaces ordinarily reserved mainly for theatrical presentations. Because of the political turmoil in Mexico City during the nineteenth-century, many dramatists premiered their works in the provinces. This situation in turn fostered the construction of several playhouses in the interior. In Querétaro, the Teatro de la República was in operation at the start of the Wars of Independence in 1810, continued through the time of Maximilian's surrender in 1867, and has been there ever since. During the Three Years' War (1858–1860) Guadalajara's Teatro Principal saw the premiere of several romantic works. Most of José Manuel Othón's plays were first staged at the Teatro Alarcón and the Teatro de la Paz in San Luis Potosí. Plays were premiered in Zacatecas at the Teatro Calderón during the Mexican-American war. Several dramatists staged their plays first in the provinces and later in Mexico City. Pablo J. Villaseñor premiered *El palacio de Medrano* and *Encarnación Rosas o el insurgente de Mescala* in 1851 at the Teatro Principal in Guadalajara and *Heroica defensa de Guaymas por las armas mexicanas* and *Clementina* in 1855 at the same theater. Peón y Contreras staged his plays first in Mérida and later in Mexico City, and Rosas Moreno, who wrote children's theater, presented his work first in Guanajuato and later in the capital city. With the exception of José Joaquín Gamboa and Alfredo Chavero who wrote plays dealing with local themes, Mexican theater during the first two decades of the twentieth century was mostly a continuation of what was staged during the last two decades of the previous century and enjoyed no significant official or private support.

It has been said that twentieth-century Mexican theater begins in the late 1920s with a shift toward the avant-garde. However, several events spearheaded by women are a prelude to the advent of experimental theater in Mexico. A movement proposing to empower Mexican authors was launched in 1921 by Virginia Fábregas and María Luisa Ocampo, who belonged to the Grupo de los Siete Autores (Group of the Seven Authors), or Pirandellos. The members of this group either wrote plays, acted in them, or lobbied public officials for financial support. During these years The Comedia Mexicana was founded by Amalia González de Castillo Ledón who, after winning the lottery, gave all her money to support the group's efforts. In 1926, under the direction of María T. Montoya and Fernando Soler, the Grupo de los Siete Autores set up a Temporada de autores mexicanos (Season of Mexican Authors) under the auspices of José Vasconcelos and Antonieta Rivas Mercado. The following authors saw their works premiered there: José Joaquín Gamboa, Parada, Diez Barroso, Francisco Monterde, A. González de Castillo Ledón, Antonio Mediz Bolio, Julio Jiménez Rueda, Nemesio García Naranjo, Carlos Díaz DuFoo, and María Luisa Ocampo. All these efforts culminated in the founding of the Teatro de Ulises (1928, 1929) by Xavier Villaurrutia and Manuel Rodríguez Lozano, among others. This was perhaps the first important renewal of twentieth-century Mexican theater. Authors like Villaurrutia, Novo, Owen, and Gorostiza, among others, brought Mexico into the mainstream of world theater in the twentieth century by translating, directing, and producing the works of dramatists such as Paul Claudel, Roger Marx, Charles Vildrac, and Eugene O'Neill.

The work of the Teatro de Ulises was continued first by the group known as Los escolares del teatro. Then Gorostiza himself founded the Teatro de Orientación, which, in three years' time (1932–1935), managed to stage the classics, Golden Age theater, and works by Mexican authors such as Gorostiza and Villaurrutia. Mauricio Magdaleno and Juan Bustillo de Oro founded the Teatro de Ahora in 1932, and Rodolfo Usigli organized the Teatro de Media Noche soon after. Generally speaking, the authors and directors of Ulises and Orientación are considered avant-garde, and the theater they authored, produced, or directed, experimental. On the other hand, Usigli and the Teatro de Ahora insisted on writing and producing works with Mexican themes. Theatrical productions in the Teatro de Bellas Artes (The Theater of Fine Arts) began in 1934 with the staging of Alarcón's *La verdad sospechosa* (The Truth Suspect).

Under the direction of Celestino Gorostiza, the Teatro de Orientación (1932–1935) followed in the footsteps of the Teatro de Ulises. Salvador Novo and Rodolfo Usigli are also associated with the Teatro de Orientación, although Usigli never wanted to be formally connected to any group. Besides the dramatists just mentioned, the names that stand out in Mexican theater during the 1930s are Juan Bustillo Oro, Mauricio Magdaleno, Rodolfo Usigli, and Xavier Villaurrutia.

In an effort to bring theater to the masses during 1941, the Grupo Proa, under the direction of José de Jesús Aceves, began staging plays for the workers' unions, an endeavor that lasted two decades. In 1943, the Teatro de México group, composed of Gorostiza, Julio Prieto, Miguel N. Lira, Conchita N. Sada, María Luisa Ocampo, and Xavier Villaurrutia, was formed. Margarita Urueta followed in the footsteps of the Teatro de Ulises and Teatro de Orientación by writing and staging avant-garde plays. The 1940s also witnessed the birth of experimental theatrical groups such as La linterna mágica of Ignacio Retes, the Teatro Estudiantil Autónomo of Xavier Rojas, and the Teatro de Arte Moderno of Hebert Darién and Lola Bravo. They all staged national and foreign plays. The Escuela de Arte Dramático

(1946) was incorporated into the Theater Section of the Instituto Nacional de Bellas Artes (INBA) when it was founded in 1947. During these years Salvador Novo helped the budding dramatists Sergio Magaña and Emilio Carballido, who would themselves become mentors of the next generation of dramatists. The playwrights who attained or continued receiving critical recognition in the 1940s include Rodolfo Usigli, Miguel N. Lira, and Mauricio Magdaleno. The development of Mexican theater was greatly enhanced in 1947 when the Theater Section of the INBA was formed. It marked the beginning of a substantial and continuous subsidy to the arts.

During the decade of the 1950s a host of Usigli's students—Federico S. Inclán, Luisa Josefina Hernández, Jorge Ibargüengoitia, Carlos Prieto, Alfonso Anaya, Fernando Sánchez Mayans, and Rafael Bernal—came into their own. In 1955, Luis G. Basurto staged what came to be one of the first box office successes in the history of Mexican theater, *Cada quien su vida* (To Each His Own), at the Teatro Lírico. Also during this time Carlos Solórzano began writing plays and theater criticism.

After the Spanish Civil War many dramatists and directors came to Mexico and made significant contributions to Mexican theater. Among them, Max Aub, Magda Donato, and Alvaro Custodio stand out. Alvaro Custodio founded the Teatro Español de México group in 1953, which changed its name to Teatro Clásico de México in 1960. Although this group presented Golden Age theater almost exclusively, it included the works of other contemporary Mexican dramatists. Mexican theater also benefited from the Japanese theater master Seki Sano, who taught and directed theater in Mexico from 1939 until his death in 1961.

The 1950s and early 1960s were years of great theatrical activity. Many Mexican authors were writing and staging plays during this time, and several critics refer to this period as the Golden Age of Mexican theater. The thematic concerns of these authors are varied: Elena Garro, Maruxa Vilalta, Héctor Azar, and Oscar Villegas are associated with the Theater of the Absurd. Nancy Cárdenas and Luisa Josefina Hernández address the theme of homosexuality, and Luis G. Basurto and Wilberto Cantón write about social problems using innovative techniques.

Although there were many dramatists writing during this so-called Golden Age, approximately 1950 to the early 1960s, the following made a continuous and successful impact: Basurto, Cantón, Ibargüengoitia, Magaña, and Solana, and groups like the Teatro Clásico de México. It was in the late 1950s and 1960s that playwrights Hugo Argüelles, Willebaldo López, Antonio González Caballero, and Vicente Leñero began to be recognized, first as playwrights and later as mentors of the dramatists of the 1980s and 1990s. Interest in directing plays appears to have blossomed in the 1960s, and most of the following new directors come from that period: Adam Guevara, Miguel Sabido, José Estrada, Hugo Hiriart, and Abraham Oceranski. In 1977 the first official theatrical group, the Compañía Nacional de Teatro, was formed.

The development of twentieth-century Mexican theater has been a joint effort by drama teachers and their students with the aid of government subsidies in the form of instruction and theater space. In one way or another, the government, through its several cultural organizations, has subsidized theatrical activities since the late 1940s. The Theater Department of the National Institute for Fine Arts (Instituto Nacional de Bellas Artes/INBA), the different cultural offices of the Mexican Institute for Social Security (Instituto Mexicano de Seguridad Social/IMSS), the Theater Departments of the National University (Universidad Nacional Autónoma de México/UNAM), and the Metropolitan University (Universidad Autónoma Metropolitana/UAM) have all contributed substantially to the development of Mexican theater since mid-century. In the 1950s, the UNAM formed student theatrical groups in the high schools. Enrique Ruelas, Héctor Azar, and Olga Harmony come from such groups. Noted directors in the 1980s and 1990s such as Juan José Gurrola, Ludwick Margules, Julio and Germán Castillo, Luis de Tavira, Nancy Cárdenas, and Jesusa Rodríguez were formed in the Teatro Universitario.

To help develop interest and talent outside of Mexico City the INBA founded and sponsored the Muestra Nacional de Teatro, a weeklong theater festival in which several young dramatists stage their works. The 1995 Muestra was held in Guadalajara at the Foro de Arte y Cultura and the Teatro Alarife, July 21–July 31, and presented eighteen plays from playwrights outside Mexico City. The UAM sponsored the Nueva Dramaturgia (New Theater) during the 1980s series by publishing and helping stage the works of several young dramatists and opened a theater, Casa de la Paz, for their presentations. Perhaps the most important government agency in the 1990s is the INBA's CITRU (Centro de Investigaciones Teatrales Rodolfo Usigli). It maintains files on all theatrical activity in Mexico. The first of a projected biennial work, *Teatro mexicano (1990–1991)*, documents all significant theatrical activity in Mexico during those years. The second volume of *Teatro mexicano* covers 1992–1993. The number and diversity of plays, playwrights, directors, choreographers, actors, and all other types of theatrical activity are truly impressive. Playwriting, acting, and directing have been taught mainly at the theater arts departments of the UNAM, the INBA, the IMMS, and the UAM and through the workshops and tireless efforts of many individual practitioners.

Among the many dedicated teachers, two stand out: Rodolfo Usigli and Emilio Carballido. Critics often refer to Usigli as the creator of modern Mexican theater or the patriarch of Mexican theater. Usigli and the Teatro de Ahora group (1932) were opposed to most dramatists and directors associated with Teatro de Ulises and Teatro de Orientación, who favored innovative experimental theater from abroad. Usigli insisted that Mexican authors should learn from the best that classical and world theater had to offer and adapt it to express Mexican reality in order to develop a Mexican theater. In the 1950s Usigli's students like Luisa Josefina Hernández, Emilio Carballido, Jorge Ibargüengoitia, and Vicente Leñero began making their mark developing regional themes with universal appeal. Emilio Carballido is not only one of the most prolific dramatists in contemporary Mexico but also a main force behind the success of Mexican theater. He collected and published three volumes of young dramatists in the 1970s and taught and assisted countless others. Carballido helped launch the careers of Hugo Argüelles, Oscar Liera, and many others. In turn, Sabina Berman, Jesús González Dávila, and María Elena Aura were all students of Hugo Argüelles.

In the 1960s, a new generation of dramatists began writing under the direction of writers such as Emilio Carballido, Luisa Josefina Hernández, Hugo Argüelles, Héctor Azar, and Vicente Leñero. After the so-called Golden Age of Mexican Theater (the 1950s and early 1960s), there was a pervasive reluctance to stage plays by Mexican playwrights or write about their work. This attitude reached its low point in 1974–1978 when many dramatists stopped writing. A cursory glance at Carlos Solórzano's weekly column confirms this theory. His critical commentaries during the 1962–1972 period in *La Cultura en México* focus on foreign theater in Mexico, theater directors (Mexican and foreign), set designers, and theater abroad. Also, according to Burgess, a lesser-known but important drama movement was that involving student theater groups during the period (1967–1973) in which the young clearly showed their disaffection for society and authority. A turning point in the development of new dramatic talent appears to have occurred in 1979. During that year, Carballido's second volume, *Teatro joven de México* (Young Mexican Theater) was published, and the Universidad Autónoma began sponsoring the Nueva dramaturgia, a program designed to publish and help young dramatists stage their plays. Only established authors like Cantón, Carballido, and Solana, or promising dramatists like Oscar Villegas and Willebaldo López, published and/or staged plays regularly in the late 1960s.

After the sclerosis of the early 1970s, Mexican theater began to flourish again in the 1980s and 1990s. Oscar Villegas and Willebaldo López, two of the most important young dramatists in the 1980s, were joined or followed by several others like Oscar Liera, Sabina Berman, Tomás Espinoza, Jesús González Dávila, Carlos Olmos, and Víctor Hugo Rascón Banda. The thematic concerns of these dramatists were varied. Liera, Berman, and Rascón Banda wrote political plays with metaphysical implications. Pilar Campesinos in the late 1960s and early 1970s expressed disaffection with the political system and suggested the need for a revolution. An important event of the 1980s was Felipe Santander's Teatro Rural and his play *El extencionista* (The Extending One). Santander is also associated with efforts to decentralize Mexican theater during the late 1980s and 1990s. With funding from the CONACULTA (Consejo Nacional para la Cultura y el Arte, or National Council for Culture and Art), he founded the CADE (Centro de Arte Dramático y Estudios, or Center for Studies of Dramatic Arts) in Cuernavaca, Morelos. At this institution he taught acting, and in 1990 his students staged his play *Mexico-USA*. During this time the works of established writers such as Rodolfo Usigli, Emilio Carballido, Hugo Argüelles, Vicente Leñero, Willebaldo López, and Oscar Liera were and are frequently staged.

Mexican theater in the 1980s and 1990s enjoyed unprecedented popularity at home and abroad. In 1984, Rafael Solana commented on the growth of this genre, observing that from two reliable playhouses in the 1920s in Mexico City, the Fábregas and the *Ideal*, the number of theaters had increased to over a hundred with both large and small stages. More recently, in reference to the biennial publication *Teatro en México 1990–1991*, which includes outstanding theatrical activity in the country, Víctor Hugo Rascón Banda cites 473 theatrical productions, 30 theater festivals, 324 theatrical directors, 171 set designers, 156 costume designers, 108 choreographers, and 191 musical composers.

Mexican theater has been regularly staged in the southwestern United States since colonial times, besides the customary student theatrical presentations in most major universities. Since its inception in 1967, the *Latin American Theatre Review* (*LATR*) has published a section detailing the performance of Latin American plays in the United States. Professional companies in cities with a heavy Mexican or Hispanic heritage such as Los Angeles, San Antonio, and New York regularly stage plays from Mexico and other parts of the Spanish-speaking world. In Los Angeles, under the direction of Carmen Zapata, the Bilingual Foundation for the Arts stages three or four bilingual plays as well as several dramatic readings during the year. During the last two years, plays or adaptations of works by Sabina Berman, Mariano Azuela, and Juan Rulfo have been staged. In the same city the Grupo de Teatro Sinergia has staged bilingual presentations of some of the works by Elena Garro, Víctor Hugo Rascón Banda, and Jesús Alberto Cabrera. Annual Latino theater festivals in

New York, San Antonio, Miami, and Costa Mesa often include Mexican plays. Mexican and Latin American theater have found a critical forum in the United States in journals such as *LATR* (published by the University of Kansas), *Tramoya* (published by Rutgers University–Camden and the Universidad Veracruzana), and *Gestos* (published by the University of California, Irvine). American interest in Mexico seems to be reciprocated by Mexican interest in American themes.

Mexican dramatists have been concerned with the flight and plight of their countrymen and their children migrating to the United States. J. Humberto Robles's *Los desarraigados* (The Uprooted Ones) and Victor H. Rascón Banda's *Homicidio calificado* (Homicide with Malice), for example, deal with the identity crisis and the abuses that Mexican Americans encounter in the United States. Plays like *Espaldas mojadas cruzan el Río Bravo* (Wet Backs Cross the Rio Grande) deal with illegal immigration into the United States.

BIBLIOGRAPHY

Arróm, José Juan. *El teatro de hispanoamérica en la época colonial.* Havana: Anuario Bibliográfico Cubano, 1956.

Careaga, Gabriel. *Sociedad y teatro moderno en México.* Mexico City: Joaquín Mortiz, 1994.

Cid Pérez, José, and Dolores Martí de Cid. Introduction. *Teatro indoamericano colonial.* Mexico City: Aguilar, 1970.

García, Genaro. *Documentos inéditos.* Vol. 15. Mexico City: n.p., 1907.

García Icazbalceta, Joaquín. "Representaciones religiosas en el siglo XVI." In *Obras: Opúsculos varios.* Vol. 1. Mexico City: n.p., 1896.

Lamb, Ruth Stanton. *Bibliografía del teatro mexicano del siglo XX.* Claremont, CA: Claremont College, 1962.

Leonard, Irving A. *Baroque Times in Old Mexico.* Ann Arbor: University of Michigan Press, 1959.

———. "La temporada teatral de 1972 en el Nuevo Coliseo de México." *Nueva revista de filología hispánica* 5 (1951): 349–410.

———. "The Theater Season of 1791–1792 in Mexico City." *Hispanic American Historical Review* 31 (1951): 349–364.

Magaña-Esquivel, Antonio. *Medio siglo de teatro mexicano, 1900–1961.* Mexico City: Instituto Nacional de Bellas Artes, 1964.

María y Campos, Armando de. *Pastorelas mexicanas: origen, historia y tradición.* Mexico City: Diana, 1985.

———. *Representaciones teatrales en la Nueva España: Siglo XVI al XVIII.* Mexico City: Costa-Amic, 1959.

Marie, Sister Joseph. *The Role of the Church and the Folk in Development of the Early Drama in New Mexico.* Philadelphia: University of Pennsylvania Press, 1948.

McAfee, Byron, and R. H. Barlow, trans., and eds. *Un cuaderno de marqueses. El México antiguo* 6.9–12 (1947): 392–404.

"México." *Escenarios de dos mundos: inventario teatral de iberoamérica.* Vol. 3. Madrid: Centro de Documentación Teatral, 1988, 87–185. Articles by scholars.

Oeste de Bopp, Marianne. "Autos mexicanos del siglo XVI." *Historia mexicana* 3.9 (1953): 112–123.

Olavarría y Ferrari, Enrique de, and Salvador Novo. *Reseña histórica del teatro en México, 1538–1911.* Mexico City: Editorial Porrúa, 1961.

Ravicz, Marylin Ekdahl. Introduction. *Early Colonial Religious Drama in Mexico: From Tzompantli to Golgotha.* Washington, DC: Catholic University of America Press, 1970.

Reyes, Alfonso. *Letras de la Nueva España.* Mexico City: Fondo de Cultura Económico, 1948.

Reyes de la Maza, Luis. *Cien años de teatro en México, 1810–1910.* Mexico City: Secretaria de Educación Pública, 1972.

———. *El teatro en México durante el segundo imperio (1862–1867).* Mexico City: Imprenta Universitaria, 1959.

———. *El teatro en 1857 y sus antecedentes, 1855–1856.* Mexico City: Instituto de Investigaciones Estéticas, 1956.

Reynolds, Winston A. "El demonio y Lope de Vega en el manuscrito mexicano *Coloquio de la nueva conversion y bautismo . . .* " *Cuadernos americanos* 163.2 (1969): 172–184.

Robe, Stanley L. Introduction. *"Coloquio de pastores" from Jalisco.* Berkeley: University of California Press, 1954.

Rojas Garcidueñas, José. Introduction. *Autos y coloquios del siglo XVI.* Mexico City: Universidad Nacional Autónoma de México, 1972.

———. *El teatro de Nueva España en el siglo XVI.* 1935. Mexico City: SepSetentas, 1973.

———, and José J Arróm. Introduction. *Tres piezas teatrales del virreinato.* Mexico City: Universidad Nacional Autónoma de México, 1976, 1–34, 149–182, 221–236.

Schilling, Hildburg. *Teatro profano en la Nueva España.* Mexico City: Imprenta Universitaria, 1958.

Spell, Jefferson R. "The Theater in Mexico City, 1805–1806." *Hispanic Review* 1 (1933): 55–65.

Suárez Radillo, and Carlos Miguel. *El teatro barroco hispanoamericano.* Vol. 1. Madrid: José Porrúa Turanzas, 1981.

Trenti Rocamora, J. Luis. *El teatro en la América colonial.* Buenos Aires: Huarapes, 1947.

◆

ARGÜELLES, Hugo (1932–   ). He was born in Veracruz, Veracruz, and studied medicine at the Universidad Nacional Autónoma de México (UNAM) for five years, theater arts for three at the Instituto Nacional de Bellas Artes (INBA), and literature for three at the UNAM, where he earned his master's degree. Argüelles has written several scripts for film and television and teaches theater arts at the UNAM. He conducts regular theater workshops in Mexico and abroad. His mentoring efforts have produced several actors, directors, and playwrights such as Carlos Olmos, Oscar Liera, Tomás Urtusástegui, and Sabina Berman. He has received numerous awards, among which are: the Juan Ruiz de Alarcón Prize in 1961 for his play *Los prodigiosos* (The Prodigious Ones); the National Theater Award in 1958 for *Los cuervos están de luto* (The Crows Are in Mourning); and the PECIME award for the film version of his play *El tejedor de milagros* (The Miracle Weaver). He also received the Sor Juana Inés de la Cruz Prize in 1981 for *El ritual de la salamandra* (The Ritual of the Salamander), and in 1983 for *Los amores criminales de las vampiras morales* (The Criminal Loves of the Morales Vampires). Several of his plays have been staged in Europe and America.

WORKS: *Los cuervos están de luto* (The Crows Are in Mourning, Orizaba, 1958). *El tejedor de milagros* (The Miracle Weaver, 1963). *La galería del silencio* (The Gallery of Silence, 1967). *La ronda de* *la hechizada* (The Watch of the Bewitched Woman, 1967). *La dama de la luna roja* (The Lady of the Red Moon, 1970). *El gran inquisidor* (The Great Inquisitor, 1973). *El ritual de la salamandra* (The Ritual of the Salamander, 1981). *El retablo del Gran Relajo* (The Altar Piece of the Great Debauchery, 1981). *El cocodrilo solitario del panteón rococo* (The Lonely Crocodile of the Rococo Pantheon, 1982). *Los amores criminales de las vampiras Morales* (The Criminal Loves of the Morales Vampires) (staged in Mérida, Yucatán, n.d.) (Mexico City: Editores Mexicanos, 1986). *Los gallos salvajes* (The Wild Roosters, staged at T. Wilberto Cantón, 1986) (Mexico City: Editores Mexicanos, 1986). *Romance, bronca y misterio de los caracoles amorosos y los muertos lujuriosos del burdel del cementerio* (The Romance, Quarrel and Mystery of the Lover Snails and the Lustful People at the Cemetery's Brothel, staged at T. Benito Juárez, 1988). *Doña Macabra* (Madame Macabre, 1989). *¿Qué comedias que adivinas?* (How Did You Guess?, staged at T. Corral Comedias Rodolfo Usigli, 1990). *Escarabajos* (Beetles, staged at Foro La Conchita, 1991). *Aguila real* (Royal Eagle, 1992). *La boda negra de las alacranas* (The Black Wedding of the Female Scorpions, staged at Festival Cervantino, 1992). *La esfinge de las maravillas* (The Sphinx of All Marvels, staged at T. La Conchita, 1995).

BIBLIOGRAPHY: Mirta Barrea-Marlys, "Argüelles, Hugo" in *Dictionary of Mexican Literature*, ed. Eladio Cortés (Westport, CT: Greenwood Press, 1992), 41–42. Alyce Golding Cooper, *Teatro mexicano contemporáneo (1940–1962)* (Mexico City: UNAM, 1962), 44–45. Ruth S. Lamb, *Bibliografía del teatro mexicano del siglo XX* (Mexico City: De Andrea, 1962), 28. Ruth S. Lamb and Antonio Magaña Esquivel, *Breve historia del teatro mexicano* (Mexico City: De Andrea, 1958). Victor Hugo Rascón Banda, "El dramaturgo y el maestro," *Proceso* 24 (enero 1994): 73–74. Rascón Banda, Rev. of *El cerco de la cabra dorada. Proceso* 6 (dic. 1993). Rafael Solana, Rev. of *El tejedor de milagros. Siempre!* 8 (April 1964): 52–54.

Mirta A. González

AURA, Alejandro (1944–). He was born in Mexico City and has won recognition as poet, playwright, actor, short story writer, and theater director. He has hosted the popular television talk show *Entre amigos* (Among Friends) since 1989. His play *Bang*, for instance, is a parody of westerns. Among the numerous awards and recognitions he has received are: Primer Premio Cultural de La Juventud (First Prize for Youth in Culture, 1969), First Prize in the Latin American Short Story (Puebla, 1972), and the National Poetry Award (1973). Along with his wife, Carmen Boullosa, he owns, manages, acts, and directs plays at a very popular theater bar in the colonial suburb of Coyoacán, Teatro Bar El Cuervo.

WORKS: *Las visitas* (The Visits, 1979). *Salón calavera* (Saloon of the Skull, 1982). *Bang* (Mexico City: Ed. Océano, 1986). *Aura y las once mil vírgenes* (Aura and the Eleven Thousand Virgins, staged at Teatro Bar El Cuervo, 1986; work coauthored with Carmen Boullosa). *El carro del esplendor* (The Cart of Splendor, staged at Estacionamientos Ciudad Universitaria, 1990). *Margarita: Sinfonía tropical* (Margarita: Tropical Symphony, staged at Sala Miguel Covarrubias, 1991).

BIBLIOGRAPHY: Ricardo Aguilar, "Aura, Alejandro," in *Dictionary of Mexican Literature*, ed. Eladio Cortés (Westport, CT: Greenwood Press, 1992), 55–56. Ron Burgess, *The New Dramatists of Mexico (1967–1985)* (Lexington: University Press of Kentucky, 1991), 128. Humberto Musacchio, *Gran diccionario enciclopédico de México: Visual* (Mexico City: O. Pedagógica, 1990), 128.

Mirta A. González

AZAR, Héctor (1930–). He was born in Atlixco, Puebla, and holds a law degree and a master's in literature from the Universidad Nacional Autónoma de Mexico (UNAM). He is a well-known playwright and director, though he is also known as a novelist and essayist. Among his many positions related to the theater in Mexico, he has been director of the Casa del Lago, chair of the Theater and Dance Department of the UNAM, and director of the National Institute of Fine Arts. In Mexico City he has founded theaters such as El Caballito, El Foro Isabelino, and La Compañía de Teatro Universitario. Azar has received numerous awards and prizes, among them: Premio Xavier Villaurrutia (1973) and an important prize at the French Theater Festival in Nancy for the staging of his play *Olímpica* in 1964.

WORKS: *La appasionata* (1958). *El corrido de Pablo Damián* (The Ballad of Pablo Damián, 1960).

Immaculada (Immaculate, 1963). *Olímpica* (Olympic, 1964). *Higiene de los placeres y los dolores* (Hygiene of Pleasures and Pains, 1967). *La cabeza de Apolo* (Apollo's Head, 1971). *La cantata de los emigrantes* (The Cantata of the Emigrants, 1972). *Los juegos de Azar* (Games of Chance, 1973). *La clase médium* (The Medium Class, 1985).

BIBLIOGRAPHY: Jacqueline Eyring Bixler, "Zoon Theatrykon: Azar y la búsqueda teatral," *Texto Crítico* 10 (1978): 42–58. Nora Eidelberg, *Dictionary of Mexican Literature*, ed. Eladio Cortés (Westport, CT: Greenwood Press, 1992), 58–59. Margó Glantz, "Teatro," *La Cultura en México* 21 (October 1964): 6. José López Martínez, "Entrevista con Héctor Azar," *La estafeta literaria* (Madrid) 565 (1975): 17–18. Humberto Musacchio, *Gran diccionario Enciclopédico visual de México* (Mexico City: O. Pedagógica, 1990), 140.

Mirta A. González

AZCÁRATE, Leonor (1955–). She is a dramatist, radio scriptwriter, and teacher. Azcárate studied linguistics and literature, then turned to writing plays and radio scripts and to teaching. She writes farces such as *La coincidencia* (The Coincidence), dramatic pieces such as *Tierra caliente* (Hot Land), fiercely violent works such as *Trabajo sucio* (Dirty Work), and socially conscious plays such as *Pasajero de medianoche* (Midnight Passenger), a primer on AIDS as well as a play. After some twenty years of playwriting, she finally began to have her works staged and published with some regularity in the early 1990s.

WORKS: *Circunloquio* (Circumlocution) (1970). *El sueño de los peces* (The Dream of the Fishes) (1976; 1st staging, 1977); in *Obras en un acto* (Mexico City: SEP-CREA, 1985), 47–74. *Un día de dos* (A Day of Two) (1982; 1st staging, 1985); in *Obras en un acto* (Mexico City: SEP-CREA, 1985), 7–46. *La pareja* (The Couple) (1982) (Puebla, Mexico: Universidad Autónoma de Puebla, 1986). *Regina 52* (1985). *Margarita resucitó* (Margarita Recovered) (1987). *Tierra caliente* (Hot Land) (1988); in *Repertorio* 4/5 (February–May 1988). *La coincidencia* (The Coincidence) (1990). *Trabajo sucio* (Dirty Work) (1992; 1st staging, 1994). *Pasajero de medianoche* (Midnight Passenger) (1993; 1st staging, 1993). Children's theater: *Fauna Rock* (1985; 1st staging, 1987); in *Obras en un acto* (Mexico City: SEP-CREA, 1985), 75–120. *Una nariz muy larga y un ojo saltón* (A Very Long Nose and a Bulging Eye) (1990). Radio scripts: *Hotel Montecarlo* (1990). *Rocio, la historia de una mujer de nuestro tiempo* (Rocio, the Story of a Woman of Our Time) (1991). *Cuatro mujeres* (Four Women) (1992).

Ronald D. Burgess

BASURTO, Luis G. (1921–1990). He was born and died in Mexico City. A lawyer by trade, he began writing drama criticism when he was nineteen. He went to Hollywood in 1942 to study cinematography. Although he wrote several film scripts, he gained recognition as a playwright and director. His work as an author, actor, and director made a significant contribution to Mexican theater. He received the Juan Ruiz de Alarcón Prize in 1956 for his play *Miércoles de ceniza* (Ash Wednesday). His social criticism and humor made him one of the most successful dramatists in the second half of the twentieth century.

WORKS: *Los diálogos de Suzette* (Suzette's Dialogues, staged at T. de Media Noche, 1940). *Faustina* (1942). *Voz como sangre* (Voice as Blood, 1942). *La que se fue* (The Girl That Left, 1946). *Frente a la muerte* (Facing Death, 1952) (Mexico City: Unión Nacional Actores, 1954). *Toda una dama* (A Total Lady, 1954). *Cada quien su vida* (Each Person with His Life, 1955). *Teatro mexicano del siglo xx* (Mexico City: FCE, 1956). *Miércoles de ceniza* (Ash Wednesday, 1956) (Mexico City: Costa Amic, 1957). *La locura de los ángeles* (The Insanity of Angels, 1957). *Los reyes del mundo* (The Kings of the World, 1959) (Mexico City: Col. Teatro Mexicano, 1959). *El escándalo de la verdad* (The Scandal of Truth, 1960). *Bodas de plata* (Silver Anniversary, 1960). *Cadena perpetua* (Life Sentence, 1965). *Con la frente en el polvo* (With Your Forehead in the Dust, 1967). *Intimas enemigas* (Intimate Enemies, 1962). *La gobernadora* (The Governess, 1963). *Y todos terminaron ladrando* (And Everybody Ended Up Barking, 1964). *Corona de sangre* (Blood Crown, n.d.). *El candidato de Dios* (God's Candidate, n.d.).

BIBLIOGRAPHY: Humberto Musacchio, *Gran diccionario enciclopédico de México: Visual* (Mexico City: O. Pedagógica, 1990), 178–179. Aurora Ocampo de Gómez and Ernesto Prado Velázquez, *Diccionario de escritores mexicanos* (Mexico City: UNAM, 1967), 38–39. Jeanne C. Wallace,

Dictionary of Mexican Literature, ed. Eladio Cortés (Westport, CT: Greenwood Press, 1992), 78–80.

Alfonso González

BERMAN, Sabina (1953–   ). Born in Mexico City, Berman has dedicated her life to the theater as an actress, playwright, and director. As a member of the Nueva Dramaturgia Mexicana movement, Berman has received numerous awards such as the coveted Premio Nacional from the Mexican Institute of Fine Arts. Although her award-winning literary production includes poetry and short stories, it is Berman's dramatic work that distinguishes her among her peers. From her first play, *Mariposa* (Butterfly) (1974), to the present, her dramatic works treat a variety of themes that, despite their seriousness, are presented with irony and humor. Among her most controversial and provocative subjects are Mexican women's struggles against the patriarchy of their society and its strong male historical figures such as Pancho Villa. Not limited to women's issues, Berman attacks the tyranny of the Church, treats world political events such as the death of Trotsky, and analyzes the causes of social ills. In her children's play *De la maravillosa historia del Chiquito Pingüica* (Little Pingüica's Fantastic Tale) (1982), she revisits Mayan mythology. Many of her plays, such as *Bill* (later entitled *Yankee*) and *Herejía* (Heresy), are performed frequently in her country and abroad.

WORKS: *Mariposa* (Butterfly, 1974). *Yoibaporlacallecuando* (AsIwaswalkingdownthestreetwhen, 1977). *El jardín de las delicias* (The Garden of Delights, 1978). *Esta no es una obra de teatro* (This Is Not a Play, 1982). *De la maravillosa historia del Chiquito Pingüica. De cómo supo de su gran destino y de cómo comprobó su grandeza* (Little Pingüica's Fantastic Tale. How He Learned of His Great Fate and How He Proved His Greatness, 1982). *Bill* (1982). *Anatema* (Anathema, 1983). *Herejía* (Heresy, 1984). *Un actor se repara* (An Actor Contains Himself, 1984). *Rompecabezas* (Jigsaw Puzzle, 1984). *Muerte súbita* (Sudden Death, 1988). *Entre Pancho Villa y una mujer desnuda* (Between Pancho Villa and a Nude, 1992), in *El teatro de Sabina Berman*, ed. Hugo Argüelles and Alejandro Hermida Ochoa (1985). *Los dientes* (The Teeth), in *Tramoya* 39 Nueva Epoca (1994): 123–133.

BIBLIOGRAPHY: Hugo Argüelles and Alejandro Hermida Ochoa, eds., *El teatro de Sabina Berman* (Mexico City: Ediciones Mexicanos Unidos, 1985). Ronald D. Burgess, "Sabina Berman's Act of Creative Failure: *Bill*," *Gestos* 2.3 (1987): 103–113. Eladio Cortés, "Berman, Sabina," in *Dictionary of Mexican Literature*, ed. Eladio Cortés (Westport, CT: Greenwood Press, 1992), 88–98. Sandra Messinger Cypess, "Dramaturgia femenina y transposición histórica," *Alba de América* 7.12–13 (1989): 283–304. Manuel Medina, "La batalla de los sexos: Estrategias de desplazamiento en *Entre Pancho Villa y una mujer desnuda* de Sabina Berman," *Fuentes* 4.8 (1994): 107–111.

Stella Clark

BOULLOSA, Carmen (1954–   ). She was born in Mexico City, studied Spanish and Spanish American literature at the Universidad Nacional Autónoma de México (UNAM) and at the Universidad Iberoamericana. She is a novelist, dramatist, and poet. Along with her husband, Alejandro Aura, she owns, manages, and acts in plays at a very popular theater bar in the colonial suburb of Coyoacán, Teatro Bar El Cuervo (The Crow's Son). Boullosa has earned several fellowships and awards, among them the INBA (Instituto Nacional de Bellas Artes) Prize (1979), the Centro Mexicano de Escritores Fellowship (1980), as well as the Salvador Novo Dramatic Prize (1977). She was awarded a Guggenheim Fellowship (1992–1993). She received the Xavier Villaurrutia Prize in 1989 for her literary work during that year and was named Distinguished Visiting Professor at San Diego State University (1990).

WORKS: *Vacío* (Emptiness, staged at T. Foro Sor Juana, 1979). *Trece señoritas* (Thirteen Young Women, staged at T. de La Capilla, 1983). *Cocinar hombres* (Cooking Men, staged at Teatro Bar El Cuervo, 1983). *X E bululú* (staged at T. Polyforum Cultural Siqueiros, 1983). *Aura y las once mil vírgenes* (Aura and the Eleven Thousand Virgins, staged at Teatro Bar El Cuervo, 1986; work co-authored with Alejandro Aura). *Propusieron a María* (They Nominated María) (Puebla: UA de Puebla, 1987). *Los totoles* (The Totoles, staged at T. Julio Prieto, 1985). *Mi versión de los hechos* (My Account of the Events, 1987). *Teatro herético* (Heretic Theater) (Mexico City: Arte y Cultura Ed., 1987). *Roja* *doméstica* (Domestic Red, staged at T. Foro Museo Tamayo, 1988).

BIBLIOGRAPHY: Ricardo Aguilar, *Dictionary of Mexican Literature*, ed. Eladio Cortés (Westport, CT: Greenwood Press, 1992), 100–101. Humberto Musacchio, *Gran diccionario enciclopédico de México: Visual* (Mexico City: O. Pedagógica, 1989), 219.

Mirta A. González

CALDERÓN, Fernando (1809–1845). He was born in Guadalajara, Jalisco, and died in Ojocaliente, Zacatecas. He was a liberal lawyer, playwright, poet, and jurist. Although some of his first plays, like *Muerte de Virginia por la libertad de Roma* (The Death of Virginia for Rome's Freedom), are neoclassic, he is considered to be one of the initiators of Romanticism and historical theater in his country. He staged his first play, *Reinaldo y Elvira*, in 1827 in Guadalajara. When he was exiled from his home state for having fought against Antonio López de Santanna in Zacatecas, he moved to Mexico City in 1837. While in the capital he became a member of the important literary circle La Academia de Letrás, where he met and worked alongside writers such as Ignacio Rodríguez Galván and Guillermo Prieto.

WORKS: *Hersilia y Virginia, Reinaldo y Elvira* (Hersilia and Virginia, Reinaldo and Elvira, 1827). *Ana Boleyn* (Anne Boleyn, 1854). *A ninguna de las tres* (None of the Three, 1854; Mexico, 1854). *El torneo* (The Tournament, 1865). *Muerte de Virginia por la libertad de Roma* (The Death of Virginia for Rome's Freedom, Zacatecas, 1882). *Obras completas* (Complete Works), 2 vols. (Zacatecas: n.p., 1882). *Dramas y poesías* (Plays and Poetry, Intr. Francisco Monterde) (Mexico City: Porrúa, 1959). *Zaido* (n.d.). *Leila o la esclava indiana* (Leila or The Indian Slave, n.d.). *Armandina, Los políticos al día* (Armandina, Today's Politicians, n.d.). *Efiginia* (Ephigenia, n.d.).

BIBLIOGRAPHY: Frank N. Dauster, *Historia del teatro hispanoamericano* (*Siglos XIX y XX*) (Mexico City: De Andrea, 1966), 12–13. Orlando Gómez Gil, *Historia crítica de la literatura hispanoamericana* (New York: Holt, 1968), 354–355. Aurora Ocampo de Gómez and Ernesto Prado Velázquez, *Diccionario de escritores mexicanos* (Mexico City: UNAM, 1967), 50–51. Enrique de Olavarría y Ferrari, *Reseña*

histórica del teatro en México (Mexico City: Porrúa, 1961), 438–440. Joseph Velez, *Dictionary of Mexican Literature*, ed. Eladio Cortés (Westport, CT: Greenwood Press, 1992), 106–107.

Mirta A. González

CAMPESINOS, Pilar (1945–). She studied psychology at the Universidad Iberoamericana and theater arts with Ignacio Retes. She is a poet, playwright, and screenwriter. Campesinos worked in different government agencies dealing with education and wrote theater for children. She received a Centro Mexicano de Escritores fellowship in 1969 and has participated in several national and international theater festivals. Her plays show the disaffection of youngsters throughout the world in the late 1960s, and some of her works suggest revolution as the answer to a stratified and deaf society.

WORKS: *Los objetos malos* (The Bad Objects, 1967) (Cuernavaca: Cihuacóatl Ed., 1980). *Verano Negro* (Black Summer), in *Teatro joven de México* (Mexico City: Ed. Mexicanos Unidos, 1979). *Superocho* (Supereight, 1979), in *Tramoya* 20 (1980): 71–104. *Más teatro joven de México* (Mexico City: Ed. Mexicanos Unidos, 1982). *Doce a las doce* (Twelve at Twelve) (Mexico City: Ed. Obra Citada, 1989). *La madeja* (The Affair, 1992). *Octubre terminó hace mucho tiempo* (October Ended a Long Time Ago, staged at T. Wilberto Cantón, 1992). *Chapadas a la antigua* (The Traditional Upbringing of Girls, 1994). *Tamalada de cenizas* (Ash Tamale Bash, 1994). *El tinglado* (The Temporary Stage, 1994). *La partida* (The Farewell), (n.d.).

BIBLIOGRAPHY: Ron Burgess, *The New Dramatists of Mexico (1967–1985)* (Lexington: University Press of Kentucky, 1991), 32–35, 141.

Alfonso González

CANTÓN, Wilberto (1923–1979). He was born in Mérida, Yucatán, and died in Mexico City. He studied law at the Universidad Nacional Autónoma de México (UNAM) and literature in Chile and in Paris. Cantón chaired the Departments of Theater Arts and Literature at the Instituto Nacional de Bellas Artes (INBA) and served as president of the Drama Critics' Guild (1955–1956). He was a playwright, poet, lawyer, essayist, and educator. Cantón is known for his incisive, deeply human social plays. It has been said that Cantón's theater along with that of Oscar Liera and Víctor Hugo Rascón Banda has contributed greatly to a new social awareness in the country. His play *Los malditos* (The Damned) was banned in Mexico City, staged in Guadalajara in 1958, and won the New York Critics' Award in 1972, and *República, Sociedad Anónima* (Republic, Anonymous Society) won the 1978 INBA Theater Prize. Other awards include: First prize in Sonora's Floral Festivities in 1942; the Juan Ruiz de Alarcón Prize for *Nosotros somos Dios* (We Are God) in 1962, and the Yucatán Medal in 1970.

WORKS: *Cuando zarpe el barco* (When the Ship Weighs Anchor, 1946). *Saber morir* (To Know How to Die, staged at T. Nacional, 1950). *Escuela de cortesanos* (School for Gracious People, 1953). *Nocturno a Rosario* (Nocturne to Rosario, 1953). *Pecado mortal* (Mortal Sin, 1953). *Nosotros somos Dios* (We Are God, 1958). *Los malditos* (The Damned, staged at T. Degollado, Guadalajara, 1958). *Tan cerca del cielo* (So Close to Heaven, 1959). *Inolvidable* (Unforgettable, 1961). *Todos somos hermanos* (We Are All Brothers, 1962). *Nota roja* (Red Note, 1963). *Murió por la patria* (He Died for the Fatherland, 1963). *Unas migajas de felicidad* (A Few Crumbs of Happiness, 1970). *Retrato dé mi padre* (Portrait of My Father) (México: Ed. Popular de los Trabajadores, 1978). *República, Sociedad Anónima* (Republic, Anonymous Society, 1978).

BIBLIOGRAPHY: Robert L. Bancroft, "The Problem of Marcela's Future in Cantón's *Inolvidable*," *Romance Notes* 14.2 (1972): 269–274. Shirley Carl L., "Reflections on the Career of Wilberto Cantón," *LATR* 13.1 (1980): 67–69. Carl L., A Curriculum Operum of Mexico's Wilberto Cantón, *LATR* 23.2 (Spring 1980): 43–53. Carl L., "The Metatheatrical World of Wilberto Cantón," *LATR* 23.2 (1990): 43–53. Rafael Solana, Review of *Nota roja*, *Siempre!* October 30, 1963: 50–52. S. Samuel Trifilo, "The Theater of Wilberto Cantón," *Hispania* 54.4 (1971): 869–875. Johm F. Tull, "El mundo teatral de Wilberto Cantón," *Duquesne Hispanic Review* 6.2 (1967): 1–7. Josepf Vélez, "Entrevista con Wilberto Cantón," *LATR* 13.1 (1979): 71–75. Jeanne C. Wallace, "Cantón, Wilberto," in *Dictionary of Mexican Literature*, ed. Eladio Cortés (Westport, CT: Greenwood Press, 1992), 118–122.

Alfonso González

CARBALLIDO, Emilio (1925–). Born in the state of Veracruz, Carballido is Mexico's most distinguished playwright. His family moved to Mexico City, where he has spent most of his life, after completing his studies in literature and theater at the Universidad Nacional Autónoma de México (UNAM). Since 1950, when he was awarded a Rockefeller Foundation fellowship, Carballido has spent many years in the United States as a visiting professor in American universities such as Rutgers and the University of Pittsburgh. He has also established himself as a theater teacher in Mexican institutions, among them the Universidad Veracruzana in Xalapa and the National Institute of Fine Arts in Mexico City.

Carballido is known as an ardent promoter of Mexican theater. Notable is his founding of the distinguished theater journal *Tramoya*, which, as a joint venture of the Universidad Veracruzana and Rutgers University, he has coedited with Eladio Cortés since 1985. He published his first play, *La zona intermedia* (The Middle Zone), in 1948, which was produced soon after his first performed play, *Rosalba y los Llaveros* (Rosalba and the Llaveros Family). Since then, his plays have appeared in numerous volumes, anthologies, and journals, and they have been translated into many languages and have been performed internationally for large audiences.

Carballido's themes tend to follow two extreme directions in relation to reality—the mundane and the magical. All his works, however, are strongly critical of social structures and contain broad humor and *costumbrismo*, as we see, for example, in *Rosalba y los Llaveros* a condemnation of the hypocrisy of Mexican provincialism, and *Rosa de dos aromas* (Rosa of Two Aromas), a contemporary look at Mexican feminism.

Carballido's versatile and prolific literary production, which includes theater, short stories, novels, and literary criticism, has been published in numerous anthologies and journals and has earned him an important place in the Mexican literary canon.

WORKS: *La zona intermedia* (The Middle Zone, 1948). *Auto de la triple porfía* (One Act Play on the Triple Argument, 1948; 1950). *El suplicante* (The Supplicant, 1950). *Rosalba y los Llaveros* (Rosalba and the Llaveros, 1950). *El viaje de Nocresida* (Nocresida's Journey, 1953). *La sinfonía doméstica* (The Domestic Symphony, 1953). *El pozo* (The Well, 1953). *La danza que sueña la tortuga* (The Dance That the Turtle Dreams, staged as *Las palabras cruzadas* [Crossed Words], 1955). *Felicidad* (Happiness, 1955). *La hebra de oro* (The Golden Thread, 1956). *El lugar y la hora* (Time and Place, 1956). *Selaginela* (1959). *Cinco pasos al cielo* (Five Steps to Heaven, 1959). *Las estatuas de marfil* (The Marble Statues, 1960). *El relojero de Córdoba* (The Clockmaker from Córdoba, 1960). *Un pequeño día de ira* (A Little Day of Wrath, 1962). *El día en que se soltaron los leones* (The Day the Lions Were Freed, 1963). *Silencio pollos pelones, ya les van a echar su maíz* (Your Feed Is Coming, You Mangy Chickens, 1963). *Yo también hablo de la rosa* (I, Too, Speak of the Rose, 1966). *Te juro Juana, que tengo ganas* (Honest, Juana, I Really Want It, 1967). *Las noticias del día* (Today's News, 1968). *Medusa* (1968). *Almanaque de Juárez* (A Juárez Almanac, 1969). *Acapulco, los lunes* (Acapulco on Mondays, 1969). *Un vals sin fin sobre el planeta* (An Endless Waltz on the Planet, 1970). *Las cartas de Mozart* (Mozart's Letters, 1975). *¿Quién anda ahí?* (Who Goes There?, 1982). *Orinoco* (1982). *A la epopeya, un gajo* (An Epic Segment, 1983). *Tiempo de ladrones: La historia de Chucho el Roto* (A Time for Thieves: The Story of Chucho the Ragged, 1983; 1985).

BIBLIOGRAPHY: Judith Bisset and Howard Blanning, "Visualizing Carballido's *Orinoco*: The Play in Two Imagined Performances," *Gestos* 5.9 (April 1990): 65–74. Jacqueline Eyring Bixler, "Carballido's *Acapulco, los lunes* and the Darker Side of Comedy," *Chasqui* 19.2 (November 1990): 3–11. Bixler, "The Family Portrait: Dramatic Contextuality in Emilio Carballido's *Un vals sin fin sobre el planeta* and *Fotografía en la playa*," *Chasqui* 14.1 (November 1984): 66–85. Bixler, Historical and Artistic Self Consciousness in Carballido's *José Guadalupe*," *Mester* 17.1 (Spring 1988): 15–27. Bixler, "Myth and Romance in Emilio Carballido's *Conversación entre las ruinas*," *Hispanic Journal* 6.1 (Fall 1984): 21–35. Bixler, "A Theater of Contradictions: The Recent Works of Emilio Carballido," *LATR* 18.2

(Spring 1985): 57–65. Becky Boling, "Espacio femenino en dos montajes de *Rosa de dos aromas* de Emilio Carballido," *Literatura Mexicana* 2.1 (1991): 165–171. Sandra Messinger Cypess, "Changing Configurations of Power from the Perspective of Mexican Drama," *Ideologies and Literature* 2.2 (Fall 1987): 109–123. Cypess, "I, Too, Speak: Female Discourse in Carballido's Plays," *LATR* 18.1 (Fall 1984): 45–52. Frank Dauster, "Carballido y el teatro de la liberación," *Alba de América* 7.12–13 (July 1989): 205–220. Dauster, "*Fotografía en la playa*: Rosalba Thirty Years Later," in *Retrospect: Essays on Latin American Literature*, ed. Elizabeth Rogers and Timothy J. Rogers (York, SC: Spanish Literature Pubs., 1987). Dauster, "*Tiempo de ladrones*, tiempo de libertad," *Crítica Hispánica* 8.1 (1986): 19–26. Nora Eidelberg, "El bosque como montaje y motivo en *El día en que se soltaron los leones*," *Texto Crítico* 14.39 (July–December 1988): 71–79. Adalberto García "Hacia una organización de las obras de Emilio Carballido: Una perspectiva cronológica" (Ph.D. diss., 1986). Delia Galván "Tres generaciones de mujeres en *Te juro Juana que tengo ganas*... de Emilio Carballido," *Discurso: Revista de Estudios Iberoamericanos* 7.2 (1990): 335–344. Malcom Scott MacKenzie, "Emilio Carballido: An Ideational Evolution of His Theatre" (Ph.D. diss., 1981). Priscilla Meléndez, "La interpretación como metáfora y la metáfora como interpretación: *Yo también hablo de la rosa* de Carballido," *Alba de América* 7.12–13 (July 1989): 305–317. Matías Montes Huidobro, "Zambullida en el Orinoco de Emilio Carballido," *LATR* 15.2 (Spring 1982): 13–25. Jorge Rufinelli, "Chucho el Roto, un hijo colectivo," *LATR* 18.2 (Spring 1985): 67–69. Candido Tafoya, "La presencia femenina como enfoque en obras selectas de Emilio Carballido," (Ph.D. diss., 1986). Diana Taylor, "Mad World, Mad Hope: Carballido's *El día en que se soltaron los leones*," *LATR* 20.2 (Spring 1987): 67–76. Helena Villacrés Stanton, "El sistema educacional como poder autoritario en *Te juro Juana que tengo ganas*...," in *National Symposium on Hispanic Theater*, April 22–24, 1982, ed. Adolfo M. Franco (Cedar Falls: University of Northern Iowa, 1985).

Stella Clark

CÁRDENAS, Nancy (1934–1994). She was born in Parras, Coahuila, and died in Mexico City. She studied theater under Luisa J. Hernández and in the United States and in Europe, and holds a doctorate from the Universidad Nacional Autónoma de México (UNAM). Cárdenas was a theater director and playwright. She was an activist who wrote on behalf of marginated individuals and directed the first play staged in Mexico dealing with homosexuality.

WORKS: *Ella se estuvo en el tapanco* (She Remained in the Attic, 1950). *Cántaro seco* (The Empty Jugs, 1960) (Mexico City: UNAM, 1960). *La vida privada del profesor Kabela* (The Private Life of Professor Kabela, broadcast by Radio Universidad, 1963). *Viaje a Cartago y pague después* (Travel to Cartago and Pay Later, staged at T. Polyforum Cultural Siqueiros, 1990). *Sexualidades* (Sexualities, staged at Casa del Lago, 1992). *El día que pisamos la luna* (The Day We Stepped on the Moon, n.d.).

BIBLIOGRAPHY: Peter G. Broad, "Cárdenas, Nancy," in *Dictionary of Mexican Literature*, ed. Eladio Cortés (Westport, CT: Greenwood Press, 1992), 140–441. Ruth S. Lamb, *Bibliografía del teatro mexicano del siglo XX* (Mexico City: Ed. Andrea, 1962), 39. Aurora M. Ocampo de Gómez and Ernesto Prado Velázquez, *Diccionario de escritores mexicanos* (Mexico City: UNAM, 1967), 62.

Mirta A. González

CHABAUD, Jaime (1966–   ). He was born in Mexico City and studied literature and theater arts at the Universidad Nacional Autónoma de México (UNAM). He is a playwright and journalist. At present he heads the Universidad Autónoma Metropolitana's (UAM) Casa de la Paz theater in Mexico City. *Tempranito y en ayunas* (Early and with an Empty Stomach) won the Agrupación de Periodistas Teatrales award in 1989, and *El ajedrecista* (The Chess Player) won the Asociación Mexicana de Críticos de Teatro award for the best Teatro de Búsqueda in 1993.

WORKS: *El cordoncillo* (The Small Cord, n.d.). *Tempranito y en ayunas* (Early and with an Empty Stomach, staged at T. Santo Domingo, 1989); *Revista Repertorio* (UA of Querétaro, January–March 1989), n. p. *Un grillo entre las piernas* (A Cricket between the Legs, staged at T. Santo Domingo, 1989). *Noche de brujas* (Witches' Eve, staged at T. Aud. Pedro Henríquez Ureña, 1991); *Revista de la UNAM* 88 (January–February 1990), n. p. *Baje la voz* (Lower Your Voice, staged at Sótano T. Carlos Lazo, 1991). *¡Qué viva Cristo Rey!* (Long Live Christ the King!, staged at T. Foro Cultural San Angel, 1992); *Revista Repertorio*, (UA of Querétaro, 1995). *El*

ajedrecista (The Chess Player, staged at T. Wilberto Cantón, 1993). *En la boca del fuego* (At the Center of Fire, staged at T. Cárceles de la Perpetua, 1993). *Perder la cabeza* (To Lose Your Head, staged at T. El Galeón, 1995).

BIBLIOGRAPHY: Victor H. Rascón Banda, Review of *El ajedrecista. Proceso* 20 (September 1993): 56–57. J. H. Interview, *El Nacional* Sec. Espectáculos 13 (March 1990): 21. Review of *Tempranito y en ayunas*, *Siempre!* 21 (February 1990): 65–66.

Alfonso González

CRUZ, Sor Juana Inés de la (1648–1695). She was born in Amecameca, State of Mexico, and died in Mexico City. Sor Juana was a poetess, playwright, feminist, and Hieronymite nun. Her biography and achievements transcend her times. Since childhood she was independent and bright. At age three she could read and learned Latin in twenty lessons when she was an adolescent. A voracious reader, she was taken into the entourage of the vicereine, the Marquise of Mancera, at sixteen. Her ability to write poetry, her talent, and intellectual curiosity won the friendship and protection of the vicereine and her husband, as well as their successors, the Marquise of La Laguna and Don Tomás Antonio de la Cerda, her husband. Often she was asked to write poems to commemorate some important event, such as the arrival of a new dignitary or the birthday of a noble. In 1667, she traded the glamour of the court for the austerity of life in a convent. Her thirst for knowledge was more important to her than being a wife, and in seventeenth-century Mexico, the only route open to a woman seeking an advanced education was the convent. It provided the security and independence that she needed in order to pursue her studies on her own. Here, she continued to write and accumulated a library of more than 4,000 volumes.

Sor Juana was an early feminist and rationalist whose achievements can only be explained by her unusual talent and the protection she received from the viceregal court. After the publication in Spain of two volumes of her work in 1889 and 1990, the Archbishop, Francisco de Aguiar y Seijas, together with Sor Juana's confessor, Father Antonio Nuñez de Miranda, apparently jealous of the nun's success, set out to silence her. Nuñez de Miranda convinced the viceroy not to interfere, unless he wanted to lose his soul. Sor Juana lost her independence and was forced to stop writing and to dispose of her beloved library. Soon after this, while aiding the victims of a smallpox epidemic, she contracted the disease and died.

Sor Juana Inés de la Cruz's literary production includes poems, letters, and dramatic compositions such as plays, *entremeses* (one-act farces), *loas* (short dramatic panegyrics), and *autos* (allegorical religious plays). Her philosophical, love, and satirical poems are among the best written during the Spanish domination of the Americas, whereas her plays, which often involved music and singing, are considered precursors of Mexican operettas. Sor Juana's prose is erudite, and her plays are religious and secular. She is the most important literary figure of the colonial period in Spanish America.

Among her plays, the *auto El divino Narciso* (Narcissus the Divine) and the comedy *Los empeños de una casa* (The Travails of a Household) stand out. In the first, she establishes the universality of God. She sets out to prove that the God of the Spaniards is the same as The Lord of Seeds of the Aztecs, the expected God of the Jews, and the Greek divinity of perfect beauty, Narcissus. Some of the scenes between Narcissus and the nymph, Human Nature, are reminiscent of Spanish mystic poetry. *Los empeños de una casa*, based on a play by the Spanish dramatist Pedro Calderón de la Barca, exposes the animosity between *criollos*, children of Spaniards born in the New World, and Spaniards.

Sor Juana Inés de la Cruz is also known for her poetry. *Primero sueño* (First Dream) is a hermetic, erudite poem reminiscent of Góngora's *Soledades* (Solitudes). In it she explores the possibilities of complete freedom for the intellect. "Hombres necios" (Stubborn Men) satirizes men's double standard toward women through the use of puns, antithesis, and clever play on words and concepts. Her love poems are either sincere expressions of her emotions ("Esta tarde, mi bien, cuando te hablaba"; "This

afternoon, my love, when I spoke to you") or rationalizations of the courting of young men and women ("Feliciano me adora y le aborrezco"; "Feliciano adores me and I despise him").

Most of what we know about Sor Juana's life can be found in her *Respuesta a Sor Filotea de la Cruz* (An Answer to Sor Filotea de la Cruz), a letter to her Bishop in which she defends her lifelong thirst for knowledge and a woman's right to learn. She backs up her arguments with quotations from the Holy Scriptures and by paraphrasing history books. Through a series of rhetorical questions and possible solutions to the limitations imposed on her because of her sex, Sor Juana indicts a society that had no place for an intelligent woman wishing an education except the convent.

WORKS: *Inundación Castálida de la única poetisa, musa décima, Sor Juana Inés de la Cruz* (Castilian Flood of the Only Poetess . . .) (Madrid, 1689). *El divino Narciso* (Narcissus the Divine) (Mexico, 1690). *Obras de Sor Juana Inés de la Cruz* (Sevilla, 1692). *Fama y obras póstumas del fénix de México* . . . (Fame and Posthumous Works of the Mexican Phoenix . . .) (Madrid, 1700). *Poesías completas* (Complete Poetry), ed. Ermilo Abreu Gómez (Mexico City: Ed. Botas, 1934). *Obras completas* (Complete Works) (Mexico City: Ed. Porrúa, 1981).

BIBLIOGRAPHY: Ermilo Abreu Gómez, *Sor Juana Inés de la Cruz. Bibliografía y biblioteca* (Mexico City, n.p., 1934). José Juan Arróm, *El teatro de Hispanoamérica en la época colonial* (Havana: Anuario Bibliográfico Cubano, 1956), 121–137. Mari Cecile Benassy-Berling, *Humanismo y religión en Sor Juana Inés de la Cruz* (Mexico City: UNAM, 1983). James A. Castañeda, "*Los empeños de un acaso* y *Los empeños de una casa*: Calderón y Sor Juana, la diferencia de un fonema," *Revista de estudios hispánicos* 1 (1967): 107–116. Rafael Catal, "La trascendencia en *Primero sueño*; El incesto y el guila," *Revista Iberoamericana* 104–105: 421–434. Enrique Cervantes, *Testamento de Sor Juana Inés de la Cruz y otros documentos autógrafos* (Mexico City, n.p., 1949). Juan José Eguiara y Eguren, *Sor Juana Inés de la Cruz*, Biblioteca Mexicana, ed. Ermilo Abreu Gómez (Mexico City, n.p., 1956). Ilse Heckel, "Los *sainetes* de Sor Juana Inés de la Cruz," *Revista Iberoamericana* 13, 25 (147): 135–140. Pedro Henríquez Ureña, "Bibliografía de Sor Juana Inés de la Cruz," *Revue Hispanique* 40 (1917): 161–

214. Juana B. Iguiñez, "Catálogo de las obras de y sobre Sor Juana Inés de la Cruz existentes en la Biblioteca Nacional," *Boletín de la Biblioteca Nacional* 2.4 (1951). Francisco López Cámara, "El cartesianismo en Sor Juana y Sigüenza y Góngora," *Filosofía y Letras* 20.39 (1950): 107–131. López Cámara, "El criollismo en Sor Juana y Sigüenza," *Historia Mexicana* 23 (1957): 350–373. Tomás Navarro Tomás, "Los versos de Sor Juana," *Romance Philology* 7 (1953): 44–50. Octavio Paz, *Sor Juana Inés de la Cruz o las trampas de la fe* (Barcelona: Seix Barral, 1982), trans. as *Sor Juana* by Margaret Sayers Peden (Cambridge: Harvard University Press, 1988). Ludwig Pfandl, *Die Zehnte Muse von Mexico* (Munich, n.p., 1946). Robert Ricard, "Antonio Viera et Sor Juana Inés de la Cruz," *Bulletin des Etudes Portugaises et de l'Institut Francais au Portugal* 12 (1948): 1–34. Ricard, "Manuel Bernardes, Sor Juana Inés de la Cruz et le Pere Kircher," *Revista da Facultade de Letras de Lisboa* 13 (1971): 5–9. Elías L. Rivers, "El ambiguo sueño de Sor Juana," *Cuadernos Hispanoamericanos* 189 (1965): 271–285. Georgina Sabat de Rivers, "Nota bibliográfica sobre Sor Juana Inés de la Cruz: Son tres las ediciones de Barcelona, 1693," *Nueva Revista de Filología Hispánica* 23 (1974): 391–401. Sabat de Rivers, *El sueño de Sor Juana: Tradiciones literarias y originalidad* (London: Tamesis Books, 1977). Sabat de Rivers, "El Neptuno de Sor Juana," *University of Dayton Review* (Spring 1983). Sabat de Rivers, *Sor Juana Inés de la Cruz y otros poetas barrocos de la colonia* (Barcelona: PPU, 1992). Rubén Salazar Mallén, *Apuntes para una biografía de Sor Juana Inés de la Cruz* (Mexico City: UNAM, 1981). Doroty Schons, *Bibliografía de Sor Juana Inés de la Cruz* (Mexico City, n.p., 1927). Kessel Schwartz, "*Primero sueño*: A Reinterpretation," *Kentucky Romance Quarterly* 22 (1975): 473–476.

Alfonso González

DÁVALOS, Marcelino (1871–1923). Dávalos was born in Guadalajara, Jalisco, and died in Mexico City. He earned a law degree from the University of Guadalajara in 1900. He was a State Congressman in 1913 and later fought in the Revolution under Carranza. He held several political appointments, including Minister of Foreign Affairs. Although he was a journalist, a short story writer, and a poet, he gained recognition as a dramatist. In *Guadalupe* he analyzes the devastating influence of alcoholism in a family.

WORKS: *El último cuadro* (The Last Painting, 1900). *Guadalupe* (Guadalupe, 1903). *Así pasan . . .* (That's the Way . . . , 1908). *La sirena roja* (The Red Siren, 1908). *Jardines tragicos* (Tragic Gardens, 1909). *Indisoluble* (Undissolvables, 1910). *Aguilas y estrellas* (Eagles and Stars, 1916). *¡Viva el amo!* (Hurray for the Master!, n.d.).

BIBLIOGRAPHY: Baudelio Garza, "Dávalos, Marcelino," in *Dictionary of Mexican Literature*, ed. Eladio Cortés (Westport, CT: Greenwood Press, 1992), 191–192. Humberto Musacchio, *Gran diccionario enciclopédico de México: Visual* (Mexico City: O. Pedagógica, 1990), 491. Aurora M. Ocampo de Gómez and Ernesto Prado Velázquez, *Diccionario de escritores mexicanos* (Mexico City: UNAM, 1967), 93–94.

Alfonso González

DEL RÍO, Marcela (1932–). She was born in Mexico City and studied literature and dramatic arts at the Universidad Nacional Autónoma de México (UNAM). She is a playwright, critic, teacher, and journalist. She received the Ruiz de Alarcón's Prize in 1970.

WORKS: *Fraude a la tierra* (Fraud to Earth, 1957). *Miralina* (1964). *El hijo de trapo* (The Rag Son, 1964). *Claudia y Arnot* (Claudia and Arnot, 1964). *La tercera cara de la luna* (The Moon's Third Face, 1965). *Trece cielos* (Thirteen Heavens, 1970). *El pulpo* (The Octopus 1970). *El teatro de la Revolución Mexicana* (The Theater of the Mexican Revolution) (New York: Peter Lang, 1994).

BIBLIOGRAPHY: Juana A. Arancibia, "Entrevista con Marcela del Río," *Alba de América* 9.16–17 (1991): 395–401. Celia Correas Zapata, "La violencia en *Miralina* . . . ," *Plural* 212 (1989): 46–52. Polly J. Hodge, "Una mirada . . . en *Miralina* de Marcela del Río," *Alba de América* (Westminster, CA) 13, 24–25, 83–93. Humberto Musacchio, *Gran diccionario enciclopédico de México: Visual* (Mexico City: O. Pedagógica, 1990), 1728. Yolanda Rosas, "Búsqueda de identidad . . ." *Discurso femenino actual* (San Juan: University of Puerto Rico Press, 1995), 307–321. Yvone Shafer, "Interview with Marcela del Río," *Journal of Dramatic Theory and Criticism* 8.2 (1994): 157–162. Carlos Solórzano, Review of *Miralina*, *La Cultura en México* 10 (November 1965): 19. Solórzano, Review of *El pulpo*, *La Cultura en México* 19 (August 1970): 14.

Alfonso González

DÍAZ DUFOO, Carlos (1861–1941). He was born in Veracruz, Veracruz, and died in Mexico

City. He lived in Madrid since he was a child and began writing there. He was a playwright, a diplomat, and a journalist. When he returned to his native country, he and Manuel Gutiérrez Nájera founded the *Revista Azul*, a prestigious *modernista* journal, in 1894.

WORKS: *De gracia* (staged at Teatro Nacional, 1885), (Mexico City: Tip. Gonzalo Esteva, 1885). *Entre vecinos* (Among Friends, staged at Teatro Ideal, 1929). *Padre Mercader* (Father Mercader, staged at Teatro Ideal, 1929) (Mexico City: Imp. Manuel León Sandres, n.d.) *La fuente del Quijote* (The Source of the Quijote, staged at Teatro Ideal, 1930). *La jefa* (The Lady Boss, 1932). *Sombras de mariposas* (Butterfly Shadows, 1937). *Palabras* (Words, n.d.).

BIBLIOGRAPHY: Aurora M. Ocampo de Gómez and Ernesto Prado Velázquez, *Diccionario de escritores mexicanos* (Mexico City: UNAM, 1967), 98–99. Humberto Musacchio, *Gran diccionario enciclopédico de México: Visual* (Mexico City: O. Pedagógica, 1990), 503. Jeanne C. Wallace, "Díaz Dufoo, Carlos," in *Dictionary of Mexican Literature*, ed. Eladio Cortés (Westport, CT: Greenwood Press, 1992), 197–199.

Alfonso González

ENRÍQUEZ, José Ramón (1945–). He was born in Mexico City and studied theater arts and literature at the Universidad Nacional Autónoma de México (UNAM), at the Instituto Nacional de Bellas Artes (INBA), and at the Real Escuela Superior de Arte Dramático in Madrid. He is a poet, theater director, dramatist, essayist, and literary critic. He has served as editor for Editorial Grijalbo, as an editorial adviser to the Fondo de Cultura Económica, and as director of publications for the University of Puebla and Ediciones Océano. Enríquez directed the prestigious Centro de Investigaciones Teatrales Rodolfo Usigli of the INBA (CITRU, or Center for Theater Research Rodolfo Usigli, 1993–1995). His play *Mother Juana* won the Premio Wilberto Cantón INBA 1987. He frequently publishes literary criticism in some of the better-known journals in Mexico City.

WORKS: *Héctor y Aquiles* (Hector and Aquiles, staged at Casa del Lago, 1980) (Mexico City: Ed. Latitudes, 1979). *Ciudad sin sueño* (Sleepless City, staged at Foro Sor Juana Inés de la Cruz, 1982)

(Puebla: U Autónoma de Puebla, 1985). *El fuego: Tres piezas* (Fire: Three Works, 1985) (Puebla: U Autónoma de Puebla, 1985). *Madre Juana* (Mother Juana, staged at Mérida, Teatro José Peón y Contreras) (Mérida: Consejo Ed. de Yucatán, 1986). *Pasarela* (Catwalk, staged at Teatro Foro Shakespeare, 1989). *Tres ceremonias: Jubileo, Alicia and Pasarela* (Three Ceremonies: Jubilee, Alice, and Catwalk) (Mexico City: UNAM, 1991). *Jubileo* (Jubilee, staged at Teatro Juan Ruiz de Alarcón, 1992). *Orestes parte* (Orestes Leaves, staged at Museo U. El Chopo, 1992). *Alicia* (Alice, staged at Teatro Bellas Artes, 1995). *La cueva de Montesinos* (The Cave of Montesinos, staged at Centro Universitario de Teatro, 1995). *La manta que las cobija* (The Blanket That Protects Them, staged at Teatro Clandestino Casa del Teatro, 1995).

BIBLIOGRAPHY: Humberto Musacchio, *Gran diccionario enciclopédico de México: Visual* (Mexico City: O. Pedagógica, 1990), 565–566.

Alfonso González

ESPINOSA, Tomás (1947–1992). A dramatist, theater critic and commentator, editor, and teacher, Espinosa was born in Mexico City and soon moved into the circle of theater and drama as a commentator and critic. He came to be one of the most knowledgeable sources of information on what would become the Nueva Dramaturgia in Mexico. He joined that group as a playwright in 1979 with a series of short plays published under the title *Ejemplos* (Examples). It was with *Santísima la nauyaca* (Blessed Be the Nauyaca), though, that he established his own particular brand of theater. His plays are excursions into fantasy grounded in reality and driven by almost unending strings of words— words that play on previous words, words that float and flow among and into each other, weaving humor, reality, and irreality into mythic worlds where the real world transforms into all manner of shape and form. In 1987, in conjunction with his job at the Instituto Mexicano del Seguro Social, he joined with Margarita Mendoza López and Daniel Salazar in beginning to compile a five-volume catalog of twentieth-century Mexican theater. He managed to complete it and a small number of additional plays before his death in late 1992.

WORKS: *El teléfono* (The Telephone, 1979); in *Tramoya* 16 (1979). *Hacer la calle* (Doing the Street,

1979); in *Tramoya* 16 (1979); in *Más teatro joven*, edited by Emilio Carballido (Mexico City: Editores Mexicanos Unidos, 1982), 173–185. *Angélica y Araceli* (Angelica and Araceli, 1979); in *Tramoya* 16 (1979). *Ejemplo* (Example, 1979); in *Tramoya* 16 (1979). *La rata* (The Rat, 1979); in *Tramoya* 16 (1979). *La televisión enterrada* (The Buried Television, 1980); in *Tramoya* 18 (1980). *Santísima la nauyaca* (Blessed Be the Nauyaca) (1980); in *Tramoya* 20 (1980), in *Antologia de teatro de Tomás Espinosa* (Mexico City: IMSS, 1993), 11–42. *Los ríos ocultos* (The Hidden Rivers, 1982); in *Danza y Teatro* 7.36 (1982–1983). *La noche de las nictálopes* (The Night of the Nocturnals, 1982); in *Antologia de teatro de Tomás Espinosa* (Mexico City, IMSS, 1993), 43–86. *María o la sumisión* (María or Submission) (1st staging, 1984); in *María o la sumisión* (Mexico City: Obra Citada, 1989), 9–43. *Pasacalles con perros* (Stroller with Dogs, 1989); in *María o la sumisión* (Mexico City: Obra Citada, 1989), 45–77. *¡Miren el sol, es gratis!* (Look at the Sun, It's Free!); in *María o la sumisión* (Mexico City: Obra Citada, 1989), 79–90. *Cacos* (Crooks) (1988); in *Doce a las doce* (Mexico City: Obra Citada, 1989), 107–122. *¡Bety, bájate de mi nube!* (Betty, Get Off of My Cloud!); in *Tramoya* 31 (1985); in *Antología de teatro de Tomás Espinosa* (Mexico City: IMSS, 1993), 87–121. *Las tribulaciones de un lagartijo* (The Tribulations of a Lizard); in *Detrás de una margarita* (Mexico City: IMSS, 1983). *Cocuyo de Lima* (Lima Beetle) (1989); in *Antologia de teatro de Tomás Espinosa* (Mexico City: IMSS, 1993), 123–153.

BIBLIOGRAPHY: Ronald D. Burgess, *The New Dramatists of Mexico, (1967–1985)* (Lexington: University Press of Kentucky, 1991). Emilio Carballido, "Introducción: Tomás," *Antologia de teatro de Tomás Espinosa* (Mexico City: IMSS, 1993), 5–7. Matias Montes Huidobro, "Bestiario y metamorfosis en *Santísima la nauyaca* de Tomás Espinosa," *Latin American Theatre Review* 16.1 (1982), 41–51.

Alfonso González

FERNÁNDEZ DE LIZARDI, José J. (1776–1827). He was born and died in Mexico City and was a novelist, journalist, and playwright. He studied law and theology and founded the newspaper *El Pensador Mexicano*, a name by which he was later known. Imbued with the liberal spirit of the thinkers of the French and American Revolutions, he criticized the society in which he lived, and for this he was imprisioned in 1813, and his newspaper shut down.

While in prison he began writing what was to be Spanish America's first novel, *El periquillo sarniento* (The Mangy Parrot). The political, social, and moral implications of his plays provide the reader with a vivid picture of society in the waning years of the Spanish colony. He is the most important literary figure in the first three decades of the nineteenth century.

WORKS: *El unipersonal del arcabuceado* (The Unipersonal of the Man Who Was Shot, 1822). *El unipersonal de Don Agustín de Iturbide* (The Unipersonal of Don Agustín de Iturbide, 1823). *El negro sensible* (The Sensible Black Man, 1825). *La tragedia del Padre Arenas* (The Tragedy of Father Arenas, 1827). *Auto mariano* (Marian "Auto," n.d.). *Todos contra el payo y el payo contra todos* (Everyone against the Simpleton and the Simpleton against Everyone, n.d.). *El fuego de Prometeo* (The Fire of Prometheus, n.d.). *La noche más venturosa* (The Most Fortunate Evening, n.d.).

BIBLIOGRAPHY: Jean Franco, "Women, Fashion and the Moralists in Early Nineteenth-Century Mexico," in *Homenaje a Ana María Barrenechea*, eds. (Madrid: Castalia, 1984), 421–430. Franco, "La heterogeneidad peligrosa: Escritura y control social en vísperas de la independencia mexicana," "Fernández de Lizardi, José J.," in *Hispamérica* 12.34–35 (1983): 3–34. Esther Hernández Palacios, *Dictionary of Mexican Literature*, ed. Eladio Cortés (Westport, CT: Greenwood Press, 1992), 223–226. María Herrera-Sobek, "The Defiant Voice: Gender Conflict in a Mexican-Chicano Pastorela," *Gestos* 6.11 (1991): 63–77. Luis Leal, "Picaresca hispanoamericana: De Oquendo a Lizardi," in *Estudios de literatura hispanoamericana en honor a José J. Arróm* (Chapel Hill: University of North Carolina, n.d.), 47–58. James C. McKegney, "Some Recently Discovered Pamphlets by Fernández de Lizardi," *Hispania* 54 (1971): 256–287. McKegney, "El payo del Rosario y la riña de Lizardi con José María Aza," in *Actas del XVII Congreso el IILI: El barroco en América* (Madrid: U Complutense, n.d.). Humberto Musacchio, *Gran diccionario enciclopédico de México: Visual* (Mexico City: O. Pedagógica, 1990). Aurora M. Ocampo de Gómez and Ernesto Prado Velázquez, *Diccionario de escritores mexicanos* (México City: UNAM, 1967), 93–94.

Alfonso González

GAMBOA, Federico (1864–1939). He was born and died in Mexico City. He was a novelist, playwright, journalist, diplomat, and theater critic. Although he is better known for some of his novels like *Santa*, a romantic-naturalistic work focusing on the life of a prostitute and inspired by Zola's *Nana*, his plays such as *La venganza de la gleba* (The Vengeance of the Land) have become classics on the Mexican stage.

WORKS: *La última campaña* (The Last Campaign, 1894). *Divertirse* (To Have Fun, 1894). *La venganza de la gleba* (Vengeance of the Land, staged in Washington, D.C., 1904). *A buena cuenta* (To Good Account, staged in San Salvador, 1907). *Entre hermanos* (Among Brothers, 1928).

BIBLIOGRAPHY: Ledda Arguedas, "Ciudad de México: Entre el mito y la política," in *La selva en el damero: Espacio literario y espacio urbano en América Latina* (Pisa: Giardini, 1989). Humberto Musacchio, *Gran diccionario enciclopédico de México: Visual* (Mexico City: O. Pedagógica, 1990), 684–685. Aurora M. Ocampo de Gómez and Ernesto Prado Velázquez, *Diccionario de escritores mexicanos* (Mexico City: UNAM, 1967), 124–125. Oscar Somoza, "Gamboa, Federico," in *Dictionary of Mexican Literature*, ed. Eladio Cortés (Westport, CT: Greenwood Press, 1992), 247–248.

GAMBOA, José Joaquín (1878–1931).

He was born and died in Mexico City. He was a playwright, journalist, diplomat, and teacher. He translated some of the works of D'Annunzio, Robert de Fleurs, Alfred Capu, and Henri Bernstein. Gamboa is considered to be one of the first to change from a realist theater into a more avant-garde one. His play *El caballero, la muerte y el diablo* (The Knight, Death and the Devil) has appeared in two English translations (William L. Mayhew, Honolulu: University of Hawaii Press 1969; Theodore Apstain, Austin: University of Texas Press, n.d.).

WORKS: *La carne o Teresa* (The Flesh or Teresa, 1903). *La muerte* (Death, 1904). *El hogar* (The Hearth, 1905). *Un día vendrá* (A Day Will Come, 1908). *El diablo tiene frío* (The Devil Is Cold, 1923). *Los Revillagigedo* (The Revillagigedo Family, 1925). *Vía Crucis* (1925). *La botella de champagne* (The Bottle of Champagne, n.d.). *Cuento viejo* (Old Tale, 1925). *Espíritus* (Spirits, 1927). *Si la juventud supiera* (If Youth Knew, 1927). *El mismo caso* (The

Same Case, 1929). *Ella o Alucinaciones* (She or Hallucinations, 1930). *El caballero, la muerte y el diablo* (The Knight, Death and the Devil, 1931). *Teatro*, 3 vols. (Mexico City: Ed. Botas, 1938).

BIBLIOGRAPHY: Herlinda Hernández, "Gamboa, José Joaquín," in *Dictionary of Mexican Literature*, ed. Eladio Cortés (Westport, CT: Greenwood Press, 1992), 248–249. Humberto Musacchio, *Gran diccionario enciclopédico de México: Visual* (Mexico City: O. Pedagógica, 1990), 685. Aurora M. Ocampo de Gómez and Ernesto Prado Velázquez, *Diccionario de escritores mexicanos* (Mexico City: UNAM, 1967), 125–126.

Alfonso González

GARCÍA PONCE, Juan (1932–   ).

Born in Yucatán, he had his academic formation at the Universidad Nacional Autónoma de México. He is well known as a literary critic and has had a distinguished career as a novelist and short story writer, having been the recipient of the Premio de la Ciudad de México and of the Cross of Honor from the Austrian government. His novels and short stories, which focus on the complexity of human relationships, have placed him among the most distinguished Mexican writers. His dramatic work remains largely unpublished.

WORKS: *El canto de los grillos* (The Crickets' Song, 1958). *Sombras* (Shadows, 1959). *Doce y una trece* (Twelve Plus One Equals Thirteen, 1964). *La feria distante* (The Far Away Fair, 1965). *Catálogo razonado* (Logical Catalogue, 1982). *Alrededor de las anémonas* (Around the Anemones, unpublished). *El día más feliz* (The Happiest Day, unpublished). *La noche transfigurada* (The Transformed Night, unpublished). *El otoño y las hojas* (Autumn and the Leaves, unpublished).

BIBLIOGRAPHY: Steven M. Bell, interview with Juan García Ponce, *Hispamérica* (April 1986):45–55. Juan Bruce-Novoa, "Drama to Fiction and Back," *Latin American Theatre Review* 16.2 (Spring 1983): 5–13. Patricia Dolores Dorame-Grajales, "Escritura y erotismo en la literatura mexicana contemporánea" (Ph.D. diss., 1990). David Johnson, "Voice, History and the Inscription of the Americas" (Ph.D. diss., State University of New York, Buffalo, 1991). José E. Pacheco, Review of *El canto de los grillos, Letras Nuevas* (July–August 1958): 45–47.

Stella Clark

GARRO, Elena (1920–   ). Born in Puebla to a Mexican mother and a Spanish father, Garro spent much of her childhood in the State of Guerrero. She studied at the National Autonomous University of Mexico, where she was an active member of Julio Bracho's theater group. After marrying Octavio Paz in 1937, she embarked upon her literary career. Losing her aspirations as an actress, she turned her love of the theater to writing plays. Garro's politics, her ambiguous residence and citizenship status, and her involvement in Indian rights have caused her a great deal of trouble in Mexico. Consequently, most of her works have been produced abroad, and many of them appeared in print long after they were written.

Divorced from Paz in 1959, Garro has subsequently spent most of her life in Europe, between Madrid and Paris, where she has been living in seclusion. In 1994, she moved to Cuernavaca, Mexico. In her fiction as well as in her theatrical production, Garro has combined a strong commitment to political and social causes with the fantastic and magical elements of Mexican life.

WORKS: *Un hogar sólido y otras piezas en un acto* (A Solid House and Other One-Act Plays 1958; 1983). *Los perros* (The Dogs), in *Doce obras en un acto*, ed. Wilberto Cantón (1967); translated by Beth Miller in *Latin American Literary Review* 8.15 (1979): 68–85. *La señora en su balcón* (The Lady on Her Balcón), in *Teatro breve hispanoamericano contemporáneo*, ed. Carlos Solórzano (1969), translated by Beth Miller in *Shantih* 3.3 (Fall–Winter 1976): 36–44; also in *A Different Reality*, ed. Anita Stoll (Lewisburg, PA: Bucknell University Press, 1990). *Un hogar sólido*, translated by Francesca Colecchia and Julio Matas in *Selected Latin American One-Act Plays* (1973). *Felipe Angeles* (1979).

BIBLIOGRAPHY: María Elvira Bermúdez, "Dramaturgas," *Diorama de la Cultura* (April 1959):4. Francisco Beverido Duhalt, "*Los perros* de Elena Garro: La ceremonia estéril," *Texto Crítico* 12.34–35 (1986): 118–135. Becky Boling, "Tracking the Feminine Subject in Elena Garro's *El rastro*," in *Latin American and Francophone Women Writers*, vol. 2, ed. Ginette Adamson and Eunice Meyers (Lanham, MD: University Press of America, 1987). Richard Callan, "El misterio femenino en *Los perros* de Elena Garro," *Revista Iberoamericana* 46.100–

101 (1980): 231–235. Callan, "Analytical Psychology and Garro's *Los pilares de doña Blanca*," *Latin American Theatre Review* 16.2 (1983): 31–35. Wilberto Cantón, "El teatro de Elena Garro: La poesía contra el absurdo," *La Cultura en México* 191 (October 1965): xv. Chelley Chitwood, "Woman's Struggle against Tradition in Elena Garro's *La señora en su balcón*," *Romance Languages Annual* 2 (1990): 378–381. Alyce Cooper Golding, *Teatro mexicano contemporáneo, 1940–1962* (Mexico City: UNAM, 1962), 30. Eladio Cortés, "*Felipe Angeles*, Theater of Heroes," *A Different Reality*, 80–89. Cortés, "*Memorias de España*, obra inédita de Elena Garro," in Eladio Cortés, *De literatura hispánica* (Mexico City EDIMUSA, 1989), 65–77. Sandra Messinger Cypess, "Titles as Signs in the Translation of Dramatic Texts," in *Translation Perspectives II: Selected Papers*, ed. Marilyn Gaddis Rose (Binghamton: SUNY Press, 1985), 95–104. Cypess, "Dramaturgia femenina y transposición histórica," *Alba de América* 7 (July 1989): 12–13. Frank Dauster, "El teatro de Elena Garro: Evasión e ilusión," *Revista Iberoamericana* 57 (1964): 84–89; also in *Ensayos sobre teatro hispanoamericano* (Mexico City: SepSetentas, 1975), 66–77. Denise DiPuccio, "The Merging of La(s) dama(s) boba(s)," *Gestos* 5.9 (April 1990): 53–63. Delia Galván, "*Felipe Angeles*: Sacrificio heroico," *Latin American Theatre Review* 20 (Spring 1987): 29–35. Carlos Landeros, "Papel de la mujer en la obra teatral de seis escritoras mexicanas," in *Actas del Sexto Congreso Internacional de Hispanistas* (Toronto: University of Toronto Press, 1980), 443–445. Catherine Larson, "The Dynamics of Conflict in *¿Qué hora es?* and *El duende*," in *A Different Reality*, ed. Anita Stoll (Lewisburg, PA: Bucknell University Press, 1990), 102–116. Larson, "Lope de Vega and Elena Garro: The Doubling of *La dama boba*," *Hispania* 74.1 (March 1991): 15–25. Larson, "Recollection of Plays to Come: Time in the Theater of Elena Garro," *Latin American Theatre Review* 22.2 (1989): 5–17. Gabriela Mora, "Rebeldes fracasadas: Una lectura feminista de *Andarse por las ramas* y *La señora en su balcón*," *Plaza* 5–6 (1981–1982) 115–131. Mora, "*La dama boba* de Elena Garro: Verdad y ficción, teatro y metateatro," *Latin American Theatre Review* 16.2 (1983): 15–22. Mora, "*Los perros* y *La mudanza* de Elena Garro: Designio social y virtualidad feminista," *Latin American Theatre Review* 8.2 (1975): 5–14. Gloria F. Orenstein, *The Theater of the Marvelous: Surrealism and the Contemporary Stage* (New York: New York University Press, 1975), 110–117. Ane-Grethe Ostergaard, "El realismo de los signos escénicos en el

teatro de Elena Garro," *Latin American Theatre Review* 16.1 (Fall 1982): 53–65. Victor H. Rascón Banda, Review of *Parada San Angel, Proceso*, August 30, 1993, 59. Rascon Banda, Review of *Entre Pancho Villa y una mujer desnuda, Proceso*, February 1, 1993, 55–56. Salvador Reyes Nevares, Review of *Un hogar sólido, México en la Cultura* 517 (February 1959): 2. Margarita Rivera Tavera, "Strategies for Dismantling Power Relations: The Dramatic Texts of Elena Garro" (Ph.D. diss. DAI 47, 6, December 1986). Lady Rojas-Trempe, "Dos escritores mexicanos dialogan sobre su teatro," *Alba de América* 8.14–15 (July 1990): 373–378. Rojas-Trempe, "Teatralización en la memoria de Elena Garro," *Crítica de Teatro Latinoamericano* 1 (1989): 135–141. Rojas-Trempe, "Elena Garro dialoga sobre su teatro con Guillermo Schmidhuber: Entrevista," *Revista Iberoamericana* 55.148–149 (July–December 1989):685–690. Patricia Rosas-Lopátegui, *"Un hogar sólido*: Pieza existencial para un público mexicano," *Alba de América* 7.12–13 (July 1989): 221–231. Lorraine Roses, "La expresión dramática de la inconformidad social en cuatro dramaturgas hispanoamericanas," *Plaza* (Fall–Spring 1981–1982) 5–6, 97–114. Carlos Solórzano, "El teatro de Elena Garro: Una nueva frescura literaria," *La Cultura en México* 167 (April 1965): xviii–xix. Susan Spagna, "The Fantastic in the Works of Elena Garro" (Ph.D. diss., 1990), Emma Susana Speratti, "El teatro breve de Elena Garro," *Revista de la Facultad de Humanidades* (San Luis Potosí: July–December 1960), 333–342. Anita Stoll, ed., *A Different Reality: Essays on the Works of Elena Garro* (Lewisburg, PA: Bucknell University Press, 1990). Stoll, "Elena Garro's Lope de Vega's *La dama boba*: Seventeenth Century Inspiration for a Twentieth Century Dramatist," *Latin American Theatre Review* 23.2 (Spring 1990): 21–31. Stoll, "The Old World vs. the New: Cultural Conflict in Four Works of Elena Garro," *Letras Peninsulares* 5.1 (Spring 1992): 95–106. Rhina Toruño-Castañeda, "Protesta contra la opresión: Categorías medulares en la obra narrativa y dramática de Elena Garro," *Deslinde* 11.35–36 (January-June 1992): 93–95. Marta Aida Umanzor de Yoshimura, "The Role of Women in the Writings of Elena Garro" (Ph.D. diss., 1991). Vicky Unruh, "(Free)/Plays of Difference: Language and Eccentricity in Elena Garro's Theater," in *A Different Reality*, Anita Stoll, ed. (Lewisburg, PA: Buckwell University Press, 1990), 38–58. Linda S. Zee, "The Boundaries of the Fantastic: The Case of Three Spanish American Women Writers" (Ph.D. diss., 1993).

Stella Clark

GONZÁLEZ CABALLERO, Antonio (1931–   ). He was born in San Luis Potosí and studied painting at the National Polytechnic Institute and art at the Escuela de Artesanías de Balderas. He is a playwright and painter and teaches dramatic art at the Universidad Nacional Autónoma de México (UNAM) and at the Emilia Carranza Acting School. Although he began his artistic career as a painter during the 1950s, he has gained recognition as a playwright and mentor of new theatrical talent. His drama *El medio pelo* (The Half-Breed) received the Drama Critics Guild award for best play of the year in 1964. Several of his plays have been filmed, and *Señoritas a disgusto* (Ladies in Spite of Themselves) was made into a soap opera. During 1989, he was honored with the Juan Ruiz de Alarcón Prize for the bulk of his theater work. In his plays he criticizes the shortcomings of provincial society, lamenting their narrow vision of the world and their lack of culture. Carlos Solórzano has classified his theater as *Teatro de costumbres* (Theater of Manners) and called some of his works *sainetes* (one-act farces).

WORKS: *Señoritas a disgusto* (Ladies in Spite of Themselves, staged at Teatro Arcos Caracol, 1960). *Una pura y dos con sal* (I Don't Give a Damn, staged at Teatro Rotonda, 1964). *El medio pelo* (The Half-Breed, staged at Teatro Jesús Urueta, 1964; made into a film.). *Los jóvenes asoleados* (The Sun-Stroked Young People, staged at Teatro Reforma, 1966). *Nilo, mi hijo* (Nilo, My Son, staged at Teatro Reforma, 1967). *Tres en Josafat* (Three in Josaphat, staged at Teatro Coyoacán, 1967; made into a film). *Las vírgenes prudentes* (The Prudent Virgins, staged at Teatro Reforma, 1969). *El increíble, extraordinario y nunca bien ponderado caso del convento de las monjas de las Palmitas o Una reverenda madre* (The Incredible, Extraordinary and Never Well Recognized Case of the Convent of the Palmitas Sisters or a Reverend Mother, staged at Teatro 5 de Mayo, Monterrey, 1969). *La ciudad de los carrizos* (The City of Reeds, staged at Teatro del Bosque, 1973). *Asesinato imperfecto* (Imperfect Murder, staged at Teatro Museo de la Ciudad, 1974). *La noche de los sin calzones* (The Night of the Naked, staged at Teatro Tepeyac, 1980). *El estupendohombre o Un viaje al centro del ombligo del Yo* (The Stupendous-Man or A Trip to the Knavel of the I, staged at Teatro de la Universidad, 1980). *Las devoradoras de un ardiente helado* (Girls Devouring a Burning Ice Cream). *Tienes que . . . o de lo contrario* (You Have to . . . Otherwise, 1982). *El mago* (The Magician). *El retablo* (The Altar Piece). *Los dos amigos* (The Two Friends). *¿Quiere usted concursar?* (Do You Want to Enter the Contest?). *R. H. (Roberto y Helena)* (R. H. [Roberto and Helena]). *Amorosos amorales* (Immoral Lovers, staged at Sala La Colorina, 1987). *El plop* (The Plop, staged at Teatro Reforma, 1992). *Vicente y María* (staged at U. Juárez de Durango, 1993). *Las vírgenes prudentes* (The Prudent Virgins, staged at Teatro 29 de diciembre 1992).

BIBLIOGRAPHY: Nora Eidelberg, "González Caballero, Antonio," in *Dictionary of Mexican Literature*, ed. Eladio Cortés (Westport, CT: Greenwood Press, 1992), 285. Edmundo Lizardi, "Todo teatro es costumbrista," *Unomásuno* 16 February 1985, 17. Sonia Morales, "*Premiado . . . ,*" *Proceso* 24 July 1989, 55. Humberto Musacchio, *Gran diccionario enciclopédico de México: Visual* (Mexico City: O. Pedagógica, 1990), 743. Aurora M. Ocampo de Gómez and Ernesto Prado Velázquez, *Diccionario de escritores mexicanos* (Mexico City: UNAM, 1967), 143. Patricia Rosales y Zamora, "Desarrollemos sensibilidad, no la importemos." *Excélsior*, Sec. Cultural 16 May 1989, 2. Carlos Solórzano, Review of *El medio pelo, La Cultura en México. ¡Siempre!* 14 April 1965, 18.

Mirta A. González

GONZÁLEZ CABALLERO DE CASTILLO LEDÓN, Amalía (1898–1986). She was born in Santander Jiménez, Tamaulipas, and died in Mexico City. She dedicated her considerable talents and energy to the advancement of theater and the fight for women's rights in Mexico. Amalia de Castillo Ledón was a jurist, a playwright, a journalist, an ambassador, and a feminist. She studied at the National University and founded the Comedia Mexicana with a 50,000 peso grant she received from President Portes Gil. She also founded the Teatro de Masas and the Ateneo Mexicano de Mujeres (1937). Castillo Ledón wrote a weekly column for the daily *Excélsior* (1946–1952) and directed the journal *Hogar* in the early 1940s. She became president of the Supreme Court and Mexico's first woman ambassador when she was named to that position in Swe-

den. She is said to have been instrumental in securing voting rights for women in 1952.

WORKS: *Cuando las hojas caen* (When the Leaves Fall, 1929). *Cubos de noria* (Pails in a Waterwheel, 1934). *Coqueta* (Coquette, 1937). *Bajo el mismo techo* (Under the Same Roof, 1955). *Peligro: Deshielos* (Danger: Thin Ice, 1957). *La mujer escondida* (The Hidden Woman, 1963).

BIBLIOGRAPHY: Beatriz Castillo Ledón, "Amalia de Castillo Ledón en el teatro del siglo veinte," *Tramoya* (January–March 1991): 76–83. Mirta A. González, "González Caballero de Castilla Ledón, Amalia," in *Dictionary of Mexican Literature*, ed. Eladio Cortés (Westport, CT: Greenwood Press, 1992), 285–286. Beth Miller and Alfonso González, *26 autoras del México actual* (Mexico City: Costa-Amic, 1978), 139–152.

Mirta A. González

GONZÁLEZ DÁVILA, Jesús (1942–   ). A dramatist, actor, and teacher, González Dávila was born in Mexico City, where he studied to be an actor and a teacher. He acted for a time, then turned to teaching, but as he prepared activities for his students, he found himself writing what amounted to short plays, which led him to more serious attempts at playwriting. His earliest works were lyrical, poetic, and symbolic. He had the misfortune, though, to begin writing in the late 1960s, a period when Mexican drama was out of favor, and Mexican dramatists were neither taken seriously nor staged nor published. After finishing his first important work, *La fábrica de los juguetes* (The Toy Factory), he stopped writing for adults and turned to children's theater. He continued through the 1970s, until he wrote *Los niños prohibidos* (Children Prohibited), a children's play whose level of violence really made it a play for adults. At that point he returned to writing for adults and quickly found success. *De la calle* (From the Street) was the first of a string of plays that have made González Dávila one of the most regularly staged playwrights in Mexico. His drama is still symbolic and very character oriented. He writes not so much stories as studies of characters who, many times, inhabit the fringes of society. They can be childlike, but they are driven by inner demons.

Almost all of his plays show the darkest side of human nature and are filled with tremendous violence—whether actual or potential—that keeps an audience in constant tension and leaves it drained.

WORKS: *La rana* (The Frog) (1968). *La venturina* (Quartz) (1968). *El camino* (The Road) (1969). *La fábrica de los juguetes* (The Toy Factory) (1970; 1st staging, 1979); in *Tramoya 11* (1978); in *Teatro joven de México*, ed. Emilio Carballido (Mexico City: Editores Mexicanos Unidos, 1980), 65–95. *Polo Pelota Amarilla* (Polo Yellow Ball) (1978). *Los niños prohibidos* (Children Prohibited) (1981); in *La Cabra* (*Revista de Teatro*) 3.38 (1981): iii–xvi. *De la calle* (From the Street) (1983; 1st staging, 1987); in *Escénica* 1.11 (1985): 52–64. *Pastel de zarzamoras* (1983); in *Trilogía: Tres obras en un acto* (Mexico City: Universidad Autónoma de Puebla, 1984), 9–48. *Muchacha del alma* (Soul Girl) (1984; 1st staging, 1985); in *Escénica* 1.6–7 (1984): vii–xxiii; in *Trilogía: Tres obras en un acto* (Mexico City: Universidad Autónoma de Puebla, 1984), 93–137. *El jardín de las delicias* (The Garden of Delights) (1984; 1st staging, 1984); in *Trilogía: Tres obras en un acto* (Mexico City: Universidad Autónoma de Puebla, 1984), 49–92. *Luna negra* (Black Moon) (1985) (Guadalajara: Editorial Agata, 1989). *Las perlas de la virgen* (The Pearls of the Virgin) (1993; 1st staging, 1993). *El talón del diablo* (The Devil's Heel) (1994; 1st staging, 1994). *Amsterdam Búlevar* (Amsterdam Boulevard) (1987; 1st staging, 1987); (Mexico City: Colección: Teatro Ibero-Americano T.I.A., 1994). *Crónica de un desayuno* (Chronicle of a Breakfast) (1987). *Tiempos furiosos* (Furious Times) (1989). *El mismo día, por la noche* (The Same Day, at Night) (1991).

BIBLIOGRAPHY: Ronald D. Burgess, *The New Dramatists of Mexico, (1967–1985)* (Lexington: University Press of Kentucky, 1991).

Alfonso González

GONZÁLEZ DE ESLAVA, Fernán (c. 1534–1601). He was born in Spain and died in Mexico City. He was a cleric, poet, and playwright. González de Eslava authored twenty-eight *coloquios* and *entremeses*, short dramatic compositions, often comical, designed to be presented between the acts of longer, more serious plays. Although he was born in Spain, his style has endured as one of the first examples of typically Mexican Spanish. Many of the words he uses—such as *tostón, gachupín*, and *mecate*—are still used in Mexican Spanish.

WORKS: *Coloquios espirituales y sacramentales* (Spiritual and Sacramental Dialogues) (Mexico City: Imp. Diego López Dávalos, 1610). *Villancicos, romances, ensaladas y otras canciones devotas* (Christmas Songs, Poems, Medleys and Other Pious Songs) (ed. Margit Frenk. Mexico City: El Colegio de México, 1989).

BIBLIOGRAPHY: Amado Alonso, "Biografía de Fernán González de Eslava," *Revista de Filología Hispánica* 2.3 (n.d.): 213–321. Anita K. Stoll, ed., *Dictionary of Mexican Literature* (Westport, CT: Greenwood Press, 1992). Frida Weber de Kurlat, *Lo cómico en el teatro de Fernán González de Eslava* (Buenos Aires: University of Buenos Aires, 1963).

Alfonso González

GOROSTIZA, Celestino (1904–1967). Born in the State of Tabasco, Gorostiza is one of Mexico's distinguished playwrights. He was a statesman and a politician, having served on the Ministry of Education and as a director of the National Institute of Fine Arts (INBA). Imbued in the life of the theater, Gorostiza was a playwright, a director, and an actor. After the Revolution, along with other dramatists, he founded several theater companies such as the Teatro Ulises and the Teatro de Orientación. Along with his colleagues Salvador Novo and Xavier Villaurrutia, he revitalized the theater in Mexico, producing world-renowned plays that he translated into Spanish.

Gorostiza's best-known play, *El color de nuestra piel* (The Color of Our Skin), is a study in prejudice caused within one family by each member's skin color. It was awarded the Juan Ruiz de Alarcón Prize in 1956. Gorostiza not only influenced the development of theater in twentieth century Mexico but also gave impulse to the growth of the Mexican cinema during its Golden Age. As a critic of both film and theater, as well as a festival organizer, Gorostiza has gained recognition as a key figure of the revitalization of postrevolutionary Mexican culture.

WORKS: *El nuevo paraíso* (The New Eden, 1930). *La escuela del amor* (The School of Love, 1933). *Ser o no ser* (To Be or Not to Be, 1934). *Escombros del sueño* (Debris from Dreams, 1939).

La reina de nieve (The Snow Queen, 1942). *La mujer ideal* (The Ideal Woman, 1943). *El color de nuestra piel* (The Color of Our Skin, 1953). *Columna social* (Society Column, n.d.). *La leña está verde* (The Firewood Is Green, 1958), in *Teatro mexicano del siglo XX* (Mexico City: Fondo de Cultura Económica, 1956).

BIBLIOGRAPHY: Miguel Guardia, "The Mexican Theater: Celestino Gorostiza," *Mexican Cultural Bulletin* (July 1935): 15. Ruth S. Lamb, "Celestino Gorostiza y el teatro experimental en México," *Revista Iberoamericana* 23.45 (January-June 1958): 141–145. Antonio Magaña Esquivel, "Celestino Gorostiza, director y comediógrafo," *Letras de México* 2.16 (April 1940): 6. Kristen Nigro, "Rhetoric and History in Three Mexican Plays," *Latin American Theatre Review* 21.1 (Fall 1987): 65–73. Isis Quinteros, "La consagración del mito en la epopeya mexicana: *La Malinche* de Celestino Gorostiza," *Latin American Theatre Review* 19.1 (Fall 1985): 33–42. Porfirio Sánchez, "Aspectos socio-psicológicos y el movimiento indigenista en *El color de nuestra piel* de Gorostiza," *Cuadernos Americanos* 258.1 (1985): 192–201.

Stella Clark

GOROSTIZA, Manuel Eduardo de (1789–1851). As a young man, he studied in Spain, where he became famous for his liberal views and began writing and staging his plays. During 1821 to 1833 he became Mexico's representative to the Low Countries, Belgium, England, Prussia, and France. He invested his personal fortune in the defense of his country and fought against the U.S. invasion at Churubusco in 1848. Influenced first by neoclassicism and later by Romanticism, his works are both didactic and sentimental.

WORKS: *Tal para cual* (Two of a Kind, staged in Madrid, 1820). *Las costumbres de antaño, Don Dieguito* (The Customs of Yesteryear, Don Dieguito, staged in Madrid, 1820). *El jugador* (The Player, staged in Madrid, 1820). *El íntimo amigo* (The Intimate Friend, staged in Brussels, 1828). *Contigo pan y cebolla* (With You, Bread and Onions, staged in London, 1833). *Indulgencias para todos* (Indulgences for All, staged in Madrid, 1918). *Virtud y patriotismo . . .* (Virtue and Patriotism . . . , staged in Madrid, 1921). *Lo que son las mujeres* (What Women Are Like, staged in Brussels, 1921). *También hay secreto en mujer* (There Is Also a Secret in a Woman, staged in Brussels, 1926). *Las costumbres de antaño* (The Customs of Yesteryear, staged in Mexico, 1933). *El cocinero y el secretario* (The Cook and the Secretary, staged in Madrid, 1940).

BIBLIOGRAPHY: Esther Hernández Palacios, "Gorostiza, Manuel Eduardo de," *Dictionary of Mexican Literature*, ed. Eladio Cortés (Westport, CT: Greenwood Press, 1992), 302–304. Armando María y Campos, *Manuel Eduardo de Gorostiza, su tiempo, su vida y su tiempo* (Mexico City: T. Gráficos de la nación, 1959). Humberto Musacchio, *Gran diccionario enciclopédico de México. Visual* (Mexico City: Sec. Orientación, 1990), 760. Aurora M. Ocampo de Gómez and Ernesto Prado Velázquez, eds., *Diccionario de escritores mexicanos* (Mexico City: UNAM, 1967), 158–159. Emma S. Sperati Piñeiro, "El teatro neoclásico en la literatura mexicana: *Indulgencia para todos* de Manuel Eduardo Gorostiza," *Revista Iberoamericana* 19.38 (1954): 326–332.

Mirta A. González

HERNÁNDEZ, Luisa Josefina (1928–). She was born in Mexico City and studied Theater Arts at the Universidad Nacional Autónoma de México (UNAM) under Rodolfo Usigli and at Columbia University. She is a playwright, novelist, teacher, and translator. She has received fellowships from the Centro Mexicano de Escritores and the Rockefeller Foundation. Her plays have won her the El Nacional and the INBA prizes. Although women in her plays are oftentimes unrealized beings and victims of their society, they are independent and assertive. Some critics view Hernández as a feminist playwright.

WORKS: *Los sordomudos* (The Deafmutes, 1950). *Aguardiente de caña* (Rum, 1951). *La corona del ángel* (The Angel's Crown, 1951). *La llave del cielo* (The Key to Heaven, 1954). *Botica modelo* (Model Pharmacy, 1954). *Los huéspedes reales* (The Royal Guests, 1954). *Los frutos caídos* (The Fallen Fruit, 1957). *Historia de un anillo* (History of a Ring, 1961). *Escándalo en Puerto Santo* (Scandal at Puerto Santo, 1962). *La calle de la gran ocasión* (The Street of the Great Occasion, 1962). *Los duendes* (The Genies, 1963). *La hija del rey o Electra* (The King's Daughter or Electra, 1965). *Quetzacóatl* (1965). *La danza del urogallo múltiple* (The Dance of the Multiple Capercaillie, 1971). *La paz ficticia* (The Fictitious Peace, 1974). *Popol Vuh* (1974). *Pavana de Aranzazú* (Aranzazú's Pavane, 1975). *Auto* *del divino preso* (Play of the Divine Prisoner, 1976). *Hécuba* (1976). *Fiesta del monte de plata o La fiesta del mulato* (Fiesta of the Silver Mountain or Fiesta of the Mulatto, 1977). *Caprichos y disparates de Francisco Goya* (Caprices and Nonsense of Francisco Goya, 1979). *Jerusalén-Damasco* (1980). *Ciertas cosas* (Certain Things, 1980). *Apocrypha* (1980). *El orden de los factores* (The Order of the Factors, 1983). *En una noche como ésta* (In a Night Like This One, 1988). *Oriflama* (1988). *Amigo secreto* (Secret Friend, 1990). *Las bodas. Zona Templada* (The Weddings. Warm Zone, 1992).

BIBLIOGRAPHY: Sylvis J. Brann, "El fracaso de la voluntad en las comedias de Luisa Josefina Hernández," *Latin American Theatre Review* 7.1 (1973): 25–31. Frank Dauster, "The Ritual Feast: Study in Dramatic Form," *Latin American Theatre Review* 9.1 (1975): 5–9. John K. Knowles, "Luisa Josefina Hernández: The Labyrinth of Form," in *Dramatists in Revolt: The New Latin American Theater* (Austin: University of Texas Press, 1976), 133–145. Alyce de Kuehne, "Pirandello en Hispanoamérica," *Revista Iberoamericana* 34 (1968): 313–322. Janice L. Krugh," Solitude and Solidarity: Major Themes and Techniques in the Theater of Luisa Josefina Hernández," *DAI* 47.6 (December 1986): 2174A. Michèle Muncy, "Hernández, Luisa Josefina," in *Dictionary of Mexican Literature*, ed. Eladio Cortés (Westport, CT: Greenwood Press, 1992), 323–332. Muncy, "Entrevista con Luisa Josefina Hernández," *Latin American Theatre Review* 9.2 (1976): 69–77. Humberto Musacchio, *Gran diccionario enciclopédico de México. Visual* (Mexico City: Sec. Orientación, 1990), 825. Kristen F. Nigro, "*La fiesta del mulato* de Luisa Josefina Hernández," *Latin American Theatre Review* 13.2 (1980): 81–86. Nigro, "Entrevista a Luisa Josefina Hernández," *Latin American Theatre Review* 18.2 (1985): 101–104. Teresa Rodríguez, "Entrevista con Lisa Josefina Hernández," *Chasqui* 16.1 (1987): 77–82.

Mirta A. González

HIRIART, Hugo (1942–). He was born in Mexico City and studied at the Universidad Nacional Autónoma de México (UNAM) and at the Escuela de Pintura y Escultura La Esmeralda. Although he began writing prose fiction, he gained recognition as a playwright during the 1980s. His play *Vivir y beber* (To Live and to Drink), a play that presents the progressive dehumanization of an alcoholic, received excellent reviews.

WORKS: *Simulacros* (Simulacres, staged at Teatro del Museo Tamayo, 1983). *Tablero de las pasiones de juguete* (Checkerboard of Play Passions, staged at Foro Sor Juana, 1984). *Ambar* (Ambar, staged at Foro Sor Juana Inés de la Cruz, 1986). *Las palabras de la tribu* (The Words of the Tribe, staged at Foro Sor Juana, 1988). *La ginecomaquia o El pabellón amarillo* (Ginecomachia or the Yellow Pavilion, staged at Foro Shakespeare, 1988). *La invención del naufragio* (The Invention of the Shipwreck, staged at Centro Univ. de Teatro, 1989). *Vivir y beber* (To Live and to Drink, staged at Teatro Benito Juárez, 1990). *120,000 leguas de viaje submarino* (120,000 Leagues of Underwater Travel, staged at Teatro de Bellas Artes, 1991). *Las aventuras de Clotario Demonax* (The Adventures of Clotario Demonax, staged at Teatro Santa Cantarina, 1993). *La representación o los peligros del juego* (Representation or the Dangers of the Game, staged at Teatro Reforma, 1993). *Descripción de un animal dormido* (Description of an Animal Asleep, staged at Teatro Santa Catarina, 1993).

BIBLIOGRAPHY: Bruno Bert, Review of *La representación o los peligros del juego, El Nacional*, December 16, 1993, 8. Ana Clavel, Review of *Tablero de las pasiones de juguete, Unomásuno*, April 14, 1984. Olga Harmony, Review of *La representación . . . , La Jornada*, December 2, 1993, 28. Hernán Lavín Cerda, Review of *Simulacros, Unomásuno*, June 15, 1983. Alegría Martínez, Review of *Las palabras de la tribu, Unomásuno*, October 24, 1988. María Muro, Review of *Simulacros, Excelsior*, May 29, 1983, 3. Bruce Swansey, Review of *Vivir y Beber, Proceso*, May 21, 1990, 55.

Mirta A. González

IBARGÜENGOITIA, Jorge (1928–1983). Born in Guanajuato, Ibargüengoitia had a distinguished career as a novelist, journalist, literary critic, and playwright. Under the tutelage of Rodolfo Usigli, he studied dramatic art at the Universidad Nacional Autónoma de México (UNAM) and later in New York, sponsored by a Rockefeller Foundation grant. His first play, *Susana y los jóvenes* (Susana and the Youths), was performed in 1954. This was followed by *Un adulterio exquisito* (A Delightful Act of Adultery) and *La lucha con el ángel* (The Struggle with the Angel), for which he received a prize at a Buenos Aires theater festival. After a negative review of a new play from

Usigli, Ibargüengoitia veered toward historical theater. His lack of success in this genre in turn led to a shift in focus to testimonial novels such as *Las muertas* (The Dead Girls) and *Los pasos de López* (López's Footsteps). The critical acclaim awarded to his fiction overshadowed his theatrical works. His plays, along with the rest of his literary and journalistic production, are highly critical of Mexican history and society, which he attacked with irony, humor, and farcical elements. Ibargüengoitia met an untimely death along with several other Latin American writers in a plane crash on the approach to Madrid in November 1983.

WORKS: *Susana y los jóvenes* (Susana and the Youths, 1954). *El rey tiene cuernos* (The King Is a Cuckold, 1954). *Clotilde en su casa* (Clotilde at Home, performed as *Un adulterio exquisito* [A Delightful Act of Adultery], 1955). *La lucha con el ángel* (The Struggle with the Angel, 1955). *El peluquero del rey* (The King's Barber, 1956). *El amor loco viene* (Crazy Love Arrives), *El tesoro perdido* (The Hidden Treasure), and *Dos crímenes* (Two Crimes), in *Tres obras en un acto* (Three One Act Plays, 1956). *Pájaro en mano* (Bird in the Hand, 1959). *Ante varias esfinges* (Before Various Sphinxes, broadcast and published in 1960). *El viaje superficial* (The Superficial Journey, 1960). *Los buenos manejos* (Good Maneuvers, 1960). *La fuga de Nicanor* (Nicanor's Flight, 1960). *El atentado* (The Assassination Attempt, 1961). *Clotilde* (1964). *El viaje* (The Journey, 1964). *El pájaro* (The Bird, 1964). *La conspiración vendida* (The Conspiracy Betrayed, 1965).

BIBLIOGRAPHY: Arturo Azuela, "Jorge Ibargüengoitia: Múltiples espejos de utopías gastadas," *Cuadernos Americanos* 4.255 (July-August 1984): 75–79. Angel Bárcenas, Review of *Tres piezas en un acto*, *Revista Mexicana de Cultura* 858 (September 8, 1963): 15. Juan Bruce-Novoa and David Valentín, "Violating the Image of Violence: Ibargüengoitia's *El atentado*," *Latin American Theatre Review* 12.2 (1979): 13–21. Jaime Lorenzo, "Historia y humor en la obra de Jorge Ibargüengoitia," *La Palabra y el hombre* 78 (April–June 1991): 287–297. Sonia Morales, Review of *Clotilde en su casa*, *Proceso*, September 10, 1990, 58–59. Esther Seligson, Review of *Clotilde en su casa*, *Proceso*, March 4, 1991, 58–59. David Jon Schuster, "A Critical Introduction to Three Plays of the Mexican Revolution: Rodolfo Usigli, *El gesticulador*; Vicente Leñero, *El juicio*; Jorge Ibargüengoitia, *El atentado* (Ph.D. diss., 1987).

Sharon Keefe Ugalde, "Beyond Satire: Ibargüengoitia's *Maten al león*," *Revista de Temas Hispánicos* 1.2 (Spring 1984): 217–229.

Stella Clark

INCLÁN, Federico S. (also Inclán Shroeder, Federico) (1910–1981). He was born and died in Mexico City. He studied electrical engineering at the University of California. He began writing plays in 1948 and wrote thirty-four of them. He gained notoriety when his play *Luces de carburo* (Carbide Lights) won first place in the Fiestas de Primavera in 1950. The Theatrical Critics Guild named his work *Hoy invita la güera* (Today, Blondie Invites) as the best of the year. His play *Detrás de esa puerta* (Behind That Door) won the 1959 Juan Ruiz de Alarcón Prize.

WORKS: *Luces de carburo* (Carbide Lights, 1950). *Espaldas mojadas cruzan el Río Bravo* (Wet Backs Cross the Rio Grande, 1951). *El duelo* (The Duel, 1951). *Hidalgo* (1953) (Mexico City: Col. T. Mexicano, 1953). *Cuartelazo* (Coup D'état, 1954). *Un caso de conciencia* (A Case of Conscience, 1954). *Hoy invita la güera* (Today, Blondie Invites, 1955). *Una mujer para los sábados* (A Woman for Saturdays, 1956). *El deseo llega al anochecer* (Desire Comes in the Evening, 1956). *El mantenido* (The Free Loader, 1958). *El honorable Sr. García* (The Honorable Mr. Garcia, 1958). *Diego le habla a la Vírgen* (Diego Speaks to the Virgin, 1958). *Cordelia o una esfinge llamada Cordelia* (Cordelia or A Sphinx Named Cordelia, 1958). *El caso de Pedro Ventura* (The Pedro Ventura Case, staged in Querétaro, 1959). *Detrás de esa puerta* (Behind that Door, 1959). *Deborah* (Deborah, 1960). *Cada noche muere Julieta* (Julieta Dies Every Evening, 1960). *El enemigo* (The Enemy, *Cuadernos de Bellas Artes*, August 1, 1960). *Doroteo Arango, Pancho Villa* (1960). *La ventana* (The Window, 1960). *Malintzin* (1961). *Aprendiendo a ser señora* (Learning How to Be a Married Woman, n.d.). *Las boinas rojas* (The Red Berets, n.d.). *Don Quijote murió del corazón* (Don Quixote Died of a Heart Attack, n.d.). *Dos mujeres y un cadáver* (Two Women and a Body, n.d.). *El seminarista de los ojos negros: Yo pecador me confieso* (The Dark Eyed Seminarian: I Confess That I Have Sinned, n.d.). *Entre alcanfores un sueño. Frida Kahlo. Hablemos de la muerte* (Frida Kahlo. Let's Talk About Death, n.d.). *Y aún hay flores* (And There Are Still Flowers, n.d.). *Joshua. La guerra de los* *dioses* (Joshua. The War of the Gods, n.d.). *La muerte de Sócrates* (Socrates's Death, n.d.). *La última noche con Laura* (The Last Evening with Laura, n.d.). *Una señorita decente* (A Decent Young Woman, n.d.). *Una noche con Casanova* (A Night with Casanova, staged at T. INBA, 1964). *Turco para señoras* (Sauna for Ladies, 1965). *Derecho de asilo* (Right to Asylum, staged in Federal Germany, 1966).

BIBLIOGRAPHY: Delia Galván, "Inclán, Federico Schroeder," in *Dictionary of Mexican Literature*, ed. Eladio Cortés (Westport, CT: Greenwood Press, 1992), 346–347. Humberto Musacchio, *Gran diccionario enciclopédico de México: Visual* (Mexico City: O. Pedagógica, 1990), 896. Aurora M. Ocampo de Gómez and Ernesto Prado Velásquez, *Diccionario de escritores mexicanos* (Mexico City: UNAM, 1967), 183. Rafael Solana, Review of *Una noche con Casanova. La Cultura en México. Siempre!* April 29, 1964. Carlos Solórzano, Review of *Hoy invita la güera. Ovaciones. Suplemento Literario*, November 4, 1962, 5. Mario Martín Ugarte, "La posición de Federico Schroeder Inclán en el teatro mexicano contemporáneo," *DAI* 32.8 (1971): 4764 (University of Southern California).

LEÑERO, Estela (1960–). She was born in Mexico City and holds a degree in sociology from the Universidad Nacional Autónoma de México (UNAM). She studied theater arts during 1982–1991 at the Centro de Arte Dramático in Mexico City, in the Centro Nacional de Nuevas Tendencias Escénicas in Madrid, and in the workshops of several known playwrights. In *Paisaje interior* (Intimate Landscape) she explores the problems of two contemporary women, a guerilla and a murderess, who have broken the law fighting for their beliefs.

WORKS: *Casa llena* (Full House, staged at Centro Universitario de Teatro, 1987) (Puebla: Universidad Autónoma de Puebla, 1986). *Todos los días* (Every Day, staged at Teatro Serapio Rendón, 1988) (Mexico: Rev. *La Orquesta* N. 13–14). *Instantáneas* (Snap Shots, staged at CADAC, 1991). *Las máquinas de coser* (The Sewing Machines, staged at Teatro El Galeón, 1990) (Mexico: UAM, Azcapotzalco 1990). *Los invitados* (The Guests, staged at Auditorio FCE, 1991). *Insomnio* (Insomnia, staged at Teatro La Gruta, 1993); Literary Supplement of *El Nacional*, 1991, n.d.). *Arroz rojo* (Red Rice, T. ITI-UNESCO, 1992). *Habitación en blanco* (Empty

Room, staged at Foro Sor Juana Inés de la Cruz). *Paisaje interior* (Intimate Landscape, staged at Teatro La Gruta, 1995).

BIBLIOGRAPHY: Victor H. Rascón Banda, Review of *Insomnio, Proceso*, April 5 1993, 55–56. Hector Rivera, Review of *Las máquinas de coser, Proceso*, April 30, 1990, 58.

LICONA, Alejandro (1953–). A dramatist, chemical engineer, television scriptwriter, and teacher, Licona was born in Mexico City, where he studied chemical engineering and worked for a time at that profession. His attempts at movie writing led him to the theater, where, in 1972, he began to find success. He continued working as a chemical engineer until he finally left that career behind and devoted himself to play writing, television script writing, teaching, and working in the video collection of the Videoteca of the Sociedad General de Escritores de México. His plays (as well as much of his television writing) are characterized by their humor, culminating in his most frequently staged play to date, *Abuelita de Batman* (Batman's Granny), a series of short sketches. His success at television writing makes it possible for him to devote increased time to drama.

WORKS: *Huélum o Cómo pasar matemáticas sin problema* (Huélum or How to Pass Math without a Problem) (1972; 1st staging, 1981), *in Teatro joven de México*, edited by Emilio Carballido (Mexico City: Editores Mexicanos Unidos, 1980), 269–301. *El diablo en el jardín* (The Devil in the Garden) (1977; 1st staging, 1980). *Cuentas por cobrar* (Bills to Collect) (1979; 1st staging, 1985), in *Tramoya* 18 (1980): 28–36; in *Más teatro joven*, edited by Emilio Carballido (Mexico City: Editores Mexicanos Unidos, 1980), 31–41. *Máquina* (Machine) (1979; 1st staging, 1980), in *Tramoya* 19 (1980): 4–50; in *Teatro para obreros*, edited by Emilio Carballido (Mexico City: Editores Mexicanos Unidos, 1985), 55–117. *Esta es su casa* (This Is Your Home) (1980), in *Raptola, violola y matola* (Mexico City: Instituto Politécnico Nacional, 1987), 84–127. *El capiro* (1981), in *El Gallo Ilustrado* 985 (May 3, 1981): 3. *Cancionero popular* (Popular Anthology) (1982; 1st staging, 1982). *La amenaza roja* (The Red Threat) (1984), in *Escándalo en Paraíso y 4 obras ganadoras* (Primer Concurso de Teatro Salvador Novo) (Mexico City: Editores Mexicanos Unidos, 1984),

169–222. *El día de mañana* (Tomorrow) (1985), in *Raptola, violola y matola* (Mexico City: Instituto Politécnico Nacional, 1987), 129–139. *Abuelita de Batman* (Batman's Granny) (1988; 1st staging, 1988), in *Abuelita de Batman* (Mexico City: Obra Citada, 1989), 9–43. *Haz de cuenta que fuimos basura* (It's Like We Were Trash) (1988; 1st staging, 1992), in *Abuelita de Batman* (Mexico City: Obra Citada, 1989), 45–68. *Verdad de Dios* (God's Truth) (1988), in *Abuelita de Batman* (Mexico City: Obra Citada, 1989), 69–105. *Castigo ejemplar a infractores de la ley* (Exemplary Punishment for Lawbreakers) (1989), in *Doce a las doce* (Mexico City: Obra Citada, 1989), 9–14. *Sólo para ardidos* (Only for the Brave) (1991; 1st staging, 1994). *Prisionero del mar* (Prisoner of the Sea) (1992; 1st staging, 1992). *El hombre de acero* (The Man of Steel) (1992; 1st staging, 1992). *Josefo el magnífico* (Josefo the Magnificent) (1993). *Todos los negros tomamos café* (All Us Blacks Drink Coffee) (1993). *El circo pirrín* (The Pirrín Circus) (1993). *Arroz con popote* (Rice with a Straw) (1993). *Los abajo firmantes* (The Undersigned) (1994; 1st staging, 1994). Television: *Entre vivos y muertos* (Between Living and Dead).

BIBLIOGRAPHY: Ronald D. Burgess, *The New Dramatists of Mexico (1967–1985)* (Lexington: University Press of Kentucky, 1991).

LIERA, Oscar (1946–1990). A dramatist, director, and teacher, Liera was born in Culiacán, Sinaloa, but did his university studies in Mexico City. He combined teaching, directing, and playwriting, and his facility for the latter led to a relatively large production in the short time that he lived and wrote. He started writing in 1979, and by 1985, he had written twenty-seven plays. Many of his works are humorous, and almost all show evidence of social commitment. Most deal with people's desires and obsessions and the games and illusions that comprise human existence. His most notorious work is *Cúcara y Mácara* (Cúcara and Mácara), a criticism of the power of the Church that many took as a criticism of religion and of the Virgin of Guadalupe, Mexico's patron saint. This occasioned protests during performances and one attack by spectators on the actors in midplay. In many cases, all the "extracurricular" activity was taken to be a part of the play, leading to a true, living drama in which spectators participated and to which they contributed, most times unwittingly. After 1985, Liera returned to Culiacán, where he died in 1990, thus ending the all-too-short career of what promised to be one of Mexico's premier dramatists.

WORKS: *Las Ubárry* (The Ubárrys) (1979), in *Tramoya* 14 (1979): 30–37; in *Teatro joven de México*, edited by Emilio Carballido (Mexico City: Editores Mexicanos Unidos, 1980), 55–64; in *La piña y la manzana. Viejos juegos en la dramática* (Mexico City: UNAM, 1982), 27–35; in *Pez en el agua* (Sinaloa: Universidad Autónoma de Sinaloa, 1990), 49–59. *El Lazarillo* (1979; 1st staging, 1979) (Mexico: Universidad Autónoma Metropolitana, 1983). *Cúcara y Mácara* (1980; 1st staging, 1980), in *La Cabra. Revista de Teatro* 3.28–29 (1981): i–xii; in *La piña y la manzana. Viejos juegos en la dramática* (Mexico City: UNAM, 1982), 101–120; in *Pez en el agua* (Sinaloa: Universidad Autónoma de Sinaloa, 1990), 77–101. *La ñonga* (The Slow One). *Gente de teatro, gente horrible* (Theater People, Horrible People). *Las fábulas perversas* (The Perverse Fables). *Los fantasmas de la realidad* (The Ghosts of Reality). *La gudógoda*, in *Tramoya* 18 (1980): 77–81. *Etcétera*, in *Repertorio* 7 (1982): 1–14. *La fuerza del hombre* (The Power of Man), in *La piña y la manzana. Viejos juegos en la dramática* (Mexico City: UNAM, 1982), 7–13; in *Más teatro joven*, edited by Emilio Carballido (Mexico City: Editores Mexicanos Unidos, 1982), 187–196; in *Teatro breve* (Mexico City: Arbol Editorial, 1984), 51–58. *El gordo* (The Grand Prize) (1st staging, 1980); in *Tramoya* 14 (1979): 38–48; in *La piña y la manzana. Viejos juegos en la dramática* (Mexico City: UNAM, 1982), 15–25; in *Pez en el agua* (Sinaloa: Universidad Autónoma de Sinaloa, 1990), 33–47. *Los camaleones* (The Chameleons) (1st staging, 1980), in *Tramoya* 14 (1979): 17–22; in *La piña y la manzana. Viejos juegos en la dramática* (Mexico City: UNAM, 1982), 37–43. *La verdadera revolución* (The True Revolution), in *La piña y la manzana. Viejos juegos en la dramática* (Mexico City: UNAM, 1982), 45–47. *El crescencio*, in *Tramoya* 14 (1979): 4–16; in *La piña y la manzana. Viejos juegos en la dramática* (Mexico City: UNAM, 1982), 49–62. *Aquí no pasa nada* (Nothing's Happening Here), in *Tramoya* 14 (1979): 49–62; in *La piña y la manzana. Viejos juegos en la dramática* (Mexico City: UNAM, 1982), 63–77. *La piña y la manzana* (The Pineapple and the Apple), in *Tramoya* 14 (1979): 63–72; in *La piña y la manzana. Viejos juegos en la dramática* (Mexico

City: UNAM, 1982), 79–88. *La pesadilla de una noche de verano* (A Midsummer Night's Nightmare), in *La piña y la manzana. Viejos juegos en la dramática* (Mexico City: UNAM, 1982), 89–100. *Soy el hombre* (I'm the Man), in *La piña y la manzana. Viejos juegos en la dramática* (Mexico City: UNAM, 1982), 121–136; in *Pez en el agua* (Sinaloa: Universidad Autónoma de Sinaloa, 1990), 61–75. *Juego de damas* (Ladies' Game), in *La piña y la manzana. Viejos juegos en la dramática* (Mexico City: UNAM, 1982), 137–171. *Las juramentaciones* (Swearing). *El oro de la revolución mexicana* (The Gold of the Mexican Revolution) (1984), in *Pez en el agua* (Sinaloa: Universidad Autónoma de Sinaloa, 1990), 135–166. *Repaso de indulgencias* (Review of Indulgences), in *Pez en el agua* (Sinaloa: Universidad Autónoma de Sinaloa, 1990), 103–134. *Bajo el silencio* (Under Silence) (1984), in *Pez en el agua* (Sinaloa: Universidad Autónoma de Sinaloa, 1990), 195–210. *El jinete de la divina providencia* (The Horseman of the Divine Providence) (1984; 1st staging, 1984), in *Escénica* 1.10 (1985): i–xx; (Culiacán: Universidad Autónoma de Sinaloa, 1987). *Un misterioso pacto* (A Mysterious Pact) (1985), in *Pez en el agua* (Sinaloa: Universidad Autónoma de Sinaloa, 1990), 211–228. *El camino rojo a Sabaiba* (The Red Road to Sabaiba) (1985). *Los negros pájaros del adios* (Goodbye's Black Birds), in *Pez en el agua* (Sinaloa: Universidad Autónoma de Sinaloa, 1990), 167–193.

BIBLIOGRAPHY: Marco Antonio Alfaro, "Un Salvaje Agresión a Actores, *Esto*, June 30, 21. Rodolfo Arriaga R. y Antonio García, "Oscar Liera. Una Semblanza," in *Pez en el agua* (Sinaloa: Universidad Autónoma de Sinaloa, 1990), 27–30. Ronald D. Burgess, "Appearances: The Sub-Versions of *Cúcara y Mácara, Chasqui* 15.1, 3–10. Burgess, *The New Dramatists of Mexico (1967–1985)* (Lexington: University Press of Kentucky, 1991). Dorothy Connell, "Theatre of Violence, *Index on Censorship* 2.2 (1982): 36–37. Renato D'Aquino Rosas, "Repudian Xalapeños la Obra 'Cúcara y Mácara,' *El Sol de Xalapa* January 28, 1981. Armando Partida, "Antología personal de Oscar Liera," in *Pez en el agua* (Sinaloa: Universidad Autónoma de Sinaloa, 1990), 5–25. Antonio Saborit, "Crónica de una Intolerancia Armada," *Siempre*, July 22, 1981, 5–10.

Ronald D. Burgess

LIRA, Miguel N. (1905–1961). He was born and died in Tlaxcala, Tlaxcala. A poet, playwright, novelist, editor, and printer, he was also a lawyer and a professor of Mexican and Iberoamerican literature at the Escuela Nacional Preparatoria, director of the National University Press of the Universidad Nacional Autónoma de México (UNAM) (1935–1938), director of the literary magazine *Universidad* (1936–1938), director of publication for the Ministry of Public Education, Supreme Court secretary, and district judge in Tlaxcala and Chiapas. He founded the Fábula publishing company, where he published the works of noted writers such as Alfonso Reyes, Xavier Villaurrutia, Octavio Paz, Vicente Aleixandre, Rafael Alberti, and others. He also founded and was the editor of *Huytlale*, a literary magazine.

Lira's production as a playwright consists of fifteen dramas, of which twelve have been staged and six published. In his theater, as in his poetry and novels, Miguel N. Lira pursued the themes and subjects of the rich folklorical heritage of his land, Tlaxcala. He dramatized the legends and customs of his people, creating a telluric theater. He also used urban themes, satirizing Mexican society and its political institutions. In 1943, Lira founded the Teatro de México Company together with Celestino Gorostiza, Xavier Villaurrutia, María Luisa Ocampo, Concepción Sada, and set designers Julio Prieto and Julio Castellanos. In the context of Mexican theater of the twentieth century, Lira is undoubtedly part of the important evolution of playwrights and companies that has brought a truly national theater to its present recognized standards of excellence in Latin America and the world.

WORKS: *Coloquio de Linda y de Domingo Arenas* (Dialogue between Linda and Domingo Arena) (Mexico City: Ed. Fábula, 1934). *Sí, con los ojos.* (Yes, with a Glance) (Mexico City: Ed. Fábula, 1938). *Vuelta a la tierra* (Return to the Land) (Mexico City: Ed. Fábula, 1940). *Carpa* (Canvas Theater) (Mexico City: Ed. Fábula, 1941). *Linda* (Beautiful) (Mexico City: Ed. Fábula, 1942). *La muñeca pastillita* (A Doll Called Pastillita, staged at Teatro Bellas Artes, 1942). *Carlota de México* (Carlota of Mexico) (Mexico City: Ed. Fábula, 1944). *El diablo volvió al infierno* (The Devil Returned to Hell) (Mexico City: Ed. Fábula, 1946). *Ella el sol y ella la luna* (She the Sun and She the Moon, 1947). *Una vez en las montañas* (Once in the Mountains, 1955). *Casa de cristal* (Glass House, 1959). *El pequeño patriota* (The Little

Patriot, 1960). *Volverán las oscuras golondrinas* (The Dark Swallows Will Return, unfinished).

BIBLIOGRAPHY: Robert K. Anderson, "Lira Alvarez, Miguel Nicolás," in *Dictionary of Mexican Literature*, Eladio Cortés, ed. (Westport, CT: Greenwood Press, 1992), 369–370. Raúl Arreola Cortés, "La influencia lorquiana en Miguel N. Lira," *Revista Hispánica Moderna* 8.4 (October 1942): 304–320. Cortés, *Miguel N. Lira, el poeta y el hombre* (Mexico City: Ed. Jus, 1977). Jeanine Gaucher-Morales and Alfredo Morales, *Epistolario de Miguel N. Lira (1921–1961)* (Tlaxcala: University of Tlaxcala, 1991). Gaucher-Morales and Morales, *Miguel N. Lira: Obra poética* (Tlaxcala: University of Tlaxcala, 1995). Gaucher-Morales and Morales, *Miguel N. Lira: Teatro completo* (in preparation). Antonio Magaña Esquivel, *Teatro mexicano del siglo XX* (Mexico City: FCE, 1956), 404–405. Jossé Luis Mayral, "Miguel N. Lira: Otro gran dramaturgo mexicano," *Orbe* (July 4, 1941). Margarita Mendoza López, *Teatro mexicano del siglo XX: 1900–1986*, vol. 1 (Mexico City: IMMS, 1987), 404–405. Alfredo O. Morales, *Miguel N. Lira: Vida y obra* (Puebla: Ed. José M. Cajica, 1972). Arturo Mori, "Teatro: *Linda*," *Ultimas Noticias* (June 30, 1941). Humberto Musacchio, *Gran diccionario enciclopédico de México. Visual* (Mexico City: Pedagógica, 1990), 1040. Aurora M. Ocampo de Gómez and Ernesto Prado Velázquez, *Diccionario de escritores mexicanos* (Mexico City: UNAM, 1967). A. Teja Sabre, "Coloquio de Linda y de Domingo Arenas," *El Universal* (June 4, 1934).

Jeanine Gaucher-Morales and
Alfredo O. Morales

LÓPEZ GUZMAN, Willebaldo (1944–   ). A dramatist, actor, director, member of the board of the Unión Nacional de Autores and of the Sociedad General de Autores de México (SOGEM), López was born in Queréndaro, Michoacán. He spent the early 1950s in a Catholic seminary in Guadalajara, Jalisco, where he discovered his attraction to theater (playing the part of a leper in a religious production). He left the seminary and spent a year studying accounting before he convinced his parents to let him go to Mexico City to study acting. Although he lived in the poorest of conditions and struggled to survive, he was driven by his love for theater and by one of his teachers, Alejandro Jodorowsky. Working on a shoestring budget (2 pesos) he entered his first play—*Los arrieros con sus burros por la hermosa capital* (The Mule Drivers and Their Burros Go to the Big City)—in a competition and won first place. Through the late 1960s and into the late 1970s, he wrote, staged, and many times acted in, directed, and managed to publish several plays that served as the first steps in what was to become *La Nueva Dramaturgia*, the new drama of a new generation of Mexican dramatists. Although most of his plays won awards, by the end of the 1970s, when Mexican plays were still being vilified, López (along with most of the dramatists who began writing at the same time) became discouraged and stopped actively pursuing playwriting. Instead, he directed his efforts to his positions in the Unión Nacional de Autores and to the SOGEM. Near the end of the 1980s he began writing again, although he continued in his more official positions. He writes socially conscious plays that portray the abuses of the poor by those in power. His plays based in Mexican culture and history—*Yo soy Juárez* (I Am Juárez), *Pilo Temirano Luca*, *Malinche Show*—were the precursors of a wave of historical dramas that would come later. He deserves credit as one of the initiators of the movement to reestablish the validity of Mexican drama after it fell out of favor in the 1960s.

WORKS: *Los arrieros y sus burros por la hermosa capital* (The Mule Drivers and Their Burros Go to the Big City) (1967; 1st staging, May 1967, Teatro Hidalgo), in *Teatro joven de México*, edited by Emilio Carballido (Mexico City: Editorial Novaro, 1973), 103–139; in *Teatro joven de México*, edited by Emilio Carballido (Mexico City: Editores Mexicanos Unidos, 1980), 115–149; (Mexico City: Ediciones INFONAVIT, 1978). *Cosas de muchachos* (Kids' Things) (1968; 1st staging, 1968, Teatro Jiménez Rueda); in *Tramoya* 1–2 (1975): 39–60; *Tramoya* 13 (1978): 4–32; *Más teatro joven*, edited by Emilio Carballido (Mexico City: Editores Mexicanos Unidos, 1982), 65–102; (Mexico City: INFONAVIT, 1978). *Vine, vi y mejor me fui* (I Came, I Saw, I Decided to Leave) (1971; 1st staging, 1975, Festival de Manizales); (Mexico City: Obra Citada, S.A., 1988). *Yo soy Juárez* (I Am Juárez) (1972; 1st staging, 1972, Teatro Independencia), in *Teatro mexicano 1972* (Mexico City: Editorial Aguilar, 1975), 31–96. *Pilo Tamirano Luca* (1973; 1st staging, 1972, Teatro Hidalgo), in *Segundo Concurso Nacional de*

Obras de Teatro: Hombres de México y del Munco. México: Sus Raíces y su Folklore 1973, 3–44. *José* (1975; 1st staging, 1976, Berkeley). *El final del lobo* (1975). *Las propiedades del cerdo* (1976). *Malinche Show* (1977; 1st staging, 1977, Teatro de Estado, Mexicali, B.C.); (Mexico: Ediciones INFONAVIT, 1980). *Y Daniela dijo no* (1987). *Tereso y Leopoldina* (1988). *Comezón de las dos* (1989); in *Doce a las doce* (Mexico City: Obra Citada, 1989), 15–35.

BIBLIOGRAPHY: Ronald D. Burgess, *The New Dramatists of Mexico, (1967–1985)* (Lexington: University Press of Kentucky, 1991). Burgess, "Willebaldo López: Mexico on Stage," *Latin American Theatre Review* 14.2: 27–39.

Ronald D. Burgess

MADERO, Luis Octavio (1908–1964).

He was born in Morelia, Michoacán, and died in Mexico City. He was a journalist, playwright, and diplomat. In Morelia he studied religion and law. He served as Mexican Consul in Barcelona. Madero was a member of the literary group Agorista, founded the daily *El Nacional*, and wrote for it for over thirty years. He holds a doctorate, Honoris Causa, from the University of Barcelona.

WORKS: *El octubre español* (Spanish October) (Mexico City: Talleres Grls. de la Nación, 1935). *Los alzados* (The Rebels, 1935). *Sindicato* (Workers Union, 1936). The volume *Teatro revolucionario* contains the following plays: *Los alzados* (The Rebels), *Sindicato* (Workers Union), and *Cuando ya no vivamos* (When We Are No Longer Alive).

BIBLIOGRAPHY: Humberto Musacchio, *Gran diccionario enciclopédico de México. Visual* (Mexico City: O. Pedagógica, 1990), 1101. Aurora M. Ocampo de Gómez and Ernesto Prado Velázquez, *Diccionario de escritores mexicanos* (Mexico City: UNAM, 1967), 204–205. Alicia G. Welden, "Madero, Luis Octavio," in *Dictionary of Mexican Literature*, ed. Eladio Cortés (Westport, CT: Greenwood Press, 1992), 389.

Mirta A. González

MAGAÑA, Sergio (1924–1990).

Born in Michoacán, Magaña was a novelist, short story writer, theater critic, and dramatist. Although he received degrees in the sciences from the Universidad Nacional Autónoma de México (UNAM), he began his literary career in 1942 with his novel *El Suplicante* (The Supplicant),

which he later adapted to the theater. This was followed by *El molino de aire* (The Windmill), for which he won the literary prize from *El Nacional*, a Mexico City newspaper.

Magaña first started writing works for the theater in 1947. His plays, which include *Moctezuma II, Medea*, and *Los motivos del lobo* (The Wolf's Motives), treat mythological and psychological themes. Dealing with Mexican historical figures such as Moctezuma, Cortés, and La Malinche, Magaña examines Mexican reality as it is reflected in its myth. In his psychological plays, in shocking scenes that can include incest and police brutality, Magaña criticizes the devastation that the real world wreaks upon the innocent and the idealistic.

WORKS: *La noche transfigurada* (The Transfigured Night, 1947). *El suplicante* (The Supplicant, 1950), in *Antología de obras en un acto*, vol. 1: 63–81. *Los signos del zodíaco* (The Zodiac Signs, 1951; 1953), in *Teatro mexicano del siglo XX*, ed. Celestino Gorostiza, III (Mexico City: FCE, 1956), 208–325. *El reloj y la cuna* (The Clock and the Cradle, 1952). *El viaje de Nocresida* (Nocresida's Journey, 1953). *Moctezuma II* (1953), in *Panorama del teatro en México* 1.1 (July 1954): 35–82. *Meneando el bote* (Shaking the Booty, 1954). *El pequeño caso de Jorge Lívido* (The Trivial Case of Jorge Lívido, 1958), in *Teatro mexicano 1958*, ed. Luis G. Basurto (1959). *El anillo de oro* (The Gold Ring, 1960). *Rentas congeladas* (Frozen Rents, 1960). *Los argonautas* (The Argonauts, 1965). *Entre bastidores* (On the Stage, 1965). *Los motivos del lobo* (The Wolf's Motives, 1966). *Ensayando a Molière* (Rehearsing Molière, 1966).

BIBLIOGRAPHY: Mario Beauregard, "Habla Sergio Magaña," *México en la Cultura* 855 (August 1965): 4. Wilberto Cantón, Review of *El pequeño caso de Jorge Lívido, Diorama de la Cultura* (August 1958): 2. Juan García Ponce, "Teatro: El pequeño caso de Jorge Lívido, Universidad de México* 12.12 (August 1958): 28–29. Miguel Guardia, "El teatro en México: *Los signos del zodíaco*," *México en la Cultura* 110 (September 1963): 5–6. Guardia, "Sergio Magaña se enfrenta con honesta valentía a una terrible diosa: La Justicia," *México en la Cultura* 490 (August 1958): 9. Juan Guerrero Zamora, "Dramaturgos mexicanos vistos desde Europa," *México en la Cultura* 757 (September 1963): 4. Malkah Rabel, "Sergio Magaña habla de *Los signos del zodíaco*," *México en la Cultura* 538 (July 1958): 9. Mara

Reyes, Review of *Moctezuma II, Diorama de la Cultura* (July 1965): 5. Carlos Solórzano, "Lo criminal y lo histórico nutren la reaparición de Magaña," *La Cultura en México* 155 (February 1955): xviii–xix. Bruce Swansey, Review of *La última diana, Proceso* 19 (February 1990): 58–59. Fernando Wagner, "Fernando Wagner elije *La Medusa* y *Los argonautas* como las mejores obras de teatro." *El Día* (May 1965): 10.

Stella Clark

MAGDALENO, Mauricio (1906–1986). Born in Villa del Refugio, Zacatecas, Magdaleno studied literature at the Universidad Nacional Autónoma de México (UNAM) and was a novelist, playwright, essayist, teacher, and biographer. He was cofounder of the theatrical group Teatro de Ahora in 1932 and held several political positions, including Secretary of Education. Magdaleno adapted or wrote scripts for at least two dozen movie pictures.

WORKS: *Pánuco 137* (n.d.). *Emiliano Zapata* (n.d.). *Trópico* (Tropic, n.d.). All of his plays were published in the volume *Teatro revolucionario mexicano* (Madrid: Cenit, 1933).

BIBLIOGRAPHY: Madeleine Cucuel, "El Teatro de Ahora': Una tentativa para hacer teatro político en México (1931–1932)," *Tramoya* (October–December 1989): 48–63. Guillermo Schmidhuber, "Díptico sobre el teatro mexicano de los treinta: Bustillo y Magdaleno, Usigli y Villaurrutia," *Revista Iberoamericana* 55.148–149 (July–December 1989): 1221–1237.

Mirta A. González

MARÍA Y CAMPOS, Armando de (1897–1967). He was born and died in Mexico City. He wrote against the American occupation of Veracruz in 1914. He was a journalist, drama critic, playwright, poet, and novelist. Together with Antonio Magaña Esquivel and Francisco Monterde he founded the Drama Critics Guild. In 1917 he founded the daily *El Universal*. María y Campos was a radio announcer between 1933 and 1938. He was managing editor of the journals *Mefistófeles*, *El Heraldo de México*, and *El eco taurino*.

WORKS: *Breve historia del teatro en Chile y de su vida tauromaca* (Brief History of Chile's Theater and Bullfighting, 1940). *Andanzas y picardías de Eusebio Vela, autor y comediante del siglo XVIII* (Adventures and Misadventures of Eusebio Vela, Author and Actor of the XVIII Century, 1944). *Crónicas de teatro de hoy: 1934–1939* (Reviews of the 1946 (Theater File. Reviews from January to December 1946, 1947). *El programa en cien años de teatro en México* (The Program in One Hundred Years of Theater in Mexico, 1950). *Manuel Acuña en su teatro* (Manuel Acuña in His Theater, 1952). *El teatro está siempre en crisis* (The Theater Is Always in Crisis, 1954). *La virgen entre candilejas o el teatro guadalupano* (The Virgin in the Spotlight or the Guadalupe Theater, 1954). *El teatro de género chico en la revolución mexicana* (Brief Theater in the Mexican Revolution, 1956). *El teatro de género dramático en la revolución mexicana* (Dramatic Theater in the Mexican Revolution, 1957). *El teleteatro en México* (Teletheater in Mexico, 1957). *Guía de representaciones teatrales en la Nueva España*; *Siglos XVI al XVIII* (Guide to Theatrical Presentations, XVI to XVIII Centuries). *Manuel Eduardo de Gorostiza en su tiempo* (Manuel Eduardo de Gorostiza in His Time, 1958).

BIBLIOGRAPHY: Silka Freire, "María y Campos, Armando de," in *Dictionary of Mexican Literature*, ed. Eladio Cortés (Westport, CT: Greenwood Press, 1992), 404. Humberto Musacchio, "María y Campos, Armando de," in *Gran diccionario enciclopédico de México. Visual* (Mexico City: O. Pedagógica, 1990), 1132. Aurora M. Ocampo de Gómez and Ernesto Prado Velázquez, *Diccionario de escritores mexicanos* (Mexico City: UNAM, 1967), 212–214.

Alfonso González

MENDOZA, Héctor (1932–). He was born in Apaseo, Guanajuato, and studied political science and literature at the Universidad Nacional Autónoma de México (UNAM) and theater arts at Yale and the Actor's Studio in New York. He is a theater director, acting teacher, and playwright who believes in the primacy of the director over the author's text. He received a Guggenheim Fellowship (1957) and a Centro Mexicano de Escritores Fellowship (1962–1963). In addition, he received the 1953 Juan Ruiz de Alarcón Prize for his play *Las cosas simples* (The Simple Things). Mendoza was assistant director for the Phoenix Theater in New York during 1958–1959. He has been a teacher at the UNAM and at Instituto Nacional de Bellas Artes (INBA) (1960–1972) and chair of the Theater Department of the UNAM in 1973. As acting teacher, he uses some of the methods of Stanislavsky and Strasberg and is credited with the formation of some of the best actors in Mexico today, such as Julieta Egurrola and Héctor Cruz. In his capacity as artistic director, Mendoza played a significant part in the Poesía en Voz Alta group (1956–1957), which is said to represent the maturity of the avant-garde, experimental theater, in Mexico. Both he and his student Luis de Tavira are considered two of Mexico's top experimental directors. He founded the Nucleo de Estudios Teatrales (NET), an acting school, in 1985.

WORKS: *Ahogados* (Drowned, staged at Teatro Colón, 1952). *Las cosas simples* (The Simple Things, staged at Teatro Ideal, 1953). *Sálpicame de amor* (Splash Me with Love, staged at Teatro de la Rotonda, 1954). *La camelia* (The Camellia), in *Revista de la UNAM* (1969). *¡A la Beocia!* (To the Beocia!, staged at Teatro de Arquitectura, 1969). *Los asesinos* (The Murderers, staged at Teatro El Granero, 1969). *Historia de la aviación* (History of Aviation, staged at Teatro Juan Ruiz de Alarcón, 1975). *Bolero* (Bolero, staged at Teatro de la Universidad, 1980). *Noche decisiva en la vida sentimental de Eva Iriarte* (Decisive Evening in the Sentimental Life of Eva Iriarte, 1984). *Del día que murió el señor Bernal dejándonos desamparados* (About the Day That Mr. Bernal Died Leaving Us Homeless, 1985). *La desconfianza* (Untrustworthiness, staged at Teatro Helénico, 1990). *Secretos de familia* (Family Secrets, staged at Teatro Santa Catarina, 1991). *Juicio suspendido* (Abolished Trial, staged at Teatro El Galeón, 1993). *Juicio final* (Final Judgment, staged at Teatro Helénico, 1993). *Misantropias* (Misanthrophies, staged at Teatro Helénico, 1993). *In memoriam* (In Memoriam, based on Manuel Acuña's life, n.d.).

BIBLIOGRAPHY: Javier Galindo Ulloa, Interview, *Unomásuno* 9 (April 1994): 11. Carlos Martínez Rentería, "Héctor Mendoza . . . ," *El Universal Cultural*. 29 (August 1994): 2. María Muro, "Treinta años dedicados al teatro," *Excélsior* 15 (January 1983): n.p. Armando Ponce, Interview, *Proceso* 5 (October 1987): 47–49. María Cristina Ribal, Interview, *Unomásuno*. 4 (May 1988): 23.1

Alfonso González

MONCADA, Luis Mario (1963–   ). He was born in Hermosillo, Sonora, and studied literatura and theater arts at the Universidad Nacional Autónoma de México (UNAM) and

Instituto Nacional de Bellas Artes (INBA) and in several workshops with Miguel A. Tenorio and Vicente Leñero. He is a playwright, actor, and screenwriter. Since 1994 he has served as director of the Centro de Investigaciones Teatrales Rodolfo Usigli (CITRU). His work in the theater is innovative in that he uses videos as well as actors to develop several planes of reality that are somehow linked together. He is recognized as a promising young playwright.

WORKS: *Poesía en voz muda* (Silent Poetry, 1984). *Cuando la soga aprieta* (When the Noose Tightens, 1986). *El destino* (Destiny, staged in Madrid, 1987). *El motel de los destinos cruzados* (The Motel of Crossed Destinies) (Mexico City: Ed. Tierra Adentro, 1992). *Exhivisión* (Exhivision, staged at Sala Julián Carrillo, 1993). *El más negro de todos los mares* (The Darkest of All Seas, staged at Teatro Santa Catarina, 1993). *Alicia detrás de la pantalla* (Alice behind the Screen, staged at Foro Sor Juana, 1995), in *Repertorio* 15 (1994), n.p.

BIBLIOGRAPHY: Victor H. Rascón Banda, Review of *Exhivisión, Proceso* 23 (August 1993): 58.

Alfonso González

NOVO, Salvador (1904–1974). He was born in Mexico City and was a playwright, poet, lawyer, teacher, literary and drama critic, and essayist and a pillar in the development of Mexican theater. Together with Xavier Villaurrutia he founded the prestigious Teatro de Ulises (1927) and was active in the Contemporáneos group. His work in these groups included translating, writing, and acting. He headed the Theater Section of the Instituto Nacional de Bellas Artes (INBA) (1946–1952) and was named chair of the INBA's School of Dramatic Art.

WORKS: *La señorita Remington* (Miss Remington, 1924). *Divorcio* (Divorce, 1924). *El tercer Fausto* (The Third Faust, 1934). *Don Quijote* (Don Quixote, 1947). *El coronel Astucia* (Colonel Astucia, 1948). *La culta dama* (The Learned Lady, 1951). *El joven II* (The Young Man II, 1951). *Diálogos* (Dialogues, 1956). *A ocho columnas* (Full Page Coverage, 1956). *El teatro inglés* (The English Theater, 1960). *Yo casta, o casi* (I Am Chaste, or Almost, 1961). *Ha vuelto Ulises* (Ulysses Has Returned, 1962). *Cuauhtémoc* (Cuauhtémoc, 1962). *In Pipiltzintzin o La guerra de las gordas* (In Pipiltzintzin or

The War of the Fatties, 1963). *El sofá* (The Sofa, 1963). *In Ticitézcatl* (In Ticitézcat, 1965).

BIBLIOGRAPHY: Eladio Cortés, "Salvador Novo y su obra". "Elementos míticos en el teatro de Salvador Novo," in *De literatura hispánica* (Mexico City: EDIMUSA, 1989), 1–14, 35–44. Michele Muncy, *Salvador Novo y su teatro* (Madrid: Atlas, 1970). Muncy, *El Teatro de Salvador Novo* (Mexico City: IMBA, 1974). Muncy, "Novo, Salvador," in *Dictionary of Mexican Literature*, ed. Eladio Cortés (Westport, CT: Greenwood Press, 1992), 467–472. Humberto Musacchio, *Gran diccionario enciclopédico de México. Visual* (Mexico City: O. Pedagógica, 1990), 1367. Kristen F. Nigro, "Rhetoric and History in Three Mexican Plays," *Latin American Theatre Review* 21.1 (1987): 65–73. Aurora M. Ocampo de Gómez and Ernesto Prado Velásquez, *Diccionario de escritores mexicanos* (Mexico City: UNAM, 1967), 254–258.

Alfonso González

OCAMPO, María Luisa (1905–1974). She was born and died in Chilpancingo, Guerrero. She studied business and became a novelist, playwright, and translator. Ocampo was one of the founders and an active member of the theatrical group Los pirandellos. Ocampo first became known in 1923 when her play *Cosas de la vida* (Aspects of Life) was staged. She was head of the Library Section of the Department of National Education.

WORKS: *Cosas de la vida* (Things of Life, 1923). *La quimera* (The Chimera, 1923). *La hoguera* (The Fireplace, 1924). *La jauría* (Pack of Wild Dogs, 1925). *Puedes irte* (You Can Go, 1926). *Las máscaras* (The Masks, 1926). *La sed en el desierto* (Thirst in the Desert, 1927). *Más allá de los hombres* (Beyond Men, 1929). *El corrido de Juan Saavedra* (The Ballad of Juan Saavedra, 1929). *Castillos en el aire* (Castles in the Air, 1931). *La casa en ruinas* (The House in Ruins, 1936). *Una vida de mujer* (A Woman's Life, 1938). *La vírgen fuerte* (The Strong Virgin, 1942). *Al otro día* (The Next Day, 1955). *El valle de abajo* (The Valley Down Below, n.d.). *La seductora* (The Seductress, n.d.). *Tres hermanas* (Tree Sisters, n.d.). *Al cabo la vida está loca* (After All, Life Is Crazy, n.d.). *Como un rayo de sol en el mar* (Like a Sun Ray in the Sea, n.d.).

BIBLIOGRAPHY: Ruth S. Lamb, "Papel de la mujer en la obra teatral de seis escritoras mexicanas," in *Actas del Sexto Congreso Internacional de Hispanistas celebrado en Toronto del 22 al 26 de agosto de 1977* (Toronto, Dept. of Spanish and Portuguese, 1980). Doris Meyer, "'Feminine' Testimony in the Works of Teresa de la Parra, María Luisa Bombal, and Victoria Ocampo," in *Contemporary Women Authors of Latin America: Introductory Essays* (Brooklyn: Brooklyn College Press, 1983).

Mirta A. González

OLMOS, Carlos (1947–). He was born in Tapachula, Chiapas, and studied at the Escuela de Arte Teatral of the Instituto Nacional de Bellas Artes (INBA) under Juan Tovar and Héctor Mendoza. He has gained recognition as a playwright and screenwriter. He was awarded a Centro Mexicano de Escritores Fellowship for 1970–1971 and 1975–1976. In addition, he received the Juan Ruiz de Alarcón Prize in 1981 for his play *La rosa de oro* (The Rose of Gold).

WORKS: *Juegos fatuos* (Frivolous Games, staged at Teatro Bellas Artes, 1968). *Juegos impuros* (Impure Games, 1969). *Juegos profanos* (Profane Games, 1970). *Lenguas muertas* (Dead Languages, 1970). *El brillo de la ausencia* (The Importance of an Absence, 1983). *El dandy del Hotel Savoy* (Hotel Savoy's Dandy, staged at Teatro Sor Juana, 1987). *El eclipse* (The Eclipse, staged at Teatro El Granero, 1990). *Final del viernes* (The End of Friday, staged at Teatro San Jerónimo, 1993). *El presente perfecto* (Present Perfect, n.d.). *Las ruinas de babilonia* (The Ruins of Babylon, n.d.). *La rosa de oro* (The Rose of Gold, n.d.). *En carne propia* (In Your Own Flesh, n.d.).

BIBLIOGRAPHY: Silvina Espinoza de los Monteros, Interview, *El Nacional* 27 (February 1994) 10–13. Humberto Musacchio, *Gran diccionario enciclopédico de México. Visual* (Mexico City: O. Pedagógica, 1990), 491. Luis Enrique Ramírez, Interview (Two parts), *El Financiero Cultural*, July 8, 1991, 74; July 9, 1991, 50–51. Victor H. Rascón Banda, Review of *Final de viernes, Proceso* 18 (October 1993): 57. Patricia Rosas Lopategui, "La exploración onírica en *Lenguas muertas* de Carlos Olmos," *Latin American Theatre Review* 27.2 (Spring 1994): 85–101.

Alfonso González

PEÓN Y CONTRERAS, José (1843–1907). He was born in Mérida, Yucatán, and died in Mexico City. After moving to the capital city he became the director of the San Hipólito Hospital. He served as senator for Yucatán several terms. As a romantic, he wrote historical dramas dealing with both the Indian and Spanish past of Mexico. His play *La hija del rey* (The King's Daughter) is based on Carlos de Sigüenza y Góngora's account of an alleged illegitimate daughter of Philip II who was sent to a Mexican convent.

WORKS: *El castigo de Dios* (God's Punishment staged in Mérida, 1861). *El conde Santiesteban* (The Count Santiesteban, staged in Mérida, 1861). *María la loca* (Mary the Insane, staged in Mérida, 1861). *Hasta el cielo* (Even Heaven, staged at Teatro Principal, 1876). *El sacrificio de la vida* (Life's Sacrifice, staged at Teatro Principal, 1876). *Luchas de honra y amor* (Struggles for Love and Honor, staged at Teatro Principal, 1876). *La hija del rey* (The King's Daughter, staged at Teatro Nacional, 1876). *Gil González de Avila* (Gil González de Avila, staged at Teatro Principal, 1876). *Un amor de Hernán Cortés* (One of Hernán Cortés's Love Affairs, staged at Teatro Principal, 1876). *Antón de Alaminos* (Antón de Alaminos, staged at Teatro Principal, 1876). *Juan de Villalpando* (staged at Teatro Principal, 1876). *Esperanza* (staged at Teatro Principal, 1876). *El conde de Peñalva* (The Count of Peñalva, staged at Teatro Principal, 1877). *La hermita de Santa Fe* (Santa Fe's Hermitage, staged at Teatro Principal, 1877). *Entre mi tío y mi tía* (Between My Aunt and My Uncle, staged at Teatro Arbeu, 1878). *Doña Leonor de Sarabia* (staged at Teatro Nacional, 1878). *Por el joyel de su sombrero* (For the Jewel in Her Hat, staged at Teatro Arbeu, 1878). *El capitán Pedreñales* (Captain Pedreñales, staged at Teatro Principal, 1879). *Vivo o muerto* (Dead or Alive, staged at Teatro Principal, 1879). *Impulsos del corazón* (Impulses of the Heart, 1883). *El umbral de la dicha* (At the Threshold of Happiness, staged at Teatro Principal, 1885). *Gabriela* (Gabriela, staged in Mérida at Teatro Peón Contreras, 1888). *La cabeza de Uconor* (Uconor's Head, staged at Teatro Peón Contreras, 1890). *Laureana: Una tormenta en el mar* (Laureana: A Storm at Sea, 1893). *¡Por la patria!* (For the Fatherland!, staged at Teatro Arbeu, 1894). *Soledad* (Solitude, staged at Teatro Arbeu 1895). *La cruz del perdón* (The Cross of Forgiveness, n.d.). *El bardo* (The Bard, staged at Teatro Rubio de Mazatlán, n.d.).

BIBLIOGRAPHY: Humberto Musacchio, "Peón y Contreras, José," in *Gran diccionario enciclopédico de México. Visual* (Mexico City: O. Pedagógica, 1990), 1524. Aurora M. Ocampo de Gómez and Er-

nesto Prado Velázquez, *Diccionario de escritores mexicanos* (Mexico City: UNAM, 1967), 286–287. Filipa B. Yin, *Dictionary of Mexican Literature*, ed. Eladio Cortés (Westport, CT: Greenwood Press, 1992), 524–525.

Alfonso González

RASCÓN BANDA, Víctor Hugo (1948–   ). A dramatist, lawyer, theater critic, movie and television scriptwriter, and teacher, Rascón Banda was born in Chihuahua, where he studied to be a teacher. At the age of twenty-five he decided to study law, beginning in Chihuahua and finishing in Mexico City. While in law school he began writing plays based on different kinds of law, as study aids. This led to further studies at CADAC (a dramatic arts school) after law school and eventually to several simultaneous successful careers: as a dramatist, as a lawyer, and as a theater critic. Rascón Banda is one of the most consistently staged and published playwrights in Mexico. He writes comedies (*Manos arriba* [Hands Up]), documentary theater (*Homicidio calificado* [Santos]), lyrical historic drama (*Voces en el umbral/La casa del español* [Voices at the Threshold/The Spaniard's House]), social works (*La fiera del Ajusco* [The Wild Women of Ajusco] later, (*La Razon de Elvira*) [Elvira's Cross]), wrestling myths (*Máscara contra Cabellera* [Máscara vs. Caballera]), and even plays in verse to be sung (*Veracruz, Veracruz*). His style is as varied as that of any of his contemporaries, but what is constant is the presence of the law. Nearly all of his plays, in one way or another, have at their center some legal question that helps to move the plot and the dramatic conflict.

WORKS: *Los ilegales* (The Illegals) (1977; 1st staging, June 1978, Universidad Autónoma Metropolitana); (Mexico City: UAM, 1980). *Voces en el umbral* (Voices at the Threshold) (1977; 1st staging Chihuahua, 1984); (Mexico City: Universidad Autónoma Metropolitana, 1983); in *Repertorio* 2.5–6: 39–69; in *Tina Modotti y otras obras de teatro* (Mexico City: Secretaría de Educación Pública, 1986), 9–48; rewritten as *La casa del español* (The Spaniard's House) (1st staging with this title, 1992). *La maestra Teresa* (Teresa the Teacher) (1979). *Las* *armas blancas* (Sharp Weapons) (1980; 1st staging, 1982); (Mexico City: Universidad Nacional Autónoma, 1990) (includes *El abrecartas* [The Letter Opener], 9–44; *La navaja* [The Knife], 45–78; *La daga* [The Dagger], 79–110; *El machete* [The Machete], 111–134). *Tina Modotti* (1980; 1st staging, April 1982); in *Tina Modotti y otras obras de teatro* (Mexico City: Secretaría de Educación Pública, 1986), 101–173. *El baile de los montañeses* (The Dance in the Mountains) (1981; 1st staging, 1982); (Mexico City: Universidad Autónoma del Estado de México, 1982). *Playa azul* (Blue Beach) (1982; 1st staging, Teatro Benito Juárez, 1990); in *Tina Modotti y otras obras de teatro* (Mexico City: Secretaría de Educación Pública, 1986): 49–100. *La fiera del Ajusco* (The Wild Woman of Ajusco) (original title, *La razón de Elvira* [Elvira's Cross], as produced in Los Angeles) (1983; 1st staging, 1985); as *Razón en Repertorio* 2.5–6: 1–38; as *Fiera* in *Teatro del delito* (Mexico City: Editores Mexicanos Unidos, 1985): 109–166. *Manos arriba* (Hands Up) (1983; 1st staging, 1984); in *Teatro del delito* (Mexico City: Editores Mexicanos Unidos, 1985), 39–107. *Máscara contra Caballera* (Máscara vs. Caballera) (1985; 1st staging, 1985); in *Teatro del delito* (Mexico City: Editores Mexicanos Unidos, 1985), 185–251. *Querido Diego te abraza Quiela* (Dear Diego, Quiela Sends Hugs) (1st staging, 1988). *Guerrero negro* (Black Warrior) (Mexico City: Obra Citada, 1988), 11–51. *Cierren las puertas* (Shut the Doors) (Mexico City: Obra Citada, 1988), 53–108. *La banca* (The Bench), in *Doce a las doce* (Mexico City: Obra Citada, 1989), 141–155. *Elena mil veces* (Elena a Thousand Times) (1st staging, 1990). *Luces de Thermidor* (Lights of Thermidor) (1st staging, 1990, UNAM). *Fugitivos* (Fugitives) (1st staging, 1992, Teatro Coyoacán). *Alucinada* (Hallucination) (1st staging, 1992, Teatro Santa Catarina). *Sabor de engaño* (Taste of Deceit) (1st staging, 1993, UNAM); (Mexico City: SOGEM, 1992). *Homicidio calificado* ([El Caso] Santos) (1st staging in English [as "Santos"], 1993, Dallas; 1st staging in Spanish, 1994). *Veracruz, Veracruz* (1994). Prose: *VHRB: De cuerpo entero* (VHRB: Full Length) (Mexico City: Editorial Corunda, 1990). Movies: *Días difíciles* (Hard Days) (1989). *Morir en el golfo* (Die in the Gulf) (1990). *Jóvenes delincuentes* (Delinquent Youth). *Playa azul* (Blue Beach) (1991). *El secreto de la Diana Cazadora* (The Secret of Diana the Hunter) (1993). Television: *Nosotros Los Gómez* (We, the Gómezes). *La navaja* (The Knife) (1993). *La banca* (The Bench) (1993).

BIBLIOGRAPHY: Ronald D. Burgess, *The New Dramatists of Mexico (1967–1985)* (Lexington: University Press of Kentucky, 1991).

Alfonso González

RETES, Ignacio (1918–   ). He was born in Mexico City and studied theater arts at the Universidad Nacional Autónoma de México (UNAM) under Usigli and under Seki Sano. He is a playwright, teacher, scriptwriter for television and the movies, theatrical director, novelist, and drama critic. He founded the theatrical group La linterna mágica (1946–1949). His accomplishments as theatrical director overshadow all of his other work.

WORKS: *El día de mañana* (Tomorrow), in *Letras de México* 1 (July 1945): 103–106. *El aria de la locura* (The Aria of Insanity, 1953). *Una ciudad para vivir* (A City to Live), in *Teatro mexicano del siglo xx* (Mexico City: FCE, 1956), 612–678. *Los hombres del cielo* (The Men from Heaven, staged at Teatro Hidalgo, 1965); *Viento sur* (Southern Wind, n.d.).

BIBLIOGRAPHY: Humberto Musacchio, *Gran diccionario de México. Visual* (Mexico City: O. Pedagógica, 1990), 1709. Aurora M. Ocampo de Gómez and Ernesto Prado Velázquez, *Diccionario de escritores mexicanos* (Mexico City: UNAM, 1967), 316. Margarita Vargas, "Retes, Ignacio," in *Dictionary of Mexican Literature*, ed. Eladio Cortés (Westport, CT: Greenwood Press, 1992), 572.

Mirta A. González

ROBLES ARENAS, Humberto (1922–1984). He was born and died in Mexico City. He studied business and dramatic art at the Mexico City College. He was a playwright and screenwriter. In Veracruz he founded the theatrical company Cómicos de la Legua. In 1962 Jorge Ibargüengoitia predicted that Robles Arenas's play *Los desarraigados* (The Uprooted Ones) would become one of Mexico's classical dramas—and it has. The play, which deals with Mexicans who migrate to the United States, received the Novedades Prize for Theater in 1956 and was filmed on two different occasions, in 1956 and in 1975. He received the Screen Writers' Guild Award for best screenplay for his *Las primeras lluvias* (The First Rains) in 1981.

WORKS: *Trampa para dos marionetas* (A Trap for Two Puppets, 1952). *Manos de lumbre* (Hands of Fire, 1952). *Dos boletos para México* (Two Tickets for Mexico, 1952). *Los desarraigados* (The Uprooted Ones, staged at Teatro El Granero, 1953). *Raíces muertas* (Dead Roots, 1954). *Esfera sin eje* (Sphere without an Axis, 1955). *El forastero* (The Stranger, 1960). *Muñeca de paja* (Straw Doll, 1963). *La voz de la tierra* (The Voice of the Land, 1976). *Romance de Epigmenio Zarsosa o Del ladino tilmado por su propio desatino* (Ballad of Epigmenio Zarsosa or The Trickster Tricked by His Own Lack of Judgement, 1980). *Perfiles de ausencia: La mujer que venció al tiempo* (Profiles of Absence: The Woman Who Defeated Time, 1981).

BIBLIOGRAPHY: David W. Foster, "Theatrical Space and Language: J. Humberto Robles's *Los desarraigados*," *Lenguas Modernas* (Santiago Chile) 20 (1993): 93–103. Adolfo M. Franco, "*Los desarraigados*: Encrucijada entre dos mundos," *Cincinnati Romance Review* 2 (1983): 90–98. Jorge Ibargüengoitia, "Review of *Los desarraigados*, La Cultura en México," *¡Siempre!* 7 (March 1962): 18.

Alfonso González

RODRÍGUEZ GALVÁN, Ignacio (1816–1842). He was born in Tizayuca, Hidalgo, and died in Havana, Cuba, while en route to a diplomatic post in South America. When he became an orphan, he went to work in his uncle's bookstore in Mexico City. He taught himself French and Italian and read extensively in Spanish literature. In addition, he studied Latin and the classics under Francisco Ortega. Along with Fernando Calderón, Rodríguez Galván is said to represent early Mexican Romanticism in poetry and in the theater. Rodríguez Galván's favorite themes are orphanhood, poverty, freedom, and glory. He also wrote about Mexico's ancient Indian leaders and directed the *Calendario de señoritas* (Calendar of Young Girls) in 1838.

WORKS: *La capilla* (The Chapel, 1837). *Muñoz, visitador de México* (Muñoz, Royal Inspector of Mexico, 1838). *El privado del virrey* (The Viceroy's Adviser, 1842). *El precito* (The Small Price, n.d.).

BIBLIOGRAPHY: Humberto Musacchio, *Gran diccionario de México. Visual* (Mexico City: O. Pedagógica, 1990), 1755–1756. Aurora M. Ocampo de Gómez and Ernesto Prado Velázquez, *Diccionario de escritores mexicanos* (Mexico City: UNAM, 1967), 332–333. Emma S. Speratti Piñero, "Lo histórico y lo antihistórico en *Muñoz, visitador de México*," *Revista Iberoamericana* 38 (1954): 321–326. Joseph Vélez, "Rodríguez Galván, Ignacio," in *Dictionary of Mexican Literature*, ed. Eladio Cortés (Westport, CT: Greenwood Press, 1992), 593–594.

Alfonso González

RODRÍGUEZ SOLIS, Eduardo (1938–). He was born in Mexico City and studied engineering at the Universidad Nacional Autónoma de México (UNAM) and dramatic art at the Instituto Nacional de Bellas Artes (INBA). He is a playwright, novelist, short story writer, screenwriter, journalist, and drama critic. During the 1964–1965 school year he was awarded a Centro Mexicano de Escritores Fellowship, and in 1964, he received the INBA Prize for his play *Banderitas de papel picado* (Little Decoration Flags). Rodríguez Solis edited the literary journal *Hojas sueltas* (Loose Leaves) and taught and directed plays in Puerto Rico and the United States.

WORKS: *Banderitas de papel picado* (Little Decoration Flags, 1964). *Las ruedas ruedan* (The Wheels Turn, 1965). *Corrido de Pepe el enamorado* (Ballad of Pepe the Lover, 1966). *Sobre los orígenes del hombre* (About the Origins of Man, staged at the University of Michoacán, 1967). *Black Jack y otra farsa* (Black Jack and One Other Farce, 1968). *Ese viejo no es un viejo, es la esperanza* (That Old Fellow Is Not an Old Person, He Is Hope, 1968). *Teatro para ser leído cuando los aviones no vuelan sobre la ciudad* (Theater to Be Read When the Planes Don't Fly Over the City, 1972). *Entrar y entrar en la galería* (To Enter and Enter into the Gallery, 1972). *Fecho notorio de egolatría pública* (Notorious Fact of Public Self-Worship, 1972). *Agua y jabón para nuestras ventanas* (Soap and Water for Our Windows, 1973). *Helicóptero de miércoles* (Wednesday's Helicopter, 1973). *Una relación cercana al éxtasis* (A Relationship Close to Ecstasy, 1974). *Las ondas de la catrina* (The Waves of the Well-dressed Woman, 1976). *La de los Kintos* (The Girl with the Money, 1979). *069 reportándose* (069 Calling, 1979). *Pas, paz pastorela* (Wham, Peace, Pastorela, 1980). *Opiniones, confesiones y lamentaciones de un verdadero payaso* (Opinions, Confessions, and Laments of a True Clown, 1982). *El encuentro de los agentes secretos* (The Meeting of the Secret Agents, 1982). *Extrema libertad a los paquidermos* (Extreme Freedom to the Pachyderms, 1982). *Guadalupe* (Guadalupe, 1983). *El señor que vestía pulgas* (The Gentleman Who Dressed Fleas, 1985). *El nido de los amantes pobres* (The Nest of the Poor Lovers, 1986). *El pequeño universo del señor Plasco y Doncella vestida de blanco* (The Small Universe of Mr. Plasco and Damsel Dressed in White, n.d.).

BIBLIOGRAPHY: Carlos Solórzano, "Review of *Sobre los orígenes del hombre,* La Cultura en México," *¡Siempre!* 23 (August 1967): 18.

Alfonso González

RUIZ DE ALARCÓN, Juan (1580–1639).

Born in Taxco, Guerrero, he was one of the major dramatists of the Spanish Golden Age. He began his studies at the Royal and Pontifical University in Mexico City but obtained the title of "Bachiller" in Salamanca, Spain, in 1602. After a few years in Spain, he returned to his native Mexico in 1608, where he earned the degree of "Licenciado" in civil and canon law the following year. He also filed all the necessary papers for a doctorate, but it is not known if the degree was conferred. Although he failed to obtain a teaching position at the university while in Mexico City, his legal background helped him secure a position as assistant to the corregidor (mayor). Ruiz de Alarcón returned to Spain in 1613, where, thirteen years later, he became Royal Court reporter. This position gave him satisfaction and financial security. After this, he published two volumes of his works in Spain at his own expense. His first volume includes eight plays, and the second, twelve. He died in Madrid.

Because Juan Ruiz de Alarcón was small in size and physically deformed in his upper torso, he endured the derisive commentaries of some of Spain's prominent literary figures. Through his works and achievements, he equaled and, in some aspects, surpassed his critics. It was during those years of searching for a position of distinction that Ruiz de Alarcón wrote. When he finally reached his lifelong quest, being named Court reporter, he

apparently lost all incentive to write. He never wrote again.

Juan Ruiz de Alarcón's contribution to Golden Age theater is unique. According to critics, Spanish Golden Age drama is characterized by an emphasis on the action, a preoccupation with the themes of "honra" and "honor," and a lack of psychological insight. Ruiz de Alarcón's theater shares the first two characteristics, but it reveals greater psychological development of the characters. Also, Ruiz de Alarcón is said to be one of the first modern dramatists to deal with morality. Writers such as Moreto, Moratín, Corneille, Molière, and López de Ayala are indebted, in one way or another, to Ruiz de Alarcón's works.

Two of Ruiz de Alarcón's best-known works are *La verdad sospechosa* (The Truth Suspect), which explores the implications of lying, and *Las paredes oyen* (The Walls Have Ears), a play with obvious autobiographical elements: Despite being poor, deformed, and unlucky, the protagonist succeeds.

WORKS: *Parte primera de las comedias de don Juan Ruiz de Alarcón y Mendoza* (First Part of the Comedies of Don Juan Ruiz de Alarcón and Mendoza) (Madrid, n.p., 1628). It contains the following plays: *Los favores del mundo* (The Favors of the World), *La industria y la suerte* (Industry and Fortune), *Las paredes oyen* (The Walls Have Ears), *El semejante a sí mismo* (He Who Resembles Himself), *La cueva de Salamanca* (The Cave of Salamanca), *Mudarse por mejorarse* (A Change to Better Oneself), *Todo es ventura* (Everything Is Luck), *El desdichado en fingir* (The Unlucky Pretender). *Parte segunda de las comedias del licenciado Don Juan Ruiz de Alarcón* (Second Part of the Comedies of Don Juan Ruiz de Alarcón) (Barcelona: n.p., 1634). The second part includes the following: *Los empeños de un engaño* (The Consequences of a Lie), *El dueño de las estrellas* (The Owner of the Stars), *La amistad castigada* (Friendship Punished), *La manganilla de Melilla* (The Scheme of Melilla), *La verdad sospechosa* (The Truth Suspect), *Ganar amigos* (To Win Friends), *El Anticristo* (The Anti-Christ), *El tejedor de Sevilla* (The Weaver of Seville), *La prueba de las promesas* (The Proof of Promises), *Los pechos privilegiados* (The Privileged Ones), *La crueldad por el honor* (Cruelty on Account of Honor), *Examen de* *maridos* (An Examination for Husbands). *Teatro completo de Don Juan Ruiz de Alarcón*, ed. Ermilo Abreu Gómez (Mexico City: Cía. Gral. de Ediciones, 1951).

BIBLIOGRAPHY: Antonio Castro Leal, *Juan Ruiz de Alarcón, su vida y su obra* (Mexico City: Cuadernos Americanos, 1943). Alfonso González, "Ruiz de Alarcón, Juan" in *Dictionary of Mexican Literature*, ed. Eladio Cortés (Westport, CT: Greenwood Press, 1992), 608–609. Julio Jiménez Rueda, *Juan Ruiz de Alarcón y su tiempo* (Mexico City: Porrúa, 1939). Aurora M. Ocampo de Gómez and Ernesto Prado Velázquez, *Diccionario de escritores mexicanos* (Mexico City: UNAM, 1967), 392–393. Walter Poesse, *Juan Ruiz de Alarcón* (New York: Twayne, 1972). Alice M. Pollin, "The Religious Motive in the Plays of Juan Ruiz de Alarcón," *Hispanic Review* 29 (1961): 33–44.

Mirta A. González

URTUSÁSTEGUI, Tomás (1933–   ). He was born in Mexico City and studied medicine at the Universidad Nacional Autónoma de México (UNAM) and theater arts under Vicente Leñero and Hugo Argüelles. He retired from medicine in 1993 but he is still an active and successful playwright. One of the most prolific playwrights, Urtusástegui has written to date ninety-two plays, sixty of which have been staged, twenty published, and eleven have won prizes. He has taught theater arts throughout the country and in Central and South America. He has also won recognition for his children's plays. Only those works that have been staged and/or published are listed.

WORKS: *Cinco monólogos* (Five Monologues, 1984). *Ponte en mi lugar* (Place Yourself in My Place, 1984). *Cuando veas la cola de tu vecino arrancar* (When You See Your Neighbor's Tail Taken Off, staged at Foro Shakespeare, 1984). *El poder de los hombres* (The Power of Men, 1984). *La canción del sapito cro-cro* (The Song of the Little Toad Cro-Cro, staged at Teatro Wilberto Cantón, 1984). *El manzano prodigioso* (The Marvelous Apple Tree, 1984). *El niño que podía leer el mañana* (The Child That Could Read the Future, 1984). *Al fin niños* (Children After All, 1984). *Profanación* (Profanation, 1985). *Venado sol, coyote luna* (Moon Coyote, Sun Deer, staged in Hermosillo, Sonora, 1985). *Huele a gas* (It Smells Like Gas, 1985) (Mexico City: Ed. Mexicanos Unidos, 1985). *Ruega por no-*

sotros (Pray for Us, 1985). *Sabes, voy a tener un hijo* (You Know, I Am Going to Have a Baby, 1985). *Y retiemble en sus centros la tierra* (And Let the Earth Tremble in Its Center, 1985). *Baldomero verdadero* (True Baldomero, 1985). *Arbol del tiempo* (The Tree of Time, 1985). *La nueva arca de Noé* (Noah's New Ark, 1985). *El fabricante de nubes* (The Cloud Maker, 1985). *Tiempo de heroísmo* (Time for Heroism, staged at Castillo de Chapultepec, 1986). *Más allá* (Farther Away, 1986). *Agua clara* (Clear Water, staged at Escuela de Arte ANDA, 1987). *Yo te quiero, tú me quieres, eso está muy bien* (I Love You, You Love Me, That's Very Good, 1987). *Sólo para hombres* (For Men Only, 1987). *Hoy estreno* (Premiere Today, staged in Guadalajara, 1987). *Hombre y mujer* (Man and Woman, 1987). *Yo sólo sé que te vas, yo sólo sé que me quedo* (All I Know Is That You Are Leaving, All I Know Is That I'm Staying Behind, 1987). *El lápiz rojo* (The Red Pencil, 1987). *Libertad de expresión* (Freedom of Expression, 1988). *Cupo limitado* (Limited Occupancy, staged at Foro La Conchita, 1988). *Apenas son las cuatro* (It's Only Four, 1989). *Drácula gay* (Gay Dracula, staged at Foro Gandhi, 1991); (Mexico City: La Cultura en México,); in *Siempre* 27 July 1994: 58–59). *La duda* (The Doubt, staged at Teatro Sergio Magaña, 1991). *Vida . . . estamos en paz* (Life . . . We Are at Peace, staged at Teatro El Juglar, 1991). *La duda* (Doubt, staged at Centro Cultural Helénico, 1991). *Ixtaccihuatl o El idilio de los volcanes* (Ixtaccihuatl or The Idyl of the Volcanoes, staged at IPN Auditorio A. Cuspinera, 1992). *Carretera del norte* (Northern Highway, staged at T. Ismael Rodríguez, 1992). *Luz del día* (Light of Day) (México: Ed. Gaceta, 1994). *Eternidad* (Eternity) (Mexico: Instituto Nacional para la Educacion de los Adultos, 1994). *Macarenazo* (Macarena Blow, coauthored with Alejandro Licona, staged at Carpa Geodésica, 1995). *Danzón dedicado a . . .* (This Musical Selection Is Dedicated to . . . , staged in Veracruz, Ver., n.d.). *Galopa, galopa* (Ride, Ride, staged at El Juglar, n.d.). *Automovil* (Automobile, staged at Casa de la Cultura in Monterrey) (n.d.). *No fornicarás* (Thou Shall Not Fornicate) (México: *Siempre*, n.d.). *Robustiano* (staged at Foro Ghandi, n.d.). *Sangre de mi sangre* (My Own Blood, staged at Casa de la Paz, n.d.). *La visita* (The Visit, n.d.). *La hoguera* (The Bonfire, n.d.). *¿Sabes? ¡Voy a tener un hijo!* (You know What? I'm Going to Have a Baby! n.d.).

BIBLIOGRAPHY: Humberto Musacchio, *Gran diccionario de México. Visual* (Mexico City: O. Pedagógica, 1990), 2110–2111. Victor H. Rascón

Banda, Review of *Sangre de mi sangre*, *Proceso* 18 (June 1992): 59. Rascón Banda, Review of *La duda*, *Proceso* 9 (March 1992): 55.

Alfonso González

URUETA, Margarita (1913 or 1918–?). A playwright and fiction writer, she was born in Mexico City on November 13, 1913 or 1918. From a well-known family of politicians, she became president of the Teatro de México in 1945. After writing soap operas and programs for television, she traveled throughout Europe, where she started writing plays that she staged upon her return to Mexico.

WORKS: *San lunes, Una hora de vida,* and *Mansión para turistas* (Saint Monday, One Hour to Live, Mansion for Tourists) (Mexico City: Ed. Quetzal, 1943). *Ave de sacrificio* (Sacrificial Bird) (Mexico City: Letras de México, 1945). *Teatro nuevo: Las máquinas devoran a una señorita llamada Rivela, o El dios laico; Graju; La mujer transparente; Angel de justicia, o el señor perro* (New Theater: The Machines Devour a Young Woman Named Rivela, or The Secular God; Graju; The Transparent Woman; Angel of Justice or Mr. Dog) (Mexico City: Joaquín Mortiz, 1953). *Duda infinita* (Infinite Doubt, 1959). *La mujer transparente* (The Transparent Woman, 1964). *Juanito Membrillo* (1964). *La pastorela de las tres Marías* (The Shepherd's Song of the Three Marys, 1964). *El hombre y su máscara* (The Man and His Mask, 1964). *Poderoso caballero es don dinero* (A Powerful Gentleman Is Sir Money, 1965). *La muerte de un soltero* (The Death of a Single Man, 1966).

BIBLIOGRAPHY: Aurora M. Ocampo de Gómez and Ernesto Prado Velázquez, *Diccionario de escritores mexicanos* (Mexico City: UNAM, 1967), 392–393. Margarita Vargas, "Urueta, Margarita," *Dictionary of Mexican Literature,* ed. Eladio Cortés (Westport, CT: Greenwood Press, 1992), 681–682.

Alfonso González

USIGLI, Rodolfo (1905–1979). Born in Mexico City, he is considered Mexico's most influential dramatist. He taught dramatic arts at the Universidad Nacional Autónoma de México (UNAM) and Yale University and served as director of the National Institute of Fine Arts (INBA). Between 1944 and 1973 he held diplomatic posts in England, France, Belgium, Norway, and Lebanon. In 1973 he received the

Premio Nacional de Literatura. As a mentor and teacher, he was recognized as the founder of Mexican theater, having influenced the careers of some of Mexico's most important dramatists. Among his disciples were Emilio Carballido and Luisa Josefina Hernández.

Like many postrevolutionary writers, Usigli advocated the creation of a national literature that would reflect his country's political and social reality. Through themes often based on Mexican history, Usigli sought to criticize and to educate his countrymen as well as to urge them to develop an awareness of their national psyche. In one of his plays, *El gesticulador* (The Impostor), for example, Usigli attacks political corruption. *Corona de sombra* (Crown of Shadows) looks back at a traumatic episode in Mexican history from the perspective of the present. Although he stressed Mexican themes, however, Usigli allowed the spectator to transcend national boundaries to a universal understanding of mankind's foibles. As a result, his plays have become classics of Mexican literature and are widely read, studied, and performed.

WORKS: *El apóstol* (The Apostle, 1931). *Falso drama* (False Play, 1932). *4 Chemins 4* (1932). *México en el teatro* (1932); translated by Wilder P. Scott as *Mexico in the Theater* (University: University of Mississippi Press, 1976). *Noche de estío* (Summer's Night, 1933). *Caminos del teatro en México* (Theater Pathways in Mexico, 1933). *La última puerta* (The End Door, 1934). *El presidente y el ideal* (The President and the Ideal, 1935). *Estado de secreto* (State of Secrecy, 1935). *Alcestes* (1936). *El niño y la niebla* (The Boy and the Fog, 1936). *Medio tono* (Half Beat, 1937). *Otra primavera* (Another Springtime, 1937); translated by Wayne Wolfe as *Another Springtime* (New York, Samuel French, 1961). *Mientras amemos* (As Long as We Love, 1937). *La mujer no hace milagros* (The Woman Cannot Do Miracles, 1938). *Aguas estancadas* (Stagnant Waters, 1938). *El gesticulador* (1938); translated by Annabel Clark as *The Gesticulator* in "An English Translation of Three Modern Mexican Plays by Rodolfo Usigli" (Ph.D. diss., University of Denver, 1971). *Sueño de día* (Daydream, 1940). *Itinerario del autor dramático* (The Dramatist's Itinerary, 1940). *La familia cena en casa* (The Family Dines at Home, 1942). *Dios, Batidillo y la mujer* (God, Batidillo and the Woman, 1943). *Corona de sombra* (1943); translated by William F. Stirling as *Crown of Shadows* (London: A. Wingate, 1946). *La función de despedida* (The Farewell Ceremony, 1949). *Las madres* (The Mothers, 1949). *Los fugitivos* (The Fugitives, 1950). *Jano es una muchacha* (1952); translated by Annabel Clark as *Janus Is a Girl* in *Translation of Three Modern Mexican Plays* (1971). *Un día de éstos* (1953); translated by Thomas Bledsoe as *One of These Days* in *Two Plays: Crown of Light and One of These Days* (Carbondale: Southern Illinois University Press, 1971). *La exposición* (The Exposition, 1955). *La diadema* (The Tiara, 1960). *Un navío cargado de . . .* (A Ship Loaded with . . . 1961); in *Tres comedias inéditas* (Three Unpublished Plays, 1967). *El testamento y el viudo* (The Will and the Widower, 1962); in *Tres comedias inéditas* (Three Unpublished Plays, 1967). *Teatro completo* (Complete Works I, 1963; II, 1966). *El encuentro* (The Encounter, 1963); in *Tres comedias inéditas* (Three Unpublished Plays, 1967). *Corona de luz* (1963); translated as *Crown of Light* by Annabel Clark in *An English Translation of Three Modern Mexican Plays* (1971) and Thomas Bledsoe in *Two Plays: Crown of Light and One of These Days* (1971). *Carta de amor* (Love Letter, 1968). *El gran circo del mundo* (The World's Great Circus, 1968; 1969). *Los viejos: Diálogo imprevisto en un acto* (The Old People: Unexpected Dialogue in One Act, 1971). *¡Buenos días, señor Presidente!* (Good Morning, Mr. President!, 1972). *Teoría y praxis del teatro en México*, ed. Sergio Jiménez and Edgar Ceballos (Mexico City: Grupo Editorial Gaceta, 1982).

BIBLIOGRAPHY: Robert K. Anderson, "Usigli, Rodolfo," in *Dictionary of Mexican Literature*, ed. Eladio Cortés (Westport, CT: Greenwood Press, 1992), 682–685. Deborah Cohen J., "Reading Toward Performance: A Critical Reevaluation of Selected Plays by Rodolfo Usigli" (Ph.D. diss.; 1992). Timothy Compton, "Máscaras mexicanas" in Rodolfo Usigli's *Jano es una muchacha*," *Latin American Theatre Review* 25.1 (Fall 1991): 63–71. Denise M. DiPuccio, "Metatheatrical Histories in Corona de luz," *Latin American Theatre Review* 20.1 (Fall 1984): 29–36. Mark S. Finch, "Rodolfo Usigli's *Corona de sombra, Corona de fuego, Corona de luz*: The Mythopoesis of Antihistory," *Romance Notes* 22.2 (Winter 1981): 151–154. Myra S. Gann, "*El gesticulador*: Tragedy or Didactic Play?" *Inti* 32–33 (Fall–Spring 1991): 148–157. Fernando de Ita, "*La danza de la pirámide*: Historia, exaltación y crítica de las nuevas tendencias del teatro en México," *Latin American Theatre Review* 23.1 (Fall 1989): 9–17. Andrea Labinger, "Age, Alienation and the Artist in Usigli's *Los viejos*," *Latin American Theatre Review*

14.2 (Spring 1981): 41–47. Catherine Larson, "No conoces el precio de las palabras: Language and Meaning in Usigli's *El gesticulador*," *Latin American Theatre Review* 20.1 (Fall 1986): 21–28. Ramón Layera, "Mecanismos de fabulación y mitificación de la historia en las comedias impolíticas' y las coronas de Rodolfo Usigli," *Latin American Theatre Review* 18.2 (Spring 1985): 49–55. Gerardo Luzuriaga, "Rodolfo Usigli y Estados Unidos," *Gestos* 7.14 (November 1992): 191–195. Mariana M. Matteson, "On the Function of the Imposter in the Plays of Rodolfo Usigli," *Selecta: Journal of the Pacific Northwest Council on Foreign Languages* 2 (1981): 120–123. Barbara Ann McFarlin-Kosiec, "An Examination of the Leadership Role of Rodolfo Usigli Through the Translation and Literary Analysis of His Play: Jano es una muchacha" (Ph.D. diss., 1986). Priscilla Meléndez, "La antihistoria' y la metaficción en *Corona de sombra* de Rodolfo Usigli," *La Torre* 4.13 (January–March 1990): 46–69. Mabel Morana, "Historicismo y legitimación del poder en *El gesticulador* de Rodolfo Usigli," *Revista Iberoamericana* 55.148–149 (July–December 1989): 1261–1275. Arthur A. Natela, "Christological Symbolism in Rodolfo Usigli's *El gesticulador*," *Discurso* 5.2 (Spring 1988): 455–461. Kirsten Nigro, "Light and Darkness in Usigli's *Corona de sombra*," *Chasqui* 17.2 (November 1988) 27–34. Nigro, "On Reading and Responding to (Latin American) Playtexts," *Gestos* 2.4 (November 1987): 101–113. Dennis Perri, "The Artistic Unity of *Corona de sombra*," *Latin American Theatre Review* 15.1 (Fall 1981): 13–19. Laura Rosana Scarano, "Correspondencias estructurales y semánticas entre *El gesticulador* y *Corona de sombra*," *Latin American Theatre Review* 22.1 (Fall 1988): 29–36. Rosana Scarano, "Metateatro e identidad en *Saverio El Cruel* de Roberto Arlt y *El gesticulador* de Rodolfo Usigli," *Alba de América* 6.10–11 (July 1988): 199–207. Guillermo Schmidhuber de la Mora, "El advenimiento del teatro mexicano: Años de esperanza y curiosidad" (Ph.D. diss. 1990). Schmidhuber de la Mora, "Buero y Usigli: Dos teatros y un abismo," *Estreno* 12.2 (Fall 1986): 6–8. Schmidhuber de la Mora, "Díptico sobre el teatro mexicano de los treinta: Bustillo y Magdalena, Usigli y Villaurrutia," *Revista Iberoamericana* 55.148–149 (July–December 1989): 1221–1227. David Jon Schuster, "A Critical Introduction to Three Plays of the Mexican Revolution: Rodolfo Usigli, *El gesticulador*; Vicente Leñero, *El juicio*; Jorge Ibargüengoitia, *El atentado*" (Ph.D. diss. 1987). Lilian E. Solhaune. "Signos lingüísticos y no lingüísticos en *Corona de luz* de Rodolfo Usigli," *Dispositio* 13.33–

35 (1988): 235–249. Ilan Stavans, "De regreso al *Ensayo de un crimen*," *Revista Iberoamericana* 56.151 (April–June 1990): 519–521. Daniel Zalacaín and Esther P. Mocega-González, "El ciclo vital heroico en *El gesticulador*," *The Language Quarterly* 22.3–4 (Spring-Summer 1984): 35–38.

Stella Clark

VELA, Eusebio (1688–1737). He was born in Toledo, Spain, and died in Veracruz. He is one of the most important theatrical figures in eighteenth-century Mexico. He was a playwright, actor, and impresario. His professional work in the new world underlies the rise in popularity of commercial, secular theater in Mexico. He came to Mexico in 1713 and spent the rest of his life there. The administration of the Coliseo (The Public Theater House) was overseen by the viceroy, who gave Vela permission and money to import professional actors and dancers from Spain. The Gaceta de México, founded in 1728, reports the staging of several of Eusebio Vela's plays, and in 1733, the journal reports that, up to that time, he had authored more than eleven plays. Apparently one of his friends took the manuscripts of three of his plays to Spain, and these were published again in 1948.

WORKS: *Tres comedias de Eusebio Vela: Apostolado de las Indias y martirio de un cacique, Si el amor excede al arte, ni amor ni arte a la prudencia, La pérdida de España* (Three Comedies by Eusebio Vela: Apostolate of the Indies and Martyrdom of a Cacique. If Love Surpasses Art, Nor Love, Nor Art to Prudence. The Loss of Spain), ed. Jefferson Rea Spell and Francisco Monterde (Mexico City: Imp. Universitaria, 1948).

BIBLIOGRAPHY: Armando de María y Campos. Andanzas y picardías de Eusebio Vela, autor y comediante del siglo XVIII (1944). Jefferson Rea Spell, "Three Manuscripts Plays by Eusebio Vela," *Revista de Estudios Hispánicos* 1 (1928): 268–273.

Ronald D. Burgess

VELÁSQUEZ TURRUBIARTES, Gerardo (1949–). A dramatist, teacher, scriptwriter, theater critic and commentator, director of Primera Llamada, and chemical engineer, Velásquez was born in Cárdenas, San Luis Potosí. He went to Mexico City on a whim and stayed

to study chemical engineering. One day he and a group of friends, looking for a particular office at the university, mistakenly wandered into a casting session for a play. From that point on, theater occupied his time and his energies. He began writing during a time when the public and producers looked down on Mexican drama, and he was one of a small number of dramatists who continued writing during the slowest period, 1974 to 1978. He can be credited with a number of firsts. He was one of the first writers of his generation to use settings in small towns, that is to say, out of Mexico City; his early works featured women as central characters; he helped lead the way in developing an interest in Mexican history as thematic material for plays (*Vía libre* and *Aunque vengas en figura distinta, Victoriano Huerta*, for example [Open Track; Although You Look Different, Victoriano Huerta]). His multilevel works are among the more difficult of the generation, and that contributed to the low number of stagings of his plays. A good example is *El cuarto más tranquilo* (The Quietest Room). It is nearly impossible to determine exactly what happens as the play twists and turns on itself somewhat in the manner of the Mexican novel *Pedro Páramo*. By the mid-1990s the obstacle to staging appeared to be disappearing, and opportunities for professional productions began to appear.

WORKS: Theater: *Ahí vienen las aleluyas* (Here Come the Hallelujas) (1969; 1st staging, 1970); in *Aleluyas para Dos Desempleos y un Tema de Amor* (Cuatro obras del Taller de Composición Dramática del IPN) (Mexico City: IPN, 1970), 85–125; in *Teatro joven de México*, edited by Emilio Carballido (Mexico City: Editorial Novaro, 1973), 51–75. *Chana volante o la jaula de los canarios* (Chana Volante or the Canary Cage) (1973); in *Tramoya* 4 (1976): 28–37; in *El Cuento* (January–February 1977): 207–214. *El cuarto más tranquilo* (The Quietest Room) (1974; 1st staging, 1975); in *Tramoya* 4 (1976): 10–18; in *Rubor helado* (Mexico City: Instituto Politécnico Nacional, 1987), 63–74; in *Punto de Partida* 49–50 (1975): 131–135. *En "El Gato Negro"* (In "The Black Cat") (1974; 1st staging, 1978); in *Tramoya* 4 (1976): 18–28. *Las viudas* (The Widows) (1974); in *Rubor helado* (Mexico City: Instituto Politécnico Nacional, 1987), 81–90. *Agua de limón* (Lemonade) (1974; 1st staging, 1977); in *Tra-*

moya 4 (1976): 37–49. *Amapola* (Poppy) (1974); in *Tramoya* 4 (1976): 49–60. *Una ciudad grande y lejana* (A Large, Distant City) (1975); in *Tramoya* 4 (1976): 72–84. *Un patio a oscuras* (A Darkened Patio) (1976); in *Tramoya* 4 (1976): 61–72. *La huerta* (The Garden) (1976). *Toño Basura* (Tony Trash) (1977). *Sobre las lunas* (Over the Moons) (1978; 1st staging, 1979); in *Rubor helado* (Mexico City: Instituto Politécnico Nacional, 1987), 91–131. *Vía libre* (Open Track) (1979); in *Rubor helado* (Mexico City: Instituto Politécnico Nacional, 1987), 19–61; in *Punto de Partida* 68–69 (1980): 56–90. *Hasta hacernos polvo juntos* (Until We Turn to Dust Together) (1980); in *Rubor helado* (Mexico City: Instituto Politécnico Nacional, 1987), 75–80; in "Diorama," in *Excélsior*, October 19, 1980, 10. *Aunque vengas en figura distinta, Victoriano Huerta* (Although You Look Different, Victoriano Huerta) (1983) (Mexico City: INBA and Editorial Katún, 1985). *No sé nada: No se nada* (I Don't Know Anything: No Swimming) (1989); in *Tribuna*, December 9, 1989, 24–25. *Una flecha en el aire (Consentida)* (An Arrow in the Air [Spoiled]) (1994); in *El centavo* 17.179 (June 1994): 10–15. *Quisiera ser un pez* (I'd Like to Be a Fish) (1994); in *Primera Llamada* 2.5 (August 1994): 16. Stories: "Aquella madrugada en Aconcá" (That Morning in Aconcá); in *Juego de Palabras* 1 (1971): 4–5. Poetry: "Ayerhoy" (Yesterdaytoday); in *Juego de Palabras* 1 (1971): 4. "Poemas" (Poems); in *Punto de Partida* 23–24 (1971): 10–24. "Todo parece que comenzó en octubre (Everything Seems to Have Begun in October); in *El Sol de San Luis*, October 18, 1971.

BIBLIOGRAPHY: Ronald D. Burgess, "Gerardo Velásquez: Pieces of the Puzzle," *Latin American Literary Review* 8.1: 5–9. Burgess, *The New Dramatists of Mexico (1967–1985)* (Lexington: University Press of Kentucky, 1991).

Ronald D. Burgess

VILALTA, Maruxa (1932–   ). Born in Barcelona, Spain, on September 23, 1932 (Hopzafel places her year of birth at 1931), Maruxa Vilalta emigrated to Mexico along with other exiled Republicans and became a Mexican citizen. It was in Mexico that she received her training in newspaper work and in literary writing. She took classes at the Franco-Mexican School, at the School of Philosophy and Letters of the Universidad Nacional Autónoma de México (UNAM) and at Cambridge University. She has been a reporter for the daily *Excelsior*,

has directed television programs such as "Mujeres que trabajan" (Women Who Work), and also has done commentary on politics, theater, and entertainment. She has traveled to Europe, the United States, and Canada.

Maruxa Vilalta began by writing novels and short stories, and the latter have been published in various dailies and journals, but it is in the theater that she has known her greatest successes. Her first work was the adaptation of one of her novels: *Los desorientados* (The Confused), an accusation directed against present-day youth, whose lives and interests wind up being destroyed and impaired by the incomprehension of their parents and by their own egotism and overblown ambitions. Her second work, *Un país feliz* (A Happy Country), develops the problem of propaganda versus reality in countries run by dictators. *El 9* (The 9) is a play about the mechanization of humanity. *Cuestión de narices* (A Matter of Noses) and *La última letra* (The Last Letter) both treat, in Absurdist terms, the problem of people whose words express love for one another while their speech and other actions are hostile and violent.

In general, Maruxa Vilalta's theater is characterized by her concerns for society and by a great mastery of theatrical form. Her work is viewed at times to be essentially naturalistic, at others absurd. Her theater is also frequently marked by violence, if not physical at least psychological. It is consistently sociopolitical, protesting the contemporary condition of mankind, but there is an underlying recognition that the sociopolitical problems are products of the individuals who also create them. Her works are often circular, ending where they began with no apparent progress or resolution for the problems presented, and thus they reinforce the notion that we cannot improve society without changing the individual, and conversely, we cannot alter the individual without revamping society, in a never-ending vicious circle of inertia.

WORKS: *Los desorientados* (The Confused), premiered in Mexico in 1960; 2nd stage performance, 1965 (Mexico City: Col. Teatro Mexicano, 1958); 2nd ed. (Libro-Mex, 1960); 3rd ed. (Eds. Ecuador, 1965); (Mexico City: FCEI, 1972). *Un país feliz* (A Happy Country), premiered in 1963 (Mexico City:

Eds. Ecuador, 1964). *La última letra* (The Last Letter) (Mexico City: Costa Amic, 1960; Mexico City: FCE, 1972). *Soliloquio del tiempo* (Soliloquy of Time) (Mexico City: Eds. Ecuador, 1964; Mexico City: FCE, 1972). *Trio (Soliloquio del tiempo, Un día loco* [A Crazy Day], and *La última letra*), one-act plays, premiered in 1964 (Mexico City: Col. Teatro Mexicano, no. 23, 1965). *El 9* (The 9), premiered in 1965 (Mexico City: Eds. Ecuador, 1965; Mexico City: FCE, 1972). *Cuestión de narices* (A Matter of Noses), premiered in 1966 (Mexico City: FCE, 1972). *Esta noche juntos, amándonos tanto* (Tonight, Together, Loving Each Other So Much) (Mexico City: FCE, 1972). *Teatro* (Theater) (Mexico City: Ed. Joaquin Mortiz, 1981). *Nada como el piso* (Nothing like a Flat) (Mexico City: Ed. Joaquin Mortiz, 1984). Anthologies and Prologues: *Antologías de obras en un acto*, selection and prologue, 3 vols. (Mexico City: Col. Teatro Mexicano, 1959, 1960, and 1965). Translation: Albert Husson, *El sistema Fabrizzi*, translated from the French by Maruxa Vilalta, premiered in Mexico under the direction of Maruxa Vilalta, in 1966.

BIBLIOGRAPHY: François Baguer, "Escena," review of *Un país feliz, Excelsior* (January 17, 1964). Grace Bearse and Lorraine Elena Roses, "Maruxa Vilalta: Social Dramatist," *Revista de Estudios Hispánicos* 18.3 (October 1984): 399–406. Joan Rea Boorman, "Contemporary Latin American Woman Dramatists," *Rice University Studies* 64 (1978): 69–80. Peter Broad, "Vilalta, Maruxa," *Dictionary of Mexican Literature*, ed. Eladio Cortés (Westport, CT: Greenwood Press, 1992), 712–715. Jeanine S. Gaucher-Shultz, "La temática de dos obras premiadas de Maruxa Vilalta," *Latin American Theatre Review* 12.2 (1979): 87–90. Sigfredo Gordon, "La escena," review of *Un país feliz, Ultimas Noticias* (January 18, 1964). Tamara Holzapfel, "The Theatre of Maruxa Vilalta: A Triumph of Versatility," *Latin American Theatre Review* 14.2 (Spring 1981): 11–18. Antonio Magaña Esquivel, review of *Un país feliz, El Nacional* (August 15, 1964): 3. "Maruxa Vilalta busca su segundo triunfo," *Revista Mexicana de Cultura* 908 (August 23, 1964): 1 1. *Medio siglo de teatro mexicano, 1900–1961* (Mexico City: INBA, 1964), 124, 163. "Reposición de *Los desorientados*," *El Nacional* (March 12, 1965): 5, (March 13, 1965): 5. "Buen momento del teatro mexicano," *Revista Mexicana de Cultura* 939 (March 28, 1965): 1 1. Review of *Trío, Revista Mexicana de Cultura* 962 (September 5, 1965): 1 1. Review of *El 9*, in *El Nacional* (October 15, 1965): 5; also in *Revista Mexicana de Cultura* 970 (October 31, 1965): 11. Sharon Magnarelli, *The Lost Rib* (Lewiston, PA: Bucknell University Press, 1985). "Esta noche juntos, amándonos tanto, de Maruxa Vilalta," *Plural* (Revista Cultural de *Excélsior*) 1.205 (October 18, 1988): 30–32. "Discourse as Content and Form in the Works of Maruxa Vilalta," *Hispanic Journal* 9.2 (Spring 1988): 99–111. "Contenido y forma en la obra de Maruxa Vilalta," *Plural* 12.192 (September 16, 1987): 77–78. Maria Luisa Mendoza, "Dos damas de vanguardia," *El Gallo Ilustrado* 173 (October 17, 1965): 4. Review of *Cuestión de narices, El Gallo Ilustrado* 222 (September 25, 1966): 4. Beth Miller and Alfonso González, eds., "Maruxa Vilalta," in *26 autoras del México actual* (Mexico City: Costa Amic, 1978), 405–417. Gloria V. Morales, "Maruxa Vilalta: Un teatro que rompe con lo tradicional," *Plural* 12.192 (September 1987): 72–75. Kirsten F. Nigro et al., eds., "*Esta noche juntos, amándonos tanto*, de Maruxa Vilalta: Texto y representación," in *Actas del Sexto Congreso Internacional de Hispanistas celebrado en Toronto del 22 al 26 agosto de 1977*, edited by Alan M. Gordon (Toronto: Department of Spanish, 1979).

Peter G. Broad

VILLAURRUTIA, Xavier (1903–1950). A playwright and essay writer, Villaurrutia was born in Mexico City on March 27, 1903. He studied at the French High School of Mexico and later attended the Preparatory. There he met Salvador Novo, Toffes Bodet, Jorge Cuesta, and other classmates who later would be recognized men of letters. He tried to study law, but abandoned it for writing. In 1927, he founded the journal *Ulises* with Novo, and when it ceased publication, the two friends founded *Contemporáneos*. These two magazines had a great impact on Mexican letters in that they attracted a group of very good young writers who formed the Ulises and the Orientación associations and aspired to revitalize the Mexican theater. Although Villaurrutia can be considered a poet, his work on the theater and as an essay writer is very important. In 1935 and 1936, thanks to a Rockefeller Scholarship, he attended Yale University, where he studied theater, acting, and dramatic theory. Upon his return to Mexico, he taught literature at the Universidad Nacional Autónoma de México (UNAM) and directed the theater section of the

Instituto Nacional de Bellas Artes (INBA). He contributed to many magazines and literary journals, among them *Letras de México*, *El hijo pródigo*, *Antena*, and *Revista de Bellas Artes*.

Villaurrutia's work in the Teatro Ulises and Grupo Orientación, along with the efforts of Celestino Gorostiza and Julio Bracho, contributed to complete change of the theater. New plays by foreign authors were staged, new points of view expressed, and the domination of the commercial theater came to an end with the foundation of a number of small experimental theaters. Villaurrutia died at age forty-seven, on December 25, 1950.

WORKS: *Parece mentira* (It Seems Untrue) (Mexico City: Imp. Mundial, 1934). *¿En qué piensas?* (What Are You Thinking About?) (Mexico City: Ed. Letras de Mexico, 1938). *Se usted breve* (Be Brief) (Mexico City: Cuadernos de Mexico Nuevo, 1938). *La hiedra* (The Ivy), in *Collection Nueva Cultura* 2.1 (1941). *El ausente* (The Absent One), in *Tierra nueva* 3.13–14 (January–April 1942): 35–50. *Invitación a la muerte* (Invitation to Death), in *El Hijo Pródigo* 6 (September 1943): 355–362; 7 (October 1943): 41–50; 8 (November 1943): 10–111; (Mexico City: Ed. Letras de Mexico, 1947). *La mujer legítima* (The Wife) (Mexico City: Ed. Rafael Loera y Chávez, 1943). *Autos profanos* (Secular Plays) (Mexico City: Ed. Letras de México, 1943). *El hierro candente* (The Red Iron), in *El Hijo Pródigo* 19 (October 1944): 44–57; 20 (November 1944): 110–120; (Mexico City: Ed. Letras de México, 1945). *La mulata de Córdoba* (The Mulatto Woman from Córdoba), in *El Hijo Pródigo* 24 (March 1945): 166–183. *Juego peligroso* (Dangerous Game) (Mexico City: n.p., 1949). *Poesía y teatro completo* (Mexico City: FCE, 1953).

BIBLIOGRAPHY: Antonio Acevedo Excobedo, "Acerca de Villaurrutia," *El Nacional* (May 8, 1966): 3. Enrique Anderson Imbert, *Historia de la literatura hispanoamericana*, vol. 2 (Mexico City: FCE, 1954), 19, 158, 159, 161–163. Enrique Anderson Imbert and Eugenio Florit, *Literatura hispanoamericana* (New York: Holt, Rinehart and Winston), 665–666. Max Aub, "Teatro," review of *Autos profanos*, *Letras de Mexico* 2 (February 15, 1943): 7. "Xavier Villaurrutia," *Mexico en la Cultura* 1–66 (April 25, 1964): 3. Angel de las Bárcenas, "Villaurrutia y la crítica", *Mexico en la Cultura* 304 (January 16, 1955): 2. Luis G. Basurto, "El teatro y la amistad in Xavier Villaurrutia," *Cuadernos de Bellas Artes* 1.5 (December 1960). Armando Cámara, "Cartas de Vil-

laurrutia a Novo," *Revista de Bellas Artes* 10 (July–August 1966), 101. Wilberto Canton, "Opina Villaurrutia: El INBA no ha hecho por el teatro mexicano lo que debería hacer," *México en la Cultura* 57 (March 5, 1950): 7. Miguel Capistrán, "Villaurrutia a Novo, Epistolario," *Diorama de la Cultura* (August 14, 1966): 3, 6. Alfredo Cardona Peña, *Semblanzas mexicanas* (Mexico City: Eds. Libro-Mex), 144–150. A. Casa Beltrdn, "*Yerro candente*, una comedia que ofrece nuevas, nobles, bellísimas posibilidades al teatro," *Así* (April 22, 1944): 37. Prologue to *Poesía y teatro completos*, ed. cit.; prologue to *Obras*, ed. cit., ix–xxx. Frank Dauster, "El teatro de Xavier Villaurrutia," *Estaciones* 1.4 (Winter 1956): 479–487. Merlin H. Forster, *Los contemporáneos* (Mexico City: Eds. de Andrea, 1964), 83–91, 125–126, 141–144. Antonio Magaña Esquivel, *Imagen del teatro* (Letras de México, 1940). *Teatro mexicano del siglo xx*, vol. 2 (Mexico City: FCE, 1956), 244–246. "Xavier Villaurrutia, dramaturgo," *El Nacional* (September 10, 1964): 5. "Teatro. Las piezas mayores de Xavier Villaurrutia," *El Nacional* (September 12, 1964): 5. *Medio siglo de teatro mexicano, 1900–1961* (Mexico City: INBA, 1964), 56–61, 73–74. Antonio Magaña Esquivel and Ruth S. Lamb, *Breve historia del teatro mexicano* (Mexico City: Eds. de Andrea, 1958), 129–131. Michele Muncy, "Villaurrutia, Xavier," in *Dictionary of Mexican Literature*, ed. Eladio Cortés (Westport, CT: Greenwood Press, 1992), 715–719.

Michele Muncy

VILLEGAS, Oscar (1943–). A dramatist and ceramics artist, Oscar Villegas is one of the first playwrights in a generation that came to be known as "La Nueva Dramaturgia" (The New Drama). Despite having relatively few plays and sporadic production, he is one of the important figures of the generation. He was born in San Luis Potosí but moved to Mexico City when he was very young. He studied visual arts and drama and began writing plays in 1966. His first plays stress language more than plot, and the fragmented structure and minimal development of individual characters make them more dark, expressionistic, imagistic views of society turned upside down than stories with a beginning, a middle, and an end. With *Santa Catarina* (Saint Catherine) and *Atlántida*, he incorporates a story, but the fragmentation, the language flow and play, and the dark view of the underside of society continue. The difficulty of staging and publishing works stopped the production of virtually all the young dramatists who began writing in the middle to late 1960s. After 1973, Villegas devoted his energies to making ceramics. He continued that activity until 1985, with a pause only in 1981, the year he finished *Mucho gusto en conocerlo* (Pleased to Meet You). He began writing plays again in 1990.

WORKS: *La paz de la buena gente* (Good People's Peace) (1966; 1st staging, 1980); in *Revista de Bellas Artes* 18 (1967): 49–64; in *Mucho gusto en conocerlo* (Mexico City: Editores Mexicanos Unidos, 1985), 9–50. *El renacimiento* (The Rennaissance) (1967; 1st staging, 1971, Jalapa); in *La Palabra y el Hombre* 44 (1967): 795–835; in *Teatro joven de México*, edited by Emilio Carballido (Mexico City: Editores Mexicanos Unidos, 1980), 11–30. *El señor y la señora* (Mr. and Mrs.) (1967; 1st staging, 1979); in *El señor y la señora y Marlon Brando es otro* (Mexico City: Instituto Nacional de la Juventud Mexicana, 1969), 3–43. *La pira* (Gang Rape) (1967; 1st staging, 1970, Monterrey); in *Juego de Palabras* 3 (1972): 26–33; in *Tramoya* 9 (1977): 4–21; in *Más teatro joven*, edited by Emilio Carballido (Mexico City: Editores Mexicanos Unidos, 1982), 11–41. *Marlon Brando es otro* (Marlon Brando Is Somebody Else) (1967; 1st staging, 1977); in *El señor y la señora y la Marlon Brando es otro* (Mexico City: Instituto Nacional de la Juventud Mexicana, 1969); in *Teatro joven de México*, edited by Emilio Carballido (Mexico City: Editores Mexicanos Unidos, 1980), 19–26. *Santa Catarina* (Saint Catherine) (1969; 1st staging, 1980); in *Premios PROTEA 1976* (Mexico City: Editorial Extemporáneos, 1977), 69–146; in *Mucho gusto en conocerlo* (Mexico City: Editores Mexicanos Unidos, 1985), 51–109. *Atlántida* (Atlántis) (1973; 1st staging, 1976, Jalapa); in *Tramoya* 2 (1976): 28–86; in *Mucho gusto en conocerlo* (Mexico City: Editores Mexicanos Unidos, 1985), 111–184. *El reino animal* (The Animal Kingdom) (1962; 1981); in *Tramoya* 23 (1982): 108–115. *Mucho gusto en conocerlo* (1981), in *Mucho gusto en conocerlo* (Mexico City: Editores Mexicanos Unidos, 1985), 185–247. *La verde de las hojas* (The Green of the Leaves) (1990); in *Tramoya* 25B (1990). *Refugio de las zonas* (Refuge in the Zones) (1990); in *Tramoya* 25B (1990). *La eternidad acaba mañana* (Eternity Ends Tomorrow) (1968; 1994).

BIBLIOGRAPHY: Ronald D. Burgess, *The New Dramatists of Mexico (1967–1985)* (Lexington: University Press of Kentucky, 1991). George Woodyard, "El teatro de Oscar Villegas: Experimentación con la forma," *Texto Crítico* 4.10: 32–41.

Alfonso González

Nicaragua

FROM PRE-COLUMBIAN ROOTS TO THE END OF THE NINETEENTH CENTURY

The Nicaraguan theater has a long and diverse history. It stretches from its pre-Hispanic roots through the missionary use of the theater, to the development of *El Güegüense*, to the formation of local theaters in the nineteenth century, and into the high periods in the twentieth century. Early Spanish missionaries found theatrical forms in existence when they arrived and viewed the theater as a useful tool for disseminating their message. *El Güegüense* proved to be a foundation stone for twentieth-century theater in Central America. During the nineteenth century a number of Nicaraguan cities built local theaters, which helped create and sustain interest in the theater, and brought in traveling groups. These traveling companies offered dramatic entertainment to the public. The twentieth century has seen a flurry of theatrical activity in Nicaragua. Playwrights such as Rolando Steiner and José Coronel Urtecho have created some innovative works. A variety of theater companies have flourished as well.

In regard to early, pre-Columbian theatrical expressions, the inhabitants of the region that we now call Nicaragua made extensive use of dance in their ceremonies. Many of these performances had religious overtones. For instance, simple dances and dances with music preceded human sacrifices. Dances with recitations of prose were a part of El Volador, a ceremony directed to the agrarian divinity responsible for the production of cacao, or chocolate. Cacao was a staple that served as a monetary exchange, as a medicine, and as a drink. The sixteenth-century chronicles have also highlighted some theatrical practices that confirm the presence and importance of drama. These practices and forms were later incorporated into the theater of the colonial period and include open-air staging near a temple, the repetition of phrases, the use of male actors to play female roles, the lack of division between public and stage, the comical suggestion that a certain character was deaf, and the celebration at the end.

In their efforts to convert the native residents and teach them Spanish, the missionaries assimilated native forms with works from the medieval tradition to achieve their goal. These resulting works were anonymous and collective in nature. They dealt with religious themes or biblical stories and were didactic. The form has come down to the present day and is cited as an example of the folklore. In recent decades a vast repertoire of such productions has been discovered. The plays assumed a variety of forms: dances, colloquies, stories, *loas* or short texts in verse that conclude with a praise of mystery or of the festival for which it has been written, and others. They were often presented during the processions of Holy Week, during the celebrations of the city's or village's patron saint, during Christmas festivities, or in homage to the Virgin Mary. After a time, they became secularized and assumed the air of popular farce. The works had obvious political and religious purposes.

Some of the works, such as *Loga de Niño Dios* (Song of the Divine Child), contain words in mangue, the language of some of the indigenous people of Nicaragua. Singing and dancing accompany some of the productions. Plays with biblical or Old Testament orientations were quite common, as were dramatizations of the conflict between the Moors and Christians (*moros y cristianos*). The pageant of the Moors and the Christians was widely represented in towns and villages stretching from the southwestern United States to Nicaragua. Although various versions of this dramatic work exist, some critics believe that the Nicaraguan version that was preserved in the village of Niquinohomo is closer than most to the original text.

In the seventeenth century, the comedy ballet *El Güegüense* arose out of the Nahualt theater. The Nahualt theater flourished from 1531 to 1768 and produced forty-two works. Written in the Nahualt Spanish dialect of Nicaragua, *El Güegüense* marks the fusion of the Spanish and the indigenous cultures and has been heralded as the beginning of an independent New World theater. The work has no known author. The plot borrows from the picaresque tradition. Its satirical nature served to subtly challenge the colonial structure in emphasizing the exploitation and corruption of the times.

The nineteenth century brought not only political changes but also theatrical development as well. Independence was declared in 1821. Around that time, the first dramatic work written by a known Nicaraguan author, *El sitio de la Rochela* (The Place of La Rochelle), by Francisco Quiñones Sunsín, was performed. It was successfully produced at the Teatro del Sol in El Salvador and was based on an episode from the French Revolution. The text, unfortunately, remains lost to this day. Around the same time, Miguel de Larreynaga wrote a comedy, *El quebrado ganacioso* (The Profitable Bankrupt). The work criticizes the ambitious businessmen of the times. It is generally agreed that it has few redeeming artistic and dramatic qualities, however.

As Nicaragua freed itself from the Spanish hold, a number of Spanish theater companies passed through some of Nicaragua's major cities and offered performances. While the types of performances varied, the majority of them had religious or colonial origins and themes, including dramatizations of the *moros y cristianos* conflict. Certain religious productions were especially popular around Christmas time through the end of the century. As their visits became more frequent, theaters sprung up in the principal cities. In Masaya, a group of actors formed a theater company, Compañía Dramática de Aficionados" (Dramatic Company of Aficionados), whose repertoire included some classical works and some contemporary ones. In Granada, a dramatic company formed by a Mr. Estrada appeared and produced some plays adapted from Molière. A Spanish company founded by Saturnino Blen traveled throughout Nicaragua and other Central American countries and offered performances. Francisco M. Flores also organized a company that produced works in León and Granada. Carlos Cucalón and his wife Mercedes founded a theater company that offered productions in León and left its mark on the city.

Some plays arose from the political ferment of the time. Luicano Hernández, a Salvadoran who was residing in Granada, wrote a work that the presidential candidacy of Pedro Joaquín Chamorro inspired. Another dramatic work with political overtones that never made it to the stage was the play *Alemania y Nicaragua* (Germany and Nicaragua). Some young Leonese are believed to have written it. The work revolves around the international diplomatic incident that occurred when Francisco Leal married Francisca Hademann, the step-daughter of Dr. Mauricio Eisentuck, a diplomatic consul from Germany. The Eisentuck family did not approve. When they made plans to send Francisca back to Germany, kidnapping attempts and fights occurred that evolved into an international conflict. Pressure from the Eisentuck family never permitted the play to be produced. As it is not available, we can only guess as to its content. It probably was a precursor of the twentieth-century Latin American documentary theater.

Other theaters sprung up to accommodate the growing dramatic activity. León dedicated its municipal theater in 1885. A year earlier, Rubén Darío read a poem in a ceremony commemorating the groundbreaking. An earthquake tremor later destroyed that theater. Around the same time, Granada set out to build a theater for its citizens. The theater opened with its first production in November 1889. This helped inspire two local playwrights, Manuel Blas Sáenz and Carlos A. García. In 1894, an explosion damaged part of that theater. It was soon repaired and functional again.

Theater groups from León and Granada also visited and presented performances in Managua, the capital city. On April 1, 1886, Saturnino Blen's company presented Rubén Darío's lost comic farce, *Cada oveja* (Each Sheep). By 1896, Managua also had a permanent, standing theater. All of this activity illustrates the importance of the theater in the lives of the citizens in the early history of present-day Nicaragua. It shows the need to produce dramatic representations. It laid the foundation for the flourishing of drama and the theater in the twentieth century. From it, one can see how the contemporary theater took root in Nicaragua.

THE NICARAGUAN THEATER IN THE TWENTIETH CENTURY

The Nicaraguan theater movement, which began timidly in the first decades of this century, reached its zenith in the 1960s and maintained its intensity through the mid-1970s, paralleling the nation's vigorous economic growth, which was sustained by its role as one of the region's largest exporters. In this opening introduction, these nine decades of theatrical activity are divided into three periods: 1900 to 1940; the era spanning 1950 to 1979, which Jorge Eduardo Arellano, in his history of the Nicaraguan theater, published in the Nicaraguan Central Bank's *Boletín Nicaragüense de Bibliografía y Documentación* (Managua, 1989, No. 58–59), calls the "golden age" of Nicaraguan drama; and the Sandanista period.

This early period is limited to the first dramatists and dramatic companies, for the most part foreign, that frequently visited Nicaragua and were responsible to a great degree for motivating the creation of national theater groups. These early efforts were brought to an abrupt halt by the devastating earthquake that struck the capital of Managua in 1931. An even greater earthquake would destroy the city again in 1972. However, while it may be true that the first quake silenced for a time the activities of the Nicaraguan theater, engaging the nation's people in more urgent tasks, it is also true that the movement emerged from the rubble with more determination and enthusiasm for establishing the basis of a truly Nicaraguan theater.

During the government of the liberal president Gen. José Santos Zelaya (1893–1911), who was defeated by the conservatives backed by U.S. troops, Nicaragua was visited by foreign theatrical companies whose repertoire included such works as *La dama de las*

Camelias (Camille), *La viuda alegre* (The Merry Widow), *La arrabalera* (The Slum Woman), and many other works brought to the stage by prestigious Spanish companies such as those directed by Paco Alba in 1900 and María Guerrero in 1910. An operetta company, directed by Carlos Obregón, also enjoyed a run of several months. The pace of theatrical activity increased significantly with the completion of the construction of the Teatro Variedades, which drew celebrated companies offering their best productions to a public eager for the chance to attend high-quality theater. One such event was a staging of *La Tosca* by the Italian opera company Odierno.

It fell to the small city of Boaco to be the site of the first theatrical activity of the period covering 1910 to 1935. Among the first authors and directors of this early stage, Ofelia Morales, founder of the Elenco Artístico company, and Father José Nieborosky stand out. The awakening of a rare dramatic vocation was not long in coming as Hernán Robleto, journalist, novelist, and playwright, organized in Managua the Compañía Dramática Nacional. Robleto's works were staged abroad as well as in Nicaragua. His most famous and well-received work, *La rosa del paraíso* (The Rose of Paradise) (1920), was produced in Lima, Peru's Teatro Municipal in 1926 to great public and critical acclaim. Included in Carlos Solórzano's *El teatro hispanoamericano del siglo XX* (Twentieth-Century Hispanic American Theater), Hernán Robleto, with some sixteen works in the genre, is considered the founder of the Nicaraguan *costumbrista* theater. His most significant works are *El milagro* (The Miracle) (1921), *La señorita que arrojó el antifaz* (The Woman Who Hurled the Mask) (1928), and *Tres dramas* (Three Dramas) (1946), which included the well-received *La cruz de ceniza* (The Ashen Cross), *La niña Soledad* (A Girl Named Soledad), and *Muñecos de barro* (Clay Dolls).

Another celebrated drama of love and infidelity of this era was *Ocaso* (Sunset), written by Santiago Argüello and staged for the first time in León in 1906. The play recounts the tragedy of a young woman who is married to an old man whom she later betrays. Another playwright who needs to be mentioned is Félix Medina, whose notable works include the historical play *Los Contreras* (The Contreras Family). This play is based on the story of the Spanish brothers who participated in one of the most shameful and painful pages of Nicaraguan history: the assassination of Bishop Valdivieso in León. Other authors who contributed to the development of a Nicaraguan national theater are: Manuel Rosales with *Andar, siempre andar* (Forever Wandering) (1930), *La danzarina trágica* (The Tragic Dancer), and *Opalos de sangre* (Opals of Blood) (1932); and Adolfo Calero Orozco with *La falda-pantalón* (The Pant Skirt) (1932), a comedy situated within the feminist current of the time. It is important to remember that feminism was a prohibited topic, a target of the provincial society of 1920s Nicaragua. In contrast, larger countries such as Argentina, Uruguay, and Chile were actively engaged in struggles over women's suffrage, female participation in unions, and women's activism in anarchist and socialist political groups. In 1973, Calero Orozco would publish a collection entitled *Cuatro obras de teatro* (Four Plays), which, in addition to *The Pant Skirt*, included the works *El diálogo o fechas en blanco* (The Dialogue or Blank Dates), *La viudita* (The Little Old Widow), and *El entierro de Juan García* (The Burial of Juan García).

It is important to note the major thematic currents of these works. They have their roots in *costumbrismo* and vernacular literature, as well as historical and anti-imperialist works. Anti-imperialism is especially evident in Robleto's *Pájaros del Norte* (Birds of the North)

(1936) and Pablo Antonio Cuadra's *Por los caminos van los campesinos* (Along the Roads Go the Peasants) (1937).

The 1920s saw a peak in theatrical production in Nicaragua that coincided with the emergence of a Nicaraguan vanguard literary movement, founded by José Coronel Urtecho, Luis Alberto Cabrales, Pablo Antonio Cuadra, and Joaquín Pasos. These and other writers, occupied with a poetic renewal movement, in tune with their European cohorts, also ventured into the dramatic genre, producing such excellent works as Pasos and Urtecho's *La chinfonía burguesa* (The Bourgeois Chymphony) (1939), a penetrating satire of the life of the bourgeoisie of the colonial city of Granada, birthplace of the vanguard movement.

The Bourgeois Chymphony is remarkable for its novel theme, for its absurd humor, and for its experiment with chained rhyming and its cacophonic effect, which tends to dispose of all aestheticism. This effect reminds one of the verses of the Argentine Leopoldo Lugones' *Lunario sentimental* (A Sentimental Moon Treatise), where the verse's harmony is violated in a search for a new aesthetic. Thus, *The Bourgeois Chymphony*, in addition to possessing a rich rhyming play, also displays absurd scenes in which the son of the rich heiress and the poet is nothing more than a sponger. According to the Costa Rican critic Alberto Cañas, the authors were ten years ahead of Eugene Ionesco and his Theater of the Absurd. Two other landmark works at the time were the vernacular *La novia de Tola* (Tola's Fiance) (1942) by Alberto Ordóñez Argüello, and Cuadra's *Por los caminos van los campesinos* (Along the Roads Go the Peasants), which is worthy of inclusion in any Latin American theater anthology. *Along the Roads Go the Peasants* recounts the tragedy of the Nicaraguan people immersed in civil wars perpetuated by the traditional parties' thirst for power, the intervention of U.S. Marines, and the endemic revolutionary activity.

These vanguard writers included in their dramatic works adaptations of classical pieces and re-creations of colonial works: mysteries, allegorical plays, pastorals, short farces, and even puppet plays. Theirs was a vast and diverse repertoire that did not reject any current or exclude any theme, striving to take in everything in an effort to renew the national theater.

Three writers who should be situated outside the vanguard movement deserve mention in this period of initiation of Nicaraguan drama: Marcial Ríos, Arturo Cerna, and Fernández Morales, whose published works include *La niña del río* (The River Girl) (1943) and *Judas*, an excellent monologue.

The second period—the 1950s, 1960s, and 1970s—is marked by the relative economic prosperity Nicaragua experienced as a result of a cotton boom, as well as the nation's integration into the Central American Common Market. During the dynastic dictatorship of the Somoza family—Anastasio Somoza García, who died in 1956, and his two sons, Luis and Anastasio—which ended in 1979, Nicaragua obtained loans and financial and technical assistance from international organizations that established the base for the accelerated capitalistic modernization of the country. This development favored the rise of the first experimental theater groups, among which the Grupo de Teatro Experimental, founded by Adelita Pellas de Solórzano, stands out. Likewise, the veteran artist Adán Castillo founded the group Talía, which in 1953 staged Jacinto Benavente's *La malquerida* (The Ill-Beloved). Another actor and orator, Henry Rivas, who years later would acquire international renown, gave a memorable presentation of the monologue *Las manos de Eurídice* (The Hands of Eurydice) and confirmed himself as a first-rate actor in Aeschylus's tragedy *Or-*

estíada (Orestes), directed by the poet Carlos Martínez Rivas and presented on the stage of the Alianza Francesa de Managua.

Deserving of special mention during this period of flourishing theatrical groups is the long-lived Teatro Experimental de Managua (TEM) under the direction of Gladys Ramírez de Espinoza, Adelita Pellas de Solórzano, and Gloria Pereira de Belli. This company (1961–1978) presented various plays by foreign authors in the auditorium of the Escuela Nacional de Bellas Artes under the direction of the painter Rodrigo Peñalba. This hall saw the staging of Somerset Maugham's *La esposa constante* (The Constant Wife) and García Lorca's *La casa de Bernarda Alba* (The House of Bernarda Alba), directed by Alfredo Valessi and later by Adán Castillo, who caused a stir with his novel application of the techniques of Stanislawsky.

Valessi has written some important works, including the unpublished *La trampa del hambre* (The Hunger Trap), a profound social commentary. However, the most consistent playwright of the period was Rolando Steiner, with his excellent re-creations of classical works such as *Judit* (Judith) (1957), *Antígona en el infierno* (Antigone in Hell) (1958), and *La pasión de Helena* (The Passion of Helene) (1963). In 1963 in Guatemala he earned the first Lope de Vega award for Central American drama for his work *Un drama corriente* (An Ordinary Drama). This work's debut in Madrid in 1964 thrust Steiner into the spotlight. Key actors in the success of Steiner's work included Carlos Morales, Esperanza Román, Mario Vidal, José Barrer and Eduardo Alvir, all directed by Tacho Sánchez, an important director on the Nicaraguan scene. Other works by Steiner include *La mujer deshabitada* (The Uninhabited Woman) (1970); *La agonía del poeta* (The Poet's Agony) (1977), based on the death of Rubén Darío; and *Trilogía del matrimonio* (Marriage Trilogy); as well as other unpublished plays.

Another group directed by Adán Castillo, La Comedia del Arte (The Play of Art) (1960–1968), enjoyed great success with *Don Juan Tenorio*, with Castillo himself in the title role, an interpretation that earned him the "Güegüense de Oro" prize, a national acting award. In addition to his acclaimed acting, Castillo was known for traveling from village to village on horseback with his company to stage performances. He died in 1973.

Among other directors of the Teatro Experimental de Bellas Artes (1960–1963), the Argentine Ricardo Quintero and the Italian Franco Cerutti, a scholar of Central American literature, who directed Eugene O'Neill's *Antes del desayuno* (Before Breakfast) and Albert Camus's *El malentendido* (The Misunderstanding), respectively, deserve special note.

A little later in the decade (1965), a group of intellectuals, professors, and actors founded the brilliant La Comedia Nacional de Nicaragua (The Nicaraguan National Drama Troupe), directed by the talented and unflagging theatrical pioneer Socorro Bonilla Castellón, a graduate of the Tirso de Molina School of Madrid. The founding of this company represents a milestone in the history of theater in Nicaragua. It has continued to stage productions for twenty-eight years, and its repertoire has included the Greek classics as well as works from Spain, France, England, Russia, Central America, and Nicaragua. Among the group's successes are *Los árboles mueren de pie* (Trees Die Standing) (1965), by Alejandro Casona; *Los verdes campos del Edén* (The Green Fields of Eden) (1966), by Antonio Gala; and *Antígona* (Antigone), by Jean Anouilh, which debuted in 1967 as part of the homage paid to Rubén Darío on the occasion of the first centennial of the poet's birth. The Argentine director Carlos Jiménez was invited for this great event; he would later go on to found the

Venezuelan theater group Rajatablas (Fearless). The performers that evening included Socorro Bonilla in the role of Antigone, Luis Adolfo Reyes as Creon, Mario González as Hemnon, Nydia Palacios as the Nursemaid, and Evelyn Martínez as Ismene. Among the troupe's other successes we might include *El amante* (The Lover), by Harold Pinter; *Las mujeres sabias* (Learned Ladies), by Molière; *Proceso a cuatro monjas* (The Trial of Four Nuns), by Vladimir Cajoli; *Seis personajes en busca de autor* (Six Characters in Search of an Author), by Luigi Pirandello; *La asamblea de las mujeres* (Women in Parliament), by Aristophanes; and *Living Room*, by Grahame Greene. Among the cast we find Blanca Amador, Mamerto Martínez, and Ruth Obregón, all deceased; Leticia Saravia, Elsa Arana, Charles Delgadillo, Carlos Pérez, Armando Urbina, and Erasmo Alizaga, who is today the artistic director of the company, as well as the great dame of the Nicaraguan theater, Pilar Aguirre.

For its part, the TEM, directed by Tacho Sánchez, won Güegüense de Oro awards for Tina Benard de Chamorro as best director, Mimí Hammer as best actress, and Gilbert Iglesias as best actor. In 1964 TEM's direction passed into the hands of the Hungarian director Estevan Isvegi, who directed works of great quality, such as *También las mujeres perdieron la guerra* (The Women Lost the War Too), by Curzio Malaparte; and *Luz de gas* (Gaslight), in which Mimí Hammer proved herself to be a first-rate actress.

In León another group was being founded, the Teatro Experimental Universitario de la Universidad Nacional Autónoma (The University Experimental Theater of the National Autonomous University), which entered the scene in 1963 with a production of *Escurial* by Michel de Ghelderode, directed by Jaime Alberdi, who won five Güegüenses de Oro for the group. Other directors included José de Jesús Blandón and Alberto Icaza, who won a first prize for the Central American region in Costa Rica with his work *Asesinato frustrado* (The Failed Assassination). Icaza also founded another group, Atelier Rubén Darío. Under Icaza's direction the group staged such memorable works as *Un fénix demasiado frecuente* (A Phoenix Too Frequent, a Comedy), by Christopher Fry, and *Una gata sobre el tejado caliente* (Cat on a Hot Tin Roof), by Tennessee Williams. The Central American University of Nicaragua also initiated a theatrical movement in 1971 with its production of *La Cenicienta* (Cinderella), starring Mario González Gramajo, who also directed the play. At the same time in Managua, Socorro Bonilla was directing the group Teatro Estudio Unan (TEU), and in León, Alan Bolt was directing another group.

Numerous high schools around the country demonstrated enthusiasm for the theater at this time as well, including the Instituto Ramírez Goyena, the Instituto Miguel de Cervantes, and the Colegio Pedagógico, all directed by Socorro Bonilla; the student troupe called El Güegüense of the Instituto Dr. René Schick; and the groups from the Instituto Bello Horizonte and the Colegio Americano Nicaragüense, founded by the teacher, actress, and orator Nydia Palacios, who directed such works as *Prohibido suicidarse en primavera* (No Suicides in Springtime), by Casona, *La guarda cuidadosa* (The Faithful Dog), and *El juez de los divorcios* (The Judge of the Divorce Court), both farces by Cervantes. Theatrical groups from Jinotega and other cities joined the movement, among them two from schools for girls stand out: the groups from La Asunción and Pureza de María, both located in León and directed by Gloria Elena Espinoza from 1966 to 1977. Perhaps of greatest significance is the fact that many of this period's teenagers today are theater directors and teachers, as well as actors, in the Nicaraguan School of Dramatic Arts.

Finally, the participation of the group from Boaco, Grupo U (1965–1970), which was founded by Armando Incer and Flavio Tijerino and counted on the drive of Ofelia Morales, deserves notice. This company presented some truly spectacular productions with works such as Sophocles's *Antígona en el infierno* (Antigone in Hell) and *Edipo Rey* (Oedipus Rex), as well as works by Lope de Vega, Calderón de la Barca, Casona, Camus, and Samuel Beckett. Although it endured just five short years, Grupo U's intense production ranks it as one of the most important in the history of the development of the Nicaraguan theater.

After the Sandinista's revolutionary triumph in 1979, there was a real euphoria about bringing to the stage different aspects of the new experience that was being lived. Many new theatrical groups came to the fore and cultivated a doctrinal theater, which was partisan in orientation and lacked aesthetic values. There was a real hostility toward the great, universal dramatic works of literature. The official theater, supported by the Ministry of Culture, encouraged these productions for their ideological value and their singular vision. They contained major shortcomings in their abuse of folkloric elements, in their obscene language, and in their insufficient props. They were sometimes produced with only two days of advance preparation. Generally, this spontaneous theater was a collective creation, with actors and actresses without artistic sensibilities but with a great deal of enthusiasm who responded, from a revolutionary perspective, to the political juncture of the moment.

While proclaiming that it was necessary to put an end to bourgeois theater in Nicaragua, the improvisation, the simplicity, and the superficiality that resulted initiated a theatrical decline. Rather than trying to offer the masses the best works of the universal theater, the quality and standards were lowered. In a year, more than forty sociodramas were performed, written by amateurs from the rural areas, the factories, the neighborhoods, and the high schools. The euphoria of the moment explains this tendency, but its proponents made the major error of believing that a theater with aesthetic values was incompatible with a revolutionary theater. At the same time, independent of this official theater, certain individual groups performed works such as *Yerma* by García Lorca, *La señora de Tacna* by Vargas Llosa, *La olla* by Plautus, *Don Juan Tenorio* by Torrilla, and children's theatrical works.

In conclusion, this brief summary of ninety years of twentieth-century Nicaraguan theater has traced the history of a vibrant movement of superior quality, advanced by theater lovers, both professional and amateur, all deserving of praise for their contributions to the cultural life of the nation. Nicaragua has produced a great number of playwrights such as Hernán Robleto, Rolando Steiner, Pablo Antonio Cuadra, Horacio Peña, Adolfo Calero Orozco, and others, all heirs to a dramatic tradition that can be traced back to the precolonial and colonial period and that anonymous first Nicaraguan play, *El Güegüense*. The Vanguard Period (1935–1942) and the Golden Age (1951–1978) are the high water marks because of the formation of theatrical groups and the quality and variety of theatrical presentations. Nevertheless, the lack of a school of drama has impeded the development of professional actors and the formation of a national company that performs for Nicaragua.

BIBLIOGRAPHY

Amante Blanco, Juan José, and Marina Galvez Acero. *Poesía y teatro de Hispanoamerica en el siglo XX*. Madrid: Editorial Cincel, 1981.

Arellano, Jorge Eduardo. Introduction. *El Güegüense o Macho Ratón*. Managua: Ediciones Americanas, 1984.

———. *Inventario del teatro de Nicaragua*. Managua: Biblioteca Banco Central de Nicaragua, 1988.

———. "Obras e intentos teatrales de autores nicaragüenses." *Boletín nicaragüense de bibliografía y documentación* 49 (1982): 119–138.

———. *Panorama de la literatura nicaragüense*. Managua: Ediciones Nacionales, 1977.

Bravo-Elizondo, Pedro. *Teatro documental latinoamericano*. Mexico City: Universidad Nacional Autónoma de México, 1982.

Brinton, Daniel G., ed. *The Güegüense: A Comedy Ballet in the National Spanish Dialect of Nicaragua*. New York: AMS Press, 1969.

Correa, Gustavo. *The Native Theatre in Middle America*. New Orleans: Tulane University Middle American Research Institute, 1961.

Cuadra, Pablo Antonio. Afterword. "Breve nota sobre el teatro nicaragüense." *3 obras de teatro nuevo*. Managua: Ediciones de la Academia Nicaragüense de la Lengua, 1957, 215–225.

Galich, Franz. "El teatro de la revolución, 1970–1987." *Revista Iberoamericana* 57 (1991): 1045–1058.

Horcasitas, Fernando. *El teatro náhuatl*. Mexico City: UNAM, Instituto de Investigaciones Estéticas, 1974.

"Nicaragua." *Escenarios de dos mundos: inventario teatral de Iberoamérica*. Vol. 3. Madrid: Centro de Documentación Teatral, 1988, 186–217. Articles by scholars.

Perez-Estrada, Francisco. *Teatro folklore nicaragüense*. Managua: Editorial Nuevos Horizontes, 1948.

Ramírez de Espinosa, Gladys. "Reseña histórica del Teatro Experimental de Managua (TEM)." *Boletín nicaragüense de bibliografía y documentación* 49 (1982): 92–118.

Saz, Agustín del. *Teatro social hispanoamericano*. Barcelona: Editorial Labor, 1967.

Solórzano, Carlos. *El teatro latinoamericano del siglo XX*. Buenos Aires: Editorial Nueva Visión, 1961.

———. *Teatro latinoamericano en el siglo XX*. Mexico City: Editorial Pormaca, 1964.

Steiner, Rolando. "Notas sobre el teatro en Nicaragua." *Encuentro* 1 (1968): 40–42.

Sten, María. *Vida y muerte del teatro náhuatl. El Olimpo sin Prometeo*. Mexico City: Secretaría de Educación Pública, 1974.

Suárez Radillo, and Carlos Miguel. *El teatro neoclásico y costumbrista hispanoamericano*. Madrid: Ediciones Cultura Hispánica/Instituto de Cooperación Iberoamericana, 1984.

◆

BONILLA CASTELLÓN, Socorro (1935–   ). Bonilla Castellón was born in Masatepe, Nicaragua, in 1935. She is considered the most famous actress and director of the Nicaraguan theater. In 1965, she founded the company Comedia Nacional de Nicaragua, the unique group that has continued to stage productions to the present day. She graduated from the Tirso de Molina School in Madrid. She has traveled widely in Europe, the United States, and South America. She has organized many poetry recitals and has served as an instructor of Drama at the National University of Nicaragua. She debuted as an actress in *Antes del desayuno* (Before Breakfast) by O'Neill, in *El malentendido* (The Misunderstanding) by Camus, and in the role of the tragic heroine Antígona (Antigone) by Anouilh.

Under her direction the Comedia Nacional de Nicaragua presented *Los verdes campos del Edén* (The Green Fields of Eden) (1966) by Antonio Gala, *Proceso a cuatro monjas* (The Trial of Four Nuns) (1968) by Vladimir Cajoli, *Living Room* (1970) by Graham Greene, *Las mujeres sabias* (The Learned Women) (1974) by Molière, *La asamblea de las mujeres* (Women in the Parliament) by Aristophanes (1975), and *Seis personajes en busca de autor* (Six Characters in Search of an Author) (1979) by Pirandello. At the same time, she founded drama groups in the secondary school such as Instituto Miguel de Cervantes, Ramírez Goyena, and Teatro Estudio UNAN. She won the coveted Nicaraguan award Orden Nacional Rubén Darío for her artistic and professional achievements.

BIBLIOGRAPHY: Jorge Eduardo Arellano, *Inventario del teatro de Nicaragua* (Managua: Biblioteca Banco Central de Nicaragua, 1988). Socorro Bonilla Castellón, "La puerta (de Rolando Steiner)," *Ventana*, 18 de junio, 1982. Bonilla Castellón, "Reseña histórica de la Comedia Nacional de Nicaragua," *Boletín Nicaragüense Bibliografía y Documentacíon* 49 (1982): 119–138.

Nydia Palacios Vivas

CALERO OROZCO, Adolfo (1899–1980). Calero Orozco was born in Managua, Nicaragua, in 1899 and died in 1980. He traveled to Spain and other European countries and the United States during his life. He has written plays, novels, and short stories and is considered one of Nicaragua's most important fiction writers during the first half of the twentieth century. He is credited with defining the Nicaraguan short story. His stories often treat the problems of the working class. His themes and language are vernacular. One of the principal traits of both his dramas and narratives is humor. His novels deal with politics, ambition, and the civil wars in Nicaragua. His first drama, *La falda-pantalón* (The Pant Skirt) (1932), is a comedy situated within the feminist current of the time. It is important to remember that feminism was a prohibited topic, a target of the provincial society of 1920s Nicaragua.

WORKS: *La falda-pantalón* (Managua: Tipografía Perez, 1922). *El diálogo o fechas en blanco* (The Dialogue or White Arrows), in *Cuatro obras de teatro* (Managua: Ediciones de la Academia Nicaragüense de la Lengua, 1972). *La viudita* (The Little Widow), in *Cuatro obras de teatro* (Managua: Ediciones de la Academia Nicaragüense de la Lengua, 1972). *El entierro de Juan García* (The Burial of Juan García), in *Cuatro obras de teatro* (Managua: Ediciones de la Academia Nicaragüense de la Lengua, 1972).

BIBLIOGRAPHY: Jorge Eduardo Arellano, *Inventario del teatro de Nicaragua* (Managua: Biblioteca Banco Central de Nicaragua, 1988), 67, 193. M. J. Fenwick, *Writers of the Caribbean and Central America: A Bibliography* (New York: Garland Publishing, 1992), 1050–1051.

Nydia Palacios Vivas

COMEDIA NACIONAL DE NICARAGUA. The decade of the 1960s called "The Golden Drama Epoch of Nicaragua" saw the flourishing of a number of theatrical groups. One of the most prominent and brilliant was the Comedia Nacional de Nicaragua (The Nicaraguan National Drama Troupe), founded in 1965 by a group of intellectuals, professors, and actors and directed by the talented and unflagging theatrical pioneer Socorro Bonilla Castellón, a graduate of the Tirso de Molina School of Madrid. The founding of this company represents a milestone in the history of the theater in Nicaragua. It has continued to stage productions for over thirty years, and its repertoire has included the Greek classics as well as works from Spain, France, England, Russia, the United States, and Nicaragua. Among the successes are *Los árboles mueren de pie* (Trees Die Standing) (1965) by Alejandro Casona, *Los verdes campos del Edén* (The Green Fields of Eden) (1966) by Antonio Gala, and *Antígona* (Antigone) by Jean Anouilh. The Argentine Carlos Jiménez debuted as director in 1967 as part of the homage paid to Rubén Darío on the occasion of the first centennial of the poet's birth. Jiménez later went on to found the Venezuelan theater group Rajatablas (Fearless). Other founders of the Comedia Nacional de Nicaragua included Mamerto Martínez, Blanca Amador, Luis A. Reyes, Gabry Rivas, Manuel Monterrey, Leticia Saravia, Esperanza Bermúdez, Bayardo Corea, Carmen Centeno, and Socorro Bonilla Castellón. Among the troupe's other successes are *El amante* (The Lover) by Harold Pinter, *Las mujeres sabias* (The Learned Women) by Molière, *Proceso a cuatro monjas* (The Trial of Four Nuns) by Cajoli, *Seis per-*

sonajes en busca de autor (Six Characters in Search of an Author) by Pirandello, *La asamblea de las mujeres* (Women in the Parliament) by Aristophanes, and *Living Room* by Grahame Greene.

BIBLIOGRAPHY: Jorge Eduardo Arellano, *Inventario del teatro de Nicaragua* (Managua: Biblioteca Banco Central de Nicaragua, 1988). Socorro Bonilla Castellón, "Reseña histórica de la Comedia Nacional de Nicaragua," *Boletín Nicaragüense de Bibliografía y Documentación* 49 (1982): 119–138. "Teatro, Bonilla Castellón," *Comedia Nacional de Nicaragua*, no. 1 (1993).

Nydia Palacios Vivas

CORONEL URTECHO, José (1906–). A poet, dramatist, fiction writer, translator, essayist, critic, and historian, he was born on February 28, 1906, in Granada, Nicaragua. Both parents came from conservative familial backgrounds. His father became involved in the liberal politics of the country. While José was still young, the conservatives placed his father in prison, where he committed suicide. At the age of nineteen, José traveled to the United States. He discovered U.S. poetry during this trip and developed a deep respect for it. In 1927, he returned to Nicaragua, where he introduced the writings of U.S. poets to others and began publishing his own poetry. He served in some political positions in the late 1930s and 1940s and served in the diplomatic corps in New York and Madrid beginning in 1948. He is considered one of the foremost men of letters in twentieth-century Nicaraguan literature.

While José Coronel Urtecho is best known for his poetry, his theatrical contributions are quite noteworthy. *La chinfonía burguesa* (The Bourgeois Chymphony), which he published in 1939 with Joaquín Pasos, combines poetry and drama. It marks a rejection of Aristotelian logic and the beginning of the vanguard movement, which sought to open the theater. The work takes popular and nursery rhymes, oral superstitions, and tongue twisters and elevates them to a more complicated level. This technique creates a playful, burlesque, and absurdist effect not unlike Eugene Ionesco, although it predates his work by at least ten years. This buffoon

opera comically undermines middle-class life. His work *La Petenera* (Petenera) follows a similar pattern. It relates the story of a young woman, Petenera, who refuses to marry the wealthy, older suitor who her parents prefer. Instead, she maintains her loyalty to a poor, young poet. The work contains the same sort of nursery rhymes and lampoons middle-class values.

WORKS: *La chinfonía burguesa* (with Joaquín Pasos) (The Bourgeois Chymphony), in *Centro* 4 (June–July 1939): 82–89; in *Tres obras de teatro de vanguardia nicaragüense* (Managua: Ediciones El Pez y la Serpiente, 1965), 9–45. *La Petenera* (Petenera), in *La prensa literaria*, September 24, 1967; in *Tres obras de teatro de vanguardia nicaragüense* (Managua: Ediciones El Pez y la Serpiente, 1965), 145–180.

BIBLIOGRAPHY: Jorge Eduardo Arellano, *Inventario del teatro de Nicaragua* (Managua: Biblioteca Banco Central de Nicaragua, 1988), 71–77. Arellano, *Panorama de la literatura nicaragüense* (Managua: Ediciones Nacionales, 1977), 129–131. Alberto Cañas, *La prensa literaria*, December 10, 1972. Pablo Antonio Cuadra, "*La chinfonía* y *La puerta* en el teatro experimental," *La prensa literaria*, December 20, 1972. M. J. Fenwick, *Writers of the Caribbean and Central America: A Bibliography*, vol. 2 (New York and London: Garland Publishing, 1992), 1054. Manuel Jiron, ed., *Quién es quién en Nicaragua* (Ediciones Radio Amor, 1986), 115–118. Carlos Solóranza, *Teatro latinoamericano del siglo XX* (Mexico City: Editorial Porrúa, 1964). Manlio Tirado, *Conversando con José Coronel Urtecho* (Managua: Editorial Nueva Nicaragua, 1983). Vicky Unruh, "The *Chinfonía burguesa*: A Linguistic Manifesto of Nicaragua Avant Garde," *Latin American Theatre Review* 20/22 (Spring 1987): 37–48.

Mark F. Frisch

CUADRA, Pablo Antonio (1912–). Cuadra was born in Managua in 1912. His mother was Doña Mercedes Cardenal, and his father was Dr. Carlos Cuadra Pasos. At the age of four, his family moved to Granada, where he was educated in a Jesuit High School and where he spent much of his early life. He worked on the family farms, farming and raising cattle, and became very attached to the land and the people. At an early age, he was inspired by the guerrilla fighter Augusto César Sandino. He initially backed General Anastasio Somoza but became disillusioned in 1946 and left Nicaragua to travel in Mexico, Spain, the United States, and South America. In 1950, he returned home, where he continues to write, edit, and publish.

Cuadra is renowned as a poet, dramatist, critic, and editor. In his works, he often focuses on the indigenous and common people, their speech, and their customs. This is the case in the dramatic work *Por los caminos van los campesinos* (Along the Roads Go the Peasants), which is considered one of the most important dramatic pieces by a Nicaraguan of this century. It draws on the dramatic style of Bertolt Brecht and severely critiques the personal destruction that civil war wreaks upon the peasants. Its characters are full and vital, and their pain and suffering are poignant. The peasants and the land suffer the powerlessness of victims. A recently discovered short play, *Death*, set in the nineteenth century, captures this same tragic sense that war brings. Cuadra employs a chorus in the style of ancient Greek drama to capture the voice and mood of the villagers and to amplify the dramatic effect. In the work, an unnamed woman cries and laments that her son is about to be executed. William Walker, against whom the town of Granada is fighting, orders the weeping woman shot so she will not suffer. Cuadra's *La pastorela* (Shepherd's Song) offers a much lighter tone and message. Cuadra integrates Nicaraguan verses, songs, and rhymes from Christmas in creating this one-act play about the birth of Jesus and the transmission of Catholicism to the Americas. In his other professional capacities, he has also contributed to the theater. For over thirty years he edited the newspaper *La prensa*'s literary supplements and also operated a publishing house, El Pez y la Serpiente. In those roles, he figured centrally in the literary and intellectual development of many of Nicaragua's writers and poets.

WORKS: *Coloquio del indio Juan de Catarina* (Colloquy of the Indian Juan de Catarina), in *Azul y blanca*, Granada, no. 18 (June 1, 1940): 12–16. *Bailete del oso burgués* (Short Ballet of the Bourgeois Bear), in *Nuevos Horizontes*, July 5, 1942, 37–51. *Por los caminos van los campesinos* (Along the Roads Go the Peasants), in *Tres obras de teatro nuevo* (Managua: Ediciones Lengua, 1957), 45–162; *Teatro hispanoamericano contemporáneo: Antología* (Mexico City: Fondo de Cultura Económica, 1964), 181–248. *La pastorela* (Shepherd's Song), in *Antología de cuentistas hispanoamericanos* (Madrid: Aguilar, 1961), 578–588; *Boletín nicaragüense de bibliografía y documentación*, no. 41 (May–June 1981): 71–73. *Death* (Death), in *Boletín nicaragüense de bibliografía y documentación*, no. 49 (September–October 1982): 34–41.

BIBLIOGRAPHY: Jorge Eduardo Arellano, *Inventario del teatro de Nicaragua* (Managua: Biblioteca Banco Central de Nicaragua, 1988), 71–77. Arellano, *Panorama de la literatura nicaragüense* (Managua: Ediciones Nacionales, 1977), 131–332. M. J. Fenwick, *Writers of the Caribbean and Central America: A Bibliography*, vol. 2 (New York and London: Garland Publishing, 1992), 1055. Manuel Jiron, ed., *Quién es quién en Nicaragua* (Ediciones Radio Amor, 1986), 119–121. U.S. Dept. of State, Bureau of Public Affairs, *Nicaraguan Biographies: A Resource Book* (Washington, D.C., January 1988), Special Report No. 174. Agustín del Saz, *Teatro social hispanoamericano* (Barcelona: Editorial Labor, 1967), 154. Carlos Solóranza, *Teatro latinoamericano del siglo XX* (Mexico City: Editorial Porrúa, 1964). Grace Schulman, Introduction, *Songs of Cifar and the Sweet Sea*, by Pablo Antonio Cuadra, trans. and ed. Grace Schulman and Ann McCarthy de Zavala (New York: Columbia University Press, 1979), xiii–xix.

Mark F. Frisch

GÜEGÜENSE, EL. *El Güegüense o Macho Ratón* is a comedy ballet, written in the Nahualt-Spanish dialect of Nicaragua. It was probably composed in the seventeenth century, somewhere in the area between Granada, Masaya, and Carazo. There is no known author, and it was transcribed by Dr. Carl Hermann Berendt in 1874. He copied it from two manuscripts owned by Juan Eligio de la Rocha, in Masaya, and brought it to Philadelphia, where Daniel Garrison Brinton published it in his Brinton Library of Aboriginal Literature, with an introduction that is still very accurate and useful. *El Güegüense* is performed popularly in Masaya in September and in Diriamba in January. The characters wear masks and elaborate costumes, adorned with chains, coins, feathers, and flowers, as well as sashes and colorful handkerchiefs. It is debatable whether the play has a moral or religious purpose, but it is certainly funny and satiric.

El Güegüense, the main character, is a traveling merchant, unscrupulous and licentious. His name comes from the Nahualt *huehuentzin*, meaning "honored elder," and there is a debate on whether this is to be taken ironically or at face value. He is accompanied by his two sons: Don Forcico, who seems to be similar to his father and supports him in all his tricks and lies; and Don Ambrosio, in reality his stepson, who is always undermining his father's authority and exposing his dishonesty. The Gobernador Tastuanes represents the Spanish authority and is the object of mockery and laughter. The Alguacil (sheriff) appears from the very beginning with the Governor, and the Escribano (secretary) and the Regidor (registrar) do not appear until the end of the play. Only one woman appears in the play, as in most pre-Hispanic theater, as mutæ personæ, Suche-Malinche, the daughter of Governor Tastuanes who is given in marriage to Don Forcico. The other characters are the mules that appear in the latter part of the play in order to show Güegüenses' wealth. The plot of *El Güegüense* is quite simple: The Governor and the Alguacil complain about the poverty of their office and demand that Güegüense pays his taxes. Güegüense constantly pretends not to understand what is being said and claims that he didn't know he had to pay taxes. This is followed by a discussion about Güegüense's possessions and the petition of Suche-Malinche's hand. After showing Güegüense's mules to the Governor and making plans for the wedding, they ride off, promising to have a great party free of charge.

El Güegüense is subject to different readings and interpretations. For Pablo Antonio Cuadra it is a very complete characterization of the Nicaraguan people. For Alejandro Dávila Bolaños it is a revolutionary message calling for popular insurrection. Jorge Eduardo Arellano has placed more emphasis on the ludicrous and risqué tones of the work. In reality, all of the above readings are valid and simultaneous, and dis-

regarding one of them would mean to lose an important referent of the text.

MAIN EDITIONS: Daniel G. Brinton, *The Güegüense: A Comedy Ballet in the Nahualt-Spanish Dialect of Nicaragua* (Philadelphia: Brinton Library, 1883). Emilio Alvarez Lejarza, *El Güegüense o Macho Ratón. Comedia bailete de la época colonial* (Granada: Cuadernos del Taller San Lucas, 1942). Alejandro Dávila Bolaños, *Teatro popular colonial revolucionario: El Güegüense o Macho Ratón. Drama épico indígena* (Estelí: Géminis, 1974). Jorge Eduardo Arellano, *El Güegüense. Bailete dialogado en español-nahualt de Nicaragua* (México City: Noriega Editores, 1991).

BIBLIOGRAPHY: Jorge Eduardo Arellano, "*El Güegüense* o la esencia mestiza de Nicaragua," *Cuadernos Hispanoamericanos* 416 (February 1985): 19–51. Pablo Antonio Cuadra; "El primer personaje de la literatura nicaragüense," *Revista Conservadora del Pensamiento Centroamericano* 74 (November 1966): 2–3. Julio Escoto, "*El Güegüense*: Expresión de la dualidad colonia. Una aproximación ideológica," *Conjunto* 51 (January-February 1982): 17–34. Carlos Mántica, "Ensayo etimológico sobre *El Güegüense o Macho Ratón*," *El pez y la serpiente* 10 (Winter 1968–1969): 89–111. Francisco Pérez Estrada, "*El Güegüense o Macho Ratón*," *Plural* 60 (1981): 43–56. Eduardo Zepeda-Henríquez, "*El Güegüense* o la rebelión del mestizaje," *La Prensa Literaria*, November 20, 1976. Alberto Ycaza, "Trato y contrato: La obra subyacente de *El Güegüense*," in *El Güegüense. Coloquio Nacional*, Jorge Eduardo Arellano, ed. (Managua: Instituto Nicaragüense de Cultura, 1992), 93–106.

Nicasio Urbina

PALACIOS VIVAS, Nydia (1939–). Palacios Vivas is a prominent director, actress, and drama instructor. She was born in Masaya, Nicaragua, in 1939. When she was twelve years old, she won the third award in the First Certamen of National Recitation of Poetry. She traveled extensively through Europe and the United States. She debuted as an actress in *Los verdes campos del Edén* (The Green Fields of Eden) in 1966, directed by Socorro Bonilla Castellón, and in *Antígona* in 1967. In 1975 she obtained a scholarship to study Spanish language and literature in Madrid. In 1982, she directed *Prohibido suicidarse en primavera* (No Suicides in Springtime) by Alejandro Casona, *La guarda cuidadosa* (The Faithful Dog), and *El juez de los divorcios* (The Judge of the Divorce Court) in 1988, both farces by Cervantes. In 1986, she received a Fulbright Research Fellowship.

Her most important contribution has been the training of many of the actors, actresses, and directors who are presently members of Nicaragua's drama companies. She founded various drama clubs in secondary schools such as "El Güegüense," a group affiliated with the Institute Dr. René Shick (1971) in collaboration with Charles Delgadillo, and groups in the Instituto Bello Horizonte (1977) and American-Nicaraguan School (1982). She is a professor of Spanish literature and drama in the National University of Nicaragua. She received the award Ciudadana Ilustre for her contribution to development of the art and culture of Nicaragua. Presently, she is a candidate for a Ph.D. in Latin American Literature at Tulane University.

BIBLIOGRAPHY: Jorge Eduardo Arellano, *Inventario del teatro de Nicaragua* (Managua: Biblioteca Banco Central de Nicaragua, 1988). Nydia Palacios, *Antología de la novela nicaragüense* (Managua: Editorial Cyra, 1989). Palacios, "Sintaxis narrativa y recursos estilísticos y morfosintácticos en la canción del oro de Rubén Darío," in *Azul y las literaturas hispánicas* (Mexico City: Universidad Nacional de Mexico, 1990). Palacios, "La novela nicaragüense en el siglo XX," *Revista hispanoamericana* 57.157 (1991). Palacios, *Técnica narrativa en Sergio Ramírez* (Managua: Universidad Nacional Autónoma de Nicaragua, 1971).

Mark F. Frisch

ROBLETO, Hernán (1885–1968). Robleto was a journalist, playwright, and novelist. He was born in Boaco, Nicaragua, in 1985. In Managua, he organized the Compañía Dramática Nacional. He is considered the founder of the Nicaraguan *costumbrista* theater, with its focus on the customs and mores of the peasants. He spent a good part of his life living in Mexico City because of his liberal ideological thought.

Several of his works deal with political themes. His famous novel *Sangre en el trópico* deals with the struggles of the Liberal and Conservative parties. The drama *Pájaros del Norte* (Birds of the North) is a re-creation of the conflict between the American Intervention Forces and the Nicaraguan national hero Augusto C. Sandino. Robleto's dramas were staged abroad as well as in Nicaragua. *La rosa del paraíso* (The Rose of Paradise) was produced in Lima, Peru's Teatro Municipal in 1926 to great public and critical acclaim. *La cruz de ceniza* (The Ashen Cross) was very well received also.

WORKS: *La rosa del paraíso* (The Rose of Paradise) (Managua: Tipografía Pérez, 1920). *El milagro* (The Miracle) (Tegucigalpa: Tipografía Nacional, 1921). *La señorita que arrojó el antifaz* (The Woman Who Hurled the Mask) (Mexico City: Talleres Gráficos de la Nación, 1928). *La cruz de ceniza* (The Ashen Cross), in *Tres dramas* (Three Dramas) (Managua: Editorial Atlántida, 1946). *La niña Soledad* (A Girl Named Soledad), in *Tres dramas* (Three Dramas) (Managua: Editorial Atlántida, 1946). *Muñecos de barro* (Clay Dolls), in *Tres dramas* (Three Dramas) (Managua: Editorial Atlántida, 1946). *Pájaros del Norte* (Birds of the North) (Managua: Boletín Nicaragüense de Bibliografía y Documentación No. 49, September-October 1982).

BIBLIOGRAPHY: Ramón Luis Acevedo, *La novela centroamericana* (Río Piedras: Universidad de Puerto Rico, 1982). Arellano, *Panorama de la literatura nicaragüense* (Managua: Ediciones Nacionales, 1977). Jorge Eduardo Arellano, *Inventario del teatro de Nicaragua* (Managua: Biblioteca Banco Central de Nicaragua, 1988).

Nydia Palacios Vivas

ROBLETO, Octavio (1935–). Robleto was born in Chontales, Nicaragua, in 1935. He is a lawyer, poet, and dramatist. He founded the journal *Ventana* with Sergio Ramírez and Fernando Gordillo, who later founded the Frente Ventana student organization that fought against the Somoza dictatorship. He was the director of the *Cuadernos Universitarios*, a journal of the students of the National University in León, Nicaragua. He has traveled widely throughout Europe and the United States. He received a Literarian Research grant for Germany in 1966, and he was awarded a Fulbright Research Scholarship in Washington, D.C. in 1990. He won the Premio Nacional Rubén Darío in 1957 and 1958. His has written many children's plays, taking folkloric themes and popular oral tales and adapting them.

WORKS: *De la guerra entre Tío Coyote y Tío Conejo* (The War between Uncle Coyote and Uncle Rabbit), staged by Comedia Nacional de Nicaragua, Managua, 1973. *Por aquí pasó un soldado* (A Soldier Passed by Here) (León: *Cuadernos Universitarios* 4.14 [September 1975]). *Tres obras teatrales de Nicaragua* (Three Nicaraguan Theatrical Works) (Managua: Ediciones Nacionales, 1977). *Teatro para niños* (Theater for Children) (Managua: Ministerio de Cultura, 1984).

BIBLIOGRAPHY: Jorge Eduardo Arellano, *Inventario del teatro de Nicaragua* (Managua: Biblioteca Banco Central de Nicaragua, 1988). Arellano, *Panorama de la literatura nicaragüense* (Managua: Ediciones Nacionales, 1977).

Mark F. Frisch and Nydia Palacios Vivas

STEINER, Rolando (1936–). A playwright and director, he is an important figure in the development of the contemporary theater. In his works, he draws on mythic themes to comment on contemporary life. His first work, *Judit* (Judith) (1957), builds on the biblical story of Judith to capture a middle-class marriage as it crumbles. His play *Un drama corriente* (An Ordinary Drama) (1963) also deals with a middle-class couple confronting the hallowness and shallowness of their marital relationship. As in *Judit*, the distinction between reality and dream blurs here. Steiner's last work was *La noche de Wiwilí* (The Night of Wiwilí) (1982). He assumes a political stance through his portrayal of the betrayal, death, and martyrdom of General Agusto César Sandino.

He has been recognized frequently for his work. *Judit* was presented in Paris in 1957 during the Festival of Nations. *Antígona en el infierno* (Antigone in Hell) received the Premio de Teatro de la Universidad Nacional. He received the Premio de Teatro Lope de Vega for *Un drama corriente* (An Ordinary Drama). He also received the Segundo Premio de Teatro de los Juegos Florales Centroamericanos de Quezalterango for his marriage trilogy *Judit, Un drama corriente,* and *La puerta* (The Door).

WORKS: *Judit* (Judith), in *Tres obras de teatro nuevo* (Managua: Ediciones Lengua, 1957), 165–213. *Antígona en el infierno* (Antigone in Hell) (León: Universidad Nacional Autónoma de Nicaragua, 1958), *Boletín nicaragüense de bibliografía y documentación* 41 (May-June 1981): 87–92. *Un drama corriente* (An Ordinary Drama) (Managua: Editorial Nuevos Horizontes, 1963). *La pasíon de Helena* (The Passion of Helen), in *Zarpa* (November 1963); *Boletín nicaragüense de bibliografía y documentación* 41 (May-June 1981): 93–95. *El tercer día* (The Third Day), in *La Prensa Literaria* (April 1965). *La puerta* (The Door), in *El Pez y la Serpiente* 7–8 (June 1966). *La mujer deshabitada* (The Uninhabited Woman) (Managua: Editorial Nuevos Horizontes, 1970). *La agonía del poeta* (The Poet's Agony), in *El Pez y la Serpiente* 10 (summer 1977): 111–163. *La noche de Wiwilí* (The Night of Wiwilí), in *Boletín nicaragüense de bibliografía y documentación* 49 (September-October 1982): 64–72; *Nicaráuac*, 4.9 (April 1983): 135–146.

BIBLIOGRAPHY: Jorge Eduardo Arellano, *Inventario del teatro de Nicaragua* (Managua: Biblioteca Banco Central de Nicaragua, 1988), 91–98, 148–151. Arellano, *Panorama de la literatura nicaragüense* (Managua: Ediciones Nacionales, 1977), 133–134. M. J. Fenwick, *Writers of the Caribbean and Central America: A Bibliography*, vol. 2 (New York and London: Garland Publishing, 1992), 1088. Anuar Hassan, "Dos grandes obras, (*Chinfonía burguesa* y *La puerta*), en el (teatro) experimental," *La prensa* (Managua), December 14, 1972.

Mark F. Frisch and Nydia Palacios Vivas

Nuyorican

Puerto Ricans constitute the second largest Hispanic population in the United States after the Mexican Americans. According to the 1990 census, there are 2.2 million Puerto Ricans living in the United States, half of whom have chosen to settle in New York. Puerto Rican migration to the United States had its greatest influx during the 1940s and 1950s when the Puerto Rican population in New York rose from 70,000 to more than 300,000. The children of these immigrants, the generation of New York Puerto Ricans of the 1960s forward who spend their formative years on the mainland, call themselves Nuyoricans. They are the bicultural and bilingual children of urban Puerto Rican immigrants who share the ethnic tradition of their ancestors but who view themselves as distinct from their relatives living in Puerto Rico. The Nuyoricans speak English and forge their roots in New York.

Theatrical expression arises from the given historic, linguistic, and social circumstances of a community. In the 1960s a new kind of theatrical and artistic expression originates among the New York Puerto Ricans in Hispanic working-class communities. This movement is coined "Nuyorican" in the very literature in which it is conceived. In his poem "Neo-Rican Jetliner/Jet neorriqueño," the poet and playwright Jaime Carrero uses the term *Neorican/Nuyorican* to refer to the cultivation of a New York Puerto Rican literature and theater in the late 1960s. Later poets and playwrights who were associated with the Nuyorican Poets' Café and Joseph Papp, such as Tato Laveira, Miguel Piñero, and Miguel Algarín, came to define the essence of Nuyorican literature and theater in their works.

The group identification as Nuyorican brings a sense of dignity, pride, and ethnic and cultural solidarity to these bilingual and bicultural writers. It is a preservation of identity against the influence of the dominant society. The thematic focus of the early Nuyorican writers is survival in the urban communities in which they live. The confusion and conflict that children of Puerto Rican immigrants experience in balancing their parents' heritage with the new popular culture results in rebellion against a normative social order that does not provide for their needs. The raw aesthetic of real life is treated through autobiographical discourses that represent the world of the underclass and criminals. Experimental and political plays reflect street life, drug addiction, prostitution, violent crime, aberrant behavior, and prison life, with the prison as a metaphorical space for Nuyorican identity.

The neologism Nuyorican designates a conscious linguistic and cultural synergy in a group that does not consider itself solely Puerto Rican but that vindicates itself with a new language and a new identity. Because Nuyorican writers convey the current reality of Puerto Ricans in the United States, their language is new: It is a mixture of English and Spanish that enriches verbal expression. Duality of language is a means of structuring the individual and collective identity of the Nuyoricans. The Nuyorican language is not legitimized by a dictionary, rules, or grammar, but it is an improvisational language without fixed forms.

Linguistic biculturalism takes its form from the code switching that validates the linguistic practices of the *barrios* in a distinctive street language that incorporates Spanish and Black English, drawing from the Hispanic and Afro-Caribbean heritage. The vulgarity represents a sociopolitical protest against the discrimination of the literate, educated classes. Linguistic cultural differentiation affirms a new paradigm for creativity. The civil rights movement and the Black and Chicano movements of the 1960s and 1970s create social transformations that enable ethnic literary productions. Nuyorican writers' self-awareness and cultural resistance in language, ideology, and identity differentiate them from mainstream America and from their island relatives in Puerto Rico. Nuyorican theatrical production dramatizes the problems of adaptation, social struggle, and cultural resistance in the daily life of Puerto Ricans.

Nuyorican writers propose to raise the consciousness of Puerto Ricans living in New York and of the larger society with respect to the unacceptable treatment of Puerto Ricans. The works of these social and political writers give visibility to ethnic discrimination, economic subordination, and poor living conditions. Nuyorican themes underscore that the Great American Dream does not materialize for all immigrants. However, not all Puerto Ricans subscribe to the Nuyorican movement. They object to the association of Nuyorican literature with desperation, hopelessness, and the rejection of island culture in favor of a culture based in New York City.

The newest generation of Nuyorican playwrights has had the opportunity of polishing their craft through higher education and the support of playwright workshops. Young playwrights, such as Richard Irizarry, Yvette Ramírez, Edward Gallardo, Cándido Tirado, Juan Shamsul Alam, and Fernando Fraguada, have not abandoned the concerns of their predecessors and still follow their language and style. They reap the benefits of a mature Hispanic theater with permanent stages, an established directorial group, and a welcoming audience. Nuyorican theater has been performed on Broadway, off Broadway, on city streets, in Joseph Papp's New York Shakespeare Festival, and at The Henry Street Settlement's New Federal Theater. New York City, the mecca of theater, has been the premiere stage for the theatrical ambitions of Nuyorican, as well as all Hispanic, theater.

Written scholarship on Nuyorican theater is surprisingly meager. In part, this is due to it being a relatively new movement, but a principal cause is the scarce publication and diffusion of these writings, which are out of print or inaccessible to readers. This hinders the task of literary critics who cannot become familiar with the works of authors who are new and unknown to the academy.

RECENT NUYORICAN THEATER

Nuyorican literature has flourished and diversified in the 1980s, but it remains a literature that addresses the issues of marginalization, oppression, and historical invisibility. The previously disguised subjects of homosexuality, the homeless, sexism, AIDS, and racism are now explored as the products of inner attitudes rather than of external politics. The sense of allegiance to New York as home is greater than the desire to return to the homeland of Puerto Rico, although the cultural tie is never relinquished. Nuyorican theater represents the problems of the community, the obstacles of biculturalism, and creative solutions for unification. The Nuyorican artists have addressed their works to a broader audience and have gained greater acceptance in the theatrical world. Their voice speaks of the familiar immigrant experience of all Americans. Hispanic and non-Hispanic theater companies are able to attract cosmopolitan audiences by virtue of the bilingual productions, the humanity of the issues, and the quality of the productions. In the fall of 1995, the Spanish Repertory Theater launched their innovative program "Nuevas Voces" (New Voices), a new series of works that document the experiences of Nuyoricans and that feature Latino playwrights and directors based in New York. Nuyorican theater continues to redefine what it means to be Latino in an ever-evolving society. Cultural identification will not fade away as long as there is a sense of common ethnicity and tradition that coexists with the U.S. experience. There are many unpublished Nuyorican plays that have earned critical and public success, but they are yet to be recognized and given literary status by the academy.

BIBLIOGRAPHY

Acosta-Belén, Edna. "Beyond Island Boundaries. Ethnicity, Gender, and Cultural Revitalization in Nuyorican Literature." *Callaloo: A Journal of African-American and African Arts and Letters* 15.4 (1992): 979–998.

———. "The Literature of the Puerto Rican National Minority in the United States." *The Bilingual Review/La Revista Billingüe* 5.1–2 (1978): 107–116.

Algarín, Miguel. "Nuyorican Aesthetics." In *Images and Identities. The Puerto Rican in Two World Contexts*, ed. Asela Rodríguez de Laguna. New Brunswick, NJ: Transaction Books, 1986, 161–163.

———. "Nuyorican Literature." *Melus: The Journal of the Society for the Study of the Multi-Ethnic Literature of the United States* 8.2 (1981): 89–92.

———, and Miguel Piñero, eds. "Introduction: Nuyorican Language." In *Nuyorican Poetry: An Anthology of Puerto Rican Words and Feelings*. New York: William Morrow and Company, 1975, 9–20.

Aparacio, Frances. "La vida es un spanglish disparatero', Bilingualism in Nuyorican Poetry." In *European Perspectives on Hispanic Literature of the United States*, ed. Genevive Fabre. Houston: Arte Público Press, 1988, 147–160.

Benmayor, Rina. "Crossing Borders: The Politics of Multiple Identity." *Centro de Estudios Puertoriqueños Bulletin* 2.3 (1988): 71–77.

Cortés, Félix, Angel Falcón, and Juan Flores. "The Cultural Expression of Puerto Ricans in New York City: A Theoretical Perspective and Critical Review." *Latin American Perspectives* 3.3 (1976): 117–150.

Cruz-Malavé, Arnaldo. "Teaching Puerto Rican Authors: Identity and Modernization in Nuyorican Texts." *ADE Bulletin* 91 (1988): 45–51.

Flores, Juan. *Divided Borders. Essays on Puerto Rican Identity*. Houston: Arte Público Press, 1993.

———, and George Yudice. "Living Borders/Buscando América: Languages of Latino Self-Formation." *Social Text* 248.2 (1990): 57–58.

Kanellos, Nicólas. *A History of Hispanic Theatre in the United States: Origins to 1940*. Austin: University of Texas Press, 1990.

Mohr, Eugene V. *The Nuyorican Experience, Literature of the Puerto Rican Minority*. Westport, CT: Greenwood Press, 1982.

Mohr, Nicholasa. "Puerto Ricans in New York: Cultural Evolution and Identity" In *Images and Identities, The Puerto Rican in Two World Contexts*, ed. Asela Rodríguez de Laguna. New Brunswick, NJ: Transaction Books, 1986, 157–160.

Morton, Carlos. "The Nuyoricans." *Latin American Theatre Review* 10.1 (Fall 1976): 80–89.

Santiago, S. "The Nuyoricans." *Village Voice* (February 1979): 14.

Zimmerman, Marc. *U.S. Latino Literature. An Essay and Annotated Bibliography*. Chicago: March/Abrazo Press, 1992.

◆

ALAM, Juan Shamsul. Juan Shamsul Alam is a popular playwright whose plays explore the contemporary problems of the "barrio" such as AIDS, alienation, and homosexuality.

Midnight Blues (1987) presents the portrayal of a patriarch whose dreams have been subverted by his own actions, reminiscent of *Death of a Salesman*. The play, set in a basement apartment, spans several hours in the life of Jackson Vega, a moderately successful businessman. His *machismo* results in the emotional abuse of his wife, Eva, and his two sons, Joe and Bobby, who are supposed to follow in his footsteps. His authoritarian actions alienate his family. At the end of the play it is revealed that his gay son Bobby died homeless on the streets after his homophobic father threw him out because he had AIDS. The character Bobby is actually a ghost who, much like a Greek chorus, serves as Jackson's conscience. After Jackson's family abandons him, he assumes a fetal position. His solitude is the only possible consequence of his lack of emotional commitment to his family. The public and critics acclaimed this play, calling the author a gifted playwright.

The play *Hakim* (1983) shows the conflict that develops between Hakim, who stays in the *barrio* to improve the living conditions there, and his friend, who leaves to improve his own condition. The sacrifice of one's culture for selfish reasons creates an unresolved tension.

Zookeeper (1989), set in Manhattan's East Harlem, presents Carlos, a character who is torn between his love for his wife and children and his responsibility toward his younger brother José, who is dying. Carlos is forced to make a choice wherein morality is the decisive factor.

WORKS: *Hakim* (one-act play), Museo del Barrio, 1983. *Midnight Blues*, staged reading at the Invisible Performance Workshop, April 1984; Malka Percal's Invisible Performance Theater, South Bronx, May 1987. *Zookeeper*, Latino Playwrights Theatre, 1989.

ALGARÍN, Miguel (1941–). Algarín was born on September 11, 1941, in Santurce, Puerto Rico. After the industrialization of Puerto Rico in the early 1950s, Algarín's family sought a better life in New York City, where they lived in Spanish Harlem and in Queens. Algarín attended New York's City College but went to the University of Wisconsin to complete his bachelor's degree (1963). He earned a master's degree at Pennsylvania State University (1965) and his doctorate at Rutgers, where he has served as professor of English literature and chair of the Puerto Rican Studies Department. As founder of the Nuyorican Poets' Café on the Lower East Side (Loisaida, the Hispanic pronunciation), Algarín has made an important contribution to the artistic and literary life of the community by providing a forum for Puerto Rican writers during the 1970s when Nuyorican literature was being defined. Algarín is also responsible for the formation of Arte Público Press in Houston, the leading publisher of Nuyorican literature, and his own publishing house, the Nuyorican Press, which issued only one book, his *Mongo Affair* (1978). Best known as a poet, Algarín has also written short stories, screenplays, and drama. He is the coauthor with Tato Laveira of the play *Olú Clemente* (1973). He has directed the Nuyorican Playwrights'/ Actors' Workshop, a service organization that develops playwrights and actors at the same time. He serves on the advisory board of the Association of Hispanic Arts in New York City.

Olú Clemente (coauthored with Tato Laveira) is a eulogy of the heroic baseball player Roberto Clemente, who lost his life in a plane crash bringing relief to Nicaraguan earthquake victims. Striving to highlight the hero's African roots, Clemente is metamorphosed into an African deity among the Siete Potencias Africanas (Seven African Powers) who are revered in Caribbean religion. Afro-Caribbean music is the background for this spiritual celebration.

WORK: *Olú Clemente*, New York Delacorte Theater, 1973.

BIBLIOGRAPHY: Eugene V. Mohr, *The Nuyorican Experience. Literature of the Puerto Rican Minority* (Westport, CT: Greenwood Press, 1982), 96–103. Carlos Morton, "The Nuyoricans," *Latin American Theatre Review* 10.1 (Fall 1976): 80–89. S. Santiago, "The Nuyoricans," *Village Voice* (February 1979): 14.

CARRERO, Jaime (1931–). Carrero was born in Mayagüez, Puerto Rico. He spent his formative years in both New York and Puerto Rico. He earned a B.A. in Fine Arts at the Inter-American University in San Germán, Puerto Rico, and a master's degree from the Pratt Institute in New York City. He studied art at Columbia University and in Florence. Having exhibited his paintings in the United States and Mexico, he now has a display in the permanent collection of the Puerto Rican Museum of Fine Arts. He has served as chair of the Fine Arts Department at the Inter-American University. In the 1960s and 1970s, he pioneered the creation of a Nuyorican consciousness that expressed the bicultural experience of those living in New York. In 1964, he gave the name *Nuyorican* or *Neo-Rican* to the literary movement of his generation in his volume of poems in Spanish and English, *Jet Neorriqueño: Neo-Rican Jetliner*. He won the Illinois Arts Council Award for his poetry. In addition to his poems, he has published novels, plays, and short stories. Carrero's work has received little scholarly attention, although he has written award-winning theater and prose works. His drama *Flag Inside* (1966) was honored with first prize in the Ateneo Puertorriqueño's drama competition. The literary journal *Sin nombre* awarded the prestigious Premio Eugenio Fernández García to the Spanish version of *The FM Safe*

entitled *La caja de caudales FM* (1978). He has served as contributing editor for the journal *Revista Chicano-Riqueña*.

Carrero writes of the isolation that Puerto Ricans experience on an individual and collective level. He recognizes that language influences Puerto Rican cultural identity and social power. The power of verbal art in a culturally alienating society is represented by the verbosity of Nuyoricans in contrast to their silent relatives on the island of Puerto Rico. Carrero credits America's lack of values and materialism with the dissolution of social and family structures within the Puerto Rican community. In *Flag Inside*, the body of Alberto, a casualty in the Vietnam War, arrives home in a coffin labeled "Flag inside." Alberto's family argues over his last wishes, not to have flags or crosses adorn his coffin, and about the morality of war. His brother Raúl rejects the war. His father Augusto, who abandoned his family for a young mistress, represents the acceptance of the values of the American corporation where he is employed. The strong Puerto Rican mother, Úrsula, has lost her family, including her daughter Lucía, who exemplifies vanity and materialism.

WORKS: *Noo Jork*, in *Revista Chicano-Riqueña* 7 (Fall 1972): 3–31. *La caja de caudales FM*, in *Sin nombre* 8 (January-March 1978): 63–99. *Teatro: Flag Inside, Capitán F4C, El caballo de Ward, Pipo Subway no sabe reír* (Río Piedras: Editorial Puerto, 1973). *The FM Safe, Chicano and Puerto Rican Drama*, ed. Nicolás Kanellos and Jorge Huerta (Houston: Arte Público Press, 1979). Plays produced: *Pipo Subway no sabe reír*, Puerto Rican Traveling Theatre, 1972. *Flag Inside* and *Noo Jall*, Puerto Rican Traveling Theatre, 1973. *The FM Safe*, Puerto Rican Traveling Theatre, 1979. *La caja de caudales FM*, San Juan, Puerto Rico, 1979. *El Lucky Seven*, University of Puerto Rico, 1979.

BIBLIOGRAPHY: J. A. Collins, "Carrero's *Cashbox FM* a Theatrical Firebomb," *The San Juan Star*, June 22, 1979, 7. Manuel Gallich, "El teatro puertorriqueño dentro del nuevo teatro latinoamericano," *Conjunto* (July-September 1978): 62–68. Juan Luis Márquez, "*Pipo Subway no sabe reír*," *El Imparcial*, May 12, 1972. Robert F. Muckley, "Introduction," *Notes on Neorican Seminar* (San Germán: Inter American University, 1972), 2. Edmund Newton,

"*Noo Jall* Opens: Set to Tour Parks," *New York Post*, August 28, 1973, 20; "*Noo Jall*: Otro éxito del Teatro Rodante Puertorriqueño," *El Tiempo*, August 26, 1973, 18–19; "*Noo Jall* Plays in City Parks," *New York Times*, August 29, 1973. Patricia O'Haire, "*Noo Jall* Lively Play," *Daily News*, August 29, 1973, 60. Asela Rodríguez-Seda, "El teatro de Jaime Carrero," *Revista Chicano-Riqueña* 5 (Summer 1977): 26–31. Norma Valle, "*Flag Inside*: Obra humana de gran valor teatral," *El Mundo*, February 25, 1973.

DELGADO, Luis. Delgado has worked with various New York theaters since 1983. He is a member of the Dramatist Guild and PRIDE (Puerto Rican Intercultural Drama Ensemble). His works include: *Halfway House, A Better Life, Tony and Son, Men Don't Cry, What Would Simon Say*, and *Papi, Loco and the Martian*. Delgado received the Roger L. Stevens Promising Playwright Award in 1993.

El Cano (The Blond Man) (1995): Danny Casiano, an ambitious, young, Puerto Rican advertising executive, is what is affectionately termed a *cano*, a Latino of fair complexion and blond hair. Because of his looks and his surname, Danny is perceived to be of Italian heritage by his bigoted Anglo boss, a misconception he passively neglects to correct. Delgado, himself a *cano*, depicts the contradictions of dual identifications faced by Nuyoricans through a mainly Spanish dialogue that is interspersed with Nuyorican Spanglish and yuppie English. The immediacy of the conflict between the acceptance of one's culture and acceptance by society resulted in rave reviews for this comedy that deeply touched New York audiences.

WORKS: *El Cano*, Spanish Repertory Theater, 1995–1996. *Halfway House* (n.d.). *A Better Life* (n.d.). *Tony and Son* (n.d.). *Men Don't Cry* (n.d.). *What Would Simon Say* (n.d.). *Papi, Loco and the Martian* (n.d.).

BIBLIOGRAPHY: Clive Barnes, "Puerto Rican Exec Learns How to Succeed in Business," *New York Post*, November 28, 1995. Ed Morales, "White Hombre's Burden," *Village Voice*, November 21, 1995.

FRAGUADA, Fernando. Part of the newest generation of Nuyorican playwrights, Fernando Fraguada continues to present in his plays the concerns of his predecessors.

In *Bodega* (The Grocery Store) (1986), Máximo Toro, the owner of a successful *bodega* in the South Bronx, dreams of someday expanding his business into a chain of *bodegas*. His wife Elena is supportive of her macho husband but wishes to return to the peaceful island life of Puerto Rico. Their rebellious teenage daughter Norma attempts to reject her ethnicity for a future as a dancer. The dreams of the family are shattered by a drug addict, a robbery, and a gun, which is symbolic of the violence of American life. The play, a successful and important comment on the Great American Dream, was very popular with audiences because of the reality of the immigrant experience. Fraguada writes from his own life experience as a former employee of a *bodega* and from a cultural construct that dictates the mechanisms of social interaction.

WORKS: *Bodega*, Puerto Rican Traveling Theater, January 1986 and May–June 1988; Centro de Bellas Artes, Santurce, Puerto Rico, January 1988; Teatro La Perla, Ponce, Puerto Rico, February 1988; University of Puerto Rico, February 1988.

GALLARDO, Edward (1949–). Gallardo's family is from Puerto Rico, but he was born and lives in New York. He left a successful acting career in Los Angeles due to his dissatisfaction with Hollywood's stereotyping of Latinos. Gallardo's *Simpson Street* (1979) inspired national interest in the Hispanic experience in New York and moved Hispanic theater out of the *barrio* and into the mainstream of American drama due to its widespread critical success around the country and abroad. This portrait of family life in a slum of the Bronx distinguishes itself from the works of the earlier generation of exiled Puerto Ricans who long to return to their native homeland. The members of Gallardo's generation know that they will have to make New York "home" while maintaining their Puerto Rican identity. Gallardo's play *Women Without Men* (1985) won first place in the New York Shakespeare Festival and Festival Latino's National Contest of Latino Plays. It was chosen from among eighty-six entries, in both English and Spanish, from throughout the United States. The play was also awarded semifinalist honors at the American Minority Playwrights Festival in Seattle (1985). In addition to his success in the United States, Gallardo's plays have garnered him international fame in Puerto Rico, Spain, Mexico, and Colombia. Considered milestones in the development of Hispanic drama, Gallardo's works have been compared to the plays of Tennessee Williams, the playwright whom he most admires.

PLAYS PRODUCED: *Bernie* (and director), New York Theater Ensemble, 1968. *In Another Part of the City*, New York Theater Ensemble, 1970. *Women Without Men*, Joseph Papp production, Public/Susan Stein Shiva Theater, 1985.

WORKS: *Waltz on a Merry-Go-Round (1975)*, in *Simpson Street and Other Plays*, ed. John Antush (Houston: Arte Público Press, 1989). *Women Without Men, (1985)*, in *Simpson Street and Other Plays*.

BIBLIOGRAPHY: *New York Times*, July 2, 1985; August 10, 1985. *Village Voice*, November 20, 1969; July 30, 1970.

GONZÁLEZ, Reubén. Reubén González is a contemporary Nuyorican playwright whose plays show the difficulties experienced by immigrant families.

In *The Boiler Room* (1987), the generational conflict between Olivia and her mother Olga is a social reality expressed at an individual level. Olga's son Anthony commits crimes, but his motive is the family's survival. Their move from a basement apartment into an upstairs apartment is a metaphor for the challenge that society presents to the immigrant family to ascend in the community and to solidify their familial unity.

WORKS: *The Boiler Room* (1987).

HISPANIC THEATER COMPANIES IN NEW YORK. Since the 1960s, Hispanic theater has flourished in New York City through the productions of major companies that are managed along traditional lines and smaller companies that follow a repertory style. Financial support has been provided by private institutions and by city and state organizations. With more than twenty legitimate theater companies in New York City, Hispanic theater is represented by The Puerto Rican Traveling Theater, Spanish Repertory Theater (Teatro Repertorio Español), International Arts Relations (INTAR), Latin American Theater Ensemble (LATE), Thalia, Café La Mama, Nuestro Teatro, Instituto Arte Teatral Internacional (IATI), Dúo, Pregones, and Tremont Arts Group. Groups that have been associated specifically with Nuyorican theater are Teatro Ambulante, Puerto Rican Bilingual Workshop, Teatro Otra Cosa, The Family, The Young Family, Acquarius, Latin Insomniacs, Puerto Rican Organization for Self-Advancement, Latino Experimental Theatre, E.T.C., Theater for the New City, Puerto Rican Intercultural Drama Ensemble (PRIDE), and Nuyorican Poets' Café.

The Puerto Rican Traveling Theater, founded in 1967 by Miriam Colón, Frances Drucker, Stella Holt, and George Edgar, pioneered the presentation of Nuyorican and other U.S. Hispanic authors. Colón, the First Lady of Hispanic theater and the artistic director of the PRTT, achieved a distinguished stage and screen presence in both New York and Hollywood and was honored with the White House Hispanic Heritage Award in 1990. Before the PRTT opened its permanent theater house in 1974 on West Forty-seventh Street in the Broadway area, it had operated as a mobile theater on the streets of Hispanic neighborhoods. The funding provided through the Summer Taskforce of Mayor John Lindsay in the late 1960s supported the PRTT in bringing its productions to the people free of charge in playgrounds and parks around New York City.

INTAR was formed in 1967 as the Latin American Art Group (ADAL) by Frank Robles, Elisa Ortiz de Robles, Max Ferra, and Antonio González. By 1977 INTAR had achieved equity status as a professional theater and is currently located on West Forty-second Street in the Broadway Theater District. Plays in English and in Spanish by classical and local writers are produced using innovative direction and settings, and INTAR is responsible for developing Hispanic playwrighting.

The Spanish Repertory Theater (Teatro Repertorio Español), founded in 1969 by René

Buch, Luz Castaños, Gilberto Zaldívar, and Frances Drucker, operates in the Gramercy Arts Theater and works as an ensemble with productions in both English and Spanish of classical Spanish and contemporary Latin American works.

Smaller companies arose under the direction of one or two individuals: Iván Acosta (Centro Cultural Cubano); Manuel Martín and Magaly Alabau (Teatro Dúo); Luz Castaños (Nuestro Teatro); Manuel Martín and Mario Peña (LATE); Herberto Dume (DUME), which later became Silvio Brito's (Thalia); Abdón Villamizar (IATI); and Oscar Siccone (Teatro 4). Marvin Félix Camillo developed the Family, a residential program for former inmates that began in workshops in the Bedford Hills Correctional Facility in Westchester County. At the Henry Street Settlement, Carla Pinza established the Puerto Rican Bilingual Workshop, which later became the Hispanic Playwrights' Workshops. The director Frank Pérez founded the Shaman Repertory Theater and the Puerto Rican Intercultural Drama Ensemble.

Joseph Papp's New York Shakespeare Theater awakened an interest in Hispanic theater by bringing productions to parks, playgrounds, El Barrio, the Lower East Side, and Queens. Hispanic theater has attained a wider recognition in the United States through the publication of plays and articles in specialized journals that feature drama, *Latin American Theatre Review* and *Revista Chicano-Riqueña*, and through the journalistic coverage of play debuts in the *New York Times*, the *New York Post*, and the *Village Voice*.

BIBLIOGRAPHY: Miguel Algarín, "Nuyorican Literature," *Melus: The Journal of the Society for the Study of the Multi-Ethnic Literature of the United States* 8.2 (1981): 89–92. Juan Flores, "Puerto Rican Literature in the United States: Stages and Perspectives," *ADE Bulletin* 91 (1988): 39–44. John C. Miller, "Contemporary Hispanic Theater in New York," in *Hispanic Theater in the United States*, ed. Nicolás Kanellos (Houston: Arte Público Press, 1984), 24–33. Miller, "Cross-Currents in Hispanic U.S. Contemporary Drama," in *Images and Identities: The Puerto Rican in Two World Contexts*, ed. Asela Rodríguez de Laguna (New Brunswick, NJ: Transaction Books, 1986), 246–253. Miller, "Hispanic Theater in New York 1965–1977," *Revista Chicano-Riqueña* 6.1 (1978): 40–59. Eugene Mohr, *The Nuyorican Experience: The Literature of the Puerto Rican Minority* (Westport, CT: Greenwood Press, 1982). Carlos Morton, "Nuyorican Theater," *The Drama Review* 20.1 (1976): 43–49. Joanne Pottlitzer, *Hispanic Theater in the United States and Puerto Rico* (New York: Ford Foundation 1988).

IRIZARRY, Richard V. Richard Irizarry is part of the next generation of Nuyorican playwrights who continues the tradition started by his predecessors.

Ariano (1988) is a dramatic account of the racial attitudes of an upwardly mobile, "yuppie" Puerto Rican who desires acceptance in the white world. Ariano is in his thirties, handsome, and light-skinned. Racial discrimination based on phenotypic characteristics, while not practiced to the extreme on the island of Puerto Rico, is part of life in America. The whiter one's skin, the easier it is to mainstream into a more privileged life. Ariano portrays the conflicts of cultural identity and values in the face of mainland racial prejudice that leads an ambitious individual to deny his family and friends. Pride in ethnic heritage, *la raza*, is the answer to racial prejudice. The dialogue of the play, which adeptly incorporates Spanish, represents the fusion of both cultures in Nuyorican speech. The public and critics responded enthusiastically to this play, which played to overflow crowds.

WORKS: *Ariano*, Off-Off Broadway, 1984; Puerto Rican Traveling Theater January 20–February 28, 1988, and January 1990; Festival of Latin American Theater, University of Puerto Rico, Spring 1990; Ninth Anniversary Celebration of El Centro de Bellas Artes, Puerto Rico, 1990.

LAVEIRA, Tato (1950–). Jesús Abraham Laveira was born on September 5, 1950, in Santurce, Puerto Rico. His family's migration to New York in 1960 coincided with the post–World War II migration process. Laveira's mother wanted her pregnant daughter to have her baby in New York, away from her husband's wrath. Laveira, a black-skinned, ten-year-old who had assumed that all New Yorkers were white, was pleased to see people of his color when he arrived at the airport. His family settled in the economically disadvantaged Lower East Side. Laveira spoke practically no English but found that his service as an altar boy in the Catholic Church gave him a sense of belonging in a society that was alien to him. He graduated from high school in 1968 and did not pursue further study. Laveira's knowledge of the community and his interest in its people led him to a social service administrative career. He worked as an assistant director at the Association of Community Services for ten years (1970–1980) and as its executive director for five more years. Laveira served as chairman of the Board of Directors of the Madison Neighbors in Action and as a board member of Mobilization for Youth, Inc. In 1973 he wrote the film *Espiritismo* (Spiritualism) for the PBS network in New York. He was honored by President Jimmy Carter at a White House gathering of American Poets in 1980. Laveira worked with the Shakespeare Festival Latino for five years and was named a commissioned playwright of the Henry Street Settlement New Federal Theater in 1983 and later the director of its Hispanic Drama Workshop. He accepts the designation Nuyorican, but he considers himself an integration of many voices, "I believe we have *cinco gorras* [five hats]: we wear the Hispano hat which answers to Latin America; we wear the Caribbean hat which binds us to Blackness; we wear the Nuyorican hat which binds to the present society; we wear a Puerto Rican hat which binds us to our country, Puerto Rico; and we wear the Latino one which binds us to this nation" (Luis, 1027). His books of poetry have been acclaimed by critics: *La Carreta Made a U-Turn* (1979), *Enclave* (1981), *AmeRican* (1986), and *Mainstream Ethics* (1988). Laveira stresses the endurance of the ethnic and cultural identity of mainland Puerto Ricans who are transforming the mainstream culture, and he highlights the bilingualism and music of his Afro-Caribbean heritage.

PLAYS PRODUCED: *Olú Clemente*, New York Shakespeare Festival's Delacorte Theater, produced by Joseph Papp's New York Public Theater, Summer 1973. *Piñones* (musical), Nuyorican Poets' Café, May 1979; Public Theater, 1979; Eleventh Street Theater, Chicago and Washington, D.C., 1980. *La Chefa*, Henry Street Settlement New Federal Theater, February 1982. *Here We Come* (musical), New York Shakespeare Festival, Summer 1982; Public Theater, 1982. *Becoming García*, Henry Street Settlement New Federal Theater, Winter 1984.

WORKS: *Olú Clemente* (coauthor with Miguel Algarín), in *Revista Chicano-Riqueña* (Winter 1979).

BIBLIOGRAPHY: Efraín Barradas, "Introducción," in *Herejes y mitificadores: Muestra de poesía puertorriqueña en los Estados Unidos*, ed. Efraín Barradas and Rafael Rodríguez (Río Piedras, Puerto Rico: Huracán, 1980). Barradas, "Puerto Rico acá, Puerto Rico allá," *Revista Chicano-Riqueña* (Spring 1980): 43–49. William Luis, "From New York to the World. An Interview with Tato Laveira," *Callaloo: A Journal of African-American and African Arts and Letters* 15.4 (1992): 1022–1033. Eugene V. Mohr, *The Nuyorican Experience. Literature of the Puerto Rican Minority* (Westport, CT: Greenwood Press, 1982), 100–102.

LIZARDI, Joseph (1941–). Lizardi was born on February 12, 1941, in Caguas, Puerto Rico. He immigrated to the United States in 1954 and taught himself English. He served in the U.S. Marine Corps from 1960 to 1964 and was married in 1972 to Linda, a secretary. He studied at Bronx Community College and in 1977 received an M.B.A. from Bernard M. Baruch College of the City University of New York. He chose to hold blue-collar jobs for most of his working life to devote time to his craft as a playwright. His plays (*El Macho, Blue Collars, The Block Party*) describe the life of factory workers, the life of his parents, in a blend of comedy and tragedy. He explores the ethnic experience in general and the Puerto Rican neighborhoods that he knew in his life. He is the author of two screenplays: *Spanish Harlem* and *The Dope War*. He was named Playwright-in-Residence at the Arena Players Repertory Theater in Farmingdale, New York in 1980. His play *The Powderroom* ranked as a finalist in the Actors' Theater of Louisville's Great American Play Contest in 1980.

WORKS: *The Agreement*, Carnegie Repertory Theater, 1970. *The Contract*, Carnegie Repertory Theater, 1971. *The Commitment*, Henry Street Playhouse, 1972. *Summerville*, West Side Community

Theater, 1972. *The Block Party*, Henry Street Playhouse, 1974. *El Macho*, Firehouse Theater, 1977. *The Powderroom, Reunion, Blue Collars*, Arena Players Repertory Theater, 1980. *Love's Comedy* (adapted from Henrik Ibsen's *La comedia del amor*), Arena Players Repertory Theater, 1981. *December in New York*, Arena Players Repertory Theater, 1982. *Blind Dates*, Plainview, New York at Old Bethpage Library, 1982. *Three on the Run*, Arena Players Repertory Theater, 1982. Also authored: *The Family Room, Love's Last Gasp, The Runaway, Save the Children, The Pretenders* (adaptation of Ibsen play), *Couples, Joggers, Then Came the Stranger*, and *A Place Along the Highway*.

BIBLIOGRAPHY: *New York Post*, May 25, 1979. *Newsday*, April 25, 1980; May 9, 1980; November 5, 1980; February 3, 1982. *New York Daily News*, November 16, 1980. *New York Times*, April 13, 1980; April 27, 1980; August 24, 1980; November 16, 1980; August 30, 1981; April 4, 1982.

LÓPEZ, Eduardo Iván. López was born in Puerto Rico and brought to the United States as a child. In *Spanish Eyes* (1982), he reveals the consciousness of bicultural identity in his character Esteban Salazar, who marries an Anglo woman, Myra. Their cultural histories, past and present, find a mutual inclusiveness that destroys defensive stereotyping.

WORKS: *Spanish Eyes* (1982).

LÓPEZ, Eva. In *Marlene* (1990), ethnic identity is the issue that plagues a group of young Nuyoricans who are becoming upwardly mobile. Leaving El Barrio means leaving the support of their common identity. The main character Sereni is preparing to leave for California to become a playwright. The death of a young Puerto Rican girl sparks Sereni's memory of the accidental death of a girl from her childhood, Marlene. The ghost of Marlene redeems Sereni's cultural identity and provides her with the subject for her first play.

PIETRI, Pedro (Juan) (1943–). Pietri was born on March 21, 1943, in Ponce, Puerto Rico, and came to the United States at the age of two. The second of four children, he was orphaned as a child and raised by his grandmother. He attended the public schools in New York City

and served in the U.S. Army from 1966 to 1968. In 1978 he married Phyllis Nancy Wallach, a translator and teacher. By the mid-1970s, Pietri was known as a poet, playwright, and stand-up comedian and was awarded the New York State Creative Arts in Public Service Grant in 1974–1975. His plays of the common people in common acts were produced at Café la Mama and the Puerto Rican Traveling Theater and by Joseph Papp at the Public Theater. On occasion, José Ferrer, the renowned Puerto Rican actor, has directed Pietri's plays. Pietri has served as literary artist at the Cultural Council Foundation in New York City since 1978 and as a consultant to the Museo del Barrio. Pietri rejects established society to write from the perspective of the underclass, with whom he identifies, and to break with social and linguistic conventions.

PLAYS PRODUCED: *Lewlulu* (one-act), Harlem Performance Center, April 23, 1976. *What Goes Up Must Come Down* (one-act), El Portón, May 7, 1976. *The Living Room* (one-act), H. B. Studio, March 15, 1978. *Dead Heroes Have No Feelings* (one-act), Manhattan Plaza, October 8, 1978. *Appearing in Person Tonight—Your Mother* (one-act), La Mama, November 8, 1978. *Jesus Is Leaving* (one-act), Nuyorican Poets' Café, December 13, 1978. *The Masses Are Asses*, Puerto Rican Traveling Theater, 1984.

WORKS: *The Masses Are Asses* (Maplewood, NJ: Waterfront Press, 1984).

BIBLIOGRAPHY: Mario Maffi, "The Nuyorican Experience in the Plays of Pedro Pietri and Miguel Piñero," *In Cross Cultural Studies. American, Canadian and European Literatures: 1945–1985*, ed. Mirko Jurak (Ljubljana: Filozofska Fakulteta, 1988), 483–489. Eugene V. Mohr, *The Nuyorican Experience. Literature of the Puerto Rican Minority* (Westport, CT: Greenwood Press, 1982), 93–95, 100–101, 105–106.

PIÑERO, Miguel (Antonio Gómez) (1946–1988). Piñero was born on December 19, 1946, in Gurabo, Puerto Rico, and died on June 16, 1988, in New York City of cirrhosis of the liver after years of hard living and drug addiction. Piñero's family came to New York when he was four years old. A few years later, his father abandoned the family of four children and a pregnant wife. They lived on the streets of the Lower East Side until his mother found a source of income. He was a junior high school dropout from the New York City public schools, but he later earned a high school equivalency diploma. Piñero, a gang leader, had constant brushes with the law for drugs, muggings, burglary, shoplifting, and petty crimes and, eventually, served two terms in prison for drug possession and for robbery. In 1971, he was sent to Sing Sing State Prison (Ossining, New York) for armed robbery. The turning point in his life came in prison when Piñero began writing and acting in Clay Stevenson's theater workshop, where he wrote the draft of his best-known play *Short Eyes*. He married Juanita Lovette Rameize in 1977, but they divorced in 1979. His one child, Ismael Castro, was adopted. The societal and personal conflicts of marginalized characters are the thematic focus of his crude, sometimes violent, dramatic production. He was honored with the Drama Desk Award, the Obie Award, and the New York Drama Critics Circle Award for Best American Play of 1973–1974 for his acclaimed prison drama *Short Eyes*, produced by Joseph Papp at Lincoln Center. Nine subsequent plays also received critical praise, making Piñero the most acclaimed dramatist of the Nuyorican school. As a principal proponent of the new Nuyorican literature, Piñero became involved with a group of Nuyorican writers on the Lower East Side and founded the Nuyorican Poets' Theater in 1974. The publication of *Nuyorican Poets: An Anthology of Puerto Rican Words and Feelings*, collected and edited with Miguel Algarín, furthered the Nuyorican literary movement. Piñero wrote screenplays for television shows such as *Miami Vice, Kojak*, and *Barreta* and had cameo roles as a drug dealer in these series and in the movies *The Godfather* and *Fort Apache, The Bronx*. He taught creative writing at Rutgers University and received a Guggenheim Fellowship for playwriting in 1982. His plays have been produced, and most have been published in his two drama collections. Some critics have considered Piñero's characters to be one-dimensional, but it is obvious that he has changed Latino stereotypes

into real individuals with personal stories. He is probably the most successful Nuyorican playwright, receiving rave reviews from mainstream critics.

PLAYS PRODUCED: *All Junkies*, New York City, 1973. *Short Eyes: The Killing of a Sex Offender by the Inmates of the House of Detention Awaiting Trial*, produced by The Family, Theater of the Riverside Church, January 1974; Broadway at Vivian Beaumont Theater, May 1974. *Sideshow*, Public Theater Annex, The Space for Transnational Arts Theater, 1975. *The Gun Tower*, New York City, 1976. *The Sun Always Shines for the Cool*, New York City at the Booth Theater, 1976; Back Alley Theater, Washington, D.C., Spring 1977. *Eulogy for a Small-Time Thief*, New York City Off-Off Broadway at Ensemble Studio Theater, 1977. *Straight from the Ghetto*, New York City, 1977. *Paper Toilet*, Los Angeles, 1979. *Cold Beer*, New York City, 1979. *Nuyorican Nights at the Stanton Street Social Club*, Nuyorican Poets' Cafe, 1980. *Playland Blues*, Henry Street Settlement Theater, 1980. *A Midnight Moon at the Greasy Spoon*, Theater for the New City, 1981.

WORKS: *Short Eyes: The Killing of a Sex Offender by the Inmates of the House of Detention Awaiting Trial* (New York: Hill and Wang, 1975). *The Sun Always Shines for the Cool. A Midnight Moon at the Greasy Spoon. Eulogy for a Small-Time Thief* (Houston: Arte Público Press, 1984). *Outrageous One-Act Plays (Paper Toilet, Cold Beer, The Guntower, Irving, Sideshow, Tap Dancing and Bruce Lee Kicks)* (Houston: Arte Público Press, 1986). Ed. with Miguel Algarín, *Nuyorican Poets: An Anthology of Puerto Rican Words and Feelings* (New York: William Morrow, 1975). *Short Eyes*, screenplay adapted from his play (Film League Inc., 1977).

BIBLIOGRAPHY: Richard Eder, Review of *Eulogy for a Small-Time Thief, New York Times*, November 28, 1977, 41. Nicolás Kanellos and Jorge Huerta, eds., "Nuevos Pasos: Chicano and Puerto Rican Drama," *Revista Chicano-Riqueña* 7.1 (1979): 173–174. Stanley Kauffmann, Review of *Short Eyes, The New Republic* 20 (April 1974): 20. Jack Knoll, "In the Oven," Review of *Short Eyes, Newsweek*, April 8, 1974, 81. Mario Maffi, "The Nuyorican Experience in the Plays of Pedro Pietri and Miguel Piñero," in *Cross Cultural Studies. American, Canadian and European Literature: 1945–1985*, ed. Mirko Jurak (Ljubljana: Filozofska Fakulteta, 1988), 483–489. Norma Alarcón McKesson, "An Interview with Miguel Piñero," *Revista Chicano-Riqueña* 2.1

(1974): 55–57. John C. Miller, "Hispanic Theater in New York, 1965–1977," *Revista Chicano-Riqueña* 6.1 (1977): 40–59. Eugene V. Mohr, *The Nuyorican Experience. Literature of the Puerto Rican Minority* (Westport, CT: Greenwood Press, 1982), 92–101, 109–115. Carlos Morton, "Social Realism on Astor Place: The Latest Piñero Play," *Revista Chicano-Riqueña* 2.1 (1974): 33–35. Edmund Newton, Review of *Eulogy for a Small-Time Thief, New York Post*, November 28, 1977, 27B. Guy Trebay, "Talking Heads: Miguel Piñero—Promises Die Hard," *Village Voice*, April 15, 1981, 63.

RAMÍREZ, Ivette M. A prominent woman playwright of the Nuyorican Theater, Ramírez explores family life.

In *Family Scenes* (1989), the acting on the stage is not the only acting because the characters themselves are actors in their family life. They live a lie fostered by the mother Margarita, who invents herself to her two children, Paula and Sophia, as a wife who has been abandoned by her husband. The discovery of the mother's deception, an invented marriage, does not improve the already unstable family relationships. The lies that helped Margarita to escape her reality are more hurtful to her family than the truth. This play received the 1989 New York Drama League Award and was designated a finalist in the McDonald's Latino Dramatists Competition held in New York.

WORKS: *Family Scenes* (staged reading), Puerto Rican Traveling Theater, June 1990.

RIVERA, Carmen. Rivera earned a master's degree in playwrighting and Latin American theater from New York University. She is co-director of the Experience Theater, a program at the Henry Street Settlement for high school students that encourages conflict resolution through writing and producing plays. Rivera, a founding member of the Latino Experimental Theater, is a playwright and artist-in-residence at the Henry Street Settlement.

La gringa (1995): The basis of this comedy is the connection between personal and ethnic identity. A young native New Yorker visits her family in Puerto Rico for the first time. After embarrassing her family with her attempt at learning to speak Spanish and her stereotyped views of Puerto Rican culture, the young woman transforms her beliefs about what it means to be a true Puerto Rican in heart, mind, and soul.

WORKS: *La gringa*, Spanish Repertory Theater, 1996.

BIBLIOGRAPHY: John V. Antush, ed., *Nuestro New York. An Anthology of Puerto Rican Plays* (New York: Mentor, 1994). Antush, ed., *Recent Puerto Rican Theater. Five Plays from New York* (Houston: Arte Público Press, 1991).

RODRÍGUEZ, Yolanda. Rodríguez is part of the new generation of Nuyorican playwrights.

In *Rising Sun, Falling Star* (1991), set in New York's Lower East Side (Loisaida), known for its drug trade, three young siblings follow in their father's footsteps and fall prey to the drug culture as pushers and users. Pedro, a victim of his own drug use and AIDS, knows he is destroying his younger brother Carlos. He gives his own life to save Carlos's in a demonstration of brotherly love.

WORKS: *Rising Sun, Falling Star* (1991).

THOMAS, Piri (1928–   ). John Peter Thomas was born on September 30, 1928, in New York to Juan Thomas, a Cuban father from Oriente Province who considered himself Puerto Rican, and Dolores Montañez, a Puerto Rican mother from Bayamón. Growing up in East Harlem, he experienced the poverty of the Great Depression. His parents worked hard to provide for their seven children, his father digging for the Works Progress Administration (WPA), his mother doing needlework. Thomas was raised to identify with his Puerto Rican roots, although he was aware of being black in a white racist society. Thomas was the eldest and the darkest of his lighter-skinned siblings, which he believed made him his father's least favorite child. His family moved to Babylon, Long Island, for a better life, but Thomas felt alienated from a family that was attempting to assimilate into the middle-class mainstream. He left home at age sixteen and returned to Spanish Harlem to sell drugs to support a heroin addiction. He followed the *machismo* code that equates strength with respect in an adolescence of petty theft, gang violence, and criminality. After traveling to the Deep South, Europe, South America, and the West Indies, Thomas concluded that blacks faced discrimination everywhere.

In 1950 Thomas perpetrated a holdup in Greenwich Village, in which he and a policeman were both shot. He served seven years in prison for attempted armed robbery and felonious assault. In prison, he began to read and write, obtained his high school equivalency diploma, trained in brickmasonry, and learned to identify with his Afro-American heritage by adopting the Black Muslim religion. He became a volunteer in the prison and drug rehabilitation programs in New York City in 1956 and worked with minority youth gangs on Long Island to calm rivalries and discourage drug use. Thomas converted to Pentecostalism and married Daniela Calo, an immigrant from Puerto Rico, on April 20, 1958. When he was thirty years old, Thomas visited Puerto Rico for the first time, where he worked with Dr. Efrem Ramírez, director of the Hospital of Psychiatry in Río Piedras, Puerto Rico, formulating a rehabilitation program for drug addicts called the New Breed (Nueva Raza). Thomas became a staff associate with the Center for Urban Education in 1967 and in that same year received the Lever Brothers Community Service Award. He was vice president of Third World Cinema Productions and trustee of the Community Film Workshop Council and of the American Film Institute.

Piri Thomas is best known for his autobiographies and autobiographical fiction (*Down These Mean Streets* [1967], *Saviour, Saviour Hold My Hand* [1972], *Seven Long Times* [1974]), in which he writes of the socially inscribed stereotypes placed on his Puerto Rican and Black heritage and of the poverty and culture conflict of the *barrio*. To finish writing his autobiography, he received the Louis M. Rabinowitz Foundation Grant in 1962. He progresses from the autobiographical into the larger collective character of urban life in his collection of eight short stories, *Stories from El Barrio* (1978). *Chago* is a screenplay about a young man who holds Puerto Rico as the foundation of his identity even though he has never visited it.

Thomas, a second-generation Puerto Rican who grew up in El Barrio, reached mainstream U.S. audiences and attracted major publishers with works that express the search for identity in the Puerto Rican community. Thomas conducts creative writing workshops, gives poetry readings to youth groups, and lectures extensively on the problems of ethnic minorities in the United States. After three marriages, he is the father of five children, and three more are children of his wife Betty, an international lawyer, with whom he travels extensively. During his visit to Cuba, he traced his father's genealogy and conducted a comparative study of the Cuban and U.S. penal systems.

WORKS: *The Golden Streets*, Puerto Rican Traveling Theater in Riverside Park, September 9, 1970; in Puerto Rico, 1972. *Chago* (n.d.).

BIBLIOGRAPHY: Edna Acosta-Belén, "The Literature of the Puerto Rican National Minority in the United States," *Bilingual Review/La Revista Bílingüe* 5. 1–2 (July–August 1978): 112–113. Wolfgang Binder, "An Interview with Piri Thomas," *Minority Voices* 4 (Spring 1980): 63–78. Mel Gussow, "Theater: A New Play by Piri Thomas" (review of *The Golden Streets*), *New York Times*, August 14, 1970, 21. John C. Miller, "The Emigrant and New York City: Consideration of Four Puerto Rican Writers," *Melus: The Journal of the Society for the Study of the Multi-Ethnic Literature of the United States* 5.3 (1978): 82–99. Eugene V. Mohr, "Lives from El Barrio," *Revista Chicano-Riqueña* 8 (1981): 60–79. Mohr, *The Nuyorican Experience. Literature of the Puerto Rican Minority* (Westport, CT: Greenwood Press, 1982), 43–60.

TIRADO, Cándido. Cándido Tirado is an innovative Nuyorican playwright who made an impact with his play *First Class* (1987).

The play is a moving portrait of two Puerto Rican outcasts surviving the ghetto wars: a young hustler and a gang leader. Apache's prostitute mother cared for the child Speedy, who had no home. Apache and Speedy are raised as brothers and teach each other the real meaning of manhood, friendship, and self-worth. Under the deceptive demeanor of a rogue, Apache holds a decent and caring persona. The working-class community that was striving to disassociate itself from street characters such as Apache and Speedy reacted negatively to this work. The play sparked controversy within the Puerto Rican community, in newspapers and on television and radio talk shows, but it was received more positively by English-speaking critics.

Some People Have All the Luck (1990) is a comedy that portrays implausible reality in the form of Carlos, a weak and unassuming individual, who communicates with a ghost, Damasia. It is easier for Ray's Cousin, as Carlos refers to himself, to develop an interpersonal relationship with an unreal woman, Damasia, than with the live Sandra, whom he hopes to marry. The intimacy with Damasia grows to the extent that Carlos believes she is real and that Sandra is imaginary. Damasia says goodbye to Carlos, leaving his death wish unfulfilled.

WORKS: *First Class*, African Caribbean Poetry Theater, June 1987; Puerto Rican Traveling Theater, May 18–June 26, 1988. *Some People Have All the Luck* (1990).

Joan F. Cammarata

Panama

When we choose to write about theater under the heading of a particular nation, it may appear that we are in fact addressing a *national theater*, the unique expression of a whole nation. Nevertheless, this monolithic appearance soon clashes with the reality of heterogeneous, often antagonistic theatrical processes that compete for a cultural space within a stratified society that has as many definitions of culture as it has races, classes, interest groups, and the like. In the case of Panama the concept of a national theater is even more problematic, given the fact that it is a country whose geographic destiny has made it a place for passage, mobility, and impermanence, and theater has not escaped the consequences of that dislocated destiny.

Moreover, in the case of Latin American countries, *when* do we begin to address the theater of a nation? Before the Conquest? After Independence? When did that which we call *nation* begin? When did its theater/theaters begin to be the representation of that concept/concepts? And furthermore, is theater the *repertory* that companies perform and only certain audiences see, which in the case of Panama in particular and Latin America in general more often privileges foreign playwrights rather than their national counterparts? Or do we address the dramatic production of national authors who often do not reach their audience/audiences since their works are not published or staged? Who and what constitute the national theater? When does it begin? These are only a few of the questions that surface as we attempt the apparently simple task of articulating the term *theater* with the name of a particular country.

In the case of Panama, those questions become even more crucial. For instance, do we begin the history of Panamanian theater in 1903, when Panama finally becomes independent from Colombia, or do we look at the cultural process on the Isthmus as a continuum in spite of the historical vicissitudes of the nation we are presently naming? Once again, what is a *national* theater in continents like ours where the process toward a so-called nationhood is hampered by the internal strife and external interference typical of colonial and neocolonial impositions? And is Sarah Bernhardt performing in the Teatro de las Monjas for the French executives and engineers of the Lesseps Canal Company Panamanian theater? But the truth is that, with few exceptions, theater in Panama until the 1930s was nearly exclusively in the hands of foreign touring companies who performed for a relatively select minority. Perhaps those international companies and the playwrights they presented inspired their national counterparts to produce the theater that was to come, and in this sense, they are part of that national history. But we must bear in mind that Panamanian theater and culture—and/or its lack of organic development—is one more consequence of the so-called destiny that is scarring its soil and its identity to this date.

Héctor Rodríguez, author of the *Primera historia del teatro en Panamá* (First History of the Theater in Panama), reminds us that since 1513, when Balboa discovered the Mar del Sur, the Panamanian Isthmus became the crucially needed route for the commerce of the time and for Spain's rise to power in the world. Mules loaded with gold and silver left their imprints as they traversed the land from ocean to ocean. Very little of those riches were to remain. What did remain was the vision of an interoceanic canal first dreamt of by Charles V. As the California Gold Rush unleashed its siren's call upon the world, Panama was once again the bridge to that dream. By 1855, the first interoceanic railroad was completed, making that route from the Atlantic to the Pacific ever more indispensable. By 1879, during the Paris Congress, Panama's destiny was sealed. After long discussions regarding the location of a canal, Panama was chosen to host it. The French immediately embarked on that project, which was to culminate ten years later in a horrible failure that cost the lives and health of workers devastated by the illnesses of the jungles. By the end of the nineteenth century, France abandoned Panama, theater was practically nonexistent, and what we are calling Panama was in fact still legally part of Colombia. With the Hay-Bunau Varilla Treaty, Roosevelt took Panama by freeing it from Colombia, thus giving Panama its independence so that the United States could build the much-coveted canal. Unquestionably, since then, Panama's destiny has been very closely tied to the interests of the United States, with great political instability ever present. Panamanian theater can only be understood as a consequence of this complex history.

In summary, with the arrival of the French, theater had a grand moment of international touring companies that entertained a minority in the midst of a tropical jungle. For the last decades of the past century, theater seemed to thrive in this scene and in this sense. With the exodus of the French, this activity diminished, only to be reactivated with the inauguration of the National Theatre in 1908, which once again hosted companies from around the world, at times surpassing the splendor of the previous epoch. By 1914, the Teatro Variedades had opened, and later in 1920, the Teatro El Dorado. These new spaces allowed for many who could not afford the exhorbitant prices of the Teatro Nacional to see the same companies in those other theaters at a later date. Nevertheless, by the 1930s the impact of the Great Depression would take its toll on Panama as well.

Elsewhere we have argued for the need to include indigenous, pre-Columbian performances as part of any Latin American theater history. Thus, in spite of what we have said above, we could argue that Panamanian theater begins with the performances and rituals of various indigenous tribes long before the beginning of the Spanish Conquest. The Cunas had several well-established performative expressions: the *Cantos de Cacería* (Hunting Chants); the Morbikuileid; and the various celebrations of puberty rituals, among them the Inna Uila, the Namake, the Ner Surba, and the El Nega. The Guaymíes also performed in La Clarida (or La Claria), La Balsería, La Chichería, and other rituals and spectacles. The invocations to the spirits in search of protection performed by the Chocoes are also part of that performative heritage amply present in indigenous cultures that enriched pre-Columbian life. It is important to note that we are not speaking of forms that are extinct but, rather, in many cases, of traditional ceremonies that have survived to this day. In the case of performances by the Cuna Indians that I have attended, there is very little influence of Occidental culture in general and of present-day culture in particular. The fact that we can speak of live, surviving indigenous expressions underlines the heterogeneous quality of a national theater as we were describing it above.

As in most of Latin America, the Conquest brought with it a European conception of theater. Nevertheless, given the need to find a vehicle for both evangelization and ideological colonization, this theater often took advantage of local indigenous practices as it utilized the appeal that performance arts exerted for local tribes to transmit religious and nonreligious doctrine in favor of the interests of the Crown and the Church. The themes and means of production were drastically modified during colonization, but above all, the ways of participation in theater for both actors and spectators were to suffer the greatest changes in the transition from pre-Columbian performance to colonial theater. Nevertheless, the communizing theatricality that is/was at the core of the Indian and Black cultures intertwined with the European tradition, and it did not disappear. The performances and dances of the Black region of Colón, the Carnavales in the provinces of Azuero, and many other such performative arts bear witness to this continuity. In the same vein, festivities profoundly rooted in the Middle Ages brought over to the New World—which shared that same communizing theatricality with indigenous forms—also continue to be practiced. Los Grandiablos, el Drama de los Reyes Magos de Macaracas, el Acto de la Pasión de Pesé, celebrated during Holy Week, are but a few of those enduring performances. In this sense, we can say that the most distant roots of Panamanian theater stem from the three cultures that converged in the Isthmus: Indian, Black, and European.

Deriving from what we have stated above, the history of Panamanian theater could be succinctly grouped into nine periods, each tightly woven with the historical circumstances of that country of transit: (1) pre-Columbian indigenous expression; (2) colonial religious and nonreligious theater; (3) Canal-inspired initial international touring activity, 1880–1900; (4) post-Independence initial brilliance, 1908–1930; (5) the Great Depression and deterioration, 1930–1940; (6) resurgence and sporadic activity, 1940–1960; (7) near disappearance, 1960–1974; (8) new resurgence and sporadic activity, 1974–1989; (9) postinvasion death and resurrection, 1989 to present.

Rogelio Sinán, one of Panama's best-known playwrights, recalls that in 1937, when he first staged his play *La Cucarachita Mandinga* (The Little Mandinga Cockroach), a production rarely survived more than one performance. It is precisely with Rogelio Sinán's (and Gonzalo Brenes's) play *La Cucarachita Mandinga* that the beginning of a national theater, written by a Panamanian playwright, with his own audience in mind, dealing with the issues of his country, can be clearly identified. Sinán, with this musical farce for children, was in fact introducing the sixth period, the first more clearly Panamanian epoch. His play stayed at the Teatro Nacional from December 1937 through January 1938, a true first Panamanian success.

BIBLIOGRAPHY

Arosemena, Julio. "Danza de la montezuma española en la villa de Los Santos." *Revista Nacional de Cultura* 1.1 (October–November–December 1975).

Avila, José. *Panorama de la dramática panameña.* Panama City: Impresora de La Nación, n.d.

Beleño, Joaquin. "Inventario cultural de las obras y de los autores premiados en el concurso Ricardo Miró," *Revísta Lotería* 176 (July 1970).

Cedeño, José. "Panorama del desenvolvimiento cultural de Panamá." Ph.D. dissertation, Universidad de Panamá, 1966.

CELCIT Panamá. Boletín del Centro Latinoamericano de Creación e Investigación Teatral (Filial Panamá) 11 (April–September 1996).

Domínguez, Daniel. "El teatro en Panamá: entre problemas, excepciones y esperanzas." *Latin American Theatre Review* 25.2 (Spring 1992): 123–127.

Gasteazoro, Carlos Manuel. *Breve historia del teatro nacional*. Panama City: Instituto Nacional de Cultura, 1974.

King, Enrique Roberto. "Arte teatral y teatro total." *La Prensa*, January 8, 1995. *Talingo*, suplemento cultural.

———. "Crisis de creatividad." *La Prensa*, September 17, 1995. *Talingo*, suplemento cultural.

Lebel, Jean Jaques. *Teatro y revolución: entrevista con el Living Theatre*. Trans. Gabriel Rodríguez. Caracas: Monte Avila Editores, 1970.

Leis, Raúl. *Cómo hacer teatro popular*. Panama City: *CECOP*, 1976.

Macias, Jesús. "*José de Jesús Martínez en el teatro panameño*." Ph.D. dissertation, Universidad de Panamá, 1967.

Mack, Gerstle. *La tierra dividida*. 2 vols. Panama City: EUPAN, 1971.

McKay, Roberto. "José Quintero está bien, contento, viviendo en Nueva York." *Revista nacional de cultura* 4 (July–August–September 1976).

Miró, Rodrigo. "Noticias sobre el teatro en Panamá." *Revista Lotería* 183 (February 1971).

Navarro, Rosa. "Manifestaciones teatrales en Panamá durante el último curato del siglo XIX." Ph.D. dissertation, Universidad de Panamá, 1953.

"Panamá." *Escenarios de dos mundos: inventario teatral de Iberoamérica*. Vol. 3. Madrid: Centro de Documentación Teatral, 1988, 218–243. Articles by scholars.

Paz, Estela. "Manifestaciones actuales del teatro en Panamá." Ph.D. dissertation, Universidad de Panamá, 1955.

Quiróz-Winemiller, Bélgica. "Teatro panameño (1970–1985): estrategias de la competencia teatral." Ph.D. dissertation, Arizona State University, 1980.

Turbyfill, Subert. *Memorias*. Panama City: Imprenta Universitaria, 1972.

———. *My Panamá Canal Theatre Adventure: The Story of Fifteen Years of Drama at the Panamá Canal*. Philadelphia: Ed. Darrance & Co., 1949.

Vázquez de Pérez, Margarita. "*La política del mundo*, primera obra de teatro panameña." Ph.D. dissertation, Universidad de Panamá, 1960–1961.

◆

BABOT, Jarl Ricardo (1946–   ). From 1967 to 1973, this playwright, poet, and theater director worked on a Master of Arts in Theatre Arts at the State Theatre Institute Anatolio Lunacharosky in Moscu. He later completed this area of specialization at the Universidad de Panamá, where he had already staged many successful versions of national and international plays. Upon his return from Europe, he directed the National Theatre School and the Teatro Taller Universitario. He was director of the Departamento de Expresiones Artísticas (DEXA) of the Universidad de Panamá, and he is pres-ently the vice-director of the Theatre Department of the School of Arts (Facultad de Bellas Artes) at that same institution.

As a writer, Jarl Babot has been drawn mainly to poetry and theater. As a playwright, he has been described as a writer of subterranean themes, an heir to Beckett and the existentialists. Yet he has explored his sociopolitical context in a Brechtian vein as well. Babot's theater is existentialist, intellectual, metaphysical. Incommunication and the absurd are ever present in his senseless dialogues, as is the play with time that does not pass and silences that operate as threats. In his plays, that verbal silence is transformed into a constant noise caused by objects that fall without apparent reason. Man is the victim of man, and he becomes an animal, an object. Truth is relative as man fights to reach an unreachable happiness.

WORKS: *El interior del pacífico reloj* (The Inside of a Quiet Clock), in *Lotería* #219 (Panama City: Ediciones Lotería Nacional, 1974). *La reina* (The Queen), unpublished, public reading performed in 1976. *El viejo león* (The Old Lion), in *Lotería* #285 (Panama City: Ediciones Lotería Nacional, 1978). *Aceite de ballena* (Whale's Oil), unpublished, public reading in 1978. *José María Candanedo*, written with Ricardo Gutiérrez, unpublished, public reading in 1979. *Las aves* (The Birds), awarded the Premio Nacional de Literatura Ricardo Miró, 1979 (Panama City: Editorial Mariano Arosemena, Instituto Nacional de Cultura, 1980). *La fiera en el jardín* (The Wild Beast in the Garden), in *Lotería* #334–335 (Panama City: Ediciones Lotería Nacional, 1984). *Preguntas en la oscuridad* (Questions in the Dark), in *Lotería* #340–341 (Panama City: Ediciones Lotería Nacional, 1985). *Historias verdaderas* (True Stories), in *Lotería* #348–349 (Panama City: Ediciones Lotería Nacional, 1985). *Imitación* (Imitation), in *Lotería* #356–357 (Panama City: Ediciones Lotería Nacional, 1985). *Aspinwall*, in *Universidad* #47, Universidad de Panamá, 1993. *Silencio* (Silence), in *Revista Nacional de Cultura* (Panama City: Editorial Mariano Arosemena, Instituto Nacional de Cultura [INAC], 1994).

BIBLIOGRAPHY: Enrique Roberto King, "Arte teatral y teatro total," *Talingo*, Suplemento Cultural de *La Prensa*, *La Prensa*, January 8, 1995. Bélgica Quiróz-Winemiller, *Teatro panameño (1970–1985): Estrategeias de la competencia teatral* (Tempe: Arizona State University, 1980).

DEL ROSARIO, Agustín (1945–   ). Born in Panama, he received his bachelor's degree in literature and philosophy from the Universidad de Panamá. He later obtained a Master of Arts in Oriental Literatures and Cultures from the Colegio de Mexico. Del Rosario was director of the *Penélope* journal for several years. In 1971 he was awarded the Premio Nacional de Literatura Ricardo Miró in Poetry with his book *De parte interesada* (Of Interested Part), published in both Panama and Mexico. He has also worked as a critic in the national media since 1970. On two different occasions he was awarded the First Theatre Prize in the Juegos Florales de Quetzaltenango, Guatemala. He also received an Honorable Mention in Theatre in the Premio Casa de las Américas, Cuba. Del Rosario headed the School of Journalism and was dean of the College of Communications, where he presently teaches.

Del Rosario excels in a theater of the Absurd that questions power relations and violence. His theater denounces a classist society, the power of the Church, and all forms of repression against people. Technically, he bases his theater on a filmic simultaneity, an episodic narrative, imaginative lighting, wildcard (or joker) characters, and a minimal amount of stage directions.

WORKS: *Los bellos días de Isaac* (The Beautiful Days of Isaac), awarded an honorable mention in the Premio Nacional de Literatura Ricardo Miró, Panama, 1965; also received the First Prize in the Juegos Florales de Quetzaltenango, Guatemala, 1972. *El bajo y el alto* (The Short and the Tall), honored with the Premio Octavio Méndez Pereira, Universidad de Panamá, 1965; published in *Colección Premio* del Departamento de Expresiones Artísticas (DEXA) de la Universidad de Panama, 1976; also in *Antología del teatro hispanoamericano*, del Fondo de Cultura Económica de México y Ministerio de Cultura de España, 1993. *A veces esa palabra libertad* (Sometimes That Word Freedom), awarded an honorable mention in the Premio Casa de las Américas, 1973; published in *Colección Premio* del Departamento de Expresiones Artísticas (DEXA) de la Universidad de Panama, 1976. *Suceden cosas extrañas en tierras del emperador Cristóbal* (Strange Things Happen in the Lands of Emperor Cristobal), awarded the First Prize in the Premio Juegos Florales de Quetzaltenango, Guatemala, 1975; published in *Colección Premio* del Departamento de Expresiones Artísticas (DEXA) de la Universidad de Panama, 1976. *Las flores del jardín de nuestra casa* (The Flowers of Our Home's Garden), unpublished, public reading performed in 1978.

BIBLIOGRAPHY: Daniel Domínguez, "El teatro en Panamá: Entre problemas, excepciones y esperanzas," *Latin American Theatre Review* (Spring 1992): 123–127. Bélica Quiróz-Winemiller, *Teatro Panameño (1970–1985): Estrategias de la compe-*

tencia teatral (Tempe: Arizona State University, 1980).

ENDARA, Ernesto (1932–). Born in Panama, he is both a playwright and a short story writer. He is also an inspector for the Panamanian Fire Department and a journalist for *El Heraldo*. All his plays have been published by the Colección Ricardo Miró as part of having been awarded the First Prize of the Concurso Literario Ricardo Miró for that year.

WORKS: *El gran rey de corazón negro* (The Great King of Black Heart, 1957). *Ay de los vencidos!* (Poor the Defeated Ones, 1961). *La mujer de sal* (The Salt Woman, 1968). *Una bandera* (A Flag, 1977). *El fusilado* (The Executed One, music by Toño Robira, 1983). *Demasiadas flores para Rodolfo* (Too Many Flowers for Rodolfo, 1985). *Donde es más brillante el sol* (Where the Sun Is More Bright, music by Toño Robira, 1990).

BIBLIOGRAPHY: Carlos Manuel Gasteazoro, *Breve historia del teatro nacional* (Panama City: Instituto Nacional de Cultura, 1974). Bélgica Quiróz-Winemiller, *Teatro panameño (1970–1985): Estrategias de la competencia teatral* (Tempe: Arizona State University, 1980).

LEIS, Raúl (1947–). Born in Panama, he is a sociologist, journalist, and grassroots educator. He is professor of sociology at the Universidad de Panamá. Leis was editor of the journal *Diálogo Social* for many years. He is a founding member of the Centro de Estudios y Acción Social Panameño (CEASPA), which he directed for several years. Leis received the coveted Nacional Literary Prize Ricardo Miró six times (four prizes and two honorable mentions in three different categories: essay, poetry, and theater). In 1982, he was awarded the Plural Prize from Mexico for his entry in the essay section. He has also been awarded the journal *Nueva Sociedad* Latin American Prize from Venezuela, in 1985 and 1992, also for his entries in the essay category.

Raúl Leis was also honored in the Juegos Florales Centroamericanos in Quetzaltenango, Guatemala, for *El fuego que nunca se apaga* (The Fire That Never Extinguishes). His play *La cantina de Pancha Manchá* was first finalist in the 1994 Tirso de Molina Prize in Spain.

Besides having won other important national and international competitions, his plays have been performed in Panama, Colombia, the United States, Sweden, Mexico, Argentina, and Central America. He has also written several screenplays and has published various books of poems and a book of short stories. His theater is strongly connected with society and political commitment, with a strong tendency toward a Brechtian aesthetic (songs, slide projections, confrontation with the audience, banners, masks). His plays are protagonized by marginal heroes where he particularly illuminates and defends ethnicity.

WORKS: *Viaje a la salvación y otros países* (Trip to Salvation and Other Countries), awarded the Premio Nacional de Literatura Ricardo Miró 1973; published in Colección Premio Ricardo Miró del Instituto Nacional de Cultura (Panama City: INAC, 1974). *Viene el sol con su sombrero de combate puesto* (The Sun Comes with His Combat Hat On), published in *Conjunto* #30, Casa de las Américas, Cuba, 1976; and in *Teatro documental latinoamericano*, vol. 2 (Mexico City: UNAM, 1982). *Lucecita González*, in *Theatre in Latin America*, vol. 7, edited by Bosele Tshwaragonang (Botswana, 1978); also in *Revista Frente*, vol. 7, Ediciones del Frente de Trabajadores de la Cultura, 1980. *María Picana*, awarded the Universidad Santa María la Antigua Prize, Panama, 1979 (Panama City: Ediciones Aspan Pipigua, 1980). *El nido del Macuá* (Macuá's Nest), awarded the Premio Nacional de Literatura Ricardo Miró 1981, published in Colección Premio Ricardo Miró del Instituto Nacional de Cultura (Panama City: INAC, 1982). *El fuego que nunca se apaga*, in *Lotería* #326–327 (Panama City: Ediciones Lotería Nacional, 1983). *Lo peor del boxeo* (The Worst of Boxing), in *Cultura Popular* 10 (Peru) (1983); and in *Praxis Centroamericana* 4 (Panama City: Ediciones CEASPAS, 1984). *Primero de mayo* (First of May), published by the author (Panama City: n.p., 1986). *Mudunción*, awarded the Premio Nacional de Literatura Ricardo Miró 1988, published in Colección Premio Ricardo Miró del Instituto Nacional de Cultura (Panama City: INAC, 1992). *No hay derecho, Señor* (There Is No Right, Lord), unpublished, premiered in 1991. *Maestra vida* (Master Life), unpublished, premiered in 1992. *Carta a Héctor Gallego* (Letter to Héctor Gallego), unpublished, premiered in 1996. *El señor sol* (Mister Sun), in *Lotería* 405 (Panama City: Ediciones Lotería Nacional, 1996). *La cantina de Pancha Manchá* (Pancha Mancha's Cantina), unpublished; under its first title *Con queja de indio y grito de chombo*, it was awarded an honorable mention in the Premio Nacional de Literatura Ricardo Miró, 1993.

BIBLIOGRAPHY: *CELCIT Panamá*, Boletín del Centro Latinoamericano de Creación e Investigación Teatral (Filial Panamá), no. 11 (April–September 1996). Enrique Roberto King, "Arte teatral y teatro total," *Talingo*, Suplemento Cultural de *La Prensa*, *La Prensa*, January 8, 1995. Bélica Quiróz-Winemiller, *Teatro panameño (1970–1985): Estrategias de la competencia teatral* (Tempe: Arizona State University, 1980).

MARTÍNEZ, José de Jesús (1929–1991). Panamanian by choice, José de Jesús Martínez was born in Managua, Nicaragua, on June 8, 1929. He died in Panama on January 27, 1991. He graduated from a naval academy in the United States during World War II. He later traveled to Europe, where he lived for ten years in Spain and Germany. He prepared a doctorate in mathematics in the Sorbonne in Paris and received a doctorate in philosophy from the Universidad de Madrid, Spain. In Panama he taught abstract algebra and mathematical logic at the Universidad de Panamá. A complex, multifaceted individual, he was a brilliant mathematician, playwright, poet, essayist, pilot, a member of the National Guard (Guardia Nacional), and a beloved professor at the Universidad de Panamá. His complete works contain more than thirty titles including his plays.

In 1976, he was chosen to represent Panama in the Conference of Non-Aligned Countries in Sri Lanka. He flew his single engine plane from Panama to Sri Lanka to undertake his duties. He directed the Centro de Estudios Torrijistas, and in 1987 he was awarded the highest distinction of the Premio Casa de las Américas in the Testimonio Category for *Mi general Torrijos* (My General Torrijos). In this book, de Jesús Martínez—Chuchú, as he was affectionately called—speaks of the Panamanian political-military figure, from the vantage point of being Torrijos's personal guard and highly respected adviser.

This author's plays show a great antireligious bent, often questioning the existence of God. He is interested in a theater that delves into the human spirit, describing new, deeper zones of our being. Constant themes in his works are the soul, solitude, death, time, the myth of Acteón, lying as an act of moral defense, the ceremony of reiteration, the impossibility of communication, the ridiculing of time and space, constant aggression, the oppressor-oppressed dyad.

WORKS: *La mentira, La venganza*, and *La parrera*, published in Madrid in 1954, n.p. *Caifás*, published in Ediciones Tareas, Panama, 1961. *Enemigos*, published in Ediciones Tareas, Panama, 1962; also in *Antología del teatro hispanoamericano*, Fondo de Cultura Económica, Mexico, 1964. *Santos en espera de un milagro*, published in Ediciones Tareas, Panama, 1962. *El mendigo y el avaro*, awarded the third prize in the Premio Nacional de Literatura Ricardo Miró, Instituto Nacional de Cultura (INAC), 1963. *La ciudad*, awarded the second prize in the Premio Nacional de Literatura Ricardo Miró, Instituto Nacional de Cultura (INAC), 1964. *La retreta*, published in Ediciones Tareas, Panama, 1964. *Aurora y el mestizo*, awarded the first prize in the Premio Nacional de Literatura Ricardo Miró, Instituto Nacional de Cultura (INAC), 1964; published in Edición del Departamento de Bellas Artes, Panama, 1964. *Amanecer de Ulises*, premiered in El Salvador in 1967. *Cero y van tres*, awarded the first prize in the Premio Nacional de Literatura Ricardo Miró, Instituto Nacional de Cultura (INAC), 1970; published by the Dirección de Cultura, Ministerio de Educación, Panama, 1970. *Segundo Asalto*, published in Ediciones Tareas, Panama, 1971. *La Guerra del Banano*, awarded the first prize in the Premio Nacional de Literatura Ricardo Miró, Instituto Nacional de Cultura (INAC), 1975, published by Ediciones INAC, Panama, 1976; also in *Antología del teatro hispanoamericano*, Fondo de Cultura Económica, Mexico, and Ministerio de Cultura de España, 1993. *El caso Dios*, 1975, unpublished. *Caifás, Enemigos, El mendigo y el avaro*, and *La venganza and La retreta* have been published in *Teatro de José de Jesús Martínez*, Editorial Universitaria Centroamericana (EDUCA), 1971.

BIBLIOGRAPHY: Jesús Macias, "José de Jesús Martínez en el teatro panameño" (Ph.D. diss., Universidad de Panamá, 1967). Bélgica Quiróz-Winemiller, *Teatro panameño (1970–1985): Estrategias de la competencia teatral* (Tempe: Arizona State University, 1980).

SINÁN, Rogelio (1902–1994). Rogelio Sinán is a pseudonym for Bernardo Domínguez Alba. He was born in Panama on April 25, 1902, and he died on September 22, 1994. He undertook university studies in the Instituto Pedagógico de Santiago, in Chile, later at the Universitá di Roma, in Italy. He graduated with a Bachelor of Arts in Literature, specializing in theater, from the Universidad Nacional de México. He was a writer, poet, diplomat, and professor of theater arts. He won the Premio Nacional de Literatura Ricardo Miró, Instituto Nacional de Cultura (INAC), several times in both poetry and the novel. His book of poems *Onda* (Wave), published in Rome in 1929, gave new visibility to Panamanian literature, introducing it in the avant-garde movement. He founded and directed the Departmento de Bellas Artes (Department of Fine Arts), which later was to become the Instituto Nacional de Cultura de Panamá. He published several books of short stories and two novels. He is the most anthologized national author and the best known outside the country.

Sinán is considered the originator of a genuinely national Panamanian dramaturgy with his play *La Cucarachita Mandinga* (The Little Mandinga Cockroach), a musical farce for children, with music composed by Gonzalo Brenes, also a Panamanian. This play has been staged innumerable times in the last sixty years. While in Mexico, Sinán organized the Teatro-Club La Quimera, which brought together artists from all of Latin America. During the 1930s and 1940s he directed theater in Panama. His contribution was a fundamental one, not only for the professionalization of Panamanian theater but also for the understanding that theater needed to be written from within the country, from within its theater. In Panama he directed his own play *La Cucarachita Mandinga*, and also *Mulato* (Mulatto), by Langston Hughes, *Las brujas de Salem* (The Witches of Salem), by Arthur Miller, and *Delito en la isla de las cabras* (Crime on the Islands of the Goats), by Hugo Betti, among others.

WORKS: *La Cucarachita Mandinga* premiered in Panama in 1937; it was published by Editora Mariano Arosemena, Instituto Nacional de Cultura, Panama, 1992. *Chiquilinga*, published by Ediciones Distribuidoras AIPSA, Panama, 1961. *Lobo Go Home*, premiered in 1976. *Comuníquenme con Dios*, unpublished.

BIBLIOGRAPHY: Carlos Manuel Gasteazoro, *Breve historia del teatro nacional* (Panama: Instituto Nacional de Cultura, 1974). Estela Paz, "Manifestaciones actuales del teatro en Panamá" (Ph.D. diss., Universidad de Panamá, 1955).

Marina Pianca

Paraguay

Theater exists in Paraguay, barely. One who speaks of drama within the country does not enjoy the luxury of movements, schools, and styles found in other countries. Paraguayan theater at any given time is fortunate to boast one or two important dramatists of any renown, either internal or external. Periods of some duration exist when no theater whatsoever was written or portrayed in the country. It is only within the past forty-five years that playwrights have demonstrated a staying power to continue dedicating themselves to the craft. Part of the reason for the underdevelopment of literature within Paraguay is found in the nature of Paraguay and the typical Paraguayan. Until recently, an extremely agrarian country, Paraguay had little in common with the cosmopolitan First and Second Worlds, where theatrical support and, as such, advances were the norm. It may be assumed that had Paraguay been either a vice-royalty of the Spanish Crown or an unlandlocked country, it would have been more open to an influx of immigrants—and hence the continual arrival of current world thought and trends. The country's inhabitants, a *mestizo* blend of native and European, were indoctrinated by Francia and other subsequent despots and dictators to satisfy themselves with minimal material goods and little education. Wordsmithing was not held in very high regard.

The earliest theater of Paraguay, as in the majority of Latin American countries, was ritualistic. The Guaraní Indians used dramatization of myths to communicate and reinforce the tenets of their beliefs within the populous. In 1595, a lyrical dramatic piece by a certain Father Alonso Barzana was presented. When the first Jesuit missionaries were given control of the area's "salvation" in 1606, they also employed dramatization of myth with purpose, in this case, the conversion to the Christian faith of the natives. This Christianization was immensely successful and was characterized by the missionaries' translation to the native Guaraní tongue of the *loas, autos*, operas, and fables used to indoctrinate the natives. The Guaraní participated in many of the celebrations as well, portraying characters during religious celebrations. During the years of *El Supremo*, all cultural undertakings, even informal guitar playing in the street, were abolished. Francia viewed such activities as belonging to the aristocracy he desperately sought to destroy. These years were a time when nothing was produced to efficiently signal a progressive way. As nothing entered the country, no outside influences could fertilize the dormant intellect of the isolated country. The theater during the years of the López, father and son, began to resuscitate itself, although not to the point of actually revealing a homegrown presence in either the writing or the production of plays. During the reign of the son, Carlos Antonio, whom Josefina Plá calls "obrero máximo de la cultura nacional," three foreigners wrote the first dramatic works of local origin. Sadly, they were nothing more than rehashed continental polemics cloaked in a veil of Paraguayan references. Written by neo-Paraguayans, these dramas were presented around the time of the War of the Triple Alliance. The first, by Ildefonso Antonio Bermejo, was *Un paraguayo leal* (A Loyal Paraguayan), which opened the door to the Paraguayan theater. Subsequent critics have seen it in a different light when it was discovered that Bermejo had written essentially the same drama in Madrid in 1949.

The second author was Cornelius Porter Bliss, a North American, whose contribution to Paraguayan letters was titled *La divertida historia de la Triple Alianza* (The Amusing Story of the Triple Alliance) and was meant to mock the collective efforts of Brazil, Uruguay, and Argentina in their destruction of Paraguay. The third effort, also recognized as the first play written in-country after the war, carried no less tributary a title—*Independencia del Paraguay, o el Doctor Francia* (The Independence of Paraguay, or Doctor France)—and was written by Benigno Teijeiro Martín, a Spaniard who counted no more than eight months as a resident of Paraguay. There was clearly no interest on the part of the majority of Paraguayans to write for the theater at this time. The rest of the day's representations consisted of Spanish *zarzuelas* and *comedias*, brought to the stage by traveling Argentine or Spanish companies.

The first play produced by an honest-to-goodness Paraguayan theater company came to pass in November 1855. It was titled *El valle de Andora* (The Valley of Andora), yet nine more years would pass before another company of its kind would grace the stage. After the Five Years' War, although numerous foreign companies continued to trample the stages of Asunción, nothing new in the way of substantial drama occurred for more than forty years. The first play written by a natural-born Paraguayan was a turn-of-the-century work entitled *La cámara obscura* (The Dark Chamber), by Alejandro Guanes. Its importance is not the content but rather that it was created at all. It inspired a generation of modernist-influenced writers to return to the theater, among them Leopoldo Centurión, Eusebio Lugo, Miguel Pecci Saavedra, Pedro Juan Caballero, and Luís Ruffinelli. Their work did not survive the ravages of time. It did, however, maintain the theater in the public eye, compelling young writers to try their hand at the craft.

During the decade 1910–1920, the expatriate Paraguayan Eloy Fariña Nuñez wrote several plays that received neither recognition nor publication. This trend to ignore has continued throughout the twentieth century in the cases of other expatriate dramatists of the status of Herib Campos Cervera and Augusto Roa Bastos (in the guise of dramatist, not novelist). Local works were impossible to stage, given that the traveling companies that roamed the country arrived with tried and true repertories.

The decade 1915–1925 gave some indication that the national theater, as yet nonexistent, was developing within the miasma of isolation. Writers such as Manuel Ortiz Guerrero found a carrot dangling just within reach for small nibbles to be taken; they knew that they were on to something, but recognition and support were simply nonexistent. A subsequent generation, consisting of Facundo Recalde, Arturo Alma, and Benigno Casaccia Bibilini, among others, continued the cultivation of the art, solidifying to a greater extent than did their immediate predecessors the substance of their works.

The greatest impediment to legitimate theater was the absence in the eyes of the dramatists of pertinent local material. *Lo paraguayo* (Paraguayan theater) was not accorded the status of the events and trends found in *el extranjero* (foreign theater). Character development, for lack of true models, was insufficient in all aspects psychological. A final blow was the leftover nineteenth-century placement of rhetoric over action, a tendency that made locally produced theater local in geography alone.

The key to the birth of a national Paraguayan theater is held in one name: Julio Correa. Correa was a complete man of the theater: actor, author, producer, director, and promoter. Writing in 1967, Roque Vallejos dedicates a meager 1.5 pages of a 58-page treatise to a section entitled "Crisis del teatro." In it he names just one representative playwright in all the history of the country: Julio Correa. Rather than appeal to a minority public of European heritage, Correa brought plays of social denunciation, written in Guaraní, directly to the people who most needed them. Although critics unfailingly point to a somewhat suspect formal structure on the part of Correa, perhaps it was this informality that so endeared his works to his public. During his roughly thirty years of renown, Correa brought the theater to towns of the interior, beginning what has been called the "national dramaturgy." Sadly enough, at his death in 1954, there was not one figure to whom reigns of succession had been extended. There had been nothing like Correa before, nor has any like him been seen since. Correa moved from town to town to provide *ceremonia, fiesta teatral*, all in the name of a people and the social equality he felt was deserved.

The decade of the 1930s was also characterized by the development of a uniquely Paraguayan form of theatrical entertainment: the *velada*, which was a combination of music, dance, poetry, tricks, and comic monologues. This form of drama followed the informal line established by Correa; it contrasted with the structured formalism commonly found in the First and Second World theaters. The awesome spirit of renewal and revitalization brought about by Correa served to awaken the Castellan-language writers. They were able to regroup, begin to form companies, and rejuvenate their portion of the stage. Ezequiel González Alsina, Augusto Roa Bastos, Jaime Bestard, and Concepción Leyes de Chaves all made contributions, albeit minor ones, during the 1940s, but the charge was headed by two young literary figures who found success both individually and in collaboration: Josefina Plá and Roque Centurión Miranda.

The 1940s and 1950s commemorate another rebirth of Paraguayan theater along a line different from that of Correa. This renaissance returned the formalism of Europe to the stage. Roque Centurión Miranda studied in Europe during the 1920s and brought the Stanislavski system to the country upon his return late in the decade. His drama was not of the populous, as was Correa's. Nevertheless, he wrote for a broad audience, employing a distinct style and content. Centurión Miranda later founded the Escuela de arte escénico in Asunción.

Josefina Plá is without doubt the predominant literary figure of Paraguay. Although Roa Bastos has garnered the lion's share of international recognition, it is Plá who to this day continues to write about all genres, tendencies, and forms of Parguayan literature. Among the variety of hats worn by the native Spaniard have been those of playwright, critic, historian, poet, and teacher. Plá first came to renown with the publication of *Historia de un número* (History of a Number) in 1949. The vast majority of her plays were not published or performed until the 1970s, in some cases, a mere thirty years after their genesis. At present she is in the midst of a four-volume opus detailing the history of Paraguayan theater. The first two tomes have been published by the Catholic University of Asunción.

Once again a war interrupted a flowering of the theater: the Civil War of 1947. After its conclusion, the first Paraguayan professional theater companies appeared in Asunción. They set down two principles around which to organize their efforts; First, theater is understandable only as entertainment; the public does not want serious drama. Second, in order to be a true Paraguayan theater, it must be so not only as regards author and actor but also as regards the characters, the settings, and the conflict. Due to this extreme appeal for audiences, the truly serious works of the period 1945–1950 remained unpublished and without debut until recent times. The same fate befell many worthy works written during the decade of the 1960s.

A continual font of controversy was the issue of language. All serious works that received their debut between 1940 and 1970, with the exception of those by Julio Correa, were written in Spanish. Some were dotted with phrases in Guaraní and one, *Casilda* by Benigno Villa, contained an entire scene in the Indian language. Ezequiel González Alsina traced a different path in *Bolí*, a play written in Yopará, the blend of Guaraní and Spanish.

A third figure stands out from the decade of the 1950s: José María Rivarola Matto. Rivarola Matto wrote along the lines of his predecessor, Correa, yet with a nationalistic air. He had the ability to mix the comic with the serious, localizing the actions in a rural atmosphere.

A new class of dramatists made itself known during the decade of the 1960s. Among its members were Mario Halley Mora, Carlos Colombino, Nestor Romero Valdovinos, José-Luís Appleyard, Ramiro Domínguez, and Teresita Torcida. Mario Halley Mora, a journalist, wrote in both Spanish and Guaraní. His dramas presented the expected social criticism of a newspaperman, focusing on the values of what he viewed as a rotting middle class. Halley Mora was not averse to the creation of heroic figures; many of his plays raise characters to the foreground as hopes for successive generations. He continues to write to the present day.

Carlos Colombino, who wrote under the pseudonym Esteban Cabañas, is best known for a stylized antitheater, founded somewhat in a devotion to plastic arts that enabled him to distance himself from a conventional reality in works such as *Momento para tres* (Moment for Three) and *La parábola del sitio más perfecto* (The Parable of the Perfect Place). Ovidio Benítez Pereira Ramiro Domínguez studied to be a lawyer, also working as teacher and director within a university. As is the case with other dramatists, Domínguez examined the relationship between the two distinct societies of Paraguay, symbolized by different languages and social perspectives. Theatrical companies in Paraguay from the end of the 1947 civil war to the present day have met with varying degrees of success. Most have been guided by an important figure in dramatic circles of the time: Compañía Paraguaya de Comedias was headed by Centurión Miranda from 1940 to 1946; Grupo de Teatro Debate was led by Josefina Plá from 1958 to 1964. Some groups have enjoyed extended success, whereas others were unable to mark a second or third anniversary.

The 1970s brought new life to the Paraguayan theater. The collective theater first popularized in Colombia by Enrique Buenaventura began to show scions in Paraguay. Tiempoovillo and Aty Nee represent the two most noteworthy attempts by companies to develop a Paraguayan voice. Tiempoovillo was founded in 1969 by students from the School of Architecture at the autonomous university in Asunción. It remains to this day the only noteworthy example of university theater. In a country desperately lacking in development of actors and writers, the university as a traditional source of new talent is nonexistent.

Tiempoovillo eventually left the University setting, striking out on its own, then, sadly, finally disbanding in 1974. During its five years of existence, however, it brought much good to the theater of the country. Tiempoovillo was created by students with no prior interest or training in the theater. In their own words, they united because theater had nothing to say to young people of the time. The group drew inspiration from the "poor theater" of Jerzy Growtowski and spent more than a year in training before debuting its first production, a nine-page play that was extended to one hour. This capability to extensively redevelop current works became a trademark of the group. Next they opted for a collective piece of their own design, *De lo que se avergüenzan las víboras* (What Vipers Are Ashamed of). The piece treated the reality of the destruction of the mythologies and structures of the various native tribal cultures of Paraguay. Unfortunately, Tiempoovillo, as had been the case with countless other companies, was unable to sustain itself, due to the lack of support from both the public and private sectors.

The most recent twenty-five-year period of history (1970–1995) has seen Paraguay better represented throughout the world of drama festivals. Numerous organizations have traveled to regional, hemispheric, and global conferences to present productions of national and world dramatists. The year 1969 saw the actuation of *Historia de un número*, the seminal work of Josefina Plá, at the First Festival of New Latin American theater in Mexico City. In 1972, Tiempoovillo brought its original creation, *De lo que se avergüenzan las víboras*, to the Fifth Latin American and International theater festival of Manizales, Mexico. In spite of some technical difficulties, the work was received warmly. The remainder of the 1970s disappoint us when compared with their explosive beginning. Tiempoovillo had disbanded, and no other theater cooperative arose to take its place. Repression under Stroessner continued, and the majority of playwrights was unable to realize the publication or performance of their works.

The 1980s brought rejuvenation once again to the Paraguayan stage. Although some groups such as La Compañía del Ateneo Paraguayo (in existence since 1941), Aty Ñee, and La Farándula ceased production, many others rise to the fore, while new organizations are born, most notably El Teatro Arlequín. Writers such as Plá, Colombino, Halley Mora, Valdovinos, and González De Valle continue their production and their interest, seeing many works published and performed. The Catholic University of Asunción introduces a theater department, whose undertakings include publication of works, a proposed theater journal, and an immense study of 400 years of Paraguayan theater, headed by Josefina Plá. The latter has already seen the publication of the first two volumes, as noted herein.

Prior to this decade, the actors guild ANDAP (Asociación Nacional de Actores del Paraguay) poorly represented its constituency, as the majority of its leaders, sympathetic to the government, had reactionary ideals. CEPATE (Centro Paraguayo de Teatro) was founded to unite everyone connected with the theater. The year 1980 saw some memorable productions, the majority of which were not written by Paraguayan dramatists, although they were supported by the multitalented *gente* of Paraguayan theater, the likes of Carlos Colombino and Edda de los Ríos. In 1981 La Farándula, a five-year-old collective that had presented plays in the National Railroad building in Asunción, closed its doors.

In 1982 Arlequín was opened by José Luís Ardissone. The theater/company would later open a second site, under the direction of Carlos Aguilera, a Uruguayan. In conjunction with a neighboring locale, the Teatro de las Américas del Centro Cultural Paraguayo-

Americano, Arlequín was able to offer an alternative to the trite costumbrist offerings of the Teatro Municipal, a theater typically closed to innovative expression. The Teatro de las Américas would undertake a partnership with the American embassy in 1984 and produce a work by North American playwright A. R. Gurney, *El comedor/The diner*. The following year the Centro Cultural brought Mexican director Alexis González to Asunción. However, this was still Paraguay, a country where free speech is, at best, an oxymoron.

The year 1989 saw the appearance of three Paraguayan representatives at the Segunda Muestra Latinoamericana de Teatro in Londrina, Brazil. A street theater group from the Catholic University of Asunción presented a Moncho-Azuaga piece entitled *Los niños de la calle* (The Children of the Street). It dealt with the ubiquitous problem of homeless street children and their unenviable fate. The second group, the Teatro Arlequín, staged a lightly Paraguanized version of Brecht's *Mother Courage*. The final representative, Actores Asociados, gave life to *Yvy Jara* by Julio Correa. This trio of plays summarizes the history of Paraguayan theater in the twentieth century: a taste of Guaraní flavor, a splash of Spanish influence, and a dash of European import.

The year 1991 witnessed the debut of a stage adaptation of Paraguay's most important prose work, Roa Bastos's *Yo, el Supremo* (I, the Supreme). Realized by the author himself, the play was subsequently delivered to Gloria Muñoz for additional revision. It was guided by the hand of Agustín Núñez, who had previously overseen dramatizations of *Pedro Páramo* and two works adapted from García Márquez: *La cándida Eréndira* (The White Eréndira) and *Macondo*. The final version was presented at the Sixth Theater Festival of Cádiz and received a good bit of recognition. The next year, also at Cádiz, Edda de los Ríos breathed life into the Néstor Romero Valdovinos monologue *Las tres monedas* (The Three Coins). This return by a Paraguayan to Cádiz may have marked the first time in history that the country was represented in successive years at the same theater festival.

Literary currents arrive late, if at all, to Paraguay. The earliest theater of the twentieth century depended on the anachronistic realism of the previous century. Beginning with Correa in the 1930s, and subsequently employed by the collective groups of the 1970s, the element of *lo mítico-folklórico*, the myth and the folklore, became an important, timeless element of Paraguayan drama. With the counterreformation of the Spanish-language writers, headed by Plá and Centurión Miranda, came a recognition of the formal European trends of the mid-twentieth century. Existentialism, the Absurd, Expressionism, Documentary theater, and Corporal theater all made inroads into the dramatic line segments of Paraguay. As few relevant dramatists were writing at any given time, it is impossible to assign "schools" to the influx of European styles. Even the South American tendencies had little success inspiring multiple disciples: The Buenaventura-based collective theater counted only Tiempoovillo, whereas the Chilean form of cooperative theater bred Aty Ñee. Throughout the cultural history of Paraguay, there have been two fundamental facts that had influenced the failure of the theater in the nation, lack of attendance and poor plays. Empty seats for both serious and frivolous drama have been the norm in Asunción. Numerous critics have eerily echoed one similar thought: For theater to survive and thrive, it must matter; to date, it simply has not been a priority of the people. It is only within the last twenty years that figures have successfully stepped forward to dedicate themselves wholly to the theater. In the past, with the exception of Correa, these efforts were brief. Nevertheless, the number who have made a career out of the theater is minute. Those dramatists of decades past were all trained for other professions and turned to theater out of love. Unfortunately, this emotional dedication cannot avoid the errors and inability that plague all amateurs, no matter what the undertaking. In a country as marked by turmoil and upheaval as Paraguay, it is no wonder that the theater, while alive, awaits life-giving contact with freedom of expression and an interested audience.

There are no journals dedicated solely to Paraguayan theater within or without the country. Nor has there been much interest from North American and European literary critics. As such, few studies on individual dramatists and cooperative groups have been written. The majority of these dramatists and groups are noted in the studies cited below, albeit receiving only one or two lines of mention.

BIBLIOGRAPHY

Alvárez González, Aurora. *Panorama de la literatura paraguaya*. Asunción: Ediciones NAPA, 1983.

Arrom, José. *El teatro de hispanoamérica en la época colonial*. Havana: Anuario Bibliográfico Cubano, 1956.

Banner, J. Worth. "Ildefonso Bermejo, indiciador del teatro en el Paraguay." *Revista iberoamericana* (February–June 1951): 97–107

Barreiro Saguier, Rubén. *Literatura guaraní del Paraguay*. Caracas: Biblioteca Ayacucho, 1980.

Benítez, Luis G. *Historia de la cultura en el Paraguay*. Asunción: Comuneros, 1977.

Bogado, Victor. "1980–1990: un decenio de teatro en el Paraguay." *Latin American Theatre Review* 25.2 (Spring 1992): 129–136.

Bruce-Novoa, Juan, and May-Gamboa, C. "Tiempoovillo: Paraguayan Experimental Theatre." *Latin American Theatre Review* 8.2 (Spring 1975): 75–83.

Caillet-Bois, Julio. "El teatro en Asunción a mediados del XVI." *Revista de Filología Hispánica*.

Cardozo, Efraín. *Apuntes de historia cultural del Paraguay*. Asunción: Biblioteca de Estudios Paraguayos, 1985.

Carmona, Antonio, and Aty Nee. "Hacia un teatro de la comunidad." *Escenario* (1981): 3.

Centurión, Carlos R. *Historia de la cultura paraguaya*. Asunción: Biblioteca Ortiz Guerrero, 1961.

"V festival latinoamericano y I Muestra Internacional." *Latin American Theatre Review* (Fall 1973).

Dauster, Frank N. *Historia del teatro hispanoamericano, siglos XIX y XX*. Mexico City: Ediciones de Andrea, 1966.

"Il Muestra Latinoamericana de teatro." *Latin American Theatre Review* (Spring 1990).

Jones, Willis Knapp. *Breve historia del teatro hispanoamericano*. Mexico City: Ediciones de Andrea, 1956.

———. "Paraguay's Theater." *Books Abroad* (January 1941): 40–42.

———. "Women in the Early Spanish-American Theatre." *Latin American Theatre Review* 4.1 (Fall 1970): 23–34.

———, and Josefina Plá. "The Guaraní Theater of Paraguay." *Theatre Annual*, 1958.

Lerman Alperstein, Aida. "El Paraguay de las últimas décadas." *Cuadernos americanos*, nueva época 3.2 (March–April 1989): 79–89.

Los Ríos, Edda de. "El teatro municipal de Asunción, Paraguay: historia y reflexión." *Latin American Theatre Review* 21.1 (Fall 1987): 109–114.

Luzuriaga, Gerardo. "IV festival de Manizales." *Latin American Theatre Review* 5.1 (Fall 1971): 5–14.

Marcos, Juan Manuel. *Nociones de teatro y cine.* Asunción: Editorial Independencia, 1976.

Méndez-Faith, Teresa. "Un nuevo programa de teatro en el Paraguay." *Latin American Theatre Review* (Fall 1988): 1160.

———. *Teatro paraguayo de ayer y de hoy.* Asunción: Intercontinental Editora, 2001.

O'Leary, Juan E. *Ildefonso Antonio Bermejo, falsario, impostor y plagiario.* Asunción: Ediciones NAPA, 1982.

Ochsenius, Carlos y otros. *Práctica teatral y expresión popular en América Latina.* Miami: Ediciones Paulinas, 1988.

"Paraguay." *Escenarios de dos mundos: inventario teatral de Iberoamérica.* Vol. 3. Madrid: Centro de Documentación Teatral, 1988, 244–283. Articles by scholars.

París, Marta de. "El teatro y los indios en el área de influencia guaranítica." *Latin American Theatre Review* 2.1 (Fall 1987): 95–98.

Perales, Rosalina. *Teatro hispanoamericano contemporáneo: 1967–1987.* Mexico City: Colección Héroes de Churubusco, 1989.

Plá, Josefina. *Cuatro siglos de teatro en el Paraguay.* 2 vols. Asunción: Universidad Católica, 1990–1991.

———. *Literatura paraguaya del siglo xx.* Asunción: Ediciones Comuneros, 1972.

———. *El teatro en el Paraguay.* Asunción: Ediciones Diálogo, 1967.

———. "El teatro paraguayo." *Cuadernos americanos*, nueva época 4 (1965): 24–30.

Rela, Walter, *Fundamentos para una historia del teatro paraguayo.* Montevideo: Jornadas de Cultura, 1955.

Reverte Bernal, Concepción. "VI festival de Cádiz, 1991." *Latin American Theatre Review* 26.1 (Fall 1992): 127–142.

———. "VII festival de Cádiz, 1992." *Latin American Theatre Review* 26.2 (Spring 1993): 171–181.

Ríos, Edda de los, and Richard Salvat. *Dos caras del teatro paraguayo.* Asunción: Agencia Española de Cooperación Internacional, 1994.

Rizk, Beatriz J. *El nuevo teatro latinoamericano: una lectura histórica.* Minneapolis: Prisma Institute, 1987.

Rodríguez-Alcalá, Hugo. *Alejandro Guanes: vida y obra.* New York, 1951.

———. *Historia de la literatura paraguaya.* Asunción: Colegio San José, 1971.

Rodríguez Medina, C. *Teatro y cine: aproximaciones.* Asunción: FVD, 1975.

Rojo, Grinor. *Orígenes del teatro hispanoamericano contemporáneo.* Valparaíso, Chile: Ediciones Universitarias, 1972.

Salazar, Ela. *Teatro en el Paraguay Literatura 4.* Asunción: Litocolor, 1981.

Saz, Augustín de. *Historia del teatro sudamericano.*

"Segunda muestra paraguaya de teatro." *Latin American Theatre Review.* 8.2 (Spring 1975): 85–87.

Seibel, Beatriz. "Romper la incomunicación: el Lencuentro regional de investigadores de historia del teatro de América Latina; Argentina-Brasil-Chile-Paraguay-Uruguay." *Latin American Theatre Review* 17.2 (Spring 1984): 73–76.

Solórzano, Carlos. "Primer Festival de Teatro Nuevo de Latinoamérica." *Latin American Theatre Review* 2.2 (Spring 1969): 60–68.

Vallejos, Roque. *La literatura paraguaya como expresión de la realidad nacional.* Asunción: Don Bosco, 1971.

Velásquez, Rafael Eladio. *Breve historia de la cultura en el Paraguay.* Asunción: El Gráfico, 1980.

Viola, Alfredo. *Reseña del desarrollo cultural del Paraguay.* Asunción: Edicíones Comuneros, 1982.

◆

ALSINA, Arturo. Alsina was an early twentieth-century playwright. Influenced notably by Ibsen, he was able to see four plays debut on stage. Alsina's works are not noted for their excellence, but rather for their existence; at a time when no Paraguayans were writing for the stage, he began a renewal of an art not practiced for thirty years by a native son or daughter.

WORKS: *El derecho de nacer* (The Birthright) (n.d.). *Evangelina* (Evangelina) (n.d.). *Flor del estero* (Flower of the Swamp) (n.d.). *La marca de fuego* (The Mark of Fire) (n.d.).

APPLEYARD, José-Luis (1927–). Born in Asunción, Appleyard was educated as both lawyer and journalist, working for the daily *La Tribuna.* Alongside his dramatic works are two volumes of poetry and one novel. In spite of a sense of linguistic elegance, Appleyard ably commands colloquial language within his works, particularly the *jopará*, a blend of Castillian and Guaraní.

WORKS: *Aquél 1811* (That Year 1811) (1971). *Cuando la patria manda* (When the Fatherland Calls) (1977). *Un momento de soledad* (A Moment of Solitude) (1981). *Tómalo de la mano* (Take Him by the Hand) (n.d.).

ATY ÑEE. Departing from the Julio Correa experience, this collective group nonetheless amplified what he had done with new sketches that included characters and styles near to the heart and reality of the Guaraní people, such as the *compuesteros*, who were minstrel-like storytellers, and the *Velada*, a particular dramatic form from the 1930s. Aty Ñee followed the lead of the Chilean-style cooperative by working with a famous dramatist, usually Alcibiades González De Valle.

WORKS: *Concierto de las picardías con el maestro Perú Rimá* (Concert of Pranks with Perú Rimá the Master) (n.d.). *Velada* (Vigil) (n.d.). (Both with Alcibiades Gonzáles Del Valle.)

AZUAGA, Moncho. Azuaga is considered the most likely to inherit Correa's importance in the annals of Paraguayan theater. His play *Los niños de la calle* (The Street Children) was chosen for portrayal by the Theater Department of the Catholic University of Asunción as a street theater piece, to be performed by a collective company. He won the only two *concursos* of the decade of the 1980s, sponsored by Arlequín and La Cooperative Universitaria.

WORKS: *Los niños de la calle* (The Street Children) (n.d.). *¡Salven a Matilde!* (Save Matilde!) (n.d.).

BENÍTEZ-PEREIRA, Ovidio (1939–). Benítez-Pereira has been one of the most daring and important dramatists of recent memory. His works take both philosophical and realistic turns, examining such symbolic failings of society as social injustices, bureaucracy, church hypocrisy, and alienation.

WORKS: *¿Dónde está?* (Where Is It?) (1971). *Paje* (Page) (1971). *Papelíos* (Little Papers) (1971). *El loco* (The Crazy One) (1986). *Como el rumor de muchas aguas* (Like the Noise of Many Rivers) (n.d.). *El ojo de la luz* (The Eye of Light) (n.d.). *¿Dónde está tu hermano?* (Where Is Your Brother?) (n.d.). *El hueco* (The Hole) (n.d.). *Jesucristo en nuestros días* (Jesus Christ in Our Day) (n.d.). *Morituri y Jurumy'yi* (Morituri and Jurumy'yi) (n.d.).

CENTURIÓN MIRANDA, Roque (1900– 1960). Roque Centurión Miranda, an actor, director, poet, and dramatist, started his dramatic career in 1925 with his play *Cupido sudando*

(Perspiring Cupid). His interest and deep devotion for the theater did not limit itself to writing plays; he was involved in acting as well as in all the physical aspects required to stage them. He encouraged younger writers to produce their plays both in Spanish and Guaraní. In 1942 he was one of the founders of the Teatro del Pueblo (The People's Theater); in 1948 he became the director of Paraguay's National School of Drama; and in 1950, together with Josefina Plá, he founded La Escuela Municipal del Arte Escénico (The School for Stagecraft). For several years during the 1930s and 1940s, in collaboration with Josefina Plá, he wrote seven plays. In 1942, *Aquí no ha pasado nada* (Nothing Has Happened Here), one of the plays written in collaboration with Josefina Plá, won the first prize of the Ateneo Paraguayo.

Also with Plá, Centurión Miranda wrote *Episodios Chaqueños* (Chaco Episodes) during the conflict with Bolivia over the Chaco region. Although many of his plays are written in Spanish, he also wrote and staged others that were written in Guaraní, the indigenous language of Paraguay. Many of these dramas in Guaraní reflect life among the common people of that country in the early 1930s, particularly the upheaval that the war brought to many Indian families. In 1933 he wrote *Tuyú* (Mud), a tragedy that deals with social justice. Centurión Miranda used his dramatic talents and produced the librettos for two musical plays in collaboration with the composer José Asunción: *Tapyi ocara* (The Country House) and *Ñandutí* (Lace).

WORKS: With Josefina Plá, *Desheredados* (The Disenfranchised) (Asunción/ Paraguay: Ministerio del Interior, 1933). *Desheredados. Inmaculada. Pater Familias* (The Disenfranchised. Inmaculata. (Family Father) (Asunción: Dirección de Asuntos Políticos y Sociales del Interior, 1942). *Aquí no ha pasado nada* (Nothing Has Happened Here) (Asunción: Imprenta Nacional, 1945). *Episodios Chaqueños* (Chaco Episodes) (n.d.). *Un sobre en blanco o Paréntesis* (An Empty Envelope, or Parenthesis) (n.d.). *La hora de Caín* (Caín's Hour) (n.d.)

BIBLIOGRAPHY: Richard F. Allen, *Teatro hispanoamericano: Una bibliografia anotada* (Boston: G. K. Hall, 1987). Frank N. Dauster, *Historia del teatro hispanoamericano: Siglos XIX y XX* (Mexico City: Ediciones de Andrea, 1966), chap. 20. Willis Knapp Jones, *Behind Spanish American Footlights* (Austin: University of Texas Press, 1966), 38–41, 51–52. Edda de los Ríos, "El Teatro Municipal de Asunción, Paraguay: Historia y reflexión," *Latin American Theatre Review* 21.1 (Fall 1987): 109–114.

CORREA, Julio (1890–1953). The son of a Polish nobleman and a Brazilian mother, Julio Correa was born in Paraguay in 1890 and died in 1953. He began his career in the letters as a poet, but soon he became known for the plays that he wrote and staged in Guaraní in 1933, a time when Paraguay was involved in the conflict against Bolivia concerning the claims that each of these countries were making over the Chaco region. Many of these dramas in Guaraní reflect life among the common people of that country and the impact that the Chaco war in the early 1930s had on their lives. Some of the titles of these plays suggest this concern about the war: *Sandía yvyguy* (Deserter); *Terejó yeby frente* (Returning to the Front); *Guerra ayá* (After the War); *Pleito riré* (After the Problem).

There are critics who consider Correa as the founder of the Paraguayan Guaraní drama. He is without doubt one of the dramatic authors who did much for the advancement of the theater in Paraguay in general and in Guaraní in particular, but he is not the first one to write plays in the indigenous language of his country. An important forerunner was Francisco Barrios (1893–1938), who in 1924 in a theater in Asunción staged two comedies in Guaraní: *Caacupé* (a town in Paraguay), and *Carai* (Lord, or Sir). A year later Barrios premiered another comedy, *Cunu'ú syry* (Everlasting Affection), which was very successful. There was a loss of interest in this kind of theater during the years following Correa's death (1953). But some twenty years later on the occasion of a drama festival in Asunción that was sponsored by the Muestra Nacional del Teatro, one of Correa's plays, *Yvi renoi* (The Call of the Land), was staged and was very well received. It seems that he has become a classic in the Guaraní dramatic tradition.

WORKS: *Nane mba'* (Our Own) (Asunción: Editorial Ortíz Mayans, 1965). *Sandia yvyguy* (Deserter) (n.d.). *Guerra ayá* (n.d.). *Terejó yeby frente* (Returning to the Front) (n.d.). *Peicha guarante* (n.d.). *Pleito rire* (n.d.).

BIBLIOGRAPHY: Frank N. Dauster, *Historia del teatro hispanoamericano* (Mexico City: Ediciones de Andrea, 1966), chap. 20. Viriato Díaz-Pérez, *Literatura de Paraguay*, vol. 2 (Palma de Mallorca: Editorial Luis Ripoll, 1980). Willis Knapp Jones, *Behind Spanish American Footlights* (Austin: University of Texas Press, 1966), chap. 4. José Monleón and Moisés Pérez Coterillo, "Entrevista con Antonio Carmona, de Paraguay," in *Popular Theater for Social Change in Latin America*, Gerardo Luzuriaga, ed. (Los Angeles: UCLA, Center Publications, 1978), 94–96 (originally published in *Primer Acto* [August 1973]). Josefina Plá, *Cuatro siglos de teatro en el Paraguay: 1544–1964* (Asunción: Municipalidad de Asunción, Paraguay, 1966), 224–225. Edda de los Ríos, "El Teatro Municipal de Asunción, Paraguay: Historia y reflexión," *Latin American Theatre Review* 21.1 (Fall 1987): 109–114. Hugo Rodríguez-Alcalá, *Historia de la literatura paraguaya* (Mexico City: Ediciones de Andrea, 1970).

GONZÁLEZ DEL VALLE, Alcibiades

(1936–   ). Born in Ñemby, González has dedicated himself to journalism as well as the narrative and theater. He had early success as a writer of *libretos* for *zarzuelas*. An extremely popular figure, González, like many others, preoccupies himself with the plight of the *campesino*, the Paraguayan peasant. González burst onto the scene in the mid-1960s with the first of a trilogy that examined the War of the Triple Alliance, *Los procesados del 70*. The two works that complete the triumvirate are *San Fernando* and *Elisa*. González experienced a rather turbulent decade of the 1980s: His play *San Fernando* was repeatedly censored by the government for his political references, and the dramatist himself was detained in 1984 and prohibited from representing Paraguay at an international theater festival.

WORKS: *Cañaveral* (Plantation) (Asunción, 1971). *Ivy reñai* (What Flows from the Earth) (n.d.). *Hay tiempo para llorar* (There Is Time to Cry) (n.d.). *Los procesados del 70* (Those Who Were Tried in 70) (n.d.). *El grito del luisón* (The Cry of the *Luisón*) (n.d.). *San Fernando* (Saint Ferdinand) (n.d.). *Nuestros años grises* (Our Gray Years) (n.d.). *Velada* (Vigil) (n.d.).

HALLEY MORA, Mario.

Mora is situated at the head of a new class of writers of the 1960s. A journalist by trade, he brings the same cynical criticism to his drama. His preferred subject has been the hypocrisy of the urban middle class. His play *El juego del tiempo* (The Time Game) was performed for the first time in 1986 by the Compañía del Ateneo Paraguayo.

WORKS: *Se necesita un hombre para cosa urgente* (Man Needed for an Urgent Matter) (n.d.). *El dinero del cielo* (Heaven's Money) (n.d.). *El último caudillo* (The Last Chieftain) (n.d.). *Magdalena Servín* (n.d.). *El juego del tiempo* (The Time Game) (n.d.). *Nada más que uno* (No More Than One) (n.d.). *Memorias de una pobre diabla* (Memories of an Unlucky She-Devil) (n.d.). *Despedida de soltero* (Goodbye to Bachelor) (n.d.). *Quince años* (Sweet Sixteen) (n.d.). *La mano del hombre* (The Hand of Man) (n.d.). *Testigo falso* (False Witness) (n.d.).

PLÁ, Josefina

(1909–   ). Born in the Canary Islands (Spain) in November 1909, at an early age she moved with her family to San Sebastian/Donosti (Spain). Before she was eighteen, the age at which she left Spain for Paraguay, she had some of her poems published in local literary reviews. In her new adopted land, she continued her literary career, and today, together with her friend Augusto Roa Bastos, her importance as a prolific creative writer as well as critic is well known beyond the borders of her adopted country. Her work and interests are not limited to creative writings in different genres. She has written nonfictional works mainly of a historical and cultural nature. She published a historical work that is a study of the role that some women played during the Conquest. This and other publications reflect her interest and concerns for the traditional role of women in Paraguay as well as pointing out the injustices committed to women in the Hispanic world. She is an accomplished ceramist who learned this craft from her Paraguayan husband, Andrés Campos Cervera (pseud. Julián de la Herrería) (died in 1937), and has written extensively on the culture of her adopted country. One of her major studies in collaboration with others is *Arte actual del Paraguay. 1900–1980* (Current Paraguayan Art. 1900–1980).

Recognized as one of the main figures in Paraguay by literary figures and critics such as Augusto Roa Bastos and Hugo Rodríguez-Alcalá, Plá has written short stories and novels and also dramatic works. Her interest for the theater has taken her to write articles and longer works in which she studies the history of the theater of Paraguay and the writing and producing of plays. She began her career as a playwright in 1927 at the encouragement of her husband and staged *Víctima propiciatoria* (The Expiatory Victim). But she did not begin to be recognized as a serious dramatic author until she began writing plays in collaboration with an already established writer and man of the theater, Roque Centurión Miranda, and with whom she wrote seven known plays.

Her ideas and ideologies that she has expressed in poetry and particularly in her novels are also found in her plays. In the comedy *Aquí no ha pasado nada* (Nothing Has Happened Here), written in collaboration with Centurión Miranda, Muriel, the main character, asserts her right to free choice to fulfill her yearnings to be a mother. In 1976 her play *Fiesta en el río* (Party by the River) received the first prize of the contest organized by Radio Charitas of Asunción. In this drama, which is not set in Paraguay but rather in medieval Europe, the theme of women's right to choose is clearly stated by the "Novio" (the fiancé). The language in this play, as well as others, is highly poetic and reminiscent of Peninsular authors such as Lorca and Casona. Another important play is *Historia de un número* (History of a Number), written in 1969 and performed in Mexico City during the Festival of the Young Latin American Theater. This drama incorporates certain basic concerns found in the ideas set forth by the expressionists and existentialists. In this work Plá delves into the theme of human alienation in a codified and legalistic society that causes the dehumanization of the individual.

WORKS: *Desheredados* (The Disenfranchised) (Asunción/Paraguay: Ministerio del Interior, 1933). *Desheredados. Inmaculada. Pater familias* (The Disfranchised. Immaculata. Family Father) (Asunción: Dirección General de Asuntos Políticos y Sociales del Interior, 1942). *Aquí no ha pasado nada* (Nothing Has Happened Here) (Asunción: Imprenta Nacional, 1945). *Historia de un número* (History of a Number) (Asunción: Diálogo, 1969). *Episodios chaqueños* (Episodes from the Chaco Borreal). *La hora de Caín* (Cain's Hour). *María Inmaculada* (Immaculate Mary). *Un sobre en blanco o Paréntesis* (An Empty Envelope, or Parenthesis), in *Teatro contemporáneo hispanoamericano*, 3 vols. (Madrid: Escelicer, 1971). *Fiesta en el río* (Party by the River) (Asunción: Siglo Veintiuno, 1977). *Cuatro siglos de teatro en el Paraguay*, 3 vols. (Asunción: Centro de Publicaciones Universidad Católica, 1994). *Cantata heroica* (Heroic Cantata) (n.d.). *La cocina de las sombras* (The Kitchen of Shadows) (n.d.). *Hermano Francisco* (Brother Francisco) (n.d.). *Los ocho sobre el mar* (Eight on the Sea) (n.d.). *Una novia para José Vaí* (A Girl for José Vaí) (n.d.). *Ah, che memby cuera*, with Roque Centurión Miranda (n.d.).

BIBLIOGRAPHY: Richard F. Allen, *Teatro hispanoamericano: Una bibliografía anotada* (Boston: G. K. Hall, 1987). Linda Britt, "Josefina Plá," in *Spanish American Women Writers*, Diane E. Marting, ed. (Westport, CT: Greenwood Press, 1990), 453–460. Lydia D. Hazera, "Signos y mensaje de 'Historia de un número' de Josefina Plá," *Explicación de Textos Literarios* 15.1 (1986–1987): 59–64. Willis Knapp Jones, *Behind Spanish American Footlights* (Austin: University of Texas Press, 1966), 38–41, 51–52. Hugo Rodríguez-Alcalá, "El vanguardismo en el Paraguay," *Revista Iberoamericana* 48 (1982): 241–255. Beatriz Rodríguez Alcalá de González Oddone, "Josefina Plá," in *Evaluación de la literatura feminina de Latinoamérica*, Juana Alcira Aranciba, ed. (San José/Uruguay: Instituto Literatura y Cultural Hispánico, 1987), 151–155. Lorraine Roses, "La expresión dramática de la inconformidad social en cuatro dramaturgas hispanoamericanas," *Plaza: Literatura y Crítica* 5–6 (1981–1982): 97–114. Celia Correas de Zapata, "Escritoras latinoamericanas: Sus publicaciones en el contexto de las estructuras de poder," *Revista Iberoamericana* 51 (July–Dec. 1985): 591–603.

RIVAROLA MATTO, José María. Rivarola Matto unite the rural with the urban, the past with the present, and provides hope for the downtrodden. *Chipi González* epitomizes this spirit of social criticism so inherent in Paraguayan writers. Rivarola Matto successfully wrote plays that operated on both a local and a universal level; although the works were populated with distinctly Paraguayan characters and dilemmas, their message may easily be applied to situations common to countries and societies like Paraguay.

WORKS: *La cabra y la flor* (The Goat and the Flower) (n.d.). *El fin de Chipí González* (The End of Chipi González) (n.d.). *La encrucijada del Espíritu Santo* (The Crossroads of the Holy Spirit) (n.d.).

TEATRO ARLEQUÍN. Opened in 1982, this theater and company produced its plays in a small *sala* in the residential neighborhood of Villa Mora. Under the direction of José Luís Ardissone, a second locale, a Taller de Interpretación, under the leadership of Carlos Aguilara, Uruguayan, was opened. In terms of repertoire, the theater alternates classical works with contemporary ones, and Latin American ones with international works. In 1989 it organized the Primer Festival Internacional de Teatro, which was attended by companies from Brazil, Uruguay, Chile, Argentina, Peru, and Paraguay.

TIEMPOOVILLO. Formed in 1969 by students from the Architecture Department of the National Autonomous University of Asunción, the group based itself on the methodologies of Jerzy Grotowski (and to a lesser extent, those of Antonín Artaud). This cooperative sought a reunification of theater and the populace, à la Correa, in Paraguay. Their first effort, *Curriculum vitae*, was a reworking of Ghelderode's nine-page drama *The Strange Horseman* into a ninety-minute play. The second play, *De lo que se avergüenzan las víboras*, was created over a period of time in which the group first studied with anthropologists, then lived with three distinct Indian tribes: one completely isolated from modern society, a second completely and tragically dependent on and corrupted by modern society, and a third somewhere in the middle.

WORKS: *Curriculum vitae* (Curriculum Vitae) (1969). *De lo que se avergüenzan las víboras* (Of That Which the Serpents Are Ashamed) (n.d.).

Enrique Martínez-Vidal

Peru

The fact that a theater exists today in Peru is nothing short of miraculous. Throughout its history, it has endured acts of God, deaths of principal dramatists, and continuous political instability. The truly dedicated (dramatists, groups, public, directors, etc.), however, have persevered and are presently very active in the proliferation of Peruvian drama on both national and international levels.

The history of this genre in Peru began long before its conquest, in the Incan Empire of Tahuantinsuyo, which not only included what is known as present-day Peru but Bolivia, Ecuador, and parts of Colombia, Chile, and Argentina as well. Although the Incan civilization was highly developed in many aspects and was the most advanced culture in South America, it did not possess a written phonetic language. As a result, little is known of this early indigenous theater. Its heritage was conserved in the oral tradition and is also detailed in many of the chronicles written to describe life in the New World. In these, the commentators mention ceremonies, dances, music, and a variety of sounds that they have observed. The most recognized of these early writers is Inca Garcilaso de la Vega. In his *Comentarios reales de los Incas* (Royal Commentaries of the Incas) he specifically alludes to the creation of tragedies and comedies that were performed on special occasions for Incan royalty and its court. He further explains that the tragedies were based on military triumphs and other heroic events or lauded past kings, whereas the comedies dealt with agriculture or other domestic matters. The theater was also used at this time to promulgate Incan philosophies and ideals.

Willis Knapp Jones points out in *Behind Spanish American Footlights* that although Inca Garcilaso uses the terms *tragedy* and *comedy* in his writings, it is probable that the performances being described did not exactly fulfill the criteria implied by these very specific terms. He also indicates that this famous chronicler compiled the information in his commentaries after he had spent some time in Spain and had observed the dramatic forms in question. Admittedly, these pre-Columbian displays may not have equaled the Peninsular masterpieces (which, incidentally, were still relatively primitive themselves), but they still possessed basic theatrical components: actors, spectators, costumes, music, dance, theme, and often a chorus. As evidenced today by many modern works, structure, plot, characterization, conflict, and other traditional elements do not necessarily have to be considered in order for a creation to be viewed as "theater."

The survival of any authentic pre-Columbian work is questionable. It was once believed that the drama *Ollantay* had been preserved throughout the centuries and had finally been transcribed some time after the Conquest. However, due to structural and thematic incongruities, this notion has been refuted. Nevertheless, there is still ample evidence that supports the existence of some form of theater in the Incan Empire. In addition to the information recorded by the chroniclers, modern-day investigators have also collected data that corroborate dramatic activity in pre-Columbian times. In *El teatro de hispanoamérica en la época colonial* (The Theater of Hispanic America in Colonial Times), José Juan Arrom frequently refers to Indian spectacles observed by the first Spaniards to arrive in Peru.

The theater rapidly took root in the New World during the colonial period, mainly due to its potential to educate. When the *conquistadores* arrived in the Americas, one of their main objectives was to convert the indigenous population to Christianity. Having observed theatrical performances by these people as well as their appreciation for this art form, the Spanish missionaries were quick to dramatize Christian doctrines in native languages to aid in the catechization process. Surprisingly, however, it was the converts to the new order who created the majority of the dramas that were used to propagate the Christian faith. Very few of these dogmatic pieces have endured the ravages of time. It is evident by the ones that still exist that the endoctrination process was still in effect as late as the eighteenth century. One of the earliest of these plays, *El auto del nacimiento del hijo de Dios* (Play of the Birth of the Son of God), was presumably written in the first decades after the conquest. Two others, *El pobre más rico* (The Richest Poor), by Gabriel Centeno de Osma, and *El hijo pródigo* (The Prodigal Son), by Juan de Espinosa, belong to the seventeenth century. The last that has been conserved is *Uscua Paucar*, penned by an unknown eighteenth-century author.

Plays were also used to celebrate religious occasions such as the feast of Corpus Christi or other important events such as the induction of a king or viceroy. In addition, they commonly served as entertainment for visiting dignitaries of Church and State.

The theater in the early part of the colonial period was performed in the open air. As its popularity increased, dramatists sought ways to make the performances more sophisticated. Alonso Hurtado's *El auto de la gula* (The Gluttony Play), created for the Corpus Christi celebration of 1563, was the first of these initial works to utilize real stage settings. It also won an award for the best theatrical contribution to the ceremony. The establishment of a competition also indicates an advancement in the development of the genre. These annual festivals led to an increase in dramatic activity and, as would be expected, an improvement in the quality of the pieces. By the beginning of the seventeenth century, Lima had become a principal cultural center and leader in the performing arts, rivaled only by Mexico. In spite of this progress, there was still no permanent place to house the growing number of theatrical productions. Finally, in 1594 the first theater, albeit primitive, was constructed in Lima. According to Jones, a man by the name of Francisco Morales and his wife rented some space from the Dominican Friars and erected what was possibly the first permanent stage in the New World. Soon after, several more theaters were constructed.

In May 1598, Felipe II closed all of the theaters in Spain, an action that played a crucial role in the shaping of the Peruvian theater in the decades to follow. Since all performances were banned in the Mother Country, a group of professional actors decided to journey to the New World to keep practicing the art. They brought with them an entire repertoire of Golden Age plays, which were very well received by the Peruvian public. These works were popular not only with theatregoers but with dramatists as well. The European influence is readily noted in their subsequent works as many writers abandoned the once popular Indian themes for classical mythology. The few native playwrights, however, remained true to their heritage and continued to write about the legends and history of their own culture. The most notable colonial dramatist was Pedro de Peralta Barnuevo (1663–1743), whose most distinguished work was *La Rodoguna*, an adaptation of Corneille's *Rodogune*.

In the eighteenth century the theater continued to flourish in Peru. More elaborate works were being written, and the writers enthusiastically experimented with a variety of dramatic forms such as the *entremés*, tragedy, and *comedia*. The first catastrophe to strike this prominent cultural center came in the form of an earthquake in 1746. Thousands of lives were lost, along with Lima s leading theater, the Royal Coliseum. In spite of this tragedy, theater lovers, still thirsting for entertainment, moved their productions to the Palacio de Gobierno in 1748. The shock of this great disaster greatly affected subsequent literary production and was followed by a period of artistic lethargy, and because of it, the theatrical repertoire was reduced to repeated performances of Peninsular authors. By 1749 the destroyed edifice had been reconstructed and was considered to be the first true theater in Lima. The inauguration of the new coliseum prompted a resurgence of dramatic endeavors in the capital. More notable, perhaps, than the plays themselves was the arrival of Micaela Villegas ("La Pericholi") to the Limeñan stage. She has been acclaimed by several critics (such as Willis Knapp Jones and Arthur Natalla, Jr.) to be the most renowned theatrical personality in the history of the Peruvian theater. The end of the colonial period gave way to neoclassical tendencies. The authors became more disciplined as they executed the Aristotelian formula to the letter, and that produced more successful results with the *comedia* than with the tragedy.

Rumblings of rebellion and revolt and revolution ushered Peru into the nineteenth century. In spite of this turbulent period, the propensity of the Peruvian theater remained unchanged in the initial decades. The neoclassical mode prevailed until well after the country gained its independence in 1821. Its presence however, did not deter the arrival of other literary impulses such as Romanticism and *costumbrismo*.

Romanticism did not flourish in the new Republic as it did in Europe and barely made it to the Peruvian stage. Many regional works exhibited Romantic undertones, but none of the successful playwrights aspired to truly embody the techniques and ideals of this movement. The two major dramatists of this period, Felipe Pardo y Aliaga and Manuel Ascencio Segura, abandoned the old themes of the Latin American Romantic drama to explore and exploit the peculiarities of one's native region.

The Romantic theater, which peaked from 1848 to 1860, was primarily sustained by Ricardo Palma (1833–1919), the most prominent Peruvian literary figure, who was then an obscure poet. It is said that he was a student of Segura and that he was encouraged by him to write *El santo de Panchita* (Panchita's Birthday), which premiered in 1859. His other works include *La hermana del verdugo* (The Executioner's Sister), *La muerte o la libertad* (Death or Liberty)(lost), and the infamous *Rodil*, which was so crude and offensive that its performance was prohibited. Palma and other writers of this era were inspired by Zorilla and Duque de Rivas. Luis Alberto Sánchez is one of the few critics who mention Romanticism in the discussion of the history of the Peruvian theater. Not only does he cite Ricardo Palma as a Romantic dramatist in *La literatura peruana* (Peruvian Literature) but several others as well, such as Manuel Nicolás Corpancho, José Arnaldo Márquez, and Carlos Augusto Salaverry. He also purports that it was this Romanticism that helped to propel the theater out of its neoclassical doldrums and further explains that Romantic efforts were hampered due to rigid censorship. The rebellion and freedom often manifested in works of this nature were suppressed by the imposition of government regulations. Another problem with the Romantic creations was that they were merely imitations of their Peninsular counterparts. They were fantasies of foreign lands and foreign people and not well received by a young Republic desperately trying to forge its own identity. The spectators, instead, rendered allegiance to the costumbrists who stayed close to home in their writings and depicted for them images of their own culture and society.

The development of *costumbrismo* in Peru has its own unique trajectory. At first the Spanish masters were imitated, but the Peruvian *cuadro de costumbres* (costumbrist scenes) soon acquired attributes that distinguished them from those of other Latin American countries. *Costumbrismo* arrived in the Republic before Romanticism. The sketches, which exclusively portrayed the Limeñan heritage, incorporated a satirical tone, and the writers themselves differed in their ideological inclinations. Felipe Pardo y Aliaga was the reactionary, a member of the upper class who embraced the Spanish culture and criticized anything Peruvian. Manuel Ascencio Segura was the liberal nationalist who represented the middle class and encouraged his public to relinquish its hold on all that was foreign. The former's first creation, *Frutos de la educación* (Fruits of Education) (1830), was the first work of significance to surface after the revolution. His other two plays, *Huérfana en Chorillos* (Orphan Girl in Chorillos) (1833) and *Don Leocadio o el aniversario de Ayacucho* (Don Leocadio, or The Anniversary of Ayacucho) (1834), were commendable but not as popular. Even though his writings accentuated the deficiencies of the Hispanic culture, and basically insulted the audience, they are still considered to be costumbrist works since they do focus attention on the mentality and customs that prevailed in his day.

Segura's theater was not without its harsh criticism of his society. He protested against the lack of encouragement given to local artists and also of the Peruvian people's tendency to overvalue everything foreign and to deride the works of their own countrymen. *El sargento Canuto* (Sargent Canuto) (1839), his first staged play, and *Ña Catita* (1845) are the most praiseworthy of his thirteen pieces. His first written play, *La pepa*, with its abominable disparagement of the army, was neither published nor presented. Critics point out that although Pardo y Aliaga realized a higher degree of artistic perfection in his works than his counterpart, it was Segura who achieved a greater popularity with the public. His works, as well as his efforts to establish a national theater, made such an impact that he is hailed by some Peruvianists as the "father," and by others as the "grandfather," of the Peruvian theater.

Although these acclaimed dramatists were classified as costumbrists, they did not hesitate to borrow forms and techniques from other schools or movements in order to indulge their artistic predilections. This inspired a dynamic theater rich in style that greatly contrasted with the austerity of that of previous decades. The polarity of these writers also contributed color and vivacity to the Peruvian stage.

The death of Segura marked another theatrical catastrophe for Peru. His last play, *Las tres viudas* (The Three Widows) (1862), was not published until 1924, which renders *Un juguete* (A Toy) (1858) as his final effort of the nineteenth century. There was no playwright during the last four decades that could fill the void left by Segura, and as a result, the genre experienced another period of lethargy that lasted until well into the twentieth century.

There are several secondary playwrights whose endeavors managed to carry the Peruvian theater through yet another recession. Among these were Carolina Freyre de James (1844–1916) and Clorinda Matto de Turner (1854–1909), two of the first women to be mentioned in the annals of Peruvian drama (Jones, *Footlights*, 264). Other writers, such as Manuel Moncloa y Covarrubias and José Santos Chocano, who were more famous for their pursuits in other genres, also made theatrical contributions. In the last years of the nineteenth century Acisclo Villarán (1841–1927) composed plays of greater significance such as *El cura de Locumba* (The Priest of Locumba) (1884), *El guerrero del siglo* (The Warrior of the Century) (1884), *La caja fiscal* (The Fiscal Box) (1886), and *Moral, virtud y urbanidad* (Moral, Virtue and Urbanity)(n.d.).

The costumbrist works that prevailed in the nineteenth century also dominated the first few decades of the twentieth. In the early years, it appeared that the efforts of two exemplary dramatists were going to revitalize the theater and give it the boost that it needed to thrive and prosper once again. The first, Felipe Sassone (1884–1959), was claimed by Luis Alberto Sánchez to be the only playwright capable of continuing Segura's legacy. He had an extensive repertoire whose production would have fostered the establishment of a well-defined theatrical tradition in Peru, which had been lacking throughout its history. However, he preferred the Madrilenian stage, and his works were produced abroad, where they gained the resounding approval of Spanish theatregoers.

This left Leónides Yerovi (1881–1917) in command of the Peruvian stage for slightly more than a decade. Influenced by Segura, this newcomer was impassioned by the *cuadro de costumbres*. However, his works were intended for entertainment purposes only and deliberately lacked the profundity and biting criticism of his predecessor's. They were enthusiastically received by the Peruvian public, and for this reason, they kept the national theater alive. His most outstanding triumphs are *Los de cuatro mil* (The Four Thousand Ones) (1903), *Tarjetas postales* (Post Cards) (1905), *Salsa roja* (Red Sauce) (1913), and *La gente loca* (Crazy People) (1914). All hope for theatrical revival was shattered by Yerovi's unexpected death at the apex of his career in 1917. This event, along with a scarcity of works and companies to perform them, plunged the theater into a dormant state from which it did not emerge until the 1940s.

José Chioino (1898–1960) was the only dramatist of any consequence to contribute to the Peruvian stage during these somber decades. His theatrical creations, characteristically costumbrist in nature, span twenty-seven years, which makes him one of the more diligent Peruvian dramatists. The most notable of these include *Retorno* (The Return) (1923), *La divina canción* (The Divine Song) (1923), *Una vez en la vida* (Once in Life) (1927), *Novio de emergencia* (Emergency Boyfriend) (1928), *La propia comedia* (The Own Comedy) (1947), and *Tabú* (1950), which received the Premio de la Municipalidad de Lima in the same year. The significance of Chioino's consistent offerings to the Peruvian theater during this lean period is irrefutable. His persistence rescued it from complete extinction and paved the way for its eventual rejuvenation in which he also played a part.

Along with the works of Chioino, the formation of two new theater companies, the Asociación de Artistas Aficionados (AAA) (1938) and the Teatro de la Universidad de San Marcos (1941), also fomented the revival of the Limeñan stage. All that was needed now was a fresh approach, something that would bring the theater into the twentieth century and up to date with that of the rest of the world. It needed daring and imaginative writers who would put the legends and myths to rest and address the metaphysical dilemmas and social crises faced by the modern-day spectator. Of equal importance was a public receptive to change and progressive enough to accept creations that deviated from traditional and historical norms.

Finally, in the mid-1940s, after centuries of mediocrity and apathy, the long anticipated rebirth of the Peruvian drama was realized. One of the main factors responsible for the notable progress being made by the genre at this time was the moral and financial support of the federal government. In 1945 it funded the Compañía Nacional de Comedias, and in 1946 it further stimulated dramatic activity by sponsoring an annual theater competition that awarded the Premio Nacional de Teatro.

The establishment of four more major theater groups within the next ten years also played a momentous role in this renaissance: Escuela Nacional de Arte Escénico (1946), which later became the Instituto de Arte Dramático; Teatro de la Universidad Católica (1951); Club de Teatro (1953); and Histrión (1956). The majority of the groups mentioned thus far are still in existence today.

Of equal importance were the playwrights themselves, who were greatly inspired by the increasing acknowledgment of the theater as a legitimate and valuable medium of expression. Between August 1946 and October 1947, three aspiring dramatists appeared on the scene, a substantial number given the paucity of writers in the previous decades. The first was Percy Gibson Parra (1908–   ) whose only dramatic creation, *Esa luna que empieza* (The New Moon), was awarded the first Premio Nacional de Teatro in 1946, along with *Don Quijote*, written by the second dramatist, Juan Ríos (1914–   ). He, unlike his contemporary, went on to produce several noteworthy pieces. Additionally, he won the Premio Nacional de Teatro four more times in the next fifteen years, which is quite impressive since his entire repertoire consists of only eight works.

The most consequential of the three newcomers, although not known at the time, was Sebastián Salazar Bondy (1924–1965). His first play, *Amor, gran laberinto* (Love, The Great Labyrinth), also premiered in 1946 and was awarded the second Premio Nacional de Teatro in 1947. During his twenty-five years of dramatic productivity, he composed ten major works and eleven brief one-act pieces, making him one of the most prolific writers in the history of Peruvian drama. His death in 1965 greatly endangered the still-fragile condition of the contemporary theater. Even today this significant loss is still felt. Critics agree that there has not been a playwright since that has been able to fill the vacancy left by Salazar Bondy.

The creations of other minor dramatists also played an integral role during these formative years. The previously mentioned José Chioino made two valuable contributions to the rebirth. *La propia comedia*, an obvious reworking of the renowned *Un drama nuevo* (A New Drama) (1847) by Tamayo y Baus, became one of his most celebrated plays, and *Tabú*, his final work, received the Premio de la Municipalidad de Lima in 1950.

Another secondary playwright of merit, Bernardo Boca Rey (1918–   ), also produced award-winning dramas. He made his debut in 1946 with *Las orejas del alcalde* (The Mayor's Ears), which was soon followed by *Un nuevo pueblo ha de nacer* (A New Town Will Be Born) in 1947. Roca Rey's dramatic efforts ceased after 1951 in spite of his considerable success. This was unfortunate and frustrating to the developing theater since it needed the strength of numbers in order to forge the foundation necessary to secure its recent position of respect in the literary world and prevent future setbacks.

Already by the 1950s the initial stage of renewal was quickly losing impetus, and the vitality of the theater was once again threatened. Of the five contemporary dramatists mentioned so far, only Ríos and Salazar Bondy remained active after 1951. Ríos made a minimal contribution to the 1950s, with his efforts comprising only two original works (*Ayar manko* [1952] and *El mar* [The Sea] [1954]) and a revision of *Los desesperados* (The Desperate Ones) (1960). Even though his offerings were sparse, they were all recipients of the Premio Nacional de Teatro. In contrast, the majority of Salazar Bondy's theatrical production was realized during these years. There is little doubt that this energetic playwright would have continued to be the driving force of the Peruvian stage throughout the coming decades. Unfortunately, he was plagued by a recurrent hepatic ailment that caused a gradual decline in his health until his death. There were no new dramatists of any significance to appear on the scene until 1958.

At this critical juncture, Enrique Solari Swayne's (1915–   ) *Collacocha* graced the Limeñan stage in time to rekindle the embers of renaissance. Although the initial impact of this newcomer was great, the scarcity of subsequent contributions left his public with unfulfilled expectations. He is not the only Peruvian playwright to have been afflicted with this lethargy. There have been many dramatists throughout the years who have vanished after writing one or two plays without ever having given their talent a chance to develop and mature. An insufficient quantity of works has historically been a contributing factor to the constant crisis in which the Peruvian theater always seems to find itself.

The 1950s ended on a positive note with the debut of Julio Ramón Ribeyro's (1929–   ) award-winning *Vida y pasión de Santiago el pajarero* (Life and Passion of Santiago the Bird Seller) (1959). Since most of his time was dedicated to the creation of renowned short stories, it is not surprising that *El último cliente* (The Last Client) (1966) is his only other dramatic piece.

The period between 1958 and 1960 represented a climactic moment in the genesis of the contemporary Peruvian drama. Not only was there a considerable amount of dramatic production but an improvement in the overall quality of the works, along with a refreshing departure from traditional themes and techniques. An increased public interest was noted as well as the emergence of the Instituto Nacional de Arte Dramático (1958) and several other private companies. The prime contribution of this fervid activity by established writers, theater groups, and the populace was its formative influence on those writers who were to come forth as beginning dramatists in the early 1960s.

Of these secondary dramatists, three are worthy of mention for their efforts to maintain the viability of the theater. The first, Arturo Jiménez Borja, a surgeon, composed his dramatic pieces entirely in verse. His deep involvement in the study of his country's folklore greatly influenced the thematic configuration of his works. His three contributions, *Pachacámac* (1958), *La creación del mundo* (The World's Creation) (1959), and *El hijo del sol* (Son of the Sun) (1964), deal specifically with indigenous myths and legends. Although these attempts are commendable, they did not advance the evolution of the contemporary drama. They lacked innovation and were too traditional, both structurally and thematically, to be anything more than minor successes at the box office.

Juan Rivera Saavedra (1930–   ), on the other hand, was more inclined to employ modern techniques and themes in the creation of his dramatic pieces. *1999* (1963) and *Los Ruperto* (The Ruperto's Family) (1965) are his two full-length dramas. In 1966 he also wrote three brief one-act plays, *Alberto el bueno* (Good Alberto), *El gran tú* (The Great You), and *¿Por qué la vaca tiene los ojos tristes?* (Why the Cow Has Sad Eyes), which utilize black humor as a literary device. The short pieces are more technically polished than the full-length works, which indicates progress in the development of his dramatic talent. He seems to have disappeared from the theater after 1966, although he was involved with the professional group Alondra.

The last dramatist of relevance to emerge during the first lustrum of the 1960s was Elena Portocarrero (1941). Her play *La corcova* (The Hunchback) (1961) was awarded the Premio de Teatro Nacional, making her the first female recipient of this coveted prize. Morris points out that this was significant not only because she was a woman but also because it demonstrated that a nonestablished writer of merit was able to obtain this prestigious award.

It is true that none of these playwrights of the early 1960s was highly productive. However, their dramatic creations surfaced at a critical period in the development of the modern theater, and for this reason, they are deserving of praise. They served to continue the renewal, and the fact that some of them even received awards stimulated other dramatic talents to make their contributions to the Peruvian stage.

The last five years of the 1960s were tormented by uncertainty. The disappearance of Ríos from the theater after 1960, along with the death of Salazar Bondy in 1965, signaled the end of an era in that the two remaining initiators of the renaissance were no longer contributing members to the cause. In addition, the output of Solari Swayne and Ramón Ribeyro, the primary constituents of the resurgence of 1958, was sluggish. This left a handful of fledgling playwrights in control of the fate of a still fragile dramatic tradition. As Morris points out, for the first time in twenty years the Peruvian theater was left without a first-rate dramatist. In deference to the optimistic inventory of months before, it was readily apparent that the recent accomplishments were indeed ephemeral, that the theater was still in a formative stage, and that renewal was still a goal, not a reality.

On a more positive note, the end of this second stage of renewal prompted the beginning of a third. The three main components of this phase, Julio Ortega (1942–   ), Alonso Alegría (1940–   ), and Sara Joffré (1935–   ), all remain active today in various facets of production and have dedicated themselves to the preservation and enrichment of a powerful, resilient Peruvian theatrical tradition.

Another important dramatist to emerge during this period was Víctor Zavala Cataño (1931–   ). He stands apart from his contemporaries in that his goals for the theater were of a different orientation. His collection of seven one-act plays is completely committed to the defense of the Andean Indian and his plight in an unjust, abusive society. He is one of a few playwrights concerned with the dissemination of the theater to rural areas of the provinces and, thus, has rightfully earned a position of distinction in the evolution of the Peruvian theater.

What distinguished this phase from the other two was an increased awareness and definition of the objectives and ideologies of the new theater. In order to modernize theatrical conventions, dramatists made a monumental effort to break with traditional structures. They entertained a more simplistic approach to plot and character. The works became shorter, and very few full-length dramas of any significance were produced. The presentation of an increasing number of foreign compositions also contributed to the totality and universality of the Peruvian stage. This, however, was not an entirely positive development since the production of more imported plays obviously implied a decrease in the production of domestic plays. In their review of the 1966–1967 season in Lima, Reedy and Morris estimated that the ratio of foreign to national plays was four to one. This is a trend that continued throughout the 1970s and 1980s and still continues to hinder the progress of this area of the theater in the 1990s.

In order to sustain the ever-growing enthusiasm for the theater, two new literary contests, Concurso Nacional de Monólogos and Concurso Nacional de Obras Teatrales en un Acto, were implemented. These encouraged writers to create the brief works that were in vogue at the time and eliminated the pressure of composing more demanding full-length dramas. Although the financial remuneration was not substantial, the winning plays were publicly performed by the Teatro de San Marcos, directed by the renowned Dr. Guillermo Ugarte Chamorro.

In addition, seven new theater companies were established, the most notable being the experimental groups Moderno and Máscara. Unfortunately, both of these disbanded some time in the 1970s. Also, the opening of two new theaters, Teatro de la Universidad de San Marcos and Teatro de Felipe Pardo y Aliaga, was tantamount to the conservation of Peru's theatrical heritage.

In October 1968, after a military coup, the Gobierno Revolucionario de la Fuerza Armada (GRFA) activated an elaborate program of social, economic, and cultural reform, which was to have serious implications for the Peruvian stage. In efforts to control theatrical production, the government rescinded all financial support and allocated the funds to the formation of the state-sponsored group Teatro Nacional Popular (TNP). The positive aspect of this action was the appointment of Alonso Alegría as director of the new company. The TNP was the object of both criticism and praise throughout most of the 1970s until its final curtain call in December 1978.

During the 1970s, Alonso Alegría and Julio Ortega, along with two newcomers, Grégor Díaz (1933–   ) and César Vega Herrera (1939–   ), were the driving forces of the Peruvian stage. It was finally becoming apparent that the efforts of the forefathers of the modern drama had not been in vain. The prognosis for the survival of the theater had gradually been upgraded from bleak to conservatively optimistic. Its future became even more promising in the next decade with the appearance of the celebrated novelist Mario Vargas Llosa (1936–   ) to the Peruvian stage.

Another phenomenon of the late 1970s and early 1980s that radically transformed the configuration of the contemporary drama was the emergence of the Collective, or Group, Theatre. As its name implies, the promoters of this dramatic form abandoned the works of individual dramatists in favor of their own collaborations. Their efforts encompassed all aspects of the theater such as the development and improvement of acting and creating skills. For this reason, they also supervised theater workshops, offered classes, and organized meetings in order to discuss the needs and the goals of the Collective Theatre.

This new dramatic approach, also referred to as the Third Theatre, was generated by Eugenio Barba, the director of Denmark's Odin Teatret, who was principally influenced by Bertolt Brecht. The Third Theatre surged in Europe, the United States, and Latin America during the 1960s and 1970s, and it was Barba himself who was mainly responsible for the diffusion of this new and exciting brand of dramaturgy throughout North and South America. His first contact with the southern continent came in 1976 when he and the Odin Teatret performed at the Caracas Festival in Venezuela. The Group Theatre was an immediate sensation and was highly appealing to other troops present who were desperately searching for a way to renovate current theatrical practices. Among these groups was the then recently formed Cuatrotablas, which is one of the leading Peruvian companies of today. Its director, Mario Delgado, was extremely impressed by Eugenio Barba, both professionally and personally, and they became close friends. The following year Cuatrotablas attended the second International Gathering of Group Theatre in Bergamo, Italy, where it was decided that Mario Delgado and his group would host the third of these meetings in 1978 at Ayacucho, Peru. It was such a success that Peru has since sponsored two more of these encounters. Not only did this have a powerful impact on the Peruvian theater itself, but it helped the country earn a position of respect in international theater circles as well.

In addition to Cuatrotablas, other major groups of the 1970s and 1980s such as Yuyachkani (1971), Quinta Rueda (1978), Setiembre (1979), Teatro del Sol (1979), Raíces (1982), and Magia (1983) were shaped and molded by this stimulating style of dramaturgy, and in the 1990s, they continue to advocate and employ its methodologies and techniques.

The main preoccupation of the Peruvian theater of the last two decades has been the growing violence and acts of terrorism perpetrated by leftist and rightist groups in Lima as well as the other provinces. Thousands of Peruvians have been indiscriminately massacred, cities have been bombed, factories have been burned, the water supply has been tampered with, and officials have been assassinated. All of these calamities have been attributed to various terrorist organizations that emerged during the 1980s in Peru. On the Right there is the Rodrigo Franco Command, an extremist paramilitary group, and on the Left, the Guevarist Tupac Amaru Revolutionary Movement (MRTA), along with the Maoist Peruvian Communist Party–Shining Path (PCP–SL). Several investigations have been conducted to examine the effects that these ferocities have had on the theatrical production of the past ten years. Juan Larco, the editor of the leftist Peruvian weekly *Quehacer*, reported in 1988 that many of the plays he observed dealt directly with rightest violence, but notably absent was any portrayal of leftist activity. He proposes that this is due to the historically leftist orientation of the theater and, hence, the expected denouncement of militaristic acts of terrorism. To criticize the undertakings of the Shining Path or the Tupac Amaru Revolutionary Movement would represent a conflict of interest. Instead of confronting this dilemma, theater people would rather not acknowledge their existence, which thus accounts for the scarcity of works dealing with the atrocities carried out by these groups. In the past five years, however, Domingo Piga indicates that there has been an upsurge of works that discuss the movement of the Shining Path.

Of equal relevance is the *teatro de guerilla*, the term designated to the collective efforts made by the members of the Shining Path. Their theater is propagandistic in nature and utilizes songs, dance, mime, and music to convey its message. Conventional stage settings are not used, and the Senderists themselves are the protagonists of their works. Their audience is comprised mainly of fellow subversives, prisoners, and the impoverished.

In the last ten years the Peruvian theater has made considerable strides. Although it may not be the leading country in dramatic output, the Peruvian theater is very much alive today. One of the most notable areas of progress has been in the dissemination of the genre to the provinces. Not only has there been an increased awareness of the existence of the theater in the more remote regions, but these have also been hosts to various theatrical events such as the aforementioned gatherings of Group Theatre. Nora Eidelburg, in a personal letter, reported an upswing of activity in these zones as of January 1994 and also mentioned that the Encuentro de Teatro Peruano would be held in August 1994 in Yurimaguas, a town in the Peruvian jungle.

Also impressive has been the improvement in the overall quality of the plays, performances, casts, and directors. Six new dramatic talents have surfaced in recent years: Celeste Viale Yerovi, whose *En un árbol sin hojas* (A Tree without Leaves) was performed in 1992 by Alondra; Alfonso Santisteban, whose *El pueblo que no podía dormir* (The Town That Could Not Sleep) was also staged in 1992 by Cuatrotablas; César de María, whose play *Escorpiones mirando al cielo* (Scorpions Looking at the Sky) was directed by Ruth Escudero in 1993; Marcela Robles; Rose Cano; and Rafael Lumett. Still active from the previous generation are Grégor Díaz, whose *Teatro peruano* was published in 1991; Alonso Alegría, who staged and directed his own *Daniela Frank* in 1993; Juan Rivera Saavedra; José Vega Herrera; and Víctor Zavala.

Outstanding directors include Rose Cano, who in 1991 directed her own translation of María Irene Tornes's *Barro*, which, according to Eidelburg ("El teatro actual en Lima en 1991 y 1992"), was an overwhelming success; Javier Valdez, who staged Lewis John Carlino's *El ángel de nieve* in July 1992; and the most distinguished director Alberto Isola, who produced and played the lead role in Roberto Cossa's (Argentina) *La nona* in 1993.

The Peruvian presence has been greatly felt abroad in the past two decades. It is true that major theater countries such as Mexico, Argentina, Venezuela, and Colombia are always accounted for at esteemed theatrical events, but there are many more who are rarely represented. The Peruvian groups fall somewhere in the middle with their frequent attendance at important theater festivals in several nations such as the United States, Spain, Colombia, and Germany. Theater activists such as Grégor Díaz and Sara Joffré regularly attend symposiums and roundtable discussions at home and abroad concerning the plight of the modern theater. In 1981, Folger's Theatre in Washington, D.C. presented the English version of Alonso Alegría's *Crossing the Niagara*. In 1988 the AAA won the Premio Ollantay, offered by the Centro Latinoamericano de Creación e Investigación Teatral (CEL-CIT), in the category of Institución de Apoyo al Teatro. This group was lauded for its support and promotion of theatrical activities including the formation of companies, theater seasons, and contributions toward the instruction, investigation, and professionalization of the dramatic arts.

Although the theater has finally attained a relative degree of consistency in Peru, it still faces many obstacles that continually threaten its security. On an economic level, it is endangered by a lack of financial support by the government. Also, many would-be spectators find it difficult to justify the expense of theater tickets in this epoch of frugality. As a result, the theater has become aesthetically compromised to a certain extent. In order to support themselves, the groups have been forced to produce works that are more popular with the public, in the hope of selling more tickets and therefore ensuring the financial success of the production. Consequently, many promising experimental works have fallen by the wayside, hindering the artistic advancement needed for the Peruvian theater to equate its development to that of leading countries.

On an individual level, there has been a decline in the number of dramatists who can earn a living by practicing the craft. Furthermore, these artists are not only in competition with foreign plays but with a growing number of collective compositions as well. Theater space is at a premium in Peru, and therefore, it is never guaranteed that a new creation will find a home on one of the national stages, which makes the writing of plays a somewhat tenuous endeavor.

The volatile political situation in Peru has exerted a substantial influence on the thematic content of current dramatic pieces and has also had an effect at the box office. Random acts of violence, bombings, curfews, and the state of emergency declared in many provinces have made it difficult for the theater to sustain its normal functions. That is not to say, however, that a valiant effort has not been made. Eidelburg gives a shocking account of an experience she had one night in a Limeñan theater. During the actuation an explosion was heard, and the audience, believing it was part of the script, remained seated. The actors, masking their fear, continued the performance. At the conclusion of the play, when a dead buzzard fell from the roof as part of the spectacle, a less intense explosion occurred. When the performance had ended, the public left the theater and entered a world of destruction and rubble. Panic ensued as the confused spectators realized what had transpired while they had been cloistered in the theater. According to Eidelburg, this had been the first attack on a middle-class district. The bombs that had exploded six and two blocks away from the theater, respectively, caused twenty deaths and 200 injuries ("El teatro actual en Lima en 1991 y 1992," 194).

In spite of this adversity, Peruvian drama has persevered and will continue to do so. Its persistent exploration of new techniques and approaches has provided it with a vitality that will endure any future calamity. The dedication and determination displayed by the actors, directors, playwrights, and public have made it patently evident at home and abroad that the goal of the Peruvian theater is excellence and that the mediocrity that has often characterized it in the past is no longer the rule but the exception.

BIBLIOGRAPHY

Arrom, José. *El Teatro de hispanoamérica en la época colonial*. Havana: Anuario Bibliográfico Cubano, 1956.

Belta, Aída. *Historia general del teatro en el Perú*. Lima: Universidad de San Martín de Porres, 2001.

Boal, Augusto. "El teatro del oprimido." *Popular Theater for Social Change in Latin America*, ed. Gerardo Luzuriaga. Los Angeles: UCLA, Latin American Center Publications, 1978, 292–311.

Cabrera, Eduardo. "XIX muestra del teatro peruano." *Latin American Theatre Review* 34 (Spring 2001): 163–166.

Cajiao Salas, Teresa. "Balance del año teatro 1972 en Lima." *Latin American Theatre Review* 8 (Fall 1974): 67–73.

Cid Pérez, José, and Dolores Martí de Cid. *Teatro indoamericano colonial*. Madrid: Aguilar, 1973.

Díaz, Gregor. "Del aparte a los espectáculos unipersonales." *Latin American Theatre Review* 24.5 (Spring 1990): 153–155.

———. "El Teatro en Lima: Lima es Perú." *Latin American Theatre Review* 19 (Fall 1985): 73–76.

Eidelburg, Nora. "El teatro actual en Lima y en Caracas a vista de pájara." *Latin American Theatre Review* 14 (Spring 1981): 87–88.

————. "El teatro en Lima en 1991 y 1992." *Latin American Theatre Review* (Spring 1993): 191–195.

Escarpanter, José A. "El VII Festival de Teatro Hispano Miami 1992." *Latin American Theatre Review* 26 (Fall 1992): 143–147.

Galt, William R., Jr. "Life in Colonial Lima." *Hispania* 33 (February 1950): 247–250.

Glickman, Enrica. "Italian Dramatic Companies and the Peruvian Stage in the 1870s. Part I." *Latin American Theatre Review* 6 (Spring 1973): 41–51.

————. "Italian Dramatic Companies and the Peruvian Stage in the 1870s. Part II." *Latin American Theatre Review* 7 (Spring 1974) 69–79.

González, Manuel Pedro. "El *Ollantay* de Ricardo Rojas." *Revista hispánica moderna* 10 (1944): 34–36.

Higgins, James. *A History of Peruvian Literature*. Liverpool: Francis Cairns Publications, 1987.

Higuero, Francisco. "Incomunicación múltiple en el *teatro breve* de Solórzano." *Latin American Theatre Review* 26 (Fall 1992): 111–121.

Hill, Elijah Clarence. "The Quechua Drama *Ollanta*." *Romantic Review* 5 (April–June 1914): 127–176.

Hoffman, E. Lewis. "Growing Pains in the Spanish American Theater." *Hispania* 11 (May 1957): 192–195.

Jones, Willis Knapp. *Behind Spanish American Footlights*. Austin: University of Texas Press, 1966.

————. *Breve historia del teatro hispanoamericano*. Mexico City: Ediciones de Andrea, 1956.

Leonard, Irving A. "Caviedes y José Hernández and the 'Underdog' a Parallelism." *Hispania* 33 (February 1950): 28–29.

————. "A Shipment of *Comedias* to the Indies." *Revue hispanique* 2 (January 1934): 39–50.

————. "El teatro en Lima: 1700–1739." *Hispanic Review* 8 (April 1940): 93–112.

Lohmann, Villena. *Historia del arte dramático en Lima durante el virreinato*. Lima: Universidad Católica, 1946.

Luchting, Wolfgang A. "César Vega Herrera: A Poetic Dramatist." *Latin American Theatre Review* 17 (Spring 1984): 49–54.

————. "Getting Better Perú." *Latin American Theatre Review* 14 (Spring 1981): 89–90.

————. "Une saison a lima." *Latin American Theatre Review* 9 (Spring 1976): 81–84.

————. "The Usual and Some Better Shows: Peruvian Theatre in 1981." *Latin American Theatre Review* 15 (Spring 1982): 59–63.

Macera, Pablo, and Matilde Torres. *Teatro peruano, siglo XIX*. Lima: Universidad Mayor de San Marcos, 1991.

McNicoll, Robert Edwards. "Impressions of Lima—Social, Literary and Political." *Hispania* 20 (1937): 69–72.

Meneses, Teodoro L. ed. *Teatro quechua colonial*. Lima: Edubanco, 1983.

Morris, Robert J. "Ricardo Palma and the Contemporary Peruvian Theatre." *Romance Notes* 15 (Spring 1973): 465–468.

Nemtzow, Mary. "Acotaciones al costumbrismo peruano." *Revista Iberoamericana* 29 (February–July 1949): 45–61.

Núñez, Estuardo. *La literatura peruana en el siglo XX*. Lima: Editorial Pormaca, 1965.

Ochsenius, Carlos, et al. *Práctica teatral y expresión popular en América Latina.* Miami: Ediciones Paulinas, 1988.

Oleszkiewicz, Malgorzata. *Teatro popular peruano del precolombino al siglo XX.* Warsaw: Universidad de Varsovia, 1995.

"Perú." *Escenarios de dos mundos: inventario teatral de Iberoamérica.* Madrid: Centro de Documentación Teatral, 228–297. Articles by scholars.

Reedy, Daniel R., and Robert J. Morris. *"The Lima Theatre 1966–1967." Latin American Theatre Review* 1 (Fall 1967): 26–38.

Salazar de Alcazar, Hugo. *Teatro y violencia: una aproximación al teatro peruano de los '80.* Lima: Centro de Documentación y Video Teatral, 1990.

Silva-Santisteban, Ricardo. *Antología general del teatro peruano.* Lima: Pontificia Universidad Católica del Perú, 2000.

Sotomayor Roggero, Carmela. *Panorama y tendencias del teatro peruano.* Lima: Herrera Editores, 1990.

Teatro peruano. Vols. 1–10. Lima: Ediciones Homero Teatro de Grillo, 1974–1985.

◆

ALEGRÍA, Alonso (1940–   ). Alegría, currently active in 1999, is one of the most diversified personalities of the contemporary Peruvian theater. He was born in Santiago, Chile, but moved to Lima, where he received his primary and secondary schooling. In 1960, while pursuing a degree in architecture at the Universidad Católica in Lima, Alegría decided to dedicate himself professionally to the theater. He had already been involved in the dramatic arts for more than a year when he formed his own troupe, Alba, and produced some of its plays. A few years later his career was propelled forward when he received a Fulbright Scholarship to Yale University, where he earned a B.A. in 1964 and a Master of Fine Arts in 1966. He then became deeply involved with the Yale Repertory Theatre, directing more than thirty plays, and the New York Shakespeare Festival. Upon his return to Lima, he worked with various groups until his appointment as director of the Teatro Nacional Popular (TNP) in 1971. During his tenure, he made numerous ambitious and creative directing attempts, to bring the Peruvian theater up to par with that of the rest of the world; some succeeded, others failed. This multifaceted dramatist has also translated three of his four works to English and has directed them as well. He wrote his fourth in English, translated it to Spanish, and produced it in Lima in 1993.

WORKS: *Remegio el huaquero* (The Buried Palace) (1965). *El cruce sobre el Niágara* (Crossing the Niagara) (Lima: Instituto Nacional de Cultura, 1974). *El color de Chambalén* (The Color of Chamberlain) (1981). *Daniela Frank* (1982).

BIBLIOGRAPHY: Robert J. Morris, "Alonso Alegría: Dramatist and Theatrical Activist," *Latin American Theatre Review* 9 (Spring 1976): 49–55. Morris, "Alonso Alegría Since *The Crossing*," *Latin American Theatre Review* 17 (Spring 1984): 25–29.

COLLECTIVE THEATRE. Also known as Group Theatre or the Third Theatre, it is one of the most prevalent dramatic forms employed by contemporary Peruvian theater companies. The surge of the Collective Theatre was an international phenomenon initiated by Eugenio Barba, director of Denmark's Odin Teatret. Instead of presenting pieces written by individual dramatists, the group members work together with a collaborator to synthesize their own creations. The motive behind this activity is that these collective efforts directly represent our history as we are experiencing it better than the plays by authors that were written years ago or that are concerned more with aesthetic principles than with current, urgent social issues.

The Collective Theatre is not considered to be a school or a movement, nor are the collaborations based on a single philosophy or ideology. It is the decision of the participants to employ the themes and techniques that best represent the inclinations of their group. There is also a strong interaction between the Third Theatre and social sciences such as psychology, sociology, and anthropology. The Peruvian groups compose and perform their works in Quechua, Aymara, or Spanish and are very careful to address the contemporary social concerns of all races that comprise their culture. The main goal of the Third Theatre is to reach as many people as possible, especially the nontraditional theatergoer. For this reason, the groups often choose to perform in plazas, market squares, sports arenas, or any place that may be available, which provides them with a mobility not offered by the conventional theater. In 1985, Peruvian groups formed MOTIN (Movimiento de Teatro Independiente), which was composed of about thirty companies from Lima and Callao. In 1990 it expanded to include members from all regions of the country and presently consists of over a hundred groups.

BIBLIOGRAPHY: Beatriz Calvo, "Reencuentro Ayacucho '88—Octavo Encuentro Internacional de Teatro de Grupos," *Latin American Theatre Review* (Spring 1990): 129–133. Elena DeCosta, *Collaborative Latin American Popular Theatre* (New York: Peter Lang Publishing, 1992). Domingo Piga, "Panorama reflexivo sobre el teatro de grupo en el Perú en la década del 80," *Latin American Theatre Review* 25 (Spring 1992): 137–149. Fernando de Toro, "El Odin Teatret y Latinoamérica," *Latin American Theatre Review* 22 (Fall 1988): 91–97. Ian Watson, "Reencuentro Ayacucho '88: The 8th International Gathering of Group Theatre," *Latin American Theatre Review* (Spring 1990): 115–127.

CONTEMPORARY THEATER GROUPS.

There are numerous currently active theater groups in Lima and the provinces, some of which are more than twenty years old. The majority of them are involved in the Collective Theatre, and many are dedicated to children's theater as well. Homero, Teatro de grillos, one of the oldest theatrical organizations in Peru, was formed in 1963 by Homero Rivera. It was originally dedicated to children's theater but eventually expanded its repertoire to include works for adults. They ceased active production in 1980 in order to commit themselves to the

promotion of other theater-related activities such as the organization of the Muestras del Teatro Peruano and the publication of a ten-volume series entitled *Teatro peruano*. Playwright Sara Joffré is the primary representative of Los Grillos and is deeply involved in the maintenance of the national theater. Another important troupe, founded in 1969, is Telba. They have presented a wide range of works by dramatists from Harold Pinter to Alonso Alegría, as well as their own collective creations such as *Made in Perú*. They are noted for their quest of a unique dramaturgy, along with coining the term *teatro urbano*. The goal of this type of theater is to recapture the history of the immediate past of the *pueblo peruano* and to situate it within the social context of the present. Also partaking in children's theater, they presented *¡A ver, un aplauso!* in 1991, which was regarded by Nora Eidelburg as an outstanding performance.

The two most extraordinary Peruvian groups of the 1990s are Cuatrotablas, established in 1971, and Yuyachkani, founded in the same year. Both of them are highly active on Peruvian soil as well as abroad. The former has played an integral role in introducing the Collective Theatre to other Peruvian groups. Its director and founder, Mario Delgado, is credited with having laid the foundation in the 1980s for the Group theatre that thrives in Peru today. The latter company, formed by Teresa Ralli and Miguel Rubio, who is also its director, is exclusively dedicated to the Third Theatre. It is also committed to theatrical investigations and organizing workshops, seminars, and publications. Some of its members have traveled to the United States, where the production of their collective creation *Adiós, Ayacucho* was praised at a 1992 conference in Kansas as well as at the VII Festival de Teatro Hispano in Miami.

BIBLIOGRAPHY: Nora Eidelburg, "El teatro en Lima en 1991 y 1992," *Latin American Theatre Review* (Spring 1993): 191–195. Sara Joffré, "III Muestra de Teatro Universitario Peruano," *Diogenes: Anuario del teatro latinoamericano* 4 (1988): 189–197. Bruno Podestá, "Del T.U.C., su evolución y sus montajes," *Latin American Theatre Review* 6 (Fall 1972): 87–90. Hugo Salazar, "Cuatrotablas, Yuyachkani y la identidad nacional," *Latin American Theatre Review* 20 (Spring 1987): 81–83.

DÍAZ, Grégor (1933–   ). Díaz is a currently active playwright. Over the years his stark, powerful portrayal of lower-class hardships has earned him the reputation of being an advocate for the Peruvian proletariat. According to Robert J. Morris, "Few, if any, of his compatriots have equalled his success as a dramatist and spokesman for the working masses" (80). His plays are thematically linked by the vivid depiction of the abuses perpetrated by the unprincipled, oligarchical "they" and the pursuit of the proletariat "we" to survive, defend themselves, unite in a common cause, and rebel against corrupt governmental powers.

WORKS: *La huelga* (The Strike) (Lima: Minerva, 1972). *Los cercadores* (The Oppressors) (Lima: Ediciones Homero Teatro de Grillos, 1974). *Los cercados* (The Oppressed) (Lima: Ediciones Homero Teatro de Grillos, 1974). *Con los pies en el agua* (With Their Feet in the Water) (Lima: Ediciones Homero Teatro de Grillos, 1974). *Cuento del hombre que vendía globos* (The Story of the Man Who Sold Balloons) (Lima: Ediciones Homero Teatro de Grillos, 1978). *Requiem para Siete Plagas* (Requiem for Seven Plagues) (Lima: n.p., 1984). *El mudo de la ventana* (The Silent Window) (Lima: n.p., 1984). *El buzón y el aire* (Lima: n.p., 1984). *Los del cuatro* (Those of the Fourth) (Madrid: Escelicer, n.d.). *Uno más uno* (One Plus One) (Lima: n.p., n.d.).

BIBLIOGRAPHY: Robert J. Morris, "The Theatre of Grégor Díaz," *Latin American Theatre Review* 23 (Fall 1989): 79–87.

ORTEGA, Julio (1942–   ). Ortega is one of two primary constituents of the third wave of renaissance writers. He began his literary career with the writing of short stories and poetry while pursuing a degree at the Universidad Católica in Lima. In 1963 and 1964 these won first place in the Juegos Florales of his alma mater. In 1964 his first poetry collection, *De este reino*, was published in the capital. A second anthology of poetry, *Tiempo endos* (Endorsed Time), and a group of short stories compiled in *Las islas blancas* (The White Islands) were published in 1966. He is also known as an exemplary literary critic. His essays on the mod-

ern novel were published in *La contemplación y la fiesta* (The Contemplation and the Feast) (1968), and various other studies have appeared in editions of *Biblioteca de hombres del Perú* (Library of Peruvian Men). In 1968 he also wrote a novel, *Mediodía*, (Noon), which was printed along with another anthology of poems entitled *Las viñas de Moro* (The Vines of Moro). He has written for a number of newspapers, magazines, and literary journals. He has been a visiting professor at Yale University, among others, and in 1980 began his professorship at the University of Texas at Austin. In 1986 Robert J. Morris wrote a significant article, "The Theatre of Julio Ortega Since His 'Peruvian Hell,' " that underscores the importance of Ortega's works in the development of contemporary Peruvian theater.

WORKS: *El intruso* (The Intruder), *La campana* (The Bell), *Perfect Soledad* (The Perfect Solitude), *La ley* (The Law), *Se vende cualquier cosa* (We Sell Anything), *Sociedad anónima* (Anonymous Society), *Como cruzar una calle* (How to Cross the Street), *El mosto de los lagares* (Must on the Wine Press), *Lázaro* (Lazarus), *Moros en la costa* (The Walls Have Ears) (all published in Lima, by the Teatro de la Universidad Católica, in 1965). *Varios rostros del verano* (The Faces of Summer) (Lima: Teatro de la Universidad Católica, 1968). *Mesa pelada* (The Bare Table), in *Revista de Artes y Letras*, 1971. *Infierno peruano* (Peruvian Inferno) (1980). *Balada de la dirección correcta* (Ballad of the Right Direction) (1982). *Aguarde su turno* (Wait your turn) (n.d.). *Pedir la palabra* (Take the Floor) (n.d.). *La bolsa o la vida* (Your Purse or Your Life) (n.d.). *El lugar del hombre en la cola* (The Place of the Man in Line) (n.d.).

BIBLIOGRAPHY: Heidrun Adler, "Julio Ortega's Peruvian Inferno," *Latin American Theatre Review* 15 (Fall 1981): 53–58. Robert J. Morris, "The Theatre of Julio Ortega," *Latin American Theatre Review* 6 (Fall 1972): 41–51. Morris, "The Theatre of Julio Ortega Since His 'Peruvian Hell,' " *Latin American Theatre Review* 19 (Spring 1986): 31–37.

PARDO Y ALIAGA, Felipe (1806–1868). He was one of two leading costumbrist writers of the nineteenth century. He received his education in the 1820s while living in Spain, which instilled in him a classical outlook that would later manifest itself in his works. He returned to Lima in 1828, where he launched a career in politics and became an eminent figure of the conservative party. He also cultivated his literary impulses in journalism, poetry, and drama and so became one of the most influential writers of the era. Upon arriving home he was immediately disillusioned by the reprehensible cultural standards of his fellow countrymen. Particularly deserving of reproach was the dismal condition of the Peruvian theater. As a theater critic, he expressed ardent disapproval of the inferior quality of local acting and theatrical productions, while lauding the performances of European companies and encouraging national groups to emulate them. He was so dissatisfied with the status quo of the Limeñan theater that he was inspired to write three plays himself in order to enrich the cultural awareness of his "provincial" compatriots.

WORKS: *Frutos de la educación* (Fruits of Education), *Huérfana en Chorillos* (Orphan Girl in Choríllos), *Don Leocadio o el aniversario de Ayacucho* (Don Leocadio, or The Anniversary of Ayacucho) (all available in *Teatro* [Lima: Universo, 1969]).

PERALTA BARNUEVO, Pedro de (1663–1743). Peralta Barnuevo, born in Lima, was the only dramatist of any consequence to emerge during the colonial period. He was an exceptional scholar and was versed in everything from French to astronomy. He became a member of the French Academy of Science, and a number of his astronomical studies were published in its journal. He also mastered Italian and Portuguese with considerable proficiency. His greatest passion, however, was the study of the language, literature, and culture of France, which is readily apparent in his writings. He wrote poetry in French, and his theatrical pieces demonstrate a significant influence of great French masters such as Corneille and Molière. Some critics, such as Irving A. Leonard, hail him as an "extraordinarily versatile genius."

WORKS: *Triunfos de amor y poder* (The Triumphs of Love and Power), *Afectos vencen finezas* (Love Conquers All), *La Rodoguna* (Rodogune) (These works, along with his short pieces, are available in the following collections: *Obras dramáticas*

[Santiago, Chile: n.p., 1937]; *Obras dramáticas cortas* [Lima: Ediciones de la Biblioteca Universitaria, 1964]).

BIBLIOGRAPHY: Irving A. Leonard, "An Early Peruvian Adaptation of Corneille's *Rodogune*," *Hispanic Review* 5 (January 1937): 172–176.

RÍOS REY, Juan (1914–   ). Ríos Rey, born in Lima, was a major contributor to the theatrical rebirth that began in Peru in 1946. In the years before the commencement of his dramatic activity, he fought in the Spanish Civil War on the Republican side in the Sierra Guadarrama. When he returned to the capital, he was exiled by the administration of Marshall Oscar Benavides. He left again for Madrid and was finally granted entry to his native land several years later. He became involved in the politics of Lima and formed a convention of writers and artists who drafted a proposal to eradicate the repressive statutes of the dictatorship. He is also a literary critic and a notable poet. In 1941 his first collection of poetry, *Canción de siempre* (The Forever Song), was published. He received the Premio Nacional de Poesía in 1948 for *Cinco cantos a la agonía* (Five Cantos to Agony) and again in 1953 for *Cinco cantos al destino del hombre* (Five Cantos to Man's Destiny).

His career as a dramatist is equally impressive. In his fourteen years of production he wrote eight major plays, five of which were awarded the Premio Nacional de Teatro. He is known as the only playwright of his generation whose creations were unencumbered by national sociopolitical influences.

WORKS: *Don Quijote. El fuego* (The Fire), *El reino sobre las tumbas* (The Kingdom of the Tombs), *Los bufones* (The Buffoons), *La selva* (The Jungle), *Los desesperados* (The Desperate Ones), (in *Teatro* [Lima: n.p., 1961]). *Ayar manko*, (*Teatro peruano contemporáneo* [Madrid: Aguilar, 1963]). *El mar* (The Sea), mimeographed (Lima: Compañía Lucía Irurita, 1954).

BIBLIOGRAPHY: Robert J. Morris, "The Theatre of Juan Ríos Rey," *Latin American Theatre Review* 7 (Spring 1974): 81–95.

SALAZAR BONDY, Sebastián (1924–1965). Salazar Bondy, born in Lima, was the foremost patriarch of the theatrical renaissance ignited in 1946 by Juan Ríos and Percy Gibson Parra and one of the most prolific writers in the history of the Peruvian theater. He first entered the literary world as a poet with his two collections, *Rótulo de la esfinge* (Sign of the Sphinx) and *Bahía del dolor* (Bay of Pain), being published in 1943. He was also known as an essayist and short story writer. During his twenty-year career as a dramatist, Salazar composed ten major works and eleven brief one-act pieces. Salazar is considered to be the most prominent and substantial writer of the theatrical rebirth. Since his death in 1965, few dramatists, if any, have equaled his talent, and none have made such a momentous contribution to the Peruvian stage.

WORKS: *Amor, gran laberinto* (Love, the Great Labyrinth) in *Teatro peruano contemporáneo* (Lima: Editorial Huascarán, 1948). *Flora Tristán*, in *Teatro* (Buenos Aires: Editorial Losada, 1961). *La escuela de los chismes* (The School of Jokes), mimeographed (Lima: Histrión, 1963). *El fabricante de deudas* (The Doubt Maker) (Lima: Ediciones Nuevo Mundo, 1964). *El rabdomante*, mimeographed (Lima: Casa de Cultura Peruana, 1965). *Ifigenia en el mercado* (Ifigenia in the Marketplace), in *Obras*, vol. 1 (Lima: n.p., 1967). *Algo que quiere morir* (Something That Wants to Die) (n.d.). *Dos viejos van por la calle* (Two Old People Walking Down The Street) (n.d.). *Rodil. No hay isla feliz* (There Is No Such Thing as a Happy Island) (n.d.).

BIBLIOGRAPHY: Robert J. Morris, "The Theatre of Sebastian Salazar Bondy," *Latin American Theatre Review* 9 (Fall 1970): 59–71.

SEGURA, Manuel Ascencio (1805–1871). Segura is the grandfather of the Peruvian theater and one of two leading costumbrist writers of the nineteenth century. He dedicated himself to dramatic pursuits after being discharged from the army as a result of wounds suffered on the battlefield. He, like his compatriots, became disillusioned by the military experience, which served as a source of motivation for his first play, *La pepa*, written around 1833. So brutal and bitter were his accusations against the army that this work was never published or performed. Although the critics agree that Segura did not achieve the technical mastery of his counterpart, Felipe Pardo y Aliaga, he was still

able to make an extraordinary impact on the Peruvian theater with his astute observations of the Limeñan people. He gained popularity by portraying the shortcomings of his society in a less condescending and insulting manner than Pardo y Aliaga. He implored his fellow countrymen to embrace their own culture and forge their own identity by rejecting foreign models. By encouraging them to accept and value the works of local authors, he did much to promote the emergence of a national theater. His death marked a steady decline in the condition of the Peruvian drama that continued until the great renaissance of the 1940s. His plays are still performed today, with the latest known production being *Las tres viudas* (The Three Widows), presented in Lima in 1993 under the direction of Luis Alvarez.

WORKS: *La saya y manto* (Skirt and Coat) (1842). *Las tres viudas* (The Three Widows) (1862). *La moza mala* (The Evil Maid) (1942). *Na Catita*, in *Teatro hispanoamericano* (New York: Odyssey, 1956). *El sargento Canuto*, in *Antología del teatro hispanoamericano*, (Mexico: Antologías Stadium-5, 1959).

BIBLIOGRAPHY: Luis Alberto Sánchez, *El señor Segura, hombre de teatro* (Lima: n.p., 1947).

SOLARI SWAYNE, Enrique (1915–). Solari Swayne, born in Lima, was a significant contributor to the renaissance of the Peruvian theater that was sparked in 1946. Like many of his compatriots, Solari left Peru upon completing his secondary education in Lima. He traveled to Europe, where he lived in Spain and Germany for several years and returned to his homeland in 1947, where he began his career as a professor of psychology at the University of San Marcos. Not much is known of the dramatist's personal life after 1969, the year in which he penned his last play. It seems that he has not been active in the theater in any capacity since then. Solari's first drama, *Pompas fúnebres* (Funeral Service) (1954), is of little importance and is yet unpublished. In contrast, his next, and most praiseworthy, drama, *Collacocha* (1958), served as inspiration and encouragement to those involved in all facets of theatrical life. After its triumphant debut, it traveled abroad and was performed at the Primer Festival de Teatro Panamericano in Mexico, where it won first prize. In 1959 it gained acceptance in Madrid and a silver plaque at the Festival Boliviano in Bogotá. It also won awards in Lima and Chile and acquired worldwide recognition, something that has not been accomplished by many Peruvian playwrights. The three-act drama is a direct result of Solari's experience in the Peruvian Andes, where he was introduced to the social, political, and economic duress under which the inhabitants lived.

WORKS: *Collacocha*, in *Teatro peruano contemporáneo* (Madrid: Aguilar, 1963). *La mazorca* (The Corn), mimeographed (Lima: Casa de la Cultura Peruano, 1966). *Ayax Telamonio*, mimeographed (Lima: Asociación de Artistas Aficionados, 1969).

BIBLIOGRAPHY: Arthur A. Natalla, "Enrique Solari Swayne and *Collacocha*," *Latin American Theatre Review* 4 (Spring 1971): 39–44.

TEATRO NACIONAL POPULAR. The Teatro Nacíonal Popular (TNP) was a theatrical organization funded by the Peruvian government in 1971 as part of a program of cultural reform. Under the direction of the talented Alonso Alegría, it produced its first play, Arthur Miller's *Death of a Salesman*, in the same year. Due to limited funds, the company was not able to present any works in 1972, nor was it able to procure a permanent group of actors. The following year proved to be more fruitful, as Alegría succeeded in establishing a fixed troupe and was able to begin steady productions. The remaining five years of the organization's activity were characterized by its leader's ambitious directing of plays such as Pablo Neruda's *Fulgor y muerte de Joaquín Murieta* (Triumph and Death of Joaquín Murieta) (1973), Lope de Vega's *Fuenteovejuna* (1974), Shakespeare's *Hamlet* (1975), John Gay's *The Beggar's Opera* (1976), Sophocles's *Oedipus Rex* (1977), the anonymous sixteenth-century Peruvian play *La tragedia del fin de Atauwallpa* (The Tragedy of the End of Atauwallpa) (1976), Beckett's *Waiting for Godot* (1978), and an adaptation of Vargas Llosa's short novel *Los cachorros* (The Cubs) (1978).

BIBLIOGRAPHY: Bruno Podestá, "Teatro nacional: Un teatro popular o la popularización del teatro," *Latin American Theatre Review* 7 (Fall 1973): 33–41. Podestá, "El teatro nacional popular del Perú: Entrevista con Alonso Alegría," in *Popular Theater for Social Change in Latin America*, ed. Gerardo Luzuriaga (Los Angeles: UCLA Latin American Center Publications, 1978), 312–324. Richard J. Slawson, "The Teatro Nacional Popular and Peruvian Cultural Policy (1973–1978)," *Latin American Theatre Review* 25 (Fall 1991): 89–95.

VARGAS LLOSA, Mario (1936–). Vargas Llosa was born in Arequipa, Peru, and is one of the most extraordinary figures in the history of Peruvian literature. He initiated his formal education in a parochial secondary school in Lima. His father, however, fearing for the manhood of his son and threatened by his growing literary interests, enrolled him in the Peruvian government's Leoncio Prado military school in Lima, from 1950 to 1952, which later served as inspiration for his celebrated novel *La ciudad y los perros* (The City and the Dogs) (1963). In 1953, a year after abandoning the academy, he initiated studies in literature and law at San Marcos University in Lima. During this period, he composed two short stories, edited a literary journal, and participated in various other writing activities. Throughout his career as a writer, he has made contributions to every imaginable literary genre as well as being a prominent critic and theoretician. He also became involved in politics and in August 1987 led the Rightist group that opposed financial reforms actuated by President García. He rapidly gained popularity and became a prime candidate for the presidential election of 1990. In the early part of the year, it appeared that he would win, but shortly thereafter his acceptance began to deteriorate, owing to the rigidity of his intended economic plan. He lost the presidency to Alberto Fujimori, a barely known candidate of Japanese descent. Due to political tension experienced following the election, Vargas Llosa left the country to reside in Spain, where he continues to write.

It is interesting to note that one of this distinguished novelist's initial literary attempts was a play, *La huída del Inca* (The Escape of the Inca), which he wrote in 1951 in Lima and directed a year later. Although not much is known about this work from a critical standpoint, it attests to Vargas Llosa's enduring interest in the drama as a literary form. His next play, *La señorita de Tacna* (The Young Lady from Tacna), was not composed until thirty years later, in 1981. It made its debut in Buenos Aires in May of the same year and in 1983 was presented in English by the International Arts Relations (INTAR) Hispanic American Theatre Company. *Kathie y el hipopótomo* (Kathie and the Hippopotamus), his second significant dramatic creation, premiered in Caracas, also in 1983. Both plays deal with the creative process and investigate how and why people relate the various anecdotes of their lives. They also address important universal issues that pervade the average society. His last play to date is *La Chunga* (1986), which gives a new twist to the concept of the love triangle by introducing a lesbian relationship. Although Vargas Llosa's dramatic output has not been immense, his three plays of the 1980s were well received and well liked.

WORKS: *La señorita de Tacna* (The Young Lady from Tacna) (Barcelona: Seix Barral, 1981). *Kathie y el hipopótomo* (Kathie and the Hippopotamus) (Barcelona: Seix Barral, 1983). *La Chunga* (La Chunga's House) (Barcelona: Seix Barral, 1986).

BIBLIOGRAPHY: Jaqueline Eyring Bixler, "Vargas Llosa's *Kathie y el hipopótomo*: The Theatre as a Self-Conscious Deception," *Hispania* 71.2 (1988): 254–261. Sandra María Boschetto, "Metaliterature and the Representation of Writing in Mario Vargas Llosa's *La señorita de Tacna*," *Discurso literario* 3.2 (1986): 337–347. Frank Dauster, "Vargas Llosa y el teatro como mentira," *Mester* 14.2 (1985): 89–94. Lucía C. Garavito, "*La señorita de Tacna* o la escritura de una lectura," *Latin American Theatre Review* 16 (Fall 1982): 3–14. Dick Gerdes, *Mario Vargas Llosa* (Boston: Twayne World Author Series, 1985). Dick Gerdes and Tamara Holzapful, "Melodrama and Reality in the Plays of Mario Vargas Llosa," *Latin American Theatre Review* 24 (Fall 1990): 17–28. Eva Golluscio de Montoya, "Los cuentos de *La señorita de Tacna*," *Latin American Theatre Review* 18.1 (1984): 35–43. Sharon Magnarelli, "Mario Vargas Llosa's *La señorita de Tacna*: Autobiography and/as Theatre," *Mester* 14.2 (1985): 79–88. Carmen R. Rabell, "Teoría del relato implícito en *La señorita de Tacna*," *Cuadernos americanos* 265.2 (1986): 199–210. Oscar Rivera-Rodas, "El código temporal en *La señorita de Tacna*," *Latin American Theatre Review* 19 (Spring 1986): 5–16. Harry L. Rosser, "Vargas Llosa y *La señorita de Tacna*: Historia de una historia," *Hispania* 69.3 (1986): 531–536.

Denice Montesano

Puerto Rico

COLONIAL PERIOD TO NINETEENTH CENTURY

The island of Puerto Rico was one of the earliest colonies of Spain. In point of fact, it might better be considered an outpost garrison of the Spanish military efforts: Its soldiers were paid out of the *situado*, a kind of tax on the profits of the Spanish colonies; the soldiers, numbering some 300 by the mid-1500s, had few amenities and neither doctor nor pharmacy; further, constant attacks from the English and Dutch privateers and armies forced the population to constant vigilance. Between 1508 and the middle of the sixteenth century the Taíno population of the island was decimated by disease and the ravages of the colonization process. The remaining native population took refuge in interior villages or was reduced to positions of servitude. There was a local diversion known as the *areyto* (or *areito*), which involved narrative, music, song, and dance—an oral theater to transmit the tribal history and traditions—which did not survive the onslaught. Nor was the *areyto* used to make it easier for the natives to understand and assimilate the Christian religion; at some point in the establishment of the Spanish Catholic culture, theatrical activities were held for the parishioners, but the purpose lacks documentation. Research has not been able to restore any authentic *areyto* works; but there is some sentiment that the Puerto Rican love of music and dance is part of this tradition that has survived.

The strategic location of Puerto Rico as a guard point between Spain and her colonies, the entry to the Indies, placed Puerto Rico in a different situation than that of the Viceroyalties. The island was considered, and populated as, a fortification against attacks of other nations; it was also the major point for restocking of supplies in the long trip across the Atlantic Ocean. These conditions were the basis of life for the small hardy colony of primarily military personnel during the first several decades. The first record of any forms of entertainment aside from sporting events (horseracing, cockfights) is contained in a report from the San Juan Municipal Cabildo (Council) to the Consejo de Indias, dated October 24, 1605. San Juan commemorated the birth of Prince Philip of Spain with festivities that included bullfights and other games. Sponsors included the guilds, government officials, and some members of the military garrison in San Juan. Further information is gleaned from a series of prohibitions decreed in 1645 by San Juan Bishop Damián López de Haro. Apparently members of the clergy had supplemented the local populace in plays of both religious and secular nature produced on Church Feast Days. In the *Constituciones Sinodales*, which the Bishop wrote, the ordained clergy were forbidden to participate in *comedias* and *autos* even if they were of religious nature and were presented on Corpus Christi or any other Church Feast Day. They forbade the Brotherhoods to pay for *comedias* with the money they had collected from the faithful; and they forbade any theatrical representations inside the church. Plays of a religious nature were permitted on Feast Days, provided they were outside the church and they were previously approved by the bishop. Various authorities assume from these strictures that plays of both clerical and secular nature were being presented with clergy acting and in churches.

The population remained small, primarily military in profession, although with a growing range of other concerns, during the eighteenth century and into the first decades of the nineteenth century. There is no evidence of either local professional or casual theater companies or of traveling companies that might have visited the island before 1811. There were, however, theatrical productions related to functions of the Church and to those of the Spanish government. Each time a king was crowned, during three of the four *Juras Reales* (Royal Oaths), in 1747, 1760–1761, and 1789, *comedias* were presented. These were often produced by different groups in the community. The government sponsored public celebrations that honored events in Spain and granted permission to perform to both amateur and professional companies. The great majority of plays presented were from the Spanish repertoire. There is a good accounting of several of these events of state. As an example, on the death of Philip V and the ascendancy of his son, Philip VI, in 1746, we learn that the brothers of the Cabildo presented *El conde Lucanor* (Count Lucanor), by Calderón de la Barca, with abundant refreshments during the intermission; the merchant class presented *Los españoles en Chile* (The Spaniards in Chile), by González de Bustos; the same night, the free mulattos presented *El villano del Danubio* and *El buen Juez no tiene patria* (The Villain of the Danube) and (The Good Judge Knows No Country), by Hoz y Mota, which was followed by a number of hand-held fireworks. Finally, the military garrison presented *Primero es la honra* (Honor Is First), by Moreto. These Spanish works provided opportunities for the various groups to exhibit not only their taste in the works chosen but also the theatrical effects, lighting with torches and mirrors, costuming, and festive events before and afterward.

GROWTH AND DIVERSIFICATION IN THE NINETEENTH CENTURY

During the first years of the nineteenth century, there was sufficient interest in the theater that several temporary structures were built in San Juan. Traveling companies performed in San Juan in 1811 and 1824. In 1822 Spanish colonial governments were authorized to impose taxes in order to finance the construction of theaters, which led to a plan for a facility in San Juan. There seems to have been a theatrical "season" during fall of 1811. A theater, probably like the Spanish *corral*, was built for that season. Amateur local actors and a few Spaniards presented three Spanish *comedias* and one *sainete*. Bishop Juan Alejo Arizmentdi opposed the performances with much the same zeal as some of his predecessors in the eighteenth century. He wrote several letters on the matter to Gov. Salvador Meléndez, he wrote a pastoral letter to all Puerto Ricans, and he informed King Ferdinand VII of his unsuccessful efforts to have the performances suppressed. Sporadic performances of various kinds were presented, sometimes for charity, during the first years of the century. Gradually, the culture of the community had grown to the outline of a colonial city, complete with merchants, an elite class of governing, military, and entrepreneurial families; and it had begun to be able to provide local information and entertainment through printing establishments (as of 1806), newspapers and theater, among others.

Theatrical events of this period, indicated by the minutes of the Cabildo of January 15,

1816, include one performance of a *comedia* that yielded 488 pesos for the Charity Hospital. In 1817, the marriages of Ferdinand VII and of his brother Charles were commemorated in Puerto Rico. There is no record of which theatrical works were performed in San Juan, but there were Spanish plays performed in Caguas and in Ponce. Also a *loa*, written by a local author, was performed in Ponce. By January 1823, amateur players in San Juan had organized a company. They performed for the season of January to April 1823 in a theater called Amigos del País. The works performed included *comedias* and *entremeses* and Spanish versions of French and Italian works. The theater had a stage, a backstage area, a curtain, a balcony with wooden steps leading up to it, four rows of seats in the balcony, boxes that were accessed through adjacent houses, lunettes, and benches in the orchestra. The growing enthusiasm of the theatergoing public can be gauged by the events at this "temporary" theater. Although it was declared a fire hazard and was to have been destroyed by the government, it was rescued and repaired, and was the site of a season in fall of 1824 and winter of 1825 of forty-one full-length plays and an equal number of *sainetes*. Most of the plays were of Spanish origin; others were translated from French or Italian. On October 1, 1824, to celebrate the first anniversary of Ferdinand VII's second restoration to the throne of Spain, the visiting Spanish professional company presented two plays, with profits to benefit the new theater to be built in San Juan.

By this time there was sufficient interest in a permanent theater that General Miguel de la Torre, governor of the island in 1824, devised a theater construction project to be financed with money collected from a bread tax and private contributions. He enlisted the cooperation of Bishop Rodríguez de Olmedo, whose Conciliar Seminary would benefit from profits from theatrical performances, and that of the San Juan Cabildo. Both bodies approved the project, which was begun in August 1824. Finished in 1832, it became the principal theater of San Juan, known then as the Teatro Municipal, now the Teatro Tapia.

Throughout the rest of the nineteenth century, a desire for theatrical entertainment grew, benefiting the productions of visiting companies and the development of local companies and stimulating the building of other theaters throughout Puerto Rico. Visiting companies are particularly important to a culture such as Puerto Rico's, which had little local tradition to build on, was only beginning an educational system in the mid-nineteenth century, and was otherwise relatively isolated from both Latin American and European cultures. The groups that came to Puerto Rico indicate strong Spanish influence and included productions of opera, operetta, *zarzuela* (Spanish musical comedy), comedy, and drama. Most of the drama was done by Spanish actors; the inclusion of local actors increased local acceptance and also stimulated local interest in theatrical production.

In 1875 the first professional company was organized. This group traveled throughout the island, then ventured abroad, visiting other Caribbean ports and some in South America. Its repertoire included plays by the Spanish authors Lope de Vega, Pedro Calderón de la Barca, and José Echegaray, as well as works by the Puerto Rican authors Salvador Brau, Alejandro Tapia y Rivera, and Ramón Méndez Quiñones.

The first recorded performance of a theatrical work by a Puerto Rican seems to be Tapia's *Roberto d'Evreux*, in 1856. There apparently was also a popular tradition that paralleled the more sophisticated plays such as that mentioned above. These were presented in open-air *corrales* and will be seen later as an influence in the theater of the *jíbaro* and in more modern popular theater. Tapia mentions one typical of this vein, *Vilorio en Bayajá y pendencia en Culo Prieto* (Wake in Bayajá and Fight in Culo Prieto).

The traditions and taste of the public in the mid- to late nineteenth century encompassed romantic and historic works, although the censorship of the day did not permit the production of works based on historic incident or action unfavorable to the Crown and the comedy of manners and customs. Works representative of the romantic tradition, as indicated by their titles, are *El hijo del amor* (The Love Child) (1872), *Lazos de amor* (Ties of Love) (1878), and *Los secretos de un padre* (The Secrets of a Father) (1880). At times these were linked to themes of liberty and heroism, as in the 1893 work *La fuerza del destino* (The Force of Destiny), based on the novel *La extranjera o la mujer misteriosa* (The Stranger or the Mysterious Woman) of the Viscount of Arlincourt. There were also works of late, or decadent, romanticism, romances with a tragic, even naturalistic twist, such as *Combates del corazón* (Battles of the Heart) (1888), by Luis A. Torregrosa, and *La voz de la conciencia* (The Voice of Conscience) (1889), by Joaquín Masferrer. Alejandro Tapia y Rivera (1826–1882), the first important Puerto Rican playwright, began writing in 1848. His liberal tendencies earned him the watchful eye of the censors from the beginning, so he used other settings and times for his works, the normal option of writers who want to get some of their message to an audience and especially in the case of dramatists. While his works may seem dated, his use of dignified actions and themes lays the groundwork for later writers. *Roberto D'Evreux* (1848) has as its theme the love of Isabel I for the Count of Essex. Prohibited from presentation because the humanization of royalty was not permitted, it was reworked and presented in 1856. *Bernardo de Palissy o El heroísmo del trabajo* (Bernardo de Palissy or the Heroism of Work) (1857) was written at the request of Román Baldorioty de Castro to uplift the people of Puerto Rico. *La cuarterona* (The Quadroon) (1867) treats the theme of love denied for differences of race, thus initiating a theme of long standing in Puerto Rico. This early treatment of the racial theme exemplifies Tapia's wide-ranging and liberal interests. The beginnings of incorporation of an indigenist theme are found in Tapia's opera *Guarionex*, written and debuted in 1854.

If Tapia served as example and stimulus for the first wave of theater in the nineteenth century, Salvador Brau (1842–1912) exemplifies the man of letters of the latter part of the century. Most of his works are of the decade of the 1870s, and all are undergirded by a liberal political philosophy, for which reason most of his works take historically allied themes as their subject. He wrote of the uprising of the *comuneros* of Spain in the sixteenth century in *Héroe y mártir* (Hero and Martyr) (1871); and he used the rebellion of the Sicilians against the French government in 1282 in *Los horrores del triunfo* (The Horrors of Triumph) (1877). Brau was also influenced by the realist tendencies of the period in *De la superficie al fondo* (From the Surface to the Bottom) (1874) and in *La vuelta al hogar* (The Return Home) (1877). He presents the problems of families of the (upper) middle class in more realistic, even popular, speech. Thus Brau represents the changes in tone and manner of theater of the nineteenth century, wherein some didacticism was present as authors explored themes relevant to the lifestyles and choices of the spectators.

Other historic themes written about in the nineteenth century include a variety of themes based on Puerto Rico's events and people. Manuel María Sama (1850–1913) wrote a dramatic one-act play, *El regreso de Colón* (Columbus's Return) (pub. 1892). María Bibiana

Benítez (1783–1875) wrote *La Cruz del Morro* (The Cross of El Morro) (1862), about the 1625 Dutch battle for the capital. Manuel María Corchado y Juarbe (1840–1884) wrote *El capitán Correa* (Captain Correa), a one-act drama that glorified the patriotic spirit of the Areciben of the title. The conservative approach continued to be very solid in Puerto Rico, which had been strengthened by successive waves of royalist refugees from Venezuela and other former colonies of Spain. Throughout the century works such as *El triunfo del trono y lealtad puertorriqueña* (Triumph of the Throne and Puerto Rican Loyalty) (1824), by Pedro Tomás de Córdova, and *Españoles sobre todo* (Spanish Above All) (1887), by Casiano Balbás, exemplify the feeling of a large part of the populace, certainly that of the ruling political and merchant class.

At the same time, the comedy of manners and customs continued throughout the century. Many of these had a moralistic tone, and some involved music, like the *zarzuela*. *Los deudos rivales* (The Rival Relatives) (1847), by Carmen Hernández de Araújo (1832–1877), was written even before *Roberto d'Evreux* but was published in 1863 or 1866 and debuted in 1879, a period more attuned to its message. Others that represent this tendency after the middle of the century are *Elección por gratitud* (Choosing Gratitude), by Felipe Janer y Soler, and the moralistic comedy *La voz de la conciencia* (Conscience's Voice) (1889), by Joaquín Masferrer.

Comedies portrayed regional and *jíbaro* themes, including several ennobling treatments of life among the outlying or more humble of Puerto Rico's inhabitants. Ramón Méndez Quiñones (1847–1889), of Aguadilla, exemplifies this aspect, with *Un jíbaro* (A Peasant) (debut 1878). The forthright and honest character of the peasant is contrasted with the duplicitous city dweller. Other *jíbaro* customs and regional events are treated as thematic material in Méndez's works. Rafael Escalona wrote works that had as principal characters both *jíbaros* and the even poorer black Puerto Rican, in comedies that favored the *bufo* humor that would be much more developed in Cuba.

As was mentioned earlier, the beginnings of incorporation of an indigenist theme are found in the opera *Guarionex*, written by Tapia in 1854, but the theme did not flourish as it did in some other Latin American environments. Most musical offerings were either imports of the Spanish *zarzuela* or imitations of these. The lighter elements of the *zarzuela* seemed to prevail over more serious treatments of politics, whether because of the element of censorship (real or implied) or because of the temperament of the local populations. The *Revista de Puerto Rico* (Review of Puerto Rico) (1880), by Fernando de Mormaechea and Félix Navarro y Almansa, dedicated to the governor, Eulogio Despujol, refers to the dismal state of the society by having the characters named for contemporary periodicals, a thinly disguised satire. Other musical reviews continued to the end of the century, with light or lightly satirical themes. Of some note is a work of 1899, *La entrega del mando o Fin de siglo* (The Change of Command or the End of the Century), by Eduardo Meireles, a Cuban actor resident in Puerto Rico. Although it obviously was concerned with a matter of considerable importance, the North American offensive and subsequent domination, presentation was suspended immediately and indefinitely.

EARLY TWENTIETH CENTURY (1900–1938): CHANGE AND UNCERTAINTY

The nineteenth-century concern with who would govern Puerto Rico was replaced with the major theme of the twentieth century, Puerto Rico's search for itself. A study of Puerto Rican theater in the twentieth century must begin with the assumption of artistic uncertainty based on the political upheaval caused by the outcome of the Spanish American War. The political changes at the turn of the century posed many questions. Hoped-for liberal changes were thwarted by the Foraker (1900) and Jones Acts (1917), which gave Congress the prerogative to annul Puerto Rican legislation and gave Congress control of customs, immigration, defense, and mail. Additionally, neither act addressed fundamental questions of democratic progress and individual human rights. In many respects the new political situation was seen as regressive when compared to the Spanish "Letter of Autonomy," of 1897, which had given Puerto Rico limited rights under the monarchy.

With the change in government from Spanish domination to that of the United States, together with those of language and cultural influence, there were to be changes in the theater. Throughout the twentieth century there has been uncertainty among the Puerto Ricans as to whether they should seek complete independence or U.S. statehood or continue the status quo, that of Commonwealth. The curious political situation is mirrored in the cultural uncertainties of groups searching for "national" feeling while a political satellite of a government whose language, culture, and values are different from those of the majority of the residents of the colony. At the same time, the lack of connection of the Commonwealth with mainland politics, literature, and educational currents perpetuated difficulties in dissemination and understanding of works in both directions.

The influence of foreign companies on the evolving Puerto Rican theater should be again mentioned, now in the context of the rapidly evolving environment of the twentieth century. The earliest companies to present works in Puerto Rico were, naturally enough, from Europe. Difficult though travel was in the eighteenth and nineteenth centuries, the island was a natural point to visit en route to the Spanish colonies, and companies were appreciated both for the works they presented and for the stimulus to local cultural growth they provided. Many of the companies took on local actors for roles and thus provided additional work in the theatrical arena.

In the twentieth century we may note several tours among the many that took place, continuing to provide the entertainment and motivation referred to above. A Cuban company presented Sardou's *Los reyes del tocino* (The Kings of Bacon), which provoked a political scandal on the second night it was performed, October 29, 1900. Beginning in December 1910, the Compañía Dramática Española presented several plays in San Juan, among them *Cyrano de Bergerac*; *El ladrón* (The Thief), by Henry Bernstein; and *El genio alegre* (The Happy Genius), by the Alvarez Quintero brothers of Spain. The company of the noted Mexican actress Virginia Fábregas opened a tour on March 20, 1912, and had to stay on the island until the end of the year due to an outbreak of bubonic plague. They thus toured the island, with productions in Mayagüez, Arecibo, Aguadilla, Huacao, and other towns. The company of the Italian actor Achille Zorda visited Puerto Rico in the summer of 1916. The company of the Spanish actress Margarita Xirgú undertook an extensive season in winter of 1924 in San Juan, with works from various countries, and continued to tour the island, finishing in July with works presented in Ponce. These visitations continued regularly throughout the first half of the century, up to the hard times of World War II.

La Compañía de Comedias Americanas de Harlem Clark (Harlem Clark's Company of American Plays) was the first company to present works in English in Puerto Rico, in 1920. *The Fortune Hunter, The Thirteenth Chair*, and *Tess of the Storm Country* are among the works presented. From this time forward, however, the course of Puerto Rican theater is inevitably linked to the U.S. mainland, and in several ways. Works are presented in Puerto Rico by mainland companies, in Spanish and in English. Because of the U.S. government policy and influence, works in English are taught and presented in Puerto Rico by the university and other groups. Puerto Rican actors are influenced by study and work on the mainland. Actors such as José Ferrer go to Hollywood rather than Madrid or Mexico to try their luck; others go to Broadway, study at Princeton and other institutions, and return to Puerto Rico for the rest of their careers.

In broad terms, we can look at theatrical development in Puerto Rico in the twentieth century in three stages. The first, from 1900 to 1938 or 1939, is that of the uncertainty of political direction and changes in artistic sensibility brought about by movements such as modernism. The plays presented seemed to portend anxiety concerning possible domination of mainland U.S. influences. And while there were many works presented in the theaters of San Juan and the provincial houses, fewer than one might expect were Puerto Rican. Further, there seemed to be a stagnation of ideas. The most that can be said of the period is that works that affirmed the two major trends at the turn of the century—lyric modernism and psychological realism or even naturalism—continued to be refined in plays that used local topics and settings. Cultural influences at the end of the nineteenth century included symbolism, naturalism, modernism, and several other "isms" of the twentieth century, including futurism, surrealism, and expressionism.

The importance of the works of the early twentieth century lies in that the drama moves away from the ideological and stylistic base of Spanish drama and that the subject becomes more social man than moral man. The heroic man of the previous century becomes the man in his quotidian situations; at the same time, the individual as unique gives way to the individual as exemplary of the collectivity. The palace gives way to the *finca* (ranch), the house, even the cottage. Even more indicative of works of this period is that they begin to use as material the conflicts of orientation as Puerto Rico assesses its political status, its social systems, its economic aims and its culture and sentiments.

Several writers show links with the previous century's romanticism in the style of Echegaray. Rafael Matos Bernier (1881–1939) wrote *Deshonra y muerte o El rescate del honor* (Dishonor and Death, or Honor's Redemption) (1903), located in England in the reign of Charles V, with Cromwell as a key motivator. The influence of Ibsen is manifest in the rebellious daughter of *El expósito* (The Foundling) (1919) by J. Espada Rodríguez. Emilio Ramírez Moll's prose drama *La vida es amor* (Life Is Love) (1929) exalts the sentiments of the protagonists Margarita and Rafael. But even here, the author begins to move toward twentieth-century criticism of customs, education, and the idea of suicide as a possible solution to difficult problems.

Political concerns are primary for many authors, some of whose works are more notable as testimony of this period of remarkable change for Puerto Rico than as literary exemplars. Eugenio Astol's *Tres banderas* (Three Flags) (1912) expresses nostalgia for the time before

U.S. domination. The three flags, those of the United States, Spain, and Puerto Rico, will be the costume of Manuela in a carnival dance wherein each young wife should represent a republic. Debuted by the company of Virginia Fábregas in 1912, it was a success due more to the emotions evoked than to innate drama of action or characters. Perhaps the first work to include Uncle Sam as a character is *Don Pepe* (Sir Pepe) (1913), by Jesús M. Amadeo, which attempts to show changes in Puerto Rico during the first twelve years of the century. Naturalistic explanations, including colonialism and repression of democracy, mar the author's lighthearted intents. Juan B. Huyke, an outspoken advocate and statesman for the good of North American government, wrote several short works with educational or political intent, including *Dolor* (Pain) (1925), *El batey* (The Porch) (1926), and *Día de reyes* (Day of Kings) (1929). One of the more interesting works of this period, by Gonzalo O'Neill, is *Moncho Reyes* (1923), a criticism of the governorship of Montgomery Reilly, popularly referred to as in the title. A *drame à clef*, the play refers to many prominent figures as it shows political corruption throughout society. Puerto Rico is represented as Borinquén, giving the work an allegorical quality. Matías González García takes on North American bourgois consumerism in the guise of a medieval legend in *Por mi tierra y por mi dama* (For My Land and My Lady) (1931), which draws on medieval legends of chivalry and idealism. And J. M. Agüero, though clearly a minor playwright, is of interest because he turned away from foreign elements and sought to incorporate local color to express political ideas in *El tío Jiribia o Un jíbaro tostao* (Uncle Jiribia, or A Real Peasant)(n.d.), showing a clear link with the works of Méndez Quiñones.

Workers' concerns were evident in Puerto Rican theater as elsewhere. While most works were more concerned with their message than the aesthetics of the drama, several of the works show interesting techniques or effects. *La emancipación del obrero* (The Worker's Emancipation) (1903), by Ramón Romero Rosa (pseud. R. del Romeral), gives a history of exploitation by the capitalist system of the worker. José Limón de Arce's play *Redención* (Redemption) (1906) shows a worker who raises his consciousness by reading a book that proposes the unification of the working class to avoid exploitation. The woman is also shown in this work as exploited by men of greater means, a theme taken up later by Méndez Ballester in *Tiempo muerto* (Down Time) (1940). Luisa Capetillo, a free-thinker, wrote protesting many of the customs of the time that subjugated women (marriages of convenience, for example) and used the theater as another way to express her ideas in works such as *En el campo, amor libre* (In the Country, Free Love) (1916).

Others who openly questioned the values of the rapidly changing society include Luis Muñoz Marín, the first elected governor of Puerto Rico, and Nemesio R. Canales, another statesman. Muñoz Marín's only play, *Despunta el alba* (Dawn Is Breaking) (1917), was written when he was only nineteen. His clear questioning of customs as detrimental to society comes through some obvious difficulties of the play as a literary work. Nemesio Canales's work *El héroe galopante* (The Galloping Hero) (1923) is a mature work that exposes some of society's flaws in a lighthearted but thoughtful work. It has continued to be presented throughout the century, a testament to the author's ability to abstract the values from the context of its original setting, the early part of the century. Other writers of the period include the Benaventian Antonio Coll Vidal and the Spanish-born José Pérez Losada, whose *La vida es ácida o Las industrias de la prohibición* (Life Is Bitter, or The Industries of Prohibition) (1925) bring current events related to Prohibition into the theater.

Returning to the definition and meaning of Puerto Rico in their works, authors such as J. P. Giordani wrote *Tragedia indígena* (Indigenous Tragedy) (1906), a romanticized version of the conquest. Likewise, Luis Lloréns Torres, the poet laureate, wrote *El grito de Lares* (The Cry of Lares) (1916) to evoke a moment of historic significance for consideration of the public. Though the protagonist, Manolo, dies, the play gives voice to the patriotic sentiments of the public: "El grito de Lares/ se va a repetir/ y todos sabremos/ vencer o morir" (The cry of Lares/ will be repeated/ and we will all learn/ to conquer or die). In spite of problems as a literary work, Morfi affirms that it was probably the most read and presented dramatic work of the early twentieth century. Its Modernist characteristics made it interesting to read, and the local color added considerably to its ideological subject matter.

Of brief mention is the work of the poet Vicente Palés Matos, whose "No-ist" work *Drama Noísta, dos actos y un epílogo* (No-ist Drama, Two Acts and an Epilogue) (1926) shows the iconoclast tendency of some sectors, including the futurists, dadaists, and surrealists. Disdaining a plot, the brief work is apparently meant to startle the audience into recognition of the banality of the theatrical experience. Gustavo Jiménez Sicardó exemplifies the writer who has moved fully into the twentieth century. Leaving behind the devices of the earlier movements, *La razón ciega* (Blind Reason) (1924) was presented in 1932 and shows the emerging link between earlier writers and the writers after 1938. Angelina Morfi makes special mention of this work, which captures the social inquietude found in other works of the early twentieth century such as *Waiting for Lefty* (Clifford Odets) and *Tobacco Road* (Erskine Caldwell) and leads logically to later Puerto Rican works such as Gonzalo Arocho del Toro's *El desmonte* (The Clearing) (1940). A number of women writers also emerged during the 1930s, several of whom continued to write well into the century. Among these are María López de Victoria de Reus, better known as Martha Lomar; Isabel Cuchí Coll, and Carmen Pilar (Piri) Fernández. Cuchí Coll is best known for her lighthearted work *La familia de Justo Malgenio* (Justo Malgenio's Family) (1963). Piri Fernández has held many key positions in the administration of theater in Puerto Rico. Her play *De tanto caminar* (From So Much Traveling) was produced during the 1960 festival.

MID-CENTURY (1938–1958): AWARENESS AND EVOLUTION

Several events in the late 1930s and early 1940s brought about significant change in Puerto Rican theater. Foremost among these are the first Certamen de Drama (Drama Competition) conducted by the Ateneo Puertorriqueño in 1938, which sought to promote works by Puerto Rican authors; and the formation of the University Theater (1939). The winners of the first competition were *Esta noche juega el jóker* (The Joker Plays Tonight), by Fernando Sierra Berdecía; *El clamor de los surcos* (The Cry of the Furrows), by Manuel Méndez Ballester; and *El desmonte* (The Clearing), by Gonzalo Arocho del Toro. All three works may be said to be manifestly Puerto Rican in their subject matter, and all three are excellent works of theater. The competition had thus assured a large measure of prestige in the face of what many felt was increasingly certain U.S. mainland cultural domination.

In 1939 Emilio S. Belaval's manifesto for a Puerto Rican theater, "Lo que podría ser un teatro puertorriqueño" (What a Puerto Rican Theater Might Be), was published in the *Revista del Ateneo Puertorriqueño*. Belaval asks for the creation of a national theater, the soul of its people and culture, which would capture the reality of Puerto Rican culture, rescue the land from its cultural usurpation, and serve as stimulus to the other arts, which find noble expression on the stage. This manifesto voiced the sense of urgency felt by many in the artistic community.

The creation of the Drama Department of the university in 1941 made possible a professional study and practice element for Puerto Rican theater. Early works staged in 1941 and 1942 were *La mujer más honesta del mundo* (The Most Honest Woman in the World), by Enrique Gustavino; Bernard Shaw's *John Doe*; and *El secreto* (The Secret), by the Spaniard Ramón J. Sender. In addition to giving theatrical background and training to those whose ambition it was to work with the theater, as presenters, as teachers, and as actors, it was the philosophy of the university administration to expose students to works universally acknowledged as important. Among the efforts of the Drama Department that played a role in Puerto Rican theater was the Teatro Rodante, a kind of self-contained stage wagon that toured the towns to reawaken the local interest in theater and bring works to places that could not sustain a local enterprise.

In addition to the Drama Department, other works were staged by the English Department, by the Department of Cultural Activities, and by local groups making use of the university facilities. The university thus played a significant role in fostering theater of the period. Additionally, in 1949 the Children's Theater of the Model School of the University became part of the Drama Department; and in 1954 a mime work was presented, thus incorporating another form of theater that had not been practiced before. The Department of Public Instruction also supported secondary drama clubs that performed both locally written and better-known works. The teachers also presented plays of good technical quality, and works were heard over the public radio station WIPR, with the Escuela del Aire (School of the Air).

Beyond the institutional efforts just mentioned, there was considerable movement of an entrepreneurial or commercial nature. The Areyto Theatrical Society was founded in December 1939 by Emilio S. Belaval with Leopoldo Santiago Lavandero for the purpose of supporting island theater and renovating the technical aspects of their presentation. Of short life, the number and quality of their presentations were exceptional, including *Mi señoría* (My Lordship) of Luis Rechani Agrait and *Tiempo muerto* (Down Time) of Méndez Ballester; others were left without presentation when the group folded. Several other companies were also founded at this time, for the most part in San Juan. The Farándula Bohemia (Bohemian Troupe) brought works from Cuba and also presented Puerto Rican works, notably the Diplo series (1940), which celebrated local character. Ponce inaugurated its theater La Perla de Ponce. The Companía Teatral del Sur (Theatrical Company of the South) became the Compañia Artística Ponceña (Ponce Artistic Company). In 1945 Manuel Méndez Ballester founded the Sociedad General de Actores, and Francisco Arriví founded the Tinglado Puertorriqueño, a company in which many of Puerto Rico's future leading actors had their first significant roles (Lucy Boscán, Madeline Willemsen, Alberto Zayas, for example).

As a group, or even generation, the authors of this period are remarkable for their excellence of thematic material, literary qualities, technical innovations, and quantity of productions, both written and produced. Manuel Méndez Ballester's work includes eleven plays. Especially in works such as *Tiempo muerto* (Down Time), his portrayal of the problems of real people and the development of the relationships of his characters in their environment mark his works as among the most sensitive in the recent development of the island as an industrial society. Likewise, Emilio S. Belaval, untiring in his efforts in essays and in engaging the energies of others to bring about productive change in the theatrical environment, also wrote many works. Unlike Méndez Ballester, Belaval's talent lay in the realm of the philosophical. *La hacienda de los cuatro vientos* (The House of the Four Winds) was presented at the First Festival of Puerto Rican Theater (1959); and *Circe o el amor* (Circe or Love) was produced for the Fifth Festival, in 1963. His works, produced throughout the decade of the 1960s and beginning much earlier in the century, provided a standard of philosophical excellence and influenced many other dramatists. He is favorably compared to other writers who used the stage to express ideas, such as Calderón de la Barca and Bernard Shaw. Luis Rechani Agrait is best known for *Mi señoría* (My Lordship), debuted in 1940 and presented again at the Instituto de Cultura Puertorriqueña in 1959 and 1968. Other works of his were presented at the Festivals of 1964—*Todos los ruiseñores cantan* (All the Larks Sing) and 1965—*¿Cómo se llama esta flor?* (What Flower Is This?). His realistic characters in situations of the period, touched with humor and understanding, were well received by the public and critics alike. Other authors who became known in the 1940s include Enrique Laguerre, certainly better known as a novelist; Cesáreo Rosa Nieves, who wrote a number of works, including the first known work to approach the theme of homosexuality—*La otra* (The Other) (1948); and Raúl Gándara, whose political commitment in his three dramas continues the line of Méndez Ballester into the years of the elections of the 1940s. To sum up this decade and its principal dramatists, it seemed clear that the efforts of the earlier proponents of the competitions were yielding fruit in quantity and quality.

René Marqués founded the group Teatro Nuestro (Our Theater) in 1950, which received critical acclaim for its use of avant-garde theatrical techniques. Going even farther in this direction, Marqués served as artistic director (1952–1956) in the Teatro Experimental del Ateneo, founded in 1952, with Emilio S. Belaval as dramatic director. Marqués's works *Los soles truncos* (The Truncated Lights) and *Un niño azul para esa sombra* (A Blue Child for That Shade) clearly show the strength of technical advances together with themes of considerable interest. Luis Rafael Sánchez formed the Teatro Experimental Acosta in 1955. Other groups of the late 1950s include Arte Teatral de Puerto Rico and La Compañía de Teatro La Máscara. On the level of the childlike and popular, a group called La Comedia de Muñecos presented the adventures of *Juan Bobo*, a folk character. At the same time, we can note that in the early 1950s Erasmo Vando founded in New York the Compañía Alejandro Tapia y Rivera, the Club Artístico de Puerto Rico, and the Spanish Musical Company. And at the military base in Aguadilla in 1951, the Ramey Theatre Guild was formed to put on theatrical works in English.

The dramatists whose works became best known during the 1950s are Francisco Arriví and René Marqués. Arriví wrote eleven plays, beginning during his period as secondary school teacher in Ponce with *Club de solteros* (Bachelors' Club) in 1940. The great variety of works, forms, and themes seem to obey only one guiding principle, that of the pursuit of issues, theatrical and social. Gender issues, race, and desire, among other themes, are pursued with art and often with great subtlety. At other times they are presented with abundant clarity, as in *Vejigantes* (Untranslatable: large masks) (1959). René Marqués (1919–1979) left an indelible imprint on Puerto Rican theater, marking changes from the beginning of his career. A man of many aspects, he studied theater in Spain and on the U.S. mainland, then began writing theater criticism in the 1940s. In 1951 he founded the Experimental Theater of the Ateneo, which presented works representative of world trends. He wrote scripts for films and worked in educationally allied efforts, and above all, Marqués wrote fourteen plays of varied thematic and dramatic content. Culture, class, and mime are the focus of *Juan Bobo y la dama de Occidente* (Juan Bobo and the Lady of the Occident) (1955); political drama in *La muerte no entrará en palacio* (Death Shall Not Enter the Palace) (1956); *Un niño azul para esa sombra* (A Blue Child for That Shadow) (1958) presents a tragic view of the upper-class Puerto Rican and political dissension combined with a very human view of the family and their complex relationships. *Los soles truncos* (The Truncated Suns) (1958) shows the tragedy of three sisters living in the past, unable to cope with the changes taking place in society around them. *Palm Sunday*, Marqués's bilingual tragedy based on the massacre of protesters in 1937 in Ponce, was presented in 1956. *La carreta* (The Oxcart) deserves special mention for the role it has played in Puerto Rican theater since its debut in San Juan in 1952. As *La carreta* preceded the festivals by a few years, it was not submitted for consideration. But it was instantly recognized by the public and critics alike for its quality. It debuted in and has played to enthusiastic audiences in New York. It has been presented in other international Spanish-speaking venues; it has been translated and produced in English and other languages. More significant for the purposes of this study, it has come to be perhaps the most popular work of local, school, and amateur theater in Puerto Rico. With its theme of survival through tragedy, strong roots, and faith in the future, it touched many sympathies in the varied audiences.

RECENT EVENTS AND MOVEMENTS (1958–1995)

From the late 1950s or early 1960s to the present, a number of regroupings of influence and effort have functioned to redirect the theater within the university and in the larger community. The Institute of Puertorrican Culture was formed, according to statute, in 1955, to create and support various forms of artistic expression in Puerto Rico. It has, in fact, supported and fomented the development and wide dissemination of theater, art, and dance. A Junta Asesora de Artes Teatrales (Evaluation Council for Theatrical Arts), from which comes the Proyecto para el Fomento de las Artes Teatrales (Project for the Development of Theater Arts), was formed in 1956. It addressed several aspects, among which the four principal were (1) to create theatrical facilities; (2) to create a national theater company; (3) to celebrate an annual theater festival; and (4) to support theater in the primary and secondary schools.

Certainly, among these are preeminent, from this point on, the annual Festivals, beginning in 1958. The plays written and produced for these Festivals have included Puerto Rico's most outstanding plays of the latter half of the century. The first Festival presented *Encrucijada* (Crossroads) (Manuel Méndez Ballester); *La hacienda de los cuatro vientos* (The House of the Four Winds) (Emilio S. Belaval); *Vejigantes* (Francisco Arriví); and *Los soles truncos* (The Truncated Suns) (René Marqués). These were not only works of exceptional quality; they also showed excellent thematic treatment of Puerto Rican themes: the immigrant family, the rural family, the interaction of class and race, and social isolation.

These works continue to be presented and appreciated as benchmarks of thematic awareness and technical excellence.

As the Festival grew, roughly doubling the number of submissions by the third year and becoming a principal event of the theater season, the professionalism of Puerto Rican theater production reached a level never before known. The Festivals began to showcase Puerto Rican dance, both traditional European style and Puerto Rican. Works as varied as *San Juan 1600*, based on Spanish music of the period, and *El brujo de Loíza* (The Wizard of Loíza), based on local legend and dance, were presented, among many others, beginning in 1961.

The Festival in itself was a key element in the restructuring of the arts in Puerto Rico. In addition, however, it seems to have acted as catalyst for other festivals, a real resurgence of theater in Puerto Rico. The San Juan Drama Festival began presenting works in English; the University Theater, the Teatro Experimental del Ateneo, and the Instituto de Cultura all worked to assist theatrical groups, such as El Tablado del Coquí, The Teatro del Pueblo in Ponce, the Little Theater, and a number of secondary school efforts. In 1961 the Programa de Teatro Escolar was initiated by Leopoldo Santiago Lavandero (Poldín). It was complemented by the Compañía Teatral de Maestros (Teachers' Theater Company) and by a traveling company of puppeteers that presented works of European theater throughout the island.

The proliferation of groups seemed the embodiment of Belaval's vision of a national theater, wherein the themes, the actors, the settings, the ideas, the aesthetics would all be Puerto Rican. Groups of high quality were formed, such as La Máscara, Teatro Yukayeque, Teatro el Cemí, Compañía Ponceña, and others. La Máscara presented varied works, including many from the international repertoire. El Cemí was a traveling theater that presented Puerto Rican works, including *El héroe galopante* (The Galloping Hero) (Nemesio Canales), *El grito de Lares* (The Cry of Lares) (Luis Lloréns Torres), and *Estampas puertorriqueñas* (Puerto Rican Scenes) (Díaz Alfardo). This group has continued to present works of high quality and has enjoyed the participation of many of Puerto Rico's leading actors. Teatro Yukayeque ("where the yuca is grown") was formed with the express idea of presenting Puerto Rican theater and has included poetry and other readings. Since incorporation in 1961, the group has gone on to include works of international recognition and has performed in a number of venues, including the Ateneo of the university. In short, both the number and quality of theatrical companies have certainly more than fulfilled the hopes of the original committees.

In 1966, in accordance with plans submitted by the Instituto de Cultura, the first Festival de Teatro Internacional took place. Several of the Puerto Rican groups, such as El Cemí, were invited to participate. Works as diverse as Arthur Miller's *The Crucible* and Alejandro Casona's *La casa de los siete balcones* (The House of Seven Balconies) were presented, together with the participation of the Ballets de San Juan. The same plans called for the extending of both the Puerto Rican and International festivals to the cities of Ponce, Maygüez, Arecibo, Humacao, Guadilla, Guayama, and Caguas. Each city, through an administrative council, would provide theatrical space and receive some subsidy for the productions. Further, in 1967 the office of Theater Development (Fomento Teatral) took steps to inaugurate a festival of experimental theater to present works of international vanguard theater. The first season included Samuel Beckett's *Endgame*. In 1981 a Centro de Bellas Artes was established in San Juan, which provides a home for the annual festivals and other activities. The processes that provided for it and its continuing governance have not been free from conflict. Chief among these are the division of activities and sponsorship and the costs of production and ticketing.

During the decades beginning with the late 1960s, a number of nontraditional theater movements developed in Puerto Rico. Some of the elements that stimulated this development were common to both the mainland United States and the island culture and, indeed, to other cultures during this period. The most obvious motivation was a feeling that theater should be more "popular," of the people, as opposed to elitist. Workshops such as Bread and Puppets, in New Hampshire, had their effect in the mainland United States and on island theater. These new movements reflect changing directions of political and social thought that were reflected in the cultural manifestations, including theater. Civil rights marches and conflicts, the Vietnam War and sociomilitary conflicts, the assassinations of President John F. Kennedy, the Rev. Martin Luther King, Jr., and Senator Robert Kennedy, and feminist, populist, and labor movements were only the outward manifestations of deeper concerns. Hippies, yippies, drugs, and antidraft popular protests were special concerns of the university communities. The Cuban revolution of 1959 was a nearby model to emulate or scorn. On a broad scale, the difference between generations, between classes and ways of thinking, was reflected in all cultural icons, from Beat poetry to *Hair*, which featured full frontal nudity, unthinkable until it was done. Additionally, universal theater had incorporated currents from sources as diverse as Jarry, Pirandello, Stanislavsky, and more recently, Brecht, Boal, and Piscator. In Puerto Rico the theater reflects significant changes during the last part of this century, which will be discussed below.

Among the first groups to indicate a different direction, still within the traditional theatrical setting, was Teatro Sesenta, under the direction of Dean Zayas and later with the Argentine Carlos Ferrari. This group evolved to become Teatro Nuestro. With a repertoire of works written by Ferrari and others, the group was among the first to try to make their audiences more sympathetically aware of social and psychological themes, including poverty and, most recently, AIDS. Other groups broke with the traditional theater and were openly opposed to theatrical conventions and artifices. Among the groups that formed during the late 1960s and 1970s were El Tajo del Alacrán, Moriviví, and Anamú. In addition to presenting themes of current interest, they tried to use techniques that would interest a working-class (or even unemployed or school-age) audience. Taking their plays to the local neighborhoods, they utilized techniques to involve the public, sometimes incorporating them in the productions. The sense of Puerto Rican identity is transmitted through language and through incorporation of local traditions and customs. The "New Dramaturgy," from 1968 on, thus represents a fluidity and openness that had not been present in the theater before. Some critics feel, however, that the movement is not of sufficient prominence to merit the designation. Many of the plays presented during this period have not been published, for a number of reasons. There are, however, reviews of many of these (see, for example, J. A. Collins's *Popular Theater in Puerto Rico: The Decade of the Seventies*). There were subsequent groups formed from this basis and strongly influenced by these, which nevertheless found the "guerrilla" aspects of these groups excessive and wanted to return to the university and public commercial and experimental theaters. With a new diversity of themes, including real problems such as racial prejudice and drug addiction, and of techniques, these groups have revitalized the theater of Puerto Rico.

Another facet to Puerto Rican theater is its presence in mainland United States, primarily New York. René Marqués's tragedy *La carreta* had its debut in New York in 1954. Isabel Cuchí Coll's lighthearted work *La familia de Justo Malgenio* (Justo Malgenio's Family) (1963) shows another side, that of promised success of the immigrant. As long as there have been Puerto Ricans in New York, there has been theater, formal and informal. An ongoing series of Hispanic Arts Festivals since the mid-1970s have given greater prominence to the pan-national Hispanic cultural presence. The Repertorio Español Theater has had a marked influence on the theatrical scene since its inception in 1969. Recently it has expanded its touring schedule and now spends several months each year bringing a wide variety of Hispanic theater, including Puerto Rican works, to high school, postsecondary, and community audiences. In a variety of community, artistic, and university settings, new presentations and standard works such as Nemesio Canales's *El héroe galopante* (The Galloping Hero), presented in New York in 1987 by the theater group of Hostos College, have made many works available. Today there are some twenty Hispanic theater companies in the mainland United States, of varying economic stability and responding to distinct interests.

New York has been both the putative and theatrical setting for recent works such as Miguel Piñeros's *Short Eyes* (1973) and for Jaime Carrero's *Pipo Subway no sabe reír* (Pipo Subway Doesn't Know How to Laugh) (1973). These works present the migrated Puerto Rican in conflictive situations. Both works were highly praised and reiterate a theme that has continued since Fernando Justo Berdecía's *Esta noche juega el jóker* (The Joker Plays Tonight) (1938), the first work on the theme of Puerto Rican migration to the mainland. Mainstream Puerto Rican theater continued to evolve, with outstanding writers such as René Marqués and Francisco Arriví on the first rung of a substantial ladder. Writers such as Luis Rafael Sánchez have attained a solid and mature reputation; and continued production of works by Myrna Casas and others of more recent reputation are many. Some themes are still concerned with the idea of what it means to be Puerto Rican. Other works consider what are now widely acknowledged to be universal social ills of the late twentieth century and human experiences and emotions related to these.

Luis Rafael Sánchez, born in 1936, was first known for his innovative narrative *La guaracha del Macho Camacho* (Macho Camacho's Beat). His concerns with both the social realities of Puerto Rican politics and daily life have evolved through two decades of presentations. As with many dramatists, the formal aspects of his works have also evolved, free from the traditional constraints of theater earlier in the century. Sánchez's theater includes *La pasión* según *Antígona Pérez* (The Passion According to Antígona Pérez) (1968), based on the classical theme but set in an unnamed contemporary dictatorship; *La hiel nuestra de cada día* (Our Daily Bitters) (1976), which portrays the embittered existence of the older impoverished generation; and *Quíntuples* (Quintuplets) (1985), a metatheatrical piece about relationships in a dysfunctional family, in which all six roles are played sequentially by two actors. Myrna Casas, director of many outstanding productions, professor in the Department of Drama of the University of Puerto Rico, artistic director of Producciones Cisne, also had several of her works come to prominence during this period. Among her works,

Cristal roto en el tiempo (A Glass Broken in Time) (1960), *La trampa* (The Trap) (1974), and *No todas lo tienen* (They Don't All Have It) (1975) are particularly outstanding. An obvious interest in metatheater and vanguard techniques and her personal quest for meaning and form give her works their special stamp. In the 1970s, a group of writers influenced by the popular movements of their youth began producing works. Among these, Lydia Milagros González, Walter Rodríguez, and Luis A. Rosario Quiles have made their presence felt in distinct ways. González's works have been written principally for the troup El tajo del Alacrán (The Scorpion's Slash) and thus incorporate themes and techniques for blue-collar audiences. Rodríguez's theater deals with themes ranging from the identity crisis of the contemporary Puerto Rican—in *La descomposición de César Sánchez* (The Decomposition of César Sánchez) (1973)—to AIDS—in *1996* (1987), a dystopian work in which society, divided internally, cannot combat the disease. Rosario Quiles's works also deal with the problems of society, some of which are seen in the protagonist of *El juicio de Victor Campolo* (The Judgment of Victor Campolo) (1973) and again in *El juego de la trampa* (The Game of the Trap) (1977).

In the decade of the 1980s there was again a period of frustration for Puerto Rican theater in the creation of the Agencia Cultural de la Administración para el Fomento de las Artes y la Cultura (AFAC) (Cultural Agency for the Development of the Arts and Culture). This impressive-sounding agency was unfortunate in its choice of works to present, primarily popular works of the mainland. Seen as a new incursion of a colonial mentality on the part of the administration, the works were not popular and, unfortunately, often were not presented well. This effort was dissolved after several years, and in the meantime, new efforts to encourage and protect Puerto Rican theater were implemented. Among these, the Sociedad Nacional de Autores Dramáticos (SONAD) (National Society of Dramatic Authors) and the Festival de Teatro Puertorriqueño Contemporáneo (Festival of Puerto Rican Contemporary Theater) both served to encourage and showcase new talent.

There are many dramatists of note and promise now working in Puerto Rico. While they have a variety of backgrounds and ideologies, all are serious about the theater as living art and about their role in maintaining its viability. The following are only indicative of the quantity and variety of talent and works. Premier Maldonado has written a theater of impressions in *Escambronado* (Done in at the Escambrón) (1982), based on class and race differences during the 1940s among the elite who frequented the night club of the title; and in *Zaguaneando en el país de los encancaranublados* (Fooling Around in the Land of Mist) (1986), which shows today's society as the result of the mixing of cultures. Roberto Ramos Perea, executive secretary of the Ateneo Puertorriqueño (Puerto Rican Atheneum) and president of SONAD, has become the most prolific and visible author of recent years. His works, such as *Módulo 104* (Module 104) (1982), *Ese punto de vista* (That Point of View) (1983), and *Malasangre* (Bad Blood) (1986), touch on themes of relevance to various sectors of society, from guerrilla politics to prostitution to the emigration of professionals to the mainland.

Writers of great promise include Aleyda Morales, Pedro Santaliz, Carlos Canales, Antonio García del Toro, and José Luis Ramos Escobar. Morales has written several shorter works, often dealing with the ambiguities of the male-female relationship. Santaliz, whose group now works in New York, writes prolifically but primarily for the occasion and not published. Canales's works reflect the corruption, drug addiction, and violence of society on the stage itself, sometimes reaching the limits expressed in the Absurd, as in Genet's Theater of Violence. García del Toro's work, such as *Hotel Melancolía* (Hotel Melancholy) (1989), is among the most literary today, justly meriting recognition in and beyond Puerto Rico. Ramos had seemed to move away from writing for the theater, but with *Mascarada* (Masquerade) (1986) and several others in recent years he has returned as a significant presence.

The major showcase of Puerto Rican theater, the long-lived Festival de Teatro Puertorriqueño (Festival of Puerto Rican Theater) sponsored by the Instituto de Cultura Puertorriqueña (Institute of Puerto Rican Culture) since 1958, has brought a wealth of plays, ballets, and music to the public. Other festivals have followed, some now in the tens and twenties of numbers of editions. Many regional or specialized festivals have taken root in recent years. Some, like the Festival Latino de Teatro (1985–), have found a special pleasure in sharing the stage with other Western Hemisphere writers. A recent survey and study of Hispanic theater in the United States (including Puerto Rico) found that of 101 theatrical companies 11 were directed by Puerto Ricans residing in the mainland United States and 17 by Puerto Ricans in San Juan within the 21 theatrical organizations surveyed there. Half the groups received some state and/or local governmental support, and one third are supported in part by NEA (National Endowment for the Arts) funds. Pan-national movements such as the Festival Latino, *¡AHA!*, the publication of the Association of Hispanic Arts, and increasingly vocal political and social movements among the various Hispanic cultures represented in the United States will be of increasing importance in the years to come. Though not without problems, those shared by all cultures in an increasingly difficult period of popular materialism and disdain for the formal arts, the theater in Puerto Rico and Puerto Rican theater in New York and other cosmopolitan areas seem strong in their foundation and assured of the possibility of future growth and development.

REPRESENTATIVE THEATERS AND PUERTO RICAN COMPANIES

The Tapia theater has been the site of regular production since its construction early in the nineteenth century. This and the Centro de Bellas Artes, which has three theaters, have been the principal theatrical locales. There are numerous theaters throughout the island, including in Santurce, Mayagüez, and Ponce.

Production companies include the University of Puerto Rico, through its Drama Department; Grupo Teatro del 60 (Theater of the Sixties); Teatro Cemí (Cemí Theater); Producciones Candilejo (Footlight Productions); Tablado Puertorriqueño (Puerto Rican Stage); Producciones Cisne (Swan Productions); Theatron de Puerto Rico (Puerto Rican Stage); Bohío Puertorriqueño (Puerto Rican Cabin); Producciones Ceiba (Ceiba Productions); and Nuestro Teatro (Our Theater).

Presenting organizations include the Ateneo Puertorriqueño (Puerto Rican Atheneum), the Centro de Bellas Artes (Center for Fine Arts), and the Instituto de Cultura Puertorriqueña (Institute for Puerto Rican Culture). The Ateneo, founded in 1876, has continued a strong program of lectures, recitals, exhibitions, awards, and theater theatrical presentations. The Centro de Bellas Artes is a state arts center with ample rehearsal areas and three theaters, the Francisco Paoli, the René Marqués, and the Carlos Marichal. The Instituto de Cultura, founded in 1955, is affected by political trends. It has the responsibility for distributing funding from the NEA and for distributing local government funding.

WORKSHOPS AND EXPERIMENTAL THEATER COMPANIES IN PUERTO RICO

The name of Rosa Luisa Márquez is intimately linked to a number of related aspects of contemporary Puerto Rican theater. She was one of the initiators of the popular theater group Anamú. Her book *Brincos y saltos* (Leaps and Jumps) (1992) is both a record of the voyage of discovery of ideas and techniques she developed and a manual for workshops using these. Márquez is also the originator of and continues to work with the Teatreros Ambulantes de Cayey (Traveling Players of Cayey). Her workshops and courses at the University of Puerto Rico, Río Piedras, have incorporated the techniques and made them now standard tools of production in Puerto Rico. Her affiliation with the ideas expressed by Augusto Boal and with those of the Bread and Puppet Theater of New Hampshire has guided much of her trajectory, but the techniques continue to evolve and spread. El Tajo del Alacrán (The Scorpion's Slash) is an experimental revolutionary theater company in which political relevance and innovative techniques are used to shock and bring awareness to audiences. Some productions have involved the public directly in the works. Grupo de Teatro Anamú (Anamú Theater Group) is an experimental revolutionary theater company that has presented works of social and political relevance in various venues and nontraditional settings throughout the island. Farándula Obrera (Workers' Troupe), a political activist theater company, was formed in the 1960s by Zora Moreno and participated in meetings, plazas, and other public forums. It had an anti-Vietnam stance and worked to demythify the political status quo and what it felt were manipulative or even exploitative U.S. mainstream economic messages. El nuevo teatro pobre de América (New Poor Theater of America), a company founded and directed by Pedro Santaliz, performs experimental populist works. He and the theater now work primarily in the poorer neighborhoods of New York. Most of the works written by Santaliz are more ideas than scripts, meant to evolve during the production and change according to the circumstances of the setting. Taller de Histriones (Mime Workshop), a pantomime company, was founded by Gilda Navarra in 1971. High-quality works in this very abstract art form have contributed to continued refinement of the public's appreciation of the theater. Navarra's book *Polimnia: Taller de Histriones 1971–1985* (1988) illustrates both the background of pantomime since Greek theater and recent productions of the company. The *mimodramas* the company has presented include *Los tres cornudos* (The Three Cuckolds) (1971), based on popular ideas dating to the Romans; *Eleuterio boricua* (Boricuan Eleutherius) (1975), based on a story of Tomás Blanco; and *Soleá* (1980), called "a dialog between jazz and flamenco music." Reviews of the works uniformly point out not just the uniqueness of the form but also the consistent high quality of the company's work.

PUERTO RICAN THEATER IN NEW YORK

Miriam Colón is an actress and director. After directing and appearing in *La carreta*, she was a founder of the short-lived Nuevo Círculo Dramático. She is associated with the Teatro Rodante Puertorriqueño (Puerto Rican Traveling Theatre), founded in 1967, which has continued to present classic and modern works, showcasing particularly the works of talented young Puerto Rican playwrights. Repertorio Español (Spanish Repertory) (1969) was founded and directed by René Busch. The company presents works of Spanish and Latin Americans in Spanish (occasionally it has audio translation available), including *zarzuelas*, classic dramas, and comedies. It has recently been more concerned with contemporary works and themes. In the past decade the company has begun to tour widely in the United States to community and school audiences. INTAR (International Arts Relations) (1966) is a concern directed by Max Ferrá. It presents works of Spanish and Latin Americans in English. Other agencies and companies are Pregones, a touring Puerto Rican Theater Collection; Association for Puerto Rican–Hispanic Culture, Inc.; and Rincón Taíno (Taíno Corner).

BIBLIOGRAPHY

Arriví, Francisco. *Areyto mayor*. San Juan: Instituto de Cultura Puertorriqueña, 1966.

Braschi, Wilfredo. *Apuntes sobre el teatro puertorriqueño*. San Juan: Editorial Coquí, 1970.

Casas, Myrna. *Theatrical Production in Puerto Rico from 1700–1824: The Role of the Government and of the Roman Catholic Church*. Ann Arbor: University Microfilms, 1977.

Canfield, Robert Alan. "Renaming the Rituals: Theatralization of the Caribbean in the 1980s." Ph.D. dissertation, University of Arizona, 1998.

Collins, J. A. *Contemporary Theater in Puerto Rico: The Decade of the Seventies*. Río Piedras: Editorial Universitaria, 1982.

Cypess, Sandra Messinger. "Women Dramatists of Puerto Rico." *Revista/Review interamericana* 9 (1979): 24–41.

Dávila López, Grace Yvett. "Diversidad y pluralidad en el teatro puertorriqueño contemporáneo: 1965–1985." Ph.D. dissertation, University of California, Irvine, 1989.

García del Toro, Antonio. *Mujer y patria en la dramaturgia puertorriqueña*. San Juan: Editorial Playor, Biblioteca de Autores de Puerto Rico, 1987.

González, Lydia Milagros. *Textos de teatro de El Tajo de Alacrán*. San Juan: Instituto de Cultura Puertorriqueña, 1980.

González, Nilda. *Bibliografía del teatro puertorriqueño: siglos XIX y XX*. Río Piedras: Editorial Universitaria, 1979.

Hill, Marnesba D., and Harold B. Schleifer. *Puerto Rican Authors: A Bibliographic Handbook*. Metuchen, NJ: Scarecrow Press, 1974.

Jones, Willis Knapp. *Behind Spanish American Footlights*. Austin: University of Texas Press, 1966.

Manrique Cabrera, Francisco. *Historia de la literatura puertorriqueña*. Rio Piedras: Editorial Cultural, 1969.

Márquez, Rosa Luisa. *Brincos y saltos: el juego como disciplina teatral: ensayos y manual de teatreros ambulantes*. Cayey, Puerto Rico: Ediciones Cuicaloca con el co-auspicio de Colegio Universitario de Cayey, 1992.

Morfi, Angelina. *Historia crítica de un siglo de teatro puertorriqueño*. San Juan: Instituto de Cultura Puertorriqueña, 1980.

Navarra, Gilda. *Polimnia: Taller de Histriones, 1971–1985*. Río Piedras: Taller de Histriones, 1988.

Pasarell, Emilio J. *Orígenes y desarrollo de la afición teatral en Puerto Rico.* 2 vols. Río Piedras, Puerto Rico: Editorial Universitaria, 1951–1967.

Perales, Rosalina. *Teatro hispanoamericano contemporáneo, 1967–1987.* Vol. 2. Mexico City: Grupo Editorial Gaceta, 1993.

Phillips, Jordan Blake. *Contemporary Puerto Rican Drama.* New York: Ediciones Plaza Mayor, 1972.

———. "Thirty Years of Puerto Rican Drama: 1938–1968". Ph.D. dissertation, University of Illinois, Urbana–Champaign, 1970.

Pilditch, Charles. "A Brief History of Theater in Puerto Rico." *Revista/Review Interamericana* 9 (1979): 5–8.

Pottlitzer, Joanne. *Hispanic Theater in the United States and Puerto Rico.* New York: Ford Foundation, 1988.

"Puerto Rico." *Escenarios de dos mundos: inventario teatral de Iberoamérica.* Vol. 4, Madrid: Centro de Documentación Teatral, 1988, 94–141. Articles by scholars.

———. *Teatro puertorriqueño en acción, dramaturgia y escenificación 1982–1989.* San Juan: Ateneo Puertorriqueño, 1990.

Rivera de Alvarez, Josefina. *Diccionario de literatura puertorriqueña.* Vol. 1. San Juan: Instituto de Cultura Puertorriqueña, 1970.

Sáez, Antonia. *El teatro en Puerto Rico.* 2nd ed. San Juan: Editorial Universitaria, Universidad de Puerto Rico, 1972.

Sosa Ramos, Lidia Esther. *Desarrollo del Teatro Nacional en Puerto Rico.* San Juan: Emasco Printers, 1992.

Vientós Gastón, Nilita. *Apuntes sobre teatro, 1956–1961.* San Juan: Instituto de Cultura Puertorriqueña, 1989.

Witte, Ann Barbara. "The Image of the United States in Puerto Rican Theater: A Point on Cultural Conflict." Master's Thesis, University of Texas, Austin, 1986.

◆

ARRIVÍ, Francisco (1915–1972). Arriví was a dramatist, theater director, poet, and essayist. After studies at the University of Puerto Rico he became a secondary teacher of language and literature in Ponce. He taught there for several years, where he wrote his first works, dating from 1940. He moved to San Juan, where he became part of the production staff for the Escuela del Aire (School of the Air) for the Department of Education. He also began directing professional works and became central to the development of modern theater in Puerto Rico. Early activities included the direction of Méndez Ballester's works *Hilarión* (1943) and *Nuestros días* (Our Days) (1944), translating works for the university theater and writing his first three-act play, *María Soledad* (1947). In 1945 he founded the Tinglado Puertorriqueño, a company in which many of Puerto Rico's future leading actors had their first significant roles: Lucy Boscán, Madeline Willemsen, and Alberto Zayas, among others. In 1949 Arriví was granted a Rockefeller scholarship, which he used to study theater techniques at Columbia University; at the same time he attended major theater productions in New York. After returning to San Juan he became programming director of WIPR, the educational radio station. Arriví was director of the theater program of the Institute of Puerto Rican Culture and, for many years, beginning in 1960, of the annual Puerto Rican theater festivals. To these notable achievements must be added Arriví's efforts, through essays and public speaking, on behalf of Puerto Rican theater. Numerous essays, especially those found in *Areyto mayor* (Grand Areyto) (1966) and *Conciencia puertorriqueña del teatro contemporáneo, 1937–1956* (Puerto Rican Awareness of Contemporary Theater, 1937–1956) (1967), contributed to increased awareness and new movement in the theater. Arriví's dozen plays explore a great many issues, both theatrical and social. Gender issues, race, and desire, among other themes, are pursued with art and often with great subtlety, as in *María Soledad*, which presents a lyric study of psychopathology in which a woman cannot reconcile her physical desires with her ideal of purity of soul. At other times Arriví presents themes with abundant clarity, as in *Vejigantes* (Masked Devils) or in *Sirena* (Siren). The former work opens with the feast of Santiago in the town of Loíza Aldea, an area in which the African component of Puerto Rico is very evident. From the music of the *bomba* to the *flamboyán*'s blood-red flowers, the sensual elements of the annual festival are emphasized in the play. In this atmosphere a masked Spaniard seduces a local woman, Toña. The Spaniard, however, marries a woman of society, while Toña lives in a room behind the kitchen. The daughter continues the history in the second act, repeating marriage to another Spaniard because she sees the mixture of races as advantageous for her future daughter. As the play develops, we view the growing awareness of empowerment in the third generation of women affected by the racial injustices and societal stereotypes. Clarita rejects her suitor from the South of the United States and, in a satisfying ending, invites her mother and grandmother to once again dance the *bomba*, recognizing the injustices of the past and the inevitable links between generations. In *Sirena* a young woman in love with her employer undergoes plastic surgery to become "white," but the North American in question then finds her boring, not exotic enough to whet his desire. The great range of themes alluded to is carried out in various theatrical styles that attest to Arriví's great expertise in the science of production as well as the art of composition. His plays are produced throughout the island; their longevity is a tribute to Arriví's ability to reach beyond the immediate circumstances and the universality of their themes.

WORKS: *El diablo se humaniza* (The Devil Becomes Human) (fantasy in one act) (n.p.) (1940). *Club de solteros* (Bachelors' Club) (1941) (San Juan,

Puerto Rico: Ed. Departamento de Instrucción Pública, 1968). *Alumbramiento* (Birth) (drama in three acts) (n.p.) (1945), debuted by the Tinglado Puertorriqueño at the University of Puerto Rico in 1945. *María Soledad* (drama in three acts) (originally titled *Cuatro sombras frente al cemí* [Four Shadows Facing the Image]), 2nd ed., pub. as *Una sombra menos* (One Less Shadow, 1947), in *Teatro puertorriqueño, Cuarto Festival* (San Juan, Puerto Rico, 1962, 12–149); also separately (San Juan, Puerto Rico: Ed. Tinglado Puertorriqueño, 1962); *Cuento de hadas* (Fairy Tale) (drama in one act, n.p.) (1949). *Caso del muerto en vida* (A Case of Death in Life) (1951) (n.p.), presented by the Tinglado Puertorriqueño in 1951 (Rev. in Collins, 64, May 29, 1977). *Bolero y Plena* (two one-act plays—*El murciélago* [The Bat] and *Medusas en la bahía* [Jellyfish in the Bay]) (1955) (San Juan, Puerto Rico: Tinglado Puertorriqueño, 1960), debuted by the Drama Department of the University of Puerto Rico, May 20, 1956. *Medusas*, pub. separately in *Asomante* 11 (April–June 1955): 88–105. *El murciélago*, pub. separately in *Asomante* 12 (January–March 1956): 71–85, partly reworked as *Muerte y transfiguración: Medusas en la bahía y transfiguración* (Death and Transfiguration: Jellyfish in the Bay and Transfiguration) (Rev. in Collins, 28, April 10, 1974). *Sirena* (Siren) (drama in two acts) (1957) (Barcelona, Spain: Ed. Rumbos, 1960), presented as part of the Fourteenth Festival de Teatro Puertorriqueño (Rev. in Collins, 4–5, October 24, 1971). *Vejigantes* (Masked Devils) (drama in three acts) (1957), presented at the First Festival de Teatro Puertorriqueño, and pub. in *Teatro Puertorriqueño* (San Juan, Puerto Rico: Instituto de Cultura Puertorriqueña, 1959), 279–401; English version in Errol Hill, *8 Caribbean Plays* (Trinidad: Extramural Studies Unit, University of the West Indies, 1978). *Isla y nada* (Island and Nothing) (poetry) (1958). *Frontera* (Frontier) (poetry) (1960). *La generación del treinta: El teatro* (The Generation of the Thirties: The Theater) (1960). *Ciclo de los ausentes* (Cycle of the Absent) (poetry) (1962). *Cóctel de Don Nadie* (Sir Nobody's Cocktail) (1964) presented at the Seventh Festival de Teatro and published in *Teatro Puertorriqueño, Séptimo Festival* (San Juan, Puerto Rico: Instituto de Cultura Puertorriqueña, 1965), 458–638 (Barcelona: Ed. Rumbos, 1966). *Entrada por las raíces* (Coming in by the Roots) (essays) (San Juan, Puerto Rico, 1964). *Escultor de la sombra* (Sculptor of the Shadow) (poetry) (San Juan, Puerto Rico, 1965). *Areyto mayor* (Grand Areyto) (essays) (San Juan, Puerto Rico: Instituto de Cultura Puertorriqueña, 1966). *Conciencia puertorriqueña del teatro contemporáneo, 1937–1956* (Puerto Rican Awareness of Contemporary Theater, 1937–1956) (essays) (San Juan, Puerto Rico, 1967). *Tres piezas de teatro puertorriqueño* (Three Pieces of Puerto Rican Theater) (for school productions): *Solteros, María Soledad*, and *Vejigantes (1968)*. *Máscara puertorriqueña* (Puertorican Mask) (Río Piedras, Puerto Rico: Editorial Cultural, 1971); includes *Bolero y Plena, Sirena*, and *Vejigantes*. *Vía Crucis* (Way of the Cross) (oratorio) (Río Piedras, Puerto Rico: Editorial Antillana, 1971). *Teatro plural* (Plural Theater) (n.d.).

BIBLIOGRAPHY: Wilfredo Braschi, *Apuntes para la historia del teatro contemporáneo* (Universidad de Puerto Rico, Río Piedras, 1952), 98–105. J. A. Collins, "*Caso del muerto en vida* Overblown, Pathetic and Fuzzy," in *Contemporary Theater in Puerto Rico: The Decade of the Seventies* (Río Piedras, Puerto Rico: Editorial Universitaria, 1982). Collins, "*Death and Transfiguration*: A Bizarre Caricature," in *Contemporary Theater in Puerto Rico: The Decade of the Seventies* (Río Piedras, Puerto Rico: Editorial Universitaria, 1982), 28. Collins, "*Sirena*: Soap without Bubbles," in *Contemporary Theater in Puerto Rico: The Decade of the Seventies* (Río Piedras, Puerto Rico: Editorial Universitaria, 1982), 4–5. Frank N. Dauster, *Ensayos sobre teatro hispanoamericano* (Mexico City; Secretaría de Educación Pública, 1975), 102–126. Marnesba D. Hill and Harold B. Schleifer, *Puerto Rican Authors: A Biobibliographic Handbook* (Metuchen, NJ: Scarecrow Press, 1974), 43–44. Willis Knapp Jones. *Breve historia del teatro latinoamericano* (Mexico City: Ediciones de Andrea, 1956), 152–153. Angelina Morfi, *Historia crítica de un siglo de teatro puertorriqueño* (San Juan, Puerto Rico: Instituto de Cultura Puertorriqueña, 1980), 421–454. Jordan Blake Phillips, *Contemporary Puerto Rican Drama* (New York: Plaza Mayor Ediciones, 1972). Josefina Rivera de Alvarez, *Diccionario de literatura puertorriqueña*, vol. 2 (San Juan, Puerto Rico: Instituto de Cultura Puertorriqueña, 1974), 128–133. Carlos Solórzano, *El Teatro latinoamericano del siglo XX* (Buenos Aires: Editorial Nueva Visión, 1961), 65–67.

BELAVAL, Emilio S. (1903–1972). He was a dramatist, essayist, short story writer, and lawyer. After graduating from secondary school in Santurce he studied law at the University of Puerto Rico, receiving his degree in 1927. Even as a youngster Belaval had evinced considerable interest in the theater, acting and producing several works, especially as a member of the first theatrical troup of the university. He held various positions in business as manager, public relations director, and chief of the Legal Department of the Puerto Rico Telephone Company, from 1928 to 1931. He then turned to private law practice for the next several years, during which time he also maintained a serious interest in writing and in the theater. Later Belaval served in various government positions, including that of associate justice of the Supreme Court of Puerto Rico, from 1952 until his retirement. At the same time, Belaval held many positions of public and artistic eminence: president of the Literature Section of the Puerto Rico Atheneum, 1939–1940; founder and first president of the Areyto Theater Group, 1940; president of the History Section of the Puerto Rico Atheneum, 1941–1942; member of the Institute of Puerto Rican Literature, 1941–1945; founding member of the Academia Puertorriqueña de la Lengua Española, 1955. Belaval's public stance and, in particular, his well-known essay of 1939, in fact a manifesto, "Lo que podría ser un teatro puertorriqueño" (What a Puerto Rican Theater Might Be), published in the *Revista del Ateneo Puertorriqueño*, are considered nationalistic. Belaval asks for the creation of a theater that would capture the reality of Puerto Rican culture, rescue the land from its cultural usurpation, and serve as stimulus to the other arts, which find noble expression on the stage. This manifesto voiced the sense of urgency felt by many in the artistic community. His own works, however, seem to partake of the universal (European) theatrical currents even when the settings are definitely Puerto Rican. These plays, produced throughout the decade of the 1960s and beginning much earlier in the century, influenced many other dramatists. Belaval's theater is philosophical, often compared to Calderón, Shaw, and Casona. *La hacienda de los cuatro vientos* (The House of the Four Winds) was presented at the First Festival of Puerto Rican Theater (1959); and *Circe o el amor* (Circe or Love) was produced for the Fifth Festival in 1963. *La hacienda de los cuatro vientos* is set in the period of frustration in the nineteenth century that produced the uprising at Lares. The play shows three generations of a family from Spain. Francisco, the son, is taken with a local creole, Tórtola Ruiz; but the idyllic romance is cursed by a sorceress, who says that his love will never survive the curse of the four winds—hatred, pride, greed, and lust—which are the inevitable result of his being a slaveholder. The second act seems to prove the curse true, as young Francisco, the only son of the couple, joins local liberals in rebellion against the repressive governor Pezuela. After his death, his father realizes he cannot blame the liberals but must join them as a reflection of his purer inner self. He then takes steps to free his slaves, who remain loyal to him; and the third act shows the more peaceful future, wherein Francisco acts as father in the wedding of two of his former slaves, one of which had been hated because he had taken part in his son's rebellion. In spite of an optimistically humanistic feeling throughout, the point is made that the steps toward a more egalitarian society are more difficult than it might seem and that hope can only be posited for the future. It is notable that in works such as *Tiempo muerto* (Down Time), Belaval's portrayal of the problems of real people and the development of the relationships of his characters in their environment mark his works as among the most sensitive in the recent development of the island as an industrial society.

WORKS: *Cuentos para colegiales* (Stories for Students) (short stories) (1922). *La romanticona* (The Very Romantic Lady) (comedy in two acts), presented in the Teatro Municipal in 1926 (n.p.). *La novela de una vida simple* (The Novel of a Simple Life) (comedy in three acts), debuted in 1935 (n.p.). *Cuentos para fomentar el turismo* (Stories to Develop Tourism) (short stories) (1936). *Cuando las flores de Pascuas son flores de azahar* (When the Easter Flowers Are Orange Blossoms) (1939), in *Areyto* (San Juan, Puerto Rico: B.A.P., 1948), 173–278. *La presa de los vencedores* (The Victor's Spoils) (comedy in one act) (1939), in *Areyto* (San Juan, Puerto Rico, 1948), 145–164. *Hay que decir la verdad* (The Truth Must Be Told) (1940), in *Boletín de la Academia de Artes y Ciencias* 8.2–3: (162–199). *Areyto* (essays) (1948). *La hacienda de los cuatro vientos* (The House of the Four Winds), in *Teatro puertorriqueño, Primer Festival* (San Juan, Puerto Rico, 1959), 173–278. *La vida* (Life) (1959), in *Teatro puertorriqueño, Sexto Festival* (San Juan, Puerto Rico, 1964), 229–357. *La literatura de transición* (Literature of Transition) (essays) (1960). *Cielo caído* (Heaven Fallen), in *Teatro puertorriqueño, Tercer Festival* (San Juan, Puerto Rico, 1961), 351–511. *El niño Sanromá* (articles) (1962). *Circe o el amor* (Circe or Love) (farce in three acts), in *Teatro puertorriqueño, Quinto Festival* (San Juan, Puerto Rico, 1963), 12–149. *Cuentos de la Plaza Fuerte* (Stories of the Stronghold) (short stories) (1963). *Agua de la buena serte, agua de la mala suerte* (Water of Good Luck, Water of Bad), in *Revista del Instituto de Cultura Puertorriqueña* 10 (July–September 1967): 26, 27–33. *Los cuentos de la universidad* (Stories of the University) (short stories) (1967). *El campo y el escritorio* (The Countryside and the Desk), in *Boletín de la Academia de Artes y Ciencias de Puerto Rico* 4.2 (1968): 445–453. *La muerte* (Death) (comedy in three acts), presented as part of the Fourteenth Festival of Puerto Rican Theater in 1971, pub. in B.A.P. (San Juan, Puerto Rico, 1953) (Rev. in Collins 6–7, October 30, 1971).

BIBLIOGRAPHY: J. A. Collins, "*La muerte* Urbane Bizarre Satire," in *Contemporary Theater in Puerto Rico: The Decade of the Seventies* (Río Piedras, Puerto Rico: Editorial Universitaria, 1982), 6–7. Piri Fernández de Lewis, *Temas del teatro puertorriqueño de hoy, El autor dramático* (San Juan, Puerto Rico: Instituto de Cultura Puertorriqueña, 1963), 155–161. Marnesba D. Hill and Harold B. Schleifer, *Puerto Rican Authors: A Biobibliographic Handbook* (Metuchen, NJ: Scarecrow Press, 1974), 52–54. René Marqués, "Apuntes para una interpretación. Un autor, un intríngulis y una obra," *Asomante* 9.4 (1953): 35–40. Angelina Morfi, *Historia crítica de un siglo de teatro puertorriqueño* (San Juan, Puerto Rico: Instituto de Cultura Puertorriqueña, 1980), 369–383. Josefina Rivera de Alvarez, *Diccionario de literatura puertorriqueña*, vol. 2 (San Juan, Puerto Rico: Instituto de Cultura Puertorriqueña, 1974), 181–187.

BENÍTEZ, María Bibiana (1783–1875). Although little is known specifically about Benítez's early life, it seems likely she spent her youth in Aguadilla and then in Ponce, where her father was attached to the Ministry of the Interior. Contrary to the scant attention normally paid to the education of young women, she seems to have read widely in the classics of the Spanish Golden Age. Toward the 1830s she lived, as a single woman, in Mayagüez, where she became known as the first Puerto Rican woman poet. Her poem "La ninfa de Puerto Rico" was published in 1832, the year of the Real Audiencia Territorial. By 1856 she was living with a niece, also a writer of poetry, and her four children in San Juan, where she continued to write poetry even after losing her sight. In 1862 she wrote the drama based on the 1625 Dutch storming of the capital city, *La Cruz del Morro* (The Cross of El Morro). In this work she combines a Romantic matter, historically based and sentimentally motivated, with a classical spirit of honor, heroism, and military pride in her country. Thus the work that initiates the historic theme in Puerto Rican history was given a suitable setting, soon to be overtaken in much more flamboyant Romantic works of the later nineteenth century. Aside from the place of this work in the history of Puerto Rican theater, Benítez's influence is seen in the works of her niece, Alejandrina Benítez de Arce de Gautier, and in the literary education of her great-nephew, José Gautier Benítez, the Romantic poet.

WORKS: "La ninfa de Puerto Rico" (*Gaceta de Puerto Rico*, 1832). *La Cruz del Morro* (The Cross of El Morro) (San Juan, Puerto Rico: Tip. D. L. Guasp, 1862), reedited and anthologized with other poetry of hers in Socorro Girón de Segura, *Vida y obra de María Bibiana Benítez y Alejandrina Benítez* (Puerto Rico, 1967), 25–66.

BIBLIOGRAPHY: Sandra Messinger Cypess, "Women Dramatists of Puerto Rico," *Revista/Review Interamericana* 9 (1979): 24–41. Socorro Girón de Segura, "Apuntes sobre la vida y obra de María Bibiana Benítez (1783–1875)," in *Vida y obra de María Bibiana Benítez y Alejandrina Benítez* (Puerto Rico, 1967), 9–66. Angelina Morfi, *Historia crítica de un siglo de teatro puertorriqueño* (San Juan, Puerto Rico: Instituto de Cultura Puertorriqueña, 1980), 155–160. Josefina Rivera de Alvarez, *Diccionario de literatura puertorriqueña*, vol. 2 (San Juan, Puerto Rico: Instituto de Cultura Puertorriqueña, 1974), 191–193.

BRAU, Salvador (Salvador Brau y Asencio) (1842–1912). A writer of many talents, Brau was a historian, sociologist, dramatist, poet, essayist, short story writer, journalist, and novelist. Due to the death of his father, at an early age he began working as clerk and assistant to a merchant. His enthusiasm led him to read a broad range of books, to teach himself French, and even to found a society of mutual education for young men of Cabo Rojo. In 1880 Brau moved to San Juan to assume the position of fiscal officer of the San Juan Treasury Department, which he held until 1889. He was elected to the Provincial Assembly from Mayagüez; was secretary of the Autonomist Party, 1889–1893; and held the position of Deputy Collector of Customs in San Juan, from 1895 to 1902. He was the official Historian of Puerto Rico from 1903 until his death in 1912. Brau's writing included positions as editor of *El Agente*, 1875–1883, and of *El Asimilista*, 1882–1894. He was an advocate of "home rule" rather than independence or statehood. He was particularly bitter about what he saw as Spain's abandonment of Puerto Rico after 1898. Numerous works of history, sociology, and politics include *El abolengo separatista* (The Separatist Inheritance) (1912); *La campesina* (The Peasant) (1886); *La caña de azúcar* (Sugar Cane) (1906); *Las clases jornaleras de Puerto Rico* (The Working Classes of Puerto Rico) (1882); and *Historia de Puerto Rico* (History of Puerto Rico) (1904). He wrote several works of poetry, some of which are collected in *Hojas caídas* (Fallen Leaves) (1909). Salvador Brau shows his place in the century, partaking of Romantic tendencies but influenced by Realism. Most of his works are of the decade of the 1870s, and all are undergirded by a liberal political philosophy, for which reason most of his works take historically allied exemplary themes as their subject. He wrote of the uprising of the *comuneros* of Spain in the sixteenth century in *Héroe y mártir* (Hero and Martyr) (1871); and he used the rebellion of the Sicilians against the French government in 1282 in *Los horrores del triunfo* (The Horrors of Triumph) (1877). Realistic traits can be seen in *De la superficie al fondo* (From the Surface to the Bottom) (1874) and in *La vuelta al hogar* (The Return Home) (1877). He presents the problems of families of the (upper) middle class in more realistic, even popular, speech. Thus Brau represents the changes in tone and manner of theater of the nineteenth century, wherein some didacticism was present as authors explored themes relevant to the lifestyles and choices of the spectators.

WORKS: *Héroe y mártir* (Hero and Martyr) (San Juan, Puerto Rico: Est. Tip. de González, 1871), and in Angelina Morfi, *Antología de teatro puertorriqueño* (San Juan, Puerto Rico: Ed. Juan Ponce de León, 1970), deb. Cía. Annexy, 1871. *De la superficie al fondo* (From the Surface to the Bottom) (San Juan, Puerto Rico: Tip. T. González Font, 1874), deb. Cabo Rojo, Cía Guerra, 1874. *Los horrores del triunfo* (The Horrors of Triumph) (San Juan, Puerto Rico: Tip. González Font, 1877), deb. San Juan, Cía Pildain, 1887. *La vuelta al hogar* (The Return Home) (Puerto Rico: Nueva Impr. del Boletín, 1877), deb. Mayagüez, Cía Astol-Prado, 1877, presented at the Fourth Festival de Teatro de Puerto Rico and pub. in *Teatro puertorriqueño, Cuarto Festival* (San Juan, Puerto Rico, 1962), 159–315; also pub. in *Colección de comedias españolas de los siglos XIX y XX* (García Rico, 1842, 1913). All his theatrical works are republished in Salvador Brau, *Obra teatral*, 2 vols. (San Juan, Puerto Rico, 1963, 1972).

BIBLIOGRAPHY: María Encarnación Caparrós, "Salvador Brau, vida y obra," (Unpublished thesis, Ed. Universitaria, Universidad de Puerto Rico, 1961). Arturo Córdova Landrón, *Salvador Brau, su vida, su obra, su época* (San Juan, Puerto Rico: Ed. Universitaria, 1949). Eugenio Fernández Méndez, *Salvador Brau y su tiempo: Drama y paradoja de una sociedad* (San Juan, Puerto Rico: Universidad de Puerto Rico, 1958). Nilda González, "El teatro de Salvador Brau," *Revista del Instituto de Cultura Puertorriqueña* 6.18 (January–March 1963): 16–24. Marnesba D. Hill and Harold B. Schleifer, *Puerto Rican Authors: A Biobibliographic Handbook* (Metuchen, NJ: Scarecrow Press, 1974), 60–61. Angelina Morfi, *Historia crítica de un siglo de teatro puertorriqueño* (San Juan, Puerto Rico: Instituto de Cultura Puertorriqueña, 1980), 71–83. Josefina Rivera de Alvarez, *Diccionario de literatura puertorriqueña*, vol. 2 (San Juan, Puerto Rico: Instituto de Cultura Puertorriqueña, 1974), 248–254.

CANALES, Nemesio R. (Nemesio R. Canales y Rivera) (1878–1923). A lawyer, poet, journalist, critic, and dramatist, Canales began studies in his native Jayuya and Utuado and continued in Mayagüez. He studied medicine in Zaragoza, Spain, but returned to Puerto Rico as the government was changing hands. He then studied law in Baltimore, Maryland, where he received his degree in 1903. Canales maintained an active practice in Ponce and then in San Juan, where he joined the law practice of Luis Lloréns Torres and others. The lawyers were also avid literary enthusiasts. Encouraged by early efforts, Canales purchased *El Día* in 1914. He also wrote for the *Revista de las Antillas*, founded by Lloréns Torres. Canales was elected to the Puerto Rican legislature, where, in 1909, he introduced a bill to extend voting rights to women. In 1922 he became assistant attorney general in the Puerto Rico Department of Justice, from which post he soon resigned for political reasons. He was also professor of law at the University of Puerto Rico, Río Piedras. He died en route to Washington, D.C. to testify at a Senate Committee on Puerto Rican–American relations. Canales wrote many essays about Puerto Rican values, political topics, and literary themes, often using pseudonyms, such as "Bradomín," "César Borgia," "Juan Bobo," "Darío," "Sor Isla," "Juan Lanas," and "Ene." Many of his articles were collected in *Paliques* (Chit-Chat) (1913). Nemesio Canales's only dramatic work, *El héroe galopante* (The Galloping Hero) (1923), is a mature work that exposes some of society's flaws in a lighthearted but thoughtful work. A somewhat complex plot pits a reluctant war hero against a lawsuit antagonist, with a young lady's affection hanging on the outcome. Only at the end, after many examples of confrontation and exposition, does the rebel prove his value: Discreet action allows him to outlast his rival. Like Shaw's *Arms and the Man*, with which it has been compared, the dialogue is the vehicle of the author, with the characters doing his bidding. It has continued to be presented throughout the century, a testament to the author's ability to abstract the values from the context of its original setting, the early part of the century.

WORKS: *Paliques* (Chit-Chat) (articles) (Ponce, Puerto Rico: n.p., 1913), and new ed. (Río Piedras, Puerto Rico: Ed. Phi Eta Mu, 1952), re-edited and augmented by biographical notes in *Nuevos paliques y otras páginas* (More Chit-Chat and Other Pages) (San Juan, Puerto Rico: n.p., 1965). *Mi voluntad se ha muerto* (My Will Has Died) (short novel) (Buenos Aires: n.p., 1921). *El héroe galopante* (The Galloping Hero) (1923), with prologue by José A. Buitrago and critical-biographical index by Antonio de Jesús (Caguas, Puerto Rico: Sociedad Literaria José Gautier Benítez, Escuela Superior, Publicaciones Caguax, vol. 1 1935), 86 also (Caguas, Puerto Rico: Sociedad Literaria José Gautier Benítez, 1935) and (San Juan, Puerto Rico: Ed. Coquí, 1967). *Obras completas, Volumen primero: Meditaciones acres*, with biographical notes by Servando de Montaña Peláez (San Juan, Puerto Rico: Instituto de Cultura Puertorriqueña, 1992).

BIBLIOGRAPHY: Marnesba D. Hill and Harold B. Schleifer, *Puerto Rican Authors: A Biobibliographic Handbook* (Metuchen, NJ: Scarecrow Press, 1974), 65–66. Servando Montaña, *Nemesio Canales, lenguaje y situación* (Río Piedras, Puerto Rico: Universidad de Puerto Rico, Editorial Universitaria, 1973). Encarnita Montes de Rodríguez, "Nemesio R. Canales, vida y obra" (unpub. thesis, University of Puerto Rico, 1957). Angelina Morfi, *Historia crítica de un siglo de teatro puertorriqueño* (San Juan, Puerto Rico: Instituto de Cultura Puertorriqueña, 1980), 278–281. Josefina Rivera de Alvarez, *Diccionario de literatura puertorriqueña* vol. 2 (San Juan, Puerto Rico: Instituto de Cultura Puertorriqueña, 1974), 282–286.

CARRERO, Jaime (1931–). Although he began schooling in Mayagüez, his family moved to New York while he was still a child, where he studied at the Art Instruction Institute of New York in 1949. Returning to Puerto Rico in 1953, he completed a degree in arts at the Instituto Politécnico in San Germán in 1957. Awarded a scholarship by the government of Puerto Rico, he again studied in New York, this time earning a Master of Arts at the Pratt Institute. He then joined the faculty of the Universidad Interamericana (previously the Politécnico) in San Germán. A multitalented person, Carrero pursued letters at the same time, often illustrating his own works with sketches and paintings. Growing up during and after World War II and in two societies, it is not surprising that his works reject classical tendencies and boldly illustrate the problems of both Puerto Rico and New York. His work shows his commitment to political and social issues of both societies, including the Vietnam War, the conflict and nostalgia of migrated Puerto Ricans, and social problems common to all modern societies. His most presented work,

Pipo Subway no sabe reír (Pipo Subway Doesn't Know How to Laugh) (1973), presents a Puerto Rican family living in New York and the problems of the young boy whose thwarted desire for a bicycle eventually leads him to cause the death of his mother, whose pregnancy was straining the family's finances and emotions. It is obvious, however, that the play presents a strong criticism of the dominant society, which foments incommunication and misunderstandings and which denigrates the societies and cultures of its migrated denizens. From *Flag Inside*, awarded the prestigious Ateneo prize in drama and presented as part of the Institute of Culture's Fifteenth Festival of Theater (1966), to his most recent works, he has shown an insistence on a rather crude, even violent portrayal of ideas in his characters. Greed, lust, and general corruption remain strong factors in his work. However, according to at least one reviewer (Figueroa), Carrero's works can lend themselves to brilliant production and a thought-provoking dramatic sense of Puerto Rican reality.

WORKS: *Noo Jork* (New York), (New York, 1972). *La caja de caudales FM* (The FM Safe) (New York, 1973), (Rev. in Collins, 90–91, June 22, 1979), (Rev. in Figueroa Chapel, June 1979, 217–218), English version in *Chicano and Puerto Rican Drama*, ed. Nicolás Kanello and Jorge Huerta (Houston, TX: Arte Publico Press, 1979). *Flag Inside* (Río Piedras, Puerto Rico: Ediciones Puerto Rico, 1973) (includes *Flag Inside* [Rev. Collins, 18–19, February 25, 1973], *Capitán F4C* [Captain F4C], *El caballo de Ward* [Ward's Horse], and *Pipo Subway no sabe reír* [Pipo Subway Doesn't Know How to Laugh] [Rev. in Collins, 214, September 6, 1973]). *Veinte mil salcedos* (Twenty Thousand Willow Groves) (New York, 1973). *Teatro: "Flag Inside." Capitán F4C. El caballo de Ward. Pipo Subway no sabe reír* (Barcelona, Spain: Jorge Casas, 1973). *Tres chapas tiene mi tía* (My Aunt Has Three Locks) (San Juan, 1974). *El lucky seven* (The Lucky Seven) (San Juan, 1976) (Rev. in Figueroa Chapel, 273–275 (November 1979). *Betances* (Betances) (New York, 1979, commissioned by the Puerto Rican Travelling Theater). *Frenesí* (Frenzy) (San Juan, 1983). *Miedo al sol* (Fear of the Sun) (San Juan, 1983) (Rev. in Quiles Ferrer, 112–115, April 27–May 3, 1984). *A cuchillo de palo* (With Wooden Knives) (San Juan, Puerto Rico: Instituto de Cultura Puertorriqueña, 1992).

BIBLIOGRAPHY: J. A. Collins, "*FM Safe* Theatrical Fire-Bomb," in *Contemporary Theater in Puerto Rico: The Decade of the Seventies* (Río Piedras, Puerto Rico: Editorial Universitaria, 1982), 90–91. Collins, "*Pipo Subway*'s Slapstick Pleases Kids," in *Contemporary Theater in Puerto Rico: The Decade of the Seventies* (Río Piedras, Puerto Rico: Editorial Universitaria, 1982), 214. Collins, "Theme, Acting of *Flag Inside* Disappointing," in *Contemporary Theater in Puerto Rico: The Decade of the Seventies* (Río Piedras, Puerto Rico: Editorial Universitaria, 1982), 18–19. Ramon Figueroa Chapel, "*La caja de caudales: FM*," in *Crítica de teatro (1977–1979)* (Río Piedras, Puerto Rico: Editorial Edil, 1982), 217–218. Figueroa Chapel, "*El lucky seven*," in *Crítica de teatro (1977–1979)* (Río Piedras, Puerto Rico: Editorial Edil, 1982), 273–275. Rosalina Perales, *Teatro hispanoamericano contemporáneo (1967–1987)*, vol. 2 (Mexico City: Grupo Editorial Gaceta, 1993), 264–265, 282, 290, 330, 333. Edgar Heriberto Quiles Ferrer, "*Miedo al Sol* de Jaime Carrero, fracaso de un buen intento," in *Teatro puertorriqueño en acción (dramaturgia y escenificación 1982–1989)* (San Juan, Puerto Rico: Ateneo Puertorriqueño, 1990), 112–115. Josefina Rivera de Alvarez, *Diccionario de literatura puertorriqueña*, vol. 2 (San Juan, Puerto Rico: Instituto de Cultura Puertorriqueña, 1974), 299–300. Ann Barbara Witte, "The Image of the United States in Puerto Rican Theater: A Portrait of Cultural Conflict." (Master's thesis, University of Texas, Austin, 1986), 150–161.

CASAS, Myrna (1934–). Myrna Casas had early schooling in Río Piedras, Boston, and Minneapolis. Secondary and university studies were in Santurce and at the University of Puerto Rico in Río Piedras, Vassar College, and the Universities of Harvard and Boston, from which Casas earned the M.F.A. in Dramatic Arts. After serving briefly in the Department of Public Instruction (1954–1955), Casas joined the Department of Drama of the University of Puerto Rico. In addition to her long tenure in this department, she has founded and been artistic director of Producciones Cisne and has acted as director, actress, and technical director of many productions. Casas has written several dramatic works and has also authored works about modern theater. Her first major work, *Cristal roto en el tiempo* (A Glass Broken in Time), debuted at the Third Festival de Teatro

Puertorriqueño in 1960. Set in an elegant older residence, it soon becomes apparent that the physical elements are only the setting for a lyrical treatment of time, disembodied voices, and a message tinged with existential anguish. *La trampa* (The Trap) (1974) and *No todas lo tienen* (They Don't All Have It) (1975) are particularly outstanding, as Casas's techniques and message become more focused. An obvious interest in metatheater, vanguard techniques, and her personal quest for meaning and form give works their special stamp.

WORKS: *Cristal roto en el tiempo* (A Glass Broken in Time) (1960), in *Teatro puertorriqueño, Tercer Festival* (San Juan, Puerto Rico, 1961), 259–349. *Teatro, Myrna Casas: Absurdos en soledad y Eugenia Victoria Herrera* (San Juan, Puerto Rico: Editorial Cordillera, 1964). "Theatrical Production in Puerto Rico from 1700–1824" (Ann Arbor, MI: University Microfilms, 1973) (photocopy of Ph.D. diss., New York University, 1973). *El impromptu de San Juan* (The Impromptu Event of San Juan) (San Juan, Puerto Rico: Ed. Universitaria, 1974). *La trampa* (The Trap) (Barcelona: Editorial de la Universidad de Puerto Rico, 1974) (Rev. in Collins 10, July 3, 1972). *No todas lo tienen* (They Don't All Have It) (San Juan, Puerto Rico, 1975). *Teatro de la Vanguardia* (Lexington, MA: D. C. Heath, 1975). *Cuarenta años después* (Forty Years Later) (San Juan, Puerto Rico, 1976). *Sueños de antaño* (Dreams of Long Ago) (San Juan, Puerto Rico, 1985) (Rev. Quiles Ferrer, 125–129, April 12–18, 1985). *El mensajero de plata* (The Messenger of Silver) (San Juan, 1987). *¡Quítate tú!* (Stop It, You!) (San Juan, Puerto Rico, 1987). *Tres obras de Myrna Casas* (Madrid, Spain: Playor, 1987), Biblioteca de Autores de Puerto Rico Collection (includes *Cristal roto en el tiempo, La trampa, Tres* (Three), *Eugenia Victoria Herrera*) (Rev. in Quiles Ferrer, 234–237, February 26–March 3, 1988) (San Juan, Puerto Rico, 1964). *El gran circo eucraniano* (The Great Ukranian Circus) (San Juan, Puerto Rico, 1988); directed by Casas as *El gran circo E.U.* (The Great U.S. Kranial Circus). *Este país no existe* (This Country Doesn't Exist) (n.p., 1993).

BIBLIOGRAPHY: J. A. Collins, "*La Trampa* Rated Superb," in *Contemporary Theater in Puerto Rico: The Decade of the Seventies* (Río Piedras, Puerto Rico: Editorial Universitaria, 1982), 10. Sandra M. Cypess, "Women Dramatists of Puerto Rico," *Revista/Review Interamericana* 9 (1979): 24–41; Casas, 34–38. Antonio, García del Toro, *Mujer y patria en la dramaturgia puertorriqueña* (San Juan, Puerto

Rico: Editorial Playor, Biblioteca de Autores de Puerto Rico, 1987) (on *Eugenia Victoria Herrera*, pp. 109–124; on scenes excised from previous versions of the play, pp. 241–245). Rosalina Perales, *Teatro hispanoamericano contemporáneo (1967–1987)*, vol. 2 (Mexico City: Grupo Editorial Gaceta, 1993), 260–261, 289, 291, 295. Edgar Heriberto, Quiles Ferrer, "Inician la XXVI temporada de teatro," in *Teatro Puertorriqueño en acción (dramaturgia y escenificación 1982–1989)* (San Juan, Puerto Rico: Ateneo Puertorriqueño, 1990), 125–129. Quiles Ferrer, "Tres obras de teatro de Myrna Casas," in *Teatro Puertorriqueño en acción (dramaturgia y escenificación 1982–1989)* (San Juan, Puerto Rico: Ateneo Puertorriqueño, 1990), 234–237. Josefina Rivera de Alvarez, *Diccionario de literatura puertorriqueña*, vol. 2 (San Juan, Puerto Rico: Instituto de Cultura Puertorriqueña, 1974), 304–306. Richard F. Shepard, "Stories of a Puerto Rican Circus at Festival Latino," *New York Times*, August 4, 1989, Sec. C, 15.

CORCHADO, Manuel (Manuel María Corchado y Juarbe) (1840–1884). Manuel Corchado began studies in Isabela but completed secondary and university studies in law in Barcelona, Spain. He practiced law in Barcelona and then in Madrid, where he remained active in literary and legal studies concerning his native Puerto Rico. He was a cofounder of *Las Antillas*, a review of scientific, literary, and political matters. Here he argued for the need of a university in Puerto Rico and wrote espousing other progressive reforms for the colony. He returned to Puerto Rico and set up a law practice but was elected in 1872 to be Mayagüez's representative to the Cortes (Parliament) in Spain. Here he argued for social, political, and economic reforms for Puerto Rico and other Spanish possessions in the West Indies. In 1879 he returned to Puerto Rico, where he became outspoken in his support of civil rights and liberties. In 1884 he lost his seat in the Cortes due to political intrigue against him, apparently promulgated by the conservative governor. Returning to Spain to defend his seat, he died there. As was often the case in the nineteenth century, Corchado considered literature—poetry, essay, and theater—as logical accompaniment to his professional career. Still in his twenties, he contributed poetry to several journals. His first drama, *María Antonieta* (1880), shows his objective to have been civil rights rather than independence. The play, an analogy for the situation in Puerto Rico, shows a maternal concern for the country rather than defiance. *Desde la comedia al drama* (From Comedy to Drama), a comedy of jealousy and emotions set in days of Carlist politics, attempts to transcend the politics with forgiveness and deeper understanding. *El capitán Correa* (Captain Correa) glorified the patriotic spirit of the Areciben of the title. Critics generally agree that Corchado's essays will outlive his dramas, but they remain interesting works, anchored in Romantic political sentiments and influenced by the best of Echegaray's techniques based on themes of honor and misunderstandings among the characters. Corchado's works, which were widely dispersed, have been collected in two volumes of his complete works published in 1975.

WORKS: *Abraham Lincoln* (essay, with José Feliú) (Barcelona: Imp. de los hijos de Domenech, 1868). *Historias de Ultratumba* (Stories from Beyond the Grave) (short stories) (Madrid, 1872). *María Antonieta* (San Juan, Puerto Rico: Impr. y Librería de Acosta, 1880). *El capitán Correa* (Captain Correa) (1885). *Desde la comedia al drama* (From Comedy to Drama) (San Juan, Puerto Rico: n.p., 1887). *Obras completas* (Two Volumes) (San Juan, Puerto Rico: Instituto de Cultura Puertorriqueña, 1975).

BIBLIOGRAPHY: Lidio Cruz Monclova, "En el centenario de Manuel María Corchado y Juarbe," *Ateneo Puertorriqueño* 4.3 (1940): 178–182. Marnesba D. Hill and Harold B. Schleifer, *Puerto Rican Authors: A Biobibliographic Handbook* (Metuchen, NJ: Scarecrow Press, 1974), 75–76. Angelina Morfi, *Historia crítica de un siglo de teatro puertorriqueño* (San Juan, Puerto Rico: Instituto de Cultura Puertorriqueña, 1980), 189–199. Josefina Rivera de Alvarez, *Diccionario de literatura puertorriqueña*, vol. 2 (San Juan, Puerto Rico: Instituto de Cultura Puertorriqueña, 1974), 378–381.

CUCHÍ COLL, Isabel (1904–   ). Although born in Arecibo, Cuchí Coll attended school in New York and then in Madrid, Spain. She traveled widely in Europe and South America, and by the time she was thirty, she had published a book of interviews with literary and artistic figures in Spain and in Puerto Rico—*Oro nativo* (Native Gold). She worked for United Press International in New York for several years and became a cultural leader of the local Hispanic community. She served as an officer of the Institute of Puerto Rican Culture for thirteen years and president of the Society of Puerto Rican Authors. Under the editorship of her maternal grandfather, Dr. Cayetano Coll y Toste, she published several biographies and histories. She has written many radio novels, not published. Of her plays, Cuchí Coll is best known for the lighthearted work *La familia de Justo Malgenio* (The Family of Justo Malgenio) (1963). This three-act farce about a typical Puerto Rican migrant family in New York gives an optimistic view of the migrated family, even when confronted with discrimination and fraud. The dialogue flows, using colloquial language and typical dialect. Other full-length plays are *El seminarista* (The Seminarian) and *La novia del estudiante* (The Student's Sweetheart). The former work, set in Spain, develops various conflict areas—generational, Puerto Rico versus Spain, secular versus religious life, as related characters are involved in the protagonist's decision. The latter work, set in Puerto Rico, may be seen as didactic, as various solutions to engagement and wedding plans are developed. Presented at the Centro Universitario at the University of Puerto Rico on October 2 and 4, 1962, it was, as Emilio Pasarell held, "very celebrated." *El patriota* (The Patriot), a short play about the life of Román Baldorioty, *Cofresí*, a one-act sympathetic view of Roberto Cofresí, a Puerto Rican Robin Hood, and several student plays complete the author's dramatic efforts. While Cuchí Coll will probably be known primarily for her incisive interviews and resulting portraits of intellectual and artistic figures, her plays show an ease of dialogue and perceptive interest in human relations that merit continued consideration.

WORKS: *El Madrid literario* (Literary Madrid) (San Juan, Puerto Rico: n.p., 1934). *Oro nativo* (San Juan, Puerto Rico: n.p., 1936). *Dos poetisas de América: Clara Lair y Julia de Burgos* (Two Poets of America: Clara Lair and Julia de Burgos) (Ciudad Trujillo, Dominican Republic, 1938). *La novia del estudiante* (The Student's Sweetheart) (New York: Impr. Azteca, 1940, 1949), (Barcelona, Spain: n.p., 1965) (San Juan, Puerto Rico: n.p., 1972). *El patriota* (The Patriot); also contains *Cofresí* (San Juan). *El seminarista* (The Seminarian) (deb. Centro Universitario, Universidad de Puerto Rico, October 2, 1962) (San Juan, Puerto Rico: n.p., 1971). *La familia de Justo Malgenio* (The Family of Justo Malgenio) (Barcelona: Ediciones Rumbos, 1963). *Trece novelas cortas* (Thirteen Short Novels) (1965). Cayetano Coll y Toste, author, and Isabel Cuchí Coll, compiler, *Historia de la esclavitud en Puerto Rico (información y documentos)* (History of Slavery in Puerto Rico [Information and Documents]) (San Juan, Puerto Rico: Sociedad de Autores Puertorriqueños, 1972). *Un patriota y un pirata* (San Juan, Puerto Rico: n.p., 1973). *The Student's Sweetheart* (San Juan, Puerto Rico: n.p., 1973). *My Puertorrican Poppa* (San Juan, Puerto Rico: La Editorial Cultural Dominicana, 1974). *El mundo de la farándula* (The World of the Troupe) (Puerto Rico: n.p., 1980). Several of her theatrical works are collected in *Teatro escolar* (Student Theater) (San Juan, Puerto Rico: n.p., 1990); includes *La muñeca* (The Doll), *Sueño de navidad* (Christmas Dream), *Cofresí*, *El patriota* (The Patriot), *El seminarista* (The Seminarian), and *La novia del estudiante* (The Student's Sweetheart).

BIBLIOGRAPHY: Sandra Messinger Cypess, "Women Dramatists of Puerto Rico," *Revista/Review Interamericana* 9 (1979): 24–41. Marnesba D. Hill and Harold B. Schleifer, *Puerto Rican Authors: A Biobibliographic Handbook* (Metuchen, NJ: Scarecrow Press, 1974), 81–82. Emilio J. Pasarell, *Orígenes y desarrrollo de la afición teatral en Puerto Rico*, vol. 2 (Río Piedras, Puerto Rico: Editorial Universitaria, 1967), 269. Josefina Rivera de Alvarez, *Diccionario de literatura puertorriqueña*, vol. 2 (San Juan, Puerto Rico: Instituto de Cultura Puertorriqueña, 1974), 449–451.

GARCÍA DEL TORO, Antonio (1950–).

He earned his bachelor's, master's, and Ph.D. in Philosophy and Letters at the University of Puerto Rico. He also studied theatrical direction at the Academia Nazionales D'Arte Drammatica "Silvio D'Amico" in Rome. He is the author of several plays, director, critic, and member of the faculty at the Interamerican University of Puerto Rico. As critic, García del Toro is best known for his *Mujer y patria en la dramaturgia puertorriqueña* (Woman and Country in Puerto Rican Drama), in which, as the title suggests, he traces the role and especially recent successful roles for women in the theater. He is also the author of many articles on Puerto Rican theater. As a director, García del Toro has been able to act on his special interests in the renewal of Puerto Rican themes and works. In addition, his work with the Taller Estudiantil de Teatro (Student Theater Workshop) has enabled the group to present many works to university and community groups since its founding in 1992, especially those works composed of scenes from plays that give a special focus to the sense of unity and diversity of Puerto Rican theater. As author, García del Toro brings values and issues of relevance to the Puerto Rican community to the stage in the situations and characters of his plays. Two of his works, *La primera dama* (The First Lady) and *Ventana al sueño* (Window on a Dream), have been awarded the "Letras de Oro" (Letters of Gold) prize in 1991 and 1993. He was awarded the René Marqués prize of the Puerto Rico Atheneum in 1986 for *Hotel Melancolía* (Hotel Melancholy) and again in 1990 for *El cisne de cristal* (The Glass Swan). Another work, *Donde reinan las arpías* (Where the Harpies Reign), was awarded the University of Puerto Rico's Drama Prize for 1990.

WORKS: *24 siglos después* (24 Centuries Later) (San Juan, Puerto Rico: Ediciones Epidaurus, 1985), 2nd ed., rev. (San Juan, Puerto Rico: Editorial Edil, 1988), includes *Guerra menos guerra igual a sexo* (War Minus War Equals Sex). *Hotel Melancolía* (Hotel Melancholy) (René Marqués Prize, 1986) (Madrid, Spain: Editorial Playor, 1989) (Rev. in Quiles Ferrer, 286–288). *Un aniversario de larga duración o El "long-playing" de nuestra historia* (A Long-Term Anniversary or The LP of Our History) (Río Piedras, Puerto Rico: Editorial Plaza Mayor, 1991). *Donde reinan las arpías* (Where the Harpies Reign) (Río Piedras, Puerto Rico: Editorial Plaza Mayor, 1991). *Metamorfosis de una pena* (Metamorphosis of a Sorrow) (pub. in *Teatro 1 (1985–1988)* [San Juan, Puerto Rico: Ediciones Epidaurus, 1991]) (Rev. in Quiles Ferrer, 145–146). *Los que se van se diviertan con las flores del camino* (Those Who Leave Enjoy the Flowers Along the Way) (pub. in *Teatro 1 (1985–1988)* [San Juan, Puerto Rico: Ed-

iciones Epidaurus, 1991]) (finalist "Premio Letras de Oro 1994–1995). *Mujer y patria en la dramaturgia puertorriqueña* (Woman and Country in Puerto Rican Drama) (Madrid, Spain: Ed. Playor, 1987). Various works collected in *Teatro 1 (1985–1988)* (San Juan, Puerto Rico: Ediciones Epidaurus, 1991) include *Metamorfosis de una pena, Hotel Melancolía, Donde reinan las arpías, Un aniversario de larga duración o El "long-playing" de nuestra historia*, and *Los que se van se diviertan con las flores del camino. Crónica de un hombre marginado* (Chronicle of an Outcast) (pub. in *Teatro 2 (1988–1991)* [San Juan, Puerto Rico: Ed. Epidaurus, 1992]). *El cisne de cristal* (The Glass Swan) (pub. in *Teatro 2 (1988–1991)* [San Juan, Puerto Rico: Ed. Epidaurus, 1992] ("Premio René Marqués 1990–91) (Rev. by Martinez Solá in *Interamericana* [June–July 1992]; 24). *La primera dama* (The First Lady) (Coral Gables, FL: Iberian Studies Institute, 1992). *Teatro 2 (1988–1991)* (San Juan, Puerto Rico: Ed. Epidaurus, 1992) contains *El cisne de cristal, Crónica de un hombre marginado, Los perros del obispo* (The Bishop's Dogs), *La primera dama, Juegos en el espejo* (Games in the Mirror), *Ventana al sueño* (Window on a Dream), and *El brindis de las cacatúas* (The Cockatoos' Toast). *Ventana al sueño* (Window on a Dream) (Coral Gables, FL: Iberian Studies Institute, 1993). *Comunicación y expresión oral y escrita: La dramatización como recurso* (Oral and Written Communication: Dramatization as a Resource) (Barcelona, Spain: Grao, 1995). *Teatro Anterior (1971–1985)* includes *La ocasión* (The Occasion) (translation of the work by Dino Terra, 1973), *Los dos sordos y la gotosa* (The Two Deaf Men and the Lady with Dropsy), *Marianela, El zapatero remendón* (The Patchy Shoemaker), *Le petit café* (The Little Café), *Juego de reinas* (Queen's Play), *Kean; un don Juan al rojo vivo* (Kean; a Don Juan in Bright Red) (adaptation of *Kean* by Dumas, the elder). *La botijuela* (The Drinking Jug) (adaptation of the work of the same name by Ramón Emeterio Betances). *Marianela* (Marianela) (n.d.) (theatrical version of the Pérez Galdós novel of the same name) (Rev. in Figueroa Chapel, 101–103).

BIBLIOGRAPHY: Ramón Figueroa Chapel, "*Marianela*," in *Crítica de teatro (1977–1979)* (Río Piedras, Puerto Rico: Editorial Edil, 1982), 101–103. Jorge Martínez Solá, "Aplaude la crítica *El cisne de cristal*," *Interamericana* (June–July 1992); 24. Edgar Heriberto, Quiles Ferrer, "*Metamorfosis de una pena* de Antonio García del Toro," in *Teatro puertorriqueño en acción (dramaturgia y escenificación*

1982–1989) (San Juan, Puerto Rico: Ateneo Puertorriqueño, 1990), 145–146.

GONZÁLEZ, Lydia Milagros.

González was educated in Puerto Rico. As a student she participated in political movements while studying literature, philosophy, and history at the university. She is one of several writers and directors influenced by the popular movements of the late 1960s. González began working in the theater in groups that produced nontraditional works in theaters, often smaller coffee houses and similar spaces, including groups directed by Pedro Santaliz. She then formed her own group, El tajo del Alacrán (The Scorpion's Slash), which moved into the areas of blue-collar workers and popular neighborhood theater. This collective theater troupe incorporated a style that engaged the audience in their works, using signs, puppets, and spontaneous audience involvement, among other techniques. Although González left the theater during the 1980s, the fifty or so players have often reappeared in roles subsequently, and the pieces, collected in the work she authored, together with notes on the collective work of the group, leave tangible tracks that others have followed. A university group recently reenacted several of these works, paying tribute to their significant themes and innovative style.

WORKS: *Gloria la boletera* (Gloria the Lottery Ticket Seller) (n.p., 1971). *Libretos para El Tajo del Alacrán* (Librettos for the Scorpion's Slash) (San Juan, Puerto Rico: Editorial del Instituto de Cultura Puertorriqueña, 1980), includes: *La historia del hombre que dijo que NO* (The History of the Man Who Said NO), *El drama de la AMA* (The Drama of the AMA), *Lamento borincano* (Boricuan Lament), *La confrontación* (The Confrontation), *The Post Card*, *El entierro* (The Funeral), *La tumba del jíbaro* (The Peasant's Tomb), *El juicio* (The Judgment), *La venta del bacalao rebelde* (The Sale of the Rebel Codfish) (Rev. Quiles Ferrer, 282–285). *La otra cara de la historia: La historia de Puerto Rico desde su cara obrera* (The Other Face of History: The History of Puerto Rico from the Worker's Face) (Río Piedras, Puerto Rico: CEREP, 1984).

BIBLIOGRAPHY: Rosalina Perales, *Teatro hispanoamericano contemporáneo (1967–1987)*, vol. 2 (Mexico City: Grupo Editorial Gaceta, 1993), 266, 282, 290–291. Edgar Heriberto, Quiles Ferrer, "Los trabajos de aficionados universitarios," in *Teatro puertorriqueño en acción (dramaturgia y escenificación 1982–1989)* (San Juan, Puerto Rico: Ateneo Puertorriqueño, 1990), 282–285.

HERNÁNDEZ DE ARAÚJO, Carmen

(1832–1877). As a young lady, Carmen Hernández received the minimal education accorded her feminine status, but she read considerably on her own and was a protégée of Father Rufo Manuel Fernández. At the age of fifteen she wrote her first drama, *Los deudos rivales* (The Rival Relatives) (1847), a five-act play that became one of the earliest native-written works to be staged in the Puerto Rican theater, this in 1879, two years after the death of its author. Little is known of Hernández's later life. At her death she left two additional works unpublished: a novel of romantic sentiment and *El catecismo bíblico* (Biblical Catechism). *Los deudos rivales* (The Rival Relatives) is set in Greece but partakes of obvious Romantic tendencies of the nineteenth century, as the three principals commit suicide at the end. However, in its sense of honor in the resolution the influence of Calderón is seen, as well as a fine sense of language. *Hacer bien al enemigo, el mayor castigo* (To Do Good to Your Enemy, the Greatest Punishment), published in 1866, is credited with introducing the moral comedy of manners in Puerto Rico.

WORKS: *Flores, o virtudes y abrojos y pasiones* (Flowers, or Virtues and Thistles and Passions) (novel) (unpub.). *Amor ideal* (Ideal Love) (1846) (Puerto Rico: Imp. del Comercio, 1866); includes *Los deudos rivales* (The Rival Relatives) (1863); repub. as *Amor ideal y Los deudos rivales: Obras dramáticas* (New York: Las Americas Publishing Co., 1956). *Hacer bien al enemigo, el mayor castigo* (To Do Good to Your Enemy, the Greatest Punishment) (Puerto Rico: n.p., 1866).

BIBLIOGRAPHY: Sandra Messinger Cypess, "Women Dramatists of Puerto Rico," *Revista/Review Interamericana* 9 (1979): 24–41. Marnesba D. Hill and Harold B. Schleifer, *Puerto Rican Authors: A Biobibliographic Handbook* (Metuchen, NJ: Scarecrow Press, 1974), 120–121. Angelina Morfi, *Historia crítica de un siglo de teatro puertorriqueño* (San Juan, Puerto Rico: Instituto de Cultura Puertorriqueña, 1980), 160–170. Josefina Rivera de Alvarez, *Diccionario de literatura puertorriqueña*, vol. 2 (San Juan, Puerto Rico: Instituto de Cultura Puertorriqueña, 1974), 736–737.

LLORÉNS TORRES, Luis (1878–1944). Lloréns Torres is often considered the national poet of Puerto Rico. Born in Juana Díaz, his life was considerably affected by the change in sovereignty from Spain to the United States, a change that took place while Lloréns Torres was in Spain, where he had gone to complete studies in Law and in Philosophy and Letters. Returning to Puerto Rico, he opened a law office with Miguel Guerra Mondragón; they were later joined by Nemesio R. Canales and José de Jesús Esteves. For the rest of his career, he combined an aggressive desire for Puerto Rican self-determination with an indefatigable effort in writing, producing over 1,000 poems in some forty years. Although he renounced affiliation with any poetic school, his creation of the "Pancalismo" (all is beautiful) school of poetry shows a clear relationship to the modernists. In 1913 he founded the *Revista de las Antillas* and later participated in writing and editing for other journals. He also theorized the nonexistence of prose, since his *panedista* (*pan*—all; *edus*—verse) philosophy stipulated that all writing was by definition poetic. In 1908 he was elected to the Puerto Rico House of Representatives, where he served for two years. He wrote only one drama, but it was among the most popular of its period, *El grito de Lares* (The Cry of Lares) (1916). The play evokes and glorifies the uprising of the title in both verse and prose. Romantic in sentiment, the protagonist, Manolo, dies, and the battle was lost at that time; but the overall feeling is one of noble rebellion and love of country, both in the abstract and in the regional sense. Luis Lloréns Torres died in Santurce on June 16, 1944.

WORKS: *América: Estudios históricos y filológicos sobre Puerto Rico* (America: Historic and Philological Studies on Puerto Rico) (essays) (Barcelona-Madrid, Spain: V. Suárez, 1898). *América* (1898). *Al pie de la Alhambra* (At the Foot of the Alhambra) (poetry) (Granada, Spain: Sabatel, 1899). *El grito de Lares* (The Cry of Lares) (Agua-dilla, Puerto Rico: Ed. Cordillera, 1927) (San Juan, Puerto Rico: Editorial Cultural, 1967). *La canción de las Antillas y otros poemas* (The Song of the Antilles and Other Poems) (San Juan, Puerto Rico: n.p., 1929). *Alturas de América* (The Heights of America) (poetry) (San Juan, Puerto Rico: Talls. Baldrich & Co., 1940) (2nd ed., Río Piedras, Puerto Rico: n.p., 1954). Virtually all works are reedited and/or compiled in *Obras completas*, 3 vols. (San Juan, Puerto Rico: Instituto de Cultura Puertorriqueña, 1967, 1969).

BIBLIOGRAPHY: Marnesba D. Hill and Harold B. Schleifer, *Puerto Rican Authors: A Biobibliographic Handbook* (Metuchen, N.J.: Scarecrow Press, 1974), 135. Angelina Morfi, *Historia crítica de un siglo de teatro puertorriqueño* (San Juan, Puerto Rico: Instituto de Cultura Puertorriqueña, 1980), 303–310. Nilda Sofía, Ortiz de Lugo, "Vida y obra de Luis Lloréns Torres" (Ph.D. diss., Universidad de Puerto Rico, 1966). Josefina Rivera de Alvarez, *Diccionario de literatura puertorriqueña*, vol. 2 (San Juan, Puerto Rico: Instituto de Cultura Puertorriqueña, 1974), 867–875.

LÓPEZ DE VICTORIA DE REUS, María (pseud. Martha Lomar) (1893–n.d.). Born in Humacao, López de Victoria received her early education in Vieques, where her father was a Customs employee. She was a primary teacher in this city until marriage in 1912. Later, in San Juan, she began work at the newspaper *El Imparcial*, where she adopted the pen name "Martha Lomar." She wrote widely, having compositions published in *Puerto Rico Ilustrado*, *Alma Latina*, *Mujer*, and *El Mundo*. Lomar published several books of poetry and three plays. After residing in New York for a while, Lomar returned to Puerto Rico, where she played an active role in civic, journalistic, and cultural affairs. Areyto, one of the several organizations that came into existence in the late 1930s and early 1940s, presented Lomar's play *He vuelto a buscarla* (I've Come Back) (1940), in which a woman undergoes a process of self-awareness and then chooses an appropriate mate from among several men who have attended her—her servant. The psychological development of the characters and related plot show the author's involvement in currents of the period. In addition, her journalistic writing seems to have given her a good command of realistic dialogue. Another play, *La hormigüela* (The Little Ant), debuted in San Juan in 1942, is historic in setting, dealing with late nineteenth-century libertarian and abolitionist ideals. Her third play, *Ese hombre se ha suicidado* (That Man Committed Suicide), remains unpublished, as do her other works, thus presenting serious obstacles to critical evaluation and their continued presence in the Puerto Rican theatrical tradition.

WORKS: *Vejez sonora* (Resounding Old Age) (poetry) (San Juan, Puerto Rico: Editorial Cordillera, 1931). *He vuelto a buscarla* (I've Come Back) (deb. 1940, n.p.). *La hormigüela* (The Little Ant) (deb. 1942, n.p.). *La canción de la hora* (Song of the Hour) (poetry) (San Juan, Puerto Rico: Club de la Prensa, 1959). *Ese hombre se ha suicidado* (That Man Committed Suicide) (n.p.).

BIBLIOGRAPHY: Francisco Arriví, "La generación del treinta: El teatro," in *Literatura puertorriqueña, 21 Conferencias* (San Juan, Puerto Rico: Instituto de Cultura Puertorriqueña, 1960), 391. Sandra Messinger Cypess, "Women Dramatists of Puerto Rico," *Revista/Review Interamericana* 9 (1979): 24–41. Marnesba D. Hill and Harold B. Schleifer, *Puerto Rican Authors: A Biobibliographic Handbook* (Metuchen, NJ: Scarecrow Press, 1974), 137. Josefina Rivera de Alvarez, *Diccionario de literatura puertorriqueña*, vol. 2 (San Juan, Puerto Rico: Instituto de Cultura Puertorriqueña, 1974), 855–857.

MALDONADO, Premier (1933–   ). Involved with more commercial theater than many recent dramatists, Maldonado represents a particular blend of large-scale works with some interesting social or psychological twists, especially in terms of reevaluation of history. Reviews in general applaud the public's appreciation of the visual and musical qualities but find dramatic depth lacking. *Escambronado* (Done in at the Escambrón) (1982), based on class and race differences during the 1940s among the elite who frequented the night club of the title, calls for nostalgic settings and choreographed dance numbers of the period. In *Zaguaneando en el país de los encancaranublados* (Fooling Around in the Land of Mist) (1983), four beggars rewrite Puerto Rican history from points

of view that differ from that commonly accepted. *Fela* was a very successful musical based on the life of Doña Felisa Rincón Vda. de Gautier, mayor of San Juan from 1946 to 1969.

WORKS: *Todo no pasa en el pasillo* (Everything Doesn't Happen in the Hallway) (San Juan, 1982). *Escambronado* (Done In at the Escambrón) (San Juan: Cultural, 1982) (Rev. Quiles Ferrer, 3–6, August 13–19, 1982). *Zaguaneando en el país de los encancaranublados* (deb. September 22, 1983, Teatro Tapia, San Juan) (Fooling Around in the Land of the Mists) (San Juan: Cultural, 1986) (Rev. Quiles Ferrer, 21–24, July 15–20, 1983). *Fela* (Hialeah Gardens, FL: F.A.M.E., 1994) (sound recording, original cast) (Rev. Quiles Ferrer, 44–46, September 12–27, 1984). *Mami Vanderbilt y Papi Rockefeller* (Mommy Vanderbilt and Daddy Rockefeller) (San Juan, 1985).

BIBLIOGRAPHY: Rosalina Perales, *Teatro hispanoamericano contemporáneo, (1967–1987)*, vol. 2 (Mexico City: Grupo Editorial Gaceta, 1993), 280. Edgar Heriberto Quiles Ferrer, "El *Escambronado* de Premier Maldonado: Devastador lujo y fastuosidad asfixiante," in *Teatro puertorriqueño en acción (dramaturgia y escenificación 1982–1989)* (San Juan, Puerto Rico: Ateneo Puertorriqueño, 1990), 3–6. Quiles Ferrer, "*Zaguaneando en el país de los encancaranublados*, de Premier Maldonado," in *Teatro puertorriqueño en acción (dramaturgia y escenificación 1982–1989)* (San Juan, Puerto Rico: Ateneo Puertorriqueño, 1990), 21–24. Quiles Ferrer, "Remembranzas de *Fela*, de Premier Maldonado," in *Teatro puertorriqueño en acción (dramaturgia y escenificación 1982–1989)* (San Juan, Puerto Rico: Ateneo Puertorriqueño, 1990), 44–46.

MARQUÉS, René (1919–1979). Marqués began his education in Arecibo, continuing at the University of Agricultural and Mechanical Arts in Mayagüez, where he earned a degree in agronomy in 1942. He had already shown an interest in drama and while in college organized, in 1940, a chapter of the Sociedad Dramática Areyto. He began writing short stories, some of which were published in the journal *Alma Latina*, and began work as an agronomist in the Puerto Rico Department of Agriculture. Though married and head of a family, he changed careers, going to Madrid to read the classics of Spanish theater and study literature. Returning to Puerto Rico in 1947, he gradually became more involved with the world of letters, becoming editor of *El Diario de Puerto Rico* of San Juan. With Rockefeller Foundation assistance, Marqués studied drama and theater arts at Columbia University in New York, where he wrote *Palm Sunday* as a class requirement. He also studied at theaters in Cleveland, Ohio, before returning to Puerto Rico. In 1950 he became a writer for the Division of Community Education and then professor at the University of Puerto Rico, Río Piedras. René Marqués founded the group Teatro Nuestro (Our Theater) in 1950, which received critical acclaim for its use of avant-garde theatrical techniques. Going even further in this direction, Marqués served as artistic director (1952–1956) in the Teatro Experimental del Ateneo, founded in 1952, with Emilio S. Belaval as dramatic director. Marqués's works *Los soles truncos* (The Truncated Suns) and *Un niño azul para esa sombra* (A Blue Child for That Shade), both of 1958, clearly show the strength of technical advances together with themes of considerable interest. Together with an aggressive interest in furthering the state of technical and artistic theater in Puerto Rico, Marqués wrote scripts for films and worked in educationally allied efforts; he wrote considerable criticism and short stories; and above all, he wrote some fourteen plays of varied thematic and dramatic content. The first work, *Palm Sunday*, was based on the police suppression of protesters in 1937 in Ponce. Successive works deal with culture clash; class (*Juan Bobo y la dama de Occidente*) (Juan Bobo and the Lady of the Occident) (1955); and political drama—the clash of ideas of Pedro Albizu Campos and Luis Muñoz Marín—in *La muerte no entrará en palacio* (Death Shall Not Enter the Palace) (1956). *Un niño azul para esa sombra* (A Blue Child for That Shade) (1958) presents a tragic view of the upper-class Puerto Rican and political dissension combined with a very human view of the family and their complex relationships. *Los soles truncos* (The Truncated Suns) (1958) shows the tragedy of three sisters living in the past, unable to cope with the changes taking place in society around them. Above all, *La carreta* (The Oxcart) gives Marqués a place

in Puerto Rican and universal theater for its theme of survival through tragedy, strong roots, and faith in the future. Its three acts show a family deciding to leave the land for economic reasons, being sucked into the slums of San Juan and leaving them for New York, and after the tragedy of the son's death, returning to the land and their extended family, fortified by the tragedy and new wisdom. Debuted in New York, it soon played in San Juan and has been translated into English and Czech and played in many countries. The basis of Marqués's work has always been the potential of humanity, and never more so than in *El apartamiento* (The Apartment), about a futuristic, overmechanized, brainless world in which the main characters are ordered to do mindless tasks and forget the outside world. At the end, they decide to leave their cocoon and search for liberation or death. Four of his works were accorded performance in the prestigious theater festivals. Further, the Sixteenth Festival, in 1982, was dedicated to him as *Homenaje a René Marqués*. A full range of symposia was combined with over fifty performances of his works during the September to March season. His works have evoked critical acclaim and public enthusiasm, making him the classic writer of his period. His influence on the subsequent development of theater in Puerto Rico is not only inevitable but fortuitous.

WORKS: *Los condenados* (The Condemned) (1942), presented as part of the XVIth Festival de Teatro, 1982 (n.p.). *Peregrinación* (1944). *El hombre y sus sueños* (The Man and His Dreams), in *Asomante* 4.2 (1948): 58–72. *El sol y los McDonald* (1950), in *Asomante* 13.1: 43–82; and as special printing (San Juan, Puerto Rico: n.p., 1957). *La carreta* (The Oxcart) (1952) in *Asomante* no. 4: (1951), nos. 1 and 2 (1952); also (Río Piedras, Puerto Rico: Editorial Cultural, 1963); and new ed., *Teatro puertorriqueño, Cuarto Festival* (San Juan, Puerto Rico, 1962), 317–563 (Rev. in Collins, 80–81, May 6, 1979, and 198–199, October 26, 1971). *Otro día nuestro* (short stories) (San Juan, Puerto Rico: n.p., 1955). *Juan Bobo y la dama de Occidente* (Juan Bobo and the Lady of the Occident) (1955) (Mexico City: Los Presentes, 1956); (Río Piedras, Puerto Rico: Editorial Cultural, 1971). *Los inocentes y la huida a Egipto* (The Innocents and the Flight to

Egypt) (San Juan, Puerto Rico: n.p., 1956). *La muerte no entrará en palacio* (Death Shall Not Enter the Palace) (1956). *Palm Sunday* (in English) (deb. in Puerto Rico in 1956), (n.p.). *La mujer y sus derechos* (Woman and Her Rights) (*1957*). *Un niño azul para esa sombra* (A Blue Child for That Shade) (1958), in *Teatro puertorriqueño, Tercer Festival* (San Juan, Puerto Rico, 1961), 17–127 (Rev. Collins 8–9, November 8, 1971). *Los soles truncos* (The Truncated Suns) (1958), in *Teatro puertorriqueño* (First Festival) (San Juan, Puerto Rico, 1959), 403–460 (Rev. in Collins, 62–63, March 25, 1977); and with *Purificación en la calle del Cristo* (Purification on the Street of Christ) (short story) (Río Piedras, Puerto Rico: n.p., 1963); and as *The House of the Setting Sun*, trans. by Willis Knapp Jones in *Poet Lore* 59 (1966): 99–131; and fragments in *Spanish American Literature in Translation* (New York: Ungar, 1963), 460–464. *Teatro* (contains *Los soles truncos, Un niño azul para esa sombra*; and *La muerte no entrará en palacio*) (Mexico City: Ed. Arrecife, 1959), and as *Teatro I* (Río Piedras, Puerto Rico: Ed. Cultural, 1970). *La víspera del hombre* (The Eve of Man) (novel) (*1959*) (Río Piedras, Puerto Rico: Ed. Cultural, 1970). *Carnaval afuera, carnaval adentro* (Carnival Outside, Carnival Inside) (1960), deb. Ateneo Puertorriqueño, 1972; presented at the XVIth Festival de Teatro Puertorriqueño, 1982). *En una ciudad llamada San Juan* (In a City Named San Juan) (short stories) (Mexico City: n.p., 1960). *La casa sin reloj* (The House Without a Clock) (Mexico City: Univ. Veracruzana, 1962) (Rev. Collins, 40–41, July 23, 1974). *El apartamiento* (The Apartment) (*1964*), in *Teatro puertorriqueño, Séptimo Festival* (San Juan, Puerto Rico, 1965), 253–377; and in *Three Contemporary Latin-American Plays*, ed. Ruth Lamb (Waltham, MA: Xerox College Pub., 1971), 4–71. *Mariana o el alba* (Mariana or the Dawn) (San Juan, Puerto Rico: Villa Nevares, 1965); (Barcelona, Spain: Ediciones Rumbo, 1966), and in *Teatro puertorriqueño, Octavo Festival* (San Juan, Puerto Rico, 1966), 499–718. *Ensayos* (1953–1966) (Río Piedras, Puerto Rico; n.p., 1966). *Sacrificio en el Monte Moriah* (Sacrifice on Mount Moriah) (Río Piedras, Puerto Rico: Antillanas, 1969). *David y Jonatán, Tito y Berenice* (David and Jonathon, Tito and Bernice) (Río Piedras, Puerto Rico: Antillana, 1970). *Teatro II* (includes *El hombre y sus sueños, El sol y los Mac Donald*) (Río Piedras, Puerto Rico: Ed. Cultural, 1971). *Teatro III* (includes *El apartamiento, La casa sin reloj*), all vols. (Río Piedras, Puerto Rico: Ed. Cultural, 1971). *In a City Named San Juan*, in *Re-*

view (Center for InterAmerican Relations), (Spring 1976). *Cuatro cuentos de René Marqués* (Four Stories of René Marqués) (dramatized presentation of "Tres hombres junto al río" [Three Men By the River], "La chiringa azul (NO TRESPASSING!)" [The Blue Kite, (NO TRESPASSING!)], "Este mosaico viejo" [This Old Mosaic], "El bastón" [The Cane]) (n.p.), (Rev. Figueroa Chapel, 175–177, March 1979).

BIBLIOGRAPHY: Ateneo Puertorriqueño, *Homenaje a René Marqués: XVI Festival de Teatro 1982* (San Juan, Puerto Rico: Ateneo Puertorriqueño, 1982). J. A. Collins, "Fitting, Poignant *La carreta* Opens Teatro Riviera's First Season," in *Contemporary Theater in Puerto Rico: The Decade of the Seventies* (Río Piedras, Puerto Rico: Editorial Universitaria, 1982), 80–81. Collins, "*Los soles truncos*: A Glorious Return to Nuestra Tierra," in *Contemporary Theater in Puerto Rico: The Decade of the Seventies* (Río Piedras, Puerto Rico: Editorial Universitaria, 1982), 62–63. Collins, "Marqués' *Clock without Hands*," in *Contemporary Theater in Puerto Rico: The Decade of the Seventies* (Río Piedras, Puerto Rico: Editorial Universitaria, 1982), 40–41. Collins, "Marqués' *La carreta* a Contemporary Classic," in *Contemporary Theater in Puerto Rico: The Decade of the Seventies* (Río Piedras, Puerto Rico: Editorial Universitaria, 1982), 198–199. Collins, "Ritual Drama Probes Shadows of Puerto Rican Identity Woes," Rev. of *Un niño azul para esa sombra*, in *Contemporary Theater in Puerto Rico: The Decade of the Seventies* (Río Piedras, Puerto Rico: Editorial Universitaria, 1982), 8–9. Frank Dauster, *Ensayos sobre teatro hispanoamericano* (Mexico City: SepSetentas, 1975), 102–126. Dauster, "The Theater of René Marqués," *Symposium* (Spring 1964); 35–45. Ramón Figueroa Chapel, "*Cuatro cuentos* de René Marqués," in *Crítica de teatro (1977–1979)* (Río Piedras, Puerto Rico: Editorial Edil, 1982), 175–177. Antonio García del Toro; *Mujer y patria en la dramaturgia puertorriqueña* (San Juan, Puerto Rico: Editorial Playor, Biblioteca de Autores de Puerto Rico, 1987), 95–108. Marnesba D. Hill, and Harold B. Schleifer, *Puerto Rican Authors: A Biobibliographic Handbook* (Metuchen, NJ: Scarecrow Press, 1974), 145–146. Tamara Holzapfel, "The Theater of René Marqués: In Search of Identity and Form (Puerto Rico)," in *Dramatist in Revolt: The New Latin American Theater*, eds. George W. Woodyard and Leon F. Lyday (Austin: University of Texas Press, 1976), 146–166. Enrique Laguerre, "Teatro experimental en el ateneo," in *Pulso de Puerto Rico. 1952–1954* (San Juan, Puerto Rico:

n.p., 1956). Eleanor J. Martin, *René Marqués* (Boston, MA: Twayne, 1979). Angelina Morfi, *Historia crítica de un siglo de teatro puertorriqueño* (San Juan, Puerto Rico: Instituto de Cultura Puertorriqueña, 1980), 455–519. Jordan Blake Phillips, *Contemporary Puerto Rican Drama* (New York: Plaza Mayor Ediciones, 1972), 89–103. Charles Pilditch, *René Marqués: A Study of His Fiction* (New York: Plus Ultra, 1977). Josefina Rivera de Alvarez, *Diccionario de literatura puertorriqueña*, vol. 2 (San Juan, Puerto Rico: Instituto de Cultura Puertorriqueña, 1974), 906–919.

MÉNDEZ BALLESTER, Manuel (1909–). Though Ballester's earliest schooling was in Aguadilla, he completed secondary school in New York, where his family resided for a while. Returning to Puerto Rico, and limited in means, he was haphazardly headed toward a career in commercial interests. While employed as an office clerk, he became concerned about the growing problems of agriculture and labor and so joined the Popular Democratic Party and was elected to the Puerto Rico House of Representatives. Later he settled in San Juan, where he devoted himself to journalism, radio, television, and teaching. Sent to the mainland in 1937 to study radio production, he was actively involved in the work of WIPR, the public educational broadcasting station of Puerto Rico. His literary involvement thus began fairly late in life, but his first play, *El clamor de los surcos* (The Cry of the Furrows), about the need for agrarian reform, based on the failure of the *colectivos* (controlled by the city-based banking industry), won first prize in a competition of the Ateneo Puertorriqueño and was presented there on December 15, 1939. From this point on he wrote and presented works on a regular basis, with several of them having won presentation rights in the festivals of Puerto Rican theater. In 1945 Ballester founded the Sociedad General de Actores, and over the years he completed work at the university and participated in colloquia on drama. Ballester's work is much appreciated in Puerto Rico for his particular combination of real-life characters and a grasp of theatrical technique that, while not particularly modernistic, shows the works to good advantage. Especially in works such as *Tiempo muerto* (Down Time), his portrayal of the problems of real people and the development of the relationships of his characters in their environment mark his works as among the most sensitive in the recent development of the island as an industrial society. Some critics feel that his most recent works may have been more ambitious than his technical abilities can delineate effectively, but they also were well attended.

WORKS: *Isla cerrera* (historic novel) (San Juan, Puerto Rico, 1937). *El clamor de los surcos* (The Cry of the Furrows) (San Juan, Puerto Rico: Imp. Baldrich, 1940). *Tiempo muerto* (Down Time) (1940) (Rev. Collins, 26–27, April 4, 1974). *Hilarión* (San Juan, Puerto Rico: Imp. Venezuela, 1943). *Un fantasma decentito* (A Really Decent Ghost) (opera, with music of Arturo Samohano) (n.p., 1950), previously known as *El misterio del Castillo* (The Mystery of the Castle) (n.p., 1946). *Es de Vidrio la mujer* (Woman Is Made of Glass) (n.p., 1952). *El milagro* (The Miracle) (1957), in *Teatro puertorriqueño, Cuarto Festival* (San Juan, Puerto Rico, 1962), 649–787. *Encrucijada* (Crossroads) (1958), in *Teatro puertorriqueño* (First Festival) (San Juan, Puerto Rico, 1959), 78–172 (Rev. Collins, 34–35, June 12, 1974). *La feria o El mono con la lata en el rabo* (The Fair, or The Monkey with the Tin Can Tied to His Tail), in *Teatro puertorriqueño, Sexto Festival* (San Juan, Puerto Rico, 1964), 21–148. *Bienvenido, don Goyito* (Welcome, Goyito) (1967), in *Teatro puertorriqueño, Noveno Festival* (San Juan, Puerto Rico, 1966), 167–295. *Arriba las mujeres* (Up with Women) in *Teatro puertorriqueño, Undécimo Festival* (San Juan, Puerto Rico, 1969), 187–301. *El circo* (1979) (pres. at Twentieth Festival of Puerto Rican Theater) (Rev. in Collins, 82–83, May 10, 1979) (Rev. Figueroa Chapel, 199–200).

BIBLIOGRAPHY: J. A. Collins, *"Dead Times Brings Life to San Juan Theater Scene,"* in *Contemporary Theater in Puerto Rico: The Decade of the Seventies* (Río Piedras, Puerto Rico: Editorial Universitaria, 1982), 26–27. Collins, *"Encrucijada*: Exercise in Hysterics," in *Contemporary Theater in Puerto Rico: The Decade of the Seventies* (Río Piedras, Puerto Rico: Editorial Universitaria, 1982), 34. Collins, "Puerto Rico's Own Godot Hits Town with *El circo*," in *Contemporary Theater in Puerto Rico: The Decade of the Seventies* (Río Piedras, Puerto Rico: Editorial Universitaria, 1982), 82–83. Ramón Figueroa Chapel, *"El circo,"* in *Crítica de teatro (1977–1979)* (Río Piedras, Puerto Rico: Editorial

Edil, 1982), 199–200. Max Henríquez Ureña, "Méndez Ballester y su teatro de símbolos, in *La nueva democracia* 42.2: 34–41. Marnesba D. Hill and Harold B. Schleifer, *Puerto Rican Authors: A Biobibliographic Handbook* (Metuchen, NJ: Scarecrow Press, 1974), 155–156. Angelina Morfi, *Historia crítica de un siglo de teatro puertorriqueño* (San Juan, Puerto Rico: Instituto de Cultura Puertorriqueña, 1980), 349–362. Jordan Blake Phillips, *Contemporary Puerto Rican Drama* (New York: Plaza Mayor Ediciones, 1972), 152–162. Josefina Rivera de Alvarez, *Diccionario de literatura puertorriqueña*, vol. 2 (San Juan, Puerto Rico: Instituto de Cultura Puertorriqueña, 1974), 975–982.

MÉNDEZ QUIÑONES, Ramón (1847–1889).

Méndez Quiñones first studied in Aguadilla, then studied secondary education and civil engineering in Spain, where he enjoyed the theatrical spectacle offered there, stimulated by sentiments of his grandfather, who was responsible for the establishment of the first theater in Aguadilla. Upon his return to Puerto Rico, Méndez Quiñones began writing short works based on rural characters and their customs. In these works he portrayed regional and *jíbaro* (peasant) themes, including several ennobling treatments of life among the more humble of Puerto Rico's inhabitants. *Un jíbaro* (A Peasant) (debuted 1878) exemplifies his works; the forthright and honest character of the peasant is contrasted with the duplicitous city dweller. Other *jíbaro* customs and regional events are treated as thematic material in Méndez's works. *Una jíbara* (The Peasant) uses the acute psychology of the peasant (the protagonist hides her husband's bad background from her father). *Los jíbaros progresistas* (The Progressive Peasants) and *La vuelta de la feria* (The Return of the Fair) allude to events of the 1882 Ponce festival and other local events. Other unpublished works include: *Un comisario de barrio* (A Local Commissioner), wherein the local population always deferred to the Spanish policies, at least in lip service, thus showing them to be very astute, and *La triquina* (Trichinosis) (about *curanderos*). *Un casamiento* (A Marriage) and *Un bautizo* (A Baptism) show local customs. *¡Pobre Sinda!* (Poor Sinda!), incomplete at Méndez's death, portrays the hard life of the slave. In addition to presenting *jíbaro* customs, he wrote in the peasant dialect, and the works have lively dialogue, proverbs, and moral and thematic concerns that surpass the merely costumbrist. Unfortunately, Ramón and his brother José were accused of causing the death of a newspaper editor; José was brought to trial, but Ramón fled and led a rather erratic life in various Caribbean theater companies until his death in Honduras a few years later.

WORKS: *Un bautizo* (A Baptism) (n.p.). *Un casamiento* (A Marriage) (n.p.). *Un jíbaro* (A Peasant) (deb. Aguadilla, October 21, 1878; pub. 1881), and in Angelina Morfi, *Antología de teatro puertorriqueño* (San Juan, Puerto Rico: Ed. Juan Ponce de León, 1970), 183–207. *Un jíbaro y una jíbara* (Peasants—A Man and a Woman) (Mayagüez, Puerto Rico: Imprenta de Martín Fernández, 1881). *Los jíbaros progresistas* (The Progressive Peasants) (Mayagüez, Puerto Rico, 1882), and in Enrique A. Laguerre and E. Melón, *El jíbaro de Puerto Rico: Símbolo y figura* (Sharon, CT: Troutman Press, 1968), 212–249. *¡Pobre Sinda!* (Poor Sinda!) (incomplete) (n.p.). *La triquina* (Trichinosis) (n.p.). *La vuelta de la feria* (The Return of the Fair) (second part of *Los jíbaros progresistas* (Ponce, Puerto Rico, 1882).

BIBLIOGRAPHY: Angelina Morfi, *Historia crítica de un siglo de teatro puertorriqueño* (San Juan, Puerto Rico: Instituto de Cultura Puertorriqueña, 1980), 90–106. Josefina Rivera de Alvarez, *Diccionario de literatura puertorriqueña*, vol. 2 (San Juan, Puerto Rico: Instituto de Cultura Puertorriqueña, 1974), 982–984. Antonia Sáez, *El teatro en Puerto Rico (Notas para su historia)* (San Juan, Puerto Rico, 1950), 69–75. Lydia Esther Sosa Ramos, *Desarrollo del Teatro Nacional en Puerto Rico* (San Juan, Puerto Rico: Emasco Printers, 1992), 33.

MORALES CINTRON, Aleyda (1955–).

Born in New York, Morales was still a child when she came to Puerto Rico; she studied in public schools and then at the University of Puerto Rico, Río Piedras. One of the group of younger writers who began composing their works within the experimental climate of the university, Morales has continued to use the theater as a primary means of literary communication. Currently director of public relations for the National Society of Dramatic Authors

(SONAD) of Puerto Rico, she continues to combine her career with new dramatic efforts. She directs her own company, El mago ambulatorio, Inc. (The Walking Wizard, Inc.), and is founder and editor of *El teatrero*, the newsletter of the Drama Department of the University of Puerto Rico. She also works with WIPR, the Puerto Rican public radio corporation. Morales has written several shorter works, often dealing with the ambiguities of the male-female relationship, as in *Estampas de mujer* (Women's Scenes) and *Espejos* (Mirrors). Another recent work shows, however, a desire to combine pyrotechnics with dramatic confrontation. *Oldies* (1994) shows various issues of society in a light and sound show stage treatment.

WORKS: *Hablemos de amor* (Let's Talk of Love) (1983). *Esos seres extraños* (Those Strange Beings) (1983). *Estampas de mujer* (Women's Scenes) (1986). *Alegoría de una mente indispuesta de silencio* (Allegory of a Mind Not Disposed to Silence) (1986). *Espejos* (Mirrors) (1987). *De pronto la felicidad* (Happiness for Now) (1980s). *La obsesión de María* (María's Obsession) (1991), (Rev. Quiles Ferrer, 231–233, October 23–29, 1987), *Oldies* (commissioned by the Instituto de Cultura Puertorriqueña and presented at the 35th Festival of Puerto Rican Theater, 1994) (San Juan, Puerto Rico: Instituto de Cultura, Colección de Teatro 3, 1994).

BIBLIOGRAPHY: Rosalina Perales, *Teatro hispanoamericano contemporáneo (1967–1987)* vol. 2 Mexico City: Grupo Editorial Gaceta, 1993), 275, 278. Edgar Heriberto, Quiles Ferrer, "Primera Muestra de Teatro Puertorriqueño Contemporáneo," in *Teatro puertorriqueño en acción (dramaturgia y escenificación 1982–1989)* (San Juan, Puerto Rico: Ateneo Puertorriqueño, 1990), 231–233.

PÉREZ LOSADA, José (1879–1937). After schooling in Spain, Pérez Losada emigrated to Puerto Rico in 1895 and found employment as an office clerk. In 1900 he founded a clerical workers' union, for which he then founded the newsletter *Los Dependientes* (The Clerks). This began a career of editorial concerns: In 1901 he joined the editorial staff of *El Boletín Mercantil* of San Juan and worked for several others, including *El Imparcial*, from 1933 to 1937. He was founder of the literary review *Gráfico* and Puerto Rican correspondent for *A.B.C.*, the Spanish paper. During the first third of the century, generally a fallow time for Puerto Rican theater, Pérez Losada showed concern in public efforts and in writing for this art. One of the founders of the Academia Antillana de la Lengua in 1916, he showed his alliance to the cause of Puerto Rican Hispanism in the face of possible English cultural and linguistic domination. He also wrote novels in the realistic tradition and poetry. His works of theater include five *zarzuelas* (Spanish opera), among which *La Cantaora* (The Diva) (1918) was probably his most successful. Works of traditional theater include *La crisis del amor* (The Crisis of Love) (1912), a comedy in three acts that affirms the values of marriage and keeping up appearances for the sake of the family and explores conflicts between romantic love and family values. Quite different is *La vida es ácida o Las industrias de la prohibición* (Life Is Bitter, or The Industries of Prohibition) (1925), debuted at the Teatro Municipal on April 23, 1912, which brought current events related to Prohibition into the theater in a wildly improbable but entertaining comedy. His writing was always elegant, even when his characters were not.

WORKS: *La crisis del Amor* (The Crisis of Love) (1912), in *Teatro portorriqueño*, vol. 1 (San Juan, Puerto Rico: Tip. Real Hermanos, 1925). *Los primeros fríos* (The First Chills) (San Juan, Puerto Rico 1915). *Zarzuelas* include *La Cantaora* (The Diva) (1918), *La Rabia* (Anger) (1912), *Sangre mora* (Moorish Blood) (1918), *Los Sobrinos del Tío Sam* (Uncle Sam's Nephews) (n.d.), *La soleá* (Solitude) (1918), and *El viaje de los congresistas* (1918) (San Juan, Puerto Rico, 1918). *La vida es ácida o Las industrias de la prohibición* (Life Is Bitter, or The Industries of Prohibition), in *Teatro portorriqueño*, vol. I (San Juan, Puerto Rico: Tip. Real Hermanos, 1925).

BIBLIOGRAPHY: Marnesba D. Hill and Harold B. Schleifer, *Puerto Rican Authors: A Biobibliographic Handbook* (Metuchen, NJ: Scarecrow Press, 1974), 180–181. Angelina Morfi, *Historia crítica de un siglo de teatro puertorriqueño* (San Juan, Puerto Rico: Instituto de Cultura Puertorriqueña, 1980), 369–383. Josefina Rivera de Alvarez, *Diccionario de literatura puertorriqueña*, vol. 2 (San Juan, Puerto Rico: Instituto de Cultura Puertorriqueña, 1974), 1182–1185.

RAMOS ESCOBAR, José Luis (1950–). Born in Guayanilla, the thirty-third child in a family of modest means, Ramos Escobar studied in local schools. After his father died when Ramos was eleven years old, he studied in Ponce. He graduated valedictorian of his class and began studies in astronomy at the University of Puerto Rico. In the turbulent years of student unrest, the war in Vietnam, and radical assaults on traditional theater, Ramos turned to the stage. He wrote his first work, *Ya los perros no se amarran con longaniza* (The Dogs Aren't Tied Up with Sausage Any More), at the age of twenty-three with Jorge Rodríguez for the Anamú theater group. At the same time he was participating in various group theatrical efforts, Ramos continued writing narrative and did considerable directing. He graduated with a B.A. degree in theater and comparative literature in 1971. In 1977 he went to Brown University, where he earned an M.A. in 1979 and a Ph.D. in 1980. Returning to Puerto Rico, he held various university teaching positions; he has now become chair of the Drama Department at the Río Piedras campus of the University of Puerto Rico. With *Mascarada* (Masquerade) (1985), rewarded with performance at the 29th Theater Festival, and several other pieces of theater he has returned as a significant presence. *Indocumentados* (Illegal Immigrants) (1989) brings an interesting perspective, that of the Caribbean basin as a source of new workers in New York. The plight of Dominicans as opposed to that of Puerto Ricans with issues such as citizenship and the right to work is illustrated in technically aggressive theater. Light play, music, and dream scenes are all utilized together with strong verbal and body language. *Geni y el Zepelín* (Genie and the Zeppelin), which was awarded the Premio Iberoamericana de Dramaturgia in August 1993, by the Universidad Santa María de la Rábida, in Huelva, Spain, was debuted in New York by the Pregones theater group.

WORKS: (With Jorge Rodríguez), *Ya los perros no se amarran con longaniza* (The Dogs Aren't Tied Up with Sausage Any More) (Río Piedras, Puerto Rico, 1973). *El lazarillo de Tormes* (Lazarillo de Tormes) (theatrical adaptation) (San Juan, Puerto Rico, 1985). *Mascarada* (Masquerade) (San Juan, Puerto Rico, 1985) (Rev. Quiles Ferrer, 242–244, May 6–12, 1988). *Indocumentados* (Illegal Immigrants) (1989) (San Juan, Puerto Rico: Editorial Cultural, 1992). *Cofresí o un bululú caribeño* (Cofresí or a Caribbean Fandango) (deb. in the University of Puerto Rico Theater, 1990). *Valor y sacrificio* (Valor and Sacrifice) (1992) (n.p.). *El olor del popcorn* (The Smell of Popcorn) (1993) (n.p.). *Mano dura* (commissioned by the Instituto de Cultura Puertorriqueña and presented at the 35th Festival of Puerto Rican Theater) (San Juan, Puerto Rico: Instituto de Cultura Puertorriqueña, Colección de teatro 3, 1994).

BIBLIOGRAPHY: Rosalina Perales, *Teatro hispanoamericano contemporáneo (1967–1987)*, vol. 2 (Mexico City: Grupo Editorial Gaceta, 1993), 281–282, 298. Edgar Heriberto Quiles Ferrer, "*Mascarada*, de José Luis Ramos Escobar," in *Teatro Puertorriqueño en acción (dramaturgia y escenificación 1982–1989)* (San Juan, Puerto Rico: Ateneo Puertorriqueño, 1990), 242–244.

RAMOS PEREA, Roberto (1956–). After completing secondary studies in Puerto Rico, Ramos Perea studied drama and acting at the Instituto Nacional de Bellas Artes in Mexico City. Returning to Puerto Rico, he studied at the University of Puerto Rico, Río Piedras. In San Juan, Ramos Perea has been an active journalist and critic. A dynamic playwright, activist for the theater, administrator of considerable breadth, he has become quite prominent while still relatively young. As executive secretary of the Ateneo Puertorriqueño (Puerto Rican Atheneum) and president of the National Society of Dramatic Authors (SONAD), Ramos Perea is very visible. His works, such as *Módulo 104* (Module 104) (1982), *Ese punto de vista* (That Point of View) (1983), and *Malasangre* (Bad Blood) (1986), have been widely presented in Puerto Rico. His works touch on themes of relevance to various sectors of society, from guerrilla politics to AIDS, prostitution, and the emigration of professionals to the mainland. Three plays are grouped as a revolutionary trilogy: *Revolución en el infierno* (Revolution in Hell), *Revolución en el purgatorio o Módulo 104* (Revolution in Purgatory, or Module 104), and *Revolución en el Paraíso o Cueva de ladrones* (Revolution in Paradise, or Den of

Thieves). Even when they are based on real incidents, such as the military confrontation in Ponce in 1937, the basis of *Revolución en el infierno* (Revolution in Hell), the plays work to show a wider reference to Puerto Rican issues in general. In the case alluded to, the particular historic incident cedes to issues of patriotism and national values, especially when a sacrifice is unlikely to yield significant gains. Some have seen this as a call to reexamine the status of Puerto Rico in the face of internal division.

WORKS: *Cueva de ladrones* (Den of Thieves) (San Juan, Puerto Rico, 1977) (Rev. Quiles Ferrer, 130–133, April 26–May 2, 1985). *El marrón menopáusico* (no translation) (San Juan, Puerto Rico, 1977). *Eran de carne quemada* (They Were of Burned Meat) (San Juan, Puerto Rico, 1978). *Fedora* (Fedora) (San Juan, Puerto Rico, 1981) (comprised of *El llanto de la parca* [The Cry of the Miser], *La mueca de Pandora* [Pandora's Sneer], and *Ese punto de vista* [That Point of View]. *Alegoría de un dilema* (Allegory of a Dilemma) (San Juan, Puerto Rico, 1982). *Revolución en el Purgatorio o Módulo 104* (Revolution in Purgatory, or Module 104) (1982) (Río Piedras, Puerto Rico: Cultural, 1986) (Rev. Quiles Ferrer, 204–207, September 12–18, 1986). *Ese punto de vista* (That Point of View) (1983), in *Cuadernos puertorriqueños de teatro breve* (Río Piedras, Puerto Rico, 1984). *Revolución en el infierno* (Revolution in Hell) (San Juan, Puerto Rico: Editorial Edil, 1983). *Revolución en el Paraiso o Cueva de ladrones* (Revolution in Paradise, or Den of Thieves) (1983). *El sueño vicioso* (The Vicious Dream) (San Juan, Puerto Rico: Editorial Edil, 1983). *Los 200 No* (The 200 No's) (San Juan, Puerto Rico: Gallo Galante, 1984). *Camándula. Historia del gran atentado* (Camándula. History of the Great Undertaking) (San Juan, Puerto Rico: Gallo Galante, 1985) (Rev. Quiles Ferrer, 187–191, June 21–27, 1985). *Malasangre* (Bad Blood) (San Juan, Puerto Rico: Gallo Galante, 1986) (Rev. Quiles Ferrer, 208–211, February 13–19, 1987; 212–216, April 24–30, 1987). *La mueca de Pandora* (Pandora's Sneer) (San Juan, Puerto Rico: Gallo Galante, 1986). *Razon de amor* (Reason of Love) (n.p.) (Rev. Quiles Ferrer, 228–230, October 16–22, 1987). *Censurado* (Censured), includes *Ese punto de vista* (That Point of View) and *El lado obscuro de las arañas* (The Dark Side of Spiders) (San Juan, Puerto Rico: Gallo Galante, 1988) (Rev. Quiles Ferrer, 231–233, October 23–29, 1987). *A puro bolero* (Only a Dance) (1989). *Golpes de reja* (Blows at the Grate) (n.p.) (Rev. Quiles Ferrer, 257–

259, February 2–8, 1989). *Llanto de luna* (Weeping Moon) (San Juan, Puerto Rico: n.p., 1989). *Teatro de Luna* (San Juan, Puerto Rico: Ediciones Gallo Galante, 1989), includes *Llanto de luna* (Cry of the Moon) and *Obsesión* (Obsession) (Rev. Quiles Ferrer, 267–270). *Mistiblú* (MistyBlue), in *Gestos* No. 10 (Nov., 1990). *Melodia salvaje* (Savage Melody) (San Juan, Puerto Rico: Instituto de Cultura Puertorriqueña, Programa de Publicaciones y Grabaciones, Colección de Teatro 3, 1992).

BIBLIOGRAPHY: Grace Yvette, Dávila López, "Diversidad y pluralidad en el teatro puertorriqueño contemporáneo: 1965–1985." (Ph.D. diss., University of California, Irvine, 1989), 249–295. Matias Montes Huidobro, "Convergencias y divergencias en *Revolución en el infierno*," *Gestos* 1 (1986): 131–146. Rosalina Perales, *Teatro hispanoamericano contemporáneo (1967–1987)*, vol. 2 (Mexico City: Grupo Editorial Gaceta, 1993), 273, 275–276, 290–291, 293, 297–298. Edgar Heriberto Quiles Ferrer, "*Camándula*, de Roberto Ramos-Perea: Historia del gran atentado," in *Teatro puertorriqueño en acción (dramaturgia y escenificación 1982–1989)* (San Juan, Puerto Rico: Ateneo Puertorriqueño, 1990), 187–191. Quiles Ferrer, "*Malasangre*, de Roberto Ramos-Perea (La nueva emigración)," in *Teatro puertorriqueño en acción (dramaturgia y escenificación 1982–1989)* (San Juan, Puerto Rico: Ateneo Puertorriqueño, 1990), 212–216. Quiles Ferrer, "*Módulo 104*: Drama histórico puertorriqueño, de Roberto Ramos-Perea," in *Teatro puertorriqueño en acción (dramaturgia y escenificación 1982–1989)* (San Juan, Puerto Rico: Ateneo Puertorriqueño, 1990), 204–207. Quiles Ferrer, "Primera muestra de teatro puertorriqueño contemporáneo," in *Teatro puertorriqueño en acción (dramaturgia y escenificación 1982–1989)* (San Juan, Puerto Rico: Ateneo Puertorriqueño, 1990), 231–233. Quiles Ferrer, "El próximo Festival de Teatro Puertorriqueño," in *Teatro puertorriqueño en acción (dramaturgia y escenificación 1982–1989)* (San Juan, Puerto Rico: Ateneo Puertorriqueño, 1990), 208–211. Quiles Ferrer, "*Razón de amor*, de Roberto Ramos-Perea," in *Teatro puertorriqueño en acción (dramaturgia y escenificación 1982–1989)* (San Juan, Puerto Rico: Ateneo Puertorriqueño, 1990), 228–230. Quiles Ferrer, "*Teatro de luna* y su *Llanto de luna*, de Roberto Ramos-Perea: Parábola de una aparente contradicción," in *Teatro puertorriqueño en acción (dramaturgia y escenificación 1982–1989)* (San Juan, Puerto Rico: Ateneo Puertorriqueño, 1990), 267–270. Quiles Ferrer, "El Teatro se hace consigna," in *Teatro puertorriqueño en acción (dramaturgia y escenificación*

1982–1989) (San Juan, Puerto Rico: Ateneo Puertorriqueño, 1990), 257–259. Bonnie Hildebrand Reynolds, *"Ese punto de vista*: El teatro puertorriqueño de Roberto Ramos-Perea," *Intermedio de Puerto Rico* 1.3–4 (1986): 61–68. Reynolds, "Las *Revoluciones* de Roberto Ramos-Perea," *Tramoya* 2 (1985).

RECHANI AGRAIT, Luis (1902–1994). After schooling in Aguas Buenas and in Río Piedras, he studied natural sciences at Harvard and Richmond Universities. His positions upon returning to Puerto Rico, however, led him into administration in the Department of Public Instruction and then in Pedagogical Investigation. He contributed many poems and stories to *Puerto Rico Ilustrado* and *El Mundo*, a daily newspaper that he edited from 1930 to 1943. Upon his retirement to Mayagüez in 1943, and stimulated by the activity in Puerto Rican theater in the late 1930s, he began writing dramas, certainly his best literary efforts. Rechani Agrait is best known for *Mi señoría* (My Lordship), which debuted September 23, 1940, and was produced for the 1959 and 1968 Theater Festivals. An authentic local politician, Buenaventura Padilla, illustrates the perils of political popularity and vested interests. In *¿Cómo se llama esta flor?* (What Flower Is This?), which debuted on April 29, 1966, at the Eighth Festival of Puerto Rican theater, dictatorship and its effects on all people are explored. The themes of commitment, the opposition of philosophy and action, of generations, are shown within a romantic story.

WORKS: *Páginas de color de rosa* (Rose-colored Pages) (readings) (Boston, MA: n.p., 1928). *Mi señoría* (My Lordship) (San Juan, Puerto Rico: Portada de Filardi, 1940); and in *Teatro puertorriqueño, Segundo Festival* (San Juan, Puerto Rico, 1960), 15–161. *Los descendientes de Poncio Pilatos* (The Descendants of Pontius Pilate) (1959). *Todos los ruiseñores cantan* (All the Larks Sing), in *Teatro puertorriqueño, Séptimo Festival* (San Juan, Puerto Rico, 1965) 45–246. *¿Cómo se llama esta flor?* (What Flower Is This?), in *Teatro puertorriqueño, Octavo Festival* (San Juan, Puerto Rico, 1966), 31–166; and (Barcelona, Spain: Ed. Rumbos, 1966). *Tres piraguas en un día de calor* (Three Ices on a Hot Day) (1970) (Rev. Collins, 42–43, June 15,

1975). *El extraño caso del Sr. Oblomós* (The Strange Case of Mr. Oblomós) (deb. April 1982, XXIII Festival de Teatro Puertorriqueño) (Rev. Quiles Ferrer, 87–91, April 8–15, 1982). *Teatro de Luis Rechani Agrait* (San Juan, Puerto Rico: Instituto de Cultura Puertorriqueña, 1991), volume I includes *Mi señoría, Todos los ruiseñores cantan, ¿Cómo se llama esta flor?* and *Tres piraguas en un día de calor* (Rev. Quiles Ferrer, 169–170, March 18–24, 1983). *¡Oh, dorada ilusión de alas abiertas!* (Oh, Golden Illusion of Outstretched Wings!) (comedy, n.p.) (Rev. Figueroa Chapel, 65–67).

BIBLIOGRAPHY: J. A. Collins, *"Tres Piraguas* Melt on Rexach Stage," in *Contemporary Theater in Puerto Rico: The Decade of the Seventies* (Río Piedras, Puerto Rico: Editorial Universitaria, 1982), 42–43. Ramón Figueroa Chapel, *"¡Oh, dorada ilusión de alas abiertas!"* in *Crítica de teatro (1977–1979)* (Río Piedras, Puerto Rico: Editorial Edil, 1982), 65–67. Marnesba D. Hill and Harold B. Schleifer, *Puerto Rican Authors: A Biobibliographic Handbook* (Metuchen, NJ: Scarecrow Press, 1974), 189–190. Angelina Morfi, *Historia crítica de un siglo de teatro puertorriqueño* (San Juan, Puerto Rico: Instituto de Cultura Puertorriqueña, 1980), 382–392. Edgar Heriberto Quiles Ferrer, *"El extraño caso del Sr. Oblomós*, de Luis Rechani Agrait," in *Teatro Puertorriqueño en acción (dramaturgia y escenificación 1982–1989)* (San Juan, Puerto Rico: Ateneo Puertorriqueño, 1990), 87–91. Quiles Ferrer, "Vigésimocuarta Temporada de Teatro Puertorriqueño: ¿Pasó hacia su revitalización?" in *Teatro puertorriqueño en acción (dramaturgia y escenificación 1982–1989)* (San Juan, Puerto Rico: Ateneo Puertorriqueño, 1990), 169–173. Josefina Rivera de Alvarez, *Diccionario de literatura puertorriqueña*, vol. 2 (San Juan, Puerto Rico: Instituto de Cultura Puertorriqueña, 1974), 1307–1309.

ROSA NIEVES, Cesáreo (1901–1974). Rosa Nieves's early training was in music, which might have been his career. While still at the University of Puerto Rico, he was named director of the ROTC Band and of the Orchestra of the university. But while still a student, he began to publish poetry, even participating in the vanguard Noísmo movement. After graduating with teaching certification and degrees in arts and education, he began teaching in Carolina and Caguas. There he published several books of poetry, while teaching and pursuing advanced studies. He completed the M.A. in

1936 and was invited to join the faculty of Hispanic Studies; he subsequently studied in Mexico, completing Ph.D. studies in 1944. He continued as professor of Spanish language and literature at the University of Puerto Rico, Río Piedras, from 1936 to 1966. He was a prolific writer of drama and poetry, based primarily on Puerto Rican history and folklore. He was granted the Award of the Society of Puerto Rican Authors in 1967. His dramatic works, written primarily in the decade of the 1940s, have been classified according to their thematic interest by Figueroa de Cifredo, including those based on history: *Román Baldorioty de Castro* (1947), which celebrated the life of the civic hero; *Brazo de oro* (Arm of Gold) (unpub.); *Pachín Marín* (unpub.); *El huésped del mar* (Guest of the Sea) (1945); and *Flor de Areyto* (Song of the Areyto) (1945), which dramatizes convivial relations between the earliest Spanish colonizers and the inhabitants of Haymanio (present Loíza). Other works are rural drama—*Nuestra enemiga la piedra* (Our Enemy the Rock) (1948) and *Norka* (1957), which presents one of his best characters in the manly woman of the title; fantastic—*Campesina en palacio* (A Peasant in the Palace) (1949); and psychological—*La otra* (The Other) (1948), the first known work to approach the theme of homosexuality in Puerto Rico. He later wrote many valuable essays, historic and critical. His constant fascination and elaboration of Puerto Rican themes provided him and his readers with many worthwhile works, always perceptive and well written.

WORKS: *Juan Bobo infantil* (Children's Readings) (Humacao, Puerto Rico, 1932). *Paracaídas* (Parachute) (poetry) (Humacao, Puerto Rico, 1934). *Tú, en los pinos* (You, in the Pines) (poetry) (1938). *La poesía en Puerto Rico* (Poetry of Puerto Rico) (essays) (San Juan, Puerto Rico, 1942) and (Barcelona, Spain: Ed. Rumbos, 1958). *Román Baldorioty de Castro* (Santurce, Puerto Rico, n.p., 1947). *Francisco de Ayerra y Santa María, poeta puertorriqueño, 1630–1708* (essay) (Río Piedras, Puerto Rico: Editorial Universitaria, 1948). *Nuestra enemiga la piedra* (Our Enemy the Rock) (drama) (1948). *Teatro puertorriqueño: Trilogía lírica* (Santurce, Puerto Rico: Publicaciones Alpha Beta Chi, 1950), includes *El huésped del mar* (Guest of the Sea), *Flor de Ar-*

eyto (Song of the Areyto), and *La otra* (The Other). *Norka*, in *Artes y Letras*, (San Juan, Puerto Rico, 1957), 13–14. *Diapasón negro* (Black Sonority) (San Juan, Puerto Rico, 1960). *Girasol* (Sunflower) (poetry) (San Juan, Puerto Rico, 1960). *Historia panorámica de la literatura puertorriqueña*, 2 vols. (San Juan, Puerto Rico: Editorial Campos, 1961, 1963). *Plumas estelares en las letras de Puerto Rico* (Stellar Writers of Puerto Rico) (essays), vols. 1–19. (San Juan, Puerto Rico: n.p., 1967). *Voz folklórica de Puerto Rico* (Folkloric Voice of Puerto Rico) (essay) (1967). *Biografías puertorriqueñas: Perfil histórico de un pueblo* (n.p., 1970). *El huracán* (The Hurricane) (unpub.). As editor, his anthologies include *Aguinaldo lírico de la poesía puertorriqueña* (Anthology of Puerto Rican Lyric Poetry), 3 vols. (San Juan, Puerto Rico: Editorial Librería Campos, 1957), and *Antología general del cuento puertorriqueño*, 2 vols. (San Juan, Puerto Rico: Editorial Librería Campos, 1959).

BIBLIOGRAPHY: Patria Figueroa de Cifredo, *Apuntes biográficos en torno a la vida y obra de Cesáreo Rosa-Nieves* (San Juan, Puerto Rico: Editorial Cordillera, 1965). Marnesba D. Hill and Harold B. Schleifer, *Puerto Rican Authors: A Biobibliographic Handbook* (Metuchen, NJ: Scarecrow Press, 1974), 202–203. Angelina Morfi, *Historia crítica de un siglo de teatro puertorriqueño* (San Juan, Puerto Rico: Instituto de Cultura Puertorriqueña, 1980), 397–405. Josefina Rivera de Alvarez, *Diccionario de literatura puertorriqueña*, vol. 2 (San Juan, Puerto Rico: Instituto de Cultura Puertorriqueña, 1974), 1409–1423.

SAMA, Manuel María (Manuel María Sama y Auger) (1850–1913). Educated first in his native Mayagüez, Sama was motivated by cultural unrest to write poetry, some of which was published at the age of fifteen. Romantic tendencies also prompted the structures of his theatrical works, the first of which, *La víctima de su falta* (The Victim of a Flaw), was presented in 1878. The influence of Echegaray can be felt in the works of Sama, which revolve around the theme of honor. His individual contribution is more felt in the area of critical anthologies of Puerto Rican poets and nascent bibliographical work. His *Bibliografía puertorriqueña* (Puerto Rican Bibliography) was awarded the Literary Prize of the Ateneo Puertorriqueño in January 1887. At the turn of the century, health concerns prompted Sama to move to San Juan, where he was elected president of the Puerto Rico Atheneum. His poetry appeared widely in literary reviews, newspapers, and anthologies.

WORKS: *Inocente y culpable* (Innocent and Guilty) (Madrid, Spain: Imp. Torrens y Navarro, 1877). *La víctima de su falta* (The Victim of His Flaw) (San Juan, Puerto Rico: n.p., 1878). *Poetas puertorriqueños* (Puerto Rican Poets) (Mayagüez, Puerto Rico: n.p., 1879). *Bibliografía puertorriqueña* (Puerto Rican Bibliography) (Mayagüez, Puerto Rico: n.p., 1887). *El regreso de Colón* (Columbus's Return) (Mayagüez, Puerto Rico: Tip. Comercial, 1892). *El desembarco de Colón en Puerto Rico y el monumento del Culebrinas* (Columbus's Landing in Puerto Rico and the Monument of Culebrinas) (essay) (Mayagüez, Puerto Rico: n.p., 1894).

BIBLIOGRAPHY: Marnesba D. Hill, and Harold B. Shleifer, *Puerto Rican Authors: A Biobibliographic Handbook* (Metuchen, NJ: Scarecrow Press, 1974), 205–206. Angelina Morfi, *Historia crítica de un siglo de teatro puertorriqueño* (San Juan, Puerto Rico: Instituto de Cultura Puertorriqueña, 1980), 171–172. Josefina Rivera de Alvarez, *Diccionario de literatura puertorriqueña*, vol. 2 (San Juan, Puerto Rico: Instituto de Cultura Puertorriqueña, 1974), 1444–1445.

SÁNCHEZ, Luis Rafael (1936–   ). Sánchez showed an early inclination to the theater. He founded an experimental theater group while still in high school in Humacao and took part in the Comedieta Universitaria at the University of Puerto Rico. Further studies in Mexico (1953–1956) brought him accolades as an actor and experience in filming. Returning to Puerto Rico for advanced studies, he began publishing short stories and his first plays. After further study at Columbia and New York Universities, he joined the faculty of General Studies at the University of Puerto Rico, Río Piedras, where he became professor of Spanish. His works continue to explore both the social realities of Puerto Rican politics and daily life. As with many recent dramatists, the formal aspects of his works have also evolved, free from the traditional constraints of theater earlier in the century. Sánchez's theater includes *La pasión Según Antígona Pérez* (The Passion According to Antígona Pérez); *La hiel nuestra de cada día* (Our Daily Bile) (1976), which portrays the embittered existence of the older impoverished generation; and *Quíntuples* (Quintuplets) (1985), a metatheatrical piece about relationships in a dysfunctional family, in which all six roles are played sequentially by two actors. Making its world debut at the Centro de Bellas Artes, Experimental Theater, it was an immediate hit for its dramatic impact and innovative technique. His topics are the conflicts between ideals and reality or, in the case of *La pasión según Antígona Pérez*, the conflicts of the individual and the collective, in this case, the government of a tyrant. Antígona is a woman imprisoned for her refusal to tell where a man is buried (so he can be condemned officially). The opposing sides, shown by characters who are one-dimensional, give a wide variety of attitudes and concerns. Music and lighting are important and used to good effect, as is often the case in this period. At the same time, the reliance on the Greek theater is obvious: the title, the fundamental opposition, Antígona's functioning as chorus to outline each act's major events, and the epic sweep of the work. Its performance during the eleventh Theater Festival certainly seems indicative of the success of the festival in showcasing major talent. The Puerto Rican Traveling Theater also toured with the work in an English translation. Sánchez's continued exploration of forms and meaning in the theater and in narrative, *La guaracha del Macho Camacho* (Macho Camacho's Beat), for example, make him the major writer of his period and, through his work at the university, a mentor of considerable influence on the younger writers.

WORKS: *Cuento de Cucarachita Viudita* (The Story of Little Widow Cockroach) (pres. Dept. of Drama, Universidad de Puerto Rico, 1951). *La espera* (The Wait) (n.p., 1959). *Farsa del amor compradito*, (Farce of a Little Love Bought) (Barcelona, Spain: Ediciones Lugar, 1960, 1st ed.), (Río Piedras, Puerto Rico: Editorial Cultural, 1976) (Rev. Collins, 46, September 19, 1975) (Rev. Quiles Ferrer, 152–154, April 17–23, 1987). *Sol 13 interior* (13 Sol Street, Inside): includes *Farsa del amor compradito, La hiel nuestra de cada día, Los ángeles se han fatigado*, in *Teatro puertorriqueño, Cuarto Festival* (San Juan, Puerto Rico, 1962), 565–648; and (Río

Piedras, Puerto Rico: Ed. Cultural, 1963) (Rev. Figueroa Chapel, 267–268, November, 1979). *En cuerpo de camisa* (In Casual Dress) (stories) (San Juan, Puerto Rico: Ediciones Lugar (1966). *La pasión según Antígona Pérez* (The Passion According to Antígona Pérez) (Hato Rey, Puerto Rico: Ediciones Lugar, 1968); (San Juan, Puerto Rico: Instituto de Cultura Puertorriqueña, 1970); (San Juan, Puerto Rico: Ediciones Lugar, 1970, 2nd ed.); (Río Piedras, Puerto Rico: Editorial Cultural, 1975, 1980, 1983, 1985, 1987); (Rev. Collins, 48, February 15, 1976). *Casi el alma* (Almost the Soul) (Río Piedras, Puerto Rico: Editorial Cultural, 1974, 1980), pub. as *O casi el alma* (Or Almost the Soul) in *Teatro puertorriqueño, Séptimo Festival* (San Juan, Puerto Rico, 1965), 379–457; both works published as *Farsa del amor compradito, o casi el alma* (1966) (also pub. as *Farsa del amor compradito* [Río Piedras, Puerto Rico: Editorial Cultural, 1976]). *Los ángeles se han fatigado* (The Angels Have Tired) (Río Piedras, Puerto Rico: Editorial Cultural, 1976). *La hiel nuestra de cada día* (Our Daily Bile) (Río Piedras, Puerto Rico: Editorial Cultural, 1976), and in *Farsa del amor compradito* (Río Piedras, Puerto Rico: Editorial Cultural, 1976). *Teatro de Luis Rafael Sánchez*, vol. 1 (Río Piedras, Puerto Rico: Editorial Antillana, 1976), includes: *Farsa del amor compradito, La hiel nuestra de cada día*, and *Los ángeles se han fatigado. Parábola del andarín* (Parable of the Walker) (Pres. Twentieth Festival of Puerto Rican Theater) (Rev. Collins, 88–89, June 5, 1979; Figueroa Chapel, 223–224, June 1979). *La guaracha del Macho Camacho* (Macho Camacho's Beat) (narrative) (Barcelona, Spain: Argos Vergara, 1982, 1st ed.). *La importancia de llamarse Daniel Santos* (The Importance of Being Daniel Santos) (narrative) (Hanover, NH: Ediciones del Norte, 1988). *Quíntuples* (Quintuplets) (Hanover, NH: Ediciones del Norte, 1985, 1989) (Rev. Quiles Ferrer, 120–122, November 2–8, 1984).

BIBLIOGRAPHY: J. A. Collins, "Antígona's Passion Wrings Hands Not Hearts," in *Contemporary Theater in Puerto Rico: The Decade of the Seventies* (Río Piedras, Puerto Rico: Editorial Universitaria, 1982), 48. Collins, "Sánchez' *Parábola*: Intriguing but Uneven," in *Contemporary Theater in Puerto Rico: The Decade of the Seventies* (Río Piedras, Puerto Rico: Editorial Universitaria, 1982), 88–89. Collins, "Sweltering Show at Arts Center," Rev. of *Los ángeles se han fatigado*, in *Contemporary Theater in Puerto Rico: The Decade of the Seventies* (Río Piedras, Puerto Rico: Editorial Universitaria, 1982), 46. Eliseo Colón Zayas, *El teatro de Luis Ra-*

fael Sánchez: Códigos, ideología y lenguaje (San Juan, Puerto Rico: Editorial Playor, Biblioteca de Autores de Puerto Rico, 1985). Grace Yvette, Dávila López. "Diversidad y pluralidad en el teatro puertorriqueño contemporáneo: 1965–1985" (Ph.D. diss., University of California, Irvine, 1989), 96–146. Ramón Figueroa Chapel, "*Parábola del andarín*," in *Crítica de teatro (1977–1979)* (Río Piedras, Puerto Rico: Editorial Edil, 1982), 223–225. Figueroa Chapel, "*Sol 13 interior: Los ángeles se han fatigado y La hiel nuestra de cada día*," in *Crítica de teatro (1977–1979)* (Río Piedras, Puerto Rico: Editorial Edil, 1982), 267–268. Antonio García del Toro, *Mujer y patria en la dramaturgia puertorriqueña* (San Juan, Puerto Rico: Editorial Playor, Biblioteca de Autores de Puerto Rico, 1987), on *Antígona Pérez*, 218–233. Marnesba D. Hill, and Harold B. Schleifer, *Puerto Rican Authors: A Biobibliographic Handbook* (Metuchen, NJ: Scarecrow Press, 1974), 206–207. Rosalina Perales, *Teatro hispanoamericano contemporáneo (1967–1987)*, vol. 2 (Mexico City: Grupo Editorial Gaceta, 1993), 273, 275–276, 290–291. Jordan Blake Phillips, *Contemporary Puerto Rican Drama* (New York: Plaza Mayor Ediciones, 1972), 177–185. Edgar Heriberto Quiles Ferrer, "Elia Enid Cadilla en *Los ángeles se han fatigado*, de Luis Rafael Sánchez," in *Teatro puertorriqueño en acción (dramaturgia y escenificación 1982–1989)* (San Juan, Puerto Rico: Ateneo Puertorriqueño, 1990), 152–154. Quiles Ferrer, "*Quíntuples*: Vodevil para dos grandes actores, de Luis Rafael Sánchez," in *Teatro puertorriqueño en acción (dramaturgia y escenificación 1982–1989)* (San Juan, Puerto Rico: Ateneo Puertorriqueño, 1990), 120–122. Josefina Rivera de Alvarez, *Diccionario de literatura puertorriqueña*, vol. 2 (San Juan, Puerto Rico: Instituto de Cultura Puertorriqueña, 1974), 1448–1453. Gloria F. Waldman, "Luis Rafael Sánchez: An Interview," *Revista/Review Interamericana* 9 (1979): 9–23.

SANTALIZ, Pedro (Pedro Santaliz Avila) (1938–). Pedro Santaliz directs the Nuevo Teatro Pobre de América (New Poor Theater of America), founded in Puerto Rico in 1968. The group was formed to dramatize the problems of the specific areas of performance, even drawing on the audience to take part in the works, either as actors or as accompanying musicians, thereby giving them a sense of control and involvement. In New York for several years now, Santaliz has done the same kind of work in the Hispanic neighborhoods of the metropolis. The popular theater has provided stimulus for other dramatic and cultural manifestations in these areas. Santaliz has written prolifically (over thirty texts were written in twenty years of performance) but primarily for specific performances and not published; in fact, he has said these should not be published, made static instead of responsive to the circumstances of their production. A number of his works have been made available through publication in a single volume, however. Originally based on a philosophy of drawing themes from the public of the moment, it has been observed that his works reflect the corruption, drug addiction, and violence of society on the stage itself, sometimes reaching the limits expressed in the Absurd, as in Genet's Theater of Violence.

WORKS: *El cemí en el Palacio de Jarlem* (The Image in the Palace in Harlem) (New York, 1969). *Güeybaná* (Güeybaná) (San Juan, Puerto Rico: n.p., 1970). *Cadencia en el país de las maravillas* (Movement in Wonderland) (San Juan, Puerto Rico: n.p., 1973) (Rev. Collins, 51, March 3, 1976). *Oda al rey de Jarlem* (Ode to the King of Harlem) (New York, n.p., 1974). *La fábula de Rico y Puerto* (The Fable of Rich and Port) (San Juan, Puerto Rico: n.p., 1974). *El caserío perfecto* (The Perfect Arrangement) (San Juan, Puerto Rico: n.p., 1976). *Serenito se cayó frente a Padín* (Serenito Fell Before Padín) (San Juan, Puerto Rico: n.p., 1976). *En la corte del Rey Bombai* (In the Court of King Bombai) (Rev. Figueroa Chapel, 161–162, December 1978). *Historia amorosa de Evaristo y Matera* (The Love Story of Evaristo Matera) (San Juan, Puerto Rico: n.p., 1981). *El teatro personal de Meaíto Laracuente* (The Personal Theater of Meaíto Laracuente) (San Juan, Puerto Rico: n.p., 1981). *El castillo interior de Medea Camuñas* (The Interior Castle of Medea Camuñas) (San Juan, Puerto Rico: n.p., 1984). *Olla* (Stewpot) (San Juan, Puerto Rico: n.p., 1985). *Teatro* (San Juan, Puerto Rico: Instituto de Cultura Puertorriqueña, 1992); includes *El castillo interior de Medea Camuñas, Las sombras del chisme, o la historia de Evaristo y Matera* (The Shadows of the Joke, or The History of Evaristo and Matera), and *El teatro personal de Meaíto Laracuente.*

BIBLIOGRAPHY: J. A. Collins, "Santaliz' *Cadencia* Mixes Barrio Oil with Water of Fantasy," in *Contemporary Theater in Puerto Rico: The Decade of the Seventies* (Río Piedras, Puerto Rico: Editorial Universitaria, 1982), 51. Grace Yvette Dávila López,

"Diversidad y pluralidad en el teatro puertorriqueño contemporáneo: 1965–1985" (Ph.D. diss., University of California, Irvine, 1989), 220–232. Ramón Figueroa Chapel, "*En la corte del Rey Bombai,*" in *Crítica de teatro (1977–1979)* (Río Piedras, Puerto Rico: Editorial Edil, 1982), 161–162. Rosalina Perales, *Teatro hispanoamericano contemporáneo, (1967–1987)*, vol. 2 (Mexico City: Grupo Editorial Gaceta, 1993), 283–284, 286, 291, 330.

SOTO, Pedro Juan (1928–). After completing secondary studies in Cataño, Soto attended Long Island University in New York. Abandoning premedical studies to complete a degree in English, he began working in New York as a reporter, contributing numerous articles to Hispanic papers—*Diario de Nueva York, Temas*, and *Ecos de Nueva York*. After serving in the U.S. Army he devoted himself to journalism and letters, earning the M.A. degree at Columbia University in 1953. Returning to Puerto Rico in 1954, he worked as an editor in the Publications Department of the Puerto Rico Division of Community Education, then became professor at the University of Puerto Rico, Río Piedras. Soto has contributed to various periodicals and literary reviews; but his most radical works are stories of Puerto Ricans, in New York and in Puerto Rico. Works such as *Spiks* (1956) and *Usmaíl* (U.S. Mail) (1958) have achieved popularity in the North as exemplary of the Puerto Rican immigrant experience. *Spiks* has been adapted for theatrical performance, in the vein of protest theater. In 1955, the experimental theater of the Puerto Rico Atheneum presented his drama *El huésped* (The Guest), which was awarded the Ateneo's prize of 1955. It is based on a story written earlier about the situation of an ailing father in New York whose grown daughters discuss various ways of coping with the issues his presence creates. He overhears their conversation and resolves the issue by committing suicide, going to join his dead wife who appears to him in a dream sequence. *Las máscaras* (Masks) presents distinct parts of the stage work alternately, telling lies about and showing real stories of a politician's life. Soto's works reveal both social and aesthetic concerns about Puerto Rican reality. *Las máscaras* was awarded Honorary Mention in the Ateneo's competition of 1958.

WORKS: *El huésped* (The Guest) (1955). *Spiks* (short stories) (Mexico City: Los Presentes, 1956) (Río Piedras, Puerto Rico: Editorial Cultural, 1973) (theatrical adaptation rev. Collins, 49, February 24, 1976). *Las máscaras* (Masks) (1958). *Usmaíl* (U.S. Mail) (novel) (Río Piedras, Puerto Rico: Editorial Cultural, 1958). *Ardiente suelo, fría estación* (Burning Ground, Cold Season) (novel) (Mexico City: Universidad Veracruzana, 1961). *El francotirador* (The Sniper) (novel) (Mexico City: Joaquín Mortiz, 1969). *Temporada de duendes* (Season of Sprites) (novel) (1970). *El huésped, las máscaras y otros disfraces* (The Guest, Masks and Other Disguises) (prologue, sketches, and related theater) (Río Piedras, Puerto Rico: Ediciones Puerto, 1973) and (Barcelona, Spain: n.p., 1974). *U.S. Mail* (Río Piedras, Puerto Rico: Cultural, 1973).

BIBLIOGRAPHY: D.J.R. Bruckner, "Puerto Rican Double Bill Mixes Comic and Tragic," rev. of *El Huésped, New York Times*, April 14, 1991, Sec. 1, 52. J.A. Collins, "Soto's *Spiks* Lacking in Dramatic Fibre," in *Contemporary Theater in Puerto Rico: The Decade of the Seventies* (Río Piedras, Puerto Rico: Editorial Universitaria, 1982), 49. Marnesba D. Hill and Harold B. Schleifer, *Puerto Rican Authors: A Biobibliographic Handbook* (Metuchen, NJ: Scarecrow Press, 1974), 206–207. Iris Thomason, *Estudio general de la obra de Pedro Juan Soto* (n.d., 1964). Ann Barbara, Witte, "The Image of the United States in Puerto Rican Theater: A Portrait of Cultural Conflict." (master's thesis, University of Texas, Austin, 1986), 134–140.

TAPIA Y RIVERA, Alejandro (pseud. Cristófolo Sardanápalo; Guamaní) (1826–1882). Tapia's early education at the private school of the Count of Carpegna in San Juan gave him a firm base, but his economic situation did not permit further studies in Spain. He therefore took a position in the Ministry of the Interior and became self-educated, reading widely and publishing in 1847 both a novel and poetry. His first play, *Roberto D'Evreux* (1848), with dignified action and theme, lays the groundwork for later writers. With its theme—the love of Isabel I for the Count of Essex—it was prohibited from presentation because the humanization of royalty was not permitted. Reworked and presented in 1856, it was the first recorded performance of a theatrical work by a Puerto Rican dramatist. His liberal tendencies earned him the watchful eye of the censors from the beginning, so he used other settings and times for his works, the normal option of writers who want to get some of their message to an audience, and especially in the case of dramatists. Deported to Spain for engaging in a duel, he was able to satisfy his thirst for Spanish culture; more important, Tapia learned about Puerto Rican history in the museums and libraries of Madrid, which led to his publication of the *Biblioteca histórica de Puerto Rico* (Historic Library of Puerto Rico). This work mentions the earliest observations of the *areyto* and other native forms of entertainment. The most prolific writer of nineteenth-century Puerto Rico, Tapia is often considered the "Father of Puerto Rican Literature" because of his pioneering efforts in virtually all genres. His liberal social concerns included the equalization of Puerto Rican government with that of the Spanish provinces and the emancipation of women; to that end he edited and published *La Azucena* (The Lily), a women's literary review (1870–1877). He participated in the commission formed in 1873 to inform the Spanish government of Puerto Rican concerns for legal reform and was editor of *El Agente* (The Agent), a liberal journal, for a brief period. He died while attending a meeting of the Society for the Protection of Intelligence, a benevolent society that sponsored study abroad for worthy Puerto Rican students. Tapia's theater, in addition to *Roberto d'Evreux*, can be thought of as classified by theme as: historic—*Camöens* (1868), which was set in Lisbon in the sixteenth century, and *Vasco Núñez de Balboa* (1872), which confirmed his tendencies toward Romanticism and tragic endings; and as social—*Bernardo de Palissy o El heroísmo del trabajo* (Bernard de Palissy or the Heroism of Work) (1857), written at the request of Román Baldorioty de Castro to uplift the people of Puerto Rico, and *La cuarterona* (The Quadroon) (1867), based on the restrictions of race and class in nineteenth-century colonial society. The beginnings of incorporation of an indigenist theme are found in Tapia's opera *Guarionex*, written and debuted in 1854.

WORKS: *El heliotropo* (The Heliotrope) (1848). *Roberto d'Evreux* (1848) (San Juan, Puerto Rico: Imp. Venezuela, 1944). *Biblioteca histórica de Puerto Rico que contiene varios documentos de los siglos XV, XVI, XVII y XVIII* (Historic Library of Puerto Rico, Containing Various Documents of the XV, XVI, XVII and XVIII Centuries) (essays) (Mayagüez, Puerto Rico: n.p., 1854), 2nd ed. (San Juan, Puerto Rico: n.p., 1945), also (San Juan, Puerto Rico: Instituto de Cultura Puertorriqueña, 1970). *Vida del pintor puertorriqueño José Campeche* (1854); also republished with a brief biography: *La Palma del Cacique; La Leyenda de los veinte años; A Orillas del Rhin* (Mexico City: Ed. Orion, 1963). *Bernardo de Palissy o El heroísmo del trabajo* (1857) (San Juan, Puerto Rico: Imp. Venezuela, 1944) (Río Piedras, Puerto Rico: Universidad de Puerto Rico, 1969). *El bardo de Guamaní* (The Bard of Guamaní), includes literary essays, *La antigua sirena* (The Old Siren) (novel), *Bernardo de Palissy o El heroísmo del trabajo* (Bernard de Palissy or the Heroism of Work), *Roberto D'Evreux, La palma del cacique* (The Chieftain's Palm) (historic legend), and *Vida del pintor puertorriqueño José Campeche* (Life of the Puerto Rican Painter José Campeche) (Havana, Cuba: n.p., 1862) (includes critique of *Bernardo de Palissy* by Román Baldorioty de Castro, pp. 140–147, and other incidental materials interspersed). *La cuarterona* (The Quadroon) (1867) (San Juan, Puerto Rico: Imp. Venezuela, 1944). *Hero* (tragic monologue) (1869), included in *Camöens* (1967 ed.). *Vasco Núñez de Balboa* (1872) (San Juan, Puerto Rico: Imp. Venezuela, 1944). *Cofresí* (novel) (1876). *La sataniada* (Satan's Song) (1878).

La parte del León (The Lion's Share) (1880) (San Juan, Puerto Rico: Imp. Venezuela, 1944). *Conferencias sobre estética y literatura* (Conferences on Esthetics and Literature) (1881). *Camöens* (1886) (San Juan, Puerto Rico: Imp. Venezuela, 1944). *Cuentos y artículos varios* (Various Stories and Articles) (1938). *Obras completas*, 2 vols. (San Juan, Puerto Rico: Instituto de Cultura Puertorriqueña, 1970). Several works published as part of the Clásicos Puertorriqueños Edil collection (Río Piedras, Puerto Rico: Editorial Edil, 1975): *Bernardo de Palissy, La cuarterona*, and *La parte del león* in one volume; *Vasco Núñez de Balboa, Camöens*, and *Hero* in another.

BIBLIOGRAPHY: Elsa Castro Pérez, *Tapia: Señalador de caminos* (San Juan, Puerto Rico: Editorial Coquí, 1964). Manuel García Díaz, *Alejandro Tapia y Rivera, su vida y su obra* (San Juan, Puerto Rico: Editorial Coquí, 1964). Marnesba D. Hill, and Harold B. Schleifer, *Puerto Rican Authors: A Biobibliographic Handbook* (Metuchen, NJ: Scarecrow Press, 1974), 209–210. Angelina Morfi, *Historia crítica de un siglo de teatro puertorriqueño* (San Juan, Puerto Rico: Instituto de Cultura Puertorriqueña, 1980), 47–71. Josefina Rivera de Alvarez, *Diccionario de literatura puertorriqueña*, vol. 2 (San Juan, Puerto Rico: Instituto de Cultura Puertorriqueña, 1974), 1489–1497. Magdalena Serrano de Matos, "El teatro de Alejandro Tapia y Rivera" (master's thesis, Universidad de Puerto Rico, 1953). Lydia Esther Sosa Ramos, *Desarrollo del Teatro Nacional en Puerto Rico* (San Juan, Puerto Rico: Emasco Printers, 1992), 30–32.

Philippa Brown Yin

Uruguay

The course that Uruguayan theater has followed since its origins is riddled with obstacles common to Latin American countries. The lack of pre-Hispanic theatrical manifestations and the subsequent imitation of European theater were principal ones. To these one might add two factors that, in addition to delaying development, transform the theater of Uruguay into a special case within Latin America. On the one hand, the city of Buenos Aires since colonial times began to model itself as the gigantic metropolis that would absorb and control the gestation, birth, and development of the national Uruguayan theater. This fact implies that up until the end of the 1940s one should speak of the River Plate theater, although isolated exceptions do exist. On the other hand, within Uruguay it is possible to observe the constant historical conflict between the great city Montevideo and the interior, that is, between the interests of urbanites and those of the country in a nation above all based on agriculture and livestock. In this sense, Montevideo exerts a powerful attraction, similar to the effect caused by Buenos Aires, and the theatrical movement of the capital eclipses the movement of the other cities. This effect begins to diminish in the last decades of the twentieth century. As a result, the independent history of Uruguayan theater is of relatively recent origin whose personality is yet in the process of molding itself according to its own characteristics.

THE FIRST ONE HUNDRED YEARS (1820–1920)

In spite of the fact that as far back as 1791 Montevideo was considered a strategic natural port, the fortress that protected it was not highly populated, and even fewer numbers included those who might appreciate and support artistic endeavors. In 1793 Montevideo boasted of a comedy house in which the first isolated and weak theatrical efforts were witnessed, comprised mostly of Spanish drama or comedy imported from Buenos Aires. In 1808, *La lealtad más ascendrada y Buenos Aires vengada* (The Purest Loyalty and Buenos Aires Avenged) by the first native playwright, Juan Francisco Martínez, was presented. The piece commemorates the triumph over the first British invasions, the brotherhood of the River Plate towns in the fight, and loyalty to the Spanish monarchy and Catholic faith. Nevertheless, the value of the work is reduced to a passing glory in the national literature as the first work created by an author of *La banda oriental* (The Oriental Band).

In the period of independence the theater, as in all River Plate literature, reflects the feeling of liberation of the people and is further used as an instrument of political propaganda. The themes concentrate on patriotic triumphs by emphasizing the hatred toward Spanish oppressors and lamenting those who died for the newly born nation, inciting unity and fraternity. These issues are expressed in cultured or popular forms. The most striking example is the poet Bartolomé Hidalgo (1788–1822), whose popular work consists of *cielitos*, dialogues, and presentations of Mayan festivals written in a mixture of urban and popular expressions. This combination sets forth a strong calling to the fight for the nation as of yet unequaled. The cultured compositions by Hidalgo lack the virtuosity of his popular works and fall into rhetorical presentations of historical pseudo-erudition, and an invocation of Latin deities within an environment of grand Americanism.

In 1838 a movement is noted in which Uruguayan authors ascribe to the Romantic creed. The first Romantic promotion reflects the conflict between neoclassicism and nature as well as American life. This confrontation represents the fight between the remains of the Spanish culture and the new French influence. These Romantic authors attempt to reaffirm a creative conscience in the national literature by emancipating themselves from Spain, although respecting the language, and orienting their works toward *costumbrismo*, comedy of local customs, and historical drama. Nevertheless, the value of the Romantic theater is inferior to the poetry. The most important dramatic work of this first generation comes from another Romantic playwright, Antonio Díaz (1831–1911). It is also fitting to point out *El charrúa* (Teatro Solís, 1858), by Pedro Pablo Bermúdez (1816–1860), because it introduces the Indianist theme, revealing the conflict between the Spanish and the natives in the River Plate region. On the other hand, the second generation of Romantics cannot or do not know how to free themselves of the decadent foreign influence, already surpassed in Europe, leaving behind an abundance of poor-quality works even when these works include some relevance in other aspects of literacy creation. Such is the case for José Cándido Bustamante (1834–1885) and his works *Reyertas Conyugales* (Teatro San Felipe, 1862), *El honor lo manda* (Honor Demands It) (Teatro San Felipe, 1865), *La mujer abandonada* (The Abandoned Woman) (Teatro San Felipe, 1876), or *Amor, dinero y política* (Love, Money and Politics) (Teatro San Felipe, 1881); Washington Bermúdez (1847–1913) and his *criollo 4 drama Artigas* (1881) or his comedy *Una broma de César* (Ceasar's Joke) (1881); and Benjamin Fernández y Medina (1873–1960) and his work *El Fausto criollo* (Teatro Nuevo Politeama, 1894).

In the final decades of the nineteenth century, the theater dealing with the *criollo* theme is greatly developed due to the rigorous impetus of the work *Juan Moreira*. One must keep in mind that the *teatro culto* of Spanish origin was dominant until the 1880s, with elegant works, *de salón*, usually acted by Peninsular actors, or works of *género chico*, the *zarzuela* and the Italian opera. Obviously, these kinds of spectacles do not awake the interest of the public, even that of Montevideo, as an audience because there is little identification with the topics presented. In that time what is considered its *own* is the environment and the gauchos, characters of the River Plate countryside. These characters, represented in the figure of Juan Moreira, live and experience the authority of the commissioner allied with foreign businessmen and thus develop a following for courage and *machismo*, creating a unique identity and conception of justice. The audience recognizes the language, type of person, dress, and customs and therefore feels able to participate in the destiny of the heroes. This association gives birth to the vitality of *Juan Moreira*, by the Argentinean Eduardo Gutierrez and acted by the Uruguayan José Podestá. The enormous popular success of the work leads to the upper class embracing the drama with great enthusiasm, although the piece lacks true theatrical and literary elements.

The gaucho, as character and theme, signals the first period of the River Plate theater.

However, even though Uruguayan authors follow the path opened by *Juan Moreira*, they soon try to distance themselves from the violence and tragic destiny of the main character given by the Argentineans. Three names merit special attention in these first moments of Uruguayan theater. Elías Regules (1860–1929), understanding the positive contribution of *Juan Moreira* to our culture, adapts the gaucho literary work *Martín Fierro* to the theater. But progress is truly marked by Orosmán Moratorio (1852–1898) in his work *Juan Soldao* (Argentina: Teatro Circo Tucumán, 1893). The value and interest of this piece lie, on the one hand, in that the setting is the Uruguayan countryside during elections in which the two parties, *blanco* and *colorado*, vie for power and in which there is a denouncement of the fraudulent victory of the authorities. On the other hand, in *Juan Soldao* one observes an improvement in theatrical technique. There is a studied variety of scenes in addition to advancements in dramatic conflict in that the protagonist is not a fatally gaucho *malo*, bad gaucho, nor does he heroically live the life of that same character. Another author, Víctor Pérez Petit (1871–1947), a great enthusiast of the national theater, finds in the *teatro gauchesco* the possibility of transforming the primitive *criollo* drama into purer expressions on an aesthetic level. In his most famous work *¡Cobarde!* (Coward!) (Buenos Aires: Teatro Onrubia, 1894) he takes a step toward the evolution of characters, and a broader and richer approach to human conflict, by presenting as a topic the difficult relations between parents and children. Nevertheless, even in this piece, there is a predominance of the traditional *machismo* of the legendary man of the countryside Juan Moreira, revealing his irresistible influence.

At the end of the nineteenth century the socioeconomic transformations of the River Plate region define the first decade of the twentieth century. The formation of a middle class brought about by a strong inmigratory influx joins the customs and lifestyles of the *criollos*. In addition, the disappearance of the feudal system, the push toward foreign trade, the forming of a consumer industry, and the transformation of archaic agricultural structures are all forces that allow the stabilization of government. Along with these modernizing effects come European ideological tendencies, bringing with them realist-naturalist aesthetics. The Uruguayan theater quickly absorbs these new forms of facing topics and human conflicts and applies them with the intention of discovering an authentic national reality. From the seeds of influence of Ibsen, Bernstein, Sudermann, Hauptmann, Giaeosa, Bracco, Dicenta, Rovetta, Benavente, and Alvarez Quinteros, there comes about a concern for the study of the characters in revealing the feelings, aspirations, frustrations, and conventionalisms of the growing middle class and in presenting a nostalgic vision of a past lost in the advances of new sociopolitical structures.

Parallel to this transformation felt mostly in the urban area of Montevideo are the concerns of the rural areas causing a special development that will later be reflected in the theater. Without ever being able to free itself from the destiny of being primarily a livestock nation, the theater, similar to the rest of the literature, reflects the *costumbrista* themes of country life, cult to courage, friction between economic classes, social protest against the perpetual subjugation to those in power, opposition between *criollos* and inmigrants, and the traditional opposition of country versus city. The rural drama overcomes the *moreirista* period and introduces a new character: the farmer. This character, who arrives thanks to foreign presence, is the figure opposite to the individualist gaucho, the adventurer cultivator of courage and absolute liberty. The farmer is the man tied to the land with deep feelings of property, ownership, and support for the laws that protect his property and social peace in the fall of spontaneous rebellion. The Uruguayan drama presents both individuals in confrontation through the feelings of honor, tradition, and private interest, though land tenancy by foreigners often transcends the issues. Conflicts are also carried through military leaders as incarnations of the past that are diluted through times and progress by the resistance to the foreign usurper of lands, the confrontation between landowners and laborers, and the threatening triumph of progress over feudal mentality. Without a doubt, this period is the most original, creative, and meritorious of the rural drama whose movement is preceded by *Calandria* (1896) by Martiniano Leguizamón.

However, the author who perfects the rural drama is Florencio Sánchez because he is able to solidify themes, language, ideas, and reality, thus harmoniously integrating the dramatic with the national. Sánchez's mature writing touches the audience by alluding to the reality of day-to-day living of the people, through the great love for the humble, those marginalized by society as well as the forgotten sinners. That is to say, Sánchez resumes and complements the issue initially presented in *Martin Fierro* and continued in *Juan Moreira* and other *moreiristas* plays. This reveals a theatrical tradition concerned with the dispossession and injustice that the characters suffered, today permanent symbols of the theater of Uruguay. Nevertheless, Sánchez's cycle of realism does not end with his death in 1910 but continues in the works of another outstanding artist, Ernesto Herrera (1889–1917). The works of these two authors compose the pinnacle of Uruguayan theater in the first fifteen years of the twentieth century. The base is formed by authors who developed their particular trajectories in Uruguay and others who blossomed in Buenos Aires by participating in the fine-tuning of the *rioplatense* theater during the period of realism such as Otto Miguel Cione (1875–1945), Ismael Cortinas (1884–1904), Edmundo Bianchi (1880–1965), and Orosmán Moratorio, Jr. (1883–1929). Among the Uruguayan authors residing in Buenos Aires, one should mention Carlos Mauricio Pacheco, Alberto Weisbach, Alfredo Duhau, and Ulises Favaro, who successfully cultivated the one-act farce of Buenos Aires.

YEARS OF CRISIS (1920–1947)

The violent events that develop in Europe cannot avoid influencing the River Plate region. While Russia begins to establish Marxist ideas in Uruguay, the socialist ideas of José Batlle y Ordóñez dominate the political scenario. Batlle y Ordóñez's ideas seem to suggest a pacifistic civil direction within a representative liberal democracy. This period marks the height of European immigration, of the economy, and of the governmental institutions. The sense of political, social, and economic euphoria culminates in the furor with which the cinema and the radio captivate the public, keeping the audience glued to their seats.

The shifting of theater to cinema leads to the closing of many Montevidean theaters, and Uruguayan authors see no alternative but to escape their disappearing market and seek refuge in Buenos Aires, whose greater population would allow for their survival. In this metropolis, the early and vigorous birth of cinema does not harm the theater; on the contrary, the cinema emphasizes and collaborates in the prestige of the theater. As a result, for a period of about thirty years, only the bravest or least ambitious playwrights remained in Montevideo. Their career possibilities were reduced to radio and public service while aspiring and dreaming that their works would soon premiere in a local theater. This immigration leads to a strong inferiority complex with regard to Buenos Aires as well as North America and devalues the concept of a national cultural product. The confidence in the capacity to create at a local level soon wanes, leading to uncertainty in the possibility of success, which in turn creates a country of passive consumers.

Meanwhile, Buenos Aires enjoys a period of great splendor where the cinema, radio, and theater reach their best moments as judged by good box office, not necessarily highest quality. Montevideo, on the other hand, finds itself without theaters, actors, directors, and national cinema and without the protection of the government. In addition, the public does not cooperate by showing great satisfaction with what Buenos Aires has to offer: a product in their own language, well-known movie stars, familiar jokes and music, a matching interest in sports, and similar historical, social, and economic circumstances. As a result, Montevideo turns into a suburb of Buenos Aires, and this city begins to count on the Montevidean public as a constant. Cultural frontiers disappear, and Uruguayan theatrical creations fall into what could be described as death throes.

During these years the Uruguayan theater does little more than depend on Argentina, which contributes to the lingering name *rioplatense* theater. The general tone of the works is comedy in search of quick and easy success, temporary as it may be, and usually written with a specific actor in mind. It is a period of theater as passing amusement, entertainment corresponding to the fleeting contentment of Uruguayan economy, politics, and society. The writer's lack of contact with drama promotes the creation of a *literary* theater with grand ideas, themes, and intentions but little chance of being presented. Here one notes the influences of Freud, Bataille, Lenormand, Verreuil, and Deval but very little of Shaw or Pirandello. Thus, the works still reflect a tendency toward realism with local and urban themes. In 1917, Francisco Imhof (1880–1937) premieres his most famous work, *Cantos rodados* (Fluent Cantos) (Teatro Solís, 1918). The fame derives from the daring, at that time, theme that bourgeois customs limit a woman's destiny by imposing arranged marriages. This work presents the union of an old man and a young woman, highlighting the immorality of such a union and the encouragement of the family. Relief comes in the guise of the bridegroom who refuses to marry. Another author concerned with the woman's situation is Carlos Salvaño Campos (1898–1955). His most highly acclaimed work, *La salamandra* (The Salamander) (Teatro Artigas, 1925), addresses the desire and the rights of women to have children. In *Don Juan derrotado* (The Defeated Don Juan) (Teatro 18 de Julio 1927) Campos shows that the generosity and strength of a woman's love are enough to save man. The defense of a woman's right to desire and search for love not found at home is the central theme of *La mujer solitaria* (The Solitary Woman) (Teatro Albéniz, 1928). Therefore, the theater of Salvaño Campos has a psychological bent and is especially concerned with moral issues in fighting for the emancipation of women.

Education enters the theater as a theme as well, thanks to José Pedro Bellán (1889–1930), following the realism trend. The themes of Bellán's works revolve around the relationships between parents and children of the urban middle class. In all of his works one perceives great human warmth, compassion, and tenderness. However, Bellán never fails to include the traditions, hypocrisy, false virtue, and injustices that vilify the human condition. In *Dios te salve* (God Save You) (Buenos Aires: Teatro Liceo, 1920), his most successful work, the lack of education appears to be the reason why the woman sacrifices herself in silence in order to keep the family together under the despotic rule of the husband.

Without education, she is unable to find an escape from the prison of her home. In *El centinela muerto* (The Dead Sentry) (1929), Bellán presents the failure of a father in not educating himself about liberty, which leads to his obsession in applying rigorous moral canons, creating only fear. Carlos María Princivalle (1887–1959) and Justino Zavala Muñiz (1898–1968) continue developing the nativist trend as well as themes of the country. Princivalle's *El higuerón* (The Fig Tree) (Teatro Artigas, 1924) deals with a problem that afflicts Uruguay even today: latifundium. His piece recounts the efforts of the son of a deceased landowner who arrives with numerous plans and innovations for the large estate and a great number of cattle. His methods fail on the estate, and likewise in his life, as he commits suicide. Princivalle's individualist and subjective solution invalidates the objective reality proposed by the work. However, the thesis is also valid in that it advocates the rational exploitation of the land by dividing the latifundium while giving testimony to a regrettably repeated and failed national attempt. Nevertheless, the most important aspect of the work lies in the realism of the setting and the characters. The veritable gallery of characters include the peasants in their moral and material stagnation; the astute and powerful laborer who, like the fig tree, *higuerón*, that devours neighboring plants, devours adjoining lands, making himself the owner with all the rights and social privileges therein; and the eternal commissioner of the Uruguayan narrative and theater, distant relative to *Martin Fierro*, the abuser of power and authority, with small-scale thieves, who looks the other way when dealing with anyone of wealth or position, not daring to intervene. Other works by Princivalle are inferior, in fact, were never premiered. Angel Curotto (1902–   ) participated actively in the theatrical scene as author and director of theatrical companies in Montevideo as well as in Buenos Aires. With a repertoire of hundreds of works, Curotto is typical of authors writing for commercial theater, especially that of Buenos Aires, where entertainment in the form of laughing theater and musical comedy of limited serious value are the norm in order to attract the greatest number of viewers. This shallowness is also apparent in the theater of Carlos César Lenzi (1899–1963) and Orlando Aldama (1904–1987) in spite of their artistic capacity that would seem to predict successful serious works.

THE NATIONAL THEATER (1947–1973)

The year 1947 is commonly accepted as the year in which the Uruguayan theater truly begins. This is due to internal and external factors. On an international level, World War II is coming to an end, but the postwar conflicts are already being felt. The world is still shaken by the impact of atomic bombs in Japan and witnesses for the first time the ideological division of nations. It is a period of profound moral, philosophical, ideological, and psychological crisis, producing anguish, fear, uncertainty, and spiritual unrest. It is also a period of political, philosophical, and artistic essays aligning themselves with Marxist and materialistic doctrines. The literary movements of this time in which Uruguay participates show a tendency toward universal human problems, following mainstream European and North American literature. In the works, anguish and loneliness reign supreme, revealing a growing interest in characters of humble origin, those marginalized and forgotten, and the denouncement of the social injustice they suffer. In the River Plate region, the regime of Juan Domingo Perón puts into practice protectionist politics, which obstruct the work of Uruguayans in Argentina by forbidding travel and creating a barrier between two countries formerly considered almost as one. Owing to these international and regional effects, the Uruguayan intellectual eliminates his dependency on Argentina, an immediate and rigorous analysis of his country up to this point hidden by the facade of the Switzerland of America. There are attempts to create a *new* culture of its own, a product of national and Latin American roots. In theater, one might add the creation of a national theater, comedia nacional, and the grouping of independent theaters under a single federation to the various social and political changes taking place. This attracts many excellent directors and actors, who put into action a prolific trend of an increasingly demanding public. In this way, Uruguay ceases to be a mere cultural consumer dependent on Argentina and evolves into a producer. For this task, realism presents itself as an adequate form in the production of a national theater, although other trends surface from time to time without ever predominating.

There are many playwrights belonging to this period, but only those who labored continuously were selected in chronological order to develop a clear profile of the author and his importance to the theater of Uruguay. Carlos Denis Molina (1916–1983) emerges as a promising talent in the vanguardist theater, greatly influenced by themes of the Spanish playwright Calderón, involving reality and fantasy. These characteristics are apparent in *La niña y el espantapájaros* (The Little Girl and the Scarecrow) (Teatro YMCA, 1944), *El regreso de Ulises* (The Return of Ulises) (Teatro del Sodre, 1948), *Orfeo* (Teatro Solís, 1951), and *Morir, tal vez soñar* (To Die, Perhaps to Dream) (Teatro Solís, 1953). However, his theater offers such a variety of styles that his later works appear superficial, which dulls the brilliance of his initial efforts and the praise of the critics and public. Juan León Bengoa (1897–1973) achieves great success through historical dramas such as *La espada desnuda* (The Naked Sword) (Teatro Solís, 1949) and *La patria en armas* (The Homeland in Arms) (Teatro Solís, 1950), describing José Gervasio Artigas, the national hero. These two works are superior due to the development of the main protagonist as well as the intelligent distribution of supporting characters. There is no sense of an epic or tragic drama but rather a historical drama of intense realism, resulting in a well-developed preparation and profound knowledge of the main character.

Andrés Castillo is one of the most important names in Uruguayan theater during this period of national development. Jacobo Langsner (1927–), a playwright of European descent bound to the theatrical life of the area, brings his best works to the national theater. Some of his works are: *El juego de Ifigenia* (Ifigenia's Game) (Teatro Solís, 1952), a contemporary Atridas myth; *Los artistas* (The Artists) (Club de Teatro, 1954), covering street life; and *Los elegidos* (The Elected Ones) (Teatro La Máscara, 1958), dealing with universal themes through novel recourses of imagination, tone, and dialogue. However, Langsner's greatest piece is *Esperando la carroza* (Waiting for the Carriage) (Teatro Sala Verdi, 1962), whereby the average Uruguayan family is superbly described using elements of the grotesque. By way of a banal dialogue that at the same time is satirical, sharp, and macabre, Langsner reveals the misery of the characters, skillfully presenting conflicts. Juan Carlos Patrón is the well-rounded intellectual and dedicated man of theater, and Carlos Maggi (1922–) writes within the theater of the Absurd, adding personal touches of his own.

Angel Rama (1926–1983) and Mario Benedetti (1920–) deserve mention, although their fame does not come from theatrical production and their dramatic experience is brief but very important. In *La inundación* (The Flood) (Teatro Sala Verdi, 1958) Rama creates an oppressive atmosphere for his characters, which allows for a brilliant dialectical and ideological game. The somber world of the clergy is presented in *Lucrecia Frangimani* (Teatro Solís, 1959), in which the author describes the anguish of a world without God. In *Queridos amigos* (Dear Friends) (Teatro Sala Verdi, 1961), Rama enters a Dantesque hell of lechery adapted to the national reality in an analysis of the middle class. In 1958, Benedetti achieves his first entry into the theater with *Ida y vuelta* (Departure and Return) (Teatro Sala Verdi). The monologue continues the theme of the mediocre middle class present in his narrative and is laden with humor, ridicule, and criticism. However, this first piece does not equal Benedetti's success in other genres. It is not until 1979 that the author's highly developed dramatic talent is discovered with the premiere, outside of Uruguay, of *Pedro y el capitán* (Peter and the Captain), a piece centered around the tense and anguished dialogue between a prisoner and his torturer.

Mauricio Rosencof (1933–), the most important contemporary playwright, is highly intuitive, expressing the act of living life itself and, unlike Conteris, keeping a distance from *literary* tendencies. Another prolific man of the theater is Juan Carlos Legido (1923–), whose literary development is dedicated to all literary genres. Despite such an intense life, Legido has the opportunity to create personally, as *La lámpara* (The Lamp) (Teatro El Tinglado, 1953) indicates. In this piece he presents the painful themes of uprooting and evasion. Many of his themes tended to follow national themes through characters, settings, and recognizable local conflicts. *Dos en el tejado* (Two on the Roof) (Club de Teatro, 1957) and *La piel de otros* (The Skin of Others) (Casa del Teatro, 1958) are the first examples of his new orientation and variations on the theme of the individual's responsibility toward society. In *Veraneo* (Summer Holiday) (Teatro Sala Verdi, 1961), Legido evokes the nostalgia of Montevideo in the 1930s, whereas *Los cuatro perros* (The Four Dogs) (Teatro La Máscara, 1964) is an intimist comedy. *El tranvía* (The Tram) (Teatro Moderno, 1965) deals with life in a small town of the interior wherein the life of a street-car worker is shown as totally dominated by the rise and fall of this means of transportation.

DICTATORSHIP TO PRESENT (1973–PRESENT)

The theater, like other forms of cultural expression, suffers terribly during the Rightist civic-military dictatorship gripping the country from 1973 to 1985. The most devastating effects include theaters closed by decree; theater companies dissolved by decree; the exile or imprisonment of playwrights, directors, actors, and technicians; and the rigid censure of thematic content. Nevertheless, the foundation of the national theater is not affected by these attacks. It is quite possible that the regime's decrees account for the notorious increase in the interest and support of the public for the national theater. This would explain the tremendous enthusiasm generated by certain works. Thus survives the theater in Uruguay until 1985, when democracy is reinstated. The playwrights of most note during this latest period are none other than those continuing their writing: Mauricio Rosencof, Carlos Maggi, Andrés Castillo, Alberto Paredes, and Carlos Manuel Varela. In spite of the tremendous political and economic crisis across the country, the theater begins to grow in cities of the interior. Already in 1985, forty-seven casts ascribe to the Movimiento teatrista del Interior, and several meetings and festivals take place far from the capital, allowing the presentation of the works of national playwrights. However, the success of these decades is too recent in nature, and owing to the paralyzing effects of the dictatorship, the analysis of the works has been delayed. More time is needed to discover and interpret the recent trends of the new generations. Nevertheless, one may anticipate a certain disdain for classical theater in favor of improvisation, collective theater, or a theater subordinated to music and bodily expression.

BIBLIOGRAPHY

Bianchi, Edmundo. "*Orgullo de pobre.*" *La escena* 110 (1920). Entire volume dedicated to this play.

Caillara, Domingo A. *Historia de la literatura gauchesca en el Uruguay.* Montevideo: C. García Editores, 1945.

Cione, Otto Miguel. "*Antes del drama.*" *Bambalinas* 188 (1921). Entire volume dedicated to this play.

Dauster, Frank N. *Perfil generacional del teatro hispanoamericano (1894–1924): Chile, México, El Río de la Plata.* Ottawa: Girol Books, 1993.

Dibarboure, Alberto. *Proceso del teatro uruguayo.* Montevideo: Editorial Claudio García, 1940.

Foster, David William. "Una aproximación a la escritura de *Ida y vuelta* de Mario Benedetti." *Hispamerica* 19 (1978): 13–25.

Freccero, Jorge Luis. "El teatro en el Uruguay." *Escritura* 12 (January–December 1987): 23–24.

Giraldi dei Cas, Norah. "Lo nacional en el resurgimiento del teatro uruguayo: 1980–1984." *Río de la Plata* 3 (1986): 121–136.

Kubhne, Alyce de. "Influencias de Pirandello y de Brechet en Mario Benedetti." *Hispania* 51 (1968): 408–415.

Legido, Juan Carlos. "Cincuenta años de teatro en Uruguay." *Revista Iberoamericana* 160–161 (July–December 1992): 841–851.

———. *El mundo del espectáculo. Enciclopedia uruguaya 52.* Montevideo: Arca, 1969.

———. *El teatro uruguayo. De Juan Moreira a los independientes 1886–1967.* Montevideo: Ediciones Tauro, 1968.

Martínez Moreno, Carolos. "*Ida y vuelta* de Mario Benedetti." *Marcha* (July 25, 1958): 17.

Mirza, Roger. "Uruguay 1998: Una intensa temporada o ante el espejo de Latinoamérica." *Gestos* 4–8 (November 1989): 165–168.

Morello-Frosch, Marta. "El diáglo de la violencia en *Pedro y el capitan* de Mario Benedetti. *Anthropos* 132 (May 1992): 79–81.

Ordaz, Luis. *El teatro en el Río de la Plata.* Buenos Aires: Futuro, 1946.

Pelletteri, Osvaldo. "*El patio de la torcaza*: Cambio y productividad en el realismo reflexivo de los sesenta en el Río de la Plata." *Latin American Theatre Review* 25.1 (Fall 1991): 51–61.

Pignataro, Jorge. *La aventura del teatro independiente uruguayo: crónica de seis décadas.* Montevideo: Cal y Canto, 1997.

———. *Diccionario del teatro uruguayo.* Montevideo: Cal y Canto, 2001.

———. *El teatro independiente uruguayo.* Montevideo: Arca, 1968.

Rela, Walter. *Diccionario de autores teatrales uruguayos.* Montevideo: Proyección, 1988.

―――. *Historia del teatro uruguayo 1808–1968*. Montevideo: Ediciones de la Banda Oriental, 1969.

―――. *Repertorio bibliográfico del teatro uruguayo 1816–1964*. Montevideo: Editorial Síntesis, 1965.

―――. *Teatro uruguayo, 1807–1979*. Montevideo: Ediciones de la Alianza, 1980.

―――. *Teatro uruguayo, 1808–1994: historia*. Montevideo: Academia Uruguaya de Letras, 1994.

Sansone de Martínez, Eneida. *El teatro de el Uruguay en el siglo XIX: historia de una pasión avasallante*. Montevideo: Editorial Surcos, 1995.

Scosería, Cyro. *Panorama del teatro completo*. Montevideo: Agadú, 1963.

"Uruguay." *Escenarios de dos mundos: inventario teatral de Iberoamérica*. Madrid: Centro de Documentación Teatral, 1988, vol. 4, 168–227. Articles by scholars.

◆

CASTILLO, Andrés (1920–   ). As a lawyer, playwright, narrator, and actor, his activity in the theater surpassed his contribution as a playwright. He founded the Teatro Universitario and was one of the initiators of the Federación de Teatros Independientes, for which he also served as a lawyer. He has published short stories and has become renowned as promoter of discussion sessions and theater competitions and has often been a delegate at theater conventions. For this constant dedication to the theater, in 1987 he was given the Florencio Cyro Scosería award by the Asociación Internacional de Críticos Teatrales, an affiliate of UNESCO. As a scriptwriter he received the *Premio Universidad de la República* in 1953 during the Festival de Cine Nacional of SODRE (Servicio Oficial de Difusion Radiotelevisión y Espectáculos) for his work *Cantegriles*. His work as a playwright took flight in 1950, and since then, he has seen twenty-five of his works on stage, ranging from original works to adaptations.

Montevideo, a city he loves deeply, is the common theme in all of his works. As a playwright, Castillo does insert himself in the current literary trend of realism because his works portray different aspects of Montevidean reality. Nonetheless, his realism also fits within the theater of denouncement upon not limiting himself to mere presentation but rather going far beyond. His works uncover original and authentic facets of the daily concerns of Montevidean inhabitants. Among the most treated themes in Castillo's work are: juvenile delinquency, as in *La cantera* and *La jaula*; social injustice suffered by the poor, *La noche* and *La bahía*; the degeneration of sports into utilitarianism, as in *Cinco goles*; and interest in the culture and traditions of the Black race in Uruguay, presented in *El negrito del pastoreo* as exclusive author with the Teatro Negro Independiente (Independent Black Theatre). It is evident that lately Castillo has shown a tendency to avoid realism in search of a combination of the grotesque and the farcical in order to more adequately express Uruguayan reality.

WORKS: *La cantera* (The Quarry) (Teatro Universitario, 1957). *Parrillada* (The Grill) (Teatro del Pueblo, 1958). *La noche* (The Night) (Teatro La Farsa, 1959). *La bahía* (The Bay) (Teatro La Farsa, 1960). *Cinco goles* (Five Goals) (Teatro Universitario, 1963). *La jaula* (The Cage) (Teatro Popular Uruguayo, 1963). *No somos nada* (We Are Nothing) (Teatro El Tinglado, 1966). *El negrito del pastoreo* (The Little Black Boy of the Shepherding) (Teatro Negro Independiente, 1969). *La reja* (The Bars) (1972). *Nostalgeses* (1986).

BIBLIOGRAPHY: Laura Escalante, ed., *50 años de teatro uruguayo. Antología II*. (Montevideo: Ministerio de Educación y Cultura, 1990). Walter Rela, *Diccionario de autores teatrales uruguayos* (Montevideo: Proyección, 1988). Rela, *Teatro uruguayo. 1807–1979* (Montevideo: Ediciones de la Alianza, 1980).

COMEDIA NACIONAL. Comedia Nacional was founded in 1947 as a culmination of crises due to the lack of artistic quality observed in the Montevidean houses controlled by commercial enterprises. To this one might add the desire of national authors to premiere their works. The combination of these factors in the mind of Justino Zavala Muñiz led to the formation of a company of actors, directors, stagehands, all of professional character and dedicated to the idea of creating a better theater for the public of their country. Considering the lack of material in terms of the integral forming of actors, and aware of the need to renew and or replenish the cast, in 1949 the School of Dramatic Arts was created.

This fundamental and defining experience is based on various components such as the artistic merit of its cast; the influence of excellent beginning directors (Margarita Xirgú, Calderón de la Barca, Orestes Caviglia, Josefina Díaz, José Estruch, Antonio Larreta, Concepción Zorrilla, Rubén Yáñez) and later directors (Alberto Candeau, Dumas Lorena, Carlos Denis, Eduardo Schinca, Jaime Yavitz, Elena Zuasti, Enrique Guarnero, Sergio Otermín, Alberto Restuccia, Federico Wolff, Nelly Goitiño, and Laura Escalante); the selectivity in the repertoire for universal and national theater; and the stage directors (Carlos Carvalho, Hugo Mazza, Osvaldo Reyno, José Echave, Adolfo Halty, Enrique Lázaro, Carlos Puig Vázquez, Carlos Pirelli, and Claudio Goeckler). The success of the Comedia Nacional has not limited itself to Uruguay but rather has enjoyed international recognition on stages in Argentina, Chile, Brazil, and Spain as well as in Paris and Rome.

BIBLIOGRAPHY: Walter Rela, *Diccionario de autores teatrales uruguayos* (Montevideo: Proyección, 1988). Rela, *Historia del teatro uruguayo 1808–1968* (Montevideo: Ediciones de la Banda Oriental, 1969). Rela, *Teatro uruguayo. 1807–1979* (Montevideo: Ediciones de la Alianza, 1980).

CONTERIS, Hiber (1933–). Although Conteris participates in all literary genres, his repertoire includes a good number of noteworthy dramatic pieces. In 1959, Conteris initiated his theatrical career with *Enterrar a los muertos* (Bury the Dead), a biblical title for his parable on the passage of adolescence to youth. *Este otro lado del telón* (This Other Side of the Curtain) presents the challenges a playwright encounters upon facing the public, criticism, actors, and the director, using a highly expressionist technique. However, the works that undoubtedly confirm the success of Conteris on stage are *El socavón* (The Cave) and *El desvío* (The Deviation). In the first work, the author imprisons several characters inside a caved-in mine, allowing the ideologically opposed characters, four miners and one priest, to discuss transcendental problems such as life, death, the human condition, and social justice. Conteris's second work, *El desvío*, deals with life's coincidences over which one has no control, causing a deviation from a perceived *correct* path. All in all, Conteris's theater is one of ideas, tending toward the literary, not the spectacle. This reveals a certain underdevelopment in terms of technical aspects and theatrical language in spite of an excellent literary talent dedicated to the projection of ideas.

WORKS: *Enterrar a los muertos* (Bury the Dead) (Teatro La Máscara, 1959). *Este otro lado del telón* (This Other Side of the Curtain) (Teatro La Farsa, 1960). *El desvío* (The Deviation) (Teatro Sala Verdi, 1963). *El socavón* (The Cave) (Teatro Sala Verdi, 1963).

BIBLIOGRAPHY: Orlando Gómez Gil, *Historia crítica de la literatura hispanoamericana* (New York: Holt, Rinehart and Winston, 1968).

DÍAZ, Antonio (1831–1911). Díaz was a Romantic playwright who composed works based on historical incidents, patriotism, and comedic *costumbristas*.

WORKS: *La corona de espinas* (The Crown of Thorns) (Teatro Solís, 1858). *Los hijos de la libertad* (Freedom's Sons) (Teatro Solís, 1860). *El capitán Albornoz* (Captain Albornoz) (Teatro San Felipe, 1860). *Los treinta y tres orientales libertadores* (The Thirty-three Oriental Liberators (1862). *El primer grito nacional* (The First National Yell) (Teatro San Felipe, 1864).

BIBLIOGRAPHY: Orlando Gómez Gil, *Historia crítica de la literatura hispanoamericana* (New York: Holt, Rinehart and Winston, 1968).

GORDON, Eduardo (1835–1875). This author develops the *costumbrista* genre through the amusement and charm of the language, characters, feelings, morality, and lifestyle of

456 ENCYCLOPEDIA OF LATIN AMERICAN THEATER

the Montevidean society of his time. His best-known piece is *Desengaños de la vida* (Life's Disillusions) (1858), although his other works show an extensive and varied repertoire of themes.

WORKS: *Desengaños de la vida* (Life's Disillusions) (1858). *Amor, esperanza y fe* (Love, Hope, and Faith) (Teatro Solís, 1859). *Deudas sagradas* (Sacred Debts) (Teatro Solís, 1860). *La fe del alma* (Faith of the Soul) (Teatro San Felipe, 1866).

BIBLIOGRAPHY: Orlando Gómez Gil, *Historia crítica de la literatura hispanoamericana* (New York: Holt, Rinehart and Winston, 1968).

HERRERA, Ernesto (Montevideo, 1889–1917). The parallels between this playwright and Florencio Sánchez are surprising. Both grew up in the interior area of Uruguay. Both were self-taught, led bohemian lifestyles, and died of tuberculosis. Both showed exceptional talent for the theater, dedicated to the trend of realism, a vigorous force in the River Plate region. Both were influenced by Russian novelists and theorists due to their great loyalty to *los desposeídos* and their sensitivity to social justice. Nevertheless, differences between the two artists do exist. Sánchez's theatrical instinct is more developed. His success was profound and shook both sides of the River Plate and later all of Latin America. His works were read in the best theaters, with the best casts and the best actors. Posterity has treated Sánchez very well, as countless commentators, critics, biographers, historians, and journalists analyze, comment, and study his life and his work. Furthermore, his pieces have continued to be performed in the River Plate region throughout the twentieth century.

On the contrary, the theater of Herrera is Uruguayan. The fewer number of works produced, only eight pieces and one sketch, dealt exclusively with the problems, surroundings, types, and passions of Uruguay. Sánchez's theater, however, shows a strong River Plate tone. Thus, Herrera has been able to enjoy success by Sánchez's side. Herrera's theater lacks stylistic embellishments, presenting and analyzing conflicts stripped of adornment. The vigorous dramatic feeling of the author and the deep technical knowledge of the modern theater come together to capture the psychology of characters, often surpassing Sánchez. Herrera himself recognized the pressing need for a national theater written as a function of the problems and idiosyncrasies of the Uruguayan people. Within this framework, which harmonized perfectly with the postulates of realism—naturalism—Herrera's works can be categorized thematically as rural or urban. The works treating rural themes are *El estanque, Mala laya, El león ciego*, and *El caballo del comisario*. Those of urban topics include *La moral de Misia Paca, El pan nuestro*, and *La bella Pinguito*.

WORKS: *El estanque* (The Pond) (Teatro Coliseo Florida, 1910). *Mala laya* (Bad Kind) Teatro Nacional, 1911). *El león ciego* (The Blind Lion) (Teatro Cibils, 1911). *La moral de Misia Paca* (The Moral of Missis Paca) (Teatro Melo, 1911). *El pan nuestro* (Our Bread) (Teatro 18 de Julio, 1914). *El caballo del comisario* (The Horse of the Commissioner) (Teatro Politeama, 1915). *La bella Pinguito* (The Beautiful Pinguito) (Teatro Mercedes, 1916).

BIBLIOGRAPHY: Carmelo Bonet, *El teatro de Ernesto Herrera* (Buenos Aires: Instituto de Literatura Argentina, 1925). Orlando Gómez Gil, *Historia crítica de la literatura hispanoamericana* (New York: Holt, Rinehart and Winston, 1968), 383–385. Ernesto Herrera, *El teatro uruguayo de Ernesto Herrera* (Montevideo: Editorial Renacimiento, 1917). Walter Rela, *Ernesto Herrera* (Montevideo: Revista Biblioteca Nacional No. 1, 1966).

INDEPENDENT THEATERS. Since the creation of the Teatro del Pueblo in 1937, sixteen additional independent troupes have developed in Montevideo, not counting those that were somewhat short-lived, and eight of those have their own theaters. El Galpón, Club de Teatro, Teatro Libre, Teatro Moderno, Teatro Universitario, Teatro Circular, La Máscara, Tinglado, Odeón, Teatro de la Ciudad de Montevideo, Teatro Universal, Teatro Palacio Salvo, and Teatro de los Talleres are the most famous. The objectives of these groups are the rejection of commercial influence on the actor and the autonomy to select the repertoire, placing more emphasis on quality than ticket sales.

The independent theater is one of the most

admirable and colorful events because each of the theaters came about as a result of the work of the cast and crew, painting, nailing, erecting sets between spectacles. These actors, with no experience, no directors, no technicians, where all was left to improvisation, timidly begin presenting a play by Casona and end up with *Los hermanos Karamazov*. These independent theaters grouped under one federation (FUTI)—Federación Uruguaya de Teatros Independientes to gain support for keeping the various theaters aligned with the ideology dedicated to the problems of the country and contemporary times. This was also done in order to avoid becoming an isolated phenomenon of a society from which it feeds and that it serves.

Among the most impressive directors of the teatro independiente are: Antonio Larreta, Atahualpa del Cioppo, Ruben Yáñez, Roberto Fontana, José Estruch, Juan José Brenta, Atilio J. Costa, Hugo Massa, Federico Wolff, Alfredo de la Peña, Rubén Castillo, Laura Escalante, Omar Grasso, César Campodónico, Ugo Ulive, Sergio Oterman, Mario Morgan, César Charlone Ortega, José Sclavo, and María E. Pons de Mendizábal.

The actors and actresses of most note in these theaters include: Juan Carlos Carraco, Dadh Sfeir, Blas Braidot, Juan Gentile, Carmen Avila, Graciela Gelos, Nelly Goitiño, Beatriz Massons, Claudio Solari, Juan Ribero, Mario Branda, Leonor Alvarez Morteo, Rubén González Santurio, Eduardo Freda, Angelita Parodi, Vilanueva Cosse, Juan Manuel Tenuta, Júver Salcedo, Rodolfo Campochiaro, Adela Gleiger, Gustavo Castro, Armando Halty, Jorge Denevi, Susana Vásquez, Mary Vásquez, Nidia Telles, Adhemar Rubbo, Luis Bernel, Marta Castellanos, Sara Larocca, Rosita Baffico, Mario Galup, Marta Oreggia, and Yamandú Solari. The value of this group and the many other names comprising it transcends their performance in the theater. These are actors who do not aspire for international recognition, nor do they expect recognition outside of Uruguay; instead, they are working in their country rather than seeking adventure in markets that are broader and better promoted.

BIBLIOGRAPHY: Walter Rela, *Diccionario de autores teatrales uruguayos* (Montevideo: Proyección, 1988). Rela, *Historia del teatro uruguayo 1808–1968* (Montevideo: Ediciones de la Banda Oriental, 1969). Rela, *Teatro uruguayo. 1807–1979* (Montevideo: Ediciones de la Alianza, 1980).

LARRETA, Antonio (1922–   ). The name Antonio Larreta is associated exclusively with the theater for his constant participation as actor, director, critic, and creator. His talent as a playwright surfaces in *La sonrisa* (The Smile), a brief study of the middle class, highly original among the works of the same period. In 1954, *Oficio de tinieblas* premiered, emphasizing the solidarity of mankind in the presence of oppression, pain, anguish, and death. This work is undoubtedly an excellent example of a well-matured *literary* theater of ideas. His next work is somewhat of a surprise to the public: a comedy of customs, *Un enredo y un marqués*, set in Uruguay's colonial period. Nevertheless, it is obvious by the amount of time Larreta dedicates to acting, directing, and founding theater companies that he is more interested in developing these than his role as playwright.

WORKS: *La sonrisa* (The Smile) (Teatro Solís, 1950). *Oficio de tinieblas* (Work of Doom) (Teatro Solís, 1954). *Un enredo y un marqués* (The Embroilment and the Marquis) (Teatro Ciudad de Montevideo, 1963).

BIBLIOGRAPHY: Juan Carlos Legido, *El teatro uruguayo. De Juan Moreira a los independientes 1886–1967* (Montevideo: Ediciones Tauro, 1968).

MAGGI, Carlos (1922–   ). Maggi is a lawyer, journalist, essayist, playwright, narrator, humorist, and movie producer. As a narrator, he has published *Cuentos de humor amor* (Stories of Love Humor) (1967) and *Invención de Montevideo* (Montevideo's Invention) (1968). His articles on customs have been collected in the volumes *Polvo enamorado* (Enamored Dust) (1951), *El Uruguay y su gente* (Uruguay and Its People) (1963), *Gardel, Onetti y algo más* (Gardel, Onetti and Something More) (1964), and *Los militares, la televisión y otras razones de uso interno* (1986). He is considered one of the most important contemporary playwrights of Uruguay. The originality of Maggi's theater rests on the constant search for innovative forms, resulting in some unconventional findings. The dominant trait is intellectualism to which is added vivid imagination, cruelty, the grotesque, and elements of the baroque as well as expressionism. All of these descriptors could be taken as evidence of the intent to avoid traditional canons of realism.

WORKS: *La trastienda* (The Back Room) (Teatro Verdi, 1958). *La biblioteca* (The Library) (Teatro del Pueblo, 1959). *La noche de los angeles inciertos* (The Night of Uncertain Angels) (Teatro del Pueblo, 1960). *La gran viuda* (The Great Widow) (Teatro Solís, 1961). *El apuntador* (The Prompter) (1963). *El pianista y el amor libre* (The Pianist and the Free Love) (Teatro Libre, 1965). After a long period of silence during the dictatorship, *Frutos* (Teatro Circular) was produced in 1985, and a new version of *El patio de la torcaza* (The Patio of the Ringdove) (Teatro El Galpón, 1967) was presented in 1986. Both works were awarded the Premio Florencio for the best national author in 1985 and 1986, respectively.

BIBLIOGRAPHY: Mario Benedetti, "Carlos Maggi y su meridiano de vida," *La palabra y el hombre* 615 (1968): 133–146. Juanamaría Cordones Cook, "Entrevista," *Latin American Theatre Review* (Spring 1987): 107–112. Osvaldo Pelletieri, "*El patio de la torcaza*: Cambio y productividad en el realismo reflexivo de los sesenta en el Río de la Plata," *Latin American Theatre Review* 24 (Fall 1991): 51–61. Louis H. Quackenbush, "Theatre of the Absurd, Reality, and Carlos Maggi," *Journal of Spanish Studies Twentieth Century* 3 (1975): 61–72.

PAREDES, Alberto (1939–). Paredes attended the El Galpón school of stage art and then studied at the Seminario de dramaturgia, whose focus is to promote the creative impulse through analysis of reality, experimentation, and discussion. The experience gave Paredes a starting point to later become the best example of dramatic authors in Uruguay today. To date, he is known for thirteen works. Paredes's theater is naturalist but imbued in the contemporary urban reality of Montevideo. This is manifested through the direct and colloquial language and constant inclusion of local, actual characters. Obviously, his theatrical creation tends to form very credible characters, not through his own style but rather through original themes. These, in turn, revolve around the reality and the identity of the Uruguayan.

WORKS: *Tan aburrido* (So Bored) (Teatro El Galpón, 1965). *Por hacerla de mentira* (Pretending to Lie) (Teatro del Pueblo, 1968). *Tres de última* (The Last Three) (Teatro Odeón, 1971). *Lo veremos triste y amargado* (We Will See Him Sad and Bitter) (Teatro del Centro, 1978). *Decir adiós* (Say Goodbye) (Teatro Circular, 1979). *Tres tristes tangos* (Three Sad Tangos) (Teatro Alianza Francesa, 1983). *Papá murió* (Dad Has Died) (Casa del Teatro, 1985). *La plaza de otoño* (The Autumn Plaza) (Teatro Alianza Francesa, 1985).

BIBLIOGRAPHY: Laura Escalante, ed., *50 años de teatro uruguayo. Antología I* (Montevideo: Ministerio de Educación y Cultura, 1990). Walter Rela, *Teatro uruguayo. 1807–1979* (Montevideo: Ediciones de la Alianza, 1980). Rela, *Diccionario de autores teatrales uruguayos* (Montevideo: Proyección, 1988).

PATRÓN, Juan Carlos (1905–1979). Patrón was a lawyer, journalist, playwright, songwriter, and scriptwriter. Blessed with a rich personality, Patrón developed his talents brilliantly in popular functions such as the carnival and the *tango*, in dramatic literature, in movie production, in which he was a pioneer, and in his professional responsibilities, which culminated in his serving as a dean in the College of Law at the University of the Republic. As a theatrical author, Patrón belongs to the Generación del Centenario, initiating himself in 1928 with the one-act play *Felicidad*, which was also awarded in the Concurso de la Sociedad Uruguaya de Autores. *Humanidad*, written in collaboration with César L. Gallardo, premiered in 1932, and *Cafetín del puerto*, written with Edmundo Bianchri, premiered in 1940. In 1944, Patrón received the Premio del Ministro de Instrucción Pública for *Compañera*, written in collaboration with Angel Curotto. But his greatest success was *Procesado 1040*, which was first presented in 1957 at the Teatro Solís to a record-breaking audience of 50,000. Later this work was filmed in Buenos Aires and translated into Russian. In 1985, *Procesado 1040* was presented again in the theater La Gaviota, and in 1963, *Almendras amargas* was shown by the Comedia Nacional, a work noted for brilliant and witty dialogue. In 1966, *El pasajero* premiered, and *Eran cinco hermanos* (1968) was written especially for the Teatro Experimental Penitenciario. His adaptation of *Compañera* for television garnered Patrón first place in a competition of national works for television. *La casa vacía* (1977) was awarded in a competition for radio theater works organized by a radio station from the Netherlands for Latin American playwrights and was selected by the Association of Authors of Uruguay to represent the National Theatre in the Certámen Iberoamericano de Obras Teatrales Juan Ruiz de Alarcón. In 1974, this work was also awarded by the Department of Education and Culture.

WORKS: *Felicidad* (Happiness) (Teatro Solís, 1928). *Procesado 1040* (Accused 1040) (Teatro Solís, 1957). *Almendras amargas* (Sour Almonds) (Teatro Sala Verdi, 1963). *El pasajero* (The Passanger) (Teatro Solís, 1966). *Eran cinco hermanos* (They Were Five Siblings) (Teatro Experimental Penitenciario, 1968). *La casa vacía* (The Empty House) (Teatro Solís, 1977).

BIBLIOGRAPHY: Laura Escalante, ed., *50 años de teatro uruguayo. Antología I.* (Montevideo: Ministerio de Educación y Cultura, 1990). Walter Rela, *Teatro uruguayo. 1807–1979* (Montevideo: Ediciones de la Alianza, 1980). Rela, *Diccionario de autores teatrales uruguayos* (Montevideo: Proyección, 1988).

PLAZA NOBLIA, Héctor (1924–). Plaza Noblia is one of the most frustrating Uruguayan playwrights owing to the thematic variety and aesthetic tendencies in his works that defy a clear profile. An inventory of his works would reveal the following: theater of realism, lyricism, Pirandellian influences, national and classical themes, monologues, one-act and three-act plays, and children's theater. The breadth of his work impedes great depth and development, although he is recognized as one of Uruguay's pioneer playwrights. Among his best received plays are *Los puros* (The Bold), a brash criticism of demagogues, and along the same lines of national themes and criticism, *Los jugadores* (The Players), dealing with large newspaper companies.

WORKS: *Ensayo N 4* (Play N 4) (Teatro El Galpón, 1953) (Pirandellian style). *Los puros* (Teatro El Galpón, 1953). *Cajita de música* (The Music Box) (Teatro La Máscara, 1954). *Alceste o la risa de Apollo* (Alceste or Apollo's Laugh) (1955). *Odiseo* (1955). *Los jugadores* (The Players) (Teatro El Galpón, 1957). *La enfermedad de Arlequín* (The Illness of Harlequin) (Teatro Taller, 1959).

BIBLIOGRAPHY: Orlando Gómez Gil, *Historia crítica de la literatura hispanoamericana* (New York: Holt, Rinehart and Winston, 1968).

ROSENCOF, Mauricio (1933–). Rosencof is a playwright, poet, and chronicler. After the death of Florencio Sánchez in 1910, the Uruguayan theater waited almost half a century for an innovative figure. This innovation came by way of Rosencof, who introduced significant changes in drama, guiding it away from the realism–naturalism tract. Rosencof was born in Florida, son of immigrant Jew parents, and moved to Montevideo, where he worked and attended night school. He found the Communist Youth Union, began his journalism career, and developed his acting in the 1950s. In 1961 he premiered at the Festival of River Plate Theatre in *El gran Tuleque*, a farcical piece that took on the popular theme of *la murga* for the first time. A year later, the Teatro del Pueblo presented *Las ranas*, a piece about life in a shantytown, which was also presented at the Latin American Theatre Festival in Cuba. In 1963 *Pensión familiar* premiered, a work that was rewritten and later presented as *La valija* in 1965 in Montevideo and at Patricio Lumumba University in Moscow. *La calesita rebelde*, for children's theater, premiered in Montevideo and later on in San Pablo, Buenos Aires, and in various cities in Italy. In 1966 Rosencof traveled to the northern part of the country and learned about the misery of the sugar cane workers. His efforts to change this unjust reality were captured in his plays such as *Los caballos*. In 1981 Rosencof published *Los caballos* in Montevideo and Spain, which premiered in Switzerland and Venezuela in 1982. Rosencof's involvement as leader of the Guerilla Movement for National Liberation Tupamaros led to his arrest and brutal torture in 1972. At the beginning of the coup d'état of 1973, Rosencof was declared a hostage of the dictatorship and remained imprisoned in subhuman conditions until his release in 1985. Nonetheless, during his thirteen years of imprisonment, his works were presented and reedited outside of the country, and Rosencof continued writing. The works of this period are *El combate en el establo, El saco de Antonio, Y nuestros caballos serán blancos, El gran bonete,* and *El hijo que espera.* In 1987 the first work written outside captivity appeared: *El regreso del gran Tuleque.* Rosencof now resides, for the most part, in Sweden.

With regard to other professional activities, it is important to mention that Rosencof founded the newspapers *El Popular* and *La Idea* and the magazine *Cuestión.* He contributes as editorialist to the Uruguayan weekly *Marcha, Brecha, Jaque, Asamblea,* and *Mate Amargo.* Furthermore, he is a member of the Editorial Board of the Spanish journal *Primer Acto.* He has participated in conferences in Latin America and Europe such as Segundo Encuentro de Intelectuales (Havana) and in the Congreso de Intelectuales (Lyón). He has lectured in the United States at Bates College, Bowdoin College, City University of New York, New York University, City College of New York, Columbia University, Tufts University, and Wellesley College, as well as in Spain, Sweden, and France.

One of the most salient characteristics of Rosencof's theater is the combination of reality/dream, dream/reality to the point that it is difficult to say which the work is based on. One notes a preference for marginalized settings from which situations of oppression are projected. In these, objects function as fetishes, as symbols of lost or desired paradises. Thus, the imagined stories seem believable by sheer force of repetition and the need to believe, and individual dreams become collective dreams. These forms of evasion and self-deceit ambush and sometimes conquer reason, a semblance of victory born of the need for survival even at the cost of insanity. In Rosencof's works, absolute victory or failure does not exist; rather, one notes a constant battle to better mankind. It should also be noted that the works cannot be categorized as before, during, and after his harsh prison experience. While certain elements are weighted toward the end, the themes and techniques are constant.

WORKS: *El gran Tuleque* (The Big Tuleque) (Teatro El Galpón, 1961). *Las ranas* (The Frogs) (Teatro del Pueblo, 1962). *Pensión familiar* (Family Boarding House) (Teatro del Pueblo, 1963). *La calesita rebelde* (The Rebellious Carousel) (1964). *La valija* (The Suit Case) (Teatro Facultad de Medicina, 1965). *Los caballos* (The Horses) (Teatro Odeón, 1967). *El combate en el establo* (The Combat in the Stable) (1985). *El saco de Antonio* (Antonio's Jacket) (1985). *Y nuestros caballos serán blancos* (And Our Horse Will Be White) (1985). *El gran bonete* (The Big Cap) (1986). *El hijo que espera* (The Child That Awaits) (1986). *El regreso del gran Tuleque* (The Return of the Big Tuleque) (1987).

BIBLIOGRAPHY: Maruja Echegoyen, Mercedes Ramírez, and Laura Oreggioni, "Liberty is . . . ," *Index on Censorship* 14.5 (October 1985): 48–50. Mauricio Rosencof, "La literatura del calabozo," in *Represión, exilio y democracia: La cultura uruguaya,* ed. Saul Sosnowsky (Montevideo: Banda Oriental, 1987), 127–140. Rosencof, *Teatro escogido I* (Montevideo: Tae, 1988). Rosencof, *Teatro escogido II* (Montevideo: Tae, 1990). Ugo Ulive, "Profile: Mauricio Rosencof," *Index on Censorship* 11.3 (June 1982): 36–38.

SÁNCHEZ, Florencio (1875–1910). Sánchez is the most important playwright of the River Plate theater. Self-taught and later a journalist, his numerous writings made him acquainted with the social and political ideologies of Europe and of his period, including literary realism and naturalism. The value of his theater lies primarily in that he abolished the sentimentalism of the tired *gauchesco* theater by concentrating on the human conflicts of the River Plate region. In this writing, these conflicts were current, profound, intense, and universal. The influence of naturalism is very strong in his works, resulting in a pessimistic tone. His works mirror the real human and social conflicts created by the transformed society of the end of the nineteenth century by the increases in population, immigration, industrialization, and the modernization of the rural economy. With regard to regional themes, Sánchez's works examine the conflicts that now surface between immigrants and *criollos*, poverty, sickness, and other topics affecting the human condition. Thus his works reveal a fresh combination of social, dramatic, and human reform. Sánchez does not advocate revolutionary social change in his work, even though he ascribed to the anarchy-socialist party line, but rather suggests clearly the need to find a just social order in which tolerance and kindness prevail toward the humble, the poor, and victims of social injustice. And so his originality transformed the theater of the River Plate and defined the parameters of twentieth-century Latin American theater.

WORKS: *Puertas adentro* (Inside the Doors) (Teatro Centro 1897). *Gente honesta* (Honest People) (1902). *M'hijo el dotor* (My Son the Doctor) (Buenos Aires: Teatro La Comedia, 1903). *Canillita* (News Boy) (Buenos Aires: Teatro La Comedia, 1904). *Cédulas de San Juan* (Saint John's Documents) (Buenos Aires: Teatro La Comedia, 1904). *La gringa* (The Gringa) (Buenos Aires: Teatro San Martín, 1904). *Barranca abajo* (Down the Ravine) (Buenos Aires: Teatro Apolo, 1905). *Mano santa* (Saint Hand) (Buenos Aires: Teatro Apolo, 1905). *En familia* (In the Family) (Buenos Aires: Teatro Apolo, 1905). *Los muertos* (The Dead) (Buenos Aires: Teatro Apolo, 1905). *El desalojo* (The Eviction) (Buenos Aires: Teatro Apolo, 1906). *El pasado* (The Past) (Buenos Aires: Teatro Argentino, 1906). *Los curdas* (The Drunks) (Buenos Aires: Teatro Apolo, 1907). *La tigra* (The Tigra) (Buenos Aires: Teatro Argentino, 1907). *Moneda falsa* (False Coin) (Buenos Aires: Teatro Nacional, 1907). *La de anoche* (That One of Last Night) (1907). *Nuestros hijos* (Our Children) (Buenos Aires: Teatro Nacional, 1907). *Los derechos de la salud* (The Rights of the Health) (Teatro Solís, 1907). *Marta Gruni* (Teatro Politeama, 1908). *La pobre gente* (Poor People) (Buenos Aires: Teatro San Martín, 1909). *Un buen negocio* (A Good Deal) (Teatro Cibils, 1909).

BIBLIOGRAPHY: Dora Corti, *Florencio Sánchez* (Buenos Aires: Instituto de Literatura Argentina, 1937). Julio Durán-Cerda, "Otra valoración de Florencio Sánchez," *Confluencia* 1 (Fall 1985): 45–52. Fernando García Esteban, *Vida de Florencio Sánchez* (Santiago, Chile: Ercilla, 1939). Tabaré Freire, *Ubicación de Florencio Sánchez en la literatura dramática* (Montevideo: Departamento de Literatura Iberoamericana, 1959). Roberto Giusti, *Florencio Sánchez. Su vida y su obra* (Buenos Aires: Agencia Sud-Americana de Libros, 1920). Julio Imbert, *Florencio Sánchez. Vida y creación* (Buenos Aires: Schapire, 1954). Nora de Marral de McNair, "*Moneda falsa*: Una nueva perspectiva," in *Festschrift José Cid Pérez*, ed. Alberto Gutiérrez de la Solana and Elio Alba-Buffil (New York: Senda Nueva de Editores, 1981). Teresinha Pereira, "O Teatro de Florencio Sánchez ou *Barranca Abajo*," *Minas Gerais Suplemento Litérario* 15 (November 26, 1982): 9. Carlos María Princivalle, *Florencio Sánchez* (Montevideo: Comisión Nacional del Centenario, 1930). Carlos Roxlo, *Florencio Sánchez y Ernesto Herrera* (Montevideo: Editorial Vila, 1915).

THEATER COMPANIES. The theatrical activity in Uruguay follows three definite directions: the independent theater composed of amateurs, semiprofessionals, and experimental groups; the official theater represented by the Comedia Nacional (National Theatre) of professional character; and the commercial theater managed by business and theatrical producers. The activity of the first two maintains an aesthetic rigor extending from the repertoire selection to the stage setting, whereas the last group generally produces foreign works, comedies, vaudevilles, and frises, satisfying their audience.

VARELA, Carlos Manuel (1940–). Varela is a playwright, professor of literature, and faculty member of the Municipal School of Dramatic Art. Varela belongs to the last generation of Uruguayan theater characterized by a new critical and revisionist position of the past and present. His works are premiered in the predictatorship period as well as during the dictatorship. Thus, Varela and many like him could not communicate through their works in the old tradition. It was therefore necessary to change the style and resort to a *masked* language. As a result, his works reveal a *hallucinatory realism* coupled with great symbolism and a unique use of time and the relations between reality, play, imagination, and dreams. The spectators of Varela's works must exert the effort to compose the images in order to capture the hidden message and must construct their own text parallel to the one offered in the setting. However, there is nothing magical in this task, given that a code was already in place for this particular generation, with a common history capable of *unmasking* and reinterpreting like accomplices. This process of construction and deconstruction is what Varela terms theory of the *espejo fracturado*, fractured mirror. The return of democracy in Uruguay meant, to Varela, the restoration of the mirror. His theater continues experimenting with form and language without abandoning the same purposes: showing the conflicts of modern man, promoting spectator participation through imagination and reflection, and appealing to audience emotional involvement.

WORKS: *El juego tiene nombre* (The Game Has a Name) (Teatro La Máscara, 1968). *Happening* (Club de Teatro, 1969). *La enredadera* (The Climbing Plant) (Teatro Odeón, 1970). *Las gaviotas no beben petróleo* (The Seagulls Do Not Drink Oil) (Teatro Circular, 1979). *Alfonso y Clotilde* (Teatro de la Ciudad, 1980). *Cuentos sin final* (Short Stories without End) (Sala Verdi, 1980). *Palabras en la arena* (Words on the Sand) (1982). *Interrogatorio en Elsinor* (Interrogation in Elsinor) (Teatro Alianza Francesa, 1983). *Crónica de la espera* (Chronicle of the Wait) (Teatro del Notariado, 1986). *Sin un lugar* (Without a Place) (1986). *La esperanza S.A.* (The Hope, Inc.) (Teatro Comedia Nacional, 1989).

BIBLIOGRAPHY: Laura Escalante, ed., *50 años de teatro uruguayo. Antología I* (Montevideo: Ministerio de Educación y Cultura, 1990). Walter Rela, *Diccionario de autores teatrales uruguayos* (Montevideo: Proyección, 1988). Rela, *Teatro uruguayo. 1807–1979* (Montevideo: Ediciones de la Alianza, 1980).

ZAVALA MUÑIZ, Justino (1898–1968). A narrator, playwright, and historian, Zavala Muñiz was a valuable participant in the political and cultural life of Uruguay. He served as Representative, Minister of Education, and Counselor of State. As founder and first president of the National Theatre (1947), he also created the Municipal School of Dramatic Art as well as the Library and Archives of Theatre. He is considered one of the greatest Uruguayan writers of the twentieth century for his narrative works. Those of greatest importance are *Crónica de Muñíz* (1921), *Crónica de un crimen* (1926), and *Crónica de la reja* (1930). His plays represent the finest contribution to the Uruguayan theater of the 1930s and the 1940s, for his continued presentation of the country on stage. Keeping within the literary tenets of realism, Zavala Muñiz's plays are strongly united to the national, social, and rural themes. His rural treatment, however, lacks *costumbrista* elements and is primarily a means of communicating ideas. Misery, ignorance, poverty, and the impossibility of salvation for the country peasants are revealed as the greatest preoccupations of this playwright. And so, the country is presented under the new aesthetic of the philosophical unrest of contemporary thought. Therefore, his realism is not photographic but rather artistic, in which characters move, imbued with meaning and symbolic suggestions.

WORKS: *La cruz de los caminos* (The Cross of the Roads) (Teatro del Sodre, 1933). *En un rincón del Tacuari* (In a Corner of Tacuari) (Teatro Solís, 1938). *Alto alegre* (Buenos Aires: Teatro Marconi, 1940). *Fausto Garay, un caudillo* (Teatro del Sodre, 1942).

BIBLIOGRAPHY: Laura Escalante, ed., *50 años de teatro uruguayo. Antología II* (Montevideo: Ministerio de Educación y Cultura, 1990). Walter Rela, *Diccionario de autores teatrales uruguayos* (Montevideo: Proyección, 1988). Rela, *Teatro uruguayo. 1807–1979* (Montevideo: Ediciones de la Alianza, 1980).

Gloria da Cunha-Giabbai

Venezuela

EARLY PERIOD

Venezuela had vestiges of an early theater with pre-Hispanic roots, the remains of which are preserved today in its dances and popular theatrical representations. This folklore represents true national values in its fusion of the indigenous, African, and Hispanic cultures that produced the modern nation. Even so, the theater in general has always shown a marked preference for its European elements, putting aside the African and indigenous influences. However, these marginalized elements continue to reappear as national themes or models.

COLONIAL THEATER

The theater developed slowly during the colonial period, perhaps because of the lack of interest on the part of the Spanish colonizers to develop the area educationally and culturally, thus controlling the occurrence of political problems. However, the colonists themselves brought theatrical elements with them in the form of religious and secular celebrations. Despite only isolated reports of theatrical activity, the developing theater is evidenced by the protests from the clergy who tried to control it. The day of the Apostle Santiago, June 8, 1600, was the first recorded permit for a play, but city records also mention theater activities earlier to celebrate various religious holidays. The construction of permanent theaters in the latter part of the eighteenth century marked its continued development and popularity.

THE EIGHTEENTH CENTURY

The chronicles record various productions of plays by the famous playwrights of Spain's Golden Age. One example is the production of Calderón's *La vida es sueño* (Life Is a Dream) in 1759. It was also in this century, in 1766, that the first theater piece written in Venezuela appeared: the anonymous *Auto a nuestra Señora del Rosario* (Drama for Our Lady of the Rosary). It represented a wide mixture of cultural elements: classical, Hispanic, local Venezuelan, sacred, and profane elements. One of the allegorical characters represents the city of Caracas.

The first building specifically erected in the middle of the eighteenth century as a theater, La Rosa (The Rose), was located in La Guaira. The first theater in Caracas, El Coliseo (The Coliseum), also called Teatro del Conde (Theater of the Count) since it was located on the street by this name, was built in 1784. It was destroyed by an earthquake in 1812. In 1831 the Teatro del Coliseo was built and was followed by the Teatro Caracas in 1854 and by many others, since a chronicler indicated that between 1835 and 1898 as many as fifty theaters were established. Visitors to Venezuela in this period reported that the public was very unsophisticated and the quality of productions very low.

The earliest dramatists were a priest, José Cecilio de Avila, who wrote *La encarnación del hijo de Dios* (The Incarnation of the Son of God), and later Andrés Bello, with *Venezuela consolada* (Venezuela Consoled) (premiered in 1804 at the Teatro del Conde), called today a historical curiosity lacking in dramatic value. It is an homage, in predominantly neoclassic style, to the doctor Balmis who introduced the process of vaccination into Venezuela. His *España restaurada o El certamen de los patriotas* (Spain Restored or Test for Patriots) (1808), obviously defended the monarchy in the fight for independence. Other authors of the first part of the eighteenth century loosely classed as dramatists were José Montenegro with the satiric verse composition called *véjamen—Véjamen en el grado del doctor Salvador Delgado* (Verse Written on the Achievement of Dr. Salvador Delgado) (1801); and Vicente Salias, whose *La medicomaquia* was also marginally dramatic.

THE NINETEENTH CENTURY

The second half of the nineteenth century, the beginning of a series of dictators, saw the production of some 300 works. Among the writers are the names Domingo Navas Spínola, Gerónimo Pompa, Heraclio Martín de la Guardia (known for dramas and *zarzuelas* on exotic themes), Guillermo Michelena, Adolfo Briceño Picón, Vicente Micolao y Sierra (the most prolific and the first Venezuelan to be produced outside the country), José María Manrique (*El divorcio*) (The Divorce) (1885), José Antonio Arévalo, José María Reina, Nicanor Bolet Peraza, Vicente Fortoul, Eduardo Blanco, Aníbal Dominici (*La honra de la mujer*) (A Woman's Honor) (1880), Enrique Coronado, Felipe Esteves, Juan José Brecca (*El poder de un relicario* (The Power of an Antiques Dealer) (1878), Manuel A. Marín (*Al borde del abismo* (On the Edge of the Abyss) (1887), Agustín Garía Pompa, José Innacio Lares (with *El recluta* [The Recruit] he anticipates the later social realism), Margarita Agostini de Pimentel, Lina López de Aramburu, and Julia Añez Gabaldón. The most important centers for theater were Maracaibo and Caracas. Also popular were the opera and *zarzuela*. The National Theater was opened in January 1881.

Venezuelan drama continued to develop at the end of the nineteenth century with the appearance of Creolism, a recurrence to native Venezuelan themes, sometimes referred to as *teatro criollo* (Creole theater). Comedies were preferred over drama, lyric forms continued to be popular, and the *sainete* (a combination of comedy and satire with emphasis on political criticism) was the most popular type of play performed. It was particularly popular for the humorous improvisations often included by the actors. Dramatists of the end of the nineteenth and beginning of the twentieth centuries were Casti Ramón López, Elías Calixto Pompa (*Un duelo literario*) (A Literary Duel), (1879), Octavio Hernández, Eduardo Gallegos, Francisco Calcaño, Aniceto Valdivia, and Eliézer Petit. Two actors of this period who gained fame outside Venezuela were Guillermo Bolívar and Teófilo Leal.

THE TWENTIETH CENTURY

During the first thirty-five years of the century the theater progressed slowly because of the influence of the repressive dictatorships of Castro and de Gómez. After the death of

Gómez, the formation of several theater groups began to accelerate dramatic activity. These groups were the Teatro Obrero (Workers' Theater), the Sociedad Amigos del Teatro (Society of Friends of the Theater), the Teatro Universitario (University Theater), the Pro-Arte Infantil (Youth Art), and the Compañía Teatral del Obrero (Workers' Theater Company). Of importance in this period also was the Ateneo de Caracas, a group of intellectuals with the purpose to advance the arts in general. The establishment of prizes for Venezuelan works also added stimulation. This period saw the continuation of the creole theater, comprising generally plays centering on or documenting local customs, lacking more universal appeal and often qualified as superficial. These were comic monologues and radio plays that often made fun of and criticized the populace and its customs. A subtype of the *sainete* was the *apropósito*, a comic-satiric work of social criticism characterized by its timeliness and daring, often based on just-occurred events.

The period between 1940 and 1950 was one of dramatic change. As a result of political upheaval, the populace gained more power in the form of more voting privileges, direct elections, and rights to strike and to organize. The decade also saw the arrival of several foreign theater professionals who greatly influenced the Venezuelan theater. Through the Teatro del Liceo (Liceun Theater), Alberto de Paz y Mateos (Spain) influenced the development of many of the theatrical leaders of the next generation. Jesús Gómez Obregón (Mexico) arrived in Caracas to teach the Stanislavski method and provided training for many professionals who developed theater throughout the country. Juana Sujo (Argentina) was an actress of stage and screen who went to Venezuela for a film and stayed to found what became the Escuela Nacional de Teatro (National Theater School). Horacio Peterson (Chile), actor and theater technician, arrived in Venezuela to work on a specific play and remained to become director of the Teatro del Ateneo de Caracas, a pivotal institution in the development of the present-day Venezuelan theater. Francisco Petrone, a famous Argentine director, spent a short time in Caracas in the early 1950s with his touring company and had a profound influence through his innovative productions. These foreigners brought about the production of types of works new to Venezuela and revolutionized the theater scene. This influence culminated in what has been called the Theater of Universal Inspiration, anticipated in the early part of the century by Rómulo Gallegos.

TWENTIETH CENTURY: SECOND HALF

Beginning around 1960, Venezuelan drama underwent more significant changes, resulting from the end of the dictatorship of Pérez Jiménez in 1958 and the consequent development of social democratism and the petroleum boom. Anticipating development beyond the creole theater, César Rengifo was instrumental in establishing the group Máscaras (Masks) (1951–1961), of Marxist orientation, with a militant intent. The new dramatists who came forth in the new democratic political climate threw themselves into a search for new themes and theatrical forms. They were also familiar with the theories of Brecht, Artaud, Stanislavski, and the living theater. Experimental theater appeared; street theater and theater festivals thrived. The development of many theater groups (documented below), the support of the national government, and the leadership of Rengifo, Chocrón, Cabrujas, and Chalbaud have brought about a true theatrical renaissance begun by the earlier impetus of the foreign dramatic specialists mentioned earlier. The high level of theatrical activity has led to numerous national and international festivals of theater held in Venezuela, an important stimulus to continued theatrical production and innovation.

The first national festival, organized by the Ateneo de Caracas, was held in 1959. Represented there were examples of the directions taken in the Venezuelan theater during the previous thirty years: the creole theater, Theater of Universal Inspiration, transitions between the two, neoclassic drama, poetic-surrealist drama, social criticism based on the country's past history, satiric comedy, and romantic comedy. The second festival, held in 1961, showed a concentration on political themes, reflecting a newfound freedom of expression. The third festival, 1966–1967, presented works dealing with generational conflicts, social disorganization, a crisis in values, and aesthetic and political problems. Other national festivals took place in 1978, 1981, and 1983. In addition, several international festivals have been held in Caracas: in 1973, 1974, 1976, 1978, 1981, 1983, and 1988.

During the 1960s a movement called the Experimental Theater developed in Venezuela (precise dates mentioned are 1964 to the end of the decade). It is described by Monasterios as a product of the confluence of the worldwide theatrical currents of the twentieth century: the ideas of Grotowski, the Theater of the Absurd, the ideas of Artaud, the idea of the happening, the documentary theater, the style of Peter Weiss in his *Marat-Sade*. This included what Monasterios has labeled "El Teatro Lúdrico" (Theater of Game-Playing). *Tric-Trac* by Chocrón, *Fiésole* by Cabrujas, *Los ángeles terribles* (The Terrible Angels) by Chalbaud, and *Bang-Bang* by Núñez are examples of these new directions. These authors and others also made use of ritual actions in the form of games and other repetitive behavior as a way to make evident and to protest the violence and social injustice prevalent in many Latin American countries in recent history (for further information on this type of theater and its use, see the issues of the *Latin American Theatre Review*). This period was followed by one that included innovations from the experimental stage, incorporated into stagings of many more foreign and Venezuelan plays produced in a more commercially viable fashion, leading to the creation of a larger theatergoing public. Also in this period the nature of human sexuality and nudity on the stage was an issue, as in other parts of the theatrical world.

A popular theater has been developed, beginning in the 1970s, with the idea of providing theater accessible to the masses in locale and in cost. The Venezuelan government has been very active in this movement, establishing some organizations and supporting others begun privately. Outstanding among these groups is Rajatabla, which has an international reputation. In 1984 La Compañía Nacional de Teatro (National Theater Company) was founded, with Isaac Chocrón as the founding director, and 1989 saw the creation of Regional Companies.

Several playwrights appeared in the 1980s, among them talented women dramatists: Perla Vonasek, with *Ella cantaba boleros* (She Sang Boleros); Carlota Martínez, with *Que Dios la tenga en la gloria* (May God Have Her in Heaven); Inés Muñoz Aguirre, with *Estados circulares* (Circular States); Thais Erminy, with *La cárcel* (The Jail), who has also written *La tercera mujer* (The Third Woman) and *Whisky y cocaína*; Alicia Alamo Bartolomé, with *Juan de la noche* (Nighttime John); and Xiomara Moreno, with *Perlita blanca con sortija de señorita* (Little White Pearl in a Young Lady's Ring) (1988) and *Geranio* (1989). The director Javier Vidal's works *Novela romántica del aire* (Romantic Novel of the Air) and *La hora del lobo* (The Hour of the Wolf) were produced in 1989 and 1990. A 1990 publication by Fundación Rajatabla, *Teatro*, includes the playwrights Elio Palencia with *Camino a Kabasken* (On the Way to Kabasken); Rubén Darío Gil with *La dama del sol* (The Lady of the Sun); and Marco Purroy with *El desertor* (The Deserter). It is also useful to name some of the actors and directors who have made the current stage in Venezuela so vibrant: Ugo Ulive, Carlos Giménez, Antonio Costante, Kiddio España, Juan Carlos Gené, Armando Gota, Herman Lejter, Humberto Orsini, Gustavo Tambascio, José Simón Escalona, and Javier Vidal; and actresses, Julie Restifo, Elba Escobar, María Cristina Lozada, América Alonso, Francis Rueda, Belén Díaz, and Pilar Romero. As is typical in most countries, many of the dramatists, actors, and directors work not only in the theater but also in film and television.

A succinct guide to begin a study of the current Venezuelan theater is *Teatro venezolano contemporáneo* (Contemporary Venezuelan Theater), an anthology of thirteen contemporary Venezuelan plays, edited by Moisés Pérez Coterillo.

BIBLIOGRAPHY

Acosta Saignes, Miguel. "El teatro primitivo en Venezuela." *400 años de valores teatrales*. Caracas: Edición especial del círculo musical, 1967.

Alvarado, Lisandro. "Música y danza entre los aborígenes venezolanos." *Revista nacional de cultura* 50 (May–June 1945): 17–37.

Antolínez, Gilberto. "El teatro: Institución de los Miku y Jiripara." *Revista nacional de cultura* 56 (May–June 1946): 113–129.

Anuario Teatral 77. Venezuela. Caracas: Consejo Nacional de la Cultura, n.d.

Arellano Moreno, Antonio. *Guía de historia de Venezuela 1948–1968*, Caracas: Síntesis Dosmil, 1971.

Arrom, Juan José. "Documentos relativos al teatro colonial en Venezuela." *Universidad de la Habana* 21–22 (1946): 80–101.

———. "Procesos del teatro venezolano de los ochenta." *Latin American Theatre Review* 25.2 (Spring 1992): 191–196.

———. *El teatro venezolano*. Caracas: Departamento de Literatura del Instituto Nacional de Cultura y Bellas Artes (INCIBA), 1967.

———. "El teatro venezolano en una encrucijada." *Latin American Theatre Review* 21.1 (Fall 1986): 79–84.

———. *El teatro venezolano y otros teatros*. Caracas: Monte Avila Editores, 1979.

———, ed. *Latin American Theatre Review* 21.2 (Spring 1988): 5–124 special issue dedicated to Venezuela.

Azparren Jiménez, Leonardo. *La máscara y la realidad: comportamientos del teatro venezolano contemporáneo*. Caracas: FUNDARTE, 1994.

———. *El teatro en Venezuela: ensayos históricos*. Caracas: Alfadil Ediciones, 1997.

Barrios, Alba Liá, Carmen Mannarino, and Enrique Izaguirre. *Dramaturgia venezolana del siglo XX: panorama en tres ensayos*. Caracas: Centro Venezolano del ITI-UNESCO, 1997.

Barrios Mora, José R. *Compendio histórico de la literatura venezolana*. Caracas: Padilla y Roig, 1950.

Bermúdez, Luis Julio, *El teatro de oriente y Guayana*. Caracas: Ediciones CONAC-FUNDARTE, 1981.

———. *Teófilo Leal y su escenario americano*. Caracas: Ediciones CONAC-FUNDARTE, 1980.

Blanco, Alexis. "Sociedad dramática: un colectivo llamado Maracaibo." *Latin American Theatre Review* 21.2 (Spring 1988): 63–68.

Brito Figueroa, Federico. *Venezuela siglo XX*. Havana: Casa de las Américas, 1967.

Calcaño, Julio. *Crítica literaria: fuentes para la historia literatura venezolana*. Caracas: Editorial Italgráfica, 1972.

Castillo, Susana D. *El "desarraigo" en el teatro venezolano*. Caracas: Editorial Ateneo de Caracas, 1980.

———. "¿Qué pasa con el teatro en Venezuela?" *Mester* 4 (November 1973): 57–58.

Chocrón, Isaac E. *Nueva crítica de teatro venezolano*. Caracas: FUNDARTE, 1981.

———. *El Nuevo teatro venezolano, tendencias del teatro contemporáneo*. Caracas: Oficina Central de Información, 1968.

———. "Shakespeare: autor para un teatro venezolano." *Revista nacional de cultura*. 154 (1962): 28–43.

———. *Sueño y tragedia en el teatro norteamericano*. Caracas: Alfadila, 1984.

Churión, Issac. *El teatro en Caracas*. Caracas: Tipografía Vargas, 1924.

Díaz Seijas, Pedro. *La antigua y la moderna literatura venezolana*. Caracas: Ediciones Armitaño, 1966.

Feo Calcaño, Guillermo. *Teatro municipal, 1881–1981*. Caracas: FUNDARTE, 1981.

Galindo, Dunia. *Teatro, cuerpo y nación: en las fronteras de una nueva sensibilidad*. Caracas: Monte Avila Editores Latinoamericana, 2000.

García Naranjo, Nemesio. *Venezuela and Its Rulers*. New York: Carranza, 1927.

Gil Fortoul, José. *El hombre y la historia: ensayo de sociología venezolana*. Madrid: Editorial América, 1945.

———. "Teatro venezolano." In *Sinfonía inacabada y otros ensayos*. Caracas: Sur América, 1931: 243–244.

Giusti, Rosa Celina. "Estudio histórico-literario del teatro venezolano en el siglo XIX y apreciación de su actualidad." *Revista del liceo Andrés Bello* 2 (October–November 1946): 34–64.

Guerrero Matheus, Fernando. *Teatro y gente de teatro en el Zulia*. Maracaibo: Universidad del Zulia, 1962.

Hernández, Alex. "El grupo actoral 80: una alternativa para la integración latino americana en el teatro." *Latin American Theatre Review* 21.2 (Spring 1988): 59–62.

Hernández Almeida, Gleider. *Tres dramaturgos venezolanos de hoy: R. Chalbaud, J.I. Cabrujas, I. Chocrón*. Caracas: Ediciones El Nuevo Grupo, 1979.

Herrera, Carlos E. "El teatro de corte histórico en Venezuela." *Latin American Theatre Review* 21.2 (Spring 1988): 17–22.

Imagen del teatro venezolano. Boletín especial del Centro Venezolano del Instituto Internacional del Teatro, Caracas, 1978.

Korn, Guillermo. *15 meses de teatro en Caracas. Agosto 1971–Octubre de 1972*. Caracas: Italgráfica, 1972.

———. *Teatro en Caracas, febrero 1978/abril 1979*. Guillermo Korn, text; Miguel Gracia, photos. Caracas: Ediciones Casuz, 1979.

———. *Unos pasos por el teatro*. Caracas: Casuz Editores, 1977.

Lasarte V., and Francisco Javier. "Significación de los talleres de textos teatrales del CELARG en la actual dramaturgia venezolana." *Revista canadiense de estudios hispánicos* 7.1 (1982): 81–88.

Loney, Glenn. "Talking to Carlos Jiménez, Creator of the Rajatabla in Caracas." *New Theatre Quarterly* 11.7 (1986): 243–249.

Martínez De La Vega, Juan. "El problema de la imagen y la palabra." *Latin American Theatre Review* 21.2 (Spring 1988): 41–46.

Matamoros, Jesús. "Los hombres de los cantos amargos." *Kena* 55 (January 15, 1967).

Mayorga, Wilfredo. "Andrés Bello, analista de la literatura dramática." *Atenea: revista de ciencia, arte y literatura de la universidad de Concepción* 443–444 (1981): 197–228.

Méndez y Mendoza, Eugenio. "Teatro nacional." *Primer libro venezolano de literatura, ciencias, y bellas artes*. Caracas: El Cojo-Tip. Moderna, 1985.

Monasterios, Rúben. "Balance del año teatral venezolano 1978." *Latin American Theatre Review* 13.1 (Fall 1979): 77–86.

———. *Un enfoque crítico del teatro venezolano*. 2nd ed. Caracas: Monte Avila Editores, 1990.

———. *Un estudio crítico y longitudinal del teatro venezolano*. Caracas: Universidad Central de Venezuela, 1974.

———. *La miel y el veneno*. Valencia: Universidad de Carabobo, 1971.

Monasterios, Rubén, and Herman Lejter. *Formación para un teatro del tercer mundo*. Caracas: Consejo Nacional de Cultura (CONAC), Imprenta Saman, 1978.

Monleón, José. *America latina. Teatro y revolución*. Caracas: Editorial Ateneo de Caracas, 1978.

———. "El II festival internacional de Caracas, 1974." *Popular Theater for Social Change in Latin America*, Editorial Gerardo Luzuriaga. Los Angeles: UCLA Latin American Center Publications, (1978): 235–247.

Moreno, Xiomara. "El grupo Teja." *Latin American Theatre Review* 21.2 (Spring 1988): 35–40.

Nigro, Kirsten F. "History Grand and History Small in Recent Venezuelan Theatre: Rial's *Bolívar* and Cabrujas' *Acto Cultural*." *The Theatre Annual* 44 (1989–1990): 37–46.

Otero Silva, María Teresa. "¿En qué punto está el teatro venezolano?" *Revista nacional de cultura* 171 (1965): 94–100.

Palamides, Costa. "Compañía nacional de teatro: el trienio inicial." *Latin American Theatre Review* 21.2 (Spring 1988): 69–78.

Palenzuela, Juan Carlos. "El teatro venezolano de los años 50." *Escena* 10 (1976): 33–48.

Pazos, Gloria. "Rajatabla, presencia y significación." *Latin American Theatre Review* 21.2 (Spring 1988): 29–34.

Peraza, Luis. "El indio y el negro en nuestro teatro." *El farol* 7 (May 1946): 2–30.

Pérez Coterillo, Moisés. *Teatro venezolano contemporáneo*. Madrid: Fondo de Cultura Económica, 1991.

Pérez Vila, Manuel. "Polémicas sobre representaciones dramáticas 1775–1829." *Revista nacional de cultura* 127 (March–April 1958): 95–104.

———. "El teatro en la Venezuela colonial." *Venezuela 1498–1810*. Caracas: Sociedad de Amigos del Museo de Bellas Artes, 1965, 69–92.

Presencia de seis dramaturgos. Gobernación del estado de Aragua. Maracas, Aragua: Ingenio Gráfico, 1980.

Rama, Angel. "A la búsqueda de nacionalidad en el teatro." *Revista escena* (Caracas) 11 (1976): 33–37.

Ramírez, José. *Vida y milagros de Antonio Saavedra (apuntes para la historia del teatro en Venezuela)*. Caracas: Patria, n.d.

Ramón y Rivera, Luis Felipe. *Teatro popular venezolano*. Quito: Instituto Andino de Artes Populares, 1981.

Rangel, Carlos. *Del buen salvaje al buen revolucionario*. Caracas: Monte Avila, 1976.

Rodríguez B., Orlando. "La enseñanza teatral en Venezuela." *Latin American Theatre Review* 21.2 (Spring 1988): 51–58.

Rojas Uzcategui, José de la Cruz, and Lubio Cardozo. *Bibliografía del teatro venezolano*. Mérida: Universidad de los Andes, 1980.

———. "Una historia desconocida." *Latin American Theatre Review* 21.2 (Spring 1988): 9–16.

Salas, Carlos. *100 años del teatro municipal*. Caracas: Consejo Municipal del Distrito Federal, 1980.

———. *Historia del teatro en Caracas*. Caracas: Ediciones de la Secretaria General de la Gobernación del Distrito Federal, 1967.

Suárez Radillo, Carlos Miguel. *Lo social en el teatro hispanoamericano contemporáneo*. Caracas: Equinoccio, 1976.

———. "El teatro de los barrios en Venezuela." In *Popular Theater for Social Change in Latin America*, ed. Gerardo Luzuriaga. Los Angeles: UCLA Latin American Center Publications (1978): 349–363.

Terrero, Blas José. *Teatro en Venezuela y Caracas*. Caracas: Litografía Comercio, 1926.

Ugarte Chamorro, Guillermo. "El teatro y los diálogos en verso de don Andrés Bello." *Revista de crítica literaria latinoamericana* 11.23 (1986): 17–26.

Ulive, Ugo. "El nuevo grupo: Sus primeros veinte años." *Latin American Theatre Review* 21.2 (Spring 1988): 45–50.

Uslar Pietri, Arturo. *Letras y hombres de Venezuela*. Caracas and Madrid: Ed. Edimé, 1958.

Valores teatrales. Caracas: Círculo Musical, 1967.

"Venezuela." *Escenarios de dos mundos: inventario teatral de Iberoamérica*. Vol. 4. Madrid: Centro de Documentación Teatral, 1988, 228–297. Articles by scholars.

Villasana, Angel Raúl. *Ensayo de un repertorio bibliográfico venezolano (años 1808–1950)*. Caracas: Banco Central de Venezuela, 1969, 1970, 1976, 1979.

Waldman, Gloria. "An Interview with Isaac Chocrón." *Latin American Theatre Review* 11.1 (1977): 103–109.

◆

ACOSTA, Ricardo. Acosta is a dramatist whose works, some of which are set in the past, emphasize the interior world of his characters, a reflection on being and existence, and the problem of alienation. He studied at New York University with José Quintero and worked professionally off Broadway. On returning to Venezuela he established the Pequeño Teatro Caracas (Little Theater of Caracas).

WORKS: *Elegía para los fugitivos* (Elegy for the Fugitives) (1965). *El asfalto de los infiernos* (Infernal Asphalt) (monologue) (1966) (Maracaibo: Editorial Universitaria del Zulia, 1967). *El baile de los cautivos* (The Captives' Dance) (1966). *Agonía y muerte del Caravaggio* (The Agony and Death of Caravaggio) (modern version of *La vida es sueño* [Life Is a Dream]) (1968). *Agua linda* (Beautiful Water) (1970), in *13 Autores del nuevo teatro venezolano* (Thirteen Authors of the New Venezuelan Theatre) (Caracas: Monte Avila Editores, 1971). *Rey Negro* (Black King) (1970). *La rebelión Túpac Amaru* (The Rebellion of Túpac Amaru) (1971).

BIBLIOGRAPHY: Ricardo Acosta, *Teatro* (Caracas: Dirección de Cultura de la Universidad Central de Venezuela, 1969).

AYALA MICHELENA, Leopoldo (1897–1962). He has been called the father of Venezuelan theater by some and also the master of the creole theater.

WORKS: *Al dejar las muñecas* (On Putting Away Dolls) (1915). *Almas descarnadas* (Naked souls). *La perra* (The Dog). *La alquilada* (The Rented Woman). *Bagazo. Emoción y eco. Las niñitas. Amor por amor* (Love for Love). *La taquilla* (The Ticket Office) (Caracas: Imprenta Bolívar, 1922).

BERMÚDEZ, Luis Julio. He is a director, author, actor, and theatrical technician. One of his works deals with the petroleum problem: *Por debajo del círculo dorado.*

WORKS: *El manto de Belisa* (The Cloak of Belisa) (1953), puppet play. *Servicio inoperante* (Out of Service) and *Por debajo del círculo dorado* (From Under the Golden Circle) (1959), monologues.

BIBLIOGRAPHY: Luis Julio Bermúdez, *Detrás de la avenida* (Behind the Avenue) (Caracas: Monte Avila Editores, 1969) (contains the two monologues and stories).

BRITTO GARCÍA, Luis. He is a dramatist, narrator, and novelist. He received the Premios de Dramaturgia Andrés Bello and Premio Casa de las Américas (1971 and 1982). He has worked with Rajatabla and El Nuevo Grupo.

WORKS: *Venezuela tuya* (Your Venezuela). *El tirano Aguirre* (The Tyrant Aguirre). *Suena el teléfono* (The Telephone Is Ringing). *Muñequita linda* (Beautiful Doll). *La misa del esclavo* (The Mass of the Slave).

BIBLIOGRAPHY: *Teatro* (Caracas: Editorial Tiempo Nuevo, 1973). *Teatro* (Caracas: FUNDARTE, 1976).

CABALLERO, Néstor. Caballero is a professor, director, dramatist, and critic. He has received numerous national and international prizes from ITI and United Nations Educational, Scientific and Cultural Organization (UNESCO). He has also gained fame as a writer of monologues and has been called the "king of the monologue." In *Con una pequeña ayuda de mis amigos* (With a Little Help from My Friends), Caballero re-creates the decade of the 1960s in the Latin American context. He presents the abyss between youthful hope and dreams of utopia and the terrible wreckage they may suffer, since utopia does not exist.

WORKS: *El rey de los Argonautas* (King of the Argonauts) (1978), Prize from El Nuevo Grupo. *La última actuación de Sarah Bernhardt* (The Last Performance of Sarah Bernhardt). *Las bisagras o Macedonio perdido entre los ángeles* (The Hinges or Macedonia Lost among the Angels). *Precios* (Prices). *Mis noches sin ti* (My Nights without You). *Con una pequeña ayuda de mis amigos* (With a Little Help from My Friends) (1983), in *Teatro venezolano contemporáneo* (Madrid: Fondo de Cultura Económica, 1991). *Algo llueve sobre Nina Hagen* (Something Is Raining on Nina Hagen). *Los hombres de Ganímedes* (The Men of Ganymede). *Dados. Gran Casino* (Great Casino). *Almanaque* (Almanac). Monologues: *Chocolat Gourmet* (Chocolate Gourmet), *La semana de la patria* (The Week of the Fatherland), *Los taxistas también tienen su corazoncito* (Taxi Drivers Also Have Their Little Hearts), *Seis monólogos para Dalila y Longanizo* (Six Monologues for Dalila and Longanizo).

CABRUJAS, José Ignacio. Cabrujas is an actor, dramatist for theater, television, and film, and director of both plays and opera. He, along with Chocrón and Chalbaud, is considered to be a prime moving force in continuing the work of César Rengifo in the development of the contemporary Venezuelan theater. These three have been called the "Santísima Trinidad del teatro venezolano" (The Holy Trinity of the Venezuelan theater). He has been instrumental in the work of El Nuevo Grupo and the Teatro Universitario of the Universidad Central de Venezuela and has been described as the renovator of the historicosocial theme in Venezuelan theater. *El día que me quieras* (The Day When You Love Me) was an offering of El Nuevo Grupo in 1979 under Cabrujas's direction and with the director taking the lead role of Pío Miranda. This character is a Communist dreamer who does not live in the present; he lives only for a future in which he and his fiancée will work the land in the Ukraine. *Fiésole* has three divisions and follows the twentieth-century fashion of the two-character play. The name *Fiésole* represents the survival of culture through the centuries since before the Romans. The text is an example of the literature of silence, found also in the work of Henry Miller and Samuel Beckett, in which the content of the words is of less importance than the sensation produced.

WORKS: *Juan Francisco de León* (1958). *El extraño viaje de Simón el malo* (The Strange Trip of Evil Simon) (1960). *Los insurgentes* (The Insurgents) (1960). *En nombre del rey* (In the Name of the King) (1963). *Tradicional hospitalidad* (Traditional Hospitality) (1963), as part of *Triángulo* (Triangle) with Román Chalbaud and Isaac Chocrón (Caracas: Editorial Tierra Firme, 1962). *Días de poder* (Days of Power) (1964), with Román Chalbaud. *Testimonio* (Testimony) (1967). *El tambor mágico* (The Magic Drum) (1970). *Profundo* (Profound) (Caracas: Editorial Tiempo Nuevo, 1972). *Fiésole*, in *13 autores del nuevo teatro venezolano* (Caracas: Monte Avila Editores, 1971). *La soberbia milagrosa del General Pío Fernández* (The Miraculous Pride of General Pío Fernández) (1974). *Acto cultural* (Cultural Act) (Caracas: Monte Avila Editores, 1976). *El día que me quieras* (The Day When You Love Me) (Caracas: Cuadernos de Difusión, 1979); (Caracas: FUNDARTE, 1983) (prologue by Isaac Chocrón and Elisa Lerner); and in *Teatro venezolano contemporáneo* (Contemporary Venezuelan Theatre) (Madrid: Fondo de Cultura Económica, 1991). *Una noche oriental* (An Oriental Night) (1983). *El americano ilustrado* (The Educated American) (1986). *Autorretrato de artista con barba y pumpá* (Self Portrait of the Artist with Beard and Pumpá) (1990).

BIBLIOGRAPHY: Leonardo Azparren-Giménez, "El americano ilustrado de Cabrujas," *Latin American Theatre Review* 21.2 (Spring 1988): 23–28. *Cabrujas en tres actos* (Caracas: Ediciones El Nuevo Grupo, 1983). José Ignacio Cabrujas, "José Ignacio Cabrujas, un teatro alucinado," *Escena* 9 (August 1976): 3–5. Isaac Chocrón, *Teatro I. (Okey, La revolución and El acompañante)* (Caracas: Monte Avila Editores, 1981). Gleider Hernández-Almeida, "Isaac Chocrón: Lo histórico y lo antihistórico," in *Actas del IX Congreso de la Asociación Internacional de Hispanistas I & II*, ed. Sebastián Neumeister et al. (Frankfurt: Vervuert, 1989), 559–566. Hernández-Almeida, *Tres dramaturgos venezolanos de hoy—R. Chalbaud, J. I. Cabrujas, I. Chocrón* (Caracas: Ediciones El Nuevo Grupo, 1979). Kirsten Nigro, "History Grand and History Small in Recent Venezuelan Theatre: Rial's *Bolívar* and Cabrujas' *Acto cultural*," *The Theatre Annual* 44 (1989–1990): 37–46. Nigro, "Pop Culture and Image-Making in Two Latin American Plays," *Latin American Literary Review* 17.33 (January–June 1989): 42–49.

Adam Versenyl, "¿Cómo se llena un vacío? *El día que me quieras* and Filling the Void in Colombian Theater," *Gestos* 7.13 (April 1992): 158–162.

CHALBAUD, Román (1931–   ). Chalbaud is a dramatist, director, and actor. He, along with Isaac Chocrón and José Ignacio Cabrujas, is considered to be a prime moving force in continuing the work of César Rengifo in the development of the contemporary Venezuelan theater. These three have been called the "Santísima Trinidad del teatro venezolano" (The Holy Trinity of the Venezuelan theater). As well as being one of the most outstanding directors, Chalbaud is also active in the movie world, having been instrumental in more than fifteen films, some of which originated in his play scripts. He has also directed many works of foreign dramatists and has participated in many television productions. *Angeles*, replete with symbolism typical of Chalbaud's work, relates the opposite poles of possibilities, such as virgin and prostitute, and continues with the message of social decomposition resulting from lack of communication, alienation, and violence. It exemplifies Chalbaud's constant interest in the marginated and indigent of his society and can be read as a religious allegory (Hernández-Almeida, 48). *Caín adolescente* deals with his vision of those who left the countryside to live in the hills around the city, a circumstance typical of much of Latin America. It was made into a very successful landmark film. *La quema de Judas* represents his search for new dramatic forms to reach the public with his constant concerns regarding the poor and the corruption of the powerful.

WORKS: As a dramatist he has staged and published *Los adolescentes* (The Adolescents), (1951). *Muros horizontales* (Horizontal Walls) (1953). *Caín adolescente* (Adolescent Cain) (1955). *Réquiem para un eclipse* (Requiem for an Eclipse) (Caracas: Editorial Landi, 1957). *Sagrado y obsceno* (Sacred and Obscene) (Caracas: Tipografía Iberia, 1961). *Cantanta para Chirinos* (Singer for Chirinos) (1961). *Café y orquídeas* (Coffee and Orchids) (Caracas: Ed. Tierra Firme, 1962). *Las pinzas* (The Pincers), first part of *Triángulo* (Caracas: Editorial Tierra Firme, 1962). *Días de poder* (Days of Power), with José Ignacio Cabrujas (1966). *Los ángeles terribles* (The

Terrible Angels) (Caracas: Instituto Nacional de Cultura y Bellas Artes, 1967) and in *Teatro venezolano contemporáneo* (Madrid: Fondo de Cultura Económica, 1991). *El pez que fuma* (The Smoking Fish) (1969) (Caracas: Ediciones El Nuevo Grupo, 1969). *La quema de Judas* (The Burning of Judas) (Caracas: Monte Avila Editores, 1974). *Ratón en ferretería* (Rat in Hardware) (1977). *El viejo grupo* (The Old Group) (1981). *Los ángeles terribles* (1967) served as the basis for the film *La oveja negra* (1987), which received the Simón Bolívar Prize at the Festival de Cine (Film Festival) in Mérida in 1990.

BIBLIOGRAPHY: Gleider Hernández-Almeida, *Tres dramaturgos Venezolanos de hoy—R. Chalbaud, J. I. Cabrujas, I Chocrón* (Caracas: Ediciones El Nuevo Grupo, 1979). Marita King, *Román Chalbaud. Poesía, magia y revolución* (Caracas: Monte Avila, 1987). Jesús Matamoros, "El pez que fuma," *Kena* 93 (July 1968): 91. Manuel Pérez Vila, "El pez que fuma," *Revista de teatro de El Nuevo Grupo* 3 (April–May–June 1968): 26–29. Edgar Quiles, "Román Chalbaud habla sobre el teatro en Venezuela," *Intermedio de Puerto Rico: Revista de teatro* 1.1 (September–October 1985): 17–20. Quiles, "El teatro es una gran mentira para decir la verdad: Continuación de la entrevista con el dramaturgo Román Chalbaud," *Intermedio* 2.1 (January–March 1986): 15–20.

CHOCRÓN, Isaac (1933–). Chocrón is a novelist, dramatist, director, critic, and essayist. Several of his theater works have been produced outside of Venezuela. He is a founding member of El Nuevo Grupo (The New Group), professor in la Escuela de Artes (Arts College) of the Universidad Central de Venezuela (Venezuelan Central University) and la Universidad Simón Bolívar, and has been visiting professor at the University of Maryland. Chocrón, José Ignacio Cabrujas, and Román Chalbaud form what has been called the "Santísima Trinidad del teatro venezolano" (Holy Trinity of the Venezuelan theater). He is director of the Compañía Nacional de Teatro (National Theater Company). The purpose of his work *El quinto infierno* (The Fifth Hell), employing the techniques of Brecht, is to pose the question, What is Venezuela? and the protagonist, Miss Betsy, is the incarnation of Venezuela. His contribution to the trilogy with Cabrujas and Chalbaud, *A propósito del Triángulo* (About the Tri-

angle), uses Pirandelian techniques in that three actors are worrying about the script that they are preparing. Chocrón's preoccupation in it is the effect of time on human beings, a preoccupation developed more fully in *Okey* and *La máxima felicidad* (The Greatest Happiness). *Tric-trac* (in *Teatro de la vanguardia: Contemporary Spanish American Theatre*, ed. Myrna Casas [Lexington, MA: D. C. Heath, 1975]) is often considered a continuation of *Asia* in that the actors play multiple characters only identified by numbers one through ten on their chests. *La máxima felicidad*, sometimes considered his best work, presents a different kind of family, one based on a concept of a life that they accept and that is revocable at any moment: Freedom of choice is the path of maximum happiness for the human being. *Clípper* (1987), with innovative staging, tells of two brothers and their intertwined careers and families and the need for the children to move out of the family sphere.

WORKS: *Mónica y el florentino* (Monica and the Florentine) (1959). *Amoroso o una mínima incandescencia* (Love or a Small Incandescence) (1961). *Una mínima incandescencia* (A Minimum Incandescence) (Caracas: Ediciones Teatro de Arte, 1962). *A propósito de Triángulo* (About the Triangle), in *Triángulo*, (Caracas: Editorial Tierra Firme, 1962). *Asia y el Lejano Oriente* (Asia and the Far East) (Mérida, Venezuela: Universidad de los Andes, 1967). *Tric-trac* (Mérida, Venezuela: Universidad de los Andes, 1967). *El quinto inferno* (The Fifth Inferno) (Caracas: Universidad Central de Venezuela, 1968). *Animales feroces* (Ferocious Animals) (Caracas: Universidad Central de Venezuela, 1968). *Okey* (OK) (Caracas: Monte Avila Editores, 1969). *La revolución* (The Revolution) (Caracas: Editorial Tiempo Nuevo, 1972). *Alfabeto para analfabetos* (Alphabet for Illiterates) (1973). *La máxima felicidad* (The Greatest Happiness) (Caracas: Monde Avila Editores, 1974). *El acompañante* (The Companion) (Monte Avila Editores, 1977). *Mesopotamia* (1980), *Simón* (1983), and *Clípper* (1987), in *Teatro venezolano contemporáneo* (Madrid: Fondo de Cultura Económica, 1991). *Suleimán el magnífico* (Suleiman the Magnificent) (1989). He also wrote the libretto for the opera *Doña Bárbara* (1967) (Caracas: Editorial Arte, 1967).

BIBLIOGRAPHY: Miguel Angel, "Chocrón o la vocación teatral," *Primer Acto: Cuadernos de Inves-

tigación teatral 235 (September–October 1990): 98–101, 103. Leonardo Azparren Giménez *"Asia y el Lejano Oriente," Revista Nacional de Cultura* 28 (1961): 101–105. Azpárren Giménez, "La revolución," *Primer Acto* 237 (January–February 1991): 128–129. Isaac Chocrón, "Tu boca en los cielos," *Hispamérica: Revista de Literatura* 14.42 (December 1985): 65–71. Edward H. Friedman, "The Beast Within: The Rhetoric of Signification in Isaac Chocrón's *Animales feroces," Folio: Essays on Foreign Languages and Literatures* 17 (1987): 167–183. Friedman, "Cherchez la femme: El lector como detective en *50 vacas gordas* de Isaac Chocrón," *Discurso: Revista literaria: Revista de temas literarios* 4.2 (Spring 1987): 647–656. Gleider Hernández-Almeida, "Isaac Chocrón: Lo histórico y lo antihistórico," in *Actas del IX Congreso de la Asociación Internacional de Hispanistas*, vol. 2, ed. Sebastian Neumeister (Frankfurt: Vervuert, 1989), 559–566. Dennis A. Klein, "The Theme of Alienation in the Theatre of Elisa Lerner and Isaac Chocrón," *Folio: Essays on Foreign Languages and Literatures* 17 (1987): 151–166. Milagro Larson, "Entrevista con Isaac Chocrón," *Confluencia: Revista hispánica de cultura y literatura* 6.2 (Spring 1991): 155–161. Kirsten F. Nigro, "A Triple Insurgence: Isaac Chocrón's *La revolución," Bulletin of the Rocky Mountain Modern Language Association* 35.1 (1981): 47–53. Leonardo Senkman, "Entrevista a Isaac Chocrón: El misterio de la familia que heredamos," *Noah: Revista literaria* 1.1 (August 1987): 779–782. Miyo Vestrini, Chocrón frente el espejo (Caracas: Ateneo de Caracas, 1980). Vestrini, "Foro con Isaac Chocrón," *O K* (Caracas: Monte Avila, 1969), 19–20. Barbara Younoszai and Rossi Irausquin, "Not Establishing Limits: The Writing of Isaac Chocrón," *Inti: Revista de Literatura.*

ELOY BLANCO, Andrés (1897–1955). A poetic dramatist, he opposed the dictatorship and was imprisoned and exiled for a time.

WORKS: *El huerto de la epopeya* (The Garden of the Epoch). *El Cristo de las violetas* (Christ of the Violets). *Abigaíl*, a biblical drama (1986). *El pie de la Virgen* (The Foot of the Virgin).

BIBLIOGRAPHY: *Teatro* (Caracas: Editorial Cordillera, 1960).

GALLEGOS, Rómulo (1884–1969). He served as president of Venezuela and is well known in Latin American literature for his novel *Doña Bárbara*. The psychological penetration evinced by his characters and his management of conflict are outstanding in Venezuelan theater. *El motor* has a psychosocial theme that is logically developed, given the attributes of his characters. *El milagro del año*, a tragedy, continues with psychological insight.

WORKS: *Sol de antaño* (Sun of Yesteryear) (1910). *La liberación* (Liberation) (1910). *El motor* (The Motor) (1910). *El milagro del año* (Miracle of the Year) (1915).

GARYCOCHEA, Oscar. Garycochea is a dramatist for theater, television, and film and an expert on mass communication. He was born in Argentina and obtained the Licenciatura en Cinematografía (Master's Degree in Cinematography) from the Universidad Nacional de La Plata. He has been active in his fields of expertise in Venezuela since 1975. Although he has received several awards, many of his works, which have been produced to acclaim, have not been published.

WORKS: *Mujeres dulces y amargas* (Women Sweet and Bitter). *Hollywood Paradise. Lágrimas de glicerina* (Glycerine Tears). *Circo de tres pistas* (Three-Ring Circus). *Prohibido regresar al Paraíso* (Return to Paradise Prohibited). *Todo está como siempre ha sido* (Everything Is as It Was) (Premio Nacional de Dramaturgia-[National Drama Award]). *A la sombra del sol* (Shaded from the Sun). *Amado enemigo* (Beloved Enemy). *Eterno femenino* (The Eternal Feminine). *Vals lento* (Slow Waltz) (Premio Nacional de Dramaturgia and Premio Primer Concurso de Dramaturgia de la Compañía Nacional de Teatro [National Drama Award and Award of the National Theater Company's First Drama Competition]). *¡Sálvese quien pueda!* (Every Man for Himself). *Go Home!. Fuego y cenisa* (Fire and Ash). *Salto mortal* (Mortal Leap). *Hembra fatal de los mares del trópico* (Dangerous Female of the Tropical Seas) (in *Teatro venezolano contemporáneo* [Madrid: Fondo de Cultura Económica, 1991]), is a comedy exploring feminine solitude through the existential anguish of three old maids who are trapped amidst Hollywood-type fantasies and historical reality.

GUINAND, Rafael (1881–1957). Guinand was a dramatist, actor, and director of the first half of the twentieth century who wrote creole theater with a humorous note. He is known as one of the best writers of the *sainete*.

WORKS: *El pobre Pantoja* (Poor Pantoja). *El rompimiento* (The Break). *Amor que mata* (Love That Kills). *El dotol Nigüín* (Dr. Nigüín). *Yo también soy candidato* (I'm a Candidate Too).

LASSER, Alejandro. Lasser is a dramatist and novelist. He has participated in the emergence of a nationalist theater through his works, which take history as a point of departure. Recurrent themes are individual liberty and conflict with authority.

WORKS: *El general Piar* (General Piar), (3rd version, 1981) (1st version [Caracas: Editorial Patria, 1946]). *Catón en Utica* (Cato in Utica) (1950). *La voz ahogada* (The Drowned Voice) (Mexico City: Editorial Moderna, 1952). *La muchacha de los cerros* (Girl of the Hills) (1955) (Madrid: Cía Bibliográfica Española, 1958). *La cueva* (The Cave) (1966) (Caracas: Ediciones Zodíaco, 1967). *Catón y Pilato* (Cato and Pilate) (1966), in *13 Autores del nuevo teatro venezolano* (Caracas: Monte Avila Editores, 1971). *Ledesma y los Piratas* (Ledesma and the Pirates) (1979); also the basis for the libretto of an opera of the same name.

LERNER, Elisa. Lerner is a dramatist, newspaper columnist, television personality, and Venezuelan embassy cultural attaché. A graduate of the Universidad Central de Venezuela, she has been an art reporter and interviewer of artists and intellectuals on television. She has received many drama prizes. *Vida con Mamá* dramatizes the lives of mother and daughter, the tense but tender relationship between two women of different generations, both demonstrating the lack of emotional communication between men and women. On another level, the play acts as a metaphor on the national level of the conflict between dictatorship and democracy.

WORKS: *La bella de inteligencia* (Intelligent Beauty) (1960), *Revista Sardio* 6–7 (1959). *Jean Harlow, Revista C.A.L.* (1962). *El vasto silencio de Manhattan* (The Vast Silence of Manhattan) (1964), for which she received the Premio Ana Julia Rojas by the Ateneo de Caracas, in *13 Autores del nuevo teatro venezolano* (Caracas: Monte Avila Editores, 1971). *El país odontológico* (The Odontological

Country), *Revista Zona Franca* 39 (November 1966). *Una sonrisa detrás de la metáfora* (A Smile behind the Metaphor) (Caracas: Monte Avila, 1969). *La envidia* (Envy) (1974). *Vida con Mamá* (Life with Mother) (1975), in *Teatro venezolano contemporáneo* (Madrid: Fondo de Cultura Económica, 1991) for which she received the Premio Juana Sujo. A monologue, *La mujer del periódico* (The Newspaper Woman) (1978), was popularized by Susan Alexander in several North American universities.

BIBLIOGRAPHY: Isaac A. Chocrón, "Prólogo," in *Elisa Lerner: Teatro* (Caracas: Monte Avila Editores, 1976). Miriam Freilich de Abadí, "Elisa Lerner: Soy una intelectual a pesar mío," *Imagen* 108 (August 1975): 56–58. Dennis A Klein, "The Theme of Alienation in the Theater of Elisa Lerner and Isaac Chocrón," *Folio* 17 (1987): 151–166. Elisa Lerner, *Teatro* (Caracas: Monte Avila Editores, 1976).

NUÑEZ, José Gabriel. He is a dramatist for theater, television, and soap operas. His work has also been published and presented in several other countries. He has received several prizes, among them the Premio Juana Sujo as best author of 1974. *La noche*, an unusual work, has as protagonists a group of fish who present a parody of humanity as perceived through the glass of an aquarium. The desolate state of human life is the result of a lack of communication between men and women, father and son, and the deadening effect of mass communication. *Madame Pompinette*, a monologue, explores the contradictions of the character and judges the political reality of Venezuela.

WORKS: *La ruta de los murciélagos* (The Route of the Bats) (1965). *Tiempo de nacer* (Time to be Born) (1965). *Los peces del acuario* (The Fishes of the Aquarium) (1967), in *Teatro venezolano contemporáneo* (Madrid: Fondo de Cultura Económica, 1991). *El largo camino del Edén* (The Large Road to Eden), in *Revista Nacional de Cultura* (August 1971). *El largo camino del Edén* (The Long Road from Eden), in *Mester* (UCLA) 4 (1973): 59–65. *Quedó igualito* (Just Alike) (Caracas: Teatro El Triángulo 6, 1975). *Bang-Bang* (n.d.). *Los semidioses* (The Demigods) (n.d.). *Parecido a la felicidad* (Like Happiness) (n.d.). *Libertad, mon amour* (Liberty, My Love) (n.d.). *La casa con el amor fuera* (House with Love Banished) (n.d.). *Memorias de un país lejano* (Memories of a Distant Country) (n.d.).

Tú lo que quieres es que me coma el tigre (You Want the Tiger to eat Me) (n.d.). He then changed styles for *Barrotes de concreto* (Bars of Concrete) (n.d.). *Antígona* (n.d.). *La vista del extraño señor* (The Sight of the Strange Gentleman) (n.d.). *Soliloquio en negro tenaz* (Soliloquy in Strong Black) (n.d.). *El señor don Juan Vicente* (n.d.). *Madame Pompinette* (n.d.). *La noche de las malandras* (The Night of the Wicked) (n.d.).

PEÑA, Edilio. Peña is a dramatist and director for theater and cinema. He has also been director of the Taller de Dramaturgia (Drama Workshop) de La Universidad de los Andes, Mérida. He has won various prizes for his works, among them the annual prize of the Nuevo Grupo de Caracas (1973); the prize of the Universidad del Zulia for *El círculo* (The Circle) (1975); Premio Tirso de Molina del Instituto de Cultura Hispánica de Madrid (Tirso de Molina Prize of the Institute of Hispanic Culture of Madrid) (1976) for *Los pájaros se van con la muerte* (The Birds Go Away with Death) (1975) (in *Teatro venezolano contemporáneo* [Madrid: Fondo de Cultura Económica, 1991]). *Los pájaros se van con la muerte* has been produced in New York and Paris as well as in Caracas. The two acts call for two actresses to play mother and daughter, and one doubles as the father later in the play. The work deals with an examination of various aspects of Venezuelan life and includes some elements of magic in the cult to the queen María Lionza.

WORKS: *Resistencia (o un extraño sueño sobre la tortura de Pablo Rojas)* (Resistence [or A Strange Dream About the Torture of Pablo Rojas]) (1973). *Los olvidados* (The Forgotten Ones) (1975). *El círculo* (The Circle) (1975) (with *Resistencia*) (Caracas: Monte Avila Editores, 1975). *Los hermanos* (The Brothers) (1980). *Más allá de las Ramblas* (Beyond the Boulevard) (1983). *María Antonieta o el rococó* (Marie Antoinette, or the Rococo) (1984). *El último regalo* (The Last Gift) (1985). *Lady Ana* (1988). *Los amantes de Sara* (The Lovers of Sara) (1988).

BIBLIOGRAPHY: Edilio Peña, *Apuntes sobre el texto teatral*, (Caracas: FUNDARTE, 1979). *Teatro* (Caracas: Monte Avila Editores, 1985).

PINTO, Gilberto. Pinto is a dramatist for theater and television, critic, actor, director, teacher of acting, and founder of theater groups. In 1986 he was awarded the Orden del Mérito al Trabajo de primera clase (Order of Merit for Work of First Class). Some works have an expressionistic cast; others show an interest in psychological and sociological implications. *La buhardilla* deals with the psychological implications of drugs and presents in an unsensational way the homosexual relationship between two women. *La guerrita de Rosendo*, starting with a historic incident, configures a theater of violence and cruelty.

WORKS: *El rincón del diablo* (The Devil's Corner) (1961). *La noche moribunda* (The Moribund Night) (1966) (Caracas: Venediciones, 1966). *La guerra caliente* (The Hot War) (1969). *Un domingo de verano* (A Sunday in Summer) (1969). *El hombre de la rata* (The Man of the Rat) (1963), in *13 Autores del nuevo teatro venezolano* (Caracas: Monte Avila Editores, 1991). *La buhardilla* (The Attic) (Maracaibo: Universidad de Zulia, 1970). *Los fantasmas de Tulemon* (The Phantoms of Tulemon) (1970). *La guerrita de Rosendo* (Rosendo's Little War) (1976) in *Teatro venezolano contemporáneo* (Madrid: Fondo de Cultura Económica, 1991). *El confidente* (The Confidant). *La muchacha del blue-jeans* (The Girl in Blue Jeans) 1981. *Lucrecia*.

BIBLIOGRAPHY: Gilberto Pinto, *Teatro* (Caracas: Monte Avila Editores, 1987).

RENGIFO, César (1915–1980). Rengifo was a dramatist and professor of drama. Rengifo, often called the father of Venezuelan theater, certainly its first modern dramatist, achieved in many creative fields as well as drama. He was a founding member of the Society of Writers and Artists of Venezuela and professor at the University of the Andes and the Central University of Venezuela. His works have received many prizes and have been translated and dramatized in many countries. *Los hombres* analyzes the real meaning of the "liberation" of the slaves, really a ploy for the oligarchs to obtain cheaper labor. In *Ezequiel Zamora*, the title character is the charismatic liberal leader who represents the dream of a better life for the populace. *Tempestad* takes place five years after the struggle and mysterious death of Zamora, presenting the result of the conflict: the devastation of houses and fields and the disillusionment of the rural masses.

WORKS: *Por qué canta el pueblo* (Why the Town Sings) (1938). *Yuma o Cuando la tierra esté verde* (Yuma or When the Earth Is Fertile) (1940). *En mayo florecen los apamates* (In May the Apamates Flower) (1943), which exists only in a fragment. *Joaquina Sánchez* (1947–1948). *Curayu o El vencedor* (Curayu, or The Conqueror) (1947). *La sonata del alba* (The Sonata of the Dawn) (1948). *Hojas del tiempo* (Leaves of Time) (1948). *Curayú o El vencedor Revista*, in *Cultura Universitaria* 8, 9, & 10 (1949). *Los canarios* (The Canaries) (1949), in *Revista Cultura Universitaria* 23 (1951). *Estrellas sobre el crepúsculo* (Stars in the Twilight) (1949) (Caracas: Ediciones de la Dirección de Cultura de la Universidad Central de Venezuela, 1967). *Harapos de esta noche* (Refuse of This Night) (1948). *Manuelote* (Big Manuel) (1950), in *Cuadernos de los Estudiantes de la Universidad Central de Venezuela* 2 (1952). *Armaduras de humo* (Armor of Smoke) (1950–1951). *Vivir en paz* (To Live in Peace) (1951). *Las mariposas de la oscuridad* (The Butterflies of Darkness) (1951–1956). *Soga de niebla* (Noose of Mist) (1952). *El vendaval amarillo* (The Yellow Wind) (1952). *Los peregrinos del camino encantado* (The Pilgrims of the Enchanted Road) (1952). *El otro pasajero* (The Other Passenger) (1956). *Oscéneba* (1957). *Muros en la madrugada* (The Walls at Dawn) (1960). *Buenaventura Chatarra* (1963). *María Rosa Nava* (1964). (Mérida: Ediciones del Rectorado de la Universidad de Los Andes, 1964). *La fiesta de los moribundos* (The Feast of the Dying) (1966). *Una medalla para las conejitas* (A Medal for the Little Rabbits) (1966), in *Revista Expediente 1* (1968). *Las alegres cantáridas* (The Happy Beetles) (1967). *La esquina del miedo* (The Corner of Fear) (1969), in *13 Autores del nuevo teatro venezolano* (Caracas: Monte Avila Editores, 1971). *El raudal de los muertos cansados* (The Torrent of the Tired Dead) (1969). *Las torres y el viento* (The Towers and the Wind) (1969), in *Teatro selecto hispanoamericano* (Madrid: Editorial Escelicer, 1970). *Esa espiga sembrada en Carabobo* (That Shoot Planted in Carabobo), 2nd ed. (Caracas: Talleres Gráficos Ilustraciones, 1971). *El insólito viaje de los inocentes* (The Unusual Trip of the Innocents) (1975–1976). *Volcanes sobre el Mapocho* (Volcanoes over the Mapocho) (1974). *Apacuana y Cuaricurián* (1975). *Roguemos todos por los inmortales* (Let Us All Pray for the Immortals) (1975–1976). *El caso de Beltrán Santos* (The Case of Beltrán Santos) (1976). *¿Quién se robó ese batalla?*

(Who Stole That Battle?) (1976). *La trampa de los demonios* (The Trick of the Devils) (1976). *Un Fausto anda por la avenida* (A Faust Walks Along the Avenue) (1979). A trilogy named by the author *El mural de la Guerra Federal*—composed of *Un tal Ezequiel Zamora* (A Certain Ezequiel Zamora) (1956–1958); *Lo que dejó la tempestad* (Left by the Storm) (1957), in *Teatro venezolano contemporáneo* (Madrid: Fondo de Cultura Económica, 1991); *Los hombres de los cantos amargos* (The Men Who Sing Sad Songs) (1959) (Caracas: Tipografía Vargas, 1970)—deals with events of 1854–1865 in Venezuela.

BIBLIOGRAPHY: Ratt Ciarlo, *Retrospectiva de César Rengifo 1931–1974* (Caracas: Por-Venezuela, 1974). Manuel Galich, "Venezuela en el teatro de César Rengifo," *Conjunto* 22 (October–December 1974): 2–9. Nelson Osorio, "La alucinación del petróleo en una obra de César Rengifo," *Hispamérica* 21.63 (December 1992): 81–87. César Rengifo, *Imagen de un creador* (Caracas: Federación Nacional del la Cultura Popular y la Asociación de Amigos de César Rengifo, 1981). Carlos Miguel Suárez Radillo, "Vigencias de la realidad venezolana en el teatro de Cesar Rengifo." *Latin American Theatre Review* (5.2, Spring 1972), 51–61. *Teatro* (Caracas: Universidad Central de Venezuela, 1967). *Teatro* (Caracas: Asociación de Escritores Venezolanos, 1970). *Teatro* (Caracas: Dirección de Cultura, Universidad Central, 1976). *Teatro* (Havana: Casa de las Américas, 1977).

RIAL, José Antonio. Rial is a dramatist for theater and television, theater critic, newspaper writer, novelist, and essayist. He was born in Spain and wrote his first plays there (lost). He spent several years as a political prisoner during and after the Civil War. He moved to Venezuela in 1950 and has since become a citizen. His plays *La muerte de García Lorca* (The Death of García Lorca) (1975) and *Bolívar* (1982) have been presented by the theater group Rajatabla. In 1983 he received the Premio Carabela de Plata de La Rábida. His program on theater criticism—"El rostro y sus máscaras" (The Face and Its Masks)—has been shown on Televisora Nacional de Venezuela.

WORKS: *Las armaduras de la goleta Ilusión* (The Skeleton of the Schooner Illusion). (1950). *La torre* (The Tower) (1951). *Nuramí* (1954). *La escuela nocturna* (Night School) (1963). *La fragata del* *sol* (Frigate of the Sun) (1982). *Arcadio* (1985). His play *Cipango* (in *Teatro venezolano contemporáneo* [Madrid: Fondo de Cultura Económica, 1991]), a story about emigrants, represents, in the author's own words in its prologue, the dream of a better world.

BIBLIOGRAPHY: José Antonio Rial, *Teatro* (Caracas: Monte Avila Editores, 1986).

ROMERO, Mariela. Romero is a dramatist for theater and television and an actress. *El juego* is perhaps her best-known work in the United States. It has been presented in translation at the University of California at Los Angeles, and several scholarly articles have been published about it. Like her other works, the number of actors in this play is small: There are parts for two women, Ana I and Ana II. It has been interpreted in various ways: as about two young girls, as representing feminist issues, as representing two facets of the same person. *Rosa*, whose title character is a prostitute, has three characters, all street people. *El vendedor*, with two characters, deals with male/female issues, as does *Esperando* (with five characters). Several of the plays exemplify the current interest in games playing as a theatrical device.

WORKS: *Algo alrededor del espejo* (Something Around the Mirror) (1966). *El juego* (The Game) (1976), in *Teatro venezolano contemporáneo* (Madrid: Fondo de Cultura Económica, 1991). *El inevitable destino de Rosa de la noche* (The Inevitable Destiny of Rose of the Night) (1980), in *Voces nuevas teatro* (Caracas: Centro de estudios latinoamericanos, 1982). *El vendedor* (The Salesman) (1981) (Caracas: Colección Cuadernos de Difusión, 1985). *Esperando al italiano* (Waiting for the Italian) (1988), in *Las risas de nuestras medusas*, ed. Susana Castillo (Caracas: FUNDARTE, 1992).

BIBLIOGRAPHY: Felix Canale, "La actitud biográfica de Mariela Romero (The Biographical Position of Mariela Romero)," *Escena* 9 (1976): 36–38. Susana Castillo, "*El juego*: Un desesperado recurso de supervivencia," *Tramoya* 20 (1980): 61–70. Isaac Chocrón, "Introducción," in *El juego*, (Caracas: Monte Avila, 1977), 7–11. Joseph Chrzanowski, "El teatro de Mariela Romero," *Revista canadiense de estudios hispánicos* (1982): 205–211. "*Esperando al italiano*," in *Las risas de nuestras medusas*, ed. Susana Castillo (Caracas: FUNDARTE, 1992). Anita K. Stoll, "Playing a Waiting Game: The Theater of Mariela Romero," in *Latin American Women Dramatists: Theater, Texts, and Theory*, ed. Catherine Larson and Margarita Vargas.

SANTANA SALAS, Rodolfo. Santana Salas is a dramatist and director. His dramatic production includes forty works, some have received prizes, and many have been produced in several different American and European countries and translated into several different languages. He has been director of the Teatro Universitario de Maracay, grupo Triángulo, the grupo Cobre, the Laboratorio de Investigación Teatral (Laboratory for Theatrical Investigation) of the Universidad del Zulia, and Teatro Universitario de la Universidad Central de Venezuela. *Encuentro en el parque peligroso* (Encounter in the Dangerous Park) contains cruelty and violent speech, employing the ideas of Antonin Artaud, as the character Pedro perpetrates murders and crimes and verbally abuses Ana.

WORKS: *Los hijos del Iris* (The Sons of Rainbow) (Maracaibo: Editorial Universitaria, 1968). *Algunos en el islote* (Some on the Island), in *Revista de Teatro El Nuevo Grupo* 3 (1968): 16–24. *Las camas* (The Beds) (Caracas: Editorial Monte Avila, 1969). *El ordenanza* (The Ordinance) (Maracaibo: Editorial Universitaria, 1969). *Los criminales* (The Criminals), in *Revista Imagen* 79 (August 1970). *Nuestro padre Drácula* (Our Father Dracula) (Caracas: Monte Avila Editores, 1969). *Barbarroja* (Redbeard) (Caracas: Monte Avila, 1971). *Babel* (Bedlam), in *Mester* (UCLA) (1973): 42–56. *La muerte de Alfredo Gris* (The Death of Alfredo Gris) (Maracaibo: Facultad de Humanidades, 1986). *La empresa perdona un momento de locura* (The Company Pardons a Moment of Madness). *El animador* (The Animator) (1978). *Gracias por los favores recibidos* (Thanks for the Favors Received). *Los ancianos* (The Old Ones). *Fin de round* (End of Round). *La farra* (The Spree). *Historias de Cerro Arriba* (Stories of Cerro Arriba). *Primer día de resurrección* (First Day of Resurrection). *Cita de muerte y amor* (A Date with Death and Love). *Baño de damas* (Ladies' Bath). *Piezas perversas* (Perverse Pieces) (Caracas: FUNDARTE, 1978). *Tiránicus* (1978). *Crónicas de la cárcel modelo* (Chronicles of the Jail Model). *Borderline. El ejecutor* (The Performer). *Moloch. Encuentro en el parque peligroso* (Encounter in the Dangerous Park), in *Teatro vene-*

zolano contemporáneo (Madrid: Fondo de Cultura Económica, 1991).

BIBLIOGRAPHY: Giménez Azparren, "El teatro de Rodolfo Santana (The Theater of Rodolfo Santana)," *Fundateatros* 3: 31–39. Susana D. Castillo, "El teatro de Rodolfo Santana," *Mester* (UCLA) 3 (April 1973): 4–53. Pascual Estrada Aznar, "Notas sobre Rodolfo Santana y su teatro (Notes on Rudolfo Santana and His Theatre)," *Fundateatros* 1 (March 8, 1970): 45–47. Rodolfo Santana, *Teatro* (Caracas: Monte Avila Editores, 1969). *Ocho piezas cortas* (Valencia: Dirección de Cultura de la Universidad de Carabobo, 1974). *Tarántula* (Caracas: Monte Avila Editores, 1975).

SCHON, Elizabeth. Schon is a dramatist and poet. Her work has been described as magic-poetic. *Intervalo* (Interval) introduced into the theatrical world of Venezuela the theater of the Absurd; other works, such as *Lo importante es que nos miramos* (The Important Thing Is That We Look at Ourselves), are examples of surrealist theater. *Intervalo* has often been produced and has been praised for its influence on other dramatists. In it the writer explores loneliness and lack of communication.

WORKS: *Intervalo* (1956), in *13 Autores del nuevo teatro venezolano* (Caracas: Monte Avila Editores, 1971). *Melisa y el Yo* (Melisa and the Ego) (1961). *La aldea* (The Village) (1966) (Maracaibo: Ed. Universitaria, 1967). *Lo importante es que nos miramos* (1967) (Caracas: Círculo Musical, 1967). *El abuelo, la cesta, y el mar* (The Grandfather, the Basket, and the Sea) (Caracas: Monte Avila, 1968). *Al Unísono* (In Unison) (1971). *Jamás me miró* (He Never Looked at Me), in *Revista Haoma* 1.2 (1967). *La cisterna insondable* (The Bottomless Well) (Caracas: Conseja Municipal del Distrito Federal, 1971). *La gruta venidera* (The Future Cave) (Caracas: Cruz del Sur, 1953). *Casi un país* (Almost a Country) (Caracas: Editorial Municipal, 1972). *El limpiabotas y la nube* (The Bootblack and the Cloud) (1973).

THEATRICAL COMPANIES. *Grupo Actoral 80.* Founded in Caracas in 1983 under the auspices of the Centro Latinoamericano de Creación e Investigación Teatral (CELCIT), its goal is to express the unity of scenic expression on the continent.

Teatro ALTOSF. Created in 1976 in Cumaná and later moved to Colonia Tovar, it has ob-tained several prizes as the best theater of the interior of the country. It has taken part in international theater festivals in Venezuela, Spain, and Portugal.

Bagazos. It was established in 1979 at the Colegio El Angel (Angel High School) of Caracas, by the educational community. It has used theater to present problems of the community, such as the work of Gerardo Blanco: *Un ciudadano llamado maestro* (A Citizen Named Teacher), *Vals en una sola pieza* (Waltz in a Single Room), *El último juego* (The Last Game), and *Mesa redonda* (Round Table).

Centro Cultural Prisma. Established in 1982, its objectives are the formation of human resources, the production of theatrical works, and exposure of the public to theatrical art. The CCP currently has its own locale, the Sala Prisma (Prisma Theater). President, Ester Kohn de Cohén; Martha Candia, artistic director.

Compañía Nacional de Teatro (National Theater Company). Created by Presidential Decree in 1984, under the directorship of Isaac Chocrón, it has been an artistic and financial success. It has presented plays by Venezuelan authors as well as works from the renaissance in Spain and England and nineteenth- and twentieth-century Europe and America: *Asia y el lejano Oriente* (Asia and the Far East), by Chocrón, *Las paredes oyen* (The Walls Have Ears), by Alarcón; *Lo que dejó la tempestad* (Left by the Storm), by Rengifo; *Acto cultural* (Cultural Act), by Cabrujas; *The Tempest*, by Shakespeare, *Una viuda para cuatro* (A Widow for Four), by Goldoni; *View from the Bridge*, by Arthur Miller.

Grupo Compas. Founded in 1955, it has presented numerous theatrical works and has shaped many fine theatrical artists. The group has as its permanent home the theater of the Alianza Francesa (French Alliance).

Contradanza. Founded in 1973, it centers its activity on theater and dance. It has carried out many experimental works, workshops, seminars, and conferences and has participated in national and international meetings. The group takes as its starting point the human body as expression of all that is artistic and intellectual.

Corso Teatro. Founded in 1982, it strives to

meet the creative problems of theater through a stable, permanent group of players. It presented *Woyzeck* by Georg Buchner in 1986 at the Festival de Directores (Directors' Festival) for el Nuevo Teatro (the New Theater), receiving the highest prize and public acclaim.

El Chichón (with the meaning in Venezuela of a hard blow on the head). Specializing in children's theater, it was formed to challenge the creative and critical faculties of children exposed to passive media. It received the Drama Prize Juana Sujo for *Canción para un pájaro* (Song for a Bird) of Alejandro Mutis and The Ollantay Prize from CELCIT.

Fundación Rajatabla (Rajatabla Foundation). Founded in 1971, it is today one of the most solid and important groups in Latin America and has an international reputation with a stable group of thirty actors. A new group of actors is being trained in the Taller Nacional de Teatro (TNT) (National Theater Workshop) (1986), a creation of Rajatabla, as is also the Centro de Directores para el Nuevo Teatro (Center for Directors of the New Theater). Its longtime director, Carlos Giménez, called its principal inspiration, has had a distinguished international career, organizing international theater festivals and directing plays in such places as New York City (invited by Joseph Papp).

Taller de Teatro Infantil Los Monigotes (Children's Theater Workshop Los Monigotes). Founded in 1975 along with the Agrupación Arte de Venezuela (The Venezuelan Art Group), it concentrates on teaching and theater for children. Director, José León. The group presents programs in the neighborhoods, in plazas, in schools, and on television. It won the Juana Sujo Prize for best children's theater for its presentation of *Cuando canta las lechuzas* (When the Owls Sing).

El Nuevo Grupo (The New Group). It was established in 1967 with the purpose of experimenting with new methods and making known the works of Venezuelan dramatists, primarily through the impetus of the outstanding dramatists Cabrujas, Chalbaud, and Chocrón. Many of their works were produced by the group as well as many works of other Venezuelan and Latin American writers. It published *Revista de Teatro* from 1967 to 1970. It was disbanded in 1988 due to financial exigencies.

Pequeño Grupo de Teatro de Mérida (The Little Theater of Mérida). Established in 1974, it is one of the few groups that have been successful in the interior of the country, having formed a stable professional troupe, a loyal public, and an honored place in the social fabric of Mérida.

Teatro Rafael Briceño. Named for the prominent actor, the theater began in Mérida in the early 1980s and sustains a high level of activity in all venues for theater. In 1986 the group received the CRITVEN award for best group in the interior of the country. The group has participated in several theater festivals and carries out workshops, classes, and conferences in the Teatro Rafael Briceño.

Sociedad Dramática de Maracaibo (Dramatic Society of Maracaibo). This theater originated in 1977 with the purposes of obtaining a theatrical location, called Sala Antonio García, and seeking a new theatrical language. The group has provided theater for children. It received the CRITVEN award for best interior theatrical group in 1983.

Taller Experimental de Teatro (Experimental Theater Workshop). This group is concerned primarily with human expressions in several ways: the study, investigation, production, and diffusion of experiences related to the necessity of establishing creative contacts among human beings. The group has produced several theater pieces and has participated in national and international theater festivals.

Talleres de Textos Teatrales del Centro de Estudios Latinoamericanos "Rómulo Gallegos" (CELARG). This group, established in 1975, has been a significant stimulus for Venezuelan theater. The texts of many dramatists have resulted from the workshops, some of which have been edited by the Colección Voces (Collection Voices) of CELARG.

Teatro Estable de Barcelona (Permanent Theater of Barcelona). This is an outstanding theater group located in Barcelona, Anzoátigui, having produced several plays and participated in national and international festivals.

Grupo Theja (Theja Group). Dating from

1974, this group is made up of professionals from all parts of the theatrical enterprise with the goal of seeking a scenic form following new patterns of human communication. It has participated in theater festivals and has received several prizes for its productions.

Grupo Thespis (Thespis Group). Established in 1981, this is a university group backed by the Cultural Extension and Division of Students of the Metropolitan University (UNIMET). It has recently begun to participate in international festivals.

Teatro Tilingo (Tilingo Theater). Dating from 1968, it is dedicated to the production of children's theater. It is the only group of this kind with a stable company and its own locale. Its successes have been recognized by the awarding of many prizes.

Teatro para Obreros (T-POS) (Theater for Workers). This group was established in 1971 in the School of Engineering of the Central University of Venezuela. The 200 members decided to move their activities to the neighborhoods, changing the name to its current one. The members are workers, employees, housewives, and professionals. They have studied the methods of Brecht, Stanislavski, and Artaud, among others. They perform in the streets and in jails. This prize-winning group has toured several countries and has participated in international festivals.

THEATRICAL INSTITUTIONS AND FESTIVALS. *Asociación de Teatro Popular Venezolano (Association of Popular Venezuelan Theater).* Established in 1974, the ATPV has as its goal to promote theater as a means of participatory education. To this end, it sponsors workshops, seminars, and conventions and publishes *Escenario* (Stage), a journal of the activity of the ATPV that also includes articles relevant to the development of popular theater. It sponsors the Festival Nacional de Teatro Popular (National Popular Theater Festival), which takes place each year in a different city.

Ateneo de Caracas. Founded in 1931, it was rewarded in 1983 by the government with its own building, which includes theaters, concert halls, a bookstore, art galleries, and rooms for workshops, seminars, forums, colloquium. It houses La Biblioteca Pública Ateneo de Caracas (the Public Library of the Ateneo de Caracas), the Centro Latinoamericano de Creación e Investigación Teatral (Latin American Center for Theatrical Creation and Investigation), Taller de Creatividad Infantil (Workshop for Youth Creativity), and the Editorial Ateneo de Caracas (Ateneo de Caracas Publishing House). It has given birth to various active groups such as Rajatabla, the Festival Internacional de Teatro (International Theater Festival), and CELCIT. Its principal goal has been dedicated to the cultural education of the public and the encouragement of artists.

Centro Latinoamericano de Creación e Investigación Teatral (CELCIT) (Latin American Center for Theatrical Creation and Research). CELCIT was established in 1975 at the recommendation of the First Encounter of Cultural Directors of Latin America, organized in Caracas by United Nations Educational, Scientific and Cultural Organization (UNESCO). It has as its primary goal the integration of Latin American theater, acting through delegations in the various countries. It publishes monthly bulletins of information; the bimonthly *Cuadernos de investigación* (Journal of Investigation); the Colección Concurso Andrés Bello, which publishes the prize-winning works in its biennial contest and various books on related topics. It has sponsored international festivals in many different countries.

Círculo de Críticos de Teatro de Venezuela (Venezuelan Theater Critics' Circle) (CRITVEN). Established in 1974, it has as its fundamental activities the awarding of bronze statues for outstanding work in the theatrical field, the encouragement of newspaper columns dedicated to theater criticism, membership in the Asociación International de Críticos de Teatro (AICT) (International Association of Theater Criticism), and the organization of symposiums on criticism within the international theater festivals held in Caracas.

Escuela Superior de Artes Escénicas Juana Sujo (The Juana Sujo Advanced School of Scenic Arts). This school was established by Juana Sujo in 1949 with the name Estudio Dramático

Juana Sujo. In 1952 she began the Escuela Nacional de Arte Escénico. The resulting school, considered the major center for dramatic arts in Venezuela, has produced many actors and actresses for theater, film, and television.

Festival de Teatro Penitenciario (Festival of Penitentiary Theater). Sponsored by the Ministerio de Justicia (Ministry of Justice) and the Gerencia de Actividades (Directorate of Activities) of CANTV (Compañía Anónima Nacional Teléfonos de Venezuela—National Telephone Company), it is an annual festival of theatrical works presented in Caracas, in the theater of CANTV. The Consejo Nacional de Cultura (National Council of Culture) sponsors workshops to teach theatrical skills to the inmates. The objective is to use theater as a way to resocialize, to direct the energies, to stimulate the creative faculties of the incarcerated.

Taller de Actor (Actor's Workshop). It was founded in 1982 under the auspices of Fundarte, Conac, and El Nuevo Grupo as a center for research and refinement of the art of acting. Its goal is to prepare the actor for a career before the public.

ULIVE, Ugo. Ulive is a dramatist, director, actor, and professor. He was born in Uruguay and lived in Cuba from 1960 to 1967. He then arrived in Venezuela, invited by Isaac Chocrón and Román Chalbaud to direct El Nuevo Grupo (The New Group). He also lived in England from 1981 to 1984. He has received awards for his work as director and as dramatist and for his work in the cinema.

WORKS: Among his plays are: *Reynaldo* (1985). *Baile de máscaras* (Dance of Masks). *El dorado y el amor* (The Golden One and Love). *Prueba de fuego* (Trial by Fire), in *Teatro venezolano contemporáneo* (Madrid: Fondo de Cultura Económica, 1991). This last play presents a reflection on the sense of an armed struggle as well as the problematic of facing the concrete problems of daily life.

BIBLIOGRAPHY: Ugo Ulive, "El Nuevo Grupo: Sus primeros veinte años," *Latin American Theatre Review* 21.2 (Spring 1988): 47–50.

USLAR PIETRI, Arturo (1906–). Born on May 16, 1906, in Caracas, Uslar Pietri is renowned as an essayist and novelist. He wrote several psychosocial plays, five of which are the most important, listed below. In particular, *Chuo Gil y las tejedoras* (Chuo Gil and the Weavers) (1960) deserves recognition for its artistic value and can be viewed as one of the major theatrical contributions of Latin American theater in the last fifty years (Marbán, 79).

WORKS: *El día de Antero Albán* (The Day of Antero Albán) (1957). *El dios invisible* (The Invisible God) (1957). *La Tebaida* (1958). *La fuga de Miranda* (The Flight of Miranda) (1958). *Chuo Gil y las tejedoras* (Chuo Gil and the Weavers) (1960).

BIBLIOGRAPHY: Jorge Marbán, *La Vigilia del Vigía: Vida y obra de Uslar Pietri* (Caracas: Editorial Arte, 1997). Arturo Uslar Pietri, *Obras completas* (Madrid: Edime, 1953).

Anita Stoll

General Bibliography

Allen, Richard F. *Teatro hispanoamericano: Una bibliografía anotada*. Boston: G. K. Hall, 1987.

Arrom, Juan José. *Historia del teatro hispanoamericano*. Mexico City: Ediciones de Andrea, 1967.

Boyle, Catherine M. *Chilean Theater, 1973–1985: Marginality, Power, Selfhood*. Rutherford, NJ: Fairleigh Dickinson University Press, 1992.

Burgess, Ronald D. *The New Dramatists of Mexico, 1967–1985*. Lexington: University Press of Kentucky, 1991.

Cajiao Salas, Teresa, and Margarita Vargas. "An Overview of Contemporary Latin American Theater." In *Philosophy and Literature in Latin America: A Critical Assessment of the Current Situation*, ed. Jorge J. E. Gracia and Mireya Camurati. Albany: State University of New York Press, 1989.

Correa, Gustavo, et al. *The Native Theatre in Middle America*. New Orleans: Tulane University Middle American Research Institute, 1961.

Dauster, Frank N. *Historia del teatro hispanoamericano: Siglos XIX y XX*. Mexico City: Ediciones de Andrea, 1966.

Eidelberg, Nora. *Teatro experimental hispanoamericano, 1960–1980: La realidad social como manipulación*. Minneapolis: Institute for the Study of Ideologies and Literature, 1985.

Foppa, Tito Livio. *Diccionario teatral del Río de la Plata*. Buenos Aires: Ediciones de Carro de Tespis, 1961.

Foster, David William. *The Argentine teatro independiente, 1930–1955*. York, SC: Spanish Literature Publishing Co., 1986.

———, comp. *Handbook of Latin American Literature*. New York: Garland, 1987.

Garzón Céspedes, Francisco, ed. *Recopilación de textos sobre el teatro latinoamericano de creación colectiva*. Havana: Casa de las Américas, 1978.

Gutiérrez, Sonia, ed. *Teatro popular y cambio social en América Latina: Panorama de una experiencia*. Costa Rica: Editorial Universitaria Centro Americana, 1979.

Hebblethwaite, Frank P. *A Bibliographical Guide to the Spanish American Theater*. Washington, D.C.: Pan American Union, 1969.

Hulet, Claude L., ed. *Brazilian Literature*. 3 vols. Washington, DC: Georgetown University Press, 1974.

Jones, Willis Knapp. *Behind Spanish American Footlights*. Austin: University of Texas Press, 1966.

———. *Breve historia del teatro latinoamericano*. Mexico City: Ediciones de Andrea, 1956.

Kanellos, Nicolás, ed. *Mexican American Theatre: Then and Now*. Houston: Arte Público Press, 1989.

Luzuriaga, Gerardo, ed. *Popular Theater for Social Change in Latin America*. Los Angeles: UCLA Latin American Center Publications, 1978.

Lyday, Leon F., and George W. Woodyard. *A Bibliography of Latin American Theater Criticism 1940–1974.* Austin: University of Texas Press, 1976.

————. *Dramatists in Revolt: The New Latin American Theater.* Austin: University of Texas Press, 1976.

Mohr, Eugene V. *The Nuyorican Experience: Literature of the Puerto Rican Minority.* Westport, CT: Greenwood Press, 1982.

Neglia, Erminio G., and Luis Ordaz. *Repertorio selecto del teatro hispanoamericano contemporáneo.* Tempe: Arizona State University, 1980.

Ordaz, Luis. *El teatro en el Río de la Plata.* Buenos Aires: Futuro, 1946.

Pellettieri, Osvaldo, ed. *Teatro y teatristas: Estudios sobre teatro argentino y iberamericano.* Buenos Aires: Editorial Galerna, 1992.

Perales, Rosalina. *Teatro hispanoamericano contemporáneo (1967–1987).* Mexico City: Grupo Editorial Gaceta, 1993.

Pérez, Renard. *Escritores brasileiros contemporáneos; biografias, seguidas de antología.* 2 vols. Rio de Janeiro: Editôra Civilização Brasileira, 1960–1964.

Ramírez, Elizabeth C. *Footlights Across the Border: A History of Spanish-language Professional Theatre on the Texas Stage.* New York: Peter Lang, 1990.

Rizk, Beatriz J. *El nuevo teatro latinoamericano: Una lectura histórica.* Minneapolis: Prisma Institute, 1987.

Rojas Garciadueñas, José. *El teatro de Nueva España en el siglo XVI.* 1935. Mexico City: Sep-Setentas, 1973.

Skidmore, Thomas E., and Peter H. Smith. *Modern Latin America.* New York: Oxford University Press, 1984.

Solórzano, Carlos. *El teatro latinoamericano en el siglo XX.* Mexico City: Editorial Pormaca, 1964.

Stern, Irwin, ed. *Dictionary of Brazilian Literature.* Westport, CT: Greenwood Press, 1988.

Suárez Radillo, Carlos Miguel. *El teatro barroco hispanoamericano: Ensayo de una historia crítico-antológica.* Madrid: José Porrúa Turanzas, 1981.

Tatum, Charles M. *Chicano Literature.* Boston: Twayne, 1982.

Toro, Alfonso de, and Fernando de Toro, eds. *Hacia una nueva crítica y un nuevo teatro latinoamericano.* Frankfurt am Main: Vervuert, 1993.

Trenti Rocamora, José Luis. *El teatro en la América colonial.* Buenos Aires: Huarpes, 1947.

Weiss, Judith, et al. *Latin American Popular Theatre: The First Five Centuries.* Albuquerque: University of New Mexico Press, 1993.

Index

This index includes names of dramatists, scholars, and individuals associated with the theater, as well as theater schools, institutions, and companies. Ordering is by the Library of Congress system, in which the period, the comma and the space are counted as letters preceeding "a" in that order respectively. This allows for the proper ordering of compound Spanish and Portuguese last names. Variant names of the same individual are usually represented in the most complete version used in the text.

About the Contributors

Mirta Barrea-Marlys is coeditor of the *Encyclopedia of Latin American Theater*. She is an assistant professor of Spanish in the Foreign Language Studies Department at Monmouth University and holds a Ph.D. from the University of Pennsylvania. She has published a book, *Jael*, on the eighteenth-century Spanish theater and has written articles on the Latin American theater. In addition, she has presented papers and published articles and book chapters on contemporary Latin American women authors, the novel and film in Spain and Latin America, and contemporary Argentine authors. She has also contributed to the *Dictionary of Mexican Literature*. Her work entitled *La obra literaria de Altaír Tejeda de Tamez* is forthcoming.

Peter G. Broad is an associate professor of Spanish and chairperson of the Department of Spanish and Classical Languages at Indiana University of Pennsylvania. He has published extensively on Mexican and Chicano literature, especially the novel *Surama* by Sergio Elizando and the works of Carlos Fuentes.

Ronald D. Burgess holds a Ph.D. from the University of Kansas and is a professor at Gettysburg College. He has published extensively on Latin American theater and is a specialist on the theater of Nicaragua. His publications include a book, *The New Dramatists of Mexico, 1967–1985*, and several articles on those and more recent Mexican dramatists.

Joan F. Cammarata received her M.A., M.Phil., and Ph.D. in Spanish Literature from Columbia University. She is a full professor at Manhattan College in Riverdale, New York, and has served as president of the Northeast Modern Language Association. Specializing in the literature of Renaissance and Golden Age Spain, she has authored the book *Mythological Themes in the Works of Garcilaso del la Vega* (1993) and has published articles on Garcilaso de la Vega, Cervantes, and St. Teresa of Avila. In the area of Latin American literature, she has done extensive research in both the colonial and contemporary periods, with her most recent publication on the work of Laura Esquivel. She is the recipient of research grants from the Andrew Mellon Foundation, the National Endowment for the Humanities, and the Program for Cultural Cooperation between Spain's Ministry of Education and Culture and United States Universities.

Stella T. Clark is professor of Spanish at Cal State San Marcos. She earned her Ph.D. at the University of Kansas.

Helena Antolin Cochrane holds a Ph.D. from the University of Pennsylvania and is a professor at Widener University. She is an expert on the theater of Honduras and has published books and articles on Spanish and Latin American literature.

Eladio Cortés is coeditor of the *Encyclopedia of Latin American Theater* and editor in chief of the *Dictionary of Mexican Literature* (Greenwood, 1992). He is also a Professor Emeritus of Spanish and former Chair of the Spanish Department at Rutgers University in Camden and coeditor with Emilio Carballido of *Tramoya*, a theater journal. He holds a Ph.D. from Rutgers University in New Brunswick, New Jersey. His major published works include *El teatro de los hermanos Machado* (1970), *El teatro de Villaspesa* (1971), and *De literatura hispánica* (1988), as well as numerous articles on Elena Garro, Elena Santiago, Altaír Tejeda de Tamez, Sabina Berman, José López Rubio, Ramón J. Sender, Salvador Novo, and others. He has also published a critical edition of *La segunda Celestina* by Salazar y Torres.

Gloria da Cunha-Giabbai is associate professor of Spanish at Morehouse College and the book review editor of the *Venezuelan Literature and Arts Journal*. She has published more than twenty articles and reviews in national and international journals in the areas of her research interests: the Hispanic essay and the prose of Latin American women writers. She is the author of five books; *Humanidad: La utopía del hispanoamericano* (1991), *El exilio: Realidad y ficción* (1992), *Mujer e historia: La narrativa de Ana Teresa Torres* (1994), *La cuentística de Renée Ferrer: Continuidad y cambio de nuestra expresión* (1997), and *Marietta: El pensamiento de Marietta de Veintemilla* (1998), and the co-author of *Cuentístas hispanoamericanas* (1996) and *Narradoras ecuatorianas de hoy* (2000).

Lee A. Daniel is professor of Spanish and chair of the Department of Spanish and Latin American Studies at Texas Christian University. He is past president of the Southwestern Council of Latin American Studies and current editor of the *SCOLAS Bulletin*. He is also vice president of the Southwest for the Spanish National Honor Society, Sigma Delta Pi. He is the author of more than thirty critical studies and three books, most recently "The Loa of Sor Juana Ines de la Cruz" and "Cuentos de Beyhuale." His current research program includes a study of imaginary literary towns in Latin American Literature and the Panamanian writer, Rosa Maria Britton.

Mark F. Frisch received his Ph.D. 1985 from the University of Michigan and is associate professor of modern languages and literatures at Duquesne University in Pittsburgh. He has published the book *La relación de Faulkner con La América Hispánica: Mallea, Rojas, Yáñez y García Márquez*. Recipient of a Fulbright Award, he lectured in Argentina in 1987. He has published articles on Elena Garro and has worked with the journal *Poe Studies* in compiling an international bibliography.

Alfonso González is professor of modern languages at California State University, Los Angeles, since 1975. He has authored several books and articles on Spanish American literature. He specializes in Spanish American and Mexican literature.

Mirta A. González is professor of foreign languages at California State University, San Bernardino. She has authored books and articles on Quevedo and Spanish American women writers. Her field of specialization is the Golden Age, but recently she has ventured into Spanish American literature.

María Mercedes Jaramillo has a Ph.D. from Syracuse University and is a professor in the Humanities Department at Fitchburg State College. She has published several articles about

Colombian theater, Colombian women writers, and Colombian literature. In 1992 she published: *El nuevo teatro colombiano: Arte y política*; she is co-author of *Y las mujeres? Ensayos sobre literatura colombiana* (1991) and coeditor of *Voces en escena: Antología de dramaturgas latinoamericanas* (1991), *Literatura y diferencia: Escritoras colombianas del siglo XX* (1995), *Antología crítica del teatro breve hispanoamericano* (1997), *Las Desobedientes: Mujeres de Nuestra América* (1999), and *Literatura y Cultura: Narrativa colombiana del Siglo XX* (2000).

Janis L. Krugh received her Ph.D. from the University of Pittsburgh, where she specialized in contemporary Latin American theater and narrative. She has published articles on indigenous cultures and literatures, the lives of Jean Donovan and Archbishop Oscar Romero, Ana Istarús's play *Madre nuestra que estás en la tierra* and her erotic poetry, and Mexican theater. She also contributed twelve entries in the *Dictionary of Mexican Literature* (1992). She is currently an associate professor of Spanish at the University of Dayton, in Ohio.

Rafael Lara Martínez is professor of foreign languages at Meredith College in Raleigh, North Carolina, and has published books and articles on Latin American literature. He is an expert on the theater of El Salvador.

Enrique Martínez-Vidal is a professor at Dickinson College in Carlyle, Pennsylvania. He has published extensively on Latin American literature and is a specialist on the theater of Paraguay.

Alfonso Montelongo is currently teaching in Puebla, Mexico. His area of specialization is contemporary Latin American literature, in particular Mexican literature. In addition, he is an expert on the theater of the Dominican Republic.

Denice Montesano holds a Ph.D. from Ohio University. Her area of specialization is the contemporary Latin American theater. She has written on the contemporary Argentine theater and on the Peruvian theater.

Michele Muncy is Professor Emeritus at Rutgers University where she taught French, Spanish, and Latin American literature. A native of Paris, France, she holds a Ph.D. in Spanish and French from Rutgers University. She is a specialist in contemporary Mexican literature and author of two books on Salvador Novo and book chapters and articles on Elena Garro, Josefina Hernandez, Emilio Carballido, Rosario Castellanos, Nellie Campobello, and many others. She is copy editor of the theater journal *Tramoya*.

Marina Pianca is a professor at the University of California, Riverside. She has published extensively on Latin American literature and is an expert on the theater of Panama. She is a contributor to the *Encyclopedia of Latin American Culture* and to the *Latin American Literary History* Project.

Lizabeth Souza Fuertes is assistant professor of Spanish and Portuguese at Baylor University and associate director of the "Baylor in Mexico" study-abroad programs. Most recently she has co-authored a manuscript on Rubén Darío. Her research includes Lya Luft and Antônio Callado, among other contemporary Brazilian novelists.

Anita Stoll is professor of Spanish and chair of the Department of Modern Languages, Cleveland State University. She is editor of *La noche de San Juan/Lope de Vega* (1988), *A Different Reality: Studies on the Works of Elena Garro* (1990), and *Vidas paralelas: El teatro español y el teatro isabelino: 1580–1680* (1993); and coeditor of *The Perception of Women in Spanish Theater of the Golden Age* (1991); *Homage to Donald Bleznick* (1995), *La puesta en escena del teatro en el siglo de oro* (1999), and *Gender, Identity, and Representation in Spain's Golden Age* (2000) as well as articles on Latin American literature and Spanish Golden Age theater.

Juan Torres Pou is assistant professor of Spanish at Florida International University, Miami. He is the author of "El e[x]terno femenino," an essay on female representation of nineteenth-century Spanish American narrative, and he has published articles in national and international literary journals on nineteenth- and twentieth-century Spanish American, Peninsular, Catalan, and Chicano literatures. He is currently writing an essay on the effects of crosscultural relations in nineteenth-century Caribbean, Mexican, and Philippine writers and is editing a collection of essays on Chicano theater.

Nicasio Urbina is associate professor and chairman of the Department of Spanish and Portuguese at Tulane University. His areas of interest include literary criticism of contemporary Latin American literature. In 1996 he won the Rubén Darío International Literary Award.

Teresa Valdivieso is a professor at Arizona State University and has published many books and articles on Spanish and Latin American literature. In addition, she is an expert on the theater of El Ecuador.

Gladys M. Varona-Lacey received a Ph.D. in Hispanic languages and literatures from the University of Pittsburgh and has taught at the Massachusetts Institute of Technology, Tufts University, and Harvard University. She is associate professor and chair of the Department of Modern Languages and Literatures at Ithaca College, where she teaches Spanish and Latin American literature. She has published in the field of Latin American literature. Her most recent publications include *Introducción a la literatura hispanoamericana: De la conquista al siglo XX* (1997) and, as coeditor, *Latin America: An Interdisciplinary Approach* (1999). She is currently writing a book on the Peruvian writer José María Arguedas.

Nydia Palacios Vivas is a professor of Spanish literature and drama in the National University of Nicaragua. She received the award Ciudadana Ilustre for her contribution to the development of the art and culture of Nicaragua.

Philippa Brown Yin teaches at Cleveland State University, where she is director of the M.A. program in Spanish. Her major research interests are contemporary Spanish and Spanish American literature. In addition to numerous professional presentations on modern theater, she has contributed chapters on the theater of Buero Vallejo for *De lo particular a lo universal*. She is coeditor of *Studies in Honor of Donald W. Bleznick* and collaborated on the *Dictionary of Mexican Literature*.